BEASTS

of the

FIELD

A Narrative History

of California Farmworkers,

1769–1913

RICHARD STEVEN STREET

STANFORD UNIVERSITY PRESS

Stanford, California 2004

Stanford University Press
Stanford, California

© 2004 by the Board of Trustees of the
Leland Stanford Junior University.
All rights reserved.

Published with the assistance of the
Edgar M. Kahn Memorial Fund.

Printed in the United States of America
on acid-free, archival-quality paper.

Library of Congress Cataloging-in-Publication Data

Street, Richard Steven.
    Beasts of the field : a narrative history of California farm workers, 1769–1913 /
Richard Steven Street.
        p.   cm.
    Includes bibliographical references and index.
    ISBN 0-8047-3879-3 (alk. paper) — ISBN 0-8047-3880-7 (pbk. : alk. paper)
    1. Agricultural laborers—California—History.   2. Agricultural laborers—
Labor unions California—History.   I. Title.
    HD1527.C2 S84   2004
    331.7'63'0979409034—dc21   2003013386

Original Printing 2004

Last figure below indicates year of this printing:
13 12 11 10 09 08 07 06 05 04

Designed by James P. Brommer
Typeset in 10.5/12.5 Caslon

For

Colonel Oscar Richard Street, USAF,

and

Mary Theresa Zaro Street

Contents

BOOK ONE   FOUNDATIONS IN CONQUEST

Chapter One

In the Nets of Heaven:
The Campesino on the Spanish Frontier   3

> California's first farmworkers are transplanted north from Baja
> California in 1769, a movement instigated by the grand imperial
> plans of two remarkable men: Padre Junípero Serra, a Franciscan
> missionary in the service of God; and José de Gálvez, a powerful
> Spanish official bent on empire. The journey is long, treacherous,
> and deadly.

Chapter Two

Bird Herders, Stirrup Boys, and Naked Winemakers:
Assembling a Labor Force   21

> Gathered on twenty-one self-contained, plantation-like outposts,
> thousands of native Californians merge field labor and survival
> skills in the service of religion and colonization. Padre Junípero
> Serra and his Franciscan brothers insist they are preparing natives
> for an independent life. They ultimately exert an opposite effect.

Chapter Three

Always Trembling With Fear:
Controlling Mission Farmworkers   38

> Unable to leave and with few individual rights, mission field hands
> are directed by an integrated system of control ranging from
> imprisonment and leg irons to whipping and public humiliation.
> Though not slaves, neither are they free.

Establishing union locals in the main stem and slave market areas of West Coast towns, soapboxers for the Industrial Workers of the World move right in among bindlemen. After winning a dramatic confrontation at Fresno, they are beaten so badly at San Diego that they completely reassess their approach, devise new strategies, and take the struggle into the fields.

List of Illustrations

xiii

Preface

Bloodier, more spectacular, and more captivating, complex, and instructive than any chronicler has imagined, the story of California farmworkers during their formative years seems fantastic beyond belief. Described by *New York Times* reporter Anthony Ripley as something that "seems as though it were put together by a heavy-handed Hollywood script writer," it is one of the great sagas of American labor—and of the American West—with Kafkaesque overtones, bracketed by death. In 1769, an overland expedition from the Spanish missions of Baja California brought the first field hands north through the desert to plant farms in Alta (Upper) California. Half of the native campesinos in the expedition died or deserted along the way. In 1913, a desperate group of harvesters, many ill from befouled toilets and unsanitary water supplies, walked out of the hop yards in Wheatland under the banner of the Industrial Workers of the World (IWW). A gun battle erupted; a deputy sheriff, a district attorney, and two hop pickers died; dozens were wounded and dozens more were rounded up; and in a well-coordinated campaign over the next six years, the entire leadership of the California IWW was arrested, tried, convicted of a criminal conspiracy, and sent to Leavenworth prison.[1]

At the time that Padre Junípero Serra established mission agriculture, California was an isolated territory, claimed by Spain. For more than ten thousand years, contact with foreigners had been impeded by the Pacific Ocean and the North American continent. Although the native population had survived well on the region's bounty, farming had not developed, nor had any entity laid claim to the entire territory and its inhabitants. As Spanish padres and soldiers and Mexican mestizos began conquering the first native populations, converting them to Catholicism and teaching them to grow and tend crops, they cast themselves as beneficent protectors. Their paternal concerns guided a supposedly hapless, child-like, and easily misled people and inaugurated a process that, 144 years later, produced a class of 120,000 farmworkers. Employed on farms stretching more than 750 miles from the U.S.-Mexico border north to Oregon, this class of people constituted the state's number one social problem and the central paradox of its booming agricultural industry.[2]

Appearing at the drop of a hat, dismissed with the flick of a finger, and em-

ployed in a glutted labor market, farmworkers were channeled through the landscape as routinely as if sending irrigation water down the furrows of a field. Their
sweat and toil allowed California farmers to specialize, industrialize, pursue the
rewards of natural advantage, tap into emerging markets, fully exploit their environment, feed millions of people in California and millions more outside the
state, and create a gigantic agricultural industry, heretofore unseen on the planet,
more important to the state even than Hollywood, gold mining, or tourism. The
same pattern was developing all across America late in the nineteenth century.
As links between field and dinner table vanished from view and people lost track
of the relationships sustaining life, agricultural expansion imposed a rural proletariat on the land. Surging up from Oklahoma through the Midwest and as far
north as Alberta, Canada, a flood of one hundred thousand harvest workers between 1880 and the 1900s annually followed the ripening tide of wheat from June
through October. At the same time, great streams of African Americans and
Italians were working a circuit running between the Florida citrus groves and
New Jersey cranberry bogs, many of them with children in tow, while sharecroppers, tenant farmers, and field hands throughout the southern cotton, sugar
cane, and tobacco belts often brought in the harvests under conditions of peonage. North, south, east, and west, the sober, self-reliant, much revered "hired
hand"—taken in and treated as part of the family, skilled in everything from land
clearing to teamstering, and revered as a cornerstone of American democracy—
passed from the scene.[3]

To confront California farmworkers during the formative years of their history is to embark on a transformative journey into the human condition. By taking the long view of that experience, I aim to provide the kind of large-scale, fine-
grained, panoramic perspective that in many ways acts like a prism—refracting
and magnifying the history of a region and industry—which is too often reserved
for the high and mighty and denied to the history of common working people.
The cast of characters would delight Shakespeare. Here is Padre Junípero Serra,
the Father of California, being carried north from the Baja California missions by
Indian field hands. Here is Count Agoston Haraszthy, the Father of California
winemaking, setting platoons of Chinese laborers to hacking out wine storage
cellars deep in the hillside east of Sonoma. Here is Claude Hankins, a fourteen-
year-old delinquent from Palo Alto, sent to Yuba City to be rehabilitated by
working on a farm, stealing a revolver and sneaking up behind an abusive foreman and blowing out the man's brains. In the San Joaquin Valley farm town of
Hills Ferry on Sunday mornings during the wheat harvest, foremen roll up to
collect bodies of farmworkers, living and dead, and haul them back to the surrounding wheat camps. Behind the cribs and bars in Oxnard at 1 A.M., two strikers confront a hated strikebreaker and shoot him dead. South of Chico, teams of
native Californians beat back an army of ravenous grasshoppers by swinging
burning burlap bags full of dung. Out on the plains near Tulare Lake, a ranch
cook strips naked, places a hollowed-out pumpkin over his head, attaches weights
to his body, slips into a pond, floats up to some geese, grabs one, then another,
by the feet, yanks them underwater and snaps their necks until he has enough to
feed the harvest crew. In a wheat field near Milpitas, a foreman catches his leg

in the gears of a threshing machine, takes out his penknife, and calmly cuts himself free by amputating the limb.[4]

To many readers, the bizarre chain of events leading field hands to assassinate a padre at the Santa Cruz mission and mutilate his body, as well as the practice of migrant workers crawling into the brake beams of boxcars to steal rides, may seem the stuff of fiction. Equally incredible are the chilling circumstances that led John Sutter to execute one of his farm foremen and impale the severed, rotting head on a pole above the entrance to his fort, or the strange and tortured logic by which growers fixed on physiological traits (short legs), racial peculiarity (tolerance for working in the heat), or ethnic characteristics (lack of ambition) that supposedly made some groups well-suited, even destined, to subordinate positions as farm laborers. Countless other incredible scenes, whole worlds, large and small, heretofore unseen or omitted from the record, appear transiently in a single newspaper clipping, for example, when a local reporter describes sugar beet workers in the Pajaro Valley, possibly the first to suffer the effects of the short-handled hoe, dragging themselves through the fields "on their knees which became so sore that blood is left as they move along."[5]

Farmwork was more than hard, unrelenting manual labor. With the exception of the grain industry, work on the fruit and vegetable farms remained static and unmechanized. Human sweat and sinews, not machines, brought in California's crops. Stooping, squatting, lifting, grubbing, and crawling about, farmworkers augmented their toil with little more than hand tools—poles, hoes, clippers, sacks, buckets, and knives, and the occasional wagon or Fresno scraper. Labor methods harked back to a traditional agrarian time even while a rapidly evolving farming system recast work along the lines of modern mass-production operations. Besides harvesting and tending crops, farmworkers engaged in a good deal of construction work as they rebuilt the countryside—raising levees, erecting trellises, clearing and smoothing land. Canal building involved a particularly intricate set of skills—scraping out the bed at the correct rate of descent and uniformity and throwing up the banks at the angle of repose while erecting a system of weirs, laterals, and holding ponds.

As outdoor workers, field hands followed the course of the sun, laboring from morning until late afternoon, and occasionally, by moonlight. Unlike mill hands, who at least toiled within protective factory walls, farmworkers, with only their clothing to protect them from the elements, endured the bitter cold of winter and the burning heat of summer. Exposed to valley fever spores, stinging gnats, blackflies, clouds of dust, pesticides of mysterious and lethal concoctions, and health-threatening diseases ranging from malaria to cholera, they worked at a steady, industrial pace, slow or leisurely labor being anathema to the industry. At day's end, they congregated in all-male camps and barracks or the odd shed, shanty, barn, bunkhouse, or outbuilding, often in tents, or frequently on piles of straw under the stars. Shelter was spartan at best and never more than rudimentary. Away from the farms, field hands holed up in crowded skid rows or in ethnic ghettos, vibrant enclaves where men relaxed, gambled, drank, smoked opium, and, all too frequently, fought one another. Although women and children worked in the fields in increasingly large numbers as fruit cutters and cooks, during the formative years of farm labor, work remained an overwhelmingly male occupation. It was also wide-ranging. Following numerous, crisscrossing, overlapping routes, farmworkers traversed a highly dispersed work environment. Farms spread through the flat Sacramento and San Joaquin valleys, clung to terraced hillsides west of Vacaville, existed tenuously behind huge levees in the delta, blossomed in recently reclaimed desert, and were constantly mutating, with some finishing a harvest just as others were beginning. Constant migration and a marginal existence kept farmworkers separated from mainstream society. Although it is hard to pinpoint exactly when it happened, these and other characteristics collectively stigmatized farmworkers as members of an outcast and "mudsill class," the lowest of the low, a segmented, nonunion labor force composed of immigrants, social misfits, Native Americans, and other dispossessed people.

With eerie redundancy, historians have described farmworkers during their formative years as victims of a "bitter harvest," members of a "caste of despair," the state's own "peculiar institution," the "cancer lying beneath the beauty, richness, and fertility of the valleys," one of the "ugliest chapters in the history of American industry." Scholar-turned–labor organizer Ernesto Galarza, a man whose word carries the weight of authoritative research and first-person experience, spoke of a "subculture within whose depths a future psychosis was fermenting . . . people by design permanently disconnected from one another and from the sources of their livelihood." Seeing crews stooped over in the fields cutting vegetables, or scurrying up and down ladders to harvest fruit, or working waist deep in the mud while building levees in fetid swamplands, contemporaries frequently commented that farmworkers performed labor that was so crude, strenuous, and energy-sapping that it was unfit for ordinary, self-respecting citizens. Heat, dust, sweat, gashed ankles, ground-up arms and hands, bad backs, aching knees, blisters, explosions, epidemics, strikes, murder, injustice, prejudice, coarse camp life, and low pay made farmwork during the formative years such a gritty, tenuous, exciting, tragic, and frequently unpleasant picture that many contemporaries compared field hands to work animals. Farmers sometimes argued that handling field hands was not unlike driving mules, as both required ample quantities of food, straw, and the occasional crack of the whip. "With the Chinese, field hands could be treated like the beasts of the field," observed the January 5, 1888, *Kern County Californian*, "and like them be removed by their drivers or herders when no longer needed."[6]

Watching farmworkers pouring their sweat and blood into the fields as they fight forward into the twenty-first century, we find ourselves admiring their virtues. We draw strength from their courage by measuring our lives with theirs, and we discover new insight into the human condition by reflecting how much we diverge from them or share common experiences. Often they seem like crowds in a Charles Dickens story. They are grumpy and dirty, loyal and diligent, thirsty and burnt by the sun. Adrift in a landscape of ordered beauty, they illustrate the human costs required to produce a geography of abundance, telling us not only about irony, suffering, misery, acrimony, disorientation, resentment, cynicism, and violence, but also about hope, tenacity, sacrifice, and generosity; about getting old, death, dreams, adventure, despair, accommodation, and transnational forces intruding on the countryside. Possessing that trait literary critics call pathos, they evoke an intense feeling of sympathy, identification, appreciation, reflection, and curiosity. In this way, they are like all the great laboring classes in history—Welsh coal miners, Russian serfs, and American slaves.

But while early farmworkers present the historian with a story as rich, worthwhile, important, and fascinating as James Boswell's *Life of Samuel Johnson* or Homer's *The Iliad* and *The Odyssey*, untangling their story presents certain unique if not daunting problems. One is the sheer mass of information: hundreds of linear feet of state and federal government investigative documents; rooms full of newspaper clippings; libraries packed with magazine and periodical articles; endless, specialized, academic studies; a labyrinth of court documents; innumerable oral histories; and countless manuscript collections scattered in twenty-two states and three countries. Plowing through these massive, widely dispersed archives was as much a physical challenge as it was an intellectual endeavor. The quest became more strenuous the farther back in time I went. One thinks of literary biographer Walter Jackson Bate's description of the void surrounding Samuel Johnson's early life, and the explosion of material confronting Bate as he plunged into Johnson's later years. It is the same for California farmworkers. The quantity and quality of information decrease geometrically as time recedes. This effect is so striking that it has caused me to imagine the data as having the shape of an inverted pyramid: a small, sharp, pointed base in the year 1769, when the story begins, and a massive, bulky structure slowly expanding upward and outward past 1913. The challenge facing the scholar of the first century of farmworker history is the reverse of what must be done for the history of the next half-century. For the early eighteenth century and before, research often assumes an archaeological feel as the deeply buried fragments, bits, and bones of farmworker history are excavated, dusted off, preserved, and pieced together. But during the late nineteenth and early twentieth centuries, the scholar can be overwhelmed, and must sift, refine, and distill from the mass of conflicting information.[7]

As I proceeded in this research, I grew acutely aware that the idea of a detailed, unifying class history raised problems and was also somewhat artificial, prone to attack and criticism. Scholars debate class ad nauseam and ad infinitum, but few, I think, would argue that by 1913 farmworkers did not constitute an important subclass of the California labor force. Class exists in California agriculture as a result of one group, farmworkers, locked into a permanent wage-earning position and sharing experiences—gang labor, uncertain employment, travel, domination, blisters, bad backs, camp life, fieldwork—under an exploitative labor system, in an industry whose interests were different and often opposed to them. Class provides unifying meaning to the disparate experiences of the many races and nationalities who toiled in California's fertile valleys from the days of the Spanish missions to the second decade of the twentieth century.[8]

To do full justice to this story, I have tried to encounter farmworkers as closely as the material allows, to reach back into their distant history and recapture some of the physical reality and the states of mind of their world. Of overwhelming importance, I believe, is the obligation to demonstrate their immense diversity and the characteristics and skills they demonstrated, as well as their similarities and differences. Early California farmworkers were often victimized, always busy people caught in a common plight, swept along by currents difficult to control, or even understand. I have tried to see things as they did, to grasp what they understood as well as what escaped them, and to always remember that, like all actors on the historical stage, they could not possibly divine the future and had no idea how things would finally shape up.[9]

Because I have rooted about in so much evidence, both unknown and familiar, and have so many stories to tell, so many anecdotes to relate, this large history has grown even larger than the one I originally intended to write. So massive are the data and the resulting narrative possibilities today as compared to a generation ago, and so good is the recent scholarship, that they extend me the singular opportunity of telling the story as a trilogy: one volume, the present, devoted to the formative years; a second volume, covering the years 1913–2000, organized around the struggle to develop countervailing power; and a third, on the photographers and photographic record of California farmworkers, 1850–2000.[10]

In my determination to be comprehensive, give fitting scope to the subject, overcome disjunction in the farmworker time continuum, and do justice to the agricultural industry, I have been especially concerned with nailing down dates, numbers, and hard facts, which are fundamental to establishing sequence. Largely because previous writers have frequently played fast and loose with chronology, I have tried to identify where, when, and why certain key developments began. I set up these signposts, label them accordingly, and return to them as they occur in the natural course of events; for example, where farmworkers were first exposed to pesticides, when they first went on strike, why they first began using short-handled hoes, how they first threshed wheat, and who invented the first cook wagon.

Just as the American West did not suddenly emerge following the Lewis and Clark expedition in 1803–6, so too California farmworkers did not spring forth as an instantaneous outgrowth of statehood, the Gold Rush, the wheat boom, or late-nineteenth-century agricultural expansion. They have been around for a long time, and a large part of their history was rooted in the history of conquest and neo-colonialism. To anchor their story, I begin with an obvious, simple, and curiously ignored question: "Who were the first farmworkers?" By beginning at the beginning and identifying the exact point at which farm labor started in California, I establish what is, in effect, a birth date. Seen from the beginning, the formative years fall into five broad, interrelated phases: a colonial and preindustrial infancy on the Spanish missions; a period of transition on the Mexican ranchos; a period of consolidation and immigration following the Gold Rush; a period dominated by bonanza wheat farming; and a mature phase under a coherent labor relations system of routinized, industrial work arrangements on specialized, intensively cultivated fruit and vegetable farms. Constantly reconfigured by immigration, markets, crops, climate, bugs, culture, government, growers, religion, microbes, technology, and politics, early farmworkers possess a surprisingly complex, dynamic, tangled, multifaceted, kaleidoscopic history that state commissioner of horticulture J. W. Jeffrey described in 1909 as "like the rainbow colors revolving upon a disk."[11]

To understand early farmworker history is to understand a process that consisted of numerous sequenced, overlapping experiences, some comparable, some distinct, that varied among different crops, regions, time periods, and racial and ethnic groups. Mission field hands, who spent most of their lives in one place engaged in basic frontier activities such as clearing land, planting crops, and chasing pests out of fields, lived an existence distinct from Japanese immigrant fruit pickers drifting between the orange groves of Southern California, the raisin grape harvest near Fresno, and the peach and apricot orchards near Vacaville. Cotton pickers pulling long sacks down furrows and living in crude barracks while working in the hot Imperial Valley experienced an environment distinct from that of sugar beet harvesters topping beets and tossing them into wagons while living in company-owned adobe homes on the cool and foggy plains around Oxnard. Early farmwork could even be a big holiday, a kind of picnic, as when families from Contra Costa and Alameda counties streamed into the Pleasanton Hop Company yards, constructed brush shelters, hung painted signs over the doorways, dressed in their Sunday best clothes, and posed for a local photographer. And it could be a living hell, as when vigilantes raided a camp of Chinese hop field-workers near Nicolaus, beat them badly, put them on a barge, and sent them downriver to Sacramento.

California farmworkers have never before been viewed this way—sequentially—as a diverse people undergoing a continual process of evolution, alteration, adjustment, adaptation, victory, defeat, and reorganization. Giving order to their disparate, constantly changing world—a world far more complicated than the archetypal one that has heretofore been described—I have been guided by the idea that narrative analysis has strength and value because it is stitched into the very fabric of life, not just forced upon an experience. I have also tried to remain true to the admonition of historian Richard White, who, in discussing the tendency among filmmakers to opt for the cinematic at the expense of accuracy, stresses the importance of remaining first and foremost a historian. The words of labor historian Melvyn Dubofsky also ring true when he observes with regard to literary pretensions in the writing of history "that narrative without power and politics is story stripped of meaning."[12]

To argue that farmworkers endured a somewhat more dramatic replay of what happened to other members of the underclass, such as immigrants and ethnic minorities, or that they were simply a variant of what happened to unskilled workers in labor's confrontation with industrial capitalism omits the uniqueness of their history. Such an argument fails to confront the massive and often insurmountable obstructions in their path: the frequent denial of their humanity; the terror, intimidation, violence, repression, and exclusionist laws; and the endless affronts to their dignity that they were forced to endure. Quite unlike most other industries, California agriculture rested in part on white supremacy, class exploitation, a dominant capitalist culture, and a bundle of stereotypes. For many early farmworkers, life and labor in the fields was a hopelessly damaging experience. It wore them out. It generated numerous pathologies. And it often degraded them. Every time they were caught out in an open field without a toilet and had to relieve themselves publicly, farmworkers suffered a humiliation that haunted them into old age. So great was the dread that old prune pickers passing through the Santa Clara Valley years after leaving the orchards would become nauseated upon catching a whiff of the ripening plums. Forced to recall child-hoods of drudgery, they would curse the time when, as children, they had stuffed themselves with plums to the point of exploding, run like crazy to escape the harvest crew, climbed up into the ant-covered trees, pulled down their overalls, held on for dear life, and in a split second fired their contribution toward fertilizing "Prune Heaven," as the valley was then known.[13]

But while the circumstances of life and labor in the fields varied in degrees of exploitation, conditions of work, dangers of physical violence, elements of coercion and reward, chances of advancement, and harshness of labor relations imperatives, and could be mitigated somewhat by the benevolence of employers, the core experiences farmworkers acquired were very similar and directed toward the basic challenges of survival and adaptation: the value of determination; the blessings of frugality; the craft of good humor; when to speak up; where to keep quiet; how to work with others; and the pleasure during a midday work break of a long, slow drink of cool, clean water. Farmworkers learned to deal with the uncertainty of seasonal employment, the ravages of a bloated labor market, the lean times every winter, the incessant travel, the meager food, the poor quarters, the firings, and the killing pace of work; the arbitrary treatment and demands of foremen; the hostile rhetoric and brutal attacks of racist demagogues; employers who did not regard them as equals; laws that held them down or omitted them entirely; and a political system that considered them only as a problem and never as a constituency. Most farmworkers not only discovered how to cope, forgive, and persevere, but also somehow succeeded in forging a culture of survival and a community of mutual struggle based on self-sacrifice and humility that carried them through the most difficult challenges and allowed them to preserve their compassion, honor, and self-worth.

Speaking powerfully to the resilience of the human spirit and involving the most fundamental of life's issues, the early history of California farmworkers can easily overstress the negative. As antidote to tensions, adversities, and crises, I have searched out what was in fact normal and central to everyday life, and I have tried to follow these routines through different agricultural districts, crops, and time periods. My main concern has been to avoid depicting farmworkers only as victims, and growers as victimizers, to factor in the larger world of each, and, above all, to keep farmworkers themselves at the center of the story. The more ephemeral facets of the farmworker story—the technological breakthroughs, marketing problems, and agricultural inventions—should not cloud our picture of the central characters in this history: the Native Californian, Chinese, Japanese, Korean, Mexican, Chilean, Indian Sikh, Irish, German, British, Italian, Portuguese, and American-born people who spent all or a significant portion of their lives working in the fields. I endorse labor historian David Brody's view of such workers as actors in their own right. The difficulty lies in discovering that path of critical empathy that genuinely enters into the mental, physical, and emotional experiences of farmworkers and sees them in the broadest possible perspective. The majority of historians have linked their accounts very closely with contemporary problems and taken a highly critical view of how farmworkers have been treated. Because they stir such great passion and virtuosity in those writers, artists, and historians who have described them, farmworkers demand a special alertness to biases that garble, falsify, and distort their history.

I have tried to compensate for such biases through an attention to context and good judgment born of long experience, extensive work, and deep friendships in both the farming and farmworking communities. The challenge facing any truly contextualized history is to build into the narrative an ignorance of outcome, to recapture and unfold the past on its own merits without reading it forward into its dramatic future. More easily said than done, the task of burrowing deep into collective history and discovering the look, feel, and sound of life in a bygone era demands a recognition that the formative phase of the farmworker story is not only distant, but very different, and requires a great effort of imagination to touch its remote experiences. Time and again I would like to have stepped in and drawn farmworkers back from the brink, away from some awful fate, some horrible misfortune, but I describe them as I see them. I like to think—borrowing a phrase from Lincoln Steffens—that "the facts have had to beat themselves into my head."[14]

I must caution, however, that I adhere to several views of California farmworkers and people like them, and these have guided and shaped my writing. I agree with Jean Mohr and John Berger that by scrutinizing farmworkers and similar people we "grasp more surely the political reality of the world." In a television culture run by corporate conglomerates hawking products, I believe scholarship of this kind, fairly presented, can nevertheless succeed in shaping society and changing the way we live. Agricultural historians will quickly see that in the interests of unified narrative, thematic advancement, historical synthesis, and straightforward exposition I have compressed some scholarly disputes about farm size and rural life in order not to bog down the reader, and also to exploit a story as profound as it is vast. As a labor historian, I have been especially drawn to the culture of the workplace, the various ways farmworkers coped with and adapted to their situation, and the complex interplay between field hands and employers. This has meant studying not just traditional labor organizations and radical unions that dominate certain phases and episodes, but also the many ethnic groups, intermediaries, associations, and individual responses. My emphasis on the normal and mundane aspects of life in the fields, and on what farmworkers actually did and how they did it, stems from my interest in the vital commonplaces of everyday life.[15]

To properly narrate this tangled story, I have adopted a perspective that is both thematic and sequential, at once topical and chronological. One chapter reconstructs a strike in a single, explosive year; another spans a generation; others unfold the story frame by frame, scene by scene, year by year, as if viewing the rough cut of a documentary newsreel. Many narrative lines run simultaneously. Some dissolve, and are bypassed or forgotten. Others reappear in different guises along the way. I assume that the reader will not necessarily be acquainted with the history of California, agriculture, the American West, or farmworkers, and therefore I provide as much information and context as is necessary for making the story clear. Wherever necessary I follow farmworkers into processing plants and packing sheds, bathhouses and saloons, hobo jungles and "slave markets." Developments in science and education, art and photography, and society and politics also figure in the course of events. And since the complete history of the emergence of California farmworkers has never been told, and one of my main purposes is to give the reader both a broad picture and a useful reference book, I have devoted considerable attention to sketching the public debate over the farm labor system, key twists and turns in the legal history of farmworkers, and those moments when the plight of farmworkers became a political issue requiring government intervention.

I use the terms "myth" and "legend" so often throughout the narrative that the reader deserves some explanation. By "myth" and "legend" I mean a significant intellectual construction that merges idea and feeling into a picture or image at variance with reality. Myths, legends, and fables abound throughout farmworker history, indeed are an important part of the story. I attempt to identify their origins and subject them to critical assessment, wherever possible dissipating inaccuracies with empirical facts. Sometimes these myths originate in a kind of pyramiding of errors. For example, scholars seeking to racialize the harvest cite the secondary work of one historian again and again, rather than the historical record, to prove that Third World immigrants always dominated the harvest, when in fact more than half of all farmworkers since the Gold Rush were American-born whites or European immigrants. Sometimes these myths are as fanciful as any spun by the most inventive novelist. One of the most absurd is the tall tale foisted on the public by Idwal Jones, a Welsh-born journalist and widely cited chronicler of the wine industry. In an astounding but unchallenged passage in *Vines in the Sun*, he described Santa Clara grower Martin Seeley importing five hundred monkeys from Panama to harvest his 1905 prune crop. "They picked well the first day. For a year they led fierce, guerilla existence in the hills, frightening a few old ladies into fits, and gradually vanished," Jones wrote, ignoring both logic and historical evidence.[16]

And last, while narrating and analyzing the history of early farmworkers, I have always tried to keep them in view as human beings—a class whose behavior, thinking, and institutions in any given era and circumstance can only be understood by visiting them in the fields and labor camps, and insofar as is possible, by seeing the world through their eyes. To comprehend something of the early history of California farmworkers it is essential to comprehend as completely as possible what it felt like to suffocate inside a thick cloud of wheat chaff while sacking grain with a threshing crew; to feel the skin on your palms dissolving from the juices seeping from the figs you were picking; and to understand the relief after a day stooped over while weeding sugar beets with a short-handled hoe, of lying on one's back on the hot, plowed earth to drive out rheumatic pain in a kind of earthen heating-pad arrangement. Such experiences underscore the fact that farmwork is after all, hard, unremitting toil. Over the years I have explored—as a photographer and journalist as well as a historian—the fields where farmworkers shed their blood and fought their battles, the graveyards of men killed in boiler explosions, the first vineyard that farmworkers planted, the deserts they crossed, the barracks they lived in, the wine storage tunnels they dug. Journeys farmworkers made, I also made, for it was a promise I had made to United

Farm Worker Union president César Chávez when we first met and discussed my project.

Although this volume will be followed by a study of the photographers and photography, I have nevertheless employed photographs and other visual material as texts in themselves, not merely as illustrations underscoring a particular point, but as documents embedded in the narrative. Images often go beyond words, and in a tome of this heft are an immensely valuable way to entice the reader further into the story.

Because many names often have multiple, incorrect, and inconsistent spellings, I have sometimes arrived at my choice after a complicated deciphering process. With the Japanese, homeland usage places the family name or surname before the given or personal name, but in California, as elsewhere when abroad, the Japanese sometimes followed Western convention and reversed them. In the text, and in note citations, I follow the most common usage, and call them what they called themselves. I follow Spanish spelling for the pre-1850 period and into the 1860s, then adopt modern English usage thereafter, for example dropping the accent mark from San José. Spanish words and phrases that have not been widely incorporated into English usage are italicized, for example *cholo* (a term used in the nineteenth century for recent Mexican immigrants, as distinct from more established, wealthier Mexican-Americans) and *atole* (mush), while common Spanish words like campesino (field hand), pueblo (town), and California place names are spelled following English custom. Generally I leave alone quoted material, even when grammar seems in need of correction, and use "[*sic*]" only when absolutely necessary.

Because the size of this volume precludes attaching a bibliography, I take care of most bibliographical matters in the Notes, where the reader will find a full citation for every source at first mention, as well as digressions, amplifications, reflections, calculations, and excursions from the main narrative. To further conserve space I have employed abbreviations and listed them preceding the Notes.

RICHARD STEVEN STREET
San Anselmo, California

Beasts of the Field

We aren't animals.
    —*Lino, Santa Cruz mission, 1812*

I am not an animal.
    —*San Juan Capistrano mission field hand, 1839*

The proprietors of large estates, have been content to herd their workmen as they would their cattle.
    —*'Transactions of the California State Agricultural Society,' 1886*

With the Chinese, field hands could be treated like the beasts of the field, and like them be removed by their drivers or herders when no longer needed.
    —*'Kern County Californian,' 1888*

The wheat grower is not always disposed to treat his employees either fairly or with common decency. They are accorded no more comfort than cattle, and are often of far less concern.
    —*'Sacramento Weekly Bee,' 1890*

Many of our farmers and fruit growers have better accommodations for their beasts of burden than for their laboring men, who have to pack their blankets about upon their backs.
    —*'California Fruit Grower,' 1892*

Men have not been used to being taken out into a field and told, "There is your bed, twenty acres of it." They will not go into a twenty-acre field with the hogs.
    —*'Transactions of the California State Fruit Growers Convention,' 1902*

The main thing about the labor supply is to muleize it. . . . The supreme qualities of the laborer are that he shall work cheap and hard, eat little and drink nothing, belong to no union, have no ambitions and present no human problems. Particularly, he should appear from nowhere, when we need him, put up with what accommodations he finds, provide his own food, and then disappear . . . until the busy season comes around again. Some sort of human mule, with the hibernating qualities of the bear and the fastidious gastronomic tastes of the goat, would be ideal, provided he is cheap enough.
    —*Chester Rowell, editorial, 'Fresno Republican,' 1913*

FIGURE I. Descendants of the mission Indians, Pedro Pablo (center) and his Luiseño head-men meeting at the *asistencia* (branch) San Antonio mission in at the foot of Mt. Palomar northeast of San Diego in 1885. Courtesy of the California Historical Society/Title Insurance and Trust Company Photo Collection, University of Southern California.

Foundations in Conquest

They live well free. But as soon as we reduce
them to a Christian and community life . . . they
decline in health, they fatten, sicken and die.
 —*Padre Mariano Payeras*

Padre, take back thy Christianity; I want none
of it; I will return to my country.
 —*San José mission Indian*

The Indians . . . crushed the Padre's other
testicle. This last act put an end to the life of
Padre Quintana. Donato, the one who had been
whipped, walked around the room with the
plural results of his operation in hand saying,
"I shall bury these in the outdoor privy."
 —*Lorenzo Asisara*

When the mission Indians heard the cry of
freedom, they said, "Now they no longer keep
us here by force."
 —*Fernando Librado*

Every day they are running away . . . three
laborers fled and if the rest who remain see that
no steps are taken to [recapture and discipline
them] I will be left with none and . . . go to
ruins due to lack of hands.
 —*Pío Pico*

In the Nets of Heaven

The Campesino on the Spanish Frontier

The first farmworkers in California were transplanted north from Baja California in 1769 as the result of the vision, grand imperial plans, and colonizing impulse of two remarkable and powerful men, Padre Junípero Serra, a missionary in the service of God, and José de Gálvez, a Spanish official who at times thought he was God. The farmworker story began two years earlier, on Saturday, November 30, 1767, a bright and still morning in San José del Cabo, the wretched, nearly deserted, scurvy ridden Spanish settlement and Manila galleon supply port planted among the cactus and rocks on the southern tip of Baja California. As the small schooner *La Laurentana* dropped anchor in deep water off San Bernabé, the long spit of sand where supply vessels landed, a skiff was lowered overboard, and Gaspar de Portolá, the newly appointed governor of Baja California, rowed ashore accompanied by a contingent of twenty-five heavily armed Catalán dragoons. The arrival of the fifty-year-old Portolá following a horrible voyage across the Gulf of Baja California from Matanchel, Mexico, stirred considerable attention and curiosity, in large part because the sequestered peninsula received few visitors, and no Spanish official had set foot on its shores in thirty years.

Portolá was met first by Ignacio Tirsch, a Jesuit padre who, after learning of Portolá's arrival, made the daylong ride from his post at Santiago mission. Soon joined by Fernando de Rivera y Moncada, the Spanish military commander of Baja California who happened to be in the area, the two learned the shocking purpose of Portolá's mission: half a world away, King Carlos III of Spain had suppressed the Jesuits, confiscated their lands and property, and ordered Portolá to expel them from the peninsula. Tirsch and the sixteen other black-robed followers of the Roman Catholic religious order, who had been working among the natives of Baja California since 1697, were to abandon their missions and submit to arrest; they would then be marched up the coast two hundred miles to Loreto, the mission, village, presidio, and supply center that was the hub of Baja California affairs. From Loreto, the Jesuits would be returned to Spain and dispersed far and wide.[1]

FIGURE 2. Field hands at San José del Cabo mission, possibly the earliest image of California campesinos, with a Philippine ship arriving to take on supplies. Watercolor by Joanne Crosby, after an original 1767 drawing by Padre Ignacio Tirsch, S.J., in Doyce B. Nunis Jr., ed., Elsbeth Schultz-Bischof, trans., *The Drawings of Ignacio Tirsch: A Jesuit Missionary in Baja California* (1972). Tirsch was the only eyewitness to have left visual evidence of life on the Jesuit missions of Baja California. Original color illustration in the State Library of the University of Prague, the Czech Republic. Watercolor facsimile courtesy Joanne Crosby, from Harry Crosby, *Antigua California* (Albuquerque, 1994).

Wasting little time, Portolá rounded up supplies, obtained mounts, and on December 6 set out for Loreto, arriving eleven days later. On December 26, Portolá arrested Padre Benno Ducrue, the Bavarian-born head of the Jesuit missionaries in Baja California, then forced Ducrue to call in all of his fellow Jesuits, who were summarily arrested as they arrived. Delayed by the task of tallying the contents of the missions and taking control of the presidio and warehouse at Loreto, Portolá kept the padres locked in their rooms and under armed guard until February 3, 1768, when he roused them before sunrise and allowed them to take the Blessed Sacrament and preside over a large mass in Our Lady of Loreto church. It was finally time to return to Spain.

Because Loreto's Indian population seemed much vexed at the expulsion, Portolá feared trouble and therefore decided to expel the Jesuits under cover of darkness. Around 11 P.M., when the padres moved down a hill from the mission to the beach, a huge crowd formed along the way. The padres had been at the center of life in Loreto; presiding over public life, weddings, baptisms, and funerals, they had been responsible for teaching reading, writing, and even singing to the local population of Indians, Europeans, and Creoles. Their loss threatened chaos.

Rushing forward, Indians and even Spanish soldiers cried out, touching and kissing the padres, kneeling and praying with their arms outstretched in the form of a cross. Some threw themselves to the ground, pleading for pardons. Still others sobbed and wept, bidding the missionaries farewell. The strongest carried the missionaries on their backs through the breaking waves to a waiting skiff. "The spectacle was so moving," Ducrue later recalled, "that it touched the heart of the governor himself, who could not restrain his tears." But Portolá would not relent. Shortly after midnight, Ducrue and the other Jesuits boarded *Nuestra Señora de la Concepción*. After two days becalmed, a wind rose, the sails filled, and the padres sailed for Matanchel. Reaching it four days later, they joined other Jesuits gathered from throughout the Gulf of California, then marched overland for seven weeks on foot and horseback, reaching Vera Cruz, a seaport on the east coast of Mexico, on March 27. They were shipped home two weeks later.[2]

The Jesuits had not yet sailed for Spain when twelve gray-robed Franciscan missionaries crossed the Gulf of California on April 1. Tough, paternalistic, celibate male followers of a Catholic religious order founded in 1209 by Francis Bernardone of the Italian town of Assisi, Franciscans were "fishers of men," who ministered to the common people rather than leading monastic or contemplative lives. Statesmen, ambassadors, teachers, farmers, explorers, emissaries, and one-man tribunals, Franciscan padres since arriving among the Indians of Central Mexico in 1523 had served as cultural and religious vanguards of conquest, securing territory for God and crown by collecting—alone, or with the help of another padre and a small military guard—thousands of natives onto self-sufficient, semi-fortified, plantation-like church communities known as missions. They were now going to move onto the sixteen former Jesuit missions and more than forty mission stations and continue converting the Indians into Christianized, potential citizens of Spain, much as the Jesuits had done. Upon landing, though, the Franciscans found that Loreto and many other missions were virtually devoid of native peoples who, fearing the Spanish soldiers, had fled into the countryside. There was no one to convert.[3]

Arriving at San José del Cabo on July 5, 1768, to oversee the transfer of power was José de Gálvez, visitador general (inspector general) of New Spain. A megalomaniac who variously believed himself to be Montezuma and the king of Sweden, Gálvez once had proposed to subdue rebellious Sonoran Indians by importing six hundred Guatemalan monkeys as soldiers. Probably the greatest Spanish expansionist in the Western Hemisphere, Gálvez was the single most powerful figure in late-eighteenth century Mexico. Gálvez, along with the Mexican viceroy Marqués de Croix, and King Carlos III, had large territorial strategies in play.[4]

Spain had regarded the Pacific Coast as part of its empire since the middle of the sixteenth century, when Spanish explorers first charted San Diego Bay and the California coastline. With unexplored territory between the Rocky Mountains, Great Basin, and Sierra Nevada Mountains still a mystery to Europeans, Gálvez and the king feared that English fur trappers, venturing south from Canada and west from Louisiana, might soon find their way to the unoccupied Pacific Coast. When Russian fur trappers began sailing east into Alaska, inevitably to make their way down the West Coast, King Carlos III ordered Gálvez to block them and everyone else. From the crude maps then available, it became clear that in order to secure Alta California—which encompassed the entire swath of land from the northern portions of the Baja California peninsula through present-day Oregon—Spain would somehow have to push its presence north.[5]

Dusting off old Jesuit plans to use the Baja California missions as springboards to establish Spanish enclaves farther north, Gálvez simply replaced the Jesuits with Franciscans. His scheme to run a string of new missions into Alta California would secure for God and king, without war or colonization, the entire Pacific Coast territory. The key to this plan was Monterey Bay. Since the voyage of Sebastián Vizcaíno in 1602–3, Spain had regarded Monterey as the best harbor north of San Diego Bay, essential for thwarting further Russian incursions. If everything went right, the Franciscans would plant their missions, teach the "neophytes" (as newly baptized natives were called) to speak Castilian, train them in agriculture, and transform them into devout disciples of God and potential taxpaying *gente de razón*, literally, "people with the capacity to reason," but in fact people fully Hispanicized in culture and thought. But as Gálvez commandeered horses, cattle, farm equipment, and supplies from the old Jesuit missions, it became clear just how difficult it would be to mount an overland expedition and how important farmworkers would be to the success of that operation.[6]

Originally believed to be a treasure trove of riches, the Baja California peninsula instead was a hot, thorny, dry land whose only commercially exploitable resources were pearls and just enough silver to keep a dozen or so impoverished miners digging. Devastated by repeated crop failures and rampant disease, Baja California not only lacked its widely rumored treasures, but it could barely feed its own. In fact, few of the peninsula missions produced enough food to keep Indians year-round; instead, natives had to be periodically released to engage in traditional hunting and gathering. To ease food pressures, Gálvez shifted large numbers of Indians by sea launch and packet boat from relatively poor northern missions like San Borja and Los Dolores to the more prosperous and agriculturally self-sufficient missions of the south, like San José del Cabo and Todos Santos. He also began revitalizing and improving Loreto. He then turned to the task of colonization.[7]

In a letter to King Carlos III on May 16, 1768, Gálvez proposed to convey the Franciscans north from the Baja California missions to their destinations in Alta California in two large, self-contained, overland expeditions supported by a naval vessels. The route was an unproven one, without landmarks. The expeditions would not have a reliable map or an experienced guide. Yet somehow Gálvez would establish a mission far beyond any other, midway up the California coast near Monterey Bay, at a remote spot that would eventually become San Carlos de Borromeo, named in honor of King Carlos III. But before reaching Monterey, the expeditions would first establish a base camp and supplementary mission on a hill near an almost forgotten bay site called San Diego de Alcalá, near present-day San Diego.[8]

Planning the route and contemplating the composition of what came to be known as the "Sacred Expedition," Gálvez made countless calculations. How many people were needed? What supplies would they require? Where would they come from? Of all such matters none was more important than picking the right expedition leaders. With a non-Indian population of no more than four hundred, few people on the sparsely populated Baja California peninsula had either the experience or drive to handle such an operation. Whoever led the first expedition had to possess a frontiersman's expert knowledge combined with a soldier's sense of authority and a priest's willingness to sacrifice and endure pain. Fernando Javier de Rivera y Moncada was the logical choice.[9]

Rivera had come to the Baja California peninsula from Compostela, Mexico, in 1742 at age seventeen and served anonymously at the Loreto garrison for nine years before being promoted to captain as the result of a power play between the Jesuits and Manuel de Ocio, the richest man on the peninsula and the principal rival to Jesuit authority. California's first entrepreneur, Ocio had enraged the Jesuits by launching silver mining and cattle ranching operations and convincing the Loreto garrison commander to run Indians out of his mining areas. When the old Loreto captain died in December 1750, the Jesuits had seized the opportunity to regain their prominence by throwing their support not to the man next in line for the Loreto command, an Ocio ally, but to Rivera. A few months short of turning twenty-seven years of age in June 1751, Rivera was appointed commandante, and for the next sixteen years, as de facto governor and judge over the civilian population, operated less as an independent representative of the crown than as an agent of the Jesuits. The Jesuits further enhanced Rivera's stature in 1853 by enticing him to accompany Padre Fernando Consag on a journey of discovery northwest of what would become San Gertrudis mission. Rivera continued to serve the Jesuits, helped them expand the missions for the first time in a generation, served as a buffer against Ocio, and allowed the religious order to maintain hegemony over the peninsula.[10]

Upon Portolá's arrival, however, Rivera had quickly redirected his loyalty. As the most senior Spanish official in Baja California, Rivera had proved a useful ally of Portolá, easing his takeover and eliminating the need for any fresh troops from the mainland. This alone would have been adequate reason for elevating him to leadership, but Rivera had one unusual distinction that made him an especially good choice, indeed perhaps the only choice to lead any journey of colonization. Besides his value as a soldier, Rivera was the most experienced explorer on the entire peninsula. Both on his own, and while escorting Padre Wenceslaus Linck of San Borja mission on a series of expeditions, Rivera had searched for new or better mission sites in the northeastern regions of the Baja California peninsula as far north as the Colorado River Delta. For all of these reasons, Gálvez chose Rivera to lead the first contingent of the overland expedition to Alta California. Juan Crespí of La Purísima mission would act as chaplain and expedition diarist. Portolá himself would lead the second contingent, tracing Rivera's steps, with the tough and pious Padre Junípero Serra leading the missionary contingent.[11]

Perhaps the greatest of all "spiritual conquistadores," the fifty-five-year-old Serra embodied the hard-edged zeal characteristic of Spain's colonization of the New World. He began his missionary crusade in 1749, when he gave up a professorship of philosophy at the University of Palma, and instead traveled to Vera Cruz, Mexico. There he joined up with Padre Francisco Palóu, a former student and friend, then walked all the way to Mexico City. Bitten by a snake or insect while on the journey, he was permanently lamed, and for the rest of his life suffered from an ulcerous and swollen leg. Serra nonetheless pursued his missionary work at the College of San Fernando, a Franciscan training center in Mexico, then in villages near Mexico City. Serra had another close scrape with death in 1758, when he was diverted from going to the Apache mission at San Sabá, Texas, just before Indians pillaged and burned it to the ground. So fierce was Serra in his devotion to the ideal of redemption through self-punishment that he wore rough hair shirts, flagellated himself to the point of bleeding (sometimes while delivering a sermon), and even burned the flesh on his chest with a lighted candle as a test of faith.[12]

Even with the king's approval and the expedition leaders chosen, the journey was plagued by bad luck and sabotage by mariners reluctant to sail. To speed things up, Gálvez eventually dispatched his personal secretary to supervise the final outfitting of the naval vessels, two large and strong brigantines commandeered from Sonora, and a smaller boat, the *San José*. Laden with all kinds of farm equipment, enough seeds and grain to feed the expedition and plant crops upon arrival, the *San Carlos* sailed in January 1769 under the command of Lieutenant Pedro Fages, having received the Holy Eucharist and full blessing at high mass with Gálvez and Serra that morning. A month later the *San Antonio*, under Captain Juan Pérez, a veteran of previous naval expeditions, sailed south for Cabo San Lucas, where it would round the tip of Baja California and head north along the Pacific Coast. In his instructions to the captain of the *San Carlos*, Gálvez summarized the whole operation: "The object is to establish the Catholic Faith, to extend the Spanish domain, to check the ambitious schemes of a foreign nation . . . no pains can be spared without offense to God, the king, and the country."[13]

Departing too late in the season, the *San Carlos* met heavy seas and winds, which forced it to tack north for one thousand miles. The *San Antonio* also made slow progress. Meanwhile, Rivera and Portolá assembled their overland expeditions. Following standard mission-planting procedures, each was careful to enlist enough soldiers for protection and to stock enough supplies to see them through the first months of travel. Most of the soldiers were experienced *arrieros* (mule drivers), adept at packing and unpacking and guiding animals across difficult terrain. They would be in charge of *bestias de carga* and *bestias de silla* (pack and riding mules or burros), and of loading and rigging the *aparejos*, or Spanish pack saddles, which draped two large pouches over each side of the burro's ribs, or held two *cacastles* or *huacales* (square crates made of small, straight tree branches notched at the corners and bound together with rawhide) on top of the saddle. Also following standard mission-building practices, both men made sure that they brought along a force of faithful, hardworking, Christianized Indians. From experience, Portolá knew that whether leapfrogging a mission twenty miles up the Baja California peninsula or one thousand miles beyond the last, if farming were to go forward during the first years of settlement in Alta California, indeed if the missionaries were to survive, they would have to rely on outsiders, on campesinos, on field hands from the existing missions of Baja California.[14]

Campesinos were essential because the first missions in Alta California would have to become self-sustaining agricultural enterprises immediately. There would be an initial frenzy of hacking down and burning brush, clearing and preparing land, and planting patches of corn, squash, melons, vegetables, and grain. This process of converting wilderness to productive fields would be no less than a desperate matter of life or death. After that there would be vineyards to plant, orchards to tend, wineries to construct, and olive presses to operate—and many other assorted farming and ranching activities—requiring large numbers of field hands drawn from among the local Indian tribes. There would be a massive amount of work building and maintaining irrigation works, storage buildings, wineries, threshing corrals, and so on. From Mexico through the American South and Southwest, Franciscan missions functioned as ongoing agricultural operations. Because they collectively employed thousands upon thousands of indigenous peoples, it was often said that next to Christianity, agricultural work was the principal lesson that the padres taught native peoples. From several centuries of this work, Franciscans knew that farm labor did not come quickly to Indian hunter-gatherers, who required instruction before understanding European-style agriculture.[15]

Already trained in the intricacies of agriculture and able to size up a situation rapidly and deploy with minimal supervision, campesinos from the Baja California missions saw nothing extraordinary when the Franciscans went among them and asked for volunteers. Many stepped forward, even if they did not entirely understand the distance and dangers involved. Of those who volunteered, though, Rivera and Portolá were highly selective, choosing only certain campesinos for the Sacred Expedition. From Rivera's experience, laborers drawn from the Guaycuras, who lived south of Loreto to about Santa Cruz Island, and the Pericú, who lived south of the Guaycuras in an area terminating at Cabo San Lucas, left much to be desired. Cochimíes, most numerous of all Baja California native peoples, who lived to the north of Loreto in a territory covering roughly two-thirds of the peninsula, were much easier to work with and far more dependable. As Jesuit historian Padre Miguel Venegas said, Cochimíes possessed a "noble nature" and pleasant disposition, and made the best field hands. In addition to being the most numerous of all Baja California Indians, the more northerly Cochimí groups also spoke a Yuman dialect that would prove useful in dealing with other natives. Accustomed to living in mission villages, most also spoke a modicum of Spanish, practiced at least the trappings of Roman Catholicism, and dressed and worked much as did other poor peoples of the Spanish colonial empire. They were reasonably acculturated and had learned various skills as *mayordomos* (foremen), gardeners, and vineyardists; they were, in short, respected and esteemed members of the mission communities. Consequently, when Rivera chose field hands for his march on Alta California, he brought along only the most loyal and trusted campesinos from Cochimí groups around the northernmost missions at Santa María and San Borja.[16]

৯৯

On February 26, 1769, a clear, bright, abnormally mild morning, a group of forty-two Cochimí campesinos assembled at Loreto, ready to trek north under the command of Captain Rivera and the spiritual guidance of Padre Crespí. The expedition was also comprised of a ragtag collection of twenty-five *soldados de cuera* (leather-jacketed soldiers), three muleteers in charge of the pack train, and the *pilotín* (shipmaster's mate), José de Cañizares, who also kept a diary. Along the route, the Cochimí campesinos would establish campsites, herd livestock, assist the muleteers, perform the drudgery of the trek, and generally prepare the way for a second expedition. Once in Alta California, those surviving the arduous journey of colonization would shift from explorers to farmworkers charged with the task of quickly establishing the agricultural operations essential for survival.[17]

Trudging north through the Central Desert, the campesinos rested with the expedition party and took on further supplies on March 22, 1769, when they reached Velicatá, the most northerly frontier outpost on the Baja California peninsula. Because of the peninsula's configuration, their route would bend just east of the San Miguel Mountains, head through the San Felipe Valley, and then continue north across the peninsula toward the Pacific Coast. Looking north from their crude thatched shelters, they could see past Pico San Miguel toward Cañon San Fernando, the first of many ravines, ridges, valleys, cliffs, deserts, and other natural barriers they would encounter along the way. Fragments of the path blazed farther north by Rivera's 1765 exploration with Padre Wenceslaus Linck disappeared toward the snowcapped southern peaks of the Sierra de San Pedro Mártir. Countless unknown Indian groups roamed the territory in between. Water was scarce, fertile farmland rare; cactus and mesquite dotted the austere landscape. A system of ancient foot trails provided the only known route. At San Isidoro Valley ten days north of Velicatá, the expedition paused for the funeral services of a campesino from Santa Gertrudis mission, the first of many to die.[18]

Breaking camp after two days, campesinos led the way north, keeping the San Pedro and San Pablo peaks in sight for the first two days. Then, unable to penetrate the mountains to the Pacific Ocean, they followed Linck's path as far as Paso de San Matías. Preceding the pack train as sappers, they used axes, spades, and machetes to cut brush, open passageways, chop down the chaparral, and create footpaths. They further served as translators and interpreters between the Spanish and various Indians they encountered along the way. When necessary, they would also serve as soldiers and guards, sometimes seizing and interrogating Indians who followed the expedition, at other times befriending them; before leaving the Sierra de San Pedro Mártir, they buried Manuel Valladares, a campesino from San Ignacio mission, second to die on the march. "His death I felt with all my heart," wrote Crespí, "for the good services he had done me all the way, acting as my interpreter." By the time they reached San Quentin Bay, the campesinos were carrying one soldier and two more of their own on litters.[19]

On their trek north, campesinos were often without access to fresh provisions, forced to scavenge for food and live off the land as best they could; Rivera made them subsist mostly on roasted mescal, a native plant, and a thin gruel of cornmeal and water. With the pack animals overburdened with supplies for the expedition party and the mission that would be established at journey's end, no one rode, and the campesinos were forced to walk the entire distance, considerably multiplying their hardship. Since they were traversing largely uncharted territory, they often found the right path through trial and error. Doubling back to try another route was common. Gradually, the ordeal took its toll. Seventy miles south of San Diego, while wandering for eight days in the mountains of present-day Ensenada, another campesino died; expedition diarist José de Cañizares noted that as they roamed among the valleys in search of water, all of them feared that they might die from thirst.[20]

On May 13, after fifty-one days on the trail, the campesinos drove their teams of oxen, mules, and wagons into the southwestern coast of Alta California. Bypassing dozens of native villages that commanded the area, they eventually halted their teams late in the afternoon, camping within a few miles of the present-day port of San Diego. They were exhausted, half-starved, dehydrated, and ravaged by scurvy, their gaunt faces, skeletal bodies, and bleeding gums evincing their ordeal. Both the animals and men could go no farther. That night, heavy rains fell, drenching everyone. Along the way, thirty of forty-two campesinos had died or deserted.[21]

Arriving in sight of the harbor early the next morning, the expedition party saw the ships *San Carlos* and *San Antonio* at anchor. The *San Antonio* had arrived in San Diego on April 11, while the *San Carlos*, which had departed from Loreto harbor a month earlier but suffered greater misfortunes, arrived on April 29. Of the ninety men who set sail on the two vessels, only sixteen were healthy enough to attend to the sick by the time they dropped anchor in San Diego Bay. Thirty had died of scurvy; twenty more would die in the coming months; and the remaining survivors were unable to work—"immobilized and in so unhappy and deplorable a state as moved my deepest pity," wrote Portolá later to the viceroy. Greeting the sailors and helping them ashore, the campesinos immediately began foraging for food and caring for the sick and dying. Meanwhile, the forty-four campesinos with the main expedition that departed Loreto on March 9 were encountering their own ordeal.[22]

ﻉﻋ

Leaving Santa María mission, Portolá and his campesinos pushed hard to reach Velicatá in one day, rather than the usual two, so that Serra could observe Pentecost. On May 14, Padre Serra said mass in a mud hut that served as a temporary church, consecrating the land as San Fernando de Velicatá, the first mission founded by the Franciscans in Baja California. Breaking camp and heading north with Portolá the following day, campesinos took turns carrying the severely crippled Serra as well as several ill soldiers. Within a few days, six campesinos became so ill that Serra administered the last rites; after one of them died, five of the most ill were left in the arroyo of Los Mártires. Descending from the Sierra de San Pedro Mártir and nearing the plain of San Telmo, another campesino deserted. Serra wrote in his diary: "At this place, one of ten Indians of San Borja, named Juan Francisco Regis, deserted. We found it out only the next day."[23]

On June 18, following several days of trying to hack their way through impenetrable tangles of brush a day's march south of Todos Santos Bay, yet another group of campesinos abandoned the expedition. Troubled by the desertions, Serra wrote in his diary:

After midday, and after eating our dinner, at one fell swoop nine Indians who belonged to our company have deserted. We sent men to go after them, but not even tracks could be found. Questioning those who still remained as to the cause of so unexpected an event, seeing that they were always given food and good treatment, and they had always given the impression of being well satisfied, the answer we got was this: that they did not know, but rather suspected that, being near San Diego, they were afraid they would be forced to stay there without hope of returning to their own missions.

Several days later, after descending from hills strewn with huge boulders, three more campesinos deserted.[24]

With their departure and the death of five others along the way, only thirty of the original forty-four campesinos on the Portolá expedition remained. Early on the morning of July 1 they joined the surviving members of the Rivera expedition and the sailors from the *San Carlos* and *San Antonio*, who were encamped at San Diego harbor, having covered the distance from Velicatá in forty-six days. Of the approximately 219 members of the expeditions, some 126 survived the journey! The combined expeditions set up camp on a small hill, near present-day Old Town in San Diego, erecting huts and a crude chapel. On July 16, the campesinos helped raise a cross and joined in ceremonies consecrating the site as San Diego de Alcalá mission, the first Spanish mission in Alta California. Almost immediately they began work on an adobe church. By all accounts mission life during those first few months was wretched. Camping in brush shelters, everyone survived not by farming and harvesting crops, but by gathering wild roots and seeds, snaring rabbits and mud hens, measuring out the meager rations shipped from Mexico, and scouring food from the nearby beach and wetlands.[25]

It was a harsh existence that exacted its toll. Digging fresh graves daily, campesinos buried sixty men by the end of July. To make matters worse, Diegueño Indians from the ranchería of Cosoy began stealing cloth and teasing and harassing the sick soldiers. On August 15, finally tiring of the Spaniards, the Diegueños attacked the mission, killing Padre Luis Jayme, and wounding another, a padre, a blacksmith, and one campesino—the beginning of a series of Indian attacks that would continue for a half century. That fall, campesinos and soldiers erected a protective stockade of poles around the mission. But they could not keep out starvation, illness, and disease. Not one picture or painting commemorates the role of the surviving twenty-six or twenty-seven campesinos as the first farmworkers in California.[26]

৵৯

Even with one mission established in Alta California, circumstances did not improve. When small crews of campesinos drawn from the San Diego group ventured out with pack trains to plant new missions, they found themselves alone on paths none but Alta California natives had ever trod, and frequently on trails never before walked by humans. Under these circumstances, campesinos sometimes grew desperate. This was what happened when fifteen campesinos joined fifty-nine soldiers, padres, and muleteers and trekked north with Portolá on July 14, 1769. Passing through the Los Angeles basin, they experienced several earthquakes, one lasting "about half as long as an Ave María," recalled Portolá in his diary. Along the way, campesinos as usual went ahead with guides from local Indian tribes to break trails. Leaving early each morning, they seldom got back to camp before nightfall. North of present-day San Luis Obispo, they turned inland to avoid the coastal mountains, then continued along the wide Salinas Valley plain, finally heading west again to reach the vicinity of present-day Monterey, where they recognized Point Año Nuevo and Point Pinos, the northern and southern landmarks of Monterey Bay, which had been noted on charts recorded by Vizcaíno on his exploratory voyages. Pressing on, they then marched all the way to Point San Pedro, near present-day Pacifica, arriving on November 1. Returning to Monterey, they awaited the arrival of the *San José*, but when the ship failed to make port in Monterey Bay (it had sunk on its way north), the whole group grew desperate. "The cold began to be felt intensely," expedition engineer Miguel Costansó confided unhappily in his diary on November 30, "and for two days the wind from the north was very strong."[27]

The next day, two muleteers requested permission to go hunting; once clear of camp they deserted and were never seen again. On the afternoon of December 3, as the expedition nervously scanned the ocean for the *San José*, the wind shifted to the south and it began to rain. Searching for shelter, a scouting party got caught in the Santa Lucia Mountains. Exhausted, suffering from diarrhea, and surviving on a diet of acorns, seabirds, and foul mule meat, the men "fell on that . . . mule . . . like hungry lions," wrote Portolá. The next day, two campesinos decided to abandon the expedition and fend for themselves; two days later the expedition headed back to San Diego without them.[28]

On January 24, 1770, the remaining thirteen campesinos returned to San Diego mission with the rest of the Portolá expedition, arriving to shouts of welcome and slaps on the back. During six months of marching through territory heretofore "untrodden by Christian feet," they had covered more than nine hundred miles, located the future site of San Gabriel mission, and reached the vicinity of present-day San Francisco Bay. Now, Portolá himself, having been on the road for nearly a year, considered abandoning the mission and returning to Baja California. Two campesinos did go south with a returning ship in February 1770, but two more arrived on March 19 aboard the supply ship *San Antonio*. With fresh supplies, Portolá recruited twelve campesinos from among those at the mission, and on April 17 took them north as part of a second expedition to Monterey Bay. On May 23, near present-day Carmel, Portolá encountered the two campesinos who had deserted him three months earlier. They rejoined the others and helped establish a presidio at Monterey, and within its walled compound, huddled together and "smelling frightfully of mules," founded San Carlos de Borromeo mission on June 3. Over the next few months, Padre Serra, who had come north on the *San Antonio*, praised his campesinos for playing a particularly significant role in establishing friendly relations with Indians from the Carmel Valley.[29]

FIGURE 3. Between September 10 and 25, 1791, a one-time cabin boy and later official artist, José ("Pepe") Cardero, sketched scenes around the Monterey presidio while the Spanish expedition commanded by Alejandro Malaspina anchored in Monterey Bay for a month of rest and recuperation. The workers in the foreground appear to be field hands but are probably not Baja California campesinos; their exact task is open to speculation. José Cardero, "Vista del Presidio de Monte Rey." Original pen-and-ink drawing in the Museo Naval, Madrid, Spain, copy in the Robert B. Honeyman Collection, Courtesy of the Bancroft Library, University of California, Berkeley.

In the sandy bottomlands near San Carlos and San Diego missions and later on the raw plains near San Antonio and San Gabriel missions (established in 1771) and at San Luis Obispo mission (established in 1772), campesinos threw themselves into heavy, backbreaking, "set-up work." This consisted of the arduous tasks of pulling tree stumps, hacking away at roots, moving boulders, digging ditches and wells, erecting brush dams across rivers, excavating diversion ditches, laying out irrigation systems, and instructing local natives in various farming techniques. When their tools broke and there were no blacksmiths to fix them, campesinos rigged repairs, lashed together implements with rawhide straps, or continued working with digging sticks and sometimes their bare hands. When water was distant, they carried it to their gardens in cowhide buckets suspended from poles resting on their shoulders. Walking among the plants, they ladled out water one precious gourdful at a time. In doing so, they established the first irrigated mission fields.[30]

Soldiers offered little if any help. Padres, some of whom had considerable farming experience, occasionally assisted in the fields. But it was the campesinos, through fanatical diligence, who cleared, planted, and tended fields and allowed everyone to just barely survive the period of initial mission building. Drought, floods, and frost wiped out most of their first crops and, even though they managed to replant everything and salvage a few bags of grain each season, campesinos continued to struggle against the poor judgment of the padres, who persisted in planting the wrong crops in the wrong places. Well into the 1770s, everyone was still living on the ragged edge, existing on roots, seeds, and nuts donated by or bartered from local Indians, and on a flimsy gruel made of boiled wheat and dried chickpeas. During the summer of 1774, conditions grew especially bad at San Carlos mission. "For thirty-seven days," reported Padre Palóu, "we were without as much as a crumb of bread or a tortilla."[31]

Overworked and underfed, campesinos declined rapidly in strength, numbers, and effectiveness. During the first years of mission building, there had never been enough of them. While the padres eventually corrected some farming problems by importing more and better tools and work animals, moving missions San Diego, San Antonio, and San Carlos to better agricultural sites, and fitting crops to conditions, they complained continuously that the lack of campesinos crippled agriculture and imperiled the mission's primary goal of attracting and converting natives and settling the land. "It seems," Viceroy Antonio María Bucareli y Ursúa wrote, "that the great progress of the spiritual conquest was only suspended by the lack of foodstuffs to maintain the Indians in the mission enough time for their instruction."[32]

The solution, some concluded, lay in the expansion of the campesino labor force. By bringing in more field hands, Franciscans hoped to increase the food supply and therefore draw more pagans to Christianity. The idea, explained Padre Serra, was that more campesinos would extend the plantings, the local Indians would "see the cornfields which appear wonderful in their eyes," and the missionaries would have "a granary to fill them [natives] with food—and catch them in the nets of heaven."[33]

Within four years of their appearance in California, campesinos became the center of a confrontation that was incited by Padre Serra himself and ultimately reached the very highest levels of church and state. Needing more campesinos and wishing to circumvent the control of Governor Pedro Fages, who Serra believed had withheld the food supplies necessary for attracting local natives as farmworkers, Serra traveled to Mexico City to present his problems directly to Viceroy Bucareli. Arriving in February 1773, Serra outlined the situation and lobbied for increased mission support. Using arguments that have since become standard for those lobbying for foreign farmworkers, Serra predicted dire consequences if he did not get the extra manpower he requested. Because of the lack of field labor, he reported, crops had dwindled or had not been planted at all, and for this reason he had failed to gather large numbers of natives at the missions and verged on failure. To further sway the viceroy, Serra on March 13, 1773, drew up a detailed report or Representación, which contained thirty-two requests covering every phase of mission life—from continued support for the port of San Blas to the removal of Governor Fages and his replacement by Sergeant José Ortega. The Representación was a remarkable document that would later become central to the case for Serra's sainthood. Campesinos figured so prominently in it that the document was, in effect, the first piece of farmworker legislation. If Serra got his way, campesinos would no longer be forced to trek north. Instead, he wrote, they "should come of their own free will." Perhaps anticipating that the end of compulsion would cause a shortfall of workers, Serra also attempted to identify new sources of labor, particularly peasants from the vicinity of San Blas, campesino boys, and even entire families of campesinos, including women and children. The latter group he proposed to maintain as family units and good examples, who would reassure and interact with native Californians and attract them onto the missions.[34]

On May 6, 1773, Bucareli granted all of Serra's requests, except for the recruitment of peasants. Governor Fages was removed, and the viceroy increased the allocation of blacksmiths, workmen, pack animals, oxen, and supplies. Bucareli then issued an even more remarkable directive, the *Echeveste Reglamento* of 1773. Named for its author, Juan José Echeveste, the Spanish official who allocated supplies to Alta California, it was essentially a temporary law increasing the annual stipend to each mission and paying salaries to soldiers in kind. But the regulation also contained provisions governing treatment of laborers. Placing all responsibility in the hands of the missionaries, the *Reglamento* ordered the padres to "serve them [campesinos] as parents love and teach their children."[35]

Implementing the declaration proved difficult. However well-intentioned and important, the *Reglamento* ultimately did little good. On June 21, a group of ten Cochimí Indian families and twelve unmarried Cochimí boys were gathered into yet another overland expedition and marched north with padres Palóu, acting superior of Alta California, and Fermín Francisco de Lasuén, soon to be successor to Serra as president of the Franciscan missions of Alta California. On August 30, 1773, they arrived at San Diego mission, where the expedition rested before setting out for San Gabriel mission, leaving one campesino family behind. On October 2, the expedition arrived at San Gabriel mission and the entire population turned out to welcome them. After an eight-day rest, the expedition continued on to San Luis Obispo mission; six Cochimí families and six Cochimí boys remained behind at San Gabriel mission to teach the native converts agriculture and "domestic arts."[36]

Placed in charge of seventy-three recently baptized local Gabrielino Indians, the Cochimí families at San Gabriel mission were immediately directed to begin digging irrigation ditches, erecting brush dams, and planting corn, wheat, and beans in the black loamy soil along the Los Angeles River near the Indian village of Yang-Na. "This affords them the opportunity to plant more grain to feed new Christians and to attract gentiles who will be much alleviated," wrote Padre Palóu, "for the Indians are very poor, on account of the small crops of wild seeds they receive from the plains."[37]

But the work did not go well. The Cochimíes could not communicate with the Gabrielinos, who spoke an entirely different language. Consequently, there was little social contact between the two groups. Young Cochimí men refused to marry local natives and disliked having to live in tiny pole huts next to the Gabrielino barracks. To make matters worse, Cochimíes were regularly denied rations and had to feed themselves from their own gardens and resources. The Cochimíes also wanted a separate mission of their own. Eventually Lasuén, the head padre at San Gabriel mission, raised the issue in a complaint to his superiors at the College of

San Fernando in Mexico City. Lasuén had marched north with these Cochimíes and felt a close attachment. But no action was ever taken to rectify the problem.[38]

꿁

Separated from their loved ones and subjected to often miserable living conditions, campesinos sometimes fled the missions, choosing instead to either live among other California Indians, or to attempt to return to Baja California. Of all those who attempted to return home, none had a more incredible adventure, or better illustrated the role campesinos played as explorers and trailblazers, than Sebastián Tarabal.[39]

In late October 1773—within weeks after arriving at San Gabriel mission—Tarabal, his wife, María Dolores, and son (in some accounts a young Cochimí boy, in others Tarabal's brother) endeavored to return to their home at Santa Gertrudis mission in Baja California. Rather than heading directly south, they struck out across the Mojave Desert on an uncharted route, keeping far to the east to avoid soldiers sent after them. Soon the escapees ran out of food and water and all but Tarabal perished. Rescued near the junction of the Colorado and Gila rivers by the Quechan Indian leader Olleyquotequiebe (known to the Spaniards as "the one who wheezes"), Tarabal was delivered to Captain Juan Bautista de Anza's expedition, then encamped near present-day Tucson, Arizona. Convinced that the region beyond the Colorado River was not impassable and seeking a direct route across the Mojave Desert from Sonora, Mexico, to San Gabriel mission (and, ultimately, all the way to Monterey), Anza had made his way north from the presidio of Altar. The captain ordered Tarabal nursed back to health, then pressed him into service as the expedition's unofficial guide and interpreter, as well as Anza's own servant, muleteer, and cook.[40]

On January 8, 1774, armed with an abundance of gifts for the Quechan Indians, Anza followed the errant field hand across the Sonoran Desert, along a route known as *El Camino del Diablo* ("the devil's road"), which reversed Tarabal's original trek. The expedition camped beside the Colorado River, several miles upstream from its junction with the Gila River, near large rancherías of Quechan Indians who raised crops of corn, wheat, beans, melons, and squash. On February 7, having established friendly relations with the natives, Anza left the majority of his animals, along with three soldiers and four muleteers, at a Quechan village and resumed his trek. On March 2, the expedition became lost while passing through the waterless sand dunes immediately west of the Yuma Crossing; in a journey later recalled as the "Heroic Ten Days," Tarabal brought Anza and his parched expedition back to their previous encampment. After resting for two weeks at a small lagoon near the Colorado River, Tarabal again set out with Anza toward San Gabriel mission. Swinging southward along the river, he took the expedition around the southern flank of the great barrier of impassable sand dunes, below the present-day U.S.-Mexico border. Cutting diagonally across the present-day Imperial Valley from near present-day Mexicali and skirting the western edge of the desert where Tarabal's wife and child had died, he guided the expedition across the valley to the foot of the San Jacinto Mountains. Discovering familiar landmarks near present-day Anza Borrego State Park, Tarabal then led the expedition to safety at lifesaving waterholes.[41]

On March 10, Tarabal halted Anza at the fork of the San Felipe Creek and Carrizo Wash at the eastern base of the Santa Rosa Mountains. Padre Pedro Font, a missionary from Mexico's San José de Pimas mission who was accompanying Anza, later recalled the site as "bad, sterile, without grass, or anything useful . . . all sandy or sand dunes with rocks on the hills." But no matter how barren, it nevertheless served its purpose as an important base of operations. Anza named the camp San Sebastián in Tarabal's honor.[42]

From San Sebastián, Tarabal led Anza west by a torturous trail that ran through Coyote Canyon, a rough place Anza described as "formed by several very high, rocky mountains, or it would be better to say, by great heaps of rocks and stones of all sizes, which look as though they had been gathered and piled there, like the sweepings of the world." Finding a pass through the mountains and then descending to camp near the present-day city of San Jacinto, Tarabal led the expedition north through what is now Riverside and Ontario, and eleven days later into the Los Angeles basin, across the Santa Ana River by means of a bridge constructed of tree branches, and at sunset on March 22, 1774, entered the gates of San Gabriel mission. Scarcely believing that the expedition had come by way of Sonora and further amazed to see the escaped campesino Tarabal at its head, soldiers and padres received Anza's people by ringing the mission bells, discharging muskets, and shouting joyfully.[43]

Scholars would later credit Juan Bautista de Anza with blazing the Colorado Trail, discovering the route through the Borrego Desert, and linking northern Sonora to Alta California. Padre Francisco Garcés, a patient young priest who had accompanied Tarabal and Anza, would be credited as the expedition's guide. As reward for this "great service to God and the king," Viceroy Bucareli promoted Anza to the rank of lieutenant colonel, missionaries praised Garcés as the greatest and most "fearless explorer of the missionary period in the Great Southwest," and state boosters subsequently enshrined both men by naming highways, colleges, and parks in their honor. But in fact, the overland route from Sonora had first been established and later retraced not solely by Anza the great explorer or Garcés the brave pathfinder, but by Sebastián Tarabal, a distraught, rebellious campesino who lost his wife, a companion, and nearly his own life escaping the fields at San Gabriel mission.[44]

Following his return to San Gabriel mission, Tarabal continued serving as a guide for at least three years, including one stint in 1776 guiding Garcés as far north as the San Joaquin Valley by way of a route approximating present-day Interstate 5. He is last mentioned in Garcés's diary of July 25, tending mules somewhere in the desert near present-day Yuma. But he apparently continued on with Garcés toward San Xavier del Bac mission, near present-day Tucson, possibly arriving there on September 17, after having traveled some three thousand miles. On the basis of Tarabal's guidance, Garcés on January 3, 1777, recommended to his superiors a new way of reaching Alta California by way of a small sailing ship brought up the Gulf of California to the Colorado River. Along the way, travelers would be cared for by missionaries and protected by troops at two small outposts established on the west side of the Colorado River, about 250 miles northwest of the nearest Spanish settlement: Purísima Concepción, a garrison in the vicinity of present-day Yuma; and San Pedro y San Pablo de Bicuñer, a village about ten miles north of present-day Laguna Dam. From there they would proceed on to San Gabriel mission and Santa Barbara mission by way of the path blazed by Tarabal, and in this way, the Alta California missions would be assured of a new link to northern Mexico, and therefore of an abundant source of campesinos, carpenters, and other workers. But on June 17, 1781, the Yuma and Quechan Indians, who initially welcomed Tarabal and the Spanish, attacked and wiped out both Colorado River outposts, killing almost one hundred soldiers and several padres, including Padre Garcés, and possibly Tarabal, who had probably continued traveling with the padre. Acknowledging Tarabal's key role in exploration and the significance of his death, Felipe de Neve, upon becoming commandant-general of the interior provinces in 1783, ordered Anza to cease styling himself the discoverer of the route to Alta California, an honor that Neve assigned to Tarabal. But Neve died the following year. Consequently, Anza continued garnering praise. Fittingly known as *El Peregrino* ("The Wanderer" or "Pilgrim"), and "Saint Sebastián," Tarabal had his contributions swept aside.[45]

꧁ꔮ

Tough, loyal Baja California campesinos like Sebastián Tarabal traveled north in substantial numbers until the mid-1770s. Wherever they went, they had to adapt to circumstances and accept without complaint the most primitive and challenging conditions imaginable. Padres devoted considerable attention to them, and in agreements planning the formation of every mission, listed them as important "items" along with bundles of colored beads and supplies of flour, saddles, tools, and other equipment. Each mission was allocated five or six families and five or six boys. Expected to serve as liaisons with local natives, these campesinos had to be able to speak several languages, including Spanish, and local Indian dialects. Teachers as well as laborers, they were required to train and instruct local Indian farmhands in the agricultural arts.[46]

Stranded on the Alta California frontier far from home, campesinos would remain in Alta California, their lives and the lives of thousands of other native field hands inextricably tied to the Spanish missions. For such men, the adventure of exploration was as significant as that of any member of the Lewis and Clark expedition of 1803–6, their sacrifices and exploits as heroic as those of Jedediah Smith and other western fur trappers in the 1820s and 1830s, their challenge as daunting as those faced by members of the American survey teams of the 1870s and 1880s. Clearing and plowing the first fields, planting the first vineyards, making the first wine, harvesting the first grain, irrigating the first crops, and training the first generation of farmworkers, campesinos from the Baja California missions more than any other group, more even than the padres themselves, were responsible for establishing agriculture in Alta California. The work they performed, the lives they lived, the obstacles they overcame, and the distance they covered undermine old assumptions about the first farmworkers and how, where, when, and why people began working in the fields of California. Separated from their families and homes and forced to march hundreds of miles overland, campesinos were essential to the formative years of the Spanish missions.[47]

Although at first glance they might seem to have little in common with later farmworkers, Baja California campesinos exhibited remarkable similarities to the braceros brought north from Mexico under government sponsorship to stem labor shortages in California during World War II, and for twenty years thereafter. Their role in averting a farm labor shortage, their long and torturous journey, their foreign origins, and the way they were brought north under an elaborate church and government program, conforms in many ways to aspects of the bracero experience. Like braceros, Baja California campesinos allowed farmers to work out the best combination of crops and farm sites without having to do farmwork themselves. Like braceros, they also decreased their master's dependence on local laborers. And they allowed farmers to proceed without having to alter their system of agriculture or their goals. During their years of toil as the principal farmworkers in the mission fields, campesinos from Baja California unknowingly established a pattern, later replicated, modified, and expanded, whereby various private, semiprivate, and official government programs would repeatedly overcome labor shortages by importing large numbers of cheap, industrious, "trained," Mexican workers.[48]

CHAPTER TWO

Bird Herders, Stirrup Boys, and Naked Winemakers

Assembling a Labor Force

On June 24, 1828, the French sea captain Auguste Bernard Duhaut-Cilly arrived at Santa Barbara mission, just in time to enjoy a celebration in honor of Saint John the Baptist. Captain Duhaut-Cilly's ship, the *Héros*, was anchored offshore, and he had taken advantage of the layover to spend a few days touring the area. While enjoying a huge feast with Padre Antonio Ripoll and hundreds of Chumash field hands, Duhaut-Cilly was at the point of walking out on an interminable two hours of what he regarded as "cruel and barbarous" bullfights when he witnessed a curious game: field hands and other natives in the middle of the mission square struggling to climb a greased pole topped with rewards of clothes and trinkets. The captain watched one man after another fail in his attempt before a young campesino from Baja California, "perfectly formed . . . of a robust constitution," managed to make it to the top and grab all of the prizes by scraping the grease from the pole and spreading ashes on it.[1]

Continuing to compete at other games, the campesino won every race, even against the very best runners. Duhaut-Cilly could not take his eyes off the young man, largely because he feared that the Chumash might harm him. Eventually, the games ended and Duhaut-Cilly sailed south to San Pedro, but he never forgot that young campesino. "A light piece of stuff was about his loins; and when he was running nothing concealed from sight the vigor and grace of his movements," he later wrote in his journal. Marveling at the young man's elegance and physical ability, Duhaut-Cilly failed to perceive the historical and demographic significance of that solitary field hand. Why, out of all the farmworkers he saw at Santa Barbara mission, was there only this one Cochimí boy? What had happened to all of the other Baja California field hands during the previous half century? And how and when had the padres managed to replace them with Alta California natives?[2]

The main reason Baja California campesinos declined as a significant part of the Alta California mission farm labor force was the expense and difficulty of transporting them north. This problem had become apparent in the late 1770s,

FIGURE 4. Second of the twenty-one California missions, San Carlos de Borromeo, founded in 1770, was located on the Carmel River about four miles south of Monterey. It was still thriving and at the height of its power as headquarters and home to Father-President Junípero Serra and his successor Fermín Francisco de Lasuén in 1827, when the British amateur painter William Smyth captured this scene. Quarters for field hands and other Indian workers are to the left of the church. Lithograph from watercolor drawing by William Smyth. Courtesy of the California Historical Society/Title Insurance and Trust Company Collection, University of Southern California.

when large numbers of campesinos died on the torturous expeditions up the barren peninsula. While field hands continued to travel north in decreasing numbers with overland resupply expeditions and occasionally aboard supply ships, their numbers dropped considerably in the 1780s. The decline caused much consternation to Padre Serra and others who depended on the campesinos not only to instruct natives in agriculture but also as interpreters, guides, foremen, and skilled artisans. With time, however, surviving campesinos married native women shipped up from Baja California, began raising families, and became part of the mestizo (people of mixed blood) population. Their sons assumed positions as loyal and trusted foremen, and their daughters married soldiers and settlers and became integrated into the mission farm labor force. Those failing to marry died off as bachelor laborers worn out by the rigors of the frontier.[3]

As the numbers of transplanted campesinos declined, the loss was offset by increasing numbers of Alta California natives, who in the eyes of the Franciscan padres, were wild, godforsaken, and backward people, in dire need of salvation. A typical view, expressed by Padre Font upon encountering the Diegueño Indians around San Diego, condemned them as "degenerate . . . ugly, dirty, disheveled, filthy, ill-smelling, and flat-faced." Other padres chimed in with observations about fornicating, worm-eating "savages" who existed at the whim of nature. By dispensing exactly what they believed natives needed—an inoculation of Hispanic civilization and an indoctrination in field-work—Franciscans sought to lift natives out of their stone-age despair and set them on the road to prosperous, self-sufficient Spanish citizenship. But contrary to this oft-repeated opinion, Alta California natives hardly existed in a state of anarchy. Descended from waves of Asian hunter-gatherers who had trekked east across the Bering Strait beginning about 14,000 B.C. and then dispersed into an unsettled continent, they were, in fact, clean, civilized, and family oriented. They organized themselves into hundreds of independent "tribelets" or groups of several hundred people uniting many extended families and totaling between 150,000 and 300,000 people, one-third of whom resided in a thirty-mile-wide strip along the Pacific Coast within range of the missionaries.[4]

With abundant natural resources, California natives did not need or practice agriculture. Living as hunters and gatherers, they adapted to their bountiful environment and benign climate according to the ecological zones in which they lived, altering the land with no tool heavier than a woman's digging stick while occasionally improving spring plant growth through selective burning of underbrush. Technologies included fishing apparatus and stone and obsidian tool manufacturing. Homes consisted of hemispherical structures of reeds and thatched grass, arranged in small clusters. Villages sheltered from two hundred to four hundred inhabitants and might include a central town, various satellite villages, and numerous outlying camps (used temporarily during hunting, fishing, and seed gathering routines). Families were monogamous (except for chiefs, who practiced polygamy) and homosexuality was common. Government was largely consensual and flowed from village elders and influential female leaders. Without horses or even any concept of domesticated livestock, Alta California Indians followed a preagricultural existence, as had been the case for centuries. And while in some years they may have suffered from seasonal shortages of one food or another, there is no indication in their mythology, their archaeological record, the records of foreign observers, or in handed-down memories that widespread hunger occurred to any significant degree.[5]

Perhaps the least questioned of all farmworker myths is that the natives who supplanted the Baja California campesinos were pressed into service against their will as captive laborers, and that they neither consented to, nor understood, their work. By this view of history California Indians submitted to spiritual conquest and became mission farmworkers as the result of a forced choice between Christ and death. One implication of this view is that Padre Serra, long promoted for sainthood, was a kind of eighteenth-century monster and therefore does not deserve adulation. Insofar as one hates and rejects oppression, so this line of thinking goes, one must also hate the man who has come to be known as the Father of California. Such an interpretation seems all the more plausible because like most myths it contains considerable basis in fact. Upon first encountering the Spanish missionaries, some natives resisted joining the religious fold. Quickly they learned the price of opposing such powerful intruders: rape, murder, execution, whippings, and intimidation at the hands of the leather-jacketed mission soldiers. This was the case at San Francisco de Asís mission, where Ohlone-Costanoan Indians who blocked padres from establishing their mission were whipped and threatened with execution. The same happened at San Luis Obispo mission; when Indians burned the mission buildings and threatened to wipe out the settlement, they were driven off by musket fire and mounted soldiers. Natives at San Gabriel mission acquiesced after being terrorized by the grisly sight of their chief's severed head "brought to the mission in triumph" and impaled on a pole in front of the chapel, in full view of the chief's little boy, a penalty for opposing soldiers who raped the chief's wife and rode out to the rancherías to go after other Indian women—in Serra's words—as if "catching a cow or mule with a lasso" in order to subject them to "unbridled lust." Violence and intimidation of inferior peoples, while entirely acceptable behavior for some western European men, was never sanctioned by the padres, who denounced forced conversion; nevertheless, it only took a few such incidents to convince unwilling converts. Reluctant, coerced, and fearful Indians no doubt comprised a significant portion of the early mission farm labor force.[6]

But while some natives were terrorized into becoming mission field hands, most arrived voluntarily, at least at first. Military force was not the cornerstone of conversion. Rather, adult natives were drawn to the missions by the allure of technology, the belief in opportunity, and the temptation of what seemed to be a superior way of life. Hispanic culture descended upon native Californians like a comet from the heavens. Expeditions brought strangers from who knows where, and no shaman could say how many more would follow or where they had come from. Spanish soldiers—armed, mounted on horses, and armored with thick leather jackets that repelled arrows—demonstrated their powers and proved to be invincible warriors, capable of riding down any who threatened them. Padres walked authoritatively among them dressed in bright vestments proclaiming entirely new and at first incomprehensible ritual practices. Spanish technology—metal, glass, and ceramics—impressed natives, signifying great spiritual power. Chieftains were intimidated, awestruck. Nothing in their power matched that of the padres, who provided natives with food and promised much more. Submission seemed to open access to incredible spiritual riches and wondrous material goods. For people whose life was never easy, the newcomers might indeed offer a better way, more security, stronger medicine, a means to offset the power of rival tribes—or so it may have seemed at first.[7]

Few natives, if any, were carried off en masse. Natives often became mission field hands after watching one of the commonest of missionary conversion tactics, wherein the padres went among sick and dying children and baptized them, knowing that some would recover and that their grateful parents would likely entrust their children's care to powerful men who seemed able to control the forces of nature. Some natives were simply "hired" through their chiefs to sow wheat in exchange for blankets, corn, and other goods, then stayed on. Some became field hands after padres enticed clan elders or young chiefs to settle on the missions; these leaders in turn brought their relatives. Each new mission provoked the curiosity of nearby tribes, and small delegations often came to observe mission life. Many were enticed to stay. Occasionally smaller, less powerful tribes—or those who for some reason were being dominated by another group—perceived the padres and their soldiers as allies against their habitual opponents.[8]

But by far the largest numbers of natives became field hands by a well-developed process known as "spiritual fishing." The initial foray was an *entrada*, an extended recruiting drive in which the padre, accompanied and protected by soldiers, met and exchanged gifts with village tribal captains. The padre then presented natives with trinkets, cloth, utensils, and blankets, and accepted offerings of feathers, hides, and food. To people who devoted most of their energy to hunting for food and preparing it, and who lacked knowledge of weaving and metalworking, Spanish trade goods proved an especially powerful lure. Such *entradas* sparked considerable interest and gave the natives an opportunity to sample Franciscan hospitality and hear the padre's exhortations. Food also proved an important means of enticing dispersed peoples to receive the Christian message. Many responded so well when offered tortillas and bread that Padre Serra begged his superiors to send him more supplies of grain and corn in order for him to "employ in farm labor the necessary number of Indians." Once Indians received the holy waters of baptism, they were required to remain and work for the common good. They could not leave without permission. Those who gave up their faith and fled soon learned that the padres would send soldiers to hunt them down and, if necessary, whip and jail them into submission. This was justified because, as the padres asserted again and again, natives suffered from all kinds of cultural, emotional, physical, and intellectual defects. Unless they were properly controlled and collected at the mission, the poor natives would revert to their lazy, godless, primitive ways.[9]

Whatever brought and held them to the missions, new converts soon found themselves formed into two general categories of laborers—inside and outside workers. Inside workers remained on the mission compound, outside workers spread across the countryside. Inside workers constructed buildings, butchered cattle, repaired tools, made shoes, tended poultry, plastered walls, and assisted the padres as pages and personal servants. They became skilled artisans and craftsmen—masons, carpenters, tanners, blacksmiths, tallow makers, butchers, and meat dryers. A few at every mission excelled at art and were employed painting murals. But comparatively few were required for these tasks. Outside laborers—field hands working in the gardens, vineyards, orchards, and fields, and vaqueros who tended sheep and cattle and raised horses, mules, and burros—were far more numerous. Vaqueros were among the most trusted outside workers, comprising about 20 percent of the mission workforce, but field hands, who accounted for approximately 36 percent of all mission laborers, were by far the most important and numerous.[10]

One of the reasons so many natives wound up in the fields was the simple matter of survival. To keep new converts, every mission padre had to develop a reliable supply of food. For the first few years after the initial period of mission building, grains and other food supplies continued to be shipped north whenever possible, but none of the missions could base its long-term survival on such costly and uncertain arrangements. So the padres immediately set about locating and developing arable land, obtaining an adequate supply of water, and establishing farms.

Natives handled these tasks. On their backs rested the success or failure of each mission. Beyond keeping everyone well fed, their efforts aimed at producing a surplus. While there was little commercial value to increased agricultural production, extra rations were very useful in recruiting forays among various tribes and in raising morale during seasonal church festivals and celebrations. Failure to establish agriculture quickly could have a significant adverse effect on converting Indians. In fact, lack of food at San Francisco de Asís in 1774 and 1775 caused large numbers of Indians to leave, and a decade later caused such problems at Santa Barbara, Santa Inés, and La Purísima missions, that at times the padres could not feed nor manage their converts. For all of these reasons, a disproportionately large number of Indian men—of necessity—became field hands throughout the mission era.[11]

Most field hands were gang laborers and had little direct contact with padres. But a few immediately became skilled horticulturalists and gardeners. Working more closely with the padres than common field hands, they established and tended gardens, planted orchards and vineyards, and pruned and trained fruit trees and grapevines. Of necessity, they devoted much of their time to protecting their crops, often using their bows and arrows to shoot wild animals that wandered into their vegetable patches. Within a few years they surrounded the gardens with brush barriers and huge prickly-pear hedges. Eventually crews of skilled native craftsmen constructed eight-foot-high walls of adobe bricks, sometimes topped with cattle horns, to keep animals from grazing in the gardens and orchards. Of the work done by Indian gardeners at San José mission, where a small rivulet allowed easy irrigation, the explorer Georg Heinrich F. von Langsdorff reported on his 1806 visit that they "kept [it] in very good order; the soil is everywhere rich and fertile, and yields ample returns."[12]

Although farmwork involved many unfamiliar activities and a radical change in lifestyle, natives quickly learned the basics. Farmworkers at San Gabriel mission progressed so rapidly during the summer of 1774 that Padre Font pronounced himself "much pleased to see how the recently converted Indians applied themselves to the plow and to their tasks." Corresponding with church superiors, Serra reported much the same. Easily adopting Spanish tools, natives were "beginning to apply themselves diligently to work: some with hoes in hand, leveling the ground to increase our crops, others digging in the garden . . . carrying the sacks to the storehouse, and doing anything they are told." Natives also contributed their food gathering traditions to the survival of the missions. Beginning their grain harvest on July 18, field hands at Carmel mission cut and threshed grain from morning to noon, moved to the beach to harvest great schools of sardines in Monterey Bay, and devoted every evening to hanging their catch out to dry according to traditional methods. "The harvesting of the wheat, thus interrupted by fishing, lasted twenty-five days," wrote Serra. "I went to watch them, and as relaxation, it was as good as seeing a theater."[13]

Adapting well to farmwork, small groups of the most skilled Indian field hands shifted from older established missions like San Diego and San Juan Capistrano to new ones such as San Buenaventura and Santa Clara, where they trained neophytes in the rudiments of agriculture much as the peninsula field hands had trained them. In this way, local natives shouldered all of the farm tasks and accepted agricultural labor as one of their principal occupations. But even if field hands could have been employed more productively, the padres would not have done so. Labor efficiency was not a priority. Field hands were employed according to a policy that on the one hand was designed to produce enough food to feed and attract them and prevent them from leaving, and on the other hand was justified on the grounds that it kept Indians busy and diverted them from sin.[14]

Land clearing was done with the most rudimentary of tools, ranging in effectiveness from machetes and axes to hand rakes, crowbars, sharpened digging sticks, animal bones, and bare hands. Plows consisted of a sturdy, forked tree branch lashed to a long, heavy wooden beam. Spanish plows were yoked to a team of oxen by means of a straight branch tied behind the oxen horns with thongs so that, instead of pulling it by their shoulders as in northern Europe, the oxen drew the plows from their foreheads. Native plowmen walked to the side of the oxen, not directly behind them, guiding their plows with one hand and driving their teams with the other.[15]

Because the plows lacked moldboards and had only small "shares" (tips) of hammered metal, native farmworkers often could not cut through the hard top layer of dry, virgin ground and had to wait until a rain had softened the soil before going to work. With these crude instruments, which were always in disrepair, they gouged shallow ruts three or four inches deep, not furrows, crossing and recrossing fields many times, so that when they finished they spoke of a field as *la cruzada*—"the crossed one." Transfixed by the sight of ten Indian plowmen in the same field, each straining to reign in a team of oxen, Sir James Douglas, an English member of the Hudson's Bay Company who was staying at Santa Clara mission, found this technique curious and tedious. He later recalled how field hands were "all following in the same direction, but so irregularly that scarcely two furrows were in parallel line [as] they met, crossed and receded according to the vagaries of the cattle."[16]

Natives broadcast wheat and barley by hand, and because they lacked harrows, covered their seeds by drawing brush or logs across the field. In some cases they soaked the grain in water overnight to enhance germination. To cultivate corn, beans, and lesser garden crops, they simply dropped seeds into furrows, sometimes using a long stick to make holes for the seeds, then stomping them in with their feet. Occasionally field hands were able to plant without even slightly cultivating the land; so fertile was the soil around San José mission that field hands one fall harvested seven thousand bushels of wheat after having simply scattered 120 bushels of wheat on the bare damp ground the previous spring.[17]

To transport crops and materials, field hands used Spanish carts, or *carretas*, odd contraptions described by one traveler as "the rudest specimen of wheeled vehicle I have ever seen." Sporting a heavy and clumsy frame that rested directly on a wooden axle and large, spokeless, not very round, wheels made of three solid pieces of joined timber, these vehicles were drawn by a long pole running from the axle to the oxen yoke, which was attached in the same manner as the plow. With so much of the cartload placed on the horns and heads of the oxen, the animals surely experienced pain and distress with every jerk and twist of the cart. When combined with primitive road conditions, field hands often had difficulty leading the oxen and driving the carts. These problems were further compounded by flimsy construction methods. Held together entirely by wooden pegs and dowels and only rarely equipped with iron-rimmed wheels, *carretas* were forever breaking down and Indians field hands were constantly repairing them.[18]

Working under the supervision of Mexican artisans in 1786, field hands at Santa Cruz mission built the first, and for many years only, water-powered gristmill (consisting of a waterwheel connected to an upright axle by means of wooden gears). *Cucharas*, or large spoons made of timber, were inserted into the mortises on the edge of the wheel; the bowls of the spoons received the water and, acting as a kind of crude turbine, forced the wheel to turn with nearly the velocity of the water rushing along the stream or raceway diversion channel. Allowing four natives to do the work of one hundred using the traditional mortar and pestle method for grinding grain, the mill was ruined in a winter flood.[19]

The mill was never repaired, leaving field hands to grind their corn and wheat using extremely primitive methods that foreign travelers found rather odd. When von Langsdorff visited Santa Cruz mission in 1806, he discovered the abandoned mill and inquired why the padres still relied mainly on native women working laboriously over mortars and pestles, or on field hands operating ox-driven gristmills. "I learned that . . . the good Padres are actuated by political motives," he wrote in his journal. "As they have more men and women under their care than they could keep constantly employed the whole year, if labor were too much facilitated, they are afraid of making them idle by the introduction of mills."[20]

Between 1810 and 1812 the mason Claudio López, working under the direction of San Gabriel mission Padre José María Zalvidea, set Indians to constructing the second water-powered gristmill. Native artisans eventually constructed water-powered mills at San Antonio, San Luis Obispo, San Jose, Santa Inés, San Diego, and Santa Barbara missions. By the 1820s most missions had added *tahonas* (mills powered by mules, horses, and burros). But even then, old ways persisted. Native women on every mission spent large parts of each day seated before their metates (curved mortar stones) grinding wheat, maize, and corn. Many had to meet production quotas ranging from an average allotment of nine quarts, which translated into about six to eight pounds of flour, to a maximum quota of sixteen pounds. On Santa Barbara mission, nine women handled duties for making flour for bread, each day grinding about thirty quarts of soaked wheat. Only pregnant women and the aged were exempt from this tedious, endless, and absolutely essential task. But even then they were not allowed to remain idle and were instead assigned some other farm-related job like washing wool, pounding *casalote* (a plant used in dyeing wool), or pulling weeds in the gardens. Nor did nursing mothers escape work; once judged sufficiently recovered from childbirth, they were required to resume grinding wheat and corn, although at a temporarily reduced production quota.[21]

Only men went into the fields. This was due in part to the nature of farmwork at the time. Consisting of heavy manual tasks, mission farmwork was classic "stoop labor," rough, backbreaking work requiring field hands to toil in a stooped position for long periods of time. Planting, sowing, hoeing, ditch digging, and land clearing were all varieties of stoop labor. The corn harvest was always dreaded. Observing men picking the crop at Santa Clara mission, Duhaut-Cilly recalled how this was a "time of joy and mirth in the fields of France," but found "no sentiment of this nature . . . shown upon the features of the Indians busied in this labor; it was simple: let them harvest little or much, they could claim only their daily pittance, and little it mattered to them that there might be anything left over." But by far the most odious and exhausting labor was harvesting wheat and barley. At San Luis Obispo, San Gabriel, Santa Clara, and San Antonio missions, where the wheat and barley crops were especially large, all able-bodied men—including those who were not normally engaged in farmwork—curtailed other duties and were required to move into fields at harvest time. They had to do so because they usually had about three weeks to complete the harvest before the heads of grain began to shatter.[22]

Although sometimes portrayed as rather leisurely, somewhat pastoral, workers, mission wheat harvesters actually followed well-established, labor-intensive techniques, even when more efficient methods were available. For example, while many European and American farmworkers by 1770 were cutting three-foot-wide swaths of wheat from an upright position with long-handled scythes, mission field hands never used them. Nor did they have other common labor-saving tools like "cradles"—bent, knifelike devices, with rows of long curved teeth projecting upward—which when swung from a standing position placed the cut grain in small clusters that harvesters could gather easily. Wading into the wheat and barley fields, mission field hands used small, heavy sickles or saw-edged iron hooks not much different from Old Testament flint sickles. Occasionally they lacked any tools at all and resorted to knives and machetes to cut the straw. Consequently, native harvesters even very late in the mission era worked all day hunched over at the waist, cutting at the rate of one-fourth to one-half acre per day, considerably less than field hands on farms in the eastern United States.[23]

When field hands did straighten up, it was to carry the cut wheat on their backs to the *carretas* for transport to the threshing corral. Crews did not use flails—long poles connected to shorter poles by rope hinges allowing the thresher to swing the shorter pole with great force against stacks of wheat, smacking the straw and knocking the grain free. Rather, mission field hands threshed by treading the cut wheat with oxen or horses. Threshing operations began when field hands drove a herd of mares into a sixty-foot-wide, adobe-walled corral, piled high with wheat straw. As the horses ran, men dashed in front of them, whooping and yelling and forcing them to turn in the other direction. When the animals tired after about two hours, field hands substituted a second team, then another team, and so on until all the grain was off the straw. Two field hands and three horses could tread about thirty bushels of wheat per day, although the animals did not tread evenly, wasting much of the grain and befouling it with their droppings.[24]

After treading, another crew then separated chaff by winnowing (tossing it as high as possible into the air) with wooden forks and *bateas* (low-sided, wooden trays). Averaging about ten bushels per day—compared to a rate of twelve to fifteen bushels on most American farms at this time—winnowing was tedious, dusty, inefficient work. Native crews did not use riddles or basket sieves, which American harvest hands shook back and forth to separate chaff from grain. Relief from the drudgery of threshing, such as it was, took the form of a blessed breeze—or better, a series of windy days that cleared the choking air and separated the straw and chaff and seed so that winnowers did not have to toss it so high or so often. On a few missions, padres located their *eras* (winnowing stations) high on the crest of a windy knoll so the constant breeze could help speed up the work.[25]

৵৹

Besides performing stoop labor, the first generation of native men brought a number of other disparate and important characteristics into the California farm-worker experience. Within a decade of joining the missions, they began growing, tending, and harvesting grapes and making wine under Franciscan supervision. In popular writing the first such experiences are mistakenly located at San Diego mission, and erroneously dated back to 1769. But in fact, natives did not become involved in grape growing or winemaking until a decade later, toward the end of the 1770s—probably sometime after May 1779—not at San Diego mission, but at San Juan Capistrano mission, when Padre Pedro Pablo de Mugártegui set six Baja California campesinos to propagating vine cuttings shipped up from Mexico or Baja California. Working closely with Mugártegui, those six men planted more than two thousand grapevines in 1781. They probably first participated in winemaking at San Juan Capistrano mission during the fall of 1784, when the first crop ripened, possibly even as early as the previous year. For the next sixty years, Indian field hands on all of the Alta California missions would be occupied at regular intervals throughout the year with the tasks of pruning and training grapevines, multiplying cuttings, planting vineyards, and harvesting grapes. They also handled all of the attendant duties of winemaking, and, in conjunction with native craftsmen, constructed and maintained vats, buildings, presses, and other winemaking facilities.[26]

Their greatest winemaking accomplishment came at San Gabriel mission, where *viñaderos* (vineyard keepers) laboring over a half-century eventually created a 170-acre vineyard, *La Viña Madre* (the mother vineyard), with approximately fifty thousand vines. At the height of San Gabriel mission's winemaking operations in the 1820s, field hands picked tons of grapes daily, hauled them to the mission winery, and dumped them down a stone ramp directly into the wine cellar vat. Groups of strong young Indian men, *muy bien bañados* (carefully washed), with their hair tied up, legs shaved, and wearing only a loincloth, climbed into the vat. As assistants dumped pickings around their feet, the naked *viñaderos* stomped the grapes. Washing frequently and using a system of poles and ropes to keep them from falling into the slippery mess, they tried to remain as clean as possible, but by day's end they would inevitably be covered in a sweet, sticky, bug-infested, fermenting purple crust. Meanwhile, other Indians tended *coras* (leather bags) which caught the juice as it ran out of the vat, then emptied the full *coras* into large stone fermentation tanks or wooden tubs.[27]

Field hands began planting olives at San Diego mission around 1798 or 1799 (some reports suggest it was as early as 1790). Although olives could be grown from seed, it is most likely that field hands planted young shoots shipped up from the Baja California missions. After tending the young plants for a few years, men began gathering the crops by striking the tree limbs and knocking the olives with long slender poles. Placing the olives in woven baskets, women carried them off to be processed. If the olives were to be used as food, the men cured them in stone vats full of a lye mixture made of water and wood ashes, or kept them in tubs of fresh water for fifteen days, changing the water every other day. Usually they pickled the olives in jars filled with salt water, sometimes with a little fennel and other spices added.[28]

Extracting olive oil was a messy affair rivaling winemaking in complexity. At first, men simply dried the olives like raisins; elderly women would pound the olives and hang them up in a fine cloth so that the oil would drip out. Sometimes they would fill cloth bags with green olives, place them in hot water, then tread upon them to force the oil out. By 1810, the mission olive groves were producing at such a rate that these traditional processing methods were no longer adequate. This led to an important change when native field hands began employing grinding mills with huge stone wheels. Dumping olives into the mills and turning the wheels by mule power, they captured the "free run" oil in tubs beneath the grindstone, then scooped out the squashed olives and placed them into strong hemp sacks. These sacks were then set in screw presses and two or three especially strong men further squashed the olives by turning a bar inserted through a slot in the screw top. As in winemaking, the olive oil process required a sanitary environment. Consequently, field hands paid special care to filter bugs and debris out of the oil and to remain absolutely clean by washing and toweling themselves repeatedly throughout the workday. Following this quasi-industrial process, field hands at San Diego mission eventually met the demand for cooking oil and lamp oil on all of the missions, with plenty of surplus left over to be sold or traded to foreigners and among the missions.[29]

By 1834, mission field hands had cultivated and were maintaining about ten thousand acres of land. They could also boast of another enduring agricultural accomplishment, although few people realized its significance at the time. This was their construction of irrigation systems. Most chroniclers of mission life attribute this work to construction crews working under the direction of skilled Mexican artisans, omitting any mention of other laborers. But almost from the moment that Baja California campesinos supervised the first dams of brush, earth, and rocks and diverted water into open ditches to irrigate fields in the 1770s, mission field hands were constantly occupied with the task of securing adequate supplies of water for domestic and agricultural purposes. And while specialized crews did supervise and direct much of the work, they often found themselves shorthanded and in need of supplementary labor, particularly when confronted with the drudgery of mixing tons of mortar and hauling rocks to construct impounding dams. At San Juan Capistrano, field hands even excavated ditches and laid a system of underground clay pipes, which distributed water to various rooms in the dormitories and shops. Occupied with such backbreaking work for years, field hands moved continually from hoeing, planting, and harvesting to canal and dam construction, and then back again.[30]

At San Diego mission between 1813 and 1816, field hands assisted artisans in building an elaborate 245-foot-long stone and concrete storage reservoir that backed up water in Mission Gorge to a depth of twelve feet. Without that reservoir, the mission could not have survived. But field hands and craftsmen did much more than merely impound water. At San Diego mission and elsewhere they laid stone for filtration systems and erected massive masonry aqueducts, often traversing miles of varied terrain and bridging ravines and creeks in order to deliver potable water to the mission quadrangles. Some efforts were truly heroic. To water San Gabriel mission's pea, wheat, and barley fields, crews equipped with digging tools of cattle shoulder blades spent most of one year excavating a ten-mile-long canal bringing water from the San Bernardino Mountains to a mission farm near present-day Redlands. At San Buenaventura mission, field hands supervised by Mexican artisans extended an aqueduct five miles from the Ventura foothills to the barrel-vaulted stone filter house beside the mission chapel.[31]

Building and sustaining these and other infrastructure elements, native men became proficient in a wide range of allied crafts and industries. They maintained complicated quarrying operations, built limekilns, crushed and burned hundreds of tons of limestone and seashells to make mortar, developed clay pipe manufacturing plants, and produced thousands of precisely fitted clay water pipes. A rudimentary form of modern agribusiness, their labors produced lush and verdant crops in the midst of what was essentially desert, and established the locations where irrigated agriculture would first impact California.[32]

Along with winemaking, olive oil processing, and irrigation, child labor also began at this time. Although the use of children in the fields did not gain common, widespread acceptance until the 1920s—and is usually attributed to the rise of Mexican family labor and the impact of the automobile as a means for carrying migrant families among crops—the roots of child labor extend back to the mission fields. Most young mission Indian girls were allowed to enjoy their childhood free of arduous farm tasks and did not go into the fields, except to assist their mothers occasionally in gathering up threshed grain. And in general, boys did not engage in fieldwork until age fourteen—but a few were always set to work. "Stirrup boys," as they were called, started as early as nine years of age walking beside the crew bosses as they rode their horses around the fields, always available to carry messages, fetch things, and generally assist in the fields.[33]

Other boys pulled weeds in the gardens, gathered olives, and chased animals out of the ripening crops. Because birds, locusts, squirrels, and caterpillars were constantly attacking mission farms, and because these pests often caused considerable damage if left unchecked, children who picked bugs off plants, snared rodents, and scared away crows and blackbirds performed work that was essential to successful mission farming. The most patient of these children served as watchmen at San Juan Capistrano mission where, perched beneath brush sunshades on top of observation towers all day, they banged on drums to drive flocks of birds out of the vineyards and orchards. For this they were known as *pajareros*—"bird-herders" and "bird-catchers."[34]

৶৯

Like their modern counterparts, mission field hands lived a barracks existence. They were initially quartered in essentially the same tule and brush shelters as those built by the campesinos from Baja California. Indian laborers started constructing somewhat better quarters—of willow-pole walls filled in with mud and covered with thatched roofs—in the late 1770s. In the early 1780s, field hands further improved living conditions by constructing communal dormitories and ten-by-ten-foot single-family apartments made of thick, sun-dried, adobe bricks. Beginning in the mid-1790s, Mexican artisans began directing native craftsmen to lay out long wings of apartments and dormitories either extending out from the sides of churches or placed close by in neat, parallel rows. At Santa Barbara mission, married field hands and other workers by 1807 were living in 252 houses located west of the quadrangle. Measuring twelve by eighteen feet, each had a door and movable window, and was stacked back to back, with their doors opening on to streets or corridors. Living space of 216 square feet was comparable to that allocated to slaves on plantations in the Chesapeake low country. With their red-tiled roofs, white stucco exterior plastering to protect against prevailing weather, interior whitewashed walls, and some arrangement for a fire pit, a 3,300-foot-long, 8-½-foot-high adobe wall surrounded everything, a huge communal orchard and garden, and stone paths leading to the dormitories, apartments, church complex, mission quadrangle, and communal kitchen, the Santa Barbara quarters were extremely well planned, warm, and safe, and marked both the first and last time farmhands enjoyed housing on a par with that of their bosses.[35]

At San Antonio mission, married and single male field hands lived in similar dormitories consisting of contiguous twelve-by-fifteen-foot rooms arranged in three wings several hundred feet long, shaped like a backward C, and enclosing the orchard. One entire wing was equipped with a corridor supported by pillars of adobe and brick and roofed with tiles, and it was here that field hands stored lumber and *carretas*. Sun-dried adobe bricks secured with adobe mortar and set on cobblestone foundations laid in shallow trenches formed the dormitory walls, with the footings extending up one foot above the original ground surface to prevent waterlogging and slumping at the base of the adobe walls. Kiln-fired tiles provided a waterproof roof, and each room was plastered inside and out and had a hearth at its center. Furniture was minimal, sometimes consisting of one or two boarded beds with rush mats, and perhaps a table of sorts. Floors were adobe, packed firmly and polished in some areas, and many rooms also sported lean-tos in the rear, presumably used as storage spaces in which to keep food, personal belongings, and on occasion, pilfered goods. Three-foot-wide doors provided a measure of privacy and security, although none appears to have had locks of any kind. Quarters also had milling stones near each doorway, indicating that food processing occurred nearby. Archaeological investigations have discovered animal bones and fire pits in the front yards, suggesting that field hands cooked and prepared meals both inside and outside their rooms and were not entirely dependent on having food prepared for them at the communal kitchen.[36]

Archaeological excavations of the San Antonio mission dormitories also disclosed that field hands possessed large stores of vessels used in food preparation and consumption, particularly coarse tableware—plates, bowls, cups, serving dishes, cooking pots—produced by mission and Mexican lead-glaze methods.

But while locally made ceramics comprised eight of ten recovered pieces of kitchenware, imported majolica and European and Chinese ceramics comprised two-thirds of the recovered tablewares. Archaeologists have theorized that this suggests that field hands in the Salinas Valley had adopted European tastes, or at least attained some level of acculturation and acceptance of European cultural values on the household level, although the predominance of imported items may also suggest nothing more than trading patterns over which field hands had little control. Dormitories also contained numerous small *braseros* (small stoves or metal fire pans), shards of green bottle glass, and fragments of clear pane glass, suggesting that some rooms had windows and numerous metal artifacts, principally iron knife and axe blades, scissors, hinges, nails, chisels, needles, hooks, and locks. An occasional dormitory room exhibited an inexplicable number of comforts, as in one dwelling that was paved with *ladrillos*—fired clay tiles, many of them decorated with circles, crosses, and diagonal lines scribed in the wet clay before firing—suggesting that the room was occupied by an Indian of some status, or that it was used for some special purpose. Ceramics in that room also consisted mostly of imported tableware, whereas most other rooms held mission pottery associated with cooking, a difference suggesting that an extended family was using the room, or that some field hands for some reason had access to European goods.[37]

Mission barracks never housed all field hands, and as late as the 1820s, farmworkers on a half-dozen missions were still living along with other natives beside the mission compounds in crowded, flea-infested villages complete with chicken yards and animal pens. Others were required, like modern farmworkers, to accept semipermanent quarters in what were, in effect, labor camps. These camps, or *estancias* (mission farm outposts), were established early on in the mission era, when it became clear that many mission sites were ill-suited to agriculture. Because their locations had often been decided for other reasons—usually by the proximity to a presidio or Indian village—only San Gabriel and Santa Clara missions could demonstrate much promise for substantial agricultural development. Most others lacked some key resource, such as arable land, a conveniently located water supply, or a warm climate suitable for growing specific crops. For this reason, the missions maintained a sprawling complex of outlying ranchos and farms, which had the additional advantage of allowing baptized Indians to remain in or near their rancherías while working for the mission. Often described as miniature missions, many *estancias* had storehouses, dormitories, homes for *mayordomos*, chapels, threshing floors, and wineries. Probably the most extensive chain of *estancias* ringed San Luis Rey mission, where eight mission farms, each specializing in a particular crop, spread over nearly one thousand square miles of what is present-day San Diego and Riverside counties. One of these *estancias*, Las Flores, had numerous tile-roofed buildings, including at least one wing with a second story, and a campanile so large it served as a navigational landmark, all arranged around a square measuring 142 by 153 feet.[38]

Located at more agriculturally advantageous sites, *estancias* were often as distant as a half-day's journey from their parent mission. The first was founded in 1774, when padres at San Diego mission opened a corral for mares and horses at nearby San Luis rancho. Most missions relied on three or four such *estancias* to provide both livestock and food crops; San Miguel mission operated six *estancias*, including a very successful bean and corn ranch; Santa Barbara mission's *estancia*, a particularly picturesque outpost, consisted of a little adobe in the middle of a well-cultivated orchard near a large ranchería, six miles distant from the mission, where field hands also grew wheat and made wine. But the mission also had numerous other lesser farm outposts, including a nine-acre vineyard with 2,262 vines and one hundred fruit trees near present-day Goleta; two other vineyards with 3,695 vines; corn and bean farms at San José and El Abajo, also near Goleta, and at San Juan Bautista and El Suazal; and wheat and corn farms at Dos Pueblos, San Esteban, Toquini, and San Miguel de Mescaltitán. Each had its own force of vineyardists, gardeners, and field hands.[39]

While some field hands and caretakers resided on the *estancias* year-round, most stayed in these agricultural camps only temporarily. Entire crews would travel out to them during June, July, and August for the wheat harvest, or in September and October to pick grapes and make wine, or for some similar job, only to return to the missions after finishing their seasonal work. At La Puente, an *estancia* nine miles distant from San Gabriel mission, more than six hundred field hands were thus employed every year, so many that Padre José Zalvidéa in 1816 built a chapel to minister to their needs. In 1791 as many as three hundred field hands—nearly half of all the Indians of San Francisco de Asís mission, where high winds, fog, and constantly drifting sand made farming nearly impossible—worked at San Pedro y San Pablo farming station near present-day Pacifica. At San Miguel mission, 190 natives worked at an even larger camp known as Paso Robles.[40]

Trudging the trails between the missions and *estancias*, native field hands were, in effect, California's first migrant farmworkers—or, more precisely, the first farmworkers to migrate between jobs. With climate and weather setting their schedules by delaying and advancing the harvest, seasonal rhythms governed their regimen. Field hands might devote most of August to harvesting wheat and storing it, spend all of September carrying shelled corn to granaries, and finish up October by hoeing weeds and cleaning up the cemetery in preparation for *El Dia de Los Muertos* (Day of the Dead) celebrations. In between farmwork, they labored at innumerable other jobs. When necessary, they cut fence rails, pitched in at the limekilns and brickyard, assisted in the slaughter yard or helped out in the soap factory. Every February, when most farmwork ceased, many would turn their attention to making candles, the principal means of illumination.[41]

In the winter, field hands excavated tree trunks and ripped out roots in the fields they were perpetually expanding and improving. While crops ripened, they repaired corrals and laid out paving stones on the floors of the threshing corrals. They also assisted in the gardens, improved irrigation systems, dug holes to plant orchard trees, and harvested and dried fruit. They also raised peas and lentils, which they gathered, threshed, dried, and stored in clay containers and leather bags. Winter to spring, mission field hands followed essentially the same seasonal sequence of farm tasks that their successors followed two centuries later.[42]

૭ટ

As the missions became established, the process by which field hands were recruited changed. Civilian communities, or pueblos, were established, the first in 1777 at San José de Guadalupe, south of Santa Clara mission, where Spanish authorities hoped that settlers would produce sufficient food to feed the soldiers and reduce their dependence on the missions and supply ships. Immediately successful, San José in 1781 was producing two thousand bushels of grain and feeding both the presidios of Monterey and San Francisco. By the summer of 1787, however, the quiet little settlement beside the Guadalupe River that had been established by Anza expedition leader José Moraga was producing such large crops of beans, wheat, and corn that the several hundred *pobladores* (founders), mestizos, and *mulatos* (half-breeds) who comprised its population could no longer keep up with the tasks of cultivating and harvesting. To help out, Santa Clara mission sent mission Indians to work in the pueblo's fields. Because the pueblo flooded every year, ruining fields and leaving hungry livestock shivering in belly-deep water, the Indians were immediately put to work helping to relocate the town and clear new fields. Within a few years, however, Fermín Francisco de Lasuén, successor to Padre Serra as president of the Franciscan missions of Alta California from 1785 to 1803, began denouncing the practice of loaning out mission Indian field hands as a "bad example." He was particularly bothered by three aspects of the arrangement. One was the way settlers employed field hands "indiscriminately for all their house and field work," thereby avoiding any hard physical labor themselves. Worse, by taking from the missions such large numbers of Indians, settlers acted as "an immense hindrance to the conversion of the pagans." Finally, Lasuén objected to the settlers' use of liquor—and other temptations of the flesh and spirit—which "scandalize them [Indians], and . . . actually persuade them not to become Christians, lest they would themselves suffer the loss of free labor." Despite these concerns, Lasuén did not terminate the arrangement, largely because such action might threaten or severely impede the very survival of fledgling Spanish colonies on the Pacific Coast. Instead, Lasuén approved a scheme whereby padres at Santa Clara mission stopped providing field hands free of charge; rather, they began renting them out for grain, hides, and other goods necessary to the financially strapped missions.[43]

The same pattern held at El Pueblo de Nuestra Señora la Reina de los Angeles de Río de Porciúncula (Town of Our Lady the Queen of the Angels), the small, isolated adobe village settled in 1781 by forty-four immigrants from Sinaloa, most of them mestizos. Given a house, lot, and fields on which to grow irrigated crops, settlers here—like their counterparts at San José—had been promised a monthly salary of ten pesos for three years, in addition to a loan of thirteen farm animals, a variety of farm tools, a musket, knife, and leather shield. Required to sell any surplus crops to the presidios at fair prices, they too found it impossible to handle all of the many farm tasks, especially construction of a dam to divert water from the river as well as digging and maintaining irrigation ditches. Within a few years San Gabriel mission began renting natives to the settlers. Working in roughly thirty-six fields covering 250 acres between the town plaza and the river, rented mission field hands quickly took over farm tasks and became the backbone of pueblo agriculture.[44]

Rented mission field hands performed approximately the same work for settlers attempting to farm at Santa Barbara, San Luis Obispo, and San Francisco de Asís missions, and after 1797, at the pueblo of Villa de Branciforte, near present-day Santa Cruz. Employed for periods ranging from a few weeks to several months and working as individuals, in pairs, and in small gangs, they chopped tules, mucked out irrigation ditches, prepared fields, harvested grain, and cultivated gardens around the governor's orchard. As the number of rented field hands increased, they began to provoke commentary from foreign visitors, who, like Lasuén, observed indolent, lazy pueblo farmers idling away the hours with a deck of cards, or drinking, gambling, and pursuing Indian women. The Russian traveler Krill Timofeevich Khlebnikov said later that settlers "do practically nothing and, if they can get Indians from the mission to work, walk around with arms folded, telling the Indians what to do." But while practical realities led settlers to rent field hands, the mission's own financial considerations also influenced the arrangement. At wages of one and a half to two reales a day (about six cents American money) or the equivalent in goods, and up to three reales a day when teamed with mules to clear rocks from fields, rented mission field hands were cheap, and their wages, kept by the missions, brought in the equivalent of hundreds of dollars per year to the mission treasury.[45]

CHAPTER THREE

Always Trembling With Fear

Controlling Mission Farmworkers

On the morning of September 15, 1786, French navigator Jean François de La Pérouse and an exploration party of eminent scientists, navigators, cartographers, and illustrators rowed through the fog of Monterey Bay to the mouth of the Carmel River. The first European visitors to Alta California since Sir Francis Drake in 1579, the men spent the next ten days observing mission life as part of a massive exploration and mapping program for the French government. After several days touring the area and taking detailed notes, La Pérouse became appalled by mission living conditions, nauseated by mission gruel, and alarmed by the sight of mission natives dressed not in European clothes or even the standard mission uniform but in ragged animal skins. But it was not just these deprivations that La Pérouse found so appalling. "Corporal punishment is inflicted on the Indians of both sexes who neglect the exercises of piety," he wrote, "and many sins, which in Europe are left to Divine justice, are here punished by irons and stocks." He had apparently reached the limit of his tolerance when he encountered a group of natives as they received a holiday gift of a cow. Quickly skinning the animal, they "croaked with pleasure," savoring and devouring the raw fat as a delicious treat.[1]

Again and again, scenes at Carmel mission suggested that for field hands life under the padres was hardly an uplifting experience. Reminded of African slaves in the Caribbean Islands, La Pérouse wrote, the "color of these Indians . . . the house of the missionaries; their storehouses . . . the appearance of the ground on which the grain is trodden out; the cattle, the horses . . . brought to our recollection a plantation at Santo Domingo or any other West Indian island." La Pérouse, whose posthumously published journals would become the basis for innumerable indictments of the treatment of the first generation of native California farmworkers, left this sojourn to Carmel mission with feelings of incredulity and pity. It was the response many people had when they saw field hands on the Spanish missions.[2]

FIGURE 5. Looking out from the courtyard at San Carlos de Borromeo mission, the artist José Cardero captured a typical scene, with Hispanic colonists and visitors from the Malaspina expedition mingling in the foreground, and the Indian ranchería in the left background. On the right, a long line of buildings served as quarters for field hands and shelter for various activities. A *carreta* stands in the left foreground. Lithograph based on a drawing made in 1791. Courtesy of the Museo Naval, Madrid. Photograph courtesy Robin Inglis, Vancouver Spanish Pacific Historical Society.

Whether they came early or late in the mission era, people who encountered mission farmworkers were often overcome with horror or dismay. George Vancouver, a British sea captain who toured San Francisco de Asís, Santa Clara, and Carmel missions in 1794, described miserable and apathetic people living in abject squalor and going about their tasks with a "mechanical, lifeless, careless indifference." Overcome by the combination of constant gloom and dreary, immutable routine he encountered at San Francisco de Asís mission in 1816, Russian naval captain Otto von Kotzebue later wrote that: "A deep melancholy always clouds their faces and their eyes are constantly fixed on the ground." An artist traveling with the von Kotzebue expedition, Louis Choris, emphasized: "I have never seen one laugh. They look as though they were interested in nothing." Under house arrest in 1826, a clerk with the Jedediah Smith fur-trapping party spent considerable time observing his San Gabriel mission surroundings. He soon found himself unable to tolerate the sight of natives working in the nearby vineyards and fields. "They are kept in great fear, and for the least offense they are corrected," he confided in his diary. "They are . . . complete slaves in every sense of the word." Again and again, from the 1780s into the 1830s, American visitors, European explorers, and even one governor of Alta California, Felipe Neve, all looked at mission field hands and agreed: A dreadful, pathetic mockery was taking place. The very institution that supposedly saved field hands had, in truth, degraded them. In the name of the Lord, Franciscan padres kept field hands in strict "bondage" and absolute "vassalage," under a "rigid system of unremitting supervision" making them "worse than slaves."[3]

Without completely appreciating it, these observers each identified one of the primary reasons for the woeful existence of mission field hands. From a life without clocks, where time was told by the changing of the seasons and by remembering where the sun rose each day in relation to the same landmark, the requirements of regular, scheduled labor must have seemed the very antithesis of their traditional way of life. And to people who did not possess tools to break the ground, did not control animals, and were accustomed to untamed nature, the simple act of becoming a field hand engaged in planting and tending crops and working in gardens surrounded by adobe walls surely was strange. Most of all, mission field hands now found themselves exceedingly closely supervised and directed, and it was this characteristic that visitors found so unforgettable—their depressingly dull lives, coupled with a tedious, immutable, and almost obsessively day-in, day-out, lifelong routine. Hardly governed by a labor relations system guided by the hand of God, mission field hands were, for their time and place, an exceedingly closely supervised class.[4]

Franciscans placed heavy emphasis on an unbroken calendar of activities, believing it was essential to fill the long days and keep everyone active and involved. To accomplish this, they employed a wide variety of rewards, punishments, and rules. And no single mechanism was more important in setting the schedule of labor, dividing the day into discernible units, and reminding field hands who was in charge than the mission bells. Field hands worked, played, prayed, ate, slept, married, and were even born and buried according to a system of bells. Suspended in modest, ground-level platforms of heavy wooden beams, or hung from tree limbs, work bells were small and plain. Issuing a loud, harsh, metallic, clanging sound that was audible fifteen miles away, work bells directed field hands into constant, diligent farm work. In juxtaposition were the large, beautifully decorated prayer bells. Often housed in elaborate towers of stone and tile, in "bell walls" adorned with cupolas, and in elaborate *espadañas*, prayer bells, also known as *esquilas* and "glad bells," called forth not only devotion, but baptisms, weddings, and deaths. Rung by the padres or teams of young boys, the prayer bells made a melodious music described by Chumash Indian Fernando Librado as like "the glorious sweet voice of God."[5]

Field hands first heard the voice of God just before sunrise, when the prayer bell woke them for mass. They continued hearing prayer bells as they trudged through the darkness to attend devotion, and again sometimes at the conclusion of services. At the sound of work bells around 9 A.M., Indians assembled in the quadrangle or some other previously designated point, picked up their tools, received instructions, and marched off to start the day's labor. They remained at their posts until a bell tolled out a lunch break around 11 A.M. Following a siesta, work bells sent them back to the fields at 2 P.M. (3 P.M. in winter), and summoned them for evening prayers at 5 P.M. An hour later the prayer bell rang them to supper. At 8 P.M. the Poor Souls' Bells announced curfew and finally, at 9 P.M., one of the *esquilas* commanded the Indians to retire to quarters. Except for Sunday, when field labor ceased and the work bells were not rung, the sequence never changed.[6]

But bells alone did not compel obedience. Over time, field hands acquired an understanding of how plants could be grown and harvested and some notion of how they fit into that process. They toiled in service to the missions and became —through supervision, religious instruction, regulated hours, and adherence to a Gregorian calendar—practically (if not entirely devoted) Christians. The greatest taskmaster of all, however, was fear of punishment.[7]

Just how much fear and how much punishment mission field hands endured has long been a matter of heated debate. Two centuries after the missions passed from the scene, farmworker activists, Chicano scholars, Indian historians, and mission revisionists continue to argue that the beautiful, beloved missions so cherished as cultural icons marking the beginnings of civilization in California were neither uplifting nor holy, and that they imposed on farmworkers the terrible, crippling, and evil legacy of colonial oppression, racial subjugation, and unending hellish work. To such assertions, latter-day Franciscans and church historians respond that natives were, in effect, children who acquired their knowledge of farm work, as they did everything else, through patient instruction from devoted teachers. They also point out that Indians overwhelmingly outnumbered the Spaniards all through the mission era, and therefore field hands, and other Indian workers, could have easily refused to work; they must have willingly gone about their business, so the argument goes, because the missions were such a vast improvement in their lives. "Few labor unions today," wrote Santa Barbara mission historian Maynard Geiger, "have even reached the working hour schedule, the fringe benefits or the social security of the California Indians."[8]

It is now possible to speak with authority on the nature of mission discipline and control. The evidence is available—indeed, most of it has always been available—and it comes down on the side of those stressing how it was impossible for mission field hands to benefit from a system that reduced them to childish dependence, prepared them for nothing, exposed them to diseases and unsanitary conditions, and gave them few, if any, individual rights. Field hands could not marry without permission, own personal property, dress as they liked, pursue their own religion, choose their line of work, hire out their labor, move about freely late at night, possess weapons, cuss, drink alcohol, or even enter the gardens to gather fruit unsupervised. The padres would not permit it. They had all the power, made all decisions, set all goals. They would not even permit field hands to raise their own children. Knowing from experience that children raised under mission guidance would be much more likely to become at least partly Hispanicized than those reared by their parents—especially field hands who had been recently converted—the padres routinely divided up families and took control of children.[9]

Teenage boys on many missions had to leave their mothers and fathers and bunk with single men in a *jayunte*, or dormitory. Similarly, all girls over age eight were required to live in a *monjerío*, a kind of monastery. There were no exceptions. That was because the padres were much less concerned about male virtue and promiscuity if they could be assured that all the women were cloistered. So important were the girls' dormitories that they were always one of the first buildings erected following establishment of a mission, usually within a year or two of founding. Fitted with bunks and sometimes with latrines, patios, and bathing pools, and holding fifty to one hundred women and girls, *monjeríos* were often crowded, uncomfortable, and unsanitary. The *monjerío* at Santa Barbara mission, for example, was forty-seven feet long and nineteen feet wide and held between fifty and one hundred women and girls. Sleeping platforms six feet wide ran the length of the two longest walls, but could not hold all the women, some of whom had to sleep on tule mattresses on the floor. A fire provided heat, tallow candles illuminated the interior, and a single, wide window high on one wall provided ventilation. When Governor Diego Borica inspected one *monjerío* in 1797, he discovered a "small, poorly ventilated, and infested" facility so revolting to his senses that in his annual report he described not being able to stomach the sight and smell "even for a minute."[10]

Young Indian girls in each *monjerío* were under the general care of a *maestra* (usually an Indian matron or wife of one of the soldiers), who "never lost sight of them" as they assisted at various tasks and kept the girls "secure from insult" and the ravages of licentious boys and diseased soldiers. Always locking the girls in at night, and delivering the *monjerío* key to the padre, the *maestras* taught the daughters of field hands and other native laborers how to sew and weave, grind corn and grain, cook, hoe, wash clothes, "keep clean," and "be like little Spaniards." In this way, girls were removed from their customary tribal traditions of premarital cohabitation. Kept immaculate of body, "educated" for matrimony, and indoctrinated in the ways of the church and crown, the daughters of mission field hands remained sequestered in the *monjerío* until they married. If they did not marry, they lived in the *monjerío* until they died. Likewise, sons of field hands who were raised in the mission dormitories quickly became accustomed to and familiar with mission rules.[11]

One of the strictest of these rules was the prohibition from riding horses. If their names were not on a list held by the corporals of the guard, young Indian men who were not vaqueros could not get near the corrals. And if they were caught on horseback, they were arrested and punished. By allowing natives to ride and control horses, missionaries and civil authorities feared that they were, in some ways, elevating them beyond their proper place, since the Spanish term for gentleman, *caballero*, was someone who, literally, rode on a horse. But the main reason for the policy was the pervasive fear that field hands who learned horsemanship would be more rebellious.[12]

Field hands were further controlled and reminded of the doctrine of God and work by certain key aspects of mission architecture. For one, they were profoundly influenced by the church structure itself, so much so, in fact, that the padres constantly labored to preserve and improve its mystique. Even the plain, adobe mission churches, with their plastered walls and their extensive decorations and furnishings, must have seemed resplendent to people accustomed to living in brush huts. On the more established missions, those with elaborately adorned churches, the feeling must have been even more intense. For some field hands, the mission church must have seemed a place of wonder and curiosity, a glorious retreat.[13]

No single architectural feature so continuously projected the aura of power as the tall bell towers. Beginning as simple *espadañas* or raised gable ends of church buildings with openings in them to hold bells, towers became increasingly elaborate as the missions prospered and expanded. Field hands could see these bell towers from miles away. Even at night, far out in the countryside, they could spot the small lanterns on top of the tallest bell towers at Santa Barbara, San Luis Rey, and San Buenaventura missions. Unavoidable, the towers served as clear marks of authority. No other symbol—not even the churches themselves—intruded into the lives of mission field hands so completely.[14]

Nearly as important to every field hand was the mission's quadrangle or central plaza. These communal areas were created by arranging all of the mission buildings around a central courtyard that included a fountain, wash trough, and sundial. At Santa Barbara, San Luis Obispo, and San Juan Capistrano missions, field hands frequented quadrangles that covered several acres, contained many workshops, and were subdivided into large patios. On other missions, like the San Miguelito *estancia*, field hands passed through quadrangles that were smaller and more intimate. Such natives enjoyed quadrangles that were cool, comfortable, intimate, and patiolike. But whether large or small, elaborate or plain, no other place on the missions was as important to native field hands and certainly none was more frequented or more central to directing their daily routine.[15]

Field hands typically received their work assignments in the mission quadrangle, and passed through at least three times a day on their way to and from mass and meals. Single men living in the dormitories were always out and about. Mornings would find them on the sunny side of an east-facing wall, where they could warm up while enjoying their meal. During lunch break on a hot day, they could be found lounging in the shade of the corridors; evenings they hung around the communal kitchen, which never closed, and served as a kind of meeting room from which they diverted themselves with music, dancing, and various games. Women washed clothes every day in the quadrangle laundry basin, or nearby, and on Sundays men played games on the quadrangle grounds.[16]

Day in, day out, Indian field hands spent more time in the quadrangle than they did in church. And because they congregated there at predictable times, doing predictable things, and because the quadrangle workshops, quarters, and kitchens were visible through doors that opened only to the inside of the courtyard, field hands were easily monitored. To further track movement, many of the larger missions employed gatekeepers to scrutinize the entrances, lock the gates at 9 P.M., and unlock them at sunrise. At San Juan Bautista mission, natives entered the kitchen one by one through a turnstile in the doorway, obtained their meals, then moved through another door leading back to the plaza.[17]

Even in church, field hands did not escape scrutiny. Although they may not have known it, field hands at San Gabriel mission were watched by padres through mirrors installed in the altar and sacristy. Those not chanting the Te Deum or singing the *Alabado* were easily noted and disciplined. Field hands were also continuously bombarded with lectures, sermons, and reprimands meant to imbue the Spanish work ethic in them. The essence of these admonitions was that indolence violated the laws of heaven, that disobedience resulted in punishment—not only in the temporal world, but in the afterlife as well—and that eternal salvation was the reward for productive, loyal service.

In the name of God, padres encouraged field hands to confess their sins. They probed their dreams and their personal lives, and asked if they had been thorough in their tasks, if they had plowed diligently, whether they had properly scattered seeds during planting. If not, they told field hands to repeat the appropriate prayers to atone for their sinful work habits. As a means of further ensuring devoted labor, the priests read all the names in the *Padrón*, the mission register containing information on everyone, and required the natives to answer to the roll call. Finally, field hands at San Luis Rey mission and several others were required (along with all other natives) to kiss the Bible or the padre's hand as they left church on Sundays. In this way field hands were further observed and checked, and those missing noted and punished.[18]

To alleviate the routine of daily labor and generate enthusiasm for their life on the missions, field hands were rewarded with numerous fiestas. These events, part of church tradition and deeply entrenched in Hispanic society, were adapted to the local situation. For example, diligent field hands who had participated in some especially arduous activity—like constructing an aqueduct or dam or planting a vineyard or orchard—were always honored in an elaborate ritual. Typically the padres and Indian assistants bearing holy water and burning incense would lead a long procession out to the new field or canal to bless it, and the people who had worked on it. Likewise, plowmen were honored every year on May 3, at the festival of San Isidro, el Labrador (Saint Isidore, the Plowman), patron saint of those who cultivate the soil. In this festival, four plowmen carried a statue of San Isidro through the fields as hundreds of field hands singing and chanting the prescribed hymns and prayers followed in a procession.[19]

The most elaborate festival of the year coincided with the conclusion of the fall wheat harvest. Reapers would ceremoniously cut the last four sheaves of grain in the field, tie them to poles in the shape of a cross, and carry them in a procession to the church. The harvesters would then receive a blessing before the congregation celebrated mass. Everyone then enjoyed a two-day celebration in which they played games, ate large meals of barbecued beef, and spent the evening singing, dancing, and relaxing around bonfires. Those field hands winning footraces, archery, or dance contests received prizes of clothing or food. Festivals broke the monotony of work and church, reinforced Christian themes, incorporated recognizable components of native culture into mission life, and transformed the missions, at times, into the equivalent of a rural carnival. They were the best compensation that hardworking field hands would receive. But they were hardly the main reason that men toiled so diligently in the fields.[20]

§ð

From early on in the mission era, field hands worked under *mayordomos, alcaldes,* and *regidores*—mission officials charged with overseeing the day-to-day field operation. Of these three, *mayordomos* were by far the most important. Overburdened by farm tasks, Junípero Serra in his Representación to Viceroy Bucareli in the spring of 1773 demanded the ability to appoint *mayordomos* because, "the Padre cannot attend personally to everything, nor would he know how to direct all the manual work that comes up, for at the monastery they did not teach him this." Obtaining this right in 1774, Serra by the 1780s had at least one *mayordomo* at every mission; on the larger missions many managers and assistants shared duties. Chosen from among the soldiers of the mission guard, *mayordomos* were often paid in kind—typically six steers and six sheep annually, approximately twenty-one quarts of corn and about three quarts of beans weekly, plus all necessary rations of candles. Those receiving wages averaged between sixty and 144 pesos per year, and sometimes were also provided with a manservant.[21]

Critics of farm labor have sometimes described *mayordomos* as abusive slave drivers, and there is some justification for this characterization. Pablo Tac, a Luiseño Indian born on San Luis Rey mission in 1822 and sent to continue his education in Italy, wrote a critical description of *mayordomos* as part of a larger document concerning mission life. One aspect that stuck in his mind was the oppressive work regimen and the role that *mayordomos* played in enforcing the schedule. Every evening, Tac recalled, these men walked through the farmworkers' quarters announcing the location, assembly place, and nature of the next day's work: "Tomorrow morning . . . the sowing [or some similar instructions] begins," followed by designation of a convenient meeting place. There was no room for lingering or malingering, stressed Tac; everyone did as told. "In the morning you will see the laborers appear in the chicken yard and assemble there according to what they heard last night."[22]

Amassing considerable power and extensive responsibilities, *mayordomos* in their capacity as general directors and supervisors of agriculture exercised great authority over field hands, in some instances, even more than the padres. Besides supervising labor, they also distributed staple foods to the cooks for each meal, oversaw food preparation and distribution, parceled out tools and locked them up, allocated clothes, arbitrated disputes, and, in cases of a padre's extended absence, essentially ran all of the mission's vital activities. When crossed, *mayordomos* could do what they wanted. At least one left his mark, as Benjamin D. Wilson, a former fur trapper and wealthy owner of Santa Ana Rancho, discovered in the summer of 1845. Wilson and an armed expedition cornered a band of Indian horse thieves led by a former San Gabriel mission field hand named Joaquin. The outlaws refused to surrender and made a stand in a dry wash along the Mojave River. Joaquin himself wounded Wilson with a poison arrow before being mortally shot through the chest. Wilson later wrote in his journal: "Joaquin laid on the ground uttering curses and abuse against the Spanish race and the people . . . some of my men . . . finished him . . . for his depredations, and outlawing, bore on his person the mark of the mission, that is one of his ears cropped off . . . The marking had not been done at the mission, but at one of its ranches [El Chino] by the Mayordomo."[23]

Although field hands were never paid for their labor, *mayordomos* found ways to reward those who were especially hardworking and industrious, or who otherwise set a good example. They might allocate small portions of tobacco or chocolate, give extra clothing, fancy cloth, or bits of colored ribbon, or allow a field hand to keep a small, private garden plot. They could provide tools if a field hand wished to do some building or create trinkets or gifts; particularly diligent field hands might receive a sheep, goat, or chicken. *Mayordomos* also controlled passes that allowed field hands and their relatives to visit native villages or to range freely in search of wild foods. Such inducements were especially useful in building a group of loyal and industrious workers.[24]

But despite the obvious power wielded by *mayordomos*, field hands generally had little contact with them. Instead, they usually toiled under the watchful eyes of *alcaldes* and *regidores*. These positions were first instituted on the missions in 1779 not as part of the labor process, but by order of Governor Felipe de Neve, who believed that native Californians suffered terribly under the Franciscans. Since assuming office two years earlier, Neve had steadily weakened the Franciscans by isolating them and undermining their power. His motives were quite genuine. Since his days as governor of Baja California, Neve had intended to help the Indians manage for themselves. In an attempt to plant a seed of self-government, teach Indians the procedures of civil life, and begin to prepare them to run the missions, Neve forced the padres to allow the Indians to elect representatives at each mission. But although they were supposedly independent of the padres and exercised certain jurisdiction over treatment and discipline, the *alcaldes* and *regidores* had no real political power. Within a few years, the padres exerted considerable control over the selection of these officials, and had transformed them from legislators to overseers, loyal crew bosses, and spies. La Pérouse called them "blind performers of the will of their superiors."[25]

Whether they were annually appointed by the padres on recommendation of the *mayordomos* or chosen in sham elections rigged to endorse only the most acculturated, favored, and trusted of the Indian men, *alcaldes* and *regidores* were essential to the mission farm labor process. Although Scottish immigrant and Los Angeles rancher Hugo Reid claimed that the *alcaldes* and *regidores* of San Gabriel mission "were chosen from among the very laziest of the community," the opposite appears true. While Reid may have been correct in claiming that some *alcaldes* and *regidores* "took more pleasure in making the others work than would industrious ones," most were chosen from among native leaders and village captains who already commanded considerable power and respect and enjoyed many privileges. These men knew all field hands by name, and were usually more fully acquainted with the Spanish language and Spanish customs than others. Additionally, they spoke the various Indian dialects required to communicate with the many different tribes populating each mission, and were able to intercede between the Franciscans and field hands. Their job, explained Pablo Tac, was to "see how the work is done, to hurry them if they are lazy, so that they will soon finish what was ordered, and to punish the guilty or lazy one who leaves the plow and quits the field keeping on with his laziness."[26]

Shedding their cotton shirts, blankets, and breechcloths in favor of fancy Spanish clothing, *alcaldes* and *regidores* often underscored their status by wielding a large staff, cane, or prod to denote their authority and move field hands along. On several missions, they also displayed huge rawhide whips, ten feet long, and "the thickness of a man's wrist." At San Luis Rey mission, the seven *alcaldes* and *regidores* who managed workers on the mission's far-flung *estancias* and farms even adopted military titles, with the chief calling himself the "general" and his underlings assuming the ranks of "captains" and "corporals."[27]

Dividing field hands into various crews and moving them about, *alcaldes* and *regidores* generally supervised everything. In fields that were so distant that it was not possible for the men to return to the mission for midday meal, *alcaldes* and *regidores* even looked after the last details of setting up the copper cauldrons and building the cooking fires in the mobile kitchens needed to feed men. Even at night, field hands could not escape supervision. *Alcaldes* and *regidores* who locked up the single men in their dormitory deposited the keys with the padre and patrolled the premises until dawn. Field hands knew not to cross *alcaldes* or *regidores*, lest they pay dearly. Exempt from most discipline and even the prohibitions against riding horses, and provided with extra provisions and the best housing, even servants, *alcaldes* and *regidores* were powerful individuals who often abused their privileges and did not hesitate to punish field hands for failing to carry out an order.[28]

Accompanying field hands wherever they drove *carretas*, the *alcaldes* and *regidores* ensured that they did not abuse, misuse, or steal the precious, wobbly wheeled vehicles. To extend their reach as overseers, *alcaldes* and *regidores* commonly operated an elaborate network of spies who kept, as Alta California Governor Juan Bautista Alvarado explained in a reminiscence, "a constant watch over . . . movements and discussions . . . reporting . . . all those who committed any criminal act, or who were remiss in the fulfillment of the obligation imposed upon them of sharing the work of the community, or who failed to carry out the orders of the padre in any other connection." *Alcaldes* and *regidores* even supervised field hands on their way to pray and attend church, and could often be found patrolling the Indian villages and mission living quarters in the minutes before mass, looking for anyone skipping out on religious service.[29]

At San Luis Rey mission, *alcaldes* supervised every phase of life, from fields to church. Visiting the mission in 1829, the Massachusetts hide trader Alfred Robinson observed field hands daily attending mass and being "driven along by *alcaldes*, and under the whip's lash forced to the very doors of the sanctuary." Visiting San Francisco de Asís mission in 1826, the British sea captain Frederick Beechey witnessed this in extreme form. Acting like "bailiffs" charged with keeping everyone quiet and in a kneeling position, *alcaldes* stationed themselves in the center of the church aisle between rows of Indians and used "goads" (prods with sharpened tips) to "reach a long way, and inflict a sharp puncture without making any noise."[30]

How could this happen? How could well-intentioned padres, who shunned worldly possessions, endured great hardships in the service of the Lord, and regarded excessive force as a mortal sin, sanction violence and brandish such total power? Padre José Señán, the president of the California missions in 1815, came close to answering these questions when he explained that missionaries who punished field hands did so, "like a natural Father of his sons." Señán and other padres regarded field hands as if they were schoolchildren with an intellectual capacity of a nine- or ten-year-old. Those who could show no ability to learn minimum work requirements as part of their "schooling" were therefore subjected to the discipline as if they were wayward children. While mitigating punishment, this hardly exempted field hands from the lash.[31]

Corporal punishment was commonplace in seventeenth-century Spain, and the practice was carried over to mission culture. Native field hands were most often subjected to the lash, stocks, leg irons, and some combination of the three. These punishments varied widely in degree of severity and regularity, depending on what the offense had been and who was handing down the sentence. But despite widely accepted tales of unmitigated brutality, mission farmworkers were generally no more ill-treated than any other colonized New World people.[32]

The first time that field hands stole anything, missed prayers, skipped church, fought or quarreled, forgot a task, or disobeyed an order, they might receive a slap or a knock on the head or several swats with a willow switch. Hauled before the *mayordomo* or the padre, they would then be admonished verbally. This was considered ample warning. A second violation brought several lashes from an instrument called *la disciplina* (the discipline), four quarter-inch-diameter sections of two-foot-long hemp or rawhide ropes, with one-inch knots every four inches, tied together around a short handle. A third violation for a slight fault such as tardiness, lying, and refusing to work might result in twelve to fifteen lashes from *la disciplina*. For severe violations—like constant tardiness and lying—field hands received as many as twenty-five lashes. Field hands who regularly quarreled or were violent got twenty-five lashes a day for nine days, and a field hand who threw a rock at or otherwise threatened a padre got thirty-five or forty lashes for nine successive Sundays.[33]

Part of what made these penalties so harsh was the randomness with which they were applied. While field hands at San Luis Rey mission in the 1820s could receive fifty lashes for a "crime" such as entering church with a dirty blanket, their counterparts at Santa Barbara mission might be sentenced to twenty-five lashes for accidentally breaking a barrel of wine. At other missions they might not be whipped at all. But some whipping practices were uniform: Field hands caught drinking alcohol, gambling, or engaging in pagan practices, and those guilty of fornication or concubinage, would be punished with twenty to thirty lashes for three successive days; field hands guilty of murder were also whipped but not executed, so long as they had only killed other natives. A small group of field hands who killed the native gardener at Santa Barbara mission in 1796 received fifty lashes and four years in the presidio prison, except for the leader, Bonifacio, who was given one hundred lashes in addition to four years in prison.[34]

Field hands often received their whippings in a public spectacle, with "the commandant [*mayordomo*] standing by with his sword to see that the Ind. who flogged them done his duty." At a set time, usually Sunday morning following mass, everyone would gather at the guardhouse, threshing corral, or on the grounds in front of the church. At San Buenaventura mission, the punishment area was a jail just east of the mission bell tower. Guilty field hands would be made to either lie face down on the ground or, more frequently, they would be tied to a whipping post or cannon. In the most violent punishments, they would have a musket tied behind their knees to immobilize them during the ordeal.

They would then be admonished for their "sins," so that everyone understood the nature of their offense, and the whipping would begin. In this way, padres hoped, news of the punishment would spread among the natives and serve as a warning with maximum effect. But plenty of field hands were not disciplined in such formal rituals or in assigned places. In fact, they often received their punishment without warning, within moments of their offenses. Field hands who fell short of their allotted tasks, who were deemed lazy, who left their plows early or quit the field before finishing their duties—and anyone not pulling the required load—would often be whipped or struck with a rod or cane the instant that an *alcalde* discovered their misbehavior.[35]

Field hands were placed in stocks and shackles far less often than they were whipped. Depending on their crime, they could be locked in either head or foot stocks, or both, for between one and three days. *Alcaldes* on some missions like San Buenaventura, which did not have stocks, employed punishment known as the "law of the Bayonne." Making the offender stand or sit next to a wall in the kitchen, the *alcalde* would plunge a bayonet into the wall just above the Indian's head, bind his hands, and then tie his hair to the bayonet. The man would remain in this painful and humiliating position for days. Once released, field hands were often further disciplined using a torturous wooden boot known as a *corma*. Recalled Fernando Librado:

> It was made from two pieces of wood which opened, and the entire foot was placed into it from the toe to heel. These pieces of wood were joined to a ring which went about the knee, and from this ring straps were attached to a belt which went around the waist of a person. Weights were fashioned to the straps. As punishment, the priests would work men and women in the fields with these weighted wooden shoes. The priests also sometimes shackled the feet of the Indians, or shackled two Indians together at the same time.

Forced to endure this for three days or more, while continuing to work in the fields or at some other activity about the mission, shackled natives were also prevented from mixing with fellow workers during the evenings. Instead, they would be locked inside the root cellar, workshop, weaving room, or toolshed.[36]

Whippings and incarcerations were not supposed to scar or permanently damage field hands in any way. But many overseers abused their power. At San Fernando mission in 1813, an *alcalde* trying to make a field hand work faster hurled a club at him, killing him instantly. For his crime, the *alcalde* received a sentence of two months in the presidio jail.[37]

Twenty years later, wealthy California landowner and mission critic Mariano Guadalupe Vallejo, whose landholdings spread like a green quilt over the valleys around San Francisco de Solano mission (usually referred to as Sonoma mission), became so disturbed by cruelty he witnessed in the fields that he wrote a confidential memo to Governor José Figueroa. At virtually every mission, Vallejo reported, he had seen natives treated so cruelly that the sight "would horrify any but the most brutal men."[38]

With a few significant exceptions, padres themselves only rarely administered corporal punishment or imposed sentences. This was not the function of the

FIGURE 6. Born sometime between 1804 and 1820 on Santa Cruz Island, Chumash Indian Fernando Librado worked in the fields and on canal construction projects at San Buenaventura mission. Interviewed by anthropologist John P. Harrington on countless occasions between 1912 and 1915, Librado provided one of the few Indian accounts of life and labor in the mission fields. Photograph ca. 1912. Courtesy of the Lompoc Valley Historical Society.

church; civil authorities held this responsibility. While such punitive sentences sometimes seemed excessive, on the whole they were reasonable by standards of the times. Most padres realized that cruel punishments undermined evangelical efforts. It was also considered a mortal sin under church law for anyone to whip a native so severely as to cause grave injury. According to the prevailing manual of pastoral theology used by missionaries, civil and church authorities were required to avoid cruel and excessive punishment, and additionally were required to treat converts lovingly, so as not to alienate them from the church. Still, abuse occurred.[39]

Field hands on San Carlos mission worked under one of the most unmerciful padres, Pedro Matias, who is alleged to have flogged them with chains for the most trivial faults. On another mission, wives of field hands suspected of practicing birth control or abortion supposedly were punished by an especially creative padre who whipped them with fifty lashes, slapped them in shackles, and shaved their heads. On Santa Cruz mission, Padre Ramón Oblés, described by one Indian as "cruel in his punishments," disciplined a young man who arrived late at his dormitory by ordering him whipped across the stomach.[40]

On mission San Gabriel, one padre was rumored to have proposed stopping natives from stealing fruit out of the mission gardens by attempting to manufacture a large, metal-jawed trap to catch them as they sneaked in at night. Another San Gabriel mission padre, José María Zalvidea, supposedly urged his *alcaldes* and *regidores* to employ the lash so often and with such ferocity against his field hands that, according to Hugo Reid, "he seemed to consider whipping as meat and drink to them, for they had it night and day."[41]

When mission farmworkers spoke outside the presence of the padres, they often described being compelled to work under threat of lash or worse. The padres themselves admitted as much. Responding to a questionnaire from Spanish authorities in 1813, Franciscans at Santa Cruz mission explained that the gardener there so feared them that he "would put the plants in the ground with the roots up, if the Padre so ordered." Continuing on, the missionaries admitted that if they wanted to punish natives at the mission, they did not have to shout or force them to submit, but rather had only to "do no more than to order them to undress . . . and they receive their lashes."[42]

~

Whatever the prods to work, mission field hands, like all farmworkers, toiled longer hours at harvest time, planting time, and during fall plowing. But they seldom if ever worked more than eight hours in a single day, or more than forty hours per week—most averaged between thirty and thirty-six hours. Additionally, field hands did not work on the twenty-four annual "saints' days" or on innumerable other occasions when the mission gathered to commemorate religious celebrations ranging from the birthday of the mission's patron saint and the feast of the Virgin Mary to Christmas and Easter. In total, field hands enjoyed ninety-two full holidays from work every year. This has led church scholars to point out that field hands worked no harder and probably far less than manual and unskilled laborers in most industries and occupations of the late eighteenth and early nineteenth centuries. They ignore, however, the many hours that religious service and instruction added to every field hand's day, extending the time required of them from well before sunrise until well after sunset.[43]

If mission field hands were not overworked, neither were they underfed. Once the mission farms were established and the starving times passed, field hands ate regularly and, according to one padre, "at all hours." They could expect three hot meals a day: at breakfast, a dipper full of *atole*, a warm gruel or mush of cornmeal or roasted barley, sometimes with milk added; at lunch, a dipper full of *pozole*, a thick vegetable soup composed of wheat, corn, peas, cornmeal, beans, and meat; and at dinner, another dipper full of *pozole*, or leftover *atole*, with tortillas, vegetables, meat, and whatever fruit was in season. "Neither salt nor fat is mixed with this *pozole*," wrote Padre Esteban Tapis, "because experience has taught us that these items do not agree with the majority and with regard to the minority who use them without detriment, neither they nor the others are denied these things if they ask for them." Indeed, during the wheat harvest, every field hand received an extra ration of one quart of *atole* or *pozole*. At San Buenaventura mission, field hands devised a kind of mobile kitchen. Suspending a clean hide across a wagon, they tied the corners to stakes, poured the hide full of *pozole*, and drove the wagon into the fields to feed men their noon rations. Foreign visitors puzzled over such meals, finding them unappetizing and a "most insipid mess." But field hands seem to have received ample amounts of food, including milk and cheese and, on religious holidays, gifts of chocolate and coffee. "That this amount of food is sufficient to sustain them to perform their necessary labors," concluded Tapis, "can be seen by anyone who has eyes and wishes to see."[44]

Gruel, soup, and rations of milk did not give field hands all the nutriments they needed—high quality protein required for growth, salts, a certain amount of fat necessary for energy, and something to break the monotony of lentils, beans, corn, and grain. These they received from other sources, from small gardens they kept at their homes; from wild seeds, birds, game, and fish they gathered on their own; and from even more extensive personal gardens that certain selected field hands were allowed to cultivate. During the sardine, salmon, and grunion runs, Indians spent large amounts of time catching fish, and whenever local crops of wild fruits ripened, they fully exploited them as well, for example the wild raspberries, grapes, and cherries that Indians gathered in the mountains above Santa Barbara mission between July and September. By far the most important source of protein were the thousands of semiwild, black cattle that roamed the hillsides and valleys about the missions. Since there were no fences in Alta California, cattle had to be guarded year-round, a chore that fell to the trusted vaqueros. Riding the range, they periodically selected good, healthy draft animals, which they trained and broke for work pulling plows and *carretas* about the missions. But their main job was driving older animals to the slaughter fields that stood on the outskirts of every mission compound. There, crews of natives deftly killed, skinned, butchered, and rendered the animals. Vaqueros then sent the beef, bones, *manteca* (butterfat), and long strips of lean back and flank meat to the mission kitchens; the heavy fat was delivered to the tallow makers, and the hides to the tanners. Goats, swine, and sheep, while never as important as cattle, also furnished limited amounts of fresh mutton, pork, sausage casings, and various other smoked and cured foods to field hands on established missions.[45]

Field hands more often received meat at San Francisco, Santa Clara, San Antonio, San Luis Obispo, San Gabriel, San Juan Capistrano, and San Diego missions, which had the largest herds; at least once a week they could count on a ration of beef (or mutton) with their midday meal. A caption scribbled on the wall of the kitchen at San Juan Bautista mission noted that as many as fifty cattle per day were killed and served at meals to the mission's 1,248 neophytes. But even during "lean times" between slaughters, field hands at some missions enjoyed steady quantities of milk, dried meat, salt pork, and cured ham, as well as various fowl such as pigeons, chickens, and turkeys. At a time when Russian peasants seldom consumed meat and French and English rural workers could not afford meat more than once per week, mission field hands benefited from high quality animal protein unavailable to many other, if not most, of their global counterparts.[46]

Physical injuries, stress, the humiliation of corporal punishment and enforced discipline, and the ravages of disease more than canceled the health benefits of this relatively abundant diet. Influenza and pneumonia epidemics, as well as outbreaks of the common cold, killed off large numbers of field hands. Dysentery, diphtheria, and typhoid—often masked by such generic names as "ague" and "bilious fever" and "fuertes dolores de cabeza" (terrible headaches)—multiplied and festered under crude and unhealthful conditions. Measles did the most damage. Unknown in California before 1805, measles epidemics swept through the missions in 1806–7, killing 372 Indians and prompting Padre Mariano Payeras to report that at La Purísima mission the scourge "has cleaned out the missions and filled the cemeteries."[47]

Mission quarters offered field hands the further discomfort of fleas, which seemed to multiply in every building. Those seeking light after sunset could find it only in the communal kitchen, the *monjerío*, the church sacristy (where candles and lamps burned constantly), or the cooking fires in their quarters. Otherwise, at night they lived in darkness. Outside of the mission plazas and quadrangles, they had neither paved walkways nor roads. They traveled on dirt paths that were dusty in the summer, slippery with mud in the winter, and often caked with the droppings of cows, dogs, hogs, goats, cattle, and fowl. As there was seldom any system of water distribution to the barracks, field hands had to troop back and forth constantly between the central fountain or pool and their quarters. The stench of eighteen hundred people relieving themselves three times each day in open latrines around a settlement the size of Santa Barbara, San Fernando, San Luis Rey, or San Gabriel missions—as with any large settlement at that time—must have been detectable for a distance of many miles.[48]

Although field hands at San Antonio mission enjoyed an elaborate aqueduct system complete with a charcoal filter that delivered water across an archway to the laundry by means of broad brick steps, they also drank from a drain that took water from a spring used by soldier's wives for washing clothes and ate crops grown in a field irrigated by water from the drain after it had been further polluted by runoff from the Indian village and plaza through which it passed. At San Luis Rey mission, where an elaborate charcoal filtration system at the wash place provided clean water for bathing, washing, and drinking, the polluted runoff was still used in the orchards and fields. On some missions, field hands certainly contracted disease through water supplies polluted by latrines, tanneries, and herds of cattle. This was clearly the case at San Francisco de Asís mission, where drinking water came from a spring-fed lake, La Laguna de los Dolores, where herds of cattle were detained while awaiting slaughter. Such water supplies were probably also breeding grounds for malaria and yellow fever, spread by the mosquitoes that were common in the swampy land along the lakeside.[49]

By far the most terrible scourges were syphilis and other venereal diseases, mainly gonorrhea. Visiting sailors, settlers, and Spanish soldiers passed the highly contagious diseases on to the wives and daughters of field hands, and through them to their husbands and babies. So many natives became syphilitic within the second generation after contact that, whenever the presidios asked for laborers, padres often refused on the grounds that they lacked enough healthy men to perform the basic tasks around the missions. "They live well free," admitted La Purísima mission Padre Mariano Payeras. "But as soon as we reduce them to a Christian and community life . . . they decline in health, they fatten, sicken and die."[50]

At San Carlos mission, field hands were attended to by a physician assigned primarily to look after the soldiers at the presidio of Monterey. On the twenty other missions, they received care from padres and the wives of soldiers, who dispensed folk remedies and experimented with what little they could glean from books. Treatments like "vomits" (induced by drinking seawater), *curanderos* (herbal potions), "sweatings," and "bleedings" often proved more fatal than advantageous.[51]

Whether they were infected with smallpox, measles, dysentery, diphtheria, typhoid, the common cold, or venereal diseases, field hands and other natives died off at a high rate. At San Carlos mission, Indians lived approximately 7.5 to fourteen years after baptism; their children survived 11.5 years after birth. In 1806, a catastrophic year, 170 out of one thousand natives died, a mortality rate nearly six times that of antebellum American slaves. Most years the death rate was between seventy and ninety out of one thousand—about two to three times that of Western Europeans. At San José mission, death rates averaged 150 to 170 per thousand between 1800 and 1802, about half again as high as those at San Francisco de Asís and Santa Clara missions. In 1813 and 1815, deaths exceeded births. Worse, high death rates were compounded by abnormally low birthrates, which dropped from around forty-five per thousand in 1820 to thirty-five per thousand at the end of the mission era, 13 years later. Although rising birthrates allowed other native populations to rebound from the impact of epidemics by replacing their losses within a generation, this did not happen on the missions. Epidemic mortality, coupled with high rates of child and infant mortality, prevented quick recovery and sealed the fate of mission field hands.[52]

In 1777, nine out of ten mission Indian children under one and a half years of age died from unknown diseases that swept through Santa Clara mission. Among Chumash Indian children brought to Santa Barbara, Santa Inés, and La Purísima missions, about one-third of the children under two years of age died within their first year, and about four of ten survived to puberty. Among children born on the missions, two of three died before reaching five years of age; three-quarters were dead by adolescence. At San Fernando mission, four of ten children under age two died; on San Gabriel mission in 1814 three out of four children did not reach two years of age. These numbers contrasted directly with children of settlers and soldiers, who could generally expect to survive at least into adulthood. But as appalling as these figures were, they did not diverge significantly from child mortality in Europe and England at this time, where four of ten children died before age fifteen.[53]

Newly converted field hands lived about twelve years after baptism. Their wives and daughters fared even worse. Dying off in disproportionate numbers (about twice that of males), they declined from a normal and balanced ratio of one male to one female at the beginning of the mission period to a ratio of 1.35 males to one female by 1834. At Santa Cruz mission, one of the missions with the greatest gender imbalance, the percentage of females dropped from 47 percent in 1797 to 31 percent in 1832. So many natives and their infants died at San Gabriel, San Juan Capistrano, and San Luis Rey missions in 1819 that the padres, finding themselves overwhelmed by calls to administer the last rites, established chapels in the infirmaries in order to speed the process. "It has been experienced that in the first years we had more births than deaths, afterwards as many deaths as births; but at present there are four deaths to three births," reported San Miguel mission padres Juan Martín and Juan Cabot on April 15, 1814. "For this malady I do not believe they have any effective remedy."[54]

With death constant, padres feared for the very survival of the missions. Promoting marriage and doing their best to offset the population decline, some padres intruded not only into the child rearing practices of field hands but also into their sexual relations as well. At Santa Cruz mission, Padre Ramón Oblés went so far as to order one infertile Indian couple to perform intercourse before him. When the couple refused, Oblés forcibly inspected the man's penis to discover "whether or not it was in good order," then tried to perform a similar examination on the woman. Horrified, she attempted to bite Oblés, then fought him off. Shackled and given fifty lashes, she was locked in the *monjerío*, given a grotesque wooden doll, and after being released, ordered to carry the doll everywhere for nine days and treat it as if it were her baby. All this time her husband was ridiculed and herded to church wearing the symbol of the cuckold, a headdress of cow horns and long, leather thongs.[55]

As the bodies of field hands and other mission Indians piled up, room to bury them grew precious. At Santa Barbara mission, a common, unmarked trench handled the overflow. Hidden in a special building at the back corner of the cemetery, the grave was reached by way of a doorway exiting the church. When Alfred Robinson happened across the site on a visit in 1828, he discovered it "crowded with a ghastly array of skulls and bones." Illinois-born lawyer and travel writer Thomas Jefferson Farnham explored it in 1846 and found the place so packed that bones had to be exhumed regularly to make room for additional bodies. Farnham probed the grounds more thoroughly, and in the mission courtyard, he stumbled upon an unbelievable sight. "Three or four cart-loads of skulls, ribs, spines, leg-bones, arm-bones, &c., lay in one corner," he wrote. "Beside them stood two hand-hearses with a small cross attached to each. About the walls hung the mould of death."[56]

⊱

Although it seems likely that field hands mitigated the shock of mission life and preserved a sense of continuity by blending old and new economic activities in their work, it is difficult to discern their actual feelings. Native field hands left behind scanty written records and oral remembrances. But in their few surviving statements, they did not have much good to say. Field hands who learned to write or who were interviewed late in life were extremely precise and detailed in their anger. Pablo Tac hated the Franciscans, military officers, and other colonialists for trespassing on native soil, and he complained bitterly of having to work in the fields to feed others, especially the soldiers. Nor did he like the way certain padres treated natives like vassals, with "the Fernando Padre . . . like a king" and natives acting as servants, pages, and errand boys. Above all, he deplored the way punishment was administered arbitrarily or without cause. "When I was a boy the treatment given the Indians at the mission was not all good," Tac complained. "We were at the mercy of the administrator, who ordered us to be flogged whenever and however he took a notion."[57]

Even more bitter, Costanoan Indian Venancio Asar told his son how Santa Cruz mission Indians were often punished by fifty lashes on their bare back. "They made them work like slaves," he said of the padres, adding "we were always trembling with fear of the lash."[58]

Among field hands who could not record their feelings, discontent surfaced in a variety of ways. One of the most common was a profound and overwhelming homesickness. Although many visitors observed and commented on this yearning for freedom, particularly among the recently converted who remembered the old ways, none left a more poignant account than the Russian explorer Otto von Kotzebue. After attending a mass in his honor at Santa Clara mission, von Kotzebue encountered groups of Indians who were leaving the mission on their twice-yearly pilgrimage to their distant rancherías. Nearby were sick and old Indians who could not undertake the long journey. Even after the boats had disappeared beyond sight, they remained by the water's edge, mournfully gazing at the distant summits of the mountains to the east, where the natives were headed. "So much does the sight of their lost home affect these new Christians," von Kotzebue would later write in his journal, that "they often sit in this situation for several days, without taking any food."[59]

Von Kotzebue did not know that the exodus from Santa Clara mission was just one of many such flights. Among the recently converted, yearning for the old ways—for freedom and home—remained strong. When work slowed down during slack times in the spring and fall, field hands and other native laborers always managed to take seasonal "vacations" and leave for two to four weeks to visit relatives. On certain missions, like Santa Barbara, the desire to leave was so strong that it became ritualized. Every Sunday anxious field hands gathered with their friends after mass at the padre's quarters to learn who had been chosen to "go on an excursion." One of five was permitted to do so and their names entered in a book "so that all may have their turn at going away."[60]

On other missions, field hands felt such a strong desire to go fishing, visit the beaches, gather wild seeds, or return to traditional hunting grounds, that they maintained a constant clamor for permission to leave. Field hands were always traveling back and forth between the missions and their tribal homes. Such field hands, leaving for short periods and returning on their own accord, were not technically runaways. But they did indicate a certain discontent, particularly when they overstayed. French sea captain Auguste Bernard Duhaut-Cilly, observing these developments in 1827–28, found in them an incipient form of resistance and strong desire for freedom that remained undiminished in strength. "The instinct of liberty is . . . crying to them," he observed of the natives, who seemed universally to detest the "monotonous" life of the missions. They seemed to long for "the poor and uncertain life of their woods and their marshes."[61]

A vivid commentary on the failure of Hispanization, these and countless other similar incidents were a clear, almost blatant, affront to the goals of the mission. Demonstrating the breakdown of one of the primary objectives of Franciscan policy—assimilation into mission society—the yearning for home revealed that field hands and other mission Indians never completely capitulated or assimilated. Maintaining elements of their culture, they constantly confronted and sabotaged the goals of the Franciscans, creating something that was neither Spanish nor Indian. Few of the first generation learned to speak Spanish and those who arrived on the missions as adults did not fare much better, particularly on big missions like San Luis Obispo, where field hands came from many different native groups and spoke more than fifteen different dialects. Even third-generation field hands, who eventually learned to speak Spanish, often understood it only imperfectly. They incorporated into their vocabulary certain key phrases, work orders, religious terms, and words necessary for daily survival, such as those describing animals, weapons, food, and tools. But only on two or three missions did very many field hands adopt the language of the padres.[62]

Did field hands ever fully comprehend Christianity? It is doubtful. With as little as eight days of religious instruction conducted in Spanish and Latin—eight days of hearing an Indian interpreter trying to convey the meaning of Catholicism, eight days of learning the mysteries of the Bible explained in unintelligible Spanish, eight days of hearing the mass in Latin—field hands could not have grasped what was happening to them. For most native field hands, total reorientation of their traditional beliefs and acceptance of the Spanish god did not occur. Much of what passed for conversion was repetition. After baptism, field hands memorized the Act of Contrition, Lord's Prayer, Ave Maria, Apostle's Creed, Ten Commandments, and seven sacraments. Every day in church, they recited their morning prayers, learning them by rote, gradually receiving each new point of doctrine. But this hardly constituted true conversion to the faith. When visitors appeared, padres would periodically trot out bands of native boys, sometimes adorned in uniforms acquired from French whaling vessels, or point to a few who could read and speak Spanish and who played musical instruments. These natives were offered as exemplars of the conversion process. But in such groups, according to one padre, "ten or twelve hardly remember what they learned the day before." If the two or three who actually memorized their music became ill or otherwise were absent, "the others, who sing only by being towed and following the rest, are stranded," the band would not be able to play, and mass would be canceled. Interviewed by the historian Hubert Bancroft in 1877, San Luis Rey mission native Julio César put it this way: "To the question whether we were taught to read and write, I reply that we were only taught to pray and recite the mass from memory."[63]

Only a core group of field hands ever became truly converted. Many, in fact, did not forsake their traditional religious customs and beliefs and were indifferent to the Christian message. Some—though it is impossible to quantify how many—inoculated Christian rites with entirely different meanings unimaginable to the padres. Continuing to practice non-Christian rituals and listening to their shamans in secret, they fended off evil, cured illness, assisted in childbirth, and strengthened family ties with hallucinogenic potions and various concoctions, charms, ceremonies, and other folk remedies. Several groups of mission field hands actually spread their native beliefs to other missions. So strong were these traditions at Santa Barbara mission that Padre Ramón Oblés confided in a letter to another padre that despite every effort to "make them forget the ancient beliefs of paganism," field hands and other native workers continued "to carry on certain pagan practices and . . . are reputed to have the characteristics of their pagan state."[64]

On the southern missions, natives developed a kind of counterreligion centered on *Chinigchinich* (Ching-ee-ching-itch), a "shaman-like hero," who advocated a strict moral code of obedience, fasting, self-sacrifice, and revenge, and emphasized both an intricate ritual and secrecy. Featuring a frightening collection of avengers, including rattlesnakes, bears, and tarantulas who maintained loyalty among followers and punished transgressors, *Chinigchinich* spread to surrounding groups, and was occasionally associated with use of *toloache*, or jimsonweed, a hallucinogenic, along with endurance trials consisting of fire walking, whipping with nettles, and being laid out on anthills. Religions such as *Chinigchinich* remained hidden among field hands. But occasionally a native would become fed up with a lecture on Christianity and reveal his true feelings and loyalties. At the end of a lecture on Satan, a native headman from one of mission San Luis Rey's rancherías exploded in anger: "See how this padre cheats us! Who believes that the Devil will leave us by the sign of the cross? If it were to be done by dancing, as authorized by *Chinigchinich*, he would depart; but that he will do so by the means which he says, I do not believe!" All of those gathered laughed and agreed.[65]

Of all the mission Indians, none maintained their culture more completely than did the Chumash at Santa Inés, Santa Barbara, La Purísima, and San Buenaventura missions. With large populations of field hands and other natives, these missions had a difficult time instructing so many converts, and more importantly, curtailing and controlling native leaders. Ceremonial leaders continued to initiate adolescent natives in the use of datura, a plant with hallucinogenic properties, and *pespibata*, a native tobacco with potent effects, both of which the Chumash believed essential to contacting their supernatural guardians. Chumash personal conduct and sexual practices also mortified padres: sexual activity continued to be practiced between unmarried men and women, and even between brothers-in-law and sisters-in-law, and between *joyas* ("jewels") or male transvestites. Some Chumash activities threatened to undermine Christian icons, especially religious practices like decorating a village enclosure with painted poles topped with feathers, or scattering feathers and seed in celebration of their god.[66]

In these and other ways, field hands developed, apparently at a fairly early stage, one of the characteristics that later farmworkers also possessed, an ability to obey their superiors (or to seem to obey them), while simultaneously going about their own lives to the extent that it was possible. By feigning obedience, while sabotaging work and forging their own unique and illegal culture—and mostly by escaping—field hands vented their discontent, resisted the padres, challenged and undermined the missions, and struggled to attain freedom. Often they paid an enormous price.[67]

CHAPTER FOUR

No Longer Keep Us By Force

Accommodation and Resistance

Among Mission Field Hands

The greatest uprising of field hands and other mission Indians occurred at Santa Inés, La Purísima, and Santa Barbara missions late in February 1824. Eyewitness accounts are sketchy, but it seems the revolt was sparked when, on the afternoon of February 21, Valentín Cota, the corporal of the guard at Santa Inés mission, brutally flogged a native from La Purísima. While violent beatings may have been commonplace on this day, it was just the spark needed to ignite discontent among an Indian population already fed up with living and working conditions and resentful of idle and inconsiderate soldiers. Upon learning of the flogging, hundreds of Chumash natives armed themselves with bows and arrows, seized control of Santa Inés mission, attacked the soldiers, and burned their quarters. Within hours, the conflict spread to La Purísima mission, and involved such large numbers of natives that there seems little doubt that field hands were among the ranks of those battling the soldiers, and that they were also among those driven from Santa Inés mission the following day. When the uprising spread to Santa Barbara mission, field hands certainly participated. There also seems little question that they were among the rebels who retreated to La Purísima mission, raised a "palisade of fortifications," again fought with the soldiers, and held out for a month before surrendering to a force of cavalry and infantry armed with small cannons.[1]

Exactly what role field hands played in the rebellion, and the range and depth of their involvement, can only be inferred by several clues, the most important of which comes from a surprising source, Padre Antonio Ripoll of Santa Barbara mission. Three months after witnessing the uprising, Ripoll reported how the day after the violence began, he had met in front of the *pozolera* "the entire population already armed, as they had assembled in front of my room in the corridor." Presumably that "entire population" included not only all of the field hands, vineyardists, gardeners, and horticulturalists on the mission proper, but those from the nearby *estancia* of Rancho Selpe, as well. According to Ripoll's report,

FIGURE 7. Spanish lancers rounding up captured Indians and herding them to the San Francisco presidio in 1816. Drawing by Louis Choris. Courtesy of the California Historical Society.

Andrés, the Indian *alcalde*, had ordered all of the *estancia* field hands to "come quickly" with their families, gather at the mission, and there await orders.[2]

Another indication of just how deeply field hands participated in the Santa Barbara mission phase of the revolt is Ripoll's observation that the neophytes were armed not only with bows and arrows, but also with "chopping knives" and machetes, common tools of field-workers. When mission soldiers surrendered their muskets in a confrontation near the guardhouse on the second day of the revolt, the rebels snatched the weapons and attacked them with their "chopping knives," wounding two men and driving the rest from the mission. There is no way to determine whether or not field hands were the ones who inflicted injury, or if they were simply bystanders to the actions of other natives. As is usually true in such cases, they most likely engaged in both activities. But there is no doubt that field hands harbored deep grievances against presidio soldiers, who every year had ruined their gardens, knocked down their fences, robbed them of their watermelons and fruit, and beaten the old men and women who cared for them. They were fed up with growing their food and being treated like slaves.[3]

Although many field hands and other mission Indians eventually returned to the missions, a large contingent—290 out of 453 and possibly including their leader, the *alcalde* Andrés—broke from Franciscan domination and settled northeast of present day Bakersfield, about one hundred miles away from the nearest mission. Relying on farming and ranching techniques learned on the missions, they grew enough food to support a thriving community. When discovered a decade later by an American fur trapping party, they were healthy and flourishing, a self-contained community of between seven hundred and eight hundred Indians with large fields of corn, pumpkins, melons, and other crops, and horses that they rode and bartered. According to the trappers, they displayed innumerable relics stolen from the missions, including "golden images and candlesticks, and . . . several thousand dollars worth in gold and silver."[4]

While those field hands who fled to the mountains won permanent freedom, most who participated in the revolt failed to secure much lasting change. The riot caused little more than momentary local havoc and exacted only minimal revenge against abusive soldiers. Field hands returned to the mission farms disillusioned by their effort to win freedom. They could not stop the whippings, random brutality, and arbitrary treatment that had given rise to their discontent. When soldiers discovered an old field hand with a blanket full of wheat near the threshing corral several days after the revolt had begun, the old man begged not to be taken to the presidio and shot, to which the soldiers replied: "Well, then we will kill you here," and promptly shot him dead. From such incidents, field hands and other mission Indians understood that collective resistance was futile. They probably suspected it long before, but now the matter was settled. They never again joined together to challenge the padres in revolt. For critics of the California missions and for activist historians, this has been hard to accept. In the general absence of organized resistance, scholars scour the historical record for other examples of dissidence. If collective protest was impossible, they say, murder was not. As a result, there is now substantial literature on the possibility that mission field hands routinely engaged in cunning assassinations.[5]

Of these assassinations, the first supposedly occurred in early February 1801, at San Carlos mission, where field hands and other Indians determined to burn the church, kill Padre José Viñals, and escape to freedom. Tipped off by an informer, soldiers surrounded the Indian ranchería where the plot was being hatched and arrested the three ringleaders before they could act. In fact, what actually happened was quite different. Soldiers did hear of a murder plot, surrounded the ranchería, and captured all of the Indians, including field hands and other laborers. But upon further investigation, they determined that the rumors of insurrection and murder were without basis. An Indian made up the story solely for the purpose of exacting revenge on rivals. If the episode reveals anything, it is that mission field hands struggled with the same petty tensions and human jealousies dividing and splitting other classes.[6]

A second, often-cited assassination plot is more complicated. This supposed example of resistance occurred at San Miguel mission two weeks after the episode at San Carlos mission, where several natives boasted of poisoning three padres, one of whom died. But the facts are again inconclusive. The first two padres stricken, Baltasar Carnicer and Juan Martín, certainly suffered some kind of poisoning, as did Francisco Pujol, who, after arriving from San Carlos mission to replace the ailing Carnicer and Martín, immediately experienced the same violent stomach pains that had stricken his predecessors. Returning to his home mission, he then endured two weeks of horrible spasms and delirium before finally expiring. At an autopsy conducted the afternoon of Pujol's death, the examining physician was only able to say "that the inside [of Pujol's abdomen] was entirely rotten and gangrened, for the stench which came out left no room for more investigation."[7]

What had killed Pujol and sickened the others? The consensus was that certainly they had been poisoned. But by whom, and with what? All of the padres had been drinking mescal before becoming ill. Perhaps the concoction had spoiled. However, another more likely culprit may have been a copper container with a lead liner. Lead contamination in distilled liquor was common at the time and it is possible that all of the padres suffered from lead residues strong enough to cause bowel strangulation. Whatever the cause of death, native field hands or mission laborers of any kind probably did not assassinate Padre Pujol, who most likely expired when fever and convulsions caused his weakened appendix to rupture.[8]

A third alleged assassination, the so-called Panto episode, which occurred in November 1811 at San Diego mission, unfolds like this. A "rigorous disciplinarian" famous for his "extreme cruelty," Padre José Pedro Panto supposedly enjoyed brutally whipping natives. Eventually, one of them fought back. After receiving 175 lashes over a two-day period, Nazario, his cook, prepared a slow-working "*yerba*" poison, which he slipped into Panto's soup just before serving the evening meal. The padre vomited and retched for thirty minutes after ingesting a few spoonfuls of the soup, but then drank a glass of warm water and quickly recovered. When he died a torturous, agonizing death on the evening of June 30, 1812, the attending priest, Padre Gerónimo Boscana, wrote in the Death Register for San Diego mission: "He [Panto] died, according to opinions, from poisoning at the hands of the cook." While some historians accept this version of events and cite it as indicative of what field hands endured and how they fought back, others remain unconvinced. Panto certainly whipped Nazario, as well as many field hands and other Indians. Evidence comes from testimony before an investigating committee in December, when the ill Panto admitted that he "had given . . . some lashes" to his cook, and from presidio sergeant Mariano Mercado, who testified that "he had heard that he [Nazario] had been given twenty-five lashes, but did not think that for such a short punishment he should have held a grudge against the said padre." At the same hearing, Nazario claimed to have received in succession fifty lashings one morning, twenty-five that evening, twenty-four on the following morning, and twenty-five that afternoon for a total of 124 lashes over two days. Nazario also said that he had been whipped earlier by Panto, while in training as a cook at San Fernando mission, and during his duties at San Diego mission. Such a harsh punishment, if administered in conformity with the style of flogging then followed in the British and U.S. navies, as well as by American slave owners, would have completely debilitated and crippled Nazario—had he survived. But Nazario's "poison," it turns out, was nothing more than a concoction made of powdered herbs (namely *escoba amarga* or "bitter broom"), a native Californian remedy for tetanus and colds. And since Panto vomited violently for a half-hour after the poisoning, he likely disgorged most if not all of the noxious substance, thereby minimizing its effect. That the poison could not have been very strong is indicated by the fact that two soldiers sampled the soup after Panto fell ill, and while detecting a very bitter taste, did not become ill themselves. Most important, church historians point out that Nazario by his own testimony had no intention of killing the priest, that he had only hoped to be fired from his position under Panto, and that Panto died seven and a half months after the food tampering. Sickened by the prank, he obviously succumbed to other causes, but most certainly was an example of the hatred that field hands and other mission Indians must have felt, and of the plots they hatched.[9]

Although these stories are clouded, in at least one instance, gardeners, field hands, and their allies certainly committed murder—cleverly, maliciously, conspiratorially, and with no regrets. Occurring just three months after Padre Panto's untimely death, the case surrounding the demise of Santa Cruz mission's Padre Andrés Quintana is complicated, difficult to decipher, and has inspired among commentators on mission history intense emotions, bitter recriminations, and heated accusations. At the core of the controversy is the principal source of information, the recollections of Venancio Asar, a neophyte at Santa Cruz mission. Asar was one of the first natives baptized at the mission and an admitted conspirator in the murder. About 1818, Asar told the story of the assassination to his son, Lorenzo Asisara, who repeated the tale when interviewed in 1877 by Thomas Savage for Hubert H. Bancroft's *History of California*. According to Venancio Asar, field hands at Santa Cruz mission cringed at the "sadistic cruelty" of Padre Quintana, who would flog them with a wire-tipped horsewhip that cut their buttocks deeply. The brutality progressed without opposition until the fall of 1812, when after beating nine luckless neophytes with the evil instrument and nearly killing two of them, Quintana announced that he wished to test a new whip on the Sunday following mass. This was too much for an Indian named Donato, one of the latest victims, who organized a meeting of fourteen men. Believing that they could not chase Quintana away nor accuse him before the Spanish authorities, they resolved to kill the Franciscan. The question was how to do it in such a way that no one could suspect that a murder had been committed.[10]

Asisara's narrative of his father's story has the conspirators luring Quintana to the orchard the night of Saturday, October 11, 1812, with a message delivered from the wife of Julián the gardener claiming that Julián was dying and needed last rites. When the padre arrived, the conspirators waiting in the orchard had second thoughts and allowed Quintana to pass through and minister to Julián. Later that same evening, there was no mercy. Again Quintana was summoned by the gardener's wife, and again he made his way to the orchard, this time with the gardener's wife following behind crying and lamenting. This time, the men ambushed the Franciscan. Lino, a *mayordomo*, grabbed Quintana from behind. "Stop here, padre, you must speak for a moment." As the assassins surrounded him, Quintana cried out, "Oh, my son, what are you going to do to me?" Lino answered, "Your assassins will tell you." As Quintana pled for his life and promised to leave the mission, the assassins covered his mouth with his own cape, bound his hands, then strangled and smothered him beneath a pear tree. In a particularly gruesome act of defiance, one of the natives then cut off one of Quintana's testicles. To disguise their crimes, the Indians then carried the padre back to his quarters and laid him in his bed as if asleep. Stealing his keys, two of the cabalists accompanied by three Indians from Santa Clara mission broke into the storehouse, stole everything, including as much silver and gold as they could carry, buried the treasure in the orchard, and then, in a ghoulish display, unlocked the *monjerío*, called the unmarried men and women outside, gathered them in the orchard, and urged them to have sex at the site of the assassination. At some point, Donato returned to Quintana's room only to discover the padre beginning to revive from the presumed fatal attack. The native responded by struggling again with the padre, crushing his remaining testicle, cutting it off, and finally, killing him. Donato walked around the room holding the padre's testicles saying, "I shall bury these in the outdoor privy." The next morning, the corporal of the guard and *mayordomo* discovered Quintana's body, but because Quintana had been in ill health and the assassins had carefully rearranged the room to disguise any evidence of struggle, no one suspected foul play. According to Asisara's account, not until two padres from Santa Clara mission arrived and examined the corpse and opened the padre's stomach to determine if he had been poisoned, did they by chance notice his mutilated genitalia. At that point they decided to hide the discovery. This is why the Death Register recorded Quintana's demise from natural causes. When Quintana was buried two days later, so the story goes, no one suspected the gardener, orchard workers, and a *mayordomo* had murdered him. At Quintana's funeral, many elderly natives cried over his grave. At that, recalled Asisara, the culprits secretly laughed and the ringleader, locked inside the padre's house, roared "like a bear."[11]

Avoiding suspicion for the next two years, the assassins were uncovered quite accidentally during the lentil harvest when a native *mayordomo* named Carlos Castro, returning from supervising crews in the cornfields, overheard two women arguing about the roles their husbands had played in the crime. Upon learning of the conversation, Padre Ramón Oblés arrested all fourteen of the conspirators. Sent to San Francisco de Asís mission, five of them were tried and convicted and each given fifty lashes a day over a nine-day period. Bound in leg irons, the men were then sentenced to between two and ten years hard labor at the presidios at Santa Barbara and San Diego. According to one legend, the murderers upon arrival at the presidios were immediately stricken with leprosy in a kind of divine retribution. Lino, the *mayordomo* who was one of the main instigators, died in the Santa Barbara presidio prison on April 4, 1817, about a year after receiving two hundred lashes. Julián, the gardener who made the pretense of being ill and who probably strangled Quintana, died at Santa Barbara presidio on November 23, 1820. Three other conspirators, Antonio, Ciriaco, and Vicente disappear from the record, perhaps moving to another mission after serving out their sentences. Venancio Asar and Donato, as well as several other participants including the gardener's wife, seem to have escaped completely any retribution because they had served as witnesses.[12]

While Asisara's version of Padre Quintana's murder is a sensational story, full of revenge and intrigue, certain parts fail to withstand scrutiny. Had Quintana been strangled or suffocated, he would have exhibited bulging eyes, a swollen tongue, bruises, or a broken windpipe. If Quintana's testicles had been crushed or mutilated, there would have been significant bloodshed about his bed, room, and on his clothing, as well as the obvious wound on his genitals. There is no evidence that any padres opened Quintana's stomach to discover if he had been poisoned. Padre José Viader had arrived from Santa Clara mission by pure coincidence on the morning of October 12, and Padre Narciso Durán had arrived on the following morning from San José mission, also by coincidence; neither ever mentioned any immediate autopsy. Most likely Quintana's genitals had been violated after he died, through smashing, but not in any way sufficient to produce an obvious wound like a double castration. Because of the suddenness of the death, Governor

José Arrillaga ordered an investigation and sent provincial surgeon Manuel Quijano to Santa Cruz mission. On October 14, Quijano exhumed Quintana's body and performed an autopsy. On October 22 he reported evidence of violence, but not of castration. He attributed Quintana's death to old age, as the padre had been so chronically ill that he could not dress himself. Perhaps the best evidence regarding what Santa Cruz mission Indians did or did not do comes from a secret investigation conducted four years after the fact. While examining various charges of Franciscan cruelty, Governor Pablo Vicente de Solá probed the Quintana case, finding that the only natives to ever accuse Quintana of using a wire-tipped whip were three of the five convicted murderers. On that basis, Solá concluded that those men had fabricated their story. Quintana may or may not have beaten natives with such an instrument, but he probably did not whip two men nearly to death. There seems little doubt, however, that he did inspire a deep hatred in a handful of mission field hands, and that he hurt several with whippings that went beyond the kind of discipline the padres officially sanctioned. As to other details of Asisara's story, the governor's investigation uncovered no evidence of a missing treasure chest, stolen gold, or an orgy. As to Quintana's reputation as a sadist, his behavior on the night of his murder suggested that he was at least interested in and attentive to the ills suffered by mission field hands. Twice he interrupted his own schedule to minister to a dying man, hardly the actions of an ogre. Indeed, even according to Asar himself, many of those witnessing the crime "cried out and pitied his fate, but could do nothing to help him because they were themselves compromised." On these grounds, there seems some basis for accepting the rumor of a political assassination to avenge ill treatment. There is also the matter of a statement Asisara gave thirteen years after he talked to Bancroft's assistant, which ignores completely the events earlier described. Finally, there is the evidence of Quintana's reputed cruelty, all of it coming from the assassins during their trials in 1814. But if the records may not support some of the more fantastic aspects of Asisara's account, they clearly verify that Padre Quintana inspired deep hatred among Indian field hands and gardeners, men and women alike, and other Indian workers, that he was certainly murdered, probably smothered, his genitals squashed, and that his murderers were later identified, tried, and imprisoned.[13]

While murders like the one in the Santa Cruz mission orchard were extremely rare, they did reveal undercurrents that were quite common. Field hands may have only rarely conspired in cold-blooded assassination plots or banded together in massive, violent revolts, but the general absence of these protests did not mean that they accepted their lot passively. Rare were those field hands, no matter how fervently they professed their loyalty, love, and obedience, who did not hold within them a sense of anger, a capability for outrage, and a longing for freedom. Such hostility represented a far greater proportion of the farm labor force than might be suspected. Whether or not that anger ever appeared, and how long that outrage would remain stifled, was the choice every field hand had to make for himself. The strain and anxiety this apprehension created could not always be contained and would, at times, flare into the open. While avoiding overtly belligerent behavior and staying put on the missions, most field hands appeared neither passive nor content, neither antagonistic nor loyal, but rather indecisive and law-abiding, often ready to pounce on the first advantage while attentive to their anonymity, ever patient, probing for ways to mitigate the bonds that held them to their holy masters. For such people, feelings and behavior invariably teetered on a fulcrum shifting between the custom of submission and the burning hope for freedom.

The same loyal, hardworking field hand who smiled cheerfully and prayed morning and evening at San Miguel mission was immediately capable of exploding in anger, reacting with violence, and stoning a missionary in a fit of rage. A recently converted San José mission native who could stoically endure a public whipping without uttering a word, would refuse to kiss the hand of the padre inflicting the punishment, throwing down his shirt and blanket and declaring, "Padre, take back thy Christianity; I want none of it; I will return a pagan to my country." The young daughter of a field hand raised under the protection of the *monjerío* and encouraged to bear children as soon as possible would abort or kill her baby when impregnated by the unwanted union with a Spanish soldier.[14]

While the majority of field hands and their families abstained from verbal or physical confrontations and did not chance the inevitable reprisals, they did so not because they were faithful but because most understood that the best way to handle their predicament was a middle course. Seizing what little opportunities opened up to them, their defiance often was not readily apparent. Seated on the floor at mass, apparently absorbed in a sermon, they scratched obscene graffiti into the stone floor. Singing in the choir, they carved idolatrous signs in the beams of the choir loft. Around the walls of churches, they drew so many Indian symbols that the padres were continually whitewashing them away. Even under the pulpit, Indians left insubordinate designs, doodling evidence revealing that their minds were not on God and Christian rituals.[15]

Defiance occasionally took a humorous turn. No farmworker better illustrated this than José Laudencio, the head gardener on Santa Barbara mission. Full of devilment, Laudencio was a renowned storyteller and prankster. One day, when the *mayordomo* told him to inform the padre in charge of agriculture that the chile peppers were ready for harvest, Laudencio decided to play a little trick. He summoned an old man who assisted him and who spoke only a few words of Spanish, and told him to say to the padre "Ave María purísima pali" or "praise the holy virgin mother of God," which was the standard introduction, to which the padre usually replied, "Bienvenido," or "welcome." Then Laudencio instructed him to say, "Padre, dame pita para amarrar tu chile." This supposedly meant, "Padre, the chiles are ready for picking." What Laudencio really told his assistant to say was, "Padre, give me a string in order to tie it to your prick." When the assistant gardener spoke these words, the padre became angry and called in the *alcalde* to take the poor man away to be punished. At the last moment, when Laudencio intervened and prayed for forgiveness, the padre pardoned all involved. But for many years thereafter the story became an ongoing joke. And whenever the words "*pita, chile*" would be mentioned, everyone would break out in uproarious, uncontrolled laughter.[16]

Too astute to challenge the padres head-on, too clever not to possess a sense of humor, farmhands like Laudencio resisted mission control with cunning as well as muscle. Other disobedient and troublesome farmworkers found equally creative ways to ridicule their superiors and express their frustrations. Some resorted to destructive and "criminal" behavior. More often than the missionaries wished to acknowledge, field hands plundered, stole, and caused malicious mischief. When food rations were scare, field hands slipped over garden walls at night and stole fruit and vegetables. They also killed and butchered cattle, distributing meat to their friends and families, sometimes feasting on the carcasses in secret, communal meals; broke into storerooms to take utensils, shoes, thread, and knives; and even stole candles out of the church.[17]

This systematic pillaging of the missions did more than supplement the diets of field hands; it augmented their clothing, improved their standard of living, and provided a gratifying revenge. Often, their actions seemed purely symbolic, as when they gorged on chocolate and enjoyed other luxuries that were often denied them, or seized mules and horses either with the idea of increasing their chances for making a successful escape or to barter with unconverted Indians. Some of their actions were downright puzzling to the padres. For example, field hands sometimes injured and abused horses and killed mules. But in reality these were nothing more than straightforward attacks on key elements of Spanish life and missionary domination.[18]

In addition to these common crimes against property, field hands regularly engaged in "silent sabotage," behavior through which they caused considerable annoyance, irritation, and exasperation. They malingered, feigned illness, dragged their feet, worked slowly or indifferently, pulled down fences, slowed down, pretended to misunderstand instructions, vandalized wagons, damaged hoes and other agricultural instruments, wandered from job sites, and worked apathetically. Many required a full day to complete work that should have only taken a morning, and a week to finish three or four days worth of tasks. Some performed careless or sloppy labor when planting, or harvested with great lassitude. Others were simply "incorrigible," refusing to do anything. Neither age nor gender, rank nor status, piety nor wickedness formed a deciding element in foretelling who might contest in these ways. Young men feigned illness; old men hid in bushes or outbuildings; new converts failed to complete assigned tasks; loyal converts balked at discharging risky jobs. Such actions rarely extended beyond individual, spontaneous deeds, and they were subtle and surreptitious, rather than open acts of defiance. Padres labled them "insolence" and "insubordination," nothing more. But taken as a whole they exacted their toll.[19]

Apathetic job performance formed an ever present irritant that confounded the padres and caused them to issue a steady stream of complaints. "They sit down, they recline, they often go away, and come back when it suits them," reported Lasuén. "They begin to ask leave on Wednesday and keep it up until Saturday." Illness—sometimes real, sometimes feigned—and absenteeism significantly reduced his farm labor force. "The healthy [Indians] are clever at offering as a pretext chronic ailments," Lasuén observed, "and they know that they are generally believed, and that even in cases of doubt the missionary dispenses them from work." Padre Luis Martínez, who ran the farming operations at San Luis Obispo mission, similarly complained of his farm laborers, "In my own experience of sixteen years in managing, I have not met one who made any improvement in his work. They are indifferent to all kinds of labor." Most frustrated of all, Padre José Altimira, founder of San Francisco de Solano mission, discovered that he could not rely on his field hands, who, "being so flighty . . . run off, wander about, forget their sacred duties, and do what they please."[20]

The frequency and intensity of these deeds—whether ridicule, sabotage, carelessness, back talk, theft, or slipshod work—ranged from mission to mission, padre to padre, and varied according to the harshness of punishment, interaction with newly converted Indians, and personal idiosyncrasies of different *alcaldes* and *regidores*. There is little doubt, however, that mission field hands, like slaves on plantations in the American South, engaged in widespread expressions of displeasure. The upshot of this behavior was that field hands, through covert resistance and on-the-job actions, demonstrated their dissatisfaction with little risk. But they did nothing to change the conditions of their lives. Eventually, many field hands reached a point where they could no longer continue. To extricate themselves from the holy embrace of the Franciscan padres, thousands of field hands determined to escape.

૪a

Mission records rarely separate field hands from others who fled. But given the frequency of escape, there seems little question that field hands comprised a large portion (if not a majority) of the first runaways. Field hands comprised all but four or five of fifteen Indians who fled San Carlos mission with the *alcalde* Baltazar in one of the earliest mass escapes, that of January 1780. And they were certainly the bulk of those involved in another mass exodus in September 1795, when some two hundred out of 872 neophytes left San Francisco de Asís, as well as a big escape the following year, when another 280 left, and a third, in 1798, when 138 ran away from Santa Cruz mission. After the mass escapes of the late 1790s, the traffic of runaway field hands became increasingly more acute. In 1817, 4,060 Indians fled the nineteen missions. By December 1825, nearly one-quarter of the adult population of Santa Cruz mission was unavailable for labor, having either fled, refused to return to the mission after visiting their rancherías, or failed to report for work due to illness, whether real or feigned.[21]

Field hands fled some missions far more frequently than others. Field hands most distant from their native rancherías and the interior refuges tended to escape in smaller numbers and far less often than those with relatives and villages nearby. Proximity to escape routes and contact with runaways congregating in the San Joaquin Valley also influenced the decision to leave. Some field hands bided their time from the moment of supposed conversion, waiting patiently as they weighed their chances for success. Others, born on the missions, watched the growing number of funerals, and, becoming alarmed by the waves of epidemic diseases, chose to escape what seemed imminent death. These fears, coupled with the energy of youth and the challenge and dangers of life on the run, prompted young men in their teens and twenties to leave in the greatest numbers. But at times it seemed that there was no identifiable reason for leaving other than that the opportunity presented itself.[22]

Questioned after being captured and returned, Indians interviewed by the San Francisco presidio commander and several soldiers candidly revealed why they had fled. Many stated flatly that they ran away from the arbitrary and sometimes crazed wrath of certain *alcaldes*. Others described fleeing savage and brutal punishments. For some there was a burning desire to see their mother, or sadness at the death of a wife or child. Some blamed excessive work, or constant sickness. Hunger and beatings were the most cited reasons. Milan, a hungry native from San Francisco de Asís mission, told investigators that he fled after being beaten for searching for clams to eat. Tiburcio, another native from the San Francisco mission, claimed that he left after he was whipped five times for crying over the death of his wife and baby. Weary of constant abuse, tired, and angry about being forced to work when ill, field hands had ample motivation for abandoning the missions by the thousands.[23]

But while field hands certainly experienced the meanness and cruelty of certain padres, they did not always flee after experiencing injustices, humiliations, and abuse. Men also readily escaped even though they were on the sick list, had been excused from labor or paroled from attending Sunday Mass, and were well fed with food especially prepared for them in their illness. Conditions and reasons for running away were as varied as the Indians and mission circumstances. Sent out to search for runaways, groups of loyal Indians would spontaneously slip away from their soldier escorts and head straight for their native rancherías. Unable to cite any specific abuses, they left unexpectedly, for no apparent reason, as the opportunity suddenly presented itself, or to go along with those more intent on leaving. Of these sudden departures during 1806, the German explorer Georg von Langsdorff could only say: "An irresistible desire for freedom sometimes breaks out."[24]

Whatever the immediate and long-term causes, thousands of field hands demonstrated their discontent with mission life by going on the run. Overall, about one of every ten field hands fled. Like runaway slaves in the American South, many struck out for distant parts, then congregated in remote areas, and formed large fugitive communities. By the end of the mission era, hundreds of runaway field hands and other neophytes from Santa Barbara, San Miguel, and San Luis Obispo missions had accumulated in a swampy area of the southern San Joaquin Valley, near what later became known as Buena Vista Lake. According to Padre Mariano Payeras, they reverted to their pagan state and fought off soldiers sent to fetch them back, forming what Payeras described as "a republic of hell and a diabolical union of apostates." With ever larger numbers of "wayward sheep" escaping into strongholds around Tulare Lake, Padre Lasuén reported that if it were not for the military guard at the missions, most of the baptized field hands and other Indians would return to their brethren in the wilderness. "The majority of our neophytes have not yet acquired much love for our way of life," he admitted. "They see and meet their pagan relatives in the forest, fat, and robust, and enjoying complete liberty."[25]

Fleeing the mission farms and setting up "maroon" colonies was an adventure of enormous dimensions, fraught with innumerable perils and uncertainties. While some runaway field hands traveled in well-organized and well-equipped groups, most escaped individually or in small groups of two or three, consisting of families and close friends from the same tribe. Usually only the most fit and motivated left. The very young, the very old, and the infirm were simply too weak to endure the dangers and physical challenges of the journey.

Flight was most perilous in the winter, when sleeping outdoors was less feasible, travel difficult, and when frostbitten feet might end the escape. Consequently, escapes tended to increase in the summer months, when climatic conditions most favored success and when the approaching grain harvest and the exertions of its attendant work provided added impetus to leave. Field hands would usually slip away under cover of night and head straight for the interior. Several groups fled San Francisco de Asís using crude boats to cross the bay. Two natives convicted of criminal activity even escaped by jumping overboard from a ship while being transported to prison at San Diego mission. Regardless of their method, escaped Indians were immediately thrust into a dangerous and exhausting adventure.[26]

Possessing few if any resources, runaways had to cover long distances quickly. The luckiest fled on horseback, carrying supplies (and sometimes babies and little children) on their backs, but many departed with nothing but the clothes they were wearing. To succeed, they needed not only the physical strength to endure the arduous trip and the stamina to keep going on swollen or bleeding feet, but also the cunning necessary to trick soldiers sent to recapture them. Mothers who fled confronted additional difficulties—including feeding and caring for children, the physical burden of carrying babies, and the inability of youngsters to keep up a fast pace. These burdens slowed them down and imposed massive demands on their energy and determination. Nevertheless, mothers ran away with so many children that in 1798, of the 128 Indians who fled Santa Cruz mission, fifty-eight were children.[27]

Exactly where runaways were headed was never very clear, because such large numbers were caught soon after escaping. Many, apparently, did not have a specific destination in mind other than leaving. Drawing on their knowledge of local terrain, runaway field hands concealed themselves in the woods, skirted swamps, waded in creeks and rivers, and used various ploys and deceptions to cover up their tracks. Quick-witted, wily, deceptive, and calculating, many evaded capture by resorting to the most extreme, clever, and desperate of measures. For example, after escaping San Diego mission on stolen horses in January 1790, two field hands secured their freedom by killing and butchering some cattle and robbing local Diegueño Indians they encountered along the way. To further assure their safe passage, they took a Diegueño woman captive.[28]

Hunger, weather, and geography plotted against success, preventing most fugitive field hands from achieving permanent freedom. Only about one out of twenty-four made good on their efforts. That such a small percentage remained free demonstrates the tremendous stamina required to succeed and the immense dangers and obstacles that stood in their way. Maroons lived a tenuous existence, far more difficult than that experienced by mission field hands. Padres and soldiers alike despised these fugitive communities, and they expended huge energy in breaking them up and bringing them back. However, rounding up maroons was hard, hot, and expensive, even though search parties usually had the help of Indians familiar with the territory. Field hands fled from armed, mounted patrols composed of soldiers, *alcaldes*, and Christian Indians that pursued them, ran them down with their horses, and if they resisted with force, shot them, or tied them to horses and dragged them back to the jail. Those managing to avoid their pursuers still faced overwhelming difficulties, especially many of the second- and third-generation mission field hands, who were unfamiliar with life in the countryside and lacked completely the skills necessary for survival. Suffering from exposure and dying of hunger, many runaway field hands voluntarily returned after a few weeks of uncomfortable independence. Such was the case of an Indian named Bruno. Claiming that he had committed some crime, soldiers from the Monterey presidio abducted Bruno, along with other Indians from San Carlos mission, in September 1787. Forced to work for no pay in the fields, Bruno fled after being beaten by a soldier. "Neither the military nor the Indians had been able to catch him in the twelve days during which he was wandering in the mountains," reported Lasuén to Governor Fages. "He has now given himself up. . . . I hope and pray that after punishing him Your Lordship will permit him to go free." Appended to the letter, Lasuén privately noted that among the farms where Bruno had been forced to work was the orchard of none other than Governor Fages.[29]

While free, field hands like Bruno sometimes engaged in amazing exploits. This was certainly the case for two natives from San Gabriel mission. After escaping, they led Jedediah Smith and his expedition from the Colorado River west across the Mojave Desert and back to the mission in September 1826. Upon their return, they were imprisoned in the mission guardhouse. As with Sebastián Tarabal a half-century earlier, the two escaped San Gabriel mission natives were denied credit for their guidance and services, and Jedediah Smith was hailed as the first American to follow in the footsteps of Garcés and Anza.[30]

Other escapees fared even worse, and some were even turned in by so-called pagan Indians unwilling to harbor field hands and face mission punishments. Even so, many runaways proved to be extremely elusive and frequently did not hesitate to fight off and even kill bands of Christian Indians sent after them. When captured, they refused to give up. And at the first opportunity, they would run away again, not once or twice, but numerous times, despite being apprehended and punished. No matter how often and harsh the punishment, they refused to capitulate. These habitual runaways were so desperate and possessed of such a "spirit of revolt" that they continued to leave no matter what the costs, caring little about the consequences of their defiance. Such escapees were celebrated by their descendants as heroes who had to be whipped until their "buttocks crawled with maggots."[31]

For the perpetually uneasy padres, the problem of large-scale desertion was deeply unsettling, just one step removed from insurgency, the deterioration and possible failure of order, authority, and religion. Runaways symbolized the very aspect of farm labor that the padres could not reconcile with their faith. Few padres were unaware of the discontent and dissatisfaction, and it made them wary about mistreating neophytes. Profoundly troubled by ever increasing numbers of runaways, Padre Narciso Durán confided to San Francisco presidio commandant Ignacio Martínez that he could not "get over the surprise of such an unforeseen occurrence by a people that appeared to be so peaceful and docile." For many padres, hardly anything separated the runaway from the revolutionary. Each one, in his own way, threatened to undermine the system. Constant reports of desertions invariably fed the Franciscan's fears of sedition, rebellion, and the decline and fall of the mission system.[32]

Runaway field hands particularly frightened Alta California governor Felipe de Neve. "The frequent flights of Christian Indians from their missions have created most serious difficulties," he warned in 1782. "The troops have had to make repeated sorties to search for them and bring them back. . . . The more often such expeditions are made, the sooner are the heathen bound to become aware of our weakness and small numbers." Over the course of his tenure as governor, this normally wary and prudent official, who prided himself on giving a present to every Indian he met, became deeply troubled over the mounting numbers of escapees. No matter how industrious, kindly, or punitive he was, he could not stem the flow of runaways. If large numbers continued to congregate in the interior, they would only coax more to leave the missions. By constantly sending out armed expeditions, the governor feared that he might leave the missions vulnerable and undefended, and possibly provoke and anger the pagan Indians.[33]

Most everyone connected with the missions understood that the effectiveness of any system designed to curb the desertions of field hands rested ultimately on both the conditions of mission life and upon local and individual vigilance. While some padres and administrators might choose to debate different strategies, particularly their role in driving field hands away through harsh and unfair treatment, nearly everyone was concerned first and foremost with achieving immediate and conclusive results. Their goal was to keep workers in the fields and souls in the mission. When field hands ran away, it was essential to bring them back. Responding to these concerns, Governor José Joaquín de Arrillaga, after serving two terms, disdained any policy that smacked of conciliation, weakness, or tolerance of runaway field hands. Defectors who held sufficient influence and leadership abilities to cause field hands to escape and fight for their freedom were dangerous. Regarding them as armed traitors, Arrillaga sent out well-equipped patrols to track down runaways, bring them back, and punish them in public spectacles. "By frequent expeditions on the part of the Commanders," Governor Arrillaga suggested, "we might be able to achieve their total conquest or reduction."[34]

Few other aspects of mission life bared the perpetual contest between field hands and mission farming, a contest that struck at the very heart of the food system, a contest that grew in scale and violence toward the end of the mission era. Padres seldom resorted to the techniques used by American slave owners, who punished mothers and fathers of runaways to strike fear among those who might be considering escape, but they were not at a loss for methods of control. Some field hands were dissuaded from leaving with threats of extremely harsh retribution. Those caught fleeing from San Buenaventura mission after they had previously fled and been recaptured were considered especially hardened individuals and placed in stocks.[35]

Spies also proved useful in curbing runaway field hands. At Santa Clara mission during 1805, when a half-dozen field hands and other Indians conspired with a pagan Indian to burn the mission and flee to the interior, spies exposed the plot and the conspirators were arrested. Five years later, spies uncovered another mass exodus and revolt, this one involving twenty-four field hands who supposedly intended, in alliance with sixteen pagan Indians, to wreak mayhem on the mission and then escape to the Central Valley. Arrested and shipped to Santa Barbara mission, the conspirators were whipped daily for nine days and then put to labor in public works. On other missions, recaptured leaders of runaway field hands were jailed and singled out for especially harsh punishment. While followers were held up to ridicule and forced to pray for forgiveness, "ringleaders" received a "sound throttling."[36]

Recaptured field hands who persistently fled the missions received especially harsh physical treatment over and above that accorded other "criminals." Second-time runaways got twenty-five lashes or two or three days in the stocks, sometimes both. Third-time offenders were dealt with even more brutally. First whipped or locked in the stocks, they would be shackled in wooden boots. Those who committed other crimes while on the loose—for example, runaway field hands who took hostages or killed cattle—endured even worse sentences. Turned over to the civil authorities, they were usually condemned to "corporal punishments" consisting of hard labor in iron shackles on public projects at the presidios for three to eight years. Leaders of groups of escaped field hands who had fought off those sent to recapture them usually received the obligatory twenty-five lashes and short terms of imprisonment. Those who killed in defense of their freedom got as many as seventy-five lashes on two occasions, plus eight months in leg irons, followed by years of imprisonment.[37]

Even when confronted with such punishments, field hands accepted the perils and persisted in their efforts to reach safe havens. This was certainly the case at San José mission in 1827, when hundreds of field hands fled with the *alcalde* Narciso, and the following year, when several hundred more fled. Together, they established a fortified village near a place known as *los tulares* (Tulare Lake) and refused to leave. When soldiers attempted to recapture them, the runaways united behind another *alcalde*, a Lacquisamne Indian named Estanislao. "I'm not going back," Estanislao explained through a courier sent to Padre Narciso Durán of San José mission. "We are rising in revolt . . . We have no fear of the soldiers, for even now they are very few, mere boys . . . and not even sharpshooters." Padre Narciso Durán shared the bad news with the commandant of the presidio soldiers: "Publicly, without reserve, they have declared themselves in revolt." After fighting several losing battles with various military expeditions, Estanislao and hundreds of others eventually were worn down under constant pursuit by soldiers and surrendered. Returning to San José mission, Estanislao then became a hunter of runaways until he died of smallpox in 1833.[38]

Far more persistent than Estanislao was Gonzalo, an Esselen Indian baptized at Nuestra Señora de la Soledad mission, who after several attempts at escaping from the padres, sometime before 1820 was whipped and then chained and shackled inside the mission jail. Determined to flee at all costs, he waited until the mission guard was asleep and, producing a concealed knife, cut off part of the heel of one foot to slip out of his leg iron. He then performed the same operation on his other heel without uttering the slightest sound. "But imagine what strength of mind he needs to begin again this cruel operation; for he has as yet gained only half of his freedom!" wrote the French sea captain Auguste B. Duhaut-Cilly a few years later. "He hesitates not; he takes off the other heel and flees, without fearing the acute pain which each step adds to his suffering: it is by his blood tracks that his escape is discovered the next day." Heading for the San Francisco Peninsula, he took refuge in the redwood forests of present-day Santa Cruz and Santa Clara counties, and after recovering from his wounds, joined a band labeled by Padre Viader as the "Insurgents." Along with three or four other Indians who came from as far away as San Diego and San Gabriel missions, Gonzalo allied with Pomponio, a notorious *alcalde* from San Rafael mission *estancia*, and began raiding settlements throughout the San Francisco Bay south to the Salinas Valley. Chased for the next three years by presidio soldiers, Gonzalo and Pomponio became the subject of innumerable folktales. One story has the two being captured at Soledad mission while infiltrating a grand fandango in the Indian quarters. Shackled, placed sidesaddle on a horse, and taken to Monterey the next day, they escaped when Pomponio feigned a call of nature. As the guard put down his lance to assist him off his horse, Pomponio "locked him with the grip of a grizzly," and Gonzalo ran him through with his own lance. The two then broke their shackles, threw the soldier's body in the Salinas River, mounted double on his horse, and headed north. While being pursued through the Santa Cruz Mountains by soldiers and settlers, Gonzalo's horse fell and injured him severely. Fearing discovery, Pomponio murdered his partner in crime in order to conceal his whereabouts, supposedly first telling him: "Ask forgiveness of God, and He will pardon you." Pomponio himself was captured at a mountain hideout near the present-day town of Novato in October 1823. Sent to Monterey presidio, he was tried and convicted on February 6, 1824, and executed in September.[39]

Neither the fear of such punishments nor the difficulties of life on the run prevented other field hands and *alcaldes* from actively resisting Franciscan domination. Aware of the severe consequences of such activities, many field hands adjusted their response accordingly. Rather than fleeing to their home rancherías and waging guerrilla war on the missions, they reacted to individual provocations by decamping for the nearby woods, plains, or mountains. Hiding out for long periods, they survived by stealing cattle, sneaking into the missions at night, and obtaining supplies and rations from friendly neophytes.[40]

Like planters in the antebellum South, padres could not understand such behavior. Asked to explain why field hands ran away, they preferred to assign blame not to themselves or to mission life but to certain Indian characteristics and defects. "Let the more intelligent Indians be asked why they run away," observed a padre at San Francisco de Asís mission, "and they reply: The same things happen to us as to every son of Adam. Naturally we want our liberty and want to go hunt for women." This belief was echoed by padres like Francisco González and Domingo Carranza of Santa Cruz mission, who claimed those who left were driven by base motives and defects of character and race. "Those at this mission cannot entirely gratify their lust because of the vigilance of the missionaries," they claimed. "Hence they run away in order to give full sway to their carnal desires."

The "call of the wild," padres said, was a compelling force that ran deep and strong in the native heart. They were not far from the mark. Well-treated, loyal field hands were not so much motivated by the desire to leave behind mission life as they were enticed by the pleasures of liberty and the pride that they could take in achieving freedom, of being themselves.[41]

≈

Slowly at first, the departure of field hands coupled with their accelerating death and declining birthrates, created a labor crisis in the early 1800s. Barely increasing between 1805 and 1821, the agricultural workforce (and the mission population in general) stagnated. This placed the padres in a dilemma. In need of more natives, the padres could no longer recruit among local tribes. The last large center of Indians, the Chumash in the Goleta area of Santa Barbara, had been incorporated into mission life in 1805. By 1821, nearly all of the Indians remaining along the coast and many of those in the nearby coastal mountains had either fled or been gathered into the missions.[42]

What saved agriculture and provided missions with a continual influx of additional natives during this period were three new sources of labor—kidnapped Indians, retrieved runaways, and hired pagans. The first two came from the inland tribes of the San Joaquin Valley and the Sierra Nevada foothills. The third consisted of those stubborn Indians who somehow managed to resist the padres, continued living according to traditional ways, and cut a deal by which they kept their freedom and traded their labor to mission padres, presidio soldiers, and, more important, to pueblo settlers.[43]

Inland natives began moving into mission farmwork in about 1789, when soldiers from Santa Barbara mission entered the southern San Joaquin Valley in search of fugitives, and 1790, when raiding parties sent out from San Francisco de Asís mission brought back large numbers of Costanoan and Coast Miwok. After that, virtually every mission, as well as the pueblo farmers in and around San José, obtained field hands and other laborers by force from the interior tribes. These operations were at first small and sporadic, but early in the 1800s they grew in scope when, professing to bring Christianity and voluntary conversion to inland natives, missions began dispatching large and well-armed detachments of soldiers and supporting Indian auxiliary. Initially led by padres, these expeditions changed from missionary to military in character and leadership around 1813. From then on, troops moved into the interior not to convert or explore, but to conduct forced labor roundups.[44]

Traversing the coastal foothills in search of "recruits," these forced labor hunts sometimes met stiff resistance, as was the case with the first large invasion of the Central Valley, a foray led by San Miguel mission Padre Juan Martín in 1804. An experienced missionary who had been at the mission for seven years, Martín had baptized 1,169 souls during his tenure, and was in search of more when he traveled into the interior near Tulare Lake. Accompanied by two soldiers, Martín was about to remove two hundred children from the village of Bubal when the headman, a chief named Chape, threatened to fight, and Martín retreated empty-handed. But even if he had been successful, it is unlikely that he could have held the young recruits for very long, as waylaid children invariably grew lonesome and returned home at the first opportunity. Explaining as much in his annual report a few months later, Martín admitted that "it is the painful experience of the missionaries that such Christians, very much attached to their Tulare homes, leave the mission, and in consequence lose the holy Mass and offend God, and hide in the Tulares region where they cannot be taken out without peril and without troops."[45]

Just how little inland natives thought of the prospect of becoming field hands, learning Christianity, and settling on the mission farms became abundantly clear the following January. When Indians from the village of Asiremes attacked and killed three neophytes and wounded a padre and soldier from San José mission as the group made its way through the Livermore Valley, a force of eight soldiers and fifteen civilians located the natives responsible for the aggression, ambushed them, and in a fierce battle, killed five natives and captured thirty-nine. Under the guise of hunting down those who had attacked the padre, they then ventured further inland and captured even more natives, marched them back to San José mission, and tried to convert them to the cause of Christianity.[46]

Because they only vaguely comprehended what was happening, captured Indians made bad converts. According to the American traveler William Heath Davis, Indians obtained in such expeditions "were guarded closely until they had become accustomed to the new life and had lost all desire to return to their native homes." According to the English ship captain Frederick Beechey, who likewise observed one of these expeditions, "If . . . any of the captured Indians show a repugnance to conversion, it is the practice to imprison them for a few days, and then allow them to breathe a little fresh air . . . after which they are again shut up, and thus continue to be incarcerated until they declare their readiness to renounce the religion of their forefathers."[47]

Not all natives who went to work in the fields were captured and subjected to forced conversion. Many arrived voluntarily, remained entirely free, and worked under a crude wage system—the first California farmworkers to be so employed. Beginning in July 1797, parties of armed men from the pueblo of San José began moving into the countryside in search of pagan laborers. Paying off the ranchería captain with a blanket, they obtained crews of twenty or more men and set them to work constructing irrigation ditches that also served as barriers to keep cattle out of the wheat fields. By August, the practice had become routine. To bring in crews of pagan Indians to harvest the entire hemp crop, all that Gabriel Moraga, the commissioner of the pueblo of San José, had to do was contact Pala, "the pagan captain" of the hill tribe of "San Antonio." While the lure of pay in goods (largely cloth) proved strong, many pagans seem to have gone to work for other reasons. Most important among these was their distaste for work on the presidios. Unable to plant their own crops or properly defend their rancherías from raiding Indian tribes while working for the soldiers, they jumped at the chance of working locally. "They are quite happy to leave off from the other projects and tasks that they so abhor," reported San José pueblo commissioner Ygnacio Vallejo to Governor Borica. After twenty additional field hands arrived in late September, a labor surplus developed, and Vallejo decided to make good use of them. Cautioning farmers and townspeople to treat pagan field hands fairly and pay them promptly, Vallejo began dispatching crews to local farmers, who promptly set them to work in the fields.[48]

By the mid-1820s, arrangements for hiring pagan field hands had spread north to San Francisco de Solano and San Rafael Arcángel missions. While far more favorably suited to agriculture than San Francisco de Asís mission, neither mission had enough field hands to bring in its wheat and corn harvests. This created an opportunity for Indian chieftains in the nearby foothills. Realizing that there was a harvest labor shortage, chieftains north of San Francisco Bay did something that would mark a key turning point in the farmworker story, something that is generally dated much later and is usually attributed to the Chinese. They became labor contractors. When the harvest was ready, chieftains would bring in large crews, set up temporary camps, and spend two or three weeks picking, winnowing, and threshing the wheat and barley. Then they would vanish with the end of the harvest season—like their successors three-quarters of a century later —not to be seen for another year. For their efforts they received neither food, wages, nor shelter, taking with them only a portion of the harvest. They were such an impressive sight as they trooped in by the hundreds to harvest wheat at San Francisco de Solano mission that everyone paused to watch. After observing several hundred of them, including women and children, during the fall of 1827, the ever present Duhaut-Cilly wrote:

> Nothing is more miserable than the people at the little camp they had pitched in front of the padre's dwelling. The men are nearly naked, and the women have only a cloak made of narrow strips of rabbit skin twisted into strings and sewed together. This garment is very warm; but being thick it serves as a retreat for an immense number of those parasitic insects so disgusting to us; for them, on the contrary, it is a kind of portable poultry-yard, where, in leisure moments, each one selects his choicest dish.[49]

Hired Indians had their greatest impact not on the missions north of San Francisco Bay, but on the pueblo farms around Los Angeles, where rancherías shifted rapidly away from their traditional hunting-gathering economy to cultivate their own crops, or those of the settlers of Los Angeles. Most were Gabrielino, Fernandeño, or Serrano Indians from the area between San Juan Capistrano, San Gabriel, San Buenaventura, and San Fernando missions. Unlike those working on the northern missions, natives employed on the pueblo farms of Los Angeles were not always hired through their chiefs or in any kind of labor contracting arrangement. Nor did they arrive and depart with the harvest. Many toiled on a year-round basis, finding work on their own, as individuals, conducting their own deals with settlers under a quasi-free wage labor system.[50]

By 1787, hired pagan field hands had become numerous enough for Governor Pedro Fages to institute a comprehensive code regulating their employment. Under his code, pueblo farmers were required to treat hired Indian field hands fairly and to provide them with adequate compensation, usually one-third to one-half the crop, as well as a blanket and meals. Enticed by this method of compensation,

California natives became a common sight on the farms around Los Angeles. In September 1795, Padre Vicente de Santa María of San Buenaventura mission, while traveling through the Simi Valley to select a site for San Fernando mission, was astounded to see crews of Indians irrigating, weeding, and chasing birds from fields of corn, beans, melons, and wheat on Rancho San José de Francisco Reyes. Santa María then headed southeast to Paraje de la Zanja, where he observed unconverted Indians tending patches of corn, watermelons, sugar melons, and beans on the rancho of Mariano Verdugo. "The whole of pagandom . . . is fond of the Pueblo of Los Angeles, of the rancho of Mariano Verdugo and the rancho of Reyes, and of the Zanja [water ditch]," he complained to Lasuén, adding that there were so many "pagans passing, clad in shoes, with sombreros and blankets, if it were not for the gentiles there would be neither pueblo nor rancho."[51]

Eight years later, Indian field hands began clearing land and planting dozens of small vineyards around the pueblo of Los Angeles, work that would have a dramatic impact on winemaking in California and on labor in Southern California. By 1812, the use of hired Indian field hands had grown to such proportions that San Gabriel mission padres Luis Gil y Taboada and José Maria Zalvidea could scarcely contain their disgust. Reporting to their superiors, the two padres complained:

> In the pueblos and ranchos . . . pagans, men as well as women, serve as farm laborers, cooks, water carriers, and in other domestic work. This is one of the most potent causes why the people, calling themselves *de Razón*, are so addicted to idleness. As the pagans labor for one-half or one-third of the product, they are constantly in the service of their masters during the time of planting and harvesting, while the masters . . . never put their hand to the plow or sickle. Hence . . . the adult Indians delay having themselves baptized, and follow their . . . pagan habits.

With commercial wine production expanding rapidly, the padres could not stop the growth of the hired labor force nor their descent into pagandom. Hundreds of Indian wage laborers were employed planting 53,686 vines in Los Angeles during 1816, and another four thousand grapevines in 1824 for Joseph Chapman, a Yankee variously described as a shipbuilder, and sailor, and one of the first American settlers in Los Angeles. As winemaking and its attendant tasks grew, hired Indian workers took over responsibility for building and maintaining irrigation canals and planting and tending all of the other pueblo crops. Without them, pueblo agriculture would surely have withered for lack of labor.[52]

૭ઌ

Toward the end of the mission era, the pace of work sped up considerably for both mission field hands and hired pagan workers, a change spurred largely by Mexico's battle for independence from Spain. As the country struggled to establish its own economy, the annual stipend of four hundred pesos that had been issued to each missionary by the viceroy of New Spain was terminated. In addition, missions now became subject to taxation and forced requisitions by the Mexican government. Left to rely upon their own resources for the first time—and with more than twenty thousand natives to feed—the padres after 1810 expanded production of wine, brandy, fruit, grains, and, most important, animal hides. Exchanged for needed goods with American, British, and Russian traders, these products generated a thriving trade between missions, with those strong in one area like grain production bartering with others specializing in goods such as fruit or cattle.[53]

To accomplish all of this, mission and pueblo field hands increased output. By 1821, dozens of stone storehouses had been filled with wheat; cellars stocked with red claret and sweet, white table wine; there were 14,973 mission cattle, 193,234 sheep, 5,772 horses, and 2,011 mules; a tallow industry; and a flourishing hide trade. So large was the hide trade toward the end of the mission era that, during the frantic two-week long shipping period every summer, field hands would have to break from their duties and join hundreds of other laborers loading hides on board ships. Piling thousands of hides onto creaking *carretas*, the backs of mules, and sometimes their own heads, the men formed a small army marching across the landscape to the ships waiting on the embarcaderos.[54]

The pace of change for field hands further increased after September 1821, when, having fought, defeated, and achieved independence from Spain, Mexico took charge of Spain's North American territories, including Alta California. Mexican control of the missions opened an era of rapid economic growth and transformation, as the sale of surplus goods to foreign markets accelerated. Numerous foreign companies quickly bid for access to California's hide and tallow industry. In June of 1822, just months before the Spanish flag was officially lowered at Monterey presidio, the English trading firm of McCulloch, Hartnell and Company obtained a three-year monopoly on the purchase of the province's surplus hides and tallow. Governor Pablo Vicente de Solá thought that, with legal trade replacing contraband, California was sure to prosper. "The poverty of the Province will disappear," agreed Santa Barbara mission Padre Mariano Payeras, "and it will be even less necessary to order items from Mexico City."[55]

As the Mexican government formulated a policy that promoted the rights of individuals over those of the church and slowly expanded the definition and privileges of citizenship, it sent a representative to select a new governor, Luís Antonio Argüello, who assumed office in 1822. But racked by political turmoil, Mexico failed to establish a firm hold on Alta California, and over the next two years did little more than develop the structure of a territorial government—a *diputación*, or provincial assembly; *ayuntamientos* or town councils for the pueblos of San José and Los Angeles; and a provincial representative to the Mexican congress. When Argüello's appointment ended in 1825, the Mexican government sent José María Echeandía north to serve as governor of Alta California. An earnest, dedicated public servant and former Army Corps of Engineers lieutenant colonel, Echeandía faced several daunting problems—settling the land, dealing with the influx of American fur trappers, controlling rebellious Spanish soldiers, consolidating government control, and exploiting whatever natural resources could be found. But his primary task by far centered on the missions and the Indian field hands living on them.

During Governor Echeandía's administration, field hands and the rest of the adult mission Indian population were supposed to inherit mission lands. Both their rights under the democratic principles of the Mexican revolution and the new government's determination to integrate everyone into Mexican society mandated the immediate emancipation of mission field hands and other Indians. To accomplish that goal, Echeandía announced a provisional plan, effective only in certain military districts (San Diego, Santa Barbara, and Monterey). Padres would be replaced by "secular" clergy, missions converted into parish churches, and control over native field hands terminated. Later known as "secularization," Franciscans and other mission defenders would come to refer to these changes as "the spoliation." For mission farmworkers, secularization ushered in the most destructive period in their entire history.[56]

Echeandía's plan called for mission field hands to join a new society. All mission land and assets, including animals, tools, and structures found on both the missions proper and on the various *estancias* and ranchos, would be annexed to existing pueblos. All would be governed by elected councils headed by *alcaldes*. Two plots of land, one for a house and one for crops, would be allocated to each family of mission Indians, along with cows, oxen, and tools needed to work the land. Once the land had been distributed, the remaining property and tools would be divided among the *gente de razón* settlers. The missionaries, now demoted to the status of parish priests, would retain rights only to their living quarters and the mission church. Everything was to be supervised by an administrator, who, bound by Echeandía's policy, would be directed by the local town councils and territorial governments, with all income used to pay the salaries of teachers and to maintain public institutions.[57]

In theory it was a good plan, one that would have transformed propertyless field hands into settled farmers. In practice, it was a catastrophe. Field hands at San Juan Capistrano mission were the first to learn of their new status when Lieutenant Romualdo Pacheco, an emissary dispatched by Echeandía, informed them during a visit early in 1826. Hearing that they were free, full, and equal citizens of Mexico, and that they were to receive land and tools, the assembled decided to take matters into their own hands. They rose in rebellion on January 22, 1826, and demanded that the corporal of the guard place the aged Padre José Barona in stocks. Shortly thereafter, they refused to return to the fields. In what may have been the first strike or job action in California agriculture, more than one hundred Indians ignored pleas to work and walked off the mission.[58]

Liberation came to most field hands on the southern missions six months later, on July 25, 1826, when Governor Echeandía issued his decree of partial emancipation. Married field hands and others who had been Christians from childhood (or for at least fifteen years), and who had some livelihood or skilled trade, were allowed to petition the commander of the local presidio, who in turn obtained information on them from the padre. If they met the required provisions of emancipation, the presidio commander then issued a written permit entitling them to travel wherever they wanted, "like a member of the Mexican nation."[59]

Sadly, most mission Indians did not make an easy transition to their newfound freedoms. Their old ways destroyed, and ill-prepared for the tenuous new society, mission Indians fell into disorganization and drunkenness. Most could not get from independence the things they really wanted—enough food, self-sufficiency, respect, land, and some way in which they might ascend in Mexican California. Those remaining on the missions often found themselves diverted away from agriculture into the production of livestock. With farming operations in chaos, the size of grain crops declined. Once abundant, food grew scarce toward the late 1820s. But these difficulties did not divert Indian field hands from their nearly universal desire for freedom.[60]

Although they may not have known very well what the future held in store for them, most field hands had little desire to continue as they had in the past. Even life on the edge of starvation seemed more appealing than captivity on the missions. But liberation extracted its price. Neglecting their prayers, skipping Sunday mass, and allowing their dress and appearance to degenerate, thousands of former field hands who could find neither work nor shelter were compelled to beg, steal, plunder, and wander aimlessly. Too many of them became, according to Frederick Beechey, "so obnoxious to the peaceable inhabitants, that the padres were requested to take some of them back to the missions, while others who had been guilty of misdemeanor were loaded with shackles and put to work."[61]

Despite such difficulties, many field hands struck out on their own. At San Juan Capistrano mission anarchy prevailed. Robbing one another and even soldiers, field hands refused to work. When padres begged them to go to work, field hands would only say that they were free, and went about their business. Field hands departed the southern missions so quickly and in such great numbers that Padre Francisco Gonzalez de Ibarra could only lament, that at San Buenaventura mission, "the crops cannot be sown at the regular time and even those that are sown are lost, for there is no one to harvest them."[62]

While hundreds of field hands experienced their emancipation in 1826 and 1827, most had to wait many years for their freedom. The delay was the result of an influx of Mexican settlers who saw mission lands as theirs for the taking. To accommodate the newcomers, Echeandía backed off his initial program and limited emancipations to those Indians who could support themselves with their skills. In 1831, just as Echeandía was formulating a new policy that would free all married Indians who had been on the missions ten years or more and all widows with minor children, a new government seized power in Mexico and Echeandía was replaced by Colonel Manuel Victoria. A ruthless, unpopular, and reactionary blowhard, Victoria halted plans for secularization, ignored the needs of mission field hands, and refused to call the territorial council into session. Instituting the death penalty for minor offenses and sending respected Californians into exile, Victoria in fact ruled in such an autocratic fashion that on January 17, 1832, several prominent Southern Californians rose in rebellion, drove him from office, and reinstalled Echeandía as governor. Unfortunately, the insurgents then proceeded to squabble among themselves for power, so in mid-January 1833, the Mexican government sent General José Figueroa north to sit as governor and continue with the task of secularization.[63]

While undoubtedly the most astute and competent of all Alta California governors, Figueroa could not surmount the turmoil caused by years of confusion, fighting, and political intrigue. Left to fend for themselves, liberated field hands further descended into chaos. That summer, two or three hundred San Gabriel mission Indians drifted into the pueblo of Los Angeles and joined other mission Indians and pagan Indians who worked in the pueblo by day and passed most of their evenings gambling and drinking. Alarmed by their wild, disorganized, and miserable condition, San José mission Padre Durán, who had twice served as president of the Alta California missions and was no friend of secularization, on July 3 reported what he observed to Governor Figueroa:

> Beyond comparison they live far more wretched and oppressed than those in the missions. There is not one who has a garden of his own, a yoke of oxen, a horse, or a house fit for a rational being. . . . For offenses which the white people consider small, or as nothing among themselves, those Indians are placed over a cannon and given a hundred blows to the naked body. . . . All in reality are slaves.[64]

Fifty miles south, field hands at San Luis Rey mission responded to news of their freedom not by drifting away, but rather by remaining on the mission. Like their compatriots in Los Angeles, these Indians also quickly descended into squalor. Drinking, fighting, gambling, robbing, and murdering one another, they went about shouting "Soy libre!" (I am free!). This so frightened Captain Pablo de la Portilla, the commissioner appointed to oversee them, that on February 10, 1833, he requested troops to protect himself and prevent anarchy. Arriving from Los Angeles to investigate, Padre Durán confirmed the sad state of affairs, finding the padre there "a veritable slave," field hands, tallow makers, and fishermen "unwilling to work," and Portilla afraid to take action against them. "With my own eyes I see the insubordination of these Indians as to the work that pertains to them," he reported to Figueroa. Again pleading for an end to secularization, Durán asserted that the state of affairs was due entirely to "lack of adequate punishment" and "having no power at hand to make them work."[65]

Figueroa ordered the arrest of a half-dozen troublemakers but refused to back off from his plan to break up the missions and distribute their land. In July, he personally selected more than sixty families for emancipation at San Diego mission, and more than one hundred at San Luis Rey mission. Calling them together, he explained that he was giving them land and water for irrigation as well as cattle and seeds, and that they could now use their agricultural skills for their own benefit. But Figueroa could not generate any enthusiasm for his plan. The Indians found little in pueblo life that was attractive and let Figueroa know that they were content to continue as before. "I was grieved to hear them renounce everything so as to remain in the servitude in which they lived," he later reported to the minister of foreign relations. Figueroa continued his attempts to entice as many as possible to leave the missions, hoping their example would inspire others to follow. But of the sixty families selected at San Diego mission, only ten accepted emancipation; at San Luis Rey mission, only four of the chosen one hundred agreed.[66]

The response of field hands and other natives at these two missions convinced Figueroa that many natives were not yet ready for freedom. He further observed that emancipation from the missions had unintentionally bound many of them in debt servitude to the pueblo settlers. Consequently, he embarked on a compromise policy. After conferring with Padre Durán, Figueroa issued his "Provisional Steps for the Emancipation of Mission Indians," which closely resembled Governor Echeandía's secularization orders of seven years earlier.

Under the new plan, emancipation would be instituted gradually, with the governor conferring with a new commissioner to decide how Indians would be freed at each mission. Only those natives who had been converted to Christianity for twelve years and who were willing to work would be eligible. Figueroa's plan initially applied only to natives on the four southernmost missions, with those at San Juan Capistrano mission first in line for emancipation because they seemed the most "civilized." During the first year of freedom, field hands would be given land, food, and other assistance, but would be required to help the mission at planting time and during the harvest, as well as at other critical times when farm labor was necessary. Emancipated Indians would be full Mexican citizens, and the land they received would be their own, with title bestowed by the governor and inherited by their children. When sufficient numbers of natives left the missions, they would be allowed to form their own pueblos and choose their own magistrates, town council members, and a *síndico procurador* (person who looked after the interests of the town). In exchange, they would be expected to participate in public works projects like digging and building dams.[67]

Almost immediately, field hands at San Juan Capistrano mission, led by their *alcaldes*, demanded control of all land in the area. They had already begun irrigating the land and using it to support themselves. Unlike their counterparts at San Diego mission, who seemed "so prejudiced and incapable of thinking that many of them refused to accept the favor," and those from San Luis Rey mission who avoided work at all costs, the Juaneños of San Juan Capistrano mission believed strongly that they had earned title to all mission land through their collective labor. When administrators ordered them to move off the mission to the *estancia* of San Mateo, they instead demanded access to the lands they had worked all along. "To stand by and watch these [the newly appointed mission administrators] take over the missions which we have built, the herds we have tended, and to be exposed incessantly, together with our families, to the worst possible treatment and even death itself, is a tragedy," exclaimed one *alcalde*. If the governor did not give them their property, the Juaneños threatened they would confiscate "all of the livestock that could be led away" and head for the San Joaquin Valley. Accordingly, on October 13, 1833, Governor Figueroa granted their petition and ordered the lands about the mission proper to be assigned to them in equal portions. Sometime in November, they formed their own pueblo and began farming for themselves.[68]

Whatever benefits field hands gained from Figueroa's plan for partial secularization, they were soon undone. Several weeks before receiving Figueroa's proposal, the Mexican legislature had passed a bill secularizing all of the missions, thereby immediately releasing thousands of neophytes from missionary control. Early in 1834, field hands and the rest of the converted natives at ten of the missions were placed under civilian administrators. Most were unprepared for freedom. At San Juan Capistrano mission, Indians often went about in "utter nakedness." Many refused to recognize the authority of the new *mayordomo*, and avoided work in the vineyards. This created huge problems for the missionary, who had borrowed 465 pesos from government officials and had promised to repay his loan in wine and *aguardiente*, the rough brandylike liquor that had become a principal product of the local economy. Without field hands, he could produce neither.[69]

As crops withered, orchards went to weeds, and cattle were left untended, the ever present Padre Durán wrote to Governor Figueroa of the disorderly state of affairs. "I myself experienced how an Indian *alcalde* presented himself before me with the demand that a certain *mayordomo* be removed and that for no other reason than because he, the Indian *alcalde* was the judge and did not want *mayordomos*," Durán explained. "Such is the situation. . . . No Padre is able to get anything out of them. . . . All is owing to the insubordination of the Indians." Conditions were no better on other missions, where only through much pleading and persuasion could the government administrator induce unruly field hands to sow a few acres of wheat.[70]

For almost all emancipated field hands, there eventually came a defining moment when, for the first time, they suddenly understood that liberty had become a distinct reality. But what did freedom mean? "When all the Mission Indians heard the cry of freedom, they said, 'Now they no longer keep us here by force,'" recalled San Buenaventura mission field hand Fernando Librado. Congregating in the woods or in secluded assembly spots and meeting secretly at night, they prayed, sang, celebrated, rejoiced, and shared in the excitement of their impending independence. In a letter to Governor Figueroa, Pablo de la Portilla, an official in charge of secularization, reported finding field hands everywhere claiming, "We Are Free! We do not want to obey! We do not want to work."[71]

By the original secularization decree, adult males were supposed to receive not only a portion of the mission land and property, but they were also to take control of all the missions and convert them into pueblos under the supervision of a civil governor. But Figueroa's secularization order of 1834 whittled down the offer of land from two plots to one, gave Indians only a "portion" of mission tools and livestock, and provided no real guidelines to define their status or enforce provisions to distribute property and land. Subsequent instructions that entrusted all surplus property to government-appointed administrators hardly helped. Consequently, for most field hands, liberation was a frightening and confusing idea, and many reacted with doubt, skepticism, and fear. None knew for certain what freedom meant, how far-reaching the changes would be, or how much it would redefine their place in society. In the absence of any comparable experiences, some field hands resorted to what they understood and were familiar with.[72]

Very old and ill field hands often dealt with the uncertainties by refusing to accept their liberty. A few responded by offering comfort and solace to their padres. That they sympathized with the same people who had for generations controlled them revealed in a very dramatic way the uncertainty and vacillation that many field hands felt on the verge of their own independence.[73]

FIGURE 8. Sometime in the mid-1860s, the photographer Edward Vischer posed Jonathan Warner with a crew of former mission Indians working as foremen and vaqueros on Warner's ranch in San Diego County. Courtesy of the Security Pacific Historical Photograph Collection, Los Angeles Public Library.

The Meaning of Free Labor

The General [Sutter] tells the Chief how many
hands he wants for the next week, and at
daylight on Monday they are sure to be there.
  —*William Dane Phelps*

You can employ any number of Indians by
giving them a lump of beef every week, and
paying them about one dollar for the same time.
  —*John Bidwell*

Any Indian . . . found loitering and strolling
about . . . shall be liable to be arrested . . .
brought to any Justice of the Peace . . . to hire
out such vagrant within twenty-four hours . . .
to the highest bidder.
  —*An Act for the Government and
    Protection of Indians*

Los Angeles had its slave market as well as new
Orleans and Constantinople, only the slave at
Los Angeles was sold fifty-two times a year
as long as he lived, which generally did not
exceed one, two or three years under the new
dispensation. Thousands of honest, useful
people were absolutely destroyed in this way.
  —*Horace Bell*

Somebody might make a fortune selling
drunken Diggers in Napa City.
  —*'Napa Register'*

They have filled our jails, have contributed
largely to the filling of our graveyards, where
they must either be buried at public expense
or permitted to rot in the streets.
  —*'Los Angeles Semi-Weekly News'*

CHAPTER FIVE

Not Free to Be Idle

Life and Labor on the Mexican

Ranchos and American Farms

One afternoon in January 1831, field hands and other workers at San Miguel mission crowded into the courtyard to hear Juan B. Alvarado, the newly appointed mission administrator, speak about their emancipation. After a vivid portrayal of the advantages of freedom and the prospect of obtaining their portion of the mission lands, he then asked them to make a choice. "Those who want to continue living with Padre [Juan] Cabot step to the left of me," Alvarado said. "Those who prefer to be free men and become owners of their own land, step to the right." Most stepped to the left, and were shortly joined by "a small minority who had not the courage of their convictions." After listening to their new status as citizens, many field hands and other workers on San Luis Rey, San Antonio, and San José missions made similar choices. Remaining loyal to the missions and their private administrators, they carried on their labor for little more than food and housing, sometimes for nothing. "It reminded me of the old Roman lady," Alvarado later recalled, "who began to weep when she learned about the death of Nero . . . [because] it was better to know one bad person than a good one unknown."[1]

But not all mission field Indians reacted to news of their freedom with empathy and vows of loyalty. Some expressed rage against the Spanish superiors and padres who had dominated them for so long. On one mission after another, field hands joined other neophytes in violating the interminable minor regulations that had been imposed upon them, and although many were still reticent about disclosing their feelings, some found them impossible to hide. Reacting against the keen personal surveillance that had characterized mission farmwork, Indians partook in wild and rebellious celebrations, feasted on barbecued meat, and left the fields strewn with rotting carcasses. By far the most common reaction was simply to withhold labor. "The Indians want the freedom of vagabonds," complained Padre Narciso Durán. "No Padre is able to get anything out of them."[2]

On San Gabriel and San Juan Capistrano missions, *alcaldes* and field hands demanded the removal of *mayordomos*, and on San Luis Rey mission, natives dis-

FIGURE 9. Supposedly 136 years of age when photographed in 1885, Victoriano, "chief of the Soboba Indians," (above) had been an *alcalde* at San Gabriel mission, and as a young man had helped establish the mission vineyard and orchards. Copy print from original glass-plate print. Born at Loreto, Baja California, Eulalia Pérez (facing page) married a soldier at age fifteen, bore three sons (one of whom survived) and came north to San Diego mission where she worked as a midwife. After her husband died, she became the *llavera* (housekeeper) at San Gabriel mission. She was 139 years of age when photographed in the 1880s. Courtesy of the California Historical Society/Title Insurance and Trust Company Collection, University of Southern California; and the Bancroft Library, University of California, Berkeley.

EULALIA PERZ, 139 YEARS OF AGE.

rupted the plowing and wheat planting schedules. Confronted with these early farmworker strikes, Pablo de la Portilla complained bitterly in December 1834: "I must suffer the pain of being obliged to suspend work for want of hands. The men have mistaken the voice of reason and even of the authority which orders the work, for they declare they are a free nation."[3]

During the first few years of freedom some field hands and other native workers from San Fernando mission petitioned for emancipation, demanded property, and in 1839 received papers that made their status official. Beginning in 1843, they obtained land and transformed it into small cattle ranches, modest orchards of pomegranates, pears, and oranges, and communal crop and livestock operations that supported dozens of Indians and their families. Receiving the first land grant issued to emancipated mission workers, an Indian named Samuel from San Fernando mission erected a house, planted a small orchard, and proceeded to grow corn, wheat, and beans. Other field hands and emancipated natives began building small living quarters near the missions. Separate from the local Mexican and Californio communities, these settlements were comprised of tule houses, adobe liquor shops, small stores, boardinghouses, and livery stables. One of the largest, Pueblito de las Flores (Little Town of the Flowers), a village on a twenty-square-mile block of land near San Luis Rey mission, had a population of thirty-two families and supported small herds of sheep and cattle, various oxen, cows, and other livestock, a large cultivated area, a vineyard, and extensive cornfields. But these were the exceptions, not the rule. Very few former field hands understood the laws of land use and ownership; they had little personal understanding of the political machinations of the outside world, and never received the training necessary for leading a free and independent existence. Ill-equipped to comprehend the idea of private property and how to bargain for and keep it, they became easy pickings for Mexican settlers and Yankee businessmen and steadily lost title to thousands of acres of land.[4]

Those field hands who dared fight for their rights usually faced retaliation and a long, drawn-out struggle. But occasionally, they won. In June 1836, a San Luis Rey mission field hand named Pablo Apis led a protest against Pío Pico, the cruel and rapacious administrator who was bent on removing field hands from Rancho Temecula mission lands, as well as the *estancias* of Pala, Agua Caliente, San Jacinto, Santa Margarita, and San Isbel, because they had the most fertile soil, best pasturage, and largest supplies of water. So desperately did Pico want these lands for himself that when Apis protested his scheme, Pico arrested him. The following year, when four other field hands persisted in demanding the land on which their families had resided for generations, Pico jailed them too. After this failed to scare off the remaining field hands, Pico attempted to outmaneuver them. On the evening of January 17, 1840, he summoned all the *alcaldes* of the mission and falsely announced that the governor had ordered all to leave, and that they should form a free town near the mission, or, if they wanted, go to Los Angeles. This was a particularly insidious scheme, since the area he told the natives to settle was arid, sandy, and lacking in resources and would force those living there to seek work in the fields. When even this attempt failed to induce the natives away from the best mission lands, Pico threatened floggings, stocks, chains, and imprisonment. As those at Temecula braced for a fight, a delegation of eleven field hands traveled to Los Angeles to plead their case before the governor. In December 1840, Governor Juan B. Alvarado assigned them at least partial control of Temecula and the other ranchos and *estancias*, and removed Pico from management of the mission properties. Those field hands and their compatriots would live on their *estancia* lands, in some capacity, for generations.[5]

Hundreds of field hands and other workers from San Diego mission endured a far more protracted ordeal when they lost title to Agua Caliente ranchería, an *estancia* astride the southern trail to California in the San José Valley of present-day northern San Diego County. In 1844, Jonathan Trumbull Warner, a native of Connecticut otherwise known as Don José Warner, obtained the property through a grant from Governor Manuel Micheltorena. Under Warner's ownership, the Cahuilla and Cupeño Indians maintained their rights to live there as before, and by all accounts they prospered. Visiting the ranchería after it had been renamed Warner's Ranch, Judge Benjamin Hayes found the Indians contented and self-sufficient. "In the huts are bushels of a nut whose kernel has the taste of a peach—a sort of plum (I was told). They make a meal of it and bread," he reported. The women ground these nuts, acorns, and wheat into meal that they sold at two dollars per *almud*. One woman did some washing for the judge at one dollar for eight pieces of clothing, while the men worked in the fields for themselves and, on occasion, for Warner.[6]

Field hands remaining on other missions recoiled in shock and horror as they were obliged to continue plowing, planting, harvesting, caring for livestock, and tending gardens to pay for the salaries of the various *comisionados, mayordomos,* and other officials appointed to oversee the mission properties. Freedom, in their minds, had meant cessation of work, the termination of punishments, and the right to obtain land, reap the fruits of their labor, and do as they liked. But with no place to go and no way to make a living, many were forced to salvage some kind of life by doing what they always had done. On San Gabriel mission, field hands were passed along, with most of the cattle and remaining tools, to Henry Dalton, a British ranchero who took charge of the mission early in 1846. Compelled to work under administrator Bernardino Guirado and *mayordomo* Andrés Duarte, field hands in February petitioned the governor with a long list of grievances against the two men. But it was already too late. By then, many had become so addicted to games of chance that they had lost their blankets and even their clothes; going about naked, they slept in straw and in the mission ruins. On other missions demoralized field hands fared little better and descended into self-destructive behavior. At San Buenaventura mission, freed natives caroused, drank, and fought incessantly. "There was sometimes trouble . . . when the Indians . . . had a big drunk," recalled a native. "When they got boisterous, the night patrol would come and drive the Indians out of the plaza like sheep, and the order would be given that if any of them got boisterous again, they would be shut up in the jail."[7]

As living conditions worsened, it became impossible for most field hands to continue on the mission farms. Whether or not they worked under avaricious or benevolent administrators, thousands of field hands resolved to test the boundaries of their supposed liberty. "Complete anarchy reigns just as though there were no government," reported Durán in September 1837 of conditions at Santa Barbara mission, where only 246 of fifteen hundred neophytes remained. "Everyone does what suits him. Grain and fruit are stolen from the fields, the cattle are killed and the hides sold. Religion alone preserves a degree of peace."[8]

If they were genuinely free, then field hands could abandon the missions where they had toiled and never go back. Walking off the mission farms therefore offered the most certain and rapid way for field hands to prove to themselves that the padres no longer governed them—that they were, for the first time, free to go about their own lives. Although some field hands would remain on the missions, most left. Within ten years of secularization, most field hands were gone. At San Juan Capistrano mission, for example, just eighty out of 861 neophytes remained in 1838; on San Luis Rey mission, only six hundred of three thousand remained in 1841; on San Francisco de Solano mission, only fifteen of thirteen hundred remained in 1835; and at San Francisco de Asís mission only fifty of fifteen hundred natives could be found eking out a living by raising corn, potatoes, and vegetables around the church in the early 1840s.[9]

Like runaways during the previous sixty years, the majority of field hands who left following secularization fled to the interior intent on abandoning farmwork in favor of traditional hunting and gathering methods. Sadly, many lacked sufficient training in the old ways and succumbed to starvation. Others became stock raiders, stealing cattle and horses from their former mission fields, and then selling or trading the animals to American mountain men and trappers. Around Los Angeles, they so terrorized settlers and provoked among them such vicious retaliatory raids that it seemed to Los Angeles prefect Santiago Argüello in 1839 that "the entire southern district is paralyzed." A small number of field hands also formed fighting bands to thwart local authorities venturing out to recapture them for labor. For the most part, freed neophytes remained near the missions they abandoned. Begging, stealing, scrounging, and beseeching inhabitants for help, they lived perilously on the edge of starvation. With no other means of supporting themselves, many continued working as field hands, either on the farms springing up around the dusty Mexican pueblos (particularly Los Angeles) or on one of the more than seven hundred private ranchos that Mexican authorities were granting to well-favored settlers. Covering more than eight million acres of land, these individual estates were fast replacing the missions as the most important social and economic institutions in the coastal zone between San Francisco and San Diego. Whatever choice they made, native field hands found their lives further transformed—and not for the better. If, under mission rule, they had worked as forced laborers and had their culture and independence systematically undermined, they at least benefited in some small ways from the munificence of padres who were charged with their care. They were at least fed, clothed, and housed. They would experience nothing close to that level of concern on the pueblo farms, ranchos, or vineyards being established by Mexican and Euro-American newcomers. Here, mission field hands would find themselves at the mercy of men willing and able to rule them with an unrestrained hand.[10]

Nowhere in Alta California did the dispersal of mission Indian field hands produce a greater catastrophe than in and around Los Angeles. The process began in July 1833, when hundreds of destitute and homeless mission natives arrived in the dusty pueblo hoping to find work. With nowhere to live, they settled in wretched conditions on the outskirts of town, a vast body of wandering, vagrant laborers whose only hope lay in the parsimonious charity of the Mexican citizenry. Angered and depressed by their plight, Padre Narciso Durán in July described their plight in a letter to Governor José Figueroa. "Beyond comparison," he concluded, "they . . . lead vicious and irrational lives."[11]

What drew mission natives to Los Angeles was farmwork. With about 170 farms, Los Angeles was emerging as California's leading agricultural region. Boasting of 112 acres of vineyards and about one hundred thousand vines, the area shipped wine and brandy as far as Hawaii and New England. It was therefore natural that mission field hands would seek employment in one of the few industries needing more laborers. Many went to work for Jean Louis Vignes, a native of Cadillac, France, who almost single-handedly established the commercial wine industry in California.[12]

Natives did not handle any skilled vineyard work; for that, Vignes paid the passage of experienced Frenchmen who labored for years grafting the imported vines onto native rootstock while they paid off their debts. But former mission field hands did just about everything else. Initially employed cutting irrigation canals from Río Porciúncula, they plowed fields three times a year, hauled vine cuttings in the winter, picked grapes and crushed them every fall, and helped Vignes build his famous El Aliso winery into one of the principal businesses and cultural centers of Southern California. During the five-year period between 1837 and 1842, Indian laborers planted more than one hundred thousand vines for Vignes and his neighbors. But even as Vignes's wine production increased and his neighbors, fur trappers–turned–vineyardists William Wolfskill and John Rowland, began shipping wine as far east as Boston, mission field hands spiraled into an increasingly miserable and degraded state. That was because, despite the agricultural boom, there were simply too many former mission Indians for all to find work.[13]

Indian field hands congregated in two settlements. The smallest was Pipimares, a cluster of huts housing Gabrielino Indian field hands, servants, and roustabouts from the Santa Barbara area. The largest was an unnamed settlement housing field hands and other laborers from San Juan Capistrano, San Fernando, San Luis Rey, and San Diego missions, which sprawled over a tract of Los Angeles city property along the banks of Río Porciúncula near what is today the southeast corner of Commercial and Alameda streets. No longer prohibited from drinking liquor as they had been on the missions, many of the Indians were addicted to *aguardiente*. Misbehaving and collapsing in the streets, they slept on doorsteps and earned a reputation as rough and dangerous laborers who loved to carouse and fight. Such behavior, according to Francisco Durán, was tolerated "provided they work and say *Amen* to everything."[14]

Most of the time, natives fought among themselves, but as the incidents of public drunkenness increased and as more field hands arrived, fearful Mexican authorities cracked down. Beginning on January 28, 1836, intoxicated natives were

arrested and assigned to work on the main irrigation ditch that tapped Río Porciúncula. Soon after, Los Angeles officials began requiring natives to carry documents indicating the reasons they had been released from work and where they
were headed; none could obtain employment without these passes. Men who
lacked documentation remained unemployed; those found loitering in public
places were arrested as vagrants, tried quickly, and after always being found guilty,
fined, and given a choice between a stint in jail or work on public projects like
mucking out the *zanja madre*.[15]

Every February and March, local farmers were required to supply laborers for
work repairing the area's vast communal irrigation system. Reluctant to force their
own hands to perform this odious task, many ranchers instead bailed out drunken
Indians and sent them off to do the work. Any jailed native could be fed into the
system. Allowed to work off their debts under an arrangement resembling legalized peonage, these unlucky field hands would toil all day—sometimes up to their
thighs in cold and mucky water—shoring up diversion dams and clearing debris
from the channels.[16]

As drunken natives were being pressed into work around Los Angeles, conditions on the missions continued to deteriorate. By 1839, Pío Pico, lord of Rancho
Santa Margarita near San Luis mission, could no longer keep his field hands.
"Every day they are running away," he complained in a letter to merchant
William Hartnell, "three laborers fled and if the rest who remain see that no steps
are taken to [recapture and discipline them] I will be left with none and . . . go to
ruins due to lack of hands." Elsewhere, so many Indian field hands left the old
missions and ranchos that Governor Alvarado feared the "great dearth of . . . laborers," coupled with alcoholism and nonpayment of debts, threatened to undermine the new order and cause "irreparable damage."[17]

As more and more native field hands left the missions for Los Angeles, residents grew increasingly alarmed at their behavior, and on September 6, 1845, met
to discuss a course of action. Following an especially violent harvest season, authorities in December issued a series of edicts that forced most Indians to leave
town. Taking their families across Río Porciúncula, field hands joined other natives and established a new community, which they called Pueblito (little town).
Five months later field hands departed Pipimares under similar circumstances
and established a second native settlement outside of town. But distance did not
free the natives from harassment. Because they continued to drink and carouse
to excess, a group of twenty-six Los Angeles citizens headed by winemakers
Vignes and Wolfskill took further action against them. "We thought that the isolation of these aborigines would prevent the committing of excess and thefts,"
they wrote to the governor of California in February 1846. "But we are sorry to
say it has proved to the contrary. . . . They steal all neighboring fences and on
Saturdays celebrate and become intoxicated to an unbearable degree."[18]

The governor failed to intervene and instead turned the matter over to the
town council, which, on May 2, 1846, placed members of the two Indian villages
under the control of an "honest warden" who instructed them to "moderate their
customs" and "thereby avoid crimes." When these measures failed, the townspeople authorized the destruction of Pueblito. Given twenty-four dollars each to

help them relocate, field hands and their families this time moved to widely scattered settlements outside the city limits. If they wished to remain in town, the council decreed they had to live with their employers. If they violated that policy, they were arrested, fined, and put to work.[19]

Meanwhile, as secularization of the missions greatly weakened the power of the Catholic Church and caused massive changes in California society, a new ranchero landowning class was expanding across the countryside, very largely on the backs of Indian field hands. About twenty private land grants had been made to retired soldiers during Spanish rule, but between 1834 and 1846 more than seven hundred private land grants were made to sons of soldiers and well-favored Californios, as well as a few favored European newcomers. About half of these were located within one hundred miles of Los Angeles.[20]

A society of all-powerful judges, employers, and military commanders, rancheros were labeled by one scholar as "grandees of the frontier California landscape," in control of vast principalities, some as large as fifty thousand acres. All these rancheros had to do was petition the governor and present a map of their desired land, then establish and mark the boundaries of the grant, more or less, often following a process that was decidedly casual. Demarcation points and property lines often consisted of little more than creek beds, large trees, skulls, or strange-looking rocks, any of which might shift or disappear unexpectedly. Some ranchos were "floating grants," consisting of a specific territory anywhere within a large, vaguely defined region. Most rancheros were equally casual about meeting land grant requirements—like actually living on their property, making improvements, and properly recording them. But most stayed and established elaborate adobe and rough timber villas. The house of Don Bernardo Yorba on Cañada de Santa Ana near Los Angeles, for example, consisted of thirty rooms and another twenty-one for servants. Many of the large landowners around Los Angeles lived in town while their isolated ranchos were operated by relatives and mestizo *mayordomos*. These ranchos housed 10 to 20 percent of the area's non-Indian population and were not nearly as grand as Yorba's estate. José de Carmen Lugo, a ranchero whose grandfather had been on the Rivera y Moncada expedition, described some early ranchos as dung-strewn places where shelter was rarely more than two crude rooms and people slept on leather cots or beds of cottonwood, if they were so lucky. On such ranchos, Indian field hands often went about "clad in shoes, with sombreros and blankets, and serving as muleteers to the settlers and ranchos."[21]

Ranchos were devoted to the care and maintenance of vast herds of cattle, which produced the principal articles of commerce for Mexican California—meat, hides, and tallow. By the mid-1840s, the hide and tallow trade would emerge as California's first export business. It was a lucrative enterprise that earned fortunes for Yankee hide merchants like Abel Stearns and attracted a wave of English-speaking foreign immigrants who would adapt to local conditions by learning Spanish and adhering to Mexican customs and usage. Many of these men would also become rancheros.[22]

To maintain smooth operations, rancheros supported entire communities of natives, including vaqueros, tanners, soap makers, harness makers, shepherds, winemakers, cooks, carpenters, blacksmiths, servants, and field hands. Of these groups, the native vaqueros were naturally the most numerous and important, but field hands, whose numbers increased at harvest time, remained integral to overall operations. Their job remained what it had always been: They produced the crops required to maintain the ranchos as economically independent hide and tallow producing communities. Without them, the ranchos could not survive or prosper.[23]

If the rancheros themselves are to be believed, former mission field hands lived happily and well as part of close-knit communities under wise and benevolent protection. "These people we always considered as members of our families," asserted Mariano Guadalupe Vallejo's younger brother Salvador. "We loved them and they loved us; our intercourse was always pleasant." Several hundred mission Indians lived at two locations on Rancho Sonoma, and they deployed to their various jobs much as they had in the mission days. They reclaimed neglected gardens, restored the mission's broken irrigation system, planted hundreds of olive, lemon, plum, orange, apple, and pear trees, and four hundred to five hundred acres of corn, beans, barley, and wheat. Their activities transformed the mission from a state of ruin into a Mecca for visitors that was noted for its beautiful, tree-shaded promenades, decorative gardens, fine hospitality, and extensive, well-stocked wine cellars.[24]

Native laborers performed approximately the same services ten miles to the west, at Vallejo's 44,280-acre estate in the Petaluma Valley. After uprooting two thousand grapevines from San Rafael Arcángel mission, they brought them twenty miles north and planted them on a low hill topped by an imposing edifice known as El Palacio (the palace). Behind six-foot-thick adobe walls and broad balconies, they tended a huge garden of squash, tomatoes, and melons and hung strings of red peppers and beans to dry in the sunshine beneath the stockade veranda.

At the old San Francisco de Solano mission, wives and daughters of field hands were kept busy catering to Vallejo's personal needs and serving his wife and sixteen children. A traveler found them everywhere about the patio of the grand house. Not accustomed to such a sight, he asked the general's wife about the Indians and was astonished by her reply.

> Each one of my children, boys and girls, has a servant who has no other duty than to care for him or her. Four or five grind corn for the tortillas. . . .
> About six or seven are set apart for service in the kitchen . . . nearly a dozen are charged to attend to the sewing and spinning; for you must know that, as a rule, Indian women are not much inclined to learn many things. . . . We give them all they need. When they are sick we care for them as though they belonged to the family. When their children are born, we act as godfathers and godmothers, and we take charge of the education of their children. . . .
> In a word, we treat the servants as friends rather than as servants.

This was the happy picture of life on the ranchos.[25]

But even then, foreign visitors saw through the pompous and usually elaborate feasts and festivities thrown in their honor and glimpsed unhappy faces among the Indians. English explorer Henry Simpson recalled Vallejo's field hands as being "the most miserable of the race that I ever saw, excepting always the slaves of the northwest coast . . . badly clothed, badly lodged, and badly fed." The observation probably came closer to reality than the version promoted by rancheros.[26]

Perhaps a total of two to four thousand Indians toiled in this way for the various rancheros. While smaller operations employed only a few former mission field hands each, the larger ranchos, like Cañada de Santa Ana, employed more than one hundred emancipated Indians. These field hands generally lived in their own village near the main house or in thatched huts, camped under trees or beside the gardens and corrals.[27]

On some ranchos, field hands went about naked or dressed in animal pelts and discarded clothing. No longer part of a communal relationship as on the missions, yet often still living on what had been mission property and in former mission quarters, they saw virtually none of the profits their labor produced. Some plunged deeply in debt to rancho stores that advanced them food and goods—most often liquor—against their wages. This system of debt peonage prevented them from leaving, as they were forever obliged to repay what they owed. And with many of them owing as much as fifty dollars while earning the equivalent of twelve and a half cents per day, few could ever hope to pay off their liability, or obtain redress for unpaid wages, unacceptable labor conditions, or brutal treatment from *mayordomos*.[28]

While most former mission field hands probably never realized that a new legal code was in place, there is fragmentary but compelling evidence that some adopted a new political consciousness and attempted to use the Mexican court system to exact justice, address their problems, and assert their rights. Rather than fleeing, striking, or refusing to cooperate, some field hands cast their faith in the new authority and found an imperfect way to resist exploitation. One of the first examples of this approach came about 1838, at Santa Clara mission, where a lecherous *mayordomo* named Vicente tried to pry field hands away from their wives. Threatening to take drastic action if the mission administrator did not remove Vicente and install a new *mayordomo*, thirty field hands drafted a public notice, signed it with thirty X's, and apparently posted it for the public to read. "We give our administrator 8 days to remove him [Vicente] and put another in his place," they wrote. "If this is not done as we state, one of two things will happen: Either this man will experience some misfortune or 30 of us men will walk off until we can meet with [local officials] making them aware of the public notices that there are on the ranch, all of them pertaining to Vicente and our wives." A second example of this evolving political consciousness came five years later, when a group of field hands employed by Pajaro Valley ranchero José de Jesús Vallejo refused to work and left the rancho. Accusing Vallejo of mistreating them, they also petitioned the local authorities, who promptly approved their claim and took action against Vallejo. Whether or not such examples made any lasting impression is unclear.[29]

&

For so-called wild Indians scattered on farms throughout California, such political action was entirely out of the question. These Indians toiled under the watchful eyes of new immigrant farmers who were laws unto themselves. Arriving before census keepers were sent out to tally their numbers, they began extending the farming frontier north and into the interior. One large group of Indian field hands laboring under these newcomers populated the coastal plateau near Fort Ross, a Russian settlement fifty miles north of San Francisco de Solano mission. Founded in 1812 and charged with growing crops to feed the huge numbers of Russian sea otter and fur seal hunters that roamed the coast from Alaska to Monterey, Fort Ross, also known as Fort Russia, needed to establish a highly productive farming operation. The Russians relied on Kashaya Pomo men from the nearby ranchería of Métini to help clear land for growing grain and vegetables and then to assist in harvesting and threshing wheat and barley. The number of Indian field hands increased dramatically after 1814, when the Russians planted a peach orchard east of the fort; as part of the project, Kashaya Pomo hands hacked away the brush and erected fences to keep the deer out of young trees. Each following year, the Russians multiplied the number and variety of fruit trees—which increased the harvest to such an extent that by 1821, hundreds of Indians were seasonally employed in various farm and farming-related activities, from drying fruit to building fences. Paid in goods—flour, tools, clothing—several dozen field hands settled in or near the fort with their families. In time, the two cultures intermarried.[30]

This symbiotic relationship proceeded smoothly until the early 1830s, when the Russians expanded agricultural production further inland, away from the fog (which the Russians called "rust" and which made farming very difficult), and over the next few years added four farms: Chernykh, Khlebnikov, and Kostromitinov, and an unnamed farm near Bodega Bay. By 1838, more than 250 Pomo field hands and other laborers worked at the Kostromitinov farm; at harvest time, roughly half of them were engaged in cutting, hauling, threshing, and winnowing the grain. At Chernykh, a peak harvest crew of fifty to seventy-five men harvested pears, cherries, and peaches and laid the pitted fruit out to dry in the sun. At Khlebnikov, Indian laborers grew grapes, which they harvested as fresh fruit and also made into a brandy flavored with the bitter cherries grown at Chernykh. The success of these new agricultural ventures required a larger number of Indian workers than were available locally. To augment the labor force, the Russians abandoned the policies of the 1820s and resorted to intimidation, kidnapping, and coercion. Sweeping into interior villages, they rounded up entire rancherías at gunpoint and took hostages—women and children—to ensure that the men would labor diligently. Spanish visitors immediately noted the shift to unfree labor. Touring Kostromitinov during the wheat harvest of 1834, Governor José Figueroa wrote in his diary how the Russians "were using, for labor, besides the settlers, some Indians from the villages whom they brought usually by force."[31]

By the late 1830s, native field hands at Fort Ross were almost entirely conscripted laborers. Miwok Indians, who had once worked for the Russians as a way to protect themselves from enslavement by Spaniards, now found themselves subjected to the very practices they had tried so hard to avoid.[32]

The use of kidnapping by the Russians at Fort Ross underscored the willingness of settlers and farmers to exploit Indian vulnerability while amassing a labor force. If the Russians sometimes whipped a man to within an inch of his life, it was excused as a way to restrain his restlessness, check any tendencies toward impudence, make an example of those who did not obey, and keep them in their place. But violence was not always necessary. Sickness and hunger were also powerful incentives to work. Harvard-educated John Marsh, California's first practicing doctor, discovered this in 1837 after settling in at Los Méganos, his huge rancho on the eastern slope of Mount Diablo, twenty miles east of San Francisco Bay. Almost immediately, Marsh noticed that the local Miwok suffered terribly from malaria. Obtaining a supply of quinine, he distributed the medicine in exchange for plowing and planting. Dependent on Marsh for relief from their suffering, the Miwok worked for next to nothing. This so impressed Marsh that he began writing letters to acquaintances throughout the United States extolling the virtues of abundant and cheap Indian labor and vast expanses of fertile land. Marsh's letters circulated widely in the Midwest and generated a significant influx of immigrant farmers. Upon arriving in California, these men followed Marsh's lead and promptly hired Indians to clear land, plant fields, and establish ranchos.[33]

In the grainfields of the Livermore Valley just twenty miles south of Los Méganos, Miwok Indians worked as "human fences"—chasing cattle away night and day, storm and sunshine—for such minimal rewards as a quarter of a beef a week. Employed under similar arrangements in the Napa Valley, natives erected their huts amid farming strips, women and children tending the crops by day, men riding along the fields at night as a "live fence" to drive out wild animals and stray cattle. So common were camps of "migratory heathens" in the Sonoma Valley at this time that, according to one traveler, they arrived during threshing season "to earn, by means of communal labor, a better living than is possible for them in the wilderness," then turned to winemaking "girt with their loin cloths only . . . and trampled out with their bare feet the mass until it was reduced to a pulp." Everywhere in fact, interior natives of Northern California were hiring themselves out to settlers and farmers—selling their labor to the recipients of huge land grants, to the administrators farming near San José mission, to General Vallejo, John Marsh, to anybody who would offer them food, clothing, medicine, or tools.[34]

છે

Of all the settlers employing Indian field hands at this time, none did so on a grander scale than John Sutter. An odd figure to occupy such a pivotal role in the farmworker story, Sutter was a German-born dry-goods merchant who abandoned his wife and five children, fled Switzerland for New York in 1834, and spent the next five years losing himself in the American frontier. After a failed series of get-rich-quick schemes, he arrived in California in 1839, where he became a Mexican citizen. Earning the favor of California governor Juan B. Alvarado, Sutter persuaded the politician of the need for an interior colony that would check the power in the northern region of Alvarado's uncle and political rival, Mariano Guadalupe Vallejo, then ensconced in Sonoma. Settling at "New Helvetia," his newly granted forty-eight thousand–acre rancho twelve miles below the junction of the Sacramento and American rivers, Sutter proceeded to establish a kind of feudal barony with himself as the unchallenged power. The first step toward this goal was to establish a one-sided partnership with local Indians. The best way to do this, he reasoned, was to prove his might. Before he even set foot on dry land, Sutter fired his nine-pound brass cannon at some trees "to show the Indians the effect of powder and shell." The blast had the desired result, and several Miwok natives from the Walagumne tribe, who had been watching from the underbrush, agreed to become Sutter's guides. Organized under a headman named Anashe, who Sutter later recalled, "was inclined to be in favor of peace, and to make terms of friendship with me," they steered him north into Nisenan Indian country and agreed to work as field hands and laborers, vaqueros, tanners, and roustabouts. For their efforts headmen received offers of cooperation and pledges to live among them in peace and were reimbursed with gifts of glass beads, brightly colored handkerchiefs, Hawaiian sugar, and blankets.[35]

Once Sutter's New Helvetia settlement was founded, the Miwok pitched camp nearby. Now living in close proximity, Sutter became aware of the rampant disease and abject poverty that characterized Indian life. Ravaged by malaria and smallpox, the Miwok wore fur pelts or nothing other than tattoos on their chins. Many seemed to possess few personal belongings besides weapons and decorations that dangled from their pierced noses. Because so many had worked on the missions and understood at least a minimum of Spanish, Sutter found it easy to organize and direct them. After the first group of Miwok had worked for a short time breaking ground for wheat, they were joined by Nisenan, and together the headmen from each tribe so impressed Sutter with their reliability that he began calling them *capitanos* (captains).[36]

Within a short time, Indian headmen emerged as the key figures in Sutter's farming operations. But these Miwok and Nisenan crew bosses were not traditional farm labor contractors. They did not make money providing food and housing for their workers nor did they charge them for their services, as would later contractors. But they did extract their price. Besides gifts and favors, they required certain concessions and privileges. The most important concession was exclusion from Sutter's ban on polygamy.[37]

With their own status considerably heightened by these special marriage privileges (and by extra gifts and rewards) grateful headmen reciprocated by feeding Sutter's egotistical tendencies. One favorite ploy capitalized on his love of pageantry. A headman would lead in a contingent of field hands carrying a full array of bows and arrows. He would then run his men through drills before finally laying their weapons at Sutter's feet. "Take these," he would say, "and with them penetrate my heart if I or my tribe betray the trust you now put in us and which we now solemnly promise to keep." In this way, they communicated the pride, power, submission, and loyalty necessary for a smooth working relationship. According to New England ship captain William Dane Phelps, who visited Sutter's Fort in 1842, the relationship between the *capitanos* and "the General" functioned seamlessly. Sutter "tells the Chief how many hands he wants for the next week," recalled Phelps in his memoirs, then "at daylight on Monday they are sure to be there."[38]

FIGURE 10. Located near the confluence of the Sacramento and American rivers, Sutter's Fort was a citadel, industrial plant, and wayside inn whose farming operations rested entirely on Indian labor. Lithograph from an 1846 drawing by Joseph Warren Revere. Courtesy of the California Historical Society.

After Anashe, Maximo, Narciso, Simplon, Rufino, and other headmen formed their alliances with Sutter, they became loyal allies and then, through their clever balancing of assertiveness and cooperation, amplified their standing. But Nisenan and Miwok field hands did not remain at Sutter's Fort merely out of obedience to their headmen. Impressed by Sutter's fabricated title, and fearing his ever present bulldog and brace of pistols, they were also kept in check by a combination of terror, intimidation, and coercion, along with monetary rewards and access to food and other resources. However, nothing was more important in compelling obedience than the massive presence of Sutter's Fort itself.[39]

Laid out on a low hill beside the American River, Sutter's Fort was the largest armed compound in the American West. To native field hands—even those who had helped create the edifice—it must have been a truly imposing presence. With thick adobe walls, the fort was designed for defense against Indian attacks and foreign incursions, but it also effectively controlled labor by funneling field hands in and out through a single, large guarded gate.[40]

Providing neither beds nor straw bedding, Sutter required his field hands to sleep with their wives and their children on bare floors in the barracks. Sutter's overseer, a Swiss immigrant named Heinrich Lienhard, was responsible for the barracks and charged with locking workers inside every night. He later left detailed descriptions of their appalling conditions: "When I opened the door for them in the morning," recalled Lienhard, "the odor that greeted me was overwhelming, for no sanitary arrangements had been provided. What these rooms were like after ten days or two weeks can be imagined." Sutter's barracks were not only smelly, uncomfortable, and flea-infested, they were unhealthy. Contagious diseases—particularly measles—spread through the quarters so regularly that Sutter had to hire a doctor to attend the needs of the ill and dying. But while the doctor was able to treat and save the lives of several field hands who were seriously injured while plowing and harvesting, he was unable to curb the spread of diseases. Because of this, field hands tried to combat the epidemics by resorting to native remedies and nightly religious ceremonies. Worried that the rituals disrupted his work force and undermined his authority, Sutter refused to tolerate the gatherings. When field hands persisted, Sutter cracked down, burning their ceremonial dance house and banishing their native medicine men from New Helvetia.[41]

Sutter consolidated his control over Indian field hands by demonstrating just how casually he apprehended and jailed runaways, and how easily he disciplined, banished, and even executed malcontents. Some of Sutter's acts were hideous. During the summer of 1845, for example, natives were terrified by the macabre sight of the severed head of Maximo's son, Raphero, rotting over the fort gateway, a sickening and unavoidable symbol of the penalty for inciting rebellion. Indians were constantly subjected to such terror; the following summer, they were forced to pass under the remains of a Miwok brave named Eusebio. Arriving at Sutter's Fort, Heinrich Lienhard later recalled seeing "a gruesome sight . . . the long, black hair and skull of an Indian dangling from one of the main gateposts." Reminiscent of intimidation techniques used by Spanish soldiers three-quarters of a century earlier, this display of a defeated enemy illustrated dramatically the price to be paid by any Indian field hand plotting to burn the wheat crop or otherwise defy Sutter.[42]

Sutter's personal army ensured further compliance. Every day field hands watched overseers drill a curious-looking force of 150 native infantrymen and fifty native cavalry. All were dressed in red-trimmed, green-and-blue uniforms purchased from the Russians at Fort Ross. Comic as they appeared, these soldiers proved to be a potent, lethal force for controlling field hands who stole cattle, injured horses, ran away, or refused to work. Never hesitant to employ them, Sutter sent his soldiers into battles against many recalcitrant native groups, ranging as far as twenty miles away from New Helvetia. As a result of these actions, scores of native prisoners, including children whose parents had been killed in these battles, were brought to New Helvetia and put to work in the fields.[43]

Whether they came to Sutter's employ through headmen or by force, New Helvetia field hands worked like slaves. They would be rented and shipped out to other farmers as partial payment for the many debts Sutter had incurred. In labor-scarce California, "perfectly guileless" field hands who would "work with a good will" proved be an extremely profitable commodity. Adults rented for eight to ten dollars per month, boys employed three days brought six dollars, and field hands and vaqueros sent off with horses commanded three dollars per day. Earning at times as much as one-third of his income from these leased laborers, Sutter would often dispatch them south to farmers around San José by way of John Marsh's Los Méganos rancho, where they arrived, according to Marsh, "as usual, dying of hunger."[44]

Sutter's field hands did not endure such hardships solely out of fear. Earning the equivalent of twenty-five cents per day under a scrip payment system, they were paid in currency consisting of tin discs with one or more star shapes cut into each. A disc with one star indicated one day's work, two stars meant two day's work, and so on. Field hands wore their discs proudly like decorations on strings around their necks. On Sundays, they cashed them in for goods at Sutter's store. One week's work earned a yard of cheap, unbleached cotton or calico. Two weeks' labor bought a plain muslin shirt or a cut of cloth large enough to make a pair of trousers. Two months' rental work at a distant rancho merited enough discs for several woolen blankets, a good stock of needles and thread, plus some liquor. Especially diligent and loyal field hands could also earn bonuses, which usually consisted of an extra allocation of cloth, sugar, or a pair of boots. Credit was also available.[45]

Field hands were additionally bound to Sutter because they depended on him for their food. Every day, when the evening dinner bell (or drum) sounded, Indians would break off work, leave the fields, and pass through the gate leading to the fort. In a procedure they followed faithfully, they first washed and cleaned themselves, then walked to a central courtyard and assembled near some hollowed-out logs, each three to four feet long. When the cooks began serving up buckets of gruel made of boiled ground barley or corn, or some other kind of mush, and the offal of slaughtered animals, field hands packed the troughs tightly to receive the food. Shouting and elbowing one another, they ate as fast and as much as they could, scooping out portions with their fingers and fighting one another for the last scraps. Witnessing the scene while visiting the fort in 1846, the Virginia-born frontiersman James Clyman recorded in his diary how Sutter's field hands "run to the troughs like so many pigs and feed themselves with their hands as long as the troughs contain even a moisture." So frenzied, raucous, and competitive were these meals that one Nisenan Indian later recalled them as inhuman, animalistic affairs that were "like a hog's feeding trough."[46]

৶৯

By 1846, Sutter's field hands had cleared and planted more than one thousand acres and were growing vast fields of corn, plus smaller plots of tobacco, rye, beans, potatoes, radishes, leeks, and strawberries. Under the direction of a German gardener, Sutter's field hands also used cuttings and seedlings from San José mission to establish a vineyard containing five to six thousand grapevines and plant small orchards of peaches, plums, and apricots. Visitors expressed astonishment at seeing long lines of field hands endlessly carrying earthen containers full of water from the river and nearby ponds to irrigate rows of lettuce, carrots, turnips, peas, cabbages, melons, and even Roses of Castile. They were also impressed by work at Hock Farm, Sutter's second agricultural operation, located thirty miles north along the Feather River, where field hands raised an earthen dam to divert river flow into a network of irrigation canals and furrows. But of all the work done by Sutter's field hands, nothing was more impressive than the intense labor native workmen expended to harvest and thresh the ever increasing wheat crops.[47]

Sutter's grain crop was so large that it became necessary to employ temporary harvesters—so-called wild Indians—who migrated in from distant rancherías. As many as six hundred came and went in a season, some staying only a few weeks or months, others remaining for the duration. Their work stretched from the beginning of the harvest in mid-June to the end of threshing in late November. These temporary harvesters regarded the work in much the same way they did the acorn harvest—as yet another in the sequence of food-related activities required for surviving another year. They would never have more than a transitory relationship with Sutter. They were seasonal employees, ready and willing to shift between their own communities and temporary encampment in Sutter's fields. These traits, which define the lives of farmworkers today, became normal and accepted characteristics for the first time among the temporary field hands flocking in to harvest Sutter's wheat.[48]

Usually at the end of a day's work, field hands would hold a great fiesta. Butchering four or five old bulls, they would gather around the barbecued carcasses, slice off portions and gorge themselves on as much meat as they desired. Habitual gamblers, they liked to pass the evenings drinking and playing games of chance. Often they would bet and lose all their clothes and blankets. When this happened, they would work the next few days entirely naked. Then, earning a few discs, they would turn them in, obtain more goods, and resume their gambling.[49]

Neither Sutter's permanent field hands nor his temporary harvesters had any access to labor-saving technology. Despite the wide acceptance of mechanical reaping and threshing equipment on farms in the eastern United States at this time, none of the machines had as yet made its way into California. Indeed, it would be a decade before grain-mowing machines and horse-powered threshers would arrive at New Helvetia. But the delay was not caused by Sutter's indifference. Quite the contrary, upon first learning of them from Captain William Dane Phelps during his visits to New Helvetia in 1841 and 1842, Sutter had immediately tried to obtain some machines, but he could not get his hands on them. Without any machines, hundreds of "wild" Indians, and "tame" Miwok and Nisenans were required for the 1843 and 1844 harvests. In 1845, when wheat harvesting, bean threshing, and all of the other farm tasks overlapped in midsummer, Indian infantrymen and cavalrymen had to be pressed into service in the fields.[50]

A shortage of tools made harvest work even more labor intensive, and forced men to improvise as best they could. Sutter had just five or six scythes, which could only be operated by the largest and strongest men. Most were not natives, but rather overland immigrants who had used the tools back home. Sickles were in such short supply that Sutter carefully allocated them only to the fittest natives. Hundreds of field hands had nothing more elaborate than butcher knives or pieces of iron barrel hoops roughly fashioned into cutting devices. Many used thin willow sticks split lengthwise, and a few who lacked implements altogether, gathered the grain by using their hands to break off the dry and brittle heads of wheat. No matter the method, it was backbreaking work.[51]

Once cut, the crop was loaded onto *carretas* and conveyed to a threshing corral. There, just as on the missions, the wheat and straw were separated by driving mares over it. In this task, field hands did benefit from one technical improvement—Sutter's threshing corral. Purchased from the Russians at Fort Ross, it had eight-foot-high redwood plank walls, rather than the packed adobe or stone *ladrillos* of mission days, and was capable of threshing two hundred bushels of grain in one day. But since Sutter did not yet have any fanning mills (devices that fed the threshed straw into an artificial stream of air), field hands still winnowed the grain as they had on the missions—by tediously tossing shovels full of wheat into the air on windy days.[52]

In the spring of 1846, Sutter's field hands became involved in the first attempt to mechanize farm labor in California. They were given thirty new American-type, heavy sodbuster plows that had been manufactured on site by Sutter's blacksmiths. Forged from thousands of pounds of surplus metal Sutter had collected from sources throughout Northern California, these modern implements dramatically increased the efficiency of plowing. In fact, field hands planted so much new land that Sutter feared he would not be able to attract sufficient workers for the coming harvest. Hoping to avert a labor shortage, Sutter in April 1847 ran an advertisement on the front page of the *California Star*: "TO MECHANICS: The subscriber wants Two Threshing Machines for wheat . . . cash will be paid for the same, on delivery at Yerba Buena or New Helvetia; for further information apply to E. P. Jones Esq., San Francisco or New Helvetia." The request, though widely read, evoked no response.[53]

Threshers may not have yet been available, but field hands that spring did receive some help from labor-saving tools. First, Sutter provided a half-dozen cradles—essentially scythes with a frame of slender rods or fingers attached behind the blades to catch and stack the cut grain. No longer required to work in a fatiguing stooped position (as they had while swinging their heavy sickles), men using cradles could cut at about the same rate as those using scythes, though they still required two or three extra hands to follow and gather the grain. The second new device, a fanning mill, vastly increased output and dramatically reduced the amount of time devoted to winnowing operations. Employing cradles and fanning mills for the first time in the fall of 1847, Sutter's field hands threshed a record twenty-two thousand bushels of wheat, nearly three times the previous year's crop.[54]

Sutter's field hands accomplished a great deal in very little time. They worked so well, in fact, that just a few years after establishing New Helvetia, Sutter began making plans for a cotton plantation. And Sutter was not alone. As he and John Marsh had been establishing feudal domains largely independent of Mexican control, others had been following them into the interior valley with similar intentions. During 1840, only about four hundred overland immigrants and former fur trappers arrived in California. But in 1841, a former schoolteacher named John Bidwell gained fame as the heroic leader of the first overland trek to California, a terrible twenty-four-week ordeal during which the thirty-two members of the expedition had to eat their mules to survive. On arrival, the group stopped briefly at Marsh's rancho, where they received a cool welcome; they then dispersed throughout the Central Valley, and each settler in turn hired native field hands and began farming. Not long thereafter, another large group trekked into California, this time from Santa Fe, and became prominent rancheros in the Los Angeles area. By 1843, the number of newcomers had doubled, and during 1844 the first wagon train of settlers rolled across the Sierra on what would become the main route to California.[55]

Two years later, perhaps three thousand Americans had arrived. Refusing to become Catholics or Mexican citizens, many nonetheless secured grants of land (while others just squatted on a tract), and, in so doing, accomplished what Spain and Mexico had failed to do—effectively colonize California. As more settlers poured in, native field hands took on even greater importance.

By mid-1846, field hands were performing well on dozens of farms from San Francisco Bay north to present-day Red Bluff. Few settlers, in fact, could imagine a future without them. Despite all of the rhetoric concerning Indian timidity, stupidity, and infantile ways, most settlers believed that "with some instruction" Indians were a useful class, "easily domesticated," who rapidly learned all of the tasks about the farm, particularly "when caught young." Of hiring practices on Rancho Chico in the northern Sacramento Valley, John Bidwell observed: "You can employ any number of Indians by giving them a lump of beef every week, and paying them about one dollar for the same time." In fact, though many rancheros were loath to admit it publicly, settlers of all persuasions—whether an American like Bidwell, a Swiss-German despot like Sutter, or even a Danish pioneer like Peter Lassen—regarded cheap Indian laborers as essential to their success. Pierson B. Reading, another former Sutter employee and Bidwell's distant neighbor in upper Sacramento Valley farming, went even further: "The Indians of California are as obedient and humble slaves as negroes in the South," he wrote. Hiring Indians "for a mere trifle you can secure their services for life. . . . They were mild and inoffensive in their manners and easily taught the duties of the farms." John Marsh added that they submitted to "flagellation with more humility than negroes," and in doing so would even choose the appropriate number of lashes and yield to the whipping "without the least sign of resentment or discontent." This quality made them better than slaves. Without them, Marsh said, "the business of the country could not be carried on." They were, in short, yet another reason for settlers to come west and begin farming in California.[56]

*

In the working out of a new code of civil rights and social status for field hands—in defining their place in a primitive capitalistic society superimposing its labor system on the old colonial system—these developments seemed to prove that American conquest would be only an interruption and minor modification of older patterns, and that the new employers would not voluntarily relinquish the control that their Spanish and Mexican predecessors had enjoyed for three-quarters of a century. Rather than expediting the transition to freedom, territorial California continued in law and custom the widely held belief that Indians existed principally in order to plant and raise crops and work about farms. Under such circumstances, Indians could hardly expect to control their own destiny. The language whites used to define territorial California, the techniques employed to undermine ideas of equality and justice, and the resolute drive to push the idea that Indians had to be controlled, revealed fears that becoming a part of the United States might restructure California and overturn existing racial practices.

While no piece of legislation explicitly spelled out the situation in those words, the course of events that began unfolding during the summer of 1846, when the U.S. Congress annexed Texas in a direct act of war against Mexico, could hardly be misinterpreted. Suddenly all of the territories in the Far West were embroiled in battle, including California. When reports of the Texas military campaign reached Commodore John D. Sloat, leader of the U.S. Pacific Squadron at Mazatlán, Mexico, he sailed the flagship *Savannah* north into Monterey harbor. Upon arrival, he learned that Captain John C. Frémont, ostensibly in California on a U.S. Army exploring expedition, had joined a group of revolutionists in the "Bear Flag" revolt. On July 7, 1846, Sloat landed 250 sailors and claimed California as a territory of the United States. Two days later, the American flag flew over Sonoma, Sutter's Fort, and San Francisco. By January 10, 1847, Sloat's successor, Commodore Robert F. Stockton, had landed troops in Los Angeles and, after a series of minor battles, secured the southern region for the United States. Under American domination, U.S. military commanders were obliged to run the territories according to the legal practices that had previously existed. Like their Mexican predecessors, U.S. leaders persisted in regarding Indians as an exploitable labor resource to be employed at planting and harvest time and then left to themselves in their rancherías. To reinforce this approach, various military officers, bureaucrats, and territorial officials issued a series of edicts that essentially acquiesced in or approved of coerced labor and cemented field hands and all other Indians into their mudsill status. Established by the Spanish missionaries, modified by the Mexican rancheros, and continued by Sutter and other settlers, the practice of using natives as the principal field hands on the farms would be shrouded in legality, made respectable, and carried over by the Americans only in slightly modified form.[57]

Field hands were first affected by a decree that Commodore John B. Montgomery, U.S. naval commander of the American forces in San Francisco, issued shortly after hostilities began. Entitled "Proclamation to the Inhabitants of California," it prohibited slavery, as did most subsequent edicts, but at the same time compelled all Indians to work. Preserving the principle of forced labor in somewhat disguised form, this notice was followed on January 11, 1847, by another, the "Ordinance Respecting the Employment of Indians." Issued by Montgomery upon the surrender of Mexican authorities, it declared that "no person whatever" would be allowed to employ an Indian without first obtaining a written release from the Indian's previous employer. Another Montgomery ordinance, issued one month later, condemned forced labor, ordered the release of all Indians held against their will, declared they should "not be regarded in the light of slaves," and asserted that they had the right to chose "their master and employer." But, as bewildered field hands discovered, these ordinances also spoke at length about work requirements, proclaiming that all Indians must have jobs and abide by the terms of written contracts. Although the military government promised to terminate contracts with abusive employers, Indians thus liberated had to find work immediately. Those who were idle and "dissolute" would be subject to arrest and forced labor "on the Public Works."[58]

Field hands quickly discovered that this policy was remarkably similar to the one Mexicans had used to keep them at work in the fields. An astute historian, James Rawls, would later explain their legal status by saying, "Indians were free, but they were not free to be idle." Montgomery's stipulation that Indians stay with their employers until they received a written discharge also had precedent, almost exactly replicating a law used to control the mobility of the rancho Indians in Los Angeles during the 1830s. Additionally, to penalize employers who enticed Indian laborers away from competitors without permission, Montgomery instituted a penalty exactly paralleling a similar law used in Mexican California; both violations drew a fine of five dollars.[59]

Field hands got a preview of how they were going to be treated—or mistreated—under this new military regime in July of 1847, when kidnappers Antonio Armijo, Robert "Growling" Smith, and John Egger went on a rampage against Indians on Yount's Farm and at Bartlett Vines in the Napa Valley. The trio next descended on natives working on William Fowler's farm, slaughtering everyone in sight. They inflicted more atrocities before traveling to the Sacramento Valley, near present-day Chico, where, after being received kindly at a Mechoopda ranchería, they attacked their hosts, killed thirteen, and secured thirty-seven Indian prisoners to be sold as slaves to ranchers. Such crimes were now supposedly illegal, punishable by fines and long jail terms, so the three men were arrested and brought to trial. Shifted from Sutter's Fort to the defendants' hometown of Sonoma, the inquiry was largely for show. Two of the judges, Sutter and Vallejo, had themselves captured field hands before, and the third judge, Lilburn W. Boggs of Sonoma, was a friend of the kidnappers. On October 26, after a perfunctory two-day hearing, a twelve-man jury acquitted the trio of murder and enslavement charges. In the aftermath, Boggs and Vallejo blamed Sutter for the outcome, claiming he had rigged the trial first by failing to obtain a proper affidavit against the men and second by failing to show up for the key phase of the trial. Whatever the reasons for failure, following the acquittal of Smith and his henchmen the military authorities never again made an effort to impede kidnapping.[60]

Field hands would be kept at work on the farms under this threat for many years. To further control the Indian population, just eight months after the Growling Smith episode, acting military governor of California, Colonel Richard B. Mason, issued a general order prohibiting native crowds from gathering on their own in any numbers. Mason also required Indians to obtain written permission from government agents before traveling anywhere in the state. The worst of all military edicts came on November 1, 1847, when acting secretary of state, Lieutenant Henry W. Halleck, and Governor Mason announced a comprehensive code governing native field hands. This new set of proclamations made natives subject to all municipal regulations and all regulations that government agents "may deem proper." All employers were required to issue field hands and all other native workmen a certificate verifying their employment. Any Indian worker "found beyond the limits of the town or rancho in which he may be employed, without such certificate or pass, will be liable to arrest as a horse thief, and if, on being brought before a civil magistrate, he fails to give a satisfactory account of himself, he will be subjected to trial and punishment."[61]

The ugly result of this confusing bundle of American military proclamations, customs, legalities, and pseudolegalities was a precarious status of half-freedom strongly resembling peonage. To be an Indian toiling on California farms under American military rule was to be, as one traveler said, "legally reduced to servitude." A rancher could shoot any Indian at the mere accusation of stealing horses or some similar act. A lord like Sutter could lop off an Indian head and let it rot like spoiling cabbage for plotting to sabotage a crop. A U.S. Army commandant like J. D. Stevenson could determine that Indian field hands were too close to the pueblo of Los Angeles and order local authorities to destroy a ranchería in a night raid. Slave-mongers like Growling Smith and former *alcalde* turned Indian snatcher José Jesús could, with impunity, slaughter dozens of family and friends and do a thriving business selling the survivors off as field hands. The *alcalde* of any pueblo could, at the snap of his fingers, detain an Indian for loitering, and if he lacked identification papers, jail him and put him to work on irrigation ditches. This left field hands but two alternatives: run away and be pursued and punished; or remain without protest and work at twenty cents per day, wages that were about one-fifth the going rate for a common laborer, when and if they were even paid.[62]

And yet this shadow of slavery was not enough. As the military extended its control and failed to end forced labor, natives found many ranchers calling for even more repressive military edicts. Idle and wicked behavior "had proved such a sad detriment to farming operations throughout the vallies [*sic*]," said certain agriculturalists, that even more coercive laws were required. Everything possible should be done to hold field hands to their jobs and require them to perform an honest day's work. Yet even as farmers and ranchers conspired to ensure and extend their tentacles of domination, events were unfolding that would radically undermine their power over field hands.[63]

In January 1848, gold was discovered at a sawmill Sutter was building on the south fork of the American River, about thirty miles east of New Helvetia. As word of the discovery filtered out, Californians rushed into the area, intent on instant wealth. Three-quarters of the houses in San Francisco were left empty, crews abandoned their ships, brickyards and sawmills shut down, and newspapers suspended publication. Native field hands were not immune from gold fever. Unwilling to labor for a pittance when a personal fortune beckoned with the turn of a shovel, they abandoned their plows, threw down their hoes, and walked off the farms in droves. That summer, most of Sutter's field hands fled, leaving only a handful of the most loyal natives at Hock Farm. But even had most stayed, it would not have mattered. With miners running amok, Sutter's Fort was in chaos; field hands that July were only able to harvest about one-third of Sutter's projected forty-thousand-bushel wheat crop. Greedy farmers and civic leaders further decimated the farm labor population by sending Indian field hands to the diggings. In a letter written in July, American consul Thomas O. Larkin advised his partners to round up all of the Indian field hands on their farms and put them to work mining for gold. By August, so many natives had departed from the farms between Fort Ross and Sonoma that Governor Richard Mason, traveling through the region, observed that "fields of wheat were open to cattle and horses; houses vacant, and farms going to waste." In September 1848, the French counsel at Monterey said of the general exodus that "lack of field hands will make it impossible to gather the harvest which is so promising this year."[64]

Field hands did not desert the farms solely in search of fortune or on orders from their employers. Many simply seized the opportunity to flee a life of violence and poverty. By the fall, only several hundred field hands remained in Northern California. Ranchers offered higher wages and other incentives to entice them to stay. But even at considerably increased pay, only older workers remained. While a handful continued on farms operated by Bidwell, Lassen, Reading, Vallejo, Marsh, and Sutter's nearest neighbor, Thomas Cordua, most simply disappeared. Facing certain ruin, farmers worried how they would survive.[65]

For some farmers, the solution to high wages and vagabondage was outright slavery. Success and the prospects of large profits drove them forward. Based on their experience that summer, farmers were looking forward to expanding prosperity, rising profits, and a bountiful harvest. And with thousands of newcomers needing to be fed, and hundreds of thousands more expected to head west on wagon trains assembling at St. Louis, St. Joseph, and Independence, Missouri, and good prospects for soon being admitted to the Union as the thirty-first state, they had ample reasons for high expectations. Throughout the spring of 1849, as the rush for gold intensified and advocates of statehood laid plans for a constitutional convention, farmers rounded up every native who was readily accessible, and some who were not. Sometimes they dealt fairly with these men, sometimes they cheated them, and sometimes they appropriated their services without providing much more than meals of boiled gruel. Traveling through California at that time, James Delavan discovered conscripted Indians toiling away on farms everywhere he went. Writing in *Notes on California and the Placers*, he described them as existing in a pitiful state, "worse than that of the Peons of Yucatan, and other parts of Mexico," a class assembled as "if they obtained their supplies from the far-famed slave market."[66]

On September 1, when delegates to the first state Constitutional Convention gathered in Colton Hall, at Monterey, to debate the terms under which California would join the Union, the farm labor situation was of uppermost concern. California's population had increased eightfold, with successive waves already on the way by land and sea. Aware of the potential profits that would certainly accrue from feeding the newcomers, farmers began lobbying for additional sources of labor. The shortage of cheap and docile farmworkers led newcomers like Texas adventurer and soon-to-be-state-senator Thomas Jefferson Green and others like him to arrive in California with black slaves in tow, and to set them to working mining claims on the Yuba River, much to the consternation of the miners. Armed with the usual assortment of racial justifications, Green and other proslavery farmers insisted that every southern staple crop could be grown in California with slaves.[67]

Although there was considerable support among delegates from Southern California for slavery, and among other delegates for excluding free Negroes, the forty-eight delegates to the Constitutional Convention, most of them elected by miners, would do nothing to compromise admission to the Union, and primarily for this reason voted overwhelmingly to include a provision in the state constitution that "neither slavery, nor involuntary servitude, unless for the punishment of crimes, shall ever be tolerated in this state." With the issue of slavery settled, discussion then turned to the matter of suffrage. At issue was the Treaty of Guadalupe Hidalgo. Ratified in May 1848, the treaty had ended the war with Mexico, ceding approximately half of Mexico's land to the United States in exchange for fifty million dollars and a promise of perpetual peace. Article 8 of the treaty guaranteed Mexican residents of annexed territories the right to become U.S. citizens if they remained in the American Southwest one year after the treaty's ratification. While open to allowing suffrage to worthy Mexicans, delegates led by former U.S. naval storekeeper Charles Botts and W. S. Sherwood of Sacramento maneuvered to deny the franchise to "the African and Indian races" by inserting the word "white" before the phrase "male citizens of Mexico." Discussing at length "the true significance" of the word "white," delegate Pablo de la Guerra, a prominent ranchero and winemaker from Santa Barbara, argued that the term referred to people of European ancestry, not merely one's skin color. "Many citizens of California have received from nature a very dark skin," he argued, but had been allowed to vote and fill public offices. "It would be unjust to deprive them of the privilege of citizens because nature had not made them 'White.'" However, if the delegates employed the term just to exclude those of African ancestry, de la Guerra had no objection. Not quite convinced, delegates discussed a measure extending citizenship rights to those Indians—perhaps no more than two hundred—who had been taxpaying citizens of Mexico. Defeating the measure by a single vote, delegates followed de la Guerra's reasoning and limited suffrage along racial and sexual lines. Only "white male citizens" of California over age twenty-one would be allowed to vote. While theoretically citizens of the state of California, native field hands—by virtue of their race—were deemed nonwhite and by that sleight of hand had their temporary disenfranchisement under territorial law made a permanent part of life under American rule.[68]

An ominous portent of things to come, exclusion signaled to growers that they could continue treating Indians as second-class citizens. Soon a case involving two settlers, Andrew Kelsey and Charles Stone, revealed exactly where Indian field hands stood in the new California society. The first to farm in what is now Lake County, partners Kelsey and Stone established their operations by commandeering local Pomo Indians and forcing them to work. Watching them vigilantly day and night, they prevented runaways by surrounding the Indian ranchería with a high fence and employing a night patrol. For disobeying any command, field hands were whipped and hung by their thumbs for several days, with their toes barely touching the ground. "Sometimes they would kill an Indian outright on the spot for some small offence," recalled neighboring rancher Thomas Knight, after whom Knight's Valley was named. "In driving them to their place they would shoot any of the old or infirmed [sic] ones by the wayside."

Starved, beaten, and worked unmercifully, field hands could endure no more, and led by Prieto and George, conspired to kill Kelsey and Stone in December 1849. According to one account, "When Stone and Kelsey were away with the vaqueros, attending their cattle one day . . . [an Indian] squaw poured water into their guns. The next morning . . . the Indians made a charge on the house. Kelsey was killed outright with an arrow . . . Stone escaped . . . to the creek and hid in a clump of willows . . . An old Indian found him and killed him with a blow of a rock on the head."[69]

While the murder temporarily freed the Pomo, it hardly changed things. Five months later, with the Kelsey massacre still fresh in the public mind, authorities demonstrated the price to be paid by field hands violently opposing their captors. The lesson came on May 4, 1850, when U.S. Army Captain Nathaniel Lyon was dispatched from Benicia to the Kelsey farm with a force of seventy-five men. Tracking down Prieto, George, and the other Pomo field hands who had revolted against Kelsey, he and his force scoured the countryside. On May 19, Lyon found three hundred Indians hiding on an island in Clear Lake. Believing them to be escapees from the Kelsey farm, his men waded into them swinging their swords "as if grass before the sweep of the scythe." After massacring one hundred of them and burning their ranchería, Lyon's troops then proceeded south and committed a second massacre, killing seventy-five to 150 Indians on a Russian River island Lyon described as "a perfect slaughter pen." In all probability, none of the 135 to 250 Indians slain in either action had taken part in murdering Kelsey or Stone.[70]

But that was not the end of the campaign of control. Even before their blood had soaked into what came to be known as Bloody Island, farmers devised a new, and ultimately more effective strategy. So cruel and exploitative was their scheme that it would stifle opposition and ensure an abundant supply of Indian field hands for the next decade. To some, it amounted to little more than slavery.

CHAPTER SIX

To the Highest Bidder

Native Field Hands and

Gold Rush Agriculture

Spring of 1850 was a prosperous time in California. Each day, shiploads of Chileans, Hawaiians, New Englanders, and Australians disembarked at San Francisco and stampeded into the gold diggings. Marysville, Stockton, Sacramento, and San Francisco were overflowing with people. Hundreds of mining camps were sprouting up across a 150-mile wide swath of the Sierra Nevada foothills between the Trinity River on the north and the Mariposa River on the south. But all was not well; there was simply not enough to eat. Voracious workmen had quickly devoured whatever small food surpluses had existed and, in a massive environmental onslaught, wiped out entire populations of elk, deer, jackrabbits, squirrels, and many other animals. Even the huge herds of cattle that roamed the ranchos became depleted so quickly that tens of thousands of cattle had to be driven in from Texas, Missouri, and Southern California to feed the hungry men. Despite California's rich agricultural regions, most provisions had to be brought in from outside the state by ocean voyage—beans from Chile, flour from Australia, vegetables from Hawaii, oranges from Mexico, jerked beef from Argentina, rice from China, and cheese from Oregon.[1]

For miners, and indeed almost anyone in Gold Rush California, fresh fruit and produce quickly became a rare but welcome addition to the standard diet of warmed-over beans and ship biscuits grubbed from a tin plate with soiled fingers. But with rancho agriculture and the remnants of the old mission farms unable to feed the population, costs skyrocketed. The price of cattle rose from about four dollars to five hundred dollars a head before eventually leveling off between $50 and $150. A spoonful of spinach cooked with bacon drippings could cost fifty cents. Flour normally worth twelve dollars a barrel sold for eighty-five dollars. Pears, when they could be obtained, sold for $2.50 each. A peach went for one to three dollars. Raisins and dried figs brought one dollar a pound, potatoes three dollars a pound, and onions as high as two dollars apiece. Apples, the most prized and expensive of all fruits, commanded up to five dollars each.[2]

FIGURE 11. Mechoopda Indian field hands during a lunch break beneath a large oak tree at Rancho Chico during the fruit harvest. Undated; courtesy of the Bidwell Mansion State Historical Park/Special Collections and Archives, Meriam Library, California State University, Chico.

Because food for both people and livestock was in such short supply, the lure of profit quickly grew irresistible. Among the thousands of newcomers to California were considerable numbers of young men who had been farmers back home. Realizing that such high food prices could make agriculture extremely profitable, many decided that raising crops would be a surer way to wealth than digging for gold. And so they moved out of the diggings and took up farming, understanding that so long as the gold held out, they were virtually assured of a continually expanding population and therefore a continually expanding market. Entrepreneurs who could quickly set up and harvest a crop—any crop—would do very well indeed.[3]

To cash in on the agricultural opportunity, men traded pistols, mining equipment—indeed anything they owned—for a yoke of oxen, seeds, tools, and equipment, or farm animals. Some leased rights to abandoned mission orchards and gardens or "rented" land from Indians in exchange for beads and pelts. Some just squatted at an advantageous spot on the outskirts of a mining camp. If the land was not on one of the Mexican ranchos, it was virtually theirs for the taking, as Indian land rights had long since been appropriated.[4]

At San Jose mission, James F. Reed, a survivor of the Donner Party who had been caught early in heavy snows in the Sierra Nevada in October 1846, assumed control of the mission properties in 1847, and after negotiating a crop-share arrangement with the padre in charge, developed a thriving business harvesting the mission's orchard and vineyard crops, drying large amounts of apples, peaches, and pears, and marketing them in San Francisco and the diggings. But while land bordering the old missions, river and ocean wharves, and mining camps was particularly favored, there were numerous centers of agricultural production, particularly on the bench and bottomlands bordering every major river. So many farmers were planting potatoes in the river bottom around Santa Cruz and the headlands of Bodega Bay, where proximity to wharves allowed them to ship out potatoes by the boatload, that a veritable "Spud Rush" began. A few newcomers anticipating markets four and five years in the future launched ambitious horticultural projects, and using fruit pits scavenged from the garbage of overland immigrants, planted the first small, commercial orchards near the mines in Yuba, Placer, and El Dorado counties. But nowhere were the rewards of farming greater than along the east bank of the lower Sacramento River. Ideally situated with outstanding soil and easy access to fresh water and markets, enterprising men in this area—later known as the Sacramento-San Joaquin Delta—created a solid string of farms. These speculative farmers were called "rimlanders" because, after cutting down and burning forests of valley oaks bordering the river, they built low levees on top of the natural riverbank to protect their small holdings. From locations near the river they could exploit access to the waterway both as a means of irrigation and as a way to ship their crops quickly to all of the population centers. For this reason they are often identified as the first commercial farmers in California.[5]

Large numbers of "wild" Indians also inhabited the delta region and, unlike the natives who had grown up around the ranchos, they did not leave for the diggings when gold was discovered. Instead, they became the primary workforce for the many new farmers in the area. One of the largest groups, Indians from a ranchería on Grand Island, went to work for a Dutch immigrant named Antonio Schwartz, also known as the Delta Hermit and Old Zwart, a veteran of the Bidwell-Bartleson Party. Although few whites could understand Old Zwart, who spoke an absurd lingua franca simultaneously mixing four different languages, including the local Indian dialects, the Indians easily understood his directions and amazed travelers by going about their fieldwork, according to journalist Edward Wilson, with "a wonderful (for an Indian) industry, whereas no one else can induce them to do anything but vagabondize and steal." Helping him reclaim a large swath of land on the northern tip of the island, Indians constructed a large vegetable garden near present-day Clarksburg, complete with an irrigation system that tapped into the Sacramento River. Quickly learning the intricacies of agriculture, they planted melons, potatoes, and vegetables, guarded the crops from animals and poachers day and night, and that summer brought in bumper crops. Sold at one to three dollars apiece, depending on their size, their melons alone earned Old Zwart thirty thousand dollars and allowed him to dominate the produce market around Sacramento. Almost anyone who could scout up a crew of Indians and had the patience and resources to wait out the first crop did well:

antisocial drunks squatting along the Sacramento farming with crews of "half-breed" children; ferrymen encamped at Montezuma Slough, who cultivated gardens on the side while waiting to ferry travelers across the river; Yankees perched on Putah and Cache creeks in crude tule huts, "pale, emaciated . . . broken down by ague and diarrheas" but growing rich selling peas at four dollars a pound; even an ancient veteran of the Revolutionary War, farming on Ryer Island opposite present-day Courtland. No matter that they lacked experience or training, that they were ill and barely able to speak, that they had only a few spades and some seeds. "Even with the imperfect plowing of the natives," commented poet and essayist Bayard Taylor, the typical farm "produces a hundredfold."[6]

Only the shortage of capable field hands stood in the way of wider success, for while some men were willing to forgo mining in favor of becoming farmers, few gold seekers—no matter how bleak the prospects—would work on farms. Mostly young men between the ages of twenty and thirty-six, miners were a fairly representative sample of the population east of the Missouri River, as varied in their trades, professions, origins, and backgrounds as the nation itself. Abandoning everything for a chance at striking it rich, they had their commitment tested by death and turmoil along the way west, no matter what route they followed. When they failed in the diggings and abandoned the mines, they would not, under any circumstances, return to fieldwork. Having left the East largely to escape the drudgery of agricultural labor, they now avoided it like the plague. The prospect of earning three dollars a day slogging through the fields planting or digging potatoes, even to plowboys accustomed to earning one-third of that in Ohio or Indiana, paled in comparison to the five to six dollars available for unskilled work and eight to ten dollars (and sometimes as much as sixteen dollars) for skilled labor. Men preferred employment as teamsters, dock laborers, loggers, carpenters, clerks, and roustabouts. Farmers nevertheless tried to hire them. For years, they placed their advertisements in the *Alta California* employment sections. "Wanted—by a farmer at San José, four or five sober and steady men, acquainted with farming," read one typical request. Such advertisements had few takers.[7]

As a result of this aversion to fieldwork, farmers constantly faced severe labor shortages. With crops and fortunes on the line in spring of 1850, Northern California farmers sought help from ranchero-turned-politician John Bidwell. Only thirty-one years old, Bidwell was already respected for his leadership on the first overland journey to California and for his subsequent agricultural achievements at Rancho Chico, one of the most successful American ranchos of the time and a prototype of the modern agricultural enterprise. While there is little doubt that early on Bidwell exploited his Mechoopda field hands, he softened his approach in later years and adopted "a kind of parental protection" over them. Still, he knew the benefits that Anglo and Hispanic settlers derived from native labor and agreed it was necessary to somehow ensure their continued usefulness.[8]

Bidwell was elected to California's first state senate as a representative and joined the legislature early in March 1850 with the specific intention of protecting farmers. He firmly believed that agriculture, not mining, would ensure the future of the state, and by serving as temporary secretary to the state senate and member of several key committees, forcefully spoke in favor of measures putting as many natives as possible to work in the fields. On March 14, as the U.S. Congress still debated whether or not to admit California to the Union as a free or slave state, Bidwell drafted An Act Relative to the Protection, Punishment, and Government of the Indians. Like most Californians, Bidwell personally opposed slavery. But with his bill, he very nearly instated it under a somewhat milder guise.[9]

Introduced by Senator E. Kirby Chamberlin of San Diego (Bidwell being ill at the time), the measure advocated the subdivision of counties into as many as ten Indian districts, each administered by a justice of the peace elected from among the Indians themselves, with all adults over eighteen years of age eligible to vote. There was a list of crimes, punishments, and defined rights, as well as a method whereby justices would resolve conflicts. In theory, Indian field hands were to be equal—if separate—from whites. But the bill failed to go far enough for some and was tabled. When a similar bill, introduced in the assembly by Contra Costa County ranchero Elam Brown, passed on April 16, both bills were sent to a three-member committee responsible for reconciling them and drafting a final version. Bidwell served on this committee, with Mariano Guadalupe Vallejo, the old ranchero and Indian raider, and David F. Douglas, a Tennessee-born southerner who had come to California after years in Arkansas, Texas, and Mississippi. Together, over two days of discussions, they hardened and recast Bidwell's original bill into a far more repressive and malevolent piece of legislation. On April 19, both houses passed the bill, slightly retitled as An Act for the Government and Protection of Indians. Three days later, Governor Peter H. Burnett signed it into law. It was the very first law enacted by the very first California legislature, meeting for the first time at the new state capital in San Jose.[10]

Characterized as an effort to aid native field hands, the new law actually provided very little, if any, protection, no government, and plenty of punishment; it also omitted many features of Bidwell's original bill, including Indian justices of the peace and Indian suffrage. Rather, the county justices of the peace held authority in "all cases by, for, or against Indian field hands, in their respective jurisdictions." Also deleted were measures protecting traditional hunting, fishing, and gathering sites and provisions guaranteeing tenure at rancherías "from time immemorial." References to the rights of Indian descendants also disappeared, as did stipulations saving Indian land "in a body" and guarantees of at least one acre of land for every Indian.[11]

Controlling and coercing work in much the same way that the Black Codes compelled freed black slaves to labor in the fields of the post–Civil War American South, An Act for the Government and Protection of Indians consisted of twenty sections, at least twelve of them designed to compel Indian labor. While some parts of the statute seemed innocuous enough (Section 15, for example, prohibited anyone from selling alcohol to Indians), others were an obvious subterfuge, such as the prohibition on setting brushfires, which in fact was aimed at eliminating an ancient hunting technique. Key sections, though, amounted to legalized peonage. One section prohibited Indians from testifying against whites in court, making it impossible for native field hands to win legal redress for mistreatment, or indeed, exercise any legal recourse at all. White justices of the peace, many of whom despised Indians, held all authority in legal cases involving Indian land claims, property disputes, criminal offenses, and child custody. By preventing Indians dispossessed from their lands from taking legal action, this section also pushed large numbers of Indians into the labor market, especially the farm labor market, exactly as intended.

Another section provided the law's unofficial name: "The Indian Indenture Act." While appearing to protect Indian field hands by prohibiting farmers and other employers from compelling Indians to work against their will (and imposing a fine of fifty dollars on anyone attempting to do so), this section in fact provided a way to obtain labor under the pretext of vagrancy. It asserted:

> Any Indian able to work, and support himself in some honest calling, not having wherewithal to maintain himself who shall be found loitering and strolling about, or frequenting public places where liquors are sold, begging or living an immoral or profligate course of life, shall be liable to be arrested on the complaint of any resident citizen of the county and brought to any Justice of the Peace . . . satisfied that he is a vagrant . . . he shall make out a warrant . . . authorizing and requiring the officer having him in charge or custody, to hire out such a vagrant within twenty-four hours, to the highest bidder . . . for any term not exceeding four months.

In other words, any farmer or employer could have an unemployed or otherwise "vagrant" Indian arrested. Once tried, convicted, and "fined" for his crime, an Indian could be bailed out and set to work for a proscribed period of time, or until he had repaid the amount of the fine and cost of bail. In effect, this made any Indian available for farm labor and, while field hands were supposed to be treated humanely and properly fed and clothed, there was no provision to enforce those provisions. And since no white farmer could be convicted of mistreatment on the testimony of any Indian, field hands obtained in this way became, in effect, slaves.[12]

Another section of the law established a system of Indian "apprenticeship" under which any farmer seeking to employ an Indian child simply had to appear before a justice of the peace with the child's "parents or friends" and show that the child had not been obtained through coercion or intimidation. That farmer would then be in charge of "the care, custody, control, and earnings of such minor, until he or she obtain the age of majority." Employing this statute, farmers could keep Indians boys until they reached eighteen years of age, girls until they reached fifteen. All that the farmer had to do was feed and clothe them, and "treat them humanely as his wards." An abusive farmer could supposedly be fined ten dollars and lose his Indians, but this never happened.[13]

With passage of the Indian Indenture Act, native field hands reached a fateful juncture. Forced Indian labor was now preserved not as a temporary expedient of American military rule or an unfortunate legacy of the state's Hispanic past, but as a permanent "peculiar institution," a necessary component of agriculture in Gold Rush California. Legalizing the peonage system that had evolved in Mexican California, the 1850 law assaulted Indian tribal and village authority, undermined Indian sovereignty, placed Indians in a subservient, dependent condition, and pushed thousands of natives into farmwork at a time of great labor shortage. In the harsh configuration of California law and custom, the role of native field hands was now clearly designated. During the shift from Mexican to American California, there would be no clear break with the past. By adopting harsh vagrancy laws and restricting nonagricultural employment by various apprenticeship statutes, white Californians not only consolidated control but effectively blocked any shift of Indian field hands away from the farms, maintained their place as landless farmworkers, assigned them a second-class legal status, forced them to work against their will, and subjected them to a system that journalist-historian Carey McWilliams described as something that "competed favorably with slavery."[14]

乎

Although native field hands throughout the state would eventually be touched by the new law, those in Los Angeles were hit first, and very hard. The center of a burgeoning wine industry since Jean Louis Vignes had established his commercial wine operation twenty years earlier, Los Angeles had, by 1850, attracted a dozen enterprising vintners, most of them Frenchmen. With more than 125 vineyards, some four hundred thousand vines, and dozens of wineries, French immigrants had so transformed the lowlands on both sides of the river that the area south of present-day Alisio Street became known as "French Town." Midway through August, the vineyards were a beehive of activity. With an almost insatiable demand for wine and table grapes bringing eighteen to twenty cents a pound in Northern California, all of the winemakers and grape growers around Los Angeles expected to make fortunes. To do that they needed a surplus of field hands. But with so many natives away in the diggings, engaged in horse raiding, or pressed into some other kind of work, a farm labor crisis appeared to be developing. Grape growers feared their crews could not pick the entire crop, or that they could not pick fast enough.[15]

On August 16, 1850, just three weeks before California was admitted to the Union as a free labor state, the Los Angeles Common Council met to see what it could do about the growing labor shortage. Town leaders turned to the new state law and cobbled together their own local version; the result was one of the most vicious and repressive laws that farmworkers would ever encounter. Under provisions of their unnamed statute, unemployed or drunk natives found about the town, or those deemed to be leading a promiscuous, wasteful, or "licentious" existence, could be immediately arrested and put to work as "chain gang" laborers. And "when the city has no work in which to employ the chain gang," the ordinance further decreed, "the recorder shall, by means of notices conspicuously posted, notify the public that such a number of prisoners will be auctioned off to the highest bidder for private service; and in that manner they shall be disposed of for a sum which shall not be less than the amount of their fine for double the time which they were to serve at hard labor."[16]

From the start, the auction system flourished because Los Angeles in the 1850s was full of just the kinds of dangers and temptations that would get natives in trouble, land them in jail, place them on the auction block, and make them easy pickings. Of all the elements entrapping natives, none was more important than a popular section of town known as Calle de los Negros, or as many called it, "Negro Alley" and "Nigger Alley." Had farmers designed the area themselves, they could not have invented a better place to concentrate native field hands in large numbers. Extending from the town plaza to Los Angeles Street at Arcadia, Negro Alley consisted of a continuous line of adobe saloons, brothels, and gambling dens. "Men and women alike were to be found there, and both sexes looked after the gaming tables, dealing monte and faro, and managing other contrivances that parted the good-natured and easy-going people with their money," observed a first-time visitor to the area. But of all the various distractions, none seemed to offer more pleasure than the cheap liquor that flowed freely from dozens of low-slung, adobe taverns that lined both sides of the street.[17]

Shortly after being paid on Saturday evenings, hundreds of field hands would arrive at Negro Alley. "Their ambition seems to be to earn sufficient money through the week to treat themselves handsomely at the close of it," observed the *Los Angeles Star*. Throughout the evening and well into the night, they would gamble, drink, fight, socialize, dance, argue, tell stories, and engage in "bestiality" and "debauchery." Few murders were ever solved, with coroners reports typically concluding "death by violence from persons unknown." Men usually did not end their carousing until sometime Sunday evening. But by late summer, when the grape harvests were in full swing, men sometimes caroused every night of the week. Passed out in alleyways, doorsteps, and on saloon floors around Negro Alley, in the plaza, and in vacant lots and along nearby streets, intoxicated field hands and other Indian workmen were easy to locate and in no condition to resist authorities. Hundreds could easily be gathered at one time. It all worked out well for local vineyardists, who needed every field hand they could get.[18]

Most Saturday and Sunday nights, the marshal and a team of deputies would appear in Negro Alley with a wagon and begin making their rounds. Paid a kickback of about one dollar for every eight Indians brought to trial, the authorities were especially diligent in scooping up all available men. After weeding out any corpses and hauling them away to what passed for a morgue, deputies began gathering the drunken field hands into a big corral near the rear of Downey Street. The groggy natives would then be left to sleep away their intoxication and in the morning be put up for sale. "Sometimes . . . we have seen the Marshal marching in a procession with twenty or twenty-five of these poor people," reported the *Star*, "and truly, it is a brave sight."[19]

The worst part of the ordeal came around 9 A.M. on Monday mornings, when the sick, sullen, and hungover men would be marched out of their cells and put on display. In need of work crews, *mayordomos* or deputized subordinates from surrounding ranchos and farms converged on the jail to purchase laborers, bidding on them as if buying mules. Sold for between one and three dollars a man, the field hands were often led from the auction chained together. They supposedly labored for one week after which they received wages equal to one-third of the price of their sale. Over the next thirteen years, thousands of natives were arrested and sold.[20]

The price of freedom was $2.50, and few if any natives had that amount of money. Of some 3,700 Indians in the Los Angeles area at the time, only 334 were identified as taxpayers with sufficient wealth to be tabulated by the 1850 census. Only three had any wealth of consequence—Urbano Chori, a farmer who held five hundred dollars in property; Roman, a farmer who had amassed some one thousand dollars in assets; and Samuel, a laborer with assets totaling $250. Virtually all other former mission Indians and so-called gentile Indians alike had nothing but the clothes on their backs. And if they did come by any money, they usually spent it by the time they wound up in jail. It was impossible for them to buy their freedom. Indeed, there is no record of a single man doing so.[21]

Once purchased, it was a simple matter to transport natives to the vineyards and wineries because most were located within easy walking distance of the pueblo. Many vineyards were actually located in the pueblo itself, as local citizen-farmers had usually begun their plantings on family lots along the principal streets. This proximity to the pueblo well served the auction system, since field hands could be immediately put to work. Usually they were harvesting grapes within an hour or two.[22]

Field hands did not always cooperate. On several occasions, according to the *Star,* "The worthy Marshal and his energetic assistant . . . opened the ponderous gates of the prison and locked up twenty-five Indians, all supposed to be drunk; but he had no sooner turned his back than, crash! went the door, and the Indians scattered in every direction, up every street in town. Jack Sware [an assistant marshal], and the Marshal, utterly confounded at the impossibility of herding off so many fugitives, stood solemnly silent." To prevent further escapes, the marshal brought in a huge pine log that extended from one end to the other of the main room and drove large, metal staples into it every three or four feet along its length. These served as anchors to which prisoners were shackled with foot-long chains. After the log and shackle apparatus was installed, no one escaped.[23]

Under these arrangements, native field hands followed a weekly regimen that was little more than a continuous drudge. "They are a miserable, squalid-looking set," reported one visitor, who found them sleeping in brush shelters and in doorsteps or in the open or packed into miserable rancherías on the outskirts of town. After three years of carnage, local authorities determined to take action. Led by Mayor Benjamin Wilson, the Common Council enacted two ordinances prohibiting the playing of *peón* (a popular card game) within the city limits and banning the sale of liquor to Indians. Those convicted were to be fined not less than twenty dollars or imprisoned for five days or both. But this had little effect. Bar owners so blatantly ignored the antiliquor sales ordinance that the *Southern Californian* identified several who were the worst offenders and demanded that the Common Council take action against them. But while the two, Vicente Guerrero and Birardo Sunega, were later arrested and fined for maintaining *peón* games and selling liquor to Indian field hands, the council nevertheless persisted. "It does not appear that the Liquor Ordinance has done much good so far," observed the *Star.* "It went into effect . . . and still the Indians get their liquor the same as ever."[24]

Despite the human costs and the hefty fines for selling liquor to Indians, few vineyardists ever objected to the arrangement. Regarding native field hands as not being legitimately part of the citizenry, they refused to acknowledge that the auctions created and perpetuated a hapless class of laborers. Nor did most local law enforcement officials seem much bothered by the system. "On last Sunday, our vigilant City Marshal and his assistants brought forty-one drunken Indians to the station house, generally on charges of drunkenness," reported the *Star*, without the slightest hint of remorse. "We do not know whether the officers are becoming more vigilant, or the aborigines more dissipated." Indeed, many officials got rich arbitrarily arresting field hands for minor offenses and then dividing up one-third of the proceeds from the auctions. "Los Angeles had its slave market as well as New Orleans and Constantinople," observed hard-drinking Los Angeles attorney Horace Bell, "only the slave at Los Angeles was sold fifty-two times a year as long as he lived, which generally did not exceed one, two or three years under the new dispensation. Thousands of honest, useful people were absolutely destroyed in this way."[25]

᠅

These conditions were not limited to the immediate vicinity of Los Angeles. They existed everywhere in Southern California. Traveling south while surveying a site for a future military post, U.S. Army Captain Edward Ord reported extensively on the way Southern California law enforcement officials sentenced offending Indians to work off petty offenses under local rancheros, thereby perpetuating the system of bondage. "It may be seen that by this law the overseer of a large rancho has but to be a 'Justice of the Peace,' and he is enabled to buy and keep Indian servants as he may want them, and to punish them at discretion within a limit," he observed. On every ranch and farm along the route of his journey, Ord discovered that "from fifteen to thirty Indians [were] permanently occupied . . . quietly labouring . . . as servants to the whites, according to the laws of this State." Like most contemporaries, he saw this as a positive good. "The system thus legalized provides labour in a hot climate where otherwise there would be none," he noted, "and being a continuation of the system to which the Indians were accustomed under Mexican rule, it works well."[26]

Farther south, Indians encountered one of the worst abusers of Indian field hands, Cave Couts. Just the type of man who would most fully exploit them under the Indian Indenture Act, the Tennessee-born Couts had also come to California in 1849 as a second lieutenant in the U.S. Army. While stationed in San Diego, he had married Ysidora Bandini, daughter of one of the wealthiest old Californio families, and, in 1852, moved to the 2,219-acre Rancho Guajome (near San Luis Rey mission), which Abel Stearns had presented to Ysidora as a wedding present. With a segmented labor force of Anglo supervisors and Indian laborers, he created a diversified farm, organized around a large adobe house with an inner courtyard, which one historian described as "a feudal manor" and another compared to "the home of a wealthy southern planter." Known to his staff as "Don Cuevas," Couts, though a drunkard, served as an Indian subagent for the Bureau of Indian Affairs, as well as a justice of the peace, positions which would seem an unfortunate conflict after he was acquitted of charges that he whipped to death two Indians and killed a Mexican who threatened him and a tutor hired to teach his children. Constantly tracking down workers who ran away to escape their indebtedness,

Couts turned to the Indian Indenture Act. If he needed labor, all he had to do was petition a local judge to "'bind and put-out' to me by indenture, the said Indians, the males as apprentices to husbandry, the females as apprentices to housewifery, for such length of time as is permitted by law." Little, if any, proof of vagrancy was required. Couts merely reported: "Said Indians are vagrant Indians having no settled habitation or means of livelihood, and have not placed themselves under the protection of any white person." With no legal recourse to appeal or any means to escape, the natives complied. Daughters as young as six years of age found themselves bound over to Couts as servants until age eighteen or twenty, in exchange for the sum of fifty dollars paid to their parents. Fatherless sons had it even worse. In exchange for as little as thirty dollars, their mothers handed them over to Couts to work in the fields for a period of three years. Those who disliked the arrangement and left did not remain free. Whenever Couts asked the court to intervene, the runaways were returned immediately and without question.[27]

Degrading laws, forced indenture, massive arrests, all-powerful rancheros, sale in the slave market, and death around Negro Alley were not the only factors that preserved old traditions of subordination and kept natives at work in the fields of Southern California. There was also liquor. At San Gabriel mission, at least three liquor shops—"devil's workshops" according to lawyer and newspaper editor Horace Bell's salty recollections—were "surrounded by a mass of drunken, howling Indians" and "did a smashing business." This was apparently not an uncommon occurrence. On the big farming operations throughout the area, taverns and shops that sold liquor provided such ready access to alcoholic beverages that drunken episodes became common occurrences among Indian field hands, vaqueros, ranch hands, and Mexican laborers. On occasion even vineyardists and growers joined in the revelry.[28]

Native field hands were further encouraged in their alcoholism by farmers and rancheros who paid not in cash but "in kind," with goods like soap, hats, shoes, cigars, calico, sugar, and shirts. The best payment was, of course, liquor—cheap *aguardiente* and raw brandy. Indeed, on some ranches, these were the only wages field hands received. Besides allowing growers and rancheros to economize on scarce capital and skim off money for their own uses, payment in liquor further served farmers in two additional ways. First, it assured them that they would always have large numbers of drunken Indians who could be arrested and pressed into work for almost nothing. Second, it bolstered an exploitative, entirely artificial farm labor market in which most workers were recruited by force and few, if any, field hands were freely employed. "In other words," wrote historian Douglas Monroy, "these were near perfect workers . . . paid little, nonviolent except toward their own, dependent on employers but needing only small remuneration . . . too narcotized to protest . . . Their addiction kept them bound to their employers and bound to die."[29]

❦

Out of their ordeal in Southern California another myth has developed, probably the least questioned of all those that concerned the lives of farmworkers during the first years of the Gold Rush. It is that native field hands on the farms of Northern California and across the state enjoyed a better life than their southern brethren. The claim does have a certain logical appeal, seeming to fit nicely with what is known about the divergent economies and societies splitting the state. It also has been fed continuously by folklore and by innumerable popular writers grappling with the farmworker saga. But this view does not square with the facts. The truth is native field hands in Northern California endured as much, if not more, than their southern counterparts.

Around Fresno, intoxicated or "delinquent" Indians unable to pay their fines were imprisoned, placed on auction blocks, and sold to the highest bidder just as they were in Los Angeles. Bringing an average price of $1.25, they were such a bargain that the *Napa Register* proposed, "Somebody might make a fortune by selling drunken Diggers [Maidu Indians] in Napa City." So devastating was the practice of buying and selling native field hands in the Sacramento Valley that one visitor was "perfectly astonished" to discover that Indians comprised the entire labor force on at least one farm. They seemed "no better than slaves," the traveler noted. "Norris is their big chief, and seems to have absolute authority over them." Such observations were so common that historical demographer Sherburne F. Cook later concluded that, at this time, native field hands "crossed from . . . peonage to actual slavery."[30]

Most auctioned natives came from the Sacramento Valley and the North Coast Mountains and were obtained not under the pretext of arrest for public intoxication or vagrancy, but were instead brutally kidnapped. Usually, entire populations would be captured at once; those who resisted were murdered outright. Survivors were labeled vagrants or "dissolute" individuals and then "apprenticed" under some provision of the Indian Indenture Act. Sold off to farmers for prices varying with their age, sex, and physical condition, they were often poorly fed and clothed, treated with contempt, and allowed to die in droves. They were most vulnerable around harvest time. This horrific practice was known but not publicly acknowledged by most of the farmers who bid regularly on native workers. One Indian agent reported such mistreatment was so widespread that it seemed to him that many farmers had "adopted the principle that the Indians belong to them as much as an African does to his master, and that they have the right to control them entirely."[31]

Occasionally one or two kidnapped field hands fled. But like their predecessors on the missions and ranchos and the alleged assassins of Andrew Kelsey and Charles Stone, they were tracked down. Those who remained free and sought justice faced innumerable obstacles. Sheriffs, constables, and justices of the peace expressed little if any concern for their distress and hardships. The cloak of legality provided by the apprenticeship laws, despite the hostile public condemnation, served to protect kidnappers and limit justice for field hands. Only a handful of kidnappers were arrested and even fewer were tried. If and when field hands brought their complaints to trial, they invariably were disappointed. Most cases ended in acquittal or were dismissed. The rare convictions that did occur usually resulted not because field hands prevailed upon local law enforcement authorities but because of the intervention of federal authorities. But even then there was a cost. Opposing kidnapers and their allies was dangerous, and Indians who did so risked reprisals, or worse. Some, after asserting their rights, disappeared and were never seen again.[32]

Children suffered the most. Classified by kidnappers according to four categories—fair, middling, inferior, refuse—kidnapped boys and girls three to four years of age went for up to sixty dollars. Indian boys who could "perform the most menial drudgery" were in great demand as field hands, stock herders, woodchoppers, and kindling gatherers on small ranches and farms. Eight- to ten-year-old boys who could drive hogs fetched eighty dollars. Handsome, "clean" girls up to twelve years of age and in "prime condition" (virgins) brought the most, often going for as much as two hundred dollars. In most cases, girls were valued as servants to lighten the work load of farmwives, and they would be assigned such household chores as cooking, carrying water, washing dishes and clothes, and tending to the younger children of the farm family. Those sold to bachelor farmers, however, often were obtained to serve both the "purposes of labor and lust."[33]

Exactly how many children were torn from their parents and sold to farmers and other employers remains open to debate. Abducted Indian children were a common, everyday sight in the rural districts around Weaverville in Mendocino County, where in 1853 one farmer reported "lots of little Diggers" working for all the farmers in the area. Three years later, Indian agent Vincent Geiger reported to his superior, Thomas Henley, that "the Indians brought in have very few children, most of them doubtless having been stolen and sold. This traffic, I am informed, is still being carried on in the vicinity of Clear Lake and Barrezesa [Berryessa] Valley." The going rate, according to rancher William Scott, was fifty dollars per child.[34]

Farther north—around Humboldt Bay and between Clear Lake and Round Valley—Indian populations were continually decimated by organized parties of slave raiders. Historians of the Round Valley, Lynwood Carranco and Estle Beard, wrote in *Genocide and Vendetta* that "Three or four thousand children were probably stolen" between 1852 and 1867. Whatever the exact numbers, it is clear that many rancherías along the north coast lost every child. Traveling with a government expedition through Yuki territory in August 1851, Indian interpreter George Gibbs recorded in his journal that many Indians had been so traumatized by slave raiders that the sight of a white man "at once excited fears and distrust." Still, farmers justified such practices, claiming that if they did not buy the children, someone else would. Kidnapped Indian children, they said, were better off living among white people on farms than among primitive native tribes. But few actually believed these tortured rationalizations. "The habit of stealing Indian children and selling them is being abused," reported the *Butte Record* on May 23, 1857. Again and again editorials would assert that kidnapping continued, indeed flourished, with disastrous consequences.[35]

Despite the considerable numbers of Indians kidnapped and fed into the state's auction systems, many farmers remained unsatisfied and wanted more. In 1854, they further shackled natives with a law prohibiting them from acquiring firearms. This law not only made natives less threatening should they resist, but it also further drove them into the ranks of farm laborers because, without firearms, Indians found it difficult to hunt wild game now widely scattered and spooked beyond the reach of bow and arrow. Emboldened by their success in banning firearms, farmers also began advocating an even more comprehensive state code to "curb the dissipation" of field hands. One provision would require Indian parents "to bind out their children to farmers and others, for a given period, so as to make them useful, and thus induct them to habits of cleanliness and industry." At first, these ideas were confined to conversations and correspondence, but inevitably their supporters grew bolder. Rural newspapers like the *Marysville Herald*, an early champion of farm interests, provided valuable leadership. Beginning in 1856 and continuing for the next four years, the paper maintained a continuous barrage of proposals meant to further strengthen the Act for the Government and Protection of Indians. Only through their passage, the *Herald* believed, would natives be made "useful to the whites" and at the same time improve their condition.[36]

❧

Not all Indians worked on farms after being kidnapped or arrested under the Indian Indenture Act. According to the superintendent of Indian affairs, about eighteen thousand native wage laborers were available for agricultural labor in the early 1850s, twice that number if adult women were included in the count. Even if these numbers were grossly inflated, which was probably the case, natives working as relatively free wage earners created a highly segmented labor pool that was hard to reconcile against kidnapped and coerced laborers. Their pervasive influence concerned farmers like Bidwell, who found them convenient yet menacing. They are "all *among* us, *around* us, *with* us," he reported to state senator J. W. McCorkle, "Hardly a farm house—a kitchen without them."[37]

On many ranches and farms, these field hands worked under arrangements that bore an eerie resemblance to mission life. South of Decoto on the east side of San Francisco Bay, natives on James Hawley's farm continued to assemble for work, rest, and meals according to the chimes of a bell removed from San Jose mission. Hung first from a limb in a sycamore tree where Decoto Road crossed over a creek and later in a frame near the Indian quarters, the bell so controlled and regulated their labor that the ranch became known as "The Bell Ranch," and the crossing as "The Bell Ranch Bridge."[38]

Nearby, Indian field hands soon became involved in what would become known as the "potato venture," one of the most significant and revealing of all Gold Rush farming exploits. Rancho de las Papas (Potato Ranch) was the largest and most modern farm in the San Francisco Bay area, headed by newcomer John Horner of San Jose mission. In 1850, Horner had planted 130 acres of potatoes, yielding thirty-five thousand bushels and a gross income of $175,000. He had also grown forty thousand pounds of onions, forty thousand cabbage plants, and fifty thousand pounds of tomatoes. In 1851, Horner had hired sixty Mormons who, in conjunction with a few Mexicans from Sonora, cleared land and planted crops, including potatoes and wheat, earning Horner a fortune. For their labor, the Mormons received a collective wage of fifty thousand dollars, about one-fifth the gross value of Horner's total harvest. When the Mormons and Sonorans all abandoned the farm for the mines in 1852, natives stepped into the "digging and delving" work and saved Horner from bankruptcy. The following year, crews of natives took over all farmwork on Horner's farm and those of his neighbors, feeding and housing themselves, harvesting four hundred thousand bushels of potatoes and fifteen hundred acres of wheat, and disappearing when not needed.[39]

Over time, the primitive way that Horner's Indians cut grain with crude cutting hooks so concerned his neighbor, New York native James E. Patterson, that he promptly purchased a grain cradle and proceeded to earn ten dollars a day harvesting wheat at four times the rate of natives. While employed using his cradle on Lyman Beard's nearby farm, Patterson began discussing with Horner ways to further increase productivity. After describing some of the reaping and threshing machines used in the eastern United States, Patterson and Horner decided that Indian labor and hand tools alone would never be sufficient to bring in the increasingly large wheat crops. Rather than lobbying for expanding the Indian Indenture Act as Bidwell had done, they proposed a daring and entirely new approach. They would build a machine—a "combine"—which both cut and threshed wheat as it moved through a field. The pair constructed a prototype with drive wheels sixteen feet high and tested it during the 1853 harvest. But frightened by the noise, the twenty-two mules pulling it bolted and tore the machine to pieces. After the accident, Patterson built a second combine with wheels only eight feet high and pulled by twelve mules. Following the harvest, Patterson gave up, but not Horner. Upon hearing of Michigan inventors Andrew and Abner Moore, who had built a combine that only worked well if the crop was ripe and dry— conditions absent in Michigan but prevailing in California—Horner invited them to bring their machine out west. Dispatching his son, Oliver, and partner, George Leland, to California in 1854, Moore disassembled the machine and shipped it to California on board a clipper ship.[40]

Cutting a twelve-foot-wide swath and looking like "the great . . . Juggernaut," as the *California Farmer* described it, the assembled machine harvested six hundred acres at the rate of twenty acres per day for farmers around San Jose mission. Employing three "skilled" Euro-American men—a driver, who guided it from behind, a front man, to raise and lower the cutting bar, and a sewer to stitch up sacks as they filled and dropped to the ground—it left in its wake long lines of bagged grain that *California Farmer* described as "resembling hundreds of large sheep." But with its twenty-horse team, the combine proved too expensive to operate. After storing the machine in a barn and spending 1855 working in the gold fields, Moore and Leland rolled it out in 1856 and attempted to harvest a large wheat field, but the novice operators failed to lubricate the bearings; the machine overheated and started a fire that destroyed the wheat field and the combine. A disconsolate Moore gave up and returned home to Michigan, but Horner and Leland persisted. Continuing to plant and harvest with Indian laborers, they tinkered with several new machines, and in 1858 displayed yet another combine.[41]

Horner and Leland's 1858 machine was essentially a copy of the Moore combine, except it featured a team of thirty horses pushing from behind rather than pulling from in front. This prevented trampling of the wheat before it was threshed, eliminated the possibility of a runaway team, and made handling the horses easier. A second version dropped the number of horses to twenty, placed two abreast, and was controlled by five drivers, each driving four horses while riding in the saddle position, "postilion fashion." A pilot, George Leland himself, perched on top of the machine, guided the apparatus as if steering a river steamer. Carrying a long pole, he also periodically reached down and cleared the cutting bars when they became choked with wild mustard and other trash. During 1860, Leland used the machine to harvest sixteen hundred acres around Alvarado. Most who saw the machine found it a ridiculous piece of equipment. "This machine is a large, unwieldy concern," wrote one farmer, "and it would not do so well in small fields as in large ones, as the stir and bustle in turning corners reminds one forcibly of tacking ship."[42]

ॐ

Failure to mechanize meant that native men, not machines, continued to harvest and thresh grain throughout the Gold Rush years. And thanks in large part to the restrictive Indian Indenture Act, many continued working for little more than food, clothing, shelter, and occasionally primitive medical care, just as they had in the past. On some of the smaller, less well-established farms, where semifrontier conditions existed, hundreds of natives worked for farmers that journalist Bayard Taylor described as "long, lothy, and sallow" people who expectorated vehemently, drank whiskey constantly, sometimes had the "shakes," distrusted "store clothes," and had an implacable dislike of trees. On John Marsh's Rancho Los Méganos, natives were still paid largely in quinine and food. Conditions were slightly better on older farms like Pierson B. Reading's Rancho San Buena Ventura in Shasta County and John Bidwell's Rancho Chico, where visitors reported Indians combining new and old farming techniques. But with white settlement encroaching on their native lands and cutting off traditional food supplies and resources, natives found field labor to be an increasingly important part of survival. Cultivating their own communal wheat fields and subsisting on meals of boiled minnows, acorn mush, salmon, and berries collected in season, they supplemented their income by working the local harvest and integrating farm labor into a seasonal circuit of hunting and gathering that often ended with a week of gambling and drinking in Marysville, Chico, and other farm towns.[43]

A variant on this arrangement developed on the Lupilloni farm near Clear Lake, where nearly three hundred natives cultivated their own fields, then trooped into the Napa and Sonoma valleys to plow, plant, and harvest in the fall and spring. Because the work was impermanent and did not provide their sole means of survival, these natives did not particularly think of themselves as farmworkers. But as spot labor shortages developed, some groups of natives threw in their lot permanently with farmers, became full-time farmworkers, and bargained for better compensation, so driving up expenses at Hock Farm that Sutter complained that his field hands refused to work for "clothing and provisions" and now demanded cash wages.[44]

A few groups of field hands entirely dictated when and where they worked. Prominent among these were Cahuilla Indians from tribes around Temecula and

San Bernardino who, at various points throughout the year, improvised an early variant form of migratory labor. Often accompanied by their families, they periodically traveled from their rancherías thirty miles north to work for Henry Dalton, the British immigrant trader and shipper who owned the 19,975-acre Rancho Azusa and a portion of San Gabriel mission. Following this routine, Cahuillas swarmed over the rancho, created a small, bustling town, and transformed Rancho Azusa into one of the most progressive and productive farms in Southern California. They planted grapevines (more than seven thousand in one year), helped dam the Azusa River, and worked on an extensive system of diversion canals. Supplementing Dalton's permanent force of twenty Indian and Mexican laborers, they also played a key role at his winery complex, where they excavated a huge storage cellar and rigged and set up winemaking equipment shipped from Mexico. Although Dalton provided workrooms and living quarters consisting of fifteen ramshackle shacks near the winery, the Cahuillas did not use them. During their forays they preferred to camp out under the trees on a low hill near the irrigation ditch about one-quarter mile north of the ranch headquarters. For their work they earned the standard wages—an occasional beef, a blanket, and a shirt to each man.[45]

While Cahuillas traveled more than sixty miles in their circuit, they did not hold the record for long-distance migration. That distinction went to a group of Northern Paiute field hands who, led by Chief Truckee (the Indian who had rescued the overland party of Elisha Stevens in 1844), departed from their homes along the eastern slope of the Sierra Nevada Mountains, and, in 1851 and 1852, traveled to farms scattered along San Joaquin River. Trading their labor for guns and horses, they worked throughout the spring and summer, departing upon completion of the fall harvests. Covering a round-trip distance of several hundred miles, Paiutes established a record for labor migration that field hands would not duplicate for another half-century.[46]

As they became accustomed to such arrangements, natives developed smooth working relationships with many farmers. In Sonoma County near the southern portion of the Russian River, Indians quickly learned what was required of them. When there was sowing, hoeing, reaping, or binding to be done, natives would install one "especially intelligent and devoted" man named Francisco as a kind of "police officer." Francisco went down to a certain spot along one bank of the river and called across to a ranchería on the opposite shore. With little more than a shout or whistle, men would then appear and "do the bidding of Francisco" for nothing more than huge kettles full of beans and peas seasoned with peppers and beef bones. When they had finished the harvest, "the account was considered squared." Then, with not so much as a thank-you, wrote Sonoma County historian Honoria Toumey, "the Indians were driven off to forage in the woods for their families and themselves during the winter."[47]

Under these circumstances, natives harvested and tended a wide variety of crops. They worked on truck farms and grain farms close to San Francisco Bay, in the fertile alluvial lands along all of the major rivers, and in the rich peat lands of the Sacramento-San Joaquin Delta. They reaped grain on the dry prairies around San Jose and the small valleys along Chico Creek, dug irrigation ditches

FIGURE 12. Beginning in 1845, Cahuilla Indians from tribes around Temecula and San Bernardino traveled from their rancherías thirty miles north to work for Henry Dalton, the British immigrant trader and shipper who owned the 19,975-acre Rancho Azusa and a portion of San Gabriel mission. Here the Cahuillas pose for a photographer in the 1860s. Courtesy of the Security Pacific Historical Photograph Collection/Los Angeles Public Library.

along Big Butte Creek, settled around Nord to drain and work the wet bogs and low spots, and furnished much of the labor on Rancho Santa Ana del Chino, at the crossroads of three immigrant trails, where Indians from a nearby rancheria handled all of the labor, women being employed during the grain harvest to winnow the wheat. Indians also gravitated to the highest point accessible by steam navigation near Hamilton on the Feather River, clumped near the tiny, diversified farms along the Marysville-Shasta Road, and along countless similar routes leading to the mines, converged on river crossings along freight routes astride the Cosumnes, Calaveras, and Stanislaus rivers and, in the San Bernardino desert, lived in rude huts while tending the vineyards and fields on Rancho Cucamonga; a U.S. Army railroad survey team venturing into the area described these Cahuilla field hands as nearly naked, ragged "serfs." Elsewhere, on modest diversified farms catering to the needs of the men tramping to and from the mines and on Mexican ranchos serving the traveling population, they worked alone or in pairs and small groups, growing vegetables, tending stock, and by their very number, inexorably transformed the landscape.[48]

Perhaps because their story so detracts from the romantic view of how commercial farming began, many commentators delete all reference to native field hands from their descriptions of the emergence of California agriculture or their accounts of Gold Rush California. Accounting for the state's achievement of agricultural self-sufficiency by 1854, and the rapid growth of a commercial farming industry thereafter, many writers commonly cite innovative American pioneers, market pressures, climate, the legacy of the Spanish mission farms, and the influence of European and French immigrants. But whether hired as wage laborers, rounded up under provisions of the 1850 Indian Act and its variants, or kept in an alcoholic state of bondage, natives comprised so much of the farm labor force that agriculture could not have continued without them. By freeing commercial farmers from labor pressures and by allowing them to utilize land for whatever specialty crops yielded the greatest profits, they played a critical and heretofore overlooked role in laying the foundations of what would soon become the state's number one industry.[49]

Native field hands themselves knew that what had been happening—their kidnapping by raiders, their addiction to alcohol, their fighting, their peonlike status, their exclusion from citizenship and the rights enjoyed by most Californians, their loss of tribal lands, their status under the Indian Indenture Act, their importance to virtually every farmer—was slowly transforming California agriculture and benefiting the farming elite. An entirely new collection of farming interests was emerging, rapidly, gropingly, haltingly, but they were emerging: the hopeful, opportunistic settlers of the Sacramento Valley, the proslavery southerners intent on establishing a plantation society, the well-established rancheros shifting away from cattle raising, the Euro-American grape growers and winemakers of Los Angeles, the spud moguls at San Jose mission, the cabbage kings of Santa Cruz, the melon magnates of the delta, the truck farmers of the mining towns, and the tenants, farm entrepreneurs, and sharecroppers everywhere. For generations before arriving in California they had labored in poverty, resigned to the limited opportunities, small markets, and dim horizons of a farming system that outside of the slave South did not call for large numbers of hired hands or supplementary labor, and which was largely a family operation. Native field hands now promised to lead them to a better life, one which, even if nothing else was involved, seemed essential to reaping the large harvests that occasionally brought riches, and at worst a prosperous, secure, and comfortable existence. Native field hands could not be ignored by farsighted farmers. They were too important and could not be lost; they would have to be held on the farms and kept at work. One way or another, they were a class that would have to be dominated.[50]

CHAPTER SEVEN

They Have Filled Our Jails and Graveyards

The Decline of Indian Labor

On a hot summer day in 1860, a field hand bent on revenge rode onto Sunny Slope, a two-thousand-acre grape-growing and winemaking operation near present-day Pasadena. Men were everywhere, as Sunny Slope owner L. J. Rose was then engaged in a massive planting project. With so much activity, the newcomer could not find the person he wanted. Instead, he started quarreling with an Indian named Juan de Diego. After insults and threats were exchanged, the newcomer jumped on his horse and attempted to ride away, but Juan de Diego would not let him escape. Quickly mounting his own horse, which stood saddled at the door to his hut, Juan de Diego rode down the fleeing stranger. At full gallop, he caught him near the winery fermentation tanks, drew his dagger, and with a backward thrust, sank it into the man's chest. Spurting blood from a wound to his heart, the newcomer fell from his horse and expired in the dust. As field hands gathered around, they fired a volley of questions: Who is the man? Is he dead? What happened? Juan de Diego, who, like other Indians of his generation was unafraid of, even accustomed to, shedding blood to settle differences, provided few answers. He was apparently never arrested for his deed. That was the outcome when one farmworker murdered another at that time on the farms around Los Angeles.[1]

Lacking any reliable system of law and order, native field hands and vineyard workers out on the farms and ranchos often resolved problems and disputes with guns and knives. Their battles earned notice in the local newspapers, which in one frightening story after another described how "two Indians succumbed beneath the assassin's knife," and so on. So common were such reports that the *Los Angeles Star* could only lament after years of continual carnage that native field hands were now becoming "a people more than half civilized," and because of that were "now exhibiting such signs of retrogression and decay as must be deplored by every humane heart." Soon thereafter, the *Star* dropped the practice of listing the names of dead Indian field hands.[2]

FIGURE 13. Indian field hands bringing in the first vintage at Sunny Slope Winery, Los Angeles, 1864. Winery owner and founder L. J. Rose seated on platform, top left. Courtesy of the Huntington Library.

Even as they were killing one another in the vineyards around Los Angeles, native field hands were also succumbing to a startling array of deadly diseases. Smallpox did the most damage, regularly sweeping through the pueblo and killing as many as a dozen natives in a single day. Epidemics spread rapidly through the ranks, often exacerbated by the opposition to immunization, and the common practice of bathing in the canals in the mistaken belief that cleanliness would help. In fact, the canals were contaminated and only further spread disease.[3]

But by far the most deadly component of Indian life at this time was the abuse of alcohol. This was certainly the case among field hands on Henry Dalton's Rancho Azusa. Hired under a system of labor barter, these men received so much per day, with the value of goods purchased from the ranch store deducted from their monthly account. Besides food, socks, cigarettes, shirts, pants, tea, and playing cards, the largest ledger item almost invariably was alcohol. Often the amount of liquor deducted was so large that field hands were required to work an extra month to pay for it all. Employed under this debt deduction system, field hands on Rancho Azusa became alcoholic wrecks. Often the pursuit of alcohol subsumed all other goals. "Indians all drunk," reported Dalton in his 1861 diary, "stole *aguardiente* from the still, all sobered off this evening, weather fair and pleasant." Matter-of-fact entries for such behavior fill page after page in Dalton's entries: "Indians merry . . . broke into the store and stole two gal. whiskey." It was the same in town, where United States Special Agent J. Ross Browne discovered that many natives were still paid in brandy every Saturday night, put in jail the next morning for getting drunk, and bailed out on Monday to work off their fine. "This system still prevails in Los Angeles," he reported, "where I have often seen a dozen of these miserable wretches carried to jail roaring drunk on a Sunday morning."[4]

Caught in an ever deepening spiral of debt peonage and with no hope of paying off what they owed, many Indian field hands simply fled. So many men left Rancho Azusa in 1862 that Dalton complained that for every man who stayed, four departed. Determined to recoup what he was owed, Dalton maintained an elaborate list of fugitives who had left without clearing their debts. He succeeded in recapturing about half of the men. Returned to Rancho Azusa, they worked until they had settled what they owed.[5]

Alarmed by what was happening, local newspapers predicted dire results. "Many are aged and infirm," reported the *Los Angeles Star*, "and are left by the government to drag out a miserable existence, living on roots and acorns when they can be obtained but . . . are fast disappearing to the silent grave for want of food and clothing." Similarly, the *Los Angeles Semi-Weekly News* exclaimed,

> The habits of the Indians are such that decay and extermination has long
> since marked them for their certain victims. They build no houses, own
> no lands, pay no taxes, and encourage no branch of industry. Their scanty
> earnings at the end of the week are spent for rum in the lowest purlieus
> [neighborhood] part of the city where scenes of violence occur, particularly
> on Saturday and Sunday nights, that would disgrace barbarism itself. . . .
> They have filled our jails, have contributed largely to the filling of our grave-
> yards, where they must either be buried at public expense or permitted to
> rot in the streets and highways.[6]

The murders, auctions, epidemics, liquor, filth, and hard labor were taking their toll. Only 219 natives remained in Los Angeles in 1860, compared with 2,014 a decade earlier. For many local vintners, who had relied on natives to farm some twenty-five hundred acres of vineyards annually, the decline was a major problem. No longer could they assume Indians would be available in almost unlimited numbers. Now they increasingly complained, as did the manager of Lake Vineyard Ranch, that "It has been impossible to hire anyone since Friday." Indeed, so many native field hands were drunk when they went to work that growers who had previously accepted alcohol abuse as a way for obtaining and keeping workers, now privately worried that "every laboring man seems to be on a grand spree; to send their souls to Heaven, or some other place." As a result, growers for the first time had to consider raising wages and competing with one another for a shrinking labor pool. "They are now paying twice the amount for day laborers paid a few years ago when Indian labor could be had as required," confided a resident of San Gabriel.[7]

Events beyond the control of the Indian population itself further reduced the native population across the state at this time, including dozens of so-called Indian wars. These campaigns, which had the support of governors Peter Burnett and John McDougal, both of whom advocated extermination to solve the "Indian problem," took the lives of 4,267 Indians between 1847 and 1865, mainly in the northern part of California. Countless thousands of others, most of them from the Wintun, Athabascan, Yuki, and Achomawi tribes, died in unrecorded clashes with farmers, settlers, and miners. Statewide, thirteen thousand natives died or were murdered between 1852 and 1860, leaving only thirty-two thousand natives alive in California in 1860, with about twenty thousand remaining a decade later. Based on these figures, some historians calculate that natives could not have handled a major or (even very significant) portion of farmwork in the late 1850s and 1860s.[8]

There is another explanation why natives supposedly ceased to be important as field hands at this time. This consists of countless anecdotal accounts of their pathological hatred for farmwork and the great lengths to which they went to avoid it. In one typical and well-known encounter, a newcomer from the eastern United States was traveling with a friend along the Atlanta Road between Santa Clara and San Jose in May 1857. At one point, a hearty-looking Indian stopped the travelers. "Good day gentlemen. Give me a 'bit,' for the love of God. I want to buy bread," he said, explaining that he was destitute. The easterner was astounded by the man's language and appearance. Mostly, though, he was offended by the request. A foreman on a local farm, the man knew there was plenty to do and not enough men to do it all, so he asked the native why he didn't look for work. "I do not like to work," the native replied. With that, he extended his hand. Startled, the easterner gave him a quarter. Displeased, the Indian rolled up his eyes and looked toward heaven. "God will repay you," he said, continuing on his way. He had no intention of becoming a field hand. Of the encounter, the easterner later wrote in his diary: "The Indians are the greatest beggars in the country. Being naturally of an indolent disposition, they avoid work, and if they can get enough to eat by begging, they had much rather do so. Feed an Indian once, and he is sure to call again next day."[9]

Large numbers of natives were undoubtedly escaping fieldwork in the late 1850s—fleeing from farmers and labor agents, foremen, vagrancy laws, and town ordinances, and indeed anyone who would want them to pick melons, stomp wine grapes, or gather grain. Their dislike for the onerous duties of farmwork was certainly real and not altogether without justification. But their opposition mainly stemmed from a desire to maintain what they could of their freedom rather than in laziness or any conscious act of opposition to farmers. In the years surrounding the Atlanta Road incident and other such encounters, many natives found their best method of survival not in withdrawing to the mountains but in roaming the countryside and living, however tenuously, according to a highly modified version of traditional hunting and gathering. They pursued this course by begging from farmers, by pilfering farm supplies, by wading into barley and wheat fields and threshing out grain and packing it off, by digging up potato crops at night for their own use, and as always, by stealing horses.[10]

But while many natives fled farmwork or were otherwise removed from the fields, it does not necessarily follow that by the 1860s they had become irrelevant as agricultural laborers. For one, the often-cited census information locating most "free" Indians near the mines has been misinterpreted. Agriculture at this time was located, when climate and soil allowed, as close to the mines as possible. Only through geographic proximity could growers overcome primitive transportation systems and sell perishable fruit and produce before it spoiled. With agriculture clumped in Yuba, El Dorado, and Sacramento counties, it is not surprising to find that native field hands concentrated there as well. Many natives in the mining areas previously thought to be miners or other kinds of laborers were in fact employed in agriculture, at least part-time.

Census data also falsely reinforces the thesis that natives were irrelevant because census enumerators conducted their surveys in May and June, several months before natives began working at grain harvesting and threshing. The census therefore missed natives who migrated in for that task. Still more problematic was the failure to identify and record native field hands in a separate racial category. Enumerators usually placed native field hands under the category "other." This practice so distorted surveys that, if the census is to be believed, absolutely no Indians worked in the fields. In fact, many natives would continue working on farms—even dominating crops and harvests in certain areas—until well into the second decade of the next century.[11]

§⌐

Indian reservations, in particular, had the effect not so much of withdrawing natives from farmwork as forcing them back into it. First initiated on a state level in February 1851, reservations had developed in 1853 under federal control after California landowners became enraged at a series of federal treaties granting 135 tribal groups large tracts of territory, amounting to one-seventh of the state of California, along with tools, provisions, and technical assistance. Forcing their representatives in Congress to block the treaties and ignore written evidence (submitted by the commissioner of Indian affairs and superintendent of Indian affairs of California, Edward F. Beale) supporting the treaties, farmers and other property owners threw their support behind an alternative system of federally funded and administered reservations scattered the length of the state. The idea was to segregate and assimilate the Indians, teach them American agricultural practices, and transform them into Christian farmers. Some of the larger Indian societies came voluntarily, enticed and otherwise lured off their tribal lands; some smaller bands were forced to move at gunpoint or were otherwise coerced. Whatever prompted their removal and relocation, agents for the U.S. Office of Indian Affairs vigorously defended the program and asserted that the natives quickly adapted to their new circumstances, learned to grow their own food, ate well, and within five years, carved out a comfortable and rewarding life for themselves. Such was the government version of events—at least at first. In fact, the reservations and smaller Indian "farms" were such an unmitigated failure that by the winter of 1860, only three remained. Of these places, wrote reservation critic J. Ross Browne in his *The Coast Rangers*, "A very large amount of money was annually expended in feeding white men and starving Indians."[12]

Mismanaged, exploitative, and riddled with corruption, reservations in 1857 never held more than six thousand to ten thousand of the state's Indians. That was because within just a few months of arriving, many Indians came to regard the reservations as something between a prison and a concentration camp— places that one special agent assigned to investigate them described as "Government Almshouses where an inconsiderable number of Indians are insufficiently fed and scantily clothed, at an expense wholly disproportionate to the benefits conferred." On Nome Lackee Reservation in Northern California, where in 1857 Indian Agent V. E. Geiger stole large portions of the grain crop and sold it, only forty men out of a total Indian population of twenty-five hundred worked at farming. The remainder, according to an investigating agent, "appeared to have no occupation whatever" and survived by roaming the countryside "gathering berries, grass seed &c."[13]

For a few years, it appeared that decent conditions prevailed on Fresno Reservation. Located on the San Joaquin River near Fort Miller, Fresno Reservation was administered by James Savage. A short, muscular man with a broad forehead, deep blue eyes, finely shaped nose, and prominent chin, Savage was one of the most controversial figures of the times, a man his admirers described as a polished and entertaining individual bearing a marked resemblance to Peter the Great, and whom his detractors described as a devil-may-care, fiery malcontent. An Indiana native, Savage had arrived in California in 1845, and after participating in the war against Mexico as a member of John Frémont's California Battalion, worked for a time at Sutter's Fort, where he dug the millrace on the American River where John Marshall discovered gold. Heading south, he soon established trading outposts along the Fresno and Mariposa rivers near Yosemite Valley, where his alliances with and against local Yokut Indians and marriages to several Indian women earned him the title "Blond King of the Tulares." Amassing profits estimated at between twenty and thirty thousand dollars a day trading Indians a pound of sugar for a pound of gold and then gambling it away just as quickly, Savage by January 1852 had developed a successful farming operation at Fort Bishop, located on what became Fresno Reservation, where he ruled as a kind of surrogate chief, alternately fighting with and defending the Indians.[14]

Although never appointed officially to run the reservation, Savage (one of two private citizens who ran reservations) refused to let that impede his work. Any field hand who defied him would be tied to a wagon wheel, whipped before the assembled Indians, his wounds dressed with axle grease, and then sent packing. With such absolute power, the reservation made rapid progress, beginning in April when Savage set twenty-five Indians to digging an irrigation canal to water a twelve-acre farm near Fort Miller. Five feet deep, and four wide, the ditch paralleled the San Joaquin River for four hundred yards and was one of the first such engineering feats in the valley. By summer, Savage's Indian field hands were cultivating 350 acres of grain and 150 acres of produce and were well on their way to becoming self-sufficient. "The Indians appeared to labor with uncommon spirit and cheerfulness," wrote one visitor, noting that along with absolute authority, Savage also possessed an unusual rapport with his field hands. "In the operation of ditching, each man was tasked, which appeared to stimulate their ambition to excel." A second visitor, equally astonished by the amount of work Savage extracted from his field hands and the huge brush fences they had erected around their farm, admitted, "We all blush for our idle habits, compared to his energy, and what he has accomplished with his Indians." A third visitor remarked that he had never seen Indians work so hard. The Indians, he concluded, "look on the farm as their hope for the future, and are planting themselves in its vicinity, in order to watch over, irrigate and cultivate it, as the season advances." In May, five groups of twenty field hands harvested 250 acres of Savage's barley, receiving as payment all the gleanings from the harvest; in July they harvested sixty acres of wheat, twenty-five acres of corn, and twenty acres of potatoes that Savage intended to sell to the U.S. Army at Fort Miller. That August, as Indians feasted on melons and corn, Savage began building extensive adobe quarters, along with a store, public meetinghouse, and a school for fifty or sixty children. "The Indians all love him," wrote another visitor, "and still he manages them in a manner that they also fear him as much."[15]

But for some Indians, the Fresno Reservation was little more than a prison. Members of the Yosemite tribe, driven out of their home, disliked the reservation rations and intense heat of the valley. In April 1851, they fled to their homes, attacked and killed a party of miners, and trekked across the Sierra Nevada to Mono Lake. With the foothill settlers fearing for their lives, a party led by Walter Harvey massacred a group of Indians at Watoka's village. Disgusted by the bloodshed, Savage caught up with Harvey, the two argued and fought, and Harvey killed Savage with three gunshots. Although California newspapers lamented his death, Indians did not. "All Yosemite Indians hated Savage, although some of the Indians of the foothills and the San Joaquin Valley near Fresno like him," recalled Maria Lebrado, a Yosemite Indian who had spent several months working on the Fresno Reservation. Whatever their reactions, Indians on the reservation would never again benefit from the administration of a man as capable as Savage. Splendid crops in 1852 prompted H. B. Edwards, the new superintendent of farming at the Fresno River Farm, to issue a glowing report. "The Indians appeared delighted with the work they had done; and the prospect of reaping a rich harvest . . . instead of living on acorns, as they had hitherto done," he reported to Superintendent of Indian Affairs Edward F. Beale in 1853. But over the next few years the farming operations deteriorated, and Fresno Reservation fell into chaotic disrepair. After crops failed in 1858, the subagent had to send Kings River Indians, who several years earlier had been forced onto the reservation at gunpoint, off to the San Joaquin River to fish and gather food and fend for themselves. And so it went. Early success gave way to starvation and anarchy. Instead of security, Indians were imperiled. Rather than enjoying a modern means of subsistence, they foraged. Soon tiring of their routines and finding the reservations to be dreary and unproductive places, they did what their predecessors on the mission had done—they fled by the thousands. Unlike their mission counterparts, however, many who fled simply returned to white society and resumed working as hired hands on commercial farms.[16]

Farmers, in fact, relied on reservation Indians as part of a more or less floating labor population. Dispatched by reservation agents to harvest, plow, and plant crops on nearby commercial farms, they occasionally endured long treks to reach their work sites. One such crew from Tejon Reservation, hired by Colonel Thomas Baker, founder and namesake of Bakersfield, probably completed the most impressive commercial farming project in the San Joaquin Valley. Since 1854 they had been working on the reservation, at the extreme southern end of the San Joaquin Valley, and had quickly made it self-supporting, with 412 field hands, including men, women, and boys farming some twenty-one hundred acres of wheat, and seven hundred acres of other grains, potatoes, pumpkins, and beans. In the summer of 1858, a crew of thirty El Tejon Reservation field hands began working around Buena Vista and Kern lakes at the south end of the valley, excavating a canal from the Kings River Slough on the San Joaquin River to Kern Lake. They also built a headgate on what remained of the old south bed of the lake, started what would become the Town Ditch, and, over a four-year period, reclaimed a large portion of the swamp and overflow lands between the San Joaquin River, Kings River Slough, and Tulare Lake.[17]

In Mendocino County, reservation Indians became a kind of private labor force for Superintendent of Indian Affairs Thomas Henley. Owner of large acreages in Eden Valley, a small depression in the mountains south of the Mendocino Reservation, his partner in this venture was Serranus C. Hastings, the first chief justice of the California Supreme Court and the state attorney general since 1851. Free to do as he pleased and with easy access to the reservation, Henley directed his sub-agent, Simmon Pena Storms, to withhold food from all natives not working, and to hire out field hands from the reservation to nearby ranchers and farmers. Most, however, went to work in Henley's own fields. Paying minimum wages and forcing field hands to buy everything from his company store, Henley milked every cent he could from them. And since most of what they bought consisted of supplies looted from their own reservation, Henley's field hands, in effect, had to work to purchase the very food and goods that they should have received free of charge.[18]

One of the most shocking examples of abuse occurred on John Sutter's Hock Farm in 1858, when field hands began demanding higher wages, the freedom to work for whom they pleased, and the right to spend their money as they liked. In retaliation, Sutter convinced Superintendent Henley that his field hands were descending into anarchy and needed supervision. On these flimsy grounds, Sutter obtained a federal appointment as a special Indian agent, which gave him broad powers to control field hands. Although the appointment violated federal government policy, it allowed Sutter to remove alleged troublemakers from his farms and order those Indians found carousing in Marysville back to work under threat of eviction. Frightened by these moves, Hock, Yukulme, Sisum, and Ollash natives capitulated completely, promised to obey Sutter, agreed to work "at reasonable prices . . . in clothing and provisions and not in money," and returned to plowing and planting Sutter's fields with seed donated by the government for their personal use. Kept at work with little hope of improving or escaping their lot, Sutter's field hands lost completely the little independence they had once enjoyed. Their only compensation besides provisions consisted of knowing that at least they would be able to live and die, as Sutter put it, on "the Grounds where they are born and where their Ancestors have dwelled."[19]

ॐ

For all their problems, addictions, and betrayals, native field hands by the late 1850s and early 1860s were playing a major role in the Los Angeles wine industry, where a core group of field hands mastered virtually every task associated with winemaking. "They understand the mysteries of irrigation, the planting season, and the harvest . . . planted all the fields and vineyards," asserted one Tennessee-born vintner. "Without them a ranchero would eat much less bread and vegetables."[20]

On the morning of January 9, 1857, their routine was suddenly interrupted when, at about 8 A.M., an earthquake struck. Joseph Edward Pleasants, a young boy attending school on William Wolfskill's farm, later recalled how the ground began to shake when "the pruners . . . had just been called to breakfast and were washing their hands at a hydrant." There were two distinct shocks, the first and longest lasting four minutes. Cattle fell to the ground, adobe buildings crumbled, dozens of people were crushed to death, and a crack thirty to forty miles long opened up near Los Angeles. Frightened, the Indians became dizzy and nauseated. "I noticed them all fall to their knees and begin to pray," recalled Pleasants. "Everyone was running . . . crying *tembler*." But the work did not end. Within a few hours the men returned to the vineyards and quickly made up for their lost time.[21]

Soon they began clearing land, the next in the sequence of their vineyard duties. Typical of frontier agricultural labor, their grub work was made all the more dangerous by the abundance of rattlesnakes and the prevailing treatment for snakebites. Field hands bitten by rattlers received a noxious ointment of equal parts of onion, tobacco, and salt. Applied to their wound, this was supposed to draw out the poison. In fact, it provided no help at all. As they dodged rattlers, natives also became involved in massive fence-building projects. Without fences, winemakers could, and did, have their vines stripped literally overnight by grazing animals and hundreds of thousands of hungry cattle that roamed the countryside unimpeded. Around the towns, where vineyards were small and unlikely to change, men did what their predecessors had done on the missions; they built ditches or, more commonly, stone or adobe walls. Farther out, where much longer fence lines were required, they constructed willow pole or brush fences.[22]

Natives planted at the rate of about one hundred thousand vines and fenced about one hundred acres per year. But they did not begin to harvest much additional fruit until about 1859, after two years had passed following the planting frenzy of 1857. At this point native field hands moved into large-scale grape harvesting. The single greatest number worked for John Frohling, a German-born winemaker, who toward the end of the summer hired 150 or more natives. Following a highly routinized regimen and dividing up responsibilities, some natives carried grapes to crossroads and dumped them into tubs, while others, known as "swampers," worked in two-man teams lifting the heavy grape tubs onto one-horse carts. From there, native teamsters took over, driving the loads to the grape-pressing area, where yet another crew weighed and dumped the grapes into a large "hopper." Compared to how grapes had been harvested during the preceding years, or how they were handled on small vineyards in Northern California, the regimen was far more efficient and well coordinated. In this way Los Angeles natives picked about nine million pounds of wine and table grapes.[23]

Winemaking was the most intense task that natives now performed. One traveler arriving at Rancho Pokamongo ("Negro Ranch") near San Fernando mission found the old black ranchero's naked and sweaty natives treading grapes with their bare feet inside a huge beef hide with a hole cut in the center, forked limbs planted in the ground at each corner, and poles running from the forks through holes in the edges of the hide to suspend the sides in a bowl shape. To prevent themselves from falling into the grapes, the men had rigged a balance stick or pole running above the hide bowl from two more forked poles. Similar scenes were observed throughout the viticultural districts, usually on marginal operations that produced low-quality wine to satisfy the local liquor shops. This did little to whet the appetite of one startled traveler who, upon watching natives toiling in the hot Southern California sun with their sweat running into the trodden juice, could only comment that "the sight . . . in no wise increased my appetite for California wine."[24]

Less primitive conditions prevailed at William Wolfskill's winery, where about sixty men working twelve-hour shifts, night and day, in about two weeks' time turned 160 tons of grapes into twenty thousand gallons of wine and four thousand gallons of brandy. Four native men did nothing but strip stems from the grapes, an extremely dangerous task as they had to push the fruit into the crusher, a mill consisting of two rotating, intermeshing grooved cylinders. Careless natives lost fingers and hands in the clanking machinery and occasionally had their entire arms shredded and ripped from their sockets. Two other men turned the crusher with large crank handles; two fed the hopper; three or four attended to the juice as it flowed from the mill; five shoveled pomace (pulpy residue of crushed grapes, stems, and seeds) into the spiral screw presses and carried off the hard, compacted pomace cakes; two or three washed, cleaned, and applied sulfur to the grapes as they were being crushed (the sulfur was used to prevent the juice from oxidizing and browning); six filled and transported barrels of juice and grape skins into 140-gallon fermentation vats, where the juice remained for one week; and three teams of five to six men each hauled the grapes out of the vineyards. There were also natives who did nothing but cleanup work. "Every night all the presses and appliances used about them are all washed thoroughly to prevent acidity," reported a correspondent for the *San Francisco Daily Evening Bulletin.* "Everything that comes in contact with the grape juice from the time the grape is bruised till it reaches the cask is kept as pure as an abundance of water and hard scrubbing can make it."[25]

The dirty work done by native field hands allowed winemakers and their French, German, Anglo, and Mexican overseers to develop a commercial operation far in advance of anything previously existing in California, spurring further viticultural advancement. With low labor costs, profit margins remained high. By the early 1860s, vintners were producing about five hundred thousand gallons of wine annually; they shipped 325,000 gallons to San Francisco. And as "Grape Growing Fever," as it was called, swept over the area, demand for native labor grew almost exponentially. Although few winemakers realized it at the time, natives were exerting an extremely important and lasting effect not only on the countryside around Los Angeles but on rural society throughout the state. In the 1860s, California had the highest ratio of farm laborers to farmers anywhere in the United States outside the antebellum South. This was the beginning of modern agriculture's reliance on an unlimited supply of farm labor, an addiction that would shape the structure of the industry for generations to come.[26]

॰

California agriculture in the late 1850s and early 1860s was growing at an incredible rate. Vast acreages in the Sacramento and San Joaquin valleys were opening up to farming as a result of droughts that killed off hundreds of thousands of cattle and bankrupted many of the big ranchos. Orchards began yielding extremely profitable crops, and wheat production was also expanding rapidly. Winemaking migrated out of Los Angeles and took root around Santa Clara, Sonoma, San Jose, and in the Sierra Nevada foothills. With truck gardening operations sprouting up around every population center, the flower industry taking root south of San Francisco, and experiments in fruit drying absorbing the growing surplus of fruit, agriculture by the late 1850s and early 1860s moved California from twenty-ninth place to twelfth place among all states in total farm production, and challenged mining as the state's prime industry. At the vortex of a specialized complex of businesses and institutions that would later become known as "agribusiness," California was growing a dazzling array of crops—alfalfa, almonds, apples, citrus, peaches, pears, plums, prunes, olives, tomatoes, walnuts, most grains, every conceivable vegetable, and almost every subtropical fruit. Among the crops that would soon be planted was the opium poppy. It was a hopeful time of great excitement and unknown opportunities. The first agricultural fairs were being held; a nursery industry was thriving; an agricultural implement manufacturing industry producing plows, reapers, threshers, headers, harrows, header wagons, and a hundred other implements was expanding over a large portion of Stockton; transportation entrepreneurs were running sailing vessels laden with fruit and vegetables from Hood to San Francisco and laying plans for a transcontinental railroad; established growers facing problems of overproduction were beginning to can large amounts of fruit; and venturesome farmers were launching countless experiments to determine what grew best and where. Would grapes do well on that southeast-facing hillside? Would peaches attain added size along that river bottomland? Could apples grow in the Pajaro Valley? How about a mixture of beans and turnips where the cattle were kept? Tea? Tobacco? Indigo? Hemp? Bananas? Nothing seemed impossible.[27]

But labor costs remained a major worry. Again and again, farmers predicted a glorious future should they find the required work force. And just as frequently they predicted dire consequences with insufficient or overly expensive labor. And always they returned to the same question: Where would they find an ample supply of cheap, docile farmworkers? Farmers had debated the question ever since the Gold Rush, but had nearly always acted individually with little or no coordination. Now, faced with declining numbers of native field hands and rapidly expanding agricultural production, a full-scale farm labor policy rapidly took shape. Becoming increasingly more important, sophisticated, well-organized, and perhaps most significant, more politically conscious, growers finally determined to use their influence to expand the labor supply.[28]

Leading the charge were *California Farmer*, the state's top agricultural publication, and the California State Agricultural Society, an organization of California's most vocal and influential growers. These groups linked up with rural publications like the *Marysville Herald* to address the question of where to find more farmworkers. Intent on corralling labor as a way of protecting and quickening the pace of expansion, these forces early in 1860 mobilized for action. Under the guise of investigating "Indian problems" in Northern California, they induced the state legislature to authorize a special committee to report on the question of Indian labor. Heading the committee was state senator J. B. Lamar of Mendocino County. The owner of large acreages and a proponent of California's agricultural future, Lamar made no secret of his desire to help farmers and other employers. Trotting out the 1850 Act for the Government and Protection of Indians and tacking on some modifications, he intended to make the law even more repressive and therefore an even more useful tool for rounding up Indian field hands. To accomplish this goal, he recommended that the state "should adopt a general system of peonage or apprenticeship." Lamar had ample support for this sentiment, although even the staunchest proponents expressed themselves carefully. Newspapers were especially clever and circumspect. Editors claimed to be interested only in advancing the welfare of natives. But frequently their true intentions emerged, as when the *Sacramento Standard*, claiming that it intended only to reverse the deteriorating condition of Indians, called for a "mild system of servitude . . . with Christian masters and . . . Christian servants."[29]

Quickly responding to Lamar's prodding, the legislature wasted little time revising the 1850 act. Dramatically expanding its scope and sanctioning many of its abuses, legislators led by wealthy Southern California ranchero Jonathan T. Warner, now called for considerably lengthening the terms of apprenticeship and also for indenturing adults. Support for the law was intense and widespread throughout the farming districts and other parts of the state, and public officials were ready to meet the demands. On April 21, a compliant Sacramento legislature passed a law that provided what farmers had wanted all along—a decisive means for controlling native field hands. According to the amended Act for the Government and Protection of Indians, adult Indians were still gathered under the usual variety of pretexts, including drunkenness and vagrancy. But in addition, any Indian who had fought in any war against whites and been captured, or even those who were simply not already "under the protection" of a white person, could also be "put out . . . as apprentices, to trades, husbandry, or other employments, as shall . . . appear proper." All a farmer had to do was take a list of Indians to any judge, who would then sign them over without inquiring whether natives consented to the arrangement or whether the farmer could "clothe and suitably provide the necessities of life for such . . . Indians . . . during the term for which such Indians . . . shall be apprenticed." Compelled to work and behave as told, Indians lost whatever modicum of independence they had previously won.[30]

What was worse, the clause from the 1850 act, ordering the presence of parents or friends during child indenture proceedings, was dropped. To obtain a native child, a farmer had merely to declare that a parent had given verbal "consent" or, lacking that permission, to present the sworn statement of anyone "having the care or charge of any such child or children." This phrase was purposefully ambiguous, allowing children to be gathered from third parties (namely, slave catchers) claiming to be guardians. Boys indentured under the new law no longer left their masters when they turned eighteen. Instead, they remained until reaching twenty-five years of age. Girls, once set free at fifteen, now worked until they were twenty-one. Young males, indentured between fourteen and twenty years of age, could be kept in the fields until they reached thirty years of age, while females could be held on farms until they became twenty-five. This pleased agricultural interests enormously. "The law works beautifully," observed the *Humboldt Times*, a strong supporter of the revised legislation. "What a pity the provisions of the law are not extended to Greasers [Mexicans], Kanakas [South Sea Islanders], and Asiatics. It would be so convenient to carry on a farm . . . when all the hard and dirty work is performed by apprentices."[31]

These codes impressed many rural critics as a revival of the "system of Indian slavery" that had existed in the days of the Spaniards. "The Indians of the country have been so long accustomed, under their Spanish masters, to be treated as menials," observed the editor of the *Sacramento Union*, the leading newspaper in the state capital and proponent of antislavery sentiment, "that we shall not expect public attention to be called to their case by any determined resistance to the decrees of the Courts." If field hands were really free, the editor argued, they ought to be able to decide where to live and how to work; dicker with farmers over employment including terms of service, rates of wages, and conditions of labor; and they should be free to take legal action against farmers abusing the relationship. But under the new regulations, he continued, natives would be forced to toil for compensation that barely kept them alive, and certainly could not sustain a family. "If this does not fill the measure of the constitutional term 'involuntary servitude,'" the editor concluded, "we shall be thankful if some one will inform us what is lacking."[32]

Contracts between farmers and indentured laborers were strict. One indenture, that of La-Ache, also known as "Jack," a twelve-year-old Indian field hand from Centerville, near Fresno, was typical. His motives in agreeing to the indenture can hardly be imagined. A facile conclusion would be that he was an orphan and like many others jumped at a chance to survive. This analysis, however, assumes that La-Ache would consciously embrace a bad deal. In this case, he might not have had any choice and may not even have understood what he was agreeing to when he made his mark on the document before the county judge. Certainly it was an unfair arrangement, even by contemporary standards. For food, clothing, bedding, medicine and "other necessities of life," the young Indian consented to work "in the capacity of Domestic Servant and general laborer, until he . . . attained the full age of Twenty-five Years." During all this time, La-Ache also agreed to surrender all his earnings to his employer, a farmer by the name of Mc-Cray, and in addition, to "serve the said McCray honestly and faithfully in all things . . . not to absent himself from said master's service, day or night, without his permission, and in all things conduct himself as a faithful and good servant ought to do." Only at the end of his service would he receive any compensation—a horse and fifty dollars for thirteen years of labor.[33]

The practice of kidnapping Indian women and children "for purposes of labor and lust," already commonplace under the original Act for the Government and Protection of Indians, now became even more acceptable—and profitable. Under the guise of the apprenticeship provision, and never with the "parental consent" that the law supposedly required, even larger numbers of Indian women and children were carried off and sold into virtual slavery on farms around the state. Once centered mainly on Humboldt and Mendocino counties, kidnapping now expanded throughout all of the Northern California counties. As dozens of "Injunmen" and "squawmen"—as the kidnappers came to be known—wreaked terror on tribes from Ukiah to Redding, the *Sacramento Union* wrote: "You may hear them talk of the operation of cutting to pieces an Indian squaw in their indiscriminate raids for babies as 'like slicing old cheese' . . . The baby hunters sneak up to a ranchería, kill the bucks, pick out the best looking squaws, ravish them, and make off with their young ones." Kidnappers would load their prisoners on horseback, two or three tied to one horse, or pile them into wagons by the dozen. Avoiding the main roads and keeping to the byways, they would then transport their captives thirty or forty miles out of the mountains to safe houses. Having seen several hundred kidnapped natives passing through the southern part of Lake County on the way to being sold to farmers in Napa, Yolo, Solano, and Sacramento counties, a miner described for the *Alta California*, "two men driving nine children; in another, two men with four children; in another, one man with two girls, one of them about fourteen years of age apparently." Kidnappers would then feed and clean their captives, give them "traveling costumes"—an old shirt or a bit of calico fashioned into a semblance of a garment—and take them to the nearest judge to be legally indentured. At this point, they would rename the natives, a formality necessary for court records. A little girl brought in from the mountains on a gray horse became Nelly Gray. A little boy brought in on a brown horse became John Brown. A dull or depressed youngster who sat in the grass pulling weeds to pass the time became Old Weedy. A thin boy became Twig. And a naked native with fresh dew on his feet from walking through the grass in the early morning became Wet Heels.[34]

By some estimates, at least one out of every four farmhouses in California's northwestern counties during the early 1860s held a kidnapped native child. People who kept them often claimed that the children were frequently "the brightest and cunningest little chaps you ever saw. They are very cheerful, laugh at jokes, and seem fond of playing practical ones occasionally on their white playfellows . . . always jolly, and always whistling." But there is ample evidence that na-

FIGURE 14. La-Ache, also known as "Jack," indentured as a field hand in 1862 for a period of twelve years, until age twenty-five. La-Ache is here photographed at the end of his indenture, about 1874. Courtesy of the Fresno County Historical Society.

tive children were hardly content with their lot. Many never forgot or abandoned their traditional ways; many never learned to speak English; and many never abandoned their desire to be free. Nothing so confounded white farmers than the "intelligent looking girl of fifteen" who, after living on a farm so long that she had forgotten how to speak her native language, nevertheless escaped at the first opportunity and, even after being recaptured, rejected her so-called family in favor of "a half-naked 'buck' with whom she is enamored." Of these developments, U.S. Indian agent Henry Bailey reported, "So far as my observation extended, contentment and apparently perfect resignation was the result [of early indenture] until manhood or womanhood was reached, when all the Indian instincts seemed to return and no influence, moral, mental or physical, could induce them to remain in the positions they had in many instances esteemed highly during their childhood."[35]

As always, whenever kidnapped field hands fought back, they failed, and often suffered miserably. As a result, in Northern California, when Round Valley farmer Elijah Potter discovered that one of three kidnapped natives tried to poison him, Potter promptly executed all of them. A similar fate befell a sixteen-year-old boy who killed Shasta County farmer Hiram Good. Apprehended shortly thereafter, he was killed by Good's neighbors. Attempts to escape usually proved equally futile. Kidnappers shot runaways—often even if they were children. Many farmers did the same or, upon recapture, gave them one more chance, all the while threatening to hang them if they ever ran away again. These were not idle threats.[36]

To those who were kidnapped and forced to work, laws prohibiting the practice, as always, must have seemed a cruel joke. Few, if any, whites who stole Indian children feared apprehension, let alone punishment. "The parties . . . boldly assert that . . . the law cannot reach them," observed an army lieutenant stationed in Humboldt County. Indeed, when the Humboldt County Grand Jury in 1861 launched a "vigorous" investigation into the matter, nothing came of it, even though everyone knew who the kidnappers were, what they were doing, and where they were doing it. Led by California Superintendent of Indian Affairs George M. Hanson, the federal government attempted to curb the practice by appointing special agents and sending them to intercept the kidnappers as they brought their captives into towns. Although this produced some arrests, local authorities invariably declined to prosecute. Because of this, Hansen called for repeal of the apprenticeship law "under cover of which all this trouble exists."[37]

When a coalition in 1862 succeeded in having the state assembly pass a repeal bill, it was thwarted by representatives from the northern counties. Even in the face of repeated protests by antislavery elements and with the country in the midst of the Civil War, California growers boldly issued one appeal after another for cheap Indian labor. "With cheap labor we could supply all our own wines and liquors, besides sending large quantities abroad," predicted one farm representative. "Turning from grapes," a joint select legislative committee observed, "let us dwell for a moment upon the production of rice, tea, sugar, tobacco, and dried fruits of every description, such as figs, raisins, etc., etc., all of which can be easily grown in the State and soon will be commenced, if we encourage cheap labor."

The solution, according to the committee, was to "harness all inferior races to work out and realize our grand and glorious destiny."[38]

It was not until four months after President Abraham Lincoln's Emancipation Proclamation that California's indenture and apprenticeship provisions came under intense attack. Glaringly incompatible with the state's professed devotion to liberty, the federal government's opposition to slavery, and the generally accepted idea that social progress was linked to free labor in a competitive society, the repressive law could no longer be defended, although many farming representatives would not listen to such logic. Condemning calls for repeal with hysterical cries of dismay, California farmers justified the repressive policies of the Indian Indenture Act on the grounds that they assisted Indian field hands by curbing their bad habits and teaching them to work with authority. A "great good had grown out of this law," argued Mendocino County senator William Holden, who used all of his power to prevent the Senate from repealing the Indian Indenture Act. But unable to justify what most by now regarded as a de facto version of the southern Black Codes, California legislators on April 27, 1862, finally eliminated the system. By then, countless numbers of Indian field hands had been victimized by the law.[39]

Some chroniclers of the farmworker story believe that with repeal of the indenture and apprenticeship statutes, native farmworkers left behind a mean and exploitative labor system and entered into a more humane existence. Even before repeal, according to this interpretation, natives were adjusting well to their new status as hired farmhands. And on at least one farm, this was indeed the case. Native field hands worked with dignity, in excellent facilities, and under a benevolent farmer for at least a generation—and the identity of that farmer in many ways fuels the misperception. The field hands were Mechoopdas and they worked for none other than John Bidwell, sponsor of the original Indian Indenture Act.[40]

None of the native field hands working for Bidwell ever experienced the repercussions of the very law for which their employer was so famous. For Mechoopdas, Rancho Chico offered such a safe and relatively comfortable haven that any native in the area with a sense of self-preservation recognized its possibilities. Life on Bidwell's rancho was not easy for the Mechoopdas. They planted, harvested, and threshed three hundred acres of wheat annually, worked in the largest orchard in the state, cleared land for a huge vineyard, made wine and raisins, built and worked in the first flour mill in the county, dried apricots, maintained hothouses for delicate plants imported from China and Japan, tended large numbers of livestock, assisted in a thriving nursery business, and generally helped Bidwell create a farm that was among the best and most productive in Northern California. Amid all of this, they also erected buildings, including a two-story adobe mansion, a barn, a carriage house, a store, an office, a blacksmith shop, a gardener's cottage, and a flour mill. And although no Mechoopda served as a foreman or supervisor on any of these projects, they were nonetheless extremely well treated. They all received regular vaccinations that saved them from various epidemics that eliminated other Butte County tribes. They also received protection from hostile whites. And in 1863 Bidwell even interceded against the government on their behalf; otherwise they would surely have been rounded up and removed with most remaining Butte County Indians to a reservation one hundred miles west in Round Valley.[41]

Exactly how many Mechoopda men and women worked for Bidwell at this time is a matter of some dispute. The U.S. census listed just fifty on the ranch—thirty-nine men working as field hands, herders, gardeners, and roustabouts, and eleven women day laborers, all but one of them between the ages of sixteen and thirty-two. The single men lived in three barracks, the single women in a fourth dwelling under a male chief named Yummarine. Because the census listed no children, some researchers have come to the mistaken impression that farmwork on Bidwell's ranch, like farmwork in general, destroyed native family life. But while this may have been true on other farms, the situation was more complicated on Rancho Chico. Local newspapers, county histories, and Bidwell's own writings mention, in addition to the bunkhouses, a ranchería organized around a large, communal sweat house. Originally located about one hundred yards from Bidwell's adobe mansion along the banks of Chico Creek, then shifted a mile to the northwest near what is Sacramento Avenue in present-day Chico, the ranchería contained large numbers of natives, including old women and young children. At least one hundred—and possibly as many as 250 natives—lived there. Such arrangements kept the Mechoopdas firmly rooted to Rancho Chico and formed them into what may have been the largest single native farmworker community outside of Los Angeles.[42]

About forty miles north, along the banks of the Sacramento River, native field hands at Pierson B. Reading's Rancho Buena Ventura continued to enjoy a relatively secure, predictable, and protected existence. With ample quarters and compensation of a pint of wheat or a loaf of blue bread per day and an old cow slaughtered for meat every week, they ate well and regularly, married, supported elderly parents, and raised large families. Because of this, there were plenty of women in their ranchería who were available for domestic work. Reading's wife, who came from a prominent Washington, D.C., family, employed them everywhere. Wives and daughters of field hands cleaned, washed, cooked, and cared for the Reading children, even accompanied them to Mt. Lassen for summers. Indian women indulged the family, served at lavish parties, and generally performed all the functions found in a large and wealthy Victorian household.[43]

But very few other native field hands experienced the civility and happiness of Rancho Chico and Rancho Buena Ventura. For them, emancipation from the Indenture Act hardly altered the day-to-day reality of life and labor on commercial farms, or the ingrained behavior, temperament, and priorities of agricultural employers. Natives working on most California farms in the 1860s earned a minimum of fifty cents a day plus food (but occasionally received up to two dollars a day and no food), with wages depending on their skill and whether or not there was a labor shortage or glut. Farms were seldom substantial enough to provide them permanent, year-round employment; consequently, large numbers of Indians continued circulating between rancherías and farms, arriving and departing at predictable times of the year as needed. Whenever the hay harvest began in the

Sonoma Valley north of San Francisco, between Petaluma and Healdsburg, natives could often be observed tramping between farms in "peaceable, docile, and in good condition," as one Indian agent explained. Still farther north, at Little Lake and Walker's Lake, three hundred to four hundred local natives cut hay every August and September, while Indians from Lake County left their rancherías every fall to work in the Napa Valley vineyards. "Harvest time has brought our valley a large number of Clear Lake Indians, many of whom, we are told, are exceedingly useful in the field, and bind equal to, or better than many white men," reported the *Pacific Echo*.[44]

Many other newspapers reiterated that theme. "The farmers needed them for labor and they worked well," reported the *San Francisco Bulletin* in October 1861. Encountering groups of natives trudging along the back roads or resting in the shade of a tree, stagecoach drivers would occasionally let them ride on the coach top to the next town. Youngsters who saw them arrive by the trainload or tramp in from the nearest ranchería or reservation to harvest fruit watched in rapt fascination as the Indians set up in a vacant field and deployed into camps. But not all natives traveled in groups; many simply came and went as they pleased. "Today I plant wheat with a boy, José," noted Los Angeles farmer Juan Bandini in his daily journal. Five days later, Bandini wrote, "José went off to the hills." Such departures were apparently a common reaction to unsatisfactory conditions.[45]

ॐ

In the early 1860s, some natives found their tasks considerably eased thanks in large part to better equipment. Gone were the crude *carretas*, the torturous ox-drawn plows, harrows made out of tree branches, and the other primitive farm tools of Spanish and Mexican origin, now replaced by American-type plows, sickles, hoes, harrows, wagons, and new agricultural implements. Some contemporaries claimed that natives could not handle farm machinery or teams of horses —that while capable enough at manipulating walking plows, they were confused by other common farm tools—but their performance proved otherwise. Contrary to popular prejudices, natives became adept at using virtually every farm tool available. Although some natives labored willingly and appeared to be treated well, in the first few years after the repeal of the Indian Indenture Act many others continued suffering abuse of the rankest sort. Some farmers continued to employ the whip as an instrument of control and punishment and did not hesitate to use it while dealing with uppity Indians. This certainly was the case in Mendocino County, where James Shores, a notorious "Indian hunter" and farmer, shot one of his Indian field hands for refusing to stand for a whipping. The field hand's chest was torn open by the buckshot, but he did not die; instead, he returned to work, but not before being whipped for disobedience.[46]

The most sensational of these episodes occurred in August 1865, and involved a native field hand who worked for Bob Hildreth, a farmer from Ukiah. Upon encountering one of his own field hands hauling barley for another farmer, Hildreth became infuriated by his independent work, stopped him, and ordered him off his wagon "damn quick." As the frightened native fled into a field, Hildreth pursued, captured the native, and roped him to a horse. The Indian pleaded for mercy. Hildreth mounted the horse, spurred it forward, and threw the Indian eight to ten feet in the air. After a few jumps, the horse—running at full speed and dragging the native—zigzagged across the road and crossed two ditches before stopping. Terribly mangled, the field hand nearly had his arms twisted off at the shoulders. Hildreth was arrested and bound over on one thousand dollars bail, but never stood trial. "So much for slavery," commented the *Sacramento Union*.[47]

A less dramatic but more specific index of how native laborers were being treated could be found in the outlying farms of Butte County, where foremen regularly cheated Indians out of their wages. Angered by the practice, Bidwell foreman Henry Gandt wrote in his diary, "They think that they are pulling the wool over the eyes of the Indian boys. They make them believe that there is fifty days in a month and when they come to pay them off they will pay them a dollar a day." Of course, fifty days' labor would only yield a month's wages. Frustrated by his inability to curtail the practice, Gandt complained, "I cannot get at those boys until they find out they are deceived." But field hands were not the only ones to be tricked. When a loyal *mayordomo* on the Cave Couts ranch near San Juan Capistrano revealed that he planned to take some time off and return to the mountains, the farm manager laid plans to replace him while he was away. "I have a man that I can recommend for his place at considerable less wages," he told Couts. So common were tricks of this kind that government Indian inspector J. Ross Browne, after encountering numerous subterfuges during the course of his travels and investigations, observed that, "If ever an Indian was fully and honestly paid for his labor by a white settler, it was not my luck to hear of it."[48]

Starving natives remained easy pickings. Near Elkhorn Station thirty miles southwest of Fresno, one group of twenty men became so desperate that they moved out of their ranchería in the foothills to work at a Butterfield Stagecoach Company station for a large, crusty, domineering settler and former army officer named John Barker. To cut his hay, an exceptionally profitable crop that Barker sold to the Butterfield Stagecoach Company to feed teams hauling passengers along the route between Visalia and Stockton, Barker paid natives one dollar a day and portions of horse meat. There were no mowing machines within one hundred miles, so the men used scythes, but lacking experience, struggled to master the work. "They would mow a few yards, stop, look at their hands, and call on another one to take their place," recalled Barker. "When the sun got up warm they would all quit work, retire to the bank of the slough and plunge into the water, come out and stick their heads under the shade of a bunch of tules and go to sleep." This continued for three days, until one morning Barker woke up and was astounded to discover that the entire tribe had migrated in and was now demanding to be fed. When a crew of Mormons appeared on the road from San Bernardino to the northern mines, Barker hired them and fired the Indians. "I gave them all the horse beef on hand and told them to get up and get."[49]

On many farms, desperate natives were assigned tasks considered too odious for white laborers. Frequently these involved massive insect control campaigns. This was an essential and unavoidable task. With the only green vegetation for miles around, new farms and vineyards quickly became magnets for pests, par-

ticularly cutworms and grasshoppers, which swarmed in from the dry countryside. Because there were no suitable poisons and modern insect control techniques were still a generation in the future, Indians were sent in to exterminate
the pests by hand. A "good brave" and his crew, it was said, could gather and
smash up to forty-two pounds of grasshoppers and other bugs in six hours. Many
Indians did not regard such work as repulsive, and on some occasions waded into
the insects with such vigor that they supposedly collected "a pile as large as any
haystack in that vicinity." Some even saved buckets of the grasshoppers to roast
with manzanita berries and minnows in great grasshopper feasts. For decades, so
long as they were available in the era before pesticides, natives all over the state
toiled away in huge bug-killing crews. Armed with little more than paddles,
branches, burlap bags, sulfured rags, smoky torches, and carts full of flaming
dung, they would frequently be employed to burn, scare, smoke, smash, or otherwise drive away insect infestations before they could threaten crops.[50]

Such unpleasant work hardly earned Indians rewards like better quarters. On
the west side of the San Joaquin Valley, where farmers were both stingy and poor,
natives often slept under the trees or in the bushes. When they did sleep indoors
their quarters consisted at best of little more than ten-by-twelve-foot enclosures
with sides of warped pine shakes, roofs of flattened oyster or sardine cans, and
some cotton muslin tacked to the rafters. "It would not do justice to the picture to
leave those muslin ceilings in this state," recalled field hand turned historian
Frank Latta. "In a few years they supported a layer of fine dust, wafted in through
the cracks between the split shakes. When the three-day northland zephyrs raced
across the Joaquin plains those muslin ceilings slapped up and down and sifted a
layer of chocolate colored material over everything in the place, including the
plate of sowbelly and bayo beans the Sky Farmer [flatlands farmer] had dished
up." Many Indians, according to Latta, did not even fare that well. "The Indians
were always more concerned about the food offered them than they were about
wages," he later told an interviewer. "I remember that a neighbor hired three of
them. . . . They soon quit the job and left without asking for their wages because
they did not get as much as they wanted to eat."[51]

Natives field hands encountered even worse conditions on Judge Serranus C.
Hastings's Eden Valley farm near Ukiah in Northern California, where thirteen
natives from a nearby ranchería were literally treated like pack mules. Farm manager H. L. Hall forced them to carry supplies over the mountains between Eden
Valley and Ukiah, a one-way trip of forty miles. For a week of this work, they
supposedly received food and clothes, but they were actually lucky if they were
even fed, and they never received so much as a shirt or pair of pants. "They were
worked naked, with the exception of deer skins around their shoulders," settler
Benjamin Arthur later recalled. "They usually packed fifty pounds if able."[52]

On Rancho Cucamonga in San Bernardino County, the seventy Indians employed during the 1865 grape harvest existed in a state of peonage. Trekking in
from Temecula and San Luis Rey accompanied by their wives, children, and often
with aged adults, they were given food and shelter, and promised a wage of fifty
cents a day, but were seldom paid in cash. On Saturday nights they would crowd
before G. W. Gillette, a tough vineyard foreman and storekeeper who conducted

the proceedings in Spanish. Calling out each man's name, Gillette reported the work he had done and the amount due, followed by the question, "What will you have?" Often the men would be in a drunken state, and when asked their names, answered "Antonio María Lugo" and "Señor Yorba," to much laughter. Money being scarce, Gillette would then pay them off with a half gallon of *aguardiente*, a pair of overalls, a fine comb, or a mouth organ. "Some chap would take mostly wine or brandy, and you knew he was going to entertain, which was verified by the sounds emanating from the rancheria far into the night," Gillette recalled in his memoirs forty years later. "Sabbath was a day of debauchery. It was a woeful file that lined up for work on Monday morning."[53]

Tricked, tormented, defrauded, and sent packing on the slightest pretext, native field hands were caught not so much in a vicious circle as in a downward spiral from which they could not escape. Much like southern blacks who failed to achieve their true liberation after the Civil War, natives in California following the repeal of the indenture and apprenticeship laws failed to win freedom from kidnapping, involuntary servitude, arrest for drunkenness, and various other devices that forced them to work or otherwise abused and exploited them. Still regarding them as property, farmers discovered that they could use existing laws to circumvent the ban on Indian indenture. So little had changed that the *Sacramento Union*, looking at the effects of repeal in August 1865, concluded it had no practical consequence in Mendocino County. Indians there were still being treated "as slaves were . . . in the South; those owning them use them as they please, beat them with clubs, and shoot them down like dogs, and no one [*sic*] to say: 'Why do you do so?'"[54]

Around Monterey County, Indian field hands arrested for such crimes as fighting, drunkenness, larceny, and urinating in public received up to twenty-five lashes, in contrast to white citizens who, for the same offense, were let off with a fine or a few days in jail. Such was the state of justice that those accused falsely of stealing horses could be shot with impunity, or, if arrested, would often be found "hung in jail yard" and "strangled in his cell"—as the Monterey County Jail Register succinctly put it—although it is unclear whether or not these listings refer to vigilante justice, retribution, or state execution. Often, one crime was compounded by another. A prime example was what happened on November 27, 1868, when José Laurencio, a thirty-year-old Carmel mission Indian field hand (employed by ranchero Honore Escolle), and his friends José Morales, Juan Alvarez, José Jacinto, and a man named Feliciano, began drinking liquor behind Girardin's Store in Monterey. Unemployed after serving ninety days in jail for larceny, Laurencio and Morales were looking to cheer themselves up. But as the liquor flowed, tempers flared, and out came the knives. Jacinto was cut on the hand, and later in the evening, Laurencio's body was discovered on the beach, dead of twenty-five stab wounds. At a coroner's inquest a few days later, no one could remember what had happened. But because Morales, along with Laurencio, were known troublemakers, the coroner assumed they had been fighting and held Morales on a charge of murder. On May 27, 1868, he was "sent to God on a rope"—executed by hanging —despite any clear evidence or testimony as to his guilt other than that he had done time in jail and been friendly, or not, with the victim.[55]

Far from offering a means of survival, field labor for such Indians was just one more nail in their coffin. Even if they had been able to foresee their fate, it would have been inescapable. Their experiences of the last generation or more—their drinking and fighting among themselves, their vagabondage and unequal status under law, their poverty and illiteracy—were slowly but certainly grinding them into extinction. Masses of native field hands were dying out—the bug smashers and grasshopper herders of the Sacramento Valley, the Mechoopdas on Rancho Chico, the grape pickers of Negro Alley, the fence builders of Los Angeles, the canal diggers of the San Joaquin Valley, the potato rooters at San José mission, the pack mules of Eden Valley, the indentured laborers of Redwood Valley, the cabbage grubbers of the delta, and the vagabonds of the Monterey Bay region. Suffering the consequences of a largely male environment, every farming region but one had extremely high ratios of native men to women. These ranged from twenty-two to one in Yuba and Tulare counties to three to one in Calaveras County. Only in Sutter County, with about one native man per every woman, was the ratio relatively normal.[56]

Indian field hands had no hope of winning much improvement in their lives, no aspiration that their diligence would bring anything better for their families and children. By the almost unanimous testimony of friends and foes alike, they were afflicted with characteristics associated with a people bordering on genocide: a vulnerability that attracted exploiters, an inability to assert independence, weak leadership, outcast status, and no political power. Those traits made them ideal laborers so far as farmers were concerned. But they were no prescription for survival. As California agriculture experienced its next spurt of growth, Indians would not be around in large enough numbers to furnish the required labor.

FIGURE 15. John Benson's threshing outfit, San Joaquin County, ca. 1875. Courtesy of the California Historical Society.

BOOK THREE

Golden Harvest

A young man, apparently a German, of about 25 years of age, went to the ranch of W. Smith, near Napa, on Wednesday, and commenced work binding grain in the harvest field. He had bound but a few sheaves when he fell down, and before any assistance could be given, expired.
    —'Napa Pacific Echo'

Oh, we were always scratching. We ate burned beef. We drank filthy water. Our bunkhouses were crowded. Sometimes we lived with the chickens and the cows. We were always dirty. We never had any money. We stank to hell.
    —Frank F. Latta

Those who tramp about the country calling themselves farm laborers, are the most complete set of loafing idlers to be found in any country . . . they are birds of passage.
    —'Transactions of the California State
      Agricultural Society'

A stouter set of bronzed athletic young men we never saw since the war closed. . . . The young men though working hard are merry as Robin Hood's gang and we take as much pleasure in writing up their chronicles as if they were tourists.
    —'Santa Rosa Republican'

All of the men searched the food for flies before eating. Every day we had pie for dinner. Before eating pie the men would turn the crust up and search for flies. We often found a fly or two under the crust. If you ate more than one fly you would surely lose your dinner within ten minutes.
    —Nick Hansen

CHAPTER EIGHT

Between the Teeth of the Cylinder

The Emergence of Migratory Labor

and Farm Technology

For wheat threshers on Richard Shaw's farm near Milpitas, a small community south of San Francisco, July 18, 1860, was unexceptional. The harvest was in full swing and, pending its completion, all other activities in and around town seemed to have come to a stop. About 6 P.M. a threshing machine finished an exhausting eight-hour shift separating grain from straw and chaff. Noisy and nonstop, the work had gone smoothly, with no machinery malfunctions. As the threshing ceased, the crew—composed not of Indians but of former gold miners—gathered at the wheat stack and prepared to return to their quarters. After a long, hot day in the field, everyone looked forward to washing up, sitting down for a big dinner, and turning in early for a much-needed rest.

Left alone on top of the thresher was crew foreman Tom Briggs, who had been instructed by Shaw to remain at the thresher, inspect it, and make sure it was in good operating order for work the next day. As he stepped onto the "feeding table" where cut wheat was shoved into the thresher, Briggs slipped on the zinc sheets, sending his leg between the teeth of the furiously spinning cylinder. Screaming in pain as the heavy mass of interlocking iron teeth mashed his bones and flesh, Briggs could not be heard over the sound of the thresher. Not until his leather boot clogged the machine's gears did anyone hear his cries and rush to his aid. With his foot destroyed and the lower half of his leg completely torn to ribbons, Briggs drew his own jackknife and began slicing away at the tendons of his leg. In the diary that he maintained for many years, farm manager Alfred Doten graphically described the accident: "He cooly cut his own foot loose, and tore the mangled mass from between the teeth of the cylinder and concave, with his own hands," the New England native wrote that night. "We took him & seated him, while under his directions we tied a handkerchief tightly just above his knee—put him in a clipper box, on some straw, & drove to Shaw's house while a man put my saddle on the fastest horse that was at the power, & rode for Dr. Spencer of San Jose."[1]

FIGURE 16. The fourth in a sequence of five progressively closer images of wheat threshing on the Green-fields Ranch, Kern County, this unposed close-up by Carleton E. Watkins, ca. 1888, conveys some of the danger, noise, and dust of mechanized threshing operations. Courtesy of Tenneco West.

Briggs lost little blood, despite having his foot and leg shredded up to the knee. "He was the coolest man there—poor fellow he laid on the bed at Shaw's in great pain, but bore it with the utmost fortitude, and would not faint," added Doten. "We took Briggs into the kitchen & placed him on a wide bench, covered with mattress & blanket & Dr. went to work—gave him chloroform—amputated the leg about 6 inches below center of the knee—took him just half an hour."[2]

Word of the accident spread quickly to outlying farms. And although no report appeared in any newspaper, the calamity became general knowledge. Farmers expressed sympathy and bitter regret. While Briggs apparently was a tough fellow, the maiming would probably prevent him from ever working again and many feared that he might become something of a public ward, unable to support his wife and children. Men who worked on nearby wheat farms gathered the following Saturday night to help their injured comrade and take up a collection. To a man, they agreed that the accident was one of the most ghastly they had ever witnessed, but none expressed surprise that it had happened. Anyone with even the slightest knowledge of the rigors of grain harvesting well knew the dangers involved. Men accustomed to rough labor in the gold mines and elsewhere accepted the risks with a mixture of resignation, determination, and calculation. They went into the wheat fields not out of any love for threshing but because California's wheat industry was expanding rapidly in the 1860s and 1870s, and work was plentiful.[3]

Most accounts of the farmworker saga ignore the vast force of men who moved from the mines to the fields when the marginal placer diggings and quartz mines they had worked suddenly played out. They describe grain harvesters and threshers as colorful characters who appeared on the scene fifty years later as railroad-riding hoboes and militant "footloose rebels." In truth, the omission has often been a deliberate one. Reading history backwards from the present, some authorities call attention to the large number of immigrant groups—Chinese, Japanese, Mexicans, Indian Sikhs, and Filipinos—who have worked in the fields. These voices infer that foreign-born minorities and colonized natives have always dominated farmwork, and that white field hands were an exception to the rule, playing only a nominal role at best. This very limited interpretation of reality ignores the vast force of men who initially dominated labor in California's emerging wheat and barley industries.[4]

ॐ

Although American-born men and European immigrants had long worked on farms around the state, they did not do so on a massive scale until the late 1850s. And while wheat and barley harvesting had always been labor intensive, the number of laborers needed had remained small because the wheat industry was restricted by drought, smut, insect infestations, disputed land titles, and inefficient machinery. But the potential for a bountiful wheat industry had always existed. The first wheat crops grown around Sacramento and in certain alluvial bottomlands in the 1850s yielded a fantastic thirty to thirty-five bushels per acre; in Alameda County, growers harvested forty bushels per acre; in Santa Cruz County, they reaped fifty bushels per acre, compared with ten to fifteen bushels per acre in the Midwest. Average yield per acre from 1852 to 1859 was twenty bushels. With easily worked soil, access to vast amounts of land, and fantastic production, commented a writer for *Country Gentleman*, "A man with a good 'ranch' in the valley, can make an independent fortune in a few years, not infrequently in one."[5]

Held back by extraordinarily heavy infestations of grasshoppers that destroyed thousands of acres of wheat in 1855, and by a shortage of separators capable of cleaning wheat befouled by mustard and weed seeds, the industry did not begin producing a grain surplus until 1856, when almost one million dollars' worth of wheat was exported and it became obvious that there were huge profits to be made. Capitalizing on the opportunity, so many farmers in a 125-mile crescent north, south, and east of San Francisco Bay planted a crop of wheat, no matter how small, that in some places like the Santa Clara Valley wheat farms in springtime would later be recalled somewhat breathlessly in the florid prose of one local historian as "like beautiful green islands in a golden sea." As California began exporting wheat, some farmers foresaw the day when the state might challenge the

Midwest as the "breadbasket of the world," and wheat would replace gold as California's main source of income. Wheat exports expanded even more rapidly during the American Civil War. When the Confederate Navy constricted California's ability to trade wheat with the eastern United States, growers made up the difference by expanding shipments to England. Hard, dry, heavy California wheat kept well in shipment and soon became a medium of exchange, as San Francisco grain merchants began using empty grain ships to transport foreign goods back to California. On this basis, a triangular trade developed: British manufactured goods to Australia; Australian coal to San Francisco; and California wheat to England. To service the trade, new wharves, docks, and warehouses were constructed. Railroad lines opened up the state's interior beyond those areas in the Central Valley previously reachable only by steamboat. In Alameda, Contra Costa, Santa Clara, Napa, San Joaquin, Solano, and Yolo counties, which together produced 75 percent of the state's wheat crop, anyone with a little land who was able to get his hands on a plow, seed, a few horses, and a wagon might do well. With more than two hundred flour mills scattered throughout the state, the saying was that men would no longer harvest gold; now they would reap the golden harvest.[6]

Blessed with wet years between 1866 and 1867, California wheat farmers grew bumper crops—twenty-one million bushels in 1868, a third of which was exported—making the state the eighth largest wheat producer in the nation. "The rivers are dotted with sails, and the winding channels among the tules are clouded with the smoke of numberless steamers threading their way through the sea of verdule [sic], loaded with the rich produce of the land," wrote grain magnate Horace Davis. "From every part of the world fleets come to bear away the treasure, and we have become one of the world's great feeders." To desperate former gold miners, the transformation of the countryside was a haven from trouble and an alternative to disaster. When California's boom economy went bust, miners split into two groups—those who determined to continue the search for gold, and those who sought other employment. Those continuing as miners followed rumors of gold strikes and rushed off to distant parts of California, Oregon, Washington, British Columbia, Alaska, South America, even Australia. Those abandoning the mines congregated in San Francisco, Marysville, and Sacramento to search for work. Within weeks their savings ran out, and thousands of men were forced to move out into the fields where, as the numbers of Indians declined, they became the dominant group on the booming grain farms.[7]

Although wheat harvesters tended to be overwhelmingly white and of European background, contemporaries described them as a remarkably diverse group coming from every class. There were restless men who habitually moved from job to job, clerks hoping to earn a stake and buy some land, businessmen who had defaulted in some venture and needed to pay off their debts, and artisans, mechanics, and tradesmen from nearby towns who were looking to supplement their income with temporary work. But there were also large contingents of Greek, Portuguese, and Italian sailors; Chilean peasants; and Irish and German dockworkers and roustabouts.[8]

Out of necessity, grain harvesters became migrant workers, coming and going with the seasons and drifting between farms and agricultural districts with the ripening tide of grain. These men walked, hitched rides, and occasionally traveled longer distances by stagecoach, railroad, or paddle-wheel steamer, looking for a few days' work. In a short time, tramping harvesters became a familiar sight on country roads. Begging meals, soliciting directions, resting beneath trees and bridges, cutting across fields, they were forever on the move. Unshaven and wearing "tattered pants and ragged shirts," the worst off among them owned nothing more than the clothes on their backs. Most carried a "bindle" or bundle consisting of a heavy blanket tightly rolled in canvas, tied at both ends, and slung over one shoulder by a length of rope. Packing all of the necessities of life inside these improvised suitcases—a razor, soap, a change of clothes, mirror, some writing paper, pencils, an address book, a Bible—they used bindles as portable beds, unrolling them each night in bunkhouses and barns, and sometimes under the open sky. Never far from their bindles, they guarded and fought over them, becoming so closely identified with their curious packages that they became known as "bindlemen" and "bindlestiffs."[9]

Bindlemen had to be jacks-of-all-trades, particularly on farms where wheat was just one of several crops. They also had to be constantly on guard, as even everyday tasks brought many dangers. Because many wheat farms were isolated and often located on Indian land, unsuspecting field hands were often attacked. This is what happened when Indians swarmed over Robert Workman's farm in Tehama County in August 1865. After slitting one woman's throat from ear to ear and beating Workman's wife, they then went after Workman's field hands. Most fled. But John "Scotch John" Banks was caught alone and shot dead in the middle of a field. His body was not found until several days later when a rescue party arrived and spotted buzzards circling his remains.[10]

Some of the riskiest work involved common jobs. Alfred Doten recalled one experience moving a sixteen-by eighteen-foot clapboard shanty from one side of the farm to another. "We were all the forenoon getting it raised up on two long, stout poles, one at each end, and each of them resting on two pair of wheels," Doten recalled.

> After dinner Emerson came, bringing Doll and Mary Blane [two horses]. Hitched on the horses and started her. Miller drove Becky and Liz [two other horses]. I drove Doll and Mary. We only got about 100 yards when one of the poles got displaced, and let one corner of the house down, racking it very badly . . . got it up after awhile and braced it, but the ground was so rough, from squirrel holes, that the house racked about badly. It came over with a big crash. I sprang off just in time to escape a smashing, for it fell directly upon the place where I stood, just missing the sterns of the horses. The descending roof nearly caught me, for I felt it brush down my back as I struck the ground running. I had a very narrow escape indeed.[11]

On most farms, work followed a predictable cycle. Specialization and differentiation of tasks quickly developed. During the off-season, men shucked corn from the previous year, ran wheat seed through fanning mills to separate out chaff and mustard seeds, prepared the seed for planting by soaking it in a solution of copper sulfate (commonly called bluestone) to kill fungus and rust, then dipped it in freshly slaked lime before sacking. Other general tasks rounded out the routine. "Commenced working today . . . building some big bins for granary . . . pretty tired at night," noted Doten in his journal. "Still hard at work . . . butchered a hog . . . busy cutting corn . . . repairing fence. . . . Took some poisoned meat along, and threw it for old Indigo's dogs, as they have been killing three of our sheep lately . . . worked trimming in the peach trees."[12]

Winter also meant plowing and sowing. During the 1850s and into the early 1860s, plowmen performed this task as they always had, by walking behind single-share American plows, also known as "foot burners." Seldom cutting more than five or six inches deep, plowmen working dawn to dusk with strong, well-trained horses might turn under three acres. Watching men plowing fields in the Napa Valley in 1859, Richard Henry Dana wrote that each followed a furrow "by little red sticks, to keep his range by, until nearly out of sight, and where, the wits tell us, he returns the next day and on the back furrow." Working almost as hard, seeders followed the plowmen, broadcasting grain by hand or by using little sowing devices, fifty to 120 pounds per acre. Eventually, the difficulty of carrying the large bags of grain over the rough, plowed ground, led to shoveling the grain from wagons. Then, sitting on boxes facing to the rear of the wagon with tubs full of grain between their knees, two or three men dipped scoopers into the tubs and spread the grain in ten-foot-wide bands. This method boosted the rate to ten acres per day. Because there were few harrows available, men sometimes hitched tree limbs and branches to teams of horses and pulled the devices over the plowed fields to cover the seed.[13]

When plowing, harrowing, and seeding finished, men who were not permanently employed endured a long period of idleness. "They may pitch upon jobs now and then and manage to subsist until haying and harvest time, and consider themselves fortunate if they can barely pay expenses," explained the *Napa Reporter*. The pace of work quickened considerably with the approach of summer when the warming weather brought the harvest to fruition. Early-ripening fields around Livermore and in the San Joaquin Valley were ready in June and July, while late-ripening fields north and south of San Francisco Bay were usually not ready until September and sometimes as late as October. By beginning in the inland areas and shifting with the ripening grain, bindlemen could work continually over a four-month period. As Doten noted: "The stragglers who are ever-ranging the country in search of a 'job,' easily find work now, at the standing harvest wages,—$2.00 per day and board. So they take up their old line of march again from ranch to ranch. . . . No one has any excuse for being idle."[14]

During the early 1850s, men swinging cradles and laying out straight, even lines of grain earned twice that of other field laborers. A few years later mechanical harvesters replaced cradlers. Cutting a little over ten acres per day—about what eight cradlemen could do—these cumbersome-looking machines were essentially wheeled platforms, pushed or pulled by a team of horses, with cutting devices geared to a drive wheel. Two models, the McCormick reaper and Hussey mower, dominated the market. Both worked so well that, within months after becoming available, *California Farmer* urged its readers to "buy the machine if you can; and if you have not the means, get them as soon as possible." In 1859, farmers bought four hundred of the "best" types of reapers, along with one hundred of the more "common" designs. The following year they purchased 690 reapers and mowers from San Francisco firms and 330 from manufacturers in Stockton, Marysville, Petaluma, and Sacramento. In 1862, when an exodus of men to new gold strikes and service in the Civil War caused a temporary farm labor shortage, farmers bought an additional five hundred mowers and 220 reapers. Farmers unable to purchase the new machines employed reaper operators who traveled between farms cutting grain on a contract basis for $1.12 ½ cents per acre, or banded together and purchased used machines, first employing them to harvest their crops, then renting them out to neighbors.[15]

Grain harvesters affected by the new technology encountered both more and less than they expected. They did not lose their jobs so much as acquire new ones. Riding through the fields rather than walking, harvesters became tenders of machines instead of laborers wielding cumbersome cradles. Cutting a field required considerable skill, and these men were expected to master it. Starting on the outer edge, harvesters worked clockwise, in concentric circles, with the horses walking through the standing grain and the harvester platform jutting into the edge of the field so that raked grain and bundles were always deposited in swaths of cut grain. Keeping their machines moving steadily, drivers often worked well into the night under the illumination of a lantern suspended from the whiffletree on the horse nearest the standing grain. Constantly adjusting the sickle to take a "full cut," they made certain that they did not move so far to one side that they skipped sections of wheat. Cutting wheat in heavy soil with a six-foot-wide reaper pushed by three horses, a driver could usually get through the shift without resting his horses, but if he was operating a larger machine that required more horses on hilly, soft, or uneven ground, he could easily overwork the animals and had to stop and rest them periodically. Machinery was always breaking down—bolts sheared off, mower bars bent, tie rods snapped, rivets popped, and pulleys ripped apart—requiring drivers to be proficient at making field repairs.[16]

Working alongside machine operators were men who raked grain off the harvester. When the grain was particularly heavy and stout and piled up quickly, four men shared this task, with none able to last more than a few hours. Standing on the harvester as it bounced over rough ground, they received a terrible jolting and retired at night with headaches and sore backs and ankles. Within a few years, however, self-rake harvesters allowed drivers to press a foot lever to activate a mechanical sweep arm that swept cut grain from the platform and deposited it in the stubble.[17]

At least nine or ten men, sometimes more, accompanied self-rake harvesters into the fields. Five or six "binders" followed the harvester with a spool of twine and a knife, gathered up the piles of cut grain, tied them into bundles, and dropped the bundles at regular spaces away from the path of the harvester. Another group of three or four men known as "shockers" picked up the bundles, carried them to designated spots along the way, and stacked them in piles or "shocks" of eight or ten bundles each (on some farms, shocks contained twenty-five to thirty bundles). From the shocks, bundles were loaded onto wagons, carried to the threshing site, and stacked. Good stackers were hard to find. They usually built four to six round stacks or two large oval stacks spaced so that the thresher could be pulled between them. Stacks might be fifteen feet high, twenty feet in diameter, and contain one hundred to 150 bushels of grain.[18]

So exhausting was binding and stacking that crews fluctuated radically in size, growing and shrinking by half as much within a few days. Ranch records from Doten's Mountain View farm on June 1, 1857, recorded the fluctuations: "Had only four binders . . . did the best we could—I was out all day looking up hands." The next day Doten wrote: "Jim Neal came to work making five binders—need five more . . . Went up to MV [Mountain View] . . . Met Henry Watson and sent him down to work at binding." On June 3 he wrote: "A Mexican came this morning, also Sleeper's man so now I have 8 binders." On June 4: "Another Mexican came to bind this morning—This makes out nine—At noon a man Williams came and I hired him . . . This makes 10 binders—a full complement." Finally, on June 5, Doten noted with relief: "The ten binders kept the reaper going straight along, so that we finished cutting the barley tonight." And so it went throughout the harvest.[19]

❧

Only crews on the largest and most successful farms threshed while harvesting because for most small farmers, the two processes were just too labor intensive to overlap. When a farmer did actually have the capability to combine the tasks, it was usually because he was using a horse-powered machine called a "groundhog thresher," so-called because it had to be staked to the ground and looked like it was burrowing in like a groundhog. Capable of threshing 150 bushels per day, groundhog threshers were slow, not very mobile, and did not clean the grain very well, which meant a fanning mill was needed to remove chaff from the seed. Within a few years, however, crews were using new, improved models. Combining a fanning mill with a thresher, these machines were first shipped around Cape Horn until agricultural machinery manufacturing operations in Stockton and Benicia began building models locally. Able to thresh about seven hundred to eight hundred bushels per day, the equivalent of what seventy men with flails could do, these machines were very expensive, with a standard Pitts or Russell separator (as threshers were called) costing five hundred dollars or more.[20]

Because threshing machinery was so expensive—especially when added to the associated costs of wagons, power drives, mules, horses, and tools—very few individual farmers could afford the equipment. Instead, custom-threshing crews handled most of the work. Moving from farm to farm, these teams stayed only a few days in any one field, threshing at five cents per hundred pounds of oats, six or seven cents per hundred pounds of wheat, and eight cents per hundred pounds of barley. Because threshing outfits arrived from one to three weeks after the harvest, men who wanted to keep working after they finished reaping, binding, and stacking had three choices: follow the reapers as they moved through the grain districts; find temporary farm jobs; or take a short vacation. Most men who intended to stay in the area did the latter, renting a room in a boardinghouse and passing their time drinking, gambling, playing, and relaxing. When the threshing outfits appeared, farmers would send out word and the men would tramp back into the fields.[21]

Once on the job, threshermen worked in crews of twenty men with just as many horses, five or six wagons, a power sweep or treadmill, and the thresher itself. There was an engineer and an oiler, each with an assistant, a pitcher, and various men to drive wagons, load and unload grain, and rake straw clear of the thresher. When a crew deployed at first light, its silhouetted movements resembled a platoon of soldiers moving into battle. "On all sides, far and near, is heard the busy rattle and hum of the various patterned [*sic*] machines . . . and everybody is extremely busy," wrote Doten.[22]

Most activity centered on the threshing site or "set," usually a conveniently located, dry place on high ground, if possible. Here, the engineer and four or five men, some of them permanent employees of the threshing outfit, maneuvered the machinery into position and staked it down. At the same time, eight to ten men employed by the farmer went through the fields loading bundles from small shocks onto wagons fitted with special racks. After filling a wagon, they moved to the threshing site. If they were going to thresh directly from the wagon they would park near the thresher, taking care to maintain the correct separation. Too near the thresher and the wagon could get caught up in all the machinery, belts, and pulleys; too distant and the men would have to work too hard pitching bundles. But on many farms, crews threshed from stacks, and when this method was used the wagons would come under the command of a man known appropriately as a "stacker."[23]

As the wagons arrived, the horse drivers swung into action. Before the advent of steam engines, there were two common ways of converting the linear motion of horses into the circular motion required to drive a thresher. Smaller threshing outfits used a "bridge," which consisted of an endless inclined treadmill of planks that revolved as the animals stepped forward and upward. Difficult to work with, treadmills tended to run away if the load was lessened or if a chain broke, forcing the poor horses to either gallop or fall. While governors and flywheels corrected this problem in later models, the great number of moving parts dissipated so much of the power that they could only thresh three hundred bushels per day. For this reason, they were seldom employed on large threshing jobs.[24]

Sweeps were more widely employed. Consisting of horizontal folding beams radiating from a vertical axle, sweeps were powered by teams of up to fourteen horses moving in a circle. As the axle turned, it transferred power through a series of gears to a "tumbling rod"—appropriately named because of its wobbling motion—connected with another gearbox on the thresher. Controlled by a driver who stood on a platform at the center of the unit, horses often walked too fast or too slow, a difficulty that produced irregular thresher speeds and commonly broke gearboxes. Because this problem was largely caused by horses stepping over the tumbling rod, larger units elevated the tumbling rod to a height of ten feet so that horses walked under it unimpeded.[25]

From his perch above the power sweep, a driver would get his team started with a crack of the whip or a shout, which set the thresher in motion. As the ponderous thresher cylinder began revolving, the machine at first gave out a sound bindlemen always described as a "deep growl," like that of a bulldog, only magnified a hundred times. As the cylinder gathered speed, the sound rose to a baritone, then a tenor, audible miles away. At this moment, threshing began. From six to eight men—with their mouths and nostrils covered by bandannas to protect their lungs from the great clouds of yellow wheat dust—pitched from each wagon onto the feeder table where a man known as the band cutter severed the binding and passed the grain bundles to feeders, who shoved them into the thresher cylinder. A series of polished steel teeth on a drum inside the cylinder whirled and meshed with stationary teeth at the front of the machine, breaking the grain free from the straw and dropping it onto a vibrating table and fan mechanism that removed the chaff and straw and delivered the clean grain out the other end of the machine. But too many bundles clogged the cylinder, and sloppy pitching lost much grain through the blower, so men were careful that each bundle went in straight and headfirst, overlapping the previous one but not piling upon it. Most important, pitchers made certain to hang onto their pitch-forks, which were terror on the concave and could cause the entire thresher to seize up if accidentally thrown into the works.[26]

As the first bundles hit the cylinder, the tenor of the thresher dropped to a lower note, the horses felt the sweep arms holding them back, the teamster's shouts rose to a higher pitch, and if all went well, the crew was off on a half-day's run, pausing only for a lunch break. "We all had to pitch in like the devil today," recalled Doten at the beginning of the 1857 threshing campaign. "The thresher kept us on the drive all the time . . . Kept feeding the stack . . . kept four teams hauling in to the stack . . . broke numerous forks amongst us today, and I had lots of repairing to do at noon."[27]

Mechanization meant that physical effort no longer entirely determined output. Production rates accelerated, and the number of field hands necessary to produce one bushel of wheat dropped. But mechanized threshing did not dramatically de-crease overall labor requirements. In fact, by increasing the speed of threshing, mechanization actually expanded the land that could be cultivated and swelled the demand for plowmen, binders, reaper drivers, shockers, general farmhands, and especially for anyone with experience operating the new machinery. "The grain crops, such as they are, afford at the present time plenty of work and good wages; so everything [sic] in the farming sections are busy," observed Doten in a letter to his hometown newspaper in Massachusetts. "The ambitious 'down easter,' the chivalric Southerner, the tall men from 'Pike,' and even the Mexicans and Indi-ans find plenty of employment at good wages."[28]

On Pierson B. Reading's Rancho Buena Ventura in the northern Sacramento Valley in 1864, for example, twenty-two men, one threshing machine, a power drive, two reapers, two wagons, and twenty-two horses finished a job in one week that had previously taken up to three months and required the services of hun-dreds of Indians. "About ten or fifteen minutes after the grain is standing in the field," remarked Mrs. Fannie Reading in a letter to her mother back east, "it is cut, threshed and sacked, ready for market."[29]

In August 1877, John Bidwell conducted the most famous demonstration ever of mechanized wheat harvesting and threshing. Sending harvesters into the fields shortly before sunrise, Bidwell directed them to run their first load of wheat through the thresher ten minutes later. Teamsters then placed the first two bags of grain on a buggy and galloped two and a half miles to Bidwell's flour mill, which promptly transformed the grain into flour. An hour and a half later, Bidwell received a portion of the flour, handed it to his cook, and at 6:45 A.M.—two hours after the reapers had commenced cutting his wheat—he and a half-dozen guests, "sat down to our nice breakfast to eat nice biscuits from the flour."[30]

Wheat harvesters often worked until well after dark, especially if they were close to finishing. At this pace, even the most experienced among them complained of their share of aches and pains. Ever attentive, Doten kept a close record of the price he paid during the hottest days of three grueling threshing seasons that "made the sweat roll." Following a long shift feeding the thresher, he reported on September 3, 1856: "Got very badly galled—two places the size of my hand, on each side, but owing to paralysis I could not feel it." On July 18, 1858, he wrote: "Last night I was troubled with inflammation of the kidneys and bladder . . . To-day I grew no better fast—PM was so sick I could hardly hold up my head . . . I did not work today because I could not." After a hard season of harvesting in July 1860, Doten spared no details in describing how the rubbing of his leather chaps had caused an abscess to develop in his crotch. "Opened it this morning," he wrote, "and fully two tablespoons full of matter was discharged from it."[31]

Perilous even to experienced field hands, threshing was doubly so to untutored laborers. In addition to the unavoidable bumps and bruises, there were also plenty of opportunities to get seriously hurt. Momentarily blinded by sun and sweat, amid the "terrible dust and din" that was part of every threshing operation, men stumbled into pulleys, fell into bull-gears, slipped under wagon wheels, and bumped into tumbling rods, escaping, if they were lucky, with a bruise; more often, men suffered a cut hand or finger, or lost a chunk of flesh from their thigh. Some men just minding their business were cut in half when hit by disintegrating drive belts. But it was not just gears and pulleys that maimed and killed. Men also faced the hazards of working with large animals. Power sweeps were especially troublesome, as horses not thoroughly broken to the work would sometimes rear and buck, wrecking equipment and injuring men. Teams pulling wagons could also inflict damage—men would be kicked to death by a mule or have their legs broken or knocked out from under them while trying to adjust the harness on a horse. When accidents occurred far out in the countryside, medical help was seldom available and men often bled to death for lack of adequate medical treatment. "There is no romance in this," wrote the journalist Samuel Bowles in *Our New West*.[32]

Another ever present if unspoken danger was the heat and pace of work. Men fainted—and sometimes died—while binding sheaves. "SUDDEN DEATH" was the headline in the *Napa Pacific Echo* for one such accident.

A young man, apparently a German, of about twenty-five years of age, went to the ranch of W. Smith, near Napa, on Wednesday, and commenced work binding grain in the harvest field. He had bound but a few sheaves when he fell down, and before any assistance could be given, expired. A *post mortem* examination was made and he appeared to have died from a rupture of the heart. His name is as yet unknown. He was dressed in grey shirt and satinette pantaloons.[33]

But by far the most dangerous place was the thresher itself. Noisy and full of moving parts, a thresher provided plenty of opportunities for accidents. Men caught their clothing in a gear and had their arms chewed to pieces or amputated. If their hair snagged on a drive belt or crankshaft, they counted themselves lucky to only lose a portion of their scalp. The most precarious location was the front end of the thresher, where fatigued men might faint, slip, or stumble, and try to brace themselves or for some reason place their hands a little too far inside the cylinder opening. The thresher teeth would pull them in, and their hand would either be shredded to bits or yanked off, sometimes to the arm socket, only to be spit out the other side of the machine as a bloody, grain-impregnated pulp. When a worker caught a foot in the thresher mechanism, a doctor would often be summoned from the nearest town to amputate the leg with no anesthetic other than whiskey. Usually, an additional amputation farther up the leg would have to be performed later. Such men counted themselves lucky. Far more common was the outcome of an accident that occurred on August 10, 1876, in Colusa County. "Dominic Deveney, a 'table man' on a threshing-machine being operated near Arbuckle, was struck by a derrick fork and thrown into the separator feet foremost," reported Colusa County historian Justus Rogers. "Both legs were torn off and Deveney died the following day."[34]

℘

Because they often left behind diaries and wrote letters home, bindlemen of this era enjoy the distinction of being the first farmworkers about which some of the intimate details of life are known. For the most part, those details are hardly pleasant. Working under the blazing sun all day in sweat-soaked clothes, bindlemen were seldom comfortable. "Oh, we were always scratching," recalled one wheat thresher. "We ate burned beef. We drank filthy water. Our bunkhouses were crowded. Sometimes we lived with the chickens and the cows. We were always dirty. We never had any money. We stank to hell." Recalled another thresherman: "Fleas were plenty, and more easily acquired than money, and indeed cling to a person longer, and far more pertinaciously than dollars. . . . Everybody has a scratch."[35]

Comfortable housing, it seems, was hard to come by. Men might bed down with animals in barns, and even the most unfortunate grain harvesters considered themselves blessed to have a leaky roof over their heads. The most fortunate might be stacked as many as a dozen to a back room in the farmer's home. They used outhouses of the most rudimentary kind (if they were available), bathed in cisterns that were usually little more than drainage basins, and continually complained of not being able to sleep because of scorpions, snakes, lice, and vermin. An all too common diary entry read: "The fleas are very troublesome here, and . . . I had rather a poor night's sleep last night."[36]

But there was seldom a shortage of food. Threshing crews ate large meals, but quality did not always match the quantity. Sanitation all too often consisted of a cook wiping off plates with his handkerchief while saying, "Supper ready again, gentlemen." Poisonings were not uncommon. Entire crews would sometimes bolt from tables writhing and vomiting after taking just a few bites. Careless food preparation was almost always the culprit. After one such episode the cook investigated and found himself at fault. "It was the cakes that did it," he later wrote. "In my hurry to get breakfast I took a small pan to mix the batter in what I used last evening to weigh out bluestone in, and a little of it was left sticking around the bottom of the pan—careless trick—It also purged Cook & Crews considerable during the day—They vomited several times this AM."[37]

Men often suffered from "barracks fever," as they called it. Lacking company other than their employer and compatriots, they idled away their off-hours as best they could. Those owning rifles and shotguns, or who had access to them, would hunt whatever animals were in season. Those owning musical instruments found themselves much in demand, as nearby farmers would often hire them for a night. Following a particularly arduous period of work, men on Saturday nights put on black faces with burnt cork and "had lots of fun with the banjo and fiddle," and occasionally, a flute. They also wrote letters home, or composed letters for illiterate fellow workers, played cards, smoked tobacco, and told stories. And they fought. One such melee, on the Triffle Ranch in Colusa County on June 23, 1869, was described in the *Colusa Sun*. "[William] Miller had a long knife in his hand, which he endeavored to use on James Dobbins and others, when Dobbins shot him, inflicting a mortal wound," reported *Sun* editor Justus Rogers. "Dobbins was arrested, and afterwards acquitted on the ground of justifiable homicide."[38]

To escape camp life, men found relief in large, daylong, outdoor religious assemblies called "camp meetings." Forming an important part of the seasonal diversions enjoyed by grain harvesters, these were odd affairs. Often held under a stand of evergreens on one of the larger ranches, these congregations would often have a restaurant fixed up for the occasion selling meals for fifty cents, as well as a fruit stand, and a dance platform. Around evening, the preachers would begin preaching, but often few paid much attention. As the men always far outnumbered the women and were starved for company, they wore out the women by asking them to dance everything from waltzes and jigs to polkas and cotillions, never allowing them a chance to rest. Singing and carrying on until after sunrise, the men would sleep for an hour or so, then sit down to a large communal breakfast before piling into wagons for the ride back to their farms, sometimes breaking out a fife and drum, playing and singing "Yankee Doodle" and other songs.[39]

A far more common and enjoyable diversion consisted of simply going to town. On Saturday nights after supper or at the end of threshing, men piled into wagons and rode as far as ten miles to visit the nearest population center, where they enjoyed various forms of recreation. They could obtain items not available on the farms, particularly tobacco, a good meal, a haircut from a barber, and better cuts of clothes. Farmers often assisted them in their shopping, providing a cash advance against their wages, or buying needed goods outright and charging them against their final wage settlement. But the real purpose underlying most such visits, though seldom admitted, was far less practical.

On many grain farms men could not get liquor, as farmers regarded this as disruptive. Nor could they gamble or even smoke, particularly since the latter too often caused fires in hay piles and grain stacks. In town, men were after whiskey, women, and fun, often in that order. Whoring, partying, fighting, singing, playing billiards, carousing as wildly as drunken sailors, and shooting their guns and the occasional Indian, they would, according to Doten, "for a short period, while their money lasts, revel in the glories of strychnine whiskey, 'choice old French Cognac,' made in San Francisco, and other delectable compounds of alcoholic drugs and hellfire." Going to great lengths to accommodate their needs, all businessmen in San Juan Bautista, according to Doten, "kept a barrel of liquor on tap in the rear of the premises for the accommodation of their patrons. The liquor was sold by the gallon and quart, but alongside the barrel there was always a glass. Their patrons, whether invited or not to do so, could go to the rear of the premises and get a drink."[40]

Drunk and exhausted men in town let old grudges surface, and in fits of rage, went at one another with ferocity. The ever attentive Doten noted the violence in his diary. "Plenty of grog drunk today, in town, & some fellows got riotous a little, of course," read one entry. Another described how, "Dutch Charley on a bender—crazy drunk and very noisy & vicious—got into a muss with Gus Rathbone—Gus threw a tumbler at his head—knocked him down and beat him badly about head & face—sobered & quieted him." Another journal entry read: "Emerson had a dispute with Frank Gallimore this forenoon—hard words were passed—and Emerson gave Gallimore the lie—Gallimore challenged Emerson to fight him, with any weapon from a 4 inch revolver, up to a double-barreled shot-gun." Doten also described how on July 8, 1857, a foreman named Elliot went searching around San Jose for a farmhand named Williams. After looking through the saloons and brothels, Elliot found Williams in the American Theater. Williams "pretended to be brushing his shoes when suddenly he caught a razor lying under the end of the counter, and made a pass with it . . . aiming to cut . . . the throat" of Elliot, who "knocked him [Williams] sprawling, and sent the razor flying across the room." The foreman then "went to stamping his head . . . gave him one or two several kicks afterwards—others now had hold of him, and Williams' life was saved—they washed the blood from his face—he was handcuffed and put in the buggy and Elliot drove off with him . . . he looked badly—his face scarred up and his head bound in a handkerchief." So common were such incidents that barkeeps in one San Juan Bautista saloon, a typical haunt for farmhands, took to protecting themselves with a nasty instrument known as the "float"—a sort of rasp, used for knocking the points off tacks protruding through the soles of boots. When two men went at one another, a barkeeper picked up the float and whacked them on the head.[41]

🙙

After the harvest, bindlemen collected their pay and scattered, leaving only a few men at each farm to work full-time at plowing, planting, and other tasks. This was the toughest part of the year. With a stake earned during three or four months of reaping and threshing, men now had to survive the winter. In the larger towns and cities all up and down the state, refugees from the wheat harvest scouted up odd jobs, mainly as laborers, roustabouts, and dockworkers. But there was never enough work.[42]

Determined to pass their time as best they could, harvesters retired to cheap hotels and working-class boardinghouses. "In all the hotels and lodging houses," recalled Doten, "were long tiers of 'bunks' for the accommodation of travelers, and the bedding consisted of straw mattresses, and woolen blankets. Every night a new lot of travelers occupied these beds, and as in these days but little attention was paid to personal appearances or cleanliness, the blankets soon abounded in varieties of the vermin."[43]

So uncomfortable were these places that men did little other than to sleep in them. By day they could be found "lounging about town . . . doing little jobs to gain bare subsistence," or making "no efforts to do anything for themselves." Upsetting to people in the rural districts, such behavior so alarmed members of the California State Agricultural Society that speakers at their 1863 annual convention condemned what seemed to be the lazy and nasty habits of unemployed field hands. "Those who tramp about the country calling themselves farm laborers," explained one member, "are the most complete set of loafing idlers to be found in any country . . . they are birds of passage." When harvest time next rolled around, though, bindlemen headed back to the fields and all was forgotten.[44]

Supply and demand largely determined wages in the grain-growing districts. During the 1867 harvest, when a slight labor shortage developed, some bindlemen attempted to capitalize on the opportunity and refused to work for wages of less than eight dollars a day. Noting these developments, *California Farmer* dismissed the complaints as the work of malcontents and attributed the assertive behavior, as always, to defects of character.[45]

Bindlemen did not always accept their lot uncomplainingly. Overwhelmed by poverty, ill health, homesickness, and other problems, former gold miners turned farmworkers sometimes saw no future for themselves and committed suicide. Drowning, knives, strychnine, morphine, and various other poisons, including powdered glass, were employed. A typical report from the *Colusa Sun* read: "The body of Thomas Brown was found on a farm adjoining John Garvey's, twelve miles northwest of Colusa. The coroner's verdict was death by shooting with suicidal intent. Brown was a hard-working farmer's hand, but had become despondent." More commonly, bindlemen protested by walking off the job. Angry over some affront, disliking a superior, tired by the exertions of work, they collected their wages and hit the road—usually alone, but sometimes en masse. Occasionally they went further. Alfred Doten once encountered an entire threshing crew on the road just north of San Jose and, after interviewing them, left this account in his journal: "All the boys . . . went up to Ralston's to work," he wrote.

> Just as they had got their breakfasts . . . and were about commencing to
> work, they struck for two dollars and half per day . . . Ralston got mad and
> swore he wouldn't pay it . . . Sneider & McCubbin [the thresher owners]
> pulled up stakes and left with all hands . . . we met the thresher and the
> boys going up towards Doc Wrights . . . a grand consultation was held,
> and at length they were induced to turn about and go down to our ranch . . .
> PM they were all here idle.

The following day, farmer Ralston replaced the malcontents with four Chileans and a relative.[46]

In Contra Costa County in 1868, grain harvesters directed their frustrations against a new technology that threatened to undermine their way of life. For at least a generation, farmers had been tinkering with "combined harvesters," highly improved versions of the machines developed and tested at San Jose in 1854 by John Horner, George Leland, and Abner Moore. In July, when Hills Ferry farmer Richard Wilson concluded that his wheat was sufficiently dry to be threshed without being stacked, he ordered his men to pitch directly from wagons into the separator, thereby eliminating one entire step in the threshing process. Buoyed by this success, Wilson discovered that, for six hundred dollars, he could add a large drive wheel to his stationary thresher, hitch it to a team of mules, and push it through his fields. Referred to as a "ground-powered separator" or "traveling harvester," Wilson's contraption, while not a true combine, nonetheless dramatically altered the nature of threshing and harvesting. Crews no longer stacked cut grain; now they pitched it directly into the thresher from the mower moving alongside. This eliminated most hand operations, as traveling harvesters required only a driver and tender, two sack sewers and assistants, and three or four roustabouts who followed the machine and hefted grain bags onto wagons. These machines became standard equipment on several large wheat farms in the San Joaquin Valley in 1869. At about the same time, Napa Valley inventor B. F. Cook developed an even more sophisticated combine that eventually became the standard for later models. A reciprocating sickle cut the grain stalks, a toothed wheel pushed the grain onto a platform, a canvas apron delivered the cut grain into the threshing cylinder, and everything was driven by a ground wheel. Cook claimed his machine cost $1.50 a day to operate, which is hard to believe, as the cost of feed for horses would have exceeded that amount twice over. But these machines were dwarfed by those being built by Washington Corners wheelwright A. O. Rix for San Jose farmer John Horner.[47]

Called Monitors No. 1, No. 2, and No. 3, the machines were introduced amid great fanfare.

> NOTICE! There will be a Public Exhibition of the Traveling Harvester
> MONITOR NO. 2, Upon the farm of Richard Threlfall, in Livermore
> Valley, Murray Township, Alameda County, on Tuesday, August 28, 1868,
> Commencing at 1 o'clock P.M. On Thursday, the 3rd day of September,
> commencing at the same hour, Monitor No. 1 or 3 will be exhibited to
> the public upon the farm of WM. Y. HORNER, near the Mission San Jose,
> Alameda County.

But what really frightened field hands were the claims that the horse-drawn combines could cut expenses in half by reducing the needed labor force. According to those claims, "Three men and twelve horses have Cut, Threshed, Cleaned, and Sacked, in good, workmanlike manner, fifteen acres of grain per day—making five acres per man—a feat, we believe, never performed in America before!" Previously, one and three-quarters acres per man had been the upper limit of productivity, with one acre per man being nearer the average. So when Horner and

Leland issued their invitation, "Come and see if our claims are well founded," bindlemen flocked in to see the new combines. They did not like what they saw.[48]

All through the harvest season, bindlemen talked of the new leviathans. Then, apparently, some decided to engage in a deliberate, calculated act of industrial sabotage as a means of making some sort of protest statement. What drove them to take this action was the success of the machines. During June 1869, Horner contracted to harvest sixteen hundred acres of wheat in Contra Costa County. After that, he planned to move into the San Joaquin Valley and harvest several hundred additional acres. Once these plans became known, field hands, fearing for their jobs and their future, decided to take action. On the evening of July 14, just after the machine had finished harvesting a sixteen-acre field "in good work-manlike manner," unknown men sneaked into a barn on the Wilder ranch, near Livermore, and set the hay on fire, burning the barn and Monitor No. 2, which was parked inside. Horner wasted no time in seeking out those responsible. "$500 REWARD: Will be paid by the undersigned for the arrest and conviction of the person or persons who caused the burning of Monitor No. 2," he announced in an advertisement in *California Farmer*. He was immediately joined by the editor. "It is to be hoped that the Farmers in that vicinity will make every exertion to ferret out the wretches—one or more—for unless a suitable punishment is inflicted now at the beginning of such outrages, not only Harvesters, but Hay and Grain Ricks, and Barnes [*sic*] and Houses will go next," the editor wrote. But despite the offer of a hefty reward and continual calls for men with knowledge of the act to come forward, no one was ever arrested. Nor did anyone ever take credit for the sabotage in any note or public statement.[49]

Although those who torched Monitor No. 2 had tried, they could not stop the introduction of combines. Monitor Nos. 1 and 3 continued working and, within a year, dozens of similar machines were operating in the wheat growing districts—and bindlemen did not hesitate to work on them. Contemporaries found this all quite extraordinary, signaling the dramatic opening of a new chapter in the farmworker story, one that propelled field hands into the modern era of industrialized farm labor relations.[50]

In a letter to the editor of an agricultural newspaper, a large-scale wheat farmer, who as a young man had worked in the harvest, attempted to explain the situation. Asking himself rhetorically if he had any fond memories of life before the coming of machines, he responded with a forceful, "No! Men of sixty to seventy years of age . . . carry the marks on their hands, as I do, of the old reap-hooks that drew blood by the merest wayward stroke, and who remember the thump, thump, thump, of the flail on the old barn floor as strong men separated the grain from the straw during the cold winter days," he said. Now he was glad "to witness the harvest scenes of to-day, where machines do the heavy labor, and the operatives ride in the shade."[51]

CHAPTER NINE

Open-Air Factories

Industrialization of Labor on

the Bonanza Wheat Farms

A few months after the Monitor arson, members of the State Agricultural Society met at their annual convention in Sacramento. As wheat prices dropped to $1.60 per hundred pounds, large-scale growers hoping that development of the grain trade with England would open new markets concluded that a pool of laborers was necessary to keep wages down and thereby reap profits from ever expanding crops, and that it was time to curb the labor gluts and shortages that had plagued them throughout the previous ten years. Hoping for some new source of help, the most aggressive farmers, in characteristic fashion, joined industrialists, real estate promoters, and other groups affiliated with the California Immigrant Union, a booster organization intent on "vigorous efforts to attract white people to fill the empty wastes of this great State." During the fall of 1869, the California Immigrant Union flooded the Midwest with pamphlets extolling the stable society, salubrious climate, and vast opportunities available in California. "In San Francisco the roses bloom throughout the year in the open air; and the olive, fig, orange and a multitude of other semi-tropical fruit trees, thrive and bear fruit one hundred miles further north," asserted *All About California*, one of the most widely circulated of these pamphlets.[1]

Although many potential immigrants remained wary of the promises these groups made, some did come west, attracted by various discount railroad tickets and immigration trains. Few were the "persons skilled in a great variety of agricultural pursuits" that the Immigrant Union and State Agricultural Society had hoped for. Instead, most were what they labeled the "wrong kind of men"—laborers, paupers, and inexperienced farm hands. Lured to the state with tales of high wages and easy labor, they arrived with inflated expectations. When they failed to find the promised land, they avoided work on the wheat farms and simply piled up in the cities.[2]

At about the same time, field hands in the Napa Valley were also being wooed by similar programs. Early in the year, the California Labor and Employment

FIGURE 17. Threshing crew and Chinese cook, near Volta, San Joaquin Valley, ca. 1889. Courtesy of the Ralph Milliken Memorial Museum, Los Banos.

Office established an office in the city of Napa and began running advertisements in the *Napa County Reporter*. "Great inconvenience was suffered last year by the Farmers of this county in consequence of a scarcity of harvest hands," read one announcement financed by local grain farmers. "The coming harvest promises to double that of last year. Farmers may save much trouble and expense by sending in their orders for help for the Barley and Wheat harvests AT ONCE . . . Stating the date which they will require men. Signed B. Fabian, Secretary pro tem." Similar advertisements continued on a weekly basis, but apparently very few men read them or sought work through the agency. At the end of the year, growers cut off their support and the enterprise ceased operations. Such was the fate of many such efforts to expand the farm labor supply through advertising and recruiting.[3]

But just as wheat growers were becoming discouraged by the failure of these recruiting efforts, an event occurred that seemed to show the state's laborers would be entirely adequate after all. In 1869, between two thousand and three thousand white laborers were discharged from their jobs building the Central Pacific Railroad. No method for assisting them existed and, as a result, the unemployed railroad workers went looking for employment, taking anything they could get. With perhaps one in five men in California already out of work, and

more than fifty thousand mostly poor newcomers in the state, the flood of displaced railroad workers added to a huge labor pool that local industries could not
absorb. The following spring, these men flooded into the wheat districts, reversing the shortage of farm hands and delighting growers with their numbers.[4]

The influx of unemployed railroad workers was only the beginning of an even
larger tide of men moving out of the cities and into the countryside. Just how
desperate, determined, and innovative some men were could be seen in the letters
they wrote to the agricultural press. "Dispirited and sick, both in mind and body,
I resolved in my own mind to start into the country, and work at anything I could
do," began a San Francisco resident identified only by the initials, NIBS.

> If I went away, there was one less at home to eat up what provisions we had
> on hand, and my family would in this respect be gainers. Besides, once in the
> country without means, I would be obliged to have something to do or else
> subsist on charity, which is entirely unnecessary for an able-bodied person
> to do in this state. So with two dollars and a half in my pocket, I took the
> steamer for Napa, and having an observant eye constantly open for the
> chance, I secured a job from a gentleman who was a fellow passenger on the
> boat, to work on his farm at anything he wanted me to do; wages $1.50 per
> day and board . . . I had never worked at aught save my trade, and never
> for less wages than five dollars per day . . . I worked ten days on this ranch,
> assisting at building brush fence, moving grain from an old barn to a new
> one and in general work . . . There was a constant change . . . I felt eager
> for work . . . for the past four months, I have been on the tramp.[5]

As the weather warmed and men grew more desperate, thousands more arrived in the agricultural districts. So many men were unemployed and looking
for work that, while tramping through the agricultural districts in Napa, Sonoma,
and Mendocino counties, NIBS observed that "in each town or place which I
visited . . . are plenty of idle men . . . Hundreds of men start out . . . monthly,
into the country seeking employment; if unsuccessful, the first day or two, they
turn back in disgust, determined as they say, to get back to San Francisco before
they go broke." Penniless, angry, and regarding many of the state's vagrancy laws
and customs with hostility, these men resented the way farmers hired them,
worked them hard, and then turned them loose.[6]

Census figures suggest that these workers were much like the displaced gold
miners who preceded them a decade earlier; they shared a common language and
ethnicity. Four out of ten were native-born Americans, and another four of ten
were immigrants from Europe or Canada. Steven V. Powers, a journalist traveling
through the countryside at this time, described these men as "runaway sailors, re-
formed street thieves, bankrupt German scene painters, who carry sixty pounds of
blankets, old soldiers who drink their whiskey and fall into the ditch." To this
mix, a farmwife added a large dose of jailbirds who "not infrequently light upon
the farmer and remain stationary for awhile." But whoever they were, they all
packed a bindle and hit the road in search of work.[7]

Both fascinating and upsetting to people, the size of this tramping class grew
to such proportions during the winter of 1872 that contemporaries continually

commented on how many men they encountered "lounging about town . . . doing little jobs to gain bare subsistence." With their meager resources, they seemed a pitiful lot. "Seeing little hopes of bettering their condition, they have sunk to the condition of nomads, without home or social ties," observed the *Napa Reporter*. "Their life is not unlike that of the soldier, who for months lounges in barracks, and then for a season is called to put forth his utmost strength in a campaign. Almost all men under such circumstances become despondent, reckless, and dissipated, and it is lamentable to observe how large a proportion of our farm laborers have thus become demoralized and degraded."[8]

The biggest influx came in 1873, when California slid into six years of industrial depression. Thrown out of work by bank collapses, business failures, financial panics, and mining catastrophes, huge numbers of men drifted across the western landscape from the Pacific Coast to the Rocky Mountains, and from British Columbia down into Baja California and Sonora. During this time, hundreds of thousands of unemployed factory hands, most of them fortune seekers, also arrived. Together with laid-off railroad workers and other laborers, they formed what writers would later call a "reserve army of unemployed" and what contemporaries referred to as "a specimen of humanity . . . new to the Pacific Coast." So many men were drifting along the Sonoma Road in Sonoma County that one farmer claimed in a single day he "could find twenty men who would be glad to work for their board." This was to have profound impact on the farm labor force. Where wheat growers once had complained to the agricultural press that "much of the grain goes to waste for want of help to cut it," agricultural leaders now admitted "the supply of laborers is generally quite equal to the demand, and sometimes considerably exceeds it."[9]

Bindlemen knew that between June and August, they could rely on wheat farmers hiring almost anyone who showed up. But they also knew that the jobs did not last. If they were going to work continuously, they would have to keep constantly on the move between farms, searching out a sequence of steady employment beginning with the first harvesting jobs and then switching to late season threshing. Some endeavored to make the most of their lot by leaving one farmer for another at the first offer of better wages; this willingness to abandon wheat farmers "in the lurch" earned bindlemen a reputation for being "unsteady and hard to keep."[10]

Because of the oversupply of labor, many towns remained full of unemployed men, even at the height of the wheat harvest. During August 1879, Marysville was said to be so packed with "besotted tramps" that a pedestrian could not cross a street or walk down a sidewalk without bumping into one of them. According to the local newspaper, these men "lounged idly around and refused to work and cursed you with stammering accent." Some resorted to begging to survive, but were unable to sustain themselves and starved or died of exposure. Although it is impossible to say how many suffered this fate, bindlemen regularly turned up on ranches, under bridges, and in haystacks. Newspapers recorded their demise. "The body of an unknown man found floating in the river at the Riley Bend, below Jacinto. No clue to his identity attainable," read an account in the *Colusa Sun* on June 19, 1878. On August 2, the *Sun* again reported, "the body of an unknown man found in the river on the Sutter County side, near Grimes' Landing." Six years later: "The body of an unknown man in an advanced stage of decomposition was taken out of the river one mile below Princeton." Unusual for its detail, one notice in the *Gilroy Advocate* announced: "FOUND DEAD. On Monday afternoon, as Mr. Grant of San Ysidro was hunting for cattle, he espied the lifeless body of a man lying on the side of a low hill in the open field separating his residence from Mr. Murdock's." The paper went on to report that, at the coroner's inquest, it was ascertained that the man had been in Gilroy a few days before his death. "He was dressed in dark clothes, appeared to be about 40 years old, was medium sized, had a fair complexion," read the death notice. "His hands were like those of a workman. His pockets contained a brass watch, a 25 cent piece and a piece of bread. No letters about him . . . When found his clothes were wet from the rains of Sunday."[11]

Most bindlemen survived the winter, but so many wandered the back roads in such dire circumstances that some Californians began wondering about what the wheat industry was doing to its laborers. To be a bindleman on the wheat farms in California, explained the *San Francisco Morning Chronicle* on September 5, 1875, was to be caught in a system that

> in many respects . . . is even worse than old-time slavery. That, at least, enabled the planter to know what labor he could depend upon in any emergency, and made the laborer certain at all times of shelter, clothing, food, and fire. Our system does neither. The farmer must take such help as he can—hunting it up when most hurried and paying whatever is demanded . . . Under our system large numbers of men are wanted for a short time; more than any farm house can accommodate; even if the employer dare trust so many strangers within his walls or admit them into his family circle.[12]

Disgusted both by the growing hordes of bindlemen and incessant demands for cheap labor, agrarian reformers began condemning the wheat industry. To them, the reliance on seasonal labor seemed to run counter to the Jeffersonian ideal, a powerful credo that held that farming formed the cornerstone of the national character. The bedrock of a true republican society, these voices argued, had always been an agricultural economy maintained by the yeoman farmer working his own land by himself, perhaps with help from a loyal hired hand living and sleeping under the same roof. "In the Eastern States," rolled out a fairly standard claim by a member of the State Agricultural Society, "farm laborers are part of the family, they eat at the table with their employers—they are self-respecting citizens of the Republic." Wheat farming ran counter to this tradition. By its size and domination of the rural economy, wheat farming promoted monopoly, undermined community life, blurred the distinction between farm and factory, and attracted considerable commentary and incessant criticism.[13]

As early as 1863, the *Napa Reporter* had compared bonanza wheat farming in California with the cotton economy of the American South, declaring both incompatible with free labor. But by far the most famous and uncompromising attack on wheat farming came from the journalist Henry George. A short, bigheaded, combative young printer by trade, George had departed his middle-class

Philadelphia home in 1855 to sail as a foremast boy to Calcutta, where he was overcome by the contrast between rich and poor that inspired his later socioeconomic
theories. In 1857, his search for work took him to California, where he struggled
against poverty for a decade, working variously as a printer, miner, author, and
newspaperman. Agreeing with Jefferson that farming was the most noble form of
labor, George argued that labor in the wheat fields was treated undemocratically;
forced to make extortionate payments to land speculators, farmers came to regard
field hands not as human beings but as cogs in the means of production. Therefore, in 1871, George urged in a pamphlet titled *Our Land and Land Policy* that
land speculation and private rent be eliminated. Continuing his attack in *Progress
and Poverty* (1879), George asked why the wheat industry had produced such a
vast disparity in wealth and power. Why, instead of a humanized landscape dotted
with little farms, homes, and people, was California's Central Valley home to a
shifting tide of bindlemen? The barriers that bindlemen had to overcome, the in-
dignities they endured, and the lives they lived were simply unacceptable. "The
equal right of all men to use the land is as clear as their equal right to breathe the
air—it is a right proclaimed by the fact of their existence," he wrote.[14]

Coming at a time of labor unrest and depression, George's views were enormously popular. But for all their anger and discontent, critics like George had
little impact. Bindlemen grew in numbers throughout the 1870s, putting a
damper on discontent and machine breaking and replacing many of the last clusters of Indian farm laborers. Assured of the necessary numbers of field hands,
wheat farmers doubled production and then doubled it again, eventually pushing aside Sutter and other Gold Rush era farmers. Beginning in 1870, they enjoyed a long period of prosperity. By 1874, they were harvesting 21,840,000 bushels
of wheat, compared to just 5.9 million bushels twenty years earlier. Six years later,
they raised their output to twenty-nine million bushels and wheat became California's largest and most profitable crop. Close behind wheat farmers, barley
farmers also increased production dramatically. From 4.5 million bushels in 1860,
they raised output to 8.7 million bushels in 1870 and 17.5 million in 1890.[15]

All this grain was earmarked not just for California consumption, but for export. Shipped to London, China, and other ports around the world, the amount
of surplus grain was staggering. In an attempt to convey a sense of the size of the
wheat crop, one journalist came up with some interesting comparisons. To export the 1872 crop, he estimated that at least seven hundred ships, each holding
one thousand tons of wheat, would be needed. Put another way, the journalist
calculated that eighteen thousand railroad cars, each holding ten tons, would be
needed to move wheat out of the San Joaquin Valley to ports around San Francisco Bay. From still another perspective, the journalist noted that 360 trains of
fifty cars, each car holding ten tons, or a single train over three hundred miles
long, would be required. Exports peaked in 1881 at nearly twenty-two million
centrals (a central was one hundred pounds; a bushel, sixty pounds), with shipments of flour passing one million barrels for the first time in 1883.[16]

Like most successful industries, wheat stimulated a number of other businesses.
Because of its extensive mechanization, it supported dozens of large equipment
manufacturing operations. Wheat also generated a huge demand for sacks, which

led growers to import huge quantities of jute from Scotland and even experiment unsuccessfully with growing their own fiber crops for a time. But the industry's greatest impact may have been felt along the rivers that bordered the vast fields of wheat. Hundreds of shipping points and landings grew up at various strategic points and, beginning in October, thousands of tons of sacked grain accumulated in huge open-air piles and warehouses, waiting to be transported to mills. A massive West Coast flour milling industry sprang up to handle the crop, as the nearly one hundred, small, water-powered mills that processed the crop in 1860 gave way to a few large, steam-powered, commercial factories. Three mill owners dominated: Austin Sperry, whose XXX brand became a market staple around Stockton; Horace Davis, whose San Francisco–based Golden Gate Flouring Mills turned out one thousand barrels of El Dorado brand flour a day in 1885; and Abraham Starr, whose south Vallejo flour milling factory was the largest in the state.[17]

Although many bindlemen found work with the small-scale grain farmers who flourished around San Francisco Bay, by far the majority worked for growers whose interests were much grander. These farmers inspired among their contemporaries emotions ranging from awe and admiration to alarm and anger. Their goal was not fine crops, but tons of grain—wheat by the boatload. These men were known as the "monarchs of the prairies," "the grain kings," and the "barons of wheat," though many Californians simply referred to them collectively as "sandlappers," and most commonly, "bonanza" and "sky farmers." Bonanza farmers were found everywhere in California, including the San Fernando Valley of Southern California, where Isaac Newton Van Nuys, a New York land magnate, harvested ten thousand acres of wheat in 1876. But most concentrated in the flat, hot plains of the Central Valley, particularly in the area from Modesto north to Willows. Here, in what many had once regarded as a worthless desert, they annually produced three-quarters of the state's wheat crop.[18]

With easy access to shipping points along the Sacramento and San Joaquin rivers, as well as proximity to numerous small railroad lines, Central Valley bonanza farmers planted ten mile tracts on each side of the rivers (ten miles being the distance that one wagon load of sacked grain could be hauled in one day). Between Merced and Stockton, they cultivated a block of wheat encompassing more than six hundred square miles. In Tulare County, they planted what was essentially an unbroken grain field encompassing the entire county. Near Turlock, John Mitchell planted between twenty-five and fifty thousand acres of wheat, storing his crop in a warehouse holding one hundred thousand bushels. Around Woodland, in Yolo County, and throughout neighboring Colusa County and north into Butte and Tehama counties, bonanza wheat farmers tended fields that literally stretched to the horizon in every direction. In Stanislaus County, grain crops were so large that former Modesto mayor Sol P. Elias recalled how "the entire country was a wavy wheat field from one extremity to the other."[19]

But though they were beautiful, such fields, complained one member of the state agricultural society, were often not farmed by locals, but "by absentee owners from their offices in San Francisco, or . . . from offices in neighboring towns." And indeed, many bonanza wheat farmers were not engaged in agriculture at all; rather they were extractive entrepreneurs who worked men and land with such intensity that they became infamous. There was Isaac Friedlander, a German-born financier, San Francisco socialite, and agricultural capitalist widely known as "the Grain King," who had made his first fortune milling flour during the Gold Rush and by the 1870s had cornered a large part of wheat shipping operations and was growing ten thousand acres of wheat north of Merced, much of it for the China market; William Chapman, a land speculator who after arriving in California in the 1860s from Minnesota began buying undeveloped land from federal and state offices and, by 1871, had amassed 650,000 acres in California and Nevada, farmed twenty thousand acres near Sacramento, played a key role developing the San Joaquin and Kings River Canal and Irrigation Company, and eventually controlled more than one million acres before losing it to Henry Miller and Charles Lux; and the 76 Land and Water Company, an absentee corporation that worked thirty thousand acres south of the Kings River. Such farmers, commented one member of the state agricultural society, were simply engaged in "a manufacturing business in which clods are fed to the mill and grain appears in carloads."[20]

In Tehama County, where wheat farms were still relatively small, five men farmed a more modest average of 9,742 acres each, while in the Sacramento Valley the *Sacramento Union* informed its readers that eighty-two men owned more than five thousand acres each, and that 502 landowners held more than 1.8 million acres, or 42 percent of the entire valley. Extensive facilities, including cottages, barns, stables, blacksmith shops, and mansions, typically served as headquarters to many operations. In the Santa Clara Valley, wheat baron Henry Miller's twelve-thousand-acre Bloomfield Ranch, located three miles south of Gilroy, was written up in the local newspaper as "a model farm complete in every respect . . . a beautiful residence and grounds rivaling in beauty some of the famous places near the metropolis . . . where from 35 to 150 men, including farm hands, ordinary laborers, mechanics, and vaqueros are kept constantly employed."[21]

But not all wheat farms were corporate enterprises. Despite renting vast portions of larger bonanza farms, many wheat growers existed in such wretched conditions that they could not even raise a potato and had to live on canned goods bought on once-a-month trips to town. Encountering one such farmer, Charles A. Nordhoff, a promotional writer and correspondent for *Harper's Magazine* wrote:

> The buildings put up . . . are . . . slight and poor . . . There is a shanty for cooking and sleeping—the farm laborer here furnishes his own bedding and does his own washing, and his equipment is usually two shirts and a pair of blankets. There is a well, and a barn roomy enough to hold the hay and barley, and the teams. The renter either has a house of his own elsewhere, or, if he is poor, his family lives in this shanty; there is no vegetable garden, there are no trees, there is absolutely nothing to make life endurable or pleasant; and the only care of owner and tenant is to get as much wheat out of the land each year as they can at the least expense.[22]

Because of the scale of wheat growing, desperate men could always find work during the fall and winter months. This aspect of wheat culture runs counter to prevailing assumptions that plowing, sowing, and harrowing demanded little manpower because of a labor-saving device invented by Manteca farmer Westley Underwood in 1861. Realizing that Missouri-built single-bottom plows were inadequate to the scale of bonanza farms, Underwood bolted three standard, ten-inch plowshares together and mounted them on a giant wooden, wheelless frame. The contraption worked better than Underwood—or anyone else—expected, largely because this area was flat as a surveyor's bench and free of rocks, trees, and other obstructions. With an Underwood gangplow, wheat farmers could plant much larger acreages. Immediately they set about copying, improving, and expanding on the apparatus. Soon it was purchased by two Stockton-area entrepreneurs, H. C. Shaw, a foundryman, and Matteson and Williamson, farm implement dealers. Patenting it, they added wheels, reversible shares, levers and gears to raise and lower the shares as necessary, and a gauge to adjust the width of the plow cuts. Known collectively as the Stockton gangplow and manufactured in large quantities, the device had numerous variations—the Sacramento-made Challenge gangplow, the San Jose–made Cronkite and Beattie gangplow and Settel and Cottle gangplow, and the Marysville-produced Oliver gangplow. Variations added six and sometimes eight plowshares and could operate even on steep hillsides.[23]

One effect of the new plows was an immediate easing of labor. A common calculation was that one man with an eight-horse team pulling a six-share Stockton gangplow and one man following them with a two-horse team pulling a seeder and an iron-toothed harrow, each working a ten-hour day, could plow and plant 150 acres of wheat in one month. This worked out to between one hour and twenty-six minutes per acre and six to seven acres per day—or about twice the previous average. With more than two million acres of wheat to plant, the saving in manpower was considerable. Advancements in seeding further pushed the trend toward mechanization. While men broadcasting by hand could cover no more than ten acres per day, and midwestern wheat planters using eight- to ten-foot-wide drills could seed about fifteen acres per day, California field hands using the latest machinery could seed up to sixty acres a day. These developments quickly linked together when farmers attached a broadcast sower to the back of a gangplow and then added a harrow behind the sower, thus integrating plowing, seeding, and harrowing into one single, mechanized operation.[24]

To contemporaries, the application of modern mass-production methods to the task of plowing was an overwhelmingly positive development. But although they considerably multiplied productivity, gangplows did not ease the work. Only men driving two-share sulky plows ever rode on their implements. And these men usually worked on smaller farms. Because of the dangers associated with riding on big gangplows, most plowmen on the bonanza farms walked behind their rigs, controlling their animals with little more than a single leather strap or braided rope called a "jerk line." In January 1874, one hundred gangplow teams, each with eight mules and a driver, were engaged in Colusa County. On some wheat farms, as many as two hundred to three hundred men and eight hundred mules were required to plow and plant a crop. A large crew would line up with each succeeding plow and team, its own width further to one side of the field than the one in front of it. Set in motion with a series of signal whistles, the collection of animals, machines, and men produced a multitude of sounds as they moved down a field—the click of buckles, the creak of straining leather, the clank of machinery, the crack of whips, the deep breathing and snorting of horses, the cries of the drivers, and birds cawing and wheeling as they swooped down on the upturned earth searching for worms.[25]

Gangplows increased the pace of work considerably. Men toiled longer hours, covered larger distances—and paid a high price for their increased efficiency. Previously, they might have suffered gashes and cuts from carelessly swung axes, sickles, and cradles, plus the usual run of mashings associated with heavy equipment and working with mules and horses. But the moment they began using gangplows they encountered what would prove to be a large and growing array of dangers. Local newspapers listed one mishap after another: men crushed and decapitated by runaway plows; men who lost arms, legs, and fingers when teams bolted and ran; a plowman trampled or plowed under when his team pivoted. Driving an eight-mule plow team with a seeder attached and a harrow behind proved to be especially perilous. Willows-area field hand Nick Hansen recalled how a close friend had been killed. "The mules were frightened and ran away. There was no way to stop those frightened animals. The mule the teamster was riding fell and the heavy sharp harrow was dragged over the mule and its rider. They were horribly mangled."[26]

From their endless trudging across fields, plowmen fashioned songs. One of the most playfully ironic went:

Don't go, I say, if you've got any brains,
You'll stay far away from the San Joaquin plains.
At four in the morning they're hustling up tools;
Feed, curry, and harness ten long-eared old mules.
Plow twenty-four miles through sunshine and rain;
Or your blankets you'll roll on the San Joaquin plains.

They'll work you eight hours and eight hours more.
You'll sleep in a bunkhouse without any door.
They'll feed you on mutton, sow-belly, and sheep.
And dock you for half of the time that you sleep.
Twenty-four hours through sunshine and rain.
Or your blankets you'll roll on the San Joaquin plains.[27]

Gangplowing and new methods for seeding and harrowing all multiplied worker productivity, which in turn expanded the acreage planted and created more, not less, work. But another innovation seemed to show initially that masses of field hands were not so essential after all. Very early in the 1870s, "self-binding" reapers replaced two binders and several shockers on each self-rake reaper by automatically gathering and tying a wire around each grain bundle. Eliminating much of the tedium and stoop work of binding, the invention spread rapidly through the midwestern wheat industry. Yet in California, these new reapers never caught on to the extent they did elsewhere, largely because self-binders were extremely complicated and demanded a greater knowledge of mechanics than most men in California possessed. Drivers had to check to make certain that their machines tied good bundles, that they did not run out of wire, and that the knotter mechanism and tension rollers that guided the wire were all functioning properly. They also had to monitor many other parts of the reaper. Even if all went well, drivers could not relax. Once in a while a skunk crossed their path, rendering the driver unfit for social purposes and forcing him to change, wash, eat, and sleep away from crewmen until his stink subsided. Then there was the problem with rattlesnakes that became bound up in the cut wheat, scaring men with their distinctive rattle and causing them to do some high and fancy stepping as they dropped their bundle and scampered away. A few men became so preoccupied with rattlesnakes that they wrapped bindings around their legs to protect themselves from bites. One year the snakes were so numerous about Mountain View that farmers were unable to secure help because the reptiles seemed to be under every bound bundle of grain.[28]

∗

Men worked with wire self-binders for only a few years. Some farms used twine binders rather than wire self-binders, with the effect that one man could perform the entire cutting and binding operation. But even this economy was not enough. With thousands of acres of grain that had to be harvested in a relatively short period of time, field hands on large-scale California wheat farms soon turned to a machine called the header, so named because it cut only the heads of grain with perhaps a foot of stalk. First introduced in the mid-1860s on farms straddling the San Joaquin and Stanislaus rivers near Durham's Ferry by four or five wheat growers whose names have since been lost to history, headers sported eight- to twenty-eight-foot-wide cutting bars, mounted on a large frame, which caught the grain and pushed it up against a reciprocating blade. Behind and parallel to the blade ran a continuous four-foot-wide belt or apron that caught the tops of the beheaded grain stalks, carried them up an inclined conveyor, and deposited them by means of a "draper spout" into header wagons—unusually designed, very broad, odd-looking, lopsided vehicles sporting one side that was six feet high and another that was eighteen inches high. Upon first seeing these wagons (also known as header barges), some writers remarked that they seemed to have been made by a builder who had started to erect a mammoth packing-case on wheels but ran out of material after finishing the bottom, both ends, and one side.[29]

By cutting only the top of the wheat straw, headers considerably sped up grain harvesting and, despite costing 50 to 100 percent more than reapers, were soon harvesting most of California's wheat crop. Although there was considerable variation in the makeup of a typical header crew, most consisted of four headers requiring twenty-four horses and four drivers, plus twelve header wagons, twelve drivers, four loaders, and twenty-four horses—a total of twenty men and forty-eight horses. Header drivers known as "header punchers" drove each header. Ensuring that the machine took a full bite of the waving heads of wheat while hugging close alongside the header wagon, punchers had to watch the right side carefully where the cut grain left the conveyor, monitor the conveyor canvas, guard against loose chains that could damage various parts and mechanisms, and constantly adjust the cutting bar according to the terrain and height of the grain. Punchers who cut straw too low added excessive bulk that took up too much space in the wagons and slowed down the threshing; those clipping too high wasted large amounts of grain.[30]

Men armed with pitchforks and known as "forkers" packed the grain as it cascaded into the header wagon, being careful not to trample it or bump their heads on the conveyor as they rounded off the top of the load. As one wagon filled, forkers climbed down and onto the next in line. Once loaded, header wagons proceeded directly to the thresher, where two or three stackers unloaded each wagon into large elongated stacks known as "ricks." Men known as "spike pitchers" fed the headed grain into the thresher.[31]

An average-sized header with a twelve-foot-wide cutting bar and three accompanying header wagons could harvest fifteen to twenty-five acres each day and keep two or three header wagons coming and going. Within a few years, however, farm implement manufacturers in Stockton, Marysville, and Benicia began producing even larger, steel-framed machines. Sporting sixteen-foot cutting bars and pushed by twenty-four-horse teams, these headers easily cut thirty-five to forty acres a day and kept six or more header wagons busy. By the late 1870s, large-scale header operations were common throughout the San Joaquin Valley. Farming an unbroken tract of land extending from the Coast Range foothills west of Graysonville to the Sierra Nevada foothills east of Escalon, Alexander Lovell "Dick" Richards used six header wagons driven by Portuguese and American workers to harvest at the unheard-of rate of 270 acres per day. On the Bayliss Ranch in the northern Sacramento Valley in 1884, a crew of thirty header drivers, ninety-nine header wagon drivers, ninety-nine loaders, assorted bosses, and twenty-four Chinese stackers cut and stacked seven hundred acres of wheat in thirty-four hours, a record for speedy wheat harvesting.[32]

Soon harvest operations assumed a well-established routine. Harvesters started by clearing a threshing circle, about five acres in size, where the thresher would be located and header wagons would be unloaded, turned around, and returned to the fields. This was usually done with one header that had a huge bag attached to the elevator spout to catch the grain and eliminate the need for a wagon. The header cut an opening large enough to accommodate a header wagon and then began widening the opening until the clearing accommodated multiple headers and header wagons. Dividing fields each as large as a mile square into nine or ten parts, harvesters established a threshing circle then moved outward in a counterclockwise direction, gradually increasing their radius until they reached the edge of the field, pausing only when changing header wagons. This method left diamond-shaped patches abutting the corners of adjoining fields, which they cut later.[33]

As the speed of harvesting increased, growers struggled to keep pace with their threshing operations. Eventually, growers turned to steam engines—especially once it was discovered that they could fuel them with wood and then straw, a convenient source of energy during the harvest. Once introduced, straw-fired engines rapidly gained acceptance. "No horses to bother with & feed," wrote one farmer. By the early 1870s, straw-burning steam engines had pushed aside horsepower thresher drives on eight of ten California wheat farms, a technological shift that took more than a generation in the Midwest. By August 1884, there were ninety steam-powered threshing machines at work in Colusa County, each threshing an average of eight hundred sacks of grain per day. Building ever larger threshers, equipment manufacturers constructed mammoth engines more than thirty-five feet long and thirteen feet high. Resembling enormous elongated frogs, these machines were capable of threshing up to three thousand bushels (or twelve hundred sacks) of grain per day, although the average was between one thousand and fifteen hundred bushels. Some of the larger Enright and Heald "tubular return" steam engines were so impressive that they were given grandiose names: Gladiator, Phoenix, Mars, and so on. Total cost for such equipment ran to five thousand dollars in 1903, which meant that only the largest farmers could afford to own such machinery.[34]

As costs increased, itinerant threshing operations—so-called traveling "steam outfits"—handled much of the work. Sometimes threshing grain at the same time it was being cut, and sometimes threshing grain that had already been cut and stacked by header crews, itinerant threshers hailed from a variety of backgrounds. Some were groups of farmers who owned a thresher and steam engine cooperatively and farmed it out. Some were independent entrepreneurs who traveled the countryside during the threshing season. And some were wealthy farmers who, once they had threshed their own crop, then hired out their machines and crews. Most charged about nine cents to thresh one hundred pounds of barley in 1893. While the rate dropped one or two cents in 1895 following several years of declining grain prices, the going rate in most of California remained nine to ten cents throughout the 1880s and 1890s. At that rate, thresher owners cleared a tidy profit, frequently earning one hundred dollars a day and as much as three thousand to six thousand dollars in a season.[35]

As a public service, newspapers kept track of the whereabouts and progress of itinerant harvest and threshing crews. Road conditions were noted, leaders of teams or crews established, schedules given, and average yields tabulated. One typical notice in the *Napa County Reporter* informed its readers: "Messers. Keyes & Walsh, after a six weeks' successful run in cleaning grain in Berryessa Valley, have come into this valley for the purposes of accommodating any parties who may desire to have grain cleaned." Likewise the *Gilroy Advocate* kept track of threshing crews in its area, announcing midway through the season that "Mr. Muir's Thresher crew, which has been engaged the last 6 weeks in neighboring fields, did its final work for the season yesterday."[36]

Albert Roselip, a fifty-year-old Prussian immigrant in San Luis Obispo County, kept his men and machinery constantly busy when not employed harvesting crops on his own Rancho Corral de Piedra. Divided into three crews, thirty-seven men worked for Roselip in 1889. Supported by various wagons, thirty-five horses, and three water-haulers, the men were fed by a cook crew, while a second support crew cared for their horses. Working on wheat farms on both sides of the Santa Lucia Mountains, Roselip's crews traveled widely, as did others in San Luis Obispo County. In 1882, one itinerant threshing crew routinely traveled 130 miles round-trip from it base in Kings County to thresh wheat at Ni-pomo. Another crew in Sonoma County traveled to twenty-eight different farms and crossed the Russian River twice in a thirty-one-day period. Yet another in Yolo County visited forty-four different farms and threshed twenty-six thousand sacks, or about five hundred sacks per day, during a fifty-two-day period commonly referred to as a "run."[37]

Usually, threshers followed a logical order based on convenience, the idea being to move deliberately from one job to the next adjoining one so as to waste as little time traveling as possible. But management abilities and efficiency varied considerably among different outfits, and some were not adverse to bragging about good runs. "BIG THRESHING.—We are informed that during the five days ending Wednesday last the machine of Deering & Co., has made the largest average run ever in the valley," read an account in the July 30, 1870, *Napa County Reporter*. "It threshed on four different ranches, (incurring a travel of ten miles) a total of 5,500 sacks of wheat—an average of over 2,000 bushels a day, with only ten pitchers employed on the stacks. Our informant tells us if any one thinks he can beat this for coin, to 'auto up.'"[38]

Crews of seventeen to twenty men driving a half-dozen teams of six to twelve horses and a thresher and engine with at least three accompanying header wagons, and nine support wagons, made up quite a cavalcade as they moved through the countryside. Newspapers often reported as they neared town and citizens routinely turned out to watch as if observing the arrival of a circus. A report appearing in the October 6, 1877, *Santa Rosa Daily Republican*, described how

> one of Captain Henry's outfits for threshing; engine, cook house and all, stopped Friday in the street by our office . . . There were nineteen men of a crew. They threshed therefore part of the season on the San Joaquin and in Yolo County . . . A stouter set of bronzed athletic young men we never saw since the war closed . . . The young men though working hard are merry as Robin Hood's gang and we take as much pleasure in writing up their chronicles as if they were tourists.[39]

Despite the reported merriment, crews found their travels not only exhausting but risky. Steam engines—with their large boilers, heavy drive mechanisms, massive frames, and huge steel wheels—could weigh as much as one ton per horsepower. And scarcely a month passed during threshing season when rural newspapers did not report some bridge accident. "Brigg's & Co.'s Threshing Engine Drops Through Milliken Creek Bridge," reported the August 28, 1900, *Napa Daily Journal* in its account of one such collapse.

> The driver, Charles Smith was slightly scalded by escaping steam, and one of his shoulders was badly wrenched. Four of the horses were considerably scratched up, but not seriously hurt. . . . A few moments before the accident one of the Briggs boys had been riding upon the engine, but he got off to fix something that had gone wrong on one of the other machines. If he had remained on the engine he would probably have been crushed.

Other reports were full of wondrous escapes by men jumping clear at the last moment, grisly details of those instantly smashed, horrible descriptions of boys irretrievably caught between a steering wheel and tender who died after hours of agony, and the elaborate operations required to pull horses and engines clear from creeks and streams. Similar mishaps also occurred when crews tried to load their rigs onboard ferries to cross some of the state's larger rivers.[40]

ℰ

As harvesting and threshing advanced and the wheat industry expanded, men flooded into the wheat-growing districts for the harvest. With the first blast of hot weather, idle dockhands, bindlemen, and other unemployed men from the cities and towns around San Francisco Bay rode weekly steamers from Vallejo, Port Costa, and San Francisco up the Sacramento River to look for work. More than five hundred men arrived each year at Joseph Cone's sixteen-thousand-acre wheat ranch near Red Bluff. An even larger number worked for Dr. Hugh Glenn, the most successful and famous wheat grower in California. Known as the "Wheat King" and often compared to Cornelius Vanderbilt, Jay Gould, and other captains of industry, the Virginia native had arrived in California in August 1849, shortly after completing medical studies in St. Louis. He had $110 in his pocket and was determined to strike it rich mining gold. Staking out a claim at Murderer's Bar, near Coloma, on the American River, he accumulated a stake of a few hundred dollars and bought an ox team to haul freight between Sacramento, Coloma, and other Mother Lode towns. With profits from that venture, he purchased a livery stable, and after a short time sold it for five thousand dollars. With this capital he returned to Missouri, and after remaining there two years, drove a herd of horses and mules to Sacramento, where he sold them for a huge profit. Selling his herding business in 1865, he began farming in partnership with Major John Briggs at Woodland in 1865. Two years later, he purchased seven thousand acres of land near present-day Willows, in Colusa County, and began planting wheat on heavy clay land previously abandoned as hot, grasshopper infested, and worthless. By 1874, he had accumulated a five-mile-wide block of fifty-five thousand acres extending north and south along the west side of the Sacramento River for twenty miles centered on the town of Princeton. On his various farms, Glenn erected thirty-two houses, seventy-seven barns, and a fully equipped central blacksmith shop that tended to the six steam threshers and sixty header wagons required to bring in his wheat crop; he also set out a two-hundred-acre vineyard of wine and raisin grapes. In 1879, Glenn reluctantly accepted the Democratic Party nomination for governor but was defeated by George C. Perkins. Returning to his ranch in 1880, he personally directed operations that shipped to England twenty-seven thousand tons of wheat worth eight hundred thousand dollars. With crops of between a half million and a million bushels of wheat, Glenn had to build his own grain storage facilities and charter his own fleet of ships to send his wheat to market.[41]

More than two hundred permanent field hands worked for Hugh Glenn, but during the harvest season an additional five to six hundred arrived to cut and thresh his gigantic crop. Attracted by Glenn's monthly harvest payroll of thirty thousand dollars, everybody knew what was required. Besides migrants and dockworkers, some of Glenn's workers were Indians from Bidwell's ranchería, who worked in exchange for being allowed to winnow the grain that the threshing machines left behind. At the time when field hands began arriving, the wharves and docks lining the Sacramento River pulsated with activity. Hoping to make as many landings as possible before the river dropped too low for navigation, boats would crowd in loaded with supplies and men. The influx of field hands was probably the largest of any farm in California, and all but a few got hired. Upon arrival, they congregated on the levee, where Glenn's foremen sized them up, assigned them to a work crew, and sent them to one of nine different divisions of the ranch. Each division was an independent unit, some as large as ten thousand acres. Run by a foreman or tenant, these divisions were home for the next few months.[42]

Although they would not begin working in the fields until the first week of July, many field hands arrived beforehand. Early arrivals helped foremen round up stray work animals, unload grain sacks, repair reapers and headers, pull equipment out of storage, erect fences, repair roads, and service steam engines and threshers. Then for the next two months, they lived in a bunkhouse, traveled each morning out to the fields, cut and threshed wheat like mad all day long, and returned each evening, taking only Sundays off. If they failed to measure up, they were discharged instantly. There was no appeal.[43]

Whether they worked for a large wheat farmer like Glenn or for a more modest grower, threshers and harvesters always rose before sunrise, got dressed, shaved and washed, then came together for their first meal of the day. Harvesting and threshing was exhausting work, and men were accustomed to receiving huge quantities of food. Breakfasts were always substantial, typically consisting of mush, platters of ham, boiled, fried, and scrambled eggs, buttered bread and biscuits, pots of pink beans, hotcakes, milk gravy, butter, jelly, and jam, all washed down with huge cups of strong, black coffee—unpercolated and unstrained. After breakfast, crews moved out into the fields. Observing them from a distance as they deployed on Glenn's farm, a writer for *Appleton's Journal* in August 1880, described seeing

> some curiously-shaped dots, moving slowly hither and thither. They seem to crawl like insects, some going north, some south, some east, and some west. After a while you will distinguish that nearly every one of these dots is of a deep-red color. A little later you recognize the awkward shape of the separator, and the broad-topped funnels of the engines. Throngs of people, most of them in wagons, yet some afoot, follow behind. After a while all of these now widely-separated groups will come to a standstill.[44]

Upon arriving in the center of a threshing circle—(usually about 5:30 A.M. or 6 A.M.)—men followed a well-established setup procedure. So immutable was the process that one local historian wrote, "Each man, as in a circus, knows what he should do." Engineers and foremen first moved the thresher into position, testing the wind with a handful of straw before locating the thresher with the cylinder opening toward the gusts. Once positioned, men then unhitched the thresher, dug out a spadeful of earth from under each wheel, and, after the thresher operator had determined the machine was level, took away the team of horses. They then blocked the thresher wheels, spread a canvas under the sack sewers to catch spilled grain, and erected a "doghouse" tent alongside the thresher to protect the sack sewers and thresher tender from the heat and dust.[45]

Crews then drove the steam engine into position about 120 feet away from the thresher and stretched the ten- or twelve-inch-wide leather gandy belt out from the separator drive pulley. A man wearing heavy gloves attached the belt onto the engine drive wheel, and once it was in place, the engineer backed his engine away to tighten the belt. Crewmen then leveled and locked the engine wheels the same as they had with the thresher. After placing a tank of water under the engine's firebox to catch and extinguish sparks, an engineer armed with a pitchfork took up position in front of the steam engine and prepared to stuff waste straw into the voracious firebox. A thresher tender then checked the belting between the engine and separator, adjusted all of the thresher's gears, and closed all the lids covering the inner works of the thresher. The outfit was now ready to thresh. Field hands called this "making set."[46]

At this point, the engineer started his fire. When enough pressure had built up to blow the steam engine whistle, the thresher boss climbed to the deck of the thresher, looked to see if the men were clear, and gave the "high ball" signal to the engineer. The engine fireman gave two short whistle blasts as a final warning, then opened the throttle slowly, brought the thresher to life, and sent an army of men into action. Bag fillers, sack sewers, and sack buckers stood at their stations near the doghouse enclosure. Feeders surrounded the stacks and arriving header wagons, ready to pitch cut grain into the thresher. A dozen or so assorted laborers and forkers deployed to various locations to assist as needed. "Everyone knew their place, and everyone had their job," recalled historian and San Joaquin Valley buckaroo Frank Latta. "Threshers were just workers in open air factories."[47]

As the headers cut and the header wagons collected the grain, spike pitchers on either side of the thresher used four-tined pitchforks to unload the stack. Of all those involved in threshing, they probably labored the hardest. Next in line, feeders pushed the cut grain along a feeder table into the mouth of the thresher. To ease their burden, they used two round, tapered, foot-long pegs, each with a leather thumb-loop at the large end. Pulling the grain toward them with a peg held in one hand, they pushed wheat into the cylinder box with the peg held in the other hand. This made their work safer and decreased the risk of losing a finger or arm in the thresher cylinder.[48]

With the thresher bucking, shaking, and rocking, there soon ensued a strange combination of sounds—grinding, brushing, rattling, roaring, and thumping—accompanied by a thin sheet of dust pouring out of every crevice. Plumes of waste chaff blew from the thresher top. Toward the rear of the machine, streams of nut-brown wheat gushed forth from two spouts. Within moments the entire machine was obscured by a thick, yellow cloud. Working within this cloud, the thresher tender kept constantly busy. Circling the thresher, sometimes climbing on top of it, he listened for any strange sounds, kept the wheels aligned, greased all of the gears and bearings, and made sure that the pitchers did not "slug the machine" or clog it up. If this happened, the thresher tender would have to then crawl inside the cylinder and clean it out.[49]

Of special concern was the thresher cylinder, which the thresher tender inspected for worn or bent teeth each morning before starting up the machine. If any teeth were broken or defective, he tightened or replaced them. He also inspected the bearings of the cylinder shaft, filed down any burrs, and made certain to keep the cylinder in balance: The cylinder and concave teeth could not contact one another, and the mechanism had to turn smoothly without vibrating. Every time he replaced cylinder teeth, the thresher tender had to remove the cylinder and rebalance it. If everything ran smoothly, the engineer could spend most of the day standing on the platform of his machine directing the overall operation. Only he and the thresher tender had the power to stop the machinery, and they would constantly keep an eye on one another for signals indicating any problems.[50]

Engineers and thresher tenders were the only members of a harvest crew whose jobs were so skilled that itinerant bindlemen could not fill them, although on large crews bindlemen frequently served as assistants, firemen, and oilers. The rest of the work was open to anyone. At least one man always served as a general "choreman" or roustabout who performed assorted tasks. Crew members, known as "tank men" if they were adults and "water monkeys" if they were boys, also had to supply water to the steam engine, which consumed about fifteen barrels of water per day. Driving a tank and team to a well, creek, pond, stock tanks, or river, these men hand-pumped their wagon tanks full of water, hauled them back to the engine, filled the engine tank, and repeated the process.[51]

Because threshing was so noisy, steam whistles signaled all that was needed—one short peep told men to stop pitching, two to resume, three long blasts for engine water, four short blasts to call in the header barges, and four long blasts to call the boss or foreman. In between signals, thresher men worked incessantly. "Not one of them is idle, or seems to wish to be," reported the *Willows Journal*. "Most of them are driving. Some are pitching, a few are feeding the separator, a few more are filling, sewing, and carrying away the bags, and some are brushing away heaps of chaff. Early in the day there is plenty of talk and laughter, but later on, as the work tells, the sun grows hot, the tongues become silent, and the hubbub of the machines alone fills the air."[52]

Straw bucks and firemen kept constantly busy, moving fast to keep the steam engine boiler stoked. On a big engine, two firemen were needed to maintain the fire. One worked as a fireman's assistant, constantly tightening the pulley belt, oiling the mechanism, keeping the thresher blocked to prevent it from creeping along, "feeling bearings and watching for that tell-tale blackspot where the dust in falling off proclaims a cast-iron box is hot." Two hands known as "straw bucks" labored as a team, one whose job was to pitch straw away from the rear of the thresher, the other (often known as a "straw monkey") whose job was to drive a straw buck team and transport straw from the thresher to the steam engine.[53]

Finally, there was the "doghouse crew." Sack tenders constantly filled sacks with 120 pounds of grain, pounded the grain into the corners with a club, and passed them to sack sewers, who deftly sewed them shut with a spring-eye needle. Then the sack bucks carried the full bags of grain about thirty or forty feet to the sack pile. "There is no suggestion of gentleness, or grace, or poetry, in the whole field," wrote a reporter for *Appleton's Journal*. "All is ingenuity, precision, order, force. A cry of admiration rises to one's lips time and again."[54]

❧

Hard as they worked, threshing crews could never keep pace. Too many men were required for such jobs as stacking and moving hay, and their efficiency dropped fast after the initial burst of work. This reality led to a plethora of labor-saving devices developed not by Stockton implement manufacturers, but rather by local farmers who, seeing problems firsthand, devoted considerable attention to solving them with homespun gadgets, innovations, and techniques. One of the most important of these labor-saving solutions stemmed from problems created when grain was harvested and threshed concurrently. Because header wagons often laid out such long stacks of grain, large numbers of men were needed to convey it to the thresher. To overcome this problem, some unknown farmer created the portable derrick table. Essentially a wooden platform, twenty- to twenty-five feet wide and thirty- to thirty-five feet long, set on the running gear of a wagon, a derrick table held three tall poles in an A-frame with a pulley at the apex. Rolled into position between or beside the stacks and at a right angle to the thresher, the apparatus was held in position with guy ropes running from brackets on the table corners. Attaching a large hay fork to the A-frame, men would pull huge parts of one stack and then another onto the platform, then rake the grain into the thresher feeder using pitchforks.[55]

In 1872, men began running a series of additional pulleys to a horse or mule to pull a four-foot-wide pitchfork called a "Jackson hay fork" full of grain along the table toward the thresher. Rapidly incorporated into threshing operations after their introduction, more than seven hundred Jackson hay forks were sold to wheat farmers during the next eight years. Each Jackson hay fork and portable derrick table combination allowed two men to do the work of eight or ten. Later models eliminated the derrick table and instead added a second Jackson hay fork and a series of pulleys so that one man driving a team of horses pulled one rake toward the thresher while another was sent back toward the stack, where it was filled with another full load of grain.[56]

Another invention that altered the way men worked was the "hoedown." Essentially a four-tined hay fork with tines bent at right angles to create a large rake, the hoedown was created by an unknown San Joaquin Valley farmer as a way to rake grain onto a thresher cylinder. A fourth innovation, the "rolling net," was the first device to handle large quantities of grain successfully. Laying the net inside the header wagon bed so that it extended over both the upper and lower sides, men fitted a long timber to the net edge hanging over the high side with a ring attached midpoint. To unload a rolling net, men drove a wagon to the stack in the usual manner but with the low side facing the feeding table. Folding the high side of the net over the low side, they tied it to the long timber, ran a long rope from the spreader ring to yet another innovation, a thirty-six-foot-high mast with a twenty-four-foot boom, known as the "Powell derrick," so-named after its inventor, Fresno-area farmer Thomas Powell. Then, by means of a horse-powered pulley, they used the Powell derrick to lift and roll the entire header load of grain out of the wagon and onto the feeding table in just a few minutes. A fifth innovation, header wagons with hinged beds that tipped toward the low side as men pulled the rolling net toward the feeding table, further increased the efficiency of stacking operations, allowing men in some cases to build gigantic stacks thirty-five feet wide, twenty-eight feet high, and three hundred feet long.[57]

Within a few years, field hands learned to handle two other innovations. One was the divided net, which could be pulled open with a jerk line, allowing men to build stacks so large that it was unnecessary to move the threshers. This advantage saved considerable time as men expended less energy resetting operations. The other innovation, the Jackson self-feeder, was essentially a conveyor belt that carried the grain into the cylinder, replacing two men and eliminating the danger of hand-feeding the thresher.[58]

Many innovations, though efficient, were initially so expensive that growers could not afford them. An Acme stacker, for example, cost $150, with the accompanying pulleys and other hardware adding an additional fifty to seventy-five dollars. And though they streamlined work considerably and eased the labor involved in threshing, these inventions forced men to work at an even quicker pace and added a new set of dangers. Stacks created by pivoting derricks and divided nets, while more compact than those formed by rolling nets, were still full of holes and voids. While setting nets, men would fall to the bottom of a stack and suffocate or expend considerable amounts of time and energy climbing out. Occasionally a grain fork would fall on them and they would be severely—if not fatally injured—by the tines. Men were also hit by swinging forks, buried under heavy loads of grain, lost fingers and arms in the rope pulley mechanisms, and were shredded and even impaled by the three-foot long, curved tines. But when measured against previous methods, the benefits of the new mechanisms far outweighed the problems. Using a net and derrick, one man with one horse could move more grain and stack it higher in a single day than ten men following older routines. The bottom line was that derricks, Jackson forks, Jackson self-feeders, rolling nets, divided nets, and hoedowns eliminated six to eight men from a threshing crew. But like harvest innovations that preceded them, these tools did not decrease overall labor needs, which continued to grow as the wheat crop first doubled, then quadrupled. Nor did they relieve the strain, exhaustion, heat, dust, discomfort, and long hours of threshing.[59]

Men routinely worked twelve to fourteen hours a day—longer, if necessary. Sometimes they did not quit until well after sundown. In a letter to the *Pacific Rural Press*, one field hand explained that he was "always busy, from about ½ past 5 A.M. until 7 P.M. and sometimes 9 P.M., before the chores were all done up." If everything ran smoothly and the equipment performed well, a normal shift lasted ten hours with only two breaks. One came after a crew had harvested about seventy acres. At that point, the distance between the headers and separators became too great, and the crew moved everything to a new site. Another break usually came sometime between 11 A.M. and noon, when a single, long blast from the steam engine whistle announced lunch. Firemen in particular welcomed the relief. Straw-burning steam engines required continuous feeding and with "little time to wipe your nose," engine tenders quickly became black with soot and needed to wash themselves. But other crewmen fared little better and were also ready for a break.[60]

By mid-morning, everyone was hungry and tired and would be worthless thereafter without a meal and a break. Because they were in no position to feed themselves, and because they were usually too far from their bunkhouses and kitchens to return for meals, farmers and custom threshers brought lunch to the men in the fields. As always, threshers demanded "good food and plenty of it," so cooks made the noon meal somewhat of an epicurean delight, always preparing hot stews or fried chicken with helpings of ham, eggs, bacon, home-baked bread, stewed tomatoes and turnips, peas, corn, slaw, fresh and dried fruit, and cookies, along with gallons of cold water, often with lemon or lime juice added. At least one day a week, cooks baked pie or cake.[61]

With so much to eat, crewmen made meals into quite a social occasion. After being fed, they would relax in the shade of cottonwoods, under oak trees, and along ditch banks. When no shade was available, they crawled beneath header wagons to escape the sun. During this "digestive time," as some called it, men talked and told stories or simply dozed off and daydreamed. These moments were long cherished by those who later remembered their days threshing wheat.[62]

On some traveling crews, men handled the cooking. No particular talent was required, and the unpalatable results of their culinary efforts earned many camp cooks the nickname of "meat burners." To avoid such results, on most crews women very quickly took over cooking. Farmwives often spent much of the year preparing just for the task of feeding harvest workers. They would put up five-gallon demijohns of tomato catsup and muscat grape juice and from thirty to forty half-gallon mason jars of "chow-chow" or "piccalilli" just to feed a crew for several weeks. They canned an average of six to eight hundred pounds of peaches and tomatoes and three to four hundred pounds of apricots, pears, and apple butter. During the harvest season, they followed a strenuous regime that, according to one thresher, "no three professional cooks would now attempt." This included rising early to bake bread, slaughter chickens, put a roast in the oven, peel potatoes, and start soup simmering.[63]

At first, women loaded their meals into horse-drawn buggies or wagons and set out as much as an hour or two in advance to deliver lunches to the fields on time. At some point they found their work considerably advanced with the introduction of cookshacks, chuck wagons, and cook wagons, as they were variously called. Exactly where and when these "mobile kitchens on wheels" originated is unknown. Some claim they were simply copied from midwestern wheat growers, others maintain that they were an entirely California creation. Whatever their genesis, they benefited field hands immeasurably. A featured part of any threshing crew, by the late 1870s the cook wagon was quintessentially arranged for the comfort of the crew, giving men, as the *History of Kern County* explained, "a cool and comfortable place to eat in; no flies to bother them, but a breeze to fan them while they eat."[64]

Field hands on dozens of different farms seem to have encountered cook-

FIGURE 18. C. J. Aydt threshing crew and cookshack, Healdsburg, ca. 1888. Note the young girl with her pet rabbits. Courtesy of the Healdsburg Museum.

shacks at about the same time. One widely accepted story asserts that threshers on J. B. Greene's San Joaquin Valley wheat farm were the first to enjoy the convenience of cook wagons during the 1874 harvest. But while Greene's threshers may very well have been the first in the San Joaquin Valley to encounter cookshacks, they were at least four years behind John Bidwell's harvest crews in the northern Sacramento Valley. Too many men were leaving during Bidwell's harvest, so his nephew, Abram, tried to cut turnover and also alleviate the harsh conditions during threshing by devising something he called a "portable boarding house." Sixteen field hands lived and ate in his "house on wheels," which was twenty-two feet long and eleven feet wide. They had a kitchen in the rear, a dining table that was raised and lowered from the ceiling by wires, and bunks that folded up to provide space during the day. Butcher wagons replenished the supplies of round steak, stew meat, and chuck roasts, while produce wagons provided fresh vegetables and fruit daily.[65]

Whether they were fed on threshing jobs in the San Joaquin or Sacramento valleys, field hands always encountered cook wagons of a standard, well-conceived design. Built out of lightweight lumber, set on wheels salvaged from a thresher, and measuring twenty or twenty-five feet long and eight feet wide, early cook wagons were often described as being "as neat as any housewife's ordinary kitchen, and . . . probably twice as convenient." A large, wood-burning stove stood in one corner; opposite it was a worktable. Staple foods such as flour, potatoes, coffee, and tea were stored under the table. Cabinets held all the necessary utensils. Later models even carried portable electrical generators. According to a Colusa County mug book,

> Serving dishes were tinware and the evaporated (or fresh) apple pies were served in the tin pie plate in which it had been baked. Sugar bowls were usually a small baking powder can and pepper and salt were likewise in cans. Syrup pitchers of glass with metal tops were always in evidence and most likely the vinegar cruet would consist of a quart whisky bottle with a notch in the side of the cork. Perishable foods had to be kept in jars covered by wet sacks.

Since the cook drove the wagon from inside, there was also usually a front window for ventilation between the stove and table.[66]

Men received their lunch in one of two ways. Either they stood at wing tables that folded down from the long windows under retractable canvas screens, or they sat at a long center table reached by means of portable stairs. Of this later, more popular cook-wagon model, one visiting Australian journalist wrote: "If one occupies a table near the center of the room this sometimes involves considerable crawling in and out, and over and under as a penalty for being late at meals." Side and end flaps furnished additional shade, and on many models screened windows afforded men a comfortable, ventilated, and sanitary place to eat.[67]

After a lunch break ranging from thirty minutes to an hour, men resumed work and continued until the engineer blew the quitting whistle. "By nightfall all seventy acres are bare; that is, not a head of wheat is left," reported a correspondent for *Appleton's Journal*, surveying the results of a day's work. "A trampled stubble higher than one's knee remains to tell the tale, but all the beauty and worth have departed, and the place is desolate. To-morrow the same scene will be enacted in another section of the same size, and a similar bustle and uproar will ensue, and a similar pile of plethoric brown bags piled very high will reward the labor of the day."[68]

౪ఎ

In their diaries and letters home, men described their work as "tolerably hard" but a hefty paycheck usually offset their exertions. Harvest wages were higher than the winter and spring labor rate. Most men earned from \$1.15 to \$1.50 per day; those on larger wheat farms also received bonus allocations of tobacco and candy. As part of their compensation, field hands were also housed in what would later become known as labor camps. This practice had long been common among custom threshing crews moving from one farm to another and on big farms where wheat fields were remote and required long journeys just to reach them. But on the bonanza wheat farms, camps developed that were larger and more complex than anything previously known.[69]

On some wheat operations, men lived in camps that were small communities. Of these, none was more elaborate than Jacinto, the tree-shaded company town that served as administrative headquarters and wheat shipping port for Hugh

Glenn's vast operations. Sprawling along the west bank of the Sacramento River twenty-seven miles north of Colusa, Jacinto had every convenience—wash houses, dining halls, blacksmith shops, barns, sheds, stables, immense grain warehouses, and other buildings, including a saloon, telegraph office, post office, hotel, two-story brick mansion, and general store. Rounding out the facilities was a complex of butcher shops, slaughterhouses, and smokehouses organized around a large kettle, four-feet across, for scalding hogs and rendering goose grease for candles.

To feed the harvest crews at Jacinto and a half-dozen outlying camps during the 1879 harvest season, Jacinto's butchering operations slaughtered 877 sheep and 120 head of cattle and produced tons of salted, cured, and smoked pork. Three full-time butchers handled slaughtering duties. An entirely separate farm produced the huge quantities of oats, barley, and corn required to feed the animals. And Chinese gardeners, living in three small shacks by the river, tended a fifty- to sixty-acre garden. Ingeniously irrigating their garden, they lifted water from the Sacramento River up and over the levee embankment by means of a waterwheel made of five-gallon kerosene cans with one end cut out, so that the wheel was turned by the current of the river.[70]

At Jacinto, men slept on feather mattresses in a bunkhouse that had formerly been Glenn's home. Elsewhere, men were not always so lucky. Camps ranged from beautiful, tree-shaded sanctuaries to raw and utilitarian places with few amenities, often without any outhouses, where the men, as one farmer admitted, "do their washing under a tree, and boil their clothes in the pot they scald the hogs in." Bunkhouses known as "boar's nests" were built out of rough, single wallboards, with rough floors, two windows, and one door. Tiers of bunks lined the walls, but otherwise they were sparsely furnished, with little more than a nail on which a man could hang his clothes. Reeking of sweat, urine, food, manure, alcohol, tobacco juice, and a dozen other unidentifiable odors or "mystery smells," the floors of such bunkhouses would become an agglomeration of grease and unidentified sticky substances that could only be attacked with a scraper or squared-ended shovel.[71]

Hot, drafty, and poorly lit, permanent quarters on many large wheat farms did have their comforts, however spare. Because custom threshers had to provide for all their crew's needs, they contrived a wide variety of accessories, such as folding tables and chairs, which made their mobile camps as comfortable as possible. As a result, traveling threshing crews seldom lacked adequate food, water, or sleeping facilities.[72]

But many wheat growers apparently regarded their field hands as not much more worthy of comfort than farm animals. This was certainly the case for one Butte County wheat farmer. On June 18, 1890, an agricultural machinery salesman told the *Sacramento Weekly Bee* shortly after encountering the man: "God in hymn and prayer, but makes slaves of His creatures. The food is worse than that fed to hogs and it is not as plentiful." Yet this apparently religious farmer could not understand why he could not induce men to remain with him. "The wheat grower," concluded the salesman, "is not always disposed to treat his employees either fairly or with common decency. They are accorded no more comfort than the cattle and are often of far less concern."[73]

FIGURE 19. "Sleeping Beauties," Vaca Valley, August 1887. Threshers often spread their beds on piles of straw and slept under the stars. Photograph by W. R. Nutting. Courtesy of the Vacaville Museum.

Because of the large numbers of horses and mules and the nearby stables and corrals, wheat camps always had problems with flies. "I worked for a month at a camp where fifty men were employed," recalled Nick Hansen, who labored year-round on a big wheat farm near Willows. "All of the men searched the food for flies before eating. Every day we had pie for dinner. Before eating pie the men would turn the crust up and search for flies. We often found a fly or two under the crust. If you ate more than one fly you would surely lose your dinner within ten minutes." But the flies also presented a certain odd opportunity. Each morning, as they gathered by the millions on the bunkhouse porch ceiling, a man arose before sunrise with newspapers doubled over the end of a stick. Lighting the paper, he held it under the flies as he walked along the porch. "The blaze singed the wings of the flies and they fell to the porch floor," recalled Hansen. Someone then swept the floor, gathered huge numbers of the still live but flightless insects, and fed them to the chickens. "You would be surprised how those chickens ate the flies."[74]

Men dealt with the harsh conditions in some unusually funny ways. On the west side of the San Joaquin Valley, Frank Latta once found shelter with a grain crew in a shack with a floor that was more or less a permanent pack of mud and dirt and walls that were so full of holes that when the wind blew it came whistling through with large quantities of dust and sand. To plug the holes, men tacked the tops and bottoms of flattened tin cans over them. But out of frustration, a jokester nailed an old sock around the inside of a particularly large hole. This became a constant source of amusement from then on because, whenever the wind blew, the sock would inflate and stand straight out from the wall.[75]

When bunkhouses became cramped and crowded, tensions rose and the younger men, especially those who were light sleepers, absolutely would not sleep in their bunks. To escape, they moved into tool houses, blacksmith shops, empty granaries, and harvester sheds. As the work continued and the men grew tired and sunburned, tensions built, and under these circumstances, anything could set men off. Recalling a typical incident, Latta described the escalating confrontation that developed one winter on the Bunker Plow Camp, near Garzas, on the west side of the San Joaquin Valley. As a young twelve-year-old splitting time between duties as a meat burner and attending school, Latta grew increasingly agitated with a mule skinner named Old Scratch. So lazy was Old Scratch that during the night he would not leave the cabin to relieve himself, instead using a knothole above his bunk, to which he had attached a short piece of garden hose that dangled into a bucket outside. Regarding him as the most aggravating, detestable man he had ever met and much agitated by Old Scratch's laziness, constant smoking, and arbitrary, overbearing, supercilious ways, Latta grew weary of breathing air saturated with smoke from the pipe Old Scratch puffed incessantly. Deathly sick from a fog of nicotine so thick that the lantern flame illuminating the cabin was a small blur at six feet, he determined to exact revenge. One morning, while Old Scratch slept and the rest of the crew was out feeding their teams, Latta built a roaring cook fire, pinned the windows shut, and stashed a long piece of flat iron outside the door. He then sprinkled pepper thickly all over the top of the red-hot stove, ran outside, shut the door, put the iron bar across it and into two brackets, grabbed his lunch and books, and ran for the barn. "From the noise and the way that cabin danced around," recalled Latta many years later, "you would think that a medium sized army tank was maneuvering inside. Just as I was riding away to school Old Scratch came headfirst through the north window with a piece of sash around his neck. He looked like a tear gas bomb had exploded in his face."[76]

But that was not the last of the youngster's pranks. Not long thereafter, he got his final revenge. "One Sunday afternoon I was resting from cutting wood behind the cabin when I happened to look up at the hose [which Old Scratch used for nighttime purposes]," he recalled. "Suddenly I was seized with an inspiration. I put the saw buck against the cabin, took a hammer and nailed the end of the hose to a rafter above the level of the knothole. I told the other three Skinners what I had done." That night everyone stayed up playing three-handed cribbage, waiting until midnight for the outburst they knew was coming. It came with a roar of oaths and a shower of quilts thrown from the bunk. But as Old Scratch bounded down intent on killing the youngster, both mule skinners stood by him with fire pokers in their hands. Old Scratch grumbled back to bed. The next morning the men removed him to Front Street in Hills Ferry.[77]

Not all such disputes ended without bloodshed. Exhausted and angry, some men simply lost control. This is what happened on the McCabe ranch near Los Banos, toward the end of a particularly grueling week, in the spring of 1888. Crammed into a small bunkhouse one man was trying to rest when another fell into a deep sleep and began snoring loudly. Unable to stand the noise and craving peace and quite after a long day threshing, a bunkmate vowed to silence the man for good. Grabbing a double-barreled shotgun, he aimed it at the snoring bunk-mate and let lose both barrels. The snorer saved his life only by awaking at the last moment. Instinctively rolling off his bunk onto the floor, he bolted for the door seconds after both charges tore holes through the bunkhouse wall inches above the spot where he had been sleeping. He was one of the lucky ones. Not long thereafter the easily irritated thresher shot and killed an equally loud but slower-moving bunkmate. Nor was that the end of the season's ranch violence. On December 4, at the end of a hard summer of threshing and hauling wheat on the A. J. Rasor ranch, three miles north of Princeton, Thomas Kern fended off an attack from spade-swinging bunkmate Manuel Silva, retrieved his rifle from an adjoining room, and shot and killed Silva. Six months later, on the Hugh Glenn ranch, a drunken Charles Strope assaulted Albert Gittner, and according to the *Colusa Sun*, had Gittner by the throat and was "fast choking him to death" when Gittner pulled out a pistol and shot Strope through the head. Arrested and charged with murder, Gittner was also quickly released when the county attorney concluded he had acted in self-defense.[78]

CHAPTER TEN

Hell's Fury and Liquid Fire

The Coarse Culture of Wheat

Harvesters and Threshers

At the start of the threshing season in early August 1874, several hundred seasonal laborers arrived on George Hoag's farm, one of the biggest agricultural operations in the northern Sacramento Valley. On their way to the bunkhouses, they looked around at Hoag's machine shops and foundries and were admiring the numerous steam engines, mowers, threshers, and wagons that were in various stages of renovation and modification. But one machine made more of an impression than any other. On display in the farmyard was a thirty-five-foot-long, thirteen-foot-high, barn-red thresher, one of the most impressive pieces of machinery that field hands would ever encounter. Built by Hoag in the shops at Jacinto and named the Monitor, it was unofficially known as "the big red grain eater." Over the next few days, fifty-six of the most experienced men found themselves separated from the others, formed into a tight crew, and assigned to work only with the Monitor. They would soon attempt to break the world record for threshing wheat.[1]

On the evening of August 7, drivers with teams of fifty mules pulled the Monitor and a gigantic twenty-five horsepower steam engine into position. Upon arriving at the threshing site, the men listened to Hoag's instruction: there was to be no respite from their work. Making camp, they then retired early in order to be ready for "the grand onslaught on the sea of yellow grain." What they did next seems fantastic even today. At sunrise on August 8, the Monitor's steam whistle sent seven headers and twenty-one header wagons out into the fields. Many years later, a writer with the Willows *Daily Journal* recalled, "Naught could be heard but the hum of the massive separator and the rattle and noise necessary among so many men, mules and headers." Everyone worked continuously; no one rested or broke for lunch or meals. If men could not continue, they were replaced, thus avoiding any delay that might result from a lack of manpower. The system worked perfectly and at sunset, the official tally showed the result of the day's work: 2,569 sacks, each containing 2.25 bushels, for a total of 5,779 bushels of

FIGURE 20. *A California Harvest Scene.* George Hoag's farm, Willows, California. Painting by Andrew P. Hill, March 1875. Courtesy of Donald Houghton.

wheat, cut, threshed, and bagged in a twelve-hour period. Hoag's threshermen had set a world record![2]

But that was not the end of the story. Proud of their accomplishment and wishing to memorialize it, Hoag's men assembled the following year to reenact their threshing operation so that a painter could commemorate the event. For an entire day, they posed for Andrew P. Hill, a twenty-two-year-old San Francisco artist, who photographed and sketched them; the next day, they threshed the field. Hill completed his painting, called *A California Harvest Scene*, the following March. George Hoag was prominent in the painting's foreground, and the Monitor filled its center, but the platoon of field hands, headers, header wagons, and ninety-six mules and horses surrounding the thresher filled most of the space. This crew soon achieved a kind of mythic status.[3]

Measuring three by four feet and bordered by a massive gessoed and gilded frame that added another foot to its outside dimensions, Hill's painting went on exhibit at Snow and May's Gallery on Kearney Street in San Francisco in April 1876. Shortly thereafter, the *Pacific Rural Press* and several rural newspapers published drawings based on the painting, and the Marcus Hawley Manufacturing Company issued a color lithograph of the scene. One reason field hands came through so strong in Hill's work was that it portrayed them in a way that professional photographers found impossible—it captured their entire working environment. Format had always been the obstacle. Harvesters sprawled across the landscape in a way that could not be depicted even on large glass-plate negatives.

Such expansive operations required a panorama, and *A California Harvest Scene* achieved that perspective. Here, sculpted in a soft, golden light, farmworkers were seen for the first time as components in a large-scale, mechanized industrial farming system that was praised as "symbolic of California agriculture" and celebrated as "a stirring embodiment of enterprise, of action, of success." One of the most important images of California farming and farm labor, Hill's painting marked an important turning point in the annals of California farmworkers, who until that time had not been considered worthy of artistic attention.[4]

Although Hill was not the only painter to capture agricultural labor in his work, he was the only one who did so without resorting to mid-nineteenth-century European art formulas. A typical artist working in this style was William Hahn. Educated in Dresden, Paris, and Naples, and inspired by landscape painter William Keith, with whom he worked briefly while in Boston in 1871, Hahn headed west in 1872, establishing his reputation over the next few years with genre paintings of Placerville, the Russian River, Yosemite Valley, and the Sierra Nevada. In 1875 Hahn painted *Harvest Time, Sacramento Valley*, a bucolic picture of field hands operating a horse-drawn threshing bee near the coastal foothills about thirty miles south of Hoag's farm. Painted in pastel hues, Hahn's relaxed, almost festive composition—with children picnicking and a bird dog bringing a pheasant to them—barely hinted at industrialized labor. Similarly, Thomas Moran's 1879 watercolor *Threshing Wheat, San Juan* was a mellow composition showing several field hands driving dozens of horses around a threshing corral in a serene valley near San Jose. In contrast, *A California Harvest Scene* was a monument to agriculture as spectacle. Including every possible facet of work, Hill drove home the point that threshing was highly regimented labor, and as a result, projected an entirely different image. He even captured one easily overlooked detail. Rather than stacking the cut grain, Hoag's men pitched wheat directly into the apron conveyor of the cylinder. This was to become the standard technique on wheat farms from this point on. But the most important characteristic distinguishing *A California Harvest Scene* from other agricultural paintings was the debate it provoked. Seeing it, Californians could not avoid discussing the nature of agriculture and its effect on land, society, and most important, on farm laborers. This debate would continue during the next few years, as Californians struggled to assess the human consequences of industrialized wheat farming.[5]

Meanwhile, the record set by Hoag's men came to be viewed as a challenge by field hands seeking fame and public recognition. As the decade progressed and the wheat industry expanded, farm laborers would become involved in even more elaborate efforts to prove their worth by threshing more grain than ever. The first of these attempts occurred on Henry Osborn's farm near Turlock in the San Joaquin Valley. Here on August 22, 1878, a threshing crew managed by J. J. Thompson of Modesto, whose men were considered to be the southern counterpart to those employed by Hoag, made a valiant effort to break the threshing record. But even though they worked with grain that had already been cut and stacked, they fell considerably short of their goal, producing 1,618 sacks of grain in nine and a half hours. It seemed that Hoag's men, their accomplishment immortalized on oil and canvas, would remain unchallenged.[6]

During 1879, another group of field hands began threshing with a new "triple return" steam engine, the Missouri Chief, largest of its kind in the state. Built by Joseph Enright of San Jose and owned by Dr. Hugh Glenn, the Missouri Chief vastly increased the amount of grain that the Monitor could thresh. On the evening of July 25, after threshing a large part of Glenn's crop, one hundred men, ten headers, thirty-six header wagons, and 130 mules and horses assembled in a large wheat field. "All the necessary arrangements were consummated," reported the *Willows Daily Journal*. "Every man was allotted his particular station and informed of the duties expected of him from which there should be no deviation."[7]

At sunrise the next morning, the horse whistle of the Missouri Chief echoed across Glenn's wheat fields, signaling the beginning of a mighty effort. As the dark smoke from the engine stack feathered into the hot, windless air, a deafening clatter ensued. With men, animals, and machines racing against the deadline, the Monitor poured wheat from its four spouts, keeping sack tenders and sewers busy. During the course of the day, crews reset the engine and thresher three times, moving it over three-quarters of a mile. Finally, as the sun set behind the Coast Range, the Missouri Chief blew its whistle once more, bringing operations to a halt, and the exhausted workers, faces gray with dust, sprawled on the ground awaiting the totals. When Glenn gave the tally, the crewmen sprang to their feet and cheered. Between sunrise and sunset, they had done something no one thought possible: They had cut, threshed, and sacked 2,748 sacks of wheat, a total of 6,183 bushels. "This showing we believe is unprecedented in the annals of farming in the civilized world," observed the *Willows Daily Journal*. Surpassing the previous threshing mark by 409 bushels, Glenn's men set a record that has yet to be broken.[8]

On October 2, 1880, Glenn's crew attempted to push the record even farther, but with tragic consequences. Under the heading "Local Matters," the *Colusa Sun* reported: "A Terrible Explosion—On Monday last, at about 11 o'clock A.M., the boiler of the engine *Missouri Chief*, running the great separator *Monitor* on Dr. Glenn's place just above Princeton, exploded, killing four men outright and badly wounding several others." According to the story, the stacks had been about half threshed when the engine firebox exploded, sending a plume of smoke into the sky that could be seen from ten miles away. The force of the blast blew the fireman, Joseph Brady, 180 feet away, tearing off his clothes and shoes, and killing him instantly. The engine was catapulted forward, and flipped onto the thresher, smashing and killing the Chinese separator, tender, and oiler, who had been resting on the tongue of the machine. The explosion also injured the engineer, and dozens of Chinese sack pitchers and straw bucks working nearby. "Chinese hats and clothing, and pitchforks, were scattered around, showing great confusion among the Chinamen," reported field hand Nick Hansen, who happened by the next day. "From the wreck to the large Chinatown of small shacks at the north end of Princeton, where several hundred Chinese lived, the road was literally covered with red and yellow Chinese papers several feet in length and about two inches in width. . . . The Chinese told me these papers were scattered there to keep the devil from getting the dead Chinamen."[9]

Throughout the 1870s, hundreds of men died annually in thresher engine explosions, and hundreds more were maimed and crippled. On July 4, 1872, the *Co-lusa Sun* reported: "A terrible catastrophe occurred at Reese's ranch, eight miles from Princeton, in which a white boy and two Chinamen were killed by the explosion of a steam cylinder to an engine carrying a separator to a threshing-machine. Many by-standers and harvest hands were injured, and the harvest machinery burned." The 1874 harvest season was an especially dangerous one in the northern Sacramento Valley: One man died on July 16, near Woodland when the boiler of the Davis and Jeffers threshing engine blew up; three more died near Colusa on September 27, when the engine driving a thresher on the Perry Pitt ranch exploded. Invariably, the explosions were caused when low water levels allowed pressure to build inside the boiler. On July 25, 1876, a boiler explosion on Pike Gupton's ranch near Jacinto killed two men, and injured three. On July 16, 1880, a boiler on the Davis and Jeffers threshing machine exploded on the Fellows farm, three miles south of Colusa, killing an employee known as Portuguese Joe. Fires were also common, even though threshing crews exerted considerable effort to prevent them by maintaining efficient spark arresters, keeping the engine away and downwind from the stacks, and by cutting large clearings to prevent flames from spreading into the standing wheat. Still, entire fields often burned. A typical headline, from the July 13, 1872, *Napa County Reporter*, began:

> WHEAT BURNED: A destructive fire occurred in some of the grain fields near Grayson, in the San Joaquin Valley, on Friday last, occasioned by a spark from the smoke-stack of a steam thresher, which was at work at the ranch of John Mingos, igniting the dry straw near by. The fire spread rapidly, destroying 200 acres of standing grain, taking in its course a large part of Frank's ranch, and fifty acres of Van Benschoten's, of Grayson.[10]

When wind-blown sparks jumped beyond the threshing site and set the countryside ablaze, threshing crews often fled in such panic that they abandoned their threshers, steam engines, headers, and header wagons. These incidents were so common and consumed so many fields and farmhouses that they eventually led thresher outfits to refuse responsibility for any damage resulting from fires. Publishing their announcements in local newspapers, threshers warned: "NOTICE TO FARMERS: The undersigned owners of Steam Threshing Machines hereby give notice that they will not be responsible for any loss or damage by fire or otherwise to farmers or owners of grain crops who employ them to thresh their grain, but will use the utmost care to prevent accidents by fires or from other causes."[11]

Besides fires and explosions, newly mechanized farm processes brought a host of new dangers. Larger numbers of men were being killed or injured in these accidents simply because steam-powered threshers had more pulleys, belts, and gears to do damage, and because the pace of work and noise levels so increased that men easily lost track of the activity around them and could not hear warning calls. So many men were hurt each week during the threshing season that accounts of carnage routinely filled the pages of rural newspapers. Men died or were injured in an infinite number of ways. Even the most minor accident could be fatal. Out in the wide expanses of the Sacramento and San Joaquin valleys medical help was distant and a gashed worker often bled to death for want of a simple tourniquet. Around Modesto during threshing season, there were so many accidents that the county hospital became crowded beyond capacity. Survivors of various manglings who managed to resume work or just hang around would be renamed "Stumpy Joe" or "Three Finger Pete." At least one became a celebrity. After losing his arm to a thresher, One Armed Hughson founded the San Joaquin Valley town of Hughson.[12]

Men faced other hazards as well. Even tasks as routine as hauling and stacking hay to feed horses were full of dangers. "Last evening, while a couple of men employed by J. F. Brown of Binghamton were unloading hay with a derrick fork, the harness on the horse F. Miles was driving broke, causing the single-tree and stretchers to fly back and, striking him on the head with great force, knocking him insensible," reported the *San Francisco Call*. "The best medical attendance was given, but he remained unconscious until his death, which occurred five hours later. He leaves a widow with six helpless children."[13]

Dust was ever present. Working in what was essentially a desert landscape, threshers in the Central Valley would sometimes break from their duties and drink from their burlap-covered water jugs as great gray clouds of alkaline powder billowed up to a height of five thousand feet, shutting off the sun, burning their eyes, clogging their nostrils, and making further labor impossible. But of all the hazards men faced while threshing, none proved to be more indiscriminate or unavoidable than the sun. Looking over blazing white summer fields, men swore they saw the horizon undulate and the distant hills lift completely off the ground, float on dancing waves of heat, then settle again, intact. On these occasions, heat had an almost metallic characteristic. It was a weight that men carried on their backs, a fiery warmth that cracked their leather boots, heated equipment to the point where it could not be touched without gloves, and baked straw so crisp that it snapped like glass filaments underfoot. "During the thrashing [*sic*] season the temperature would run above 115 degrees for weeks at a time," recalled Frank Latta. "The light reflected from the stubble in all directions until a person was almost blinded."[14]

Burned by the sun, men became dizzy and sick. Some fainted; others simply dropped dead. Pitchers, who worked the hardest, were most prone to sunstroke, but anyone could become afflicted. Many field hands who saw their fellow workers struck down were careful to keep a gallon jug of water wrapped in a wet gunny sack nearby. If the outside was kept damp, the water stayed cool and potable. But not everyone was so careful, and often even those who sipped regularly sweated so profusely that they became dehydrated. Notices of their misery dotted the pages of the rural press during threshing. "A man driving a grain wagon from Farmington to Stockton was found lying on the sacks insensible from sunstroke, but with proper applications soon recovered," reported the July 31, 1886, *Pacific Rural Press*. "Four deaths have since resulted from the intense heat near here."[15]

One of the hottest harvests in the Sacramento Valley occurred in June 1876. With a huge crop, high wages, and plenty of work, men of all backgrounds and races found it easy to land jobs. But many were unfamiliar with the rigors of threshing, and when the temperature in the shade began to hold steadily between ninety and 104 degrees, dozens of these men succumbed to heatstroke; in one week, seven wheat threshers died in Colusa County. So dangerous were conditions that on June 15, all threshing ceased. But even after the weather cooled somewhat, newcomers still continued to perish from the heat. Typical of them was Willis King, a twenty-two-year-old from Michigan, who died on the Dibble Ranch near Dayton. "Deceased was a fine young man of exemplary character and had only been in this state about six months," reported the June 30, 1876, *Chico Enterprise*. "The body was taken in charge by Hallet & Love and brought to their rooms, where it was put through a process of embalming, after which it was put in metallic casket and shipped last Monday by express to his father, Hiram King, Jonesville, Hillsdale County, Michigan."[16]

Despite its prevalence, heatstroke was not the worst—or even the most common—hazard of steam threshing. Inexperienced hands were cautioned to go easy when working on a steam threshing outfit for the first time, and to wear lightweight clothing to protect themselves from the heat. To ward off chaff and dust and protect their lungs, experienced threshers wore veils of wet handkerchiefs, and if they could obtain them, dabbed themselves with wet sponges. Some men draped gunnysacks or damp flour sacks over their heads. All of which helped very little. Threshing was dirty work that clogged nostrils and gave men horrible, hacking coughs. Recalled Frank Latta, "The dust from the cylinder poured out in . . . a cloud" so that, after a couple of hours, he was so covered with sweat and debris that he "could not be distinguished from an Indian."[17]

Adding to the discomfort of threshers were huge swarms of black gnats. Men were often so bothered by the pests that they tied their gloves over their shirtsleeves and lashed their pant legs to their boots to ward off the pests. This kept the insects out, but added considerably to the men's discomfort. Many preferred simply to tolerate the insects and ignore the remedy. But for everyone, threshing was a fatiguing job that left them sweat-soaked and sore to the bone.[18]

৪৯

During the workweek, threshing crews had little time to relax. Meals and sleep were their main forms of recreation, with perhaps a bet or two on who would sew the largest number of grain sacks the next day. But when a crew finished "threshing out a farm" and moved equipment to a new location, the mood changed. Wherever they were, threshing crews looked forward to the end of the workday. At that moment, as the engineer blew the steam from the boiler, the entire crew would bring buckets, capture the hot water, and take baths. But while this helped relieve some of the daily pressures of hard harvest labor, it usually was not until late on Saturday that the men finally had time to themselves. This was when they received their wages and decided how to spend their free time. Mechanics sometimes worked overtime, overhauling and oiling machinery, readying it for use on Monday, but to most men Saturday nights provided a chance to play.[19]

Because banks were usually far away, field hands were sometimes paid in cash. More commonly, though, they received checks. Whatever the method of payment, men had no difficulty spending their hard-earned income. The strict regulation of their day-to-day work lives left many field hands craving excitement come the weekend. As Chino farmer Richard Gird explained: "Everybody must stop work . . . and indulge in some sort of foolishness." Embracing a culture largely based on drinking, whoring, gambling, and brawling, many wheat harvesters and threshers on the bonanza farms—along with canal diggers, mule skinners, and other field hands—pursued a lifestyle resembling that of other common laborers. Setting them apart from most of society, their leisure activities paradoxically provided them with shared experiences that provided release, and afforded them a way to vent their feelings and cope with the harshness of life in the fields.[20]

Of all the state's harvesters and threshers, none played harder or longer than men employed on Hugh Glenn's ranch. At Jacinto, men wishing pleasures of the flesh could find them in boatloads of prostitutes shipped up from Sacramento. The going rate was $2.50 in gold per woman per hour. When prostitutes were unavailable, men improvised. They would hold a "stag dance," complete with fiddlers and violinists, in which men danced with one another, with those men wearing hats playing the role of women as dance partners, a tradition carried over from the mining camps. Almost the entire upper floor of the Jacinto Hotel was a dance hall given over to these activities. Liquor flowed by the bucket, and many men simply spent Saturday nights drinking in the camp's two or three saloons or under the locust trees surrounding the hotel. Often they would continue drinking until they were broke, had exhausted their credit, or passed out.[21]

Gambling was by far the favorite pastime. Men bet on almost anything: how many sacks or piles of wheat or how many mules or horses were in a field, and whether or not and when it would rain. Everyone enjoyed cards. Bunkhouse poker games could involve high stakes and run all night long. In fact, some card sharks took jobs as harvest hands just to have the opportunity to harvest the paychecks of other workers. At Jacinto, Dr. Glenn himself was known to participate in these games, which on at least one occasion became serious enough to result in murder. Following the incident, the killer was jailed, tried, and convicted, but while a gallows was being constructed, Governor William Irwin pardoned the man. According to rumor, the governor granted him a reprieve on the grounds that the murdered man was a card sharpie and "needed killing."[22]

Whenever they could, harvesters and threshers in the northern Sacramento Valley headed for Willows. Founded when the Central Pacific Railroad finally pushed its line through the area on the way to Oregon, Willows stood in bold relief on the treeless plains beside a spring-fed waterhole sustaining a clump of willow trees after which the town was named. A typical wheat town owing its entire existence to the grain crop, Willows shared many of the characteristics of raw mining camps and tough lumber towns of the West. Along Main Street stood a row of hastily built, crude wooden structures, a bank, hardware store, some livery stables, a butcher shop, a shoe store, several hotels, and a few cafés and rooming houses. Streets were unpaved, sidewalks were raised and uneven plank structures, and there were no shade trees or lawns. And because the town lacked a sewer system, refuse collected in low spots and open cesspools that emitted a sickening stink in the August heat and had to be cleaned late at night by the "sewer wagon gang." But none of this bothered field hands on the surrounding wheat farms. Bored, sunburned, exhausted, and starved for female companionship and other diversions, they regarded Willows as a welcome alternative and change from the humdrum isolation of threshing and camp life.[23]

On Saturday nights, hundreds of harvest workers flooded into town. Many who had grown accustomed to cleaning their clothes by hitting their trousers against a wagon wheel to knock the dust out certainly were attracted by the happy prospect of a hot bath, a haircut, a trip to the Chinese laundry, some fresh underwear, and perhaps a can of Union Leader pipe tobacco. But the real lure was less practical; men prowled the town streets in search of women, whiskey, and card games—usually in that order. They found all three in great abundance among the twenty-five saloons and gambling dens lining one side of Main Street, and the numerous brothels, housing some seventy-five women, on the opposite side.

Crowded and dirty with card-strewn floors, a typical Willows saloon was curtainless, lit by a single, large coal oil lamp, and adorned only with cobwebs that hung limply from the ceiling corners. Flies buzzed lazily about or perused the sticky floor; in the darkened corners there were always a few souls who could go no farther and had been laid out for the night in drunken repose. Here men with names like Bib Tex, Misso, Broken Back Sam, Little Rex, and Rough House Jack gathered at the bar and card tables. Laughing, singing, and tossing down liberal amounts of liquor, they shot their pistols to their heart's content, wrestled with one another, fought and debated, made their rounds until the early morning hours, and then passed out in streets, alleys, fields, or vacant lots. Newspapers matter-of-factly reported these debauches. "Charles Wilsey and N. J. French, while wrangling over a game of cards at Willows, came to blows, when Wilsey was shot through the mouth," read one account in the *Colusa Sun*. Another described how "in a row over a gambling game at St. John one McCommins stabbed 'Dutch Jake,' *alias* Jake Hamming, in the head and abdomen. McCommins escaped." In Modesto, one hundred miles south, field hands frequenting saloons between I and J streets were regularly poisoned by adulterated liquor. "Hardly a night passed during which some derelict who floated in from the country to enjoy a rest from labor or a season of joy was not fleeced in a game of cards, robbed and beaten up, or plied with liquor until he became insensible and his pockets picked by the light-fingered gentry," wrote Sol P. Elias.[24]

Conditions were just as drab and dangerous in Traver, Nelson, Princeton, Firebaugh, Hanford, Goshen, Maxwell, Wheatville, Williams, Dutch Corners, and dozens of other Central Valley wheat towns. Turlock, for example, at one time had as many saloons and bars as it did private residences; Traver, a wide-open town, boasted ten saloons and gambling halls and two houses of prostitution, each with between fifteen and twenty women. As with Willows, the men who flocked into these towns hardly ever strayed far beyond the saloons and bars, making them convenient targets for all kinds of exploitation. In Traver, the streets would be clogged on Saturday nights with hundreds of men staggering up and down the sidewalks barhopping and trying to keep track of all of the gambling games that were running; at least one infamous card game ran for two weeks nonstop, using up two hundred packs of cards. "The drunkenness would increase as the day advanced," wrote the town historian. "Crowds would assemble where an exciting game or other excitement was in progress, and not only fill the building but would extend clear out across the sidewalk and compel pedestrians to detour out in the street." Cases of delirium tremens were common, and every week sufferers from the "jim jams" (alcohol poisoning) were sent to County Hospital, at least one of whom died while tramping back to town. In Newman, scores of field hands tottered and swayed up and down the street downing concoctions such as "Sheepherder's Delight," "Hell's Fury Smooth Stuff," "Squirrel Poison," "Tarantula Juice," and a particularly high-test libation known as "Liquid Fire." One odd benefit of these brands of liquor was that after a few sips, field hands could seldom conduct much physical activity beyond an initial bend of the elbow. "Apparently, it was too lethal," recalled Frank Latta. "Victims became paralyzed before the fighting stage developed." And while such an effect probably saved more than a few men from reckless confrontations, too much of the stuff could be fatal. "I remember that after one of these excursions 'Whitie' Evans died of acute alcoholism," Latta confirmed. "I also saw two others fall dead of the same affliction. One of these fell as he was entering and I was leaving a restaurant, and the other fell as I met him a quarter of a mile north of the Bunker Plow Camp, part of a quart bottle of 'Squirrel Poison' in his coat pocket."[25]

As with their predecessors, many field hands discovered too late that fatigue and alcohol could combine with deadly results. Such was the case on September 20, 1889, when Paul Miller and Robert McMartin were sparring in a Maxwell saloon. Tired from a week in the fields and inebriated on some local concoction, Miller picked up an old pistol that he believed to be unloaded. Pointing it at McMartin, he playfully said, "I will shoot you," and pulled the trigger. Unknown to Miller, someone had loaded the weapon. When he pulled the trigger, the pistol discharged a bullet into McMartin's chest. Before he died two days later, McMartin exonerated Miller, and on that basis, Miller was tried and acquitted.[26]

With men exhausted from a hard week of threshing, it sometimes took very little to provoke a quarrel. Men regularly scuffled over the slightest insult, demolished barrooms over minor disputes, and shot it out over the most trivial matter, as when Joseph Casey shot and killed Daniel Matheson in Gould's Saloon on January 1, 1890, in Williams. "The trouble originated in a game of cards," reported the *Colusa Sun*. "Matheson lived nearly four days after being shot." While awaiting trial on March 30, Casey attempted suicide by plunging a sharpened iron hook into his neck, making an ugly gash, but was sewn up and on May 27 was tried, convicted of murder, and sentenced to life imprisonment. Often the reasons for these bloodbaths were but dimly perceived by the survivors the next morning. And though most fights were caused by indiscriminately flaring tempers, some were ongoing. For example, in Firebaugh, thirty miles north of Fresno, a field hand named Lou McElvaney, who was described as "wild as a cat," regularly squared off against a powerful black field hand. Under the influence of Sheepherder's Delight or Firebaugh Firewater, the two men battled long and often, in fact, every time they met—and their clashes frequently lasted for hours before ending in a draw. "Lou tried for that Negro's scalp every time they met," recalled Latta. "He never could lick that big Negro, nor could the Negro down Lou."[27]

No group of carousing field hands had a worse collective reputation than those in and about Hills Ferry, a grain-shipping depot and raw collection of shacks, often referred to as "the most sordid, dirty hole" in California and "a Sodom if ever there was one," located astride the San Joaquin River just north of the Stanislaus–Merced County line. Attracted by the town's fifteen saloons—in particular by the Oasis, an establishment whose staff of three dozen women had a reputation for exquisite pleasures of the flesh, the Pink House, so named not because it was in fact painted pink but because its temptations included six beautiful young women, and Ah Gun's, a Chinese bordello—men poured into town from wheat farms and sheep-shearing camps as distant as thirty miles away. In their written recollections, residents relate one incident after another—murdered field hands lying in the dust for most of a day, bloated and drawing flies, until the coroner removed them; barkeepers who shot field hands for small offenses, and were later absolved of any crime on the grounds of self-defense; and random violence between field hands, including an incident that resulted in the last legal hanging in Stanislaus County.[28]

The most notorious saloon in Hills Ferry was The Jeannette. Located near the docks and owned by John Henchy, it consisted of a saloon and dance hall with a loosely built bar. At least two notorious murders occurred here. One involved the town marshal and was sparked when the marshal accidentally shook the bar and an enraged Henchy threatened to kill him. Believing this was a joke, the marshal shook the bar again; without hesitation, Henchy pulled out a double-barreled shotgun and fired two loads into the marshal, killing him instantly. Bound over for trial, the saloon keeper was released because all of the witnesses were afraid to testify against him. A few years later, Henchy shot Lou McElvaney, the well-known bar fighter from Firebaugh, after McElvaney wrecked The Jeannette in retaliation for Henchy's abuse of a bar girl. Afraid of confronting McElvaney at close range, Henchy ducked out the back of his bar, went next door to the Old Globe Saloon, borrowed a shotgun, returned to The Jeannette, called out, "Look out," as he stepped in through the back door, and let go with both barrels. "Everyone ducked but Lou and he lost the side of his head," recalled Latta. "Witnesses of the shooting were all saloon bums, and all favored Henchy. With this made-up testimony, Henchy was freed." He continued tending bar at The Jeannette for another ten years.[29]

Collecting these stories, a correspondent for the *San Francisco Morning Chronicle* amplified the theme of mayhem and portrayed Hills Ferry field hands as "tough characters," given to "robberies, ruffianism, and crime." According to his October 21, 1883, report,

> The crack of a pistol was a familiar sound and the cry of agony and despair of some poor victim as he received the assassin's knife was an almost nightly occurrence. The upturned face, cold and white, of a shearer or woodchopper or some other who happened to be possessed of money, would frequently startle the man who had happened to step aside from the beaten track, stumble across the victim of revenge or avarice, stiff in death.[30]

Because so many men passed out in the streets, gutters, and vacant lots of Hills Ferry on Saturday nights, local citizens in 1881 took action to curb the growing problem. Tired of paying the police to collect drunken field hands and put them in jail, city councilmen required that all saloons in town maintain small back rooms with rows of shelflike bunks, running two or three high along a wall. Here, barkeepers laid out drunk field hands after they became paralyzed with booze and "over celebration." But often, before the men were left to sleep it off, the barman would roll them over and go through their pockets, taking what few dollars they had retained, if any, hence the term "rolling rooms."[31]

A far different—and more menacing—campaign developed in Modesto. Rather than making barkeepers responsible for policing drunks, Modesto citizens improvised their own justice. Bit by bit, sometimes with marked informality and wide consensus, townspeople joined together to clean up their town. The most famous vigilante action of the bonanza wheat farming era occurred in August 1879, when a masked mob known as the San Joaquin Valley Regulators rode into Modesto and pushed every prostitute, confidence man, and criminal out of town. The following year, vigilantes drove gamblers and prostitutes from Hanford, fifty miles south of Modesto; this action was so successful that vigilante action was never again necessary. Reform took a more gentle form in Willows on June 18, 1881, when the town council passed a law closing all saloons on Sundays. All but the saloon kept by Al Allen complied. Staying open all Sunday, Allen made a haul and then happily paid a ten-dollar fine. This raised such an uproar that Allen's wife was fined twenty-five dollars, and Shasta, the saloon manager, fined the same amount. After ten merchants were arrested for violating the Sunday law at Maxwell, the practice of serving liquor effectively ended.[32]

Whether they went on a bender in Modesto, Willows, Traver, or Hills Ferry, field hands usually partied well into Sunday morning. That afternoon, those who could sobered up on a folk cure of vanilla extract and Worcestershire sauce or recuperated by dozing in the sun, loafing in front of the brothels, talking with prostitutes, enjoying a big meal, and generally lounging around. But many would be so sick and in such a deep alcoholic trance that they were unable to stand up, let alone return to the farms and prepare for the next day's work. So on Sunday afternoons, foremen would drive into town with several header wagons, hunt for the crews that they had dropped off the night before, and take them back to the bunkhouse to sleep off their alcoholic binges. They called this "the weekly cleanup."[33]

During most weekly cleanups, foremen followed the same routine. Frank Latta, who often drove a hay wagon into Newman to collect field hands, recalled how he first searched the back alleys on the east side of town behind Front Street, where he would collect all those sober enough to stand. He then employed these men to help him load the "limp, bloated, and rolled victims into the wagon." Next, he searched the rolling rooms, then made the rounds on the west side of the tracks, looked into a rooming house known as The Lancelot, a dance hall called the Bella Union, and finally the town's "sporting houses." Before departing, the foreman checked the names of those he had collected against his crew list. After discovering that Missouri Pete, Texas Slim, Tennessee Jack, Red, and Windy were missing, he recruited enough new workers to round out the crew. "Generally the trip home was much quieter than the one to town," Latta remembered.[34]

Drunk threshers in every wheat town returned to work under similar and sometimes even more curious circumstances. On Monday mornings around Chico, men were collected under an arrangement resembling the slave market roundup a generation earlier in Los Angeles. Having been arrested for disorderly conduct, they would summarily be hauled before the local police court and given a sentence of "ten days or ten dollars." Having blown their cash in town the night before, few men could pay their fines, but foremen and farmers always bailed them out.[35]

ଜ୍ଞ

Winters were always a difficult time for threshermen and other field hands, who struggled to survive until the next harvest. One farmhand with thirteen summers in the fields told investigators for the State Bureau of Labor Statistics that, in order to survive, he and others labored "in any way to keep soul and body together." To do that, some packed up and headed for the mines or the warmer climate of Baja California and Mexico. But most stayed in California, piling up (as they always had) in the cities. If they were lucky, they found work on the docks around San Francisco Bay. Many ate in soup kitchens and flopped in boardinghouses, all the time wondering if they would survive until the spring. Many strung together odd jobs as a way to earn a little money and keep a roof over their head.[36]

The spectrum of jobs taxed a man's abilities. Simi Valley farmhand Charlie Havens listed the following work, which ranged from roofing to planting, during a one-week period in the winter of 1889:

6000 shingles	$16.50
Labor for hauling them from Hueneme	$2.50
1 day shingling	@$1.50
7 ½ hours labor	$2.25
6 Hours Labor	.90
One man plus team/ploughing ½ day	$1.50
Grubbed cactus—2 hours	.30
" " 2 ½ hours	.38
2 men hauling cactus and stones	$4.00
Digging holes for trees, setting stakes for trees, setting them out, binding them with sacking [to protect them from animals]	
was ordinary work 10 hours	$1.50
2 men and teams to San Fernando to pick up trees	$4.00
Hoeing around trees (per hour)	.15
hoeing grape cuttings (per hour)	.15
Harrowing 2 acres twice (per acre)	.25
rent/2 horses for a trip to Santa Paula	$3.00 [37]

One of the oddest of these jobs was "herding" jackrabbits in the San Joaquin Valley. Because rabbits moving in from the surrounding countryside so devastated young orchards and vineyards, men formed businesses and traveled from one farming community to another organizing "rabbit drives." Enlisting the aid of as many people as they could, rabbit drivers set up large corrals with long wings made of several thousand feet of four-foot-high fish netting held in place with crude poles and supporting lath. Early the next morning they would direct long lines of boys to beat the bush with sticks as men on horseback rode behind them. Driving the rabbits ahead, they then closed the netting behind the frenzied animals, funneling them into a narrow pen, then directing others to club the rabbits to death. A good, early morning rabbit drive lasting less than two hours could net one thousand rabbits, and there are records of some drives lasting forty or fifty consecutive days, with forty thousand to fifty thousand rabbits slain. On one rabbit drive near Shafter, three men caught about twenty-five hundred rabbits. "Five hundred were scalped for the one-and-one-half cent bounty, 380 were placed in coops and at least 1,500 were turned loose," reported the *Shafter Progress*. "It was necessary to free all not needed immediately because they would injure themselves if kept penned." With so much carnage, there was an abundance of meat, so drovers usually sold some of the bludgeoned rabbits to local farms for hog and chicken feed, barbecued what they could eat in one sitting, and shipped large quantities of rabbit meat as far away as Mexico, Canada, and England. Often the killing achieved such proportions that great piles of carcasses were simply left to rot where they fell. No one thought this cruel or unusual, and most saw it as part of the tough fight for survival. Invariably, someone took at least one photograph, with a sea of dead rabbits in the foreground, and the proud, exhausted hunters, led by their field hand drovers, arranged proudly in the background, with rabbits dangling from fences in strings, like a fisherman's catch. In the washed-out sky of one photograph, a participant wrote, "THE OLD TIME JACK RABBIT DRIVE, in the days of Frank Hunt, Cliff Metcalf, John Linville, Pete Ruiz, Nannie Rowe—These Rabbits were shipped to San Francisco for TAMALE Purposes," he wrote. Then, unable to resist a joke, the man added: "Johnny Medina says, 'No Meat Shortage Here.'"[38]

Another odd but important off-season job was herding geese in the northern Sacramento Valley. Because so much wheat-growing territory had once been "goose land," gigantic flocks of migrating geese settled in like clockwork every September 18 and stayed until April. Growers calculated that, in a twelve-hour period, a single flock of geese, fattening on grain left behind after harvesting and on seeds planted for next year's crop, could devour the equivalent of ten acres of wheat. To combat the devastation, squads of unemployed harvesters armed with shotguns patrolled the fields on horseback firing into the flocks night and day. Riding special "goose horses" that did not flinch at gunshots and following paths cleared through the center of each wheat field, goose herders by constant harassment kept geese on the move and prevented extensive damage. Glenn alone hired from thirty to forty men to herd geese on his farm, spending thirty thousand dollars one year on their salaries, ammunition, and horses. With buckshot whizzing about and falling from the skies, there were numerous accidents. Plowmen would be hit, horses and mules killed and maimed. Although goose herders generally did not aim at killing geese, some achieved a local fame for killing sprees, among them noted fowl hunter Paddy Lord and his five-man crew. During the winter of 1877, Paddy and his assistants killed seven thousand geese on Frank Moulton's wheat farm near Chico. "We never picked them up," he recalled. "We shot them and just let them lay right where they fell." But some goose herders collected the birds, picked the down, and sold it for fifty to seventy-five cents a pound for pillows and featherbeds in Willows, often netting an additional thirty dollars a month.[39]

Because so much grain fell from the threshers and was left behind beneath the stack, a small number of field hands always found off-season work cleaning up the grain at the threshing sites. This hand cleaning salvaged large plump grain that was often used for seed the following year. On many larger wheat farms, men also shifted from threshing into maintenance and repair work. With sixty headers, 180 header wagons, six threshers, six steam engines, 130 gang plows, and one hundred harrows, Hugh Glenn's big operation provided plenty to keep field hands busy assisting skilled mechanics in one of five machine shops throughout the winter. Those who were not adept with tools could always find lots to do feeding and caring for livestock, renovating the work facilities and other structures, building and repairing levees, clearing land for new fields, and even chopping wood.[40]

Besides goose herding, rabbit driving, wood chopping, and helping out with general repairs, men also found off-season work hauling straw out of the fields. Typically three or four men, sometimes assisted by boys, were hired to pitch the straw into header wagons, then drive to a central dump and unload it in piles as large as thirty feet high. "Rattlesnakes in the straw dumps were sometimes forked on the wagon at my feet," recalled Latta, who worked as a straw hauler while in high school. "Barley beards [heads of barley] crawled inside a bandanna handkerchief tied tightly around my shirt collar, inside my belt and trousers, stuck in my undershirt, gouging me everywhere, in my socks, drawers, hair, ears, in my mouth and under my tongue. . . . Even today, when a soda jerk sets a can of straws in front of me for my malted milk it spoils my appetite." Of all the off-season jobs, this one was universally considered to be the most unpleasant, disagreeable, and disgusting "man-made purgatory" ever conceived. Usually it lasted several months.[41]

Far greater numbers of men found work transporting bags of grain to river landings, warehouses, railroad depots, and flour mills. This was usually good for two months of income, and while not as unpleasant as hauling straw, "swamping," as it was called, was hardly easy work. To begin, men loaded six to nine tons of grain on two, or sometimes three, wagons, carefully laying out the sacks in such a way that they would not break on the rough ride. If sacks in the lower tiers broke, the entire pile could become unbalanced and fall. With swampers manning the brakes on these ponderous wagons, teamsters drove loads over the narrow, rutted roads, bellowing out a continuous chorus of cusswords to guide their teams of up to ten mules or horses. On a big wheat farm, a half-dozen slow-moving grain-hauling teams might be kept in constant motion lumbering between the threshing sites and distant warehouses. After enduring a long and exhausting journey over dusty, deeply rutted roads, grain haulers frequently would not make it back to the threshing site before sundown. The trip from Dick Richards's farm to Stockton took several days; from the more distant ranches of Turlock the minimum time for a round-trip was three days. Along the way every logical stopping point became a halfway house, or "Five Mile House," as they were called, where men camped and watered their teams. But frequently they did not make it that far.[42]

Once at the grain warehouse, teamsters and swampers unloaded their wagons, building huge stacks, some of which contained twenty thousand tons or more of grain. During a threshing season, they might deposit seven thousand sacks full of grain in a Willows warehouse during one twenty-four-hour period or work nonstop, day and night, for one hundred days unloading grain at the Hills Ferry docks. At the height of grain hauling, newspapers reported so many teams lined up at big shipping points like Turlock that on an average day local stables had to provide enough hay to feed six hundred mules and horses. With animals and wagons everywhere, the stench from manure would drift for miles around town. As many as three parallel lines of grain haulers might extend from the front of each warehouse several blocks outside of town, causing a giant traffic jam that brought all work to a standstill and forced grain haulers to wait for days before unloading. In Traver, lines of wagons sometimes stretched for a mile from the three grain warehouses far outside of town. "At such times a team would take its place at the rear of the column and be two days working its way up to the front where the wagons could be unloaded," reported the *San Francisco Morning Call* on December 9, 1880. "We see the dust-begrimed mule skinner at the rear of the long string of animals . . . with drooping shoulders partially shaded from the scorching sun by his broad-brimmed sombrero." Grain haulers impatient to unload would pull up directly alongside the railroad and load it directly into cars. During 1886 and 1887, Traver shipped thirty-six thousand tons of grain this way, an amount unequaled by any other shipping point in the country.[43]

Grain haulers had to be careful. Most of the wagons were pulled by teams of mules, and men were regularly kicked, stomped, crushed, and mauled by the cantankerous animals. Some mule skinners overcame this problem by sharpening both ends of an iron spoke from an old buggy wheel. Carrying this with them, they would hold it out when the animals attempted a squeeze job, and if one began kicking, would floor the animal with a hard blow behind the ear. Men most feared working with teams raised from wild mustang mares. Trying to place a harness on them and then attach jerk lines, they were often kicked as they walked behind the team. With long hooves, mules could inflict heavy damage. Even a glancing blow could cut through a heavy leather hat and open a hole in a man's skull. Men kicked by mules often did not die immediately. Realizing how badly they were injured, they would sometimes hitch a team and drive or be driven twenty miles to the nearest doctor. Sometimes under chloroform anesthesia, sometimes not, they would have bone splinters picked out of their brain and a flap of skin sewed in place over the hole in their skull. With little more than three weeks' rest, they would have to return to work. Then one day they would begin complaining of a bad headache and fall over dead.[44]

In addition to being maimed and killed by mules, men were often hurt while driving a load of grain sacks. Not only were crashes and collisions involving one or more wagons common, but serious accidents also occurred when loads shifted, end boards broke, axles cracked, teams bolted, and deep ruts caused wagons to lurch and toss drivers forward into the wagon wheels. Men thrown from their wagons and knocked cold would lie in the road until a passerby found them. Men whose arms were broken in accidents often had no choice but to continue on to the loading docks, unload their wagons, then drive themselves to the nearest doctor to have their arms set. Even standing on the docks while unloading grain could be dangerous. Men stepping into a coiled rope would become entangled and pulled into the water as a steamer barge drifted out and either drown or lose a leg. Hundreds of grain haulers were injured and killed every fall and winter in these accidents, most of which went unreported. But some were so spectacular that they earned headlines in local newspapers. "MANGLED CABEZA," began one account in the *Chico Enterprise*. "TERRIBLE," shouted another. "Hubbard A. Sublette . . . about three miles east of Vacaville . . . was thrown from a wagon loaded with sheaves of grain, and in his descent he fell upon an upright pitchfork, the tines running entirely through his body." A headline in the *Napa County Reporter* screamed "ACCIDENT," and announced:

> On last Thursday a teamster whose name our reporter failed to learn while coming over the grade near the summit between Napa and Berryessa, let his team get out of the track, and the team and wagon went over the grade. The wagon was heavily loaded with wheat. The team and wagon went down a distance of about twenty-five feet. The horses were very much injured, and the wagon nearly ruined. The driver, by some unknown means, escaped without injury.

Of an accident near Germantown in Butte County, the *Colusa Sun* reported how Edward Pieper, an employee of Eppinger and Company, was thrown from a wagon as the team bolted. "He clung to the singletree and was dragged about a hundred feet, when he let go and fell under the wheels, one going over his breast and another his neck, killing him instantly."[45]

§a

Field hands offered few protests about their circumstances, for the most part accepting danger and tragedy as just part of the job. But in return for their willingness to risk life and limb they demanded their pay on time and in full. Paydays were rarely simple affairs, however. Before they were paid, those employed on Hugh Glenn's wheat farm had to clear their debts with the bookkeeper-cashier at the Jacinto store. This often resulted in quite a surprise, as the cashier would first check the time cards foremen kept on each worker, and then look through the books of the various local businesses to determine if a man owed anything to the company store, saloon, or hotel. If he did, that amount would be subtracted from his paycheck. Frequently, men discovered that they owed more than they were due. But even if this were not the case, men sometimes had a hard time collecting. After all debts were deducted, the men received not cash or a check, but a draft drawn on a Sacramento bank; if they wanted to cash this draft for its full value, they had to travel to Sacramento, a distance of seventy miles. Since most men did not have the time or means to make the long trip, they had no choice but to sell their checks back to Glenn's bookkeeper-cashier at a discount of 10 percent, an arrangement that earned the bookkeeper a tidy sum of about $150 a month. As a general rule, after paying their bills and subtracting the cash discount, men did not have sufficient funds to leave the Glenn farm. Instead, they would have to go back to work and wait until the next payday.[46]

Men hated the arrangement. They believed it unfair and exploitative, and many grew angry and resentful. Dr. Glenn's "M.D" they said, did not stand for

"Medical Doctor," but rather for "Mule Driver." Pushed particularly hard during the 1880 threshing season, they grew more resentful when he told them, "Boys, I want you to hurry up all you can. I am paying twenty dollars an hour for interest [on borrowed money for wages]." Two years later, they were further angered by Glenn's labor practices upon learning that the wheat baron had promised his foremen a huge cash bonus rumored to be ten thousand dollars if they pushed the men hard enough to meet the unheard-of goal of harvesting one million bushels of wheat. Determined to get their due, the men struck for higher wages and won a raise from $1.50 to $1.80 per day. But that did not settle the matter. Over time, these extraordinary practices took a toll on Glenn's reputation and ultimately, they led to his demise.[47]

Huram Miller was an old friend of Glenn's from Missouri who, arriving in California in 1874, had worked for Glenn first in the fields, then running the company store at Jacinto for a time. In January 1883, Glenn fired his bookkeeper for drunkenness and Miller returned to Jacinto to take the fired man's place. But before Miller's arrival, Glenn's new mistress, known variously as Carrie B. Posten, Miss Posten, and "The Rosebud," had moved in with Glenn and taken charge of the paycheck deductions, quickly enriching herself by strictly enforcing the 10 percent rebate system and pocketing most of the rebates. Almost immediately, Miller clashed with Miss Posten over these matters and offered to resign. Glenn interceded and asked him to stay, but nevertheless supported his lover's call for a larger discount rate. "I told them that I supposed they wanted me to get more money from the laborers by way of discount," Miller later testified. "Miss Posten said that was just what it meant and that she wanted me to work for her interest . . . and not so much for the interest of the men."[48]

Animosity between Miller and Posten continued to build until the evening of February 9, when Miller arrived for dinner at Glenn's mansion drunk and insulted Posten in Glenn's presence. According to Miller's later testimony, this enraged the wheat baron, who imprisoned the bookkeeper in an upstairs room and beat him severely, as an armed Posten monitored the proceedings. Miller also claimed that Glenn then threatened to kill him if he told anyone what happened and ordered Miller to cease all mention of the discounted pay system. This was their last conversation, as Miller left Jacinto immediately.[49]

For several days, Miller sulked around Colusa County before returning to Jacinto supposedly to sell all his possessions so that he could leave the area permanently. But on the morning of February 17, Miller spotted Glenn standing on the porch of the camp's two-story frame hotel and walked up behind him carrying a shotgun. What next happened is the source of much disagreement, both among contemporaries and subsequent historians. According to press accounts, Miller aimed his weapon at Glenn and fired one barrel from a distance of about ten feet, deliberately assassinating the wheat baron with a blast of No. 12 goose shot just above the right ear. But according to some trial testimony and Miller himself, Glenn attempted to wrestle Miller's gun away from him as they met. In the struggle, Miller had accidentally shot Glenn; in this scenario, Glenn's death was not murder but manslaughter—an accident.[50]

As the hotel keeper and bartender bandaged and carried Glenn inside, another employee hitched a nearby buggy and drove to Willows for a doctor. Eight other men led by farm superintendent R. M. Cochran armed themselves with rifles and took off on horseback in pursuit of Miller, who had fled on foot. In a wheat field about a half-mile west of Jacinto, they caught up with Miller and shot him through the right leg. Miller was immediately taken to Willows, and from there to Colusa, the county seat, where he was held without bail. At the time of his capture, Miller supposedly told Glenn's men, "Boys, you won't blame me as much as you do when you hear it all. I have been treated like a dog—yea, worse."[51]

Dr. Hugh Glenn died that night, apparently without regaining consciousness. He was fifty-eight years old. Obituaries stressed his key role in developing the wheat industry and agriculture in the upper Sacramento Valley. A typical lament stressed: "It seems one of the most inscrutable mysteries of Divine Providence that the life of the best and noblest so often be sacrificed by the most worthless." But these sentiments were not shared by Glenn's men, who regarded him as a ruthless, aristocratic land gobbler. If he could have used slaves, they said, he would have done so. Plenty felt Glenn got exactly what he deserved.[52]

Even so, everyone from Jacinto accompanied the coffin to Willows on February 20, in what newspapers described as the largest assembly in the area since the Gold Rush. Farmers, businessmen, and politicians including Governor George Perkins, cattle and land baron Charles Lux, and other California dignitaries attended Glenn's burial at Mountain View Cemetery in Oakland. Carrie Posten was notably absent. Miller's trial did not begin until June 23, a delay caused largely by the difficulty of seating jurors at harvest time. After two weeks, the trial ended in a hung jury because Miller managed to portray Glenn as a womanizing, ruthless employer who had beaten him badly.

Not until a second trial concluding on October 21 was Miller convicted of premeditated murder and sentenced to life in Folsom Prison. By that time, Glenn's friends had become so angered by the attacks directed against him that they embarked on an eight-year campaign to memorialize him and wipe from the records any mention of him as an oppressive and hated employer. They succeeded in the fall of 1891, when the state legislature created a new county, splitting off the northern section of Colusa and naming it Glenn County. Ironically, the honor came just nine months after Huram Miller was paroled from Folsom, his petition strengthened by the signatures of 135 citizens of Colusa (now Glenn) County.[53]

Nowhere did Glenn's memorials mention that his men suffered under a discount pay system, that many hated the wheat baron, or that a former field hand and close friend had murdered him in large part for what he had done to his workers. Also omitted from the memorial was another pertinent fact, one that is essential for charting the course of field hands on the wheat farms at this time, and that surely also contributed to worker discontent. Field hands on Glenn's farm had been among the first to be replaced by a combined harvester. This had happened during the 1880 harvest, when Glenn brought up a new combine from Stockton, tested it for several weeks, and pronounced it "a charm."[54]

Convinced that he could considerably reduce harvest costs by switching to combines, Glenn sent a thresher by riverboat to Stockton the following year, where the Houser and Hines Agricultural Works converted it from a stationary threshing machine to a combine. Drawn by thirty-two mules hitched four abreast and powered by two drive wheels weighing one thousand pounds each, the new

FIGURE 21. Sacramento Valley, ca. 1890. By the 1890s, horse- and mule-drawn combined harvesters had reduced the size of harvest and threshing crews from twenty-one or more men to four or five. Courtesy of the California State Library.

machine saved considerably on labor. With just one combine, Glenn had been able to eliminate six stackers, three pitchers, one straw buck, an engineer, a boiler tender, and several assistants, including the two tank tenders, from the normal complement of threshing crew members. Lowering harvest costs from three dollars to $1.75 per acre during the 1882 season, Glenn replaced an entire platoon of field hands with just a few combines.[55]

৯৯

Several years earlier, field hands around Stockton had encountered the first modern combines. Most accounts credit Stockton implement builders Matteson and Williamson with ending the brief reign of the "traveling harvester" in 1876, when the company built the Centennial combine. A cumbersome, five-ton machine, the Centennial combine was based on a patented design acquired years earlier from rival implement builders Marvin and Thurston. Field hands cut the grain just as they did with an ordinary header. An apron then carried the grain to a separator mounted on the right-hand side of a platform behind the cutting bars. Threshing "on the move," the Centennial combine eliminated most of the men who had previously tended the thresher. Now, grain poured into sacks that men sewed shut and dropped on the ground. Wagons followed at any time, carrying the wheat to a central stack. There were no header wagon drivers or sack stackers.[56]

Manufactured with interchangeable parts that lowered the cost of maintenance, the Centennial combine required just four or five men to operate—a driver, lever-tender, sack-sewer, a man with a pitchfork to keep the apparatus from clogging, and a roustabout to fill in as needed. Cutting a nine-foot swath, one Centennial combine harvested fourteen hundred acres that year without any problems. This inspired several other implement manufacturers to build their own versions. Each had progressively larger cutting bars of twelve to twenty-two feet, cut between twenty-two and thirty-six acres per day, and required teams of twenty to thirty-five horses or mules. One of these new designs, by Daniel Houser and David Young of Durham's Ferry, united a header and separator in a single unit. Drawn by fourteen horses and cutting a sixteen-foot-wide swath, it harvested 640 acres near Farmington, also with a four-man crew. After six years of testing, two Houser combines worked the 1884 season; fifty-six were in operation the following season. Another combine model, manufactured by Stockton banker-turned–implement builder L. U. Shippee, was pushed, not pulled, by a team of twelve horses, weighed only two and a half tons, cut a twelve-foot wide swath, and required only five men, the extra hand being employed as insurance to prevent the machine from clogging. But these were hardly the only combines in operation. As news of the Centennial combine and Shippee machine spread, dozens of San Joaquin Valley wheat farmers and inventors scavenged parts from wrecked threshers and headers, bolted them onto frames, and added cleaners and drive wheels to create their own custom combines. After 1882, a dozen different manufacturers produced the machines in Stockton and San Leandro. Most were pushed by teams, not pulled. Their utility was settled at the September 20, 1883, California State Fair, when, in a trial witnessed by two hundred farmers, a Shippee combine pushed by ten mules bested a Houser combine and a Powell combine, each pulled by fourteen mules. In October 1885, the Stockton Combined Harvester and Agricultural Works and the Houser Combine Works merged into one gigantic operation in an attempt to corner the market. By 1898, they had manufactured between five hundred and six hundred combines. The first of these appeared in Colusa County on June 2, 1889, where it harvested and threshed a field near Germantown.[57]

Combines cut the size of an average threshing crew from twenty-one or twenty-two men to just four or five—a pilot, teamster, crew captain, and sacker or two. On some models, two or three men handled all of the work, a phenomenal savings in labor. Further efficiencies were achieved by running a team of grain haulers behind the combines, eliminating the teams of stackers who had once carried grain away from stationary threshers. Yet for all these changes, very few field hands protested against combines, went on strike, or sabotaged them. Quite the contrary, many hailed the machines because they eradicated the most odious threshing tasks. Men who had once toiled long hours beneath the hot sun now sat under umbrellas or rode in canvas doghouses. Combines also enclosed the separator and delivered the chaff and straw to within a few inches of the ground so that no dust choked and bothered the men or the horses.

Piloting a combine was no easy task. Some men used a long whip, reaching out to the lead mules and flicking the rumps of any slack "hay burners." A few carried a box of smooth stones about the size of a bird's egg and tossed them underhand at the collar harness of any slow-moving animals. Around Rio Vista, drivers began using BB guns to pep up loafing animals, firing shots from one hand while holding the lines of twenty-six animals in the other hand. But most drivers simply re-

FIGURE 22. In the Tulare Lake basin and elsewhere in the San Joaquin Valley, steam-powered combines supplanted headers and horse-drawn and mule-powered combines in the early twentieth century. Photograph ca. 1900. Courtesy of the Huntington Library, San Marino, California.

sorted to shouts and commands and a language that was colorful and got results. "It was a mixture of handed-down Mississippi river boat, Civil War, mining, water front and 'mule license' accumulated vocabulary," wrote agricultural journalist F. Hal Higgins. "The user prided himself on an unabridged flow of vocal prodding of his mules that would last a long full breath with no repetition of words."[58]

Driving combines was dangerous, and there was plenty of opportunity to be maimed or killed. Accidents caused by the teams of horses and mules were common. The animals could become startled and bolt, or the combine could hit a bump; either way, men would be thrown to the ground and run over by the pusher team. "Horrible Death by a Combine," shouted an August 6, 1885, *Stockton Independent* account of a gruesome accident that took the life of teamster Charles Mosher on James Barnhardt's ranch about three miles north of Stockton.

Mr. Mosher was driving twenty-three mules, attached to a Houser harvester, when the animals became unmanageable and ran away, dragging the heavy harvester after them. When the mules stampeded, three men who were on the machine, were thrown to the ground, but were not injured. A few seconds afterward Mosher, who was in the driver's seat, fell among the mules, and before he could extricate himself from his dangerous position, one of the front wheels of the harvester passed over him, crushing his shoulders and skull in a shocking manner and killing him instantly. Two of the mules were also drawn under the harvester and crushed to death, and the machine was badly damaged. Dr. Young, the Coroner, and his deputy, W. K. Richards, went to the scene of the accident and took charge of the mangled remains of the unfortunate man and brought them to the morgue in this city. The deceased was a native of New York, and was 41 years of age at the time of his death.[59]

Just in the course of bumping over the fields, no matter how careful or attentive they were, combine operators would bang a shin, bump a forehead, or mash a toe. The most frequent accidents happened when a man placed his hand on a gear or drive belt and had a finger ripped off. But while it was virtually impossible not to suffer lacerations, scrapes, and bruises, or to have close calls with wheels and gears, men unanimously preferred riding combines to working on traditional threshing operations. Frank Latta later recalled that as soon as combines appeared, "It was impossible to hire a crew of men to work on a stationary outfit."[60]

What happened to displaced field hands was hardly of much concern to most bonanza wheat farmers, who had little choice but to integrate the new machines into their operations quickly. Years of overcropping, shallow plowing, and farming the same fields without allowing them to lay fallow, rotating in new crops, or using fertilizers had exhausted the soil and caused yields to decline. Unable to increase production, growers scrutinized their costs, looking for other ways to improve their profit margins. Combines cut, threshed, and sacked between twenty and forty acres per day, and with drastically reduced crews, saved from forty to eighty dollars a day in wages. According to advertisements from the Stockton Combined Harvester and Agricultural Works, the largest combine maker in California, the Shippee combine reduced harvest costs to less than three cents per bushel, "placed the grain in the sack at less cost than the old system," saved three bushels an acre over and above heading and threshing "sufficient to pay the cost of harvesting," and prevented the loss of grain that usually remained on the ground when a stack was threshed. "It will pay for itself in one season's run," promised one advertisement.[61]

As they experimented with the combines, growers further examined labor costs. In one widely published statement, Merced wheat grower C. H. Huffman reported that, after firing his threshing and harvest crews and switching to a combine, harvest expenses declined by 75 percent. In another commonly cited testimonial, Tulare grain grower D. Spangler cut his harvest expenses by one-half to two-thirds after switching to a combine. Other farmers commonly reported harvesting by combine at $1.50 to $1.75 an acre, sometimes as low as one dollar an acre, compared to three to four dollars under the previous header and stationary threshing system. The best accounting from Colusa County in 1889 and 1890 found profits of $13.15 to $17.14 per acre, based on a tidewater price of 1.4 cents per pound, with the main variable being yield per acre, which fluctuated from 939 pounds per acre in 1890 to 1,224 pounds per acre the previous year. By 1884, combines had replaced headers and stationary threshing operations on about fifty thousand acres of wheat in the San Joaquin Valley. So popular were the new machines that five years later, as wheat production topped forty million bushels and California became the second leading wheat-growing state, the *Sacramento Bee* observed of harvesting and threshing around Lodi, "The old style thrashing [*sic*] machine will soon be a thing of the past. There are only about two or three running in this vicinity."[62]

But the prediction was premature. Outside of the San Joaquin Valley, where the 3.5 million-bushel crop of 1883 pushed farmers to adopt combines quickly, a more complex situation prevailed. For most of the 1880s, large-scale wheat growers were the only ones who could afford combines. A new Harvest King combine with a fourteen-foot cutting bar, for example, cost fifteen hundred dollars in 1893. And depending on the size of their combine, farmers also needed enough grain-hauling wagons ($105 to $125 each) to keep the work flowing, as well as between seven and eighteen teams of horses or mules (at twenty-eight to fifty dollars per team), which made for considerable additional expense. But within a few years, the advantages of combines became so apparent that groups of eight to ten farmers began pooling their funds and borrowing from friends, neighbors, and relatives to buy combines, each member of the group then contributing a team of animals. In this way, combines steadily spread from the bonanza wheat districts into outlying areas, where small-scale wheat farmers earned additional income hiring out their machines to neighboring farms.[63]

Combines harvested and threshed about 10 percent of California's wheat crop in 1880, and about 25 percent in the early 1890s. By 1913, Holt Manufacturing Company, which had replaced Houser as the dominant manufacturer of combines, claimed that 90 percent of California's wheat crop was being harvested by about three thousand Holt combines.[64]

♨

Even as men were gradually adjusting to horse-powered combines, the last and most sensational episode in the mechanization of grain harvesting was unfolding. Beginning in the 1880s, field hands had repeatedly heard rumors of monstrous steam-powered tractors, literally "iron horses" that worked twenty-four hours a day, drastically reduced expenses, and eliminated the need for large numbers of mules, men, and horses. But no one saw any working models until January 1871, when the Tide Land Reclamation Company imported a three-wheeled vehicle known as the Thompson road steamer from England. Weighing two tons, rated at twelve-horse power, and running on rubber tires fitted with steel treads, it consumed a half-ton of coal per day while pulling loads as large as thirty tons at speeds of two to six miles per hour. It was cumbersome, bulky, and problematic. As one field hand summed up: like a "steamboat hunting for water."[65]

The following June, a successor called the Hydesteam engine, built by Marysville inventor John Hyde, attracted considerable curiosity but also proved too ponderous. Four years later, field hands at first laughed as Hyde's improved machine arrived at Sumner Station in east Bakersfield, then grumbled in amazement as it was fired up and made its way west through town, followed by almost the entire population of Bakersfield, to haul tools and perform various tasks on William B. "Billy" Carr's Kern Island Farm, about seven miles to the southwest. Eventually, the machine was consigned to the freighting business between the railroad terminus and the mines of Inyo County, where it promptly replaced an entire crew of mule skinners and created new opportunities for those able to master its new technology. On large land-clearing projects near Bakersfield, a single Hyde steam engine began doing work normally requiring dozens of men driving

"Fresno scrapers" (highly improved slip scrapers with runners and long handles used for dumping loads). Towing a bar of railroad iron, the wagon ripped out weeds and, with an immense rake, gathered them into piles for burning. A single steam engine with a gang of plows attached tilled eight to ten furrows at once, averaging about thirty acres per ten hours "without turmoil or trouble and with a 3rd of the expense that would have attended the same operation if performed by 15 pairs of horses and the number of men necessary to manage them."[66]

In 1880, field hands in the northern Sacramento Valley were even more flabbergasted to see a three-wheeled, San Jose–built steam engine towing six header wagons, each fully loaded with three hundred sacks of wheat, on regular runs between Willows and the Princeton River landing. A seventh wagon in the train held 615 gallons of water and one and a half tons of coal for the engine. Operating flawlessly and hauling thirty-five tons at three miles per hour—about twice the weight that a team could haul—these machines so impressed local growers the following year that they bought six other steam wagons to haul wheat between Orland, Riceville, Olympia, and the McIntosh River landing. Running wagons day and night, with "an immense and flaming light," a number of growers predicted that they would soon be able to eliminate nine out of ten field hands assigned to grain hauling duties.[67]

During the abnormally hot summer of 1885, field hands were having trouble finishing the harvest because so many animals on each combine crew were dying from heatstroke. To overcome this difficulty, Tulare County farmer George S. Berry began building a self-propelled steam combine. Stripping down and redesigning a twenty-five-horsepower straw-burning Mitchell and Fisher steam boiler, Berry mounted it on a frame, placed five-foot-wide drive wheels in front, and added smaller steering wheels to the rear. The device was large and cumbersome, measuring thirty-eight feet wide and nearly just as long. Seeing it run backwards, with the rear wheels doing the steering, local field hands regarded it as a joke. But a year later, as the wheat crop in Tulare County neared harvest, Berry decided to test his contraption. Everyone for miles around took the day off from work and joined people from all parts of the state to watch the demonstration. At sunrise, Berry started his engine and began cutting a twenty-foot-wide swath. Moving at about three miles per hour—about twice as fast as a horse-drawn combine—he kept at it all day, and by nightfall had harvested, threshed, and sacked 160 acres of grain. Spectators had witnessed the first steam-propelled farm machine, forerunner of the modern tractor, and a world record for a single day's combine harvesting; those who had bet against the "unwieldy abortion," as some labeled it, ended up losing large amounts of cash.[68]

The following year, field hands on the neighboring farm of J. J. Cairns began working with another steam combine built by Berry. With the cutting bar extended to forty feet, it cut 160 acres a day but still required a large crew—an engineer, two firemen, two water bucks, a sack-sewer, a sack tender, a separator tender, a steersman, and a grain hauler. By 1888, men employed by Merced wheat farmer Frank Archibald, Livingston farmer John Blivens, and Marysville farmer Frank Curtis also began harvesting with Berry steam combines, as did dozens of others supplied with Berry combines built under license by the Benicia Agricultural Works. Soon, Daniel Best of San Leandro bought out Berry's design and began manufacturing an improved steam-powered combine. Although models with cutting bars ranging in size up to twenty-five feet were available, he and rival implement manufacturer Benjamin Holt sold mainly smaller machines with fourteen-foot-long cutting bars. Although expensive at between three thousand and five thousand dollars each, when measured against the cost of thirty-two mules or horses required to pull a combine plus their upkeep, farmers calculated that they could raise much of the price of a steam combine by selling their animals. And since the smaller machines only required a crew of about seven men—a driver, fireman, cutter bar operator, two grain haulers, water hauler, and a coal, wood, or straw hauler—a wheat grower could also expect to reduce his wage bill substantially and the cost of feeding and housing field hands.[69]

Steam combines, like their horse- and mule-powered predecessors, were not without problems. Despite wire-mesh smoke guards and other devices designed to reduce sparks and embers, they presented a great fire hazard. And since some would only burn coal or wood, tenders had to be constantly nearby, as neither fuel was readily available. Nor would they work well in the early morning if there was dew on the grain or fog or mist in the air. These shortfalls somewhat blunted the spread of combines, restricting them to the hot, flat interior valleys. In fact, only on the west side of the San Joaquin Valley, where a huge fleet of "land dreadnoughts" worked the reclaimed Tulare Lake bottom, did steam combines completely dominate the wheat harvest. Otherwise, they offered less dramatic gains over their horse-drawn cousins. While steam-powered combines did not reduce labor requirements as sensationally as their inventors hoped, they did considerably increase the rate of work. For example, a Holt combine with a twenty-seven-foot cutting bar could harvest twelve hundred sacks of grain per day, roughly three times that of a horse-drawn combine; a Best machine could thresh and sack about one thousand bushels per day. However, these advantages required many years before they produced enough savings to offset the huge initial cost. As a result, very few field hands immediately began working on steam-powered combines. Out of about 2,060 combine crews in the late 1890s, only sixty labored on steam-powered machines, most of them on the very largest San Joaquin Valley wheat farms. Whatever the comparative advantages of horse versus steam power, the advantages of combines were well proven. By 1900 they accounted for 67 percent of the state's grain harvest.[70]

≈

But even as they basked in the glow of their new status as tenders of machines and semipermanent workers, many field hands were coming to understand that their lives as laborers had gotten about as good as it would get. In the early 1880s, grain brokers in Argentina, Russia, Canada, India, and Australia unleashed a flood of wheat on the world market, driving the price below $1.50 per central. In 1883, the price of wheat fell below $1.50 for the first time; by 1890, it was down to $1.33 per central. Wheat prices—and the California wheat industry—never recovered. Old combine drivers and their crewmen were forced to supplement their income by moving from the San Joaquin Valley to new locations like Ventura County to thresh other crops, like lima beans.[71]

Ventura County lima bean harvesters were, in fact, the only field hands other than grain harvesters who successfully mechanized. The whole process had developed quickly. Initially little more than a barley and bean growing region, Ventura County emerged as a center of lima bean production after 1875, when Jefferson Crane planted a crop that yielded more than one ton per acre. Selling for as much as five to six cents a pound, the crop returned a handsome one hundred dollars per acre, although the average was more like fifty dollars, far more than the twenty-dollars-per-acre return for barley, and set off a lima bean planting frenzy. With financing from banker Achilles Levy, farmers built a wharf at Port Hueneme and began shipping lima beans out by the boatload. By 1890, nearly forty thousand acres of lima beans were in production. But as production skyrocketed to five hundred thousand sacks in 1902, growers confronted a bottleneck when they began harvesting their crop in the fall. At first, field hands pulled the plants by hand, then separated the beans from the vines by beating them with flails and tossing them into the air. When this method proved too slow, they attached two six-foot knives to the back of a sled and drove it through the fields, cutting down the crop. Left to dry, the beans were then gathered and, beginning in 1883, fed into modified grain threshers. Following the same procedure as their counterparts in the bonanza wheat fields, lima bean threshers harvested, sacked, and hauled hundreds of tons of lima beans well into September, with the bulk of the crop being threshed on contract by custom outfits traveling between farms.[72]

Lima bean threshing provided little refuge for obsolete wheat threshers. By the time bonanza wheat farming went into decline around the turn of the century, it was just one segment of agriculture. As California dropped from the second-largest wheat producing state in 1890 to sixth in 1900, and wheat production dropped from a high of forty million bushels in 1889 to a low of six million bushels in 1909, more and more men worked as stoop laborers in intensively cultivated vegetable farms, vineyards, orchards, and fruit ranches across the state.[73]

This agricultural industry had actually existed since the Gold Rush, but it had expanded rapidly following completion of the transcontinental railroad in 1869. Entrepreneur farmers near Vacaville, Sacramento, Fresno, Placerville, and in other communities along the path of the new transport lines began cultivating irrigated fruits and vegetables not for a local market, but with an eye on exporting specialty crops like peaches, apricots, pears, and oranges—crops that eastern farmers could not produce with the same degree of output and efficiency. To protect their crops from natural and man-made threats, fruit and vegetable growers developed complex protective mechanisms—including some of the earliest efforts at frost control—the likes of which had never been seen before. Besides curbing insect infestations, increasing yields, ensuring quality, and perfecting marketing strategies, the new fruit and vegetable farms also sought to secure a labor supply. People were needed in far greater numbers than ever before, and more than any other group, Chinese immigrants filled that need. In doing so, they established themselves as the ideal against which all subsequent farmworkers would be measured and, with few exceptions, found lacking.[74]

FIGURE 23. Chinese wheat threshers (the doghouse crew), San Joaquin Valley, ca. 1878. Courtesy of the Huntington Library, San Marino, California, C. C. Pierce Collection.

BOOK FOUR

Immigrants from the East

The employers of the Chinese laborers invariably
agree that they are excellent workmen. They never
have, like whites, a Sunday spree and a "blue
Monday." They are always "on hand" at the time
agreed upon; always sober and industrious. . . .
And they prove most trustworthy laborers.
    —*Charles L. Brace*

They like the Chinaman because he is their slave,
and they can sit in the shade and drive him as the old
Southern overseer did the negro in the cotton field.
    —*J. W. Gally*

If you can get them this year, you can get them next
year and the year after, if you treat them well and pay
them. They become attached to your place and stay
with you.
    —*George Roberts*

Irish fill the almshouses and prisons and orphan
asylums, Italians are among the most dangerous of
men, Jews are unclean and ignorant. . . . There are
few Chinamen in jails and none in the poor houses.
There are no Chinese tramps or drunkards.
    —*Lee Chew*

In the celery and asparagus and vegetable fields [the
Chinese] were eternally chattering of the time when
they would be able to buy . . . enough to secure ease
and plenty back home.
    —*Forrest Crissey*

Chinese . . . readily move, like armies, come when
called for, and depart when their mission is
accomplished.
    —*'Pacific Rural Press'*

They will sleep on a board, cook with a brazier, live
upon rice and tea, desiccated vegetables . . . and eat
the very best they can.
    —*Benjamin S. Brooks*

The Chinese labor machine . . . is perfect.
    —*'Fresno Republican'*

CHAPTER ELEVEN

Trustworthy Laborers

Chinese Infiltration into

Irrigated Agriculture

Early in August 1868, Presbyterian minister and sometime journalist Augustus W. Loomis visited a hop plantation along the American River ten miles east of Sacramento. He was touring California farming districts on assignment for *Overland Monthly*, the leading regional magazine in the Far West. The hop harvest was in full swing, and Loomis counted between fifty and seventy pickers, "in the garb of the eastern Asiatics, working steadily and noiselessly on from morning till night, gathering, curing, and sacking the crop." In March 1869, in an extremely influential, widely read article entitled "How Our Chinamen Are Employed," he expanded his observations, reporting how "on many ranches all the laborers are people whose muscles were hardened on their little farms in China, and who there learned those lessons of industry, patience, and economy which render them of incalculable service."[1]

Wherever they went in the agricultural districts of California at this time, journalists found Chinese field hands. North of San Francisco in the Sonoma Valley, they were spotted clearing fields and hillsides of chaparral, hacking away all the wood down to the roots, piling debris, and hauling it to market to be sold as fuel. South of San Francisco in the Santa Clara Valley, twenty Chinese were observed tending a cider mill, running machinery that turned out little strawberry baskets, sorting and boxing apples, picking apples, and gathering grapes. Landing near present-day Seal Beach in Southern California in February, a crew of Chinese from San Francisco attracted considerable attention as they went to work cleaning and maintaining irrigation ditches for the Anaheim Union Water Company, which had taken over from the Los Angeles Vineyard Society. Earning $97.17 each per month, plus board, they proved so invaluable that, when not needed, the water company hired them out at ten dollars per day to farmers. A much larger group also earned extensive notice and commentary when they flooded into the Pajaro Valley. Newspapers reported they were so desperate that they worked for promissory notes redeemed only after growers sold their crops. It was the same on the

FIGURE 24. Chinese onion seed harvesters, Morse seed farm, Santa Clara County, ca. 1902. Photograph by Mrs. Alice A. Hare. Courtesy of the California Historical Society.

big wheat farms, where the Chinese worked with a combination of stoicism and military organization. "John [Chinaman] spreads a dirty tent in some corner of the field near water, sleeps on the ground . . . and lives on rice of his own cooking, and will soon be indispensable to our wheat-growers," wrote wheat magnate Horace Davis, perhaps the most influential of all commentators on the California grain industry. It was not an isolated opinion. "Were it not for the Chinamen in the state," observed one promotional tract, "one-half of our luxuriant harvest would annually rot in the fields for want of hands to gather it."[2]

On the basis of such observations, many chroniclers of the farmworker saga have concluded that shortly after arriving, the Chinese immediately dispersed to farms throughout the state and took control of labor on California's fruit and vegetable farms. "Most of the California grain was plowed and planted, harvested and bound by the Chinese. Two-thirds of all vegetables were cultivated by them," wrote one scholar. From these claims has arisen a central myth of the farmworker story, one holding that Chinese immigrants moved onto farms by the thousands, took the places of native field hands, and became "the initial foreign-born saviors of California agriculture." By the end of the 1860s, so unfolds this rendition of events, Chinese field hands so dominated agricultural labor that the state's growers were "almost totally dependent" on them and in this way perpetuated the cheap labor market that had developed on the backs of native field hands. According to this claim, "the same rationale of peonage and compulsion" that developed around native field hands was applied to the Chinese. From the Gold Rush forward, so unfolds this analysis, an arrogant attitude toward "inferior" people of color was coupled to a heritage of forced labor and passed along not only to the Chinese but to all subsequent ethnic immigrant groups.[3]

Certainly, these theories hold true for at least some groups of Chinese. But like so many ideas advanced about California farmworkers, this one is mostly untrue. In no segment of commercial agriculture were Chinese laborers ever a majority—or even a significant minority—at any time. They seldom dominated a harvest, controlled only one or two farming districts, and monopolized labor in just a single crop—strawberries. But there is no doubt that they played a crucial role. Their journey to the farms and fields was far more complex than has been described, and it dates back farther than most historians realize—to before the emergence of bonanza wheat farming and the beginning of commercial agriculture, to pre–Gold Rush California.

૪૭

Even before they arrived in California, Chinese peasants attracted attention as potential farm laborers. They appear to have been discussed for the first time in the spring of 1848, when a merchant who had once lived in China foresaw the crucial role that an adequate supply of labor would play in unlocking California's agricultural potential. The merchant wrote to U.S. Consul Thomas O. Larkin, explaining that "any number of . . . agriculturalists and servants can be obtained . . . willing to sell their services for a period to pay their passage across the Pacific." Eight months later, as the first contingents of Chinese disembarked in San Francisco, they again attracted attention, this time as a way to hold down farm wages. "If white labor is too high for agriculture," wrote a correspondent for the *Alta California*, "laborers on contract may be brought from China, or elsewhere, who if well treated will work faithfully for low wages." Even before California became a state, Chinese immigrants were seen as an excellent source of farm labor, useful both for keeping white field hands in line and replacing dragooned Indians. The Chinese, however, had other ideas.[4]

Chinese immigrants at first expressed little interest in fieldwork. Like their midwestern and East Coast predecessors, the adventurers who crossed the Pacific Ocean in the first years of the Gold Rush intended to earn their fortune and return home. In pursuit of that goal, eight out of ten headed for the gold diggings, where they soon constituted the largest single ethnic group. But it was not just the lure of quick wealth that kept the Chinese away from fieldwork. There was also the matter of the background of the two of ten who did not make a beeline for the mines. Most of these early Chinese immigrants were merchants and members of the gentry. Quiet and deferential men, they sought respectable business opportunities and were completely unsuited for—and uninterested in—hard labor. For them, farmwork was unthinkable.[5]

Not until 1852, when Chinese began pouring off the clipper ships into San Francisco, did people of the type required by the state's farmers begin to arrive in large numbers. Most of these immigrants were peasant farmers from Kwangtung province, particularly the barren hill district of nearby T'oishan, and the relatively well-off but crowded Pearl River Delta. Like the adventurers and gentry who had preceded them, they also had a tradition of emigration, mainly to the British colony of Hong Kong and the Portuguese colony of Macao. When news of the California Gold Rush reached them, thousands unable to eke out a living in their villages left China seeking *Jinshan* ("Gold Mountain" or "Country of Gold").[6]

When this second wave of Chinese immigrants poured into the state, "bearing long bamboo poles across their shoulders" and wearing "new cotton blouses and baggy breeches . . . slippers or shoes with heavy wooden soles [and] broad-brimmed hats of split bamboo," they seemed perfect candidates for farmwork. In part, this notion was based on the assumption that the Chinese were ill-prepared to do much other than grub work and had to move immediately into agricultural work. And although farmers as a group were naturally receptive to the idea of employing them, farmers of the Sacramento-San Joaquin Delta, in particular, clamored after these contingents. To delta-area farmers, the Chinese seemed more than a source of cheap and abundant labor, more than a way to hold the line on wages. They were a blessing that arrived at exactly the right time.[7]

Thick with malaria-carrying mosquitoes, crisscrossed with unpredictable sloughs and channels, and tangled with dense vegetation, three-fifths of the delta was submerged, and the rest was subject to periodic flooding. But the soil was the best in California—a rich, black, peat soil, running eighteen to forty feet deep —and had already earned fortunes for those delta farmers who had been established at the beginning of the Gold Rush. When the federal government in 1850 passed the Swamp Land Act and announced plans to turn over large portions of delta swampland to California, and the state, in turn, began selling the land, the only obstacle to successful farming seemed to be the large numbers of laborers necessary to drain, dike, clear, and level the area. The labor was going to be extremely unpleasant, as the delta was inhospitable and dangerous to those unfamiliar with its ways. Given the shortage of Indians and the general aversion of whites to fieldwork, many farmers naturally looked to the Chinese. "We have amongst us several thousand of the inhabitants of China . . . ready to . . . settle down and turn our waste lands into beautiful fields," explained the March 3, 1852, *San Joaquin Republican*, "and no better class of men could be chosen to develop the agricultural resources of the Tulare Valley."[8]

In March 1852, state senator George B. Tingley, a Whig from Santa Clara County, introduced a bill to import Chinese reclamation workers. Under this arrangement, farmers proposed to pay for the passage and upkeep of Chinese field hands, who would then be obligated to work until they fulfilled the terms of their agreement. "There is ample field for its [*sic*] employment in draining swamp lands, in cultivating rice, raising silk, or planting tea," argued one senator. "For these special objects, I have no objection to the introduction of contract laborers, provided they are excluded from citizenship; for those staples cannot be cultivated without 'cheap labor'; but for all other branches I would recommend its exclusion." Many confused Tingley's bill with the so-called coolie trade, then still flourishing, in which coolie brokers bought Chinese men at $120 to $170 each in Hong Kong and sold them upon arrival, if still alive, for $350 to $400, to sugar plantation owners in South America and the West Indies. Others protested it as "a system of modified slavery resembling Mexican peonism." California miners were particularly adamant in their opposition, arguing the law would bring thousands of competitors into the already crowded diggings, while at the same time allowing wealthy farmers to develop a monopoly over the best land. "The man who is so simple, or so mole-eyed, as not to see that these would be the first consequences of the measure, is either to be pitied or despised," proclaimed the *Alta California.*[9]

Although passed by the California assembly, Tingley's bill was labeled a "moral evil" by Governor John Bigler and soundly defeated in the Senate. In a state where mining interests still were predominant, agriculture as yet lacked the clout to implement the kind of farm labor importation program that would one day become commonplace. Yet the episode had more than passing significance. Not only was it the second farm labor importation scheme, it also marked the beginning of a controversy over Chinese labor that would fester for a generation before eventually swelling into a virulent form of racism.[10]

But even as the debate raged in the senate, Chinese gangs began working for delta farmer Reuben Kercheval. An Ohio native who had come to California to mine gold in 1849, Kercheval soon abandoned those plans after exhausting his funds and instead joined his uncle, Armstead Runyon, farming a 320-acre plot some twenty miles downstream from Sacramento near present-day Courtland. Because the land was close to the Sacramento River and therefore subject to frequent flooding, Kercheval spent the profits from his first crops erecting a series of flimsy levees. When these were washed away by floods in the spring of 1852, he tried to enlist his neighbors in a cooperative effort to raise the levees. Failing at that, he gathered a crew of Indians and Kanakas and set them to work. But needing more men, he turned to the Chinese.

Taking over a large portion of the work, the Chinese superimposed their levees upon the outer edge of the existing natural levee and constructed twelve miles of barriers, thirteen feet wide at the base and a yard wide at its crest. With no dredges, they used only shovels and wheelbarrows to raise the barrier, obtaining their loads from the land side of the levee because they had no way of scooping sand out of the riverside. Foremen armed with revolvers patrolled the levee crests and prevented men from tossing stumps into their wheelbarrows to fatten the 13.5 cents they earned for every cubic yard of earth they moved. Within one year, at a cost of about twelve thousand dollars, they had completely surrounded Kercheval's farm. During the next three years, as Kercheval planted the dry ground to grapevines and fruit trees, neighbors duplicated these efforts. In this way the Chinese "jest growed" the levees for eighteen miles until they enclosed the entire northern end of Grand Island, creating out of a bog what was probably the most ideally situated and profitable commercial farming district in the entire state.[11]

As they were raising levees for Kercheval on Grand Island, Chinese field hands also moved north into Sonoma County, where they planted four thousand grapevines (possibly the white grape variety Palomino) for William McPherson

Hill's Glen Ellen Winery, and east into the San Joaquin Valley, where they bound and threshed grain on John Wheeler Jones's farm between Stockton and the Stanislaus River, as well as on several other unnamed grain farms. Scattered information clearly indicates they also worked on farms in the prime farming districts of Sacramento, San Joaquin, and Yuba counties during this time. For some reason, the only Chinese that census enumerators officially listed as working on farms in these three counties were cooks—eighteen in Sacramento County, thirty-five in Yuba, and eight in San Joaquin—but newspaper reports clearly identify other Chinese laborers on farms in and around Fresno and San Jose.[12]

It was not long before their work attracted the attention of *California Farmer* editor James L. Warren, a prominent and influential Massachusetts nurseryman and leader of the State Agricultural Society who, in one of his first editorials, enthusiastically endorsed the state's destiny as "a large grower of Cotton, Rice, Tobacco, Sugar, Tea, and Coffee." With Indians dying out and many white immigrants still preoccupied with the diggings, Warren wondered in an 1854 editorial, Who would provide the labor to secure that agricultural destiny?

> At the South, this is the work of the slave, but slavery cannot exist here. California is a Free State—her citizens have spoken it—human progress has uttered it—God has said it. Then where shall the laborers be found? The Chinese! And everything tends to this—those great walls of China are to be broken down and that population, educated, schooled and drilled in the cultivation of these products, are to be to California what the African has been to the south. This is the decree of the Almighty, and man cannot stop it.[13]

From this and other similar writings arose the myth that the Chinese possessed a multitude of physical attributes that, according to one state assemblyman, would allow them "to settle in the Tules and work in the mud among the mosquitoes and frogs." Besides the similarity between the kind of "peasant labor" they had performed in their native China and the work California farmers needed done, growers claimed the Chinese made good candidates for fieldwork for one other reason. It was a well-known "fact," they said, that the Chinese were not as susceptible to malaria as white field hands. Based on this line of thinking, several big swamp reclamation companies made plans in 1856 to import Chinese laborers and put them to work on thirty-six thousand acres of delta land.[14]

Chinese laborers soon attracted the attention of the Los Angeles Vineyard Company, a cooperative of German settlers that was attempting to clear, level, fence, plant, and irrigate half a million grapevines in the dry, sandy land along the banks of the Santa Ana River in Anaheim, twenty-six miles southeast of Los Angeles. In September 1857, the society spent one-third of its expenses attempting to construct a six-mile-long irrigation canal from the Santa Ana River to the colony. To lower subsequent costs, the society employed sixty Mexicans and Indians from the Pala Reservation, paying them fifteen to twenty dollars per month, but according to Mrs. Amalie Frohling, wife of one of Anaheim's founding settlers, the Indians "played cards or slept . . . let the teams stand . . . disregarded the necessary work, let the ground crack after irrigating, and heeded no persuasion, only made merry, play, sleep, dance, feast, steal chickens, do nothing until the last cent was gone." As problems mounted, a committee of society members met on July 23, 1859, to obtain information about Chinese labor. Shortly thereafter, three of the colony's leaders headed to San Francisco and returned with thirty Chinese field hands. Paid eighteen to twenty dollars per month plus room and board, the Chinese were remembered by Mrs. Frohling as "industrious, peaceful, never drunk and . . . cleaner than the Indians." They proved ideal laborers, and several became well known. "Sam, one of the Mongols," recalled Mrs. Frohling, "was in our household for ten years. He spoke only Spanish and was a perfect farmer. He had a great love for horses."[15]

From Los Angeles, Sonoma County, the San Joaquin Valley, and the delta, Chinese farmworkers fanned out into the surrounding countryside. Little is known of their initial movements, but an 1861 legislative committee found that, of fifty thousand Chinese in the state, 1,200 had moved onto the farms. "They work for us; they help us build up our state, by contributing largely to our . . . farming," observed the committee in its report the following year. And although they are curiously unmentioned in any 1863 newspaper accounts, Chinese field hands reappear in the historical record in September 1864, when Benjamin Davis Wilson brought eleven men south from San Francisco to harvest fruit, wine grapes, and citrus at $1.20 per day on his Rancho Santa Anita. A year later, when the Chinese appeared in the Pajaro Valley fifty miles south of San Francisco, newspapers announced the event with great fanfare. "ARRIVAL OF CHINAMEN," shouted the *Pajaro Valley Times* as a contingent of twenty laborers trooped into town on April 28. "Chinamen in the harvest field," echoed the *Monterey Gazette*. The men would help growers overcome a labor shortage and replace Indians who had been demanding two dollars a day, the newspapers explained. Their wages of one dollar a day, added the newspaper, would soon "surely be reduced."[16]

Even more exciting was the arrival of sixty Chinese field hands in the Salinas Valley the following week. Rolling through in a wagon train carrying seven tons of food and equipment, they were headed for Milpitas Rancho. Manuel Luco, owner of the rancho, had hired them through Ah Yuk, a San Francisco Chinese labor contractor, to divert water from the San Antonio River to Big Gulch, near a site by the old mission. But the project proved too much, and after three weeks of digging, they gave up. On the road north, the editor of the *Monterey Gazette* met the "cadaverous looking" crew near San Juan Bautista. Asked why they had quit, the men could only say as rendered by the *Gazette* reporter, "too muchee sand, too muchee workee."[17]

Four months later and one hundred miles to the north, the *Solano Press* reported, again quite breathlessly, that numerous "Celestials," the first of 163 who would enter the fields there that year, were "discovered" in Pleasants Valley, a frost-free, early agricultural district at the base of the coastal mountains west of Vacaville. William Smith and other growers had hired the men to harvest vegetables planted between the rows of young vines and fruit trees. Two weeks after that, the *Pajaro Valley Times* reported, "Loads of Chinamen are arriving almost daily in Watsonville for the past few weeks." Elsewhere, travelers gave equally distorted reports of "armies of Chinese" swarming through the orchards about

Yuba, Lake, and Sonoma counties; in fact, no more than several hundred were employed. Chinese field hands hired to build long runs of mortarless stone walls in Tehama County attracted a considerable amount of admiring commentary. Similar accolades accompanied the Chinese entry into Santa Clara County during the July 1868 grain harvest. "There is a large force of Chinamen employed in our harvest fields, at prices which will be a saving of many thousands of dollars to the farmers of this county," reported the *San Jose Mercury*. "In fact, but for Chinese labor, it would be impossible to secure the present crops, as there are but very few white laborers to be had." One month later, after "a strong force of Celestials" rebuilt a ruptured dam on the Stanislaus River, thereby allowing local farmers to divert water and irrigate their fields, the *Tuolumne City News* credited them with saving all of the orchards and vineyards around Knight's Ferry.[18]

Traveling through the Sacramento Valley at this time researching his book *The New West*, Charles Loring Brace was particularly impressed by certain idiosyncrasies of Chinese custom and behavior. In his characteristic form of literary tourism, he wrote,

> Sometimes I see these Eastern laborers with their broad hats leisurely working in the fruit gardens, as if in a tea-plantation. Sometimes they are binding sheaves behind the American reapers . . . always busy yet never hurried; clean, social, sober, polite, with an expression, it often seems to me, of half contempt for this western hurry and barbarism. I have seen a whole gang, after a day's work on a farm, washing themselves all over with warm water, which they keep ready for their return, as carefully as a company of gentlemen, and I was assured this was their daily habit.[19]

ஐ

By early 1869, the Chinese had earned a reputation for organization, stamina, and stoicism coupled with an unmatched willingness to toil under disagreeable conditions. Admiration for these characteristics focused attention on their labor whenever it was encountered, and was further reinforced by an "exotic" appearance. With their conical, wide-brimmed "high-binder" hats of woven straw and black felt, tight skullcaps, braided queues (pig tails), black and tan trousers, and double-breasted summer coats of blue silk or cotton, Chinese field hands were easily distinguishable from other farmworkers, quickly attracted attention, and often became objects of ridicule. "The Chinaman is not pretty to look at," observed the *St. Helena Star*. Personal habits added to such fears. Anything even slightly sensational—particularly their food, religion, temples, celebrations, and love of firecrackers—also inspired derision. One Ventura resident admitted years later, "I was scared of the Chinese. When you saw a Chinaman you were scared." Coupled with the extensive discussion of the benefits and liabilities of Chinese immigration and the attributes and defects of Chinese as a people, this heightened awareness reinforced the general misimpression that the Chinese were taking over the bulk of farmwork and exerting an overwhelming impact on the countryside.[20]

Hard numbers told a different story. Roughly six out of ten Chinese—about thirty thousand men—still toiled in the mines. Thousands of others found work in San Francisco, where they comprised half of the men in the boot and shoe trade, woolen mills, cigar factories, and the garment industry. Others found employment as domestic servants, became fishermen, opened shops and laundries, or became gamblers or opium salesmen. Only in Tehama County did a majority of the Chinese population (64 percent) work on farms. Of the 15,014 laborers on farms statewide in 1870, only 1,637, or about 11 percent, were Chinese. Counting many of the "unspecified" Chinese laborers as field hands and expanding the definition of farmworkers to include census categories like "garden laborer," "works on farm," and any "laborer" living in a farm household, the total number of Chinese field hands could still not have been above twenty-three hundred, or about 15 percent of the total farm labor force (18 percent if the figures are confined to the six counties where the Chinese farmhands were concentrated).[21]

Measured according to their proportion of the total farm labor force, Chinese field hands were most important in Sacramento, San Mateo, and Alameda counties, where they constituted, 45.4, 25.2, and 24.5 percent of all farmworkers, respectively—mainly on the most productive and rapidly developing row crop farms. By concentrating in certain areas and on particular farms, Chinese field hands multiplied their impact, in some cases, far beyond their numbers. For example, while comprising only 7.9 percent of all field hands in Solano County in 1870, Chinese were fully 25 percent of the farmworkers in Vacaville Township, Solano's principal farming area. Similarly, while they were only 8.3 percent of the population of Tehama County, they comprised the entire labor force in Deer Creek Township, and on Henry Gerke's big, diversified farm. And while, numerically, they were a distant second to the seven hundred European and American-born field hands listed in the census, the 622 Chinese field hands in Sacramento County nonetheless comprised the largest single group of Chinese agricultural laborers anywhere in California. Similar patterns held for Alameda and San Mateo counties, where 350 and 180 Chinese field hands, respectively, comprised 25 percent of the farm labor force in each place. In Santa Clara and Solano counties, Chinese field hands made up 11.6 and 7.9 percent of the farm labor force, respectively, while they accounted for just 4.1 percent in the Sonoma County.[22]

જ્ઞ

Had the Chinese been unavailable, farmers would not have lost any crops or been prevented from developing any agricultural district; at worst they might have had to raise wages or accommodate to local labor shortages. But in one area, that of farm and camp cooks, the Chinese did exert an early, overwhelming influence. Chinese immigrants started working as farm cooks almost as soon as they moved into the rural areas, and over the next half century, they would acquire a well-deserved, almost legendary status as trusted and influential employees. "Every ranch had its Chinese cook who ruled with an iron hand over the ranch kitchen," observed Colusa farmer L. W. Wigmore. Compared to field hands, Chinese farm cooks earned higher wages and led a more stable life. In fact, it was not uncommon for these men to remain with their employers for life—or at least for several decades. There are numerous examples of young men going to work as farm

FIGURE 25. Chinese cook and ranch management, McClung ranch, Kern County, 1888. Photograph by Carleton E. Watkins. Courtesy of Tenneco West.

cooks in the 1860s and remaining until after the turn of the century, when they returned to China as old men.[23]

On family farms, Chinese cooks catered to the immediate family as well as to the permanent field hands. It was their responsibility not only to prepare meals, but also to act as all-purpose servants, household managers, and, occasionally, as figures of authority. So reliable, popular, and essential were some China cooks that they were consulted on important business matters and treated like members of the family. Given control over considerable sums of money or access to credit accounts with merchants, they ordered and paid for various materials and services without oversight and bossed subordinates, including white laborers. The most skilled and fluent in English rose to commanding posts, and would frequently be left to run daily operations when their employers were absent.[24]

On small farms, China cooks often resided beneath the same roof as the family they served. On very large farms, they would often have their own quarters, a small building in the ranch yard usually called the "China house." Whatever their status and accommodations, they were always the last to bed and, along with the threshing crew fireman, the first to rise. Frequently the final sound anyone heard in the evening was that of the China cook grinding coffee or chopping firewood.

"You're just cleaning up and then you start lunch," recalled John Dong, a Chinese farm cook on the Cowell ranch near Santa Cruz. "After lunch, I'd take about an hour off. That was all. Then I'd start dinnertime. I'd have dinner at five-thirty or six o'clock." For his efforts, Dong earned fifty-five dollars a month plus room and board, a very high wage. Most earned between thirty to forty dollars a month, although some particularly desperate farmwives offered up to sixty dollars. Young Chinese laborers thus found it highly desirable to become cooks and went to great lengths to obtain these jobs, often showing considerable initiative in doing so.[25]

Despite their trusted status, Chinese cooks would often remain nameless. Even after working on a farm for many years, a Chinese cook still might not be called by his proper name. Because their names so baffled white foremen and farm owners, many Chinese were renamed with similar sounding names— "Who" instead of "Woo," for example—or nicknames like "Hot Cakes." But when confronted with names like "Wu-Gow," "Wen-Hao," "Wong Gee," "Wu-Gan," or "Ah Sing," farmers simply gave up and resorted to "Jim the Cook," or some such moniker. It was very common for Chinese farm cooks to take the last names of the families who employed them; in this way Yuen Yeck Bow, a cook on the William Ellis farm near Marysville, first became "China Jack," then "China Jack Ellis," and finally "Jack Ellis." And "Wong Gee," a sixteen-year-old who went to work on the Morehead farm west of Chico, and remained there for sixty years, became "Gee Morehead."[26]

Cooks usually led solitary lives. Unlike Chinese field hands and urban laborers, they worked far away from their compatriots and could not easily visit the nearest Chinatown. Because they often resided under the same roof as their employers, their daily interactions required many to learn English and become very Americanized—to a point. As a general rule, they took great care to master traditional American dishes, though many also took pleasure in introducing their employers to Chinese fare. But their willingness to adapt to their new surroundings rarely diminished their yearning for Chinese companionship.[27]

Cooks might occasionally be allowed to bicycle into town for a Sunday afternoon in a Chinese pool hall or café, and those on neighboring farms would take turns pedaling to visit one another. As further proof of loyalty to their culture, there are numerous examples of China cooks continuing to wear their hair in long queues and dressing in traditional black clothes, and no matter where their farm was located, most made sure they celebrated Chinese New Year in the San Francisco Chinatown.[28]

People who knew Chinese cooks enjoyed reeling off stories about their personality quirks, their struggle with the language and culture, and about tricks played on them, and the jokes they played on their employers. Mostly, they recalled the central role that they played in farm life. They most commonly spoke of how industrious and mysterious they were. A mule skinner named Gene Kay grew fond of telling a story about Hung Woo, a Chinese cook who worked on the Jacobs ranch southwest of Guernsey in the San Joaquin Valley. The cook had not been on the ranch more than two weeks when he dazzled everyone with a series of roast goose dinners. As none of the mule skinners and plowboys had been hunting and knew of no one else who had, they asked Hung where he got the geese. "Me ketchum," was all he said. After the third meal, the men could not contain their curiosity, and when they left for the field one morning, Kay hid in the barn and watched Hung Woo all day. Shortly the cook emerged from his shack, looked around, and slid into the willows bordering a large pool fed by Jacobs Slough. Following him, Kay watched Woo strip naked, weigh himself down with a heavy gangplow belt, then slip a hollowed-out pumpkin over his head. The pumpkin had peek holes cut in it, and it allowed Woo to wade into the slough and sneak up on bands of geese he had lured in with wheat seeds. Once beside a feeding goose, he grabbed it by the feet and pulled it under the muddy water and broke its neck before it could squawk. Soon he did the same to another goose. After three had disappeared, the pumpkin started back toward the bank. That evening, Kay confronted Woo with what he had witnessed. The cook told him it was an old Chinese method for catching geese that his forefathers had used for thousands of years. "You break his neck and hold him between your knees while you catch one more," was all he said. Hung Woo would later be remembered by Frank F. Latta as "one of the most famous Chinese cooks ever to burn meat in a [San] Joaquin [Valley] plow camp."[29]

Many Chinese cooks became best friends with their employers and children, whom they came to regard as family. Caring for them as part of their general duties, they went to great lengths, carving little wooden wagons and gadgets for favored boys and delighting them by flying beautiful kites and shooting off long ropes of firecrackers on their birthdays. They would remember birthdays and present their employers with gifts of silk handkerchiefs, ginger in quaint green jars, bags full of lichee nuts, and unusual cakes. Those able to return to China for a brief visit often came back with lovely musical clocks and similar gifts that became treasured family keepsakes. For this, Alfred Doten fondly recalled one Chinese cook as "first rate . . . smart, industrious, & a capital cook . . . honest and with principles that would do credit to a Christian." Another farmer described his Chinese cook as "one of the wonders of this new country." When they died or moved on, they were genuinely missed. And when they departed for China, their old employers remembered them and maintained regular contact through the mail. "What a blessing he was," recalled one Stockton farmwife of her Chinese cook after he left for a higher-paying job at a neighboring ranch. "What bread and coffee and nice broiled steak he gave us, and no fuss nor noise."[30]

China cooks remained important until well into the early part of the twentieth century. For example, on John Schutz's diversified farm in Fresno County, enumerators from the 1900 census counted fourteen Chinese cooks, nine of whom could not speak English. Having come to California as young men barely out of their teens, roughly half were now in their late thirties, one fifty-five years old, and the rest between forty and forty-five years of age. Each Chinese cook was placed in charge of a different labor camp, feeding a total of 324 field hands. They also fed Schutz and his family and supervised two Chinese truck gardeners who supplied the farm with fresh produce on a year-round basis. But their responsibilities were not unique. Miller and Lux, the vast farming and ranching operation whose holdings spread across the Central Valley and into Nevada and Oregon, employed forty-nine Chinese cooks by the 1880s, so many that the historian of the company, David Igler, wrote, "For Miller and Lux, the Chinese as a race were cooks." Regarded as far superior to any other nationality, hundreds of Chinese cooks retained their jobs on dozens of large farms long after Chinese field hands had ceased to be an important part of the farm labor force.[31]

ℬℬ

Another segment of agriculture where the Chinese exerted a strong early influence was on farms operated by their fellow countrymen. Here, they represented virtually 100 percent of the farm labor force. This was no small matter. Beginning in the 1860s, Chinese truck farmers, tenant farmers, and vegetable peddlers were a considerable force in California agriculture. They first appeared in the mining camps, where they generally leased town plots and corners of abandoned mining claims to grow Chinese vegetables to meet the unique food needs of their fellow countrymen, as well as the populations of San Francisco, and the mining camps of the Sierra Nevada foothills. As more of their countrymen arrived and spread beyond the mining districts, Chinese tenant farmers and various cooperative arrangements followed, expanding both the size of their operations and the number and variety of the crops they grew. By the mid-1860s, there were several hundred of them in Sacramento, scattered throughout the delta and in various locations around San Francisco Bay. Typically working in partnerships of three to six individuals—in contrast to white farmers, who tended to farm alone—the Chinese tended plots of five to twenty-five acres, but in Alameda County ran operations as big as forty to sixty acres. Some of the most prosperous and stable members of the Chinese community, they were one of the few groups whose success and sedentary life allowed them to take wives and raise families.[32]

Chinese field hands usually made working and tenant arrangements with their compatriots through the intercession of various merchants and contractors, and only rarely after being contacted directly by farmers themselves. One of the most famous and interesting of these arrangements involved a man named Jim Jack, also known as "Poison Jim," a Chinese jack-of-all-trades, former field hand, and ace "squirrel poisoner," who, in spring of 1864, hired several dozen Chinese laborers to pick wild mustard in the fields between Hollister and San Juan Bautista.[33]

Convinced he could make a fortune harvesting what was essentially regarded as a nuisance weed, Poison Jim and his crew spent the next several months gathering, drying, separating, and bagging mustard seed, which they then stored in a warehouse in San Juan Bautista. That fall, when the mustard crops in Europe and South Africa failed, a Frenchman in the condiment business paid Poison Jim thirty-three thousand dollars for the mustard seeds his crew had harvested. This single act established California's wild mustard business, and the following year, Chinese field hands returned to work not only for Poison Jim (now known as "Mustard Jim") but also for dozens of other Chinese and white farmers in the Salinas, Pajaro, and San Juan Bautista valleys.[34]

Mustard was not the only burgeoning agricultural industry cornered by the Chinese at this time. Along Coyote Creek and the Guadalupe River between San Jose and Santa Clara, farmers were emerging as prime suppliers of fruit and produce for the San Francisco market. Just a short wagon ride from the city and able to grow crops year-round, truck farmers in the Santa Clara Valley specialized in celery, peas, cauliflower, cabbage, potatoes, and above all, strawberries. During peak production in May, the Santa Clara Valley shipped forty thousand pounds of strawberries per week. But sometimes it achieved phenomenal production levels of sixty thousand to seventy thousand pounds.[35]

Chinese farmers seized this opportunity by banding together in groups of five or six to lease or sharecrop five- to twenty-five-acre plots of land. Sharing both the risks and profits, they planted the Longworth Prolific variety of strawberries, as well as blackberries, raspberries, and gooseberries. Many further increased their returns by planting onions and lettuce between the rows of berries.

And though these farmers did much of the daily maintenance work themselves, they could not do it all. Hired hands were always needed to help with the harvest. According to the *Alta California* at least six extra men were needed to pick ten acres of strawberries. For the half-dozen or so berry farmers of the late 1860s, this meant an annual harvest labor force of about 186 men. Thus the success of Santa Clara's Chinese tenant farmers rested to a very large extent on their ability to exploit their compatriot connections and use them to obtain the hands required to work their fields and pick their berries.[36]

About 145 Chinese men from the San Jose Chinatown worked in the strawberry fields. Contracted by Chung Kee, the self-appointed mayor of Chinatown, they would assemble each morning and wait for the berry growers along the east bank of the Guadalupe River just north of San Carlos Street. When the growers arrived, the workers climbed into the wagons and headed off to the fields carrying their tea, rice, matting, and other supplies, including opium. As the demand for harvest hands swelled and growers placed orders through one of the Chinese dry goods store owners, more men poured in from San Francisco, sent by the Chinese Six Companies, a coordinating body of Chinese district associations that ran a huge network of intermediaries in California and China and held a near monopoly on U.S-bound immigrants. Arriving by rail, barge, and horse-drawn wagon, they mixed with locals and moved into rudimentary farm labor housing, often bunking with their employers. As they arrived, some landlords began restricting their tenants' work practices, allowing them to add more men only on Fridays and Mondays. In this way they hoped to preserve local mores, particularly the prohibition on Sunday work. At least one landlord required his tenant to sign a lease that banned him from hiring "quarrelsome or lazy or incompetent Chinese."[37]

Chinese field hands kept at this from early June through mid-September, five days a week, earning about $1.50 for ten hours of work. After the harvest was over, a small portion of them remained on the farms. Like the migratory mustard harvesters of Monterey, they would follow this routine for several decades. Doubling and then tripling in numbers, they became so important that the *Alta California* would assert: "It would be impossible to grow the berries profitably without Celestial help," while a traveler would later observe that, "In picking fruit they are indispensable. If anyone is willing to break his back picking strawberries he can have their place."[38]

By the late 1860s, Chinese field hands were working on hundreds of other small

truck farms throughout Northern California. On some of these farms, their status
as field hands was considerably blurred by a unique cooperative arrangement in
which a business leader or contractor formed a company and field hands bought
shares at a certain price—or more commonly, acquired them in exchange for work.
With the capital amassed by pooling resources, the company rented land that the
group proceeded to farm collectively. By electing a boss and designating their own
leaders, field hands had a direct say in farming operations. "Certainly it is a marvelous system for giving the poor man a start," observed journalist Forrest Crissey.
"Every field hand felt that he was working for himself . . . and this motivated the
men to push themselves harder than if they were mere hired hands."[39]

Of all the Chinese field hands in California at this time, the ones who played the
most important role in commercial agriculture worked some fifty miles north of
San Francisco near the town of Sonoma. The man they worked for, Agoston Haraszthy, was one of the great figures of California agriculture. A Hungarian refu-
gee who left his native country in 1840, Haraszthy had first settled in Wisconsin,
where he helped found the community that became Sauk City. Ultimately
thwarted by harsh Wisconsin winters, he headed for California in search of a better climate for growing fine, European wine grapes. He experimented with viticulture while serving as county sheriff and a member of the third state legislature in San Diego in 1852, and continued his attempts while holding posts with
the U.S. Mint in San Francisco from 1854 to 1856. Shortly after being forced to
resign from the U.S. Mint in January 1857 because of false charges of fraud, Haraszthy turned his entire attention to winemaking and began searching for a place
in Northern California where the combination of soil, climate, and access to markets would allow him to produce first-class wines. Haraszthy found what he was
seeking at the Vineyard Farm, two miles east of the Sonoma town plaza, close
to the old mission, where Mariano G. Vallejo had once held forth as de facto
provincial governor.[40]

Owned by pioneer winemaker Julius K. Rose, the Vineyard Farm consisted of
a winepress house, brandy distillery, and other structures, along with a vineyard
containing fifteen thousand grapevines. Spreading over lowlands and hills, the
property included parcels in the Mayacamas Mountains east of the existing vineyards, an irregularly shaped tract to the southeast, and was crossed by Arroyo
Seco, a ravine fringed with willows, sycamores, and cottonwoods, which cut south
toward Sonoma Creek. Dotted with hillside springs and tiny creeks and bathed
by cooling breezes off the San Pablo Bay, the property was indeed picturesque—
and full of potential. The condition of the vines, which yielded some forty thousand pounds of grapes, the profits to be made selling those grapes as fresh fruit in
the nearby San Francisco market, and most important, the crude but potentially
good wine being made by Rose, all convinced Haraszthy to purchase the property
in January 1857. He called the property Buena Vista ("Beautiful View").[41]

Placing his son Attila in charge, Haraszthy prepared to move onto the property
that summer. He had grand plans; on Buena Vista, Haraszthy intended to intro-

duce modern winemaking methods and equipment, plant hundreds of fine European grape varieties, and move past the limited local market in bulk red wines for the miners by branching out into brandy and even champagnes—in short, he dreamed of creating a viticultural Garden of Eden, the seat of California winemaking. At that time, the center of California wine production was 350 miles south, in Los Angeles, where the first vineyards outside the missions had been planted in the 1820s and a handful of vintners annually produced 162,000 gallons of mostly sweet wines. Several hundred acres of vineyards also spread over the Santa Clara Valley, where a colony of French immigrants led by Charles Lefranc and Louis Pellier were beginning to produce some vintages; there were also small but well-established vineyards in Santa Barbara, El Dorado, Mariposa, Sacramento, Napa, and Alameda counties. At the time of Haraszthy's arrival at Buena Vista, California's wine industry was at a point economists call "takeoff," where some energetic, pioneering entrepreneur could seize on the state's great natural advantages of climate, cheap land, and access to markets and take it to a higher level.[42]

Haraszthy had plenty of work to do. He needed to bring hundreds of acres of raw, snake-infested terrain into production as vineyards; construct a winery; excavate wine storage caves; build wine barrels; make wine; and ship a large portion of his first grapes to San Francisco for sale as fresh fruit. And besides building his winemaking operation, he also wanted to plant corn, almonds, walnuts, peaches, and wheat. With few men from around Sonoma available and willing to handle the work at Buena Vista, Haraszthy turned to well-known San Francisco contractor Ho Po, who assured the Hungarian it would be no problem bringing crews up from the city to the Sonoma embarcadero. From there it was but a short wagon ride to Sonoma Plaza, and from there a brief walk to Buena Vista.[43]

Chinese laborers jumped at the opportunity to obtain long-term employment, and Ho Po sent one hundred men to Buena Vista in January 1857. On arrival, their first order of business was to establish a camp, as no housing yet existed. Moving into the oak groves east of the vineyard, they built their own bunkhouses. Called "China cabins," these quarters featured cookhouses with chimneys constructed of flattened tin cans.[44]

Even as they were settling in, they began planting rooted cuttings of fine European grape varieties, which Haraszthy's sons, Gaza, Attila, and Arpad, had brought up from Crystal Springs by boat. Using shovels and heavy iron bars, two-man crews dug holes twenty inches deep and two feet in diameter, being careful to throw the surface soil to one side, the subsoil to the other. Following them, a group of planters placed a vine in each hole, one man spreading the roots, the other raking in first the subsoil, packing it, then the top soil, finally tamping the hole firm. By May, the Chinese had planted 16,850 grapevines on eight-foot spacings—thirteen thousand of the vines on twenty acres of Haraszthy's property, and the rest on property owned by friends who had settled nearby. Among the varieties they planted was zinfandel, a European red, never before grown in California on a commercial scale, which soon become the state's favorite wine grape. After more than tripling the acreage of wine grapes in Sonoma, the Chinese then established a viticultural nursery. That summer, they picked several tons of fresh grapes for the San Francisco market and harvested grapes for Haraszthy's first wine crush.[45]

FIGURE 26. Ho Po (sometimes spelled Hoe Poe), a San Francisco labor contractor who furnished workmen to the Buena Vista Winery in Sonoma, ca. 1870. Courtesy of the Wine Institute, San Francisco.

During the fall, Haraszthy turned to the task of creating underground wine cellars, although there is some question as to whether or not Chinese laborers were involved. The first such cellars in Sonoma County—perhaps the first in California—they would eventually hold forty thousand gallons of wine at a cool, uniform, year-round temperature between fifty-five and sixty degrees. Two side-by-side arches marked the entrances to the caves, which were carved deep into a hillside on the eastern edge of Haraszthy's property. A description of the cellars, published in the *Sonoma Democrat*, reported completion of "a tunnel, 100 ft. deep, made into a hillside." The article described the tunnel as seven feet high and twenty feet wide, but did not mention the laborers. Drawing on the example of later Chinese tunneling through the Sierra Nevada while building rail lines for Southern Pacific, one might assume the Chinese did the same, only earlier, at Buena Vista. Complicating matters is another description of these cellars published the following year by the California State Agricultural Society. Once again the type of labor is not specified. But the wage scale of forty dollars per month was far too high for Chinese laborers.[46]

While it is debatable whether or not Chinese built these first wine caves, there is little doubt concerning their excavation work at Buena Vista after the fall of 1858. As they expanded existing cellars so Haraszthy could store his first year's vintage, Chinese laborers also began quarrying rock for a champagne cellar and for the foundations of a palatial Pompeian-style villa Haraszthy was constructing on a knoll overlooking the valley.[47]

Haraszthy's wine cellars were only the first of many momentous construction projects carried out by the Chinese. Soon after the 1858 harvest the Chinese erected a press house large enough to accommodate all the equipment—including a crusher, fermenting tubs, and barrels—necessary to manufacture wine. Haraszthy's winepress was a major advancement. On the other side of the Mayacamas Mountains, the Charles Krug winery was still making wine by trampling grapes under foot and fermenting them in rawhide bags. Although Krug the following year would visit Buena Vista, become inspired, and borrow Haraszthy's old cider press to make the first significant lot of commercial wine in the Napa Valley, neither Krug nor anyone else in California had in mind anything approaching the massively energetic modernization program under way at Buena Vista.[48]

Kept constantly at work, the Chinese chiseled and blasted away for most of the next ten years, adding a third cellar just west of the other two in 1862. Though originally planned as a four-hundred-foot-deep excavation, crews on this cellar project stopped after hitting a seam of quartz at 150 feet; still it was the deepest wine cellar anywhere in California. As they worked, the Chinese raised a huge pile of excavated rock. In 1863, they used that rock to build a new press house. Measuring fifty-four by sixty-four feet, the building had a large, arched entryway facing north toward Arroyo Seco. The new building insulated the adjoining tunnels from extremes of heat and cold with thick rock and mortar walls ensuring a constant temperature inside. Large doors at either end allowed Chinese to deliver wagon loads of grapes to the second floor by means of a narrow road cut into the hillside. Inside the press house was a steam-powered grape crusher capable of crushing fifty thousand pounds of grapes per day, the first such device in the valley. The winepress, located on the first floor opposite the fermenting tanks, was a large wooden structure capable of exerting two hundred thousand pounds of pressure. Processing operations also exploited the hillside location. Pomace went out a door into waiting wagons, permitting the pressed juice to move from one place to another without pumping; juice and must drained down from the crusher through trapdoors into huge redwood vats on the first floor.[49]

Quarrying, tunneling, and vat work comprised but a portion of what the Chi-

nese did at Buena Vista. During the summer of 1860, Haraszthy formed the Sonoma Tule Land Company, with himself as president, and filed a claim on eight
thousand acres of marshland along the north end of San Pablo Bay. Setting a force
of Chinese to draining the land and building ten miles of earthen dikes, he then
brought in steam-powered plows and had them cultivate the land for rice, hemp,
tobacco, and asparagus. By the mid-1860s, Chinese field hands had transformed
Buena Vista into a showplace of California agriculture, where soil, sunshine, labor policy, creative enterprise, and the growing wine industry harmonized in beautiful, productive symbiosis. When Haraszthy established the Buena Vista Vinicultural Society in 1863 and issued six thousand dollars worth of stock to outside
investors, the Chinese became part of a modern agricultural estate, owned by corporate shareholders and managed by a board of trustees, like a mill or mine.[50]

Much of what the Chinese did at Buena Vista necessarily centered on planting
grapevines; 16,850 in February and March 1857; forty thousand in 1858; thirty thousand in 1859; seventy thousand in 1860; 135,000 in 1861. During the spring of 1862,
the Chinese in addition to their other duties began building hotbeds and cultivating grapevines—some three hundred different varieties—as well as small lots of
almonds, olives, oranges, lemons, pomegranates, chestnuts, and figs. By fall, the
Chinese had over three hundred thousand rooted vines ready for sale and distribution. Sold, given away, and otherwise distributed to other winemakers, those
varieties—including many that were wholly new to the state—became an important and indispensable part of the viticultural rootstock of the state. That fall, the
Chinese planted twenty-nine thousand vines for a total of 332,000 vines, right on
target with Haraszthy's plans to plant one thousand acres at Buena Vista.[51]

At first, the Chinese planted vineyards in the flat, valley floor. But in 1863, Ha-
raszthy sent Ho Po's men to chopping out the snake-infested, sloping hillside of
Lovall Valley, east of Sonoma, which Haraszthy had purchased from Thomas O.
Larkin. Here, occasional rains and steep drainage would cause vines to grow under
stressful conditions, and the unobstructed southeastern slopes would provide maximum sun exposure. On July 22, a reporter for the *Alta California* found thirty
Chinese hard at work under Attila, "grubbing oak saplings on a pretty steep hill."
The men chopped down the wild holly and manzanita, cleared away the dense
undergrowth, yanked out tree stumps, hacked away at the madrone, then piled up
the debris and burned it. Because the hillside at first could not be plowed, the men
did everything by hand, largely with spades, axes, saws, and mattocks. It was backbreaking monotonous work—more akin to construction than farm labor—but the
Chinese attacked the slopes in a well-organized fashion, and by the following
spring had scoured them clean, trenched them for water runoff, and formed terraced ledges on which vines could be planted. Next, they lined off the clearings
into fields, then shovel-plowed, cross-plowed, and subsoiled the land with two-
horse plows. Finally, they marked the vine rows and set grape stakes every eight
feet. They would return to the slopes and plant them the following spring.[52]

When not busy clearing land, propagating vines, or quarrying and excavating,
the Chinese had plenty else to do. In the winter they pruned the vines. March
through July, they plowed between the vine rows, first one way, then the other.
In July and August, they used sickles to cut the tops off the vines to a height of

six feet. And every fall, from mid-September through the beginning of November, they concentrated on the harvest and crush. It was exhausting work made even more difficult by the steep hillsides and the rattlesnakes that sometimes crawled up into the shady portions of the vines to rest.[53]

Always on the lookout for snakes, harvesters feverishly picked into wooden boxes, fifty pounds each, loaded the boxes thirty-five per wagon, and delivered them to the press house. A "good Chinaman," it was said, picked an average of fifteen hundred to two thousand pounds of fruit per day, a rate that would later become the industry standard. They also made wine at Buena Vista, becoming the first Chinese to handle every phase of the process, including removing the grape stems and crushing the grapes, fermenting the juice, wracking it off, filling and corking wine bottles, even wiring champagne caps.[54]

Based on measurements of their labor, Haraszthy created individual standards for each work day—"summer pruning" by sickle at the rate of twenty-five hundred vines per day, crushing twenty-five hundred pounds of grapes per day; or staking and digging 180 grapevine holes and planting 492 vines. With their high work performance, the Chinese established an almost unattainable norm. In many ways, it is fitting that these practices should have developed at Buena Vista, where Chinese laborers did so much to influence California's modern agricultural landscape.[55]

✍

Reported widely in national magazines and newspapers and chronicled in traveler's accounts and various formal and informal "fact finding" delegations, Chinese accomplishments at Buena Vista quickly became known. The *Alta California* called the Chinese a farmer's dream—easy to hire, easy to fire, easier to manage than anyone else, quiet, honest, dependable, highly organized, seemingly possessing a great capacity for tireless, unremitting labor, "industrious, obedient, and easily taught to perform every description of labor required of them." Even more important in establishing their value as prime field hands was Haraszthy himself. A prolific writer, and a frequent public speaker before various civic and business groups, he often discussed Chinese field hands in speeches to farmers and the general public throughout Northern California. Concerned with the high cost of labor, Haraszthy spoke at length about Chinese field hands on September 30, 1862, at the state fair in Sacramento. Elected president of the California State Agricultural Society in April, he took advantage of his position as the titular head of the state's farmers and on the opening day of the fair delivered his opening address to a huge crowd assembled in the hall of the pavilion. Only one thing worried him, he explained—the mounting call for excluding Chinese immigrants. As he had been saying for years, the Chinese who worked for him and for other winemakers in Sonoma were good for California agriculture. By accepting labor that white men would not do, the Chinese contributed to the state's prosperity not only as workers but as major consumers of the state's products. One member of the state senate had calculated that Chinese workers spent about $1.5 million dollars a year in California, Haraszthy noted. "Why then," he asked, "does an unfriendly Legislature drive these people out of our country?"[56]

While delighting in detailing the role the Chinese played in allowing him to expand operations unimpeded by labor shortages or problems, Haraszthy did much more than talk. When he first brought the Chinese to Buena Vista, he had armed himself with a revolver to defend himself and the Chinese from threats by local white laborers. When the legislature passed a law imposing a tax of $2.50 a month on every Chinese in California, Haraszthy led the effort to repeal the law. When he finally completed the new champagne house in 1864, he immediately erected a large dwelling for the Chinese. So highly did Haraszthy think of Chinese field hands that he would not only oppose all efforts to restrict immigration from China, he would also devise and lobby for a recruitment program, modeled after similar efforts developed by several southern states, which would draw in large numbers of Chinese. Such policies were necessary, he believed, because farmers would not be able to prosper without the Chinese, or people like them. Certainly at Buena Vista, Chinese labor had only advanced Haraszthy's drive to improve wine productivity and quality. In September 1859, wines made by Chinese field hands won six awards, including a grand prize silver cup for the best wine. The lesson was clear. "We must employ partly Chinese laborers," he told his fellow farmers. "With this labor we can compete with any part of the world."[57]

As word of their abilities spread, the Chinese moved out from Buena Vista, hiring out first to Charles Krug and Jacob Gundlach, two German immigrants who were also attempting to establish themselves and who would soon become major figures in the wine industry. Attracted to these and other opportunities, Chinese field hands between 1857 and 1861 began furnishing a supplementary source of labor to grape growers in the Sonoma and Napa valleys, north to Mendocino County, and east into the Central Valley orchards around Vacaville. Besides their work in the vineyards and wineries at Krug, Gundlach, and Buena Vista in Sonoma, they also assisted in the first wine production in Healdsburg at Chambaud Winery, in Yountville at Occidental Winery, and at several other wineries where they worked as cellar bosses and "cellar rats." By spring 1870, they had also moved five miles east into the Glen Ellen vineyards of Dr. J. B. Warfield, where they were observed "liberally sprinkling sulphur on the vines to protect them against mold," and sometime thereafter, into the Chauvet Winery, also in Glen Ellen, where one of the most famous of all Sonoma Valley Chinese, Young Moon, along with a Chinese assistant, worked his way up from field hand to became and expert in blending and distilling brandy.[58]

Although it is doubtful that their expanded influence in Sonoma surpassed in importance what they were doing at Buena Vista, there seems little doubt that the Chinese allowed winemaking and grape growing to prosper throughout the entire valley. Between 1856 and 1869 they planted most, if not all, of the county's 3.2 million grapevines, thus allowing Sonoma to increase wine production from a few hundred gallons of wine to nearly three hundred thousand gallons. Due very largely to the Chinese, Sonoma now verged on wresting the lead in wine acreage and production from Los Angeles. The Chinese also played a key role in improving wine quality by ripping out old mission grape vineyards and replanting them with Riesling, Muscatel, Traminer, Black Hamburg, Cabernet Sauvignon, Chardonnay, and other fine French and European varieties. Their contribution did not go unnoticed by the state legislature. "Our vineyards could be cultivated and vastly increased by Chinese labor," acknowledged a state committee. Seeing a bright future for an industry that might one day rival that of Europe, it drew a parallel, then made a prediction: "The wine crop of France in 1849 was valued at $100,000,000 raised on an area of 250 miles in length by 32 in breadth. California contains 188,981 square miles, so that if only one twenty-fifth part of her area should be planted with vineyards, she would have an amount equal to France. But this cannot be done without cheap labor furnished by Chinese."[59]

That Chinese laborers at Buena Vista were part of the opening phase in the industrialization of the countryside is not a fact preserved in wine lore. Other than the undeniable marks in the limestone cave walls that the Chinese made with their pickaxes, the Chinese of Buena Vista are largely omitted from official wine industry accounts. But at Buena Vista, Chinese field hands participated in something that was part investment opportunity, part experiment in fine European-style winemaking, and part lofty effort at establishing a great horticultural community. At Buena Vista, the Chinese left a mark not only in the horticultural world of climate, soil, and grape variety, but also in the realm of labor. No skill apparently was beyond their comprehension, no task so odious they would not accept it. "I can show a haystack made by them . . . my grain was bound and harvested by Chinamen; my vineyards and orchards were planted, pruned and cultivated, ten plows were driven and my wine made by them," explained Haraszthy in an address to the Sonoma County Agricultural and Mechanical Society in 1860.[60]

Yet, despite these glowing testimonials, Chinese field hands and winemakers did not remain in the wine industry and vineyards of Buena Vista for very long. After laboring faithfully at Buena Vista for a generation, a tiny pest, the phylloxera vine louse, brought it all to a disastrous end. Having destroyed most of the vineyards in Europe, it somehow appeared at Buena Vista, probably transported among the vines Haraszthy had imported with such great hope and fanfare in 1862. As the louse proceeded to munch its way through the vine roots around Sonoma, the Chinese tried their best to fight it. For years, they ripped out vines by the thousands, propagating new ones and replanting them year after year. But they could not stem the ravages of the pest. Unable to maintain productivity in the face of the onslaught, Haraszthy left Buena Vista in 1867. The Buena Vista Vinicultural Society continued to struggle with phylloxera for another decade, finally selling the pest-ravaged property in 1878 to a wealthy San Franciscan who transformed it into a private country estate.[61]

Elsewhere, though, California farming was booming. For twenty years the vintners of Sonoma and Los Angeles, truck farmers of the delta, mustard entrepreneurs of San Benito, berry sharecroppers of Santa Clara, lords of the old Mexican land grants, and squatters on a few acres of unclaimed dirt had been hampered by the lack of labor, resigned to the difficulty of finding help, even to the realization that their crops might not be harvested for want of harvest hands. Now everywhere they looked a savior had appeared to them, one who could allow them to exploit their opportunity. Farmers could no longer deny the Chinese. They admired them; they tried in every way to obtain more of them. If ever California was to attain its potential as a fruit-growing state, predicted a writer for

The Nation in 1864, it would be because of the "introduction of Chinese skill and the moderate aspirations which are behind it." Chinese field hands, the writer concluded, were the wave of the future.[62]

A well-traveled California journalist tried to explain the situation to the public. There was a new force, he wrote, huge and strangely exciting, loose in the agricultural districts of the state. A higher standard seemed to have been imposed for farmwork. "The employers of the Chinese laborers invariably agree that they are excellent workmen," he said. "They never have, like whites, a Sunday spree and a 'blue Monday.' They are always 'on hand' at the time agreed upon; always sober and industrious . . . and they prove most trustworthy laborers." Hereafter that sobriety, industry, and trustworthiness would be increasingly devoted to the great task of transforming the state's raw landscape into productive farms.[63]

CHAPTER TWELVE

Bought Like Any Other Commodity

China Bosses and Gang Labor

Well before they became field hands, Chinese working for the Central Pacific Railroad demonstrated the most amazing abilities and work habits. Organized into gangs of twelve to twenty men under a boss, they handled much of the heavy grading, cut and fill work, and logging required to lay tracks through the treacherous Sierra Nevada. On April 28, 1869, Chinese and Irish crews built ten miles and fifty-six feet of track in less than twelve hours, beating the old record by more than two miles. To meet construction deadlines, Chinese drillers often labored through winters, living and working by lantern light while burrowed beneath the snow in a labyrinth of tunnels, relying on shafts cut in the snowdrifts for oxygen and light. To cut routes along dangerous cliffs at Cape Horn, fourteen hundred feet above the north fork of the American River, Chinese "powder monkeys" hung in wicker baskets, swaying and scraping against the mountain while pounding holes in the cliff face; after tamping in black power charges, they were hauled up just before the gorge was exploded. Constantly in danger, Chinese crews in the Sierra Nevada were caught in avalanches that wiped out entire crews and buried men so deeply that their bodies were not recovered until the snow melted and the rubble was removed the following spring.[1]

In the summer of 1869, when work was completed on the transcontinental railroad, thousands of these gang laborers were released from work. Tired and looking for jobs, they joined almost fifteen thousand Chinese peasants who arrived that year, and together they poured into the state's agricultural districts. The largest numbers headed for Stockton. Gateway to the southern Mother Lode, the San Joaquin Valley, and the Sacramento-San Joaquin Delta, Stockton had the third-largest Chinese population in California after San Francisco and Sacramento. Known as Sam Fow or "third city" in the Cantonese dialect (San Francisco was Dai Fow, the big city; Sacramento Yee Fow, or second city), Stockton boasted three geographically and culturally distinct Chinatowns. Largest of the three, the Channel Street settlement, so-named because it was conveniently lo-

FIGURE 27. "Breaking of the Foot Levee on San Joaquin River, Four Miles South of Stockton, April 18th, 1894." Lithograph from a sketch by F. E. Howell, *Harper's Magazine*.

cated near the head of the Stockton channel, sported wood-frame hotels and rented shacks, had easy access to the docks, and was dominated by Heungshan Chinese. Second-largest was the Washington Street Chinatown. Located four blocks south, between El Dorado and Hunter streets, the Washington Street Chinatown had developed when all of the Sze Yup Chinese from Guangdong's T'oishan district left the Channel Street settlement following a disastrous fire in 1862. A third settlement, known as the Mormon Slough Chinatown, began as a squatter's camp for fishermen but soon evolved into a thriving industrial complex with truck farms, laundries, and fish-drying facilities.[2]

Packing into the Channel Street and Washington Street Chinatowns, newly arrived immigrants and Central Pacific construction hands piled up on one another. Desperate for work and extremely familiar with the various techniques involved in reshaping the natural environment, they were thus perfectly situated late in 1869, when a former mining engineer turned land developer named George Roberts formed the Tide Lands Reclamation Company and launched a project that would forever alter the course of California's agricultural development and prove the value of mass Chinese gang labor. Like many of his generation, Roberts sought to discover and exploit the fruits of California's natural advantages, particularly those in areas like the delta where, through the application of engineering science, he might create an orderly and productive landscape out of a seemingly chaotic miasma. Having already purchased huge chunks of the unowned redwood timberlands of the north coast and having filed for large portions of public land during the years 1868 and 1869, Roberts was looking for similar speculative opportunities elsewhere when he noticed that delta farmers were not only perfectly situated and could outproduce other farmers but had been able to escape the crop-killing droughts. Envisioning the potential of both selling and farming reclaimed swampland, Roberts quickly issued 120,000 stock certificates in his new company and went to work buying up the delta. To avoid the acreage limitations imposed by the Swampland Reclamation Act, Roberts paid "dummy entrants" to make claims in their own names and then sell or assign him title to their parcels. After the acreage limitation on the purchase of swampland was rescinded, Roberts seized on the opportunity and acquired 250,000 acres of so-called overflow lands in the Yolo Basin, the Sacramento-San Joaquin Delta, and Suisun Bay. He then transferred 120,000 acres to his company and launched his first reclamation project on Twitchell Island, a thirty-six-hundred-acre, tule-covered expanse of virgin swampland opposite Rio Vista, at the southwestern end of the delta.[3]

Compared to the magnitude of previous land reclamation projects, the undertaking proposed by Roberts was mammoth in scope and vision, completely without precedent in California, and fraught with organizational, logistical, engineering, and labor problems. On the basis of previous experience reclaiming nearby islands, levee builders assured Roberts that he could secure his property from ordinary floods and high tides with levees raised three feet above the surface of the natural embankments, plus another two or three feet of freeboard. Intent on enclosing the entire island with such a levee system before selling it, Roberts initially spent huge sums trying to cut costs and increase efficiency by mechanizing operations. But after testing ditching machines, "floating wheel dredges," and peat excavators, he discovered that they were ineffective and, suddenly confronted with the task of mobilizing a labor force, abandoned the machines in favor of gangs obtained through China bosses. Among the wealthiest, most influential, and respected members of the Chinese community, China bosses were modern entrepreneurs, part foremen, part businessmen, who identified a need, provided a service, and filled a void in the primitive labor market. Spanning the gap between the sites of labor supply and demand and bridging the political, cultural, and economic gulf separating growers and agricultural laborers, China bosses organized work crews, provided transportation, supplied food and board, advanced wages, negotiated pay rates, set working conditions, and supervised the general terms of employment—usually securing agreements with little more than a handshake. Collecting and distributing salaries, they brought order and predictability to a chaotic farm labor market. They did not require substantial amounts of capital to get started, and when they did need financial backing it was always readily forthcoming from Chinese merchants, community leaders, and sometimes even from local growers who advanced money and supplies on credit. The only real prerequisite to being a boss was an ability to speak English and sometimes several Chinese dialects. But successful China bosses also needed to understand the sequence of crops, anticipate labor needs, know when and where to scout up work, and figure out how to move large numbers of men efficiently around the countryside.[4]

Scooped up upon arriving in Stockton—often before they had rested or eaten a meal—unemployed railroad workers and recent immigrants hardly viewed China bosses as odd. With some precedent in the Chinese countryside, where intermediaries made their money by holding men in place rather than guiding their mobility, the relationship with superiors was deeply ingrained in them; it was instilled in them by everything they heard as boys growing up in rural China, by district associations, and most of all, by the pragmatic realities of life in California. Saddled with the imperative of paying off their debts and meeting their obligations, men knew the difficulties they faced on their own, and it is quite probable that everyone in a gang appreciated the value of a contractor and respected the role he played in finding work. A long way from home, in a strange and at times hostile land, and unable to speak the language, field hands followed a system that fed them, sheltered them, got them jobs, and sent their bodies home after they died.

The arrangement was not equivocal. With little say in the terms under which bosses worked them, field hands never saw any account books (if indeed bosses ever kept any) and were frequently in no position to demand their wages directly from a farmer. Should they dislike the terms of employment or otherwise have any grievances, there was no mechanism, formal or informal, for resolving them. Contractors were answerable to no one other than their financial backers, employers, and their district or clan association. If any field hand malingered, talked back, fomented disorder, failed to work diligently, or in any way displeased a grower or contractor, he could be sent packing without pay at a moment's notice.[5]

Within days of being contacted by Roberts, bosses rounded up the required workers, organized them under subcontractors, then directed each subcontractor to report to a foreman. The bosses received general directions and a lump sum payment. Assuming responsibilities for paying, housing, and feeding the men, they also provided them with prostitutes, transportation, and mail while enforcing discipline, supervising fieldwork, and ensuring compliance with provisions of the agreement with Roberts. It was all very easy. "We go to some of the Chinese merchants or business men, and tell them we want to give a contract for a certain number of miles of levee," Roberts explained to a U.S. Senate committee investigating Chinese immigration in 1876. "They will contract, then, sometimes in large and sometimes in small bodies of land. Sometimes the contracts are for five, six, seven, or eight hundred or a thousand [cubic] yards, and sometimes, with one individual, as the case may be." Always, Roberts stressed, the contracts were executed with great "executive ability," as the China bosses—eager for the commission they would earn from their men and for the income they would garner supplying rice, tents, and other goods—had no problem rounding up men. What Roberts especially liked about the arrangement, besides the fact that he did not have to feed and house his men, was the complete reliability of the contractors. "If you can get them this year," he observed, "you can get them next year and the year after, if you treat them well and pay them. They become attached to your place and stay with you." This made them, in his opinion, "better than the Swede, and the Swede is the best worker."[6]

As they moved onto Twitchell Island, the Chinese surely must have felt a vague familiarity with their surroundings. Coming from the Pearl River Delta, many had grown up in similar surroundings, while virtually all had glimpsed the area from the deck of steamboats while traveling to the diggings and railroad construction camps. Dread and apprehension must surely have greeted most of them as they poured out of the steamers into the rotting tules and bulrushes that constituted the improvised ship landings. One solid block of peat, Twitchell Island snaked in every direction, divided into countless swamps, disappeared into impassable tangles, and was completely cut off from human habitation. But Chinese laborers had little time to reflect on their situation. Immediately organized into gangs of between forty and one hundred men, each gang with a cook or two and a laundryman, they dispersed around the island. With no settlement or housing other than a few crude sheds, the men spent considerable time erecting tent camps on elevated spots as their bosses met with engineers, walked the levees, staked off sections, estimated their costs, bid on the work, and concluded contracts.[7]

Almost immediately, an industrial time and discipline regimen was established. Days were long, parceled out to extract as much work as possible. A standard day began around 5 A.M., when the laborers awoke to a work bell that signaled the beginning of a rigid routine. First, they had to clean and care for the horses and ready their equipment. Following a 5:45 A.M. breakfast, they were on the levees by 6 A.M. From that point on, they kept to a strict schedule. With only a fifteen-minute morning break, they worked straight through to noon, and following a one-hour lunch break, labored until 6 P.M. After tending their horses and cleaning themselves, they ate dinner at 6:40 P.M., and after that were free to visit, write letters, and put their tools in order. Meals were served promptly, and those tardy for meals went hungry. This meant, on average, a twelve-hour workday, with about one hour and fifteen minutes off to eat and rest. Workers who missed part of their work shift would not only be docked wages but charged for their food and board, typically a half-day's food and board for a half-day missed.[8]

Raising levees on Twitchell Island was hard, dangerous work. The first step, called "grubbing," involved clearing a thirty-foot-wide strip of land along the riverbank. This meant cutting trees, hacking down brush, and dragging away debris. A slow and laborious process, grubbing was perhaps the single largest part of reclamation work. As in all land-clearing projects, stumps proved difficult and often required teams of mules (oxen being too heavy for the saturated land). A common way to grub out stumps was to undercut them, whereby men chopped away at the roots and excavated underneath, causing stumps to collapse into the excavations.[9]

With the land grubbed clear, men next turned to embankment work. After damming the sloughs, cutting drainage ditches, and building floodgates, diggers began excavating a "borrow pit" on the inside of the levee. Clad in slickers and rubber waders and working in synchronized fashion amid swarms of mosquitoes said to be dense enough to snuff out the flame on a candle, gangs of Chinese cut out blocks of peat with special shovels known as "tule cutters," "tule knives," and "peat spades." At first, they simply piled the peat blocks in the area of the levee line. But as the levees rose in height, a production line was established that aimed at accomplishing the maximum in the minimum amount of time. Wheelbarrow operators led the way, picking up the blocks and transporting them up slope by means of narrow plank ramps built on pilings sunk into the levee side. On top of the levee, "peat fitters" took over, lifting the blocks out of the wheelbarrows, fitting them together, and tamping them firmly in place so as to make the levees watertight.[10]

As the levees rose to a height of several feet, the men periodically readjusted the ramps, adding more planks, reinforcing the pilings, and keeping the angle of ascent as gradual as possible. Men encountered the worst part of their work just before completion of a section, when the levee neared its maximum height. At this point, the diggers would be ten or fifteen feet below the levee crest. Splattered with mud and sloshing through muck, they would have to shovel the peat into wheelbarrows that now stood at eye level. Wheelbarrow pushers would slip and fall while winding their way up a series of increasingly long plank switchbacks to dump their loads. On particularly steep inclines, pulley systems were rigged on the lip of the levee, with a bit of security provided by ropes running down around belts of men scaling the incline.[11]

Men died in droves while building the levees on Twitchell Island. Many caught malaria, some died of dysentery, and some simply gave out from the strenuous, body-sapping toil. Most died in work accidents. Wheelbarrow men fell and were crushed by their loads, diggers in the pit below were buried under avalanches of debris or crushed by runaway wheelbarrows, and men assigned to undercut large trees were squashed when the heavy stumps broke loose and fell on them. Many reclamation workers drowned after falling into the river. Nevertheless, Chinese laborers persevered until they completed each levee segment, then moved on to the next section and repeated the process. Impressed by their determination and organization, landowners could only marvel at "those sturdy little Orientals."[12]

Once Roberts had raised his levees, a group of absentee investors from Kentucky bought the island, and in the fall of 1870, when the interior had dried out, set many of the Chinese to clearing the land, breaking the peat sod, and readying it for farming. This was probably more difficult than prairie busting, which had challenged many pioneer settlers in the Midwest. First, the Chinese had to remove the thick stands of tules. Burning proved to be the cheapest and quickest method, but it too was extremely dangerous. Chinese peat burners would dig holes in the turf, drop clumps of straw into them, and ignite the straw. But the high organic content of the peat often caused it to ignite along with the tules. A few large fires smoldered until winter rains extinguished them.[13]

After burning the tules, the Chinese plowed the land—another difficult task. Because the virgin peat was too soft for horses to walk on and the sod was so tangled with woody tule roots that it could not be cut with ordinary plows, the Chinese developed the first of several specialized pieces of delta farming equipment, a heavy sod breaker with two sharp knives attached known as the "tule buster." Crews ran tule busters across the peat at least three times before they were finally able to sow it to wheat that fall. But working diligently, they managed to prepare one thousand acres for farming and planted both a wheat crop and vegetable patch that together earned the absentee owners some seventy thousand dollars in 1872.[14]

On Twitchell Island, the Chinese had been pitted against some of the most difficult agricultural conditions in the state, and their spectacularly successful work dramatically increased the almost insatiable demand for their labor as well as the power and importance of China bosses. As reclamation companies contracted with them, bosses moved ever larger numbers of men into the delta—even as the first "steam-shovel" dipper dredges arrived. Seeking to speed up their work, reclamation companies continued to employ Chinese long after the arrival of dredges. On Roberts Island, for example, thirteen hundred Chinese employed by Joel P. Whitney operated as many as two hundred scoop and slip scrapers to reinforce nearly fifty miles of peat block levees erected in 1875 by two giant dredges, the Samson and Goliath. In Tulare Township just south of Roberts Island, Chinese field hands employed by Thomas "Land Hog" Williams worked in conjunction with dredges to build some very distinctive levees. Crews ranging in size from "hundreds" to up to three thousand men cut peat blocks and stacked them not in the usual massive barrier but in two parallel rows, twenty-five feet apart, and well back from the river, then filled in the space between with alluvium and clay scraped from the interior with small gangplows, single-horse scrapers, two-horse Fresno scrapers, and large scrapers pulled by as many as fourteen horses. With two long handles extending back, these devices required their operators to bend over nearly double as they tilted and adjusted the handles and dumped each load of earth. Even after crews had been replaced by clamshell bucket dredges (giant barges with huge buckets that scooped earth from the riverbeds and swung their loads by means of a long boom over the levee) and suction dredges (which sucked up sand and river-bottom muck and deposited it via a floating pipeline), much work remained. Chinese crews still had to level out sags and cracks in levees, and during winter floods often had to creep along the levee tops to sandbag "scour holes" and line them with riprap. Many drowned in these efforts, and for their sacrifices, employers would later recall them as "the best field men that we have." Such diligence, loyalty, and self-sacrifice earned no death benefits. When drowned field hands were fished out of the Sacramento River they received a quick funeral and ignoble burial in the Stockton Rural Cemetery. Such bravery did not allow even a few to break free of levee work and land clearing or ever earn the forty-five-dollar monthly wage, plus room and board, paid to so-called skilled white workers. High-paid, skilled positions building docks, barns, and bunkhouses always went to a varied lot of white workers, drifters, and roustabouts, despite their propensity to pack up and leave after a few weeks on the job.[15]

As levee work proceeded, the logistics of transporting so many Chinese strained the abilities of delta steamship companies, whose mates constantly struggled to figure just where to stop for men who could not speak enough English to make their destinations known. Finally, boat operators hit upon the scheme of putting a Chinese "runner" onboard each boat to announce approaching docks and landings in Chinese. The mate would tell the runner that they were approaching some remote dock or "China landing." The runner would then scurry below deck to the "China cabin," shouting "Hop Sing landing," "Mow Sang landing," "Sang Wah landing," and "China Ranch landing." He then rounded up the men who wished to go ashore, and brought them up on deck. When the boats called, whole populations rushed to the wharves. The workers would disembark quickly, loading goods or baggage from the dock, exchanging gossip, news, and rumors, while departing field hands would board. As quickly as possible, the ship would head off out into deep water for the next stop. With hundreds of ships plying the delta waters, thousands of reclamation workers could come and go in this way with great ease and efficiency.[16]

Although reclamation workers generally received one dollar a day or thirty dollars a month, without room and board, surviving pay records for laborers on Roberts Island show wages were no simple matter. Apparently, the rates they received were not uniform throughout the islands; some were paid according to a progressive scale. Determined to finish its reclamation project on schedule, for example, the London-based Glasgow-California Land Reclamation Company, Ltd., which in the winter of 1876 bought Roberts Island from Whitney and instituted this policy to reward loyal workers and keep them on the job. One day of work on Roberts Island usually earned one dollar. Two days earned $2.25. Four days earned five dollars. Another system pegged pay to productivity by instituting work quotas. To calculate what they had earned and provide a measure of productivity, levee workers left a column or pyramid of untouched dirt in the middle of each pit. Measuring these columns every four or five days, China bosses would use an abacus to calculate the cubic yards of earth moved, and their wages were tied to their productivity. "Our engineer measures the work, the Chinamen measure it, and we seldom have any disagreement," explained George Roberts in 1876 to the U.S. Congress, Joint Select Committee to Investigate Chinese Immigration. "They are very accurate in their measurements." By the mid-1870s, perhaps four thousand reclamation workers were employed under such arrangements, making them the first piece-rate workers employed on a large scale.[17]

Under these circumstances, exploitation ran rampant. On some islands, the Chinese would be employed to build levees out of peat soil when, in fact, the ground was clay. Landowners preferred clay because it made better levees, but they would lure the Chinese under pretext that they would be digging and moving peat. This saved them considerable amounts of money, as the going rate for moving the much lighter peat was 7.5 cents per cubic yard, as compared to 13.25 cents for the much heavier clay. Another form of abuse originated among the Chinese themselves and stemmed from dishonest bosses. In one famous case, workers on Grand Island entrusted their entire earnings, in sums of twenty to two hundred dollars to their foreman, Ah Jack, only to lose everything—some six thousand dollars—when the man disappeared with the cash. This was not an entirely uncommon occurrence. Contractors, apparently, were always disappearing with payrolls.[18]

Alert to various fraudulent pay methods and always suspicious of their foremen, field hands did not tolerate crooked contractors and were not afraid to take action against them. To minimize theft, they demanded that landowners inform them when contractors were paid. So informed, they would place the subcontractors under surveillance and prevent them from fleeing with their payroll. On many occasions, however, they went further. Several times on Twitchell Island, field hands confronted foremen who had withheld their pay, tied them up, and extracted their wages. After doing so, they called in George Roberts himself, turned the foreman over to him, and saw him run off the island. In March 1878 two hundred field hands contracted to work on Union Island revolted against "Land Hog" Williams when, upon arriving, they discovered that there was work sufficient for forty men. Enraged and disappointed, they threw their labor contractor into the Sacramento River, and then ran Williams and his staff off the island. Twenty-five of the "ringleaders" were arrested by Sheriff Thomas Cunningham the following day, but they refused to identify others involved. Only after a second armed expedition under County Constable Ben Kohlberg surrounded the 142 Chinese remaining on the island did they identify their leaders, who were promptly arrested and taken to jail in Stockton.[19]

If the Chinese were sometimes uppity, they were also inventive and developed a variety of contraptions to compensate for the harsh environment, among them "tule shoes," large, snowshoelike, woven tule mats attached to the hooves of horses. Some accounts of agricultural technology claim that these devices originated a generation later, invented by white celery growers working the peat bogs around La Cienega near Los Angeles. Like many other myths and distortions, this one is not entirely inaccurate. In their zeal to exploit their fertile bog land, celery growers did use "peat shoes," as they called them, but they did not invent the devices, and instead borrowed them after the Chinese had perfected them in the delta. It is not difficult to see why the Chinese created such gadgets. Working in the soft peat soil, they regularly struggled to control horses that became bogged down, panicked, and thrashed about as they pulled scrapers, often injuring themselves and their drivers. Sometimes a poor horse was sucked under and the men could not extract the animal. To overcome this problem, the Chinese first fashioned oversized horseshoes out of ash planks, the idea being to spread the weight of the animals. Ten inches long and eight inches wide, these, the first tule shoes, had a one and one-half inch thick webbing and were held to special studs underneath the hooves on the front legs of each horse. Thus equipped, horses made a poor showing on dry land, clumping along heavily. But once they learned to wear the devices, they could work in bogs without floundering. All they had to do was swing each leg out in a wide circle to avoid tripping. Allowing horses to move slowly over otherwise impassable ground, the shoes worked so well that the Chinese rapidly modified and improved them. Replacing the ash with iron rings about twelve inches across, they joined them to ordinary metal horseshoes by means of metal supports, creating what were in effect oversized horseshoes that quickly became standard on horses employed by all farmers working in bog lands.[20]

Less than a decade after first moving into the delta, China bosses and field hands alike could look back on numerous accomplishments. No group outside railroad construction exerted such influence on the landscape, supervised such a large number of workers at one time, shed so much blood and sweat, endured more difficult working conditions, or contributed more to the advancement of agriculture. Thanks to the army of Chinese gang workers, bayous were being drained, farmland protected, and agricultural projects launched on a scale heretofore thought impossible. To some growers, it seemed that the Chinese were as essential to their prosperity as the rich delta soil, literally agents of transformation excavating the past and raising the earthworks of industrialized agriculture with every scraper full of soil. "How is it that we can compete with the granaries of the world?" asked a fan of the Chinese. "By Chinese cheap labor . . . This class of laborers, these mud-sills, are at the bottom of our success, and I challenge contradiction. We have reclaimed a million acres and more of swamp, overflowed, and tule lands, where the Chinamen stand up to their waists in soft-tule marsh throwing up this dirt. This land produces seventy-five bushels of wheat per acre." The developments trumpeted by this spokesman were real and even more impressive than he described them—and they were being duplicated in dozens of other agricultural districts throughout California.[21]

డ్

Agricultural expansion in the 1870s was different from the Gold Rush boom. While California's growing population was going to ensure steady growth, a new, even more important, transformative engine promised more. This was the completion of the transcontinental railroad. When the Central Pacific Railroad and its offshoot the Southern Pacific raked together a network of feeder lines, farmers for the first time were presented with the chance to assemble their fruit and vegetables by the trainload, rather than by the wagon load. Although vast amounts of fruit spoiled when shipped east in cattle cars, boxcars, and ventilated cars, it was clear to everyone that the new transportation system would eventually reconfigure the countryside. Able to ship crops to cities like Tucson, Denver, Laramie, and Albuquerque in just a few days, Chicago in 120 hours, Philadelphia in seven days, and Boston in nine days, fruit and vegetable farmers everywhere in California began exploiting the opportunity to reach new markets by embarking on a spectacular program of growth.[22]

Some changes were immediate and dramatic. In Placer County, a played-out mining district astride the Central Pacific tracks in the foothills east of Sacramento, farmers around Newcastle converted mining flumes into irrigation canals and planted more than forty-seven thousand fruit trees between 1868 and 1870. On Union, Staten, and Bouldin islands in the delta, and on the nine-thousand-acre Pierson tract between Walnut Grove and Courtland, Chinese tenant farmers developed a thriving fruit and vegetable operation. Elsewhere, efforts were no less dazzling. In a frenzy of planting, growers converted land that was once considered marginal or worthless and brought fifty-eight thousand acres under irrigation by 1870. Fruit shipments shot up from three boxcars sent east from Yolo County during the summer of 1869 to seven hundred boxcar loads shipped annually from a half-dozen counties a year later. By the end of the decade, growers were sending fruit east at the rate of more than ten thousand boxcars per year. In one town after another, trains chugged out of sidings decorated in bunting, streamers, flags, and canvas signs typically proclaiming, "Strawberry Special," "Peach Express," "California Ventilated Fast Fruit Special," and "Porterville Oranges: First Carload of Washington Oranges from the Central California Citrus Belt. Best Oranges in the World."[23]

Because none of this could go forward without a system that rounded up labor, agricultural expansion outside of the delta amplified the power of a whole new aggregation of China bosses—bilingual former field hands aspiring to move up in life; China goods dealers and noodle parlor operators capitalizing on their central position in the community; hotel managers who ran one or two crews of twenty to forty men and supplied job information; store owners who operated from the front porch; boardinghouse proprietors and laundry operators doing their business in back rooms; agents of the Six Companies and "high bossee men" who divided up the countryside into spheres of influence; anyone with links to district leaders, knowledge of the farm labor market, or connections with growers; and above all, clever and energetic men who saw the moment and seized the opportunity. The managerial contribution of the China bosses is, in fact, one of the keys to understanding of the nature of agricultural development. For the first time in California history, an intermediary class of contractors exercised an influential role on the course of events. By moving into labor contracting, these men hoped to be in position to handle ever larger numbers of former railroad laborers and newly arrived immigrants. Their work assembling field hands in a labor-starved industry, distributing them as needed, competing with one another for jobs and men, overseeing gangs in the fields, and creating a layer of countervailing power paralleled the rise of padrone labor among Italian, Greek, and Mexican contractors elsewhere in the United States and became the essential link in the chain of agricultural development.[24]

The speed with which China bosses executed their move into the agricultural districts outside of the delta was long remembered by contemporaries with awe, disbelief, and grudging admiration. Responding to the desperate appeals of Los Angeles winemakers, a San Francisco China boss rounded up a six-man crew, loaded the men into a freighter, and sailed south to Anaheim in February. Lodged in excellent quarters with their own cook, the men worked steadily for the next six months unclogging irrigation canals and putting them in working order. Paid a total of $538, the China boss earned even more by renting out each of his men to local farmers at the unheard-of rate of $10 a day. In July, just as the San Francisco boss and his men returned north, a rival provoked considerable commentary when he brought a large crew into the Pajaro Valley. Determined to secure a foothold and please his employers, this boss cut quite a different, far less lucrative, but ultimately more long-term deal. Realizing that there would be plenty of work once agriculture became established, but that farmers were in a precarious financial state, this boss agreed to bring in the harvest in exchange for little more than food, lodging, and promissory notes redeemable only after growers sold their crops.[25]

The flow of men picked up in January 1870, when Jon Tim, a China boss for John Bidwell, assembled a crew in Chico and set them to plowing fields, pruning grapevines, and digging up cottonwoods; on the basis of his performance, Tim became a trusted ranch manager who supervised dozens of crews throughout Butte County. By May, the Chinese who had arrived in the Pajaro Valley the previous year were "busily engaged in hoeing and plowing" the hop yards around Watsonville. At about the same time, railroad construction bosses brought more crews out of the Sierra Nevada to Knight's Ferry on the edge of the Sierra foothills and to Benjamin Flint's San Justo Rancho near San Juan Bautista. Hired by Abraham Schell, a freethinking German immigrant winemaker at Red Mountain Vineyard near Knight's Ferry, one crew of railroad veterans terraced the hillsides and planted 275 acres of wine grapes, spent most of the winter blasting and excavating a cavernous system of underground wine storage vaults, and with loans from Schell, bought lots, erected homes, and settled into a small Chinatown. Another crew planted and cultivated sugar beets on Flint's San Juan Bautista ranch. After sending their crop north to be processed at the California Sugar Beet Company at Alvarado, the first sugar beet factory in the United States, they established the nucleus for a thriving Chinatown in San Juan Bautista.[26]

By the summer of 1870, census enumerators identified 180 Chinese field hands in San Mateo County, mostly in the truck farms of First Township just south of San Francisco; and 145 in Santa Clara County, mainly in Santa Clara and San Jose townships, where the berry industry was concentrated. Another 350 were tabulated in Alameda County, chiefly Washington Township, around the old San Jose mission and in the plains between San Francisco Bay and the coastal foothills. There were also 163 Chinese in the early fruit district of Solano County, primarily in the Green and Vaca valleys. Counting those in the delta, some sixteen hundred Chinese were identified by census takers as working on farms throughout the state, although the number could easily have been double or triple that official figure.[27]

Early in 1871, a "brigade of Celestials" built an irrigation canal in Ventura County. A few months later, when Bakersfield growers began planting cotton, previously cultivated only on a small scale, local newspapers launched a campaign to bring Chinese laborers into the southern San Joaquin Valley. Late that summer, Chinese were spotted harvesting wine grapes in the Napa Valley, digging a canal alongside Mexicans on the west side of the San Joaquin Valley, and scrambling through the vines harvesting hops on Orrin Smith's ranch near Watsonville.[28]

These incursions proceeded without incident until August 5, 1871, when a China boss arrived on the W. H. Coe hop ranch in Santa Clara seeking a contract to pick several hundred acres of hops. Apparently the boss had been attracted by the high wages Coe and his partner, Isaac Bird, offered to overcome a labor shortage. But before a contract to provide most, if not all, of Coe's hop pickers was negotiated, a fight broke out between a white field hand named Woods and his sister. When Woods began beating her, the China boss intervened in an attempt to stop the abuse. He grabbed Woods and when the man still would not stop his attack, the China boss struck the laborer repeatedly on the back and head. This saved the woman but infuriated Woods, who now turned his rage on the China boss. Not wanting to continue fighting, the China boss attempted to flee, but Woods ran him down, caught him by the queue, and struck him behind his head several times with his fist. The China boss died within minutes. Woods went into town and gave himself up to authorities, but was never prosecuted. It had all happened too fast for the other Chinese present to intervene on behalf of their compatriot.[29]

Some Chinese moving into the ranks of farm labor at this time did so to escape urban violence. This is what happened on October 26, following a savage riot that left nineteen Chinese residents of Negro Alley in Los Angeles dead of gunshots and hanging from lampposts. Fearing for their lives, several dozen Chinese abandoned cooking, laundry work, and vegetable gardening and fled out of town to work alongside Indian and Mexican field hands for L. J. Rose at Sunny Slope Winery, the largest and most modern winery in Southern California. "The two factions soon fraternized and had a fine time trying to teach each other a few words of their respective languages, of which mixture they made a fine jargon," recalled the Bavarian-born Rose in his memoir *Sunny Slope*. "The Chinamen adapted themselves readily to their new surroundings, were absolutely dependable and honest, rarely losing a day and seldom quitting their jobs, easy to get along with in every particular, housing themselves in quarters that one-third their number of Caucasians would rebel against." But while they seemed ideal workmen in every respect, with bosses who were able to iron out most problems, their narrow escape from the Negro Alley violence marked them deeply, and they refused to tolerate any abuse. "On rare occasions a Mexican struck one of them; in an instant every Chinaman in sight or within calling distance—perhaps half a dozen—would be on top of the lone adversary, clawing with might and main," recalled Rose. "As they were not naturally vicious, their onslaughts did little damage, sufficient, however, to teach the assailant to be sure the next time he started anything with one of them that no other Chinamen were around."[30]

Despite their efficient work habits and willingness to accept even the most grueling assignments, the Chinese were increasingly harassed. Still, as the hostility grew and the violence continued into the winter and spring of 1872, the Chinese did not back off. On May 24, when a wheat farmer near Red Bluff killed a Chinese field hand, apparently for no reason, Chinese incensed by the act cornered the farmer and beat him to a pulp. That summer they ignored additional attacks and began clearing land for new vineyards in San Mateo, Los Angeles, Anaheim, and Napa. Elsewhere they bided their time. Waiting until farmers faced some crisis and were desperate for labor, they moved in and secured contracts. Many farmers complied immediately.[31]

One of the largest farming companies to hire Chinese at this time was the Sacramento Sugar Beet Company. When the company failed to obtain enough white workers to plant its first crop, China bosses moved in and planted eleven hundred acres of sugar beets using new, twelve-row seed-sowers. At about the same time, Chinese were also observed south of Bakersfield on Kern Island planting cotton for the newly formed California Cotton Growers and Manufacturers Association. Throughout the spring, the Chinese continued irrigating, weeding, and thinning the huge Sacramento Sugar Beet Company crop, and in June, 350 Chinese moved into the company's fields, attacked the sugar beets—according to one observer—like a small army moving into battle, and disposed of the crop without the slightest problem. Three months later, near St. Helena, one hundred Chinese began picking hops for five cents per pound. In October, when they began picking wine grapes, the *Napa County Reporter* carried a humorous story that inadvertently suggested their ever widening importance. A team of horses pulling a load of grapes near Oakville Grade became frightened by an approaching train and bolted straight for the railway crossing. Describing how the train conductor succeeded in keeping the animals from colliding with the train by throwing pieces of bark and wood at them, the newspaper only mentioned in the last sentence that the Chinese apparently had been working in the grape harvest. "Several China-men with their tails flying also joined in the exciting race," observed the paper, "and for a while it was doubtful which pulled the most, they or the locomotive."[32]

As the Chinese dispersed, self-made San Francisco economist and journalist Henry George became alarmed at their growing importance and launched an attack. Already well known for his campaign against bonanza wheat barons, George felt equally strongly about the Chinese. Passionately arguing that land monopoly created undemocratic societies by producing unparalleled poverty topped by a few rich land barons, George saw Chinese "cheap labor" at the base of this unfair feudal structure. First in *Progress and Poverty* and then in *Our Land and Land Policy*, he blamed the Chinese for many of the state's problems. Comparing Chinese field hands to black slaves, he warned in one attack after another that they constituted a serious threat, for they were "simple barbarians," the new "peons" for big farmers, with "habits of thought rendered permanent by being stamped upon countless generations." Mincing no words, he predicted, "What the barbarians enslaved by foreign wars were to the great landlords of Ancient Italy, what the blacks of the African coast were to the great landlords of the Southern states, the Chinese coolies may be, in fact are already beginning to be, to the great landlords of our Pacific slope." Such, he wrote, was the "blight that has fallen upon California."[33]

Endlessly cited, George's scapegoating analysis became gospel to those who blamed Chinese field hands for whatever woes befell the countryside. His proposed solution—exclusion of the Chinese on the grounds that they were "utter heathens, treacherous, sensual, cowardly, and cruel"—would become a rallying cry for racist elements. But George's rhetoric, much like the violence of the previous two years, did not stop the Chinese. Early in 1873, China bosses from Chico, realizing that there was much work to be done, visited every farm or ranch around Llano Seco, a new farming area opening to cultivation in the northern Sacramento Valley. Upon arriving, they walked the bare ground with farmers, noting the lay of the land and the amount of brush and trees to be removed. Usually they would estimate the number of men required, calculate the time it would take to complete the project, then make a verbal bid. Once hired, they swarmed in with their crews, set up camp, and, moving tirelessly over the landscape as a kind of migratory land-clearing operation, cleared a few hundred acres, then readied it for grain planting.[34]

One hundred and fifty miles south, at Los Banos, a crew of more than 370 Chinese hired by the Miller and Lux cattle business organized into thirteen gangs to extend the San Joaquin and Kings Canal sixty-seven miles west across the valley to Orestimba Creek. Their work, the first big land-moving operation outside of the delta, would create the largest irrigation canal in the American West and open another 160,000 acres to irrigation. With each man paid twenty-seven dollars per month (a portion of which contractors Ah Yung and Ah Yah retained to cover food and housing), the Chinese payroll in August topped ten thousand dollars, nearly twice that of skilled Italian and Portuguese carpenters, whose monthly wages ranged from eighty to one hundred dollars. In another typical project later that year, sixty Chinese employed by Dr. George Griffith on the Parrot Land Grant in Butte County cleared more than three thousand acres of land and prepared it for wheat, enclosing the entire farm with a wire fence, the first such structure in the county.[35]

If China bosses had planned it, they could not have devised better advertisements for their work. Some crews deployed so effectively, that it was not unusual for one thousand men to be on the job within a few days after a grower put out the call for help. As a result, China bosses experienced a sensational growth in power and influence. So great was the demand for their services that some bosses literally grew fat on the profits earned supplying field hands to farmers around the state. One of the biggest, both in a literal and figurative sense, was Chu Muk, a gigantic man with a thriving business on Sacramento Street in San Francisco. Through Muk, thousands of field hands found employment on farms in Stockton, Sacramento, and Fresno, as well as in Alaskan salmon canneries. Closely supervised by an extensive network of Muk's foremen, field hands shifted between industries as the work requirements and seasons dictated, and in this way overcame to some extent the seasonal nature of their work. But Chinese field hands were in such demand that whites soon entered the contracting business. One of the largest Anglo contracting firms, the San Francisco employment service of Sisson and Wallace maintained extensive contacts with dozens of China bosses and apparently deployed and kept track of men through a web of Chinese subcontractors.[36]

Moving into the countryside, China bosses won and kept jobs by underbidding competitors. They had always done so, but now they settled on a standard pay scale of one dollar a day without board, cementing the wage by holding to it for many years regardless of the season or skill. This was considerably less than the average wage of $1.25 for Mexicans and $1.50 for white laborers, both of whom required an average additional expenditure of sixty cents for board. A general rule held that a grower could hire four Chinese for the price of two whites or Mexicans.[37]

Although the Chinese certainly understood that they received smaller wages than whites, they did not see themselves as "cheap laborers." Possessing a Confucian exuberance for life coupled with a fanatical devotion to purpose and a love of work for its own sake, they mentally converted wages in California into purchasing power back home. "Whatever you do there," one brother said to another as he was about to leave China, "you can earn more than here." The goal was steady employment. Describing this orientation while recovering from an exhausting day of stoop labor, one immigrant wrote to the editor of the *Watsonville Pajaronian* with a simple explanation. "Work," he said, "is more honorable than idleness."[38]

Thrifty living multiplied the earnings. With no one else to support in California, a steadily employed bachelor field hand could live on about eight to ten dollars a month, sometimes as little as fifteen to thirty cents a day. After spending another two dollars for board, one dollar for clothing or a pipe, and two dollars for recreation, he could, if lucky, save ten to fifteen dollars each month, thereby mentally converting the value of savings into the expanded purchasing power and higher social status money brought to wives, children, and families back home. And those wages did in fact become a significant factor in the economic life of China's Sze Yap region, where living costs were considerably lower than in California. There, a family could live comfortably on seven to fifteen cents a day, and even the smallest savings sent home could make a considerable difference.[39]

To maximize their savings, the Chinese economized on expenses by always congregating by themselves, separate from any Mexican or white field hands, in clean but rudimentary camps. Under these circumstances, China bosses stretched their resources as far as possible. Describing their activity around Vacaville, one old farmhand recalled: "You give them a cabin to live in and a little place to raise their garden, and they'd work for you." Making do with whatever was at hand, bosses packed their men into chicken coops, barns, and stables, transforming the buildings into dormitories and fashioning kitchens out of tents and pole and timber sheds. "They will sleep on a board, cook with a brazier, live upon rice and tea, desiccated vegetables . . . and eat the very best they can," observed San Francisco resident Benjamin Brooks. Not all Californians understood this orientation. One Ventura County woman who saw the Chinese squatting on their haunches in the countryside, cooking rice over an open fire amid piles of manure with big blowflies everywhere, could scarcely contain her revulsion. "We were not thinking of them as fellow mortals," she confessed years later, "but as a new and interesting species."[40]

With time, China bosses dispelled the misconceptions gained from these first, impulsive glimpses. Drawing closer, observers invariably would be surprised at the lengths to which men went to make their temporary quarters into welcoming places that fully exploited whatever resources were available. Food being one of the major rewards from a hard day of labor, observers invariably noted how camps were organized around some kind of communal cooking area. Traveling with their own cooks who specialized in Chinese foods, work crews often ate their meals from a single, huge, communal pot. Visitors would find men in the evenings ladling out dippers full of steamed pork and vegetables, devouring pans of fried noodles, and washing it all down with cauldrons of freshly brewed tea. With men sitting on logs or rocks, joking, talking, and smoking their corncob pipes after the meal, such camps were far from the foul and depressing places that many farmworkers would later endure.[41]

With near-complete control over field hands, many bosses could not resist the temptation to take advantage of their workers as some had done in the delta. There were many opportunities for small frauds and swindles beyond the nickel-and-dime operations associated with feeding, housing, and transportation. Men were required to clear all of their expenses before receiving their earnings, often at a considerable markup in price, plus a fee of fifty cents to one dollar for finding their work. There were also charges for opium, liquor, prostitutes, tobacco, mail delivery, and letter writing, none of which was open to negotiation. Apparently these added up. Reflecting on the amount of money some China bosses raked in from all the different rackets, the *Pacific Rural Press* reported in August 1884, "Several have grown rich in the business."[42]

Angered by such exploitation, field hands continued to retaliate against corrupt bosses. One famous fight pitted Nom Kee, a Vacaville contractor who attempted to flee with a large payroll, against two members of his crew. Catching up with Kee on a back road, the two field hands proceeded to pummel their boss and, when he drew a pistol to protect himself, disarmed and shot him with his own weapon. Another case involved a contractor named Ing Cue and a crew of seven men who had been harvesting a vineyard east of Rutherford in the Napa Valley. At the end of the season, the men calculated what they were due and submitted a bill for $280. Obtaining the wages in cash, Cue quietly slipped down to Oakville and wired his ill-gotten wealth to San Francisco. But before he could depart the valley, his crew caught up with him, contacted the police, and had him arrested on charges of embezzlement. An even more famous case involved a boss named Ike, who, like Ing Cue, apparently kept all of the wages he collected for his crew. When a crewman named Ah Yung demanded his pay, the two men argued. Ike then drew a revolver and shot and killed Ah Yung. Ike disappeared with the funds, presumably back to China. Commenting on a rash of such incidents, a Napa Valley newspaper could only say: "The average Chinese has as much regard for human life as a rat."[43]

ℒ

Despite the abuses, the boss system was a nearly ideal arrangement. Presenting huge advantages to growers, it allowed them to minimize wage expenditures, stabilize labor relations, and assure an ample supply of tractable workers. According to the editor of the *Fresno Republican*, through their bosses Chinese field hands could be "bought like any other commodity, at so much a dozen or a hundred," and "this elimination of the human element reduces the labor problem to something the employer can understand." From the grower's standpoint, the editor concluded, "The Chinese labor machine . . . is perfect." By employing Chinese, growers avoided not only the expenses but the headaches and responsibilities of feeding and housing field hands. "The food, management or care of the laborers would give them no trouble," observed the *Kern County Californian* of growers employing the Chinese. "No preparation for them would be needed." With bosses, field hands "could be treated like the beasts of the field, and like them be removed by their drivers or herders when no longer needed."[44]

There was also the matter of convenience. A half-century later, the journalist Alice Prescott Smith vividly recalled in *Sunset* magazine how, during the grape harvest, gangs of Chinese would pack into various Chinatowns waiting to find work. With the crops quickly ripening, growers would become desperate, but the Chinese bided their time until a grower hitched up his wagon, headed into town, and grabbed the first contractor in sight. "John, you find me fifty men. Come Thursday," he would say. The "square brown man" would consider the question, dicker over price, and just as the grower gave up hope, reply "All lite, I get em." Nothing more was required. Within a week, "fifty replicas of John Chinaman" marched in with mess kits, tents, and bedding. Living in the fields, they worked like locusts, picked the crop, then melted away.[45]

In some of the emerging agricultural districts, where new growers were unfamiliar with rounding up and supervising large numbers of field hands, China bosses aggressively emphasized their role as intermediaries. American Fruit Company manager L. C. Lee once recalled in an interview for the Survey of Race Relations how the Chinese were completely under the control of their contractors and went about their tasks with a military efficiency. "No individual worker or gang will ever come to me. I cannot go to the field and give orders . . . but must issue all orders . . . to the spokesman," explained Lee. If he had any difficulties, the contractor handled the matter. "Everything comes through this one man."[46]

Often repeated with minor but creative variations, these themes became common as larger numbers of Chinese made their way onto more farms. "Why tolerate grumpy whites and their tendency to walk off the job?" asked growers at their annual conventions. With the Chinese, when the work was done a grower simply dismissed them and they vanished, only to reappear when next needed. As the editor of the *Pacific Rural Press* explained, the "Chinese . . . readily move, like armies, come when called for, and depart when their mission is accomplished."[47]

So great was the role of China bosses that some contemporaries credited them with making possible California's rapid transition from a mining stronghold to an agricultural leader. "Without these useful workers, California would at this day be scarcely more than Nevada—a great mining-ground, whose wealth all flows away," wrote Charles L. Brace in *The New West*. "With Chinese labor and the immeasurable advantages of climate, the California farmer is able now to compete in the markets of the world with the farmers of Illinois and Indiana, and the peasants of the Black Sea." A corollary belief among later students holds that the emergence of commercial farming and the transition from wheat to fruit and vegetable farming would have been delayed at least twenty-five years had the Chinese not been available. "They were a vital factor, one is inclined to state *the* vital factor, in making the transition possible," wrote Carey McWilliams in *Factories in the Field*. The assertion is a common one among those seeking to spotlight the role of the Chinese at this time, but it has the flaw of most such ideologically oriented claims: It is history based on wishful thinking rather than facts, with just enough basis in anecdotal evidence to seem correct.[48]

∮∂

Only in one farming enterprise outside of delta land reclamation (Santa Clara strawberries) and one vineyard venture (Buena Vista Winery) did the Chinese actually dominate the farm labor force. But in one industry, tobacco farming, China bosses did indeed briefly monopolize field labor and by all accounts advanced the interests of their crews in the face of considerable hostility. China bosses were attracted to tobacco culture by a very special figure in early farming, James D. Culp. A New York native who had come west in 1859, Culp settled in Gilroy, a small farm town sixty miles south of San Francisco, where, after years of experimenting, he patented an improved process for curing California-grown Havana tobacco leaves. In 1872, Culp brought together a group of San Francisco investors, sold them on his new process, raised $250,000 in capital, and formed the American Tobacco Company. He then announced plans to build a cigar factory in Gilroy and to plant tobacco on his ranch near San Felipe, on the border between Santa Clara and San Benito counties. He soon merged his company with the Pacific Tobacco Manufacturing Company to form the Consolidated Tobacco Company. After purchasing a building on Rosanna Street, Culp erected a brick cigar factory near the railroad siding on Monterey Street. Although he had not yet gone into full production, Culp vowed that his cigar factory would be the world's largest, capable of producing two million cigars per month. His plans set off a frenzy of tobacco planting on the farms around town that immediately attracted the attention of China bosses.[49]

China bosses became involved with Culp because he offered them work both in his factory and in his fields, and because there was not enough white labor in the area to handle all of Culp's operations nor those of his neighbors. Days before the cigar factory opened, China bosses from San Francisco brought in 140 men. But not just any men. These men all had one common characteristic—very small fingers—because Culp believed that attribute essential for rolling the little *cerut* cigars he first produced. Culp apparently made a special trip north to San Francisco specifically to solicit the services of these small-fingered Chinese.[50]

Any Chinese laborer could find work in the area (with or without the intervention of a San Francisco boss) either on Culp's San Felipe tobacco plantation or on neighboring tobacco farms. Hundreds of unemployed Chinese headed for Gilroy apparently on their own. Upon arriving, all they had to do was visit one of two rival Chinese contractors in town—Ah Tyng, who had his headquarters near the cigar factory on Monterey Street, and Ah Quin, whose business was on the corner of Church and Sixth streets. Neatly dividing up the labor market, Ah Tyng supplied men to Culp's factory, Ah Quin to Culp's tobacco farms.[51]

The Havana tobacco grown by Culp for making cigars and the Florida variety he cultivated for chewing purposes required different growing practices, harvesting dates, curing times, and cultural techniques, thus the agricultural operations performed by the Chinese were spaced out, providing a long period of steady employment. During March, bosses directed men to transplant the young seedlings, tediously pushing each one individually into the soil. Throughout the summer, they weeded and irrigated the plants. Because tobacco plants produced three crops during a season, bosses were busy supervising harvest crews from mid-June through early October. At various other times they supplied men to Culp's nine large curing houses. Here, Chinese worked from late summer into the fall sweating, turning, and racking the leaves, and hauling loads of finished tobacco to the factory for processing.[52]

No single operation occupied them for very long; often during that first year, bosses shifted workers daily between various tasks, moving from a field where they were setting out plants in the morning to a curing shed where they stripped leaves and bulked away cured tobacco in the evening. Although there were white foremen and overseers, only the Chinese actually handled tobacco and only the bosses directed men. That was because constant exposure to the leaves had a toxic effect and no white men in Gilroy would at first touch the plants on a daily basis.[53]

Within a few years, China bosses at Gilroy were supervising several hundred men who grew, harvested, and cured a million and a half pounds of tobacco annually. That was enough to make two hundred thousand cigars per month and pack ten thousand pounds of smoking and chewing tobacco for shipment, and it went a long way to establishing the business of tobacco growing in Santa Clara and San Benito counties. In fact, on the basis of how well the Chinese worked,

Culp announced plans to add a second story to his factory, erect a three-story brick building in the rear of the old one, and expand cigar production considerably. At the same time, farmers around town expanded tobacco growing until the Gilroy area became essentially one large tobacco plantation. But while good for the local economy, it did not please many whites in town.[54]

᪾

Simmering just below the surface, racial hatred and xenophobia ran deep in Gilroy, as it did throughout much of rural California, where sporadic individual outbursts of violence, and on several occasions, large-scale riots, had taken the lives of many Chinese. "The poor Chinaman has been kicked from pillar to post till he hardly knows if he has a right to live," commented the *Napa County Reporter* late in 1872. But before then, no one in rural California had attempted to organize an anti-Chinese movement, mobilize the public on a large scale, or drive all Chinese from the fields and out of the state. That was about to change.[55]

The impetus for change was a national financial panic. As businesses failed during the fall of 1873, thousands of unemployed men swarmed into farming districts in search of work. Commercial farmers regarded this as a fortunate development, providing them with unlimited numbers of field hands at a moment when they needed all of the laborers they could hire. Instead of a perpetual labor shortage, growers now had exactly what they always wanted—a surplus of desperate men competing for jobs. But for the Chinese, the appearance of the unemployed classes was not so fortunate. With tramps lounging about the sidewalks and saloons of every farm town while China bosses were apparently able to find their crews plenty of work, many whites became jealous and blamed the Chinese for their problems. Following a pattern that they repeated on countless occasions over the next generation, men gathered to rant against the "Yellow Peril" and plan their moves, often singing a popular song:

> His drinks are A-1 and his prices are low
> His motto is always 'The Chinese Must Go!'
> So call on your friends, workingmen, if you please
> Take a good solid drink and drive out the Chinese.[56]

At first, Chinese field hands were not physically harmed. Bosses were threatened with boycotts, and farmers who employed the Chinese received delegations demanding that they dismiss them and hire whites or suffer the consequences. Soon enough, though, the threats turned to violence. Mobs cornered Chinese field hands, cut off their queues, and brutally beat them. A few resorted to even more violent acts. On January 24, 1874, after issuing ultimatums to farmers in the Napa Valley, anti-Chinese agitators set fire to two large hay barns on Terrill Grigsby's winery near Napa City. A field hand awoke to the sound of crackling flames and sounded the alarm. Unable to save any of his belongings, Grigsby watched helplessly as two hundred tons of hay burned, along with seven horses, a large quantity of harnesses, many wagons, buggies, several reapers and mowers, and a header. "The fire was probably the work of an incendiary," concluded the

Napa County Reporter. It was also a mistake. Grigsby, who had arrived from Missouri in 1852 with a wife and seven children, did not yet employ Chinese.[57]

After the Grigsby burning, unemployed men began boldly attacking Chinese field hands throughout the state's agricultural districts. Many assaults took place away from population centers and were not covered by the press. One such incident occurred on the west side of the San Joaquin Valley, in the vicinity of Los Banos during the summer of 1874. Someone murdered a Chinese field hand and threw his body in an irrigation canal. The body floated several miles downstream before it was discovered. Pulled from the water, it was briefly examined by a justice of the peace and, after a brief inquest, thrown back into the canal. Discovered again a few miles further downstream in a different county, it was again pulled out, subjected to another inquest, and again thrown back. "There is no telling how many inquests might have been held over that dead Chinaman if he had been able to stand the hot weather," commented San Joaquin Valley historian Frank F. Latta many years later.[58]

Although their reputation as cheap and efficient laborers went a long way to blunt the surge of hostility, China bosses soon determined that a class of laborers under such constant attack had to be able to dispel any doubts about their abilities. And so bosses everywhere pounced on the tendency of white laborers to pack up and leave. They had plenty of opportunities. Whenever white field hands made a week's wage and "felt the urge of crime or vice," or news of a new gold or silver strike crossed their path, they "wanted an adventure," as the saying went, and skipped out. They would throw down their hop sacks, drop their grape boxes in the middle of a field, or without notice stroll away from picking peaches. This was a major headache for all growers, particularly wheat farmers, who discovered that if one or two white men quit during threshing it often stopped the entire operation.[59]

All that China bosses had to do was wait for the desertions to begin and then offer their services. Staying as long as required, the Chinese on more than one occasion took over from departing crews and bound wheat by moonlight to bring in the crop before the impending November rains. For these reasons, they became indispensable to many grain farmers and to fruit growers who had initially been hostile to them. "They have found no labor so well adapted to their needs as the Chinese," reported the *Bakersfield Californian*. "The Chinese laborers are perfectly satisfied if they can obtain work for two or three months of the year . . . The rest of the year, even if they pick up no odd jobs . . . they can subsist for a few cents a day."[60]

By late 1874, the Chinese had earned a reputation as steady laborers who never struck, grumbled, or walked off the job. As they proved their worth, the Chinese assumed an almost legendary status. In Alameda and Santa Clara counties and in Georgiana Township in Sacramento County, there are many descriptions of "pig-tailed yellow gardeners" dominating farm work with their "ant-like labor," and around Sonora in Tuolumne County, there are accounts of orchards "swarming with Celestials." But it is impossible to determine from these reports exactly how much of the workforce they comprised at this time. Only one thing is certain: from this point forward the Chinese forced their advantage. China bosses completely took over many farms, running day-to-day operations while landowners left for long vacations. On one farm twelve miles south of Sacramento, a farmwife later recalled how "none but the Chinamen are employed. . . . One Chinaman has been employed six or seven years and acts as interpreter and foreman. . . . The owner will have nothing to do with any other laborers, because he finds in these faithfulness and obedience—qualities which he looks for in vain in any other race."[61]

Realizing the opportunities presented by these attitudes, China bosses considerably expanded their control of hillside terracing for vineyards, rock wall construction, brush grubbing, land clearing, canal digging, fencing, and other farmwork requiring mass gang labor. So many men became China bosses that growers could literally order crews like seed, tools, and other farm supplies. Adding to that efficiency was the extremely competitive nature of contractors, who often jostled and maneuvered with one another for jobs. Nowhere in California at this time did bosses exert a greater impact than in Anaheim. With a thriving local Chinese population second in size only to its German residents, bosses there had a huge reservoir of labor to draw from. To solicit men, bosses ran large advertisements in the Anaheim newspapers. "NOTICE," began one typical announcement in the January 9, 1875, *Anaheim Gazette.* "China laborers in all departments can be found and employed at WANG LUNG's Wash House on Center St., to wit: Good cooks, laundrymen and all other business. See WANG LUNG, agent of SEE YUP Company for Information." Another Anaheim contractor in his advertisement urged farmers seeking Chinese field hands to consult: "Employment office of Gee Wau Co., Los Angeles St., Anaheim."[62]

During 1875, Wan Yup, an agent for the See Yup Company, who operated his contracting business out of his washhouse on Center Street in Anaheim, supplied eighty-five men to the Cajon Water District, which was building an irrigation canal running sixteen miles along the Santa Ana River from Bedrock Canyon to the Anaheim Union Receiving Reservoir. Another one hundred workers came south from San Francisco through the Grange Labor Association. Beginning work on March 27, they spent the next eight months quarrying rock, erecting huge rock walls, and excavating and moving land. The work took them through eight miles of hard sandstone and shale and included a cut chiseled several hundred feet long and ten feet deep through solid rock. Covering their activity on a daily basis, the *Anaheim Gazette* reported their progress, including many fossil discoveries, the number of flumes crossing gulches, and a recurrent problem with rodents that burrowed into the soft mesa fill, causing water to break through at such a rate that the Chinese for a time could neither kill the rodents nor fill the holes fast enough to keep water in the ditch.[63]

On November 13, 1875, after excavating the first eight miles of the canal, most of the Chinese were discharged. The following morning, seventy of them were spotted camping beside the Anaheim railroad depot waiting for a train to Los Angeles. Meanwhile, a small crew remained behind to enlarge the head of the ditch, bore a tunnel, and build 2,640 running feet of flumes and more than five thousand feet of subsidiary ditches. They continued to supply the muscle power driving forward all of the "heavy rock work" as the project stalled and restarted and was completed three years later by the Anaheim Union Water Company. After finishing the digging, a dozen Chinese stayed on to maintain the canal. But none was present at a huge barbecue and canal opening celebration on November 6, 1878. When speakers praised all present for having seen the project through to the end, none mentioned the Chinese. Nor did the president of the water company when he closed the ceremony with a brief history of the canal.[64]

As they were digging their way toward Anaheim, the Chinese were also expanding their role in the Napa Valley, still largely an enclave of white labor. That orientation changed several weeks before the 1875 grape harvest, when three hundred Chinese laborers arrived in St. Helena, where they had been contracted to pick wine grapes, only to find the harvest delayed by cool weather. Unable to return to San Francisco, they settled in a field on the south side of town, digging three wells and scrounging up building materials. A labor boss named Wah Chung happened by as they squatted in their camp and, finding them destitute and verging on starvation, promised to feed them in exchange for a cut of whatever wages they earned. The men had little alternative and agreed to the deal. Later someone asked Chung how the arrangement worked. Quite well, he replied; in addition to receiving a lump sum to cover wages for the harvesters he provided to the growers, he also received a finder's fee from each man, and additionally collected money for food, blankets, clothes, and other essentials.

After the harvest, most of the men remained with Chung. That winter they began pruning grapevines and cutting hillside terraces. Quickly the demographics of the grape harvest changed. Mexicans, Indians, and Chileans still worked here and there, but they were on the way out. White field hands, who were no longer an overwhelming majority, continued working in every vineyard but two or three. But on operations where massed crews were necessary, white men simply could not displace Chung's crews, who took control of most of the big jobs around the valley.[65]

That winter, China bosses also made further inroads on John Bidwell's ranch, where they replaced whites who had broken a contract to dig up trees and stumps in an old orchard. Settling into quarters in town, they commuted to Rancho Chico each morning; after finishing the job, many were hired on as permanent field hands. Working for wages of about half that of whites and two-thirds of what Indians received, they became an integral part of Bidwell's farm labor force, joining a small group of Chinese already on the farm. And though comprising only 16 percent of Bidwell's farmhands, they exerted a disproportionate influence by specializing in specific tasks. Soon they were harvesting all of Bidwell's fruit, handling all of the nursery tasks in his ornamental garden, and growing all of the vegetables for Bidwell's force of about four hundred permanent field hands. However, they did not work in Bidwell's cannery or in his large, fruit-drying factory, jobs Bidwell reserved for thirty to forty white women, young girls, and schoolboys from town. Nor did Chinese work in the flour mill, grain fields, dairy, hog farm, almond orchard, or in haying and seeding—tasks white men and Indian laborers still dominated.[66]

By far the greatest success of 1875 occurred in the Central Valley, where China bosses were overwhelmed with requests for men to plant thousands of acres of new vineyards. The largest project centered on the Natomas Land Company, a massive, industrial-type grape-growing operation launched by Horatio P. Livermore sixteen miles northeast of Sacramento. Originally hired to plant 110 acres of Muscat and Flame Tokay grapes in the red volcanic soil sloping back from the east bank of the American River near Folsom, as was often the case, large numbers of Chinese remained behind to irrigate the vineyards during the summer and to harvest existing Muscat vineyards in the fall. Although they stopped making raisins that fall when Livermore abandoned the operation (owing to frequent early rains), the Chinese picked up additional work establishing what came to be known as the "Shipping Vineyard," a three-hundred-acre, ultramodern, irrigated table-grape operation centered on a giant packing house that sprawled for a half-mile on both sides of a railroad spur line. Here, they did everything from making lug boxes and packing grapes to loading the packed fruit carefully onto railcars and sending it east to market weeks ahead of grapes harvested in the Napa and Sonoma valleys. While most workers left after the harvest season, several large gangs remained. Establishing a small China camp, they pruned grapevines and cleared additional vineyard lands.[67]

෪

As the Chinese spread further into the California countryside, the nation slid further into depression, and that winter even more unemployed men went looking for work, swamping privately supported almshouses. With agriculture sagging and industries shutting down, wages fell and the standard workday increased to ten hours or more. Newspapers such as the *Alta California* saw the problem as a normal part of the business cycle and called for additional municipal lodgings where board would include water, black bread, and salt fish, and where tramps could sleep on blankets spread on the floors. But for many, the economic downturn was grist for the anti-Chinese movement. That spring, letters blaming the Chinese for these economic ills began appearing in rural newspapers throughout the state. On March 30, 1876, the *Marin Journal* claimed that most Californians believed of the Chinese field hand:

> That he is a slave, reduced to the lowest terms of beggarly economy, and is no fit competitor for an American freeman; that he herds in scores, lives in small dens, where a white man and wife could hardly breathe, and has none of the wants of a civilized white man. . . . That American men, women and children cannot be what free people should be, and compete with such degraded creatures in the labor market.[68]

The first indication of just how serious the situation was came on April 3. Following mass marches by anticoolie clubs in San Francisco, the California legislature empowered the San Francisco Board of Supervisors to send a delegation to Washington, D.C., to lobby Congress to terminate legal Chinese immigration under the Burlington-Seward Treaty of 1868. The second and more significant indication of mounting hostility toward Chinese field hands came a few days later, when state senator Creed Haymond had a resolution adopted, amid great fanfare, calling for the appointment of a special California senate committee to investigate Chinese immigration. The timely creation of the highly publicized investigating committee in the midst of growing anti-Chinese furor was a Democratic ploy, although Haymond, the appointed chairman, was a Republican. With an eye on the November elections, Democrats wanted to see to it that the "Chinese Question" was kept alive, as it was an issue likely to appeal to the state's voting population, one-half of whom were foreign-born. With four of its members from San Francisco and only two from rural areas, the committee was weighted heavily toward urban interests. In fact, no committee member had even the slightest acquaintance with field hands and the work they were doing.[69]

Over the course of fifteen days of hearings beginning on April 11 in San Francisco City Hall, a parade of witnesses appeared before the committee. Of the forty-one Americans called to testify, four were clergymen, one was a farmer, one a lawyer, five were "experts" on the Chinese (rendered so by virtue of having spent varying lengths of time in China), five were municipal police officers, five were special Chinatown police, one was a judge, and the remainder consisted of eleven public officials, two journalists, two manufacturers, an expressman, a dealer in marble, a ship's captain, and a mate on a "coolie ship." Selected for their predictable testimony, these witnesses had prepared and rehearsed their answers long before the committee began its hearings. Like the committee members, all but one or two knew nothing about farm labor or the role that the Chinese were playing in agriculture. Most of their testimony centered on the urban problems of prostitution, gambling, opium smoking, and secret societies.[70]

With their highly negative testimony, the string of witnesses reinforced the picture of the Chinese as an unmitigated evil causing the Pacific Coast, in the words of one man, to "become a Botany Bay to which the criminal classes of China are brought in large numbers." Not coincidentally, Chinese field hands experienced a sudden upsurge of hostility during and after the two-week investigation. For example, during the hearings the California legislature passed a so-called cubic-air law to regulate the amount of space allocated tenants of lodging houses to ensure livable standards; and a few days later, the San Francisco Board of Supervisors passed a "queue ordinance" requiring law enforcement authorities to shave the hair of all Chinese prisoners in the county jail. On April 31, the state legislature banned Chinese from working on irrigation and reclamation projects. For the most part, these new laws were not strictly enforced. While a few Chinese field hands found sleeping in boardinghouses were arrested in midnight police forays enforcing the new "cubic-air law," virtually none lost his queue or was dismissed from his irrigation or reclamation job.[71]

Much of what happened to Chinese field hands during 1876 seems to have been the work of the Order of Caucasians, a white supremacist group based in the Sacramento Valley and sometimes known as the Caucasian League. Established at the time of the committee hearings "to protect white labor," embodying many of the vicious features of the Ku Klux Klan, and modeled after a similar anti-Chinese society in San Francisco, the Order of Caucasians spread quickly throughout the agricultural districts. The Order of Caucasians led an anti-Chinese rally in Red Bluff in April and organized another in Marysville during May. Hundreds of new members joined over the summer, and dozens of "anti-coolie" meetings were held in farm towns from Monterey to Chico. Most were peaceful, resulting in nothing more than verbal denunciations and appointment of so-called Fourth of July Committees. But toward the end of the summer, the Order of Caucasians moved beyond talk and instigated a well-coordinated wave of attacks that continued well into the fall.[72]

Chasing "Celestial hop heads" off small farms around Healdsburg, Red Bluff, and Marysville, Order of Caucasian zealots also harassed and threatened the Chinese in rural areas throughout the state. While Order of Caucasian followers were not behind every attack, their widely publicized activities soon inspired imitators, and a rash of anti-Chinese incidents followed. Yet even in the midst of this violence, the Chinese easily found plenty of jobs simply by showing up at the right time. A typical incident, reported in the July 1, 1876, *Gilroy Advocate-Leader*, involved a robust young white "bummer" sitting on the porch of the local hotel complaining that he had been seeking work for a week but could find none on the surrounding farms, all on account of the Chinese. "They are ruining this coast. They are making all the money and taking it out of the state," he said. "Here I have been for a week, trying to get work, but cannot. It is all on account of the Chinese." Suddenly a farmer offered him employment hauling hay at twelve dollars a week and board for the summer, an excellent wage. "Well," said the man, cleaning his fingernails and cursing the Chinese, "I don't believe I care to go about going out today." A few hours later, the *Advocate-Leader* saw a crew of "Celestials" meandering down the road in a cloud of dust toward the haying job. "While we are strongly in favor of anti-Chinese, we cannot but say that the 'bummers' in California have brought the damning curse of the coolie trade upon themselves. Such men as the one above cited have been the cause of bringing to this coast the Chinese we now have. Why? Because the bummer cannot be depended upon."[73]

෨

The worst incidents of anti-Chinese violence occurred not in Northern California but in Southern California near Anaheim. For years, the area southwest of Anaheim had been known mainly for its inhospitable, swampy environment. But owing to the richness of the peat soil, free-flowing artesian wells, and the nearby Santa Ana River, about thirty thousand acres of the Anaheim lowlands between the new and old river channels emerged as a center of Southern California agriculture, renowned for gigantic pumpkins and record harvests of corn, alfalfa, and potatoes. Besides its productivity, the area had nearby wharves and river access, which made for easy shipping of produce up and down the coast. It also possessed two other characteristics. First, it was subject to periodic flooding during the rainy season, so much so that every farmhouse supposedly kept a boat handy as a means to escape rising waters. Second, most of the early residents were devout Methodists and Mormons who held frequent prayer meetings in tent churches. It was said that the head of every household was capable of delivering a sermon on a moment's notice. These two elements, religion and flooding, combined to give the area its name—the "Great Gospel Swamp."[74]

For twenty years, a mixture of races and classes had shared farmwork in the area. Packing into Anaheim in such great numbers toward the end of the fall grape harvest, they were such a sight that they attracted the scrutiny of Polish journalist Henryk Sienkiewicz, who would later win the Nobel Prize for his novels *Quo Vadis* and *Trilogy*. Describing the autumn grape harvest in Anaheim, Sienkiewicz wrote that these were "days of joy and celebration" when "the town was packed with the vineyard hands. There is nothing more picturesque," he continued, "than the sight of these people, composed partly of a sprinkling of Mexicans, but mainly of Cahuilla Indians, who come from the wild mountains of San Bernardino to earn some money by gathering grapes. They scatter through the streets and market places, called *Iolas*, where they sleep in tents or under the roof of the sky."[75]

Until about 1876, Chinese field hands had comprised just a small part of this influx, but as the Great Gospel Swamp expanded as a farming area, labor demands outstripped the local population of Mexicans and Indians, especially at harvest time. Drawing on the growing reservoir of Chinese laborers, Sin Si Wau (also known as Sin Tin Wo), described in the *Anaheim Gazette* as a "sub-agent for one of the Chinese Companies," stepped into the breach. Operating out of a laundry, Wau, who had arrived in town ten years earlier, supplied laborers to laundries and restaurants, but did most of his business with Great Gospel Swamp farmers. Early in 1876, he provided crews to J. B. Raine, a prominent local businessman and owner of a drain tile factory and grocery store, who was establishing a twenty-acre hop ranch. Setting poles, planting vines, weeding and tending hops, Wau's men worked so well that when the harvest rolled around late in August, Raine asked him to send a second crew. Having done so on countless occasions, Wau must have been surprised when he and his men arrived at Raine's ranch to find crowds of hostile white laborers.[76]

Local settlers and laborers had begun to turn on the Chinese for several reasons. First, the area, for all its prosperity, still harbored pockets of struggling homesteaders, some of whom were barely able to eke out a living and so were inclined to look for a scapegoat to blame for their failures. Second, the Great Gospel Swamp did not have a Chinatown or any local Chinese. Consequently Sin Si Wau's field hands were regarded not only as foreigners but also as outsiders. Why should they be employed when local whites could not find work? This question was soon to have dire consequences for Sin Si Wau's men.[77]

At first, Wau's crew picked hops with little interference. Then one evening as they rested inside their bunkhouses, white hooligans rode onto Raine's farm, surrounded the bunkhouses, then chased the Chinese outside and held them at gunpoint. Sin Si Wau's men watched in horror as the vigilantes demolished their quarters and destroyed their personal possessions by throwing them into the dirt and riding their horses over them. "The action," reported the *Anaheim Gazette*, "was occasioned by the refusal of Mr. Raine to employ white labor unless he could obtain it as cheaply as Chinese." But the violence did not have its intended effect. Local white field hands found hop picking too difficult and would not do it. None ever arrived to take the place of the Chinese, although Raine offered to employ any who showed up. Understanding this, Sin Si Wau's crew simply lay low. After a few days holed up in their bunkhouses, feelings against them subsided. Returning to the fields, they made quick work of the crop, bringing in all of the hops within a few weeks.[78]

Shortly the violence spread north to Grand Island in the delta where, a few days after the Anaheim confrontation, a Chinese field hand got into a fight with Thomas W. Hill, an employee of the James Balsdon ranch. Hill struck the Chinese field hand with a bottle, killing him instantly, but—as had happened so often in the past—was not tried on the grounds that he had acted in self-defense. A few days later the growing antipathy toward the Chinese surfaced in the Napa Valley, where residents began making equally loud and threatening noises against the Chinese during the grape harvest. Supposedly some three thousand white schoolboys were waiting to work in the vineyards. "Help our boys against encroachments of Chinese coolies in competition for labor," wrote one man in a letter to the *St. Helena Star*. "In the battle of life and struggle for existence on this Coast, let the fitter race, the higher type of humanity survive." From past experience, the Chinese understood this was largely rhetoric. Growers and winemakers would never hire boys because they had to be fed and housed, in contrast to the Chinese who handled those matters themselves. Furthermore, very few (if any) schoolboys could match the productivity of the Chinese. Harvesting grapes in the burning heat on steep slopes—or even in the flat benchlands adjoining St. Helena—was man's work. For these reasons, despite loud opposition from some groups, Chinese field hands did not fear the protest. They had seen and heard it all before. Again biding their time, they quietly moved into the vineyards, harvested the crop, and continued to win favor with winemakers and grape growers throughout valley. By fall, they had significantly expanded their role in the vineyards and had even taken over most of the work picking hops around St. Helena.[79]

Just how deeply the Chinese had infiltrated the valley soon became clear. Although a racial taboo prevented winemakers from mentioning that skilled Chinese "cellar rats" were assisting many of Napa's best winemakers, word leaked out. For example, there is little doubt that the Chinese played a key role that fall at Henry Pellet's Manzanita Vineyard Winery near St. Helena, even though, as was often the case, no one directly mentioned them. Evidence came in the form of a work accident. On September 15, a Chinese laborer caught his finger in the cogs of a grape crusher. The digit was badly mangled, and the man was taken to a local doctor, his blood literally becoming part of that year's vintage. He was not the only Chinese laborer involved in winemaking. In reporting the accident, the *St. Helena Star* mentioned the victim was "one of Pellet's Chinamen," the implication being that many other Chinese were working the crush that fall at Manzanita Vineyard Winery and elsewhere.[80]

CHAPTER THIRTEEN

The Chinese Must Go!

Community, Chinatowns, and

the Anti–Chinese Movement

On October 18, 1876, a special committee of the U.S. Congress, formally designated the Joint Special Committee to Investigate Chinese Immigration, opened hearings in San Francisco. The government suggested that a proper hearing would be more dignified than the vicious attacks and accusations that had been occurring sporadically for the past six months. Witnesses could be called, a record compiled and published, and in this way investigators would get at the truth about field hands and Chinese labor in general. But while the committee established its inquiry with great regard for the trappings of objective investigation, it was, in fact, hardly an open-minded inquiry.[1]

Through sickness and cancellation, the more moderate committee members dropped out, and the supposedly impartial six-man tribunal transmogrified into a rabidly anti-Chinese inquest. Led by Senator Aaron A. Sargent and Representative William A. Piper of California, both of whom were honorary members of the Anti-Coolie Union of San Francisco, and Senator Henry Cooper of Tennessee, the committee was rounded out by Frank Pixley, a fanatic, bullying San Francisco city attorney and raging anti-Chinese editor of *The Argonaut*. Throughout the proceedings, Pixley acted like a prosecuting attorney, presented himself as the representative of the entire city of San Francisco and leaned heavily on the testimony of carefully primed, if dubious, witnesses. Not to be outdone, Representative Piper enjoyed tormenting witnesses when he was not contradicting them or digging up dirt on the Chinese. But neither man could match Senator Sargent. Possessing a marvelous ability to expand and drag out testimony unfavorable to the Chinese, Sargent viciously cut short (and in some cases, excised entirely) anything he did not find to his liking.[2]

As in the state hearings six months earlier, Chinese field hands themselves never spoke. Instead, the committee relied on "expert" testimony from a variety of questionable sources. One of the most widely cited witnesses was Thomas H. King of San Francisco. Introduced as a merchant with experience in China, in

FIGURE 28. Chinese New Year's Dragon, sponsored by the Hop Sing Society, First and C streets, Marysville, date unknown. Courtesy of the Community Memorial Museum of Sutter County.

fact his business acumen consisted of helping to embezzle immigration funds in Hong Kong. King's testimony was fascinating not only for its many untruths, but also because his language was often illiterate to the point of unintelligibility. Even more problematic was Charles C. O'Donnell, a physician who had been charged with an abortion murder six years earlier but released for lack of evidence. Soon to achieve fame as the first great anticoolie orator of the city, O'Donnell falsely asserted (among other things) that there were at least 150 Chinese lepers running loose in the streets of San Francisco.[3]

Nearly a week passed before Chinese field hands were specifically mentioned, but when they were, an extremely influential man stepped forward to defend them. He was San Francisco attorney H. N. Clement, a representative of the Six Companies. Contradicting the general anti-Chinese tone of the proceedings, Clement pointed to the experiences of A. Luck and Company, a large fruit-shipping firm. According to Clement, the firm "could not ship a car load of fruit East if it had to be picked and packed by white laborers." He was asked why. "Because . . . a white man who lives with his family, and has to support them, cannot live and work for a dollar a day." Clement was not alone in praising Chinese field hands. Many farmers who employed Chinese showed up to register their opinions as well, including Santa Barbara farmer Colonel William W. Hollister, owner of seventy-five thousand acres of prime farmland. Telling the committee that "the Chinese should be allowed to come until you get enough here to reduce the price of labor to such a point that its cheapness will stop their coming," Hollister pointed out that there was "common sentiment and feeling in favor of the Chinamen" among the state's farmers, who regarded them as "the only thing that the farmer can rely upon at all." Echoing Hollister's statements, John M. Horner, who paid his Chinese workers one dollar a day, praised them as reliable and explained that every farmer around San Jose employed them. "Why not tear up the railroads, blow up the steamboats, stop the stages, kill off the horses, and destroy the telegraphs, etc., so that white labor could take their places," he asked an astonished Senator Sargent. To the surprise of committee members, about half of the witnesses spoke favorably of the Chinese. Some of the strongest testimony came from Benjamin Brooks, attorney for the San Francisco Chinese, who accused most of the anti-Chinese of being "bummers." Asked by Sargent to define a bummer, Brooks replied: "A bummer is a man who pretends to want something to do. . . . If there is a building being erected, or a dog fight, or a man falls down in a fit, or a drunken man is carried off, it is necessary for him to be there to see that it is done right." Even more of a surprise to Sargent, Piper, and Cooper was the action of ailing Republican Chairman Oliver P. Morton of Indiana, who had been too ill to travel to the West Coast and had relinquished the committee chair to Sargent. Collecting the testimony of Hollister, Clement, and others, Morton's assistants published his notes as a kind of minority report strongly favorable to the Chinese. Suggesting that they should be allowed to become citizens, Morton asserted that their "difference in color, dress, manners, and religion have, in my judgement, more to do with this hostility than their alleged vices or any actual injury to the white people of California."[4]

Finally, after accumulating almost thirteen hundred pages of testimony and hearing 129 witnesses, the committee ended its hearings early in November. Based on the information it had gathered, the committee eventually issued a bulky three-hundred-page report the following February; it did not echo Senator Morton's sympathetic view. Entitled *Chinese Immigration: Its Social, Moral and Political Effect*, the document was little more than a hatchet job on the Chinese. And with ten thousand copies distributed to the general public, various memorials and condensations sent to leading newspapers around the state, and copies rushed to every member of congress and every state governor, the hefty, five-pound tome was widely read and cited.[5]

Opinions conformed exactly to prejudices. When a five-page majority summary urged the government to restrain the great influx of Asiatics and renegotiate the Burlington Treaty with China, no one was surprised. As newspapers published long discussions of the "Chinese Question," all of the anticoolie clubs and labor organizations in San Francisco cheered. Elated by the committee's hearings and its preliminary recommendations, they now believed that their voices were being heard in high places. Pouring into the streets, they turned out for great, noisy torchlight parades and rallies, hailing the hearings as the first step in a program to drive Chinese laborers from the state.[6]

To such men, Chinese field hands seemed a cancer, deadly and menacing. One anti-Chinese journalist wrote:

> In this view of the question, coolie labor is worse than the African slavery . . . For the Southern planter was commonly a gentleman of refinement, intelligence and humanity, and it was always his intent to look after and care for the health of his slave. The average employer of coolie labor in this state is not a man of education nor of much humanity, nor has he any interest in the health or life or comfort of the coolie. His sole motive is to obtain the greatest quantity of work at the lowest compensation. If one coolie sickens and dies he can always get another.[7]

Anti-Chinese groups saw only one solution, aptly summarized in a single phrase: "The Chinese must go!" Reiterating this motto continuously, these activists grew rapidly in strength and power and, sustaining a semicoherent but potent political organization, attacked not only farmers and the "moon-eyed nuisance that was the Chinese," but capitalists, corrupt politicians, land monopolies, and the railroad "octopus." Their ranks multiplied that winter, largely because the Consolidated Virginia Mines of the Comstock Lode, having exhausted the diggings, announced it would pay no dividend, thus accentuating a deepening economic panic and causing the worst financial crisis the state had ever faced. That winter, hundreds of businesses folded and more than fifteen thousand men lost their jobs in San Francisco alone. With unemployed men tramping the country roads and linking up with groups like the Order of Caucasians, anticoolie zealots easily added to their numbers in rural California.[8]

By now, Chinese field hands knew that it was only a matter of time before hostile words and malicious thoughts turned into something more. Field hands at the Simpson Thompson nursery at Soscol five miles south of the town of Napa—the most important nursery in the valley—were the first to feel the wrath of the unemployed masses when, early in January 1877, tramps forced the nursery owner to dismiss his Chinese and hire whites in their place. A month later, the dozen Chinese employed tending gardens and orchards and working in the nursery at John Bidwell's Rancho Chico came under attack. Although comprising only a small part of his overall labor force, they were singled out by a particularly vitriolic anti-Chinese leader, George H. Crosette, editor of the *Butte Record*. Whipped to a frenzy by Crosette's editorials, local members of the Order of Caucasians threatened to kill Bidwell and run the Chinese off his rancho. After burning his soap factory, carpenter shop, and hay barn, the mob sent him a threatening letter: "Sir, you are given notice to discharge your Mongolian help within ten days or suffer the consequences." When Bidwell refused, they set fire to the ranch of a nearby widow, Mrs. Patrick, who had leased her orchard and garden to some Chinese tenants. As the Chinese attempted to extinguish the blaze, they were driven off by gunshots. They lost not only their dwelling and personal property worth fifteen hundred dollars, but six horses which were burned alive in the barn.[9]

Following the Patrick arson, Chinese field hands throughout the northern Sacramento Valley became targets of a reign of terror. On March 5, 1877, they were burned out of a ranch house near Nord and again shot at as they fled. The next day, field hands living in the rear of a Chinese laundry on Chico Creek were also burned out, and over the next few days, several arson fires were extinguished in both the new and old Chinatown sections of Chico. But the most violent act occurred on the evening of March 14, when four Chinese field hands (Ah Lee, Ah Gow, Sue Ung, and Ah Yuen) were murdered in their bunkhouse on the Christian Lemm ranch (in some accounts identified as the Simmons ranch) just off Humboldt Road on Big Chico Creek, two miles east of Chico. According to newspaper reports, five intruders had broken into a small cabin serving as a bunkhouse and shot the Chinese, then doused their cabin with kerosene and set it on fire. Two horribly burned and wounded field hands escaped. One died on the way to Chico; the other somehow managed to lie low until the intruders left. In shock, he reported the crime to Lemm, and the next day stumbled into Chico and reported the crime to the Chico Chinatown night watchman.[10]

Most citizens of Chico were appalled. Anticipating more trouble, Bidwell attempted to protect the Chinese in the area by forming a Committee of Safety and arming 200 men with rifles to patrol Chico and curb the anti-Chinese elements in the area. Meanwhile, local police offered a one-thousand-dollar reward for the arsonists and murderers. Sacramento and San Francisco Chinese followed the investigation closely, as the four victims belonged to the Nin Yung Company, one of the original six clans that had affiliated in San Francisco. Demanding swift justice, members of the Six Companies raised money to pay several detectives who began their own independent search for the murderers. Although working incognito, the detectives were immediately exposed by the local newspapers, and their presence served to fan the flames of hatred. The situation soon became so tense that, according to the *Oroville Mercury*, "Every business man in Chico goes about armed, day and night, and woe to the man or set of men who attempt any violation of law."[11]

On March 27, five suspects in the Lemm ranch murders were arrested, along with seven others accused of various related acts of arson and assault. The arrests came as the result of the capture of Ned Conway, a "dark, low-browed moronic young man" with a "mean streak." Tailed by detectives, Conway was apprehended as he deposited a threatening letter in a Chico post office. Interrogated for two days, he eventually identified seven other henchmen, five of whom later confessed. Published in the *Chico Enterprise* on March 30, the confessions of Thomas Stainbrook, Henry C. Wright, Adam Holderbaum, H. T. Jones, and Charles Slaughter disclosed the motives behind their actions.[12]

Members of the Council of Nine, a subgroup within the local Order of Caucasians, the men admitted that they had plotted to institute a county-wide reign of terror to drive the Chinese from the farms and fields. Under cover of darkness, the men had made their way to the Chinese camp on the Lemm Ranch. Intent on merely robbing the field hands, Ned Conway, Charles and John Slaughter, Eugene Roberts, and Stainbrook held the Chinese at gunpoint as they searched for money. Finding none, Roberts then suggested they each shoot one Chinese laborer. Although several men objected and Stainbrook withdrew outside the bunkhouse, others did not hesitate. Roberts then took a small bottle of kerosene from his pocket, drenched the clothes of the dead Chinese, and one of the Slaughter brothers struck a match and lit the bodies on fire.[13]

With some local citizens threatening to take matters into their own hands and lynch the men and others threatening to release them from jail, the Chinese would not have the satisfaction of seeing their attackers tried in Chico. The whole gang was shipped under armed guard to Oroville, the county seat. "It was an exciting time in Chico when the parties charged with murder and arson were marched from the town hall, guarded by soldiers, to prevent either a breakout, or a lynching, with fixed bayonets to entrain for Oroville," a local reporter later wrote. "A weeping crowd of wives, mothers, and sisters watched their loved ones taken away, perhaps forever. . . . Even the spectators and the guards had tears in their eyes." Apparently no one in the crowd publicly mourned the dead Chinese; nor did the local newspapers cover their funerals.[14]

Following the arrests, field hands were not freed of threats and intimidation. Although six men were indicted by a grand jury for arson, and five for arson and murder, scattered acts of violence continued. As the men went on trial in May, Bidwell's carpenter shop was torched. But the Chinese did secure a certain measure of justice. Pleasant Slaughter, the third Slaughter brother, described as a half-breed who "looked as Indian as Sitting Bull, with an utterly impassive face and ophidian eyes," confessed to burning Bidwell's soap factory and was convicted and sentenced to ten years in prison. The Chinese also took some satisfaction a few weeks later, when Conway, whose confession broke the case and who had been segregated from the other prisoners lest he be murdered, received two years in prison. Stainbrook, Roberts, and Charles and John Slaughter were given life sentences, and H. T. Jones, who refused to confess, was sentenced to 20 years.[15]

But still Chinese field hands were not safe in Chico. Those working for Bidwell were again threatened, and when they refused to leave, Bidwell's soap factory was torched for the third time. After an arson fire destroyed one of Bidwell's barns and anticoolie elements began boycotting Rancho Chico and falsely accusing Bidwell of being the first to import Chinese farm laborers to California, the Chinese so feared for their lives that they would not leave the farm. They faced even worse threats in Roseville, Grass Valley, and Colusa, where during a period of a few weeks, arsonists torched their settlements, burning them to the ground and sending men fleeing into the countryside.[16]

☙

Despite the wave of attacks in 1877, the Chinese never retreated; they had too much at stake to withdraw. All had endured a horrible ocean passage every bit as dangerous as the more famous wagon-train migration that brought white settlers west. Speaking through interpreters, old Chinese would communicate a shudder of horror when asked to recall the overseas journey and disembarkation. Bewilderment, disorientation, and suffering were persistent themes, as were descriptions of being treated like cattle, starving, vomiting from seasickness, and seeing friends swept overboard in raging storms. Men went insane after being confined below deck for weeks; a few resorted to murder and mutiny. Cramped quarters evoked the most commentary. Steerage forced everyone into the same common misery. Reporters of the time were aghast at what they discovered. "The space assigned to each Chinaman is about as much as is usually occupied by one of the flat boxes in a milliner's store," observed a writer for the *San Francisco Examiner*. "If a few barrels of oil were poured into the steerage hold, its occupants would enjoy the distinction so often objected to of being literally 'packed like sardines.'"[17]

Because historians have tended to diminish parallels with the horrible "middle passage" of the African slave trade or the trauma of the great Jewish migration, the dangers that Chinese immigrants suffered have never become deeply imprinted in the American mind. But whether they traveled on sailing vessels operated by China traders or faster steamships of the Pacific Mail Ship Company, contemporaries did not miss the similarities. One headline in a single issue of the *New York Herald* shouted: "Slavers in the Pacific—The Coolie Trade— Dreadful Scenes on Board a Coolie Trade Ship. Worse than Slavery. Death a Relief—Barbarous Treatment of the Coolies—Bound and Beaten—Fortunate Relief —Fearful Tales of Suffering." One newly arrived immigrant put it best: "I ate wind and tasted waves for more than twenty days."[18]

On arrival, disoriented men gazed in silent wonder at the new land whose fame had reached them and whose riches they hoped to exploit. Stashed in the back of their minds or written on slips of paper were the names and locations of various friends, relatives, and clan members who had preceded them and who might be able to offer assistance. Some came with Chinese-English phrase books. "You must not strike me," read one often-repeated phrase. Others were: "He came to his death by homicide" and "He was shot dead."[19]

As ships docked, customs officials boarded and tallied passengers. Once counted, men poured off forward gangways, often bending under the weight of their belongings. Separated into groups of ten to thirty men, they were perfunctorily examined by doctors, who asked the first of a seemingly endless stream of questions that would determine their fate that day: "Are you ill?" "What's that scar?" The men shuffled on, some marked with colored chalk—"Sc" for scalp, "X" for medical problems. Next came the customs inspectors: "What's your name?" "Can you read?" "What's in that bundle?" There were questions about crime, smuggling, relatives, and family insanity. Then a second tier of doctors detained those with obvious symptoms of contagious diseases. Those who were sick or gave the wrong answers were sent back.[20]

Finally released through the wharf gates into the light, they would be met by fellow countrymen. "Over here! Don't stop!" yelled countrymen in their native dialects. Piling onto wagons, the new immigrants quickly disappeared into the "Little China" quarter of San Francisco. Their journey had just begun. Expanding westward and northward along Stockton, DuPont, and Sacramento streets and blurring into the surrounding city, San Francisco's Chinatown was the heart of Chinese California, the hub of trans-Pacific migration, and the first stop for every immigrant.

To exhausted travelers, Chinatown must have seemed a familiar and reassuring place in a strange and at times unfriendly society. Walking its streets, newcomers found a crowded, thriving, colorful complex of shops, gambling halls, opium dens, restaurants, temples, theaters, brothels, lodgings, and communal organizations, as well as thousands of their countrymen, "all in their native costume, with queues down their backs." Chinese grocery stores catered to their needs, goods cascaded onto the sidewalks, familiar odors of Cantonese foods wafted through the air, and the sound of men speaking in their native dialects surrounded them. Those who could read were further enticed by signs: "The hall of approved medicines of every province and of every land," read one sign above an apothecary shop. "Fragrant almond chamber" and "Fragrant tea chamber," beckoned them into restaurants. "Opium dipped up in fractional quantities, Foreign smoke in broken parcels, No. 2 Opium to be sold at all times," read another sign, painted on red cards and displayed in the window of an opium den. Everywhere they went, men found Chinese vegetable peddlers "carrying two deep baskets of greens, fruits, and melons, balanced on their shoulders with the help of a pole."[21]

After a few nights of rest in a boardinghouse or the back of a shop, immigrants met a local emissary from the Chung Wai Wui Koon, the Chinese Consolidated Benevolent Association, popularly known as the Chinese Six Companies or just plain Six Companies. The most important and influential group in the Chinese community, the Six Companies was comprised of six (later eight) powerful clan organizations—Sze Yup, Sam Yup, Yeog Wo, Ning Yeung, Hop Wo, and Yan Wo—each representing a home district or clan and run by members of the Chinese-American power elite.[22]

Back home, in a variant of the indenture system that two centuries earlier had brought Englishmen to the American colonies, Chinese field hands had borrowed money for the trip to California from Hong Kong merchants connected with one or another of the different associations. Eight of every ten men arrived under "credit ticket," financial obligation to one of these organizations, a heavy investment and considerable burden that would organize and guide their lives for years to come. Signing contracts under the eye of an agent of the Six Companies, each immigrant was required to work for a specific period, during which time the man's ticket and transportation debts to the Six Companies were deducted from their wages. Without exception, they would be required under penalty of family dishonor to repay that debt, plus interest, as soon as possible. To do that they first linked up with one of the district or clan representatives. Once fed and rested, they would disperse to labor as directed. In a strange land where they could not speak the language, men had no choice but to accept the arrangement that fed and housed them, found them work, collected and paid their wages, loaned them money, and provided them with an informal postal service. Once on the job, expenses such as food, clothing, and housing would be deducted from their wages, leaving workers little once they fulfilled their obligations. It was a tight system of control from which immigrants could not deviate, and it was under these arrangements that thousands of men became field hands and moved into the countryside under the supervision of the China bosses.[23]

Some immigrants never left San Francisco and were contracted to wash clothes, roll cigars, or toil in other Chinese-owned business. But within a few days after arriving, clan and district representatives sent large numbers of newcomers to rural Chinatowns scattered throughout the farming districts. If field hands thought that they would escape control by the Six Companies once they reached their destinations, they were speedily disabused of such notions. Moments after they arrived, a China boss met them, issued orders, and laid down rules as to how they would be dispatched—so many men for each boardinghouse, so many for each crew, so many to this or that farm. The local boss or contractor and the San Francisco clan representative would agree in advance on a number of field hands that were needed for a particular job or season, somehow balancing the influx of new arrivals with the demand for laborers. The arrangement worked so well that there was seldom a surplus of Chinese field hands in any farming district, but it gave individual field hands little control over their destination or the terms of their employment. Few Chinese immigrants were fluent enough in English or familiar enough with American labor practices to break free and make their own arrangements with farmers, although some always managed to do so.[24]

For the most part, it was a nearly inescapable situation. Before any laborer could board a ship bound for China, he was checked by a district association official to make sure all his debts were paid and his financial obligations fulfilled. Even if the man was completely clear, the district associations required the payment of a special exit tax before they would issue the license that permitted a field hand to leave. Exit tax money went to support the activities of the Chinese Six Companies.[25]

Field hands attempting to flee back across the Pacific Ocean without repaying their debt or obtaining permission from their district or clan association usually could not make it past the wharf gate. And if they did, their troubles had only just begun. Lawyers and strongmen retained by the Six Companies tracked down wayward field hands and brought them back on phony theft charges. Once returned, the field hands would be sent out to work and closely watched until they had finished making their payments. But not all were able to do so. Occasionally, a man burdened by debt would take his own life rather than return to a life of loneliness and despair in the fields. This was apparently the case with one Coulterville field hand who in September 1866, slashed himself with a razor across the abdomen, then lay down to die. So determined was he to end his life that after friends discovered him, sent for a doctor, and placed the razor on a table, the man struggled up, grasped the razor, slit his wrists, and soon expired. "He preferred to die rather than live owing his neighbors," commented the *Mariposa Gazette*.[26]

Most Chinese agricultural workers possessed a singular consciousness of duty that prevented such desperate acts. Some had bunked with neighbor boys, as many as thirty per room, while working on subsistence farms in their home village. At school, they had learned how "the great Emperors of China ruled with the wisdom of gods and gave to the whole world the light of high civilization and the culture of our literature, which is the admiration of all nations." They felt that they were men of destiny who had arrived in California for a specific purpose. They were less certain, however, about the exact nature of that duty, or how long it would take them to achieve success.[27]

Men held few illusions about their work or their place in American society. "Chinese treated worse than dog," one man warned newcomers, while another told an interviewer, "Oh, it was terrible, terrible. . . . The hoodlums, roughnecks and young boys pull your queue, slap your face, throw all kind of old vegetables and rotten eggs at you." A third, who had achieved enough to marry and raise a family, later cautioned his son, "This is a white man's country. You go back to China when you make your money, that is where you belong. If you stay here, the white man will kill you."[28]

Letters home emphasized the disillusionment many immigrants felt upon arrival. California, they warned, turned out not to be the much desired "Golden Mountain," but rather an ever increasing pile of debt. "From the proceeds of a hard day's toil, after the pay for food and clothes, very little remains," warned a representative of the Six Companies. Underemployed and frequently injured, men, no matter how brave or determined, seldom achieved their goal of twenty-six days of work per month and consequently often found that they could not garner the earnings they expected. Farmworkers who returned to China in their later years, it was said, were worn out by their years stooping, sweating, and worrying in the fields. Yet they did not stop coming. And once in the state, they did not stop working.[29]

To a large extent, Chinese field hands measured their success according to their ability to return home. When did they make the first trip? How many trips did they make? How long did they remain? Did they marry? Father a child? Retire? Returning to visit their homeland in sizeable numbers, they crowded outward-bound ships each autumn and winter, and the inward-bound vessels during the spring. From 1852 to 1870 (including some good, average, and prosperous years), sixty-four Chinese departed California for every one hundred who arrived. Altogether, 91,027 left the state in those eighteen years; between 1870 and 1875, forty-four left for every one hundred who stayed. In some years (1864, 1866, and 1867) more departed than immigrated—but only by a slim margin.[30]

When they died, most field hands were too poor to warrant a large ceremony. While men of stature were buried following processions through the streets accompanied by gifts of food, fireworks, bands, and crowds of mourners, field hands, with their limited funds, were laid to rest in swift, simple, and quiet funerals, ending when friends placed a small roasted pig on top of the grave so the deceased could have something to eat on his way to heaven. But sometimes the funeral of a popular field hand or well-known labor contractor would become an elaborate public affair involving the entire local Chinatown. This is what happened on January 12, 1894, when Lea Hau, a fifty-three-year-old field hand, was accidentally killed on Captain Gustave Niebaum's Inglenook Winery in the Napa Valley. Working with six other men clearing a field of eucalyptus trees, he had been pulling on a rope as another field hand had sawed off a large limb. When the tree trunk cracked, everyone ran, but Lea Hau slipped, and the tree crashed down on him, breaking his back and killing him almost instantly.

At a funeral held two days later, hundreds of mourners and members of the Chinese Masonic Order marched in a long procession between two Chinese bands "making a hideous noise." Ten wagons carried mourners, and an eleventh carried roast pig, roast chicken, rice, and burning punk. Accompanying the hearse were fifty men, all wearing red-and-white armbands. At the grave site, fellow workers stepped forward, as many as twenty at a time and, following ritual, bowed three times, sank to their knees, took out small vessels filled with gin, and spilled them on the grave. Then the high priest, a basket in his hand, delivered a short oration and was joined in chorus by everyone present. During all of this, men lit hundreds of candles and incense sticks, distributing them to every tomb in the graveyard; they also burned papers covered in Chinese characters as Hau's grave was being covered. All then gathered up the edibles, left for Chinatown, and there feasted late into the night. "Taking all in all," commented the *St. Helena Star*, "a Chinese funeral is quite an interesting affair."[31]

Even in death, many field hands did not sever their links to home and family. Believing that their spirit would not find eternal peace unless they were laid to rest in their native soil, many made arrangements with Chinese benevolent societies to be buried in a shallow grave marked with a burial brick identifying them and their home village, so that eventually they could be shipped home to China for reburial. About seven years after they died, sometimes sooner, they would be dug up by migratory "bone pickers." The skeleton was then prepared in accordance with a well-established sacred ritual. Dipping the bones in a bucket of brandy and water, the pickers first polished them with a stiff brush until they almost shined, then laid them out in such a way as to reconstruct the skeleton in a tight fetal position, with leg bones and finger bones of each hand, as well as the bones of their feet, placed in separate small bags. Lastly, they packed the bones, with skull on top, inside a tin can or a small, eighteen-to-twenty-one-inch-wide wooden box lined with an oilcloth or heavy canvas. Boxed by the hundreds and accompanied by supervisors, "dead Celestials" headed for Hong Kong and transshipment to Kwantung province in such great quantities that San Francisco newspapers announced their departure as if reporting so much freight.[32]

It would be a mistake to overestimate the importance of this orientation, to deduce, as some might, that Chinese field hands were diverging from the usual immigrant configuration, a far-eastern antithesis of Polish immigrants and certain other European settlers of their century. It hardly follows that because they prepared to return, that because they yearned for their village homes, they would make any sacrifice to achieve their goals. They were not Arcadian zealots, answering to voices that whispered of a summons to responsibility and heroism. They did not come on a divine mission, following a preordained path that would carry them to a magnificent end. Few sheltered any misconceptions about California. "The Chinese were in a pitiable condition," one old field hand later recalled. "We were simply terrified; we kept indoors after dark for fear of being shot in the back. Children spit upon us as we passed by and called us rats." Six Companies spokesmen stressed: "Expensive rents, expensive living . . . wages are low, yet they are compelled to labor and live in poverty, quite unable to return to their native land."[33]

Understanding that exhausting labor awaited them, only the hardier peasants traveled east. The aged and ill, the very young, and the unambitious stayed home. And those who did come often did so after being well informed of what to expect. The huge investment and need to borrow heavily provided agriculture with the hardiest, most adventuresome, desperate, and determined of China's masses. Carrying them through the trauma of departure, ordeal of steerage, rigors of work, and dangers of racist attacks, those qualities would also help them establish vibrant Chinatowns in virtually every California farming community.[34]

ॐ

Most rural Chinatowns were located in the least desirable sections of town. Arriving in Fresno, field hands flopped in the area west of the Southern Pacific Railroad switching yards, adjacent to Fresno's main business district, where, according to one reporter, a low row of wooden boardinghouses, noodle parlors, gambling rooms, herb shops, and little stores crowded along Tulare Street "as clearly cut out against the encompassing desert as a row of bathing houses on a beach." Merged into the edges of Fresno's Chinatown and encircling it was a larger slum area or "criminal reservation," as the *Fresno Republican* called it, of inexpensive lodging houses, saloons, and general stores. Slot machines, lewd peep shows, and card games were featured in the saloons; brothels were either part of the saloon business or closely affiliated. Nearby, where Elm Avenue entered town and along McKinley Avenue, was the Chinese cemetery. "By way of this street and the railroad reservation a turbid tide of evil humanity flowed into Mariposa Street from across the tracks," recalled an unsympathetic, but not untypical, Fresno writer.[35]

In many farm towns, Chinese field hands found themselves in boardinghouses lining a single dilapidated street. "What an accumulation of filth," commented an otherwise sympathetic farmhand upon visiting the Chinese quarter in Newman. Field hands in Santa Ana's Chinatown found rooms in the backs of laundries and a series of "junky redwood shacks," while Calistoga field hands disappeared into a section the local weekly newspaper described as "blackened with the smoke of 1,000 fires and greasy with the rubbing of 1,000 shoulders . . . dank and dismal holes into which the sun never penetrates."[36]

Field hands in Knight's Ferry took refuge in shacks in the perpetually flooding bottomland along Main Street. Those lodging in Princeton and Jacinto disappeared into camps sprawling along the west bank of the Sacramento River levee. According to one account, during the winter, when the high-sided header wagons were not in use at Jacinto, the Chinese would tip them over and live underneath. Around Isleton they laid over in unnamed, unincorporated settlements casually referred to as China camps, China landings, and China ranches. Packed into a two-block section of Colusa, the Chinese section of town was said to have air thick with the sweet, blue smoke of burning joss sticks. In Willows, Chinese field hands sustained a settlement that by the mid-1880s consisted of numerous boardinghouses, laundries, and stores that supplied the surrounding Chinese camps with native foods and goods.[37]

San Jose Chinese relocated several times over the years before leasing land from John Heinlen, an affluent white businessman. Residents of "Heinlenville," as this Chinatown became known, protected themselves from intolerant white citizens with a ten-foot-high picket fence and locked gates. Chinese field hands around Watsonville congregated first in an unnamed Chinatown along Maple and Union streets on the west side of the Pajaro River, and later in Brooklyn, their second Chinatown, essentially a labor camp on the east side of the Pajaro River bridge. One of the largest and most colorful of all rural Chinatowns, the Watson-ville settlement was so cramped that it could expand only by adding second stories to buildings and wedging new two-story structures in vacant lots between existing structures. Elsewhere men found quarters in unnamed enclaves and provisional communities invariably described by newspaper reporters as "a jumble of huts" and debris, where pigs wallowed in the streets and ducks waddled around in an "awful odor." Often such camps were transitory settlements that lasted only until the local landowner or authorities booted men off the property.[38]

Whatever community they passed through, Chinese field hands seldom en-joyed anything beyond the most rudimentary living conditions. Sometimes build-ings were constructed of old shingles, broken packing boxes, and flattened kerosene cans. In Salinas, a two-story former dance hall served as a boarding-house for forty-seven laborers who worked for contractors Ah Sing and Yee Get. Surrounding houses were dark, poorly ventilated, in decline, and according to the *Salinas Democrat*, "nestled together as a brood of frightened chickens." Run-down and arranged helter-skelter, the enclave reminded locals of "a western town af-ter the advent of a tornado." Similarly, in Santa Ana, the Chinese section was de-scribed by the *Santa Ana Evening Blade* as "one big dwelling and a row of smaller shacks." Rooms in these dirt-floored shacks were said to be "barely large enough for a miserable bunk."[39]

Chinese quarters in Sacramento were described in great detail by thirty-seven-year-old Russian physician Nikolai Sudzilovskii, who toured the area in 1891. Dis-covering windowless boardinghouses that were "mere huts and lean-tos that are plastered with long, vertical, red signs in Chinese," Sudzilovskii was so appalled that, in his memoir, *Around California*, he included a long and detailed account.

> These inhabitants of the Celestial Empire live in a far from Celestial man-ner. Someone who has had occasion to peek at the midships of the German and English steamers that transport emigrants from Hamburg and Liverpool to New York will have some idea of how the Chinese live on shore. Imagine the lowest and smallest possible room, all the walls of which are hung from top to bottom with navy bunks. Each of these bunks is the apartment of a Chinese. The filth and stench are unbearable, especially at night, when all the lodgers gather and each lights his stinking opium pipe.[40]

Quarters in other rural Chinatowns were just as crowded. If a standard four-room frame house served as a boardinghouse, the proprietor or contractor would sleep in one downstairs room with his family (if he had one). The rest of the rooms were generally set aside as bunk rooms with only a small kitchen area for eating and preparing food. During cold weather, the place by the stove would often be-come a prime sleeping area because it remained warm more or less continuously. Usually the remainder of the rooms would be double—and sometimes triple—decked with bunk beds. When the harvest was in full swing, field hands would use bunk rooms night and day, often sleeping in shifts as they rotated through.[41]

Chinatowns in Merced, Stanislaus, Calaveras, Tuolumne, and Mariposa coun-ties consisted of three-walled shacks, each one added to the sidewall of its prede-cessor. Surrounded by white-owned businesses, Vacaville's Chinatown boasted houses shingled with flattened tin cans. Packed close together, these tin buildings would clatter from rain in the winter and turn into baking ovens in the summer. According to legend, Chico's Chinatown was crisscrossed with secret tunnels, supposedly used for nefarious purposes ranging from gambling to drug smuggling. The tunnels were, in fact, nothing more than a series of interconnected basements in which Chinese stored goods, escaped the heat, gambled, smoked opium, and hid from vigilantes. Napa's Chinatown, situated on a frequently flooded, low-lying strip of land between the Napa River and Napa Creek, consisted of three rows of low frame buildings separated by a walkway containing a barbershop, gambling dens, and mercantile company. One local historian described Tehama's Chinatown as a "honeycomb" having "no semblance of architecture."[42]

Constructed of tinder, dry wood and jammed together at odd angles, buildings in rural Chinatowns burned regularly. With everything packed closely together and constructed of unpainted wood, the slightest accident could set off an inferno impossible to extinguish. St. Helena's Chinatown burned twice, the first time in 1884, when a fire in the second story of Quong Loon High's store spread rapidly, destroying three China stores and lodging houses, the second in 1898, when a fire in the rear of Foo Doo's store spread to eight buildings, including a Joss House (Chinese temple). Carelessly tended cooking fires seem to have caused most of the conflagrations. One blaze, which leveled the entire Stockton Chinatown in September 1887, started in an adobe and sheet-iron shed used by Chinese delicatessen owners to roast and barbecue pig. When a cook dropped a ladle of fat on the fire, an instantaneous surge of flames engulfed the shed and spread quickly to surrounding buildings, burning them to the ground. On July 12, 1877, a fire leveled the entire Colusa Chinatown, between Seventh and Eighth streets. "One Chinaman was roasted to death," reported the *Colusa Sun*. After more wooden buildings in the Chinatown burned on January 13, 1879, the county board of trustees banned any further construction of wooden buildings and required that all structures be rebuilt of brick. Ten days later, the *Sun* reported, "Two Chinamen burned to death in the Chinese quarters at Princeton." Another blaze, which leveled thirty-five buildings in the Chico Chinatown in August 1886, began when a Chinese butcher accidentally dropped embers from his pipe into the hay of a stable. About forty buildings in the Salinas Chinatown burned after someone upset a kerosene lamp; bedlam ensued when the fire found caches of firecrackers, pistols, and ammunition stored in basements and alcoves, causing sporadic explosions and hampering attempts to extinguish the blaze. Always in the charred rubble and smoking ruins, firemen found the remains of some field hand unable to escape.[43]

❧

Surrounded by these vibrant and austere firetraps, sojourners joined with friends and relatives to form loyal familial groups. In Bakersfield, loyalties to home villages and clans proved so great that Chinese field hands could not mix and instead split into two separate settlements. These associations continued even when they moved out of town into the countryside. For example, in the Sacramento-San Joaquin Delta, Heungshan Chinese dominated orchard work north of

Courtland in Sacramento County, while those from T'oishan commanded row crop work on farms south of Rio Vista, to the east in San Joaquin County, and in Salinas as well. Similar patterns developed in truck gardening, where crews tended to be composed of related groups, but such associations hardly represented the only means of community cohesiveness. Chinese field hands encased themselves in a variety of protective institutions aimed at preserving their dignity and self-respect amid a hostile society.[44]

Essentially smaller versions of their urban counterparts, rural Chinatowns served as geographic sanctuaries where ethnicity, language, and cultural practices were held in common and where the amenities of traditional Chinese life were readily available. Organizations called tongs (originally antigovernment movements back home) formed in California among unrelated immigrants as a means of self-protection, comfort, and mutual assistance. Tongs soon carved out territories, challenged the Six Companies, wrestled control of segments of Chinese California away from them, and extended their reach into the opium trade, gambling, and prostitution. In some areas they were particularly strong, for example in Santa Cruz County, where nine of ten Chinese belonged to the Chee Kong Tong. Occasionally work on ranches would be interrupted when a so-called tong war broke out between rival organizations. According to a witness to one such incident on the Joseph Cone ranch near Red Bluff, field hands who had been employed building rock walls would "scatter across the hills like a bunch of inebriated loons and Cone wouldn't have any stone manipulators until the difficulty was resolved."[45]

Because of the high price of immigration and the harsh life that they found upon arrival, Chinese men typically came to California alone and lived solitary lives. Many could not afford the luxury of a wife, either stateside or in their homeland. With a ratio of fourteen men to every one Chinese woman (twenty or thirty to one in Fresno's Chinatown), Chinese field hands instead sustained a thriving sex industry. Throughout the state, census investigators calculated that in 1870, six of ten Chinese women were *lougeui* (always holding her legs up) and *baak haak chai* (hundred men's wives). As late as 1880, about two in ten Chinese women still worked in the profession. Although some Chinese women worked as freelance prostitutes, and a few entrepreneurial-minded women even ran their own operations as madams, most were controlled by the tongs of San Francisco. Organizing prostitution on a statewide basis, the Hip-Yee Tong imported six thousand Chinese women between 1852 and 1873, and netted about two hundred thousand dollars from their work.[46]

Field hands had no problem finding prostitutes. San Francisco's Chinatown alone had sixty-eight houses of prostitution in 1885. If they were willing and able to pay, men frequented prostitutes in high-class bordellos. Because most could not afford them, many turned to low-class brothels or "cribs." Located in dark back-alleyways, cribs were simply cubicles, approximately twelve feet wide by fourteen feet long, sparsely furnished and with bars or heavy screens across a small window. Crib workers were among the most oppressed, exploited, and powerless of all Californians. Wearing cotton blouses and trousers, the worst off among them peered out from the windows hawking their wares, promising pleasure for twenty-five to

FIGURE 29. Ah Gun, slave girl imported from Canton to San Francisco in 1879, lost in a card game in Aurora to a Hills Ferry bar owner, whom she was rumored to have poisoned in 1893. Ah Gun operated her own house of prostitution in Newman until she died at age ninety-five. Photo courtesy of the Frank F. Latta Collection, Sky Farming, Huntington Library, San Marino, California.

fifty cents, sometimes calling out as recalled in one contemporary account: "Two bittee lookee, flo bittee feelee, six bittee doee." Such women supplied more than sex. Field hands visited brothels as part of a general round of worldly and spiritual activities that might include shopping for gifts, getting a haircut, an evening at the theater, smoking opium, gambling, and even attending church.[47]

Other recreational activities followed the cycles of farming. Throughout the harvest season, when the men lived on farms or in labor camps, they would try to spend Saturday nights and Sundays in the closest Chinatown. For men facing years of toil before they might be able to return home, the lure of recreation was strong. Many found an outlet in gambling. When interviewed for the Survey of Race Relations in 1922, one elderly Chinese man who had been in California most of his life looked back on his experiences in the fields and asked rhetorically,

> Do you realize what our situation is here? We come over here a lot of young men, eager about life, and then we work most of the time. What's there to do when work is over? There is no family to go to. The Chinese are not welcome in the theaters. They have to live in Chinatowns. . . . So, because there is no recreation, no way out, the Chinese go to the gambling houses. They are not necessarily gamblers at all, but they want some place to go and they watch the excitement. That is why there are these gambling places.[48]

Gambling was such a popular diversion that it did not take much to get started. Field hands joined or quickly set up games practically anywhere—in the back rooms, "gaudily furnished and highly ornamented" cellars, and across beds in boardinghouses. They played mahjong, fan-tan, and *baakgapbiu*, a game resembling keno; they also gambled with dice and dominos and played lotteries. Although these games generally ebbed and flowed according to the crops, many were ongoing. Field hands seeking bigger stakes frequented formal gambling halls and contacted professional gamblers; census takers counted at least one or two of each in every rural Chinatown or farming community. Observing that gambling was virtually nonstop in the local Chinatown, the *Napa Register* complained in July 1887 that, if white residents of Napa opened similar institutions, they would be immediately arrested and prosecuted. "You are right, neighbor," the *St. Helena Star* replied, "and if we're not greatly mistaken, and we are pretty sure we're not, there is a big game in full blast in our Chinatown which goes on without interruption by anyone."[49]

Field hands generally gambled the most in the days just before the Chinese New Year, when it was their custom to settle all debts. Hoping to accumulate enough money to pay off outstanding bills, many field hands instead found themselves owing even more. To survive, they had to turn to Chinese moneylenders. Every year, countless men toiled just to pay off their debts at exorbitant interest rates. More than anything else, gambling losses kept field hands tied to labor contractors, who often doubled as moneylenders. Occasionally the losses and debts became too much for them, and fights—even murder—would result. But usually field hands involved in such incidents would have their cases dismissed for lack of evidence when no witnesses would testify in court.[50]

Although most Chinese gambling houses were hidden away in basements and nondescript structures, those in Fresno's Chinatown were notorious, gaudy places, brightly illuminated with glow lamps and Japanese lanterns festooned over the doors. "Gambling tables are displayed before open doors and prohibited games are run while the police pace up and down without molesting anybody," complained the *Fresno Morning Expositor*. "Stud poker is the game mostly played, but the Chinese lotteries and [fan-] tan games also flourish in their accustomed haunts." Gambling establishments were typically protected by multiple security systems. At the street entrance, a guard would signal anything suspicious by pulling on a long cord stretching to an alarm in the inner "gambling den." Inside, a large iron door with a peephole protected the inner room. As often as not, by the time the police made it inside, all of the gamblers had departed through hidden exits in the cellar and roof. Only a few old and bewildered men would be left behind smoking their pipes.[51]

Occasionally raids on the Fresno gambling establishments met with stiff resistance. After wading through a shower of rocks, bricks, and bottles from the surrounding rooftops in October 1899, Fresno police battered down the heavy iron door of one Chinatown establishment, seized four hundred dollars, arrested thirty-six men, and marched them off to jail in groups of four with their queues knotted together. But in a jury trial, all were released because by the time police had made it through the door, everyone had been alerted by the guards and no one could be observed in the act of gambling. The steel door had held long enough for the men to put down their cards and take up their opium pipes. Those few who were arrested in such raids would be fined ten dollars each and immediately released to resume their recreation.[52]

In nearly every raid on a gambling hall, field hands would be found not only with cash and lottery tickets but with opium. Depending on the source, between one-third and one-half of all Chinese in California at some time used opium, which, until 1909, was not against the law. By all accounts, it was readily available. Contrary to many accounts, field hands did not have to descend into dingy basement dens to "hit the pipe" or otherwise hibernate in holes without ventilation to become—as one writer put it—"creosoted like timber, or smoke-cured hams, so that they survived when otherwise they should have died." Chinese merchants carried opium and sold various kinds and grades openly, even advertising it on signs above the entrance to their stores. They also carried opium pipes, stems, bowls, and other paraphernalia and set aside a place—usually a back room or corner—where men could relax and enjoy the drug. There would be chairs, trays, opium pipes, and bunks for them to recline on. Because opium was expensive—about $1.36 an ounce, compared to six cents a pound for rice—men enjoyed their opium according to a certain social ritual. They would first carefully unwrap their packet of opium and, using a long needle, place it in the pipe bowl. Lighting it, they inhaled deeply, a step called "mounting the dragon" to ride into better worlds from the grind they lived. Despite periodic raids, few were ever arrested for their habits, and when local communities occasionally launched efforts to "clean up" the practice, merchants posted sentinels around town to warn of approaching police.[53]

Although opium smokers seldom caused problems, occasionally a field hand would overdose, with disastrous consequences. One such case occurred on May 10, 1887, in the Riverside Chinatown. While bathing in a bathhouse on Monroe Street, a field hand named Ling Gee stabbed a fellow field hand, Quong Sing Yee. As the only murder in Chinatown up to that point, the case attracted considerable attention when it went to trial. Doctors testified Gee had been "loaded up with opium" and that his health was so bad that he would not have lived very long. Concluding that Gee had been under the influence and probably did not know what he was doing, the jury recommended life in prison, to which a cowering Gee responded with "exclamations of joy and all morning was in a hilarious state of mind, crowing like a duck, cackling a la Bramah and giving an excellent imitation of a sick cat."[54]

Next to gambling and smoking opium, field hands enjoyed playing the lottery. Tickets were sold all over town, to all kinds of people. In 1899, the *Fresno Republican* counted eleven companies and twenty-five individuals selling lottery tickets. "The beauty of the whole Chinese lottery system is its simplicity," observed the September 14, 1894, *Fresno Daily Evening Expositor*. "A child can play Chinese lottery, notwithstanding the 'abracadabra' look of the characters and squares on the tickets." To place their lottery bets in Fresno, field hands walked to the rear of the Tong Duck Company building or one of any number of stores and businesses. Like gambling dens, each had a room constructed specifically for lottery activities and boasted heavy iron doors or bars protecting the chambers in which drawings were conducted. Field hands could count on four daily drawings—at 2 P.M., 4 P.M., 8 P.M., and 10 P.M.[55]

Despite the lure of gambling and the need for female companionship, field hands probably passed most of their leisure time in Chinese stores, restaurants, businesses, and barbershops, which were the center of life in most rural Chinatowns. Here, men purchased a variety of goods—firecrackers, books, magazines, tobacco, herbal medicines, vegetables, and incense—unavailable elsewhere. Many Chinese merchants were also connected to *jinshanzhuang* (Golden Mountain firms), which had close links to Hong Kong businesses and provided a way for field hands to send letters and money home. But the real value of Chinese stores was as social centers. Every store had a back room where men clustered around a stove to warm themselves on cold days, told stories, drank tea, recalled happier days back home, played chess and checkers, read Chinese and local newspapers, heard of jobs, and found out what was happening in Chinatown. As one man explained, "We communicate . . . otherwise we're alone. You know nothing."[56]

Every store had a bulletin board and an unofficial postal drop where men could send and receive letters. They consulted public notices written on tablets and posted outside or found interpreters nearby to conduct negotiations and help them deal with English-speaking employers and businesses. Stores also provided lodging. When boardinghouses were full or when men were strapped for cash, they would pack into the back rooms of stores and do their own cooking. This considerably benefited store owners who, acting as labor contractors, charged field hands not only for jobs, but also for room and board.[57]

Field hands remaining in Chinatown during the fall celebrated the Harvest Moon Festival, similar to American Thanksgiving. Other festivals also punctuated the year, but none was bigger than Chinese New Year, which occurred in late January or early February. The 1883 New Year's celebration was described by the *Fresno Weekly Republican* as a "wild, weird melody of the Chinese violin, of the tam and *yangteeshuldabaloo* float in the evening air until about 4 o'clock in the morning, when the last musician falls under the table in a state of helpless intoxication." Considerable pomp and anticipation accompanied the event, but for most celebrants, the greatest excitement came in a midnight fireworks display featuring "firecrackers strong enough to knock a mule down at 100 yards."[58]

Weeks in advance, newspapers informed field hands: "CHINESE NEW YEAR. Will be celebrated by a grand Discharge of fire crackers at the store of Quong Loon High Company in Chinatown Next Sunday at 4:00 P.M. Citizens generally invited to witness it." Each day thereafter another event would be announced. A notice in the *Winters Express* read: "The Chinese request all who will have teams on the streets next Tuesday from 3:15 to 4 o'clock, to care for them while they have their jubilee with fireworks." As field hands and other Chinese crammed into the boardinghouses in the days before the festivities, even gambling halls would shut down after midnight and turn their gaming tables into temporary bunks. Stores stayed open, beautiful lanterns would be hung in doorways and on balconies, merchants received friends and distributed candy, laundrymen and vegetable peddlers handed out lily bulbs to patrons, and Chinatown engaged in *Dah Faw Hom Muy*, a general cleanup.[59]

With businesses decked out in flags, banners, and shrines, butterfly-shaped kites dancing high overhead, and all kinds of food and entertainment in abundant supply, Chinese New Year's celebrations attracted huge crowds of field hands, who would for a brief period rub elbows with Chinese gentry and various nationalities streaming in from outlying communities. The sound of firecrackers, the gongs and drums of Chinese bands, and the odors of incense, opium, and roasting chickens and pork all made for a glorious celebration. Dozens of men would always be arrested for violating some prohibition on fireworks, and more than a few fires would be attributed to Chinese pyrotechnics. "New Year is a great event for the Chink," wrote the *Ventura Free Press*. "He dresses up in good clothes, if he has any, throws care to the wind and enjoys himself to his heart's content. His debts are paid and if he has anything left over he plays fan tan and blows it all in."[60]

At New Year's celebrations, field hands dealt with the isolation and oppression of life in California by fervently embracing old-country traditions and displaying their distinctive identity. Men came in search of fortune, but failing to find it, were forced to accept a life of toil in a strange land. In truth, California was not their home, nor would it ever be. Their language, customs, even common, everyday items like clothes remained distinctly Chinese. So few Chinese adopted American-style dress that as late as 1868 one Chinese official visiting San Francisco estimated that 99 percent still wore their traditional clothing. Nor did they cut their queues, an act that one sympathetic Californian likened to abandoning the star-spangled banner.[61]

❧

Chinese immigrants were in fact remarkably clear about their values and aspirations. At government hearings, they would express (through representatives of the Six Companies) strong local aspirations; they wanted to accumulate a "stake" and maybe some property. But even as they described these goals, they would often let slip larger and more complex dreams—ones that encompassed their old life in China. On occasion, they revealed a vision commonly found among people who have been forced to leave their homeland—a conviction that they would one day return and that their stay abroad was only temporary. Overhearing them, one journalist reported how "in the celery and asparagus and vegetable fields [they] were eternally chattering of the time when they would be able to buy . . . enough to secure ease and plenty back home." Lee Chew, who came to San Francisco in 1860 as a sixteen-year-old, recalled many years later in an autobiography published in the *Independent* magazine, how he had been inspired by stories of men who returned to his home village and "took ground as large as four city blocks and made a paradise of it. He had gone away from our village as a poor boy. Now he returned with unlimited wealth, made in America."[62]

When interviewers met them much later in their lives, field hands would invariably produce a packet of memorabilia that included some family photographs and letters. The old men would say the mementos reminded them of their failure, loneliness, and what they had left behind. Such men revealed that they had originally hoped to achieve through farmwork at least five goals: first, they would pay off debts from the voyage; second, they would accumulate a stake; third, they would return home, either permanently or temporarily; fourth, they would buy some land near their native village and take care of their aged parents; and fifth— inevitably—they would ensure the survival of their family and be honored by their communities as a "Gam-Saan-Haak" (a wealthy and respected traveler from the Golden Mountain).[63]

To hear them talk about it, the perilous sea voyage, the years of ill-paid field labor, and the self-disciplined, frugal living had little or nothing to do with establishing a new life in California. As most interviewers learned, such sacrifices were entirely incidental, if not irrelevant. Chinese field hands saw immigration not as a rejection but rather a defense of their traditional way of life, a way to provide for it and preserve it amid political and economic disaster; such men were known as sojourners. Always looking toward home, they occasionally revealed to interviewers a tension common among people who feel the tug of two worlds— an uncertainty that leads to fear of losing an old identity and of never quite attaining a new one. As one man put it, "I have one foot in this country, and one foot in China."[64]

CHAPTER FOURTEEN

More Manpower from a Pint of Rice

Sugar Beets, Short-Handled Hoes,

and Chinese Exclusion

One afternoon in the summer of 1877, a group of Chinese was returning from the fields around Gridley, a small farm town beside the Southern Pacific Railroad tracks thirty miles south of Chico. With plenty of work on surrounding ranches, the men had established a small but thriving Chinatown just south of Libby's Cannery and, keeping to themselves, fit well into the community. So they were surprised when, upon reaching the outskirts of town, police stopped them. A local constable had earlier been robbed of eight dollars by some Chinese, and the field hands, being the first spotted after the crime, were caught in a crude dragnet. Questioned and tortured unmercifully for hours, the men would not admit any guilt or knowledge of the crime. Absolutely insisting on their innocence even after being strung up by their arms, they were let down for a brief time, then strung up again. Finally, more dead than alive, they were released several hours later. Their consistent denials had finally convinced authorities that they were not guilty of the crime.[1]

By the late 1870s, it seemed that wherever the Chinese went in the farming districts, they were tormented and harassed. Many watched helplessly as farmers employing them were threatened with arson and had their barns burned down for refusing to dismiss them. Violent confrontations were common. In one incident after another, members of the Order of Caucasians, zealots from the Workingman's Party, young boys, and lawless tramps attacked Chinese with impunity. Their efforts were so successful on farms around Healdsburg in the Sonoma Valley that the *San Francisco Call* reported, "It may be said that Chinamen, as laborers, are almost unknown." But even as the campaign against them mounted, Chinese field hands in certain areas like the delta remained largely untouched. Working on isolated islands and physically cut off from the wandering mobs and anti-Chinese zealots, they were employed by landowners who valued their industry and who saw no other way to farm than with Chinese field hands. By the end of the summer of 1877, however, they too were threatened. "Notice is heare

FIGURE 30. Chinese farmworkers stacking hay using a California derrick and fork, Stockdale ranch, five miles southwest of Bakersfield, 1888. Photograph by Carleton E. Watkins. Courtesy of the Library of Congress.

given to all men who owns lands on the Sacramento River is heare ordered to dispense with Chinese labour or suffer sutch consequences as may follow within tenn days," read a letter to Stockton area farmers. "We have heaved and puked over Chinese imposition long a nuff," the letter concluded. "Good-by John Long Taile."[2]

Delta growers initially stood fast against such threats. Like their counterparts in the Salinas and Pajaro valleys, they were heavily dependent on the Chinese and inclined to leave them alone. Meeting in Courtland, one group of sixty farmers, including such leaders as O. R. Runyon and V. J. Sims, berated the "thieving, cowardly tramps, who wander around, systematically lying, plundering, exciting, and threatening," then declared their admiration for the "sturdy, sober and industrious" Chinese. But following several mysterious barn fires, their resolve dissipated. After a few more fires, fifty of the sixty farmers who had originally resisted anti-Chinese agitation met in Isleton to reconsider their stand. They now pledged neither to rent land to the Chinese nor hire them to work in their fields. However, there is no evidence that they actually implemented these policies or dismissed any Chinese already employed.[3]

Of all the incidents during the summer of 1877, the worst by far occurred during the hop harvest in the Gospel Swamp near Anaheim. As usual J. B. Raine had guarded against any delay in picking by contracting with local labor boss Sin Si Wau far in advance. A crew of ninety Chinese hop pickers arrived early on Monday, August 1, expecting to be employed for fifteen to eighteen days. Instead, they encountered a well-organized blockade. On Tuesday, August 2, local residents notified the Chinese that they would not be allowed to enter Raine's hop fields. Local workers were in dire circumstances, they said, and many families, unable to find work since the previous year's campaign against the Chinese, had been subsisting on nothing but potatoes and bread. But not all local residents agreed with the anti-Chinese campaign. Writing to the *Gazette*, one man asked indignantly,

> Who on earth are these 'swampers,' or any other class or body of men, that they should be allowed in their impertinence to dictate to any other person or persons whom they shall or shall not employ? . . . Let the people of Gospel Swamp, Anaheim, or any other place, sanction such action even by inaction or silence, and the next notice may be that the grape-growers may not hereafter be allowed to hire Mexicans to prune their vines, not Chinamen, nor Indians to gather the fruit; and then why not go a little further and serve notice that no office of honor, trust or profit . . . shall be held by any other than an American born, or an Irish naturalized citizen?[4]

Opposition to Chinese field hands was so strong that, within a few days, they encountered hostility not only from Gospel Swamp residents, but also from normally tolerant citizens of Anaheim and from citizens of Los Angeles as well. Publishing a letter in the *Anaheim Review* addressed to "Vineyard Men and Employers of Chinese Generally," anti-Chinese elements threatened not only the Chinese and anyone who employed them, but Raine specifically. Raine met with a delegation of anti-Chinese zealots, explained the nature of the work, and announced he would annul his contract with Sin Si Wau and hire sixty white workers. Locals in turn promised that if the necessary number of white men did not show up, they would allow Raine to employ enough Chinese laborers to make up the difference. This arrangement was soon put to the test.[5]

When picking time came around on Monday, August 15, only thirty of the sixty whites who had signed up to harvest hops appeared for work. Unable to tolerate the heat and the pace of the harvest, half of them quit after just a few hours, and the rest immediately struck for higher wages. Sin Si Wau then brought in his crew to take up the slack and Raine fired four of the strikers. As they passed each other on their way to and from the fields, one white field hand threw a potato that struck one of the Chinese in the back. The assaulted Chinese hop picker drew a pocket pistol and fired a shot at the white man. He missed, and before he could take a second shot, Raine disarmed him. Just as quickly, the Chinese hop picker drew a huge and heavy navy pistol and fired another shot before again being disarmed. No one was injured, but the confrontation was too much for residents of the Gospel Swamp. "They told the Chinamen to leave," reported the *Anaheim Gazette*, "and their command must have been very emphatic, because the Mongolians in their haste forgot to take their cooking utensils with them. These the settlers smashed into smithereens. And so endeth the second chapter in this conflict of races."[6]

Within a few days, all of the Chinese were replaced by white workers and Gabrielino Indians from Los Angeles. But after a liquor salesman arrived on August 25 and began selling whiskey, the Indians went on a long bender and "high old jamboree." They continued to drink after the liquor salesman made a second visit on the following day, "so that," as the *Gazette* reported, "the Indians got enough bug-juice to render them helplessly inebriated." White hop pickers took advantage of the labor shortage by striking for higher wages on Monday, August 29. Firing them, Raine eventually brought in the harvest by September 5 with the remaining whites and sober Indians. After finishing the harvest, all of the Indians headed into town. Camping on the edge of the railroad yard near the *Gazette* office, they waited to catch a train back to Los Angeles.[7]

More trouble came that winter, when a rabble mob opposed to large landowners, government corruption, banks, and Chinese immigrants formed the Workingman's Party. Led by red-faced, arm-waving demagogue Denis Kearney, the Workingman's Party pursued the Chinese with a dogged hatred. In fiery speeches to workers in meeting halls and vacant lots, Kearney used his extraordinary oratorical power to hammer home his message to men made receptive by their own dire economic circumstances. With a shrill and extreme rhetoric, Kearney's movement labeled the Chinese an unmitigated curse, and soon extended its presence far beyond San Francisco into agricultural districts from Redding south to Salinas. "Chinamen are not citizens in any sense of the word," said one rabid Kearney supporter. "They do not grant us the miserable boon of letting their heathen carcasses manure our soil, but ship the bones of their dead to the land of Confucius for final internment [*sic*]."[8]

Surpassing and supplanting the Order of Caucasians as the most violent and vociferous anti-Chinese group in the state, the Workingman's Party quickly won the support of prominent urban, rural, and political leaders, many of whom, such as potato magnate and Santa Cruz developer Elihu Anthony, could hardly be classified as workingmen. And while Kearney's sandlot oratory made him the symbolic chief of the anti-Chinese forces, his speeches were by no means unique. Racism permeated the unemployed masses. Thrown out of work and seeking scapegoats, desperate men gathered in taverns and on street corners and, often inspired by liquor, concocted a vast assortment of anti-Chinese songs and poems. One popular verse went:

> Yu can take a Chink away from 'is hop
> 'Is lanterns an' gals an' pigs an chop
> You can dress 'im up in yer Christian clo'es
> Put texts in 'is head an' hymns in 'is nose
> But yu'll find, when he's actin' a dead straight part
> He's a chinaman still in 'is yeller hart.[9]

Already under attack by Kearney's followers, and by what some called "the tramping elements," Chinese field hands in 1878 suddenly found themselves also targeted by members of yet another activist group, the Patrons of Husbandry, more commonly known as the Grange. With its grandiose economic schemes, fraternal opportunities, mysterious rituals, and harsh criticism of American corporate economic practices, the Grange was on the rise everywhere in rural California, particularly among angry tenant farmers plagued by indebtedness, tax problems, and the vagaries of the international grain market. Championing small, family farmers, a network of 231 local Granges with a total membership of fifteen thousand, most from California's northern wheat-growing counties, joined the anti-Chinese movement, often condemning the Chinese as one of many sources (along with the railroad, land, and tax issues) of an undemocratic rural society. They further agreed with Kearney that cheap coolie labor was an aid to monopolists—particularly the railroads and big landowners, who were their archenemies. Grange members supported resolutions demanding taxes on Chinese vegetable peddlers, advocated laws forbidding the Chinese from wearing queues or carrying baskets or bags suspended from poles across their shoulders, and called for banning further immigration of "this scourge to western humanity and civilization." To many Grange leaders, Chinese field hands represented an "overshadowing curse which are sapping the foundation of our prosperity, the dignity of labor, and the glory of our State."[10]

Chinese field hands were not without their defenders. Prominent among them were the more wealthy and educated members of the agricultural elite, men like J. P. Johnson, owner of a San Francisco employment bureau; university-educated Sacramento wheat growers James Chiles and George Swingle; Wheatland hop grower D. P. Durst; Fresno peach farmer P. W. Butler; and Selma raisin grower T. C. White. Holding public office and participating fully in the state's political process, these men championed the precepts of scientific farming and rejected blanket attacks on bankers, capitalists, and railroad barons. Members of the State Agricultural Society, the oldest and most prestigious farm organization in California, they diverged significantly from Grange members on almost every question. Rarely praising Chinese culture or individual Chinese, they instead regarded them as a resource. And believing that cheap labor was essential to profitable, large-scale farming, they viewed the Chinese as absolutely essential to keeping costs down. While sometimes passing resolutions urging restrictions on further Chinese immigration, they did so halfheartedly in order to avoid being branded pro-Chinese.[11]

To actually harm the Chinese, single them out for attack, or to blacklist those who employed them, they believed, was to commit economic suicide, depreciate property values, cause crops to go unplanted and unpicked, and force banks to foreclose on mortgages. For these reasons, while seeming to go along with anti-Chinese statements, members of the State Agricultural Society frequently criticized the Grange along with other anti-Chinese extremists, labeling them "idlers," "loafers," and followers of Kearney. "The writers dip their pens in gall, and slash away diatribes against the bug bear John Chinaman, and would have us believe he is the plague of the nation," grumbled one member of the State Agricultural Society. "They simply argue from one set of facts and ignore another." More succinctly, a farmwife put it this way in a letter to the *San Francisco Post*: "Our fruit will rot; we must have help to pick it at once, and so we are compelled to hire Chinese."[12]

Commentators on the anti-Chinese violence of this era have routinely stated that it marked the beginning of the end for the Chinese in rural California. From this seemingly logical conclusion has grown yet another myth of the farmworker story, one holding that the attacks took their toll on the Chinese, drove them from the agricultural districts, or forced them to withdraw voluntarily. And while there is ample anecdotal evidence to support such a view, the truth is that Chinese laborers were much more affected by the hostility in cities and mining districts than they were by anything that occurred on farms around the state. Denied work in San Francisco and Sacramento and chased out of the gold fields (where their numbers in the three main mining districts declined from twenty-four thousand in 1880 to 9,500 in 1890), battered and frightened Chinese men were forced to unite defensively and seek employment in the countryside away from unruly mobs. During the summer and fall of 1877, Chinese field hands streamed into the farming districts in record numbers. Rather than driving the Chinese out of agriculture, the anti-Chinese movement actually sent more of them into farmwork than ever before.[13]

Seeking employment, many Chinese now moved onto tenant farms operated by their compatriots in the delta, the Sonoma and Vaca valleys, and in the Sacramento Valley around Colusa. The pattern of work on these farms differed considerably from that on farms operated by white growers. Employers were often former field hands who, after years of work had come to an arrangement with a landlord. Many had formed partnerships with five or six fellow Chinese to work a plot of land, and then upon becoming successful, expanded and began hiring newly arrived Chinese to do the work they had once shared.[14]

Recent immigrants found their countrymen hard taskmasters, but working alongside them, they learned what to do and how to do it properly. They also enjoyed many advantages. One was steady employment. On tenant farms in the Sonoma Valley, they worked continually, handling everything from clearing and planting land to harvesting crops. And when not working, they would hire out— or would be hired out—to neighboring farmers. They also enjoyed protection and companionship, since Chinese tenant farmers functioned much like surrogate heads of extended families, housing and feeding men and watching over them for years at a time. A final advantage of working for Chinese tenants was safety. Field hands on such farms remained largely unaffected by and unaware of the campaigns against them. On potato farms run by Chinese tenants in the delta, the major disruption in the lives of Chinese field hands was not racist sinophobes or night riders but tired steamer pilots who, arriving late at night, would roust men out of a bunkhouse and march them along a narrow landing and across an even narrower gangplank to load a crop while still half-asleep.[15]

The Chinese work ethic was a powerful weapon against racism, earning Chinese laborers such wide support from farmers and members of the agricultural community that they were often able to blunt or avoid intimidation entirely. Typical was the work done by a fifteen-man crew under Sam Long, a China boss near Santa Paula in Ventura County. Entirely on their own initiative, Long and his crew cut mustard and separated out seed at the rate of twelve hundred pounds per day, threshing out the seeds onto sheets with flails. This netted each crewman two dollars a day and a profit of several hundred dollars for Long. Impressed by the undertaking, the rabidly anti-Chinese *Ventura Signal* sent a reporter to observe the men. "The Chinamen, though a nuisance in many respects, have their uses," conceded the *Signal*. "They certainly give us some wholesome lessons in industry and economy."[16]

Nowhere at this time did the Chinese exert a greater impact on the land and on agriculture than in the Salinas Valley. Full of festering sloughs, the valley was still largely devoted to wheat growing. But if the lowlands could be drained, the deep black, alluvial soil might sustain a variety of fruit and row crops. To accomplish this, the firm of Carr, Vanderhurst, and Sanborn in 1877 decided to hire a crew to clear and drain a five-hundred-acre tract of land north of Salinas. Using many of the same techniques their compatriots had used on Twitchell Island, Chinese reclamation workers slogged through waist-deep slime and muck and fought off swarms of mosquitoes to grub out brush and trees that clogged the channels, used gigantic peat spades to cut the bog into blocks, then hefted and dragged the blocks into levees with large steel forks and hay-bale hooks. Next they excavated six miles of drainage ditches. In this way, they quickly transformed a mosquito-infested miasma once worth twenty-eight dollars an acre into prime farmland selling at four times that price. Contracting to reclaim more land, the Chinese next began diverting part of the Salinas River into the Alisal Slough, an ancient river channel, thereby bringing water to drought-stricken land between Salinas and Castroville. This would allow farmers to irrigate fields in some of the most fertile land on the west side of the Salinas Valley, thus opening up an entirely new area for farming. Hundreds of Chinese went to work on the canal before heavy rain broke the drought and farmers scrubbed the project. But that was hardly the end of the story.[17]

Having created some of the most valuable farmland in the entire state, many Chinese field hands now abandoned their status as day laborers and began working for themselves. China bosses developed a reclamation-lease system much like the one they operated in the nearby Pajaro Valley, whereby they grew and harvested crops rent-free for several years in exchange for ditching and draining land and readying it for agriculture. One of the most successful reclamation bosses was Sam Kee. In exchange for cutting down and grubbing "all timber and other trees and underbrush" and burning "all underbrush unfit for firewood," Kee obtained all rights to a one-hundred-acre tract owned by David Jacks near present-day Spreckels. (Kee also earned a considerable bonus selling the firewood back to Jacks at $1.25 a cord.) Soon two other Chinese contractors concluded similar leases with Jacks, agreeing to plant whatever the landowner wanted while also promising as a condition of their lease to kill off entire populations of gophers and ground squirrels "infesting" the land. Under this arrangement, the Chinese within a few years leased more than one thousand acres from Jacks alone and concluded similar arrangements to reclaim and farm hundreds of acres owned by other Salinas Valley farmers.[18]

Although such arrangements appeared to be generous, for the Chinese it usually meant years of continuous and exhausting labor. Little of what they did at first involved farming because during the first year crews often did nothing but chop down brush and trees and cut, split, and stack firewood and haul it to town or out to farms and ranches. Once they cleared the land they turned to "muck work," and during the second year dug drainage canals, built dikes, and dried out the land. Only during the third year would they actually begin working as field hands, plowing and cross-plowing, then planting a first crop, usually potatoes or some other tuber that had to be dug up during harvest, thus helping to further break up the soil. Finally, during the fourth year they turned to true farmwork. Planting, cultivating, and harvesting a variety of crops, they worked at a frantic pace, driven hard by white employers who now had to recoup most of their investment from profits earned during the final year of their leases.[19]

For Chinese field hands, the end of 1877 marked a year of exhausting work. They had moved into new areas and new types of labor, and despite the violence against them, their setbacks had been few and minor. No other group of farmworkers had ever provoked such wide commentary, inspired such a bizarre combination of hostility and admiration, or established such an unattainable standard. By almost unanimous agreement, Californians now considered Chinese field hands the key to agricultural success and prosperity. "If we had not the Chinese," argued the Reverend Otis Gibson, a Methodist minister and head of the church's San Francisco Chinatown mission school, "our famous fruit ranches would be turned back into pasture grounds." With such endorsements, few if any Chinese field hands could foresee a day when it would all come to an end, when they would be excluded entirely from California, and when they would be replaced by another group of Asian immigrants. For the moment, the work was proceeding too well, opportunities were too great, and the rewards too tangible to think much about anything else.[20]

ৡৡ

Early in 1878, the Chinese assumed an even larger role in the sugar beet industry, once again basing their success on a superior work ethic. Having supplied labor to grow beets at the first sugar beet plant in California at Alvarado in 1870, and the second one in the state in the Sacramento Valley in 1873, they now played a key role growing and harvesting sugar beets after the California Sugar Beet Company shut down its Alvarado factory, moved to Soquel, near Camp Capitola, and erected a new, three-and-one-half-story beet processing factory. Of the two hundred men employed at the factory during the fall sugar beet season, 145 were Chinese. Under an arrangement that became common, white Pajaro Valley farmers provided the water, land, and sugar beet seed, and the Chinese supplied the labor to plant, thin, harvest, clean, top, and load beets. Typically, Chinese contractors agreed to raise the beets at seventy cents per ton for Chinese farmers who presold them to the sugar beet company at a contracted price of four dollars a ton. Even less the one-dollar-a-ton shipping costs, that left a remarkable profit. By handling both ends of the harvest, Chinese field hands thus formed the cornerstone of the sugar beet business, becoming so important that, by the end of the year, growers and factory managers acknowledged that without them, the entire industry would crumble.[21]

By monopolizing sugar beet work, China bosses were betting on the tenacity of their people. Beet cultivation was backbreaking labor, a process that had remained unchanged and unaffected by technological improvement since Napoleonic times. After the ground had been ploughed and seeded, sugar beets sprouted quickly, with plants sending up four or more shoots. Workers then went through the fields cutting out all but a few beet plants, leaving clumps standing ten or twelve inches apart, while another group of workers, often on their hands and knees, would pull all but the largest plants from each clump. This was called "blocking," and had to be done quickly. Thinning immediately followed blocking and involved removing all but one in the cluster of plants. Hoeing followed blocking and thinning by a few days, and consisted of removing weeds to within six or eight inches of young plants. Two or three hoeings were required to loosen the earth and remove weeds. Most of the work was done between May and July with one of the most awful tools in the history of farm labor, the short-handled hoe, a sharp-bladed implement with a six-inch-long handle. Also known as *el cortido* (the short one), the short-handled hoe is usually dated much later in the farmworker story and assigned to Mexican and Japanese beet and lettuce thinners after the turn of the century. There is no direct evidence describing Chinese using short-handled hoes at this early date, but that may be because it was simply taken for granted. Indirect evidence arises out of complaints that the California Sugar Beet Company employed only Chinese and not white men in the fields. Seeking to explain why this was the case, farmers pointed to the miseries of beet thinning, which "was of such a nature that only Chinamen could be obtained to do it." To properly thin beets, men had to "work on their knees which become so sore that blood is left as they move along." This could only have been true if the Chinese had been crawling and pulling young plants by hand or, more likely, not using long-handled hoes from a standing position.[22]

If beet thinning was exhausting, beet harvesting was torture. Beets were first loosed from the soil in late summer or early fall by a horse-drawn implement known as a "lifter." Then field hands took over, using a special "beet knife," a kind of machete with a square tip carrying a forward-facing prong. To lift the sugar beet out of the soil, a field hand stabbed the prong tip of his beet-knife into the beet and pried it loose. Then, inverting the sugar beet and holding it in one hand, he lopped off the leafy crown with one deft chop, piled all the beets together in one row, roots up, clear of the furrows where the wagon wheels ran. Accidents were commonplace. Many workers sliced hands open, chopped off fingers, and even hit arteries and bled to death. Beet pitchers then followed, grabbed the beets two or three at a time and threw them into the wagon where beet loaders grabbed them and stacked them carefully like cordwood in the wagon. The stacking was necessary to prevent any beets from falling out of an overloaded wagon.[23]

As they were taking over sugar beet labor, Chinese field hands also continued to gain ground in the Napa Valley. The 1877 vintage had mostly been sold, and a nearly ideal spring growing season was promising to yield a huge and highly profitable harvest of more than four tons of grapes per acre—an 1878 crush of two million gallons. To take advantage of the bounty, growers had embarked on a massive planting campaign, and Chinese field hands became central to their effort. The Chinese had already won many jobs in the valley by simply demonstrating that, when hired, they would relieve growers of the torture of having to fight to extract an honest day's work from lazy bindlemen and inexperienced locals. As California farmers generally did not hold tramp laborers in very high regard, it was easy enough for Chinese to find jobs through local bosses. Among these legendary characters were Kong Sam Kee, who ran a laundry on Lincoln Avenue in Calistoga and would later populate the pages of Robert Louis Stevenson's memoir *Silverado Squatters*; Quong Goon Loong, who sold "China goods" in St. Helena's Chinatown; and Wah Chung, a full-time contractor, also in St. Helena.[24]

By early summer it became apparent that the local Chinese population could not possibly meet the industry's needs. This opened up opportunities for China bosses and labor agencies in San Francisco. Among these were Grosett and Company, an employment office at 623 Clay Street in the heart of the city's Chinatown. Grosett and Company's advertisements in Napa newspapers conveniently omitted the word "Chinese," but it was well-known that a note sent south to them on the railroad would bring gangs of Chinese workers on the first northbound train. Attracted by jobs hauling and moving stone for the two-foot-thick walls of the huge Occidental Winery that Terrill Grigsby was building, as well as considerable work planting new vineyards and building other wineries, about seven hundred Chinese field hands poured into the valley during May 1878. The *St. Helena Star* saw them coming and exclaimed: "The tide of Chinese migration has turned this way."[25]

Hundreds more Chinese arrived in August for the hop harvest and, after finishing, stayed over intent on harvesting the grape crop. Many worked through the winter pruning grapevines. Others, having finished excavating the Beringer Winery cellar in St. Helena, turned to cutting tunnels into the nearby limestone hillside. For the next two years they drilled, dug, blasted, scraped, and carted away thousands of tons of debris, punching three wine tunnels deep into the rock.[26]

From their work during the 1878 wine grape harvest, yet another stereotype developed, one that linked their success to certain physical attributes. The Chinese were repeatedly said to be "naturally well-suited" to grape picking, tunneling, pruning, and other elements of stoop labor. "The best hand in the grape field by all odds is the little Chinaman," the *San Francisco Wine Merchant* reported. "He grows close to the ground, so does not have to bend his back like a large white man." With their compact physique, stubby and "supple" little fingers, and "stolid industry and genius for plodding," the "little brown men" could easily "squirm," "slither," "squat on their haunches," and "bend . . . to a painful angle." This supposedly allowed them to work far more easily among vines pruned to within a foot and a half of the ground, as was the practice until the mid-1880s. Chinese field hands worked so well that, according to one editor, they were better even than mules and horses—plus, they didn't kick and bite.[27]

When the rains came early and horse-drawn wagons could not get into the vineyards, Chinese field hands proved especially useful. On countless occasions they sloshed through the mud, hefted lug boxes full of grapes onto their heads, and carried them to wagons waiting on the nearest passable road. Whether they were picking grapes or clearing brush, no one could match their output. "I have watched Portuguese and Chinamen on a ranch where a little squad of each was employed," wrote a reporter for *Overland Monthly*. "I have noticed how carelessly the Portuguese heeded instructions, and how . . . the Portuguese went down on the nearest seats . . . and how invariably . . . the Chinaman's hoes went on faithfully."[28]

Chinese field hands never completely took over vineyard work in the Napa Valley, but only because there were not enough of them. Whites continued working among the grapevines, often alongside the Chinese and in competition with them, and as always continued to handle the bulk of all work. Crews of Germans would march into a vineyard like an army, each man carrying nothing more than a small, sharp, hooked knife and a gourd full of wine, and work just as hard, if not as efficiently, as the Chinese. There was, in fact, little difference in productivity separating the two. Neither height nor dexterity nor stamina allowed the Chinese to infiltrate the Napa Valley. Rather it was their hunger for work and the way their labor bosses effectively organized and directed them that gave them an advantage. But while the Chinese were being blindly praised for picking the wine grape crop, they still remained largely omitted from accounts of winemaking itself.[29]

Even though vintners praised them for not "drinking and [for their] general steadiness and adaptation for the work," their role as wine blenders, fermentation masters, general roustabouts, pomace shovelers, and assistant winemakers still remained a carefully guarded secret. With Napa's reputation for quality just becoming established, the valley did not in any way want to jeopardize its position by mentioning the Chinese. To do so would inevitably—if unjustifiably—raise issues of cleanliness, disease, and immigration policy, which might, in turn, impede sales. Knowing all too well what Denis Kearney and his followers were capable of, no vintner wanted to chance opening the industry up to boycotts or other threats. It was at this point that *Harper's Weekly* stepped into the picture and shattered the stereotype of the Chinese as little more than plodding grape pickers.[30]

From a reporter's visit the previous year, *Harper's Weekly* had developed a long and detailed portrait entitled "The Vintage in California," that went a long way toward establishing the Napa Valley as the premier winemaking region in America. To illustrate the October 5, 1878, issue, the magazine commissioned French-born artist Paul Frenzeny to do a pencil drawing of a typical winemaking scene. Often working from existing photographs, Frenzeny was known to take artistic license, borrowing and pasting elements from multiple scenes to achieve his desired compositions. Employing this technique to produce his picture of winemaking, Frenzeny's work showed Chinese field hands playing a prominent role in gathering the Napa vintage. But what most angered winemakers was that Frenzeny also showed them—quite inaccurately—stomping the grapes with their bare feet![31]

Napa winemakers had long since discarded that technique and prided themselves on their modern and highly sanitary winemaking procedures. So concerned with cleanliness were some of the valley's wineries that they hired Chinese to stand alongside conveyor belts and pick out unripe grapes, stems, leaves, and other debris as the grapes were transported inside the winery to be crushed and fermented. Now it seemed not only that their reputation for innovation and quality was being tarnished but additionally that the woodcut might link their product to Chinese hands![32]

FIGURE 31. "The Vintage in California—At Work at the Wine Presses," October 5, 1878. Lithograph by Paul Frenzeny. *Harper's Weekly*. Image from the author's collection.

To a man, Napa's winemakers denounced *Harper's Weekly* and demanded that the magazine immediately drop all further references to the Chinese. Unable to restrain his anger at Frenzeny, a writer for the *San Francisco Call* proclaimed: "He has libeled the state . . . The tendency of such a picture is not likely to weaken the prejudice which some Eastern dealers have endeavored to create against the wine produced in this state." There was little truth to the claim. Two-thirds of California's five-million-gallon annual vintage actually sold within the state, while slightly less than one million dollars in wine sold annually to markets in the eastern United States. Hence, California wine merchants had little or nothing to fear from the *Harper's Weekly* drawing. Still, the image of "dirty Oriental laborers, reeking with perspiration" while stamping dirt and various unmentionable pollutants from between their yellow toes into the vintage was too much for most California winemakers to stomach.[33]

Just as winemakers feared, the widely circulated *Harper's Weekly* image became a rallying point for anticoolie groups intent on driving Chinese field hands out of the Napa Valley. It was not long before Chinese working at Terrill Grigsby's Occidental Winery, the focus of hostility for several years, felt the first wave of attacks. After threatening them repeatedly throughout September and October, anti-Chinese forces struck early in November, burning down the barn that served as their bunkhouse in the middle of the night. But the Chinese would not leave, nor would Grigsby fire them. They spent that winter living in tents and sheds and beneath trees as they put the finishing touches on the winery. To them, the only goals that mattered were those of work and income, and they would not be driven off.[34]

In January 1879, tough-looking tramps appeared in the Napa Valley. Beating several Chinese on sight, they sent threatening letters to various growers, warning them to dismiss the Chinese; to underscore their intent, each letter contained a match—the unspoken threat of arson that was a powerful persuader. Initially confident that the area's more responsible citizens would head off the campaign if for no other reason than for its danger to property and business, vintners at first ignored the tramps. But when Charles Krug received threats, he dismissed all but six Chinese from his workforce of forty-six men. Wandering the streets, unemployed Chinese field hands now found their friendly gestures toward children misinterpreted as the overtures of "filthy Chinese beasts, who seem to lust after tender children." Everywhere, it seemed, the tide was turning in favor of Chinese exclusionists.[35]

A few months later, copies of a new state constitution containing several anti-Chinese proposals began circulating throughout the farming districts. These resolutions had grown out of the State Constitutional Convention in Sacramento, where the Workingman's Party had garnered one-third of the delegates and used this control to introduce a series of provocative anti-Chinese measures. Among other things, the new constitution would segregate Chinese neighborhoods and terminate any Chinese employed by state, county, or local governments. Almost immediately, Denis Kearney stumped the rural districts, urging support of the document. All loyal Californians should repudiate the "long-tailed lepers from Asia," as well as perpetrators of land monopoly and cheap labor, he argued, and vote for the new constitution. Although some audiences agreed that the Chinese ought to be barred from further immigration, most listeners seemed to think that those already in the state ought to be allowed to stay and work.[36]

The new constitution and the arguments presented by Kearney supporters that it would produce a "healthier society" were calculated to win the broadest possible support and give the Chinese no time to react. Adopted in May, the new constitution was further bolstered via a referendum against further immigration passed in September of that same year with 94 percent of the vote (150,000 to 9,000). The measure soon came to the attention of national politicians who took up the matter in Washington, D.C. Congress shortly passed a bill prohibiting Chinese laborers from settling in the United States, but because it violated a previous treaty giving them the right to immigrate, President Rutherford B. Hayes vetoed it. Momentarily protected, Chinese laborers continued to immigrate. Commented one newspaper: "Said Denis, 'the Chinese must go'; but still does the queue cumber the land."[37]

The failure of the national campaign came as a real shock to anti-Chinese elements, but what especially upset them was the way China bosses and laborers seemed to be shedding their docile ways. This new militancy surfaced in dramatic fashion during the 1880 fruit harvest in Santa Clara. At the time, it was common for China bosses to receive half of the fruit picked in lieu of wages, but now they demanded a two-thirds share. In support of this, virtually every Chinese gang in the valley went out on strike. Their near-monopoly control of field labor made them hard to resist. While tallying just 8 percent of the Santa Clara population, the Chinese comprised 70 percent of the harvest labor force in the principal fruit growing areas of the county. They therefore had no problem completely shutting down the harvest. "Where any gang had left," reported the *San Francisco Bulletin*, "it was found impossible to secure other Mongolians to replace them, and the growers were compelled to treat with their old hands before they could get any at all."[38]

The strike rattled the farming community. Traveling through the area a few years later, a reporter found the Chinese in absolute control. "A person who desires to go into this [farming] business, must consult the Chinamen," he reported. "If they think the increase in production will be greater than the market can stand, he will get no labor. If the Chinamen decide that the new acreage will not overstock the market, he will get all the labor he wants." But it was not just the magnitude of the strike or its outcome that captured the attention of growers, agricultural leaders, and journalists. For the first time, the Chinese had shut down an entire agricultural district. This was not the passive behavior they expected from the Chinese, and growers were left wondering, How had they done it? What did it mean? And who was next?[39]

It was not difficult to see why the Chinese asserted themselves. Besides the specific demands and immediate goals underlying their action, there was also a basic question of power. Sometime in the late 1870s—though it is impossible to say exactly when and where this realization materialized—China bosses and farmworkers began to sense that, in many agricultural areas, they held the upper hand. Santa Clara was a test. If they could exploit their numbers in Santa Clara, they realized they could do the same throughout the state. Growers had only to glance at a map of the state's farming districts to see what the Chinese might do. Although whites still comprised the majority of California's twenty-eight thousand field hands, the Chinese constituted as much as one-third of the farm labor force in three counties. In several key townships within those counties, they completely dominated farmwork.[40]

In Sacramento County's Georgiana Township and Alameda County's Eden Township, Chinese field hands held down nine of ten jobs, while in San Joaquin County's Union Township, also a traditional stronghold, eight of ten farmworkers were Chinese. On Staten and Bouldin Islands in the delta the Chinese comprised virtually the entire farm labor force. They also made up half of the farmworkers in a new farming area, Solano County's Vacaville Township, where, in contrast to white pickers who required small, wheelbarrow-like orchard trucks with a flatbed to haul their harvest out of the orchards, the Chinese picked directly into two baskets, suspended them from poles across their shoulders, and simply walked to the end of an orchard row to dump their load. This technique allowed growers employing the Chinese to avoid purchasing orchard trucks, thereby saving considerably on expenses; it also worked well on the terraced hillside orchards west of town that produced the earliest fruit.[41]

Chinese field hands also played significant roles in several other new farming districts, among them the fruit belt around Marysville and the hop yards near Wheatland, both in Yuba County, the orchard district between Auburn and Rocklin in the foothills of Placer County, and even in Colusa County, the state's leading wheat growing area, where they comprised about 8 percent of all field hands. At about this time, the number of Chinese in the wine-producing districts also increased dramatically, doubling from 473 to 904 in Sonoma, and nearly tripling in the Napa Valley from 263 to 905. In Fresno County, a relatively new but rapidly expanding grape-growing area, their numbers increased from 427 to 753, while in Los Angeles the numbers of Chinese working on truck gardens and in the new orange groves around Riverside jumped from 239 to 1,169, the most dramatic increase anywhere. Overall, the percentage of Chinese engaged in farm labor in agricultural counties increased from between 3 and 20 percent in 1870 to between 5 and 28 percent in 1880.[42]

As the range of their work expanded, so did the power wielded by Chinese field hands and bosses, and a few apparently began testing the boundaries of what they could do. Nearly fatal consequences resulted from one of their first and most reckless actions. Stranded in a remote labor camp during the September 1880 grape harvest in Lodi, Chinese field hands ignored "Keep Out" signs and stole fruit and produce from the neighboring McFarling ranch. They had been doing this for several years, but McFarling had grown tired of the losses and warned that he would shoot the next man who trespassed on his property. The grower loaded his shotgun with a painful but not deadly combination of rock salt and bird shot and waited by the edge of his orchard. That night, two Chinese pickers crept in to steal fruit. Ordered to halt and surrender, they attempted to run away, but McFarling shot both of them. After recovering, the men attempted to have McFarling arrested, but local authorities refused. Labeled thieves, the Chinese were told that they had gotten what they deserved and were then ordered to leave town. Several weeks later while picking wine grapes in Napa County, the men obtained a warrant, and authorities there hauled McFarling into court on charges of attempted murder. These charges were dismissed three weeks later, after Mc-Farling pleaded guilty to a lesser charge of assault with a deadly weapon and paid a twenty-five-dollar fine. It was the first time that Chinese field hands had ever obtained a legal judgment against a farmer.[43]

Chinese field hands could look back on many triumphs as the 1880 harvest season closed. They had won several victories, and their setbacks had been few and minor. No group of farmworkers had ever before behaved with such unity, exerted such influence over agriculture, or extended so much control over the farm labor market. They were in a confident mood as they settled in for the winter and prepared to expand the gains they had made. During the previous two years, Chinese had immigrated to California in ever larger numbers. And with thousands more now leaving the played out mining districts in search of employment, they converged on the rural areas in such volume during 1881 that they created an extreme overabundance of farm labor and took control of an increasing number of farms, crops, and agricultural activities. Farmers noted the influx. "In all the fruit orchards there are nothing but Chinese; everywhere in the farms around Marysville, all the fruit farms, particularly are entirely cultivated by Chinese; all the bottom land is cultivated by Chinese . . . there is no white labor there at all," reported one farmer during the proceedings of a court case. "I went down to the orchard. There were forty Chinamen, picking, pitting and drying apricots; every place swarms with them."[44]

Of all the new tasks that the Chinese performed at this time, cutting and drying fruit may have been the most important. Growers were producing a surplus, and when the local market and refrigerated shipments could not accommodate it all, many apricot, plum, and peach farmers diverted much of their crop (particularly smaller and substandard fruit) into the dried fruit market. Seven pounds of surplus plums yielded one pound of dried prunes, which sold for twenty-five cents a pound in the East. This was considerably better than the three to four cents per pound that fresh fruit brought, or the twenty-five to thirty dollars a ton canneries paid. The problem was that drying fruit required a huge labor force. Although fruit growers had traditionally hired women and children to cut and dry their crops, it was often impossible to get them out to remote farms. Only the Chinese would camp out next to the sulfur sheds and live in tents for the duration of the harvest. Consequently, on many of the more remote farms, Chinese field hands comprised entire drying crews.[45]

Chinese field hands fit easily into the ebb and flow of this labor market. Becoming important not just as pickers but also as ranch hands, irrigators, and canal diggers, they handled everything from plowing fields and cleaning out chicken sheds to pruning and planting fruit trees. On the larger fruit ranches, they frequently toiled alongside white farmers-turned–field hands. Some were general roustabouts who worked year-round, but more often they were dismissed and rehired as necessary. The value of Chinese contract workers was apparent in the reactions of one grower who, describing why neighbors preferred to hire Chinese rather than white field hands, told the *Pacific Rural Press* that it was "because he is their slave, and they can sit in the shade and drive him as the old South overseer did the negro." Few growers actually disputed such comparisons.[46]

Farm diaries are full of entries about Chinese crews coming and going as the work tempo dictated. A sample of entries from January through December, 1881, on the Walter Allen citrus and grape farm near Pasadena reads:

> Two Chinamen in morning, two Chinamen in afternoon, ploughing barley field . . . two Chinamen picking up and burning rubbish all day . . . Fong sewed 8 ½ sacks, about 9 acres, of oats . . . Chinaman picking roots all morning, 5 Chinamen in afternoon . . . Wet all day, no work outside, Chinamen all lost the day . . . Chinamen all lost day . . . Chinamen all lost day . . . 13 Chinamen & self putting in 8,000 vines, Zinfandels, Bergers, and Charbonne . . . picked oranges all day . . . Chinamen 3 cutting weeds & mending fowl coral & cleaning out fowl houses all afternoon . . . Chinamen hoeing young orchard . . . Chinamen 4 men picking oranges & lemons all day . . . paid off 12 extra Chinamen . . . two new Chinamen came . . . went to town got extra Chinamen . . . got extra Chinaman . . . Chinaman paid off 8.[47]

Although most Chinese laborers in the citrus and other farming industries around the state continued to find work under China bosses, many newcomers now found jobs the same way that other immigrants did—they tagged along with relatives. Those who worked for fellow countrymen in the orchards about San Jose simply brought along their newly arrived family members or pals from home. On farms leased by Chinese contractors, it became common for an entire crew to be comprised of men from the same district in China, often from the same village. This produced extremely cohesive and well-organized crews and further strengthened their bargaining power. So large and strong were Chinese crews moving into Anaheim to work on the Cajón Canal in December 1881 that, when threatened by fifty white men, one hundred Chinese simply closed ranks and defied them. Faced with such resolve, the whites backed down.[48]

Many Chinese who immigrated during 1881 immediately went to work in the hop fields of Sacramento, Sonoma, and Mendocino counties. Hop production had increased fivefold since the industry began a decade earlier, and harvesting required huge numbers of laborers for an extremely short period of time, far more per acre than vineyards or orchard work. So large were some of the hop farms that harvest labor requirements always exhausted the available labor supply in neighboring communities, even when the entire population of a hop-growing district helped to bring in the crop. With an immense acreage to be picked, all of it ripening from mid-August to early September, hop growers took great care to integrate Chinese laborers thoroughly into their operations. Soon Chinese laborers were playing a key role in expanding hop acreage and were busy year-round cutting and transporting thousands of hop poles, erecting elaborate trellises, stringing miles of trellis wires, planting and training vines, suckering (cutting runaway shoots) twice a year, pruning vines in winter, building hop curing houses, and weeding, plowing, irrigating, harvesting, and baling hops. So important were the Chinese that growers went so far as to number hop picking boxes in Chinese and English, a practice that allowed them to calculate piece-rate payments more easily and identify who was responsible for any dirty hops rejected at the kiln. Those workers could then have their pay cut or adjusted.[49]

In addition to the advantages of their numbers and work habits, Chinese field hands also spread quickly throughout the countryside at this time because of a dire shortage of laborers in certain new agricultural districts. This was particularly true in the desert lands of the southern San Joaquin Valley, where farmers around Bakersfield were diverting water from the Kern River and building a vast network of dams, irrigation canals, and lateral canals. The work required hundreds of men who could correctly manage the water delivery system, but in labor-starved Kern County, farmers had trouble finding qualified white workers, so they scoured the Bakersfield Chinatowns for irrigators. Irrigation work was very complicated and largely unsupervised because too much or too little water—or water at the wrong time—could ruin a crop or make a field a muddy mess. Farmers therefore always selected the most loyal and dependable Chinese men. "Chinamen were used as irrigators until they became hard to shake out of the bamboo jungle in Bakersfield's China Town," recalled Kern County farmhand-turned-author Calhoun "Cal" Collins in his book *The McKittrick Ranch*. "They did their own cooking on the ranch and could get more man power out of a pint of rice than I could out of a quart of beans."[50]

Many Chinese irrigators in Kern County were former railroad construction workers who had arrived in Kern County around 1873 to grade and excavate tunnels through the Tehachapi Mountains southeast of Bakersfield. More than fifteen hundred remained behind once the tracks were complete, forming a huge labor reservoir for farmers. Hired through San Yick, who ran a store and several other businesses in town, Chinese irrigators found most work with area alfalfa farmers, who grew huge quantities of hay needed to feed the herds of Kern County's gigantic beef and dairy industry. Each field was watered by distribution ditches radiating off at right angles from a main canal and feeding into fields of ten to fifteen acres surrounded by levees or low ridges. First raising the water level in the ditch by inserting moveable boards, then opening a side gate from the main canal, Chinese irrigators would cut out a section from the ditch and flood the area between each check (a field surrounded by a low levee) to a depth of one foot. After irrigating one field, they cut out part of the next levee, allowing overflow water into the next check until the entire field was flooded. The work, which required men to stand knee-deep and barefoot in cold water for many hours under the hot sun, was painfully uncomfortable. Yet a good Chinese irrigator under this system could water two hundred acres a day. "They were natural irrigators, and it was quite a show to watch several rush to a break in a canal that some pesky gopher had started to stop it quick before the whole bank washed away," recalled "Cal" Collins. "They would chatter like a bunch of sparrows in a brush pile, and jump around with their shovels like a bunch of ants pulling in all directions trying to move the same bug. You would see their canteen of water or tea sitting on a levee in the hot sun, and not in the shade where us puny white people would place it."[51]

Besides watering alfalfa, Chinese field hands also found work cutting and stacking it. Under the excellent growing conditions in the southern San Joaquin Valley, alfalfa was cut four or five times each year between May and November, each cutting usually harvesting two and a half to three tons per acre. On the Collins ranch, Chinese alfalfa cutters worked as part of a semipermanent force. Using four mowers, seven wagons, two horse rakers, and one derrick fork, twenty-five men and twenty-six horses could harvest about forty to sixty acres a day. When they were any distance from farm headquarters, the men camped out, sleeping on the ground with a chuck wagon and dining wagon to attend them in what came to be known as a "haymuckers camp." Typically, the Chinese drove the rakes and worked on the derrick stacks but did not operate mowers, drive wagons, or supervise stacking operations.

The derrick stacks were gigantic. Built with California derricks and forks able to lift five hundred pounds, they were commonly one hundred to three hundred feet long, twenty-five to thirty-five feet high, and twenty-five to thirty-five feet wide, and contained anywhere from one hundred to 750 tons of alfalfa. Chinese contractors around Bakersfield also seem to have done a land-office business hauling alfalfa out of the fields to an alfalfa press at Poso Station, where they baled and loaded it on railroad cars for shipment to ranches as far away as Los Angeles.[52]

By the end of 1881, Chinese field hands had become so important to the success of crops statewide that growers were absolutely terrified by the possibility that they might lose them. While that possibility had, only a year earlier, seemed a remote and unfathomable possibility, now the prospect was a very real one. The U.S. Congress was deeply embroiled in arguments over the Chinese Exclusion Act. Closely following the debate, growers flooded local newspapers and agricultural journals with their opinions. These letters were remarkable documents—abounding in long and elaborate analysis and candid admissions. Some actually called for immigration restriction: "Far better it is that every orchard and vineyard in the state should go to destruction than that we should continue to import the Mongolian and ruin our children," argued one writer. "If nobody had Chinamen, nobody else would need Chinamen." Others, like hop grower Daniel Flint took a different tack, and maintained that without the Chinese, "hop culture would be unremunerative on account of the high wages demanded by white labor in his absence."[53]

Protesting that the agricultural industry would never again find such a class of people as industrious as the Chinese, the plea published by one prosperous peach grower in the *Pacific Rural Press* read: "It is difficult to see how the present fruit crop, which is bringing such fine prices, or the immense grape crop now ripening, could be handled at all without Celestial aid." Commenting on the issue in a note appearing in the December 10, 1881, issue, one Pajaro Valley grower known for his stance against Chinese immigration chimed in that the entire agricultural industry seemed "afraid of being ruined if the Chinese teat is pulled out of their mouths." The debate seemed fairly evenly split. But two Chinese cellar rats soon changed the minds of many farmers who had previously supported celestial labor.[54]

৶৯

Wong Ah Wing and China Ah Loy, employees at Occidental Winery, brutally murdered foreman Eddie Butler after Butler twice refused to pay the men eighty dollars in back wages. On December 12, 1881, Wing and Loy broke into Butler's home late one night, intending to rob him. When Butler discovered them, they killed him with a hatchet, stabbed him with a knife, and then attempted to make the murder look like suicide by shooting him with his own pistol and placing the weapon in his hand. The coroner's jury initially brought in a verdict of death by suicide, but skeptical detectives investigating the case launched a murder investigation and dragnet after discovering the hatchet under Wing's bed. Arrested in San Francisco in January 1882 along with two other Chinese field hands, they were brought to St. Helena two months later and held for trial. On March 10, China Ah Loy, despondent and refusing to confess to murdering Butler, hanged himself by his queue before he could be put on trial.[55]

Following Loy's suicide, Chinese field hands became more demanding and assertive in virtually every farming district. "Vineyards at work—teams scarce and even Chinamen are exceedingly independent and dictating their own terms, if they will work at all," complained the *St. Helena Star* on March 31. A few weeks later, Chinese farmworkers in Colusa demanded the same wages as whites, a development that so alarmed local Caucasian workers that they formed the American and European Labor Association, announced plans to import girls from the East Coast and boys from Europe to replace the Chinese, called on members to patronize only those businesses that did not employ "Mongolian labor," lobbied for passage of a bill restricting Chinese immigration, and vowed "to relieve the county of its pestiferous and insolent Mongolian colony, who had now assumed to dictate the wages at which any of their countrymen should be employed."[56]

The spurt of Chinese assertiveness lasted until April 21, 1882, when Wong Ah Wing's trial concluded after two days and the jury found him guilty of murder. That night, Wing attempted to hang himself but did not succeed. Sentenced to twenty-two years in San Quentin Prison, he remained front-page news into late summer when one of the prosecution witnesses, Ah Chuck, was murdered in San Francisco. This supposed retaliation immediately earned headlines and transformed the original murder case into a symbol of the uncharacteristic but apparently growing militancy of normally placid Chinese field hands.[57]

As the Occidental Winery murder case played out, growers confronted their worst fears. In March 1882, the U.S. Congress presented to President Chester A. Arthur a Chinese immigration bill that, among other things, suspended immigration of Chinese laborers for twenty years and called for creation of an internal passport system as a way to identify those in the country illegally. Finding the provision for internal passports both unreasonable and a violation of the 1880 revision of the Burlington Treaty, President Arthur vetoed the bill. When Congress could not muster sufficient votes to override the veto, it altered the bill slightly, changing the period of suspension to ten years and eliminating the internal passport provision. To the shock and dismay of many California farmers, President Arthur signed the long-feared Chinese Exclusion Act on May 6.[58]

A radical and dramatic departure from the policy of open, laissez-faire immigration instituted under the 1868 Burlington Treaty, the innocuously titled "Act to Execute Certain Treaty Stipulations Relating to Chinese" was the first immigration law to single out a specific ethnic group. The legislation initiated a new era of restrictive immigration policy requiring those entering the United States to have official identification certificates issued by the Chinese government. It also suspended naturalization of any more Chinese, paved the way for exclusion of other Asian immigrant groups, and imposed severe restrictions on immigration from southern and eastern Europe. But it did not apply to field hands in the United States as of the November 17, 1880, treaty with China, or to Chinese laborers who entered the country by August 4, 1882, a month and a half after the Exclusion Act went into effect. Chinese who met these requirements could come and go under an elaborate identification system by which collectors of customs at U.S. ports compiled lists of Chinese laborers sailing for foreign destinations and furnished them with certificates of identification and so-called return certificates. These certificates included "all facts necessary for the identification of each of such Chinese laborers." Upon returning, they would present their certificates for comparison against a permanent record maintained at the custom collector's house. If the information matched, they were allowed back into the country. If not, they would be denied entry. Furthermore, any Chinese found to be in the country illegally would "be caused to be removed there from . . . after being brought before some justice, judge, or commissioner of court."[59]

On August 8, Chinese seamen on board the American steamship *City of Sydney* were officially denied entry when they attempted to land in San Francisco. They were the first Chinese to be excluded on the grounds that they were laborers and lacked the proper certificates of identification. Ten days later, while the men languished on board, a San Francisco law firm retained by the Six Companies filed the first challenge to the law. Acting on behalf of a cabin waiter who had immigrated to California six years earlier, the law firm argued that the detention deprived the waiter of his liberty in violation both of the Constitution and the Burlington Treaty. Three weeks later the court agreed, holding that a Chinese laborer working on an American merchant vessel could not lose his residence in this country simply because he stayed a few hours in a foreign country. Other challenges to detention policies soon clogged the courts, and a swelling resentment against the new law swept through the Chinese population, quickly becoming a burning hatred. Hoping to pressure the U.S. government to reconsider its law, some mainland Chinese proposed to discriminate against American interests in China, boot their legation out, and leave only a consulate behind. To this, the *St. Helena Star* remarked "Go ahead, pigtail; guess we can stand it."[60]

Out of the 1882 Chinese Exclusion Act has grown a central myth of the farmworker story, that the "small-handed workmen in pigtails now trooped from the vineyards," orchards, fields, farms, and ranches "that for thirty years had known their ministering." Anecdotal evidence supporting the mythical exodus of Chinese field hands can be traced to California newspapers, which declared that the new law heralded the beginning of the end of Chinese immigration and all of the evils and controversy it brought. Rural newspapers reported extensively on the successful use of Indians to pick hops in Sonoma County at $1.50 a day, where they were described as "excellent workers who spend their money here." But growers protested that, with the loss of the Chinese, the demand for labor would far exceed supply as a very large acreage of orchards and vineyards came into bearing.[61]

Despite legends to the contrary, there is no hard evidence that the law caused Chinese to embark on a general exodus from the California farming districts. To the contrary, many more seem to have rushed into California before the August 4 cutoff date. Immigration records show thirty thousand Chinese laborers arriving in 1882, bringing the total number in the state to 105,000. And even after August 4, they did not stop immigrating. Instead, Chinese field hands began circumventing the law almost immediately. By simply altering their stated profession to "student" or "trader," dressing appropriately, and keeping quiet, field hands quickly discovered that they could easily pass through the port of entry. When stopped, they appealed to various district associations. "Witnesses" would then appear at their immigration hearing and testify that the men were indeed "tourists" or "merchants" and therefore not subject to the ban. When these efforts failed, men filed writs of habeas corpus through district associations, an action that entitled them to a hearing by a judge or commissioner appointed by the court. More than 85 percent of those filing such writs after being denied admission would eventually be allowed to enter the state. One of them, a Chinese laborer who had been living in the United States at the conclusion of the 1880 treaty but who had left for a return trip to China before the 1882 act, won the right to return without presenting the laborer's certificate as required under the act, thus establishing a precedent that others employed.[62]

Many Chinese, unable to challenge the law legally or circumvent it, found another way to immigrate through an arrangement known as the slot system. Under the slot system, children born to Chinese residents of the United States during return visits to China could enter the country unrestricted. Men who returned to California and claimed they had begotten a child while abroad in effect created a slot on their family tree. Chinese who wanted to immigrate to California bought these slots for huge sums of money, often agreeing to repay merchants and district associations at exorbitant rates. Such an immigrant only had to produce a single witness to verify his identity, and once verified, could then bring in a wife and child. Peasants entering under a bogus familial identity were known as "paper sons," and were often accompanied by another man known as a "paper brother." Women also took advantage of the loophole, although in smaller numbers, coming to the United States as "paper daughters."[63]

Meanwhile, out on the farms, Chinese field hands finished the 1882 harvest much as usual. Streaming into Vacaville, they went to work for Chinese fruit agents and harvested and packed a large portion of the crop. In September, they breezed through the Napa wine grape harvest. Underbidding everyone, they also picked much of the Sonoma hop crop, accepting wages of $1.12 per hundred pounds, compared to $1.50 paid to others. After they dug, sacked, and loaded the entire Sonoma potato crop for eight to ten cents a sack in November, grateful growers praised them endlessly. "Were it not for the Chinamen," one grower said in late fall, "potato raisers and grape growers of Sonoma County would not be able to harvest their crops." So busy were the Chinese that they apparently turned down huge wages in the remote Pope and Berryessa valleys where the hay crop lay rotting in the fields for want of men to bind and stack it.[64]

✢

As they concluded the season and settled in for the winter, Chinese field hands in the Napa Valley and other winemaking regions found their lives dramatically influenced by catastrophic events in Europe. In less than ten years since its first appearance, the root louse phylloxera had destroyed half of the vineyards in France and threatened to kill off all that remained. As prices and demand for wine increased, a "wine boom" swept across the state. Nudged along not only by the lure of profits but also by capital from the state's bankers and businessmen-financiers and by the state legislature—which created the Board of State Viticultural Commissioners (a nine-member commission charged with working in concert with the University of California to disseminate scientific information regarding grape growing and winemaking)—vintners embarked on a frenzy of activity. Planting tens of thousands of acres of grapevines and launching winery construction projects of vast proportions, vintners opened up dozens of new grape-growing districts and built hundreds of new wineries, fourteen of them just in the Napa Valley. By the end of the decade, only thirteen of California's fifty-four counties did not have wineries, wine production had more than quadrupled, and vintners were turning their attention to setting standards and establishing marketing organizations to ensure the quality of their wine and further increase sales.[65]

The boom created plenty of opportunities for winemakers, but it had an even greater effect on Chinese field hands, who in 1883 found the greatest demand for their labor in the Napa Valley. Rushing in to plant grapevines in March, April, and May, they found so much work that many settled in the valley on a permanent basis. Hundreds more Chinese arrived to pick blackberries in July, even more came for the hop harvest in August, and by September they were pouring off the northbound trains to pick grapes in such great numbers that a labor surplus developed. By early October a writer poking around St. Helena for the *San Francisco Chronicle* reported, "You come on the trail of the Chinese, which is all over this paradise, as over every other winery." The latter observation is significant, further indicating that Chinese laborers were no longer just field hands engaged in planting, tending, and harvesting grapevines but apparently had worked their way even further into winemaking. According to the *St. Helena Star*, by fall at least forty of them were working as semipermanent cellar rats at the Charles Krug winery, where they earned the standard one dollar a day without board.[66]

Outside of Napa Valley, Chinese from San Francisco who had provided labor for earlier vineyard-planting projects now branched out. With grape growers planting more than one hundred thousand acres of vines around the state, they found plenty of work. But they made perhaps their greatest impact opening up new grape-growing districts in the Central Valley. Many of these field hands were miners who, during the fall and winter slack season, escaped the snow and found work clearing vast swaths of land. With nothing more than pry-bars, axes, saws, plows, and horse-drawn wagons, the work was slow going. At the rate of a few acres a week, crews cut and stacked brush in huge piles, burned it, and hauled rocks to the edges of fields, erecting "China walls" so sturdy that many stand even today.[67]

As a result of their wall-building activities, even larger numbers of Chinese field hands became established in Tehama, Butte, and Colusa counties. Living in a Chinatown in Red Bluff, they found work in orchards on the Star Ranch north of town, where they built waterwheels on the Sacramento River and kept young orchards and seedlings alive through the broiling summer heat by conveying water in large tubs that they carried on their shoulders and heads. A few miles below Red Bluff on the west side of the Sacramento River, several hundred Chinese established a large settlement. Huge China gardens on the east side of the Sacramento River provided plenty of work for field hands, and crops of peanuts, squash, corn, and other vegetables earned Chinese tenant farmers such large profits that they were able to purchase much of the property occupied by the Chinatown. Adding to the general prosperity was a thriving gambling district frequented not only by local field hands, miners, and sheepherders, but also by the county's two professional gamblers. Although the Chinese seem to have arrived largely without incident, one exception was the town of Princeton. Objecting to the expanding Chinatown growing along the banks of the Sacramento River, unknown assassins cornered a Chinese field hand late one night, killed him, and threw his body in the river. Perhaps in retaliation, a Chinese cook on the Hunter farm, near Funk Slough, set fire to the ranch house, burning it to the ground.[68]

Farther south, in Tehama County, Chinese field hands settled in Vina. A small settlement, founded on March 1, 1871, when Henry Gerke, the largest farmer in the area, donated a one-hundred-acre site to the Central Pacific Railroad Company, the town had grown slowly at first, gaining distinction mainly for its all-night high stakes gambling. But avoiding its vices, the Chinese settled on the north end of town, straddling the railroad tracks between Deer Creek and China Slough. Packed into three square blocks of stores, restaurants, and boardinghouses, they created a kind of giant farm labor camp, not unlike the camps at Jacinto and on other ranches near Redding, Chico, and Los Molinos. From this base of operations, they generally made themselves invaluable not only to Gerke, but also to several other neighboring farmers.[69]

For the next decade, Vina grew apace with the prosperity of the surrounding farms And the Chinese, who called the place home, continued to work on those farms without incident until the winter of 1881, when somebody came in from the ranch office with news that former California governor and Southern Pacific Railroad magnate Leland Stanford had just purchased Gerke's nine-thousand-acre ranch and renamed the ranch Vina, after the nearby town. Quickly the Chinese learned that Stanford was embarking on an ambitious plan to buy more land, expand existing winemaking and grape-growing operations, and establish a huge estate rivaling the great wine châteaus of Europe. Stanford further intended to retire at Vina and planned to spare no expense acquiring the latest technology, hiring the best personnel, and developing his new property. In place of the small, crude wine cellars Henry Gerke had excavated, Stanford planned a huge, two-story fermenting house, a gigantic distillery, a massive storage cellar capable of holding two million gallons, a cooperage where barrels would be made, a machine shop, water-powered winepresses, a twenty-five-thousand-gallon water storage tank, incandescent lights, redwood and oak storage tanks, and a bonded warehouse the size of a city block. The winery buildings would be kept cool with two-foot-thick brick walls covered by hop vines. Inside, light, dry wines would be made from the finest European grape varieties. Everything was to be carefully and scientifically planned, every effort exerted to make Vina successful, no expense spared in hiring sufficient labor.[70]

Learning of all this work, China bosses quickly mobilized. They knew a good opportunity when they saw one. Realizing the amount of labor that would be required, they contacted the ranch manager and told him they could supply unlimited numbers of men; name the number and they would come. The ranch manager took up their offer and within a few weeks, additional crews came up from San Francisco and down from Red Bluff. As they disembarked at the railroad depot, China bosses met the men and escorted them into Chinatown. Exhausted and anxious, the men could hardly wait to begin. "Me quick go wuk," one resident ranch employee recalled the Chinese pleading. "No goda money live."[71]

As word got out that there was a massive amount of work being done, more

Chinese poured into Vina. Over the next few months the influx of men had a huge impact on the Chinatown, which suddenly expanded from a few ramshackle buildings into a bustling community of boardinghouses, gambling houses, opium dens, restaurants, "China gardens," and China goods stores. Although these businesses catered primarily to the Chinese, many also served a substantial white clientele. Soon Vina acquired an even worse reputation for vice and wild behavior, and its Chinatown became an exotic attraction for all kinds of bachelor field hands seeking entertainment.[72]

But Chinatown's prime purpose was still as a residential community for the Chinese working at Vina, who, except for a handful of cooks, did not live on the ranch. Instead, they packed into the back rooms of stores and sheds, and into several large bunkhouses including one that doubled as a gambling house, which Chinatown leaders had purchased thirty miles south in Walnut Grove and hauled in on skids and by railcar.[73]

In the fields, the Chinese worked under the direction of vineyardists and winery workers imported by Stanford from Bordeaux, France, in the early months of 1882. At their direction, the Chinese split into several large crews and each day followed a strict schedule. They began at 6 A.M., paused for lunch from 11:40 to 12:45, and stopped work at 6 P.M., sometimes resuming an hour later if necessary. They followed this routine six days a week, taking Sundays off. Beginning in March, a half-dozen crews ripped out the mission grapes grown by Gerke and began setting out six hundred thousand grapevine cuttings. These supplemented the Zinfandel, Berger, Trousseau, and Blau Elbe grapes already on the property, and included European varieties such as Charbonneau, Riesling, and Malvoisie, as well as some Sultana raisin and Catawba table grapes, all shipped up from the Sunny Slope Vineyard in San Gabriel. By May, crews had planted 428 blocks of vines, each measuring 552 by 152 feet, with fourteen hundred vines per block, spaced eight feet apart and separated by sixteen-foot alleyways running north and south and thirty-two-foot avenues running east and west.[74]

At the same time that they were establishing new vineyards, Chinese crews were also raising a granite dam on Deer Creek about three and a half miles from ranch headquarters. This was to become the centerpiece in an elaborate irrigation system. Besides damming Deer Creek, Chinese field hands were busy excavating a canal large enough to carry eighty thousand gallons of water per minute. Subdividing it into ten smaller ditches, nine of them running through the vineyard and controlled by floodgates, they extended the tenth beyond the vineyard two miles and further subdivided it into twenty field ditches to irrigate five hundred acres of alfalfa. About three hundred men were employed in these jobs. Around June, some of them paused from these duties to cut the first alfalfa crop, one of five cuttings they would make each year in order to feed the Vina farm animals. A few months later, other crews harvested and dried $175,000 worth of fruit in Gerke's old orchards. Upon completion of that task, all the crews moved into the grain fields to harvest and thresh the wheat and barley crops and bring in the fall alfalfa. They would follow this routine for most of the next decade.[75]

Sometime that fall, the Chinese harvested grapes in the existing seventy-five-acre Gerke vineyard. As no wine would be made at Vina for several years, they had to pick and pack the grapes for sale to Sacramento wine merchants. To accomplish this, they again divided into teams under a French foreman on horseback. Pickers paired off in two-man teams; one man cut the grapes, while the other separated them by quality, loaded them into fifty-pound boxes, and took them to wagons. Chinese teamsters also divided up tasks, with drivers handling the horses and swampers stacking the grape boxes. At the headquarters another Chinese crew weighed the arriving grapes and sent them to the railroad siding, where yet another crew loaded them for shipment south. Once finished, the men turned flocks of sheep loose in the vineyards, allowing them to eat all of the foliage, thereby inducing dormancy and removing various bug pests. A month later, the Chinese crews turned to winter pruning. While some gangs trimmed the orchards, others went through the old Gerke vineyards and the newly planted Stanford vineyards and cut the vines low to the ground, like little bushes. But instead of burning the vine cuttings they trimmed eight hundred thousand of them into eighteen-inch-long canes, carted them off to a nursery, and stored them in moss and sand pits for planting the following spring.[76]

By year's end, the Chinese had built some 150 miles of canals and were operating a vineyard measuring a little more than two miles wide and three miles long, the largest vineyard in the world. Within a few years they would be cultivating almost three million grapevines. This year-round employment caused Vina's Chinatown population to swell to more than one thousand people. Extending their gardens, the Chinese began catering not only to Vina's Chinese and white populations, but to Chico's as well. With a sense of permanence and of responsibility, few men left, and as Vina prospered, Chinese field hands put down permanent roots. One of them, China Joe, a particularly gregarious English-speaking field hand in charge of Stanford's poultry, soon became well known. Serving as the unofficial guide for journalists, he drove visitors on buggy tours, telling jokes and passing out cigars along the way.[77]

China Joe and other field hands seemed comfortable and secure as the 1882 harvest season closed, but their apparent contentment masked deeper problems and lingering discontent. On November 10, in the vineyards operated by the Natomas Land Company seventy miles to the south, Chinese field hands bundled against the cold trooped into the vineyards armed with shovels, axes, saws, chains, winches, and digging bars. They were going to plant a new vineyard, one rivaling Vina in size. Working throughout the fall and winter and into the following spring at eighty-five cents per day, they followed their usual labor-intensive land-clearing procedures. By March 23, 1883, they had planted 965 new acres of grapes to complement the already vast "Shipping Vineyard," so named because most of its grapes were Flame Tokay, Seedless Sultana, Black Ferrara, Emperor, and other fresh table-grape varieties that could withstand railroad shipment to eastern markets. Then, just as they were supposed to begin grafting choice European wine-grape varieties onto ten-year-old Mission grapevines, they walked out of the vineyards and went on strike. With operations completely shut down, vineyard managers were forced to concede to their demands. Chinese field hands would now receive $1.25 a day, exactly what their white counterparts earned.[78]

At the Natomas Vineyards, Chinese field hands had acted totally out of character, and the behavior startled grape growers and other farmers throughout the state. Incidents like these reminded them how vulnerable they were to job actions at harvest time. As the effects of the Exclusion Act slowly began to be felt and the farm labor market tightened, the tide of surplus labor, which had run so strongly in favor of growers for a generation, now turned against them. "Never . . . has it been more difficult for farmers to find help than now," reported the June 22, 1883, *Napa Register*. "From every quarter comes the cry, the harvest is great, but the laborers are few. . . . Where is the help needed to gather the crops coming from?"[79]

Debating the labor question in light of what had happened at Natomas, some growers authoritatively asserted that they had nothing to fear. And as Chinese field hands went about their business over the next few months, growers calmed down considerably. But even as they were noting appreciatively in their diaries how the Chinese still came and went with the precision of an army, all was not well. Trouble was brewing in the hot, flat, raisin vineyards around Fresno.[80]

CHAPTER FIFTEEN

Snapping Their Fingers in Our Faces

Human Pesticides, Labor Shortages,

Child Labor, and the Response to Exclusion

One day in the summer of 1883, a foreman rushed in from the vineyards outside of Fresno to give farmer John Hyde Braly some bad news. An onslaught of army worms, nearly a mile long and a half-mile wide, was moving out of the adjoining hogweed and wild sunflower fields and into Braly's two hundred acres of grapevines, devouring everything in its path. Braly told his foreman to go over to the hardware store and buy two dozen spades and shovels, hurry back to the vineyard, hitch up all of the plows, take all of the Chinese field hands to the vineyard, and immediately cut a ditch on the west side where the worms were entering, then fill it with water. "Meanwhile, I went over to Chinatown and hired a dozen or more Chinamen and scurried them off to the fight," recalled Braly in his memoirs, *Memory Pictures.* "I next went to the stores and bought all the little scissors they had, at twenty-five cents a piece." Braly intended the Chinese to wade into the worms and snip them in half one by one.[1]

Moving into the vineyards, the Chinese quickly discovered that they could not handpick the squirming larvae quickly enough to stem the assaults. Deployed into crews, some men whacked the vines with sticks, causing the worms to fall onto sheets of paper spread below, while others collected the worms and poured them into pans of coal oil. Joined by the ditch diggers, they labored together late into the night and were just beginning to make progress when thousands of the worms reached the ditch, fell in, and drowned, creating a bridge of dead worms over which thousands more passed. Wriggling forward, they now advanced in such great numbers that all of the Chinese ditch diggers redeployed. After clearing the ditch, they stood by with their shovels smashing worms and breaking up "worm bridges" until dawn. Over the next several days, the Chinese snipped, smashed, squashed, poisoned, burned, and diverted worms by the millions, buying Braly enough time to visit all of the surrounding poultry farms, round up every turkey in the area, and bring them back to his vineyards. Turned loose to

FIGURE 32. Chinese unloading wine grapes into the crusher, Fair Oaks Rancho, San Gabriel Valley, ca. 1885. Courtesy of the Huntington Library, San Marino, California.

munch on the worms for the next month, the turkeys relieved the now exhausted Chinese from their battle.[2]

By the time they saved Braly's grapes, Chinese field hands had become a familiar sight in the raisin vineyards around the state. They had started working in commercial raisin operations in the 1860s when small crews in the Sacramento Valley and near Los Angeles, Riverside, Davisville, Woodland, and San Diego harvested and dried Muscat of Alexandria and Gordo Blanco grapes. But because Muscat grapes had seeds that many people found objectionable, and raisin production therefore remained small, very few Chinese found work in the young industry. In fact, they might have remained uninvolved with the raisin industry entirely had it not been for a bizarre sequence of events set in motion by a Sutter County rancher named William Thompson.[3]

Born in Bristol, England, in 1816, Thompson had come to Yuba City from Carlinville, Illinois, in 1863. Hoping to enjoy the delicious hothouse-grown grapes he had eaten as a child in England, Thompson in the spring of 1872 had obtained three cuttings of Lady de Coverly grapes from Erlanger and Barry, a Rochester, New York, nursery. Grafting them onto Muscat vines, Thompson planted them on his 240-acre grain ranch ten miles west of Yuba City. After losing two vines the following year when the Sacramento River overflowed its banks and washed them away, Thompson pruned the surviving vine back to three short canes and allowed it to grow without a trellis. When the vine failed to produce grapes, Thompson gave up. Left to grow wild, the vine produced fifty-six pounds of seedless, oblong, lime-green grapes in August 1875. A week later, Thompson displayed several clusters of the luscious fruit at the seventh annual Marysville Fair. Labeled "Thompson's Seedless" by a clerk, the grape—which made perfect raisins —immediately caused a sensation. After the name was formally changed to Thompson Seedless by the Sutter County Agricultural Society, neighbor John Onstott obtained several cuttings, grafted them to existing rootstock, and in 1882 established nurseries in Fresno and Los Angeles. Onstott then began propagating the variety by supplying growers throughout the San Joaquin Valley and Southern California. Soon, cuttings from Thompson's original vine were planted around Fresno and as far north as Sutter County, where Onstott himself established a one-thousand-acre vineyard. Constructing a packing house and installing a stemmer, which used brushes to remove stems from the dried grapes, Onstott expanded his operations and almost single-handedly established the market for Thompson Seedless raisins in the East. By 1885, he was hiring as many as five hundred men from mid-July through September, as well as four Chinese cooks to feed his large force of workers.[4]

News of the grape spread rapidly, and soon raisin growers, realizing that the raisin crop matured earlier and cured easier in the hot landscape around Fresno, began abandoning traditional raisin growing areas and varieties and rapidly shifted production to Fresno. With less than ten inches of rain per year, and none during the months of June, July, and August, Fresno's hot, dry climate allowed growers to produce raisins on a scale heretofore unseen. So handsomely did Fresno's climate reward raisin growers that ten or fifteen acres of vines would usually produce enough income to support a family and meet mortgage payments on the land.[5]

As production increased, California quickly pushed aside Spain as the main supplier of raisins to the U.S. market. Shrewd land developers offered many Fresno-area farmers the chance to tap into this "raisin mania." Obtaining a large block of former wheat land and then leveling it for cultivation, William Chapman, for example, named his development the Central California Colony, divided it into twenty-acre "vineyard lots," then hired an engineer and crew of workers to scrape out a latticework of canals and ditches connecting the lots to a source of water. Between 1875 and 1877, Chapman sold hundreds of acres of colony land to a wide variety of settlers, including immigrants, doctors, teachers, merchants, and engineers. Settlers with common ethnic or geographic origins clumped together in the Scandinavian Colony, Nevada Colony, and Armenian Colony. When the colony movement peaked, thirty-four colonies with names like Temperance Colony, Easterby Rancho, Muscatel Estate, and Washington Colony extended over thousands of acres of the San Joaquin Valley as far south as Bakersfield. Outside of the colonies, large-scale operations also took root. One of the first, that of the Butler Vineyard Company, shipped six hundred tons of raisins in 1886;

a few years later A. D. Barling Company harvested enough raisins to fill eighty-three railroad cars. Within the space of a decade, Fresno changed from rural backwater to the "raisin capital of the world." The transition, however, was not always an easy one.[6]

For aspiring raisin barons and small-scale raisin farmers alike, the reality of farming proved a shocking experience. Land was the largest initial expense—favorably suited but unimproved "raisin land" cost between forty and one hundred dollars per acre, while established raisin vineyards with buildings and bearing vines ran as much as $350 per acre—but that was only part of the cost of doing business. Growers also had to purchase vines at about twenty dollars per acre. A house and barn for packing raisins added another twelve hundred dollars. Expenses further mounted when furniture ($500), equipment, wells, and pumps ($100), wagons and tools ($350), horses ($200 each), cows ($50 each), raisin trays for a twenty-acre vineyard ($174), and packing boxes ($116) were added to cultivation costs, planting costs, and land leveling and pruning expenses. Then, after having expended those sums, a grower still had to wait three years before harvesting a crop, and four or five years before full production began.[7]

If they did not know it at first, most prospective raisin growers soon discovered that harvesting and drying operations were completely beyond their abilities, other than perhaps as managers. And then there was the need to harvest before the fall rains, which could turn raisins moldy and make them fit for sale only as hog feed. As a practical matter, growers aimed at getting their raisins dried and boxed as soon as possible, but when hundreds of Thompson Seedless vineyards matured in the late 1880s, labor demands around Fresno skyrocketed. After waiting years for the first commercial harvest, growers knew that the profits from that crop constituted the difference between meeting their mortgage payments and losing their land.[8]

As raisin growers prospered, the Chinese figured prominently in their economizing calculations. There were already plenty in the area. Some had worked on the Fresno Canal, the Centerville Ditch, the Fowler Switch Canal, and on countless smaller canals, lateral ditches, headgates, levees, and other structures. Moving easily into the vineyards, they at first concentrated on planting, pruning, and cultivating, working smoothly and without incident during the winter of 1882–83, shaping the vines with just the right number of spurs and canes to produce the largest number of high-quality grape clusters. Then during the late summer harvest of 1883, as large numbers of young vineyards reached commercial production, a labor shortage suddenly developed. With raisin production increasing tenfold, it became clear that the local Chinese labor force, although easily available through Sing Long Chung Kan Kee Company in Fresno, would be inadequate.[9]

Determined to avert the impending disaster, one of Fresno's largest raisin growers, Gustav Eisen, who would later be referred to as "The Father of the Raisin Industry," dispatched foremen to scour the countryside for Chinese pickers. Finding none, he began looking in nearby towns. Working his way north, Eisen's men searched as far as Stockton. At the last moment, China bosses there agreed to help.[10]

Early one August morning, Chinese laborers from Stockton boarded a train for the five-hour journey to Fresno. Wearing blue blouses and wide basket hats called *mows*, the men quickly funneled through the Fresno Chinatown, climbed into wagons, and rode out to Eisen's vineyard. There they set up camp as efficiently as a platoon of soldiers. Although few if any had ever harvested raisins before, it only took a few hours of instruction before they learned the required techniques. Then, early the next morning, they marched into Eisen's three-year-old Muscatel de Gordo Blanco Vineyard (he had not yet planted Thompson Seedless) and spent the next month working among the low-growing vines.[11]

At first everything went well. The Chinese picked clusters of the amber-colored fruit and placed them on wooden trays, each measuring three feet wide by three feet long, then set the trays between the vine rows, carefully off-setting and tilting them so that the grapes caught the sun's rays and dried more efficiently. After about a week, they returned to the vine rows in two-man teams, placed empty drying trays on top of full ones, flipped the trays over together, lifted off the empty tray, and then allowed the grapes to dry for another week. After several weeks of constantly bending over, standing up, and walking forward to the next tray in one-hundred degree heat, Eisen's raisin harvesters left the fields with sore backs and stiff, aching knees.[12]

The routine only slightly softened toward the end of the harvest, usually about nine days later, when all the grapes were dried and had turned from amber to a dark purple color. At this time the Chinese again went through the vineyards, this time dumping the raisins into large "sweat boxes," carefully adding a sheet of manila paper between each layer. Finally, they collected all of the sweat boxes, took them to a cool building and allowed them to stand for several weeks to a month, at which point they began packing them for sale and shipment to market. In this way, Chinese laborers saved Eisen's harvest and earned him a tidy profit— but they also exacted their price.[13]

Few could match the Chinese in speed and efficiency. Realizing that growers like Eisen were in no position to bargain, the Chinese exploited their advantage and demanded wages of $1.50 per ton, the equivalent of $1.50 a day, the same rate that white men earned. Eisen gave in immediately, much to the dismay of his fellow growers. "The Chinese labor, which was once considered the great pillar and blessing of the vineyard interest, is now appearing in a new light," noted a grape grower writing to the *Fresno Republican*. "We are at last near that point when Chinese labor will be as expensive as that of the white man."[14]

৵৯

Coming on the heels of the 1883 Natomas strike and coinciding with growing concerns about the Chinese Exclusion Act, the Eisen vineyard wage demands seemed to signal an abrupt change in the behavior of Chinese labor. And growers in characteristic fashion did what they would always do in such circumstances— they looked for replacements. The first to respond with a practical program for replacing Chinese workers were the owners of the Haggin and Carr Ranch near Bakersfield. Determined to grow cotton on a scale comparable to farmers in Georgia and Mississippi, James D. Haggin and Henry Carr in the spring of 1883 had planted one thousand acres of the crop between present-day Wible Road and Kern Island Road, then immediately launched an ambitious scheme to counter Chinese militancy. Traveling to St. Louis, agents for Haggin and Carr attempted to lure one thousand black workers to the California fields with exorbitant promises of wages of twelve to fifteen dollars a day, plus free transportation. Only one hundred took up the offer, many of them women and children. "It was a wonderful arrangement for us, since the meat was furnished, as well as our housing and use of animals," recalled William Henry Pinckney, who was twelve years old when he arrived with his father and mother. "They even brought around sacks of flour and dropped them off on the door steps. It cost us nothing."[15]

The workers did not long remain on the farm, however. Housed in hot, uncomfortable little shacks while chopping and cultivating the cotton crop, they lasted less than two weeks, despite signing a contract to work for one year. "Most of the colored people who were brought to California . . . were city folks who were probably no good in the first place and didn't want to work," Pinckney later explained. Deserting to a man, they left one thousand acres of cotton choked with weeds. Floundering in bankruptcy, the growers plowed under their crop, replanted the land to sugar beets, and frantically searched for Chinese replacement workers.[16]

Nervous growers throughout the state noted the Bakersfield cotton catastrophe as they had the problems in the Natomas grape and Fresno raisin harvests. That fall, as reports of other Chinese strikes, slowdowns, labor shortages, and pay increases trickled in, growers panicked. Where could they find the laborers they needed? Large numbers of unemployed men were moving through the farming districts, but growers dismissed them as of no use. "Great burly men, dirty, but fat, and otherwise well conditioned, well able to work and earn an honest livelihood, comprise the grand army of tramps," reported the *Fresno Expositor*. But they were as unreliable as ever, deserting on the slightest pretext. They could not match Chinese workers.[17]

Clogging the editorial pages of rural, urban, and agricultural publications with their letters, growers offered only bitter complaints. Nostalgic for the days of Chinese gangs who "require no further coaching" and could be "ordered" like so many shovels and other tools, one farmer observed in the pages of the *Pacific Rural Press* that the end of an era seemed at hand. Now the Chinese "fully realize the advantages they hold under the operation of the exclusion act," he warned. Another grower explained to readers of the *San Francisco Call*, "Since the stop has been put to Chinese immigration, the labor question has undergone, and is still undergoing, a material change. The competition with Chinese cheap labor has disappeared to a great extent, although in many cases in a rather different way from what had at first been expected."[18]

More pleas and remonstrances followed, and as they had on several occasions in the past, some growers blamed their labor problems on the nature of commercial agriculture. The *Sacramento Bee*, which was emerging as a leading advocate of rural reform, blamed everything on poor working conditions. "The trouble lies with the growers themselves, who neglect or refuse to provide white help with the commonest of accommodations," the newspaper asserted. "If the labor of picking hops has no charm for the Caucasians, it is because of the employment of Chinese and by their own selfishness in denying decent treatment to white men. If the hop growers, who can well afford to do so, will do their share in elevating both labor and the lot of the laborer, they will need neither to depend upon coolie slaves nor to go out of business."[19]

Joining the growing chorus of critics calling for structural changes in agriculture, a small minority of farm leaders, as well as members of the newly created California State Bureau of Labor Statistics, now began to argue that the only way they could secure a reliable supply of labor and deal with declining numbers of ever more militant Chinese was by breaking up large farms. Their notion was to subdivide land into 160-acre parcels, creating healthy agricultural communities with comfortable cottages, little gardens, and shorter workdays, where families on small orchards could handle most of the work, and when done, help their neighbors. "These bind the laborer to the farm," thus inducing "loyalty" and "conservatism," argued W. J. Sanborn, an early agricultural reformer, in a report to the California State Bureau of Labor Statistics in 1883.[20]

Despite the prominence of those advocating reform, most large-scale farmers regarded such ideas as premature if not downright silly and impractical. Rejecting fundamental change, they frankly admitted that their farming operations were based on the employment of large numbers of people who were available for a short period of time, at low pay, and under adverse conditions. Of their many proposals for replacing the Chinese, the most common involved child labor. Although children had labored in agriculture on a limited scale since the Spanish missions, their numbers had always remained small. Not until the summer of 1877, when John Bidwell had constructed his large, steam-powered, fruit-drying furnace on his Chico ranch and began drying much of his own fruit crop, did his shed manager, Mr. Chapman, begin hiring large numbers of children. That year, between fifty and one hundred boys and girls between ten and twelve years of age worked alongside women cutting, peeling, pitting, and drying peaches. Watched over by a timekeeper, the women earned $1 to $1.35 per day, the children seventy-five cents.[21]

Drawing on Bidwell's example, some growers insisted that a huge, untapped labor pool existed in the local grammar and high schools around the state, and that boys and girls could be hired by the thousands to take up the slack not only in the sheds and dryers, but in the fields as well. But when they presented the idea at agricultural society meetings, growers who had previously hired schoolboys from the cities proceeded to shout them down, relating one mishap after another to illustrate the folly of employing children to do men's work. Nevertheless, growers continued to discuss the subject, their proposals and schemes constituting the first sustained efforts to employ children systematically in the fields on a large scale. But they were hardly the only suggestions for dealing with the problems posed by changing farm labor relations.[22]

More than any other proposal, growers favored encouraging larger numbers of non-Asian immigrants. By bringing in more men, they could maintain—if not increase—the oversupply of labor, keep the Chinese in check, and hold wages down. But who would come? When a few growers advocated importing help from the states east of the Rocky Mountains, most laughed off the idea by citing the desertion of black cotton workers around Bakersfield and then pointing out that field hands beyond the Mississippi River earned at least $1.50 and sometimes more than two dollars a day. For this reason, growers began looking overseas for new sources of cheap labor.[23]

Among those who might replace the Chinese, only European peasants were believed to possess the ideal combination of experience, drive, and motivation, and to be available in large enough numbers. Portuguese laborers, Italian families, and Mexican campesinos were the most frequently mentioned substitutes, but any and all prospective farm laborers were considered. Returning from a tour of Switzerland, Germany, and Scandinavia, an agent for the California Immigrant Society delighted members of the Santa Clara Viticultural Society by reporting that large numbers of men could easily be brought to California. "Once assure the outsiders that they can get steady employment," wrote the editor of the *Pacific Rural Press*, "and they will come as fast as we need them."[24]

ॐ

When nothing tangible came of these efforts, some Chinese began demanding higher pay in several farming districts. Wage rates, long fixed at one dollar a day without board, rose in 1884 to $1.25 without board on many farms, and $1.50 in several farming districts. Chinese field hands also dramatically raised their wages in the orchards and vineyards of Lake County just north of the Napa Valley. Blaming such insolence on the labor shortage caused by exclusion legislation, the *Lakeport Bee-Democrat* warned,

> If we read the signs of the times aright, Chinese in the little towns through-
> out our state are gathering a store of wrath. . . . The Restriction Act cuts off
> competition among themselves and in a little town such as Lakeport, there
> are just enough of them to keep out such white labor as our families need.
> Consequently we are at the mercy of these heathens. Each month that goes
> by adds to their importance in their own eyes. Still upward is the demand for
> wages. . . . Besides this, they are insolent in the extreme and in every way
> show that they are complete masters of the situation.[25]

Chinese militancy in the Napa Valley during 1884 seemed even more ominous and threatening. "Chinamen are gradually increasing the price of their labor," reported the *St. Helena Star*. "Those fellows who were pleased to obtain $1 per day, raised to $1.10 are in many instances now demanding $1.15 and it may not be long before $1.50 is required for a day's work." Two weeks later the *Star* reported Chinese demanding $1.25. "There is no telling to what extent they'll go when vineyards get in a pinch!" predicted the newspaper. "We urge vineyardists not to encourage the heathen in their demands." But the caution had little effect.[26]

For all their alleged arrogance and demands, Chinese field hands were hardly engaged in a widespread attack on prevailing wages. Outside of Napa and Lake counties they continued to take work that no one else would accept. Nothing better demonstrated their resolve than what they did in July 1884, when another wave of army worms threatened a crop, this time munching their way through John Bidwell's farm. Once again toiling as human pesticides, Chinese field hands marched into the slithering mass, gathering and killing worms by the millions. Elsewhere, Chinese workers also moved into the Mendocino County hop harvest in large numbers; in September 1884, over twelve hundred of them passed through Sonoma bound for the hop yards around Ukiah. According to the *St. Helena Star*, every train headed to the Cloverdale hop yards that fall was packed with Chinese.[27]

At about the same time, Chinese field hands also seemed to be thriving around Anaheim. Besides the well-established Sin Si Wau, two other Chinese contractors were in business, Sin Tin Wo and Sin Kong Wo. According to the *Anaheim Gazette*, Sin Si Wau's men were earning thousands of dollars in wages mucking out old ditches and excavating new ones for the Anaheim Union Water Company. They earned so much that the *Gazette* observed: "Times are lively and business brisk in Chinatown. Games, big and little, are the order of the day and the order of the night." The only other place that the Chinese seem to have flexed their muscle so successfully was on the Haggin ranch south of Bakersfield. Late in August, a "large force" of Chinese hop pickers there demanded an advance on their pay and walked out of the fields. When inexperienced pickers brought in to replace them could not handle the work, the Chinese quickly won a modest increase and resumed harvesting.[28]

As the winter of 1884–85 approached, fruit growers around the state were clearing and planting so much land that thousands of Chinese who might otherwise have spent the season unemployed now managed to secure work well into the following spring. Newspapers and farm diaries of the time describe crews of Chinese working from dawn to dusk cutting wood, burning brush, hacking down poison oak, yanking out stumps, plowing, terracing, and planting in Napa, Butte, Monterey, Placer, and Los Angeles counties. But again, work did not always proceed smoothly. Just as they had during the previous year, a few Chinese began demonstrating an increased independence of spirit and behavior. In April, Chinese on Juan Bandini's Los Angeles rancho apparently became so defiant that they were discharged and replaced with more complacent Chinese. Similar incidents occurred throughout the summer until, during the August hop harvest, Chinese pickers near Sacramento refused to dry any hops picked by other crews; only they could harvest the crop.[29]

This "arrogance" unnerved many growers. But for all their contentiousness, when the wine grape harvest rolled around in Northern California that September, the Chinese were still the laborers of choice, and the China bosses knew it. Advertising in the *Sonoma Index-Tribune*, one labor agent proclaimed: "HO-TELS, RANCHES, AND FAMILIES—Will Get the BEST CHINESE HELP, at 403 Sutter St., San Francisco. Fong Co." Two months later, every grape grower in Sonoma County had apparently accepted their offer. Filling entire trains, hundreds of Chinese began "arriving daily from San Francisco to engage in picking the grapes."[30]

For all the wage increases and expanded opportunities, however, Chinese field hands still found it difficult to save money, economize on expenses, and send funds back home. In addition to fees owed to labor bosses and basic living expenses, they were also vulnerable to innumerable unexpected threats, sometimes at the hands of their own countrymen. Stories abound of Chinese robbers targeting field hands at pay time. In one late-night attack, four Chinese entered a bathhouse in Princeton, beat all the field hands, and robbed them of $235. In another attack, two Chinese broke into the hut occupied by a fellow countryman on a farm two miles south of St. Helena. Tying, gagging, and blindfolding him, the robbers then ransacked the man's hut, stealing a two-hundred-dollar certificate of deposit, and two hundred dollars in wages. Withdrawing the certificate of deposit the next morning, the two were long gone before the field hand managed to untie himself and inform police.[31]

Even when they avoided thievery, Chinese field hands often came up short. Farmwork was casual labor, meaning that men were hired by the job and were, except for those few permanent employees who worked year-round, constantly on the move. Because they worked outdoors, they were also subjected to the vagaries of weather, halting entirely for winter, but shutting down also when fields were muddy and impassable. Farmer's daybooks and journals were filled with notations of such interruptions, of Chinese being dismissed after completing a job, of six-man crews cut in half, of men being added for a week or two. Sickness and work accidents also ate away at a man's income. Strained muscles, lacerations, and bruises sustained while harvesting meant lost days. Bones broken by kicking mules and feet crushed by wagon wheels could lay them up for longer periods, if not cripple them for life.[32]

During the course of their work, the Chinese were buried under collapsing haystacks, gored by enraged bulls, suffocated beneath shifting piles of potatoes, sliced by wayward plows, crushed by overturned wagons, and run over by speeding trains. Newspaper reports invariably gave only the skimpiest details of such accidents. "A Chinaman employed by Mrs. T. H. Ink in Pope Valley carelessly allowed his team to run away," went one typical newspaper report. "By some means the plow passed over him, cutting his head in a fearful manner." Another report disclosed: "Wednesday evening R. G. Eubank brought a Chinaman from his ranch suffering with a broken leg. He was cutting wood, and as near as can be learned, a log in some manner rolled on to him. He was sent to San Francisco Thursday morning." On December 24, 1887, the *Kern County Californian* reported: "A Chinaman was killed on the ranch of Philo D. Jewett north of town last Tuesday. He was driving a load of hay, and the team taking fright, he fell off, landing beneath the wheels of the wagon, which passed over him, breaking one of his legs and fracturing his skull. He died soon after." A report in the June 17, 1889, *Colusa Sun* was especially gruesome. "An infuriated steer attacked a Chinese on H. D. Blodgett's place near Princeton," the report began. "The steer pinned him to a post with his horns, broke three ribs and crushed in the side of his head, from the effect of which he died."[33]

Just getting to work could be dangerous. Stuffed into overloaded wagons driven at a rapid rate by sometimes drunk farmhands, men were thrown out and badly hurt when wagons overturned on sharp corners or hit ruts and other obstacles in the road. Trains could be equally dangerous. According to one ghastly accident report in the *St. Helena Star*:

> Wednesday morning as a passenger train from San Francisco was nearing
> St. Helena the engineer saw a Chinaman walking on the tracks over Sulphur
> Creek bridge and promptly sounded the warning whistle and signaled down
> brakes. The Mongolian for some reason did not heed the warning. Just as he
> was leaving the bridge he was caught by the engine and pitched off to the side
> of the track about 30 feet ahead. The Chinaman's head was split open and one
> hand was completely torn off while the arm was horribly mangled. . . . The
> Chinaman had ample time and opportunity to save himself but was so seized
> with fright that instead of jumping to one side he ran ahead of the train for
> 20 or 30 feet until the engine hit him. The jury returned a verdict of accidental death and exonerated the engineer from all blame.[34]

Realizing that growers accepted no legal responsibility for on-the-job accidents—or for injuries incurred while traveling to a farm—Chinese field hands often continued working even after sustaining terrible wounds. In a rare and valuable report on such resolve, the *St. Helena Star* described how "an extremely bright young Mongolian" employed chopping wood for a local vineyardist had sliced his finger open to the bone, causing it to bleed profusely. Walking over to the vintner, he held up his mangled finger and said in his best English, "You gottee little flou' sack?" Aware that his employer would at best provide room and board during a period of recuperation, the man did not want to stop working. A rag bandage, a little rest in the shade, and he was ready to go, although it is unlikely he could have continued working as before.[35]

℀

Despite their grit and determination, Chinese field hands could not overcome the growing movement that had been quietly building against them for years. In January 1885, officers from the Anti-Chinese League in Ventura County began denouncing Chinese field hands for stealing work from local whites. Such sentiments next surfaced among members of the Chico African Methodist Episcopal Church, who in May successfully petitioned Mayor John Bidwell to deny Chinese field hands access to land needed to expand their local Chinatown. Over the next few months Chinese field hands experienced various new forms of intimidation. In San Jose, Stockton, and Modesto, new laws banished Chinese laundries from downtown areas. At the same time, Chinese field hands around Calistoga and in Knight's Valley became targets of a campaign of intimidation by groups threatening to burn barns and property on farms that did not dismiss their Chinese laborers and hire white men. On July 15, the *Colusa Sun* reported that Frank Van Weizer "shot and killed a Chinese vegetable peddler at Germantown without any provocation whatever."[36]

In October, the Chinese came under attack as they finished picking hops in the Napa Valley. When a farmer named J. H. Allison discovered that the Chinese on the Dowdell ranch had stolen a buggy cover and were using it as a tent, Allison and his sons went on a rampage. Finding their property, they attempted to remove it, but the Chinese resisted. When one of Allison's sons struggled with two Chinese hop pickers and "was about to be brained," the farmer shot one of the Chinese and sent the rest scurrying off the farm. "Mr. Allison gave himself up and is out on bail," reported the *St. Helena Star*. "Clearly a justifiable case."[37]

After the attack, Chinese field hands around St. Helena increasingly became the object of harassment. Almost anything they did provoked response from hostile whites. Their mere presence in town sometimes led to retaliation. For months, citizens had been complaining about the large numbers of field hands inhabiting the local Chinatown just south of the stone bridge over Sulphur Creek. Workers had first settled there in 1868, when the area had been outside of the town limits, but as their numbers grew and as their proximity to townsfolk narrowed, tensions rose and citizens began demanding that they leave. For example, after police searched the entire Chinatown, arrested a "Mongolian" field hand for stealing ducks from a nearby farm, and put him in jail for twenty-five days, anti-Chinese zealots used the incident as proof of Chinese thievery. Similarly, when local juveniles surrounded and shoved a Chinese field hand into the mud as he walked through town one evening, the town newspaper, while condemning the attack, also cited it as just one more reason for removing a menacing presence that detracted "materially from St. Helena's reputation for neatness and good order and depreciates the value of adjoining properties."[38]

A few days before Christmas, 1885, hundreds of St. Helena citizens convened a series of meetings and formed local chapters of the Anti-Chinese League and Anti-Coolie League. Dedicated to moving Chinatown outside the city limits, "but not by any unlawful means," the groups raised several thousand dollars to buy the existing property as well as a new tract farther out of town where the Chinese could relocate. Still, even staunch anti-Chinese proponents like the editor of the *St. Helena Star* emphasized that they did not advocate driving the Chinese out of the valley. Were Chinese field hands to leave, the paper argued, "it would be impossible to gather and care for the grape crop," as white laborers could not be found either in large enough numbers or at low enough wages. Should the Chinese all leave at once, warned California labor commissioner John Enos, "the farmers, orchardists, and vineyardists" would suffer "great loss and hardship."[39]

On December 18, the owner of the Chinatown property ordered the Chinese to vacate their premises, but they refused. The stand precipitated a rash of violence against the Chinese. Confrontations continued over the next few weeks, and as the Chinese began fighting the eviction in court, citing among other things long-term leases to their property, tensions reached a breaking point. On the afternoon of February 4, 1886, a mob of several hundred anti-Chinese zealots assembled in a pasture and marched toward the St. Helena Town Hall to the sound of tooting whistles, ringing bells, and a large drum. By the time they arrived on the outskirts of town, the streets were deserted. Having heard the commotion, the entire Chinese community bolted the doors to their shanties, closed their shutters, and disappeared inside. Several Chinese shop owners were finally induced to come out and listen to speeches, and then everyone marched away into the gathering twilight. But the Chinese would not budge. The refusal fueled local anti-Chinese sentiments and led the *St. Helena Star* to reverse its opposition to boycotts. Now advocating a new tactic, the editor wrote, "A sure way to get rid of them is not to employ them. We should get employers to sign a pledge not to employ them."[40]

౾ஐ

As these confrontations grew, another sensational murder case fueled the anti-Chinese campaign. On Monday, January 19, 1886, a farm cook named Ah Tai Duc murdered Captain Jesse Wickersham and his wife Sarah, both aged fifty-three, in their Skaggs Springs farmhouse about twenty miles west of Cloverdale in the Sonoma Valley. Firing at the couple through a partly opened kitchen door as they sat down for dinner, Duc then fled with eighty dollars. When the crime was discovered by a neighbor three days later, Mr. Wickersham still sat at his accustomed place at the dinner table, biscuits on his plate, a pie on the table, with a tablecloth wrapped around his head. His feet were in a pool of dried blood. He had five buckshot wounds in the back of one ear and another gunshot wound in his side. Mrs. Wickersham was found in her bedroom, "in horrible condition," having apparently been shot through her side as she fled the dinner table. A piece of cake had been placed on the pillow beside her, a curious act that newspapers claimed was a Chinese custom to exorcise evil spirits from the bodies of the dead.[41]

With a three-day head start, Ah Tai Duc was long gone before law enforcement could mount an effective dragnet. Reports circulated that the "Murderous Mongol" had been spotted in Fresno, and dozens of Chinese field hands and cooks matching his description were hauled in and questioned by police around the state, aided in part by a one-thousand-dollar reward offered by the Chinese Six Companies. But Ah Tai Duc had already fled the country. After confessing his crime to a relative in Cloverdale on Tuesday morning, he caught an early train south to Marin County, crossed the bay to San Francisco, and on Wednesday boarded the steamship *Rio de Janeiro* bound for China. Intercepted when his boat docked in Japan two weeks later, Ah Tai Duc was detained by the ship's captain, transferred to Hong Kong, and held for extradition. But he never stood trial, nor did anyone ever find out why he had murdered the Wickershams; as law enforcement officials sailed for China, Ah Tai Duc hanged himself in his jail cell. But from that point on, China cooks were never regarded with the same reverence. Ever suspicious, some farm owners worried that their loyal servants were plotting to murder them. On Grand Island, one farmer went so far as to have his Chinese cook arrested and charged with poisoning a jug of water with strychnine as revenge for some reprimands.[42]

Even as word of Ah Tai Duc's fate reached Sonoma, Chinese field hands throughout the valley were encountering the wrath of hundreds of fearful and paranoid white citizens. At two large anti-Chinese meetings, the first ever in the area, speakers grossly exaggerated the number of Chinese in Sonoma to more than fifteen thousand (when the U.S. census counted only about one thousand), then used these inflated numbers to force growers around Santa Rosa and Glen Ellen to fire large numbers of Chinese field hands. Meanwhile, the Chinese also came under attack in the neighboring Napa Valley, where opposition was strong and growing. "No one has any love for a Chinaman or a mule," explained the *Napa Register*. "White men or even black men and horses will displace them very easily as soon as the change can be effected." Discharged in large numbers following the end of the grape-pruning season, fired Chinese congregated in nearby towns with little chance of obtaining more work. Observed departing for San Francisco on every train, many of them were so destitute that they snagged rides on the railroad car brake beams. In uncharacteristic fashion, a few of the most desperate even resorted to stealing food and goods.[43]

Until that winter, most of the opposition there had consisted of scattered acts of violence against individual Chinese. A half-century later, a Sacramento Valley grower told agricultural historian F. Hal Higgins a story about the kind of violence inflicted upon the Chinese by a farmer who had lost ten dollars in gold pieces while crossing his field. Missing the money, the farmer returned and told his Chinese field hand to look for the coins. About a week later, the farmer learned from a local prostitute that a Chinese field hand had gone on a spending spree with a ten-dollar gold piece. "The rancher immediately went home, got a rope and his hired man and went out and located the Chinaman," he recalled. "Flindee kleepee," replied the field hand. "Whereupon, the rancher and his man tied up the finder and left him swinging until cut down a day later by a passerby for burial."[44]

Chinese field hands encountered hostility of a new kind in January, 1886, when leaders of Denis Kearney's International Workingman's Association fanned out into the San Joaquin Valley. Holding mass meetings in Lodi, Tracy, Lockeford, and Stockton, they formed new chapters of the Anti-Coolie League and enlisted the support of hundreds of politicians and local leaders, including many leading businessmen who, even as they signed petitions against the Chinese, continued to employ them as field hands and cooks. League members then announced plans for a statewide boycott of the Chinese, their products, and their employers. In Turlock, they ordered the Chinese to move out of town and settle on the north side of East Avenue, between present-day Alpha and Minaret streets. To move, the Chinese knocked the floors out of their shacks, lifted them on their shoulders, and walked them to their new site.[45]

Anti-Chinese elements in the northern Sacramento Valley found hundreds of followers among angry crowds of unemployed white laborers who had been congregating in Orland, Biggs, and Gridley. Focusing their anger on John Bidwell, principal employer of Chinese in the area and a staunch supporter of Chinese immigration, they demanded that he fire all of his Chinese. But Bidwell resisted. Steadfastly declaring, "I am wholly opposed to the unlawful, cruel and outrageous treatment going on in this state against the Chinese," he refused to dismiss his Chinese unless he could find white laborers to work at the same rate. This so angered members of the local Anti-Chinese Association and other sinophobic groups that they expanded their attack and launched a statewide boycott of Bidwell's products. Within a few months, he had lost thousands of dollars in sales and business.[46]

During February, anti-Chinese clubs were formed in Sycamore, College City, and Colusa, and their members "pledged themselves to introduce white labor in place of the Chinese and to patronize only white laundries and white vegetable and fruit peddlers." Others did more than talk. On February 6, members of the local anti-Chinese organization targeted crews of Chinese field hands working about twenty-five miles northeast of Sacramento in the small hop-growing town of Nicolaus. Notified that they had ten days to leave or suffer the consequences, the Chinese stayed put. After two weeks passed without further incident, they let their guard down. Then, while asleep in their bunkhouses at 3 A.M. on the night of February 18, they were surprised by masked vigilantes. Forced out of their beds, forty-six Chinese were driven at gunpoint to a wharf on the Feather River and there loaded onto a barge and deported downriver as vigilantes and a large crowd of onlookers applauded and celebrated. The hop workers arrived near Sacramento that evening. Of their ordeal, historian Charles J. McClain wrote that it "rivaled in contempt for law some of the outrages then being perpetrated in the southern states by the Ku Klux Klan."[47]

One week later and forty miles north, Chinese field hands on the H. Roddan hop farm near Wheatland were dragged out of their bunkhouses at midnight by thirty masked men and forced to watch as an old Chinese farmhand was pistol-whipped and a bunkhouse burned to the ground. Eventually freed and allowed to disperse, a few of the men the next day attempted to retrieve their possessions but were not allowed to do so. When they returned to town, the Chinese community posted guards to watch over Chinatown day and night until feelings calmed.[48]

When these attacks occurred, Chinese vice consul at San Francisco, Cheng Ping, had been in Red Bluff investigating the violence. Three days after the Wheatland episode, he visited both Wheatland and Nicolaus, interviewed deportees, and arranged for their safety. But he did not stop there. Along with his secretary and a somewhat mysterious figure, San Francisco investigator and former deputy U.S. Marshal W. J. Burns, Cheng Ping decided (probably after consulting with local Chinese leaders) to go on the offensive.

Taking legal action intended to force the federal government to better protect Chinese laborers, Cheng Ping arranged for John Sing, one of the Nicolaus deportees, to appear in the U.S. District Circuit Court of California on March 8. Swearing out a complaint, Sing charged vigilante leader Thomas Baldwin and fifteen other men of conspiring to expel him and forty-five Chinese from the town, thereby depriving them of their right to equal protection under the law. Acting on this complaint, Circuit Court Justice B. N. Bugby issued arrest warrants for Baldwin and his conspirators. Four days later, Deputy U.S. Marshal J. C. Franks arrested Baldwin and transported him to Sacramento to stand trial. The action was unprecedented.[49]

Soon word of the court proceedings spread through the anti-Chinese movement, and on March 16, a large and boisterous crowd crammed into Bugby's Sacramento office for the hearing. Representing the accused were former Attorney General A. L. Hart and Grover Johnson, a leader of the anti-Chinese movement. Standing for the Chinese field hands was Sacramento attorney A. C. Hinkson, on retainer to the Chinese Consul and Six Companies and, in the absence of official government representatives, charged with presenting the government case. Hinkson proposed to prosecute Baldwin and the others under Section 5519 of the Revised Statutes of 1875. Part of the Civil Rights Act of 1871, the statutes made it a crime to conspire to deprive anyone of their right to equal protection under the law.[50]

Three years earlier, in *United States v. Harris*, the United States Supreme Court had overturned the conviction of a group of white Tennessee citizens who had been imprisoned under the statute for murdering one black man and violating the civil rights of several others held in police custody. The statute, according to the Supreme Court, applied only to private conduct. Citing this decision, attorneys for Baldwin and the vigilantes demanded that Bugby immediately release their clients. Hinkson argued that, under Article VI of the Burlington Treaty, Chinese immigrants living in the United States were entitled to the same privileges as all citizens.[51]

As the case wound its way through various hearings over the next few weeks, the Chinese consul replaced Hinkson with well-known San Francisco attorney Hal McAllister. At a hearing before circuit court Judge Lorenzo Sawyer on March 30, McAllister conceded that Section 5519 had been declared unconstitutional, but then argued that the circuit court had voided it only insofar as it applied to actions of United States citizens against other citizens. In this case, prosecution rested entirely on different and ample constitutional premises and on treaty obligations, specifically the 1868 treaty guaranteeing Chinese immigrants "all rights, privileges, immunities, and exemptions" enjoyed by American citizens, and the 1880 treaty, which pledged that should Chinese immigrants meet ill treatment, the United States would "devise measures" to protect and secure their rights.[52]

During the hearing, speculation ran rampant on how Sawyer would rule. "The Chinese are basing high hopes on the result," commented a reporter for the *San Francisco Evening Post*. "If the prayer for the writ is denied and the petitioner remanded, it will open the way to retaliatory arrests in every town in the state from which the Chinese have been evicted." Dismissing this assessment as he read his half-hour opinion, Sawyer found that Section 5519 did, in fact, apply to the kidnapped Nicolaus field hands. "If Chinese laborers, or Chinese of any other class, now either permanently or temporarily residing in the territory of the United States, meet with ill treatment at the hands of any other persons," concluded Sawyer, "the government of the United States will exert all its power to devise measures for their protection, and to secure to them the same rights, privileges, immunities, and exemptions as may be enjoyed by the citizens or subjects of the most favored nation, and to which they are entitled by treaty."[53]

While overjoyed by the decision, Chinese field hands in the town of Nicolaus were still not completely vindicated. Sawyer's associate, Judge George M. Sabin, dissented from the decision, and following the official ruling issued a minority opinion. Believing that the matter was of "too vast consequence to be finally determined by a subordinate court" Sawyer passed the question along to the United States Supreme Court. In the meantime, he released Baldwin on his own recognizance and suggested the government refrain from prosecuting anyone or pursuing any other such cases until the higher court ruled.[54]

As news of the arrests and court action was being reported, a huge anti-Chinese convention featuring attorney Grover Johnson got under way on March 10 in Sacramento. Although the majority of delegates to the convention called for eliminating the Chinese only through legal and peaceful means like boycotts, there was a small but strong contingent from San Jose that advocated nonlegal techniques; they fully supported what the vigilantes had done in Nicolaus and Wheatland. After forming a new organization called the State Non-Partisan Anti-Chinese Organization, the convention called for the absolute end of Chinese immigration, the prompt removal of all Chinese, a ban on hiring Chinese workers on state public works, an end to purchasing any fruit or vegetables grown by the Chinese, and a boycott of all employers who hired Chinese laborers, particularly John Bidwell. Opposed to such measures, Bidwell attended the convention, attempting to inject reason into the increasingly hysterical proceedings. At one point Bidwell found himself next to Denis Kearney at the speaker's podium. After listening to Kearney attack the Chinese, Bidwell could no longer contain his anger. "All right, Mr. Kearney," he said, "send the Chinese. Next thing is, the Irish will have to go." At that point Bidwell stormed out of the convention, labeling it "a disgrace to civilization, the State and the nation."[55]

Within a few days, the effects of the boycott began to be felt. As the *Colusa Sun, Butte Record, Chico Enterprise*, and other newspapers endorsed the boycott and businesses throughout Northern California vowed not to purchase "the products of the Asiatic slave labor of that ranch," it became just a matter of time before Bidwell was forced to release his Chinese. Initially, Bidwell fought against the boycott with the Law and Order Committee of One Hundred, also known as "the Hundreds," although there is no evidence that more than a handful of people ever belonged to the organization. Enlisting the aid of prominent Chico citizens, he pointed out in letters to the local press that his payroll contributed substantially to the local economy, and that a boycott could throw many men out of work, hurting innocent families. Just to demonstrate his resolve, Bidwell kept some Chinese working even after they had completed their contract.[56]

What finally drove off most of the Chinese was a series of death threats against Bidwell, followed by an arson campaign that cost Bidwell another barn with ten thousand dollars' worth of hay inside. A few days after the fire, Bidwell dismissed all but fourteen of the forty Chinese still working on the ranch. Those kept on were needed to hoe and weed gardens and fields and were deemed absolutely essential. But even their presence continued to anger the rabidly anti-Chinese *Chico Enterprise*, which contended that soon they would be picking cherries and peaches, much to the detriment of white laborers. Chinese field hands in fact did continue working until their presence threatened to ruin Bidwell. Finally, after another arson fire destroyed Bidwell's soap factory (the fourth such attempt on the factory), they became too much of a liability. With the boycott slicing deeply into his business and a half-dozen buildings torched, Bidwell in early April 1886 discharged nearly two hundred workers. Among those released were the fourteen remaining Chinese.[57]

After the Chinese left Rancho Chico, Bidwell took on the local anti-Chinese movement. Always active in politics, he now attempted to negate the effects of the boycott and other anti-Chinese activities and to bring Chinese back to work on Rancho Chico by meeting with the governor and appealing to local church leaders. Bidwell's biographer Rockwell Hunt would later summarize these developments by claiming that the anti-Chinese movement had been shattered almost single-handedly by Bidwell's "steadfast adherence" to principle and his devotion to "right and justice." But in fact, even though Bidwell continued to speak out in favor of the Chinese, he never again hired them.[58]

Over the next two months, Chinese field hands were harassed and driven out of thirty-five communities around the state. When the anti-Chinese boycott eventually faded in the summer of 1886, it was less because of Bidwell's efforts than the results of a ruse instituted by Major W. J. Burns, the mysterious and secretive police operative who had been working closely with the Chinese Six Companies to initiate a campaign of disinformation. Announcing to newspaper reporters that he intended to publish the membership rolls of anti-Chinese groups, Burns frightened a number of zealots by describing an elaborate (but certainly false) plan. In it, the federal government would arrest and prosecute up to five thousand of them, holding them in a three-hundred-acre lot next to Folsom Prison while they awaited trial. To expedite prosecution of Chico boycotters, Burns also announced that he would record the names of those boycotters who owned property that the government could confiscate. As to constitutional questions, he asserted confidently that the U.S. Supreme Court would soon smooth out the technical details of the plan and that arrests were scheduled to begin around June. The ploy intimidated anti-Chinese boycotters and drove them into the shadows, although it did not end their anti-Chinese activities or change their minds.[59]

Outside of Chico, Chinese field hands seemed to fare little better. Anti-Chinese Leagues continued holding meetings, and cities continued passing ordinances against Chinese businesses. The populations of some rural Chinatowns, like that of Santa Rosa, declined precipitously—from six hundred in January 1886 to about one hundred three months later. But as winter gave way to spring, growers again mobilized in support of the Chinese. Assessing life without them, few liked what they saw, and they now determined to defend their workers as best they could.[60]

৯৯

As the anti-Chinese movement played out, the California State Bureau of Labor Statistics stepped into the fray. Opening hearings in April 1886 the bureau questioned several San Francisco employment agents about the number of white laborers who would be available during the harvest season. Two of these agents estimated that about one of eight farmhands were white and the rest Chinese. After the bureau published the figure in its annual report, writers cited it widely without assessing its reliability. From this information another myth developed, one that both contemporaries and subsequent commentators seldom questioned. Accepting and perpetuating the seven-eighths figure, an entire generation of farmers concluded that the Chinese had so completely taken over farm labor that their loss would ruin the entire agricultural industry. Repeated so often that it assumed the status of fact, this view ignored much better information indicating that, outside of Sacramento and Yuba counties and a few select crops, the Chinese did not constitute more than four or five out of every ten field hands.[61]

Chinese field hands were certainly dominant in many areas, as indicated by figures compiled by the Bureau of Labor Statistics. For example, whereas a decade earlier there had been very few Chinese on farms in Mendocino and Yolo counties, there now were four thousand and two thousand, respectively, during the hop harvest. In Los Angeles County, they numbered two thousand; San Joaquin County employed nine hundred. But it was not just their numbers that seemed to make the Chinese so irreplaceable. According to San Francisco employment agent J. P. Johnson, white workers just would not work for $1.25 a day—even with board. In fact, they would not work at all. Instead, they griped, demanded better housing, better food, and higher wages. Harvesting with them, warned the owner of another employment bureau, required that "a change would be . . . necessary." Even more bluntly, a speaker at the California State Agricultural Society Convention charged that Chinese labor had caused growers to become callous. "The proprietors of large estates," he claimed, "have been content to herd their workmen as they would their cattle." With the Chinese, they no longer had to worry about humane working conditions. This was why growers in Vacaville and St. Helena continued hiring Chinese.[62]

Besides the savings on expenses, growers defended Chinese field hands because of the key role that they were playing as fruit packers. Besieged by London merchants complaining that good and bad dried fruit were regularly mixed together, and by eastern fresh-fruit merchants angry at receiving boxes of spoiled fruit covered with one layer of good fruit, growers tried to ensure uniform quality through random sampling and close supervision. Many found that the best way to maintain quality was to hire Chinese. "The Chinese have always been regarded as the best packers," explained the U.S. Immigration Commission. Coupled with certain physical characteristics and personal habits, their work as fruit packers seemed to make them absolutely essential. Observers constantly commented on Chinese adroitness. Recalling how "practically all the labor performed in the preparation of citrus fruits for market was done by Chinamen," one citrus packing house manager remembered being "much impressed, especially by the dexterous manner in which the fruit was wrapped in paper and placed in the boxes by these Chinese packers."[63]

In Fresno, the Chinese dominated the small raisin-packing sheds. Women and children had initially handled these tasks, but this had changed under raisin grower Minnie F. Austin. Owner of the one-hundred-acre Hedge-Row Vineyard, Austin had settled three miles south of Fresno in the Central California Colony in 1878. With three other women, all former teachers, she acquired five twenty-acre lots and developed them into the most successful and profitable raisin operation in California. In 1885, with her land in full production, she packed six thousand boxes of raisins; the following year production reached seventy-five hundred boxes. Fearing the effects of rain, Austin acquired the first air-blowing raisin dryer. She also began purchasing crops from neighboring vineyards and marketing them under her own label. Selling more than twenty thousand pounds of raisins, all of them carefully packed in boxes, fancy ornamented paper bags, and small cartons, Austin discovered that Chinese packers demonstrated an agility and patience that few others could match. While most white men could not pack more than six boxes per day, Austin's Chinese packers supposedly had "expert fingers" and routinely packed nine to twelve boxes per day.[64]

Employed at $1.15 per day compared to $1.75 for white labor, Chinese laborers saved Austin and other growers considerable sums. But not all turned to the Chinese. Farming more than one thousand acres of vineyards, A. B. Butler employed 225 Chinese grape pickers, but, unable to find enough to handle his packing, hired a mixed crew of 450 white men, women, and children. Because his sheds were located outside of town, Butler chartered a train and transported everyone to and from his sheds every morning and evening. Few other packers adopted his solution. Unable to obtain Chinese, most shifted packing operations from the fields into town and hired local women and girls. Erecting twenty-two packing houses along the Southern Pacific Railroad tracks in Fresno and the neighboring towns of Fowler, Selma, and Malaga, packers employed upwards of four hundred workers at the height of the grape harvest. But while claiming to be "strongly and decidedly opposed" to the Chinese, they nonetheless held them as a standard by which labor was measured and employed "floor walkers" (supervisors) to monitor their work; they further ensured work on par with Chinese by paying a piece rate calculated by "the amount a Chinaman usually will do in a day."[65]

So valuable were the Chinese, in fact, that they now found themselves being defended by growers everywhere. A favorite defense stressed that the Chinese were simply a tougher lot than white field hands. "If those men who employ Chinese would dare treat white men the same way, no doubt they would do it, but thanks to God the white laborer will not stand it and they discharge him," noted one state senator. "The trouble is only this; he will not work for 80 cents a day and board himself. The Chinaman will." Then there was the matter of the unreliability of white labor. "If those who come to the farmer for employment would forsake the whiskey bottles," explained the *Pacific Rural Press*, "what farmer would hire the Chinaman." Such words were often coupled with praise of Chinese reliability. "I have never yet been able to get a white man that could pack my fruit and pick my berries in a satisfactory manner," wrote Newcastle fruit grower George D. Kellogg to another fruit grower in April 1886. With complete confidence, Kellogg had his Chinese "teach new white help on the ranch how to pick and pack my fruit." So dependable were his Chinese that if Kellogg had any special concerns, he merely had to "instruct his man." All instructions would be relayed, and the whole crew would comply.[66]

Some growers felt so strongly about the Chinese that they publicly condemned anti-Chinese boycotters as violent anarchists who fomented class warfare and engaged in "masked barbarism." A few even went so far as to compare them to German socialists, Russian nihilists, and "chattering French communists." More common, though, were responses like those members of the Mendocino Hop Growers Association, who professed to be sympathetic to the anti-Chinese cause, but emphasized that business overruled personal feelings. Explaining their opposition to the anti-Chinese movement, they proclaimed, "That what is here we own and we have a perfect right to use it as we think best, and while we deplore the presence of the Chinese in our midst and that they have come into competition with white labor, still our necessities, owing to losses in the hop business in previous years, compel us to use any and all honorable means to retrieve these losses." Therefore, the association declared, it would continue to employ Chinese and physically oppose with force and firearms anyone who tried to prevent the association from doing so. It was an extraordinary turn of affairs.[67]

№

Nowhere in California at this time did Chinese field hands play a more important role than they did around Vacaville. So essential were the Chinese in the area that in 1887, when local fruit growers published their promotional tract *The Vacaville Early Fruit District*, a dozen colored lithographs depicted Chinese field hands engaged in every aspect of agriculture. Faithfully derived from San Francisco publisher and photographer W. R. Nutting's photographs and accompanied by an essay by *Pacific Rural Press* editor Edward J. Wickson, the colored lithographs showed that the Chinese were thoroughly integrated into the farm labor force. Cutting apricots, toting full buckets of fruit suspended from poles laid across their shoulders, driving wagons loaded with fruit boxes, and posing on ladders, Chinese were shown as part of large, racially mixed crews. On a typical fruit-drying operation there would be a half-dozen Chinese interspersed among white men, women, and children. Around Vacaville, Chinese field hands seem to have been thoroughly accepted, despite the occasional threats and outbreaks of violence against them.[68]

Vacaville Early Fruit District also revealed that the Chinese were hardly dominant. Not one colored lithograph and not a single surviving Nutting photograph shows a crew entirely composed of Chinese. If these visual documents are accurate—and there is no reason to doubt them—most work on fruit-drying operations was in the hands of local men, women, and children, supplemented by Chinese and tramps or floating laborers drifting in for the harvest.[69]

Besides showing Chinese immigrants fully integrated into harvesting operations, the *Vacaville Early Fruit District* lithographs also inadvertently captured Chinese farmworkers at the moment they were being subjected to study and retraining by the rural counterpart of the industrial efficiency movement. Just as Frederick Taylor and others studied the work process of Slavic immigrants in steel plants around this time, teams of university scientists and industry researchers were exploring ways to harvest and pack peaches and apricots more carefully. And since Vacaville sold so much of its crop to eastern markets, it was imperative that the industry eliminate mistakes that caused fruit to spoil. After scrutinizing harvest procedures in detail, investigators made a number of discoveries. One of their first centered on the simple act of picking fruit. By carelessly yanking fruit from stems, Chinese pickers often removed too much flesh. During transit, these large stem holes furnished entry points for mildew, molds, and rot, which often caused entire boxes of fruit to deteriorate rapidly. To solve the problem, China bosses were remonstrated to have their men remove fruit more carefully. They were not to tug at it. Rather, Chinese field hands learned to pick fruit by a slight upward twist. They were also cautioned never to pick overripe fruit, never to drop any basket or fruit "even a few inches," and to press the individually wrapped fruit "firmly . . . together" so that it would not bruise while being hauled by wagon over bumpy roads to the train depot. Through these and other methods, Chinese field hands around Vacaville became the cornerstone in what was essentially the first effort at systematizing harvest and packing operations and shipping out individually wrapped and graded fruit.[70]

By the summer of 1887, the peach, plum, and apricot crops in and around Vacaville had grown so large that it was impossible to sell them entirely on the fresh fruit market. To absorb the surplus, virtually every Vacaville grower dried part of their crop. Statewide, dried fruit shipments nearly equaled those of fresh fruit. So when the harvest began, the entire community (including families from nearby towns) mobilized and moved into the orchards to nail up fruit boxes, drive fruit wagons, pick, pack, and dry fruit, or perform some other chore associated with the fruit industry. "In this way," wrote *Pacific Rural Press* editor Wickson, "the family secures an income which cuts quite a figure in the year's receipts. The climate is such that very slight shelter is required during the summer, and dwelling in tents is very comfortable. Cot beds and hammocks for sleeping out-of-doors among the trees and vines are [a] common sight."[71]

So great was the need for labor in Vacaville that Anglo children, some as young as four, commonly worked in the drying yards alongside Chinese field hands. They can be seen in dozens of Nutting's photographs, and although their presence constituted a kind of on-site day care, children as young as eight and nine years of age were also valued workers. Their small size and agility proved particularly important in fruit drying yards, where they could make their way between long rows of trays to turn and rotate fruit. But children also worked at other tasks. Paid on a piece rate of fifteen cents a box, children as young as six packed peaches in Luther Harbison's Vacaville orchard. According to Wickson's text, boys "easily" earned a dollar a day cutting fruit or laying it out in drying yards. He wrote:

> Either men or women with nimble fingers can earn two-dollars a day at cutting fruit by the 100 pounds. One young woman is known to have made two dollars and a half in a single half-day, and a ten-year-old boy to average a dollar a day. . . . But families of undisciplined hoodlums are avoided by all fruit growers, as they spoil more fruit and hinder the earnest workers more than they are worth. School children from the cities are totally worthless unless in charge of some parent or teacher whom they are accustomed to obey.[72]

While Chinese field hands did not dominate the Vacaville early fruit district, they were an important enough part of the mixed workforce to be defended by one of the largest, most prosperous, and active of all grower groups, the Vacaville Fruit Growers Association. Fearing that a hasty and violent expulsion of the Chinese would cause a labor shortage and ruin them, the association in March and April 1887 took aggressive action whenever the Chinese were threatened. Meeting to counter mobs and vigilantes, association members promised to use "shooting Winchesters to protect our property and laborers" and appealed to "brother fruit-growers, the directors of the Fruit Union, San Francisco newspapers, and every good citizen of California to help prevent the Chinese from being driven away." Soon trustees of the California Fruit Union endorsed the Vacaville growers, claiming that violence against the Chinese threatened to ruin them and that they, too, would resort to force if necessary to defend their field hands. "Several hundred Chinamen find continual employment here from one year's end to another, simply because they stick to business," wrote the *Vacaville Reporter* at the conclusion of the harvest season. "Good, steady, sober men will find it an easy job to supplant John, who is wanted—in China—by the citizens of the United States."[73]

❧

What happened in Vacaville was not unique. Elsewhere in the state, the Chinese were also protected by other adamant farming associations. Grape growers from St. Helena went so far as to hold a pro-Chinese meeting, and when several uninvited anti-Chinese agitators arrived, attacked them with such vigor that, according to the local newspaper, "only the presence of the [police] officers prevented serious trouble." Members of the Santa Clara Horticultural Society, supported by local packers and businessmen, vowed that they would "not submit to any interference by any man or set of men in [their] business." They, too, would protect their Chinese by any means necessary.[74]

By late summer, Chinese field hands could see tangible results from these mobilizations on their behalf. Knowing they could count on the agricultural industry and the Chinese consul of San Francisco to intervene on their behalf, many Chinese breathed a sigh of relief. As various local chapters of the Grange—once anti-Chinese itself—sponsored "anti-boycotter meetings" and groups such as the Fruit Growers and Citizens Defense Association emerged to protect Chinese farm labor, anti-Chinese activities sputtered and, after a last brief flurry of parades and speeches, passed from the scene. Although humanitarian statements often motivated the defense of Chinese field hands, sound economic motives invariably played the leading role. A fruit district like Newcastle, in Placer County, with three hundred thousand peach trees, needed nearly fifteen hundred workers to bring in the harvest; most of them had come from outside the county. Once residents of farm towns realized that they would be adversely affected by attacks on Chinese field hands and boycotts of those employing them, these communities bonded together to prevent economic hardship. Certain elements of the agricultural industry were so afraid of labor shortages that they predicted "depreciation of property value, loss of crops, foreclosures of mortgages" and other catastrophes would follow if the labor glut ended. Also revealing was the discovery by Napa anti-Chinese groups of something Chinese field hands already knew: even the most vociferous anti-Chinese advocates continued patronizing Chinese, even as they publicly campaigned against them.[75]

Perhaps more than any other group of Chinese field hands, those employed at Vina saw the movement against them weaken and wither in the face of growing opposition. In August 1886, the *Red Bluff People's Cause*, one of the most vehement opponents of the Chinese in Butte County, demanded that Leland Stanford dismiss all of his Chinese. Although under threat of boycott, Stanford rebuffed and ridiculed the newspaper in a long and angry letter to the *Sacramento Record-Union*. "The Chinaman is entitled to the same just treatment, while in our country, as any other foreigner, or as any other citizen," he said, laying plans to hire 140 Chinese grape pickers and packers and thirty-five Chinese cellar rats that summer. "Whether white men shall be preferred to him in employment is a question of humanitarianism and private interest."[76]

ga

With violence on the wane, the Chinese continued to disperse throughout the agricultural districts. During April 1886, about three hundred Chinese moved into the Pajaro Valley. With berry growing expanding rapidly across the sugar beet fields that had been abandoned after the Soquel sugar beet factory had shut down after six years of operation, the Chinese found plenty of work, and by late spring had achieved absolute domination of labor in the strawberry, raspberry, and blackberry fields around Watsonville. Meanwhile, Chinese field hands in the Vacaville fruit district assumed an even larger role, and by early summer, according to the *Vacaville Judicion*, there were more than fifteen hundred men handling every aspect of labor in the cherry, apricot, and peach orchards. Chinese field hands also further expanded their hold on wine grape and hop picking in the Napa and Sonoma valleys at this time. Streaming out of every train that arrived during the September harvest, thousands of Chinese field hands fanned out through the vineyards and hop yards, some even traveling as far as Sacramento under contract at $1.02 per hundred pounds of hops, a rate newspapers labeled "exorbitant." Reflecting on these developments, the December 24, 1886, *St. Helena Star* could find little evidence of anti-Chinese activity and plenty to indicate that Chinese had returned to the brazen and impertinent behavior of the previous year. "Now they are saucy," the newspaper reported, "independent, defiant, snapping their fingers in our faces."[77]

Whatever collective benefits Chinese field hands derived from this newfound support, greater tolerance for individual assertive behavior was not among them. According to the January 21, 1887, *St. Helena Star*, an "uppity Celestial" was "laid up for repairs" after talking back to a foreman on the James Dowdell farm. Growers, it seemed, were willing to defend their workers only if those workers remained docile and compliant. Just a month and a half later, Chinese field hands were forced to face a harsh reality when, after a year of appeals and arguments, the U.S. Supreme Court finally issued its ruling in the Nicolaus kidnapping case. On March 7, the high court rejected efforts by Chinese Six Company lawyers to invoke Section 5519 of the Revised Statutes of 1875 to protect the forty-five Chinese rounded up and deported from Nicolaus. At the mercy of local law enforcement personnel, many of whom strongly supported the anti-Chinese agenda,

Chinese field hands in the northern Sacramento Valley soon felt the practical effects of the decision excluding them from protection under federal law. As happened in the past, a spectacular act of violence rekindled a reign of terror.[78]

Late on the evening of April 6, 1887, a Chinese cook, Ho Ah Hueng, also known as Hong Di, shot Julia Billiou, the well-liked wife of a prominent farmer near St. John in Colusa County. Mrs. Billiou had just finished supper with her two daughters and a hired hand, Billy Weaver, when the sixteen-year-old Hueng entered the kitchen and shot her through the heart. When news of the murder reached Chico, "a fever of excitement" enveloped the population and citizens launched a massive manhunt to apprehend Hueng. Several Chinese field hands found around Chico's Chinatown and the vegetable gardens in Butte were caught in the dragnet, detained, searched, questioned, and roughed up by police and bullies alike. One frightened Chinese field hand was shot in the back and killed by posse members as he ran from a cabin. In the nearby mountain town of Magalia, an old vegetable cultivator said to know Hueng's whereabouts was "necklaced" with a rope and tortured by vigilantes until it was clear that he had no information. On the John Bowers farm a third field hand, also an old man who knew nothing about the suspect, was strung up and let down five different times and nearly killed by a mob.[79]

The reign of terror continued for six weeks, fueled by the belief that Chinese field hands throughout the area knew where Hueng was hiding and were actively protecting him. Rumor had it that they were moving him through the Chinatowns and Chinese gardens with the goal of eventually finding him employment picking crops or perhaps even cooking for some unsuspecting farm family. In fact, Hueng had received little support from his local Chinese, who offered a two-hundred-dollar reward for his apprehension, or from the Chinese Six Companies in San Francisco, which offered five hundred dollars. When apprehended by a traveling salesman in a wheat field south of Chico on May 22, the emaciated murderer had for three of six weeks cowered in a granary near Billiou's farm, subsisting on water and raw wheat grains.[80]

Jailed in Oroville and then transferred to the county jail at Colusa two days later, Hueng further inflamed public opinion by claiming that he had nothing against Mrs. Billiou, a kind woman who had taught him to read and write, and who was his closest friend in California. He had only been acting in self-defense. According to Hueng, Billy Weaver had taken advantage of Mr. Billiou's many long absences on business trips to San Francisco and carried on a torrid love affair with Mrs. Billiou. After Hueng had stumbled on them having sex in a barn shortly before Christmas, Weaver had told Hueng that he was going to kill him before Mr. Billiou returned. When Hueng shot Mrs. Billiou, he claimed he had actually been trying to kill Weaver—and, in fact, Hueng had shot him first. He had only hit Mrs. Billiou accidentally with his second shot when he had prematurely discharged his rifle as he prepared to finish off Weaver.[81]

Incensed by the story and the denigration of Mrs. Billiou's character, friends of the Billiou family vowed to avenge the murder and restore their family's good name. Hueng, they said, had actually intended to murder the entire family, except for Mrs. Billiou's twelve-year-old daughter, whom he planned to rape before robbing the home and vanishing back to China. During the brief trial in Colusa, Hueng's defense attorney quit without notice and his successor was denied an extension and no more than a few minutes to confer with his client. Anger toward Hueng only grew stronger when a Colusa jury found credible evidence of extenuating circumstances and sentenced him to life in prison. On July 7, at midnight, Hueng was lynched by an angry mob described by the local newspaper as "wild with excitement and delirious with joy."[82]

Revealing just how vulnerable Chinese farm laborers still were, Hueng's lynching convinced Chinese government officials that there was little hope of completely protecting field hands and other laborers—not only from the waves of violence in California, but also from even more vicious attacks throughout the American West. Scores of Chinese laborers were being randomly murdered by vigilantes in Rock Springs, Wyoming, while others were burned out and threatened by mobs in cities from Seattle to Los Angeles. With so much violence against the Chinese breaking out, Chinese officials determined it was necessary to curb emigration. Negotiating a new treaty, they agreed that if the United States would assure the safety of its citizens, then China would prohibit further immigration and also prevent field hands from returning to the United States unless they had family, property, or outstanding monetary claims. This last stipulation became a sticking point, and talks dragged on. To make matters worse, the Chinese and Americans could not agree on what new steps, if any, the U.S. government should or could take to better protect resident Chinese field hands and other laborers. As both governments argued, Chinese field hands realized that immigration was going to be reduced, if not completely eliminated, and that this would dramatically decrease the oversupply of labor and further increase the bargaining power of farmworkers. Among the first to capitalize on this development were sugar beet workers in the Pajaro Valley, who raised wages from $1.25 to $1.75 a day to hoe, block, and thin the crop.[83]

℘

Midway through the summer of 1887, a severe labor shortage developed in many agricultural districts around the state, causing thousands of dollars' worth of fruit to rot on the trees. As in the past, growers tried to recruit substitutes for the Chinese, loading up wagons full of schoolboys and bringing them out to their farms. Families, women, and children figured so prominently as supplemental labor in the August peach and grape harvest in the area around Winters that the *Winters Express* hailed the development not as an impediment but an opportunity that would enhance family gatherings and community cooperation. "Our youth and women are getting all the work they can do," boasted the newspaper. "We believe their employers will be better satisfied at the close of the season's work than if they had employed Chinese exclusively." But this was just talk; Chinese field hands around Winters named their price. Rather than diminishing their importance, the labor shortage enhanced their bargaining position.[84]

By mid-September, growers were in a state of panic. Then something happened on a Colusa ranch that sent cold shivers through the northern California countryside. On the evening of September 12, Lee Ying, a Chinese cook, attempted to murder his former employer, Stewart Harris. Ying had worked for Harris since 1883, but had been discharged at the end of August. Enraged, he lay in wait for Harris and attacked him late one night as Harris returned home. Although cut badly about the head, Harris managed to flee to Colusa. Ying was arrested and bound over for trial. Coming just two months after the Billiou murder, the attack seemed to suggest a dark and dangerous side to the Chinese that multiplied fears arising from their wave of strike activity and Chinese murder cases from the previous years. Now, with the Chinese striking, demanding higher wages, and murdering their employers, growers sensed that the balance of power had tipped against them. No matter how many women and children they hired, they could not restore the status quo. Further proof of the tilt against them seemed to come toward the end of the month, when Chinese in Sonoma struck a hop ranch and obtained a raise from $1 to $1.25 a day. Additional evidence came a week later, when Chinese commuting each morning from the little Chinatown in Rutherford to work alongside French, German, and Italian workers at Inglenook Winery became angry when paid fifty cents a day less than their Euro-American counterparts. Walking out of the vineyards, they obtained a raise from $1.25 to $1.50 per day. Observing these events, both the *St. Helena Star* and the *San Francisco Merchant* reported a "general agitation" among Chinese field hands everywhere. "The shrewd Chinese have grasped the situation and are demanding an increase in the wages," observed the *Star*.[85]

"They have become arrogant and self-important, and this not withstanding the fact that they are receiving $1.25 to $1.50 a day—a large increase of their former wages," reported the *San Francisco Merchant*. "They strike if a white foreman is put over them, if a Chinese foreman urges them to work faster, if they do not think they are getting enough pay." According to the *Sacramento Bee*, some Chinese even resorted to fraud. Paid by the weight of their pickings, hop harvesters now began dropping rocks and dirt clods into their hop bags. As Chinese militancy increased, nervous growers and agricultural leaders met in their annual conventions that fall and weighed their choices. Confident in their horticultural skills, growers like Pomona Valley farmer J. W. Sallee now worried that their workforce, not insect infestations, would be their downfall. "I believe in fig culture provided that we can be assured of abundant cheap labor to handle the crop," he told members of the Pomological Society meeting in November 1887.[86]

Faced with declining numbers of increasingly militant Chinese, many growers fell into a state of despair. "They have found no labor so well adapted to their needs as Chinamen," explained the January 5, 1888, *Kern County Californian*, "and while there is to be no further increase in the supply, the demand for it, owing to the immense additional area that is every year being devoted to their line of production, is constantly augmenting."[87]

Soon growers had even more to fear. During the wave of anti-Chinese violence, U.S. attorneys from California, Wyoming, and Washington had written the Department of Justice complaining that they could not convict white rioters and secure justice for the Chinese because of prejudiced juries. Now they were joined in this complaint by the federal judges of San Francisco, Ogden Hoffman and Lorenzo Sawyer. Frustrated with the huge backlog of Chinese habeas corpus cases clogging the courts, Judge Hoffman wrote California representative Charles N. Felton in January of the "importance that something should be done to relieve the courts of the intolerable nuisance and obstruction to their regular business caused by the Chinese cases." As these events were unfolding, the Chinese government, appalled by continuing violence against its citizens and frustrated by the failure of the U.S. government to protect them, volunteered to end emigration of laborers for twenty years if the U.S. government would protect existing laborers from further attacks. On March 12, Chinese and U.S. diplomats signed a new treaty incorporating these main points, but as protests against the treaty mounted in China, Congress drafted another exclusion law. Named after its sponsor, Democratic National Campaign Chairman and Pennsylvania congressmen William Scott, the Scott Act slammed the door on Chinese field hands and other laborers seeking to return, even if they possessed reentry visas; the law also prohibited any new return certificates, voided all in existence, and permanently forbade the immigration of laborers instead of just suspending immigration for twenty years, as originally intended.[88]

Led by John Bidwell and prominent Sacramento Valley hop grower Daniel Flint, growers quickly mobilized a last-ditch campaign to overturn, repeal, or modify the Scott Act. Growers and agricultural leaders across the state strongly supported Chinese demands for more liberal provisions for the return of Chinese laborers with property in the United States. Without such concessions, they complained, they would be "forced to stop operations." Their campaign largely rested on the lobbying efforts of Secretary of State Thomas Bayard, who criticized the bill as a "mortifying" effort to scuttle a treaty. Over the summer, Bayard would attempt to persuade President Grover Cleveland to veto the legislation.[89]

ஃ

As anti-Chinese legislation was taking shape in Washington, D.C., German-born Claus Spreckels—the so-called Sugar King—arrived in Watsonville. Having been pushed out of Hawaii by planters resentful of his control over political and economic affairs on their island kingdom, the tall, heavily muscled Spreckels had spent a year in Austria studying the latest sugar beet technology. Engaged in a struggle for survival with the newly formed Sugar Trust, Spreckels had to either establish a presence on the West Coast or be driven out of the refining business. Upon arriving in California, he had traveled throughout the state searching for the best site for an ultramodern sugar beet processing plant. Of fourteen sugar beet processing plants built in the United States, only one, Ebenezer H. Dyer's old factory at Alvarado, remained in operation, but Spreckels was determined to succeed where his predecessors had failed. Shrewdly playing Watsonville off against Salinas, he extracted substantial concessions from the Watsonville city leaders, including land donated for the mill site. In January 1888, he organized the Western Beet Sugar Company and began erecting a huge, $350,000 processing plant. The largest such facility in North America, the Western Beet Sugar Company would pump an estimated fifty thousand dollars a month into the Pajaro Valley. It also supported a myriad of industries: farm machinery, livery stables, and draymen required for the agricultural side of operations; lime mined and transported from the hills around Santa Cruz for the sugar processing; feedlots where beet pulp was fed to cattle; seed companies; and a railroad for bringing in machinery and shipping out refined sugar. But its major impact was on row crop agriculture. Contracted to grow at least twenty-five hundred acres of beets and supply the factory with 350 tons of beets per day, compared to just sixty tons per day at the old Soquel factory, sugar beet growers expected far greater and more predictable incomes than they had earned with any other crop.[90]

With so much at stake and immigration restriction on the horizon, Watsonville growers vowed to do their best to attract and hold Chinese field hands by providing housing both for those already in the valley and for the huge numbers who would soon arrive. The problem was that the existing Maple/Union Street Chinatown could not possibly hold all of the anticipated newcomers. "If there should be an increase in Chinese laborers in this valley there will have to be an increase in the size of Chinatown," observed the *Watsonville Pajaronian*. And so John T. Porter—owner of much of the land planted to sugar beets, a major stockholder in the company that supplied two million board feet of lumber to the new factory, and the owner of the old Watsonville Chinatown—devised a novel solution.[91]

Foreseeing the day when Chinese field hands would spill outside of the Watsonville Chinatown limits, Porter, backed by a committee of prominent citizens, in summer 1888 relocated the Chinese living in the Maple/Union Street Chinatown—along with their boardinghouses, cafés, laundries, gambling dens, opium parlors, and various other buildings. Shifting them to a new and larger site that Porter also owned east of town, just across the Pajaro River bridge in Monterey County, the move left them beyond the jurisdiction of the Watsonville town council, whose attempts to regulate gambling, prostitution, opium smoking, and the open cesspools created by Chinese laundries had always been minimal. The jurisdiction also removed the Chinese from control by the far more hostile Santa Cruz County Board of Supervisors, who had always favored anti-Chinese sentiments. This arrangement allowed the town to exploit Chinese field hands while at the same time escaping responsibility for any problems they created.[92]

Years later, some Watsonville residents concocted a mythical version of events. Boasting that they had driven the Chinese out of town as part of an effort to reclaim the streets for Caucasian humanity, they dressed up the invented account by claiming that a mob had literally picked up the Chinese and bodily removed them. This myth gained further credence when the Chinese themselves adopted it as an example of early prejudice, racism, and discrimination. But the story had no basis in fact.[93]

As Watsonville ensured its labor supply, other communities debated what to do. As usual people split into two schools of thought. The *Sacramento Bee* stressed smaller, ten- to twenty-acre family farms and an end to large-scale agricultural operations. Ever critical of large-scale agriculture, the *Bee* asserted:

> The remedy . . . must be found in the subdivision of the large tracts. In a community of small orchards there will be no question of labor arising to

imperil the rewards of industry. The women and children on the small orchard will pick and pack the fruit and then help their neighbors, to be in
turn helped by them. The man with hundreds of acres . . . is bound to find
himself embarrassed at every harvest by the difficulty of securing help. Give
us homes and plenty of them among the trees and vines and we will hear
no more the cry that the exclusion of Chinese is an injury or menace to the
fruit industry.[94]

Closely aligned with the idea of solving the farm labor problem by restructuring agriculture was the belief that by improving working conditions, building better bunkhouses, and raising wages, growers could entice plenty of white laborers
into the fields. They would not remain, warned the *Kern County Californian*, if,
like the Chinese, they were forced to live like hogs and work until they could no
longer stand up. "They must be well fed and comfortably and decently lodged,
and . . . in all regarded as capable, intelligent, trustworthy, and self-respecting
members of society."[95]

As they had in previous years, most growers rejected such ideas as the halluci-
nations of impractical reformers, know-it-all newspaper editors, and nonfarmers.
Faced with the loss of Chinese field hands and seeking to discover new sources of
cheap labor for the 1888 harvest, some growers turned to Indians. Tribes from
Nevada, in particular, found plenty of work in the Rancho del Paso hop fields
southeast of Sacramento during August, and they pleased hop growers so much
that they vowed to use them to eliminate Chinese labor entirely. According to
the *Sacramento Record Union*, "Captain John, a Paiute chief, arrived one day last
week with 50 of his tribe (bucks and squaws), and others will follow as soon as
their services are required. They are broad-shouldered, and most of them over six
feet in height. The Indians spend all their money for beads and watermelons."
Similar reports of Indians filling in for declining numbers of Chinese filtered in
from farming districts throughout the state.[96]

Other growers dusted off long-shelved schemes to import black contract laborers from the southern states. One of the first to adopt this course was Rio
Vista farmer E. J. Baldwin, who gained wide press coverage on April 16, when
he brought in seventy-eight "experienced" black laborers from Georgia and the
Carolinas. News of his apparent success quickly spread, and within a few weeks
the Santa Clara County Viticultural Association and growers around Fresno also
began importing black field hands. Seeing an opportunity, two labor agents,
F. M. Quimby of the Missouri Pacific Railroad and R. A. Williams of the Mem-
phis and Little Rock Railroad, devised an ambitious scheme. "As the south has
tens of thousands of negroes who can barely make a living," explained Quimby in
an interview with the *Pacific Rural Press*, "we conceived of the idea of contracting
for negro help here and shipping them out to take the place of the Chinese."[97]

Within a few weeks, several hundred black field hands were working for dozens
of California growers. Under terms of their employment, agents paid their transportation costs and growers agreed to hire them for at least one year, paying $15 a
month to the men, $10 to women, $7.50 to boys, and $5 to young girls, while also
providing food and board. Field hands were to repay the $60 cost of transporta-
tion in installments of two-thirds of their monthly wages. This arrangement ap-

FIGURE 33. Local men, women, and children in the Kraljevich apricot drying yards, Campbell, ca. 1890. Courtesy of the California History Center/DeAnza College, Cupertino.

parently worked well at first, with blacks on the farms around Fresno described by the *Pacific Rural Press* as making "capital field hands." But as in the past, few stayed very long. Finding the work disagreeable, the pay unacceptable, and the conditions impossible, they did what their predecessors had done. At the first opportunity they slipped away, with the majority heading for the nearest city.[98]

Of all their strategies to replace the Chinese in 1888, growers placed the most faith in yet another elaborate labor recruitment program, this one to employ Anglo children on a massive scale. Unlike past efforts, these new schemes extended to local schools. Eager to assist farmers, several school districts adjusted their summer vacation schedules to accommodate harvest labor requirements, thereby making large numbers of children available at just the right times. Even schools that did not close down entirely or alter their vacation schedules issued special passes to students who were headed out to the fields. Students as young as twelve could take up to three weeks off to work in the orchards and drying sheds. Although only a few hundred children worked under these arrangements, the use of the pass system became a common practice. Around St. Helena, for example, out of 261 students, forty would be absent and laboring in the nearby vineyards during the fall grape harvest.[99]

By far the largest number of boys—close to one thousand by some estimates—arrived in the fields through an ambitious program launched by the State Board of Trade. Under this arrangement those seeking harvest work were guaranteed a certain pay rate, usually at least one dollar a day, provided wholesome food, and given good housing, usually in clean tents or bunkhouses. Collected in Marysville, Los Angeles, Sacramento, and San Francisco, the boys were transported to agricultural districts by the Southern Pacific Railroad at half-fare rates; upon presentation of a certificate from a farmer at the end of the season, they were returned home for free. Although some farmers immediately refused to employ any children whatsoever, many changed their minds late in July when one of the first groups to be sent out, a crew of "forty white lads" from Sacramento, broke a strike by Chinese hop pickers near Roseville. So remarkable was the large force of boys—supplemented by women, girls, and "maidens" employed in the Jean Baptiste Portal Vineyard near San Jose—that a photographer traveled out to the vineyard at the beginning of the harvest. With the women attired in long dresses and bonnets or bandannas and the boys in white shirts and vests, the crew posed amid full lug boxes, with an authoritative foreman on one side displaying a gigantic cluster of grapes. Unconcerned that children were working in the fields, the July 21 *Pacific Rural Press* ran the image on its cover. "The large boxes used for gathering are an intimation that the fruit is abundant, and the weight of the box can be inferred from the wearisome countenance of the young man who evidently tires of balancing it upon his shoulder, even while the photographer is at his work," observed the newspaper. "It is inspiring work when the crop is large. . . . It is hard work."[100]

By early August 1888, a dozen groups of children ranging in number from twenty to seventy-five, were working in Tulare, Kern, Yuba, Butte, Santa Clara, and Yolo counties. Pleased with the results, many observers praised the so-called Boy Experiment. Newspapers enthusiastically described child laborers who were proving "more trustworthy than the Chinese," boy hop pickers who outworked men, children earning "neat little sums" of up to forty-five dollars during the harvest season. Girls and boys employed by one Elmira grower worked so well that he said he "would not give one of his white girls for a whole shed full of Chinamen." But for every one of these reports, there were dozens describing catastrophes and failures. Unprepared for long hours of hot dusty labor and primitive living conditions, and having signed up for work assuming that they were going out on a kind of picnic, many children grew homesick, quit, and took the next train home. This is exactly what happened at Vina, when forty boys from San Francisco were brought in to replace striking Chinese grape pickers. "Finding the job was not as soft a thing as they expected, the boys left in a body . . . boarded the Oregon Express and returned to their homes," reported the *Chico Chronicle* on August 11. The lesson seemed obvious. "It will not do to expect these workers to bunk in haystacks or feed on salt pork and crackers," warned the *Sacramento Weekly Bee*.[101]

Within a few weeks, it became obvious that most children employed as harvest hands were too "full of mischief and frolic," too unmanageable, and required too much care, organization, and supervision, as well as better food and housing.

"They want quarters in which they can preserve the decencies of life, want meals cooked for them and want opportunity to pass their resting hours as become civilized people," observed the *California Fruit Grower*. "This does not suit some fruit growers, who consider only the fruit and the immediate profit." As the *Sacramento Weekly Bee* explained, growers "did not want to pay $1.00 a day and board when they could get Chinamen for less." According to one grower, only about 65 percent of the children he hired ever proved good and reliable workers. Most Chinese field hands thus kept their jobs "as against both men and boys because they always [fed] themselves and [slept] in their own tents."[102]

Despite these setbacks, growers did not abandon schemes to attract cheap labor. During the peach and nectarine harvest, farmers around Vacaville placed advertisements aimed at Anglos in newspapers throughout the state and succeeded in attracting hundreds of families. Although some came from as far away as Los Angeles, most resided locally. Arriving in horse-drawn wagons from Vallejo, Winters, Sacramento, and Fairfield, newcomers clogged the train depot and Main Street. They handled roughly three-quarters of the harvest work around Vacaville in the summer of 1888, largely replacing the Chinese. So many congregated about town that the *Pacific Rural Press* announced, "It seems as if all the laboring people in California had come to Vacaville to get work. The roads are lined with men, from 2 to 12 in a bunch, hunting work. There are families that have come 300 miles to get work cutting fruit. From 5 to 20 men apply for employment every day at the large packing sheds."[103]

Newspaper reporters described the harvest as a kind of holiday. Arriving with their own tents and camping gear, families set up in the orchards "just as if they had gone to the country for an outing." Soon a kind of ritual became institutionalized. Simi Valley resident Everett "Joe" Delano Chavez recalled:

> When we reached our teens we would work in the drying field. The pitted fruit would be laid out in wooden trays, stacked on railroad trolleys, and rolled into concrete bunkers for curing. Pots of sulfur would be lit and allowed to burn overnight. In the morning, they would be rolled out. I hated this part of the process because the smell and the sulfur residue was so strong you would choke . . . After curing, the trays would be laid out in the sun for drying. The next step was to work in the pitting shed—this was where all the young men wanted to work because this was where all the girls were. One would deliver fruit and trays, pick up full trays, and boxes that were full of pits, and in the process flirt with the girls. We worked hard but we also had fun.[104]

Piece rates made novices into efficient workers. Paid so much per basket or tray, not by the hour, families worked as a unit, pooling their labor and sharing their income. Commenting on this pay method, peach grower William Parker explained to the *Chico Enterprise*, "by this means all foolishness and play is avoided, as everyone is prompted to excel his neighbor . . . payment by the day or hour will never make fruit-raising profitable, as the natural instinct of the worker is to take things easy, especially where a lot of young people are brought together."[105]

※

From this point on, whenever the harvests swept through their agricultural districts, hardworking white families would increasingly move into the fields and fruit-drying yards, earning vital supplemental income. This pleased the *Pacific Rural Press*, which predicted that family labor would bring greater profits, drive expenses down, and relieve them from the burden of providing food and housing. Nor did they have to worry about labor shortages and haggling with the Chinese. With the influx of families, growers could assume that "there will be two or more available summer laborers next year where there is one this year."[106]

Also diminishing the labor crisis of 1888 was the arrival of French, Portuguese, and especially northern Italian immigrants from Genoa, Turin, and Lombardy. Hired through "padrones" (literally "masters" or "owners") who acted as employment brokers, most worked under a form of "compatriot exploitation" whereby, in exchange for money and various forms of debt peonage, the padrone bridged the legal, lingual, class, ethnic, and racial terrain separating newcomers from employers. This system further swelled the ranks of farmworkers with large numbers of immigrants who, preferring to stick together while employed mainly by fellow countrymen, earned a reputation as some of the hardest working, lowest paid, least troublesome laborers in farming and farm-related industries, including cannery labor, gardening, and nursery work.[107]

Concentrating in specific agricultural districts, these immigrants exerted a profound impact, creating what amounted to ethnic enclaves. One such clustering could be found at Charles Lefranc's New Almaden Vineyard and Winery. Astride Guadalupe Creek in the Santa Clara Valley, New Almaden Vineyard by 1888 was not only the largest vineyard of good Bordeaux grapevines in California, it was also a little slice of France. That year, visiting journalist William Henry Bishop found it operated entirely by French workers. "An Alsacian foreman showed us through the wine cellars," Bishop later wrote. "At other places the surroundings are exclusively Italian or Portuguese. One feels very much abroad in such scenes on American soil. The foreigners from Southern Europe take naturally to wine-making."[108]

While the Italians played a key role in the vineyards and wineries throughout the San Joaquin and Napa valleys, they made their most profound and lasting mark on the fifteen-hundred-acre Truett sheep ranch astride the Northern Pacific Railroad line, four miles south of Cloverdale in northern Sonoma County. Hundreds of ambitious, fair-haired *contadini* (plain folk) had moved there in 1881, when Genoese banker Andrea Sbarboro announced plans for a cooperative vineyard and winery. Although Sbarboro's idea was that the settlers would work for room and board, wine for personal consumption, wages of thirty-five dollars per month, and stock in the company, the immigrants had something else in mind. Attracted less to the semiutopian ideal than to the prospect of earning wages and applying their experience as vineyardists and winemakers, the Italians refused to accept stock in the company over cash. Forced to reorganize as the Italian Swiss Agricultural Colony in 1885, Sbarboro raised capital by selling shares to outside investors. Hired at a daily rate plus room and board, the Italians then proceeded to plant the hillsides, battle grasshopper plagues, and erect the world's largest wine vault, a five-hundred-thousand-gallon subterranean tank cut into the solid rock. Working through various immigrant societies, the Italians funneled more and more laborers into the colony and soon produced an excellent vintage under winemaker Pietro C. Rossi. Naming their winemaking facility Asti, after a vineyard town in the Italian province of Lombardy, they eventually formed an Italian Workingman's Society of Mutual Relief and an Italian Labor Society, whose functions were to provide funds in case of illness and death and to hold various festivals. By 1888, Asti resembled a slice of old Italy where, at the height of the harvest season, entire families of pickers worked in the fields while their babies slept in empty crates at the end of the vineyard rows. So thoroughly Old-World was Asti that, after writer Frank Norris visited, he described it as a little slice of Italy, accessible at a cost of three dollars, "by means of a one and a half hour trip to Sonoma County."[109]

For all that they accomplished in 1888, the clusters of European immigrant vineyardists, railcars full of southern blacks, tribes of Paiute Indians, families on holiday, and children on summer vacation hardly presented a permanent solution to the labor crisis. Most whites were too demanding of better pay, blacks too given to running away at the first chance, families available only for brief periods, children too much in need of supervision and good housing, and Indians too far in decline as a population to be of much use. Wheatland growers learned this lesson during the late-August hop harvest. Despite soliciting every possible source of labor for miles around, they still could not break Chinese domination. Of about seven hundred field hands working on the hop ranches around town, the *Marysville Appeal* estimated the majority were still Chinese, "though as many whites as will work are given places."[110]

✑

On October 1, 1888, as the harvest season tailed off, President Cleveland signed the Scott Act into law. Anti-Chinese groups immediately held mass demonstrations throughout California, and the Democratic State Central Committee even fired off a one-hundred-gun salute in celebration. Not to be overshadowed, the chairman of the Republican State Committee called for an even stronger law that would require all Chinese to register and carry certificates of identification under penalty of immediate deportation. For Chinese field hands, the law was a catastrophe. Certificates of identity issued under the 1882 act were voided, a provision that proponents of the Scott Act had hoped would accelerate the depopulation of Chinese communities in the United States. This meant that about twenty thousand field hands and other immigrants who had gone home for a visit and were in China when the law was passed were now prohibited from returning to California—even most of those who were already en route back.[111]

On September 30, the day before the act went into effect, the collector of customs for the port of San Francisco allowed returning Chinese to enter the country, but they would be the last. Chae Chan Ping, who had lived in California from 1875 to 1887 and who had obtained a laborer's return certificate from the collector of the port of San Francisco before departing for China, was among hundreds of Chinese field hands and other laborers possessing return certificates who were denied reentry when the steamship *Belgic* made port on October 7. Informed of the action, the Chinese consul hired San Francisco attorney Thomas Riordan, applied for a habeas corpus writ, and chose Ping—who had left China on September 7 and had been at sea when the Scott Act went into effect—as the man to serve as the test for the new law. Circuit court Judge Lorenzo Sawyer heard arguments before a packed courtroom on October 12 and 13. The atmosphere inside the courtroom when both sides met to debate crackled with hostility. On behalf of Ping, a battery of attorneys attacked the law, though their arguments had little impact on Judge Sawyer.[112]

Tension built as Sawyer considered the case. On October 15, amid much "weeping and wailing" by the Chinese, Sawyer rejected Ping's appeal and found the law constitutional. The legal decision of exclusion had the effect of military defeat, and the Chinese reacted with great emotion. "Their great hope that the new exclusion law would be killed [has] received its death blow," observed a reporter for the *San Francisco Evening Bulletin*. At the same time, anti-Chinese forces present for the decision rejoiced. Many agreed with Dr. Charles C. O'Donnell, the anti-Chinese firebrand who had once opposed the Chinese on grounds that they introduced leprosy into the state: "I have been preaching the anti-Chinese gospel for great many years, and I tell you it's quite pleasant now to know that the battle is about over." Now, he suggested, the next order of business should be the removal of Chinese field hands from the entire state.[113]

Inevitably, the Chinese appealed. On the same day that the court issued its decision, attorneys filed notice that they would take the case to the U.S. Supreme Court. To pursue their appeal, the Chinese Six Companies hired two additional lawyers, George Hoadley, the former Democratic governor of Ohio, and James Carter, a well-known east coast lawyer familiar with the appeals process. Contending that Chinese field hands and others caught in China upon passage of the Scott Act had a vested right to return, lawyers maintained in their briefs that such a right could not be taken away by mere legislation. Termination of a treaty did not strip away rights previously granted under it.[114]

The drama and significance of the case riveted public attention to the courtrooms. Chae Chan Ping was, after all, a case of major consequence, one that had countless implications. One of the basic processes of democracy was on exhibit— the right of a group to appeal a law that it deemed tyrannical or evil. Lawyers representing the Chinese had challenged the Scott Act, and representatives of the government were going to defend it. As the appeal wound its way through the courts over the next several months, leaders of the agricultural industry speculated on what might happen should the Scott Act go into effect.[115]

On May 13, 1889, Supreme Court Justice Stephen Field issued his decision. While conceding that the Scott Act certainly violated earlier treaties with China, Field in a long and carefully worded opinion found the betrayal of no legal consequence. While a definite moral shame originated in disregarding solemnly undertaken treaty obligations, Field observed, it was not the purpose of the court to censor or pass judgment on the morality of governmental policy. Solely concerned with the constitutionality of the new law, he found it entirely legal, if reprehensible. Under its provisions, he explained, Chae Chan Ping was an alien, and the United States as a sovereign nation had the absolute power to exclude him and anyone else, much as it excluded paupers and criminals. While Ping might have reason to feel abandoned and while he might bring suit to retain or administer his property, if he had any, he had no right to return. Chae Chan Ping and thousands of men like him had to stay in China. They would never be allowed to return to California.[116]

CHAPTER SIXTEEN

Worn Out, Bent, and Discouraged

Chinese Labor (Almost) Disappears

from the Fields

The mood in California's farming districts in 1889 was thick with apprehension. Field hands and farmers alike were jittery, wary of one another, contentious. A wave of Chinese strikes had begun early in the harvest season, when China bosses in Ventura moved in to cut and pit apricots for ten cents per pound, undercut the local whites who would not do it for less than 12.5 cents, then promptly struck to raise wages to fifteen cents. Widely reported in the *Pacific Rural Press*, this opening salvo had the effect of a declaration of war. Posting "No Chinese Wanted" signs, growers across the state dismissed even reliable China bosses of long standing and had field hands arrested, jailed, and fined as much as ten dollars merely for using profanity. One Santa Clara County landowner specified in her farming leases that "no immoral institutions or any Chinatown or undue congregation of Chinamen" would be permitted, and that tenants could not have "pig pens, Chinese women, opium dens or gambling" anywhere on her property. So determined was prominent Sacramento Valley hop grower S. D. Wood to replace the Chinese that he solicited five hundred white hop pickers through advertisements in the July 25, 1889, *Marysville Appeal*. He was successful, but few other growers found the necessary replacements. "Chinamen seem to be the only help," complained the *California Fruit Grower*, adding "this class of help have become scarce and high-priced."[1]

A month later, when the Fresno raisin harvest began, nervous growers unable to come up with new sources of labor had no choice but to hire Chinese. Recognizing their advantage, the Chinese then proceeded to ignore threats to replace them with unemployed whites, launched numerous strikes, and raised wages on dozens of ranches. Growers also tried and failed to replace Chinese laborers during the September grape harvest in the Napa Valley, where the Chinese again exploited their advantage and raised wages. It was all too much for the *Kern County Californian*. Looking back on the year, the newspaper could scarcely contain its anger. "Next year," the paper predicted, "the industrious Cal-

FIGURE 34. Chinese field hand irrigating a ditch in an Inglewood orchard, ca. 1900. Photo by Isaiah West Taber. Courtesy of the California State Library.

ifornia boys will 'raise' most of the Celestials in the state by doing nearly all the light farm work."[2]

As labor problems expanded the following year, anger and frustration swept through the agricultural districts. Acting in response to local conditions and capitalizing on spot labor shortages and bumper crops that left growers vulnerable, China bosses, according to the *Pacific Rural Press*, began engaging in "slowdowns," "endeavoring to run bluffs," and "manifesting industrial discontent" that raised wages from $1.25 to $1.50 a day for picking fruit. When slowdowns and job actions broke out in the Newcastle fruit district, the paper observed of the Chinese that, "very few seem to be trying to save motions or to hurry." Some Chinese leaders, in fact, advocated large-scale actions to raise wages statewide. Among them were spokesmen for the Six Companies, who declared in a widely reprinted message that they would raise wages for all their field hands by year's end. Marveling at the "intelligence," "shrewdness," and "industriousness" of China bosses like Big Jim, Wing Tai, Sing Woo, Hoy Hop, and others, a reporter for the *Fresno Evening Expositor* observed that growers now deeply resented the power and militancy of the "heathen hordes." So angry was one Fresno raisin grower after agreeing to pay the unheard-of wages of two dollars a day that he vowed: "I shall never employ a Chinaman on my ranch again, if I can help it." Adding his two bits, an angry citizen proclaimed that, if raisin growers could not flourish without the Chinese, then "it would be better for the industry to go."[3]

Nowhere during 1890 did growers feel labor pressures more acutely than in Sonoma County. Requiring at least one thousand pickers to harvest hops near Cloverdale, prunes in Santa Rosa, and blackberries in Sebastopol, growers who for many years had relied almost entirely on Chinese labor now grew desperate and brought in children from the Boys and Girls Aid Society in San Francisco. "Hop picking is not necessarily hard work," explained hop grower L. E. Rickseller in a letter to the *Santa Rosa Daily Republican*. "With a few men to shake the trees and handle the full boxes, little boys and girls ten years old could do the prune gathering as well as anyone." Housed in a summer camp and supervised by a "camp counselor" who instilled discipline and order, the children lived much like they did on a summer outing, which was probably why the experiment worked when most others failed. However, when growers secured several hundred teenage boys from employment offices in San Francisco and attempted to duplicate the Sebastopol effort at Fowler in the San Joaquin Valley, they met with dismal failure. The boys were undependable, raided neighboring melon patches, and generally made a nuisance of themselves when not working. Characterized in a local newspaper as "hoodlums and thieves," they were promptly sent back to the city.[4]

Eventually these strains had to explode in some kind of conflict. The first of many confrontations occurred at Chino, in Southern California. In 1891, the imaginative and ambitious San Bernardino Valley farmer Richard Gird used capital garnered through sale of rich silver mining properties in Tombstone, Arizona, to purchase Rancho Santa Ana del Chino. Gird divided his land into city lots and small farms, established the *Chino Valley Champion* newspaper, and, with the support of local officials, appealed to Claus Spreckels to build a sugar beet factory. After negotiations broke down, he turned to Henry Oxnard, a prominent sugar refiner in Nebraska and Colorado. Completed on August 20, 1891, the Chino sugar beet factory inaugurated the beginning of commercial sugar beet refining in Southern California. Soon the sleepy little town of Chino awoke, in the words of one local newspaper reporter, "to the metallic clatter of money . . . more men, women and children, more schools, more churches, more society and general improvement and prosperity all along the line." By September 18, the factory was processing more than three hundred tons of sugar beets a day and paying local growers $3.50 to $5.50 per ton of beets. Earning returns of between $28.37 and $47.98 per acre, growers predicted Chino, with its long processing season (from September to February) would soon become the beet sugar capital of the world. Unable to hire enough local labor to plant, thin, and harvest eighteen hundred acres of sugar beets, Chino growers brought in Chinese who had been digging tunnels and canals around Upland, Cucamonga, and Alta Loma. From the moment they arrived, the Chinese came under attack.[5]

During mid-April, 1891, shortly after California passed its own stringent version of the Chinese Exclusion Act, unemployed white laborers began tramping the countryside outside of Los Angeles. Seeking jobs and blaming the Chinese for taking work and lowering wages, they became enraged when a crew of twelve to fifteen Chinese began thinning and cultivating sugar beets on a farm rented from Richard Gird. A few days later at about 3 A.M., while the Chinese were sleeping, a mob of forty unemployed men raided their camp. Brandishing guns, the mob, identified by the *Chino Valley Champion* as "indignant farmers," ordered the Chinese to leave. "The Chinese did not seem disposed to follow the directions," reported the newspaper, "and they and their belongings were unceremoniously pitched into several large four-horse farm wagons and escorted to the limits of the Gird Ranch." From there, other vigilantes transferred the Chinese into larger wagons, drove them south, and dumped them in the brushland outside of Pomona.[6]

This type of violence would not long remain isolated to the beet fields of Southern California. Another attack occurred on May 8, when a Chinese field hand returning home after work in the vineyards around St. Helena was surrounded by small boys and local bullies. Police who came to his rescue found the victim displaying the usual cuts and bruises from such attacks, but also discovered the man had been badly mauled about the nose and mouth. Investigating, they found that a woman, not content with seeing the man beaten, had set her dog on him when the thugs were done. But not all of the violence came at the hands of whites. With fat payrolls, China bosses became easy marks for robbers of all types, including fellow Chinese. This was apparently the case on July 9, when a horrible murder occurred on the Morgenstern and Milzner ranch west of Vacaville. Someone crushed the head of a China boss with a large rock and stole a five-hundred-dollar payroll. Although police suspected a Chinese field hand who had left the ranch that evening, it took them four years to track him down. Discovered in Oakland, he was brought back to Vacaville but released for lack of evidence. Remarked the *Vacaville Reporter* of the incident: "It is said that murder will out. It is not always true."[7]

Two weeks later, the Chinese confronted more bad news. With newspapers reporting a "vast army of idle men everywhere looking for work" and nearly "ten men for every job," growers began hiring them to replace or supplement the Chinese, often with disastrous consequences. Describing his "sad experiences" to a meeting of Vacaville fruit growers, J. A. Webster warned that in hiring any and all who arrived at his ranch he had found "many . . . drunken men, whose highest motive has been to procure money to prolong life's debauch." Fearing such problems, growers as always looked for more stable sources of labor. Along the banks of the American River, east of Sacramento, the Lovdal brothers and Menke hop yards replaced Chinese field hands in August with four hundred Paiute Indians and two hundred white families. Streaming out of "wagons containing all their household utensils and equipment," the newcomers set up camp along the riverbank, with the white families living in tents and the Indians improvising shelters made of bushes, discarded hop poles, and hop vines. Earning $1.75 to $2.25 per day and boarding themselves, the Indians received lavish praise. "Squaws and girls are the favorites," explained one reporter, "as they pick cleaner than the Chinese, though slower in operation." To the north, Wheatland hop growers were apparently so committed to replacing the Chinese that they raised wages from between ninety cents and one dollar per one hundred pounds of hops to $1.10. "The days for Chinamen in the Wheatland hop-yards is over," declared the *Wheatland Four Corners*. "Every year the crews are made up of more desirable people."[8]

Because the replacement of Chinese field hands in Sacramento County had occurred peacefully, did not grow out of pressure from anti-Chinese groups or unemployed laborers, and apparently had the complete and enthusiastic support of growers, the action attracted considerable attention. Curious about what had happened, the *Sacramento Bee* dispatched a reporter who found all was not what it seemed. Dozens of small encampments surrounded each field, each composed of a different group of Indians and white families, while on the periphery, clumps of destitute tramps and bindlemen slept under the stars with little more than a blanket for shelter. From a distance, the encampments appeared "picturesque" and decent, but up close they reeked; there was no sanitation system. The work was apparently as rough as the living conditions. When asked, "How are you getting along?" one sixteen-year-old girl replied: "My hands are awful sore. I made 75 cents yesterday." An unemployed printer was having an even tougher time. "I started working early yesterday morning in the hopes of making a stake," he explained. "I got up at four o'clock, and went into the field. I never worked so hard in my life; went without meals, and when night came and I weighed my hops, I had only picked thirty-five pounds. Hell, I can drink more hops in my beer than I can pick."[9]

On close examination, these experiments actually offered mixed results and few other growers attempted to duplicate them. Looking back over the 1891 harvests in October, the *St. Helena Star* could see little change in the labor force. "Many more Chinese are being employed . . . this year than last," reported the paper. "Cull times and low wages are the causes assigned for this condition of things." On the other hand, these early efforts to replace the Chinese offered models that anti-Chinese forces could follow and espouse. And combined with a U.S. Department of Agriculture study that found there were plenty of people both willing and available for farmwork, assertions of ample labor appeared to have been verified. Adding fuel to the smoldering fire, the *California Fruit Grower* warned that the Chinese were beginning to move into the fruit business on the same scale as they had done in vegetables, and the *Fresno Republican* asked of the raisin business, "What would become of our product if it were known the country over that it passed into the hands of the filthy Chinese?"[10]

During January of 1892, hoodlums, robbers, and bullies broke into Chinese barracks around St. Helena, ransacked the Chinese camps, and stole goods and money. None feared arrest. Chinese who complained were often beaten; those who went to the police seldom received justice. When one Chinese field hand defended himself against a man who knocked him down and pummeled his face on a farm near Rutherford, authorities summarily dismissed the case, claiming that the field hand was at fault.[11]

As violence mounted, many growers saw an opportunity to eliminate the increasingly troublesome Chinese. The difficulty behind such a plan became clear in June 1892, when two hundred Fresno raisin growers met "to discuss the labor situation." Fed up with China bosses, T. C. White suggested that he and his fellow growers sell grapes cheaply to the wineries or leave them to rot on the vines rather than raise wages another penny. Thus inspired, Fresno area growers set harvest wages at $1.15 per day and vowed to boycott the Chinese and hire only white laborers. But after the first day of harvesting, "Half [of the whites] . . . quit, some saying the work did not suit, others that they had a better job," one frustrated grower recounted of his experience. "Before the second day half the others came for their money," he added. One day later, he gave up and headed to Fresno to contact a China boss. "My grapes must be picked," he stressed, "and while I am in favor of giving the Americans a chance, I cannot afford to lose my raisins." Even though the boss demanded $1.50, far above the agreed-upon wage scale, the desperate grower did not hesitate to pay. Nor did others who found themselves in a similar situation. Commenting on these developments, the *California Fruit Grower* conceded that "vineyardists, though willing to hire white men, cannot afford to do so."[12]

During spring of 1893, attacks against Chinese field hands intensified. One of the worst incidents occurred in the celery fields south of Los Angeles. The area had developed as a center of celery production in 1890, when D. E. Smeltzer, a slight, stoop-shouldered Michigan farmer, found wild celery growing in a peat bog near the Santa Ana River. A year later, Smeltzer and E. A. Curtis planted the first celery crop, but the crop failed. Determined to succeed, Smeltzer and Curtis brought in Chinese gardeners from Los Angeles in 1892 and set them to digging drainage canals to Alamitos Bay. Once drained, the marshlands rose in value from ten or fifteen dollars to four hundred dollars an acre, and the Earl Fruit Company moved in to try planting celery again. But in trying to hire laborers for its Rancho La Cienega celery operations, the company discovered that local residents, known variously as "tule rooters" and "swamp angels," absolutely would not go into the celery fields. After a year struggling with local farmworkers, the company contacted a China boss who agreed to rent eighty acres of land for $325, if the company would advance him $125 against the first harvest, and furnish all of the seed, supplies, horses, and implements required for working the land. Moving into shacks rented from D. E. Smeltzer, the Chinese began working late in March.[13]

Chinese domination of celery harvesting presented few problems so long as white laborers rejected it as "muck work." But after the industry became established and land values rose, local field hands who had once refused to go into the celery bogs changed their minds and began demanding jobs. When the Earl Fruit Company refused to hire them in the spring of 1893, the men held loud "indignation meetings" and resolved "to wipe out the almond-eyed Mongols." They began by stealing celery knives and other tools from Chinese workers; when that failed, they formed a mob, and late one night stormed into the Chinese camp. The *Anaheim Gazette* reported:

> They poured coal oil on the walls and set it blazing in several places. The Chinese, awakening at the . . . light, rushed out to extinguish the flames, only to be fired upon by the midnight marauders. The bullets flew thick and fast and upon examination the next morning the building looked as though a small army of Indians had made an attack upon the premises. The Chinamen remained in the house during the night, but beat a hasty retreat in the morning, resolving never to return to the celery field again.[14]

Following the attack, the Earl Fruit Company hired armed guards to protect the Chinese in the fields. Local police patrolled the Chinese camps with huge watchdogs, and the Orange County Board of Supervisors offered a reward of fifty dollars for the arrest and conviction of the criminals. With that, the violence ended. But long after the guards left, the dogs remained. Chained at the doors of the Chinese shacks, they frightened off strangers and protected celery workers from other attacks. In June 1893, the Chinese harvested the first of 1,250 carloads of celery. The area known as Smeltzer (now part of present-day Huntington Beach) soon became a company town with barracks for the Chinese, a huge barn for teams of fifty horses, a small hotel, a blacksmith shop, store, and telephone office. Recalled one celery grower, "it wasn't long before everyone was raising celery and hiring Chinese."[15]

Shortly after the attacks at Rancho La Cienega, Chinese field hands confronted another major problem—a new exclusion law. State and federal representatives incessantly protested that the Chinese Exclusion Act of 1882 was on the verge of collapse, while anti-Chinese groups complained that hordes of Asians were waiting for the act to expire and were about to inundate the country. The Chinese had been able to fight off several radical bills calling for an absolute ban on immigration. But they could not stop the Geary Act, named for the Democratic congressman from Sonoma, Thomas Geary, who was one of its chief sponsors. Passed on May 5, 1893, and signed into law ten days later, it placed even more restrictions on the Chinese by creating America's first internal passport system and forcing Chinese field hands and other Chinese laborers residing in the United States to obtain a certificate of residence. Those failing to do so by May 15 of the following year faced arrest and deportation following a period of hard labor not to exceed one year.[16]

Chinese field hands protested the new law through their tong leaders and bosses, asserting that this was the first time undocumented residence in the United States had been made a crime. The Geary Act, they claimed, violated the Bill of Rights and cast a dark shadow over the right of residence. Because it required immigration officers to photograph all Chinese immigrants, the Geary Act created a legal presumption that Chinese were all in the United States unlawfully. On these grounds, representatives of the Six Companies denounced the measure as cruel and degrading. Soliciting a one-dollar contribution from every Chinese living in the United States, the Six Companies vowed to retain eastern lawyers ("the best that money can hire") and fight the law all the way to the Supreme Court. In the meantime, they encouraged Chinese laborers to disobey the Geary Act. In the spring of 1893, the *Watsonville Pajaronian* reported that Chinese in the area seemed to be universally ignoring the law and were "not rushing for the registration office."[17]

Not all Chinese field hands followed the advice of the Six Companies. Many bosses, permanent farmhands, and farm cooks weighed the injustice of the Geary Act and advice of family and regional associations against their own interests and experiences and sometimes came down on the side of registering. Such men, however, were always in the minority. By some estimates, eight of ten Chinese refused to register.[18]

As the deadline for registration approached, so many Chinese field hands had failed to register that growers feared entire crews might be deported. But it was not just the bosses who feared the consequences of civil disobedience. Local business interests, particularly those involved in agriculture, feared ruin. Mass deportation of Chinese field hands from agricultural districts like the Pajaro Valley, where they did virtually all of the work in the sugar beet and berry fields, would leave agriculture "considerably crippled for some time," as the local newspaper explained. For this reason growers, large landowners, and Watsonville town leaders united with local China bosses and the Chee Kong Tong, opposed the call for civil disobedience, and urged field hands to register.[19]

In Watsonville, Chinese field hands became confused by the abruptly changed strategy and requested a meeting to determine a course of action. On April 10, 1893, Watsonville businessman John T. Porter addressed a mass meeting in the Brooklyn Chinatown. Warning the assembled field hands that they could cause huge losses to the town—not to mention to themselves and their community— Porter urged them to register. Because feelings ran so high, a delegation composed of Porter and two prominent Chinese businessmen traveled to San Francisco to discuss the issue with Chinese vice consul Frederick Bee and representatives of the Six Companies. They got nowhere. Despite their pleadings, very few Chinese field hands registered. The *Watsonville Pajaronian* on May 25 reported that hundreds of Chinese field hands had fled to Canada and Mexico rather than register under the Geary Act, and that China bosses seemed either unwilling or unable to provide more men.[20]

Chinese field hands refused to register for the Geary Act out of a real sense of outrage, but they also refused because of their faith in, and loyalty to, the Six Companies, which declared the new law was unconstitutional, and would be proven so. They would quickly be disappointed. When the Geary Act became effective on May 6, the Six Companies launched its legal attack. By prearrangement with federal authorities, three Chinese laborers chosen in advance by Six Companies lawyers were arrested by the U.S. marshal for the southern district of New York on the charge of being in the United States without certificates of residence. Two were immediately brought before the district court judge and ordered deported. Within hours—and before the other laborer, Fong Yue Ting, could be arraigned in district court—Chinese Six Companies attorneys petitioned for habeas corpus writs on behalf of all three men, arguing that the registration provision of the Geary Act was unconstitutional.[21]

In California, the legal proceedings had little, if any, immediate impact. As Fong Yue Ting and the other men were being arraigned, Chinese field hands were blocking sugar beets, thinning lettuce, weeding strawberries, planting grapes, clearing fields, and picking oranges and lemons. But while work kept them busy, it did not prevent them from following the case. The Six Companies appealed to the Supreme Court after the courts dismissed the writs and ordered the petitioners remanded to the federal court. On May 10, the Court consolidated all three cases into one, *Fong Yue Ting v. United States*, and convened a special session to hear oral arguments. Five days later, the court upheld the constitutionality of the Geary Act by a vote of six to three. The deportation proceedings, as the court interpreted them, were hardly criminal actions; deportation itself was not a punishment but rather a way to force the return of aliens failing to live up to the conditions of their residence in the United States. From this ruling, field hands understood or were soon told that, if they were arrested and deported under the Geary Act, they were not entitled to trial by jury or protection against unreasonable search and cruel or unusual punishment, as well as other provisions of the Bill of Rights.[22]

Chinese field hands in Watsonville were reported to be enveloped by "great big hunks of gloom." In Ventura, they became hysterical and, according to the *Ventura Free Press*, panicked; when Company D of the local National Guard unit paraded through Chinatown they feared they were about to be marched to the wharf and shipped back to China. In response, they "scattered in all directions, tumbling pell-mell into houses, barring the doors and extinguishing the lights." In July, these fears were diminished somewhat when field hands learned that a federal appeals court had ruled that none of them would be deported without a trial by jury and due process. Their fears eased further when it became clear that no one would be deported simply for failing to register. Then, on November 3, Congress amended the Geary Act, extending the deadline for registration and broadening the definition of who was a laborer and therefore subject to the law. Forced to recant its previously defiant stand, the Six Companies now began encouraging field hands to register. Within a few months most Chinese field hands had complied.[23]

On the supply side of the labor equation, the Scott Act was highly ineffective. Viewing the legislation as unfair and discriminatory, workers labeled it *keli* (tyrannical law) and began employing various well-established subterfuges, including attempts to disguise themselves as sons of merchants, bookkeepers, students, returning shopkeepers, and so on. Aware of these deceptions, immigration officials initiated an elaborate process to weed out Chinese laborers, interrogating all who arrived unmercifully: "What do you come back for now?" "When you went to China, why did you not take a certificate of identification with you?" "What was your reason of your haste for your departure to China?" "How many bridges are there that cross the river at Santa Cruz, in the town, or near the town, wagon bridges?" "What is the name of the river, the stream of water?"[24]

Men could expect to be questioned about their income, business partners, products, location, and reasons for returning to China. Often the questions were so detailed that even men who had, in fact, run businesses could not answer correctly and were therefore deported. Even if a man passed the exam, relatives would be asked the same questions, and any discrepancies could result in deportation. Every answer was recorded, and files cross-referenced to other immigration cases. To survive their interrogation, immigrants turned to their "coaching books." Purchased in China and memorized during the long voyage across the Pacific Ocean, coaching books contained answers to commonly asked questions. Immigrants claiming to be paper sons or paper daughters filled in bogus information. Since they were to provide the burden of proof, field hands exerted great energies and huge sums of money to obtain these books, showing that they were indeed businessmen or wives and children of businessmen, and therefore exempt from exclusion. Books could be fifty pages long and contain answers to several hundred questions. Most immigrants destroyed their books by tossing them overboard the day before arrival.[25]

To circumvent the grueling immigration process, some Chinese began entering California illegally by way of Mexico. The journey was both expensive and dangerous. Transportation and smuggling fees often ran as high as $150 to $200 and usually came with a high interest rate for repayment. Even men who could afford the trip (or who could borrow the sum) were not guaranteed a successful passage. According to one legend, smugglers would unload the men from ships into small dinghies at Ensenada and would always take plenty of large rocks with them so that, if they saw any immigration authorities, they could tie a rock to the Chinese and throw them overboard, thus disposing of the evidence. From Ensenada, men quickly departed by boat for the border town of Tijuana and from there were guided along smuggling paths by foot into California.[26]

Chinese coming in by way of San Felipe in Baja California followed an even more elaborate and perilous route. Landing near the southern end of the Colorado River Delta, they headed north for the Mexicali Valley, near present-day Calexico, where they rested briefly, sometimes obtaining work before continuing on. They next hired a guide who took them north through the desert along a volcanic outcropping that later became known as Cerro El Chinero (China Hill). Many did not survive the trek.[27]

Once in California, Chinese field hands and others who had arrived illegally were relatively safe. By disappearing into the Chinese community, they were difficult to identify. After the summer of 1893, "illegal" and "undocumented" Chinese farmworkers would help perpetuate the tradition of cheap, abundant farm labor well past the time when Chinese field hands supposedly faded from the scene. Local newspapers delighted in telling stories about them taking flight at the appearance of immigration authorities. One such story, from the *Oxnard Courier*, described how, while passing through Oxnard and Port Hueneme examining immigration certificates while trying to ascertain the whereabouts of the well-known Chinese Wong Wing, U.S. Deputy Chinese Inspector J. P. Putnam was looking for Wong in some sheds with Constable Fred Lynn when Putnam saw a shoe protruding from beneath a stack of hay. "Accordingly, giving Fred the wink, he [Putnam] thrust his cane suddenly into the little pile of hay, eliciting a smothered Mongolian squeal, and Wong Wing was ignominiously dragged forth," reported the *Courier*. "He claimed good faith when asked for certificate of landing, but could not produce it, stating it was in Los Angeles. To that place he was accordingly taken, and it is yet to be learned whether he will be shipped back to China at an early date, a circumstance most probable."[28]

ቆa

Just as the fear surrounding the Geary Act dissipated, Chinese field hands confronted an even greater problem. During the summer of 1893, the panic on Wall Street that had begun earlier in the year deepened, initiating a catastrophic economic downturn. Lasting four years, the depression caused 580 banks to fail (seventy-five in California) and forced sixteen thousand businesses to close; two of five western transcontinental railroads were left insolvent. People fortunate enough to remain employed watched their pay drop 20 to 50 percent. In California alone, fifty thousand men were jobless; more than seven thousand were out of work in San Francisco. Soup kitchens, the favored method of relief and a sure index of economic health or malady, overflowed capacity.[29]

All over the state, unemployed and homeless men took over empty buildings, commandeered entire trains, camped out in warehouses, and established shanty-towns. Those who could wrote letters to farmers soliciting work, and their advertisements dotted the pages of rural newspapers: "SITUATION WANTED—An experienced man in fruit culture wants a place on ranch. Sober, industrious, and has family. Address H. Dennis, Redlands post office. References given," read one solicitation in the *Redlands Citrograph*. "Competent and experienced ranch hand, with family, desires place on ranch or will take orchards to care for by the year. Address Chas. Simmons, Redlands," read another. Men took to the road everywhere. The *Sacramento Bee* reported:

> Tramp, tramp, tramp, the tramps are marching. They are coming into the State from the East, from the North, and from the South. They are flocking on freight trains. . . . They are not altogether an undesirable class. . . . The majority of them . . . appear to be men of honest intentions, but rough, determined, sadly in need . . . they are simply looking for work and for food. It is probable that most of them come from Colorado, where the closing of the silver mines has placed the people in desperate straits.[30]

When the various harvests commenced that summer, unemployed men moved out into the agricultural districts. Trudging along Fourth Street in Sacramento headed for the orchards, such men were astounded to find gangs of Chinese laborers holding their blankets, cooking utensils, and bags of rice, and waiting to be carried to the fields in wagons provided by growers. Outside of town, unemployed men found an even more depressing situation—crews of Chinese swarming through the orchards and fields. As they searched for work or handouts and found none, the unemployed became increasingly frustrated and turned their anger on the Chinese. Some offered themselves for hire in place of the Chinese at the same wages, others began grumbling and organizing. "White men and women who desire to earn a living," observed the *Los Angeles Times*, "have for some time been entering quiet protests against vineyardists and packers employing Chinese in preference to whites."[31]

Beginning in August, unemployed men attacked Chinese field hands in dozens of different farming districts stretching from the Napa Valley south to Los Angeles. Lasting well into September, this six-week rampage was bitterly recalled by older Chinese years later as "the driving out." One of the first incidents occurred on August 24, when a Chinese field hand inching a wagon down Glass Mountain in the Napa Valley rounded a turn and was met by two drunk Euro-American laborers in a cart. Some jeering remarks followed, and the field hand made the mistake of shouting back. One of the drunks got out of the cart, dragged the field hand to the ground, and beat him over the head with a metal bucket. The drunk then got back into his cart and drove away with his cohort. The *St. Helena Star* reported that the incident resulted when the Chinese field hand had threatened to kill the two men in the cart. Reading the account, C. T. McEachran, the St. Helena grape grower who employed the battered Chinese laborer, wrote a long letter to the editor of the *Star* disputing the account. He emphasized that

> this Chinaman has been with me five years. I know him to be sober, peaceful and industrious. Is it probable such a man would wantonly assault two white men? I have heard before of the vicious sheep who attacked the innocent man. The tracks of the wheels in the road as examined by myself and others at the time show that the Chinese was not the aggressor and the circumstances in the case warrant that it was an unprovoked attack on the Chinaman because he was a Chinaman."[32]

Exactly what happened that day remains a mystery, but it does seem clear that it had nothing to do with labor competition or any organized campaign to drive out the Chinese and was more inspired by prejudice and liquor. The white men fled the area and the accused Chinese field hand was released from jail. But that did not mean he or his countrymen were now safe. As the wine grape harvest got under way, Chinese field hands were soon targeted by a group of restless unemployed men calling themselves the "White Labor Union." Before long, Chinese field hands working for prune and wine grape growers around Napa Valley were being confronted by roving bands of union members demanding that they leave so that white men could take their places. In a series of confrontations, Chinese crews were driven out of several vineyards and prune orchards. According to the *Pacific Rural Press*, most attacks followed a similar pattern. Agitators who claimed to be workingmen but who were in fact "low tramps and bummers" would "go at night to a Chinese camp," throw the laborers out of bed, march them to the nearest railroad, and put them on the first outbound train, justifying their mob actions on the grounds that the federal government had failed to enforce the Chinese Exclusion Act properly. But their true motive, according to the *Pacific Rural Press*, was nothing more than "a beastly taste for violence and plunder."[33]

Some of the biggest confrontations occurred in the rapidly expanding Southern California citrus industry, particularly around Riverside, which owed a very substantial part of its success to large numbers of Chinese field hands. At first living mainly on the citrus ranches, the Chinese did not attract much attention until 1878, when *Riverside Press and Horticulturalist* editor James H. Roe noted a small number in town who were "models of peaceable industry." During the winter of 1880, the Chinese expanded from Riverside into the citrus farms in Los Angeles, Orange, and San Bernardino counties. Scholars of the citrus industry hold that these men exerted very limited social impact, did not mix with other racial groups, and labored "only as seasonal workers," but surviving records suggest a more complicated situation. When the Duey Woo Lung Company astounded local citrus growers by suggesting that the Chinese could combat infestations of cottony cushion scale by going through the groves and hand washing the leaves of every orange tree, the Chinese received widespread attention for the first time. By 1885, they had established a thriving Chinatown in Riverside. Covering seven acres in the Tequesquite Arroyo, and known as "Little Gom-Benn"—after a village in southern China—the Riverside Chinatown had a permanent population of three hundred to four hundred, many of them living in what locals referred to derisively as "rookeries" (shacks with tiers of bunks ascending to the ceilings on all four walls) while they worked as cooks, irrigators, pruners, and general field hands on nearby ranches. But during the apricot, raisin, grape, and citrus harvests, more than two thousand Chinese arrived, most of them settling into a tent city sprawling along Pine Street west of Brockton Avenue. As one citrus grower explained, "Poor John spreads a dirty tent in some corner of the field near water, sleeps on the ground, works by starlight, and lives on rice of his own cooking." Visitors to the citrus belt now constantly commented on the Chinese. The poet Charles Warren Stoddard found hundreds in the Riverside orchards and packing sheds, "washing and brushing and sorting oranges, chattering and laughing as they worked under the direction of an American inspector," sometimes even toiling through the night. One manager of an orange packing operation at this time later recalled how, during the harvest, he would arrive at a large tree or some barn where "a number of Chinese men are squatting around a huge pile of freshly picked oranges. Deftly they sort out the different sizes and pack them in a box standing on end after which the full boxes are carried to a peculiar-looking press where one end at a time is pressed down and nailed."[34]

The Chinese worked without incident in the region until Monday, August 28, 1893, when the Colton cannery, which employed several hundred Chinese "tinners," notified workers of a 25 percent cut in wages. Although the two hundred whites accepted the wage cut without protest, the Chinese did not and quit en masse. Without their critical skills, the cannery was unable to function and had to rescind its wage reductions. The action should have won the thanks and praise of white workers. But instead their bravado at the Colton plant served only to anger unemployed whites.[35]

Four days later, during a drenching downpour, Chinese field hands working in the citrus orchards around the small Riverside County towns of Mentone and Crafton were rounded up in the middle of the night, driven out into the countryside, and "told . . . to start walking." Within a few hours, Chinese field hands in the nearby town of Redlands also came under attack by a crowd of four hundred men who swept into Chinatown. According to popular accounts, the Chinese armed themselves with picks and hammers from the local hardware stores and barricaded themselves inside packing plants and labor camps to avoid this forced eviction. Eventually they were "driven out" in a blaze of gunshots and "unmercifully harassed" by mobs that looted their homes and burned their buildings to the ground. But in fact this version of events is not even close to what actually happened. The real story was much less dramatic and resolved itself in a much more complicated way.[36]

On the night in question, unemployed men passed resolutions urging mob actions, then marched through the Redlands Chinatown pounding on walls and ordering the Chinese to leave within two days. Protected by locked and bolted doors, most Chinese were able to avoid any confrontations, but several were captured by the mob. Just as they were about to be hauled into the streets and pummeled, the mob learned that the Redlands police had arrested their ringleader and that many citizens had come forth to block any violence. Leaderless and drenched from the rain, the men disbanded with plans to gather again in two days and make good on their threats, but by then, Redlands citizens had mobilized to defend the Chinese. With one hundred special police standing guard, militias from Redlands, San Bernardino, Riverside, and Pomona alerted, the National Guard at the ready, and *Riverside Press* editor E. W. Holmes waging a daily editorial battle against the rioters, Chinese field hands had little to fear from the "anarchistic agitators" and "hoodlums," as the local press called them.[37]

It was not long before the Chinese in Redlands faced a new and ultimately more dangerous threat. Surprisingly, it originated not among the illegal undertakings of vigilantes but in the legal actions of the local police chief and Riverside sheriff. While opposed to vigilante justice, these law enforcement leaders were not opposed to the orderly departure of the Chinese and so they began calling on every man who knew a Chinese field hand to file a complaint and have him arrested for failing to register under Section 6 of the Geary Act. A *Los Angeles Times* reporter who covered the earlier mob action and had noted the generosity with which deputies had fed, housed, and protected the Chinese, observed: "But little did they suspect that those with them at that hour were evolving plans to rid the city of them, though in a legal way." And the following day: "Plans are completed for issuing warrants for the arrest of all Chinese here tomorrow."[38]

Within a few days, more than one hundred Chinese had been rounded up by the sheriff under what became known as "the Redlands Plan." Chinatowns throughout the San Bernardino Valley were raided and farm cooks hauled out of labor camps and dragged naked out of bathhouses screaming and kicking and placed in the round-up wagon. Brought before a local judge, they were promptly convicted and ordered deported for being found without a certificate of registration. So frightened were residents of Riverside's Chinatown that all four hundred residents fled to the Santa Ana riverbottom, where they hid in the willows for nearly a week. Many more Chinese left to avoid the dragnet as the local press crowed loudly about "the purple coated celestial heathens" fleeing from the wrath of an "aroused citizenry." Redlands became famous as the first California town to find a way to expel its Chinese legally. Within two weeks, the town boasted: "There are not now in Redlands . . . more than fifty Chinamen, whereas there were before . . . not less than two hundred. Another batch of warrants will perhaps drive the balance away."[39]

Seven of nine Redlands Chinese arrested by U.S. marshals were eventually deported, and according to the *Redlands Citrograph*, the tactic of exhorting the citizenry to come forth and swear complaints had "spread in nearly one week to nearly all Southern California." Although lack of funds for prosecution and a crowded court calendar prevented the U.S. attorney general from implementing the deportation scheme on a large scale, it nevertheless hit the Chinese hard. One citizen of Los Angeles was so enthusiastic over the deportations that he announced he would contribute ten thousand dollars toward ridding Los Angeles of "the Mongolian evil," while the Cahuenga Farmers Association offered to pay the deportation expenses of every Chinese field hand it employed. Inspired by these developments, mob attacks spread north from Orange County. Within a few days, Chinese field hands in Compton were forced to barricade themselves into packing sheds, where they worked and slept until the end of the harvest. They dared not venture out lest they be caught alone on the streets and beaten by mobs.[40]

Of all the violence against the Chinese in 1893, probably the worst occurred in Selma, a small San Joaquin Valley farm town located about ten miles south of Fresno and, again, it involved the Earl Fruit Company. On August 11, the company fired all of the women in its Selma packing shed, then brought in crews of Chinese men from Fresno, ostensibly because they were superior packers. The following day a "raging mob" of about one hundred unemployed men converged on the Unger Opera House in Selma and organized an anti-Chinese league, then ordered the Chinese to close all of their businesses, abandon their work in the vineyards, and withdraw from town by September 1. Upon issuing their ultimatum, they marched on the Earl Fruit Company packing plant and demanded that the company dismiss all of its Chinese and rehire the women. Although the company complied and the Chinese fruit packers and most other Chinese field hands left town immediately, a dozen or more laborers along with several businessmen remained in the local Chinatown. Angered by this apparent act of defiance, a local labor contractor named T. R. Vinzent, who had been supervising a crew of forty bindlemen picking raisin grapes in his brother's vineyard, took matters into his own hands.[41]

Around 11 P.M. on August 13, terrified Chinese field hands watched from behind locked and barred doors and windows as Vinzent's crew, wearing masks made of wheat sacks, began marching on Chinatown. Ignoring warning shots by Deputy Marshal H. P. Gay, Vinzent's band pushed past a line of police officers, ransacked the Chinese quarters, stole more than three thousand dollars in goods and money, then rounded up all of the Chinese and began marching them toward the town of Fowler, five miles distant. All of Selma's Chinese field hands and fruit packers would have been deported if Marshal Gay had not enlisted the help of Constable W. M. Spencer and a dozen police officers. When Vinzent ignored Spencer's order to stop, the officer drew his pistol, fired a bullet through Vinzent's hat, and promptly arrested him. Panicked by the gunfire, the mob set off on the run for Fowler with nine Chinese in tow. Quickly organizing a mounted posse, Constable Spencer overtook the mob, arrested twelve men, returned the Chinese to their heavily damaged homes, and placed Chinatown under extra guard. Vinzent was convicted for inciting a riot and kidnapping. Given thirty days in jail after the jury recommended "extreme mercy," his sentence so angered anti-Chinese zealots that one of them set fire to a Chinese laundry, burning it to the ground.[42]

In the vineyards around Fresno, more violence flared in the wake of the Selma incident. Determined not to pay $1.40 a day to harvest raisin grapes, two hundred growers held a secret meeting and again adopted a pay rate of $1.15 without board, or seventy-five cents with board. Vowing to hire only white field hands, they then descended on the Fresno Chinatown, seized several wagons full of Chinese, put them on the next train out of town, and rounded up one hundred unemployed men. That evening, the unemployed mob began marching through the city streets waving American flags, shouting "for predominance of white labor," and vowing, "On to Chinatown." That night, masked men raided the R. H. Metzler vineyard near Del Rey, peppering the Chinese camp with bullets, breaking into the barracks, dragging the Chinese outside, and beating several residents badly. Eleven of the Chinese who attempted to flee were captured, robbed, and marched off to Fresno. Local businessmen managed to stave off a similar attack on the Fresno Chinatown only after holding a large public meeting in which they agreed to establish a "free labor bureau," hire the unemployed at $1.15, and "submit to the teaching of green hands, in order to favor white men."[43]

While these measures curbed violence in the immediate vicinity of Fresno, they did not help unemployed whites find stable positions. Abandoned once the harvest ended, they congregated as always around Fresno's Courthouse Park, hoping to be picked up for day jobs. Nor did these measures stop anti-Chinese attacks in the outlying districts. Over a period of several weeks early in September, fifteen different Chinese barracks were attacked. Near Kingsburg, unemployed men hung the effigy of a Chinese laborer, labeled "Wun Wing," from a telegraph pole near the train depot and organized a boycott of Earl Fruit Company, the sole packer in town. During a raid on one remote camp, two Chinese field hands who dared to resist were shot and killed.[44]

☙

All but a few small farmers denounced the anti-Chinese violence, and most townspeople refused to participate. Simple economics, it seems, was the more powerful dictator of behavior than prejudice. Given the spectacular growth of irrigated agriculture and its importance to the state and countryside, both *Pacific Rural Press* editor Edward J. Wickson and *Los Angeles Times* owner Harrison Gray Otis agreed: Driving out the Chinese, "mainstay of the orchardist," perhaps a long-term goal, was undesirable, costly, difficult, and unwise. While it was only natural to prefer white help, the Chinese should not be pressed too hard. No sane orchardist would trust the task of harvesting his crop to "sandlot hoodlums and agitators" or a "class who are of less value to the country than the Chinese themselves."[45]

Of all the farming districts in California, none espoused this view more strongly than Stockton, which bragged that not a single Chinese field hand was driven out of the nearby fields—or the Sacramento-San Joaquin Delta—during the 1893 mob actions. Perhaps more than anywhere else in the state, Stockton Chinese remained intimately connected to the local economy. Everyone in town understood their debt to the Chinese who, early in the year on Bouldin Island, had harvested the first commercial asparagus crops in the delta, initiating the start of a new and highly profitable industry. Regarding the Chinese as an asset who threatened no one and benefited all, Stockton citizens were of the nearly unanimous opinion that "no Chinese were taking jobs as in the Fresno vineyards" and that "nine-tenths of the businessmen wanted the Chinese to remain here." For these reasons, Stockton workingmen broke with the general campaign against the Chinese and strongly rejected the kind of violence that had occurred at Fresno,

Selma, and Redlands. Stockton union officials even went so far as to issue a press release stating "that the various labor organizations of the city of Stockton are opposed to any and all violent measures of ridding the state of Chinese."[46]

Elsewhere in the state, Chinese field hands were not so lucky. In Sonoma and Mendocino counties, they were again forced out of the hop yards in favor of white laborers, families, and some Indians. A newspaper reporter for the *Santa Rosa Democrat* claimed that the Chinese had been turned away, ostensibly because they traded almost exclusively with Chinese merchants who, at the end of the season, sent their remittances to Chinese wholesalers in San Francisco and ultimately to China. By firing the Chinese, hop growers put more money in the hands of Sonoma and Mendocino County businesses. "Even now the merchants of Ukiah begin to feel the difference," wrote the journalist. "The white pickers spend their money in the cities and towns as do the Indian pickers for that matter, and one hop man says it will make a difference of $10,000 to the county."[47]

Anti-Chinese attacks continued into the winter, fueled largely by the deepening national economic depression and large numbers of unemployed men searching the state for any kind of job, no matter how demeaning. On December 30, 1893, about two thousand gaunt and hungry bindlemen in Chico arrived outside a hiring hall at 6 A.M. Shivering and stomping their feet against the cold, they stood in line until after 3 P.M. Eventually hired to clear land for ten days at one dollar a day and board, the two hundred who obtained jobs counted themselves lucky to snag even that scrap of work. Thirty miles south at Vina, conditions took a nasty turn in February 1894, when Jane Stanford assumed control of the estate following the death of her husband and immediately dismissed more than 150 field hands—including French vineyard workers and others who had worked on the ranch for more than a decade—but retained all of the Chinese. Angry at their ill treatment, the dismissed men one evening crept up on Mrs. Stanford's private railroad sleeping coach and sprayed it with bullets. Newspapers downplayed the incident, carefully noting that Mrs. Stanford "was not scared" and claiming that the entire episode was nothing more than a "harmless discharge of revolvers by revelers which caused no terror." When Mrs. Stanford still refused to rehire the men, fire the Chinese, or rescind her wage cuts, the unemployed men became even more violent. Only after the rabble-rousers departed did Chinese field hands return to their routines.[48]

Such incidents temporarily forced Chinese field hands to accept extremely low wages in 1894. In some areas, they worked for as little as fifty to seventy-five cents a day. But in doing so they only provoked greater hostility from whites who could not survive on such small pay. The frustration soon returned to Southern California, where the appearance that spring of Chinese field hands in the orchards around La Verne infuriated unemployed men. First hired to sort oranges for citrus grower Marcus Sparks, the Chinese quickly moved into packing sheds in Pomona and San Dimas as well. Initially they worked without incident, but on March 3, when they started picking oranges around Anaheim, mobs of unemployed men attacked them and drove them from the orchards. Under police protection, the Chinese returned on March 14 and skirmished with unemployed men near Rivera in Los Angeles County. Again protected by police, the Chinese then continued working in the fields, reclaiming a large portion of "tule land" and planting it with alfalfa.[49]

On March 23, Napa Valley grape grower John Dowdell discharged all of his Chinese and replaced them with twenty unemployed men from St. Helena. Two months later, Chinese field hands near Vacaville were attacked by unemployed men who were passing through the area on their way back from a mass rally in Washington, D.C. The unemployed men were members of Fry's Army from Los Angeles and Kelley's Army from San Francisco, two militantly organized groups of unemployed men who had left California six hundred strong with plans to rendezvous with Jacob Coxey's Army and thousands of other unemployed men. They had traveled to Washington, D.C., intent on forcing Congress and President Grover Cleveland to create public works jobs and address the problem of mass unemployment. Now returning from their two-month journey with little more than the clothes on their backs, they were disembarking from trains in the Vacaville marshaling yards when they noticed Chinese field hands in the area.[50]

Tired and angry after the long journey and thoroughly infected with the "Chinese Must Go" slogan, they descended on Vacaville for a weekend rally to persuade growers to fire Chinese field hands and instead hire unemployed whites for the cherry and apricot harvests. But after one grower donated money and food and a dozen others offered jobs, none of the unemployed showed up for work. Instead, they moved south to Winters and set up camp. Growers thought the confrontation had ended, but around 9 P.M. on May 18, the men returned and began attacking growers employing Chinese field hands. "The first place reached was the Wilson ranch, where they broke open the house," wrote the *Vacaville Reporter*. "At Wm. Thissel's, five men with masks on drew guns and pistols on him . . . they could hardly be induced to refrain from burning the house. At Brinick's, Hathaway's, Mrs. Blake's, Tucker & Tubbs', Smith's and all down the valley they carried things with a high hand, forcing Chinese . . . to leave their places and come with them."[51]

When word reached Vacaville that the mob intended to burn the town, a mounted force of about fifty growers and Vacaville residents armed with shotguns, pistols, and rifles assembled at 4 A.M. to intercept the mob. "The whole crowd was finally arrested," reported the *Sacramento Bee*, "and including the Chinese . . . are in custody." After being marched en masse into Vacaville, the Chinese were released while each unemployed rabble-rouser was required to post a five-hundred-dollar bond. When none could make bail, they were marched to county jail in Fairfield; all eighty-four members of the unemployed mob were tried in Fairfield at the end of the month and acquitted.[52]

Chinese field hands were understandably shaken by the verdict, but many no doubt took some measure of solace from what happened next. Fearing that violence might erupt again, growers and a number of prominent Vacaville citizens took matters into their own hands. To protect the Chinese, they formed a Law and Order League, hired San Francisco detective Charles L. Foster, and sent him into the hobo camps along Putah Creek disguised as a tramp. Using information he gathered while undercover, Yolo County authorities arrested ten of the "more vicious" vagrants on the Yolo County side of Putah Creek and shipped them to Woodland for prosecution. Vacaville authorities also began weeding out some of its most prominent anti-Chinese agitators by giving them two hours to leave town and advising them not to return. Those who refused were immediately arrested.[53]

Almost everywhere they went in California during the summer of 1894, Chinese field hands were greeted by increasingly hostile men and angry mobs. Around St. Helena, they endured a system of continual harassment (known locally as "mauling") and could not show their faces in town without fear. "Assaulting Chinamen is too common a practice by the ruffianly men and boys," commented the *St. Helena Star*, "and we hope for the credit of our fair town . . . a man calling himself a heathen may walk the street without fear of abuse from the man calling himself a Christian."[54]

To counter the wave of attacks and ingratiate themselves with growers, China bosses in the northern Sacramento Valley adopted unusual and drastic measures. As the harvest season commenced in Butte County, they made their first move. "The cunning chaps are now offering to employ white men in the orchards, paying them $1 a day and board," reported the *Sacramento Bee*. Actually, the offer made good business sense. Having leased several thousand acres of orchards in the vicinity of Marysville, Vina, Red Bluff, Oroville, and Willows, including a large part of the Bidwell ranch, as well as a cannery, fruit driers, and other properties in the northern fruit belt, the Chinese could not safely provide all of the labor required for their enterprises. But while they offered to hire anyone, few whites responded to their proposal. Only the most desperate or unprejudiced men would work for China bosses.[55]

When the national Pullman strike shut down all railroad traffic from June 30 to July 7, and growers pulled fruit out of refrigerator cars and hauled it back to their orchards for drying, Chinese field hands around Winters moved onto the farms, worked alongside bindlemen and white families from neighboring towns, and brought in the harvest without incident. One month later, when the hop harvest rolled around in Yolo, Sutter, and Sacramento counties, the Chinese comprised but a small portion of the thirteen thousand laborers working in the hop yards. The *Sacramento Bee* reported: "The white man, his wife and children, the little yellow man . . . the almond-eyed mongrel and the Paiute buck and his squaw from the sage brush plains of Nevada mingle like one picturesque family moving among the trailing vines in the hop yards." With the surplus of labor, pay rates fell. Chinese field hands now picked hops for 70 to 75 cents per 100 pounds, compared to 80 to 85 cents for white field hands and the $1 to $1.10 that they had received the previous year. To compensate for their plummeting pay rate, the Chinese worked even harder, averaging three dollars per day, still roughly double that earned by white hop pickers.[56]

Wage cuts did not always go unchallenged. On September 16, 1894, at the Pleasanton Hop Company hop yards in Livermore Valley, the Chinese diverged spectacularly from their pattern of accommodation and instead participated in one of the earliest interracial farm labor strikes in California agriculture. Owned by San Francisco capitalist E. R. Lilienthal, the Pleasanton Hop Company spread over twelve hundred acres of alluvial soil on a tract once known as Rancho

FIGURE 35. Local harvest hands dressed up in their Sunday best for a local photographer outside their brush shelter at the Pleasanton Hop Company, Livermore Valley, ca. 1895. Courtesy of the Amadore-Livermore Valley Historical Society.

del Valle. Described as the largest hop growing operation in California, the company had been formed in 1892 and, according to newspaper accounts, was "equipped with every modern invention applicable to hop culture and to facilitate the labor from the time the soil is plowed until the hops are ready for market." Harvesting one thousand to two thousand pounds per acre, the company shipped hops on such a massive scale that entire trainloads of bailed hops would depart Pleasanton bound for the eastern states, some eventually shipped to London, where the hops fetched premium prices.[57]

About thirty men worked year-round tending and cultivating vines in the Pleasanton Hop Company yards, but as many as twelve hundred picked and processed the crop at harvest time. Hundreds of men cured and baled hops in three batteries of large hop-drying kilns, others drove wagons full of hops out of the fields to the train yard, but most labored in the fields. Attracted by printed circulars advertising good camping grounds, free water, and a match of the previous year's wage of $1.10 per one hundred pounds of hops, about four hundred Chinese field hands gathered with an equal force of Portuguese, 125 Paiute Indians, and families from as far away as Davisville and Oakland. Settling into a giant brush and tent camp along both sides of Hopyard Road, with each ethnic group occupying its own section, the work was described by the *San Francisco Call* as "more like a big picnic than anything else." With grocery wagons, a butcher shop, restaurant, and bakery wagons, the Chinese were relatively comfortable here, within easy walking distance of the fields, about a half-mile from the train depot.[58]

But two weeks into the harvest the company suddenly announced, following the lead of the Oregon Hop Growers Association, that it was lowering pay rates to eighty cents per one hundred pounds. With the hops ripening rapidly in the one-hundred-degree heat, everyone calculated their chances and astonished the hop company by rejecting an offer of ninety cents per one hundred pounds. Joining the Portuguese and white laborers, Chinese walked out of the hop yards at dawn under the leadership of former miner John Williams. "By 8 o'clock every division and every nationality, except a bank of Paiute Indians numbering 125, had joined the big strike and left the fields," reported the *Sacramento Bee*. Not only did the Chinese refuse to abandon their Portuguese allies, they issued their own demands: They would return to work only if they received their old wage, and if the Portuguese were rehired. But with the countryside overrun by tramps, bindlemen, and groups of unemployed, and with hundreds of local families available for picking, the Pleasanton Hop Company had no problem hiring replacements. Within two days, eight hundred strikebreakers arrived, some from as far away as Sacramento. With armed guards standing by to prevent any protests, the Chinese, along with the Portuguese and local whites, could only watch helplessly as the strikebreakers moved into the hop fields and began working alongside the Indians.[59]

Although the Pleasanton hop strike ended without violence, Chinese field hands continued to experience a string of attacks throughout the fall and winter. Even around Vacaville, where growers had supposedly rooted out the last vestiges of anti-Chinese activity, the Chinese found themselves under assault. Early in November 1894, a group of 150 "marauding tramps . . . organized in squads with captains and lieutenants" traveled from one farm to another, ordering growers to discharge all Chinese field hands. If someone refused, they marched onto that grower's property, rounded up the Chinese, and moved them out forcibly. To emphasize their resolve, they cut down dozens of fruit trees. The *Pacific Rural Press* urged readers to protect the Chinese "from these cormorants, the tramps," by any and all legal means.[60]

⁂

As even more unemployed men poured into the countryside in 1895, wages in many areas declined to less than one dollar a day, and a glut of employment agencies sprang into action. Providing jobs for a fee, they ran their advertisements in agricultural papers throughout the state. "FARMERS, ATTENTION!" read an advertisement in the July 20, 1895, issue of *Pacific Rural Press*. "DO YOU WANT TO EMPLOY ANYBODY? If so, we furnish Farmhands, Teamsters, Men and Wives etc. promptly. No charges to employers. Send in your orders to J.F. CROSETT & Co., Employment Agency, 628 Sacramento Street, San Francisco, Cal." Nowhere did the glut have more effect than in the Pajaro Valley, where early in the year gangs of Italian, Portuguese, and Mexican laborers, who had long avoided the sugar beet fields, suddenly gained control of nearly 30 percent of the fieldwork. Ironically, they did so by utilizing a technique that the Chinese often had employed successfully: they underbid everyone. Whereas Chinese gangs had used their monopoly control to dominate 98 percent of the sugar beet contracts and drive the rate for raising sugar beets up from 70 cents to $1.06 a ton, Italian padrones in the southern part of the valley worked for $1 per ton, and Portuguese along San Juan Road raised beets for $1.04. But it was not just that the labor surplus was undermining Chinese power. The Chinese were being challenged on all fronts. A group described as "Spaniards" (actually Mexicans) even had the audacity to move into hop picking east of Watsonville, where the Chinese had long held a near monopoly of the harvest labor force.[61]

To counter inroads into hop harvesting, China bosses met their competitors head-on. In exchange for two-thirds of the crop, free use of the land, and access to all necessary hop-drying and bale-pressing equipment, they concluded five-year sharecrop leases to harvest, dry, cure, and deliver 190-pound bales of hops. But when it came to sugar beet production, the bosses took a different tack. Realizing that production was declining around Watsonville and that more productive beet land was about to open around Castroville, China bosses abandoned their contracts and brought several hundred field hands into a run-down section of Castroville along McDougall Street. Soon the area earned a reputation as the liveliest Chinatown in the Monterey Bay region. On Saturday nights during the sugar beet harvest, crews streamed in, gambling and carousing until well after midnight. "All the alluring games which prove so attractive to the Mongolian laborers and so destructive to his purse . . . run full blast," reported the *Salinas Index*.[62]

But the Chinese did not stop at Castroville. Closely watching the sugar beet fields creep south into the Salinas Valley, where irrigated crops promised higher yields per acre, a group of bosses early in 1896 signed contracts with Salinas Valley growers, tying up as much acreage as possible. Late in the year, when the cost of shipping sugar beets from Castroville to Watsonville for processing exceeded one dollar per ton, Claus Spreckels announced that he would close the Watsonville mill and build a new factory on the banks of the Salinas River. In response, hundreds more Chinese trooped out of Watsonville, this time bound for the new sugar beet plant and the unincorporated community growing up around it, now known appropriately as Spreckels. With growers engaged in the monumental task of converting some nineteen thousand acres of wheat, barley, and oat fields to sugar beets, roughly forty-two men would be needed to plant, cultivate, and harvest for every one man formerly employed in the grain industries. Having anticipated these huge labor requirements, China bosses at the end of 1896 were well positioned and looking forward to the 1897 planting season. But on October 6, when a large contingent of unemployed men came south from San Francisco and Oakland, it became clear that the Chinese would not be the only source of labor in the sugar beet fields of the Salinas Valley.[63]

Arriving with a huge sign on their four-horse wagon exclaiming, "Ho! For Salvation Army Colony," the men settled at Fort Romie, a 519-acre "sugar beet colony enterprise" operated by the Salvation Army near Soledad, at the southern end of the Salinas Valley. Within a few days they began breaking soil and preparing the land for planting. Soon joined by additional settlers, they began erecting cottages and a store, and by June had planted 150 acres of beans, potatoes, and sugar beets. But drought conditions and a faulty irrigation system impeded their progress and in the spring of 1899 many began working in the mammoth, five-story, $2.5 million Spreckels factory. Moving into the company town or relocating to Salinas and commuting to work on the new trolley line, they tended beet machinery, hauled beets, and shoveled beets into the sluice boxes alongside the plant. Hundreds of others became sugar beet contractors or went to work in the fields.[64]

It was not just the mass arrival of unemployed whites that prevented the Chinese from dominating labor in the Salinas Valley and elsewhere. The simple fact was there were not enough of them to take control. At the beginning of the 1899 sugar beet thinning season in the Santa Maria Valley, the Union Sugar Company, having just erected a new factory, could not find enough Chinese. Tacking up posters around town and placing advertisements in local newspapers, the company announced:

> Five hundred men, women, and children wanted to work in the beet fields of the Santa Maria Valley. Men with their families can come and camp in the fields in which they work, where wood and water will be furnished free. The work of thinning beets will begin in about two weeks and extend over a period of possibly three months. Children can earn from 75 cents to $1 per day, and adults from $1 to $1.50 per day. Payments will be made as work progresses. People are required to bring tents, or covered wagons, and camping outfits, on the score of economy. The work is of such a character that any boy or girl over eight years of age can do it. Work can be contracted for by the acre or by the day. Address M. Fleisher & Co., Santa Maria, Cal., sending number of persons that will come, so that places to work can be reserved for them.[65]

Census figures explained why farmers panicked. Most Chinese field hands tabulated in the 1880 census of the Monterey Bay region (Santa Cruz, Monterey, and San Benito counties) were in their twenties; now in 1900 most averaged fifty-seven years of age. In other counties, most Chinese field hands were in their late forties. Along with pioneer farmers like John Bidwell, who died in 1900, Chinese immigrants were growing old, and laws like the Scott Act made them unable to replenish their numbers with younger men. Old Chinese field hands, working in the shadow of the newest, largest, and most advanced sugar beet processing factory in the world, struck newspaper reporters as sadly ironic reminders of a bygone era. "Chinese labor is rapidly becoming scarcer," lamented a writer for the *Watsonville Pajaronian*. "The exclusion act has kept out immigration of young Chinese, and most of those who were in California when the exclusion act was passed have reached an age where they are unable to give a full day's labor."[66]

As the numbers of Chinese field hands continued to decline, sugar beet growers briefly placed their hopes in the hands of a local inventor, Isaac Sutter. Lured by a twenty-five-thousand-dollar prize offered by the German government, Sutter had created a machine that plowed beets, carried them to a cutting device, topped them, and then dropped them in neat rows on the ground. Described by the *Watsonville Register* as "more successful in harvesting beets than any other machine that has come under observation," Sutter's device, according to the newspaper, did as much work in one day as thirty field hands. But while the machine could have become one of the earliest examples of mechanization outside of the wheat industry, it did not have much effect, at least immediately. Locked in a patent dispute, Sutter expended considerable funds and several years defending his rights and, consequently, very few machines were built immediately and very few men replaced.[67]

Aging Chinese who remained in the Pajaro Valley found plenty of work on the berry and vegetable farms, and in newly planted apple orchards that, by 1900, established the Pajaro Valley apple industry on such a sound basis that Watsonville shed its nickname of Sugar City and became known as Apple City. Hundreds of Chinese planted, pruned, irrigated, and applied pesticides during the winter and spring, picked the apple crop in the fall, and after the industry began producing a surplus, found work in huge fruit-drying operations. Stripped to the waist and sweating profusely, the Chinese often worked twelve hours a day processing apples, dominating labor so completely that apple dryers in Watsonville became known as "China Dryers." Chinese workers also made boxes, tended sulfur fires used to cure and dry the apples, regulated the oil, coal, and wood fires in the brick kilns, and removed the dried apples from the kilns and packed them once they had cooled. Because early September apple drying wedged in nicely between various other seasonal industries, many Chinese drifted into town after picking fruit in the Central Valley. Remaining in Watsonville until the last dehydration work finished in December, they then moved north to the salmon canneries of Alaska or west to the Monterey sardine canneries, thus extending their employment well into the winter.[68]

As they diversified their work around Watsonville and followed sugar beet production into the Salinas Valley, the Chinese exerted—despite their declining numbers—a profound impact on several of the state's other agricultural districts. So great was their role washing and sorting oranges in the Fay Packinghouse in Casa Blanca near Riverside that on the night of February 29, 1896, fifteen masked men carrying shotguns rode up to the facility, dismounted, and broke open the packinghouse doors. Discovered cowering behind a stack of packing boxes, a Chinese laborer named Ah Chinn dove through a glass window and raced for the police station. Before the police arrived, the masked riders hauled the seven remaining Chinese from their hiding places, tacked a note on the packinghouse door warning against rehiring any Chinese, and drove their captives to the outskirts of Corona. "Make tracks," they said as they dumped the men beside the road. "We don't ever want to see you in Riverside again." But the threat had little effect either in Riverside or elsewhere in California. When a devastating freeze hit C. P. Adamson's vineyard near Rutherford in the Napa Valley three months later, the Chinese arrived in force, cut out damaged canes and dead bud wood, gathered the cuttings into great piles, burned them, and then spread the ashes under the remaining vines. So dirty and fatiguing was the work, and so easy would it have been to ruin Adamson's vines with careless cuts, that Adamson and neighboring grape growers refused to trust white workers, Indians, or any other group with the task. Two months later, when growers began rooting out tussock tules around Ukiah, the work proved so hot and difficult that only the Chinese would do it. "They'd cut them off and then they'd plow," recalled rancher Chester Bishop, whose father hired Chinese to cook and handle chores about his farm. "All horse power and man power. We'd have a sixteen inch braking plow. Four horses. One guy driving the horses and the other guy holding the plow. They'd turn this land over. They'd have to disk. They'd disk one way and then they'd cross-disk the other way. They'd just chop the land all to pieces . . . Called it the China Field."[69]

As the surplus of unemployed men grew, intensive agriculture, having expanded into a fifty-two-million-dollar industry, turned to them on a massive scale. The process began in mid-June 1897, with the apricot harvest on the Goodyear ranch four miles west of Winters. The ranch had only twenty-two regular Chinese laborers and could not pick and process the fruit fast enough, even working the Chinese from 5:30 A.M. to 6:30 P.M. But by advertising for white pickers, paying them five cents more, and working them only seven hours per day, the ranch managed to hire an additional twenty men from nearby towns, as well as eighty women and children to cut and dry the fruit at seven and a half cents per box. Two months later, hop growers in Wheatland employed a similar technique. Describing the hop harvest as a "veritable picnic," they placed advertisements in the *Sacramento Bee*, *Sacramento Union*, *Wheatland Four Corners*, and other newspapers and attracted a conglomerate force of more than one thousand bindlemen, unemployed teamsters, teenagers on a lark, and families from nearby towns. People arrived in such numbers, in fact, that many had to be turned away; some even clipped ads and applied for work by mail. Paid not by the hour but according to a "sliding piece rate" of eighty cents per one hundred pounds the first week, eighty-five cents the second week, and ninety-five cents the third week, all became efficient workers, since their pay hinged entirely on their productivity. One month later, the labor surplus reached such proportions that Fresno grape growers only had to frequent Courthouse Park, where hundreds of men waited for work. "The men are of all ages, from saucy-looking little 16-year old boys to men of many years, whose hapless look tells of ambitions departed and their resignation to circumstances which have turned them out on the highway during old age," reported the *Fresno Daily Evening Expositor*. "At frequent intervals during the day wagons drive up . . . and load up with twenty or thirty of the eager laborers."[70]

Even after industrial depression ended and full employment returned in 1898 and 1899, growers in their newspaper advertisements described the harvest as if it were a picnic. "We want you now. Come quick! Bring outfit, or board in a private family or hotel," read one advertisement in the *Maywood Colony Advocate*. "100 men, women, boys and girls wanted at Maywood Colony to pick and cut fruit." Testifying before the U.S. Immigration Commission, Wheatland hop magnate E. Clements Horst told an investigator that the goal of the advertising campaign was to play one group off against another. "We get as many white men as we can," he explained, "and fill up with orientals." Piece-rate payment systems made large numbers of unemployed men, as well as local families, women, and children, no matter how inexperienced, into efficient workers. And the use of the "bonus" or "holdback" of ten cents per one hundred pounds of hops picked, or ten cents for every day worked, paid at the end of the harvest, held workers on the job.[71]

Attempts to operate with a mixed labor force did not always function smoothly. Working on Don Duering's vineyard near Larkmead just south of Calistoga in February 1899, whites who had passed out after sharing a big jug of wine at lunch awoke to discover money missing from their wallets. Blaming their Chinese coworkers, they beat them horribly. So common were such assaults in the Napa Valley that, according to the *St. Helena Star*, any mistreated Chinese who dared to speak up could expect to be violently attacked.[72]

୬ୈ

As growers attracted larger numbers of white, Mexican, and black workers, the Chinese declined to about 10 percent of California's 67,493 field hands in 1900. While hundreds of Chinese were no doubt driven out of the fields by sinophobic groups, most of this decline was simply the cumulative result of the 1882 Exclusion Law, the 1888 Scott Act, the 1892 Geary Act, and a 1902 federal law indefinitely extending the Chinese Exclusion Act. So devastating were the effects of twenty years of immigration restriction that, when Pomona citrus grower Fred Palmer in his memoir tried to recall the Chinese after the turn of the century, he could remember just two old irrigators. Huddled in a shack hidden away in the immense orchard owned by neighbor Seth Richards, they went about their business all but forgotten.[73]

From a peak of 75,183 in 1880, the number of Chinese laborers in California fell to 45,753 just twenty years later. Los Angeles County lost more than one thousand Chinese between 1890 and 1900; Alameda County's Chinese population fell from 455 to 360; Colusa County's from 169 to 43; Lake County's from 469 to 82; Santa Clara County's from 763 to 670; Sonoma County's from 202 to 148; Yuba County's from 124 to 25. In the same time period, Stanislaus County lost 44 percent of its Chinese population and San Francisco County 46 percent. Napa County lost half of its Chinese. Happy with the trend, Humboldt County officials boasted it had no Chinese left, "making it a fine place for Americans." Of the Chinese in Orange County, a resident observed: "There were practically none . . . just a few gardeners who have gradually returned to China or have died . . . They seem to be entirely gone."[74]

There were significant exceptions to the pattern of overall decline. Depending on the county, the Chinese still ranged from 4 to 52 percent of the total farm labor force in these years—and in some counties, their numbers actually rose. For example, in Sacramento County, between 1880 and 1900, the numbers of Chinese working in the fields grew from 240 field hands to 1,165. Perhaps reflecting the rapid expansion of agriculture in the San Joaquin Valley, the Chinese there increased both the percentage and absolute numbers of their population engaged in field labor, expanding their numbers in Fresno County from 23 to 403, and in San Joaquin from 471 to 917. But Chinese field hands also increased significantly in Solano County, where they nearly doubled from 240 to 417. Put another way, one of three Chinese in the Sacramento and San Joaquin valleys and one in five in the San Francisco Bay area counties (Napa, Sonoma, Mendocino, Contra Costa, and Santa Clara), still worked as field hands. In Butte, Contra Costa, Fresno, Kern, Placer, Sacramento, San Joaquin, Santa Clara, Sutter, Tehama, and Yuba counties, where the Chinese comprised between 10 and 20 percent of the agricultural labor force, they were the second-largest single group of field hands. The Chinese also remained concentrated in certain crops, for example, nurseries, flower, and seed farms in Santa Clara County, where they outnumbered whites and others until about 1910.[75]

The reasons why the Chinese faded from the scene are numerous and complex, and not always the result of restrictive immigration legislation, the anti-Chinese movement, or the resulting demographic collapse. A resurgence of malaria, for example, certainly contributed to their fate. Common in the mining camps of Gold Rush California, the disease had seemed nearly extinct when it had reappeared in the 1880s east of Sacramento, in the Newcastle District of Placer County, where growers converting the old mining ditches and flumes of the Bear River Ditch system into irrigation canals inadvertently created the kind of swampy environments that bred mosquitoes. During the summer months, great swarms of mosquitoes plagued orchard workers. Newcastle grower-shipper Harry Butler recalled seeing white field hands lying in clumps "with severe chills . . . stricken with the disease." As word got out, whites began to shun the county. To bring in their crops, growers like Butler turned to Chinese labor, claiming—with no evidence— that "Orientals apparently were not susceptible." Working the Placer fruit harvest, many Chinese field hands became infected, and although it is impossible to say how many suffered, there seems little doubt that they paid a heavy price.[76]

Bloody and protracted tong wars also contributed to their demise. Pitting "highbinder" or fighting tongs against one another, tong wars killed and maimed countless Chinese field hands. Unlike the more traditional, service-oriented family and regional tong organizations, fighting tongs were comprised of militantly organized bands of criminals and killers. Fighting tong members vied for control of Chinatown gambling and drug operations, and occasionally labor contracting and its associated businesses. Three of the most violent of these tongs were the San Francisco–based Hop Sing and Suey Sing tongs, which were allied against the third, the Sacramento-based Bing Kong Tong Society. After fighting for years they left behind them a long record of crime, extortion, murder, mayhem, and vendetta.[77]

Although largely confined to urban areas, vendettas often spilled over into the countryside. One such vendetta, in which three were killed and two more badly wounded, was front-page news in the *Fresno Republican* of April and June, 1899. At other times hatchet men or *boo how doy* (salaried soldiers) became so brazen that they marched into stores and approached China bosses openly to demand money. Probably the most sensational vendetta occurred during the spring of 1900, when three Hop Sing and Suey Sing hatchet men—Lee Sing Park, Toy

Yock, and Willie Yee—were sent north to Sonoma County to ferret out and murder Hom Hong, a China boss and highly respected member of the Bing Kong Tong Society. As Hong supervised a crew of six field hands grubbing out weeds on Wilson Finley's hop ranch five miles east of Santa Rosa, the trio of assassins jumped out of a carriage firing their weapons. Hong was shot five times through his head and heart. Turning to the surviving field hands, Park exclaimed: "There's one [bullet] left for anyone who testifies against us." He then threw his weapon into the hop field, and with his cohorts, fled the scene.[78]

The three assassins had nearly made it back to the San Francisco Chinatown when they were apprehended in a police dragnet at the Ferry Building. During the police investigation, a problem developed with the interpreter used in interrogating the men who had witnessed the assassination. Forced to use a local Chinese interpreter, Sheriff Wallace Ware suspected that the man had been contacted by the two offending tongs and was alternating between rewards and threats to keep the men from talking. To uncover the fix, he employed the son of a Christian missionary, fluent in Chinese, who sat in on one interrogation disguised as a county clerk. Overhearing the interpreter's double-dealing, he informed Ware, who bounced the interpreter off the bookcases in his office and immediately secured cooperative testimony from the witnesses at the trial a month alter. Willie Yee was convicted of first degree murder and sentenced to life imprisonment. He drowned himself several months later in a laundry vat at San Quentin Prison. Toy Yock copped a plea of second degree murder. And Lee Sing Park was offered a sentence of manslaughter but refused and was sentenced to life imprisonment. A few years later, Ware encountered Park in prison and asked him why he had not accepted the offer of a manslaughter plea; he was astounded to discover that Park's lawyer, paid ten thousand dollars on the morning of the trial and under orders from a local tong boss, had never conveyed the offer. Park was released from prison following a hearing. Disappearing into the San Francisco Chinatown, he was never seen again.[79]

Murder also took its toll on Chinese field hands. Rural newspapers were full of accounts of Chinese killing one another for reasons that could be but dimly perceived. A typical murder story in a Colusa newspaper described a field hand found murdered in his bunk on a ranch south of town. Who had killed the man, or why, remained a complete mystery. A similar puzzle surrounded a murder on the Laban Scearce ranch, also south of Colusa. Charley Taing, a popular Chinese field hand, confessed to the deed. A petition to commute his punishment signed by hundreds of Colusa county citizens delayed his execution for three years. On January 17, 1880, Taing attempted to hang himself in his cell, only to be cut down at the last moment. He was finally executed by hanging on January 30. But despite being baptized on the morning of his execution (and presumably confessing to a priest), Taing never explained his crime. Other murders, however, followed typical homicide patterns. While in town to gamble and enjoy themselves, Chinese field hands got caught in fights and were stabbed and shot. Or, cooped up on remote ranches, they became exhausted and despondent, and in such circumstances some small affront would touch off a fight. This was apparently the case on May 10, 1890, when the remains of two Chinese field hands named Chung and Toy were discovered at their camp near the Finnel ranch, south of Chico Ferry Landing. "The body of Chung lay across a doorway with his throat cut, nearly severing his head from his body," reported the *Colusa Sun*. "The body of Tay lay on a cot, his throat cut and his skull split open." The men had been caught while chopping wood for a dinner fire. A third member of the camp, Ah Won, was missing and suspected of committing the murders for some reason that the newspaper could not guess.[80]

But the main reason why the Chinese faded from the scene was simply old age. Worn out and crippled by decades of stoop labor, possibly infected with recurrent malaria from their seasons picking fruit in Placer County, some elderly Chinese field hands could not feed or take care of themselves. History texts would later describe these old men as a "bachelor society," but many in fact were married back home. Caught in California, they would have been more properly described as men without families. Confined to rural Chinatowns that had become little more than giant warehouses for aging men, many lonely Chinese field hands lived out their last days in barracks where a reporter for the *San Francisco Chronicle* found them—"plenty of old, worn out, bent, diseased and discouraged Chinese farm laborers." Those men, it was said, were crippled by their years stooping and sweating and working in the fields. "We worked like mules," they were fond of saying. Those who lived alone in the back room of a store or some shack or cottage often died with neither family nor friends to comfort them. Sometimes their bodies lay for days before being discovered.[81]

As the bodies piled up, reporters spared no details. Obituaries sometimes read like mystery stories. One account in the September 25, 1896, *St. Helena Star* described how:

> Lee Jim, a Chinaman working on the Hitchcock place north of St. Helena, was found dead in his room. He was found in a terribly decomposed state, having evidently been dead four or five days. The coroner was at once notified and Wednesday morning an inquest was held on the premises. Phillip Lonney, who works on an adjoining farm was the only witness. He testified that he went to Lee Jim's cabin Tuesday to get him to assist him with some work but could not find him about the place so he came to town and inquired among the Chinese to learn of his whereabouts. No one knew anything about him so he went to Mr. Cole's place and with that gentleman went to Lee Jim's cabin and finding the door locked forced an entrance through a window into the kitchen, back of which was the Chinaman's room. Again they were compelled to force their way in and upon getting the door open found him lying dead on the bed. The jury returned a verdict of death from natural causes. Lee Jim was 57 years old.[82]

Sacramento–San Joaquin Delta Chinese hung on the longest. Unlike most farming districts, which catered to a single crop, the delta offered such a wide variety of crops that Chinese men could work, within a twenty-mile radius, in potato, asparagus, onion, and bean fields, on hay and grain farms, in orchards and vineyards, and even in truck gardens. They could weed fields in March, irrigate them in April and May, harvest cherries, peaches, pears, grapes, and apricots from

June until October, and fill in the winter months by pruning fruit trees and grapevines, repairing ladders, or working as levee repairmen for the Pierson Reclamation District.[83]

Blessed with ample work, Chinese field hands transformed parts of the delta into old-world enclaves even as they were declining in every other agricultural district in the state. This is why Chinese populations in San Joaquin and Contra Costa counties, portions of which bordered the delta, increased significantly after 1900. Packing into a half-dozen "wooden communities" (so named because of their wooden shingle and lap-board construction) along the Sacramento River between Walnut Grove and Rio Vista, Chinese field hands lived in bunkhouses where fifty cents a day bought a bed and meal; five dollars a month rented a small room with two beds and a stove. Local merchants acting as labor bosses provided credit, allowing men to postpone payment until they received their paychecks. "All kinds of Chinese help for farmwork can be secured on short notice by applying to or addressing Toy Goon, Hop Lee Jan, Front Street, Rio Vista, Calif.," read a typical advertisement.[84]

In Tulare Township, which served as shipping center for the town of Tracy, Chinese field hands worked for their countrymen in massive truck gardening enterprises. Elsewhere, they banded together in syndicates, hiring themselves out directly to growers or moving in from Stockton for one or another of the harvests. While they worked on Mildred Island in San Joaquin County, Sherman Island in Sacramento County, and Byron Tract and Union Island in Contra Costa County, they lived in camps that mirrored fully outfitted towns, ate in comfortable dining tents, were fed by a professional staff of cooks, and used a full complement of farm animals and implements. But once their assignments were completed, the men moved on to a different island or back to one of the wooden communities. A few English-speaking Chinese foremen always remained behind to watch over the camps, earning for their lonely work between four hundred and six hundred dollars a year. Because of their relatively high income and stability, these men were among the few Chinese who married. Able to establish families, they frequently provided living quarters not only for their wives and children, but also for other farm laborers in extended family arrangements.[85]

Of all the Chinese field hands in the Sacramento Delta, probably none survived as long or established themselves more successfully than those from Zhongshan district of China. For two generations they had lived in Walnut Grove, side by side (though not very happily) with Sze Yup Chinese. Retaining their original dialects and only rarely mingling, the two groups even pursued different occupations, Zhongshan specializing primarily in orchard work in the northern delta, while the Sze Yup worked row crops in the reclaimed swamps around Rio Vista to the south. Their differences would eventually come to a head.[86]

In 1924, a Zhongshan merchant built a one-story store and saloon beside an asparagus and celery packing shed on the wharf just north of Walnut Grove. Soon thereafter two other Zhongshan merchants erected a gambling parlor and boardinghouse next to the store and saloon. After the Chinese section of Walnut Grove burned down the following year, Zhongshan Chinese decided to separate from their Sze Yup brethren. When their leader, Lee Bing, along with six other

Chinese businessmen, financed construction of a restaurant, second boarding-house, dry goods store, two additional gambling halls, and a town hall, two hundred Zhongshan field hands packed up and moved out of Walnut Grove, settling a mile upstream at the new site. At first they called their settlement Lockeport, after Sacramento merchant and pear grower George Locke, whose heirs owned the town site and leased it to the Chinese. But they could not properly pronounce Lockeport, which usually came out as "Lakpo." So they shortened it to Locke, or as they said, "Lockee."[87]

After becoming established, Zhongshan Chinese in Locke wasted no time protecting their town. To prevent fires, they immediately hired a night watchman known as a *bok bok*. Walking the streets and yards, he signaled that all was well by knocking a stick against a wooden box every half hour. Secure among their own kind, the original Walnut Grove Zhongshan were soon joined by a semipermanent migrant labor force of another two hundred Chinese who arrived from other areas in the delta. During the fruit harvest, as many as fifteen hundred Zhongshan and other Chinese field hands would crowd into Locke. To meet their needs, merchants embarked on a building boom, adding bunkhouses, restaurants, houses of prostitution, a hotel, bakery, barbershop, candy store, flour mill, and slaughterhouse. From these beginnings, an all-Chinese community emerged. Visiting Locke in the 1920s, a Baptist missionary was amazed. "This looks like China," he later wrote. "It sounds like China. It smells like China. And it is China."[88]

Chinese cannery workers also survived long and well in the delta. Like field hands, they found plenty of work and, in contrast to the way they were treated elsewhere in the state, they were not relegated to only the worst jobs. Instead, they handled "floor work," cooked fruit or vegetables in huge vats, carted canned products to warehouses, and wielded heavy equipment, tasks normally reserved for white men. They also pitted, cut, pared, and sorted fruit, jobs traditionally delegated to white women. Of course, they also did traditional "China work"—soldering tin cans ("tinning") and cleaning up around the canneries—but of all that Chinese cannery workers did, nothing quite matched the regimented labor they performed in the big asparagus processing plants. At the Isleton cannery, for example, Chinese laborers worked with an efficiency unmatched anywhere else in California or the United States. Employed year-round, sometimes on a piece-rate basis, sometimes by the hour, Chinese cannery workers in the delta earned relatively high wages of about $2.50 a day—occasionally as much as $4—compared to $1 to $1.67 elsewhere. As a result, they were considerably wealthier than most other agricultural workers, and were also able to settle in relatively stable communities; some even married and raised families.[89]

෴

During their years in the California fields, Chinese laborers faced down prejudice, pestilence, and protest with hard work and loyalty. They were routinely abused by citizens and their fellow countrymen alike, yet still they came in search of the prosperity that eluded them in their homeland. And ultimately—ironically—what sealed their fate was a misguided attempt to help them.

For two generations, Chinese immigrants had always been detained upon arrival in California in a dark, cramped, two-story shed at the Pacific Mail Steamship Company wharf in San Francisco. As many as four hundred to five hundred Chinese would be packed into the shed at any given time, where they waited for inspectors to examine them and evaluate their claims. Sometimes it took as long as six months to complete the process. "No matter how comfortable he is made in the shed," wrote a group of San Francisco Chinese merchants, "he is virtually a prisoner and more or less deprived of exercise and liberty of action." As a result of these and other ongoing complaints, the immigration service in 1910 constructed a new, escape-proof, isolated processing center on Angel Island in San Francisco Bay.[90]

For field hands attempting to immigrate under guise of forged papers, this was a disaster. Intercepted by immigration officials climbing on board their ships, those with well-forged documents proceeded ashore. But the remainder were transferred to a small steamer and ferried to the new facility. Although this was meant to make the waiting period more tolerable, Angel Island became a kind of Ellis Island of the West Coast—a place where dreams could be shattered before they could even begin. As part of a new screening process, immigration officials now boarded boats before they docked to review travel documents. Those with legitimate (or well-forged) papers were allowed to proceed ashore. Everyone else was transferred to a small steamer and ferried to Angel Island. There, they were given medical exams and fumigated, and those afflicted with common parasitic diseases like trachoma, hookworm, and liver fluke were immediately separated out to be sent back to China. Field hands sentenced to deportation for illegal immigration from Mexico, Canada, or Hawaii were also held at Angel Island until transport could be arranged.

Those who passed their physical were packed into locked and guarded detention barracks to await their immigration hearing. At any given time, between two hundred and three hundred men, and thirty to fifty women, were detained on the island. To prevent men from being coached before their hearing, none was allowed visitors, and all had their packages routinely inspected. With only small, fenced, outdoor recreation areas for sunlight and fresh air and a weekly, supervised trip to the island storehouse to select needed items from their baggage, the detainees were completely isolated inside their second-floor barracks. Doors were kept locked, and a barbed wire fence surrounded the enclosure, preventing anyone from escaping.[91]

Languishing in their bunks and spending their waking hours daydreaming and worrying about their plight as they waited up to two years, some field hands reached their limits and went insane; others committed suicide. Many vented their anger, frustration, and desperation by carving hundreds of poems on the detention center's walls. Undated and unsigned for fear of retribution, their poems were vivid impressions of their voyage to California, their longing for their families back home, their outrage and humiliation at the treatment accorded them upon arrival, and their utter failure to make it onto the farms of California.[92]

Anger, loneliness, frustration, bitterness, homesickness, and disappointment were recurring themes in their poems. Vivid metaphors about braving waves big as mountains and encountering laws harsh as tigers studded many poems. Others recalled parents and the moment of departure, their inability to sleep, and the tears that constantly welled up inside them. Many prayed merely to return to China to become a farmer again. Expressing his sense of helplessness, one fifteen-year-old immigrant wrote of his cramped quarters:

I, a seven foot man, am ashamed I cannot extend myself.
Curled up in an enclosure, my movements are dictated by others.
Enduring a hundred humiliations, I can only cry in vain.
This person's tears fall, but what can the blue heavens do?[93]

As word of the ordeal trickled back to China and the effects of immigration restriction unfolded, fewer and fewer men attempted to make the trip. With the Chinese declining in numbers and their Chinatowns burning, growers became nostalgic, profusely eulogizing the Chinese as perfect field hands—men who were available in large numbers, who lived on rice, slept under the stars, never complained, toiled like pack animals, and disappeared once their work was completed. Many wondered if their advertising campaign could ever fill the labor void caused by the declining Chinese. "We have degraded a certain class of labor," explained H. P. Stabler to his fellow fruit growers, "and there is not a man who lives in any agricultural locality who wants to get in and do this work." Other growers posed the same proposition. "Americans can not go out in the hot sun and stoop over the vines all day when the thermometer is probably 115 degrees in the shade," asserted one grower. "Our American sons won't do that." Another put the matter this way: "The young men in the East have . . . not been used to being taken out into a field and told 'There is your bed, twenty acres of it'. . . . They will not go into a twenty-acre field with the hogs."

As the labor situation worsened, growers reiterated the same question, and answered it the same way: "Will the white people do the work? Anyone with experience knows that they will not."

This invariably led to another question: "Where will we find the workers to harvest the crops?" The answer was nearer at hand than most realized.[94]

FIGURE 36. Japanese crew, Leffingwell ranch bunkhouse, ca. 1913. Courtesy of the Huntington Library, San Marino, California.

寄贈　　　北米合衆國加州ロースアンゼルス郡ホエッテヤ　近藤氏ノキヤンプ
　　　千九百十一年四月撮影　　　　　　　　　　　長川寫眞師

BOOK FIVE

Japanese Farmworkers

You asked a Chinaman about a Japanese, and
they cussed and they said 'They're no good this
and that, dirty and all that.' You asked a Japanese
about a Chinaman, and the Japanese laughed.
    —*Luke Cikuth*

We piled them up in those days. There would
be about twenty-five or thirty Japs in a house
about twelve by thirty feet.
    —*George Moore*

There comes a sudden threat of rain in the
drying season, and the [raisin] trays must be
stacked at once or the crop will be irreparably
[damaged]. Instantly the costs of Japanese labor
rises to blackmail prices, regardless of previous
contracts.
    —*Fresno fruit grower*

If a man hired twenty Japs . . . for a certain
price, and his next door neighbor offered them
ten cents a day on the day they were to report,
he would get them. Contracts meant nothing
to them. So they got the reputation of being
unreliable and tricky; contract breaking meant
nothing to them.
    —*Ben Walker*

The Japanese have been plentiful . . . and they
are unreliable. They are apt to strike or to jump
a job when most needed.
    —*'Watsonville Pajaronian'*

They are cunning—even tricky. They have no
scruples. . . . They are clannish and have such
a complete understanding among themselves
that they can act promptly and in unison in
an emergency.
    —*G. H. Hecke*

CHAPTER SEVENTEEN

Running from Vine to Vine

Japanese Farmworkers and the

Beginning of Labor Militancy

On his way from British Columbia to Texas in 1907 to collect information for a series on the Japanese in the United States, *Collier's Magazine* West Coast correspondent Will Irwin sat on a bench in the shade and jotted down notes as Japanese field hands arrived in Fresno for the grape harvest. "They tumbled by scores from every train," he wrote, "little, clean, chattering boys, carrying their worldly goods in straw telescope hats." Hardly any appeared to be more than twenty-one years old. "In face and manner," Irwin continued, "they gave the impression of the adventurous, wandering, eager youths that they are." All Friday night and into Saturday, Irwin watched as they clogged the sidewalks, halted traffic, and assembled in long lines to board wagons at the loading docks. Not until Sunday morning did their numbers diminish. Burdened with provisions, grape trays, and blankets, the last of them pulled out that afternoon. "By Monday morning," concluded Irwin, "the . . . vineyards . . . about Fresno were polka-dotted with the straw hats of Japanese pickers."[1]

When the first handful of Japanese immigrants made their way to Fresno in 1890, they were turned away by hostile white men. But the following year, about thirty settled into a ten-block-long neighborhood of brick buildings near Chinatown. By picking the fall and winter citrus crop in Tulare County, traveling to Salinas and Oxnard to thin and harvest sugar beets during the spring and early summer, and filling in the winter with odd jobs and domestic work, they quickly achieved relatively stable year-round employment. As more of them settled in Fresno in the years that followed, they established a thriving Little Tokyo. About one thousand worked in the 1897 raisin harvest; their numbers grew to about four thousand in 1900, and over five thousand in 1902. Only about half of these workers resided near Fresno, with the remainder traveling from as far away as Los Angeles, Sacramento, and San Francisco. But together, Japanese locals and outsiders comprised more than half of the raisin harvest labor force by 1900, and they al-

FIGURE 37. Japanese field hands arriving in the orchards on bicycles, ca. 1912, Los Angeles. Courtesy of the Huntington Library, San Marino, California.

lowed Japanese bosses to divide up the vineyards into districts and push aside Greek, Armenian, Portuguese, and Chinese field hands.[2]

Working with astonishing speed, the Japanese quickly earned a reputation as men who, according to Fresno farmwife Mrs. G. W. Aiken, would "come bright and early, and work like Trojans, running from vine to vine, scarcely taking a breath." So dominant, efficient, and attentive to "living up to their contracts" were the Japanese that Sun Maid Raisin Growers Association secretary Frank Smith considered them "a necessity" and did "an immense amount of business through the Japanese." Acknowledging that without them, the raisin industry would wither and die on the vine, Smith and others were so dependent on the Japanese that, in 1899, the *Fresno Morning Republican* wrote that the Japanese had raisin growers "on the hip."[3]

Technological innovation contributed to Japanese success. Long hindered by the tedious process of removing seeds from Muscat raisins by hand, growers in 1896 perfected a "seeder" that moved raisins between two large rolling pins. Placed side by side, one roller flattened the raisins and pressed the seeds to the surface while the other brushed them away. As important to the modernization of the raisin industry as the cotton gin was to that industry, the raisin seeder eliminated the need for careful packing and cosmetic presentation. Now, seeded Muscat raisins could be packed in bulk in twelve-ounce cartons, much like raisins made from Thompson Seedless grapes. This change would have important consequences not only for marketing and packing, but also for vineyard labor. Careful handling during the harvest and drying process had previously been the rule for Muscats, as laborers were exhorted to preserve whole grape clusters. With the seeder, this was no longer necessary and mass production techniques could be applied. Whereas growers had previously paid by the hour to ensure careful handling, now they could pay by the piece rate. By 1900, they had almost completely abandoned wage payment. Capitalizing on the incentive to push themselves, Japanese harvesters who were paid from two and a half to five cents a tray earned three or four dollars a day. Increased productivity more than compensated for higher pay. Harvesting an average of 1.3 acres of grapes daily in 1890, Japanese harvest crews pushed output to three acres in 1902, and a phenomenal eight acres in 1908.[4]

What the Japanese did in the vineyards around Fresno differed little from what they accomplished in other crops and other agricultural districts throughout California. At the height of their power and influence in 1909, about thirty thousand Japanese worked on farms in the state and accounted for about 42 percent of the farm labor force. Although they never constituted a majority of the field hands, they nonetheless held commanding leverage in certain areas. They were at least half of the farm labor force in eleven prime agricultural counties (Alameda, Fresno, Kings, Monterey, Orange, San Benito, San Joaquin, San Luis Obispo, Santa Barbara, Santa Cruz, and Tulare), and dominated field labor around the towns of Vacaville, Watsonville, Oxnard, Walnut Grove, Florin, Fresno, and Santa Paula. They also dominated agricultural labor on farms over 360 acres. Most important, the Japanese monopolized labor in certain key crops, comprising eight of ten sugar beet workers, nine of ten berry pickers, six of ten grape pickers, half of all vegetable cutters, and nearly all of the state's asparagus workers and nursery tenders.[5]

By their numbers, the Japanese forced a reconfiguration of the agricultural labor market from its earlier two- and three-tiered structure—with Indians on the bottom, Chinese occupying a middle position, and whites on top—to a four-tiered structure dominated by the Japanese. This increased complexity impeded class cooperation and created independent farm labor markets, each insulated from one another. Certain regions and certain jobs remained off limits to the Japanese, who made up only seven of every one hundred field hands on grain farms, for example, and held down virtually no positions on dairy farms. Nor did they ever find much work as teamsters, plowmen, or cultivators using teams of horses. White field hands, who were considered to be more "adaptable" and "skilled," continued to dominate these segments of agricultural labor.[6]

Filling the labor void left by the dwindling numbers of Chinese, the Japanese allowed California agriculture to continue expanding, unimpeded by labor shortages. But the transition from one Asian workforce to another was neither smooth nor simple. Initially greeted by growers as another easily manipulated racial minority, the Japanese quickly dispelled that notion, breaking sensationally with the past by picking up on the brief flurry of Chinese militancy in the 1890s. Japanese field hands were the first to initiate and secure collective bargaining agreements systematically on a widespread basis, the first to establish functioning ethnic labor unions, and the first to be condemned by growers. Assertive, ambitious, and upwardly mobile, they capitalized on their solidarity, demanded and broke contracts, altered and improved working conditions, boycotted and confronted growers, engaged in organized slowdowns, withheld labor at key planting times, walked out during harvests, participated in interracial strikes, set minimum wages, and initiated the first efforts at large-scale farm labor organization. Prevailing opinion of them in the radical press of the time was that they were formidable opponents. According to one organizer, Japanese field hands would "work . . . until all idle labor is out of the field, then just when the crop is ripest, when the work must be done, they walk out, making demands for better wages, or shorter hours."[7]

To Japanese farmworkers, agricultural labor was not something to be accepted but rather a rung on the agricultural ladder. And direct action and ethnic solidarity were the means to climb that ladder.

છે

Before immigrating, most Japanese field hands, like their Chinese counterparts, had lived in rural hamlets and worked as part of a highly labor-intensive, small-scale farming system. During the Meiji era (1868–1912), this stable peasant society began to unwind when the imposition of a land tax designed to finance the government undermined traditional communal patterns in favor of private property rights, nearly doubled the number of tenant farmers, and threw rural society into a state of extreme flux. At the same time, village populations exploded, life expectancy rose, living costs skyrocketed, and living standards declined. When market fluctuations, poor harvests, and natural disasters occurred, peasant families lost everything; many were forced to mortgage or sell their property to pay their debts and taxes. By the 1890s, some three hundred thousand men had joined the ranks of propertyless laborers. Heading to the cities in search of work, they became rickshaw men, longshoremen, even pirates. Considered the lowest stratum of unskilled labor, their remittances to families in their home villages nonetheless moderated the distress in the countryside and saved their mothers and fathers from starvation.[8]

Soon, inspired by tales of those who had found plentiful work abroad, peasants were seized by an emigration *netsu* (fever). With thirty thousand contract laborers in Hawaii and a small contingent establishing a silk farm as early as 1869 in California, men listened intently to news of those who had left. After 1885, when the Japanese government began to allow citizens to emigrate legally, peasants hearing fantastic reports of men earning two dollars a day in Hawaii and California could not stay put. Adventurous firstborn sons, not yet responsible for the care of their elderly parents and accustomed to earning the equivalent of fourteen cents per day, begged their parents to sell off their possessions, mortgage their property, scrape together whatever funds they could muster, and book them ocean passage. Those unable to raise the forty-five dollars required for third-class ship fare and another thirty dollars for expenses once they arrived, sought help from one of two sources: mutual credit associations in their home villages, which pooled funds to aid one member; or moneylenders in the cities, who loaned money to entire groups. Excluded from inheritance by virtue of their unlucky birth order, resolute second- and third-born sons—as well as those subject to military conscription—also sought opportunities outside their native villages. Men would later tell investigators that they left for California believing that it "was a large country . . . the best place . . . to succeed."[9]

Few Japanese sought religious or political freedom or had any desire to become Americans. Known as *dekaseginin* (sojourners and "birds of passage"), only about eight of one hundred who became field hands ever intended to remain abroad permanently. Much like the Croats, Slovaks, Serbs, Poles, and Italians who were moving into the steel mills in the eastern United States at this time, and the Chinese before them, Japanese immigrants saw their adventure as temporary. They would stay a few years—long enough to save money and buy land back home, care for aged parents, and restore lost social position—and one day return in triumph to their home villages. Also like the Chinese, but not European immigrants, most came alone. Twenty-seven of thirty Japanese immigrants during the peak years of immigration were men, roughly two out of three were single men, and half were under twenty-five years of age.[10]

For every Japanese field hand, the long sea journey was an ordeal not easily forgotten. One Issei, as first-generation immigrants were known, told an interviewer how he had been "packed into the ship in one big room . . . with no privacy, no comforts, no nothing," not even a trip above deck during the two-week passage. "We were like silkworms on a tray, eating and sleeping and wondering what the future held for us." The *San Francisco Call* in June 1902, described a ship named the *Potter* unloading one cargo of 24,494 sacks of sugar and another of several hundred Japanese who perched together on top of those sacks "much in the fashion cattle are imported only with less regard to the health and comfort of the Japs." Crowded bunks, ill-smelling decks, foul washrooms, continual noise, poor ventilation, stale air, fumigation daily by smoking peppers "for sanitary reasons," open toilets (consisting of planks suspended over the rear deck), and miserable and meager rice meals dealt out from huge kettles into dirty tin cups or bamboo plates compounded the misery of steerage.[11]

By the time they reached port, many Japanese field hands were ill and disoriented. Walking down the gangplanks and stepping onto the docks with purple passports, overflowing anxiety, and dreams of big wages, they were shocked and overwhelmed by what they encountered. None of their previous experiences had prepared them for the Customs Wharf, where they were separated into dozens of lines, examined by doctors, and questioned by inspectors. If they managed to avoid detention for some misstatement or quarantine for some suspected disease, they then made their way into San Francisco. "I shall never forget how depressed my heart became as I trudged through those littered streets, with rows of pushcarts . . . and the deafening noise," one field hand later told an interviewer for the Survey of Race Relations. "This was the boasted American freedom and opportunity."[12]

Upon leaving the Customs Wharf, Japanese immigrants found waiting for them not only a strange and hostile environment, but also the friendlier faces of Japanese immigration agents and representatives of various prefecture organizations. A welcome sight after the misery and uncertainty of the voyage, these representatives often mediated between the new arrivals and immigration officials. As immigration became more routine, Japanese community leaders began checking steerage conditions, publishing Japanese-language newspapers, and providing reliable information on various aspects of immigration and employment. They also circulated pamphlets explaining immigration laws and offering homely advice on proper behavior to laborers in California. One of the most popular pamphlets, *Manga Yonin Shosei* (The four students' comic), was a 112-page bilingual hardbound publication by Henry Yoshitaka that used cartoons to depict and explain problems that laborers frequently encountered. Largely autobiographical, it traced the sometimes hilarious story of Kiyama and three of his friends after they arrived in California in 1904.[13]

No such coaching books guided the initial contingent of Japanese field hands: four indigent *hinsei* (student-laborers) from Wakayama prefecture and two nurserymen who arrived in California during the winter of 1887–88. The four *hinsei* rode a river steamer fifty miles into the delta, disembarked at Rio Vista, and settled on the G. W. Thissell and Brinck brothers' ranches near Winters. The Winters fruit district needed men who could pick cherries in April; apricots and peaches in May; plums, pears, and grapes in June; and later varieties of fruit, grapes, and pears into November. Able to put down roots and work continuously during the fall and winter on hundreds of small local farms, the men did not have to migrate to other areas during slack periods. The two nurserymen, meanwhile, headed south to tend thousands of fruit trees and grapevines on the Grover Company's large nursery along Porter Gulch in the Santa Cruz Mountains. The ease with which these two groups of men found steady work and established themselves as members of the larger society soon inspired countless men back home to immigrate.[14]

When sixty Japanese immigrants picked fruit in the Suisun Valley of Solano County and several hundred others began working on land-clearing projects in the Sacramento Valley in 1889, Naotaro Yoneda, a merchant who had immigrated the previous year, saw an opportunity and opened a boardinghouse and trading center on the banks of the Sacramento River at a place soon dubbed Yoneda Landing. In 1890, as the Japanese worked their way into the Fresno vineyard district, a group of thirty laborers found lodging in Vacaville, where they earned one dollar a day. Another group sailed north by boat to Cuttings Wharf, moved into the Sonoma Valley, and became the nucleus for one of the first and largest concentrations of Japanese field hands in California.[15]

Chinese field hands did not greet these first Japanese with open arms. On June 24, 1890, the two groups clashed on the S. D. Bristow ranch near Vacaville. Accused by the Chinese of breaking a large fruit tree limb, a Japanese field hand took offense, and after pointing out the guilty Chinese, exploded in anger. "A brief wordy war took place, until the Jap could restrain himself no longer, but sailed into the Celestials a la Melican man [*sic*], and as the eight came at him, he sent them to grass with all the ease of [John L.] Sullivan. Three of them were so badly used up Wednesday morning that they were unable to work. Good for the Jap," reported the *Vacaville Reporter*. "You asked a Chinaman about a Japanese," recalled one apple grower of these first contacts, "and they cussed and they said, 'They're no good this and that, dirty and all that.' You asked a Japanese about a Chinaman, and the Japanese laughed . . . They didn't pay any attention to them anyway."[16]

Over the next two years, as more Japanese laborers arrived, made contact with those who had preceded them, and went to work, headlines breathlessly announced their arrival: "Japanese Rapidly Supplanting Chinese," shouted the *Sacramento Bee* on May 20, 1891. "They are more Tractable and Find Life Luxurious on a Dollar a Day." Eight days later, the *Vacaville Reporter* described a workforce of 150 white men and women, Japanese, and Chinese, picking cherries in W. W. Smith's orchard. Although such early accounts invariably stressed their diligent work habits, the Japanese quickly shattered the prevailing illusion that they were stamped from the same mold as the Chinese. When an acute labor shortage developed in Pleasants Valley in June 1891, the Japanese struck for higher wages, demanded a raise from $1 to $1.15 per day, and brought the Chinese out with them; the action threw the entire Vacaville fruit district into turmoil. Eventually, white strikebreakers from Sacramento moved in, but not before growers lost considerable quantities of fruit, fired all of the Japanese, and replaced them with white pickers.[17]

Growers learned no lesson from the strike, and by late summer of 1891, the Japanese had spread farther east and north, finding jobs picking peaches in the Newcastle fruit district and pears in the orchards near Marysville and Biggs. Working alongside Paiute Indians, white families, and a few Chinese in the Lovdal brothers hop yards near Sacramento that August, they won the praise of hop magnate Daniel Flint. Speaking to a reporter, Flint pronounced himself, "very well satisfied with the Japanese experiment." He particularly liked the way the Japanese carried the correct "housekeeping utensils" and their tendency to "herd together." Similarly pleased, another grower noted, "As the Exclusion Act crowds out the Chinese, the Japs seem to come in and take their places."[18]

Early in 1892, something happened in Watsonville that would have monumental significance for the Japanese of California. That spring, about a dozen Japanese headed south from San Francisco to cut and clear trees for a land reclamation project on the Sawmill Ranch near the Pajaro River. Their leader, fifty-seven-year-old Sakukō Kimura, was a somewhat mysterious, bilingual labor contractor, or *keiyaku-nin*. Immigrants were not completely unfamiliar with men of his kind. In Japan, bands of field hands led by similar headmen had been roaming the countryside for decades, selling their labor to the highest bidder.

Kimura was a masterful organizer, so adept at directing labor that, toward the end of the year, a number of growers asked him to bring in more field hands. Soon his Pajaro Valley bunkhouse became a general rendezvous point and labor agency where growers needing extra help, farmers needing firewood cutters, and tanners looking for tanbark choppers all hired men. Wisely moving operations to Watsonville, Kimura rented a house, named it the Tao, and created a kind of club. For an annual fee of three dollars, unemployed field hands could bunk there and cook their meals during the winter, although they had to provide their own bedding. So successful were field hands under Kimura that, within a year, about 250 of them were using his facilities, each paying him five cents out of every dollar they earned to provide jobs and housing. Since the five-cent commission constituted Kimura's only salary, he soon realized that it was to his advantage to solicit work for his men and eliminate periods of unemployment. Kimura soon began underbidding everyone and supplying ever larger numbers of Japanese laborers to farmers around Watsonville. Contracting to grow and harvest sugar beets for seventy-five cents a ton compared to the usual rate of $1.20 offered by the Chinese, Kimura quickly struck a deal. In a move that foreshadowed later developments, Kimura soon raised his price to one dollar a ton.[19]

Besides jobs and housing, Kimura also provided for mutual help in case of sickness, injury, or death. Whenever a member of the club died, everyone was required to contribute a fifty-cent assessment toward the funeral fund. After deducting funeral expenses, any surplus was then sent to the parents of the deceased field hand. Witnessing more than two hundred men and women join the funeral procession of one club member, Stanford University historian Yamato Ichihashi observed that "certainly it was a funeral more than a farm laborer could ever expect to have." According to the Japanese newspapers, contributions typically totaled more than two hundred dollars, with a surplus of one hundred dollars—suggesting that at least four hundred men belonged to the club.[20]

When the advantages of the arrangement became apparent, three more keiyaku-nin appeared on the scene and organized clubs of their own—the Higashi, the Hirabayashi, and the Matsuaka. Patterned on Kimura's Tao, they had a total membership of 390 and, along with the Tao, dominated farm labor around Watsonville. With 640 of 750 Japanese field hands in the Watsonville area belonging to one of these clubs, the keiyaku-nin found that they could easily set wage rates. Even during the busy berry and apple picking season between April and November, when hundreds of Japanese flooded into the area from San Francisco and doubled the Japanese population, keiyaku-nin still controlled more than half of the field hands around Watsonville. This meant that they were able to set wages at $1.50 per ten hours of work during the harvest season and $1.25 at other times. But their ambition did not stop there.[21]

Moving into sugar beet contracting, an area long dominated by the Chinese, keiyaku-nin expanded their power by developing an intelligence service, querying growers, analyzing and forecasting labor requirements in the surrounding agricultural districts, and devising ways to keep their men constantly employed. This earned their men steady work and more income, but also increased their expenses. By 1899, men paid annual club dues of five dollars. Under this system, observed the Watsonville Pajaronian, Japanese field hands made a "steady encroachment" on positions formerly dominated by the Chinese.[22]

৪৯

Soon, inspired by the success of the Watsonville clubs, dozens of Japanese students, brothel owners, and even former foreign service officers (working out of the Tokyo Club and boardinghouses in Sacramento, Vacaville, Fresno, and other towns) became keiyaku-nin. Part of a much larger labor contracting system that sent men into jobs throughout the American West, keiyaku-nin seemed to reincarnate all the best qualities of the China boss. At the mere threat of rain or frost or early ripening of fruit, all a grower had to do was send a foreman to town or to the nearest Japanese camp. Immediately the required number of men arrived and went about their jobs with the speed and efficiency of an army platoon deploying for action. Shouldering all responsibilities for recruiting, paying, and supervising field hands, *keiyaku-nin* also handled transportation, feeding, and housing. After the harvest was over, a grower merely paid the contract price. With that, the *keiyaku-nin* rounded up their men and moved them along to the next job. "These bosses were miniature godfathers," wrote David Mas Masumoto in his recollection of Japanese life in Del Rey. "They took care of the workers and their families, located housing and employment, advised and educated naive immigrants about the ways of California agriculture."[23]

All that was required to get started as a *keiyaku-nin* was a working knowledge of farming, some contacts with growers, reasonable fluency in English, and connections with immigration agents and boardinghouse operators. By the summer of 1892, *keiyaku-nin* were also running crews in Solano County, where growers praised the convenience of contracting their labor needs to them for the entire season. "Japanese labor is taking the place of Chinese in this section," reported the July 16 *Vacaville Reporter*. "It is said to be more reliable and more intelligent. The Japanese are the 'Yankees of the East' and look down upon their celestial neighbors." A year later, *keiyaku-nin* moved into the Colusa County orchards, the hay fields around Florin, and the hop yards near Wheatland. Watching them work alongside the Chinese, reporters described the Japanese as younger, quicker, and more agile.[24]

For most Japanese immigrants, labor contracting was a purely economic venture, the quickest path to what they really wanted: property ownership. Arriving in California at the rate of fourteen hundred a year, Japanese immigrants fell into the embrace of the *keiyaku-nin* through an extremely well-organized system. At the heart of the arrangement were boardinghouse operators and immigration agents who rounded up the newcomers at the docks, fed them box lunches of rice balls and dried plums, and provided a place to rest, charging about thirty cents a day for their services. Often men arrived with the business card and address of a particular boardinghouse operator who catered to immigrants from their district. Once the men had settled in, the boardinghouse operators loaded them onto boats and rail cars and, in exchange for a finder's fee or commission, funneled them off to work under *keiyaku-nin*. At the height of their power and influence, *keiyaku-nin* employed about thirteen thousand railroad section hands; twenty-two hundred sawmill workers in Oregon and Washington; another thirty-six hundred salmon canners in Alaska, Oregon, and Washington; and several thousand miners and steelworkers scattered between Utah, Wyoming, and Colorado. But by far their greatest influence was on farms throughout California.[25]

Japanese immigrants had no real options other than to follow the *keiyaku-nin*. Few spoke English or understood American labor practices, so they needed an intermediary simply to survive. Required to honor their obligations, they had limited options once they arrived. During their first three or four years of employment, most immigrants readily agreed to split their wages, paying 40 percent of their net income to the *keiyaku-nin*, who remitted the money along to the appropriate backers; the remaining 60 percent was spent on food, lodging, transportation, and employment fees. Eventually, after settling their debts, men would be free to toil as they pleased—at least in theory. They might then shift between cannery work in the fall, domestic work in winter, and harvest work in the summer, with perhaps a stint here and there as a sawmill worker or railroad section hand. But in reality, wherever they went and whatever they did, Japanese laborers could not escape the *keiyaku-nin*. Few found work without them.[26]

Described by the *Sacramento Bee* as efficient, ambitious, "cleanly, [*sic*] amiable, and industrious, having many virtues and few vices," Japanese immigrants initially established a reputation as reliable laborers—people who "stayed on the jobs" and "bucked up" under the most intolerable conditions. Predictably, they were often compared to other groups, particularly the Chinese, over whom they seemed to present numerous advantages. One was their supposed speed, particularly as fruit packers. "The Japanese are fast," recalled one Santa Cruz fruit grower. "The Japanese are faster than even white men. Yes, I used to have four Japanese workmen turn out a carload every day. Every blessed day they'd do five, six hundred boxes. Each one would do over a hundred boxes. They were fast as lightning."[27]

Between 1893 and 1894, *keiyaku-nin* exploited these qualities—both real and perceived—to the fullest. Underbidding everyone, they replaced Chinese crews working at one dollar a day around Florin by taking the same jobs for seventy-five cents a day; white field hands earning $1.25 to $1.75 a day and Chinese earning one dollar a day in the Santa Clara Valley were displaced by Japanese willing to work for fifty cents a day without board. In some areas, they pushed aside all competition by hiring out crews for as little as thirty-five to forty cents a day for twelve to fourteen hours without board when no other field hands would work for less than one dollar. A favorite tactic was to move in at the first hint of trouble among white crews and guarantee a smooth and successful harvest. Rural newspapers were continually impressed. "These cunning Celestials have been quick to take advantage of favorable conditions for securing an advance," observed the *Sacramento Bee* after several *keiyaku-nin* shipped in crews to replace complaining white hop pickers. "They work for small pay, and in every competition which is now open to them on equal terms they are the winners," added the *Pacific Rural Press*.[28]

෴

During this time, the Japanese encountered many of the same problems that Chinese laborers had faced for years. In fact, they were often mistaken for Chinese by uninformed citizens. Accused of taking jobs from white workers, they were commonly threatened and attacked by unemployed mobs. The violence was at first attributed to a generalized racism, but as time passed and the Japanese established themselves as separate from the Chinese, *keiyaku-nin* became the single greatest source of conflict. Admired at first, the *keiyaku-nin* emerged as a major source of concern in May 1895, with the arrival in the Livermore Valley of N. Sato, a thirty-three-year-old *keiyaku-nin*, described by the *San Francisco Call* as "a shrewd little Jap," and R. Fujimoto, similarly described as "a shrewd little fellow." Obtaining men from a boardinghouse in San Francisco, Sato and Fujimoto quickly pushed aside all local help, gained control of about half the Japanese laborers in the valley, and obtained a contract to provide one hundred field hands to the Pleasanton Hop Company.[29]

Sato's activities caused an uproar. For several years, Pleasanton residents had handled all of the off-season work in the hop fields and constituted a large portion of the hop pickers annually required to bring in the local crop. Small area farmers relied on hop picking wages to pay for their land and finance their farms, families who worked in the hop fields substantially augmented their income, and even school children had their vacations adjusted for "this light work." Now, with a key source of revenue diverted into the hands of two *keiyaku-nin*, citizens called a mass meeting and threatened vigilante action. To defuse their anger, local authorities called upon the state government to investigate.

Prompted by the Pleasanton appeal as well as growing concern over the number of Japanese entering the United States by way of Victoria, British Columbia, State Labor Commissioner Edward L. Fitzgerald and U.S. Immigration Commissioner W. L. Stradley arrived in June to investigate. Immigration by way of Canada had come to Fitzgerald's attention toward the end of May, when large numbers of Japanese had landed in San Francisco bearing Canadian immigration certificates and then gone directly to a farm in Fresno. Rumors soon circulated that more than eight hundred Japanese were waiting to immigrate from Victoria, putting the situation in Pleasanton and the greater issue of Japanese labor on the front pages.[30]

Determined to stop the influx, Fitzgerald and Stradley issued subpoenas to eighty local farmers and Japanese laborers. Threatening to arrest those who refused to obey their summons, the commissioners began investigating how the *keiyaku-nin* had worked their way so quickly not only in the Livermore Valley, but also into Vacaville, Fresno, and the Pajaro Valley. "Both wish to secure facts and statistics to show the dangers arising from unrestricted Japanese immigration," reported the *Call*, "so that Congress will take hold of the matter before it is too late."[31]

Convening in the Pleasanton Courthouse on Tuesday morning, June 4, Fitzgerald's hearings probed the growing importance of the *keiyaku-nin*, the pattern of their move into agricultural labor contracting, the tactics they employed, and the arrangements under which Japanese laborers came to California. Covered on a daily basis by the *San Francisco Call*, the hearings earned headlines when Sato, the first subpoenaed witness, fled to San Francisco and disappeared. As the hearings proceeded, one Pleasanton farmer described how Sato and Fujimoto had taken control of the hop fields by underbidding competitors with contracts to tend fields at twenty-two dollars per acre, compared to twenty-eight dollars for white labor. Other witnesses described how the *keiyaku-nin* had employed the same technique to obtain sugar beet contracts in the Livermore Valley. Sato also agreed to allow a foreman to terminate a contract if he deemed the work unsatisfactory and had also waived rights to secure unpaid wages through a mechanic's lien. "In other words," reported the *Call*, "all legal protection is waived by the contractor for the Japanese, all of which is illegal."[32]

Angry at this discovery, Commissioner Fitzgerald asked, "How in the name of common sense can white laborers compete with such a labor system?" On Wednesday, June 5, Fitzgerald and a federal agent visited the Sato labor camp at the Pleasanton Hop Company. Conditions were shocking. "Dozens of laborers were seen in all directions working among the vines," reported the *Call*. "They were all Japanese, not a white man being seen for miles." Moving inside the large barn where Sato housed and fed his men, the commissioners observed "a truly oriental scene" consisting of one hundred bunks, one above the other, "like mill-pan shelves in a dairy." A dozen "low-browed coolies" rolled out of their bunks as the commissioners approached, standing and staring at the commissioners, "whom they recognized as enemies." The general appearance of the men and the place was "more forbidding than any Chinese camp on the planet," wrote the *Call*. "Those who were not at work bore unmistakable signs of a recent debauch, and their absence from the fields was caused by inability to work."[33]

Tongues were still wagging at the Fitzgerald exposé when Fujimoto took the witness stand and was questioned about how and where he obtained his men. Denying any illegal activities, Fujimoto claimed not to have been in league with boardinghouse operators in San Francisco or to have written to Japan for laborers. Unconvinced, the commissioners obtained lists of his men, compared them with passenger lists from recently arrived steamers, and concluded that Fujimoto's men had probably signed contracts long before arriving. But as the commissioners continued to probe these matters, critics challenged the value and cost of the inquiry. Forced to defend himself, Fitzgerald released figures showing that the investigation had cost less than thirty dollars thus far; he then went on the offensive, claiming that San Francisco *keiyaku-nin* had already contracted to harvest most of the Fresno raisin crop for fifty to seventy-five cents per day without board, and had shipped in about two thousand men in boxcars from San Francisco. With *keiyaku-nin* moving so many men into the fields, the commissioners reasoned, they could only fill any future labor orders by contracting more men in Japan and British Columbia. Therefore, customs officers would have to "watch every incoming steamer."[34]

By Saturday, June 8, it was obvious that the investigation was going to raid incoming steamers for evidence. While searching the newly docked steamer *China*, Deputy Immigration Commissioner A. H. Geffeney found an envelope addressed to K. Shiono, who operated a boardinghouse in San Francisco. Written by a hotel keeper in Yokohama, the note read in part, "The following persons will sail. . . . Please meet them as I am sending them to you." When hearings resumed on Monday, the commissioners confronted Shiono with this information. After being promised immunity from prosecution, Shiono provided the names of several Sacramento Valley and Alameda County *keiyaku-nin* with whom he did business. One of them, a man named Nichiuchi, had arrived on the steamer *Peking City* on May 14 and promptly had taken twenty men to Vacaville and 150 to A. T. Hatch's ranches near Suisun. "This was the first positive evidence of a contractor having gone to Japan and returning with cooly laborers," observed the *Call*. At the same time, field hands at the Pleasanton Hop Company, having learned through the press how Sato had signed away their rights, walked out on strike. "Even if they receive their pay now, the gang, numbering about seventy-eight, will as likely as not pack up their belongings and start out for the orchards and vineyards," reported the *Call*. "As there are but few coolies in this City, the places of the strikers will have to be filled with white men."[35]

On Tuesday, commissioners finally tracked down Sato, the "wily boss contractor of Pleasanton," and interrogated him relentlessly. Asked for some background, Sato volunteered that he had worked for ten years on his uncle's farm in Kobe, Japan, never earning more than thirty dollars a year. Arriving in San Francisco in the spring of 1893 with twenty-eight dollars in his pocket and no idea where to go or how to obtain work, he had been sent to Pleasanton by a boardinghouse keeper on Stevenson Street. Working briefly as a field hand for $1.10 a day, he had, by virtue of his ability to speak English, become the designated *keiyaku-nin* for Alameda County and, in February 1895, began supervising one hundred field hands who cultivated 296 acres of sugar beets for fifteen dollars an acre.

Sato seemed to be cooperating with the investigation, but when confronted with testimony from his bookkeeper describing how he profited by employing men straight off the steamers and began charging them as much as half their wages for the service, Sato became sullen and withdrawn. Grilled over the next four hours, he could not explain how he rounded up such a large number of Japanese without soliciting them in San Francisco. The mood of the interrogation steadily deteriorated, and eventually Sato refused to answer any further questions. The inquiry ended when Sato flew into a rage and stormed out of the hearing room, vowing to get even with those who had told lies about him—especially his bookkeeper.[36]

Frustrated by Sato's uncooperative and erratic testimony, commissioners Fitzgerald and Stradley sought more conclusive evidence, and on June 12 detained all steerage passengers arriving from Japan on the steamer *Peru*. Questioning those passengers whose papers listed them as students, they discovered most had strong, callused hands, suggesting that they had done hard labor with hoes and shovels, not pens and pencils. Nevertheless, each claimed to be a good Christian, bound for the Japanese missions in San Francisco. "The stories told by the Japs who desired to land yesterday caused Mr. Stradley to believe that not one out of six spoke the truth," reported the *Call*. Unable to prove that they were contract laborers, Stradley allowed them to disembark. A few days later, he obtained what seemed to be damning evidence when the steamer *Walla Walla* arrived from Victoria, British Columbia. Discovering what appeared to be a labor contract between one of the immigrants and a farming company, Stradley wrestled it away from the man, and then discovered another contract held by a young boy from Kobe. Translated into English and published the following day in the *Call*, the documents specified the terms under which the Nichibeichi Emigration Bureau sent men to California, often by way of British Columbia, complete with certificates stamped with the official government seal and a guarantee of work. Additional letters of introduction not only provided the name and address of a Vacaville *keiyaku-nin* who promised them work but also directions to his office and detailed instructions about how to answer questions at the Customs House.[37]

Commissioners immediately shifted their inquiry to Vacaville, where they subpoenaed testimony from a dozen fruit growers and all of the local labor contractors. Convened in the Vacaville Courthouse on Monday and Tuesday, June 17–18, the hearings drew huge crowds that spilled out of the courthouse onto the sidewalk and street. Sworn testimony from Vacaville growers quickly established that between six hundred and eight hundred Japanese were already employed in the area, with the *Call* reporter adding that "during the day and evening dozens can be seen in the stores and post office." Asked to explain why they had turned to the Japanese in such a large way, one grower after another had a similar tale. When they hired through employment offices in San Francisco, all they ever got were lazy unreliable white laborers and "hoodlums," who, earning a few dollars, "goes [*sic*] off to town, and after a drinking debauch is [*sic*] unfit to work for several days." J. G. Gates, who farmed one hundred acres of peaches and apricots, complained that he "had to go to town every Monday morning with a header wagon and round up his men in order to get them to work." In contrast, Gates explained, the Japanese worked steadily through the week, "Sundays and all," and while they "cannot do as much nor as fast work as the white men, they are as regular in their habits as a clock."[38]

At the conclusion of the first day of hearings in Vacaville, the Japanese mobilized to prevent damaging testimony. Hiring every buggy in town, "Japanese Paul Reveres" sped up and down the length of the Vaca Valley warning *keiyaku-nin* to be careful of what they said. "About daylight these messengers came straggling back to town, dusty and weary, but out of the 800 Japanese in the Vaca Valley," reported the *Call*, "there is not one that had not been well coached as to what he should tell if called by the Commissioners." One *keiyaku-nin* went into hiding, apparently fleeing to San Francisco, others "took to the bush," where they remained until the investigation concluded. When the Japanese discovered that an investigator was driving out to the Henry Brinck ranch in Pleasants Valley to round up S. Nichiuchi, the *keiyaku-nin* implicated in earlier testimony as the kingpin of Japanese farm labor around Vacaville, local Japanese quickly mobilized. A Japanese hotel keeper, a Sacramento Valley *keiyaku-nin*, and a recently arrived field hand quickly hired a team and raced seven miles to Brinck's ranch and warned Nichiuchi. Arriving just after Nichiuchi had left for Sacramento, the investigator threatened to arrest the entire Japanese crew. "In a few minutes the man was found in an orchard," reported the *Call*. Hauled back to Vacaville to testify the following morning, Nichiuchi was cross-examined unmercifully, but the heavily perspiring *keiyaku-nin* denied bringing men to Vacaville under contract from Japan and was set free at the end of the hearings. "No doubt remains in the mind of any one," concluded the *Vacaville Reporter*, "but that it is the fact that the Japs are in many cases brought into this country under contract in violation of the law, but as in the case of the Chinese investigations it is a hard matter to prove it."[39]

On Tuesday evening, Immigration Commissioner Stradley returned to San Francisco and composed a memo to Congress warning that unrestricted Japanese immigration posed an imminent danger. He also threatened to arrest those *keiyaku-nin* guilty of obtaining coolie laborers, and to deport two or more of them. To support Stradley, State Labor Commissioner Fitzgerald began preparing a massive investigation of Japanese immigration. Hearing of such developments, the Vacaville Japanese became extremely agitated, "almost beside themselves with fear and anxiety," reported the *Call*. "They fear deportation more than any violence that might arise from anti-cooly agitation."[40]

☙

Once the hysteria following the investigations had passed, the *keiyaku-nin* embarked on an aggressive program of expansion. "Wanted—Work on ranches for 20 Japanese. Address Frank, post office box 108, Vacaville, Cal," read one advertisement in the *Vacaville Reporter*. Other stories in the newspaper hinted at the growing importance of the Japanese around Vacaville. On July 9, the *Reporter* described a serious accident on the Charles Laird ranch, in which a Japanese cook was burned seriously while preparing supper for a crew of Japanese peach pickers. "It seems he was using coal oil to light the fire, when the can exploded, burning his hands, legs and feet seriously," reported the newspaper. "He was taken to the county hospital. The house was burned down."[41]

As more Japanese moved into the countryside that summer, they earned praise for removing a considerable amount of uncertainty from an otherwise chaotic farm labor market. "They are now to be found singly and in colonies all over the coast and have become a very important factor in our California labor system," reported the *Pacific Rural Press*. But even as they were being praised in print and winning converts, the Japanese continued to demonstrate an independent spirit that left growers stunned and angry. Japanese hop pickers soon became infamous for one particularly clever trick. Paid by the pound, they discovered that they could easily increase their income by rising early, as soon as there was enough light to work. Picking furiously, while the leaves were still moist with dew, they added considerably to the weight of their first bags of hops. "When everything is dry during the heat of the day," observed the *San Francisco Call*, "they quit work and drink wine."[42]

With about eight thousand men under their control statewide in 1896, *keiyaku-nin* enjoyed unprecedented success, winning one contract after another. Few local field hands objected to their work until January 1897, when a group of men known as the Whitecap Gang began attacking Japanese in the Vacaville area. In one of the most sensational incidents, a group of six Japanese laborers were surrounded and tortured, even as the farmer who had hired them attempted to leave to contact the police. Six men wearing gunnysacks over their heads drove the Japanese from their hiding place behind the barn, marched them into a field, and told them to run for their lives. "Seven pistol shots were fired after them to accelerate their departure," reported the *Sacramento Bee*. "A rope was put around each of the little brown man's neck and their captors started for a big white oak tree." When the farmer returned, the gang threw a rope around his neck, saying, "a man was never better than the men he employed." After much pleading from his wife and children, the farmer was released, but the still-noosed Japanese were forced to march to and from a big oak tree several times. Eventually the gang was satisfied, and the Japanese were allowed to leave. As they packed and departed, they were told if any ever returned, the gang "would hang them and leave them for the Coroner to cut down." As proof of their intentions, they poisoned the farmer's dog and burned a barn on a neighboring ranch.[43]

Although the sudden onset of violence briefly frightened the Japanese, they were quickly rescued by a posse of local farmers and townspeople, and the incident was soon forgotten. No other attacks occurred outside of the Vaca Valley. Able to resume their business, the *keiyaku-nin* embarked on a period of rapid growth beginning in the summer of 1897. Soon they were operating on a grand scale. Working out of Los Angeles, one *keiyaku-nin*, Charlie Mura, achieved local notoriety by coordinating dozens of subcontractors who provided thousands of laborers to growers as far north as Santa Paula and as far south as San Diego. Mura's counterpart in Northern California, San Francisco's Hori and Company, sent crews to growers throughout the Sacramento Valley. On a smaller scale, *keiyaku-nin* carved out specialized spheres of influence, dividing regions among themselves. Around Selma, a *keiyaku-nin* named Mr. Kawamoto supplied labor to every peach farmer in the area; in Colusa County, Naotaro Yoneda, now in business nearly a decade, supplied laborers for land clearing, providing them in such numbers that Yoneda Landing eventually grew into a community of some 130 permanent residents and some fifty buildings, commonly referred to by whites as "Jap Camp." Elsewhere, *keiyaku-nin* joined together to form large, interlocking operations that set pay rates and controlled employment standards in entire agricultural districts and crops. Eventually, a network of some three hundred *keiyaku-nin* distributed field hands to every agricultural district throughout the state.[44]

The arrangement could be very profitable. In the Santa Clara Valley, for example, local Japanese bosses controlled about one hundred to two hundred men each during the busy season. Housing them in flimsy bunkhouses, they required field hands to provide their own bedding, but otherwise fed them at cost and sheltered them free of charge. "The bosses received orders from the local farmers for so many men, and distributed them accordingly," wrote Yamato Ichihashi after visiting the camps. For this service, the bosses received daily a five-cent fee from each man, earning them a daily commission of five to ten dollars above the profit earned from boarding men. Bosses employed by larger growers might earn as much as forty to sixty dollars a month above this commission through retainer fees; unlike camp bosses, these *keiyaku-nin* also acted as foremen.[45]

By controlling their workers' lives so completely, the *keiyaku-nin* had plenty of opportunities to manipulate circumstances in their own favor. Some let their greed run wild, squeezing out everything they could get; at the very least, most turned a tidy profit. By spending as little as possible on food and housing, *keiyaku-nin* could pocket the difference between what they claimed to be the price of goods and what they actually cost with no one being the wiser. They also earned considerable sums by selling their men everything from clothing and tobacco to boots and other necessities, usually at considerable markup. If their men gambled, as most did in the absence of other diversions, representatives of the *keiyaku-nin* played the "house" and took a large cut. Some *keiyaku-nin* also collected an "interpreter's fee" of one dollar per month; others tagged on an additional five cents per day for up to twenty days for "office expenses" like remitting funds to Japan and other "sundry services," including medical help, even when none was provided. It was a double (sometimes triple) billing technique one Japanese labor guidebook described as "tantamount to compensations paid to thieves." From these various practices, a few *keiyaku-nin* pocketed between twenty and forty cents from every dollar that their field hands earned.[46]

Besides the nickel-and-dime operations, *keiyaku-nin* were not above skipping town without paying wages, a practice field hands called "*mochinige*." Since *keiyaku-nin* were unregulated, there was little to stop them from absconding with entire payrolls, a considerable temptation since the payroll for a single large crew provided enough for a man to retire comfortably. So common were these incidents that immigrant guidebooks warned field hands that it was best to send someone along when *keiyaku-nin* traveled into town to cash their payroll checks. One Japanese newspaper, *Shin Sekai*, became so alarmed with cases of *mochinige* that it contacted the Japanese consulate and other immigrant organizations. After identifying dozens of "immoral" and "corrupt" *keiyaku-nin* and calling on other Japanese to blacklist them, the newspaper attempted to curb their activities by suggesting field hands obtain photographs of corrupt contractors and forward them for publication, along with their home addresses in Japan, actions that might lead to their identification and eventual arrest. Japanese field hands benefited little, if at all, from these exposés. Led from one place to another, frequently traveling great distances between jobs, they did not live in permanent quarters. Additionally, men were often strangers to one another despite having sometimes come from the same prefectures in Japan. Under such conditions, they found it difficult, if not impossible, to break free.[47]

❧

During the course of a year, Japanese field hands might work on a dozen different farms, travel hundreds of miles, and sandwich in many jobs outside of agriculture. One field hand, Mike Masaro Iwatsubo, later described how he picked grapes in Fresno; peas and tomatoes in San Leandro; celery in Huntington Beach; strawberries in Gardena; and corn, potatoes, onions, and barley in Venice. Later that year, Iwatsubo took a trip back to Japan for his father's funeral, then returned to chop wood in Sacramento during the off-season. Another man recalled one year in which he thinned and harvested sugar beets in Oxnard, cooked for a crew in Suisun, mined coal in Colorado, harvested sugar beets in the Pajaro Valley, and worked as a bootblack in New Mexico. Others specializing in fruit and vegetable packing described a circuit that took them from asparagus sheds in the delta and cherry packing operations in Lodi to raisin packinghouses in Fresno and apple dryers in the Pajaro Valley. Field hands in Santa Clara followed a well-defined circuit: They picked strawberries in Alviso from April to June; moved to the middle and southern part of the valley to harvest apricots, pears, and prunes between July and August; shifted to Fresno to harvest grapes during September and October; then returned to Santa Clara for whatever work was available before winter planting. Of this constant shifting about, an old Japanese field hand later recalled: "In my early life, I remember moving, moving, moving."[48]

As they traversed the countryside, the *keiyaku-nin* initiated a number of innovations, among them a massive stockpiling of bicycles in their camps. So many of their men used bicycles to pedal to and from the orchards around Riverside that the most frequent reason they were arrested other than for gambling was for bicycle riding violations—riding on the sidewalk, operating a bicycle at night without lights, or rolling through a stop sign. One California state investigator, J. Vance Thompson, visited eighty Japanese camps and found at least half of them stocked with bicycles. Impressed by their mobility, he explained in a report to his supervisor how, at daybreak, hundreds of men would mount their bicycles and pedal out to work. "Owing to close proximity of Japanese camps on the beet and fruit ranches; their excellent mobility due to ownership of bicycles . . . and their regular headquarters in several towns, they are in a position to mobilize much faster than the white population," he observed. Growers loved the arrangement. As one explained with undisguised admiration: "It seems . . . that the Japanese are a good deal better organized than the owners of the vineyards."[49]

Boardinghouses and small hotels provided rest stops along the migratory circuit. Usually located near the Chinese sections of farm towns, early Japanese lodging facilities and labor clubs typically consisted of little more than run-down wooden buildings, back rooms of stores, and basements outfitted with dormitory-style double bunks. When the Japanese population grew and various Japantowns became established, boardinghouses multiplied in number. By 1907, Japanese merchants operated more than ninety-two boardinghouses in Los Angeles. As the years went by, these places grew larger and more elaborate, and some began specializing in lodging men from specific prefectures. Whatever their nature, these quarters served as hubs for the transient population. Prices were modest. A comfortable room with a real bed and pillow slips—not a bunk—cost ten to fifty cents a night; during the winter, when unemployed field hands packed the boardinghouses, rooms went for five to fifteen dollars a month. Some boardinghouses also served meals at ten to fifteen cents per sitting, although men generally ate in nearby restaurants. "In brief," wrote Yamato Ichihashi, "they can supply everything that farm laborers want."[50]

Men got more than food and shelter during their stay in boardinghouses. They also got jobs. Simply by taking a room, field hands came in contact with men who shared their knowledge of jobs, advised one another which growers and keiyaku-nin to avoid, learned where work was easiest or steadiest, discovered who paid the most, and gleaned information about various agricultural districts. Boardinghouse proprietors also played an active role, sending men out to surrounding farms and collecting fees of one to three dollars per man from keiyaku-nin and growers alike, thereby earning considerable income beyond what they obtained from renting rooms.[51]

Out on the farms, housing was not so well developed. "Living conditions . . . were terrible," Garden Grove farmwife Mrs. C. C. Violett later admitted to Survey of Race Relations investigators. Often temporary workers had no shelter at all. "They slept in the fields with what they had on," recalled one old field hand. "They drank river water brought in by irrigation ditches." At other times Japanese laborers camped in barns, chicken sheds, corn cribs, feed storage rooms, old shacks, and washhouses, cooking their food over an open fire outside the building. Occasionally they would be given a blanket. If not, they made do with what was at hand, fashioning mattresses out of straw and grain sacks and making beds by lining up boxes and placing planks on them. This seldom concerned farmers. "The Americans who owned the ranches . . . couldn't afford to put much in buildings," recalled one Japanese field hand, "and they thought the Japanese, because of the way they lived in Japan, with their flimsy houses . . . didn't need much shelter."[52]

If they were lucky, the Japanese settled in crude labor camps consisting of a bunkhouse, kitchen, and dining room. Usually managed by *keiyaku-nin*, such places housed anywhere from 25 to 175 men. If the observations of contemporaries are any indication, many of these camps ranged between spartan and barely habitable. Visiting one camp near Fresno, a reporter for *Shin Sekai* described it as being totally unfit for human beings, "worse than a dog and pig pen. Rain and moisture seep down from the roofs. Winds blow nightly through all four walls. It's like seeing beggars in Japan living beneath bridges. No one, not even dirt-poor peasants, wants to live in such unpleasant and filthy surroundings." Another camp, portrayed in a Japanese guidebook, was even worse. "Twenty to thirty Japanese sleep alongside each other in field sheds on the edge of fruit orchards," the book reported. "These sheds . . . have no beds. Men sleep with bedding on straws spread over dirt floors." Of Japanese bunkhouses on the Earl Fruit Company camps near Smeltzer, a grower later explained to an interviewer: "We piled them up in those days. There would be about twenty-five or thirty Japs in a house about twelve by thirty feet."[53]

Life in these camps did not vary significantly from any labor camp before or since. Before daybreak, men rose amid a clash of noise and confusion as they slid from their bunks and stumbled in the darkness for clothes and boots. Wincing from the aches and pains of yesterday's labor, dressing was often a painful ordeal itself. During the heat of midday no one ventured into camp quarters, which reeked of stale food, sweat, cooking oils, men's breath, and ever present dust. In the evening the men crowded inside to eat dinner and gulp huge quantities of cold water. The hours before turning in were spent relaxing, cleaning up, quarreling, writing letters, and gambling. Gradually men drifted off to sleep, and tranquility slowly returned. The night passed with bodies turning restlessly, men coughing, snoring, breaking wind, waking from dreams and nightmares swatting at mosquitoes and other insects, and rising to attend to "nighttime duties."[54]

Malnutrition was a recurring problem. Although *keiyaku-nin* provided basic provisions, they seldom supplied the hearty diet needed to satisfy men working strenuously for hours on end. Men survived on skimpy, tasteless, monotonous meals. Breakfasts consisted of little more than flour dumplings in a soup seasoned with a little salt known as "*suiton*." All too often, men ate dumplings again for dinner, often accompanied by rice balls. "Vegetables were unheard of," one field hand recalled of camp meals. Consequently some resorted to picking edible weeds like shepherd's grass, a spinachlike plant, which they boiled and added to their diet. Lacking soy sauce, a few men seasoned their bland dumplings, rice balls, and mystery soups with sauce made from burned flour, sugar, salt, and water. Those picking fruit or grapes also supplemented their diets with whatever crop was at hand. Men who could afford to do so purchased luxury items like tea, sugar, and eggs on their own.[55]

Camp life could be fatal. Using kerosene-fueled lamps and cooking on wood or kerosene stoves, camp cooks were constantly burning down their cookshacks and bunkhouses. Cooks themselves experienced many close calls. "Last week a Jap was preparing to cook supper for a gang on the ranch of W. J. Pleasants," began one report in the *Vacaville Reporter*, "and in order to hurry the fire up, poured oil out of a 5-gallon can which ignited and exploded. The poor fellow was terribly burned."[56]

Fire was not the only danger. With no law enforcement around, justice was improvised. Men caught stealing were thrashed and mauled, in some cases seriously. Gamblers and various confidence men also prowled the camps, ready to fleece laborers in card games. More commonly, bandits and robbers preyed on the men. Paid in cash regularly and living far out in the countryside in isolated camps, field hands made easy marks. Eleven grapevine pruners living in a bunkhouse on the Mattei vineyard near Malaga just south of Fresno were assaulted on February 16, 1899. The yield, according to press accounts, was relatively meager: two watches and two hundred dollars. Because the field hands were so frightened, they were not of much help when police arrived. All they could remember was that both assailants were not Japanese, that they wore masks, that one was big and bearded with a gash over one eye, and that his partner was smaller. Whether or not they were the same men who raided a Japanese bunkhouse on the Briscoe ranch a few miles west and took sixty dollars from field hands remains unknown. Apparently a gang of men was going from one camp to another, singling out the Japanese as easy targets.[57]

Days were long and demanding. After eight to ten hours of hard labor, field hands returned to their bunkhouses grimy, "tired out and limp as a rag," so exhausted that they could not bend over to use the toilet; some such men later recalled how, during beet thinning season, their lives seemed to compress tightly into their hoe handles. During the raisin harvest around Fresno, sweat-drenched field hands told of working "day in, day out," seven days a week, laying out bunches of grapes and using one arm as a towel to wipe away sweat as the temperatures rose and the vineyards became "as though . . . paved with hot iron boards." Around Madera, famous for its wind, men struggled against both heat and blinding sand and dust storms. Most tedious of all, the Japanese (like the Chinese before them) often acted as human pesticides, picking insects such as cutworms off vines with their fingers. "We would drop them into a pot of oil," recalled one old field hand. "That was a common practice."[58]

Eventually the poor food and water, primitive living conditions, constant migration, and fatiguing labor wore men down; many became ill and died. The Sacramento Betsuin *Book of the Deceased*, maintained by the Sacramento Buddhist temple, contains information on ninety-nine Japanese men in their twenties and thirties, many from Aichi prefecture, who died either in Sacramento County hospitals or at one of two Japanese clinics between 1900 and 1902. "Sickness" and heatstroke are listed as the general cause of deaths, with beriberi (caused by deficiency of vitamin B-1), pneumonia, and tuberculosis being the most commonly mentioned specific illnesses. Japanese consular statistics confirm the general outline, with tuberculosis, pneumonia, typhoid, and "intestinal disorders" (diarrhea and diseases of the digestive system) taking the highest toll, followed by accidents and homicides, and finally suicides. A similar pattern emerges from cases reported to the Butte County Infirmary, where fifteen of twenty-nine Japanese field hands admitted for treatment between 1900 and 1910 were diagnosed with "fever," the remainder for sore feet and arms, pleurisy, lame backs, lung problems, and various weapons-related injuries (a knife wound, self-inflicted knife wound from an attempted suicide, and a gunshot wound in the foot). But if the number of advertisements in the Japanese immigrant press praising medicines for curing gonorrhea was a fair indication of the health of Japanese field hands, then venereal disease must have also been a fairly common ailment. The *Shin Sekai* carried countless advertisements for "Ritanol for Gonorrhea." Costing $2.50, only one bottle was required; ads promised the concoction would eliminate the curse, as well as other "private diseases," in forty-eight hours.[59]

For many field hands, the effects of constant labor were more insidious and not so easily measured. Worn out and in need of rest, desperate men often checked themselves into hospitals, but unable to pay their bills, they soon found themselves on the street again and, still ailing, headed straight for a free meal and bed at the local rescue mission. Usually they recovered quickly and resumed work, but if they were tormented with some lingering affliction like malaria they could find themselves unable to regain their strength. When this happened, men often became bitter and depressed. Disillusioned with the gap between the California they had imagined and the California they encountered and inheriting much of the prejudice, racial slurs, and discrimination once directed at the Chinese, they grew weary of the taunts and lowly jobs. Regretting their decision to leave home and family behind, many returned to Japan. In some years, ships carried more Japanese home than to California. Other years, for every two arriving, one returned. Unable to return home, many Japanese resorted to suicide. A despondent Shinnosuki Nishibi left his quarters at Vina early one morning saying that he wanted to be killed and "dynimoted" [*sic*] and drowned himself in a nearby creek. A Butte County field hand slashed his throat but survived. K. Takegawa, a field hand on the H. M. Watson farm near Vacaville, hanged himself in a tree on Walker Ridge southwest of Vacaville. Searching his pockets, officers discovered fifty cents, a razor, a receipt for a money order drawn on a Vacaville post office, and a Japanese newspaper. Although the exact reason for his suicide was never given, newspaper accounts attributed it to insanity. Several days earlier, Takegawa had set fire to the cutting shed on the Watson farm and placed a pan of burning sulfur in the bunkhouse after barricading the doors shut to prevent sleeping men from escaping. Breaking down the doors, field hands had chased him into the mountains, where he wandered for several days before committing suicide.[60]

꽃

But for all their sickness, exhaustion, and disappointment, most field hands chose to remain in California. On the harvest circuit, they had little time to play or relax. But between jobs and on Saturday nights after receiving their paychecks, they would leave their camps, pile into wagons, and pour into the nearest Little Tokyo or Japantown. By 1900, dozens of these communities existed in California, one in virtually every farm town. Usually located near old Chinatowns and frequently taking them over, Little Tokyos were lively, self-contained, densely populated, rural ghettoes, neatly segregated from the surrounding society and usually occupying at least several city blocks. This was the case in Winters, Fresno, San Jose, Sacramento, Vacaville, Bakersfield, Chico, and Yuba City. One exception was Riverside, where the Japanese quarters were dispersed in clusters throughout the city. Field hands working around Watsonville found Japantown located just across the Pajaro River from the declining Chinatown, while those coming in from the fields around the San Joaquin County town of Holt frequented a block of buildings on the east side of the railroad tracks just outside of town bordering Whiskey Slough. Among the most compact rural Japantowns were those in Salinas, which snuggled up against an existing Chinese section, and the Little Tokyo section of Los Angeles, which spilled over into the old "Negro section" and Chinatown. Stockton's Japantown was interspersed among Jewish, Italian, and Russian-owned businesses along El Dorado and Center streets. Several Japantowns also maintained Buddhist temples, the one in Marysville being the most elaborate.[61]

Touring the Japanese section of Vacaville, a reporter for the *Fresno Tribune* painted a not very pretty picture of a place where "extensive laundries, large general merchandise stores and employment agencies elbow each other at ever[y] turn" in "true oriental style." Besides the numerous pool halls, ice cream parlors, and "ubiquitous Japanese bank," what most captured his attention were the buildings in the very center of town. "The rooms are tiny and dingy," he wrote. "One building contains twenty-six rooms and houses twenty-six families. All the members . . . work in the fruit fields and live, eat and sleep in the same room. The post office does a money order business approximating $80,000 a year, 75 percent of which goes to Japan." Of the Japanese section of Colusa, which overlay an existing Chinatown, one old Japanese washroom owner later recalled vividly that it

> started with a barber shop between 5th and 6th on Main Street, the Uyesugis operated a grocery store. . . . Further down . . . was a single story tin house, which furnished rooms and meals to farmworkers. In later years the building came under 'new management' as a house of ill-repute. Next door was the Watanabe Pool Hall and Boarding House, followed in line by Fujimoto's boardinghouse and tofu . . . shop, the Toyo Company, often called the 44 Cigar Company because of the huge overhead sign, operated by Toriumis, and Ide's boardinghouse next to the old Chung Sun Grocery. Directly across the street from the Toyo Company was a two story boardinghouse, known as the tin house because of its tin roof, run by the Obas, later by the Kasais. On the corner, opposite Chung Sun, was the Sun Laundry owned by Mr. and Mrs. Ogi. On Seventh Street north of the alley were the 'American Restaurant' operated by the Masunagas and later sold to the Kusunokis, the Kojima Candy Store, and the Nakagawa General Merchandise.[62]

Venturing into Japantowns, field hands found a mixture of small businesses—theaters, barbershops, laundry and pressing shops, clothing and shoe stores, groceries, pool halls, and vegetable stands, drugstores, toy shops, furniture stores, and hotels, vulcanizing shops, and vegetable gardens—all catering to their basic needs. Although one Japanese diplomat claimed that the "filthy, winding alleyways crisscrossing each other" in Walnut Grove were typical of rural Japantowns, few contemporaries agreed. Unlike Chinese field hands, who were constantly attacked for living in quarters so foul that they threatened public health, the Japanese escaped

FIGURE 38. Japanese section of Fowler, ca. 1910. Courtesy of the Hutchinson Collection, Fresno County Historical Society.

such criticisms. Watsonville's Japantown was described by the local newspaper as "opulent." According to a California State Labor Commission investigation in 1896, most Japantowns "were as good as or better than ordinary immigrant quarters in the west, and better than the immigrant quarters of eastern cities. From the point of cleanliness and sanitation," the commission concluded, "their condition was superior to that of other races similarly circumstanced."[63]

A welcome change from the austere surroundings of their field camps and the dominating presence of labor contractors, Japantowns were a place where men could relax in the shade, rise at their leisure, and retire late. Whereas the crowded, meager conditions of camp life and the incessant migration between farms tended to fragment and isolate Japanese field hands, Japantowns provided a sense of community and retreat, plus plenty of diversions. Much like wheat harvesters, Japanese field hands followed a fairly predictable routine upon arrival. First stopping to secure a room in a lodging house or hotel, they would change into clean clothes, drop their soiled ones off at a laundry, then head for a Japanese-style bathhouse, a social center for relaxation and a place to exchange news and gossip. The typical community-style bathhouse was a simple structure, its corrugated iron sides and roofing blackened on the outside with smoke from the unceasing fires within. The bath (*furo*) itself was made entirely from sheet metal. Like a pot of water, it sat on top of a stone foundation and was heated by means of an excavated fire pit that constantly burned logs, twigs, and orchard trimmings. Portable wooden grating that rested on the bottom of the bath and lined its sides prevented men from burning themselves on the metal tubs, which became extremely hot. Entering the bathhouse, field hands would strip, sit on benches in the tubs, and soak in water up to their necks for as long as they liked.[64]

After washing away the grime and sweat, men put on fresh, clean clothes, and then visited a store. Usually homesick for Japanese food, men liked to purchase tins of canned salmon and large quantities of rice. Returning to their boardinghouses, they made "extravagant" rice balls covered with slices of salmon. Dressed in traditional kimonos, they would sit on straw mats and feast on the improvised sushi. Those flush with money favored meals in restaurants catering to their needs. Japanese restaurants were some of the first businesses that developed in Little Tokyos. Offering hearty meals of traditional Japanese foods, they were loud and crowded places, packed with field hands and other laborers, including Mexicans, blacks, and various other ethnicities.[65]

Field hands also congregated in pool halls, the third most numerous business in the Japanese quarter behind boardinghouses and restaurants. Important social havens, pool halls were places where men could renew old friendships. Because many of these establishments combined other functions as well—including barbershops, bathhouses, restaurants, and bars—they were places where field hands could forget (for a while, at least) their pains and troubles, sometimes by partaking of cheap wine and whiskey (a gallon of wine, enough for a cheap high for several men, cost them only twenty-five cents). But field hands found another diversion in pool halls: the *shakufu*, or barmaids, who served men familiar foods and spoke Japanese with charm, warmth, and traditional deference. Without wives or sweethearts and outnumbering Japanese immigrant women by a ratio of twenty-four to one in 1900, the men craved female companionship. The pool hall was one of only two places where they might have such contact. The traditional house of ill repute was the other.[66]

Very few descriptions exist of Japanese houses of prostitution, let alone of the prostitutes themselves. While the Japanese consulate of the time admitted that there were 161 Japanese prostitutes in California in 1898, unofficial sources estimated there were at least three times that number, most of them innocent country women lured to California under false pretenses as part of an organized traffic in women. Sold to Japanese pimps, they were put on display so that it was not uncommon for field hands to stroll down an alley past cages full of women wearing wreathlike ornaments on their heads and dressed in gaudy red garments. These women were known as *nihonjin-tori* and catered only to other Japanese, leaving white customers to prostitutes known as *hakujin-tori*, and Chinese customers to women known as *shinajin-tori*. According to one Japanese reporter, during the 1908 grape picking season around Fresno, fifty or sixty *nihonjin-tori* worked in crude hovels reached by way of a path behind China Alley. "When evening sets in," the writer observed, "they show off their 'wares' by leaving the doors open and wearing bright grotesque Japanese and Chinese garments with cribs by their sides." Vacaville had at least four such houses of prostitution. One of them, a yellow cottage behind Sam's Club on the bank of Ulatis Creek, was known as the Banks of the Wabash, and featured two Japanese and two white madams. A second brothel was run by a Frenchwoman named Fanny, married to a Japanese man; two others were located in downtown Vacaville. Field hands willing to pay a higher price could also frequent more traditional houses of prostitution. One Fresno brothel operated by a Japanese who went by the name of Lee Troy offered men free wine, beer, and tea while they waited, played cards, and chose their women. So successful and famous was the establishment that Fresno Christian and Buddhist ministers banded together into the Moral Reform Association and unsuccessfully attempted to close down the establishment and have Japanese prostitutes arrested.[67]

More than any other diversion, Japanese immigrant laborers enjoyed gambling. So great was the temptation that a Japanese labor handbook cautioned men against the risks of cards, dice, and other traditional Japanese games of chance. "As a laborer in the countryside," the handbook began, "you will toil from dawn to dusk with only shots of whiskey and cigarettes to enjoy. Beware of gambling! Why did you leave your home and cross the wide Pacific to endure hardships in this foreign land? It was of course to enrich your family and benefit the homeland. . . . Then, why try to forget your long days of toil by gambling?" The answer may have been no more complex than human nature. Of all the ways they had to pass their time and help them forget their dull routine, gambling was simply the most amusing diversion.[68]

Japanese immigrants lost an estimated several million dollars a year in games of chance—perhaps much more. In Fresno alone, nineteen gambling houses, many of them controlled by Chinese entrepreneurs, raked in an estimated two hundred thousand dollars per year from Japanese raisin and grape pickers. Lotteries ran twenty-four hours a day, and people of all races and backgrounds participated. According to the *Fresno Republican*, three thousand dollars in gambling profits went to San Francisco bosses each month; unlicensed gambling operations in Watsonville extracted forty-five thousand dollars a month from field hands during the sugar beet season. According to Mojiro "Charlie" Hamakawa, a longtime store owner in Winters, Japanese field hands there had no problem finding games of chance, since all of the restaurants on the north side of Putah Creek "were just fronts for gambling houses."[69]

Because they loved gambling, Japanese field hands were frequently caught in well-publicized police raids. Rounded up and marched off to jail by the score, they would then be summarily fined and released. Aside from the lost wages, they seem to have suffered few ill effects from their gambling forays, although occasionally those who felt cheated would retaliate against professional gamblers, occasionally murdering them. But they never slacked off from their addiction to gaming. With few other recreational outlets and endless hours in the fields, Japanese field hands supported a thriving, if illegal, gambling industry in every agricultural district.[70]

Whatever their motivation, men preferred two games in particular—*baahk gap piu*, literally "fools cards," a Chinese game similar to modern-day keno, and *shiiko*, known more commonly as fan-tan. Field hands lost entire paychecks at these games, and some continued to play on credit even after they had spent all of their money. When *keiyaku-nin* arrived to haul them away, field hands would immediately ask for an advance or beg them to wait just a little longer until they won their money back. On Sunday evenings, they would be seen walking back to the farms along the railroad tracks or sleeping by the side of the road, dead broke and in some cases, shoeless. But a week later they would be back in town again trying to win what they could not earn through hard labor.[71]

Poverty was not the only danger of trips to town. Drunken and defenseless men were often preyed upon by thieves and occasionally even kidnapped and pressed into working in Alaskan salmon canneries. Several small riots occurred in San Jose, apparently when field hands approached by Alaskan cannery pressmen hauled out knives and slashed away. Interracial violence between different groups of laborers was another common occurrence. On February 12, 1897, Japanese field hands on a bender in Hanford "started to clean out Chinatown" in response to some perceived affront but were prevented from doing so by local police, two of whom were injured in the fighting. Another similar incident took place in Vacaville on July 18, 1903, when a young white boy and a Japanese field hand scuffled, the Japanese field hand was severely cut and soon returned with a dozen friends intent on beating up his assailant. "Other whites then took a hand and a general mix-up seemed imminent," reported the *Vacaville Reporter*. "By this time Constable Stadfeld was on the scene and succeeded in putting a stop to further demonstrations of a warlike nature. The officer tried to get the Jap to swear out a warrant for the man, but this he would not do, so no arrests were made."[72]

❧

A casual observer in the first months of 1900 might well have concluded that the Japanese, now having established a network of *keiyaku-nin* and Japantowns throughout California, were doing nothing but following in the footsteps of the Chinese. A census enumerator in the Pajaro Valley captured part of the change in his tally of a crew of strawberry pickers: There were nine old Chinese strawberry pickers whose average age was fifty-one; next to them was a crew of eight Japanese averaging twenty-one years of age. But it was not just that the Chinese were old and dying out and the Japanese were young and arriving in increasing numbers that led to the shift.[73]

Aiming to take over as much work as possible and then raise wages, *keiyaku-nin* convened statewide just before the 1900 sugar beet harvest and agreed to set wages at $1.25 per day for ten hours, and to contract with growers at a rate of $1.60 per ton of sugar beets with a minimum guarantee of ten tons per acre. They also agreed to boycott any grower who refused to accept the rate and to censure any *keiyaku-nin* who failed to keep to the agreement. In this way, they expected to eliminate harmful competition and regulate the contract price to their advantage. Around Fresno, *keiyaku-nin* divided up the grape district into various jurisdictions, then jealously guarded their territories against encroachment, sometimes developing loose alliances, sometimes fighting each other. With these tactics, *keiyaku-nin* began to create in the sugar beet and raisin districts what American trade unions called a "closed shop," meaning a place where no one could work without their approval.[74]

When labor shortages developed in 1901, growers quickly mobilized. To head off Indian field hands who had raised wages by 50 percent in the Owens Valley, about 150 growers pledged to stand firm on a rate of $1.25 a day for harvesting hay and one dollar for general farm labor. Around Davisville, twenty miles west of Sacramento, almond growers were reported "searching every nook and cranny . . . in vain to get white men to do this urgent work and are now driven to the extreme of employing any one they can get, be he white, Chinese, or Jap." Around Sacramento, hop growers noted what had happened in Inyo and Davisville and set wages at ninety cents per hundred pounds. Reflecting the general paranoia over labor shortages and manipulative field hands, the *Los Angeles Times* asked of state and federal leaders: "Will they tell us where we are to procure laborers for our orchards and ranches? . . . They are perfectly aware that every year thousands of dollars worth of fruit and grain spoil because help cannot be procured to harvest it."[75]

Recognizing the power they now wielded, *keiyaku-nin* in June 1901 launched a wave of job actions that raised wages throughout the early fruit districts. But just one month later, circumstances suddenly turned against them. On July 24, the Employer's Associations of San Francisco locked out thirteen hundred teamsters and attempted to break the Drayman's Union by hiring scabs. When one hundred Oakland teamsters joined the strike, perishable foods began to spoil on the docks. Soon fifteen thousand longshoremen, seamen, and teamsters from San Francisco joined the strike. With plenty of jobs for scabs and thousands of union men out of work, an odd cross-migration developed. Farm hands poured into the San Francisco Bay Area to load and move crops and goods, and at the same time, more than one thousand teamsters streamed out of the city and into the countryside looking for work on the hop farms and peach ranches between Wheatland and Marysville. On the Horst brothers hop ranch, two hundred unemployed teamsters formed a union, struck, and raised the piece rate from ninety cents to one dollar per one hundred pounds of hops. The situation worsened as Paiute Indians poured out of a string of boxcars, having been transported to Marysville and Wheatland, according to the *Sacramento Evening Bee*, "at the same rate as is paid for transporting cattle."[76]

When nine railroad carloads of Japanese disembarked at Wheatland to work in the immense Horst brothers hop fields, they found the camps glutted not only with teamsters, but Indians, local families from nearby towns, and hundreds of unemployed men drawn from as far away as Red Bluff by advertisements placed in newspapers all over the state. Barred from Wheatland by a "whites only" policy, they sought work in nearby hop yards at eighty cents per hundred pounds, a cut of ten to twenty cents from the previous year's wage; they also found work on fruit ranches in San Joaquin County for just $1.50 a day, when the previous wage had been $2 to $2.50.[77]

Given the unexpected labor surplus and growing anti-Japanese sentiments, no one expected the *keiyaku-nin* to flex their muscles as extensively as they did around Davisville during the almond harvest later that year. Contacted in August by Davisville grower George W. Pierce, Sacramento labor boss Shi Kubo sent eleven men to work for $1.25 per day without board. Although previously unfamiliar with almond harvesting, the Japanese worked well the first day. On the second day, though, Kubo pulled his men out of the orchards and demanded twice the normal pay. As labor was again scarce and white almond harvesters were getting as much as $2.50 a day, Kubo probably calculated that he had the upper hand. But he failed to take into consideration Pierce's personality and resolve. Owner of twelve hundred acres of prime farmland, Pierce was a stubborn, innovative, second-generation farmer who often worked alongside his men while running the almond huller in his packing shed. He was intimately involved in every phase of his farming operation, which he was carrying on for his father, and would not surrender any control. Instead of giving in to Kubo's demands, he immediately fired the labor boss, drove into town, contacted the *Davisville Enterprise*, warned his fellow farmers, and then went searching for replacement labor. Hiring five white laborers at $1.25 a day, he filled out his crew with ten Chinese field hands obtained at the same wage through the offices of Wing Hai, a Chinese grocery store owner who doubled as a China boss.[78]

Undeterred by their failure at Davisville, *keiyaku-nin* launched a series of job actions around Fresno in August and September. During the first month of the raisin harvest, when most of the crop was ready, *keiyaku-nin* concentrated on obtaining as many jobs as possible. But when the size of the crop decreased after the second month, they began pulling crews out of well-worked vineyards. Sending them on to the next job, they left behind only a skeleton crew, often charging the exasperated grower an extra fifty to seventy-five cents per day for each man. Growers hated the practice, which extended the harvest and left them vulnerable to rain. But that was not the worst of it. Once on the job, *keiyaku-nin* began demanding raises and often walked off the job (at the height of the harvest, if necessary), to secure the wage hikes. When they struck, they usually won because recalcitrant growers who fired them found themselves threatened with a boycott for the next season's harvest, while those who capitulated were quickly assured of labor. Sometimes that threat was all that was required to obtain better wages and working conditions.[79]

By the time the *keiyaku-nin* stopped their attack that fall, growers were in a state of shock. Complaining that they could not control the Japanese, some tried instead to thwart them by proposing a labor bureau that might restore the oversupply of labor. Though frightened by the wave of *keiyaku-nin*–led strikes, many growers worried that, should teamsters again succeed in blocking the loading and shipment of crops as they had done in San Francisco, they might become more ambitious and, building on their success, unite with farmworkers and use their power to build a union capable of controlling agricultural production throughout the state. To prevent that from happening, growers called for "a general law proscribing a closed season for strikers during the gathering and movement of crops." Since crops were harvested year-round, the law would have effectively outlawed farm labor strikes and undermined the *keiyaku-nin*; it would have also insulated farmers from labor unions forever. Though they lobbied hard for the legislation throughout the fall, growers could not get it past urban and labor-oriented representatives. For years thereafter, they would recall the 1901 harvest as an example of their extreme vulnerability and what field hands might do should their power go unchecked.[80]

As the labor shortage continued into 1902, growers took stock of the labor situation. Whereas earlier the editors of the *Pacific Rural Press* had advocated agricultural reorganization as a way to solve the labor problem, now they adopted a more realistic view. "It is a commercial necessity," the *Press* explained in a January editorial, "that to make some lands yield anything to their owners there must be a large supply of people who are willing to do hard work at prices which the traffic will bear." When the cherry and apricot harvest began in the early fruit district around Winters, growers suddenly confronted the practical matter of dealing with a labor shortage. Despite wages of $1 to $1.75 a day and appeals for men, women, and children, growers found that they could not obtain enough harvesters and soon found themselves again dealing with *keiyaku-nin* rushing into the area. Compounding the labor crisis was a dramatic upsurge in Japanese immigration. The number of Japanese immigrants to the West Coast for most of the 1890s had averaged about fifteen hundred per year, but the number had risen to 2,230 in 1898, of which fifteen hundred were farmworkers. On May 28, 1900, the *Sacramento Bee* reported Japanese arriving at the rate of one thousand per month. By the end of the year, 12,635 were in California, ten thousand of them young men between the ages of twenty and thirty. But it was not just that the *keiyaku-nin* suddenly had more field hands to offer at a time when growers needed them. Their hand was now dramatically strengthened when the United States annexed the kingdom of Hawaii. Suddenly the *keiyaku-nin* had a new type of immigrant, some thirty-four thousand Japanese plantation workers who had been imported to Hawaii. With considerable experience working as contract laborers under industrial-style agriculture on Hawaiian sugar plantations, these men as residents of U.S. territory did not have to undergo the difficulties of crossing a border and could easily immigrate to the mainland.[81]

During the summer of 1902, newspapers reported the arrival of entire shiploads of Japanese immigrants, the first of some thirty-two thousand who would arrive from Hawaii over the next four years. Observing two hundred Japanese disembarking in San Francisco from the steerage of the steamer *China*, the *Sacramento Bee* reported:

> They came from Honolulu and the Hawaiian Islands, where they had been working on the plantations. This influx of coolie labor from the Hawaiian Islands is alarming the immigration authorities, but they state that they are powerless to stem the tide. . . . The immigration officials are unable to deny the Asiatics landing because of their coming from a Port of the United States. In addition . . . the Oriental liners carry large numbers of contract laborers from Japan to Honolulu. On her last voyage the *Hongkong Maru* landed over 400 Japanese from Honolulu.[82]

Brought in by corrupt immigration companies, many newcomers were immediately disappointed. In one well-known case, the Meiji Emigration Company promised thirteen men wages of $2.50 a day harvesting fruit and hops in the

Central Valley. However, they never earned more than eighty cents a day. Scraping together their meager savings, many returned to Japan that winter, their plight widely reported in the Japanese-language publication the *Sacramento Daily News*. Those who stayed had no choice other than to seek out *keiyaku-nin* and hope for better luck. These immigrants, the U.S. Industrial Commission reported, "are more servile than the Chinese, but less obedient and far less desirable. They have most of the vices of the Chinese, with none of the virtues. They . . . are, as a class, tricky, unreliable and dishonest." The editor of the *Watsonville Pajaronian* put it another way: "The Japanese have been plentiful . . . and they are unreliable. They are apt to strike or to jump a job when most needed."[83]

But despite this questionable reputation, the power of the *keiyaku-nin* expanded as more plantation workers poured down the gangplanks. Over the next few years they would benefit from one of the few times in the history of California agriculture when anything other than a glutted labor market ever existed. Attractive jobs in railroad construction and industry offered higher-paying work to thousands of white men who otherwise would have been part of the farm labor force. So noticeable was their absence that one grower in 1902 complained that "there is not a [white] man who lives in any agricultural locality who wants to get in and do this work." German immigrant and Woodland grower George Hecke, who in 1916 would be appointed to the State Commission of Horticulture and would subsequently serve as the first director of the California State Department of Agriculture, reiterated this complaint. Addressing the thirty-third California State Fruit Growers Convention, Hecke pointed out that harvest work was dirty, dangerous, and unpleasant, and that "intelligent and reliable white labor is no longer content to engage in menial [farm labor] occupations."[84]

Placing growers at a great disadvantage, the 1902 labor shortage presented the Japanese with countless opportunities. Moving quickly to fill the holes, *keiyaku-nin* began hauling crews of newly arrived plantation workers everywhere. "We see altogether too many Jap teams traveling the streets of Vacaville, and the highways of Vacaville township," complained the *Vacaville Reporter* early in the harvest season. But the *keiyaku-nin* did more than expand their influence. Within months, the "tricky" and "cunning" men were up to their old subterfuges. As fruit ripened, they went to work for a few days, but knowing that they could find better wages elsewhere, broke contracts and forced growers to choose between meeting their demands or watching their crops rot. Sometimes a slowdown was all that was needed to convince a reluctant grower. For example, during the Sonoma County berry harvest in June, *keiyaku-nin* contracted to pick at a certain piece rate then lessened their pace until the grower, faced with a rapidly ripening crop, raised his pay rate. On another farm, *keiyaku-nin* brought in two hundred men at $1.25 a day without board over a two-day period then managed to slow down their work and place the harvest in such jeopardy that they obtained six separate wage increases, eventually settling for two dollars a day. Thereafter they contracted for more work than they could perform and drove their men twice as hard.[85]

As the August hop harvest neared, the Japanese moved into Wheatland prepared to extract as much as they could get from growers who, as the result of a 52 percent drop in European hop production, had seen hop prices rise from eight and one-half cents to twenty-eight cents a pound. As hot weather ripened their unusually large crop, and growers worried that "it will be impossible to secure sufficient white labor for the season's work," Daniel P. Durst hired a crew of seventy-five Japanese, who immediately demanded a raise from the standard ninety cents per one hundred pounds piece rate and ten-cent "bonus" to a flat rate of one dollar a day. Two days into the harvest, when Durst refused their demands, the Japanese walked off the job. Rather than giving in, however, Durst brought in two hundred bindlemen and townspeople, and according to the *Marysville Daily Appeal*, "endeavored to induce others to do likewise." But within a few days, these groups also struck for the same deal. Dismissing these strikers too, Durst then attracted so many white replacements with newspaper advertisements that two days later he was forced to post signs stating, "No more pickers required."[86]

A month and a half after failing at Wheatland, *keiyaku-nin* contracted to pick a Madera County vineyard at the high price of $1.50 per ton, then quit suddenly and moved to another company for slightly better pay, causing a huge loss to several growers. Near Oleander, Japanese grape pickers stalled repeatedly and raised their wages from eighty cents to four dollars a day. Throughout Tulare County, *keiyaku-nin* practiced a particularly exasperating variation on the slowdown. One grower later recalled,

> At the beginning of the season they were picking table grapes, which was slow, careful work, and they soon found they could make more if they picked by the pound. So they went to the grower and told him they wanted to be paid by the pound. The man agreed to their terms, then when the height of the season came on and the grapes were thick and the picking not so particular, they decided they could make more if they picked by the box.[87]

Looking back a few months later, one Fresno grower related one horror story after another for readers of *California Fruit Grower*. "About the third day you see a falling off of pickers, the fourth day another falling off, and they keep falling off until there are only two or three left," he explained. "Where have they all gone? To hold down other jobs."[88]

The problem was that the *keiyaku-nin* were overly ambitious and deserted at the slightest opportunity. "The fact of the matter is," he continued, "they take more work than they can satisfactorily do, and in order to hold the contracts the bosses string out the men." For raisin growers, the policy was disastrous. "Only those who understand the situation can fully sympathize with the vineyardist in his anxiety to get his grapes dried," one grower concluded. "The least delay brings broad visions of stacking and unstacking, at a cost of from 50 to 75 cents per hour for each little man." So thoroughly infuriated were some growers with these tactics—particularly at the approach of rain—that they swore they would never talk to another Japanese so long as they lived.[89]

To escape these pressures during the September prune and peach harvest, Santa Clara County growers again pressed "city boys" into work. But even with wages ranging up to $2.25 a day and railroads offering a two-thirds rate cut to groups of fifteen or more field hands, growers lost large quantities of fruit. After one Tehama grower lost a fruit crop valued at thirty thousand dollars, the

Marysville Record Union carried a long article detailing the crisis. "Fruit Rotting in the Valley Orchards: Thousands of Tons Going to Waste Because Pickers Cannot be Had," shouted its headlines. "Reports coming in from all over this Section of California make it evident that the problem before the people is not the raising but the harvesting of fruits. The pear crop is practically all on the ground in most localities, and the prune crop in Colusa and other communities will be only half-saved."[90]

Conditions were indeed dire, reported the *Sacramento Bee*: "Millions of figs are reported from all around to be falling from the trees to rot while in many sections peaches are being fed to hogs or left to decay. Plums, too, are going to waste. . . . In some districts acres of melons have been left to lie on the ground." Desperate and frightened, one Fresno raisin grower told assembled members of the California State Fruit Growers Convention: "If I had one million dollars, I would not plant another vine unless I knew some solution for the labor question."[91]

By fall 1902, wages had risen 25 to 50 percent since 1900. To most, the lessons seemed clear. A direct relationship existed between labor supply, wages, and working conditions. During years of abundant labor, wages bottomed out and conditions deteriorated; when labor was scarce, wages rose, workers struck, and conditions improved. Given the option of employing five hundred people to pick a crop over a four-week period, or hiring one thousand workers to harvest a crop in two weeks' time, growers always preferred the latter, when it was practical. It was therefore essential, growers reasoned, to restore and maintain a labor glut. University of California agricultural economist R. L. Adams made this a key point in his 1912 textbook on farm labor relations. "When labor is abundant, there is, in the ordinary sense, no labor problem," he wrote. "Competition among laborers . . . results in greater ease in procuring men when wanted, less necessity for providing accommodations, and reduction in the wage scale."[92]

Meeting in their annual conventions at the end of the year, California fruit and vegetable growers wondered if they could survive another year of strikes and job actions. Unlike mine operators or steelmakers, growers produced so-called nondurable goods, products that spoiled if delivery to market was delayed. They could not shut down their operations and wait out the *keiyaku-nin*; the lockout, a standard response of industrialists, would not work. Even a slight delay in picking hops, wine grapes, or cherries could cause a disaster. This vulnerability created an intense paranoia. As one farmer explained: "You can not bank the fires of a cow, or padlock the hen. There is no modern Joshua to command the harvest sun to stand still. A shutdown on a farm means the loss of a year's labor and probably the loss of the farm."[93]

Holding to these views and angered by their brash and callous tactics, nervous farmers shed their earlier enthusiasm for the Japanese and lined up unanimously against them. Speakers at the twenty-seventh California State Fruit Growers Convention, meeting in Pioneer Hall in San Francisco in December 1902, scrutinized what Sacramento fruit grower H. P. Stabler described as an "unprecedented scarcity of . . . help" coupled with a wave of labor militancy. Longing for the days of the "patient, docile, and generally reliable" Chinese, growers discussed ways to induce immigration from the East and Midwest or to amend or undo restrictive Chinese immigration laws. But more than anything else, they discussed the increasingly arrogant Japanese. "Aside from being very unsatisfactory laborers, my experience has been that they break up my trees, steal my chickens, and eat them down by the side of the creek in the night time," complained one grower. "They seem to do everything they ought not to do, and nothing that they should do." Another farmer, a realist not wishing to concede anything to the Japanese, recommended forming growers associations, much like the National Association of Manufacturers. "It seems to me that a vigorous effort at organization might bring something out of this almost hopeless situation—organization seems to be the only hope," he argued. But at least one speaker did not wait for others to act and immediately fired all of his Japanese. "I could not control the people at all," he explained, "so I bade good by [sic] to the Japs."[94]

Eventually the hysteria died down. "Notwithstanding the fact that much talk had been heard about a shortage of help, there was not a person present who knew of any serious loss of crops from that cause," reported the *Placer County Republican*. Nevertheless, after the 1902 harvest season, the *keiyaku-nin* were depicted in the California press as tough fellows, a little greedy, perhaps, but determined, competent in what they were doing, extremely well organized, and a bit underhanded. "The Jap is a fairly good fellow, but too smart," one grower explained to the Farmer's Institute meeting in Newcastle's Good Templar's Hall in March 1903. "He is thoroughly organized and takes advantage of the unorganized condition of the growers to demand excessive wages." Asked about such accusations, some *keiyaku-nin* later said that they had taken the offensive to capitalize on a tight labor market and to shake field hands out of their *dekaseginin* orientation. But this was probably an afterthought. More likely, they started the campaign on impulse, with each *keiyaku-nin* responding to unique local conditions. When they realized their power, they grew bolder. At Oxnard, in Ventura County, they would come together and systematically challenge agriculture and the sugar beet industry on a scale heretofore unseen in California.[95]

CHAPTER EIGHTEEN

Blood Spots on the Moon

The 1903 Oxnard Sugar Beet Workers Strike

In 1897, Congress passed the Dingley Tariff Act, which imposed a heavy duty on imported sugar. One year later, Chino sugar magnate Henry Oxnard seized the opportunity and decided to add a second sugar beet processing factory in California. After scouring the state for a suitable site, he settled on a forty-eight-thousand-acre tract astride the Santa Clara River in Ventura County, about sixty-seven miles north of Los Angeles. The soil was unusually deep and fertile and the deepwater port city of Port Hueneme was just a few miles to the west. Returns from lima beans and grain farming had been steadily declining, and local farmers, many of whom had been growing sugar beets and shipping them south to Oxnard's refinery at Chino, were ready to plant on a large scale. All of these conditions suggested a bright future for the Oxnards and their American Beet Sugar Company. Even the ocean fog seemed advantageous, allowing the crop to grow without irrigation. Prospects were so good that the Oxnards decided to construct the "model sugar factory of America"—a mammoth, ultramodern, superefficient, three-million-dollar plant that would make all previous facilities look primitive. Groundbreaking ceremonies for the new factory drew more than four thousand invited guests on February 5, 1898. Listening to speeches, dancing, and touring the area, the crowd consumed three thousand pounds of beef, one thousand loaves of bread, and a large supply of barbecued rabbits.[1]

To overcome the shortage of local construction materials, the innovative Oxnards developed their own quarry and cement manufacturing plant, then built a temporary railroad line from Montalvo down the dry Ventura riverbed to the factory site and transported more than nine hundred railcar loads of machinery needed for the project. Overseeing everything, engineer Wilhelm Baur watched his men like a hawk from a glass observatory atop his office, instantly dispatching messengers to summon and discipline foremen found to be performing unsatisfactorily. When the work was finished on August 19, 1898, the factory was the second largest sugar processing plant in the United States and resembled a small

FIGURE 39. Japanese field hands hauling sugar beets to the Pacific Sugar Company factory. Date unknown. Courtesy of the California Historical Society/Title Insurance and Trust Company Collection, University of Southern California.

city. Besides the factory itself, Baur had erected a sixty-by-one-hundred-foot, two-story boardinghouse, office buildings, storage bins, water and oil tanks, kilns, evaporation and settling ponds, and other assorted structures. Rising above the valley floor, the factory's 175-foot tall smokestacks instantly became prominent landmarks visible twenty miles away.[2]

In some ways, the American Beet Sugar Company was built better than expected; in other ways, considerably worse. After a disappointing first season, the factory began to show excellent results. The average dollar return per acre of beets rose from $48.35 in 1897 to $59.01 in 1901, while the factory registered a corresponding increase in "tons of beets produced." By 1903, the factory was refining nearly two hundred thousand tons of beets and guaranteeing contracts for twenty thousand acres of beets at $3.75 a ton for beets with 12-percent sugar content, and bonuses for every additional percent of sugar content, figures that brought an average $4.75 a ton for most growers. Paying $1.5 million to growers for beets, and seventy-five thousand dollars a month to factory workers, the beet factory also operated a seventy-five-hundred-acre experimental farm. Staffed by professional agronomists, most with considerable experience growing sugar beets in Europe, the farm employed all of the latest implements, installed a vast drainage system, pioneered deep plowing methods, laid out more than four miles of railroads to deliver beets to the factory, perfected techniques of crop rotation that increased yields substantially, and worked out a way to plant earlier, thereby moving up the harvest date from July to May.[3]

As their business grew, the Oxnards became involved in countless social functions and in financial matters of the region. Besides helping to found the Bank of Oxnard and serving on the boards of various civic organizations, they ingeniously promoted the cattle industry, which thrived on a diet of surplus sugar beet pulp mixed with straw and molasses. To protect the town's residents and raise funds for its fire department, the Oxnards held a great benefit ball and special factory tour, bringing more than one thousand guests from Los Angeles and raising thousands of dollars. So grandiose and important were the Oxnards and their sugar beet factory to the Santa Clara Valley economy that, when Southern Pacific Railroad built a branch line from Burbank, local leaders appreciative of the millions of dollars that the factory annually pumped into the area named the station—and later the town—Oxnard.[4]

About three thousand people resided in Oxnard, virtually all of them dependent either directly or indirectly upon the sugar beet industry. So promising was the factory as a source of employment that, in 1899, hundreds of residents of Port Hueneme loaded their possessions onto wagons and relocated in such numbers that their former town was depopulated; even buildings as large as rooming houses were pulled by mule teams over log rollers four miles to Oxnard. At the height of the harvest, seven hundred men worked in the factory, mostly at racially and ethnically segmented tasks. For hundreds accustomed to battling the glutted local labor market while following the harvests every summer from Saticoy to Santa Paula, often camping out under the stars with their families in tow, promise of continuous work in one location and a roof over their head proved especially alluring. Because so much of the machinery came from Germany and so many key engineering positions were staffed by Germans, for example, it was often remarked that the factory was "practically run by Germans." White foremen, supervisors, office employees, and maintenance workers handled most skilled positions, while Mexicans, immigrants from several Louisiana sugar factories, and hundreds of merchants, fishermen, artisans, and laborers from the area handled most of the unskilled labor.[5]

Work was hard and every bit as dangerous and exhausting as labor in a steel mill. As in many steel mills, machinists often arrived at dawn and departed after dark. Men became exhausted, lost concentration, and were maimed and killed in horrible and grotesque accidents. Mechanics attempting to make repairs were smashed by falling debris, decapitated by loose pulley belts, or caught in sugar mixers and crushed by revolving mixer arms. Limekiln operators had their arms shredded by cogwheels. Boiler tenders who climbed ladders to inspect gauges or adjust gears fell into vats of boiling sugar and were scalded. Janitors sweeping the floors stumbled into open elevator shafts and plummeted several stories to their death. Teamsters arranging beet nets at the beet dump, one of the most risky jobs, were routinely killed when teams spooked and entire wagon loads of beets fell on them or the wheels of the runaway wagon crushed them horribly; laborers employed forking sugar beet pulp down into bins lost their footing, were caught by a flood of water and washed down into the pulp shoot and out through the flumes into the waste pulp ditch. As always, coroners invariably concluded their investigations by exonerating the American Beet Sugar Company of any blame.[6]

At the height of the sugar beet harvest, Oxnard was as wild as any Central Valley wheat town. On Saturday nights or on rainy days, factory hands crowded the sidewalks. Mixed in among them would be crews of thirty or forty men, each from various barley or bean threshing outfits. Starting at the plaza and all the way down Main Street to Saviers Road, workers went from one drinking establishment to another. A favorite spot was the sidewalk outside the saloon on the southwest corner of A and Fifth streets. With a little stage at the back and the door open so that anyone could see the dancing girls performing, it always attracted large throngs. Taking advantage of the traffic, prostitutes frequented the area, dressing in flashy dresses and hats loaded with plumes. Nearby, the two blocks between Sixth and Eighth streets intersecting Saviers Road accounted for the bulk of Oxnard's fights and murders.[7]

As Oxnard developed, a strict social dividing line bisected and segregated the town, creating two entirely different worlds. German and Irish farmers, Jewish families, and local businessmen lived on the west side, which boasted substantial buildings, at least one mansion, the principal hotel, the town plaza, the newly constructed Santa Clara Catholic Church (built on land donated by the Oxnards), the Women's Christian Temperance Union, the *Oxnard Courier* newspaper, and various other upstanding enterprises ranging from dry goods stores to the telegraph office. Also living on the west side were officials and managers of the American Beet Sugar Company, who retired each evening to the Colonia Clubhouse, a kind of private hotel, complete with smoking rooms and dining halls, which the company officials described as "a model of a modern owl's nest, where the heads of departments will rest from toil." Permanent factory employees also enjoyed a free reading room with plenty of chairs where they could lounge and browse an extensive library or read the latest newspapers from Ventura County, Los Angeles, and San Francisco.[8]

On the east side of town, field hands concentrated in an enclave that extended between the alley south of Fifth and Sixth streets and Saviers Road. Early on, this was the habitat of tramps, and the local newspaper, disliking the men, complained often that they were infesting the town and were as worthless as field hands. While local whites and bindlemen tried their hand at thinning sugar beets in the spring of 1899, they were a dismal failure. Obtaining jobs through a "Free Labor Bureau" operating out of an Oxnard storefront, they were unable to keep up with the pace and often walked out before fulfilling their contracts. To save their crop, growers turned to Mexican crews from Santa Barbara, China bosses from Ventura and Port Hueneme, and *keiyaku-nin* from Watsonville and Riverside. As early as February 4, 1899, China bosses had met to capitalize on the opportunity. But it was the sight of Japanese passing through Santa Paula on their way to Oxnard that touched off heated debate. "Nearly every west-bound passenger train has had a load of them," observed a reporter for the *Santa Paula*

Chronicle, who counted nearly one thousand Japanese. As concern for the influx grew acute during the summer, the *Oxnard Courier* attempted to counter alarmist reports in the *Ventura Free Press* and angry street-corner talk in town by assuring its readers that virtually all of the Chinese and Japanese would depart after the beet thinning season; none would work in the factory, none would purchase property in town, and they would not become a permanent presence. But within a few months, the newspaper recanted. "The not unexpected has happened. The COURIER has feared from the start that the large force of men required to properly thin and care for the large acreage of beets could not be had when wanted." Now growers would be "compelled to employ all kinds of labor, Japanese, Chinese, or whatever, or see their crops ruined." With only fifty local Chinese available, the *keiyaku-nin* again sprang into action and shipped in two thousand Japanese, mainly from Watsonville. Like the Chinese, they settled on the east side of town and immediately established their own quarter.[9]

For local blue bloods, the Japanese quarter—known as the "tenderloin" and "Japtown"—quickly became a source of concern. If the *Oxnard Courier* was to be believed, knife fights and murders soon became everyday occurrences. "JAP WAR IN OXNARD," "CUTTING AFFRAY IN JAP TOWN," were typical headlines feeding the view of the Japanese section as a den of wickedness. Headlines like these, always run in uppercase, bold type, only made citizens more nervous about the Japanese culture, which seemed literally foreign even to those accustomed to immigrant neighborhoods. In particular, people could not understand why the Japanese crowded together. "With so much unoccupied land all about us," mused one town leader, "there is absolutely no necessity for 1,000 to 1,500 Japanese and Chinese cuddling themselves up in a half dozen measly, low, stinking and dirty huts with all kinds of pitfalls and dark alleys where murder can be committed in broad daylight without detection."[10]

Although few locals understood it, the Japanese section was a fully functioning community. Here field hands gained easy access to everything they required. Cafés, pool halls, and opium dens catering to the small Chinese population all were located conveniently nearby, as were boardinghouses and various stores furnishing food, clothes, and shelter to laborers (often at inflated prices). Most important, this was where one went to find work. If a man wanted a job thinning or harvesting beets he went to the Laborer's Headquarters building at the corner of Seventh and A streets, where *keiyaku-nin* operated a large contracting business. Or there was Joe Baba between Fifth and Sixth streets, or George T. Hara and Company on Saviers Road.[11]

Very little is known about the *keiyaku-nin* operating around Oxnard at this time, except that nine or ten of them annually ran crews of one hundred or more men. These men, along with a few Japanese businessmen, comprised a substantial middle-class society distinct from the more than two-thirds (68.2 percent) of Ventura County Japanese who worked in the fields. Whatever protection Japanese laborers enjoyed, whatever job security they gained, whatever wages they earned came through these *keiyaku-nin*, not the American Beet Sugar Company.[12]

❧

Since 1900, *keiyaku-nin* had, on several occasions, protected or advanced the wages of local field hands, and because of their assertiveness around Oxnard, and their general uppityness throughout California during the preceding years, were increasingly regarded with suspicion and distrust. Though beneficial to field hands, their power and independence was seen as a threat to the agricultural industry. Believing that there was a notable difference between Japanese, Chinese, and Mexican field hands and fearing that, as the *Oxnard Courier* put it, "the Jap is a fighter from way back," sugar beet factory officials complained about how *keiyaku-nin* delayed work and squeezed farmers "at a time when work is plenty and workers scarce."[13]

Pressures to eliminate the *keiyaku-nin* had begun building early in January 1902, as the beet factory prepared for its largest run ever. With a record 18,600 acres of sugar beets in the ground, farmers had employed all the latest technology to establish their crop. At great cost, several of them used giant, stationary, steam-traction engines and plows imported from England to prepare their land for planting. But mechanization only went so far. Hand labor was central to sugar beet production. "The sugar beet is a hoe crop in the true sense of the word," wrote the *Beet Sugar Gazette*. "The hoe . . . must not be spared in the cultivation of this crop."[14]

Once the planting had been done, hand laborers would take over and remain at the center of operations. Within the space of six to eight weeks, from mid-March to mid-May, the entire sugar beet crop had to be blocked and thinned. No machines could perform the work. Unlike wheat farmers, who according to John D. Spreckels, "were accustomed to scratch the ground up a little bit and put in wheat and go back to town in the back of the saloon and play cards," sugar beet farmers had to perform numerous hand-labor operations to raise their crop. "There has never been anything invented that will thin and weed beets," sugar trust agent Chester S. Morey told a congressional committee investigating the sugar beet industry in 1912. "It is gardening on a large scale. . . . So that over all those long fields must be gone across on the knees of some man, woman, or child."[15]

Although conventional wisdom held that only immigrants and minorities would perform beet thinning, sugar beet growers, uneasy over the size of their huge crop and the perennial shortage of workers, continually experimented with different groups. This led to curious experiences, most of which were duly reported in the *Oxnard Courier*. When one prominent farmer hired an Irishman to thin his beets, the gentleman explained that he had never thinned beets but supposed it was like hoeing potatoes. As the grower watched him closely, the Irishman grew restless and angry. When the grower came out for the seventh time to instruct the Irishman in the art of beet thinning—it seemed impossible to teach him how to cut the rows straight and leave any beets for maturing—the farmer exclaimed in disgust, "Oh, you've got wheels in your head." "Yes," said the Irishman, "an th' wheels in me had an th' rubber in your neck wu'd make a foine bicycle."[16]

To increase the efficiency of hand operations, growers experimented with different kinds of beet hoes, bending and shaping them to various angles in an attempt to decrease the effort required to use them and to increase the efficiency of each swing. During February 1902, Thomas Ruiz, who operated a blacksmith shop in Ventura, and Al Espinosa, a Mexican beet contractor, patented and introduced one of the most promising of these devices, consisting of a detachable, curved steel hoe that could be strapped to the hand and drawn through the soil while leaving the fingers free to pull beets or weeds. It is impossible to sort out whether or not this device was an attempt to improve on existing short-handled hoes or merely a step toward the initial introduction of that infamous device. Still in prototype form, it presented considerable promise, but was not yet available in sufficient numbers to influence the impending blocking and thinning operations. This meant that, as usual, sugar beet growers would require the labor of more than one thousand field hands.[17]

While cultural practices defied mechanization, the industry did make progress eliminating hand labor at harvest time by deploying the Eifer and Nauman riding beet plow. Invented by a local blacksmith and farmer, it was much lighter and more efficient than other devices, easily adjustable to work in hard and soft ground, and introduced for the first time that summer. Dividing crews in two, foremen sent one group in behind the beet plows to lift, top, and pile beets, and a second behind the topping crew to load the beets into a wagon for transportation to the factory beet dump. The new beet pulling device allowed beet plowers to ride rather than walk behind the plow and more quickly and easily lift beets from the ground two rows at a time. But while speeding the harvest, it did not eliminate the need for large numbers of field hands deployed under contractors.[18]

Unable to mechanize cultural practices and only slightly able to increase harvest labor output, sugar beet company officials well aware of how the *keiyaku-nin* had amassed power and raised wages in other agricultural districts feared that they would try similar tactics once on the job in Oxnard. In March, the presidents of the Bank of Oxnard and the Bank of A[chilles] Levy, with backing from several prominent businessmen, beet growers, and officials of the American Beet Sugar Company, raised fifty thousand dollars in capital, formed the Western Agricultural Contracting Company (WACC), and settled on a plan to eliminate the *keiyaku-nin* and bring the entire labor contracting business under their control. Although it has sometimes been described as a union of company-backed and financed contractors, the WACC, unlike most company unions that at least offered some benefits to workers, provided none; its only purpose was to set one group of contractors against another, to break the *keiyaku-nin*, and hold down labor costs.

Moving quickly, the WACC rented quarters in the American Beet Lodging House then immediately signed beet thinning and topping contracts with the one-thousand-acre Patterson ranch. Within a few weeks, the WACC had signed up 307 field hands, obtained contracts with a dozen other farmers, and secured the services of an additional 150 men as insurance should the thinning work come in all at once. "Contract your topping to a responsible company, who have ample capital and experienced men," read WACC advertisements in local newspapers. "We will be pleased to submit you prices. Call and see us before closing your topping contracts, or write and our representative will call."[19]

From its inception, the WACC was closely watched by growers throughout the state. As the first labor organization of its kind, it seemed to present a ready solution to growing problems with *keiyaku-nin*. The WACC's operation was, in fact, extraordinary. To obtain the required laborers, salaried WACC representatives in San Francisco, Fresno, and Los Angeles scoured their territories for men. During early April, with more than five thousand acres of sugar beets ready for thinning, the WACC brought in 443 Japanese and 175 Mexican field hands from San Francisco, San Fernando, Riverside, Los Angeles, Selma, Fowler, and Fresno. To house them, it established a string of thirty-eight labor camps, some of them containing more than one hundred men and resembling small villages, at strategic points from Port Hueneme north to Carpinteria, south to Camarillo, and east as far as Somis and Santa Paula. Daily payroll at thinning time amounted to an enormous eleven hundred dollars per day. With seven thousand acres under contract by April 26, the WACC did not confine its activities to Oxnard and soon began shipping beet thinning crews as far away as Chino and Los Alamitos.[20]

By all appearances an overwhelming success, the WACC had succeeded in filling jobs and holding down wages, particularly during late April, when panic-stricken farmers considered offering as much as seven and eight dollars an acre for thinning. At one time, the WACC assisted a number of desperate farmers by gathering two hundred men in a day and a half. "It is indeed hard to estimate what would be done without this large force of men, all of whom were under-experienced overseers," explained the *Oxnard Courier*.[21]

In June, just as the sugar content of beets reached 12 percent (the minimum for harvesting), George E. Herz, an authority on sugar beet growing who had supervised the American Beet Sugar Company's experimental farm, purchased a controlling interest in the WACC. Although the company was already well established, Herz's leadership nonetheless proved effective when the sugar beet factory, "like a fierce Grendal of old, spitting fire and steam," roared into action. Supervising about one thousand field hands, the WACC harvested roughly half of the 190,000-ton sugar beet crop that year. By completing their contracted jobs and never skipping town with wages, WACC contractors seemed very different from their Japanese competitors. It was an impressive performance, marred by only one minor problem. Midway through October, as the harvest wound down, the WACC lost parts of several Mexican crews when men abandoned beet work to pick over the straw and dust left beneath lima bean threshers after they had moved on. They could hardly be faulted. Yielding $2.50 to $3 a day, "bean setting," as it was known, not only paid more than sugar beet harvesting, it was also far easier.[22]

Through connivance, backroom dealings, and intimidation, the WACC in its brief existence had succeeded in taking over more than 90 percent of Oxnard's sugar beet contracting business. But early that fall, as it laid the basis for expanding its operation, the company suffered a temporary setback and minor scandal when cofounder and president Hugh W. Bryson ran into financial and legal difficulties and was arrested as the result of embezzlement committed by a woman he had taken up with. Meeting quickly, stockholders forced Bryson to resign, then elevated Herz to president. When the WACC convened its next meeting on December 17, Herz announced plans to go after the remaining portion of the labor force aggressively, and to eliminate the *keiyaku-nin* and other independent contractors. WACC leaders had no idea that the Japanese had foreseen just such a move and were already preparing a counterattack.[23]

≠∂

On March 1, 1903, more than one thousand Japanese departed from their labor camps and boardinghouse communities to begin the second season of beet thinning under the WACC. Riding in wagons bound for the sugar beet fields around Oxnard, they passed the American Beet Sugar Company factory's stinking holding ponds. Just as they reached the fields, the first rays of dawn caught the limekiln smokestacks, accentuating the smudge and grime on their sides. They arrived for work in a disposition as dark and foul as the odor wafting off the sludge ponds.[24]

Two months earlier, they had discovered that the WACC had lowered the rate for thinning beets from six or five dollars per acre to between $4.25 and $3.75 per acre (in some cases, as low as $2.50 per acre). Their discontent grew as beet growers made it known that they would not negotiate wages with other contractors. Forced to secure employment through the WACC, the Japanese found not only that their wages had been lowered without their say, but also that they now had to pay a fee to the WACC and a percentage of their wages to WACC subcontractors who employed them. Even more humiliating, they would have to accept scrip payment for merchandise and store orders redeemable only at the company-owned Japanese-American Mercantile Store. Since the store routinely marked up goods as much as 60 percent, field hands would now be forced to pay $1.20 for a seventy-five-cent pair of shoes, for example, a gouging that further ate into their already lowered wages.[25]

In a meeting with sugar beet growers, a group of sixty Japanese field hands, many of them from among the ranks of 120 boarding students who had been recruited in San Francisco by labor contractor Y. Yamaguchi, complained that the WACC in earlier meetings had misrepresented working conditions and lied about wages. Demanding restoration of the original arrangement promising them $1.50 per day, the men threatened to strike. But WACC leaders and officials of the American Beet Sugar Company stood firm, announcing that all Japanese field hands would hereafter come under supervision of the WACC's so-called Jap department, run by an Ibaragi prefecture native, former Oxnard *keiyaku-nin*, and Japanese-American Mercantile Store manager Inosuke ("John") Inose.[26]

With beet thinning about to accelerate, Japanese field hands challenged the WACC. Led by Kōzaburō ("Joe") Baba, an experienced *keiyaku-nin*, and San Francisco contractor Yamaguchi, the Japanese formed their own farm labor organization. On the following Saturday, men still at work thinning beets under the WACC accepted their pay envelopes without a hint of protest. Instead, Yamaguchi wrote to the *Oxnard Courier* succinctly explaining their position. "Many of us have families, were born in the country, and are lawfully seeking to protect the only property that we have—our labor," he began. "It is just as necessary for the welfare of the valley that we get a decent living wage, as it is that the machines in the great sugar factory be properly oiled—if the machine stops, the wealth of the valley stops, and likewise if the laborers are not given a decent wage, they too, must stop work and the whole people of this country suffer with them."[27]

Most Oxnard newspapers predicted the Japanese would not carry through with the threat. And even as their recruitment drive accelerated, local farmers ignored what the *Oxnard Courier* called "the ignorant, and . . . irresponsible" *keiyaku-nin*, preferring to deal with "reliable American contractors" who could provide men at lower wages. Too weak to pose a serious threat, according to the paper the Japanese were "in the hands of people whose experience has been only to obey a master rather than think and manage for themselves." Furthermore, the paper predicted, they could expect little support from outside the area.[28]

Yet industrial warfare was closer at hand than most realized. The protagonist was Colonel J. A. Driffill, one of a tight-knit group of veteran sugar beet officials whose power and influence radiated throughout the Oxnard community. A close personal friend of Robert Oxnard, the stiff, militaristic forty-three-year-old Driffill had worked his way up through the ranks at the Chino sugar beet refinery before coming to Oxnard, where he supervised every sugar beet "campaign," as each season's harvest was described. Meeting with growers, local officials, and his subordinates early in 1903, he urged them to support the WACC. By the time the Japanese stated their intentions, Driffill had put everyone on notice that he was not about to tolerate farmworker militancy, and a few days later, as beet thinning neared, issued an unambiguous threat. "I have heard that you have a scale of prices which is detrimental to the interests of the farmers," he told Baba and Yamaguchi, "and the interests of the farmers are our interests, because if you raise the price of labor to the farmers and they cannot raise beets at a profit, we will have to take steps to drive you out of the country and secure help from the outside—even if we have to spend $100,000 in doing so."[29]

❧

When the Japanese left the Oxnard fields, they did so without the support of organized labor; their as yet unnamed union had acted alone. Profoundly conservative and thoroughly racist, the American Federation of Labor (AFL), despite lofty appeals for working-class unity "irrespective of creed, color, sex, nationality, or politics," in actual practice did not embrace all workers and followed an increasingly obsolete philosophy. Known as "pure and simple unionism," "craft unionism," and "business unionism," this philosophy, which also featured high dues and large strike funds, made the AFL ideologically and temperamentally ill-suited to the technological changes that, for example, cost the AFL virtually its entire membership in the glass industry, where skilled glassblowers were rapidly replaced by machines, and the cigar industry, where machines also ate away the AFL base among skilled cigar makers. Its greatest failure was in the steel industry, where the once strong Amalgamated Association of Iron, Steel, and Tin Workers faded from the scene under the impact of mechanization.[30]

While craft unionism generally made the AFL a bad fit for California's unskilled farm laborers, it was racism more than anything else that truly separated it from Japanese and other ethnic farmworkers. To most AFL leaders, Japanese immigrants—indeed, all Asian immigrants—were filthy, diseased, and "degraded people," so impossible to organize that, according to Gompers, "all efforts to elevate them to a higher standard have proved futile." Keeping Asians out of the labor movement (and out of the United States) was as important to Gompers and the AFL as the eight-hour day and overtime pay, so important, in fact, that AFL leaders had championed restriction throughout the 1890s. Gompers himself wrote one of the nastiest racists tracts of the restrictionist campaign. Entitled *Some Reasons for Chinese Exclusion: Meat vs. Rice, American Manhood Against Asiatic Coolieism, Which Shall Survive?* it was a broadside against the "Asian-hordes," essentially the same message as his presidential report to the 1901 AFL convention, in which he said that "every incoming coolie means . . . so much more vice and immorality injected into our social life" with the inevitable "degenerate" effects of miscegenation between Americans and Asiatics.[31]

If anything, Gompers, the AFL, and the California labor movement regarded Japanese immigrants as a greater blight than their Chinese predecessors. Nowhere was this sentiment stronger than in San Francisco, the most thoroughly unionized city in the United States, where brewers, plumbers, and bricklayers won significant concessions from management in their trades, a "skilled aristocracy of labor" emerged, wages rose 30 percent higher than in Los Angeles, and the San Francisco Building Trades Council, wielding considerable political clout through the Union Labor Party, elected two of its candidates mayor. Using his power to protect his base, Building Trades Council leader Patrick McCarthy poured his union's energies and resources into an anti-Japanese campaign that pumped a steady stream of propaganda before the public and rallied support for restrictive legislation. Maintaining that Japanese workers were unlike "ignorant" immigrant workers from Eastern Europe who could be taught the fundamentals of unionism, the trades unions painted a picture of treacherous Japanese dominated completely by *keiyaku-nin*. "I have learned that a Jap can live on the smell of an oily rag," explained California labor leader Walter MacArthur at the founding AFL convention. Incapable of being Americanized, they would never make good union members and, as a "menace" to honest workingmen, should be excluded from labor unions and prevented from immigrating.[32]

Hostile to the Japanese, organized labor demonstrated only passing interest in the agricultural sector. In late August 1901, after eighty-five Fresno raisin packers struck for higher wages, the AFL issued a "federal charter" to 350 members of the Fruit and Raisin Packing House Employee's Union. Although such unions usually dissipated quickly, an organizer on loan from the California State Federation of Labor led a strike that won a wage increase during the 1902 raisin harvest. At about the same time, an organizer affiliated with the Federated Trades Council of San Jose set up locals among packinghouse workers in San Jose and Santa Clara County and chartered Fruit Worker's Union Number 10,770. But after forming a labor bureau to secure some measure of employment regularity and serve as a clearinghouse for labor, the new union made only one demand: a wage of two dollars a day in the packing sheds. While the two unions appeared to win some concessions, neither survived beyond the end of the year. Their principal legacy, insofar as Oxnard's workers were concerned, was to alert growers to the growing restlessness of labor and lead some to conclude that everything possible must be done to prevent any contact between city workers and organized labor.[33]

When the Japanese looked for help outside of Oxnard in March of 1903, only labor unionists in Los Angeles seemed at all sympathetic. And while this interest may have seemed odd on the surface, in fact the Los Angeles labor movement differed radically from its counterparts nationally and in San Francisco. In 1902, it had teamed up with Socialists to run a Union Labor Party ticket that came in third in the mayoral campaign, their candidate winning about 17 percent of the vote. For the next decade this alliance remained firm, as the labor council supported political candidates under various party labels. With its Socialist leadership, the Los Angeles County Council of Labor, though entirely composed of Anglos, remained far ahead of the rest of the labor movement in extending its hand to working people of color, as well as Mexican political refugees and Mexican workers on strike against "El Traque," the city's electric railway system. When the Oxnard sugar beet workers appealed for help, the council did not hesitate.[34]

Intent on doing what they could to advance the cause of labor solidarity, Fred C. Wheeler, an officer in the Los Angeles Brotherhood of Carpenters and Joiners, who had been nominated by the Socialists for state senator and ran for mayor in 1900, and John M. Murray, a craft unionist long active in the Labor Party movement, took the train north to Oxnard. Wheeler and Murray provided leadership during the initial phase of organization and remained in town until the Japanese had met with their Mexican counterparts, formed the Japanese-Mexican Labor Association (JMLA), elected leaders, and established an office. Signing up all five hundred or six hundred of the Japanese who had been brought down from San Francisco by Yamaguchi, the JMLA quickly gained the sympathy of substantial numbers of residents in Oxnard, especially the merchants who had lost considerable trade as a result of the WACC scrip payment policy and arrangements with the Japanese-American Mercantile Store.[35]

❧

Elected JMLA secretary in mid-February 1903, Yamaguchi quickly emerged as an eloquent and forceful spokesman for his organization. For two weeks, as the wet fields began to dry out and the beet plants sprouted, he held nightly meetings, addressed crowds of beet workers, and led labor parades and gatherings that drew attention to the cause. Described as "most demonstrative" and an "eloquent chap" who "stirred up considerable enthusiasm," Yamaguchi quickly ran into trouble. Rumors circulated that, as a result of Yamaguchi's agitation, his principal rival, John Inose, had been threatened. "It is thought," wrote the *Ventura Independent* on March 5, "that a killing or two may yet result from the present agitation."[36]

On these grounds, and to "quiet troubled spirits," Sheriff Edmund McMartin arrested Yamaguchi on Sunday, February 28. Charged with inciting to riot and held under a five-hundred-dollar bond, Yamaguchi was tried two days later. Defended by Judge W. E. Shepherd of Ventura, he was promptly acquitted. Once free, he was back on the streets talking to beet workers. Over the next four days, Yamaguchi held street meetings and initiated an active organizing campaign designed to double the JMLA's membership. He also distributed circulars and mailed literature to farmers and merchants "of a tone to excite their sympathy with the labor union and for the purpose of getting contracts."[37]

The JMLA was now well on its way, but it still faced one major problem. Japanese field hands and *keiyaku-nin* did not hold a monopoly over farm labor in the area. That was because Oxnard's farm labor force was composed of several different groups. The smallest group was the Chinese, who made up only about five of every one hundred field hands. Far more important was Ventura County's Mexican population, nearly half of which (47.6 percent) worked as field hands; around Oxnard they accounted for roughly one in five sugar beet hands. Unlike the Japanese, who were mostly single migrant men and recent immigrants, many Mexican field hands were second-generation Californians, with families, permanent residences, and a long history in the area. Some Mexican families considerably supplemented their income by allowing so many children to leave school and work in the fields that when census takers moved through in late May and early June, they complained that they could not make an accurate count because too many schoolchildren were absent. But even with all the work, life in the sugar beet fields remained a drudge, and some young men simply could not endure it. This was apparently the case with Lee Valenzuela, a twenty-four-year-old field hand. After coming to Oxnard from Los Angeles, he had failed to make ends meet. Lonely and despondent, Valenzuela sat in the alley between A Street and Saviers Road, took several swallows of carbolic acid, and died in a short time "by the old carbolic acid route."[38]

By the time Wheeler and Murray arrived, the WACC had created a "Mexican department." Run by Ventura agricultural machinery expert and community leader Albert Espinosa, the department was tacit admission of the importance of Mexican field hands in the Oxnard sugar beet industry. To counter the WACC's efforts among the Mexicans, the JMLA also devoted considerable attention to the Mexicans. Electing local labor contractor J. M. Lizarras as secretary of its Mexican branch, the JMLA sent him into the Mexican community on an aggressive organizing drive.[39]

Lizarras, a stocky, almond-skinned man, did not have to look far to find Oxnard's Mexican beet workers. He had only to stroll down Saviers Road from the Japanese quarters on the east side of town toward Chinatown, where Mexican field hands packed into a lively rural ghetto known as Sonoratown or the "Latin quarter." A rough place, Sonoratown at first glance would seem an impossible and unlikely location for Lizarras or anyone else to conduct a successful farm labor organizing drive. Oxnard leaders had nothing good to say about the place. Repulsed by the profusion of gambling parlors, houses of prostitution, boardinghouses, and saloons, they constantly scrutinized and condemned Sonoratown as a strange, disreputable, "rip-roaring slum," thoroughly "contaminated" with "riff-raff" and numerous "Mexicans and others loitering around." According to many residents, Sonoratown exerted a "damning influence on her neighbors" and prevented many people from settling in town.[40]

Nor was Sonoratown safe. Robberies, murders, and drunken brawls always made sensational copy, as did shootings between rival labor contractors, which

FIGURE 40. Adobe housing constructed for Mexican field hands by the American Crystal Sugar Company, Oxnard. Courtesy of the Minnesota Historical Society.

sometimes wounded innocent bystanders. These occurred frequently enough for Mexican field hands and labor contractors there to acquire a not entirely undeserved reputation as hard drinking, tough customers who sliced and carved one another in an instant. Ever alert, the *Oxnard Courier* never failed to report the more sensational and violent events. "TWO MEN BURNED TO DEATH," began one grizzly account of Mexican field hands, jailed for drunkenness, who incinerated themselves after lighting a fire in an attempt to escape from their locked jail cell. Other stories reinforced the picture of Mexican lawlessness. "MEXICANS IN BLOODY BATTLE," "MEXICANS GORE ONE ANOTHER WITH POCKET KNIVES," "SHOOTING AFFAIR," "SHOT BY A BEAN THIEF," "ANOTHER SHOOTING AFFRAY ENDS FATALLY," "TWO CONTRACTORS ROBBED AND BEATEN," "UNKNOWN MEXICAN FOUND SLASHED IN THE FACE WITH A KNIFE," "A LITTLE ON THE RACE WAR," and "CARD GAME THAT TERMINATED IN BLOODSHED," shouted typical headlines. Perhaps the worst story described the sad fate of Ignacio Avila, an "energetic and reliable beet laborer, and well thought of by contractors." Avila's body was discovered early one Saturday morning in the Pacific Lumber Company yard. He had seventeen stab wounds, four to the heart.[41]

But if the dangers of Sonoratown impeded Lizarras in any way, it was not evident. Working his way through the boardinghouses and bars, Lizarras was able to go about his business largely free of harassment, perhaps because most local authorities gave him little chance of succeeding. More important, he had close connections to, and the support of, other Mexican contractors. This would prove particularly important. Mexican contractors not only provided employment, housing, and loans to their workers, they were also deeply involved in many aspects of civic life, especially the annual Mexican Independence Day celebration, held on September 16. With so much money and stature to lose should the WACC succeed in sweeping them aside, they proved natural allies. Within a few days, Lizarras had enlisted most Mexican contractors in the JMLA. With the contractors came three hundred of their beet hands.[42]

By early March, Lizarras and Yamaguchi had signed up about eight hundred men, whereupon they turned their attention to the remaining five hundred Japanese and Mexican field hands; their intent was to recruit the entire labor force. Conducting discussions in both Japanese and Spanish, with English serving as the common mode of communication, they continued to recruit members as beet thinning neared. On Saturday, March 6, they paraded through the streets of Oxnard in a show of strength and unity. "Dusky skinned Japanese and Mexicans march through the streets headed by one or two former minor contractors and beet laborers four abreast and several hundred strong," reported the *Oxnard Courier*. "They are a silent grim band of fellows," it continued, "most of them young and belonging to the lower class of Japanese and Mexicans." By Saturday evening, nine of ten beet hands—more than twelve hundred workers, including many Chinese—belonged to the JMLA. From this strong base, the JMLA presented *keiyaku-nin*, Mexican labor contractors, and sugar beet hands alike with an opportunity for action.[43]

Later commentators would claim that when Yamaguchi and Lizarras began mounting their opposition, they were attacking the fundamental nature of capitalist agriculture, that their effort was, in effect, a class struggle. But they would not assault the heart of the existing relationship between major capitalist interests in the county. To the contrary, both the JMLA and its leaders accepted the existing employment arrangement, differing with their employer only on the question of pay and supervision. The JMLA was a profoundly conservative, defensive organization led by labor contractors who demanded not a raise in wages but a return to the old rates and restoration of their right to negotiate directly with growers. That was the extent of its goals. The JMLA did not seek a social system better than the one it had; at no point did it ever attack the scheme under which beet hands labored or accuse anyone of treating men as less than human beings. "It . . . will be simply a question of whether the Japanese-Mexican labor classes will control labor," the *Oxnard Courier* wrote of the strike issues, "or whether it will be managed by conservative business men."[44]

Despite the conservative demands—elimination of the WACC, restoration of the previous year's pay rates, and a return to the system of independent Japanese and Mexican labor contracting—growers refused to meet with JMLA leaders or even discuss the issues. Most believed that, given the obstacles of different tongues, temperaments, and social environments, the union could not possibly last any length of time. Meanwhile, reporters, editors, and publishers eager to sell copy did their best to manufacture stories about JMLA members being anarchists and revolutionaries. At least one newspaper predicted some kind of confrontation, even though violence was certainly not among the objectives or tactics espoused by the JMLA. "Oxnard is up against labor turmoil, and blood spots are gathering on the face of the moon as it hovers over the sugar town," wrote the *Ventura Daily Democrat*. "The Japanese-Mexican labor union has inspired an enmity and opposition that threatens to terminate in riot and bloodshed." The prediction proved accurate.[45]

෪

On Sunday afternoon, March 7, JMLA members broke up a nonunion crew discovered sneaking into the beet fields by way of a riverbottom road. That evening JMLA members, most of them Mexicans wearing masks, visited a contracting company on Charles Donlon's ranch, cut the guy ropes of the tents housing field hands, and forced the crew of eighteen men to leave and return to Oxnard. Another JMLA group carried out a similar action against a camp on Al Hosiet's sugar beet farm. By Monday morning, March 8, JMLA members were distributing union literature on dozens of sugar beet farms, leading the *Oxnard Courier* to report: "Such proceedings are reprehensible, illegal and calculated to inspire distrust of the union's purity of motives." Exaggerating the actual events, the *Courier* also claimed that JMLA members were scaring and haranguing nonunion members.[46]

Violence was hardly among the goals of Yamaguchi, Lizarras, and the JMLA. Indeed, as JMLA leaders asserted firmer direction among the strikers, such confrontations diminished. Nevertheless sugar beet officials, reiterating that Lizarras and Yamaguchi were "anarchists" and "revolutionaries," placed armed guards around many labor camps, then prodded authorities to take action against picketers. On Wednesday afternoon, Ventura County sheriffs responded to a trumped-up complaint from Patterson ranch manager John Roupp and arrested K. Obata and K. Yoshinari, two JMLA representatives, after they attempted to induce beet thinners to leave the fields. Even the *Oxnard Courier* had to concede that there was little justice to the arrests. "The laws of California are such that this could not be considered a trespass as the Japanese went through open gates, did not steal anything, break down fences, spoil crops, hunt or any other of the features enumerated by the law to constitute a trespass," admitted the newspaper.[47]

Much to the dismay of the American Beet Sugar Company executives, the two JMLA officials were acquitted at trial on the following Saturday. Not long after, sheriff's deputies began escorting beet thinners into the fields. With the arrests and the support of armed guards and law enforcement, Oxnard's sugar beet officials expected the strike to collapse. But with the strike less than a week old, the JMLA had time to produce leaders from within its ranks to replace the arrested leaders and to develop a smooth and cohesive organization that, according to one observer, functioned "like that of a railroad office or an army in the field." From the beginning of the conflict, the JMLA carried the main responsibility for strikers' relief, opening a restaurant, paying medical expenses, sharing funds, and providing mutual assistance. Each ethnic group had its own relief committee that, though supposedly only loosely organized and run by so-called uneducated immigrants, operated with remarkable efficiency.[48]

While they were feeding and caring for strikers, Lizarras and Yamaguchi also established a system of information and communication at their Oxnard headquarters that was the epitome of class harmony and determination. Using a huge, recently drawn wall-sized map of the Santa Clara Valley, strike leaders located and kept tabs on various sugar beet farms. Next to each farm they tacked up the latest information on the location of labor camps, number of men employed, and the proportion who supported the strike. Lizarras and Yamaguchi efficiently dispatched secretaries, sent out messengers, deployed pickets, and responded to various emergencies. Holding frequent executive committee meetings, union members gathered around a large table, beginning each discussion in English, hashing it out in their respective languages, then stating their conclusions in English. "Respect for order was a marked feature of these meetings," recalled John Murray in his account of the strike, "each nationality keeping silent while the other had the matter before it for discussion and decision."[49]

No one could have dreamed that the organizing campaign and strike would work so well. Although cool weather prevented the rapid growth of the twelve thousand acres of beets and delayed the onset of most thinning work until around April 1, the strike nevertheless severely disrupted thinning operations on four thousand acres of early maturing beets. Realizing the advantage they enjoyed, union leaders requested a mass meeting with growers at Pioneer Hall in Oxnard on March 21, "for the purpose of discussing labor conditions and making known the true status of their affairs."[50]

Fred Wheeler and John Murray were to be in charge of the union side of the meeting. With nothing to lose, the WACC, growers, and sugar beet factory officials agreed to attend. "It certainly will do no harm . . . to come together and exchange pleasantries and state their individual positions to the public," reasoned the *Oxnard Courier*.[51]

Gathering shortly after the JMLA paraded through Oxnard for the second time, the audience in Pioneer Hall was packed with Mexican and Japanese field hands and contractors, with perhaps a dozen farmers present. With Colonel Driffill presiding over the growers, Wheeler addressed the audience for fifteen minutes, telling the farmers "you have the beets and we have the labor and want to work directly with you. We are members of the American Federation of Labor and are here to stay. It is bread and butter to us and we will deal directly with the farmers."[52]

Throughout the meeting, Wheeler fielded dozens of questions. Several elicited responses suggesting that the JMLA was a profoundly conservative labor union. For example, in response to a question about whom growers should negotiate with, Wheeler explained that they should contact Japanese and Mexican contractors just as in the past. The union would not intervene in any way, other than to insist on wages of $1.75 per day. Perhaps most revealing, however, was the question regarding "troubles" between various contractors; Wheeler claimed ignorance of the matters, but Lizarras stepped forward, admitted that there had been certain problems, and claimed that they had been settled amicably through a process of drawing straws. Apparently, contractors had been fighting over who was entitled to receive contracts offered to the union, and no method had been developed to satisfactorily resolve the problem. All that Wheeler could add was that any contract dispute would be decided by Lizarras or Yamaguchi.[53]

Mild as these arrangements were, neither growers nor local police would accept them. Determined to break the union, Oxnard police arrested Lizarras and Yamaguchi the next day, just as the two were addressing a street meeting in Oxnard. While the two JMLA leaders were being held in jail on five-hundred-dollar-bond each, growers attempted to further undercut the union by forming a second company union, the Independent Agricultural Labor Union (IALU), a group of fourteen Japanese contractors who tried to pass themselves off as an alternative to the JMLA. Headed by what the *Ventura Daily Independent* claimed were "some of the most influential and best-educated of the Japanese residents of Oxnard," IALU claimed it was striving "to secure and maintain harmonious relations between employers and employees of agricultural labor," while also eliminating abuses suffered by contract laborers. In fact, though, IALU was a strikebreaking organization. Conceived, financed, and controlled entirely by sugar beet growers and run by none other than WACC's John Inose, it neither calmed nor stabilized labor relations and served only to inflame and anger the JMLA.[54]

With beet thinning about to resume, the WACC placed advertisements in Japanese newspapers in San Francisco and Los Angeles, hoping to bring in more labor than was actually needed. But the JMLA, upon learning of the plan, intercepted the men and convinced them to join the strike. To circumvent the JMLA, the WACC then tried to bring scabs to Oxnard and unload them behind a screen of armed guards. But the union somehow got to these men as well, and many simply escaped through railroad car windows and joined the JMLA. According to the *Ventura Free Press*, "by the time these men reached Oxnard they were on the side of the union and against the Western Agricultural Contracting Company."[55]

Growers were furious. On March 21, Port Hueneme sugar beet grower Henry Fraho inflamed the already tense situation by announcing that he would hire nonunion men "if he chose to do so." Much agitated and bolstered by the large numbers of newly arrived supporters, JMLA members vowed to physically prevent the men from ever reaching Fraho's ranch. Expecting trouble, Constable Charles Eason deputized Charles Arnold, a local sugar beet farmer active in the WACC and known as a hotheaded nonunion type, who promptly purchased two revolvers and vowed to hire only nonunion men on his farm. Part of Arnold's job as a strikebreaker was to ensure that the laborers got away from Oxnard unharmed. "Trouble was expected," predicted the *Ventura Free Press*, in one of the few understatements of the day.[56]

❧

Early Monday morning, March 23, the WACC sent a wagon load of laborers and their provisions from boardinghouses in the Chinatown section of Oxnard to Fraho's ranch. Packing into the streets, a noisy crowd of JMLA members blocked the wagon and attempted to induce the men to desert the WACC. Asking the scabs if they were union men and hearing them say yes, they belonged to the new IALU, JMLA members attempted to place a union sign on one wagon. Some scabs objected and struggled with the JMLA members; at this point, a Japanese beet hand rushed out of the WACC store with a double-barreled shotgun, intending to prevent the JMLA from placing its sign on the wagon.

Suddenly Perfecto Ogas, later identified as a "big Mexican, one of the union men," slipped behind the Japanese man and took the shotgun from him. A melee ensued and Deputy Constables Arnold and Al Hawkins joined in the struggle. At this point, another Japanese field hand rushed out of the WACC store, stepped up to Ogas, and deliberately shot him through the neck. Retreating into a doorway, the Japanese man then shot at JMLA members, who returned fire, wounding two scabs in the wagon.[57]

With that, a "general fusillade" erupted. More than fifty shots were fired. "Guns and revolvers were poked out of windows and discharged regardless of aim or consequences," reported the *Oxnard Courier*. Dropping beneath the bed of the big beet wagon, the deputies fired back. Later Arnold would claim that he spotted one Mexican JMLA member in an alleyway with two pistols leveled at him. Exchanging gunshots point-blank, he ducked behind a wagon wheel, dodging five shots before chasing the assassin and losing him behind a building. When the smoke of the brief battle had cleared away, four men were found wounded. The worst off was Luis Vásquez, with a bullet to his groin (in some accounts, his bladder); less severely injured was Manuel Ramírez, hit in the leg. Two unnamed Japanese were also wounded, one in the nose (in some accounts, the wrist), the other in the arm. "How many more stole away and secreted themselves is unknown," commented the *Oxnard Courier*, suggesting even larger numbers of men may have been injured.[58]

The sound of gunshots brought most of Oxnard's citizens to the scene within minutes. "The street was crowded with a motley throng of Orientals, Mexicans, and Americans," reported the *Oxnard Courier*. "Oriental faces peered anxiously from doorways and windows, every vantage point was filled with spectators and the excitement grew apace." Within an hour both the Ventura County sheriff and deputy were in Chinatown. Also on the spot were at least three newspaper men, *Ventura Democrat* editor E. F. McGonigle and *Ventura Free Press* editor L. F. Webster, who arrived later that day; and George Dennis, representing the *San Francisco Call* and *San Francisco Examiner*, who arrived two days later.[59]

All sorts of rumors filled the air. Reports that a hundred men had engaged in a pitched battle, fired two hundred shots, killed a dozen field hands, and wounded countless others finally resolved themselves into the story of five men being wounded and forty or fifty shots being fired, with some twenty field hands and scabs participating in the riot. "The fiasco showed that there are many fire arms being carried contrary to law," concluded the *Oxnard Courier*, with considerable understatement, "and that a dangerous condition of affairs exists."[60]

With armed deputies patrolling the streets of Oxnard and local citizens fearing "serious trouble," March 24 passed quietly. According to the *Oxnard Courier*, "the various clans, while watching each other closely, were quiet." Late in the afternoon, Ogas was taken back to Oxnard at his own request, while Vásquez slipped into a coma from which doctors said he would not recover. Out in the fields, about sixty nonunion men thinned sugar beets, twenty of them on the Patterson ranch. About three hundred JMLA members also found work with various sugar beet growers. Meanwhile, newspapers outside of Oxnard did their best to manufacture stories and headlines about bloody clashes. These stories invariably laid blame for the violence entirely on the JMLA.[61]

Perhaps the most sensational, inaccurate, and antiunion reports appeared in the *Los Angeles Times*. Describing for its readers how "agitation-crazed striking Mexicans and Japanese" led by "loud-mouthed and lawless union agitators" and "trouble making" Mexicans had inflamed "ignorant peons," the *Times* reported that the union had attacked "independent workmen" and precipitated a "pitched battle" in which dozens of beet hands had been hurt and "thousands gone wild." According to the newspaper, Japanese and Mexican JMLA members had terrorized the town, shooting and murdering innocent bystanders who simply wanted to fill beet thinning jobs that strikers had abandoned. Somewhat more balanced in its analysis, the *Oxnard Courier* admitted, "It is practically impossible to load all the blame on any one, or a small set of persons, with any degree of accuracy, though one or two culprits may be located and punished." Around town, however, most Anglos and many officials singled out JMLA's attempt to place its union label on the wagon load of scabs as the root cause for the riot. Only one newspaper, the *Ventura Independent*, condemned the WACC. Finding "the root of the evil" in the hundreds of restless Japanese laborers from San Francisco and Fresno that the WACC had imported, the newspaper accused the WACC of failing to control the newcomers.[62]

ॐ

As rain squalls moved through Oxnard on Wednesday afternoon, Colonel Driffill along with several civic leaders attempted to calm matters and bring the various parties together at JMLA headquarters in the Cottage Hotel. Leading off the discussion, Lizarras insisted on being able to bargain directly with local farmers, and failing to achieve that goal, threatened to remove the entire union membership out of Ventura County to work elsewhere, thus dooming the entire Oxnard sugar beet crop. Faced with an impending catastrophe, WACC secretary George Herz, after expressing regrets about the violence, offered to surrender two thousand of the seven thousand acres of contracts he held if the union would only return to work and leave WACC men alone.

With more than thirteen hundred men compared to about sixty in the WACC, the JMLA was in a strong position. Rejecting the compromise proposal, the JMLA vowed that it would not end its strike until the WACC's monopoly had been broken and all farmers had signed contracts with the JMLA. Ridiculing the WACC, the union came up with its own compromise, offering to provide labor in proportion to the number of men each organization represented, a proposal that would have effectively given JMLA complete control of the fields. Although the *Oxnard Courier* found the meeting "productive of very little," the *Ventura Daily Democrat* disagreed, reporting that the union had mounted a strong front, "clearly demonstrating to the ranchers that they controlled the labor necessary to do their work, and without their services beet crops must perish."[63]

That night, Vásquez died in the Ventura County Hospital. As a result, passions were once again rekindled. Among union members, the feeling was that, had the police done their duty, "many arrests would have been made among the occupants of the company's housing from which the fatal volleys of bullets came." Soon a rumor began circulating among Mexican members of the JMLA that Charles Arnold instigated the violence, fired the first shot, and was therefore responsible for shooting Ogas, Vásquez, and Ramírez. Vowing to kill him, a gang of angry Mexicans began searching for Arnold on Thursday morning, March 26. Warned of the threat, Arnold immediately fled to Justice of the Peace W. H. Harris's office, where, according to the *Oxnard Courier*, "a number of white men kept guard, surrounded by muttering, half-drunk natives." So infuriated were JMLA members with Arnold that, later in the day, JMLA union member Christian Trajo, assisted by attorney W. E. Shepherd, swore out a warrant charging Arnold with attempting to murder Ogas. On these grounds, Arnold was placed under arrest and taken to the county jail in Ventura pending the outcome of a coroner's inquest. A few hours later Shepherd swore out a second warrant charging a beet thinner named T. Cato with "murderous assault on M. Ramirez."[64]

As this was transpiring, Lizarras and Yamaguchi resumed negotiations with WACC representatives. Meeting at the sugar beet factory at 9 A.M., they again refused to accept any WACC contracts. Demanding a minimum of five dollars an acre and a high of six dollars an acre for sugar beet thinning—rates nearly double that of the WACC—the JMLA agreed not to harass WACC men, insofar as they could control their members. Following the meeting, the WACC attempted to test the agreement by moving a Japanese crew from its Chinatown bunkhouse out to the Hill brothers' ranch. The effort quickly attracted a large crowd of union members and spectators who completely intimidated and "terrorized" the WACC men.

At this point, Murray proposed a scheme to arrest every nonunion man who showed up and charge them with complicity in the riot. Although Justice Harris dismissed the idea as flimsy and refused to issue any of the required John Doe warrants, his decision was of little consequence. When the time came for the WACC men to climb into their beet wagons and ride to the fields, only five appeared, even though Sheriff McMartin and his deputies had cleared the streets and JMLA attorney Shepherd, who had placed himself in the street between the scabs and union members, had ordered his union members to stand clear. So fearful were the remaining scabs, explained the *Oxnard Courier*, that they preferred "to make a rear exit."[65]

With just twelve men at work, the WACC prepared to obtain an injunction against the JMLA, but soon ran into an unexpected opponent. Responding to union requests, the Japanese consul at San Francisco sent a representative to Oxnard. Hoping to arbitrate the dispute, the diplomat immediately discovered that anti-WACC feelings ran deep and that it would be wise to get the idle and angry men away from Oxnard to Riverside and other places, beginning with fifty men on Friday, and followed by others as fast as possible. Completely panicked by this idea, the WACC now found itself backed into a corner. With warm weather bringing the beets on fast, WACC had little time left. "Every man . . . is needed to save the beet crop," wrote the *Oxnard Courier*. "It needs instant attention or the factory won't run this year. If the men leave, or any great number of them, the ranches will grow up in weeds. The only thing to do, apparently, is for the beet raisers to take matters into their own hands and disregard the Western Contracting Company entirely and all other interests and deal directly with the men."[66]

Three days later, on Monday, March 30, after hearing testimony from ten eyewitnesses, a coroner's inquest into the death of Luis Vásquez announced its findings. Exonerating Charles Arnold from any criminal responsibility, the decision of the Anglo jury meeting at Reilly's Mortuary seemed to help the WACC. Most witnesses testified that Arnold had not shot Vásquez. Of these witnesses, the most important was John Connelly, driver of the sugar beet wagon, who saw everything close-up and testified that Arnold never even unholstered his revolvers. Concurring with this testimony were police who had examined Arnold's revolvers after the shooting and found them fully loaded and unfired. One Mexican witness seemed to exonerate Arnold as well. Wounded at the riot, Manuel Ramírez now claimed that it was a Japanese strikebreaker in the WACC wagon who had shot him in the leg. However, in reaching its decision, the coroner's jury did not hear testimony from about forty other Mexican and Japanese field hands brought to the inquest by J. H. Murray.[67]

Commenting on this omission, some observers claimed that this was evidence of a cover-up, a gross miscarriage of justice. In fact, it was not. While several Mexican witnesses gave exactly the same testimony, all having seen Arnold first open fire on Ogas, none claimed to have seen Arnold shoot Vásquez. Since the inquest did not probe the shooting of Ogas, who was rapidly recovering, but dealt with assigning responsibility for killing Vásquez, the information was deemed irrelevant, more properly a matter for the police, and the witnesses were never heard.[68]

About 5:30 P.M., as it considered reconvening to hear the additional witnesses, the jury objected to hearing further testimony. "They were ready to render a verdict," observed the *Ventura Independent*, "and did not care to longer participate in a farce having for its purpose revenge upon parties evidently not at fault." At that point, all other witnesses were dismissed. Around 8 P.M. the jury reconvened and issued a decision clearing Arnold of any complicity in Vásquez's death, finding that he died "as the result of a gunshot received at the hands of some party unknown to us . . . during a labor riot at Oxnard."[69]

Angered by the verdict, JMLA members may have attempted to exact revenge on Arnold. At least, that is one interpretation given to what happened about one hour later, when Charles Garcia, a foreman on Arnold's farm, was shot at while returning from Oxnard with a payroll for Arnold's nonunion sugar beet thinning crew. Near the Arnold ranch, three masked men jumped from behind some bushes and opened fire on Garcia, hitting one of the horses pulling his buggy. "That the 'union' element is still intent upon reaching or taking vengeance upon Arnold was once again evidenced," wrote the *Ventura Independent*. "Whether or not the assailant thought the occupant was Arnold, or that the intent was to kill Arnold, or that the intent was to kill Arnold's team is, of course, a matter of surmise."[70]

Following the attack, the WACC on April 1 relinquished contracts to thin five thousand acres, only retaining contracts on the eighteen-hundred-acre Patterson ranch, which was owned by the American Beet Sugar Company. Several developments other than the violence and inquest had forced WACC secretary George Herz to sit down and hammer out a settlement with JMLA attorney W. E. Shepherd. For one, Oxnard was at this time trying to incorporate as a town, and civic leaders feared that any unresolved labor conflict would undermine or delay that move. There was also an impending visit from President Theodore Roosevelt, who was scheduled to tour the sugar beet factory on May 16 with Henry Oxnard, Governor George Pardee, and Colonel Driffill. Should the strike remain in effect on that date, Roosevelt's visit would have to be canceled, causing great embarrassment. A third reason for settling was the effect the strike was having on local business. Hard hit by the strike, the Wonder Store, heavily dependent on beet workers for its trade, had shut down operations, and other businesses had been forced to likewise cut back heavily on their hours and lay off employees. Also pushing growers to settle was the huge financial burden the WACC faced for hiring armed guards. Working on a margin of forty cents per acre, the organization simply could no longer afford to provide guards to protect its workers from JMLA pickets.[71]

After four weeks of industrial conflict, it became apparent that the JMLA would not crack. Stronger than ever, the union's relief organization was handling all needs smoothly. Following the riot on March 23, statewide support and sympathy had propelled the union forward until a change in the weather amplified its position. When the rain ended and the fields dried out, growers suddenly faced the prospect of either thinning nine thousand acres of beets or seeing their crops go to weeds. Furthermore, at least another two thousand acres remained to be planted. All of this work had to begin immediately. Growers and factory officials had run out of time.[72]

ૐ

As they returned to the fields, JMLA leaders rejoiced. They had broken the WACC monopoly, sent Herz and Inose packing off to Utah in fear for their lives, and achieved all of their original goals. Not only had Japanese and Mexican field hands and contractors united in one of the first big, successful farm labor strikes, they had done so by overcoming the very strong ethnic divisions that had previously impeded success, contradicting the general view that seasonal farmworkers always accepted their lot uncomplainingly. But there was one additional element separating this strike from all others. Recognizing that sugar beet growers could not even raise a crop if their sugar beets were not properly thinned, Oxnard field hands had seized the opportunity, hit growers at a point of extreme vulnerability, and won an overwhelming victory.

But what, if anything, had really changed? Issei historian Yuji Ichioka argues that it is not clear that the union itself actually negotiated contracts for thinning. If it did, then the JMLA was, in fact, functioning as a true labor union. If not, then the small independent contractors simply continued dealing with growers separately as usual. The only real change, according to this line of thinking, was that now they would do so in accordance with terms and wages of the negotiated settlement.[73]

This was also the thinking of the *Oxnard Courier*. Unconvinced that JMLA had effected any changes of consequence, the newspaper published a detailed analysis of the proposed strike settlement. Maintaining that the lot of common field hands, in whose interest the strike had been conducted, would not be improved one iota by the elimination of the WACC, the newspaper argued that the men who would gain by the collapse of the company were the smaller Japanese and Mexican contractors, who were the real inspiration of the union.

What does the union ask? That the farmer contract through it, with independent contractors. In the first place, the union, or central organization, has to be supported. There is a Japanese and Mexican branch. Each has its officers drawing good salaries. If this doesn't take off as great a percent as the Western Agricultural Contracting Company, we miss our guess. Then the contract goes to the contractor. Say he has half a dozen jobs. It is not likely that they will be located adjoining so that he can personally oversee them, but it is likely that the jobs will be separated as far as Hueneme and the Las Posas. How is he going to manage? His Japs can't be trusted to work without supervision. He either sublets again to the head of a gang or hires a foreman, which amounts to the same thing. If this sort of scaling is not as bad as any condition labor has felt to date, we miss again.[74]

Although the JMLA did not eliminate any *keiyaku-nin* or Mexican contractors, there is nonetheless considerable evidence that it did handle all negotiations for beet thinning and harvesting during 1903. In a brief account of Yamaguchi's sudden departure from Oxnard for Japan on April 18 to look after his dying father, the *Oxnard Courier* interviewed Yamaguchi and published some very revealing information. According to the newspaper, Yamaguchi had signed contracts on behalf of the Japanese branch of the JMLA for 1,165 acres of sugar beets, an increase of fourfold. With his departure those contracts would be turned over to the new Japanese branch secretary, H. Otomo.[75]

≈

The JMLA's success would have far-reaching implications. Since the California labor movement had heretofore regarded agricultural workers as impossible to organize, the Oxnard sugar beet strike raised several obvious questions: If sugar beet workers could form a union, then might other farmworkers do the same? Would the labor movement actively organize them? And if so, would current union members accept farmworkers into their fold? As the *Oakland Tribune* explained, the Oxnard strike had suddenly "brought the matter to the front." Following the lead of the JMLA, Hayward labor leaders met to consider organizing their local field hands and formed a mutual assistance club to assist in the task, but nothing appears to have come of the effort.[76]

Another issue the JMLA raised centered on whether organized labor would now reverse its position and unionize field hands belonging to a despised racial group. Oxnard strike leaders Wheeler and Murray convinced local labor councils in Southern California that the time had come to ditch past policies. Under the auspices of the Los Angeles County Labor Council, the two Socialists pushed through a carefully crafted resolution that praised the Oxnard strikers and called on the AFL to organize farmworkers "regardless of race or national distinction." The resolution was, according to the *San Francisco Examiner*, "the first time that a labor council had put itself on record as in any way favoring Asiatic labor."[77]

Buoyed by this support, JMLA leaders changed the name of their organization to the Sugar Beet Farm Laborer's Union of Oxnard (SBFLU) and appointed Joe Baba president. They then did something that, given the well-known anti-Japanese sentiments of organized labor, seemed incomprehensible. They applied to AFL President Samuel Gompers for membership. Given his pathological and long-standing antagonism to Asian labor, Gompers's response was entirely predictable. Agreeing that the new union deserved status in the AFL, Gompers wrote to Lizarras on May 15, placing only one condition on affiliation. "Your union will under no circumstance accept membership of any Chinese or Japanese," Gompers declared. "The laws of our country prohibit Chinese workmen or laborers from entering the United States, and propositions for the extension of the exclusion laws to the Japanese have been made on several occasions."[78]

Reading Gompers's words, Lizarras must have been devastated. Although offered membership for himself and for his entire branch of the union, Lizarras chose not to sell out. Composing a long and thoughtful reply, he took Gompers to task.

> We beg to say in reply that our Japanese brothers here were the first to recognize the importance of cooperating and uniting in demanding a fair wage scale. They were not only just with us, but they were generous when one of our men was murdered by hired assassins of the oppressor of labor, they gave expression to their sympathy in a very substantial form. In the past we have counseled, fought and lived on very short rations with our Japanese brothers, and toiled with us [them] in the fields, and they have been uniformly kind and considerate. We would be false to them and to ourselves and to the cause of unionism if we accepted privileges for ourselves which are not accorded to them. . . . We will refuse any other kind of a charter except one which will wipe out race prejudices and recognize our fellow workers as being as good as ourselves. I am ordered by the Mexican union to write this letter to you and they fully approve its words.[79]

Lizarras was not the AFL's only critic. Noting that Gompers's decision had left highly organized, highly motivated, militant Japanese to fend for themselves against both growers and trade unionists, labor newspapers in Chicago and Los Angeles belittled the AFL leader, calling for a more inclusive policy. Contacting the AFL executive board in Washington, D.C., the Los Angeles Central Labor Council pointed out that the Japanese in Oxnard had proven "their courage and manhood," and having emerged from their ordeal "with unbroken ranks," were obviously worthy of organization and inclusion in the AFL. Long a thorn in the side of Gompers, the *American Labor Union Journal* let fly with the strongest criticism.

> There are between forty and fifty thousand Japanese in this state, who hold the balance of power among the field workers, and nothing can be effectively

done without their cooperation. In such warfare to raise race prejudice is unpardonable folly, a folly for which President Gompers must soon answer to the unions of southern California who are unanimous in demanding recognition for brother wage workers, the Japanese.[80]

Disregarding such criticism, the AFL and Gompers would not budge. Nor would California labor leaders. Even those who did call for organizing the Japanese were ultimately less concerned about sugar beet workers as exploited minorities than with defending white workers from potential harm. Nothing more clearly demonstrated this than the fact that the Los Angeles Labor Council followed its Oxnard-inspired resolution with another calling for exclusion of Asian immigrants from the state. Even Andrew Furuseth, the Pacific Coast Seaman's Union leader and member of the AFL Executive Council who had dedicated his life to ending the quasi-serfdom of American sailors and who took a strong class approach to most labor matters, showed no sympathy for the Japanese at Oxnard. "We are in favor of Japanese being organized and Chinese being organized," Furuseth was fond of saying during the debate over SBFLU, "but we want them organized in Japan or China, not in the United States."[81]

❧

Despite their failure to obtain AFL membership, Oxnard's Japanese and Mexican field hands did not fold. Catapulted to statewide prominence, the *keiyaku-nin* and Mexican contractors appeared to be real competitors to organized labor, as well as a distinct force in California agriculture. Not only did they gain the upper hand over Oxnard's sugar beet growers, they had ended the era of placid farm labor relations, established a basis for interracial action, and inaugurated a struggle that would grow over the next century. But for all their success, they did not get through the 1903 sugar beet thinning season without problems. As abusive as ever, some contractors did not appear to have much changed their behavior in the wake of the strike. Declining to pay their men the agreed-to union rate, these contractors instead continued to exploit and mistreat field hands by skipping town with payrolls and otherwise shortchanging men as brazenly as always. One of the most notorious of these men was Alberto López. Refusing to pay Thomas Rubalcaba for a week of thinning beets, López on May 15 became angry when Rubalcaba confronted him and demanded his wages after finishing work on Saturday. Screaming, "This is the way I pay my men," López suddenly drew a pistol and thrust it into Rubalcaba's stomach. Defending himself, Rubalcaba lunged at López and, as the two fought, the pistol discharged sending a bullet through Rubalcaba's hand into López's leg. Four days later, Rubalcaba appeared in court with his fist in a sling. The evidence being in his favor, he was discharged. As for López, the *Oxnard Courier* reported that he was "laid on the shelf for repairs and won't be able to appear for trial for some little time."[82]

As the thinning season gave way to harvesting, though, the number of such incidents declined. During June, SBFLU members found their position enhanced considerably, not so much by their victory as from a dire shortage of labor. The apricot harvest was in full swing, and large numbers of men normally available for beet harvesting remained occupied picking fruit and drying it. Because of this, sugar beet contractors could muster only enough crews to supply the factory with fourteen hundred tons of beets per day when the factory needed twenty-one hundred tons to operate with maximum efficiency. With labor so dear, contractors were able to charge the maximum. They had little reason to shortchange their men or abscond with payrolls; for the first five weeks of the harvest, everyone seemed happy. What nobody could predict was that, as the labor shortage eased, old tensions would reemerge. Many sugar beet workers remained angry over the violence they had suffered and the injustice they had endured before and during the strike. All that spring and summer, they nursed festering hatred toward many local officials. Some laborers, still refusing to accept the coroner's inquest exonerating Charles Arnold from murder charges, frequently taunted and occasionally still fought with police and sheriff's deputies.[83]

One source of dissatisfaction was a campaign by Oxnard authorities to clean up the town and eliminate vice, thereby "removing obstacles" to growth, investment, and prosperity. Beginning in July, local police began raiding dozens of gambling joints, saloons, and various "undesirable businesses" in Sonoratown, sending sugar beet workers scurrying and jailing people the *Courier* labeled "tough customers." Under these circumstances, it did not take much to ignite the laborer's hidden rage.[84]

About 11 P.M. on the Fourth of July, an intoxicated Mexican beet thinner named Manuel Sepúlveda started a scuffle in front of a pie wagon near Gammill and Dominick's meat market at the corner of Fifth Street and Saviers Road. Arriving on the scene, Deputy Sheriff Charles Russell arrested Sepúlveda and attempted to take him off to jail. Just as they reached the sidewalk, a second Mexican field hand knocked Russell down with a blow to the back of his neck; six others then jumped on the deputy, smashed a beer bottle over his head, and began dragging him into the gutter. Sepúlveda then wrestled away Russell's pistol, stuck it in the lawman's stomach, and pulled the trigger several times, only to hear it misfire. Breaking free, Russell jumped behind the pie wagon. Moments later, Sepúlveda hit him with a grazing gunshot in his back. Lunging for Sepúlveda, Russell regained his pistol and began firing at Sepúlveda and the other Mexicans.

Over the next five minutes, the men fought a running gun battle that moved the length of Fifth Street. Reloading three times, Russell fired twelve shots, wounding three Mexicans—and possibly a fourth—before staggering for cover and calling for help. When order returned later in the day, Ventura County Sheriff Edmund McMartin and Deputy Sheriff William H. Reilly, armed with Winchester rifles, arrested all of the wounded Mexican field hands, two of whom they found still lying in the street seriously injured. But Sepúlveda, who had started the shooting, along with one of the gang who jumped Russell, made a clean escape. They were never seen again.[85]

Five weeks later, someone tried to assassinate John Inose who, after fleeing Oxnard, had been hired to run contracting crews for the American Beet Sugar Company around Salt Lake City. He had returned to Oxnard that summer to visit friends when, around midnight on August 11, after enjoying an evening at a "Japanese resort" on Saviers Road, he was observed leaving the building by way of the back door with another Japanese man. Soon the two were heard arguing loudly. A shot rang out, and Inose was discovered by the night watchman with a gunshot wound to his chest. When asked who had shot him, Inose stated that he believed he was going to die but could identify his assailant. Asking for a paper and pencil, he wrote the name of W. W. Tokeda (in some accounts Tekato), a contractor active in the JMLA. Arrested a few hours later in the Simi Valley where he was directing several gangs of harvest hands, Tokeda produced an alibi and was released. Meanwhile, Dr. Dumont Dwire operated on Inose and extracted the bullet. "While the Jap has rather a crooked hole through him and does considerable groaning, it is not thought to be a dangerous wound," reported the *Oxnard Courier*. "No matter who did the shooting it was no doubt another eruption of the trouble generated here among the beet workers last spring."[86]

While feelings remained strong well into September, support for the union slowly withered. One reason that SBFLU declined was the overabundance of labor. As the Ventura County peach, apricot, bean, and walnut harvests ended, large numbers of men who knew little of the strike or union crowded into Oxnard in search of work. So far behind schedule were labor contractors that they hired every one of them at top rates. Thus, large numbers of men who had never supported or been involved in the strike benefited from its outcome. Another key reason that the SBFLU declined was its failure to obtain AFL membership. Lacking that affiliation, the union had little to offer its members and could play no role in setting future harvest wages or establishing hiring practices. A third reason was that by now the WACC had passed from the scene. With much of the WACC's work picked up by Tomiyama Company, the union born of opposition to WACC lost its main reason for existence.[87]

By the end of the 1903 sugar beet harvest, *keiyaku-nin* were once again operating on their own, with no union involvement. Placing advertisements in local newspapers, they solicited work for the coming year. "Japanese Labor Contracts. And all kinds of help furnished. Joe Baba Co. Saviers Ave. North of 5th," read Joe Baba's announcement in the *Oxnard Courier*. By December, labor contractors had completely returned to their former individualistic approach. At least three had also moved beyond their original function of furnishing labor. Leasing five hundred acres near Port Hueneme, Tomiyama Company along with Tokuyama and Yoshioka companies began growing sugar beets, barley, and lima beans. "The scheme is pure profit sharing," commented the *Oxnard Courier*, "The Japs are good farmers and there are educated, intelligent men at the head of these companies."[88]

Exactly when the Oxnard *keiyaku-nin* abandoned the union and went their own way is unclear. Although Oxnard strike historian Tomás Almaguer has theorized that they continued working with the SBFLU for several years, there is no convincing evidence of any activity after late summer. Reporting on the SBFLU, the *Oxnard Courier* explained on December 25, 1903: "We are informed that the labor unions of last campaign are almost dissipated, that all parties are sick and tired of the experiment and hope that nothing of the sort will occur to disturb the peace of the rest of next season."[89]

Although both the WACC and SBFLU were effectively gone, sugar beet growers continued to support various methods to weaken both field laborers and *keiyaku-nin.* This meant that even though Japanese provided most of the labor for the sugar beet industry not only in California, but also in Idaho, Colorado, Montana, Utah, and Oregon, growers determined never again to allow them to accrue such power. Hoping to reassert control, impede any further challenges, and eliminate their dependence on hand labor, growers began experimenting with new beet pulling and topping machines. The first of these rolled into the Oxnard fields on September 12, 1904. Consisting of a two-wheeled wagon with a sharp knife about four to five inches wide, the device shaved off the tops of the beets, caught them between two cone-shaped rollers, and carried them over an endless apron to the back, where it deposited them in a neat row. "One man and a team does the work that usually requires four horses and about five men and does it better," reported the *Oxnard Courier.* "With the advent of this machine," predicted the paper, "the great question of beet topping labor which makes gray hairs come long before their time will be practically done away with forever."[90]

But as with previous attempts, nothing much developed from mechanization at this time. Try as they did, growers could not replace the thousands of men required to bring in their crop. Nor could they curb the violence that pervaded their industry. Often their laborers could not get along with one another, and occasionally growers got caught in the middle. This is what happened on September 22, 1904, when William D. Suytar, a prominent thirty-nine-year-old sugar beet grower, attempted to act as a peacemaker. Stepping between two of his laborers who had become engaged in an altercation over some trifling work matter, Suytar grabbed a double-barreled shotgun just as one man pointed it at the other. As Suytar pulled the barrel down, the shotgun discharged both cartridges of number 15 buckshot into his groin. Taken to Bard Hospital, Suytar died that evening, leaving behind a wife and three sons.[91]

In addition to this type of random violence, problems with the *keiyaku-nin* lingered long after the strike. As a result of the strike's success, all kinds of men set up as contractors in the hopes of securing some piece of the emancipated labor market. Bathhouse operators and store owners, for example, realized the natural advantages they enjoyed operating establishments where large numbers of men congregated. But differing little from previous contractors, they continued to cause dissatisfaction among workers as they attempted to outdo one another with promises of loyal and efficient crews and cheaper costs. Eventually Japanese field hands made a desperate attempt at getting rid of these contractors. Forming the Japanese Cooperative Contracting Company (JCCC) in February 1906, they attempted to establish an alternative contracting organization. Although it was not a union, the JCCC did advertise itself as representing longtime Japanese sugar beet workers who wished to work directly with growers and avoid the abuses and exploitation of the contracting system. "Don't make your agreement with other contractors, because we laborers have been depressed by them," read the JCCC's advertisement. "We trust them no more."[92]

If the JCCC ever did any business, it was not reported in the local press. Within a month it was dead. But old resentments persisted. For years, Oxnard field hands remembered who had done what to whom, and many vowed revenge. In particular, they had grown to hate the town's night watchman, Andrew Murray

McNaughton, who often arrested or harassed them as he patrolled late at night. Men also disliked him for the role he had played in arresting strike leaders and for his zealous tracking down of drunk field hands and backing up of local law enforcement raids on farmworker quarters. They eventually got their revenge. About 3 A.M. on March 23, 1906, two Mexican field hands cornered McNaughton in an alley behind the Chinese cribs. Whether they were looking for him or had been caught in some crime is not known. Shooting him repeatedly, they left him to die in the dusty street.[93]

CHAPTER NINETEEN

Exact Everything Possible

'Keiyaku-nin,' Mexicans, Sikhs,

and the Quest for Labor Stability

The reaction of California farmers to Japanese organizing activity was entirely foreseeable. "The halo of the Jap has vanished," asserted the September 19, 1903, *Vacaville Reporter*.

> He is no longer looked upon as a philanthropist who comes to California from the Orient for the benefit of the orchardist. He is understood more fully and is recognized to be possessed of all the fruits of any white labor, mingled with some of those of the Chinese and supplemented by some peculiarly his own. . . . The Chinaman is yearly a scarcer quantity and the Jap is in control; he knows it, moreover, and does not hesitate to manifest his power by a generally arbitrary manner, which however much it may be resented must be tolerated in fact. When it suits him to work in Vacaville, he does, and mighty near his own terms. When he hears that he can get higher wages at some distant point, he quits and leaves his employer to get along the best he can.[1]

Such reports revealed a predictable amalgam of fear, anger, and calculation—in short, the typical response of any employer confronted with organized workers. Growers realized that the Japanese were going to be a force and there was no way to keep them from advancing their interests, but that power might be softened and mitigated; the industry might absorb them, render them less threatening, and keep them in their place. The first move toward that goal was to reassert control over the labor market, to demonstrate to the Japanese that growers could do without them and easily find replacements. Led by Yuba City fruit grower H. P. Stabler, growers began their counterattack at the 1902 California State Fruit Growers Convention in San Francisco, when they formed the California Employment Committee. Resurrecting old plans, they raised thirty-five hundred dollars for a campaign that would induce "desirable workers of the East" and "farmer lads" to migrate west.[2]

FIGURE 41. Japanese field hands, Marysville, ca. 1902. Photograph by Clara Smith. Courtesy Arne Svenson, New York, N.Y.

Four "experienced fruit-men," led by Davisville almond grower George W. Pierce and his son, kicked off the blitz in Missouri during the winter of 1903. Lecturing in small towns throughout Nebraska, Iowa, Michigan, Missouri, and Illinois, the two men planted articles in local newspapers, presented stereoscopic views of "scenic and industrial California," and distributed one hundred thousand copies of a promotional pamphlet, *Grasp This, Your Opportunity*, which extolled California and the possibilities for work and happiness there. Audiences ranging in size from 250 to one thousand people turned out to hear the talks. At the conclusion of the campaign, California's growers hoped that the Japanese would be held in check by a migrating force of some ten thousand men.[3]

If they followed the recruiting campaign at all (and it is more likely they did not), the Japanese would quickly have realized that they faced no threat. Only 917 people were placed in harvest jobs, even though farm employers had listed more than nine thousand jobs with the California Employment Committee. Almost immediately upon arriving, the newcomers encountered a campaign against them. According to historian Michael Kazin, organized labor "was practically unanimous" in its hostility. Stressing that, contrary to what the growers were saying, the state was overrun with workers, short of jobs, and suffering from systemic unemployment, union leaders attacked the farm labor importation scheme in brochures, advertisements, and mass meetings.[4]

Although none of the state's fruit growers would admit it, their scheme to induce a cross-country migration failed largely because of its ridiculous premise: that young men who worked as family-housed hired hands would give that up for life in labor camps around California. Addressing the state fruit growers convention a few years later, a grower who had once been a farmer in Minnesota explained that California farmers had a bad reputation in the Midwest and ought to concentrate on improving housing and working conditions if they wanted to attract more labor. In his home state of Minnesota, the man explained, laborers lived indoors "and are treated as children of the house." Out West, it was different. The grower related a conversation he had once had with a field hand who, after spending a season in the orchards of Southern California, returned to the Midwest disgusted. Upon being hired, the laborer recalled, he had been told to "to take his blanket on his shoulder and go into the stable to sleep." Even stronger evidence had come from the farmer's son, who had traveled to California to learn the fruit business and settle down. Within six months, the young man had returned home, explaining "that he had not been treated much better than a dog by his employers."[5]

∮৯

Even as the California Employment Committee agents were entertaining audiences in Iowa, Japanese field hands were marshaling their forces for action. Following the successful confrontation at Oxnard, they initiated strikes in a variety of farming communities—apricot orchards near Hayward, peach orchards of Sutter County, and raisin vineyards around Fresno. In the orchards near Hayward, a crew of apricot cutters walked off the job and demanded a raise from eight to ten cents an hour. Fired immediately, they were easily replaced by whites from Oakland. In Sutter County, the outcome was different. The *Pacific Rural Press* observed: "They asked for a raise of 15 cents a day. They were being paid $1.25 a day and demanded $1.40. The fruit was ripening rapidly and the little brown men had their employers in a corner which they were not slow in realizing . . . Their demands were promptly met." And without ever using the words "labor union," *keiyaku-nin* around Fresno tied up the raisin grape industry and secured contracts specifying wages, hours of labor, and rates of work, in effect creating a union shop.[6]

At the end of 1903, state horticultural commissioner Ellwood Cooper looked back and concluded that growers had harvested their crops with "excellent results." Nowhere did he mention the turmoil to be found in the fields across the state. Beneath the positive rhetoric, however, lurked deep uncertainty and panic. Wherever growers looked, they saw Japanese success, and so they began to consider additional ways to augment the farm labor supply. Among their plans was an expanded program to have local schools close during grape picking, thereby freeing up schoolchildren to work in the harvest. Additionally, growers proposed to take on truants and juvenile delinquents. By removing them from their urban environments and inculcating them with a good dose of work in the fresh air and

FIGURE 42. Claude F. Hankins, age fourteen, sentenced to sixteen years in San Quentin Prison for murdering a foreman on the Boles ranch, Marysville, July 20, 1904. Photograph by Clara Smith. Courtesy of Arne Svenson, New York, N.Y.

sunshine, so this line of reasoning went, growers would reform young criminals while bringing in the harvest. To this end they began placing advertisements in San Francisco newspapers. But a sensational murder case soon dissuaded growers from these beliefs, discrediting the entire idea of supplementing the farm labor force with juvenile criminals.[7]

The case centered on fourteen-year-old Claude F. Hankins, who on July 20, 1904, shot and killed George Mosse, a middle-aged foreman employed on the Boles ranch six miles east of Marysville. Widely covered in the Marysville and San Francisco newspapers, the trial that October unfolded as one long indictment of farm labor conditions, especially for young city boys. Hankins claimed that after being sent from Palo Alto to the Boles ranch by his sister "to break him of bad associations he had formed," he had been abused by Mosse, who had whipped him and taken him into the orchard to commit "a crime against nature." After Mosse "told him that he would just as soon cut his head off as he would whittle a piece of wood," the homesick and terrified youngster went to Mosse's room, took Mosse's pistol from his bureau, crept up behind him, and blew Mosse's brains out. Hankins then robbed Mosse of seventy dollars and fled to Marysville, where he was arrested in the Eagle Hotel.

Supporting statements and testimony from several field hands (including another boy who had traveled from San Francisco) also described Mosse as a monster who had abused them. They also had little good to say about George Thompson, who owned the ranch where the murder had taken place and was then considered one of Marysville's leading citizens. "We were slaves on that ranch," testified Charles N. Dray, who had worked there the previous year. "My brother was forced to sleep in the chicken house until he ran away. Many times my mother sent for me to come home to San Francisco, but Thompson, the man I was working for, would not let me go. He never paid me a cent until I received a pass from my mother to come home, and then he gave me a dollar for the year's work." Moved by the testimony, jurors initially informed the court that they could not deliver a verdict against Hankins. Only after the judge threatened to lock them up until they came to a decision did the jury reach a verdict of guilty of second-degree murder. Disregarding the jury's recommendation of extreme leniency, Judge E. P. McDaniel on November 6 sentenced Hankins to sixteen years in San Quentin.[8]

After the Hankins case, a sense of doom and impotence crept into discussions of labor supply. With child labor increasingly discredited, it seemed that inevitably the Japanese would continue to amass power. They seemed too well organized, even bold, and at times dangerous. When a burglar had attempted to plunder their boardinghouse at Fourth and A streets in Marysville at 2 A.M. on November 3, 1904, Japanese field hands had swarmed out of their bunks armed with guns, knives, clubs, and other weapons. Firing at least one shot, they had chased the intruder up Fourth Street. "The noise attracted Officer Single," reported the *Marysville Daily Appeal*, "and he nabbed the fleeing man."[9]

To many growers and citizens of the rural counties, such actions were further evidence of the assertiveness of Japanese field hands. And with labor scarce, the Japanese did indeed seem to exploit every opportunity. After they worked the 1904 season picking citrus around Pomona, the manager of the Indian Hill Citrus Union lamented how, "owing to the scarcity of labor for a time last season, we were compelled to resort to Japanese for picking." Those "saucy, debonair Japs who like to work in a white starched shirt with cuffs and collar accompaniments," complained the *California Fruit Grower*, were now as "merciless," "tricky," and "cunning" as any disciple of AFL President Samuel Gompers. Not to be outdone, the *Los Angeles Times* complained, "The little brown traders know how to get as much for their product as the traffic will bear." One result of their actions was clear: harvest wages rose dramatically, from one dollar for eleven hours in 1889 to $1.40 or $1.50 for ten hours in 1903; pay for nonharvest work like sugar beet thinning jumped from four dollars an acre in 1890 to five dollars a decade later.[10]

❧

Keiyaku-nin succeeded so completely in their campaign that they next set their sights on California's newest agricultural region, the Imperial Valley. Wedged between the Colorado River, Mexican border, and coastal mountains in the extreme southeastern portion of California, the region was one of the more forsaken in the state. Here, the labor supply was so short and the working conditions so stark, that growers welcomed the Japanese, despite their growing reputation for militancy—along with anyone else who sought work in the fields—with open arms.[11]

The Imperial Valley's remarkable transformation had begun in 1901, when the California Development Company dug a canal from the Colorado River, bent it south into Mexico around an expanse of impenetrable sand hills, ran it for a few miles along the U.S.-Mexico border, dropped it into the dry bed of the Alamo River, then turned the water north; on May 14, 1901, a series of fingerlike canals began irrigating hundreds of desert farms. As construction roustabouts camping in large tent cities built a latticework of feeder canals and lateral lines, other laborers erected hundreds of buildings, roads, packinghouses, icehouses, and railroad sidings required to make the valley function as a farming area. Even before farming could begin, a classic land rush started. "Some arrived on the desert with stiff collars and derby hats—but they did the quick change act and compromised with the desert sun immediately," wrote the valley's first historian, Otis B. Tout, in his book *The First Thirty Years in Imperial Valley*. "Many families arrived with all their belongings on one wagon, pitched tents, boiled beans and went to work without further ado to reclaim the desert."[12]

Where open desert once stood, the new towns of Heber, Holtville, El Centro, Brawley, and Westmorland took root. Settlers soon discovered that table grapes, grapefruit, apricots, cotton, yams, wheat, alfalfa, asparagus, Irish potatoes, peanuts, and beans all did well in the irrigated desert, but melons—cantaloupes, especially—were an ideal crop for growers seeking immediate return on their investment. The area's potential and the possibility for great profit were evident. The one unanswered question was: Where would Imperial Valley farmers get their laborers?[13]

Realizing that growers could not come up with enough laborers from among the local Indian and Mexican populations, *keiyaku-nin* from Los Angeles stepped into the breach. Moving into the valley on a large scale for the first time during the spring melon harvest of 1904, a group of *keiyaku-nin* began working not only as field hands for white-owned farms, but also as tenants and sharecroppers on Japanese-owned melon ranches. It was just the beginning. Japanese numbers grew during 1905, and pleased growers called on Congress to repeal all restrictive immigration laws, something the *Oakland Tribune* condemned as "a request for . . . servile labor." Perhaps because of all the attention, stories about the Japanese and their effect on life and labor began to multiply, and newspaper reports made the entire state witness to the alleged ill effects of their presence.[14]

Rumors abounded. One involved an influx of "strike-prone" Japanese workers about to sweep into California from pineapple plantations in the Hawaiian Islands, bringing with them a tradition of discontent and belligerence that was even stronger than that of their California brothers. This point was driven home by local newspaper reports out of the Pajaro Valley, where several *keiyaku-nin* failed to provide all of the promised laborers during the 1905 apricot harvest, leaving growers desperately short. Watsonville apple grower Luke Cikuth later recalled that "you couldn't depend on the Japanese . . . no matter what kind of contract you made, you couldn't depend on them. If you needed some Japanese, you'd say you needed well, twenty of them to go to work, to pick apples or whatever you wanted them to do. They'd say all right, they'd come. The next morning probably you'd have two or three."[15]

Another story circulating at the time held that the so-called Japanese invasion of the orange and lemon industry of San Dimas had ruined the little citrus community. According to this tale, the Japanese were solely responsible for the town's ill fortune, vacant buildings, run-down appearance, and general decline. Where a large number of white families had once worked and supported many beautiful and substantial buildings, reported the *Oxnard Courier*, "the Japanese had superseded them in the labor, but were living in tents, purchasing their supplies from foreign dealers." As a consequence, property values fell. "It does seem strange," observed the newspaper, "that men whom we would suppose to have the best interest of a community at heart, would for any reason give a foreign non-home builder and non-consumer the labor that rightfully belongs to a free-born, country-loving American. Yet they are doing it, and San Dimas is not the only town in Southern California that is feeling the effects of this state of affairs."[16]

Despite these scare tactics, by 1906, about five thousand Japanese field hands were working regularly on farms in Southern California. But their importance was hardly confined to the agricultural districts around Los Angeles. According to a California State Bureau of Labor study conducted the previous year, Japanese at this time comprised about four of ten field hands statewide. After analyzing the relationship between Japanese militancy and landownership, the bureau proposed, as others had in the past, to end the dependence on Japanese field hands by "cutting up the large holdings, putting small farms on the market at reasonable figures, and making an especial endeavor to attract men with families who can raise crops." Cognizant of these sentiments, the Japanese did nothing to inflame public feelings, instead quietly going about their business throughout the summer. Labor relations thus remained calm. Nonetheless, grower associations still searching for ways to curb the power of the *keiyaku-nin* transported several railroad carloads of Indians and *cholos* (recently arrived Mexicans) from Arizona and New Mexico to California at a special rate of $2.50 cents per man.[17]

After beginning uneventfully, the 1906 harvest season was interrupted in August when *keiyaku-nin* struck peach growers near Vacaville. Having originally contracted to deliver gangs at $1.25 a day, they then held out for and obtained $1.75. On October 12, *keiyaku-nin* running a walnut harvest crew on the H. R. Owen ranch in Santa Barbara pulled their men out of the orchard demanding an increase in their piece rate. Later that day, Owen dismissed the *keiyaku-nin* and brought in local whites. Angered by the strikes, community leaders in the Santa Clara Valley drafted a number of measures designed to undermine the *keiyaku-nin* and, in December, the once sympathetic San Jose Chamber of Commerce launched what it called "a gigantic advertising scheme" to employ children in the orchards and attract five thousand white laboring families into the Santa Clara Valley. According to the *San Jose Mercury*, the scheme would minimize the need for hundreds of "yellow skinned pickers" and put the *keiyaku-nin* out of business. But as with all such strategies, nothing of the sort developed. No families ever arrived and, as the apricot and cherry harvests commenced the following spring, the *keiyaku-nin* were as much in control as ever.[18]

Even as plans to undermine Japanese labor were coming to naught in San Jose, *keiyaku-nin* around Vacaville came under scrutiny when State Commissioner of

Labor W. V. Stafford issued a report suggesting that the Japanese had a strangle-hold on field labor in the area. The implications were ominous: *keiyaku-nin*, asserted Stafford, had forced local fruit growers to bow to their wage and price demands and dictated working conditions as they pleased. They had also doubled their numbers in the area to around two thousand at harvest, taken over the city of Vacaville, and held virtually every fruit grower at their mercy.[19]

By committing his findings to paper, Stafford's report created a stir in California's agricultural circles. Finally, someone had gone beyond anecdotal evidence and detailed the insurgence of Japanese labor contractors and their men. A flurry of anti-Japanese violence followed. Of all the attacks of 1906–7, though, the most serious came from organized labor in San Francisco. Field hands and *keiyaku-nin* alike had long known that San Francisco labor leaders feared and loathed them. So it came as no surprise when, after capturing control of city hall and putting their candidate, Eugene Schmitz, into the mayor's office in 1905, organized labor went on the offensive. Representatives of more than one hundred labor unions led by Olaf Tveitmoe and Andrew Furuseth of the Seaman's Union, along with Patrick McCarthy of the Building Trades Council, created the Japanese and Korean Exclusion League (JKEL), which called for extending the Chinese Exclusion Act to include all Japanese and Koreans and advocated a boycott of Japanese workers and businesses and segregated education. Growing into a strong coordinating organization whose principal role was to harmonize opposition, monitor legislators, and supply statistics and information to further the goal of exclusion, JKEL in October 1906 succeeded in forcing the San Francisco School Board to transfer all of the city's Japanese students to a school in Chinatown. But anxious to avoid a diplomatic crisis with Japan, the federal government intervened immediately. In an attempt to overturn the San Francisco segregation order, the U.S. attorney general sued the city and then deployed troops to protect the children. What next happened, while not directly aimed at curbing the power of the *keiyaku-nin* or replacing Japanese field hands, had that effect for all practical purposes.[20]

Early in February 1907, Congress buckled under to pressure from the JKEL, by then renamed the Asiatic Exclusion League (AEL), and authorized President Theodore Roosevelt to amend immigration statutes and bar all Japanese immigration from Hawaii, Canada, and Mexico. The move drew predictable fire from farmers. Worried about labor shortages and rising wages, growers put aside their gripes with the *keiyaku-nin* and protested loudly against any federal plans to restrict the Japanese. "We are wholly dependent upon Japanese labor," explained a Fresno fruit grower in a letter to the *San Francisco Chronicle*. "If they are excluded, we shall have to give up our farms and go out of business." Even more resolute in their opposition were the *keiyaku-nin* who flooded the Japanese Foreign Ministry with protests. "We Japanese here are gravely concerned with the amendment, for it will greatly impede our economic progress," wrote Abiko Kyūtarō, the most influential and well known of all *keiyaku-nin*. On February 20, two days after Congress authorized the president to amend immigration laws with Japan, Kyūtarō and other *keiyaku-nin* organized mass protests of field hands and other laborers in Los Angeles and San Francisco.[21]

It would prove to be a losing battle. On March 14, 1907, President Roosevelt by executive order terminated further Japanese immigration; by the following summer, American and Japanese diplomats had secretly negotiated an accord, known as the "Gentleman's Agreement," which ensured the effectiveness of the executive order. In it, the Japanese government pledged to issue passports only to merchants, students, diplomats, tourists, and Japanese residents of the United States. Parents, wives, and children of those residents were eligible for passage as well. The U.S. government, in turn, agreed to allow entry of all Japanese falling into these categories, while reserving the right to deny entry to laborers with passports issued for any destinations other than the United States.[22]

᠅

The first in what would become a long series of legally imposed restrictions on Japanese immigration, the Gentleman's Agreement struck a severe blow against agriculture just as growers were losing large numbers of unskilled workers to high-paying jobs rebuilding San Francisco following the 1906 earthquake. Unanimously opposed to the agreement, the farm press leveled a barrage of criticism at Roosevelt, but toward the end of the year a consensus of negative opinion toward the Japanese reemerged among leaders of the agricultural community. The change in attitude was remarkable, given the industry's vehement early opposition to restriction. Where they had once admired the Japanese and welcomed them as model laborers, growers increasingly began to sing a different tune as the year went on. Often able to command wages as high as three dollars a day, Japanese field hands were no longer cheap labor; in fact, they were actually "the highest paid farm labor in the United States."[23]

As the debate over Japanese exclusion raged on into the fall, Colonel John P. Irish, an Iowa-born journalist who had edited both the *Oakland Times* and *Alta California* before investing in farmlands of his own, addressed the California State Fruit Growers Convention. In a long speech attacking proponents of racial exclusion, Colonel Irish advanced a new theory of the farm labor market—one that welcomed anyone—especially Chinese and other Asian peoples. To Irish and many others, it appeared obvious that white labor alone would not completely meet the needs of farmers. During the 1907 harvest season, it had been difficult, if not impossible, he pointed out, to obtain the required number of white men "at any price." (Surveying the labor market that year, the California State Bureau of Labor Statistics discovered that labor was so scare that one in four growers employed children.) With labor dear, bindlemen had begun to challenge the authority of foremen and managers. They routinely walked off jobs, demanding better food and housing, and in general misbehaved at least as badly as the Japanese. Irish explained how he had attempted to stabilize his workforce by offering white harvesters forty dollars a month with room and board, but turnover had remained high and he had been forced to hire a succession of men. "He works a month, takes his $40, goes to town, throws it down his throat, and that is the last of him," Irish asserted.[24]

Whom could they employ? As the convention threw the question to committees and opened it to discussion, several growers worked themselves into a panic. Where and how could they get not only the "cheapness of the labor" they required, but also "fidelity and dependability?" For some the answer was already evident. Mexicans, commented the *California Fruit Grower*, "are plentiful, generally peaceable, and are satisfied with very low social conditions." As Irish saw it, Mexicans were useful, but the Japanese were still by far the best of all possible immigrant groups because they had the three characteristics essential for any group of farmworkers: desperation, uprootedness, and lack of organization. They did not necessarily want to become citizens or even assimilate; all they really needed was to work. "If the rural industries of California, the foundation of all prosperity, require this Asiatic non-competitive labor—a labor and form of immigration that we don't have to assimilate," he told his audience, "we are not committing that hard task to our sons and daughters, to our grandsons and granddaughters, and our descendants."[25]

To enhance the availability of all immigrant labor, Irish proposed a completely open immigration policy, one that restored the labor glut. "Any raisin-grower in Fresno will tell you that you may pay white men $5 a day to work in that temperature and at that stoop-over task and they may work one day and that is all," Irish continued. "You can't pay them wages enough to make them stick to it and save your property. . . . It has been tried by the raisin-growers of Fresno for twenty-five years, and no man there has yet succeeded in getting reliable, long-legged, long-backed, white men who will work all day in a stoop-over position, or squat with heads down, in a temperature of 110 degrees, and save the raisin crop."[26]

The assertion was completely untrue. As always, white field hands continued to outnumber the Japanese, a fact verified by the California Bureau of Labor Statistics. But despite the numbers, the state's growers loudly seconded Irish's claims. What was true of raisin grapes was also true for other crops, they said. For example, a spokesman for the sugar beet companies observed whites would not thin sugar beets. Why? Because they were too high-strung: "A man who is high-strung," the grower explained, "could never work beets, because there are five miles of row to every acre, and if a high-strung man would look down those rows . . . he would be distraught. He could not see the end. It takes a certain mental attitude or . . . line of thinking and physical equipment to do this work."[27]

৯৯

Growers became reconciled to the Gentleman's Agreement in part because the immediate labor crisis many had predicted in the wake of its passage did not occur. Initially, this was due to novel efforts at mechanization that were taking place around the state. Some of the most innovative developments came from Segundo Guasti at the Italian Vineyard Company in Southern California.

Guasti had immigrated to California from Italy in 1881, eventually settling in Los Angeles, where he obtained work as a coal shoveler in the Southern Pacific yards. A few years later, he became a fry cook at Hotel d'Italia. Marrying the hotel owner's daughter in 1884, Segundo built a house and started a small winery to supply his father-in-law's restaurant and to sell to the city's growing Italian population. Noticing that several small vineyards seemed to be thriving in the rich orange districts east of Pomona and Ontario, he traveled out to the Cucamonga Desert in 1900, rounded up fifteen hundred acres, and bought the land for sixty thousand dollars with capital supplied by three partners. By 1903, his Italian Vineyard Company was thriving. With four square miles of vineyards, it had displaced both Vina and Natomas as the largest contiguous vineyard in the world.[28]

In 1904, Guasti erected a huge winery on the edge of his vineyard. The main building, six hundred feet long and one hundred feet wide, was divided into three ground-floor cellars, with a fourth giant cellar in the basement. In total, the winery held five million gallons of wine in aging barrels, and its fermenting cellars could process one million gallons. In addition to his winery, Guasti built a company town that bore his name. With a school, clubhouse, large social hall, library reading room, grocery store, fire station, bakery, and church named San Secondo d'Asti, the town of Guasti was home to 250 permanent Italian, Spanish, and French workers and foremen. During the annual grape harvest from late August through November, Guasti hired nearly twelve hundred temporary laborers—Indians, Mexicans, and African-Americans who camped out south of the railroad tracks, seldom mixing. "They preferred it that way," recalled one harvest hand. "Worked together, fine, but evenings with the wine flowing, they wanted to be among their own." About 250 to 300 Japanese pickers rounded out the harvest labor force. "The owners of the vineyard are possessed of the Californian's usual dislike and distrust of Japanese," observed a writer for *World's Work*, "but it is next to impossible to get together enough white laborers who are willing to go out in the hot acres and stay on a job that is merely temporary. The pickers, are, therefore, furnished by the Japanese contractors, who establish camps in the vineyard, where are often to be found whole Japanese families, the women and children adding to the picturesque squalor of the bivouac."[29]

Following traditional harvest practices, the Japanese, Mexicans, whites, and African-Americans carefully packed the grapes in boxes, nailed them shut with a lid, and stacked them eight to ten boxes high at the end of each vineyard row, where white teamsters and wagon drivers gathered and hauled them to the winery. At any given time, fully one-third of the harvest labor force would be busy loading, transporting, and emptying boxes rather than picking the crop. Dissatisfied both with his dependence on field hands and the inefficiency of traditional harvest techniques, Guasti in 1907 purchased twenty miles of narrow-gauge railroad track, forty gondola cars used for hauling coal, and a fifteen-ton locomotive called the *Italia*, complete with a brass bell used to announce its arrival at the winery. Used for the first time that August, the railroad considerably streamlined the harvest and dramatically cut labor requirements as men simply dumped their grapes into the gondolas as if they were loading coal. At the winery, the gondolas would be tipped sideways, sending their cargoes cascading directly into great concrete troughs, where men pitchforked the grapes onto chain conveyors feeding the grape stemmers and crushers. In the vineyards, tracks could be picked up and relaid as different vineyard blocks ripened. Gone were the crews of swampers, wagon drivers, and box distributors who did nothing but deposit thousands of boxes ahead of the picking crews.[30]

FIGURE 43. Dreyfus winery, Center and E Street, Anaheim, 1894. Courtesy of the Anaheim Public Library.

With everyone except the engineer cutting and pitching grapes into gondolas, Guasti was literally able to make wine by the trainload. Late in the afternoon, as gondolas of grapes stacked up and men scurried to dump them, the Italian Vineyard Company seemed more like a moderately sized manufacturing plant than a farming operation. Out in the vineyards, workers still performed much the same daily movements and exertions as did workers in a Pittsburgh, Pennsylvania, steel plant. With the temperatures topping one hundred degrees, the work took its toll. By late afternoon the rails would become too hot to touch and the first boxes of grapes dumped into the gondolas would sizzle as the juice hit the hot metal gondola sides. Commented one old-timer of the arrangement: "With the heat reflecting off that sandy soil, it was like working in a foundry." Within two years, both the Great Western Vineyard Company north of Reedley and El Pinal Winery south of Stockton were operating their own narrow-gauge vineyard railroads. But just as growers were considering adopting these and other ways to cut their labor requirements, a new group of immigrants moved into the fields to help preserve the status quo.[31]

❧

Known variously as "Hindoos," "Muslims," and "Punjabis," the newcomers were, in fact, mostly Sikhs from the Punjab area of northern India. Opposed to the strict caste system and corrupt social, economic, and political practices in their home country, Sikhs had arrived on the Pacific Coast earlier in the decade to escape persecution and British colonial rule. After arriving in British Columbia, some drifted south and settled around Yuba City and Marysville, where they found work on the railroads and in the lumber mills. Those with agricultural experience naturally moved into field labor and were soon employed extensively on farms in the northern Sacramento Valley. Because they looked different—most wore traditional turbans and kept their beards and hair uncut—Sikhs attracted considerable attention and were labeled "rag heads," or "the turbaned tide." Labor leaders often described "Hindoo" immigrants as "unspeakably filthy and in nearly every instance suffering from dangerous and incurable diseases."[32]

Almost immediately Sikhs began undermining Japanese field hands and *keiyaku-nin*. During the spring of 1907, four Sikhs traveled to George Pierce's farm looking for work. Impressed by their initiative, and by their robust physical appearance, Pierce hired the men to excavate drainage ditches, cut, saw, and stack firewood, burn orchard prunings, shovel and haul manure, and attack various chores and tasks around the farm for $1.25 per day. Pleased by their wages, which compared well with railroad work and other forms of common labor (and far outstripped the ten to fifteen cents per day they could earn back in Punjab), the Sikhs became regular workers on Pierce's almond ranch, completely replacing the Japanese and eliminating all but one or two white crew bosses. These men may have been the first Sikh field hands employed on California farms.[33]

Outside of Davisville and the northern Sacramento Valley, Japanese field hands were at first not adversely affected either by the Sikhs or the Gentleman's Agreement. Arriving ahead of the immigration deadline, 30,824 Japanese (double that of the previous year) created a large reserve of laborers. Drawing on this supply, Fresno *keiyaku-nin* during August held out for higher wages, announcing that if they did not receive the unheard-of wage of $2.50 a day to harvest the raisin crop they would let the grapes rot on the vines. "What one Jap said all Japs said, and there was no help to be had," reported the *San Jose Mercury*. "And the grape growers took their medicine. If the weather is favorable the growers this year will probably have a little money left after paying their help. If the rains come and the extra trimming is required they will lose money. Either way is perfectly satisfactory to the Japs. It will be $2.50 a day just the same."[34]

But it was not the same. Thoroughly angered by their excessive demands, growers again determined to stop the increasingly assertive Japanese. First banning them from the vineyards, growers then brought in a "small colony of full-blooded Sikhs" and two thousand Greek immigrants from Los Angeles and San Francisco. Many of the Greeks were familiar with raisin drying, having performed the same work back home. Succeeding beyond everyone's expectations, the replacement workers broke the back of the strike and inspired the California Bureau of Labor Statistics to observe that the "Greeks have proven satisfactory and have been a positive influence in driving the Japanese out of this district."[35]

Encouraged by the victory, growers began retaliating against the Japanese with several clever tactics. Still angry with the Japanese for the way they had treated him six years earlier, Davisville almond grower Pierce now got his revenge. Aware that late frosts had cut his yield and that an infestation of red spider mites would further diminish his harvest, Pierce sold his entire unharvested almond crop to J. Tanaka, an unsuspecting Sacramento *keiyaku-nin*. The agreement earned Pierce

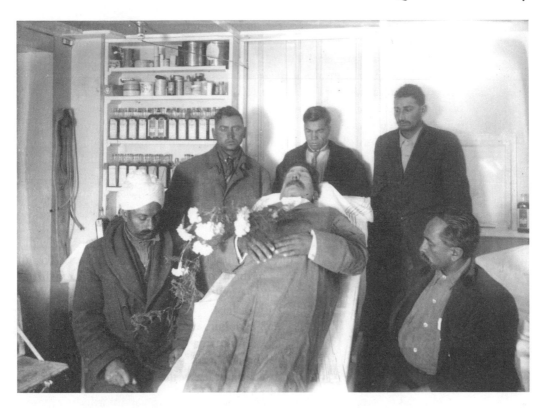

FIGURE 44. Sikhs gather around the corpse of a fellow field hand, Marysville, ca. 1905. Photograph by Clara Smith. Courtesy of Arne Svenson, New York, N.Y.

six hundred dollars, but after harvesting the crop and paying his crew, Tanaka earned exactly $3.39. "Pierce's actions," wrote agricultural historian David Vaught, "revealed just how unforgiving a horticulturalist could be if his authority in his orchards was challenged."[36]

Growers may have welcomed the new immigrant classes as a substitute for unruly Japanese workers, but most of the field hands already in the state—regardless of ethnicity—viewed them as a threat. Closely monitoring the situation in Vacaville, white field hands near Live Oak, ten miles north of Marysville, decided that they would not let Punjabi Sikhs become established in their community. On the evening of January 28, 1908, they attacked a camp of Sikh orchard pruners, beating and terrorizing the men, burning the camp to the ground, and robbing them of about twenty-five hundred dollars before driving them out of town. When Governor James N. Gillette ordered a perfunctory investigation of the incident, the Live Oak district attorney defended the rioters by claiming that the Sikhs "dressed funny," had been raiding henhouses, and exposed themselves to women and young girls. When the Sikhs attempted to have two of their attackers prosecuted for robbing them, dozens of townspeople swore that the accused men had not been at the camp. Summarizing the incident, the *Sacramento Bee* observed, "All is quiet today and there will be no more trouble if the Hindus keep away."[37]

With the arrival of East Indians, a new element had been introduced into agricultural labor relations. Soon competing with the Japanese for jobs in the melon fields of the Imperial Valley, Sikhs caused *keiyaku-nin* to realize that their days as the dominant group in the fields were numbered, that they could be replaced, and that growers might increasingly undermine their strongholds by bringing in other laboring groups. For their part, growers were content. "I do not believe that the Imperial Valley is a white man's country," exclaimed one Brawley farmer, "and I am willing to hand it over to the Hindus and the Japanese." Such statements led some Japanese to side with lawless elements and taunt Punjabi immigrants as "English slaves" and "poles," the latter term a disparaging reference to their height. But they could not stem the "tide of turbans."[38]

Outside of Fresno, Japanese contracting began to attract academic scrutiny. Around Watsonville, where four *keiyaku-nin* supplied about 650 men to farmers in a district embracing some one hundred square miles, Stanford University historian Yamato Ichihashi visited in the summer of 1908 and found labor relations thoroughly systematized. He later wrote:

> When the season . . . began to slack, the "outsiders" first withdrew, and some of its members also migrated whenever it was found advantageous to work elsewhere. To assist these migratory laborers, the secretary studied the situations in the neighboring districts, if he did not know them already; in fact, he often arranged with employers of such districts for the employment of his men before the members were allowed to move, and in this case he collected the five-cent commission. More often, however, in order to obtain accurate information from the latter he communicated with the bosses of such localities, who were more than glad to furnish the information because they had to secure a labor force fluctuating with the seasonal needs of their respective districts . . . Thus the club members kept on going from . . . place to place until there were no more jobs; then they returned to their clubs to spend the winter, doing such casual jobs as they could pick up in their residential district.[39]

Alarmed by such organization and power, one of three vineyardists surveyed by the U.S. Immigration Commission listed *keiyaku-nin* as a significant problem and "complained of strikes by Japanese to compel them to pay higher wages." One dried fruit grower recalled, "There comes a sudden threat of rain in the drying season, and the trays must be stacked at once or the crop will be irreparably damaged. Instantly the cost of Japanese labor rises to blackmail prices, regardless of previous contracts." Another explained: "If one quits or is disciplined, they are all likely to quit." There seemed no end to the strikes and no way to combat the *keiyaku-nin*. Although growers in Sonoma County and other agricultural districts around San Francisco Bay got around the Japanese by arranging to have railroads transport pickers from the cities at half-cost, most others placed their faith in larger numbers of Sikhs and new sources of foreign labor that might become available following the opening of the Panama Canal in 1914. All through the spring of 1909, growers discussed how the canal would bring in more hardworking Italians, Portuguese, and other "good, sturdy, peasants of Europe." Rural newspapers like the *Fresno Morning Republican* also mentioned "Mexican peons" as possible replacements because, when no longer needed, they would "go back to Mexico" and "walk if necessary."[40]

During the summer of 1908, farm labor took yet another dramatic turn in the Imperial Valley. For three years, growers there had worried little about the labor supply; they had instead been preoccupied with overcoming a disastrous flood caused when a headgate on the Colorado River broke in November 1905. When the break was finally closed in the fall of 1907, the flood took another six months to abate. Even before the land dried out, farmers launched a get-rich-quick cantaloupe rush, and in an attempt to recoup their losses of the past two years, shipped 644 railcars of cantaloupes to eastern markets in May and June. Lured by fantastic profits from the scheme, they then prepared to grow a bumper crop of the melons in 1908. As a result, the valley filled with cantaloupes—acreage shot up from twelve hundred acres to more than ten thousand—too many for the available labor force of Coachella Indians and Japanese. As the harvest neared, growers began to worry that their crop would rot in the fields because they could not entice men to work under the valley's harsh and remote conditions.[41]

With several thousand field hands required for the harvest and everything riding on their ability to get the crop out of the fields, farmers contacted labor agents in Los Angeles, who brought in eighty "college boys" and forty "Hungarians." Arriving before the harvest, the newcomers piled up around the pool halls and rooming houses in Brawley and El Centro. Some became impatient. Before the picking began, about twenty of the "college boys" returned to Los Angeles complaining that they had been charged fees for nonexistent jobs and had been left to starve on the streets. Their stories were published in the *Los Angeles Times* under the headline "Boys Starve Down South Seeking Jobs That Don't Exist." As a result, the two labor contractors—E. J. Palau and C. M. Dunnick—were arrested for running an unlicensed business. Meanwhile, Imperial Valley growers housed and fed every transient who arrived, and still they could not find enough men to "pitch melons." Even rounding up hundreds of Mexicans from the "Mexican colonies" on the fringes of Imperial and El Centro, they still found themselves short of labor. Now desperate, they appealed reluctantly to local *keiyaku-nin*, who brought in between five hundred and six hundred Japanese from Los Angeles. Additionally, when several *keiyaku-nin* offered to not only harvest cantaloupes, but grow and cultivate the melons as well, a half-dozen growers hired them on a tenant and sharecropping basis.[42]

After a promising start, the first large-scale cantaloupe harvest quickly deteriorated. Not only did growers lack market connections with all but a few of the large cities in the East, but they directed their inexperienced crews to pick, pack, and ship all the melons in the fields indiscriminately. As a result, worthless melons were packed along with good ones. This shortsightedness destroyed the market for mid- and late-season cantaloupes, so when the bulk of the crop ripened during the first week of June, it appeared that many growers would have to leave most of the melons in the fields. Suddenly lacking a market for their crop, some growers abandoned the harvest and began discharging pickers; their timing could not have been worse. Unemployed laborers were piling up in El Centro, and when cantaloupe grower C. A. Carr arrived in town to secure labor on Monday morning, June 8, "a gang of loafers" ignored his offer of work. But seeing him hire a crew of Japanese, they became enraged. As Carr drove several wagon loads of Japanese over the railroad tracks on the way back to his farm, the gang attacked the caravan, overturned one wagon, and caused a team driven by one Japanese field hand to bolt. "It was a lucky chance that the driver, when thrown, escaped being crushed by the wagon wheels," observed the *Imperial Valley Press*.[43]

After delivering the men to his farm, Carr returned to town and swore out complaints against seven of the attackers, who were promptly arrested. The *Imperial Valley Press* reported:

> Of the seven arrested only three were identified positively as assailants of the Japs. One, a bootblack who had no interest in the question of pickers' wages and only got into the affair because of lack of sense, was fined $5 by Justice [Otis] Tout. The two others were fined $15 each, and one paid his fine and the other went to jail for 15 days. The Japanese Consul General at San Francisco telegraphed to Sheriff [Mobley] Meadows to ask what steps were being taken to protect the Japanese laborers from attacks in Imperial Valley. He was assured that they would be amply protected, that none had been hurt and that rioters had been punished.[44]

But outside of El Centro, Japanese field hands and tenant farmers continued to be attacked. On one farm, unemployed whites overturned and demolished a half-dozen wagon loads of cantaloupes. With much of his harvest smashed and left to rot in the dust, the Japanese farmer was unable to harvest his crop and meet his contracts. Later that evening, a mob of about sixty unemployed men visited the El Centro office of melon grower L. M. Lyon and demanded work, threatening to burn his packing sheds "if they were not provided for at once." The city marshal and his deputies were called to the scene and dispersed the crowd, then deployed throughout the town to keep watch over the melon sheds. Four days later, at nearby Meloland, a new packing shed owned by the Interurban Melon Growers Association mysteriously burned to the ground, severely injuring two melon packers from Pomona.[45]

While most growers decried the arson, violence, and crop losses, leaders like *Pacific Rural Press* editor E. J. Wickson were encouraged by at least one aspect of the cantaloupe harvest. Whereas the industry had for some time worried about where it would find labor, the influx of unemployed men seemed to have resolved this problem in the Imperial Valley. "There is one piece of good luck which often comes to California farmers, and that is that whenever they become much alarmed lest their labor supply be short for some coming crop, time brings a solution of their difficulty," wrote Wickson in July. "Either the crop is so short that few men are needed, or some other business slacks up and sends a lot of labor afloat and it blows itself into the rural districts."[46]

There was no shortage of labor in Davisville that August, when Sikhs took over even more work on George Pierce's almond farm. Mousha Singh and Bogosin Singh, having worked through the winter, gained Pierce's confidence, moved out of common labor, and began taking on more skilled work such as pruning, irrigating, and cultivating. At Pierce's behest, the two men contacted Shaam Singh, a Vacaville-based Sikh contractor, who brought in thirty more Punjabi men for the monthlong harvest at $1.25 a day, less food and board expenses. Eliminating the *keiyaku-nin* and providing a compliant and able labor force, the Sikhs in one stroke solved Pierce's problems, efficiently brought in the harvest, and earned the grower his largest returns ever. Moving into newly constructed bunkhouses, the Sikhs completely replaced Japanese and white laborers and took over positions as gang bosses. For the next nine years, Pierce and other area growers relied on Shaam Singh and his contacts in the Sikh community to secure an uninterrupted supply of field hands.[47]

Elsewhere Sikhs also continued to make inroads. When the Japanese became scarce in the Monterey Bay region during the 1909 season, for example, about 150 Sikhs began harvesting sugar beets; they also found work in the beet fields around Visalia and Oxnard, sometimes gaining a foothold by hiring on for as little as fifty cents a day. At about the same time, Sikhs moved into the celery, potato, and bean fields near Holt, two miles west of Stockton, and the orange groves of Southern California, especially around Pomona.[48]

While East Indian Sikh laborers generally resorted to wage cutting to gain a foothold in harvest work during 1909, they would often equalize wages through slowdowns once on the job. In at least one case, when a farm owner near Los Angeles attempted to establish the work rate for hoeing beans, Sikhs threatened the pacesetter and forced him to slow down. Similar confrontations occurred in nearby celery fields, where Sikhs performed the exhausting task of transplanting tiny celery seedlings. In one instance, an Italian boss shouted at his workers constantly and succeeded in urging them to speed up. But each time he stopped his exhortations, the Sikhs resumed their own slower pace. This wore out the boss, and the crew was eventually left alone to find its own pace to finish out the day.[49]

❧

Keiyaku-nin did not accept these developments easily. Unsettled by the Sikhs, they struck at growers where they held the greatest leverage, strategically aiming their blow at the newest and most vulnerable segment of commercial agriculture, the recently established sugar beet industry around Hamilton City in the northern Sacramento Valley. At the start of the harvest in mid-July 1908, *keiyaku-nin* began breaking their contracts and shifting their men from Hamilton City and the area around Chico into the peach harvest near Yuba City. Left in a fix with thousands of acres of ripening sugar beets and no one to harvest them, the Sacramento Valley Sugar Beet Company (SVSBC) scrambled to round up crews of inexperienced Indian Sikhs, but never quite succeeded in replacing the departed Japanese. One foreman noted that the Japanese could not be blamed, as SVSBC was only offering ten cents per hour for thirteen-hour days in the shadeless fields. By shifting to the peach orchards, the Japanese earned $1.50 or more for ten or eleven hours work and taught the SVSBC a lesson.[50]

A month later, the Japanese retaliated against the Fresno raisin grape growers who had broken their strike and lowered wages the previous year. Several months before the 1909 harvest, a group of fifty-three *keiyaku-nin* organized themselves into the Central California Contractor's Association and set a rate of $1.65 per ton of grapes. But despite vows to punish corrupt bosses and keep its workers in line, the association could not hold everyone to the agreement. As the harvest neared, three *keiyaku-nin* from Hanford arrived in Fresno and signed contracts to harvest grapes for $1.25 a ton on the nine-hundred-acre M. F. Tarpey ranch. Association leaders immediately appealed to all Japanese field hands not to work for these "traitors." They also appealed to Japanese Association of America secretary Kuma Toshiyasu, who, after failing to persuade the newcomers to break their contract with the Tarpey ranch, expelled two of the contractors from the Hanford branch of the organization.[51]

At the height of this conflict, *keiyaku-nin* received unexpected support from a group of Japanese socialists led by Takeuchi Tetsugorō. A member of the Social Revolutionary Party who had fled Japan to avoid being drafted into the army, Tetsugorō had arrived in Fresno after working first in labor and peace movements around the San Francisco Bay and then as an agricultural laborer around Vacaville. On August 20, he formed the Fresno Labor League (Furesno Rōdō Dōmeikai) and enlisted a large and enthusiastic group of grape pickers. Friendly sources estimated that roughly half of Fresno's four thousand Japanese grape pickers joined the league; less sympathetic authorities put the figure lower, but admitted that at least one thousand grape pickers had joined. Not an organization of contractors, the Fresno Labor League held the interests of the laborers above those of the *keiyaku-nin* and supported the Central California Contractor's wage rate.[52]

Just before picking season, the Contractor's Association deployed picketers at the Sunnyside trolley line, which ran east to the Tarpey ranch. When the *Fresno Morning Republican* reported that the three-rogue *keiyaku-nin* had received death threats, the Fresno police sent officers to guard the area. Meanwhile the Fresno Labor League assembled picket crews and began roaming the countryside, obstructing efforts by the mutinous contractors to recruit Japanese field hands from as far away as Fowler. Members of the Fresno Labor League were so successful that not a single Japanese field hand signed on to work for any of the insurgents.[53]

While Fresno Labor League members celebrated Labor Day, their opponents were gathering momentum. Recalling an incident from two years earlier, when Japanese men were hired to replace white women employed at the California Canning Association plant, the *Fresno Morning Republican* denounced the league, proclaiming that citizens were "determined to put their foot emphatically down upon Jap labor where it threatens to take the bread from the mouths of their womankind in the city." Gathering in Courthouse Park to hear speeches, listen to a band, and socialize, crowds heard State Senator George W. Cartwright "in plain and forcible language" brand Tetsugorō and other members of the Fresno Labor League and the Contractor's Association as "little yellow . . . menace[s] to the nation at large and the laborers in particulr [*sic*]."[54]

Faced with little support and considerable hostility, the Contractor's Association strike sputtered along. Meanwhile, Tarpey had little trouble bringing in his crop with Mexicans, Sikhs, and Koreans provided by the rogue *keiyaku-nin*. In desperation, Tetsugorō visited the Tarpey ranch and attempted to negotiate a deal to take over the harvest, while the Contractor's Association offered to lower its wage demands and finish the harvest. Neither landed a contract. In a fit of anger, Tarpey refused to ever again hire any Japanese laborer, regardless of affiliation.[55]

After the harvest concluded, Tetsugorō and the Fresno Labor League remained active for a time, publishing a weekly Japanese language newspaper, *Rōdō* (Labor). On the eve of the 1909 grape harvest, the league held a convention in Fresno's Japantown and bombarded three hundred field hands of all stripes with speeches by Japanese socialists and activists from San Francisco, Los Angeles, and Sacramento. But while Mexican and Italian radicals vowed to cooperate with league members, nothing much came of the promise. Shunned by other Japanese leaders and organizations and unable to branch out or establish an English periodical, the league on September 14 stopped publishing *Rōdō*. Toward the end of the year, Tetsugorō traveled to San Francisco to challenge one of his critics in a public debate. Instead, he wound up seriously injuring the man in a knife fight. Forced to spend most of his time defending himself in court, Tetsugorō so exhausted the Fresno Labor League's funds that he ceased being an effective organizer.[56]

ॐ

As the Gentleman's Agreement began to take effect late in 1909, life became even more difficult for Japanese laborers and *keiyaku-nin* trying to maintain dominance in the fields. Only 3,275 men officially immigrated from Japan that year, and of those, two out of three were classified as nonlaborers—professionals, students, and the like. As with the Chinese before them, Japanese laborers did not completely cease immigrating as a result of restrictive laws. They were simply forced to find another mode of entry.

Thousands continued to arrive illegally from Mexico, stepping off vessels as they stopped briefly in Acapulco, then making their way to Mexico's northern provinces, especially Sonora, where they crossed into California. "Where are the Japanese . . . that have come to Mexico, and did not remain in that Republic?" asked the U.S. commissioner general of immigration. "The almost irresistible conclusion is they found their way to the United States. . . . None of the ships that brought laborers to Mexico took one Japanese passenger back . . . and yet there are at present hardly 2,000 Japanese in the whole Republic of Mexico. The conclusion is forced on me that . . . fully 80 percent deserted immediately after their arrival and went to the United States." United States newspapers reported as many as five thousand Japanese arriving in one month. A common subterfuge was to purchase a railroad ticket for passage to Canada, and then to simply get off wherever they wanted. Many would make their way into the vineyards around Fresno. "They have ninety-nine chances out of a hundred in their favor to remain in the country," concluded the commissioner general.[57]

As the Japanese continued to pour in and the *keiyaku-nin* continued to exercise their power, a troubled apprehension settled over the vineyards around Fresno. With 65 percent of California's forty-two thousand Japanese working in agriculture, *keiyaku-nin* still held tight reins over field hands. To Fresno farmers and public officials alike, Japanese domination seemed to be the spearhead of a threatened social revolution that would leave raisin growers at the mercy of Japanese contractors. A series of unrelated events seemed to confirm that fear. Moving into vineyard pruning—work previously dominated by Italians—*keiyaku-nin* in 1910 gained absolute control over the Selma vineyard district just south of Fresno; by the end of the harvest season, a single Japanese contractor, Mr. J. Kawamoto, provided every grape picker and pruner in the area. At the same time, other *keiyaku-nin* did not ignore Indian Sikhs as they moved south into Fresno. Aware that Sikhs had been used to undermine their position in the northern Sacramento Valley, *keiyaku-nin* quickly organized the newcomers into crews and used them to supplement declining numbers of their own countrymen. Elsewhere in Fresno County, *keiyaku-nin* struck again and again at the most opportune moment. Going after one grower, they walked out six times in two days, raising wages from $1.25 to $2 an hour. To head off similar threats, farmers throughout the raisin district began paying the two-dollar rate. One Scottish immigrant working in the vineyards for the first time observed that while white grape pickers toiled from 8 A.M. to sunset for $1.75 a day, Japanese pickers put in an eight-hour day at a piece rate that earned them five dollars. "At that time," he added, "the Japs had camps . . . while the whites were invited to enjoy the hospitality of a shady tree."[58]

By the end of the year, the issue of Japanese labor had grown to such proportions, and become so controversial, that the legislature instructed State Commissioner of Labor John D. Mackenzie, a conservative Republican from San Jose, to conduct a full-scale investigation. Sending a four-page questionnaire to hundreds of farmers, Mackenzie obtained information on wages, working and living conditions, and race relations. From this information, Mackenzie drew six lessons: (1) the farm labor situation had developed over a long time and had become so entrenched that it could not be changed; (2) crops could not be harvested using only white labor; (3) any change in the farm labor situation would necessarily wreak havoc with agricultural transportation, marketing, and sales; (4) the continued development of intensive agriculture required an assured supply of labor from outside the state; (5) the shift from grain to specialized fruit and vegetable farming had been the event that had caused agriculture to become dependent on a labor supply larger than what was available in the state; and (6) the main problem with the farm labor system was the seasonal nature of employment. Released to newspapers late in May, the report provoked such an uproar that Governor James Gillett rejected it before copies could be printed and distributed. "It would almost seem that its conclusions were derived from interviews with large landed proprietors, who would, by the employment of Orientals, create much the same conditions that existed in the Southern States before the war, viz: A landed aristocracy and a vast body of servile laborers," wrote the *Vacaville Reporter*. "This is something no true American wants to see repeated. And we do not believe it essential to the development of the vast horticultural and viticultural industries that the fairest portions of our great state should be handed over to hordes of Chinese, Japanese or Hindoos."[59]

Nowhere in California at this time did growers feel labor pressures more strongly than in the cotton fields of the Imperial Valley. Cotton had always seemed perfect for the wide, flat spaces and hot climate of the state's interior valleys, but it was not until 1910 that growers launched a massive planting program. After harvesting their first commercial-scale crop that fall, growers expanded acreage rapidly and began calling the region the "Egypt of America." Upon discovering that the Durango variety of cotton was even better adapted to the climate of the Imperial Valley, growers built five cotton gins and planned for huge profits when prices soared in the wake of Egypt's cotton crop failure. Their main problem, as always, remained isolation. Outside of El Centro, Brawley, and Holtville, candles and kerosene lamps still illuminated most shelters, such as they were. And even permanent settlers did without schools, churches, doctors, newspapers, hotels, and other luxuries for years after the first cotton gins were built.[60]

Because any cotton picking force would have to live under frontier conditions in the blistering heat, field hands continued to be in short supply. With demand for cotton on the rise, cotton growers found that, although they could grow bumper crops, they could not so easily pick them. And although Japanese had been working for some time in the lettuce and melon industries there, cotton growers apparently did not even consider hiring them. Unlike melon growers, who would hire anybody, cotton farmers wanted a specific type of laborer, preferably "experienced" Mexicans or black field hands from the south. As picking season approached, cotton growers placed advertisements in all of the daily newspapers in Arizona, New Mexico, all of the southern states, and several Mexican border cities. "SEEKING SOUTHERN HELP," began one advertisement. "Wanted—1000 cotton pickers, for Imperial Valley, California. Wages, $1.00 per 100 pounds. Picking begins September 1. Colonists rates will be in effect on all railroads. Joseph R. Loftus Company, the California Cotton People, El Centro, California."[61]

By September, the *Imperial Valley Press* was reporting how "every inbound train during the present week has brought to the various valley towns people who have been attracted hither by the lure of news about the new cotton district. For more than a month past parties of Negroes from the South have been arriving and have scattered out to the various plantations."[62]

But the steady stream of blacks into the valley did not satisfy growers, who continued searching for labor in all directions. About thirty Indians from Arizona went to work in mid-October, but were found somewhat lacking. "Their scheme," wrote the *Imperial Valley Press*, "is to get enough cotton in a sack to make a comfortable cushion, and then sit down on the sack and pick the bolls within reach, holding a branch with one hand and carefully extracting the lint with the other." Sikhs arrived from the San Joaquin Valley, but they too proved ineffective. The first who arrived quickly abandoned the cotton fields to clear ditches and, upon accumulating funds, moved into cotton farming. As growers had predicted, Mexican campesinos who crossed the border at Calexico proved to be the best. Experienced pickers, they easily sacked 150 to 250 pounds per day, earning up to $2.50 a day for picking one hundred pounds. Many would return to pick cotton again the following year, a development that did not sit well with some valley residents. As they settled into the "Mexican colony" near the town of Imperial and into the "Little Mexico" section of El Centro, the *Imperial Daily Standard* on October 29, 1910, could not help commenting that "cotton picking time is attracting a doubtful looking bunch of all shades and kinds."[63]

Mexican field hands were just another of the mass of people sucked in by the opening of the Imperial Valley. But the influx was never enough—even in conjunction with Sikhs, Japanese, and white field hands—to satisfy cotton growers. The perceived shortage led to early efforts to mechanize using a crude, horse-drawn, cotton picking machine imported from Texas in September 1910. Reporting on the event, the *Imperial Valley Press* predicted that the "difficulty in obtaining laborers this year" as well as "the importation of hordes of undesirable people and the citation of troublesome social problems" would be overcome by the new picking machine. The paper later had to report how the machine bogged down to a crawl that could not match a crew of "laxadaisical [*sic*], experienced Mexican pickers."[64]

 formula ornament

As growers in the Imperial Valley were crying for any and all types of labor, officials of the SVSBC at Hamilton City became so fed up with the Japanese that during 1910 they spent considerable time and money scheming to eliminate them—or at least diminish their power. When beet thinning season approached and SVSBC began worrying that sugar beets would come up too suddenly, the company in desperation contacted a Japanese banker in Sacramento and asked him to provide crews. The banker recommended two *keiyaku-nin*, both reliable and financially secure. Company president Hamilton promptly offered one of them a high-paying contract believing the arrangement would protect the SVSBC, "if anything will." Writing to his banker in Los Angeles, he predicted confidently, "I do not believe we will have difficulty with thinning labor at least." Just how badly Hamilton had miscalculated soon became apparent. Problems began just after the start of beet thinning in March, when *keiyaku-nin* notified every foreman on the SVSBC's Moorhead, Gienello, and Bell ranches that they had withdrawn their men. They charged that, upon going to work, they had found the fields hopelessly choked with weeds, thereby nullifying their contracts. Company foremen immediately visited the sugar beet fields and acknowledged the problem.[65]

Realizing that if the company delayed beet thinning it would lose much of its crop, *keiyaku-nin* quickly took advantage of the situation. They renegotiated their contract, canceling their piece-rate arrangement in favor of a flat rate of $1.50 per day. And because there was now too much work for the number of men available, the *keiyaku-nin* brought in fifty additional Japanese workers from San Francisco. But even with the added manpower they could not catch up. Nor did they want to. Instead, *keiyaku-nin* shipped in a crew of slow and inexperienced Indian Sikhs. As the Sikhs went to work, shocked and dismayed SVSBC officials pondered what to do next. Recognizing the seriousness of their predicament and desperately in need of men to thin one thousand acres of weed-choked sugar beet fields, company officials went in search of labor in San Francisco, Sacramento, Stockton, and "all small towns along the line." They found none.[66]

Without any railroad construction, cannery work, or harvesting to draw men away from the fields, the SVSBC blamed the shortage of field hands on the *keiyaku-nin*. The only solution, they concluded, was to search far and wide for more laborers. "We have got to get some other nationality," wrote Hamilton to his labor manager late in March. "We might as well go to the expense necessary to get Mexicans in here now . . . I hope you will be able to send us a couple of car-loads of Cholos."[67]

The campaign commenced in Los Angeles, where an SVSBC agent scouring the downtown area for labor found that the best he could do was to sign up 150 *cholos* at $1.75 per day without board, considerably more than what the SVSBC paid to the Japanese. But so determined was the company to teach the Japanese a lesson and break their power that it laid plans to bring the men north by cattle cars. When the men refused to travel by cattle car, the company considered shipping the men up by boat, then dropped that idea to avoid losing them in San Francisco, where it was assumed they would jump ship. To prevent the *cholos* from abandoning their railcars before arriving on company land, the company stationed armed guards on board the train. But this had little effect. "As the train came through the San Joaquin Valley," recalled one SVSBC supervisor in a letter to President Hamilton, "Mexicans jumped out of the windows at each town the train stopped at."[68]

Arriving at Hamilton City, the Mexicans proved to be inexperienced and slow. So many abandoned the fields that the company fell behind its thinning schedule. Hoping to make up the difference, SVSBC again tried to bring in Italians from San Francisco, Indian Sikhs from Sacramento and Marysville, California Indians from Tehama, and even a few old Chinese—"the greatest conglomeration of thinners one could imagine," reported Hamilton. Still, the company was plagued with weedy fields. Even with between 280 and three hundred beet thinners on its payroll, Hamilton admitted, "we have been up against it, and some of the beet fields have suffered for want of thinning, because labor could not be procured in time."[69]

News that the sugar beet fields were not going to be thinned, and possibly would have to be plowed under, terrified officials of the SVSBC. At the last moment, they beat a strategic retreat. Fearing disaster, the company discharged all of its Mexican and Sikh workers and contacted the Mori Company, the largest Japanese contractor in Sacramento. Having held out for higher wages, Mori now agreed to coordinate a half-dozen smaller Japanese contractors and provide one hundred experienced sugar beet thinners at the unheard-of wage of two dollars per day. Soon the wage of two dollars a day and board became the industry standard. With the Japanese now completely in control, few growers dared bolt because, as the *Monterey Cyprus* explained, without the Japanese, "not a sugar beet would be planted or harvested thereafter."[70]

Angry with the Japanese and thoroughly disillusioned by their experiences during 1910, SVSBC officials shifted tactics during 1911. Abandoning labor recruitment, the company attempted to create a stable labor force and undermine the *keiyaku-nin* through an elaborate program of corporate welfare designed to attract the best elements of the workforce. Their initial move was to show that the SVSBC respected and appreciated its field hands, and that it wanted to make their work as comfortable as possible. Although sugar beet thinning would not begin until spring, officials decided to commence their campaign before winter ended. Concentrating at first on the general conditions all men encountered upon passing through Hamilton City, the SVSBC announced it was planning to construct a model worker community. The hope was that word of what was under way would get out and field hands disgusted by what they encountered elsewhere would flock to the area in large enough numbers to render the Japanese irrelevant.[71]

Foremen and employees of the sugar beet factory were the first to benefit from these plans. When they arrived in February to ready the factory for the upcoming harvest, they discovered the company had instituted several new benefits. There was an accident insurance system, new cottages for married couples, a restaurant, a rooming house, and three separate bunkhouses for Greek, Italian, and Austrian factory hands. Complete with ventilation systems, "first class grub and rooms with good beds, pillows, linen etc.," and cool "sleeping basements," the quarters rented for one dollar a week, with restaurant privileges going for $23.50 per month. The transformation in Hamilton City was amazing. From a ramshackle, somewhat seedy, and backward settlement, the city took on the appearance of a neat and comfortable company town. With such modern conveniences, it was expected that labor turnover among factory hands would cease.[72]

Turning to field hands, the company devoted a great deal of money and energy to improving the circumstances under which they lived. Even more than wages, what seemed to play into the hands of the Japanese and prevent white field hands from laboring in the northern Sacramento Valley were the miserable living conditions in the sugar beet camps. Besides the heat, dust, flies, mosquitoes, and isolation, the company concluded that field hands were repelled by the often vermin-infested, unscreened shacks, contaminated water supplies, and filthy or nonexistent toilet facilities that only the Japanese would endure in exchange for high wages. Determined to eliminate this situation, SVSBC overhauled its housing, established a network of tent camps, equipping each block of tents with clean toilets and plenty of fresh, cold water. The SVSBC also hired a physician fluent in several languages and experienced in treating malaria. Visiting men on regular rounds, the physician provided services at only a minimal charge. Additionally the company employed a Portuguese cook who supervised a staff of other cooks at the various camps, and a full-time gardener and several assistants who provided the cooks with fresh produce from the company's Hamilton City gardens.[73]

But if SVSBC officials thought they had undermined the Japanese by creating ideal working conditions, they were soon disabused of such notions. As ambitious and comprehensive as their labor welfare programs were, they failed to lure and hold white sugar beet thinners and harvest hands. Unable to attract large numbers to properly thin their crop, the company tried to stagger its planting so that all of its sugar beets did not mature at the same time. But the measure was too little too late. Company president E. C. Hamilton admitted as much. "The system as a whole," he explained in a long and candid letter to one of his foremen, did not make "the least bit of difference in our getting or keeping any better class of labor." As a result, the company once again found itself calling in *keiyaku-nin* to thin their crops at the unheard-of wages of three dollars per day.[74]

♨

As they were winning the battle in the northern Sacramento Valley, the Japanese were also flexing their muscle in the south. Moving into San Benito County in 1911, just as it emerged as a center for commercial seed production, *keiyaku-nin* set up shop in a pool hall, barbershop, and small grocery store owned by Kichigoro Tanimura at the southeast corner of the city of San Juan Bautista. Providing employment for nearly half of the town's 282 Japanese (many of whom could be found bathing together after work in the large Japanese-style bathhouse behind the San Juan Bautista grocery store), the *keiyaku-nin* over the next two years gained control of labor (including a small group of newly arrived Koreans) employed by the local seed companies, including Ferry-Morse Seed Company, the largest in the state. The following year, *keiyaku-nin* continued their campaign. When white citrus pickers walked out of one Sacramento Valley orchard demanding $2.25 per day in early November, *keiyaku-nin* moved in for $1.75; when another group of whites earning two dollars a day struck for piece rate, *keiyaku-nin* broke the strike for $1.75 an hour. These actions so angered white orange pickers around the Central Valley town of Lindsay that, when large numbers of Japanese arrived a few weeks later, the whites chased them from the orchards and packing plants. Loaded into wagons and deported to the outskirts of town, the Japanese were "invited to vamoose." Shortly thereafter, in the small citrus town of Dinuba, the Japanese struck and obtained a raise in wages, prompting the *California Cultivator* to complain that growers were now "having trouble with Jap laborers in both orchards and packing houses."[75]

By the end of 1912, the Japanese had pushed up their wages 50 percent over the rate paid in 1900. Around Vacaville, about eight hundred Japanese earned between $1.85 and $2.25 a day picking fruit, compared to $1.60 for Mexicans whose work rate, according to growers, was only 70 percent of an average Japanese worker. "They got the reputation of being tricky," recalled *Fresno Republican* editor Ben Walker in a 1923 interview with historian Yamato Ichihashi.

> They weren't dishonest, you understand. It's just that they went by a different code of business than we went by. If a man hired twenty Japs in the old days for a certain price, and his next door neighbor offered them ten cents a day more on the day they were to report, he would get them. Contracts meant nothing to them. So they got the reputation of being unreliable and tricky; contract breaking meant nothing to them.[76]

But it was not just that the Japanese—through organizing, strikebreaking, and aggressive negotiating—drove wages higher. Paid by the piece rate, Japanese field hands through sheer hard work earned more than anyone else. Ten hours picking raisin grapes around Fresno on piece rate earned them as much as four to six dollars per day, compared to whites averaging three dollars, Germans and Russians

$2.50, and Mexicans and East Indians about two dollars. Piece rate differentials were equally pronounced in the sugar beet fields, where Japanese beet toppers averaged seventy-five cents per day more than Mexicans and Sikhs. In the hop industry, where the Japanese were "quick and worked longer hours than did the whites," many Japanese earned three dollars per day (about one dollar per day more than whites). All of this translated into a larger monthly income that, according to the Japanese Association of America, averaged $101.91 with room and board and $130.66 without, compared to $97.22 and $128.32 for whites. The annual income of Japanese field hands was also higher, averaging $366.65 a year with board, and $427.18 without, compared to Italian field hands, next highest, who earned $312.67 and $385, respectively.[77]

As they advanced their wage rates, drove out rivals in Fresno, taught a lesson to sugar beet growers in the northern Sacramento Valley, and caused the state of California to launch yet another investigation, the Japanese were also struggling to bring organization to their compatriots 250 miles to the south in the fledgling citrus industry of Southern California. Here, they would eventually achieve their greatest triumph, dominating harvest labor in the most profitable, colorful, romantic, and spectacular segment of California agriculture.

Handle the Fruit Like Eggs!

The Japanese Shift from

Field-Workers to Farmers

After the turn of the century, no segment of agriculture seemed more open and attractive to Japanese field hands than Southern California's citrus industry. Unlike the sugar beet industry, whose dominant images were the factory smokestacks and laborers slaving in shadeless fields, citrus culture suggested something higher and finer. With its ornate shipping crate art depicting dark green groves, fragrant blossoms, and carefully cultivated mission architectural traditions, the citrus industry exemplified California's greatest agricultural potential. It embossed on the American mind an image of Spanish fiestas, annual citrus fairs, and happy workers gathering "golden globules of health" beneath the snowcapped peaks. In fact, the image was not so fanciful. Having benefited from—and, to a very large extent, influenced—the American dietary shift from traditional European foods such as potatoes and wheat to Mediterranean or subtropical fruits, the Southern California citrus industry in the twentieth century was entering a period of rapid and sustained growth. With tens of thousands of employees and millions of dollars in revenues and wages, the industry ranked among California's largest and most important enterprises. As such, it exerted a massive influence on the state's development. "Citrus built more than Southern California's agricultural wonderland," wrote citrus industry historians Ronald Tobey and Charles Wetherell. "Citrus built the foundations of the region's economic modernization before the great flood of defense funds began in World War II."[1]

Citrus farming started in California when oranges and lemons from the Baja California missions were planted in Alta California, possibly as early as 1769, although the first definite mention of citrus did not come until 1793, when George Vancouver observed some thick-skinned, sour oranges growing in the garden at San Buenaventura mission. The first orange grove of any size, some four hundred trees, was planted at San Gabriel mission about 1804, but substantial plantings did not begin until 1834, when Luis Vignes used seedlings from San Gabriel mission to set out the first private grove of orange trees, or 1841, when William Wolf-

FIGURE 45. Japanese field hands washing oranges, Arlington Heights Fruit Company, ca. 1910. Courtesy of the Huntington Library, San Marino, California.

skill became the first commercial grower. Although the Gold Rush created a huge market for oranges, expansion of plantings proceeded slowly, with only seventeen thousand orange trees and 3,700 lemon trees in the state in 1867, almost all of them in Southern California. Citrus culture did not really become established until 1873, when Luther and Eliza Tibbets planted winter-ripening Washington navel oranges near Riverside, and 1876, when A. B. Chapman of San Gabriel began cultivating the summer- and fall-ripening Valencia orange. At about the same time the thornless Eureka lemon was introduced from Sicily and the Lisbon lemon from Spain. Following completion of Southern Pacific's route to New Orleans in 1881 and Santa Fe's competitive line in 1885, a frenzy of citrus planting swept through Southern California. On February 14, 1886, the first train loaded with oranges left Los Angeles bound for the East Coast. Thereafter, citrus expanded rapidly, fueled first by the introduction of the ventilated boxcar and then by development of refrigerated boxcars and icing stations, and construction of several massive irrigation systems around Riverside. Following the slogan "Oranges for Health, California for Wealth," a class of well-educated, wealthy, genteel midwestern and eastern entrepreneurs settled around the city of Riverside, which emerged as the wealthiest town in the United States per capita. As citrus culture spread west to Pasadena, Azusa, and Duarte and south to Covina, Ontario,

Pomona, and Redlands, a new group of commercial growers entered the industry. Developing large enterprises, they perfected spraying, fumigation, and orchard heating techniques, employed modern business methods, and introduced scientific farming based on information developed at the University of California's Citrus Experiment Station.[2]

By 1913, the Southern California citrus industry extended throughout a vast, crescent-shaped, frost-free belt stretching from Santa Barbara through portions of Ventura, Los Angeles, Orange, San Bernardino, and Riverside counties. Shipping thirty thousand railroad carloads of oranges eastward, the region led the nation in orange, grapefruit, and tangerine production, and produced about 90 percent of the nation's lemons. Sixty percent of the state's crop was sold through the California Fruit Growers Exchange, an agglomeration of 131 separate packing-houses and seventeen district associations that became one of the biggest fruit marketing organizations in the United States. The exchange employed the most advanced marketing techniques, pioneered standardized packing procedures, and emerged as a leader in every phase of farming—from irrigation and pest control practices to refrigeration and the use of citrus by-products. Constantly searching for ways to improve its performance, the exchange even purchased lumber mills and stands of timber in Northern California in order to ensure an adequate supply of low-cost wood shook necessary for making orange crates. Perhaps most important, the exchange created a field department that conducted scientific experiments and provided members with horticultural advice that yielded huge gains in productivity. All of these measures placed the citrus industry in the forefront of modern corporate agriculture.[3]

Employing every race and nationality including Indians, Chinese, and Italians, the Southern California citrus industry never experienced a shortage of labor. Citrus growers constantly received letters from men and women as far away as Colorado and Virginia besieging them for employment. "Dear Sirs," began one such letter to the Duarte Monrovia Fruit Growers Exchange from a recently arrived Los Angeles resident. "I beg to apply for a position as a grove hand on your orange grove, for a young man of 19 years of age. I can secure excellent references from places, etc. where I have been employed in the East. I expect a moderate salary to start, and have had no experience in the orange or lemon business before, but am willing to learn."[4]

Despite such petitions, experienced Japanese field hands—not enthusiastic but inexperienced white men and boys or Mexican, Chinese, and Italian field hands—overwhelmingly dominated harvest work in the citrus industry. Initially, their appearance in the citrus groves of Southern California did not proceed smoothly. On March 29, 1904, a Japanese crew arriving to work for the American Citrus Company near Highland was attacked and forced to return to Riverside by armed white laborers. Six months later, a group of Japanese grape pickers was chased back to Riverside from Cucamonga. On January 14, 1905, a crew of Japanese citrus pickers was attacked near Corona. Loaded into wagons, they too were sent back to Riverside, but refused to press charges against their attackers. Two months later, a group living in tents on Santa Fe Railroad land at the foot of Michigan Avenue in Glendora aroused such antipathy that trees in orchards where they worked were cut down. One night, someone tied all of their tent ropes to a freight train that pulled down every tent as it chugged down the tracks. Nevertheless the Japanese remained. Moving into the Alosta Hotel, they took over the top floor, keeping pigeons on the roof.[5]

Taking over more work in the lemon and orange groves, the Japanese were praised by the manager of the Indian Hill Citrus Union early in 1906 as "very satisfactory and far more reliable in every way than the average white man or boy." By 1909, they were, in fact, so dominant in the citrus industry that, when investigators for the U.S. Immigration Commission visited twenty-three Southern California citrus ranches, they found that the Japanese controlled labor on eighteen of them and played an important role on the other five. By 1910, the Japanese held down about six of ten picking jobs; in 1915, a force of seven hundred Japanese picked and packed virtually the entire twenty-one-million-dollar Washington navel orange crop, held down seven of ten jobs in the orchards around Riverside, focal point for the citrus industry, and filled about one of four positions washing, sorting, and grading fruit in the packing sheds.[6]

Simple economics dictated the reliance on Japanese labor. Profit ruled. Innovative as they were, citrus growers had little control over costs of transportation, fuel, fertilizer, farm machinery, or pesticides. Net return therefore remained relatively small—between 4 and 10 percent—in the years from 1890 to 1912, with market fluctuations determining the exact profit margin. And so, after achieving breakthroughs in marketing, sales, and production, citrus growers turned their attention to labor costs. The goal was to make workers as productive as possible, pay them as little as possible, and keep them happy but disunified. Holding the cost of labor steady per box of fruit was the triumph of the economizing effort. From that perspective, field hands were subject to the cold and calculating standards of efficiency and expense cutting. Under the calculating regime, citrus growers, like steelmakers, aimed at multiplying their output in relation to expenses. Cost per box was the core of the matter, but had significance only to accountants, the variables being productivity and earnings measured across a given period of time. The Japanese were simply believed to be the most capable of meeting productivity standards.[7]

♮ॐ

More so than others, Japanese employed by the Limoneira Company felt the exertions toward labor efficiency. Founded by Nathan W. Blanchard, Charles McKevett, and Wallace Hardison with money earned in the 1860s from Pennsylvania oil and Sierra Nevada lumber operations, the Limoneira Company (in Portuguese, literally "place of the lemons") was, from its inception in 1893, a pacesetter in every aspect of farming. Limoneira Ranch began as a 412-acre lemon farm near Santa Paula, but through the individual holdings and activities of its three board members, the company soon exerted control far beyond the home ranch, wielding power on the boards of land, lumber, banking, farming, and water companies throughout northern Ventura County. Under the direction of Charles Collins Teague (commonly referred to as C. C. Teague), a Caribou, Maine, businessman who had come west to work for his uncle, Wallace Hardison, Limoneira quickly expanded into a model citrus ranch, one of the dominating enterprises of California's early citrus industry.[8]

Embracing modern horticultural practices, Teague—who had worked his way up from labor foreman to general manager by age twenty-five—initially followed accepted industry policies like providing dormitory housing for single white field hands and cottages for supervisors and married men. This initial force of several hundred men was employed clearing land, planting citrus groves, and harvesting intercropped beans and pumpkins. In 1897, a crop surplus forced Teague to employ all of the married women and their daughters (one as a cook, the rest in the packing shed) to ensure a timely harvest; these women were paid merely by increasing their husbands' paychecks. Because all permanent hands were occupied elsewhere on the farm, Teague then had to hire Chinese and Mexicans to pick his lemons. As he expanded operations to 2,902 acres in 1906, Teague found that such makeshift measures would not work. Limoneira required at least 250 workers at peak harvest time and so, with no viable alternative, he turned to the Japanese.[9]

After watching workers scout up accommodations in Santa Paula and seeing many pitch tents among the orchards, Teague determined that housing was one key to assembling and keeping a stable labor force. He quickly decided to provide them permanent, high-quality, inexpensive housing that tied workers to Limoneira and ensured their loyalty, while also providing him with a means of control. To further stabilize his labor force, Teague attempted to create a community. Concluding a contract with local keiyaku-nin, Teague donated materials and land for two modern dormitories to house single Japanese men and six small houses for Japanese families. With rooms renting for seventy-five cents per month, the dormitories—located south of a huge packing shed and costing five thousand dollars each to construct—were equipped with kitchens and bathing facilities, with each room reached by means of an outside stairway. Each dormitory contained a living room, dining room, large kitchen with Japanese cook, and twenty sleeping rooms upstairs, and four downstairs. A forty-by-twenty-seven-foot bathhouse held the toilets, showers, and washrooms, and in the center, a large concrete bathing tank, ten by ten feet by three feet, filled with three hundred gallons of water heated by a wood- and oil-fed boiler. Well built and relatively comfortable, these model facilities proved so successful in holding the Japanese that, seven years later, Limoneira constructed another Japanese dormitory and six additional cottages with outside cold water and toilets. Complete with a library and barbershop, the complex looked more like a small village than a labor camp.[10]

As a result of Teague's success at Limoneira, Japanese citrus hands throughout Southern California increasingly enjoyed the benefits of similar efforts at corporate paternalism. The change affected thousands of men who, shifting from winter harvest work in the Washington navel orange groves to the summer and fall harvest work in Valencia orange groves, lived at least part of each year in racially and ethnically segregated grower-housing. But their housing never measured up to that provided for white workers. Employed by district and local exchange associations, whites always enjoyed the best camps, many of which included blacksmith shops, stables, and offices, even such amenities as private baths in addition to cottages and huge barracks. In 1906, Rancho Sespe constructed a seven-thousand-dollar two-story dormitory for its single white workers. Measuring eighty by forty-five feet, it had a large living room, public and private dining rooms, kitchen, washrooms, three bathrooms, three toilets, a linen room, and twenty separate sleeping rooms on the top floor. Each sleeping room measured eight by thirteen feet, with a large window, and was furnished with an iron bed, mattress, two clean sheets changed twice a week, clean towels daily, two blankets in the summer and three in the winter, one pillow, one pillow cover, one bedspread, one chair, one table, and a closet. The living room was furnished with a large card table, a large library, a billiard table, and a large wood-heating stove. For dues of twenty-five cents per month, residents received several dozen newspapers and magazines. A Japanese cook, waiter, and janitor took care of feeding, cleaning, and laundry. A similar arrangement prevailed on the C. W. Leffingwell ranch. Located near Whittier, at the gateway to the La Habra Valley, the Leffingwell ranch camp was designed by Pasadena architects Greene and Greene. Providing many of the comforts of home, including a piano, Victrola, billiard table, card tables, rocking chairs, writing tables, a large supply of books and newspapers, and plenty of ink, each dormitory featured twelve-by-twelve-foot sleeping rooms, dining rooms, a clubhouse, a library, showers, and hot and cold water and was said to resemble a modest hotel. The nearby Japanese bunkhouse, where sixty-five packinghouse workers prepared their own food, could not compare.[11]

Corporate paternalism also benefited about twenty-three hundred Mexicans who worked in the citrus groves of Southern California in 1912. Escaping economic disruption and declining opportunities on the haciendas of rural Mexico, they left their homes in Michoacán and Guanajuato, and followed the railroads east to Texas. In El Paso, the U.S. Public Health Service provided a rude welcome by subjecting all Mexican immigrants to medical examinations, spraying them with disinfectant, and delousing them. Once across the border, they made contact with contractors, then worked their way west through a series of mining and construction jobs or rode the Southern Pacific all the way to California. Arriving on the Thomas Robertson citrus ranch in the Simi Valley, Mexican families from Sinaloa settled into a comfortable company town with a store and small schoolhouse, recreational facilities, a park shaded with eucalyptus trees, and quarters that included small garden plots. Those moving into the groves around Rialto, Highgrove, Casa Blanca, Riverside, Upland, Azusa-Foothill, and Arlington Heights settled near Japanese camps. In the *barranco* (gulch) on the Leffingwell ranch, forty-five to 125 single Mexican laborers bunked in an apartment-like building with a communal shower and French cook, while married Mexicans shared ten or twelve buildings behind the packinghouse. On Rancho Sespe, Mexicans built their own houses on land allotted from the company. "The plan of other large ranches in building houses for Mexicans and charging them rent does not seem to us to be as good a system as it does not give the Mexicans the same feeling of permanence," explained ranch manager W. H. Fleet to the *California Citrograph*.

> In cases where Mexicans employed by us have not the ready cash to buy lumber to build the house, we buy it for them, and deduct usually $10 a month from their wages until the bill of lumber is paid for. If a Mexican

leaves the employment of the ranch before he pays the entire lumber bill he loses his equity in the house. We then allow some other Mexican family to move into the building and take up the payments where the other occupant left off. But when we discharge one of them we return to him his equity unless he sells the house to some other Mexican.[12]

On the fifteen-thousand-acre Chase plantation operated by Ethan Allen Chase south of Corona, Mexican families settled into a feudal enclave of thirty-six adobe houses. Most houses had a room ten by ten feet, with piped-in water, and a second screened porch six feet by ten feet. Four were more elaborate—two with two bedrooms and a bathroom between them, a dining room, parlor, kitchen, and screened porches front and rear; and two measuring twenty by twenty feet, with four rooms, and screened porches. The foreman's house had four bedrooms, bathroom, dining room, hall, parlor, kitchen, and screened porches. Nearby was a large communal garden and a complex of barns and out-buildings where the Mexicans kept their horses, chickens, and pigs. Near the lemon-packing shed, an old, loyal Mexican family occupied a detached concrete blockhouse measuring fourteen by twenty feet. Divided into two rooms, each measuring fourteen by ten feet, the house boasted a garden twenty-five by forty feet. In such camps, with ornamental plants, shade trees, roses, lawns, and wisteria vines, the sense of strangeness quickly gave way to a sense of home. Men sent for families or returned to bring them north. An extended social network of aunts, uncles, cousins, and friends developed. People opened small stores in nearby towns, and mutual aid societies put down roots. "The children of the employe[e]s have ample room for play and grow up amongst beautiful and healthful surroundings. They are regularly transported to and from school under the care of a competent stage driver," wrote citrus scientist A. D. Shamel. "Amidst such surroundings, is it any wonder that peace and contentment reigns?"[13]

Such facilities, which typically rented for five to eight dollars a month, were described succinctly in citrus company business ledgers as "white camps," "Mexican camps," and "Jap camps." With their operating expenses carefully worked into overall production costs—along with water, chemicals, fumigation, and fertilizer—labor camps were always strategically located at various points around the ranches where they decreased the amount of time required to reach the groves and thereby further contributed to the efficiency of operations. But not all, or even a majority of field hands, lived in well-designed housing. For every one enjoying the benefits of corporate paternalism, two lived in abject misery. That was because not all citrus growers held paternalistic attitudes toward labor or subscribed to corporate welfare as a way of building a loyal workforce. Citrus ranches were expensive ventures, requiring a large initial investment, and several years before newly planted trees came into production. For these reasons, many struggling growers saw no reason to expend large amounts of money on workers' housing. Many found justification for this attitude in *Farm Management*, a leading textbook by agricultural economist Richard L. Adams, who advised that good housing was a waste as harvest hands were "unappreciative of attempts to provide livable surroundings" and therefore were "best cared for with some cheap shelter where they can flop."[14]

This is what the Japanese—as well as Mexicans and whites—encountered on many isolated citrus ranches. Often housing facilities were little more than run-down structures where crews might find "plenty of clean hay to sleep on" or a few rows of sturdy frame cabins, buttressed by clumsy chimneys and lined up along a dusty road with no porch welcoming them. Inside, men heaped their meager belongings onto a few beds, perhaps a decrepit chair or two, and a rickety old table. Outside were muddy shower stalls, some with gravel floors, and outhouses that only occasionally were both sanitary and sufficient in number to meet the needs of the camp population. Encountering one such place, a rancher addressing the 1902 meeting of the California State Fruit Growers Convention told his fellow growers that he found men forced to sleep "in the loft over the horses' mangers, under the shake roof that rattled in every breeze," without even a stove to dry their wet garments. "How many ranchers house their men as he does?" he asked. "I myself have been offered the side of a rail fence and a five-gallon coal-oil can to cook my meals on, laboring in California."[15]

ॐ

Whatever the housing conditions, Japanese citrus workers saw no accompanying change in their daily regimen. When the winter-ripening Washington navel orchards were overlain with heavy frost or fog, crews often had to wait at the orchard's edge shivering until the conditions improved. Pickers received no pay for this "wet time," as it was called. Those who chose not to wait quickly became drenched with freezing dew; some fell off wet and slippery ladders. On such days, oranges were like ice balls and, after a few minutes, a picker's hands would become frostbitten and ache until the sun climbed high enough to warm them. Adding yet another layer to old racial ideologies, the *California Citrograph* argued that Japanese field hands (and later Mexicans) were well suited to these conditions, while "the white man sidesteps . . . picking whenever he can grab something just as good or a little better."[16]

Of all winter work, the Japanese found no aspect of citrus labor more odious or detestable than smudge pot duties, which were based on techniques developed in the 1850s, when Placer County growers built small fires beneath their fruit trees to heat their orchards on frosty nights. From then on, growers sought various ways to protect their crops from freezing temperatures. One grower boiled thousands of gallons of water in massive kettles then dumped it into his irrigation furrows. Another covered his trees with cloth blankets. On the Irvine ranch, workers burned hundreds of bales of wet straw in an effort to create a temperature inversion and save the fruit. By 1900, Japanese crews on most ranches resorted to hanging wire baskets full of soft coal on the lower limbs of trees. When the temperature hit thirty-three degrees Fahrenheit, a watchman would sound a general alert, fire whistles would be blown in certain combinations of long and short blasts, and men would turn out to light the pots. One man drenched a basket with coal oil and a following man ignited it with a torch. Within twenty minutes, a good frost crew could light thousands of baskets and raise the orchard air temperature several degrees. Crews would remain active until the threat of a freeze had passed. At times during the winter, so many wire baskets would be burning in the groves around Riverside that a thick acrid smoke would lie over the county and it would appear that the orchards were on fire. With the advent of the telephone system and oil fired smudge pots, mobilization became more efficient. Daily weather forecasts would be telephoned to packinghouses throughout the citrus belt, and local packinghouse managers would notify growers of frost predictions. Growers lacking telephones received frost reports from boys on bicycles employed by the packinghouse managers to pedal out to each ranch. When the temperature dropped thirty degrees, eight-man squads on standby in various dormitories would be alerted and move into the orchards filling and refilling the pots from horse-drawn oil-tank wagons. During the Great Freeze of 1913, when temperatures in Southern California hovered between twelve and twenty-two degrees Fahrenheit from January 5 to 9, thousands of men taxed the limit of their endurance. The Arlington Heights Fruit Company employed two hundred field hands from its three labor camps and kept them busy lighting 150,000 smudge pots and burning more than six rail-tank cars of oil. "The oil heaters would burn out completely during the night and they had to be refilled the next day," recalled C. C. Teague in his memoir. "This required much labor and the men were required to work day and night with almost no sleep. Everyone connected with the operation was ready to drop with fatigue and loss of sleep and only the loyalty of our men saved the crop." On a big ranch like Limoneira, where management invested $182 an acre for frost control, crews might burn twelve thousand gallons of fuel oil and forty tons of coal in one night. Whatever the method for combating frost, by sunup a dense, black cloud of sooty smoke would linger over the orchards, and all outdoor activities would cease. After several days of this work, men would leave the orchards soaked and stained with oil and coal, coughing up gobs of black soot.[17]

During the summer harvest, when temperatures typically shot over ninety-five degrees, the Japanese and others faced a different set of hazards. Blinded by sweat, men often reached too far for fruit and fell from ladders. Few left the orchards without some strain, sprain, gash, bruise, cut, or broken bone. Making them even more uncomfortable and contributing to their misery was "black smut," the excretion of the black-scale insect. Proliferating on branches, the smut rubbed off on citrus pickers, covering them from head to foot in a brown filth. But even when conditions were normal enough, harvesters could not avoid being gashed by the green thorns on lemon trees, stuck in the eye by small branches, or bitten by the ants that crawled into their ears, noses, eyes, and hair. Many also suffered from heatstroke. Few citrus pickers of any nationality or ethnic group ever recalled harvest work with humor or affection. "Concerning orange-picking as an occupation," wrote one man in the *Industrial Pioneer*, "it cannot be denied that for those who relish outdoor life in a generally pleasant climate it has its advantages. The surrounding scenery is often inspiring, and the golden fruit, vividly set off against the dark green of the trees, is a lovely sight. But orange picking," he cautioned, "is an occupation requiring considerable strength and agility, which bars the employment of women and children. After a day's toil the 'orange glommer' is usually 'all in,' and has not much stomach for romantic reflections."[18]

Citrus harvesting was hard labor that required physical strength and agility as well as mental concentration. Ladders weighing as much as seventy-five pounds, had to be shifted at least four times per tree, which meant men had to climb their twelve-foot height hundreds of times each day. Carrying sizing rings and clippers, they balanced precariously, grabbed an orange or lemon with one hand, snipped its stem, then reached for the next piece of fruit. Picking lemons on Lemonita, the Leffingwell's ranch, two crews went through the groves every four to six weeks. The first crew used a 2 ⅝-inch picking ring and harvested only fruit that would not pass through it; the second crew picked with a smaller, 2 ⅛-inch ring and harvested all of the fruit that was just starting to color. The most common lemon picking ring, called the No. 8 ring, was a 2 ¼-inch ring, generally used on lemons picked for storage. As labor costs rose, the crews were combined and instructed to use only a single-sized ring. Whatever the procedure, men repeated these motions until they had a full load (about sixty pounds). Scurrying down their ladders, they would sink ankle-deep into the soft soil as they waddled toward the lug boxes and dumped their loads of fruit. Then they would scurry back up their ladders and repeat the process.[19]

য়৯

While hours and routine remained largely immutable, the Japanese found that other aspects of harvest labor underwent dramatic change over the years. As one agricultural adviser put it, "The way to solve the labor problem is to organize the farm business so well, that the labor program on the farm is universally effective." And so, under the leadership of agricultural scientist G. Harold Powell, that is precisely what citrus growers did. By analyzing every aspect of orchard work, they streamlined fruit picking operations, profoundly altering the way Japanese worked.[20]

Perhaps more than any other group of field hands, Japanese citrus pickers were subjected to detached and analytical scrutiny. Beginning in 1904, Powell, his colleagues at the U.S. Department of Agriculture (USDA), and various university and industry researchers studied citrus growing from top to bottom. As a result of their findings, growers made numerous adjustments and initiated a series of labor practices that altered fieldwork habits. Besides minimizing damage to fruit, ensuring fruit quality, and combating decay, these labor practices also increased the speed and efficiency of harvest work, decreased dangers faced by workers, and increased production rates.[21]

Almost immediately after entering the citrus industry on a large scale around 1905, Japanese field hands noticed that growers devoted a great deal of attention to the layout of ranches and orchards. No detail was too insignificant. Were groves too far from housing? Were trees so far apart that workers wasted time carrying ladders between them? Were newly planted orchards laid out so as to permit maximum speed in harvesting? Were the brambles and deadwood in older trees properly pruned in order to make the fruit more accessible to pickers? Did the access roads run crosswise to the irrigation furrows, bumping the loaded boxes free from their restraining ties as they were hauled out of the groves? Were roads leveled to avoid unnecessary jostling? All of these measures altered the work environment, cumulatively easing labor for the Japanese and making them more efficient.[22]

Ultimately, no single problem was more devastating—or more preventable—than blue-mold fungus. Entering the fruit through mechanical injuries to the skin of the fruit, blue-mold fungus was caused by such basic and easily avoidable mistakes as clipper cuts, stem punctures, scratches, and bruises. Millions of dollars of fruit was lost every year as a result of these injuries. Consequently, industry leaders devoted considerable attention to developing harvest procedures designed to minimize these problems. "Great care must be taken in picking fruit," warned the *California Cultivator* when it reported these discoveries. This was to have important consequences for Japanese field hands.[23]

To achieve the necessary supervision, industry leaders relied on *keiyaku-nin*, who took on added responsibilities as field foremen, admonishing pickers to "handle the fruit like eggs!" and warning them not to pick fallen fruit, throw fruit about, or leave boxed fruit in the sun too long. Clippers came in for special attention. To reduce scratches, all workers were required to use a special type of clipper with rounded ends. Each picker was usually provided two pairs of clippers. While one pair was in use, the other was inspected and adjusted by the blacksmith, and in this way kept in good repair. "As a result of this and other like attention to the details of picking it is a well known fact that the lemons . . . are handled with practically no clipper cuts or other similar mechanical injuries," wrote A. D. Shamel. "Consequently, the crops arrive in the markets with little or no crop loss from decay and consistently bring the top prices." To guard against fingernail nicks, *keiyaku-nin* enforced industry requirements to wear soft cotton gloves; to minimize nicks, they made certain that crews inverted fruit boxes and dumped out any debris, dirt, or nails left in fruit boxes. Many assigned identification numbers to pickers, stamped those numbers on filled boxes, and inspected randomly selected boxes of fruit, computing the percentage that had long stems, stems pulled from the fruit, or that were in some way unacceptable. San Antonio Fruit Exchange manager Peter Dreher directed *keiyaku-nin* to place an identifying ticket at the bottom of each box so that inspectors in the packinghouse might discover "who is a drone or who does sloven work." Provided with such information, *keiyaku-nin* maintained elaborate lists summarizing each worker's performance. Those pickers who consistently injured fruit were fired. In this way, according to the *California Citrograph*, a good *keiyaku-nin* could reduce the percentage of defective fruit from between 3 and 9.22 percent to between 0.40 and 0.71 percent of the total harvest. "The placing of the quality of a man's work down in black and white," reported the paper, "without doubt promotes better work."[24]

Of all the innovations employed by the Japanese and other citrus workers at this time, none was more fundamental than the Canterbury fruit picking sack. Replacing cumbersome buckets and baskets that bruised and cut fruit and were difficult to carry into the trees, the Canterbury sack—invented and named after Redlands citrus grower Ellison Canterbury—was nothing more than a canvas tube with a harness that fitted over a worker's shoulder and neck. The mouth of the tube, held open by a wire expansion ring, was attached to the worker's arm just below the wrist. Left free to use both hands, pickers using the new sack quickly cut oranges or lemons at the stem and flipped them into the mouth of the tube. When the sack filled, they emptied it simply by unhooking the bottom and allowing the contents to fall out by gravity into a collection box. Various modifications improved the original design, broadening straps, allowing men to adjust sack capacity and carry the sack in different ways. This produced a radical change in harvest work by eliminating wasted motion and cutting down on fatigue. As a result, Japanese workers fell off ladders less often and, more important, picked at a faster rate. Best of all, the sack reduced damage to fruit. "Probably 50% of the decay which now comes out of the profits of the industry will be done away with, when this improved sack is generally [employed] throughout the citrus belt," observed the *California Citrograph*.[25]

Japanese citrus workers also received welcome boosts from a number of other work-related changes. One was a pair of special gloves that used a strap to hold a pair of clippers in place. Using these gloves, men not only were able to cut lemon and orange stems cleaner, they could also use both hands for climbing and picking and no longer lost time climbing down ladders to retrieve dropped shears. A second invention consisted of a pair of canvas sleeves which, when slipped over a picker's forearms and fastened at the wrist by means of snaps, protected the picker from the thorns that scratched and tore at his arms as he harvested citrus. A third timesaving device was a new style of packing box. Extensive time and motion studies showed that the optimum picking box was larger, longer, and narrower than those commonly employed. Immediately converting to the new boxes, the Covina Orange Growers Association concluded that "the boxes of larger capacity would pay for themselves in a short time."[26]

Ladders also came under scrutiny. After experimenting with many designs, growers discovered that the best was the simple three-legged tripod ladder. With the third leg consisting of a long, rounded pole on hinges that could be let down through the branches to rest on the ground at the base of the tree, it worked best for citrus and most other tree fruit. Three-legged ladders were also easy to carry and stack in wagons. The fifth innovation consisted of teams of young men who raced around the orchards in light, two-wheeled sulkies carrying cans of cool water to the pickers. Simple as it seemed, the use of water boys contributed to the health of citrus workers more than any other single innovation by ensuring that men did not suffer dehydration or heatstroke. Two final innovations centered on picking procedures. First, after carefully studying the harvest, growers discovered that it was most efficient for crews to pick two or more rows on each side of a wagon and for each individual worker to handle a section consisting of four trees. Second, to avoid confusion over pickers' names, growers instituted a system of numbering whereby each picker placed his number with chalk on each box he picked. "This plan makes it possible to locate the picker whose work was poor at any time until the tag is removed from the tree," wrote Sierra Madre Citrus Association manager F. G. Webber. "Daily inspection of at least one box of each picker's fruit is necessary to determine percentage of clipper cuts, long stems, green fruit, or injuries from the brush and litter in the boxes."[27]

ஐ

As they adjusted to these changes, Japanese citrus pickers also encountered new wage policies. Here, the industry's rule of cold, rational calculation prevailed. Studying pay rates closely, many citrus growers concluded that neither field hands working for hourly wages nor those employed on a piece-rate payment system were entirely satisfactory. Paid on an hourly basis, crews sometimes malingered—although by closely supervising crews, *keiyaku-nin* minimized the loafing. Paid on a piece-rate basis, they were more efficient and supposedly required little supervision, but often tore through groves in a reckless fashion, picking only that which was easily accessible, leaving plenty of "shiners"(fruit that was high in the branches and difficult to reach), and damaging trees and excessive amounts of fruit. For these reasons, growers adopted the ideas of G. B. Hodgkin, a leader in the industry, who explained in the *California Citrograph*, "Nothing could be more deadly to efficiency than a hard and fast wage scale." Various citrus associations came to the same conclusion. "The payment of pickers by the day, instead of by the box, is preferable from the standpoint of securing careful and proper work, as box or piece labor usually puts a premium on quantity," advised the manager of the Riverside Orange Company. "Careful inspection of the character of the work secured under the two systems of labor payment has shown conclusively that the pickers working by the day do on the average much better work. On the other hand, good work can be secured under either the box-payment or day-payment plan if the labor is properly supervised."[28]

The best method of payment, according to growers and Japanese pickers alike, was to combine an hourly base rate of pay with a piece-rate "bonus" rewarding quality work and speedy pickers. This was known as the "Quality and Quantity Bonus System." To achieve that goal in 1905–6, managers at the Indian Hill Citrus Union in Pomona paid Japanese crews nineteen cents an hour plus a bonus of 6 percent if defective picking was held to under 1 percent; in 1910, they increased wages to twenty cents an hour with a 10 percent bonus. Crews employed by the San Gabriel Valley Farm Labor Association also received a base wage, but their ten-cent-per-day bonus kicked in only if less than 1 percent of the picked fruit was defective; the bonus dropped off to four cents if 2 percent of the fruit was unacceptable; and one cent if 3 percent was defective. If defective picking was over 4 percent, no bonus was paid. Under this system, pickers had an incentive to pick carefully and also to maintain productivity, and the association was able to eliminate poor quality work as well as slowdowns. "Aside from assuring . . . proper handling in the field," explained H. O. Easton, manager of the Placentia Mutual Orange Association, "we find this method . . . is a big help in speeding up the work and permits us to get by with fewer pickers than we would under the straight hour system."[29]

Japanese pickers tried to take advantage of these fluctuating wage policies by working, whenever possible, in the best groves. Although harvesting was difficult in all orchards, pickers knew that young groves with small trees produced big fruit that was easy to reach, while old orchards with big trees produced smaller crops. To compensate for such differences, growers began adjusting their piece and wage rates so that pickers working in orchards on rocky, hillside slopes received higher rates then men working in well-situated orchards on flat, fertile plains.[30]

By surpassing white, Mexican, and Chinese citrus pickers in quickness and reliability, the Japanese allowed growers to multiply output without increasing pay.
For this, they earned lavish praise from citrus company managers, who claimed
that the Japanese not only worked more quickly, they also seemed more conscientious. Carefully placing boxes of picked fruit to cool all night in the shade before being loaded the following morning, Japanese pickers won acclaim for using
special fruit wagons with platform springs to transport citrus to the packinghouse.
Seldom did one see any Japanese lagging behind, recalled Garden Grove citrus
grower M. B. Allen. "We always got one-third to one-half more pounds to the
picker," he explained, "because our [Japanese] boss didn't smoke himself and he
didn't allow any smoking in the fields."[31]

With the new gloves and shears, plenty of fresh water, a Canterbury fruit picking sack or some similar device, a system of bonuses, and combination payment
systems, Japanese field hands picked up to seventy boxes of fruit a day, whereas
their counterparts using pails, baskets, or buckets without special clipper gloves
and wage arrangements averaged only about forty. And by using the gloved clipper
and picking sack, field hands fell off their ladders far less frequently than men following older techniques; as a result, they produced fruit that was much freer of
clipper cuts, bruises, and stem punctures, and therefore less likely to decay while
in transit to market. In 1904, the California Fruit Growers Exchange had lost 21
percent of its fruit in shipment. Within six years, as a result of these and other
measures (including new packinghouse machinery and considerable changes in the
way packers handled fruit), the exchange cut losses to 7 percent and earned an additional $1.5 million; a few years later fruit losses dropped by half again. Each time,
the improvement was due in large part to the diligent labor of Japanese citrus pickers, who literally saved the exchange and its members millions of dollars.[32]

℘

The Japanese also saved considerable amounts of fruit through their diligent pest
control work, and in doing so became some of the first field hands exposed to
the dangers of pesticides. So long as citrus production had remained a small, isolated business, concern over insects had not played a prominent role in citrus culture, but as orchards spread over hundreds of square miles, ecological impacts
multiplied until they caused serious financial loss and prompted growers to experiment with various types of insecticides. At first, these "kitchen concoctions"
did not present many problems. Sprayed, sponged, washed, sprinkled, drenched,
flooded, and otherwise applied to citrus groves in ample, if not liberal, doses to
kill orange thrips, black scale, red scale, or some similar plague, they left behind
fairly benign residues of black tobacco leaf, boiled blue gum (eucalyptus) leaves,
distillate emulsion (light oil and water), blended shark oil, whale oil, and kerosene
and some other petroleum base to provide adhesion. Along with sulfur dust to
control mildew (which was seldom used in citrus), these materials usually dissipated by the time pickers arrived to harvest fruit many weeks, if not months,
later. While residues could make workers itch like crazy, irritate their eyes, and
occasionally cause breathing problems, they did not kill or permanently harm

FIGURE 46. Spraying a fruit orchard, ca. 1910. Courtesy of the Pat Jacobsen Collection of Fruit Crate Label Art.

anyone. Fresh air and a bath usually relieved most of the symptoms. Other than temporary discomfort, citrus pickers of the 1890s faced little if any threat from these homemade pesticides.[33]

By 1912, all that had changed. Regarding pesticide spraying much as they did insurance, and concerned with producing big, juicy, shiny, unblemished oranges and lemons, citrus growers added to their arsenal a nasty synthetic concoction known as Paris green, a pigment made of copper, arsenic, and lead arsenate. Applied in ever increasing amounts, lead arsenate became the leading all-purpose poison in the citrus industry before the advent of DDT. Dangerous even when applied at normal application rates, lead arsenate was a source of great concern to scientists who knew that it caused "eczema, keratosis, peripheral neuritis, disturbances of vision, and neurological symptoms hitherto obscure." But if early spraying charts and anecdotal recollections are any indication, lead arsenate, London Purple, Rex Lime, bordeaux mixture (lime and copper sulfate), and many other similar combinations of ingredients, seldom were applied at "normal" rates. Typically, growers would boil up a mixture of blue-gum sprouts in a galvanized iron tank full of water, dump in a pint of carbolic acid or some other material to "strengthen" and "intensify" it, then, after the morning dew had evaporated, send in a crew of Japanese to spray the concoction from a Giant Tryplex spraying machine through Bean Mist nozzles with 250 pounds of pressure. The process was laborious. Hand-operated pumps put out only four hundred gallons a day and spray rigs seldom sported more than two seventy-five-foot lengths of hose, so it took a long time to spray an entire orchard. Oversprayed trees often died; others produced spotty, poorly colored fruit. Spray crews generally followed the dictum: better to overspray than to stop short and see the crop consumed by insects or covered in mildew. But they had trouble even reaching the tops of large trees when spraying from the ground. This led to the construction of special spraying towers or platforms. Some were little more than stacks of picking boxes, crudely nailed together; others were well-built, iron-pipe frames. Rising ten to fifteen feet above the wagon bed, they had a platform for the sprayer and could be adjusted to the height of the trees being treated. Standing atop the tower, a man operating a long spray rod directed his spray to the tops of the trees and down the sides of the trees. Increased pumping pressures of up to four hundred pounds allowed tower sprayers to reach the tops of trees in the next row.[34]

Given the toxicity of lead arsenate, its widespread and liberal use, and the various other poisonous compounds thrown into homemade mixes, there seems little question that pesticide spraying exposed the Japanese—along with Mexicans and Anglos—to a host of physical hazards. But in the absence of full-scale health emergencies, toxified orchards, and mass poisonings, any problems resulting from pesticide spraying were probably confused with influenza—if not by the Japanese themselves, then surely by public health officials. The same was true of fumigation, a key aspect of citrus pest control that developed in 1885 and 1886 in an effort to control red scale and red spiders, which for a time threatened to destroy large acreages of oranges in Southern California.

To combat the infestation, citrus growers and a group of University of California scientists designed a heavily braced boom, placed it on a large Ohio cultiva-

FIGURE 47. Nighttime fumigation, ca. 1910. Courtesy of the Huntington Library, San Marino, California.

tor, and with a system of ropes and pulleys, dropped a heavy, airtight canvas tent over a tree. Crews then deposited a tablet of solid cyanide in an earthen cup containing a mixture of water and sulfuric acid at the base of the tree, closed the tent, and scurried for safety. In 1891, crews near Tustin perfected a new procedure to deliver a dose of highly poisonous hydrocyanic gas. After estimating the appropriate dose of poison, a man placed a delivery hose under the tent and the crew pumped in gas from a vaporizing machine known as a "Cyanofumer," which generated chemicals in the field. One hour later, the crew removed the tent and moved to the next tree, being careful not to damage limbs when lifting off the tent. Gradually, the process improved and fumigation companies took over the work. Most crews consisted of five men—three to lower and adjust the tents, a foreman who measured the tree size and estimated the dose, and a machine operator who placed the hose under the tent and delivered the fumigant. Believing that the process was less destructive to trees when the temperatures remained low, companies at first fumigated only at night or on cloudy days. But upon discovering that fumigation worked best on hot days, crews began fumigating nonstop, night and day, most of the work being done on a contract basis by custom fumigation companies. To protect applicators, regulations were soon established governing fumigation procedures, the most important being the requirement that tents touch the ground on all sides to prevent excess leakage, that all work cease when the wind was strong enough to move the tent walls, and that fumigation companies file extensive records of their work with the county agricultural commissioner.[35]

As all of this was happening, Japanese field hands and *keiyaku-nin* in the citrus industry and throughout California were diligently applying themselves to the task of improving their lot. For some, the wise words received by a friend or relative before leaving for California spurred an almost fanatical devotion to purpose. Among the most common advice was the admonition against carnal temptations that impeded success. "Those 'blanket carriers' are a good example of failures," a friend cautioned Kazuo Miyamoto before he left for the Central Valley. "Do not become one of them. The one thing you should not do is play pool and join the crowd that goes to Chinatown over the weekends. Sooner or later you may be drawn into games of chance." Carrying that advice with them, field hands found that by avoiding gambling, liquor, opium, and prostitutes, they could save enough money to move out of wage labor.[36]

As they shed their *dekasegi* orientation and reliance on common labor, such men became quick and eager students of American culture, with many purchasing and wearing American clothing, studying and learning English, even celebrating the Fourth of July each year. Before federal law excluded them from doing so in 1906, more than four hundred Japanese on the West Coast became naturalized U.S. citizens. Unlike the Chinese, who seldom patronized non-Chinese stores, the Japanese regularly bought supplies at white-owned businesses and moved freely outside Japantown. "The Jap . . . runs restaurants, barber shops, billiard halls, saloons, groceries, dry goods and ready made clothing stores in the city of Watsonville," observed the *Santa Cruz Surf*, "and operates buses and delivery wagons in the adjacent territory." Most important, the Japanese were becoming farmers.[37]

Besides pride, ambition, a desire to achieve a sense of place and belonging, and the quest for the obvious financial rewards that came with success, Japanese were attracted to farming in large numbers because their government allowed farmers and businessmen—but not field hands—to summon their wives from back home. By 1911, about three thousand field hands, *keiyaku-nin*, and other Japanese had become farmers; compiling information on 490 of them, the U.S. Immigration Commission discovered that 259 had begun as field hands and had been in the United States about eight years. "These people did not intend to stay as laborers," explained an investigator for the Survey of Race Relations.[38]

Japanese farmers climbed out of the fields by employing one of three methods: contracting, sharecropping, or leasing. Contract farmers received the necessary tools, seed, fertilizer, and other necessities from landowners, then supplied all needed labor and purchased materials on credit; once the crop was sold, they received a price fixed at so much per acre, usually for at least two years, regardless of output. Contracts often shifted from acreage farmed to crop production in the third year. While some barely broke even and their income varied with the weather, market, soil, and plants, most Japanese contract farmers generally earned more than they could as field hands. Sharecropping differed from contract farming in that the Japanese received a certain portion of the crop—usually half of its value when sold—for essentially the same work as they performed as contract farmers. They were then free to sell that portion for their own negotiated price. Compared to contract farming, sharecroppers assumed fewer risks and could also earn greater profits.[39]

Under leasing arrangements, field hands and *keiyaku-nin* pooled resources and formed farming companies, assuming full responsibility for all aspects of production. So popular was this method that in 1905 the *Sacramento Bee* complained of dozens of "little brown men crowding out white laborers and getting hold of ranches." Around Penryn, the site of a utopian citrus colony founded in the late 1880s by sheep rancher, reclamation entrepreneur, and agricultural colony enthusiast J. Parker Whitney, Japanese farmers leased such large acreages that at harvest time in 1912 it was "common . . . to see twenty fruit wagons lined up at the fruit house with a Japanese driver on each wagon." Most leased from the Producer's Fruit Company, a Chicago-based firm, or from the local Penryn Fruit Company. For all practical purposes, Japanese lessees were independent farmers whose enterprise could bring greater yields and cash returns than contracting or sharecropping. But because they typically paid more than anyone else, and made extensive improvements, Japanese lessees quickly became the preferred tenants and, by 1910, gained control of 60 percent of the orchards and 75 percent of the fruit in the Newcastle District. As they expanded their leasing into Solano and Yolo counties, their success led opponents to complain that they aimed only at immediate returns. At a meeting attended by two hundred fruit growers and shippers in Vacaville in November 1909, one speaker after another accused the Japanese of pruning their trees for maximum production, trying to "get all he can from the orchard, leaving it exhausted the following year," and ignoring the long-term health or quality of fruit.[40]

With minor variations, *keiyaku-nin* and other bosses followed similar paths into agriculture. At the end of a season—if they did well with a vineyard lease, or after four or five years if they had a long-term lease on a portion of a large farm planted to melons, vegetables, or grain—they cleared their debts, earned a nice profit, paid their rent, expanded operations, and shed their wage earner status. In the Vaca Valley, Japanese employed these methods to gain control of 65 percent of the ranches by 1907. But in some agricultural districts the rush into farming backfired. Around Santa Clara County, for example, so many *keiyaku-nin* moved into strawberry farming in response to exceptionally high 1907 market prices that overproduction occurred and they failed to turn a profit until 1910, when many converted their berry patches to truck gardens. Such reversals of fortune were characteristic of sharecropping and contracting and caused the acreage controlled by the Japanese to drastically fluctuate from year to year.[41]

Of all *keiyaku-nin* turned farmers, the one who most completely mastered these various arrangements was Kinji Ushijima, the "Potato King," whose success unfolded like a Horatio Alger story. The son of a relatively prosperous farmer in Japan's Fukuoka prefecture, Ushijima had arrived in California in 1889 at age twenty-six with less than one thousand dollars in funds. Working as a field hand near Stockton, Ushijima gained a reputation as a speedy potato picker who, owing to "unusually short legs," worked so fast that taller and less industrious whites stole sacks of potatoes from his rows to even the score. "When this happened," wrote one commentator, "the Japanese never winked an eyelash but kept on smiling."[42]

After living frugally for a number of years, Ushijima next became a *keiyaku-nin*. Soon, with funds earned from contracting and with additional funds from his family back in Japan, he purchased fifteen acres of barren, half-submerged lowlands in the San Joaquin Delta. After draining the land and constructing dikes, he planted potatoes, onions, and asparagus. The potato crop thrived in the rich peat soil, earning him a fortune. To exploit the opportunity, Ushijima shortened his name to Shima, then formed partnerships with other Japanese and purchased more land. Rapidly expanding his farming operations, he used a fleet of a dozen steamboats, barges, tugboats, and launches, all bearing the name Shima, to transport his potato crops to San Francisco. By 1910, Shima and his associates owned 420 acres and rented another eighty-three hundred. Two years later, he controlled ten thousand acres of potatoes valued at half a million dollars, and was commonly referred to in the press as the Potato King. The following year he bought fifteen hundred acres of King Island at a cost of $225,000, sank $75,000 into reclamation work, harvested twenty-eight thousand acres of potatoes, and within a few years controlled 85 percent of the California crop. Eventually, more than five hundred people worked on his farms, which included ventures as far away as Mexico, Oregon, and Korea.[43]

Shortly before he died on March 27, 1926, Shima published a book of verse, *The Best of Another World*, which was an apt summation of his life in California and his rise from field hand to potato magnate, and of the fifteen-million-dollar farming enterprise he left behind. Among the pallbearers at his funeral were Stanford University president David Starr Jordan and San Francisco mayor James Rolph Jr. Describing his intelligent business practice of selling potatoes when prices were high and storing them when prices were low, the *San Francisco Chronicle* praised Shima as a model farmer. His success, wrote the paper, "pointed to the opportunities here to anybody with pluck and intelligence."[44]

Although Shima was by far the most celebrated of all Japanese *keiyaku-nin*–turned-farmers, he hardly stood alone. In fact, so many Japanese were moving into farming around this time that not even official government watchdogs could keep track of them all. In 1900, when federal census data measured farm proprietorship, only twenty-nine Japanese leased land in California; ten years later, the number had jumped to 1,816. In 1905, Japanese leased 35,258 acres, sharecropped 19,572.5, contracted for 4,775, and owned 2,442 acres. Five years later, they had increased land ownership eightfold to 16,980 acres, more than doubled their leasing to 89,464 acres, and more than doubled sharecropping to 59,399.5 acres. But despite the considerable gains these numbers reflect, they may, in fact, considerably underestimate the extent of Japanese farming. When the *Nichibei Shimbun* (Japanese-American News) studied the matter in 1910, it found that the Japanese owned, leased, sharecropped, and rented a total of 194,742 acres of land—roughly 20 percent higher than the 99,524-acre figure given by the official census.[45]

Besides steadily increasing the amount of land they either owned or controlled, Japanese farmers also multiplied the value of the crops from a few million dollars in 1900 to $16.2 million in 1909. By the end of the decade, Japanese farmers also dominated certain crops. For example, they grew 88 percent of California's strawberry crop, 60 percent of the state's cantaloupes and sugar beets, 51 percent of the fresh table grapes, and most of the tomatoes, onions, celery, and berries; they also controlled ten percent of the fruit and vegetable land in Los Angeles County. While they owned or leased only about 13 percent of California's cultivated land, the Japanese nevertheless accounted for nearly 21 percent of the dollar value of the state's crops.[46]

Once established, Japanese farmers protected and advanced their positions in much the same ways as their white counterparts—by joining together to share information and resources. For example, on February 20, 1910, when the Placer County Growers and Shippers Association called 250 of its Japanese tenants to instruct them (through interpreters) in the necessity for and various ways of producing uniform, high-quality fruit, the Japanese reacted by creating their own "protective association" to ensure compliance and deliver fruit that met or surpassed all standards. But soon they were doing more than simply instructing members in the best methods for spraying, picking, packing, and shipping produce. Apparently they began sharing and comparing lease arrangements; once association members learned the going rate, they began demanding cash rents and various concessions from the Shippers Association. Many jumped their leases and boycotted uncooperative growers. "Trouble," reported the *Placer County Republican*, "has reached crisis." Equally alarmed, the *Pacific Rural Press* denounced the "exorbitant" demands of what it called the "Japanese labor union."[47]

But Japanese field hands and *keiyaku-nin* did much more than seize opportunities to lease, rent, sharecrop, or otherwise muscle in on established farmers. Years of living economically in preparation for the time when they would move toward landownership left them with a strong sense of frugality and determination to succeed. What had been rubbish to white Californians, the Japanese habitually gathered and made useful. Discarded oyster and sardine tins would be melted down into tin and solder, or cut and flattened into shingles and siding for their farmhouses and dwellings. Others weeded crops wearing shoes of red canvas bean sacks and fed their vegetable patches with fertilizers made of old bones they gathered and ground up into a fine powder. They approached farming the same way, interplanting sweet potatoes, asparagus, tomatoes, eggplants, and melons between the rows of young trees and vines to maximize the land's output in the crucial first year. In time, each small conservation combined to equal a large savings. "They take a place, and leave it in better condition than they found it," recalled *Fresno Republican* editor Ben Walker. And because their farms were labor intensive and because many of them planted permanent crops like vineyards and orchards, which required a minimum of three or four years to mature, the Japanese often left their own farms and migrated between the crops to supplement their incomes as field hands. When it came time to harvest their first small crops, they commonly did the picking themselves, hiring only a few men and relying on colleagues and relatives for help. So determined were a few Japanese field hands turned farmers that for years they existed almost completely on the potatoes they grew and made into something called "*battera*," a potato batter fried like a pancake, then rolled and stuffed with sweet peas and other vegetables.[48]

Through these and other methods, former field hands and *keiyaku-nin* created the most productive, efficient, and tidy farming operations in California. "There is no disputing the fact," noted Modesto mayor Forrest Crissey in his book *Where Opportunity Knocks Twice*, "that the Jap . . . is making more net profit from a small holding of twenty to forty acres [than] the representative farmer . . . is making from his one-hundred and sixty acres." Seconding this assessment, the California State Board of Control reported, "Where he has taken over lands that were in use before his time he has almost always, if not always, put them to a far higher use and made the farms more valuable than they were before."[49]

Japanese field hands and *keiyaku-nin* seemed particularly adept at converting marginal land to fertile fields. On the west slope of the Sierra Nevada, southeast of Fresno near Lemon Cove, they discovered some cheap "hog wallow," long avoided by whites as apparently worthless. Realizing that it was in the thermal belt, they bought the land for a pittance, terraced it, planted citrus orchards and vineyards, and created what amounted to an entirely new fruit district. North of Vacaville, they moved into the hot, rattlesnake-infested canyons, planted their orchards on terraced hillsides, and there grew fruit that ripened two weeks ahead of that grown on the valley floor. After harvesting their own crop, they would then travel down into the valley and hire out as pickers. By 1913, they leased or owned between one-third and one-half of all Vaca Valley fruit farms. They also transformed the alkaline land south of El Monte into rich celery fields, hauled away rocks from the San Gabriel Valley's hillsides and planted fruit trees, erected the first lettuce packing shed in Hollister, introduced peas to Visalia, developed the watermelon industry around Dinuba, pioneered truck farming at Delano, planted bush peas on the hillsides at Pismo Beach, and started the garlic industry in the San Juan Valley. Around Stockton, Japanese farmers using careful fertilization methods so dramatically increased their yields that they pushed out established Italian farmers. Perhaps most important of all, the Japanese brought rice cultivation to California on a commercial scale. Although not the first to grow rice, they were the first to do so successfully. By combining techniques perfected at the USDA with lessons learned from centuries of rice growing in their homeland, Japanese farmers discovered that the very conditions that spoiled the land for most forms of agriculture in Colusa, Sutter, Yuba, Glenn, and Butte counties were perfect for growing rice. For that accomplishment farmers thanked one K. Ikuta, the "Rice Wizard," who realized that the abandoned hardpan soil between Williams and Marysville prevented water from seeping below the soil surface and was therefore perfect for growing rice on a large scale.[50]

Once field hands and *keiyaku-nin* became established as farmers, they usually settled into distinct communities separate from the bunkhouses and bachelor quarters found on the farms and in rural Japantowns. One of the earliest of these farming settlements sprang up on the shallow hardpan "hay land" around Florin, ten miles south of Sacramento. Moving into the area in 1902, Japanese took control of harvest work as usual by undercutting Chinese already on the job. They also took over labor in the Florin box factory, which manufactured the crates and baskets required for shipping grapes and berries. With about one thousand men working in the strawberry harvest between April and July and about half remaining behind to pick the grape crop through September, the Japanese quickly gained experience. Within a few years of learning the rudiments of strawberry culture, they set up cooperative farming companies, moved into farming, and with their savings began leasing, renting, and purchasing farms from white landowners. Attracted by prospects of having worthless land converted to productive vineyards and strawberry fields and of earning more through rent than they could by selling the crops themselves, white farmers readily agreed to sell, rent, lease, or sharecrop their land. By 1909, about 150 Japanese had taken control of 2,360 acres, or about one-third of the farmland around Florin. Four years later, they were producing one-third of the Florin-area strawberry crop and running all but one business in town.[51]

Of all the Japanese who became farmers in the early twentieth century, perhaps none was more influential than Abiko Kyūtarō, who had landed in San Francisco with one dollar in his pocket in 1885, but by working at a series of menial jobs, financed his own education at the University of California, Berkeley. After graduating, he operated a laundry and restaurant before becoming a *keiyaku-nin* in 1902. Quickly developing the largest labor contracting business in California, he supplied labor to beet growers as far away as Colorado and Utah. Wealthy and established, he returned home to marry, then brought his new bride to California. Through his newspaper *Nichibei Shimbun*, the leading Japanese daily on the West Coast, he next launched an aggressive campaign to overturn the bachelor lifestyle that dominated among immigrant Japanese. Using his newspaper to promote a Japanese-American community rooted in agriculture, he decided to create a model Japanese farming settlement. In 1906, he founded the

American Land and Produce Company. Purchasing thirty-two hundred acres of land "good only for hay and jack rabbits" near Livingston in the San Joaquin Valley, he divided the tract into forty-acre lots and persuaded Japanese immigrants to settle there permanently. Planting grapes, fruit trees, and alfalfa, the colonists constructed a system of irrigation canals and ditches that tapped into the Merced River. By 1910, the settlement had 1,571 acres of permanent crops, one hundred acres of hay, and five hundred acres of alfalfa. Within eleven years of its founding, Yamato Colony (as the settlement came to be known) was home to forty-two settlers who annually produced 260 carloads of fruit in addition to alfalfa and hay.[52]

At Yamato Colony, Florin, and dozens of other farming clusters, the Japanese established agricultural associations, or *nogyo kumiai*; these included the Association of Japanese Sugar Beet Growers, the Placer County Japanese Farmers Association, the Japanese Agricultural Association of California, the Japanese Farmers Association of Turlock, and others. Essentially mutual-support systems, these groups coordinated crop production, fixed prices, exchanged information, provided financial assistance, arbitrated disputes, stabilized rents, helped men purchase food and supplies in bulk, and established marketing organizations. Responsible to either the *Zaibei Nihonjin Degō Kyogika* (United Deliberative Council), which coordinated Japanese associations in Northern California, or the Nanka Chuō Nihonjinkai (Central Japanese Association of Southern California), which supervised the southern part of the state, Japanese farming associations formed an integrated network that assisted farmers in growing, shipping, and selling fruits and vegetables throughout California.[53]

Success angered racists and fed old fears, inspiring among the anti-Japanese movement a new complaint—that by moving into farming the Japanese were rising too quickly. According to the Asiatic Exclusion League, the Japanese controlled the equivalent of a five-mile-wide strip of prime farmland running over 750 miles from Oregon south to the border with Mexico. Left unchecked, the Japanese would dominate California's agriculture within ten years and make white farmers as extinct as the "whooly [sic] rhinoceros." Acting on these fears, California Democrats beginning in 1910 repeatedly called for legislation banning the Japanese from owning land. But in the spring of 1913, Governor Hiram Johnson along with California Attorney General Ulysses S. Webb finally acted on these fears and drafted an act barring noncitizens from owning land or leasing it for longer than three years, the latter provision discouraging many from planting crops like grapes or fruit trees requiring a long-term commitment. Signed into law on May 19, the Webb-Henry Bill—popularly known as the Alien Land Act of 1913—became effective on August 10, despite strong opposition and threats of military action and boycotts from Japan. Although the new law ostensibly applied to "aliens ineligible for citizenship," it in fact applied only to the Japanese and their farming companies, along with Indian Sikhs, and was designed to reverse Japanese movement up the agricultural ladder. This meant that if a Japanese farmer died, he could not leave his property to his family if they were noncitizens. While some farmers returned to Japan in disgust or abandoned orchards and vineyards in favor of one-year crops like vegetables, others rapidly implemented measures to evade the law, even before it went into effect. By transferring land titles and leases to American-born children, or to some one hundred quickly formed corporations whose stock was controlled by American-born Japanese, most Japanese continued farming and escaped the economic consequences of the law, which, while humiliating, had limited economic effect.[54]

ৡৢ

By becoming farmers, Japanese men hoped not only for financial gain but also to become accepted into American society, to transform themselves from *dekaseginin* to settlers. Initially, though, most were forced to hire and associate with other Japanese. Many pointed to racial loyalty as the reason for these associations, but the true cause was that most whites simply would not work for Japanese farmers, who had a reputation as tough taskmasters and demanding employers. Even though Japanese farmers generally paid their men 10 to 15 percent above the prevailing rate, most whites simply considered working for a minority group an unthinkable humiliation.[55]

Socially shunned by their non-Asian counterparts, Japanese farmers soon began to capitalize on a provision of the Gentleman's Agreement that allowed Japanese natives to immigrate in order to join a parent, spouse, or child already residing in the United States. Those with families immediately brought them to California. And because newly established bachelor farmers who returned home could not return to California, these men often enlisted the services of friends and relatives back home to arrange marriages, or they might hire a *baishakunin*, a marriage broker. "As soon as a Jap can produce a lease," reported the *Sacramento Bee*, "he . . . sends a copy . . . back home and gets a picture bride." Exchanging photographs and personal information with women from the same prefecture—the same village if possible—and similar socioeconomic backgrounds, these men married by proxy and their new wives left for California on the next available ship. As a result of these practices, 66,926 Japanese women eventually immigrated to California in the years after restriction (5,581 by 1910), outnumbering male immigrants by a ratio of two to one.[56]

In 1910, researchers for the Immigration Commission reported that, around Newcastle, more than half of the Japanese tenant farmers had wives who had "migrated to the area recently in most cases." Not all were picture brides. Many were wives who had been left behind when men originally immigrated; they arrived with children of all ages in tow, from youngsters and grown sons to daughters who had reached adulthood in their father's absence. Japanese farmers hardly offered their wives and children a life of luxury. Conditions were crude at best. Dusty, windblown fields, where the drifting sand piled up in storms "so fierce that chickens were buried as they sat on their eggs," hardly offered an enticing setting to begin married life, remembered one bride. Quarters frequently consisted of unfinished, makeshift wooden huts "boxed up" of rough boards or shakes. Sometimes a single room functioned as a living room and bedroom, with a shedlike lean-to tacked on for cooking and eating. Oil lamps provided illumination. Furniture consisted of tables of old planks cobbled together with a few rusty nails. Mattresses could be little more than onion bags stuffed with straw.[57]

Newly established Japanese farmers readily assumed that their imported wives and children would contribute substantially to the workload. At harvest time, families routinely worked sixteen hours a day, seven days a week; a family of four was usually able to handle all but the harvest on a twenty-acre fruit farm. Women worked endlessly—"as good as the men," according to one Newcastle grower— dividing their time between *hatarite ita* (laboring) and *asonderu* (keeping house); eventually, raising children became part of the mix as well. Rising before dawn they would prepare breakfast, then go into the fields to pick tomatoes, sack onions, or lay out clusters of raisin grapes. Traveling through the farming districts, *Century Magazine* writer Konrad Bercovici could not help but notice "the squat forms of the diminutive little women grubbing out the earth, moving slowly about as they sat on their heels, frequently with children strapped to their backs." From a distance, Bercovici observed, "they look more like giant bugs crawling along the paths than human beings."[58]

After an average ten hours of stoop labor, Japanese wives would return to their houses so tired and sore that they could not sit down to use the toilet. The first thing they would do was start a cooking fire and prepare dinner for their husband and harvest crews. Often they had to haul buckets of water from wells. After the evening meal they would sort tomatoes, pack raisins, and tend to various household chores, particularly washing. During harvest, when the local Japanese Association would bring in crews, the women were expected to cook for them and do additional chores like laundry. "We worked from morning till night, blackened by the sun," recalled one picture bride, who seldom finished her chores before midnight or 1:30 A.M.[59]

For some women, the isolation and unending labor were just too awful to bear. Many attempted suicide. Reporting the tragic demise of one woman, the *Oxnard Courier* went into some detail explaining exactly what had happened and why. "Weary and tired of life in a foreign country, little Mrs. Kotune Togohara, wife of a Japanese laborer, committed suicide by hanging Wednesday evening at the Len Richardson ranch near town," explained the newspaper. Returning to the labor camp at about 6 P.M., the woman's husband found her still warm body suspended from a tree limb near their tent. "Not realizing that life was extinct, Togohara summoned Dr. Potts of this city, but upon the doctor's arrival he pronounced the unfortunate woman dead. The Coroner's jury yesterday morning returned a verdict of suicide."[60]

Most Japanese brides fought through their loneliness, and with time, family obligations and pride in accomplishment overrode whatever disillusionment and tensions originally stemmed from marriage by proxy. Most brides soon acquired at least the rudiments of the English language. Unity and trust developed, divorce seldom intruded, hard work prevailed, and family labor became the norm. Children grew up loyal, highly valued, and closely supervised. Their birth gave new meaning to the struggle for American residency, prompting ever larger numbers of Japanese field hands to climb the agricultural ladder and become farm operators.[61]

Within a few years, the hard labor bore results. First covering their dirt floors with wood, Japanese farming families would gradually add a room or two, perhaps even a stone fireplace and a kitchen, erect a tankhouse, and construct a windmill. The model Japanese farmhouse thus became a three-story structure with a large water-storage tank on the top floor, a living or storage space beneath it, a ground level room, and a large windmill nearby. Soon, Japanese farming colonies began building schools to educate their American-born children. Thus through marriage and farming, Japanese field hands and *keiyaku-nin* finally were in a position to increase their numbers without immigration.

As a result of these developments, by the summer of 1912, Japanese field hands were beginning to lose their dominance as farm laborers. Although some five years would pass before Japanese farmers outnumbered field hands, contemporaries already understood the implications of what was happening. California state commissioner of labor statistics John D. Mackenzie in his annual report that year observed, "the moment this ambition [landownership] is exercised, that moment the Japanese ceases to be an ideal laborer." Determined to stem the outflow of field hands, some agricultural leaders joined anti-Asian elements and proposed to further restrict Japanese property rights. The theory behind the move was that, by preventing Japanese field hands from even thinking of acquiring land, they would be forced to remain harvest workers and thereby preserve the labor surplus. But many growers did not support anti-landowning legislation. For one, arrangements with Japanese renters and sharecroppers were so favorable that they did not want to in any way jeopardize that relationship. For another, they could see that they were not going to suffer any significant labor shortage; even as the Japanese were moving out of farm labor into farming, growers were finding access to increasingly large numbers of bindlemen.[62]

FIGURE 48. Seldom photographed while on the move, California bindlemen remained largely undocumented on film until 1935, when Dorothea Lange captured this timeless image of a bindleman packing his "balloon." Copyright the Dorothea Lange Collection, Oakland Museum, City of Oakland. Gift of Paul S. Taylor.

BOOK SIX

Bindlemen

The road is one of the safety valves through which
the waste of the social organism is given off.
—*Jack London*

Just one thing leads to another and it goes on until
the first thing you know, years have gone by. You're
sitting in a jungle somewhere and you decide, well,
I'm going to quit, I'm not going to do this anymore.
—*Hood River Blackie*

It was no trouble at all to round up a crew. We'd
just drive to where they lived, sometimes in a
lean-to under the gum trees, and recruit a crew
in short order.
—*Joe Terry*

I learned to lie fully clothed on top of the covers,
wrapping myself in clean newspapers. Instead of
sheep, I counted the shufflings, mutterings, cuss-
ings . . . I noted . . . belches, groans, farts, incipient
snores . . . a crescendo of tubular coughing, bibu-
lous slurping, snorting, and snoring, a vomit, and
many stringed cot creaking. After a climax of
nighttime yells, partition pounding, and cries of
protest, brief intermission [was] called by the night
clerk. Then on again, till the dawn's early light
brought the quiet of windless exhaustion.
—*Len DeCaux*

You have a sudden and severe attack of 'wanderlust' . . . and before you realize the fact you are
headed for the nearest freight yards . . . and you
don't know where you are going to go next or when
or why nor where you are going to sleep tonight
and don't care a damn either.
—*'Industrial Worker'*

California has passed laws for the protection of
migratory birds, but it can not pass laws for the
protection of migratory workers.
—*'San Francisco Bulletin'*

CHAPTER TWENTY-ONE

Blinky Joe, Red Mike, and Hobo Sam

Bindlemen on the Move

One Saturday evening during the orange picking season, a young bindleman named Fred Thompson approached the company store on a ranch near Lindsay, a small town astride the western foothills of the Sierra Nevada. Born in St. John, New Brunswick, young Thompson had drifted through Canada and the American West. On his way back from working on a nearby water project, Thompson had stopped off to pick oranges before heading north to Oroville. Thompson had counted himself lucky to secure the position, because it was one of the rare farm jobs available during the winter and spring months and attracted more "orange rustlers" than could be hired, a fact accentuated by growers who solicited labor as far away as Stockton, Fresno, and Sacramento. Forced to buy his own picking sacks and clippers, Thompson was dog tired after pushing himself to the limits of his endurance to fill twenty boxes a day at ten cents each. Now, aching from head to foot and nursing blistered hands after spending a week scrambling up and down ladders, Thompson joined his fellow workers outside the company pay shack.[1]

The men were hungry and craving a night's relaxation in town. Dreaming of getting their hair cut and washing in steaming hot baths, perhaps enjoying a meal of "bacon and" at George's Place, a local eatery whose flaming red sign announced the best twenty-five-cent meals in town, they were in a foul mood when a foreman appeared and signaled the men to quiet down. "Don't get excited," he yelled. "Wait your turn." Soon a confrontation developed. As the foreman attempted to pay everyone not in cash but in scrip notes redeemable only at the ranch store, Thompson and the rest of the orange pickers shouted back with catcalls and obscenities. Having been forced to submit to a hold-back system in which growers wishing to keep them until the end of the harvest concocted excuses to avoid paying them, many recognized the deception. Whenever the foreman tried to entice someone to accept a slab of bacon or a two-dollar pair of shoes in partial payment for what was owed, the men pushed forward. "Give us our wages!" they shouted. "We'll break your head!" As the workers became more

FIGURE 49. Bindlemen hopping a train. Alcohol-induced watercolor recollection by R. Dibbs Ginther. Courtesy of the Washington State Historical Society.

resolute, their show of force eventually wore down the foreman. "Take it easy," he shouted. But Thompson and the men were in a foul mood. "Stop stalling," they bellowed, shaking their fists. "We worked hard." Finally collecting his pay, Thompson left and vowed never to return. It was a promise that countless other bindlemen also made after encountering parsimonious or fraudulent growers while tramping through California's agricultural districts.[2]

&a

Present since the Gold Rush, transient laborers like Thompson expanded dramatically in numbers after the turn of the century. "All along every country road, under almost every tree, there were the evidences of these homeless citizens," wrote socialist author Morrison Swift in *What a Tramp Learns in California*. Newspaper reporters and other observers further suggested that bindlemen—often called fruit tramps—"were thicker than hops" at harvest time, "infested" every rural county and agricultural district, harvested every crop, and were found "in all parts of the state and in all seasons . . . on every road, tramping back and forth."[3]

Like their predecessors nearly a half-century earlier, these men had, for various reasons, abandoned societal mores and taken to a life on the road as a means of survival. Filling the void created as the Japanese moved up and out of farm labor, and the Chinese and native Indian populations died out, bindlemen became so essential to the prosperity and growth of California agriculture that they should have earned the respect and admiration of their fellow citizens as well as the gratitude of farmers and rural communities. But this was not the case. Despite their central role, they remained social outcasts. Among farmworkers, no group—with the possible exception of the Indians—was more exploited or ill-treated, no group was more misunderstood or taken for granted by the agricultural industry, and none led a more perilous or mobile existence. Towns passed laws designed to keep bindlemen on the move. Citizens saw them as a sinister presence to be avoided at all costs. Railroad authorities chased them along the lines. Constables drove them from their camps. Judges convicted them of vagrancy. Newspapers dismissed them as "transient cattle," condemned them as "spineless, low-down creatures," labeled them "human drones," characterized them as "shiftless, improvident, and unreliable," and denounced them as "only the poorest class of white labor" and jailbirds who "fall by the wayside soon after they get into the city." Infamous labor detective Allan Pinkerton judged them "things to be dreaded, shunned, driven and despised." When the Stanford University department of education tested two hundred bindlemen in 1914, it found one in four "feeble minded," as did Reed College, using similar testing criteria that year, as did common laborer turned sociologist Nels Anderson in his seminal 1923 study, *The Hobo*. Regarded by many citizens as a menace undeserving of sympathy, they were a class to be avoided at all costs, worth hiring only as a last resort. According to some, they were best handled with a swift boot kick, a blast of rock salt from a double-barreled shotgun, or a large dose of strychnine. "I have no sympathy to waste on him," explained one grower in a letter to the *Pacific Rural Press*. "His place is on the chain gang." Only foremen and others who knew them up-close understood bindlemen, emphasizing that the conditions they endured in their nomadic existence amounted to a "vicious" example of "industrial oppression on a large scale."[4]

Who were these farmworkers? What propelled them into the countryside? Why did they remain on the move? Curious about their habits, crimes, encampments, and movement, journalists met the public clamor for information by writing hundreds of stories documenting, sensationalizing, and trivializing bindlemen. None was more memorable than the portrait produced by Jack London. Drifting about the country during 1903 and 1904, he struck up conversations with several exceptionally literate and colorful bindlemen, sought them out in jails and lodging houses, made his own sojourn through "beggerdom," and to everyone's surprise, lived to tell his tales, as often as not describing men who were as fascinating as they were pitiful. From his experiences, he concluded that most bindlemen were cast-offs and misfits, unable or unwilling to fit in. "The road," he wrote, "is one of the safety valves through which the waste of the social organism is given off." It was a common impression.[5]

From such popular perceptions, a myth developed, yet another of the many that obscure the history of California farmworkers. It is that California bindlemen were a unique and peculiar class of workers, people not found anywhere else in the country. Alone among American workers, they were said to have "a sort of gypsy spirit within them." In fact, the truth was quite the contrary. As itinerant workers, California bindlemen were typical. Mass population movements were common early in the twentieth century, as men constantly shifted between cities and farms, states, and regions. At various times between 1900 and 1920, as few as a half-million laborers and as many as three or four million men tramped about the United States, holding as many as twenty or more different jobs in one year. So familiar were these transient workers that *Solidarity*, the radical publication of the Industrial Workers of the World, observed how "every industrial center, and every industry . . . has its quota of these wandering slaves."[6]

Of all drifting laborers at this time, those who most closely resembled California bindlemen were the 125,000 to 200,000 migratory wheat threshers and harvesters who swarmed through the Midwest every summer. Four or five months elapsed from the time they began running the first reapers and binders in mid-June until they separated the last bushel of wheat in early October. Along the way they worked on dozens of farms, with the average job lasting between nine and twelve days. "They reached our neighborhood in July," remembered the novelist Hamlin Garland, "appearing like a flight of alien, unclean birds, and vanished north as mysteriously as they appeared. Some carried valises, others had nothing but small bundles containing a clean shirt and a few socks."[7]

California bindlemen led an equally dramatic, difficult, and highly mobile existence that set them off from their Chinese and Japanese predecessors in the fields, whose well-ordered communities contrasted dramatically with the cruel and heartless world that bindlemen inhabited. Theirs was a world that lacked ordinary social institutions; it was a distinct subculture where survival depended upon fortitude and wit, where death occurred without sentiment and usually led to an unmarked grave in a potter's field. Bindlemen often went days without food, weeks without an adequate place to sleep, and months without satisfactory clothing. They "more or less could expect to never obtain economic security, a family, or community attachment," explained *Solidarity*. Life was an endless, repetitive, often meaningless drudge. "In California," wrote Jack London, "a man may pick berries in Siskiyou, peaches in Santa Clara, grapes in the San Joaquin, and oranges in Los Angeles, going from job to job as the season advances and traveling a thousand miles ere the season is done."[8]

At first glance, bindlemen seemed to share few attributes with one another besides their mobile lives, but in fact as a group they were remarkably uniform. Not all transients were bindlemen. As the *Hobo News*, *Solidarity*, *Industrial Worker*, and other close observers of itinerant life were quick to point out, there were important distinctions between bindlemen, hoboes, tramps, and bums. And while the lines between each group were not always clear-cut, with men of the road drifting between all three worlds, each generally remained separate from the other, followed different rules, adhered to different values, and did not particularly get along.[9]

What distinguished bindlemen and hoboes from tramps and bums was a willingness to work. A common saying went: "A hobo is a migratory worker. A tramp is a migratory non-worker. A bum is a stationary non-worker." But there were further shades of difference. Dr. Ben Reitman, a Chicago physician who traveled as a bindleman early in the twentieth century, gave this interpretation: "The hobo works and wanders. The tramp dreams and wanders. The bum drinks and wanders." Another distinction stressed that hoboes and bindlemen went on the road to work, while tramps and bums worked to live on the road. Unlike bindlemen, tramps and bums made little contribution to farm labor in California. And while these derelicts drifted among bindlemen and were often lumped together with them by casual observers, they essentially regarded work as a waste of time and energy.[10]

California bindlemen were workers first and migrants second, and they followed a lifestyle designed to further their pursuit of jobs. Engaged in a perpetual internal migration—as opposed to immigration from a foreign country—they were anything but idle. At one time or another, many bindlemen toiled as miners, loggers, and fishermen, and labored in sugar beet factories and quicksilver mines; farmwork was only a part of their annual circuit of jobs. Because of the seasonal nature of their work, bindlemen shared a common goal with migratory and field-workers who had come before. The idea, wrote *Industrial Worker*, was "to dig in and work like Hell in the summer" so that, "when the fall comes you may be even with the game." To earn that stake, bindlemen traveled considerable distances. "They know just when to hit the various places, and they follow it up," explained West Coast radical George Speed to the Commission on Industrial Relations. "They understand that part of it well themselves."[11]

In 1914, University of California economist Carleton Parker studied 222 bindlemen in California and several western states and gathered a wealth of information about their migratory patterns, work habits, lifestyles, and backgrounds. Parker quickly discovered that most bindlemen had their last job in a different area of the state, that two of ten had last worked outside of California, that 86 percent had not been born in California, and that half of his sample had been in the state six years or less. A few followed work circuits entirely within the borders of the Golden State, but many more added detours into the Pacific Northwest, even into midwestern states, "never remaining for more than a few days in any one place, completely independent and roving and working at their own will, tied to no particular location."[12]

Parker also found bindlemen to be overwhelmingly of European background, dividing almost evenly between American-born (48.4 percent) and immigrant (51.6 percent). Among the immigrant component, men from Germany, Ireland, and Sweden dominated; a much smaller component came from southern European countries, principally Italy. About 55 percent of all immigrant bindlemen had been in the United States for more than five years, and about six of ten had become citizens. Most spoke English, had shed their old world traditions, and were in the prime of life, between twenty and forty years of age. Only one of ten was married. As *Solidarity* observed: "The floater is almost always a compulsory celibate. He is either unmarried or his family life has been permanently broken up." Unlike coal miners, textile workers, or steel mill workers, bindlemen could not participate in raising a family, regularly attend church, build permanent friendships, or maintain attachments to home. While about 12 percent of all bindlemen had some regular contact with relatives, only 36 percent ever wrote to family members, and four of ten had ceased writing to or maintaining any contact whatsoever with relatives. As a result, union newspapers were always filled with advertisements from wives and children seeking information about "the whereabouts of our father." Many such families were almost destitute. Their ads pleaded, "If any person has knowledge of the whereabouts of my husband and father of our three children, please contact his desperate wife."[13]

Most bindlemen had some training or skill, with half of Parker's sample claiming a profession. Slightly over half (55 percent) had left school before age fifteen, while 26 percent had never attended school at all—numbers comparable to the educational levels of industrial workers in the East. Four of ten had been on the road less than six years, three of ten between six and fifteen years, and two of ten more than fifteen years. Most worked an average of seven days before moving on, compared to ten days for construction workers, fifteen to thirty days for lumberjacks, and thirty days for cannery workers. Underscoring the transitory nature of their employment, just one in five bindlemen managed to work more than ten months of the year. The temporary nature of their employment directly affected their wages, as few bindlemen earned more than three hundred dollars a year.[14]

Exactly why bindlemen hit the road and drifted with the harvests was a question that puzzled and upset many observers, including even some of the growers who hired them. While it was easy enough to understand what drove Japanese and Chinese immigrants across the Pacific Ocean and into the fields of California, it was not so clear why those already in the country took to the road. "I have often wondered," wrote one correspondent for the *California Citrograph*, "what degree of despair it must take to drive a man to plow the fields, or pick fruit . . . and then have no reward, but the right on Sunday to sit on the curbstone of some village that is little more lively than a cemetery."[15]

A variety of circumstances caused men to give up on conventional society and become desperate enough to tramp the countryside. Boredom, family problems, the death of a loved one, difficulties in school, ethnic discrimination, personality flaws, crises of identity, and fear of punishment for some crime all played some role in driving men to drift with the crops. Carleton Parker placed heavy emphasis on biological causes. In his opinion, men became bindlemen as the result of "a biochemical defect of one kind or another—e.g., an idiosyncratic geneotropic lack of nutritive elements, or a defective function of the endocrine gland or a masked food sensitivity."[16]

Bindlemen themselves cited less unwieldy and condescending explanations, often stressing alcoholism and women. They offered these explanations again and again in interviews and letters to newspapers, but nowhere more succinctly than on a wooden grave marker in Caliente, Nevada, which said of the anonymous person beneath:

A woman frail.
And a glass of ale.
Made a horse's tail of me.

For a small group of impressionable people, the flood of writing romanticizing life on the move—especially Jack London's articles and Josiah Flynt's *Tramping with Tramps*—undoubtedly served as a catalyst. Older bindlemen also sometimes used exciting stories to entice younger men to join their ranks. Some bindlemen, like Hood River Blackie, who worked the harvests and a string of seasonal jobs for most of his adult life, began migrating about California in the mistaken impression that it was "a tramp's paradise," a place of eternal sunshine and glowing colors where you "could sleep out of doors every night and throw your shoe into an overhanging orange tree and bring down your breakfast." Later in life, Blackie looked back and still could not be more precise about why he followed the harvests. "Just one thing leads to another and it goes on until the first thing you know, years have gone by," he recalled.[17]

Some reasons bindlemen chose to drift with the harvests were not so difficult to discern. After examining the problem closely, the *Napa Weekly Register* explained: "There are those in the great army on the road, who have been brought to their present state of dependence by sickness, accident, or that ill-starred luck which often times persists in standing in the path of the best-intentioned of men." Anyone, it seemed, could wind up on the road. After scrutinizing the situation closely, the U.S. Commission on Industrial Relations identified all kinds of circumstances—industrial modernization and the introduction of new machinery, accidents, occupational disease, immigration, and periodic economic depressions—that fed the ranks of the unemployed and caused hundreds of thousands of men to "gradually sink into the ranks of migratory and casual workers." Fired or laid off from their jobs, or unable to find work after migrating to California in response to one of the state's gigantic promotional campaigns, they hit the road, permanently or temporarily, believing that it was "better to starve to death in a warm country than a cold one." Seldom seeing their hopelessness as anything other than a temporary expedient, they all hoped one day to escape their predicament and settle down, although when interviewed by Parker, seven of ten admitted that they never expected to ever settle down and intended to continue drifting. For them, becoming migrant farmworkers was a logical response to underemployment as well as unemployment.[18]

Of all the many reasons for their drifting, none was more important than the peculiar economic reality underpinning life in California and the American West. Every one of the region's dominant industries outside of agriculture—lumber, railroad construction, fishing, mining—was highly seasonal, with peak employment in summer and autumn, and minimal opportunities in winter and spring. Overall, one of four California workers could expect to be unemployed at least three months of the year and in certain industries men fared far worse. One of two lumbermen were unemployed at least two months annually; eight of ten cannery employees were out of work at least three months of every year. Even manufacturing followed seasonal patterns, employing 119,688 men in January and

161,072 in August, a swing between minimum and maximum employment that was greater in only five other states.[19]

With unemployment so widespread, California became a "state of summer employment," where men were always looking for work. Touring the California countryside and later writing about his experiences, the English radical Charles Ashleigh found jobs so highly seasonal that no one could expect to work throughout the year. "The result," explained Ashleigh, "is the existence on the coast of an immense army of unskilled or semi-skilled workers, with no fixed abode, who are forever engaged in an eternal chase for the elusive job."[20]

৯৯

Bindlemen were forever on the move between the state's widely dispersed agricultural regions. From early ripening grapes in the Imperial Valley to fall apple crops four thousand feet up in the Sierra Nevada, men meandered California's highways and back roads in search of harvest work in the state's two hundred different crops. Some also found seasonal employment as roustabouts, mule skinners, and squirrel poisoners. But wherever they went, few did so entirely by foot. To travel about, bindlemen of the early twentieth century did what their predecessors had done a generation earlier. They rode trains. Few could afford train fare, considering what they earned in the fields. Bindlemen therefore viewed it as their privilege to "beat their way" on the railroads free of charge, the term "beat" meaning that they stole their rides and thus had "beaten" the railroad out of a fare.[21]

Riding the rails, bindlemen were able to reach a much wider range of agricultural districts than any other farmworkers. Consequently, every aspect and dimension of railroad operation figured in their lives. Train schedules, routes, and technology, the physical layout of tracks and switching yards, and the people who worked on the railroads all became everyday concerns. Bindlemen learned not only how to ride the rails, but also where to catch trains, who to trust, and who to avoid. By fully exploiting the railroads, bindlemen became the most mobile element of the agricultural labor force.

At certain times of the year railroads were, according to Charles Ashleigh, "alive with men tramping the ties, under the burning sun." On December 19, 1892, the *San Francisco Chronicle* reported bindlemen organized in gangs of forty to two hundred men, commandeering Southern Pacific boxcars throughout the state "as if they owned them." Travelers were always commenting on them. Robert Louis Stevenson once saw two of these "land stowaways," as he called them, whip suddenly from underneath the cars, and take to their heels while his California-bound train was parked in the yards at Elko, Nevada. Wealthy John Hays Hammond even brought one from the brake beams into his private car to have dinner and conversation with him and novelist Rider Haggard as their train sped across the Sacramento Valley. "There is hardly a working man," reported the March 18, 1909, *Industrial Worker*, "who has not beat his way on freight trains."[22]

Like sailing the ocean, beating one's way on trains was full of dangers, many of them fatal. Bindlestiffs had to be daring and physically fit. The best were regarded with awe and deference. Experienced bindlestiffs bragged about their feats, built reputations, and developed considerable pride in their abilities to steal rides and make time. Some claimed with understandable exaggeration that they "could ride on the side of a boxcar dressed as a Swift premium ham or the trademark of Old Dutch Cleanser."[23]

Packing their ever present bindles, men were limited as to where they could stow away on trains. The first axiom of train riding was to travel light, and every successful bindlestiff learned quickly to take only what was necessary. One test of an experienced bindleman was his ability to roll and compress his belongings into a "bindle" of no more than thirty-five pounds, the weight he could sling over one shoulder and heft aboard a slow-moving freight train; this was called "packing a balloon." Drawing on lessons learned from the previous generation of men on the move, bindlemen pared their bindles down to an extra heavy coat, or "benny," which doubled as a pillow or bedcover, high-topped boots, a couple of big wool blankets, some soap, a knife and razor, some coffee, bread, potatoes, a little sugar, a pot or kettle, and a sheet of canvas. To effect repairs, men usually also carried an awl, some heavy thread, and a buckskin. Tied snugly with heavy rope or cinched firm with two or three wide belts, bindles went everywhere their owners went. "Each possessor of a perambulating bed hugs close his treasure," wrote Morrison Swift in *What a Tramp Learns in California*. "He does not take his watchful eyes off it either day or night. When he moves down-town to the pool hall the bed goes with him, and when he comes back . . . so does the bed."[24]

Climbing on board an ordinary freight or "rattler" ("nailing a drag," as it was known), was the most common means of transport for bindlemen. If they had connections with switching-yard operators, bindlemen simply asked about the next fast freight, found an empty freight car or boxcar, sprung the door open, and crawled inside. But if the switching yard was being patrolled by railroad police or the trains were moving, stealing a ride became more complicated. A bindleman had to hike outside the switching yards, hide by a culvert or water tank, wait under bridges and behind trees, and catch the train there as it started out. Old bindlemen in their autobiographies and memoirs stress that this was a far more dangerous task than most people realized. Properly boarding a moving train was a skill not easily taught, and there was no room for error or second chances.[25]

To hop a moving freight, a bindleman looked for a grade where the freight train would have to slow down and he could grab a handhold and swing on board. Walking over the land, he scrutinized it closely for uneven spots and hidden obstacles; this was particularly important if he was going to board a train at night. He then cinched his bindle tight to his back and waited for the train to approach. Allowing a quarter-mile of cars to pass by, he judged the train's speed, and kept an eye cocked for a string of boxcars. As the train passed, he began running alongside, holding out a hand to feel for a ladder or step. Once he found a handhold, he grabbed it and dove forward, the motion jerking him and slamming his body against the side of the train. He then had to scramble for the safety of a protected spot. If he was lucky, he would find an empty boxcar where he could escape the wind and weather and maybe make a sleeping nest out of discarded straw; if it was a hot day, he could sit in the open door, dangling his legs and enjoying the scenery. But because boxcars were not always open or available, men rode every variety of railcar. The most successful learned to ride trains, as one bindleman explained, "the way an Indian brave could ride his horse: they could hang onto belly, neck, rump, and get there."[26]

To ride undetected, bindlemen crawled into dozens of spots in, around, and under the train. To escape detection, they burrowed into the soft coal of an engine tender box or ducked down among the machinery strapped to a flatcar. In midsummer, men naturally headed for the refrigerator cars, where they could lie down on top of the ice, chip away pieces to suck on, and keep cool even when the temperature outside topped one hundred degrees. Men also found shelter in the "blind baggage" vestibules between the engine tender and the front end of the baggage car and in cramped battery boxes located halfway back on the Pullman coaches. This latter hiding place was less than desirable, since the battery boxes tended to contain battery acid, which ate away at men's clothes and skin. More daring bindlemen rode in ways that now seem unimaginable. A great "train barnacle" who went by the name of "Frisco" once rode the cowcatcher of the Golden State Limited from Redding to Fresno. "Open yer mouth and she'd blow you wrong side out," Jack London said of riding the front of the engine. It was like "riding the nose of a great steel projectile hurtling like a comet through flying sawdust and frightened planets." Men also rode on top of passenger or mail cars—a cold hell if the weather turned foul—and wedged themselves into the undercarriages of railcars, called "riding the rods," or the maze of brake beams, struts, and springs holding the wheels to the trucks; this was something only the most experienced bindlemen attempted. Usually a man with a big pack could not ride the trucks and rods. But a thin man traveling light could stretch flat and ride like a kipper frying on a grill. Leon Livingston, a bindleman who rode the rods out of Modesto one summer, never forgot the experience. "Soon my eyes were filled with dust so that I could not open them," he later wrote. "My ears were becoming deaf from the grinding and whirling noise. My mouth and throat were as dry as parchment." Worse, he swallowed a plug of tobacco and became ill as the train sped along.[27]

When the boxcars, blinds, cowcatchers, and battery compartments were full or otherwise off-limits, bindlemen rode the "death woods," the narrow planks above the couplings of a boxcar. Or they rode the couplings themselves and bumpers (large railroad ties bolted to the ends of railroad cars). Perched there, one foot on each bumper or coupling, the cars bouncing up and down, shaking and swaying from side to side, the men had to ignore aching wrists, the wind shooting between the cars, and the burning cinders blowing back from the engine while holding on to their bedroll. If they survived, they seldom rode the bumpers and couplings more than once.[28]

Occasionally bindlemen attempted to bluff their way onto passenger cars, usually with predictable results. When one group boarded cars at Napa Junction on a Santa Rosa–bound train, in October 1895, a violent clash developed. "Conductor Gates ordered them off the train," reported the *Napa Daily Journal*, "but they refused to go and attacked him, using stones and clubs. Other conductors and trainmen came up, and for some minutes things were dangerously lively, but at last the tramps were beaten off. Gates was somewhat used up and several windows were smashed in the melee."[29]

So difficult and dangerous was train riding that, with rare exceptions, it remained an overwhelmingly male subculture. When three female bindlestiffs were spotted "beating their way" through the Sacramento Valley on a fall day in 1893, the *Sacramento Bee* considered it front-page news. "They are said to be honest women, who are in search of employment," explained the *Bee*. "There are three of them who are said to be headed for Sacramento . . . They are without means and starvation stared them in the face . . . It was a decidedly bold thing for women to do . . . At one place, it is reported, a tramp insulted one of the women, when the three sailed in together and gave him a trouncing that he will remember for many and many a day." Such female train riders tended to be hard-bitten and liberated; usually they were divorced. Asked about life on the road, one advised that if you kept your mouth closed and your legs crossed you might live to talk about your adventure.[30]

༃

Riding the rails was a perilous business. Bindlemen suffocated in the engine gases of slow freights in long tunnels, died in train wrecks, and were swept off or decapitated by low trestles, walkways, and bridges. Sleeping in the sun while riding the tops of swaying boxcars, they rolled down the pitched roofs and off into space—"hitting the highball for heaven," it was called. Seated in a boxcar doorway, they had their legs amputated when the train lurched and the big doors snapped shut like a guillotine. Curled up in a pile of straw at one end of a boxcar full of lumber, they were smeared against the bulkhead when rough switching in the yards or heavy application of the air brakes catapulted the lumber load against and through the car ends. Bindlemen also had their clothes ignited by sparks while clinging to the top of a dining car and lost their grip while trying to put out flames. Riding long distances on cold nights in granite-filled gondolas, bindlemen often froze to death. Others died after being trapped inside empty refrigerator cars.[31]

Jumping off a moving train also took its toll. Cuts, bruises, sprains, and broken bones were common, but more serious injuries—even death—could also result. Many bindlemen met their end by "dropping off" at night and slamming into a sign, telephone pole, bridge abutment, cow, or some other object they had failed to detect. Because of these and other dangers, few bindlemen ever retired from life on the road without some near-death experience. No matter how careful they were, bindlemen would eventually step on a broken ladder rung, lose their grip, miscalculate a handhold, catch their foot, or snag their clothes on something. In a moment of exhaustion, they might slip on a wet board. Those "lucky" enough to dodge death and suffer a major injury usually found themselves miles from medical help. One bindleman by the name of John Rodgers was boarding a train at Napa Junction in December 1893, when he fell under a train wheel and lost part of his foot. "He had no money or friends, and he was allowed to come to Vallejo on the train," reported the *Vallejo Chronicle*. "Officer Smith was on the train and he took the unfortunate man to Tull's drugstore, where the wound was dressed. The wound bled profusely, and the bone of the foot, having been crushed under the wheel, there is a chance of blood poisoning. After having the injury dressed, Rodgers was given quarters in the city jail." Whether or not he recovered was not reported.[32]

Few injured bindlemen were so lucky. What happened to many was truly horrible. Falling under a train's wheels, they had their legs amputated and bled to death, or they were chopped to pieces. Eventually someone would discover their remains, the coroner's office would scrape up the corpse, and the rural press would matter-of-factly print an epitaph. "Last night a tramp fell from a car, the wheels passing over his head, crushing it, splattering his brains along the rail," read one such report in the *Fresno Morning Republican*. "No inquest."[33]

Another headline, from the August 31, 1906, *Marysville Daily Democrat*, read, "Fearfully Mangled Body Found Today: Unknown Man Meets Awful Death; Remnants of Body Scattered Along Track Near Reed Station." The article then went on to describe how some poor bindleman, apparently riding the brake beams of a train on the Roseville route to Marysville, was run over and literally ground to pieces. When discovered by the section foreman, the man was nothing more than a "conglomeration" of flesh, bones, entrails, shoes, clothing, gravel, and dirt; a piece of his head was found in one place, and one hundred yards away, both arms, with fingers and toes scattered along the tracks. No identifying information was recovered, although the coroner did find a letter postmarked Springfield, Illinois, and a picture of a young lady. "The man was about 25 years old, had light hair and wore two suits of clothing," reported the *Democrat*. "The body was gathered up by scoop shovel and placed in a basket, after which it was brought to the morgue . . . and was later buried in the city cemetery."[34]

A gory death followed by a hasty burial—often with a blanket for a coffin, in a shallow, stone-topped, nameless grave—was the final reward for most bindlemen killed aboard trains. Nationally between 1901 and 1905, 23,964 men were killed and 25,236 injured by trains; about one in three of these incidents occurred on western railroads. Crews did not report every death or injury, largely because the procedure and paperwork were too time-consuming. As one knowledgeable railroad man pointed out in 1907, "There is hardly a railroad line in this country but what has private graveyards on its own right of way." Bindlemen often sang about meeting their maker along the rails. One popular song had a conductor saying:

> It's only a bindle stiff ye hit—
> Sent another bum to hell
> Had I better report it?
> I guess I might as well
> No, con, don't make out no report—
> Let's plant him by the steel
> This bum's bound for an unknown port
> And tracks will make it real[35]

Unable to continue moving about on trains or remain at work, bindlemen who survived railroad accidents "retired" to the cities. Hobbling about on stubs capped with wooden pegs five inches below his groin, old "Joe No Legs" and others like him sold pencils, begged, and told anyone who would listen of the accident that gave them their name.[36]

Despite the multitude of dangers, bindlemen remained on the road because it proved to be such an efficient way to travel. Men regularly crossed vast amounts of territory. Hopping express fruit trains bound for eastern markets, men could move from Winters to Boston in six days. Within California they made even better time. A freight caught in Corcoran near Bakersfield at 1:30 P.M. would arrive in Fresno at 4 P.M.; another freight caught north at 8 P.M. would be in Tracy by 2 A.M. One more ride would make Oakland by sunrise. The cannonball out of Redding covered the two hundred miles to Sacramento in six hours. Moving west from Yuma, Arizona, to Los Angeles, any average "train bummer" could routinely cover the 250 miles in twelve hours. A favorite north-south run was on board the Shasta Limited, the "fast devil" from Portland. Crawling implacably up through the Siskiyou Pass, it then rushed into California, highballing it all the way from Red Bluff to Sacramento.[37]

Bindlemen beating their way cost railroads plenty of money beyond lost fares. Bindlemen accidentally burned boxcars by building small fires while trying to keep warm, ruined fruit by prying open reefer car doors and leaving them open, stole tools, hefted batteries from their compartments, broke locks to gain access to buildings, tossed freight off flatcars to make room for themselves, ripped up carriages and other transported goods in order to find bedding, and closed off angle-cock connections on brake lines to stop a train.[38]

Besides the damage they did to railroad property, bindlemen were also responsible for countless fires in barns, shacks, grainfields, and buildings along their routes. Newspapers in the Napa Valley maintained extremely close and detailed tabs on fires attributed to bindlemen and if their accounts are accurate and typical, then bindlemen (usually accidentally) caused considerable damage each year, usually when their campfires got out of control. One disastrous conflagration, in September 1889, consumed the entire wheat crop on the C. H. Holmes ranch in Knight's Valley, west of Healdsburg. After extinguishing the blaze, several travelers and neighboring ranchers pursued, caught, and roughed up three bindlemen before sending them on their way considerably worse for the experience. Yet another group of fires was caused by bindlemen sleeping in barns. One of the largest of these fires exploded across the C. A. Richards ranch two miles southeast of St. Helena in August 1888. A group of bindlemen cooking dinner apparently failed to contain their campfire, which somehow got away from them, consuming Richards's barn, fifty tons of hay, horse harnesses, and farming machinery worth two thousand dollars. One of the more gruesome fires destroyed a barn on W. L. Hooper's ranch in Knight's Valley in November 1892. Sifting through the smoldering ruins, investigators discovered human bones and a melted whiskey bottle. On this basis investigators concluded that a drunk bindleman had fallen asleep while smoking and had been consumed in the fire. And so it went. Granaries, farm animals, hogs, hay, fences, and machinery commonly burned in fires attributed to careless bindlemen traveling between jobs.[39]

Because they vandalized property and caused so much damage both inside and outside of the agricultural districts, railroad authorities relentlessly waged war to prevent bindlemen from riding trains or residing on property adjoining company lines. "Town clowns," as local police were known, could be just as nasty. Consequently, wherever they went, bindlemen feared arrest, if not for drinking, fighting, trespassing, or disturbing the peace, then for some other trumped-up charge. Often there was no reason at all, other than their presence in a community. Passing through Vacaville looking for work in July 1889, a group of bindlemen lay down to rest on a pile of straw while waiting for some promised jobs on a nearby ranch. The *Vacaville Reporter* reported them dozing off, "dreaming of the sweet bye and bye with the hopes of better things," just as "eagle-eyed officers" happened by. Rousting the men out of their sleep, Constable Frank Long, assisted by Deputy G. L. Parker, hauled them off to "the calaboose" where the crime docket later read: "arrested for sleeping."[40]

In any town a cop might stop a bindleman at any time, take him in for questioning, beat him up, and throw him in jail. One old bindleman recalled how he was regularly arrested by deputies on the grounds that they did not like his looks or objected to his clothes. Sometimes town marshals would swoop down on bindlemen, "cleaning them out" from around train depots and moving them along the lines with a "liberal dose of lead." To push men along, authorities would often cite the need to protect the health of the community from diseased men. Sometimes all it took to bring down the wrath of town authorities was a loud celebration or a late-night round of song. After one group of bindlemen was discovered passing a bottle around while trespassing in a boxcar full of hides parked on a siding by a tannery near Napa in December 1893, the local police department showed no mercy. "It was found necessary to load the aggregation upon a truck and escort them to the jail," reported the *Napa Register*. "Between times our reporter learned that their names were Blinky Joe, Red Mike, Hobo Sam, Comical Jim, and Santa Claus."[41]

Every bindleman with more than a year on the road knew that communities differed widely in their policies toward them. Some were entirely welcoming. For example, stranded in Oceanside, a bindleman could mooch a beef stew and sour beer dinner at several saloons in exchange for scrubbing floors. And while moving through Los Angeles and the San Joaquin Valley, men learned that police rarely bothered train riders. Other towns also recognized that bindlemen were necessary and tolerated them so long as they stayed on the outskirts and did not actually venture into the respectable sections.[42]

On the other hand, there were a few farming districts that broke with the general invitation to all sources of labor and firmly closed their doors to bindlemen. One was the Yulupa Valley in Sonoma County, where the *Santa Rosa Daily Republican* reported that "there is no place . . . where a tramp finds less encouragement, less food and less opportunity for employment." Of all the places that bindlemen passed through, Colton, on the east side of Los Angeles, was the most hostile. There town police scrutinized every train and handed out a six-month jail sentence to any bindleman whom they did not beat. Bindlemen usually dropped off trains before entering the Colton switching yards, tramped around the town, and caught the same train on the fly as it pulled out on the west side bound for Los Angeles. Similarly, others would go hundreds of miles out of their way just to miss "San Berdu," as San Bernardino was also known, because of random police sweeps that could catch hundreds of bindlemen in the railroad yard. "That is how San Berdu built its courthouse and its schools," claimed one old bindleman of the fines imposed. But San Bernardino and Colton were not the only towns bindlemen learned to avoid as they beat their way. Tramping through the Napa Valley, for example, bindlemen detoured around Rutherford, where they encountered an aggressive policy of herding men along and routing them from resting spots.[43]

Often, there was no way to predict how people would react. A community like Turlock, for example, could be confusing. Because bindlemen played such an important role in the local harvest, the town extended many courtesies to them as they passed through. Turlock businessman John Mitchell even went so far as to hire a cook to bake beans and bread, which he then fed free of charge to bindlemen frequenting the hobo hotels on West Main Street. Bar owners also extended courtesies to bindlemen, providing each man who was out of work with at least one free drink per day. At the same time, however, Constable Jim Parker and Deputy George Spires took advantage of bindlemen hungover on the free booze by patrolling John Mitchell's barns and the haylofts around "Cannibal Street" and the "Barbary Coast" where bindlemen slept, often arresting men in the morning as they awoke. The officers then fined each man up to three dollars and turned them loose, only later to return and arrest them again.[44]

Vagrancy was the most common charge against bindlemen. Section 647 of the California State Penal Code, as amended by the legislature in April 1892, specified that "every person (except a California Indian) without visible means of living, who has the physical ability to work and who does not seek employment nor labor" could be arrested as a common vagrant, jailed up to six months, and fined. Additionally, the law stated that every person who roamed from place to place without any lawful business, every idle or dissolute person who wandered the streets at late or unusual hours of the night and every person who lodged in any barn, shed, shop, or outhouse without the permission of the owner could also be arrested as a vagrant. In a town like Pomona, vagrancy statutes were taken so seriously that between 1888 and 1911 vagrancy vied with intoxication and disturbing the peace as the most common crime. "It has . . . been remarked on more than one occasion," observed the *Sacramento Bee*, "that if Christ were to come to the Golden State, He could be and probably would be jailed as a tramp under our vagrancy laws."[45]

Rural newspapers warned readers to lock their doors against bindlemen, while editorials encouraged peace officers to arrest bindlemen quickly and criticized judges for being too lenient on them. Routinely denying jury trials to vagrant bindlemen, many rural communities ultimately devised onerous provisions resembling the regulations used to keep Indian field hands in check during the Gold Rush. For bindlemen, this meant that no matter where they were arrested or how unjust their arrest or the charges against them, they could not get a public defender or trial by jury. Even in those rare instances where they could obtain a lawyer and were granted a hearing, they rarely received more than five or ten minutes in court.[46]

Because vagrancy laws were so frequently used against them, bindlemen understandably feared the police, courts, and civil authorities throughout the state. They learned that a constable, deputy sheriff, or policeman upon noticing them could, after a few questions, label them "bums" or "suspicious characters" and slam them in jail. "No one can tramp about the country without feeling the effect of the vagrancy law," wrote Ben Reitman. "If a boy keeps going, he will be arrested for vagrancy on an average of once every six weeks; and it is during one of these stays in jail that he makes up his mind to go home or become a criminal. It is much easier to do the latter . . . the vagrancy law makes many tramps criminals." Often bindlemen were charged with crimes someone else had committed, this being a way some police departments solved cases. Quickly tried and found guilty, the innocent bindlemen would be sentenced to long terms in jail and the cases closed. Distraught and driven to despair, at least one bindleman arrested in October 1891, for a crime he had not committed, hung himself in the St. Helena jail with strips of cloth torn from a blanket. Some men went insane while in jail and were committed to the state asylum.[47]

In many agricultural communities, the very first person arrested every year was a bindleman. Usually jailed for vagrancy, his arrest would be announced in the local newspaper as a warning to all bindlemen in the area. Local police found this an easy way to establish the town's tolerance level. But the vagrancy statute had other uses as well. Quite often, police used vagrancy statutes as a way to keep bindlemen on the move without arresting them. Some officials were more enthusiastic about the technique than others. In Marysville, for example, men were initially welcomed during the hop harvest, but town authorities maintained a vigilant eye. When growers became overwhelmed by hop pickers from every destination, police began arresting bindlemen for passing forged checks and for stealing bindles, coats, pants, and boots. Even after the harvest was over, the town would be full of idle men, some of them so bad off that they would break into a bunkhouse locker for a watch or suit of clothes, or walk off with a horse collar from the pavilion stable. Fed up, police would conduct roundups and raids, informing any idle men "to go to work or get out of town."[48]

When bindlemen began piling up in Marysville in November 1911, the chief of police blamed a spate of robberies and crimes on the newcomers and directed Marshal C. J. McCoy to begin cleaning "suspicious" and "bad looking characters" out of the camps along the Yuba River. Within a few days, thirty bindlemen were in jail and the camps had disintegrated, even though there was no hard evidence linking migratory workers to the crimes. Two years later authorities repeated the sweep, driving almost two hundred bindlemen out of town and arresting 596 men between July 1 and October 1. Asked to choose between beating their way or staying in jail, most left town immediately. Those not departing immediately were "given a taste of prison fare," then allowed to choose between a heavy sentence or a suspended one contingent on their departure. This was called "floating the men." Employed regularly, it was primarily an effort at avoiding jail costs after rounding up scores of bindlemen. A floater who returned to town would be immediately arrested. While lawyers and courts frequently questioned the legality and morality of this system of internal deportation, thousands of homeless men were nevertheless shuffled along to the next town by law enforcement officials who preferred to pass the problem to another jurisdiction.[49]

Asked to choose between jail and hitting the road, most bindlemen took the next train out, and pleased by the periodic sweeps and roundups, newspapers praised police for cleansing their communities of drifters. "The officers in . . . town have taken this manner of getting rid of the tramp element," wrote the *Napa Register*, "thus saving much expense to the county." But getting run out of town was the least of what bindlemen faced at the hands of law enforcement. Arrested for vagrancy, they were often subjected to various county workhouse schemes and programs. Around Pomona, where men regularly dropped off trains along the main route to San Francisco, communities strongly supported such measures. "Southern California needs a whole flock of chain gangs," proclaimed the editor of the *Pomona Daily Times* in January 1889. Around Fairfield, a popular jumping-off point along the state's main east–west railroad line, men arrested for vagrancy were set to repairing and paving roads on a bread and water diet; bindlemen arrested for vagrancy in Stockton broke rock while serving out their sentences. On April 27, 1896, the *Sacramento Bee* suggested that in times of farm labor shortage growers might naturally turn to a system in which vagrant bindlemen would be supplied to pick fruit at public expense. "It must certainly come to this sooner or later," argued the *Bee*, "and the sooner the better for all concerned, even the tramps, and vagabonds themselves."[50]

During the farm labor shortage of 1902, rural authorities did toy with the idea of allowing growers to pay the fines of bindlemen arrested for vagrancy in exchange for their work in the harvest. But it was not until bindlemen—jailed as vagrants in San Bernardino early that year—were actually forced to work off their sentences in the fields that the issue was resolved. Angered by the program, local citizens protested to the San Bernardino Superior Court, which considered the matter and ruled the local vagrancy law violated the California constitution. "The Court holds," reported the *Sacramento Bee* in February, "that if roaming about from place to place, without any lawful business, was a crime, that any man, no matter how wealthy, traveling about the country seeking health or pleasure, without any lawful business, was guilty of committing a crime, and under definition of the offense . . . was guilty of being a vagrant."[51]

Not everyone agreed, though, and even after the court ruling, bindlemen arrested for vagrancy continued to be put to work. As late as October 1909, Yuba County deputy sheriff Steven Howser was supervising work crews of vagrants who were "given a chance to earn board and lodging" and "get in and dig for their keep." Justifying his action on the grounds that chain-gang labor would hold down the commission of crime and save the county money, Howser also predicted that bindlemen would give Yuba County a wide berth as a result of his program. "Vagrants and petty larceny thieves will commence to steer clear of Yuba County," he told the *Marysville Evening Democrat*, "and their absence will be appreciated."[52]

ℬ

Bindlemen called being arrested "being vagd." It was the most common "crime" in California, accounting for about one in three of all convictions in 1906, and one of ten during 1909–10. That most vagrants were bindlemen is suggested in the fact that one of three men arrested for vagrancy had not been in the county where they were arrested for more than one month, and that half had not been in the county where they were arrested beyond one week. At one time or another, a large proportion of the state's bindlemen probably spent time in jail on vagrancy charges, usually for two or three days, but occasionally for as much as two weeks or a month. The net effect of such harassment was to generate and reinforce among most bindlemen profound antisocial attitudes. "After a few such experiences," explained Charles Ashleigh, "a man becomes embittered, and loses respect for the law."[53]

The experience of going to jail was humiliating and demeaning. County jails were notoriously unsanitary. Recalling his stay in a dark, vermin-infested facility, one bindleman told the Commission on Industrial Relations that he had nothing to do other than to "lay on a bunk and sleep in a little dark cell and have no physical exercise to speak of." In Sacramento, jailed vagrants got sixty days in clean, well-ventilated cells holding a few men each. But if imprisoned in the Imperial Valley, they might receive ten days in a crowded, seven-by-nine-foot cell with sixteen bunks, often with thirty men, a single toilet, and mattresses placed on the floor. Those incarcerated in San Joaquin County received between five and ten days and also slept on dirty mattresses on the floor. If jailed in Santa Clara County, bindlemen served five days for vagrancy and were fed and housed for 10 ½ cents per day, while those jailed in San Diego were allocated 37 ½ cents per day. Reporting on thirty-three bindlemen held on vagrancy charges in the Monterey County Jail in February 1902, the *San Luis Obispo Breeze* noted that there were cots to accommodate only twenty-five men, the rest being forced to sleep on the floor. Of these prisoners, the newspaper observed: "They are honest working men and boys who are simply out of employment."[54]

Before entering their cells, bindlemen were usually searched by a desk sergeant, and their age, sex, and nationality recorded. Salient details noted in police logbooks were place of birth, scars, hair color, eye color, complexion, weight, height, tattoos, gold teeth, bracelets, rings, diseases, past arrest records, and profession. Personal items would be taken from them and sealed in an envelope, and the men were compelled to wash. Often they would also be sprayed with some disinfectant. When they finally got out, bindlemen serving time for vagrancy were often worse off than before. In his book *Passage of the County Jail* (1920), Stuart Queen described a bindleman released from a vagrancy term as having no money, no job, no friends. "His muscles are soft from idleness," wrote Queen, "his skin is sallow, and his lungs are filled with stale prison air."[55]

Bindlemen knew that they were most likely to be arrested as vagrants in certain rural counties. In 1906, the worst "vag" counties were Fresno, Los Angeles, Monterey, Placer, Santa Clara, Sacramento, San Bernardino, Solano, and Ventura, which together accounted for 54 percent of the state's 2,880 vagrancy arrests. Bindlemen also knew that they were more likely to be arrested as vagrants at certain times of the year. From March until September, when they were needed to tend and harvest crops, they were arrested far less often than during slack times from October through April. In the Southern California Washington navel orange growing districts, vagrancy arrests reversed the general pattern, relaxing during the winter to facilitate the flow of harvest workers, increasing during the summer as labor requirements declined.[56]

Besides the unceasing fear of arrest and ill treatment by police and railroad authorities, bindlemen also faced other threats along the tracks. On occasion, the threats came from other workingmen—as when two bindlemen boarded a train leaving the station at Napa in July 1890 and began "bumming" money from passengers. Seeing them, members of a local threshing crew became incensed. A brawl developed, with the fight moving up and down the car. The battle became so furious that several passengers were nearly thrown out the windows. Eventually, one bindleman jumped off the front of the car, and the other jumped from the rear, with nearly fatal results. "When he jumped off he was between the train and a car, which was standing on the side of the track" reported the *Napa Daily Journal*, "and came very near being thrown under the wheels, as the train was moving rapidly."[57]

More often, bindlemen clashed with authority figures like police and labor bosses. Because many conductors and other railroad personnel allowed bindlemen to ride unmolested, and because most town authorities could or would not keep them off the lines, railroad companies hired their own private police. These hard-nosed "cinder dicks," "bulls," and "shacks" (brakemen), as they were known, often followed a policy of fierce intimidation. A typical technique was to let the train pull out, then stop it on an isolated spur somewhere down the tracks and make the rounds gun in hand collecting fares from anyone found stowing away. If a man could not come up with the ticket price while riding from Bakersfield to Fresno he got a night in jail. "In the morning a judge asked you about your origins, destination and family," recalled one bindleman. "You might not get out of town without a run in with railroad bulls, and might have to hitch a ride."[58]

If their memoirs and reminiscences are accurate, bindlemen commonly endured beatings, shootings, and extortion at the hands of railroad authorities. A few of these enforcers were notorious brutes who thought nothing of tossing a man off a train traveling at sixty miles per hour. One of these men was a character known as "Gila Monster," a vicious shack who roamed Southern Pacific's sunset route from Yuma to Los Angeles and was rumored to have killed twenty-five men between 1914 and 1917. Another was "Mac the Knife," who while working around Fresno was said to have charged bindlemen the exorbitant fare of ten cents per one hundred miles and twenty cents a night. Yet another such individual was "Big Red," a brakeman who liked to lock men inside boxcars and nail doors to reefers shut until the end of a run.[59]

Bindlemen commonly planned their travel in such a way as to diminish or avoid encounters with railroad authorities. They had good reason for taking such precautions. While all shacks and railroad bulls were not the ogres that they were often made out to be, many were indeed tenacious, sadistic killers who hunted bindlemen, often terrorizing them with the heavy lanterns they carried. Surrounded by thick protective wire, these lanterns made for nasty weapons. Bindlemen had their noses smashed, heads bashed, and front teeth knocked out by bulls wielding these devices. Occasionally, bindlemen planned and took revenge, but such attacks only fueled the anger and determination of some shacks and bulls, who would then retaliate with escalated violence. Shacks and bulls employing such tactics were given a wide berth, and bindlemen frequently identified their whereabouts in signs on water towers. "Pay or hit the grit," a warning might read.[60]

One bindleman who left a particularly detailed account of his encounters with railroad detectives was Henry McGuckin, who traveled throughout California and the Pacific Northwest for more than a decade. On one occasion, McGuckin was riding the front end of a fast passenger train when a hard-boiled railroad detective booted off a gang of bindlemen. As the train started up, the men all climbed back on board; within one mile the train again stopped and the detective returned, evicted the stowaways, and warned someone would likely get hurt. "We climbed back on as the train pulled out," McGuckin recalled,

> and in five minutes, the door to our boxcar was flung open, and out came 'Hard Boiled,' a big 45 in his hand. He fired a shot in the air and pulled the cord to stop the train. But we had cut the cord, so nothing happened. Then I could see the dick was crazy mad, so we went hand over hand out on the engine water tender. For almost too long we hung there with our fingers clutching the edge of the tender, our bodies and legs whipped by the wind, hanging in space, and that train wasn't going less than 60. Well, most of the boys had jumped before the train reached top speed, and when the conductor sent his brakeman over the tender to stop the train, we dropped off. My arms were like sticks, and my fingers flattened-out like pancakes. I was skinned up too.

It was a long time before McGuckin could stand up and walk.[61]

Railroad bulls and town authorities were not the only characters that bindlemen encountered on their travels. Outlaws and bandits routinely preyed upon them, especially during harvest times, when trains were loaded with migrant workers and most every man's pocket was packed with wages. Heavily armed and well organized into gangs known as "pushes," the robbers would pass from one car to another or lurk about the rail yards, methodically pillaging each bindleman they encountered. This is what happened to John Pache, a bindleman employed on a farm two miles south of Yuba City. Walking along the railroad tracks near the cannery, he was attacked by three men who beat him severely and robbed him of fifteen dollars. "There is no clue as to the identity of the robbers, and they will probably never be apprehended," reported the *Marysville Daily Democrat*. "There was no protection from these blood suckers," cautioned William Dimmit, a bindleman writing in the socialist publication *Industrial Pioneer*.[62]

Bindlemen had few defenses against these "hijacks," "stickup men," and "vampires of the road," since appealing to authorities typically earned no sympathy, and if they fought back, they could be killed. Some were robbed and murdered in their sleep. This is apparently what happened to Burge and Homer Emmert in November 1904. Making their way north from Bakersfield they were discovered by railroad bulls on a Sunday morning near Strathearn Station along the main coast line of the Southern Pacific in Simi Valley thirty miles north of Los Angeles. One brother was thrown off the train, and the other jumped clear, and they

were both observed by residents camping for the night near the water tank awaiting the next freight train. Monday morning a merchant making his usual trip to
the station with the mail discovered the bodies of both men lying across a switch.
Summoned to investigate, the coroner determined that they had been brained
with a big club that was found near the bodies. Although the sheriff notified all
officers in towns along the coast to look out for and arrest "all suspicious looking
characters," authorities held out little hope of apprehending whoever was responsible for the crime. "Robbery must have been the motive . . . as the pockets
of both men had been rifled of their contents," reported the *Oxnard Courier*.
"Death must have come instantly, for there was no evidence of a struggle."[63]

෩

By the time they reached age forty, most bindlemen were worn out; only one in
five remained on the circuit after this age. Unlike old men in the steel industry
who might turn to sons and daughters, or aged coal miners who could at least
earn a little money picking slate in the coal breakers, old bindlemen had no way
to earn money once their days on the move were over. While a Japanese field
hand could fall back on kin and prefecture associations for support, or borrow
money from *keiyaku-nin*, bindlemen lacked any safety net. Unable to ride trains,
aged bindlemen who did not die under lonesome and pathetic circumstances usually ended up in the urban skid rows, forced to sell their possessions to obtain
money to live. If they were lucky, someone from the "Mission of Living Waters"
or some similar rescue mission would try to retrieve their bodies and thereby save
their souls. Few bindlemen were rescued. Living out their last days as stubble-
faced men sprawled on a stoop, they begged for scraps or existed on handouts.[64]

Most did not even make it that far. Eventually the killing pace, exhaustion,
work, and bad food exacted a toll. Drifting from crowded, lice-infested bunkhouses and crude labor camps during the summer to humid flophouses and rescue missions in the winter, bindlemen were constantly exposed to unsanitary surroundings. When the California Commission of Immigration and Housing
studied bindlemen one summer it found them a "pathetic and melancholy lot."
Half were in "fair to bad" physical condition, and one in five were "unclean in
their clothes or body."[65]

Other observers were distressed by the number of men who had rasping,
wheezing, or persistent hacking coughs. Inevitably they contracted some disease
or passed it along. "The floating laborer acts as a distributing agent for many diseases," reported the commission's sanitary adviser after analyzing health records
throughout California. "They bring into the rural districts . . . venereal diseases . . .
typhoid . . . small pox . . . and in this way the dysentaries are carried from South
to North." Often men died from minor infections or afflictions that most people could survive. Whatever the causes of their death, countless bindlemen would
be found in their bedrolls all alone at the end of a switching yard, in a barn, or
beneath a trestle. They would be buried without even a name on the wooden
cross marking their grave, and coroner's inquests invariably concluded that they
had expired of "exposure, old age, and malnutrition."[66]

CHAPTER TWENTY-TWO

As Rotten as Ever

Jungle Camps, Slave Markets,
and the Main Stem

As they beat their way by railroad, bindlemen learned to live with dirt. Dust, wood sparks, and other debris soiled and burned their clothes. Railcars added their mix of dust, splinters, and grease. Rainstorms drenched and shrunk their coats, the sun bleached and faded their shirts, and various snags along the way—branches, barbed wire, and tools—ripped and shredded their pants. Cut off from polite society and living a rugged and transitory existence, most migrant bindle-stiffs wore the uniform of drifters. There was no way of avoiding it. "A man cannot spend continuous days and nights in his clothes, beating trains, fighting soot . . . sleeping anywhere, and maintain a good front," wrote Jack London.[1]

Contrary to the common belief that bindlemen hated to wash, most actually took great pride in personal hygiene and did their best to remain clean. Frequently delousing themselves by bathing in rivers and boiling their clothes, they cut each other's hair, mended their socks, and tried to keep as neat as possible. "This picture you see of the hobo with the patches all over his coat and pants and all that does not fit . . . it was a matter of pride to keep a pretty good pair of pants and shirt and decent shoes so you could go, you know, be cleaned up and go looking for a job," recalled Hood River Blackie to an interviewer at the California State Railroad Museum in Sacramento. "I've even known them to carry some really nice clothes in a packsuit and maybe get to some town and clean up and walk up town. You'd never dream that was a hobo."[2]

No matter how conscientious bindlemen were, no matter how often they washed their clothes or how attentive they were to personal hygiene, after a month on the road their bindles became repositories for lice. As a result, many lodging places, knowing the vermin-infested state of their packages, refused to allow the men or their bindles on the premises. Like the ancient Chinese proverb, most bindlemen had too many lice to feel the itch. "All they possessed," recalled the tramp author Morrison Swift, "were the things they stood in." Road weary

FIGURE 50. Bindlemen dining in the municipal lodging house, Fresno, ca. 1913. Courtesy of the Pop Laval Collection, Fresno, California.

and usually in need of a decent change of clothing, bindlemen were "seen as stray dogs . . . and everyone knew it," explained Fred Thompson.[3]

Stiff, aching, and filthy from travel, bindlemen could not anticipate what conditions would greet them on the farms. A recurring dream, some admitted, was that upon arriving they would collapse into a clean bed heaped with soft pillows and freshly laundered sheets. Some got their wish. Although later commentators would assert that while working the harvest bindlemen drifted between camps ranging from bad to atrocious, the situation was in fact far more complex. Housing conditions varied from farm to farm and even among individual agricultural districts. Many farms went to great lengths to design, build, and operate labor camps that, while plain and utilitarian, nevertheless adequately sheltered field hands. A few even went so far as to pick sites that were sheltered and aesthetically pleasing, sometimes even sacrificing valuable land to construct substantial dormitories, complete with outhouses, a kitchen, showers, and recreation facilities. Methods and materials, along with designs and locations, changed over time, ranging from clapboard structures set on posts driven into the ground and framed structures on brick foundations to adobe homes with whitewashed walls and neat cottages with large communal gardens.[4]

Working around Fresno, bindlemen gravitated to the estate of M. Theo Kearney, an enigmatic, well-groomed social gadfly who was often referred to as the "Raisin King of California" and the "Prince of Fresno." Few bindlemen ever actually met or saw the imperious, ruthless, autocratic, overbearing Kearney. But all who worked for him reaped the benefits of his vision. A wheeler and dealer, Kearney in 1874 took control of a development known as the Central California Colony, and through aggressive advertising methods, sold west Fresno desert land to hardworking colonists, thereby transforming it into a veritable garden. With profits from sales, and from foreclosing when the settlers could not meet their payments during the depression years of the early 1890s, Kearney then purchased Fruit Vale Estate, and in 1889, just as the raisin industry was emerging, embarked on a grand scheme to develop a raisin empire. By 1900 he had organized the California Raisin Growers Association and constructed an ultramodern, 5,400-acre farm. Connected to Fresno by an eleven-mile-long avenue complete with two graceful curves to interrupt the monotony of the drive and some fifty thousand ornamental shrubs and trees, Fruit Vale Estate was so beautiful and sported so many comforts and innovations that bindlemen must surely have thought that they had died and gone to farmworker heaven when they traveled on the long boulevard and first caught sight of the farm. A cross between a small city, European château, and factory farm, Fruit Vale Estate boasted innumerable buildings, including a carriage house, icehouse, water tower, brandy distillery, winery, creamery and milk skimming plant, railroad spur, cooperage plant, windmills, stables, wells, underground meat storage and wine cellars, blacksmith shops, packing sheds, assorted barns, a two-story adobe headquarters building, and a number of small cottages for seventy-five permanent employees. Bindlemen bunked in one of several large, two-story dormitories with wraparound verandas and screened porches that were probably the best farmworker housing in the state. Within easy walking distance, men found everything they needed—a grocery store, post office, "tea house," landscaped park, "refreshment room," garden, even a five-hundred-foot grapevine arbor tended by Japanese field hands.[5]

Every August and September, more than five hundred bindlemen and locals worked at Fruit Vale harvesting raisin grapes. For two dollars per month, a man could sleep in a private room with an iron bedstead, woven wire and spring bottom mattress, sheets, and pillow; three dollars bought the same accommodations with electric lights and slightly more ornamental furnishings. All of the rooms were cleaned daily, and men had their clothes and laundry washed for free. Men who did not want to pay for a room were given a bed of dry hay and access to washrooms free of charge. A bell roused the men out of their beds each morning and summoned them to a large and hearty breakfast prepared by a staff of Chinese cooks. They could also snack in the central dining room at all hours of the day or night. Every morning they washed in the exquisite luxury of hot showers. Those wishing to drink liquor, gamble, and carouse traveled to town on Saturday evenings by means of Fruit Vale's daily wagon service and returned on Sunday afternoon.[6]

Bindlemen could also find good food and housing at the Sacramento Valley Sugar Beet Company (SVSBC), which housed men in comfortable camps, provided unlimited access to a company dining room, and fed them substantial meals supplemented by fresh produce, poultry, and pork. At least once a year, usually at Christmas or Thanksgiving, bindlemen would also be treated to a turkey dinner with all the trimmings. So important was the welfare of farmworkers that a supervisor who reported directly to company president E. C. Hamilton personally looked after their camps, maintaining them in sanitary and attractive condition, making sure that all lumber, wire, fencing, and stove wood was neatly stacked, and that everything was in a "ship-shape manner."[7]

Doing almost as well were bindlemen working in the southern San Joaquin Valley for Henry Miller and Charles Lux, two German immigrant cattle and land barons. Known as the "Clemenceau of the San Joaquin Plains," Miller, who had changed his name from Heinrich Kreiser shortly after arriving in the United States in the early 1850s, hired between eight hundred and one thousand bindlemen to harvest the grain crops required to feed the vast herds he ran on dozens of ranches and farms scattered over nearly one million acres between Los Banos and the Tehachapi Mountains. As a condition of employment, Miller's bindlemen accepted close supervision. Because Miller was a stickler for detail, bindlemen often found themselves corrected and disciplined by detailed written guidelines Miller passed along as he toured his operations by buggy. For example, a man wearing loose-fitting long sleeves while operating a mowing machine would be called over and ordered to roll them up to prevent them from getting caught in the mower blades. Those who failed to obey instantly or who did not completely carry out such orders were fired. But bindlemen who heeded the instructions benefited considerably.[8]

Miller believed that nothing was more critical in maintaining a stable and productive labor force and minimizing turnover than good food and housing. To that end, Miller constructed first-class bunkhouses, equipped them with all of the latest conveniences, and required laborers to keep them immaculate and sanitary. Men daily wiped and cleaned all implements and stored them under cover in screened cabinets. Following Miller's standing orders, they also washed their clothes once a week, bathed daily in horse troughs or nearby canals, and swept out their bunk rooms regularly. If anyone found bedbugs, they were directed to "pour scalding water over the floors, walls, and blankets."[9]

Bindlemen employed by Miller also ate exceptionally large and well-prepared meals. On every one of Miller's camps, cooks provided plenty of vegetables, which Miller believed made men "more contented" and attracted a better class of workers. On Buttonwillow headquarters ranch, fifty to seventy-five bindlemen could buy various luxuries on credit from a ranch store and enjoyed a big Sunday meal once a week. Chinese cooks baked bread in Dutch ovens and regularly spread out meals of beans, pork, dried apples, prunes, milk, and butter. Even stray bindlemen could always count on a meal, as it was the custom to set five or six additional places in case someone straggled in for dinner, which was very common.[10]

Because meals were so large and well prepared, bindlemen behaved boisterously at dinner, grabbing their share the moment it hit the tables. They also frequently enjoyed meals supplemented with wild game. When work slowed on the Miller and Lux ranch near Firebaugh, the foreman would send men into the countryside to catch feral hogs. Back at the ranch, the animals were put in a pen, fed scraps, and, when good and fat, slaughtered for some special occasion.[11]

Midway between the SVSBC and the Miller and Lux empire, and about thirty miles east of Fruit Vale Estate, bindlemen could also find relatively good facilities at the Great Western Vineyard Company located in the Kings River bottomland five miles north of Reedley. Believing that the best way to attract and keep good men and get the most out of them was to treat them well, Great Western management built and maintained five neat, sanitary labor camps, each fitted with washtubs and hot showers that harvesters were required to use regularly. Strategically placed throughout the company's two thousand acres of vineyards and responsible for all work in the surrounding four-hundred-acre block, the camps further enhanced efficiency by eliminating time wasted traveling to and from work. "Although the buildings for the hands were constructed years before the law was passed requiring employers to provide certain specified housing and sanitary conditions for their employees, the Great Western Vineyard Company had their buildings fitted up far better along those lines than the law now requires," wrote Reedley farmer and local historian John C. McCubbin early in the century. Bindlemen found it extremely easy to reach the camps. Upon arriving in Reedley, all they had to do was step off one train, wait a few hours, and take another train north on the Santa Fe Railroad spur line running directly to the California Wine Association's Wahtoke Winery. Bindlemen then had only to stroll along two wide avenues lined with rows of fig trees. At the end of each avenue was a camp. "Everything around the grounds at the camps, including the implements and work stock, always presented the same neat clean appearance that was to be found throughout the entire vineyard," wrote McCubbin.[12]

But on many other farms, living conditions were scandalous. All too often, farm labor camps were ugly, decrepit, and dirty. Shower facilities might consist of a pipe running from a water tank to a cubicle surrounded by burlap sacks suspended from posts. To wash themselves, men waded through mud and stood on a few rocks under a tin spray device or counted themselves lucky to bathe among the mosquitoes in irrigation canals and ditches. On many jobs, men slept, as the *California Fruit Grower* explained in March 1912, "under a tree or in a bunk attached upon a wall." Men also slept in tents, lean-tos, or in crude structures fitted with tiers of bunks so dirty that men complained they were "engaged in perpetual warfare against lice."[13]

It was a rare pleasure to find a camp whose bunkhouse did not reek of body odors, where men did not feed on rye bread greased with sowbelly, where a large percentage of occupants were not down with dysentery, and where dishes and utensils were not dirty. So miserable was most field labor housing that it was denounced not only in the pages of the general press, but in agricultural publications as well. Even a journal like *Technical World*, normally concerned with more bookish matters, told its readers how "dirt and wretched misery . . . prevailed in a great many of the western fruit camps." Elaborating further, it reported how, "migratory workers leave one camp only to go to another of the same kind . . . spend the best part of the year in temporary shacks, vermin infested bunkhouses, in leaky tents, or under the open sky." Confirming these conditions, the California

State Bureau of Labor Statistics found that one in five labor camps was "very bad," while a bindleman testifying before the U.S. Commission on Industrial Relations explained: "I have been in camps where we would have a big clean up in the morning and we could fill two or three dishpans with flies . . . that would fall off the roof of the tent . . . the boys say that camps is just as rotten as ever."[14]

On most farms there was no alternative to bunkhouse fare. Growers recognized that hearty meals were essential to productive labor, and devoted considerable effort to raising livestock and grain necessary for feeding large numbers of men. On Rancho Tapo in Simi Valley, purchased by the Patterson Ranch Company of Oxnard in 1904, men were spread out in a dozen different camps and required an entirely separate ranch division devoted to feeding them. Numbers and weights of "animals killed for the ranch table," as company correspondence put it, rose and fell according to the harvest season and feeding demands. Ironically, these workers were not directly involved in farming. Engaged in subsidiary work supporting the American Beet Sugar Company, they raised horses, hogs, and mules, along with hay, grain, and vegetables, to feed workers at other ranches, often driving a herd of hogs from the Hare Camp on Rancho Tapo to Oxnard for butchering. But their operations were so large that they in turn required an entirely different subsidiary feeding operation to sustain their work supporting the main operation growing sugar beets and lima beans in Oxnard.[15]

While the quantity of meat on Rancho Tapo and other farming operations was never lacking, it was usually cheap. Bindlemen did not know it, but efforts to economize on food were due in large part to well-publicized studies by University of California economist Richard L. Adams, who, having already analyzed the economics of employing Japanese and Chinese laborers, turned to what he called "white laborers, or hobo or tramp laborers." Seeking to identify the attributes contributing to their docility, availability, and reliability, he dissected the costs of employing them and discovered that one-quarter of all expenses went for board. As a result, most bindlemen sat down to meals doled out according to a strict formula, devised by Adams, that aimed not so much at providing nutritious or delicious food as saving money by avoiding "foreign flavors," "elaborate meals," and "unfamiliar dishes." Because the largest of all expenditures was typically for meat, bindlemen seldom enjoyed a meal with roast beef or fried steaks, but instead were usually given meat in a stew. This allowed growers to utilize bones and other unsavory parts that could be easily disguised in gravy and sopped up with bread. Generally bindlemen also ate meat substitutes, like eggs, milk, dried fruit; and packinghouse by-products like hog jowls, oxtails, pig's feet, sausages, "the lesser cuts," and lamb tongue.[16]

On some farms, bindlemen ate in dining halls where cooks cut down on food costs by trimming bread into half and quarter slices, because it was less wasteful than setting out uncut loaves, using soup bones twice, turning surplus and uneaten meat into hash, working leftover bread into puddings, and feeding the men drippings from fat rather than lard. Bindlemen were also denied certain foods that growers believed had a deleterious effect on productivity. For example, on many farms men were served lettuce and onions only at dinner, because Adams and other University of California economists claimed those foods had "sedative effects" that made men lethargic and worthless as field hands. Nevertheless, meals could often be the highlight of a hard day and hungry bindlemen would often begin assembling for dinner ten or fifteen minutes before a meal. When the doors to the dining hall opened on the Bellevue ranch, eight miles south of Bakersfield, men would rush forward and elbow one another for seats. "There was no 'You first, my dear Gaston,' or 'Please pass the biscuits,'" recalled one roustabout. "It was a case of joining the rush and grabbing food for yourself or you went hungry."[17]

ℰℯ

Because they were so poorly treated on the farms, so unwelcome and uncomfortable in rural towns, and so unable to afford lodging while on the move, bindlemen spent much of their time between jobs and train rides in rest stops and gathering points known as "harvest hotels" or, more commonly, "jungle camps." Jungle camps were located in shady thickets, under bridges, on the outskirts of towns, at division points, near railroad switching yards and junctions, next to refuse dumps, beside streams, close to water towers, and in dry creek beds away from public view. One government investigator discovered a permanent jungle camp on the outskirts of nearly every farm town in the San Joaquin Valley. Traveling south by train from Mount Shasta through Redding, radical journalist Jack Gaveel observed that the number of jungle camps increased as one moved into the Sacramento Valley, "until the whole state is covered with their wretchedness, a living condemnation of capitalist civilization." Echoing these observations, the *Industrial Worker* found that "wherever there is a railroad line through a farming or grain country, at every junction may be seen the jungle gangs."[18]

Some camps were small, well-kept, "one tomato can" affairs containing a dozen or so men. Others, like the big camps at Bakersfield, Porterville, Petaluma, Santa Rosa, and Hobo Hot Springs along Southern Pacific Railroad's main line were, in effect, huge rural slums spread out over a mile of woods and housing one hundred to six hundred men. Reeking of "hobo perfume"—a pungent mixture of wood smoke, decaying rubbish, coal, creosote, and human waste—such camps sent forth an odor announcing their presence far beyond the line of sight. Whether large or small, bindlemen always stocked jungle camps with extensive collections of junk: utensils fashioned of old kerosene and lard cans, frying pans made of broken shovel blades, benches constructed from split telephone poles, tables fashioned of boxcar doors set upon railroad ties. But the most useful tool was a soup can with the label still on it, which could serve as a coffee pot, coffee cup, or drinking cup—the paper label providing insulation to prevent the hot can from burning a man's hand.[19]

At the center of every jungle camp, bindlemen placed a large kettle or "boiling can," often referred to as "the true melting pot of trampdom." Kept perpetually simmering over a low fire, the pot typically contained a "mulligan stew" consisting of a basic gruel of boiled wheat and supplemented periodically with bacon rinds, purloined vegetables, old potatoes, soup bones, scrap meat "bummed" from a butcher or slaughterhouse, or perhaps a rooster or two rustled from a nearby chicken coop. A common fare was "hoboes delight"—alfalfa greens and bacon rinds. Heated, cooled, left standing, and replenished over a period of days, the soupy mush was generally served in the evening and often tasted, in the words of a correspondent for the *Industrial Union Bulletin*, like "shoe heels and cowhide with a few chips of birch thrown in for seasoning." When it reached the consistency of moldy muck, the concoction would be tossed and the kettle washed thoroughly. Before starting another stew, bindlemen would then fill the pot with water, bring it to a boil, and perform a combination laundry, bathing, and delousing operation.[20]

Although most bindlemen regarded jungle camps as temporary homes, a few used them as semipermanent, year-round residences, returning whenever out of work. Some communities were so well established that bindlemen elected "mayors" to oversee their operation and enforce rules. To wait out the winter, men might head for Goshen Junction, a jungle sprawling over one mile in the thickets beside the railroad tracks near the town of Goshen in the Central Valley. But if bindlemen wanted to continue working, they could also use jungle camps as work camps. For example, in the Imperial Valley each winter, hundreds of men flooded the jungle camps around El Centro and spent the season picking carrots, lettuce, tomatoes, and eggplant. According to Hood River Blackie, a man could "live good in a hobo jungle on $10 a week."[21]

Over time, each jungle camp developed its own code of acceptable behavior and means of enforcement, usually through various committees of bindlemen assigned to oversee specific aspects of daily life. While the "spud and gump" committee rustled up food, others cleaned the camp and gathered information on train movements. As in western logging and cow camps, in order to share a meal, a man had to contribute either food or work: "rent" consisted of a few minutes chopping wood, gathering brush, or washing pots. Those who did not abide by "the code of the road," as jungle laws were called, were labeled "jungle buzzards" and promptly kicked out.[22]

Unlike most other places, bindlemen felt in control while in the jungles. At the very least, they felt loosened from the constraints of traditional society and free to be themselves. Far from being anarchistic, "every man to himself" places, jungle camps provided a sense of camaraderie and fellowship that bindlemen seldom found elsewhere. Men passed their leisure around a communal kettle and campfire, swapping stories and trading information on jobs, wages, and train routes. Strangely, men could live for days together in the jungle camps and share a boxcar for long distances without ever learning each other's real names. Instead, they used "monicas" (monikers) or "noms de rail" based on localities, trades, and personal characteristics, as in California Pete, Frying Pan Jack, Lantern Jaw Mike, Sailor Jack, Scoop Shovel Scotty, Boxcar Bertha, Whiskey Joe, Sheepherder Charlie, Big Pete, Dirty Shirt Bob, and so on. Such names allowed bindlemen to drop all of the obligations of neighborly relations and maintain a degree of anonymity many of them craved.[23]

Bindlemen further separated themselves from the rest of society by using a unique version of the English language meant to confound any outsiders who heard it. The dialect of bindlemen combined the slang of countless immigrant and ethnic groups, a strong railroad vocabulary, and innumerable strange and vivid terms and original expressions. For example, bindlemen identified roving bandits as "yeggs," black men as "shines" or "dingies," inexperienced wanderers as "boomers," and railroad section hands as "snipes" or "jerries." Speaking of various aspects of train riding, they might announce their intention to "grab a rattler," meaning they were taking a slow freight. Or they might "gloom the belly of a drag," meaning they were going to ride the rods on a boxcar. Only a bindleman knew that a "blinky" was a one-eyed traveler, a "winky" a one-armed transient, that "mitts" described a one-armed man, that a "scissorbill" was a bindleman lacking in class consciousness, and that a "slave" was a wage earner. Other colorful words included "cans" (police stations), "crumbasses" (janitors in camp bunkhouses), "flops" (temporary shelters), "nags" (clothing), "punk" (bread), "dingbats" (tramps who were homeless, helpless, and harmless), "gay cats" (rookie bindlemen), and "the coast" (all territory west of the Sierra Nevada).[24]

Given the lack of enduring friendships and the absence of female contact, it is not surprising that the sex life of bindlemen deviated from early twentieth century heteronormative patterns—that it was anything but "normal." And given the masculine élan that characterized bunkhouse life on the farms, it was not surprising that foremen, ever vigilant for any odd or troublesome men or anything out of the norm, reported how on occasion they caught men having carnal relations with mares and sheep, a discovery that led to humiliation and immediate dismissal without pay. Just how common such sexual practices were is impossible to guess. That bindlemen were anything but "normal" seems confirmed by the extensive commentary on their homosexual activities. "Every hobo in the United States knows what 'unnatural intercourse' means," wrote Josiah Flynt in 1899, "talking of it freely, and according to my finding, every tenth man practices it, and defends his conduct."[25]

A large and apparently well-recognized homosexual subculture was sufficiently visible among bindlemen that journalists and university investigators could find it easily, although popular prejudices required commentators to always preserve the anonymity of homosexual bindlemen and to label their sexual preferences as "degenerate." Although there are no statistics, homosexuality among bindlemen was probably as fully developed as it was among the general population in New York, Chicago, or New Orleans, where the press reported it without alarm as a source of interest, not a threat. A well-known facet of life in prison, in West Coast lumber camps, and among sailors, homosexuality was acknowledged as being common among bindlemen for essentially the same reasons it was common elsewhere—because bindlemen were essentially outcasts (not quite degenerates) and because the all-male environment made it possible. That men might be born that way was neither accepted nor much considered.[26]

When Carleton Parker studied homosexuality as part of his larger inquiry into bindlemen, he found the practice quite common and attributed the phenomenon to environmental factors, especially harsh living conditions. Despite legal prohibition against oral sex and mutual masturbation, homosexuality was so widespread among Parker's sample of bindlemen that he described it as a greater "menace" than the ill effects of bad sanitation and malnutrition. To Parker, a reformer, same-sex relationships among bindlemen revealed a "vice," something acquired, not innate, a condition that could be treated, if only the correct diagnosis could be made. Bindlemen interviewed by University of Chicago sociologists at about the same time also supplied considerable amounts of impressionistic and anecdotal information about either having homosexual relations themselves or knowing of men who had homosexual partners. They told stories about railroad bulls catching men making out in the bushes and throwing them into the slammer together, and of how, on cold nights in the jungle, men moved close together, and how a man might wake up in the middle of the night with someone's legs wrapped around him. They also supplied a considerable lexicon of homosexual terms, including various categories of homosexuals or "fruiters," for example, "wolves" and "jockers," older men who had intercourse with boys known as "lambs," and men who liked to be "drained," that is, have oral sex. Some men happily admitted a preference for "boy-bumping" (having anal sex with young and inexperienced "punks" who sold their services to older men rather than working). "Give me a clean boy every time," declared one man who had been away from his wife for twelve years. "I'd rather go fifty-fifty with a fellow than to stay with the best woman in town." As a bindleman explained to a sociologist posing as a fellow traveler, "There's more people doing it than you think—it's natural."[27]

Bindlemen on occasion discussed homosexuality in their memoirs. William Edge, who hoboed with his friend Slim for more than a year, sharing beds, jobs, and saloons, rejected another companion after discovering his new partner was a "fairy." But others had an entirely different experience. Some sang about it. Before it was cleaned up, "The Big Rock Candy Mountain," one of the most famous of all hobo folksongs, described a boy being lured in by a wolf/jocker with promises of "cigarette trees," "lemonade springs," and "soda water fountains." Taking to the road as a teenager, John Worby had his first erotic adventures with a bindleman. Later he described a classic wolf/jocker-punk encounter in his book, *The Other Half: The Autobiography of a Tramp*. "I was beginning to marvel at the queer way in which this young man spoke," he recalled.

> His train of speech was getting more and more affectionate . . . and when he kept endearing me with his words, and caresses, I began to get a queer sensation which I could not for all the world of me account for. It was a sort of a soothing thrilling feeling which seemed to urge itself on as soon as he touched me. It seemed as if I didn't want him to take his hand off my thigh and when at last he did take it off I had a feeling of utter loneliness. I had never experienced anything like this before and the fact that I was with a man made it all the more difficult to explain.[28]

Besides homosexuality, bindlemen participated in other behaviors that gave outsiders pause. Most damaging among these was drug use. Although a few bindlemen were "snow birds" and used heroin or morphine, life in the jungles made it difficult to sustain a drug habit that required close and regular contact with a supplier. Easily identified by police, and frequently arrested for petty theft, "morphine fiends," as they were called, would usually be charged, quickly released, and then sent on their way "in order to get rid of them," as the Marysville police logbook noted. About three of one hundred bindlemen admitted to using opium and cocaine. Alcohol, however, was a different matter.[29]

By most accounts, everyone in the jungles enjoyed liquor, in almost any form, whether cheap wine, local rotgut whiskey, "fighting licker," or "alky" (an alcoholic concoction of dubious origins). Another popular concoction was "Skat" or "joy water," also known as "China gin," so named because bindlemen purchased it in Chinatown. Laced with opium and flavored with a few cigar butts that gave it an amber hue, the beverage was very popular. "A sip makes one feel perfectly like a millionaire," reported the *Marysville Evening Democrat*. "One drink is a full fledged promise of a crying jag, while two drinks constitute a guaranteed admission to any bug house in the state." When Carleton Parker studied bindlemen in 1914, he found that three of four were alcoholics, while another study of 482 bindlemen found that four of ten listed their main vice as drinking. Jungle camps always had their "canned heat brigade members," who settled for a little cheap Sterno (cooking fuel) and their "bay horse jockeys," who drank bay rum.[30]

Whatever the type of alcohol they ingested, bindlemen stretched out around a jungle campfire, intoxicated and rocking with laughter, could be a very convivial assembly. Occasionally, however, drunken tempers could rise and fights would break out. When a big brawl broke out in the jungle camp near the Napa railroad depot in the summer of 1895, local constables were called. "Some of them fought savagely before they would submit to arrest," reported the *Napa Daily Journal*. "They had been fighting among themselves before the officers got to them and one of their number was badly beaten up."[31]

An uneasy truce existed between bindlemen in their jungles and citizens of nearby communities. That did not mean that they were entirely welcome. Bindlemen were tolerated as a necessary part of agricultural society so long as they stayed within the confines of their camps. But frequently, town folk took action against the men. Around Marysville, where the number of bindlemen so proliferated at times that one local newspaper claimed "it is hardly safe for the people to be on the streets after nightfall," residents on July 22, 1901, formed a Citizens Protective Association (CPA) "to rid the community of the hundred or more denizens of the willows who have been in camp there during the past month." Over the next few months, the CPA raided camps along the Bear and Yuba rivers, driving their residents off and destroying everything. Elsewhere in the state, jungle camps were attacked and wrecked, as citizens shot up every utensil in sight, stomped the smaller cans used as drinking cups, removed the frying pans, scattered firewood, and burned any shelters. These tactics deprived bindlemen of necessities essential for life and caused them great hardships. But they were never successfully driven from the thickets.[32]

To alert and direct fellow travelers away from such inhospitable communities, bindlemen employed a generally agreed-upon set of symbols, a "modern hieroglyphics," "rolling graffiti of the road," and "boxcar art." Largely unseen by the average citizen, bindlemen knew where to look for symbols—on water tanks, fences, chicken sheds, gates, signs, telephone poles, bridges, boxcars, warehouses, train stations, and even trees. By deciphering them, bindlemen instantly learned not only the location of certain jungle camps and the attitudes of local police but also such important information as train schedules or the whereabouts of a friend who had passed by recently.[33]

By grouping stones in a specific fashion, a bindleman could leave a message for those who followed that a certain farm was a good or bad location to seek handouts. Markers for a welcoming, secure jungle camp might be signified by scribbling a chalk circle on a fence or post, with a line to the right or left showing the direction to go. A picture of a comb with its teeth warned of a vicious dog. Four symbols arranged in one sequence meant that a bindleman was entering a town that prohibited liquor but gave out free meals and had friendly police and a tolerable rescue mission. A slight rearrangement of the same symbols warned of a town that had saloons but where handouts were rare and the cops mean.[34]

❧

There always came a time each year when the rains commenced, work stopped, the jungle camps became uninhabitable, and no one could safely ride the trains. At this point, bindlemen ceased their perambulations and headed for the city. A few found employment on fruit ranches, but even for men accustomed to wintering in the cities, the adjustment was sometimes difficult. One man, known only as "Quizzy," passed November 1891 through January 1892 on a fruit ranch near Suisun. At first he found it a "lonely island" and longed for the city with its lights, noise, crowds, and diversions. Work consisted mostly of pruning fruit trees, and Quizzy was a "veritable greenhorn" compared to "professional" pruners. "The first week my hands were greatly blistered, my fingers twinged with pains akin to rheumatism, my face showed evidence of vicious upper-cuts given by mischievously bent limbs, while my body felt sore from the frequent falls from the ladder," he recalled in a letter to the *Solano Republican*. But gradually he and other men learned the various pruning techniques and the different ways of trimming apricot, plum, and peach trees. "The occupation of an orchard is a healthy one, a life free and unfettered by anxieties incidental to city vocations," continued Quizzy.

> The ruddy glow of health beams on his countenance, his muscles are hardened by honest toil; he rises fresh and sprightly as the plumaged rooster gives the bugle calls . . . he has nothing to embarrass him and he has unequaled opportunities for studying nature. While at work good-natured jokes go around—time does not seem tedious. His appetite gets no bitters—he eats healthily and devours pie with an avidity that would put a Missourian into the shade. At night yarns are told interluded with exaggeration, songs are warbled and a hand of cards occasionally indulged in. On Sundays some of the 'goody' boys, like the village blacksmith, are seen in the church pews, while others suffering from the arrows from Cupid's bow pay their 'fair ones' a visit . . . I very much prefer the 'hayseed's' lot with coarse jumper and overalls to that of a city 'tough' who has to economize by living on coffee and sinkers and one fifteen cent 'square' a day.[35]

Only a small percentage of bindlemen ever passed the winter pruning and handling other chores. Most headed for the nearest farm town or to a big city.

Unemployed, "rich in suntan and experience," and clutching fifty to seventy-five dollars of carefully accumulated savings, bindlemen often purchased tickets and "rode the cushions" to San Francisco, Los Angeles, Sacramento, Fresno, Stockton, Marysville, and other West Coast cities. Surviving the winter as best they could, they piled up in that section of town commonly known as "skid row," alongside drifters, bums, hoboes, unemployed construction workers, loggers, steam shovel men, locomotive engineers, vagrants, cripples, "defectives," "gutter drunks," and other seasonal workers.[36]

The most prominent skid rows were the Mission District and the Tenderloin in San Francisco and the unnamed area just south of Main Street and the financial section in Los Angeles. But by the turn of the century almost every city had its section of cheap lodging, inexpensive meals, lurid entertainment, booze, dope, sex, and companionship. Bindlemen had their own colorful names for these areas. They referred to them as the "pig market," the "flop house district," "hobohemia," the "main stem," and the "main drag." The terms were appropriate. Arriving tired and with a small stake, bindlemen found exactly what they needed to wait out bad weather and unemployment—cheap shelter and food, and a vast array of diversions and services devoted solely to the needs of homeless, unemployed men. At the turn of the century, about twenty-five thousand bindlemen "laid up" in the Los Angeles skid row, three thousand in Sacramento, and thousands more in Fresno, Redding, Marysville, Bakersfield, Stockton, Oakland, and other locations. Here, during the winter months they "hibernated" on the cheap, keeping body and soul together by measuring out forty to sixty cents a day, and parceling out their savings only on what was absolutely necessary.[37]

Throughout skid row, bindlemen moved among a dense network of inexpensive hotels, dormitories, boardinghouses, secondhand stores, poolrooms, pawnshops, movie houses, cafés, lunchrooms, honky-tonks, parks, "blind pigs," "barrel houses," "slop joints," "greasy spoons," nickelodeons, peep shows, houses of prostitution, street hawkers, military recruiting stations, tattoo parlors, card rooms, dance halls, burlesque houses, workingman's stores, dives, and rescue missions. Mingling with other denizens of the area—pimps, prostitutes, pickpockets, and "freaks of all descriptions who operate on the street corners"—bindlemen survived the winter quite well in the main stem, although every year police would find a few apparently murdered and robbed of their stake.[38]

Owing to San Francisco's mild climate and central location, bindlemen were especially fond of its flophouse district, which was wedged south of Market Street between the docks and the Mission District, with Bryant Street to the south, First Street to the east, and Sixth Street on the west. Far removed from the middle-class suburbs out in the Sunset and Richmond districts on the ocean side of the city, and spreading out below the Victorian mansions on Nob Hill and Russian Hill, San Francisco's flophouse district developed as a separate enclave in the 1860s when winter rains and snows drove thousands of gold miners into Bay Area towns. By 1871, it had become a refuge for unemployed field hands and other seasonal workers. According to the *San Francisco Opinion*, migrant workers annually shifted from the rural areas into San Francisco "to come back the next season like so many ragged crows." Boasting almost half of the city's lodging houses, the flophouse district south of Market Street was, by 1883, winter home to some five thousand men who, according to one newspaper, looked "poverty-stricken, ready to commit suicide."[39]

Although bindlemen were driven out of the area with everyone else when it burned in the 1906 earthquake and fire, they quickly returned after it was rebuilt. By 1907, San Francisco's flophouse district had eighty lodging houses, fifty-one secondhand stores, and countless saloons, pool halls, movie theaters, missions, and union halls. By 1910, some 24,500 bindlemen wintered in the area. Four years later, between thirty thousand and forty thousand men lived "south of the slot," as it was known. In 1914, federal investigator Peter A. Speek interviewed district denizens and was amazed by the varied population of "down-and-outers." Finding men everywhere, he reported to his superiors that the area was "blackened with the human mass."[40]

Upon arriving in town, the first thing a bindleman did was obtain shelter. There were many choices. If the weather was mild and a man was broke, he could sleep in newspaper beds on park benches until the rains came or it turned too cold. If a man had only pennies to spare, he went to a "barrel house," purchased a mug of stale beer, and with his mug obtained the right to sleep on the floor in the sawdust. A man might also spend an entire afternoon in the Cesspool, the Beer Can, the Hobo Retreat, or some other saloon. If he could afford five cents a day, he slept in a basement dormitory or a "bull pen," where facilities consisted of smelly, insect-infested, blanketless hammocks stacked closely together with little regard for privacy.[41]

Ten cents bought the most common form of lodging—straw bedding and a blanket, often in the same cramped facility as the "five center." Full of bedbugs and "broad gauge rats," the ten-cent-a-night flophouses were frequently investigated by state and local governments. One such investigation, by J. Vance Thompson of the U.S. Industrial Relations Commission, focused on several flophouses south of Market Street. Venturing into the Marshall Hotel, Thompson discovered 132 men in "foul and stiffling" air, sleeping in little nests of newspapers, coats, and blankets, side by side in rows upon the floor. Next door in the Grant Hotel, Thompson recorded 187 men living under similar conditions; in another section of the same hotel, 211 men were found "sleeping upon the window platform and so closely packed on the floor as to make passage between them impossible." All total, Thompson found twelve hundred men in the area (seven hundred in the upper floors, five hundred in vacant stores) "with a constant stream of newcomers." Men could be heard coughing throughout all parts of the buildings, and in one stairway Thompson found a "Mexican peon . . . in the last stages of consumption . . . coughing and spitting all over the floor." He described conditions as generally "putrid" and "unspeakable."[42]

Sleeping in these hot, smelly, noisy, vermin-infested flophouses was a challenge to all but the most comatose bindlemen, and it inspired some graphic descriptions. Of these portrayals, none surpassed the one written by Len DeCaux, a prominent labor union publicist in the 1930s, who, a generation earlier as a young bindleman, had worked as a seasonal laborer and wintered in the main stems of several West Coast cities. In his memoir, *Labor Radical*, DeCaux recalled the revolting scene before him when he lit a match to examine the surroundings in one flophouse.

> The sheets bore marks of bedbugs killed in battle, readily telling of missions accomplished. Other-colored splotches testified to the victims' manhood. On the pillow, a crushed cock-roach—plus marks of sweat, hair, grease, and dried saliva. I removed the linen and shoved it under the bed. I wrapped myself in the blanket . . . too dark to tell tales. Later I learned to lie fully clothed on top of the covers, wrapping myself in clean newspapers. Instead of sheep, I counted the shufflings, mutterings, and cussings, as each cubicle was occupied. In this tune-up, I noted the remarkable acoustics of the . . . tin partitions . . . the symphony [of] winds . . . belches, groans, farts, incipient snores . . . a crescendo of tubular coughing, bibulous slurping, snorting, and snoring, a vomit, and many stringed cot creaking. After a climax of night-time yells, partition pounding, and cries of protest, brief intermission was called by the night clerk. Then on again, till the dawn's early light brought the quiet of windless exhaustion.[43]

If a bindleman had a little bigger stake, he could move up the hierarchy of main stem housing to the "fifteen center"—a clean blanket, locker, and straw mattress, usually in a large dormitory-type room, with as many as two hundred other men. Twenty cents rented a corrugated iron cubicle six feet wide, seven feet high, and eight feet long, with a thirty-inch-wide central-access aisle. Usually furnished with a chair, locker, clean sheets, a cot, and topped with wire netting to admit light and circulate air, these cells were known as "muzzle loaders" because they were so confined that bindlemen could climb in only from the front end.[44]

After settling into their lodging, bindlemen next sought out places to eat. Here, prospects improved, because flophouse districts abounded with "slop joints," "greasy spoons," "lard pots," and other varieties of working-class cafés. Boasting hearty fare and low prices one-eighth the price of a meal in an uptown lunchroom, many displayed their offerings—strings of raw sausage, sides of bacon, raw red steaks, and wire baskets of oysters—to attract bindlemen and lure them inside. A typical restaurant, a place like the Ideal Café or Queen Coffee House, provided a dinner of pig snouts, liver and brown gravy, kidney stew, or baked beans for as little as ten to fifteen cents. Such places were not white-tile and marble cafeterias. Instead, they were often dark, with windows opaque with steam and dust. While the cooking may have been "lardaceous, oleoginous, and blubbery," as one bindleman recalled, it was also ample and nutritious, allowing men to eat often and at all times of the day and night.[45]

Once settled into their flophouse-café circuit, bindlemen tended to mundane tasks and needs. If their teeth were bothering them they headed to the local office of Dr. Painless Parker, or his counterpart, a dentist who ran a thriving chain of tooth-pulling parlors. If they wanted to save some money, they went to one of the many barber colleges, which, forever needing heads upon which to allow students to practice, offered a haircut and a shave for free. Next, they might stop at an outfitting store to replace their boots or buy some cheap clothes and gloves. Only then came the decorous havens of rest and recreation—tattoo parlors, fortune tellers, card parlors. For bindleman so inclined, the main stem provided a sumptuous array of pleasures designed to distract his mind and relieve him of both tensions and cash.[46]

Sex was readily available to those wishing to purchase it. For men denied female companionship while on the road, practically the only chance for sex with a woman came while holed up in the main stem. In San Francisco, bindlemen could sample women found in lodgings several blocks east of Union Street, along Morton Street, as well as eighty-four non-Chinese houses of prostitution lining eight blocks of Chinatown and a big prostitution operation, the Municipal Crib, at 620 Jackson Street, which maintained ninety rooms. The largest house of prostitution available to bindlemen was the Nymphia Club, a three-story, U-shaped building first opened for business in 1899. Inside, men found 450 cell-like compartments, roughly seven feet high, seven feet long, and five feet wide, each containing a bed, chair, and wash basin. On the door of each was the "nom de crib" of the woman inside—"Blondetta," "French Erma," "Mexican Maria," or "Blackie Satin," for example.[47]

At the "Mexican bargain basement," prices began at twenty-five cents. After that, the cost of pleasures escalated according to the race of each prostitute. Few could afford the so-called French girls on the third floor, who brought a premium price of one dollar. Although wealthy clientele frequenting the higher class establishments were protected somewhat from diseases by pimps who had their girls examined every week by a doctor, bindlemen frequenting lower-class houses of prostitution seldom enjoyed such protection before 1911, when San Francisco's short-lived Municipal Clinic examined and treated prostitutes.[48]

Most bindlemen, however, preferred to pass their time in less carnal pursuits. Nursing their stakes, economizing in every way except for food and lodging, they spent little on luxuries or entertainment. If the bindlemen's own accounts are accurate, they devoted most of their time during these slack months not in the nickelodeons, burlesque parlors, card rooms, or houses of prostitution, but in more mundane pursuits. Men became adept at idling away the hours talking, arguing, getting the "straight stuff" on jobs and working conditions, frequenting the public library, sunning themselves in sheltered areas, listening to fiery sermons of preachers and the revolutionary speeches of soapboxers, or just sitting for hours on park benches reading discarded papers, drinking, and generally making everyone's business their own.[49]

When bindlemen ran short of money, they supplemented their income by taking odd jobs as dishwashers, waiters, hotel porters, and even potato peelers, or they turned to the rescue missions. Common in the main stem, missions did a thriving business dispensing "soap, sleep, soup, and salvation," as bindlemen were fond of saying. Signs in train yards advertised their service: "Free Meal and Night's Lodging: Rescue Mission." San Francisco alone had twenty-three such establishments in 1910. Each morning, afternoon, and evening, a long line of ragged and disheveled men—a combination of bindlemen out of money, bums on the lam, and other refugees waiting out the winter—would assemble at the "Sally" (Salvation Army) the "Willy" (operated by Good Will Industries of the Methodist Church), or at some similar mission. Pouring into the "Whosever

Will" mission, or some similarly named mission, these men each received a free meal and a night's lodging, but not before witnessing an hour-long sermon or pep talk by a young preacher, occasionally accompanied by some devout woman.[50]

Because men sat through prayer meetings in a daze between sleeping and waking, virtually all missions had attendants called "bouncers" whose job was to shake and harass bindlemen who had fallen asleep. Pretending to be saved, bindlemen mostly regarded the whole arrangement cynically, calling it "coffee and" —coffee, rolls, and a bed; coffee and prayers; coffee and God. But if they were hungry enough and destitute enough and spring was still a long way off, bindlemen happily kneeled down for a "plate of greasy water and a dessert of prayer." Christmas breakfast was always a crowded affair. Thousands of bindlemen would line up outside the missions, filling the streets to the point where riots nearly occurred. "The hungry people were waiting for the breakfast the whole night," recalled a twenty-four-year-old Danish immigrant who had been in the United States for seven years, most of them on the road. "Got for breakfast rotten fish, could not eat it; two slices bread and coffee—bread was all right. The mission wanted the men to come for dinner, for parading through the streets." The following morning the Dane left to pick oranges in Southern California.[51]

Holed-up in southern San Joaquin Valley farm towns for the winter, bindlemen fared much better than their compatriots elsewhere in the state. That was because when they hit rock bottom they could as usual turn to Henry Miller. Concerned with preserving the goodwill of the bindlemen who crossed his property and worked on his ranches, and acutely aware that they might respond to poor treatment by opening cattle gates or setting fire to haystacks, Miller always treated bindlemen kindly during the off-season. Knowing this, bindlemen who saw Miller enter a bank would line up outside. When he emerged, Miller would usually have a large bag of coins with him, which he would then hand out two bits at a time, as bindlemen, hats in their hands, replied: "Thank you, Mr. Miller," or "God bless you, sir." A few called him Santa Claus.[52]

Bindlemen got more than handouts from Miller and Lux. Without exception, if Red Lizzard, Spoonbill, Seldom-Seen Murphy, Gunneysack Swede, Holy Joe, and other bindlemen appeared at any of the Miller and Lux ranches during the fall and winter, they would receive supper, a place to rest, and a good breakfast in the morning. Attracted by these rewards, hundreds of bindlemen would emerge from jungle camps, barns, bridges, and clumps of willows around supper time on a cold and foggy evening, work their way toward one of Miller's ranches, and make a beeline for the dining hall. Those departing from boxcars in Bakersfield hotfooted it to the Panama Ranch, then headed for Deep Wells, and last of all, Buttonwillow Ranch, before climbing back on board a northbound train. Sometimes as many as two dozen men would be on hand for a single meal, a luxury that Red Lizzard recalled as having "no equal in life's poker game for a man without a pair." Because of this policy, Miller never had to worry about labor shortages and could always manage to bring in his crops, even while neighboring farmers were complaining that they could not find any men. Eventually, men discovered that by moving from one of Miller and Lux's ranches to another they could make "the grand whirl" in a regional circuit of Stanislaus, Merced, Madera, and Kern counties, and thus survive the winter without going hungry. Some hit Miller and Lux's "entire reservation," eating their free meal then moving on to the next ranch. Some followed what they referred to as the "inside whirl" or "southern whirl," and stayed in the southern part of the valley. "Hitting one or two of the Miller and Lux cattle camps west of Madera," recalled Frank Latta, "the Stiffs had a good meal and spent the night at the old Columbia Ranch. Next they hit Poso Farm, Dos Palos Ranch, Santa Rita, Delta, Hereford, Midway, Canal Farm, Fremont, and McPike. This last left them at Newman, where they could ride the brake rods or a gondola car back to Firebaugh and begin all over again."[53]

Because ranch cooks refused to prepare extra meals for the stragglers, bindlemen learned to eat leftovers, wash their dishes themselves, or eat from dirty plates on a first-come, first-served basis. Chinese cooks supervised the meals and, according to Joseph Matthews, would run off any bindlemen "if they attempted to crowd in among the [permanent] work hands." Rumor has it that plates were nailed to the tables, leading someone to eventually christen this the "Dirty Plate Route," a name that stuck and became synonymous with migratory labor in the southern San Joaquin Valley.[54]

After dinner, full-time employees returned to their jobs or retired to their bunkhouses, while the unemployed bindlemen headed back to the barn or jungle camp where they were holed up. Men seeking employment might talk up a foreman, snag a job chopping wood, and work long enough to "choke off a piece of booze money." So well known was the routine that it inspired songs and poems. One of them, by Reedley farmwife L. L. Wright, went:

He made a dash for Miller's hash
On the banks of the San Joaquin;
The hash was hot, the hobo cold,
Though his clothes were ragged, his ways were bold
For he swore a lot, so I've been told,
On the banks of the San Joaquin.

Another verse, written by an anonymous bindleman, stressed the value of the Dirty Plate Route in thwarting discontent:

Here's to Uncle Hank, who lets us satisfy
The belly chiefly, not the eye.
Keeping the barking stomach wisely quiet,
Less with a neat than a needful diet
For he, from sad experience knows,
The hungrier man gets, the more dangerous he grows.[55]

Outside of the San Joaquin Valley, bindlemen did not have the luxury of knowing that no matter how bad things got, they could always find food and shelter. As the season wore on, men low on cash would arrive at a bakery early in the morning and offer to sweep it out in exchange for a sack of stale rolls and yesterday's leftovers. If they became desperate enough, bindlemen resorted to thievery, but for the most part, they stole only what they needed to survive. Usually bindlemen stole goods, not food. They might snatch clothing left out to dry on a clothesline and try to pawn it, or they might lift rubber boots from a clothing store while a partner tried to divert the proprietor's attention, then run like the devil only to be tripped up and held for the police. In Marysville, two cold and desperate bindlemen in need of a coat simply walked into a stable in December 1905 and asked for a coat hanging on a peg, claiming it belonged to one of them. After the coat's owner appeared, someone remembered that the bindleman had been seen about town wearing old coats. Arrested for working a "flim flam," as the police blotter noted, the bindlemen were sentenced to sixty days in the county jail. Another desperate group of bindlemen near the town of Napa broke the lock on the kitchen leading to the Palace Hotel in September 1889, stole the cook's key, walked in, and helped themselves. "The merchants should remember that sneak thieves are very plentiful at the present time and that those that hang out their goods in front of their stores take desperate chances," warned the *Marysville Daily Appeal*.[56]

Desperate men often worked together to increase the odds for success through a tactic known as "swarming" or "bumming." Packing into the front of a store where goods were displayed, they distracted the proprietor's attention so that one of them would walk off with a pair of shoes or a hat. When a group of eleven bindlemen pulled this at the City Cash Store in downtown Napa on a rainy winter afternoon, the clerk spotted one of them leaving with a pair of rubbers, chased him down, grabbed him by the nape of the neck, and proceeded to drown him in the gutter by scooping up handfuls of mud and muck and shoving it down the man's throat. The clerk nearly killed the bindleman, relenting only when the entire Napa police force turned out and attempted to arrest every bindleman in town. Taking to their heels, the men fled to the train depot, where they put up a tough fight before being arrested.[57]

If desperate enough, some bindlemen would steal almost anything. Often they tried to take items that would not be missed. Around Stockton, they discovered that they could always make a good haul appropriating food left on Chinese graves following a funeral. Another way they could forestall starvation was to sit down for a big meal, eat as much as possible, and then refuse to pay, announcing that they were broke. Usually men this desperate would be forced to wash dishes and sweep up. But when one bindleman refused to pay for his dinner in a Chinese restaurant in Selma, the angry owner grabbed him, demanded payment, and took the bindleman's coat as a forfeit. As the men fought, the bindleman proceeded to smash out the café windows. As a result, the proprietor called police and had the bindleman arrested, which may have been exactly what he wanted. For the next two nights he had a warm cell and plenty of food.[58]

Occasionally a bindleman would become so desperate as to steal and forge checks, usually with disastrous consequences. This was what happened to Thomas Gordon, a twenty-two-year-old unemployed tinner from Colorado. Arriving in Wheatland to pick hops in July 1906, Gordon found the work too difficult. Broke and needing new boots and clothes, he stole three checks from the Horst hop camp. Forging the ranch foreman's name on two of the checks, he aroused considerable suspicion while attempting to pass the checks in town. Arrested before he could leave, he was found with a train ticket for San Francisco.

Gordon pled guilty and was sentenced to three years in San Quentin Prison. He apparently had done the same thing in Oroville.[59]

Bindlemen who were extremely bad off might apply for relief at a local jail. In many towns, sheriffs would allow desperate men to sleep in vacant cells, usually in exchange for a few hours' work chopping wood, washing floors, or the like. After finishing their chores, they would be allowed to stay the night, and in the morning they would be fed breakfast before being "cut loose." But jail lodging sometimes backfired, as when men would be kept in jail and tried for some unsolved crime. More than a few innocent bindlemen served long prison terms after being "apprehended" in this way.[60]

As a last resort, famished and cold bindlemen would "pling for grub" (beg for food). This was also known as being forced to "panhandle," so named because men often used a frying pan to collect change. Bindlemen did not apologize for begging. "I was a worker and had a right to live," recalled William Z. Foster of his days on the road. "If no job was to be got, then someone who had food must give what I needed." Almost every flophouse district had its share of panhandlers. But bindlemen would also beg at farmhouses and in residential areas of rural towns if necessary. Many trudged from one door to another all day long asking for something to eat. This was called "banging for a lump." So many bindlemen went from door to door around Fresno in March 1882, that, according to the *Fresno Weekly Expositor*, one annoyed citizen bought bakery tickets for bread loaves and handed them out when panhandled. In this way "his dollars [purchased] twenty loaves of good bread, instead of eight drinks of whiskey, as before." Occasionally, men employed extreme measures to attract sympathy, like eating grass or cardboard to demonstrate how bad off they were. One bindleman drew up a handbook assessing the most easily approachable groups or "marks." Married women, prostitutes, and nuns were the best bet, he advised, while wealthy men and ministers were to be avoided. Other bindlemen perfected their storytelling abilities to theatrical proportions, adjusting their stories, killing off parents, throwing in injuries and sickness, and creating false and romanticized tales of woe as needed. With these yarns, they would "strike" citizens for a dime or a quarter from a street corner.[61]

Whatever the season, bindlemen could always earn a meal doing chores on farms near railroads. The routine was well established. Usually a pile of unsplit wood was stacked near the kitchen door. Whenever a bindleman asked for a meal, he would be shown the woodpile and set to chopping and splitting. If the woodpile was full, a bindleman would be set to other chores like raking the yard or sweeping the garage. A hot meal was always served on the back porch, never in the house. "My mother would prepare a hot meal and serve it on a tray which was passed out the back door," recalled "Swede" Righter of bindlemen passing through the Santa Clara Valley. "I think my parents felt 'but for the grace of God go I,'" recalled Simi Valley resident Mary Pollock Daily, who would sometimes sit with the men as they ate their meals following chores at her father's farm. "Sometimes the guys were a little scary. But my mother would explain that they had been on the road, so they couldn't get baths, and they were probably people just like ourselves."[62]

FIGURE 51. Bindlemen at work in the citrus groves around Corona, ca. 1906. Courtesy of the Huntington Library, San Marino, California.

As the weather turned milder with the approach of spring, bindlemen would begin to look for harvest work. But even if they knew general crop patterns and had made the agricultural circuit before, finding employment was not easy. There was no reliable source of job information, so that even when work was abundant, finding it was a hit-and-miss proposition. Unlike the Chinese and Japanese, bindlemen could not rely on labor contractors to secure positions, and the free labor clearinghouses that did cater to bindlemen were, for the most part, short-lived or inefficient. The first of these, opened in July 1895 by the California State Department of Labor, promised growers and other employers a register of ten thousand to fifteen thousand men to draw from. The service relied on a dual card system to track its men; employers were asked to fill out one card for each hired man and another for each man who was fired or otherwise left their position. The idea was that, with this information, the bureau could get an idea of who was hiring, how long jobs lasted, and why men left. "In a very short period of time," reported the *San Francisco Call*, "the commissioner will be able to tell who is deserving of help and who is not. The former will be able to secure other positions, but the latter will be blacklisted. Within a few months only tried men will be sent out by the bureau with recommendations."[63]

Few bindlemen took advantage of the service. With no clients, the Bureau of

Labor Statistics soon abandoned the project. Federal efforts were no more successful. During 1907, progressive politicians aiming to cut unemployment created the first federal agency designed to redistribute labor. Called the Division of Information and located within the U.S. Department of Commerce and Labor's Bureau of Immigration, it was charged with collecting and disseminating reliable information and acting as a clearinghouse for bindlemen and other seasonal laborers. But outside of a few eastern states, bindlemen remained largely unaffected by the new bureaucracy. As for private and philanthropic efforts, they came and went, seldom lasting very long or having much impact. If any bindlemen in California ever consistently obtained jobs through these sources it was not reported.[64]

Because they had so little systematic information, bindlemen as often as not scattered into the farming districts based on rumors, habit, hunches, and instinct. As a result, many would arrive too late to find work. For example, every fall hundreds of bindlemen who had holed up in San Francisco would tramp into the Napa Valley long after the peak harvest. With little prospect of employment, they would either have to return to the city or hop a train for another agricultural district and hope for the best. By the early 1900s, waves of bindlemen were moving out from the cities each spring in such numbers that the West Coast became what Peter A. Speek described as "something like a highway for migratory laborers." Packing into depots and parks, they made the best of their situation and moved along as rumor took them. "We travel around from place to place," explained one bindleman to a reporter for the *San Francisco Bulletin*, "and get work where we can find it."[65]

Upon arriving in a farm town, men would congregate around the pool halls, parks, or along Main Street, a saloon, or hotel where local farmers were known to come looking for men. This was as true in Marysville, Biggs, Richvale, and Chico as in Winters, Knights Landing, Newman, or any of a dozen other farm towns. Early or late in the season, the same chaotic scene would unfold every morning. Clutching their bindles, men stomped their feet, spat, and milled about, talking and laughing and smoking cigarettes while they waited for work. Every so often, a farmer would pull up with a wagon. "Who wants work?" he would shout. The farmer and the bindlemen eyed one another for several minutes, sometimes negotiating wages, but usually not even raising the subject. There would be so many men in town and in the nearby jungle camps that when the grower lowered the wagon door, or motioned toward his farm, men would elbow and push one another as they rushed forward. "It was no trouble at all to round up a crew," recalled Ventura County lima bean grower Joe Terry. "We'd just drive out to where they lived, sometimes in a lean-to under the gum trees, and recruit a crew in short order."[66]

Faced with a choice between starving, blindly chasing after an elusive job, running the gauntlet during the morning shape-up in a small farm town, or fighting among themselves for winter work in the citrus groves, thousands of bindlemen sought an alternative to this chaotic situation. They prowled a peculiar section of skid row known as the "slave market" or "stiff town." Aptly named, the slave market catered to the bindleman's quest for work in various seasonal industries. San Francisco's slave market was especially well developed and provided a number of mechanisms for securing jobs. Among the most important were private employment agencies. About 350 private labor agencies operated in California at the turn of the century, mostly in the slave market areas of San Francisco, Los Angeles, Sacramento, Fresno, and Stockton, although at least one labor agency could be found in every farm town. Somewhat resembling labor contracting services, labor agencies were actually hybrid organizations that, although acting as intermediaries, seldom if ever intervened on behalf of employees. Nevertheless, so chaotic was the labor market and so desperate were bindlemen that labor agencies did a thriving business supplying men to farms, lumber camps, construction projects, and other seasonal industries throughout California.[67]

Bindlemen found labor agencies packed into old shipping offices, on rundown street corners, or in warehouses adjacent to train stations. Crowding the streets nearby, they would rendezvous there and mill about. On the street, labor agents placed folding blackboards with their ever changing list of jobs. On the sidewalk outside the San Francisco labor agency of Meyers and Young, bindlemen found jobs listed in red, blue, and yellow chalk, with each color designating a different category of work or a different industry. Inside, men scrutinized more blackboards. For men waiting for a particular job, or with no place to go, there would usually be some rude chairs and tables where they could sit and rest. Several hundred men could fit inside the larger labor agency offices, waiting patiently for a labor agent, also known as a "man catcher," "straw boss," or "shark," to shout news of some new job listing.[68]

Throughout the day, bindlemen would come by, lounge about the agency offices, or bunch together inside, stacking their bindles in a back room as they waited for jobs. This was a common routine wherever bindlemen laid up. "Suntanned, brawny men, most of them in early manhood or in the prime of their life, dressed in blue overalls or khaki pants and blue cotton shirts . . . are standing in knots around the doors of the employment sharks, watching the requirements chalked up on the blackboards outside," wrote Charles Ashleigh. So many men crowded around the labor agencies in the Los Angeles main stem during July 1909 that the *Industrial Worker* characterized the throng as "thicker than the flies on a piece of bad meat on a hot summer's day."[69]

Bindlemen turned to labor agents in such numbers that one of two at some time found farmwork through their services. Some agencies were free; but most charged a price. For farmwork around Sacramento, bindlemen in San Francisco coughed up $1.50 to $2 a job. Around Fresno they paid $1 to pick grapes, and those in Los Angeles paid $2.50 to $3 to work on farms in the Imperial and San Fernando valleys. Average cost of obtaining farmwork through a labor agent statewide in 1906 was $2.09, which meant that bindlemen had to work one day just to earn enough money to pay for the cost of obtaining their job. Nevertheless, many bindlemen considered it a bargain, as did many growers. Needing men in a pinch, the Glenn ranch near Willows merely contacted the Wide Awake Employment Agency in Sacramento, and within a day or two, a crew magically appeared. Other farmers followed the same procedure. "We telephone the . . . agency to send a certain number of men for a certain class of work," explained Wheatland hop magnate E. Clements Horst, "and they send the men out."

Sometimes the arrangements were quite impressive, as during 1886, when San Francisco labor agencies sent two thousand fruit pickers to Solano.[70]

Bindlemen hated and distrusted labor agencies, regarding them as corrupt predators and "swindling shops" where, as the *Industrial Union Bulletin* put it, "the unsophisticated workingman was fleeced most unmercifully." The greatest abuse, everyone knew, was fee splitting between foremen and employment agents. After obtaining complete control of recruiting labor for a particular farm, labor agents falsified working conditions to scrape up crews, then sent them to a foreman who worked the men for a day and fired them. The agents could then round up and send along another crew, and another, and another, splitting the fees exacted from bindlemen with their coconspirators, and making a little extra by charging for transportation. The practice was so common that a standing joke among bindlemen was that sharks made them pay for every job they got, as well as every one that they did not get. One song, "Coffee And," ridiculed the practice by telling the story of a man who tried to collect his wages after being fired from a job purchased through an employment agent, only to learn that the clerk had deducted fees for roads, schools, hospitals, along with a poll tax, and that the poor bindleman now owed the company fifty cents.[71]

Fee splitting was just one of many ways traditional society threatened, cheated, and exploited bindlemen, further evidence of just how far away they were from the freedom and rights enjoyed by most other citizens. Everywhere bindlemen went at this time, they encountered reminders of their outcast status and obstacles to full participation in American life—in the jungles around Goshen, the flophouse districts of San Francisco and Los Angeles, the slave markets of Fresno, Stockton, and Newman, the Dirty Plate Route, the Salvation Army rescue missions, and most oppressive of all, in the halls of the California legislature where, around the turn of the century, bindlemen were neglected, excluded, and marginalized.

CHAPTER TWENTY-THREE

The Privilege of Quitting

Death, Discontent, and Alienation

Late one Saturday evening in August 1897, a bindleman appeared at a Napa Valley farmhouse and begged for supper. He ate heartily, then asked permission to sleep in the barn, saying that he was sick and too old to sleep outside. A few hours later he complained of being ill and said that his stomach hurt him. Given a warm breakfast, the bindleman seemed to get better and said he would go up to the valley to look for work the next morning. No one paid much attention to him until evening, when he was found still in the barn. Again fed and allowed to occupy the hayloft, he broke into a sweat and was given a dose of ginger. This relieved him somewhat and the next morning he again ate breakfast. In the afternoon one of the farmhands went to the barn and found the bindleman taking his last breath. A doctor was summoned, but it was too late. Within an hour, the bindleman died. "The man's name is unknown," reported the *Napa Daily Journal*.

> He said that he was a native of Sweden . . . He said that he . . . had worked in orchards in the Suisun Valley. No letters were found on his person, but among his effects was found a gray coat with blue cuffs and collar and brass buttons, also several newspapers, one a *S. F. Chronicle*, dated December 17, 1880, another a *Vallejo Chronicle* of July 25, 1897. He was perfectly bald, wore blue overalls, a white muslin shirt, brown straw hat and brogans, and was quite neat.[1]

As desperate as such men were, they knew very well not to count on anyone other than themselves, to live by their own muscle and wits, and to expect nothing from society. At the bottom of the social heap, bindlemen had no labor unions to bargain for them, no district or fraternal organizations to provide mutual benefits, no bosses or *keiyaku-nin* to speak on their behalf and ensure a minimal safety net. They frequented no lodge or church other than the rescue missions, nor did they exert any influence over local or state government. No state senator or representative regarded them as a part of his constituency. No mayor turned to them

FIGURE 52. Valencio Gonzalez, found dead in the orchards near Santa Paula, Ventura County, ca. 1910. Courtesy the Ventura County Coroner's Record of Violent Deaths, Ventura County Museum.

for support. No politicians solicited money or help from them or counted on them for votes. Only marginally literate, few bindlemen could meet the 1894 California state requirement of competency in English as a prerequisite for registering to vote. Even those who were able to read and write well enough to register to vote rarely remained in one place long enough to establish residency.[2]

But it was not just that bindlemen were too poor, too mobile, and too marginalized to exert much impact on the political process. They were also excluded from equal protection under the law simply because they were farmworkers. According to most accounts, systematic exclusion from social and labor legislation did not occur until much later, when debate began over whom to include in the Wagner Act, Social Security Act, and other New Deal measures. But in fact, exclusion of agricultural workers from labor protection laws began in January 1897 with the passage of California Assembly Bill 75, a law giving laborers the right to secure unpaid wages by placing liens on property. Designed to prevent employers from deferring wages until completion of a job (when some excuse would be found for withholding full or partial payment), the bill had strong urban support from the building trades and construction worker's unions, but was vehemently opposed by rural representatives who—exerting disproportionate power in Sacramento and controlling the state senate—demanded that agriculture be excluded from coverage in exchange for their votes. Faced with a choice between seeing the legislation completely fail and enacting a watered-down version of the law, urban legislators agreed to the deal. As a result, bindlemen defrauded by unscrupulous farmers and labor contractors had no legal recourse. "Now I ask," said Woodland field hand William Walsh in a letter to the *Sacramento Bee*, "is not . . . work done on that farm a benefit to the farm? Why should not the laborer get his wages which he honestly earned?" The answer was that there was no politically beneficial reason to help bindlemen (or any other farmworkers) even if, as some argued, "improvement of working conditions would attract better labor and encourage laborers to work harder."[3]

From this point forward, virtually every piece of state and federal labor legislation would contain some clause denying benefits and coverage to farm, cannery, and packinghouse workers. To justify these exclusions, rural leaders amplified a form of agricultural exceptionalism stressing that the production of perishable fruits and vegetables made growers highly susceptible to labor strife. According to this line of thinking, farming was so different from other forms of business that it should not be held to the same standards, responsibilities, and constraints as manufacturers of durable goods. Agriculturalists celebrated in 1899, when the California legislature excluded farmers from a law limiting work to no more than eight hours per day. Over the next two years, they pressed their claim of agricultural exceptionalism by opposing even the most basic forms of social and labor legislation. When the 1901 state legislature considered a bill making counties responsible for the care of indigent, ill, aged, and homeless citizens, rural leaders inserted a clause stating that only citizens who had resided in a county at least three consecutive months were eligible. This effectively excluded bindlemen and other transient workers. Disgusted with these and other developments, the *San Francisco Bulletin* later observed: "California has passed laws for the protection of migratory birds, but it can not pass laws for the protection of migratory workers."[4]

৯৯

At the turn of the twentieth century, California bindlemen found themselves forsaken by a state government hardly noted for being compassionate. What mattered most to the state's politicians was business. Since the Gold Rush, no other state had been more subservient to the dictates of big business, and one business in particular exercised greater power than any other. As the largest landowner, largest employer, principal engine of economic growth and richest corporation in the American West, Southern Pacific Railroad maintained a stranglehold on California state politics almost from its inception. The head of Southern Pacific's political department was much more powerful than any governor, and the company's "invisible government" corrupted politicians, influenced elections, and exercised greater leverage than any other entity in the state. By controlling appointments to the railroad and banking commissions, buying the votes of state legislators, directing political functionaries in every county, influencing judges and publishers, squashing all challengers, and reaching into every corner of society, the railroad earned the dubious nickname of "the octopus."[5]

Not until the financial panic and depression of 1893 did a swelling wave of resentment propel small farmers and capitalists to unite behind the Populist Movement (or People's Party) and challenge the Southern Pacific machine. Populists preached reform, fought against the big capitalists, won large numbers of followers, and instituted many legislative processes that eventually made politics more responsive to constituents, but they never really attacked the fundamental nature of capitalist agriculture, expressed much sympathy for bindlemen, or had any significant following among transient workers. Unconcerned with marginalized groups, Populists did not reject the use of hired labor or advance programs meant to restructure farming or stabilize and humanize farm labor relations. Their brand of rustic radicalism, in fact, ignored or dodged such issues in favor of middle-class reforms and governmental supervision of business.[6]

By the turn of the century, Populism was beginning to lose what little grasp it held on the political psyche of the working class. But in Los Angeles and other parts of Southern California, where resentment toward the state's political corruption was on the increase, middle-class socialism was becoming a significant force. Statewide, Socialists won 12 percent of the vote in 1910. A year later, campaigning for public ownership of utilities, prison and hospital reform, social welfare, public housing, workmen's compensation, increased regulation of industry, and the expansion of social services, Socialists nearly succeeded in electing the mayor of Los Angeles and did elect candidates to town councils, school boards, and other city posts in Eureka, Santa Cruz, and San Bernardino. Yet for all their egalitarian rhetoric, Socialists advanced no practical program for helping seasonal and transient workers.[7]

The Socialists of 1911 were discontented intellectuals, labor leaders, and progressive politicians who embraced socialism because they were seeking a convenient weapon of protest. But other than a cooperative of Russian Jewish chicken farmers in Petaluma and the Llano del Rio cooperative colony in the Antelope Valley north of Los Angeles, their major contribution to the cause of the dispossessed consisted of Edwin C. Markham's epic poem, "The Man With the Hoe." Inspired by Jean Millet's painting of a brutalized French peasant gazing up exhausted from his labor, the lavishly illustrated poem, which first appeared in the *San Francisco Examiner* on January 15, 1899, called for a redeemed agricultural economy free of dehumanizing economic oppression. Though signifying that at least some Californians were sympathetic to the plight of bindlemen, such poems hardly constituted a program to aid the most exploited members of society.[8]

There is little evidence that bindlemen ever touched the consciousness of more than one or two California politicians. Nor was concern for bindlemen prominent in the minds of the progressive leaders who were at the time energizing the entire country and dictating policy for both major political parties. Exactly what the Progressives wanted to create was somewhat ill-defined—perhaps a political culture devoid of class orientation, perhaps an altruistic society that aimed at solving the problems of urbanization and industrialization, perhaps a state that ameliorated somewhat the harsher aspects and more glaring defects in the socioeconomic system. On the national level, Progressives called for restraining business and curbing the evils of bigness. In California, Progressives were represented by wealthy, college-educated young men from the urban upper middleclass. In 1907, these men formed a statewide reform movement that coalesced as the Lincoln-Roosevelt Republican League in opposition to Governor James N. Gillett's gubernatorial administration. Eager to participate in politics by peacefully modifying existing institutions, the lawyers, editors, publishers, educators, clergymen, and independent businessmen who made up the league—like their national counterparts—defended capitalism as a general concept and rejected socialism in most forms. They criticized big corporations and monopolies and favored moral and political reforms that would democratize the political process and mitigate the worst effects of entrenched interests.[9]

The group gained a foothold in 1908 by electing enough members to the legislature to enact a direct primary law. As a result, league reformers and their allies transferred control of party nominations from machine-controlled conventions to voters, assumed control of the Republican Party, and selected San Francisco assistant district attorney Hiram Johnson as their candidate for governor. In a hard-hitting campaign, Johnson employed his very considerable oratorical skills to unleash a torrent stressing the single theme of "kicking the Southern Pacific out of politics." Although his Democratic opponent, Theodore Bell, discussed a wider array of reform issues, including a "New Deal, a Fair Deal," Johnson won the 1910 election, largely because the Socialists pulled thousands of votes away from the Democratic Party.[10]

Some recorders of the farmworker story have concluded that bindlemen and other field hands benefited substantially from Johnson's policies, which demarcated the end of a corrupt era in California politics. The supposition stems from the many fights that Johnson and the Progressive movement fought on behalf of working people and against "special interests," from their attempt to balance the interests of labor and business, and from the assumption that their moral sense extended into every corner of society. And the conjecture does have a certain plausibility about it. Common working people were favored by more than one hundred pieces of labor legislation in 1911, the most important being the Workman's Compensation Act and the institution of the Industrial Safety Commission. President Theodore Roosevelt was so impressed with the California Progressives that he characterized their program as "the beginning of a new era in popular government . . . the greatest advance ever made by any state for the benefit of its people." Despite strenuous opposition from both urban and rural employers, during the winter and spring of 1911, Progressives enacted such an unprecedented number of laws and established so many agencies to further the causes they championed that, in his study of California labor legislation, historian Samuel Crockett described the 1911 session as a "landmark of legislative achievement."[11]

Of all that the Progressives accomplished during the first two years of Hiram Johnson's administration, only two programs even remotely affected bindlemen. One was the Public Employment Office Act, which provided jobs for a few thousand men in and around San Francisco and Los Angeles but left private employment offices to operate unregulated and did little to mitigate the evils of the slave market or the chaos of seasonal hiring. The other was the establishment of the California Commission of Immigration and Housing (CCIH). The CCIH was almost entirely the creation of one of the most selfless of all California Progressives, Simon J. Lubin. Heir to a Sacramento department store chain, the passionate, brilliant young Lubin had graduated from Harvard in 1903 with a degree in economics but had also taken time to study philosophy under Josiah Royce. He then spent two years as a settlement-house worker among the Irish poor in South Boston, and another two years in settlement work on the Lower East Side of New York City. In 1908, Lubin returned to California and took a leading role in the Progressive cause.[12]

Despite four years of exposure to slum life and the problems of various immigrant groups, Lubin was appalled by conditions he encountered among farmworkers in the Central Valley. During 1911, he began discussing with Johnson his ideas for improving the lot of farmworkers and for attacking rural poverty. Concerned that the opening of the Panama Canal would induce a flood of immigrants to California, rather than to eastern seaports, Lubin in June 1912 drafted legislation for a statewide plan to deal with the impending influx. Convincing Johnson to appoint a special committee to study the matter, Lubin found that conditions in many California cities indeed were beginning to resemble those in New York and Boston, and therefore constituted an appropriate concern for any state agency. His solution was a permanent Commission of Immigration and Housing, which would "prevent the dreadful conditions of poverty" resembling those endured by immigrants in the eastern cities of the United States. Established later that year and authorized to investigate the "condition, welfare, and industrial opportunities of all immigrants arriving and being within the state," the commission proceeded to study agricultural labor requirements, schemes to settle immigrants in rural areas, and ways to assist them in finding work. Given the power to conduct public hearings, even to subpoena witnesses, the commission was also directed to survey the educational needs of new immigrants, compile and supply lists of immigrant children to school districts, establish Americanization and assimilation programs, and inform public officials of any violations of the laws governing the employment of women and children.[13]

In stark contrast to Lubin's success, certain immutable political realities impeded most other Progressives from demonstrating much concern for bindlemen and other migrant workers. By far the most important of these factors was the rural vote. With rural areas figuring prominently in Hiram Johnson's Progressive coalition and growers in the Southern California citrus belt and San Joaquin Valley comprising the very heart of his support, Johnson was more concerned with farmers paying high freight rates than he was with politically insignificant bindlemen and other workers who provided farmers with a captive labor force. Willing to sacrifice casual workers for the larger good (and the support of rural votes), Johnson and the Progressives carried forward the by-then decade-long tradition of exclusion. Every piece of social or labor legislation they proposed contained some clause denying benefits and rights to bindlemen and other farm laborers and packinghouse workers. Such exclusion, wrote labor historian Robert Knight in *Industrial Relations in the San Francisco Bay Area*, "reflected not only the strong political influence of agricultural and food processing interests, but also labor's willingness to accept a compromise."[14]

Bindlemen and other farmworkers were first excluded from Progressive legislation just two months after Johnson became governor, sacrificed for what the Progressives believed was a greater good—a law prohibiting women from working more than eight hours a day or more than forty-eight hours in one week. Twenty-five states already had eight-hour laws for women. In California, though, rural interests claimed that the perishable nature of their crop made it necessary to work both men and women longer than eight hours per day and demanded in exchange for their support some stipulation protecting agriculture. To get the bill through the rural-dominated senate, Progressives did what politicians had always done in California; they inserted a provision stating that the law "shall not apply to nor affect the harvesting, curing, canning, or drying of any variety of perishable fruit or vegetables." With that exemption, representatives of the California State Federation of Labor, who had been the bill's strongest backers, overcame strenuous opposition from other industries, and on March 22, 1911, Governor Johnson signed it into law.[15]

Two years later, when Progressive politicians proposed workmen's compensation and employer's liability laws so significant that California State Federation of Labor president Paul N. Scharrenberg described them as "the greatest achievement of the fortieth session of the legislature," the California State Fruit Growers Association mobilized agricultural interests in opposition. Arguing that small farmers might have to forfeit their land and crops to compensate the relatives of "some field hand" who died while working for them, or "support for life" some transient who had become injured on their property, they again succeeded in having the senate committee exclude agriculture from coverage. "The farmer in California is exempted," wrote *Fresno Bee* editor and Progressive politician Chester Rowell, "and if his employee falls and paralyzes himself for life, that employee is to make his own living and bear all the loss."[16]

Not long after exclusion from workman's compensation legislation, a cook on the Lowe and Hennigan ranch near Woodland began preparing a meal for a crew of Japanese sugar beet harvesters employed by the Sacramento Valley Sugar Beet Company (SVSBC). The cook had been hired just the day before, and was unfamiliar with large-scale kitchen work. In an attempt to reignite a smoldering fire, the cook threw some kerosene on the coals. Immediately engulfed in flames and screaming for help, the cook was saved by two field hands who rushed into the kitchen and extinguished the blaze with pans of water. Horribly burned, the cook was sent to a sanitarium in Woodland and required the constant attention of physicians and a trained nurse. At first, company president William Baker diligently paid the cook's expenses, but, he noted, the company did not have to do so, and the payments would not continue indefinitely. The cook only lived a few days, negating the argument over liability, but in internal communications Baker made it clear that SVSBC would not provide similar assistance to field hands or other employees injured on the job.[17]

℘ℨ

Excluded and ignored by politicians by virtue of their status as farmworkers, bindlemen (like rivermen, lumberjacks, cowpunchers, and other illiterate and semi-literate Americans who lived transiently) formulated their own unique culture of opposition. Most of that culture has since dissipated, but the pieces that survive suggest the rigors of life on the road did not obliterate creative dissent. With a huge reservoir of experiences to draw from, bindlemen sustained a folk culture that helped them counteract political exclusion, stabilize their uncertain life, and create bonds among strangers. Stretched out on their bedrolls at night or waiting in the shade of a tree for a train, men with names like Horse Blanket Blackie, Pork Chop Whitie, Short Line Red, and Boxcar Shortie told lies, spun tales, shared yarns, sang songs, and recited proverbs and epic poems. These compositions provided bindlemen the opportunity to transcend (at least symbolically) the inevitable restrictions of their environment and to vent their feelings and frustrations.[18]

Of the endless stream of stories that bindlemen told one another along the harvest route, the most common were about road experiences, with an emphasis on hostile brakemen, fights, cinder bulls, town clowns, and skid-row habitués of various talents. Many stories boasted of narrow escapes and harrowing adventures; others dwelled on lost loves and families left behind. Ultimately, a few became "hobo classics," known to all. Especially popular in this womanless society were innumerable variations on the story of the seduction of the lady of the farmhouse by a bindleman asking for a meal. The plot was the same, with the details changed slightly. The bindleman gets a generous sample of the lady, her cooking, her husband's clothes, and the advice: "If you ever come around here again my husband will shoot you full of holes. And if he doesn't, I will."[19]

Even more unique than their words was their rich folklore of song. Unlike coal miners of the time, whose balladry also reflected adverse living and working conditions, bindlemen did not sing of religion or tradition. Rather, bindlemen sang from memory or they made up verses and adapted them to popular ballads and religious hymns. Theirs were songs of parody and despair, restlessness and alienation, natural disasters, labor actions, and home. One of the best, "The Mysteries of a Hobo's Life," by T-Bone Slim, was set to the tune "The Girl I Left Behind." The third verse went:

> I grabbed a hold of an old freight train,
> And around the country traveled.
> The mysteries of a hobo's life,
> To me were soon unraveled.[20]

Vocal songs—as opposed to instrumental music—had the great advantage of being carried in men's minds, which meant they could not be confiscated or curtailed by foremen or employers. Some compositions were alert, caustic rhymes lamenting a way of life that cut all moorings to home and family. But in addition to expressing desires for a life left behind, compositions mocked virtually every institution in society. In "Hallelujah, I'm a Bum," a popular folksong set to the tune of the religious hymn "Revive Us Again," down-and-outers from all walks of life sang:

> O, why don't you work,
> Like other men do?
> How in the hell can I work,
> When there's no work to do?
>
> Chorus: Hallelujah, I'm a bum
> Hallelujah, bum again,
> Hallelujah, give us a handout—To revive us again.

It then continued:

> O, why don't you save,
> All the money you earn?
> If I did not eat,
> I'd have money to burn.
> O, I like my boss—He's a good friend of mine.
> That's why I am starving. Out on the bread-line.[21]

Within this lyrical tradition, no composition better expressed the longing for a better life than "The Big Rock Candy Mountain," in which, after years on the road, Iowa Slim finally reaches bindlemen's heaven:

> Where the ham and eggs grow on trees,
> And bread grows from the ground,
> And the springs spurt booze to your knees,
> And there's more than enough to go around.
> Where the chickens crawl into the skillet,
> And cook themselves up nice and brown,
> And the cows churn their butter in the mornin',
> And squirt their milk all around.
> You never change your socks,
> And little streams of alcohol,
> Come a-trickling down the rocks,
> The boxcars are all empty,
> And the railroad bulls are blind.
> There's a lake of stew and whiskey too,
> You can paddle all around 'em in a big canoe.[22]

In poetry even more than in song, bindlemen recorded their anger and alienation. Transient poets sometimes mocked religion by relating a story as if it were a verse from the Bible; at other times, they employed rhyming verse to lament life on the move. And just as bindlemen had their epic poems, so too did they have their poet laureates. Among the most famous were Robert Service (1874–1958) and Joe Hill (1879–1915).[23]

A Scottish bank clerk who immigrated to Canada in 1890, Service spent the next twenty-five years stumping across the American West as far north as the Yukon Territory. During this time he washed dishes, dug tunnels, did time as a "cow juice jerker" (farm laborer) in Canada and an orange picker, orange washer, sandwich-board man, gardener, and handyman in Southern California. During the fall and winter of 1897, Service subsisted in Los Angeles, where his routine included evenings in the public library. Here, Service wrote some of his first verse. In 1908, his writings were collected in *Songs of a Sourdough*, which included his most famous work, "The Cremation of Sam McGee." Among his semiauto-biographical tributes to the vagabond life, "The Men That Don't Fit In" stands as a defiant celebration of the freedom of the road:

> There's a race of men that don't fit in,
> A race that can't stay still,
> So they break the hearts of kith and kin,
> And they roam the world at will.
> They range the field and they rove the flood,
> And they climb the mountain's crest,
> Theirs is the curse of the gypsy blood,
> And they don't know how to rest.[24]

Joe Hill's legacy extends far beyond his bylines. Born Joel Hagglund in a musically inclined Swedish family, Hill fled a life of grinding poverty when he and his brother immigrated to the United States in 1901. After stints as a porter and rigger, the twenty-two-year-old spent the next ten years wandering the country in search of work. Somewhere along the way, he became known as Joe Hill. In 1906, he was in San Francisco, where he wrote a sharp and compassionate account of the earthquake and fire. Arriving in San Pedro in 1910, Hill went to work on the docks unloading cargo as a member of crews that were a mixture of many ethnic groups, including Swedes, Mexicans, and Italians. A loner, who never drank alcohol nor smoked, Hill had a passion for music, often playing the piano at Sailor's Rest Mission. From a table in Malgren's Hall he sketched cartoons and wrote articles for both Swedish and American newspapers. Mostly he wrote songs and poems, many of them on the backs of laundry tickets and envelopes. "A pamphlet, no matter how good, is never read more than once," he wrote in a letter to a radical publication,

> but a song is learned by heart and repeated over and over, and I maintain that if a person can put a few cold, common sense facts into a song, and dress them up in a cloak of humor to take the dryness off of them, he will succeed in reaching a great number of workers who are too intelligent or too indifferent to read a pamphlet on economic science.[25]

Hill proved this theory during the Southern Pacific Railroad strike of 1910, when he wrote a short, daring, and catchy song about a famous strikebreaker. "Casey Jones the Union Scab" soon became a favorite among bindlemen. Well aware of the conditions of the working class, Hill began using his songwriting as a weapon in the battle for a more just society, publishing dozens of songs and poems that expressed the trials and tribulations of life on the move. Such standbys as "Mr. Block," "Preacher and the Slave," and "Scissor Bill" were soon being sung and recited on picket lines, from soapboxes, and in union halls and jail cells. One of his most widely sung tunes, "The Tramp," included the lines:

> If you will shut your trap,
> I will tell you 'bout a chap,
> That was broke and up against it too for fair;
> He was not the kind to shirk.
> He was looking hard for work,
> But he heard the same old story everywhere.
>
> Chorus: Tramp, tramp, tramp, keep on a-tramping,
> Nothing doing here for you;
> If I catch you 'round again;
> You will wear the ball and chain,
> Keep on tramping, that's the best thing you can do.
>
> He walked up and down the street,
> 'Till the shoes fell off his feet;
> In a house he spied a lady cooking stew,
> And he said, "How do you do,
> May I chop some wood for you?"
> What the lady told him made him feel so blue.
>
> Chorus: Tramp, tramp, tramp, keep on a-tramping,
> Nothing doing here for you;
> If I catch you 'round again;
> You will wear the ball and chain,
> Keep on tramping, that's the best thing you can do.[26]

In 1914, Hill was convicted of murdering a grocer in Salt Lake City and sentenced to death. In the wake of the judgment, his songs and poems gained even wider fame. Facing down a firing squad on November 19, 1915, Hill supposedly asserted, "Don't mourn for me, Organize." Whether this final act of defiance is true or not, Hill quickly became a labor martyr and was later immortalized in a song by Alfred Hayes and Earl Robinson as the man "who never died."[27]

Bindlemen like Robert Service and Joe Hill did more than vent their anger in poems and songs. Natural, instinctive rebels, they called for work slowdowns, quickie strikes, and delays, and proposed a campaign of organized opposition. "Many a time riding the trains or sitting around jungle fires we heard rumors about a proposed organization of agricultural workers," recalled radical propagandist Ralph Chaplin after a year in the harvest fields. "We listened greedily. There were dark hints, knowing glances, and an occasional song or poem." On occasion, it amounted to more than idle chatter.[28]

The first time bindlemen struck California farmers in the twentieth century was late in the summer of 1902, when "a bunch of young fellows from town" joined a rowdy group of bindlemen who were picking prunes east of Fresno and walked out demanding $1.50 a day; a few weeks later, again capitalizing on the tremendous rush of harvest, they struck a second time and won an increase in wages to two dollars a day. Bindlemen did not lead that strike, but they participated in it, and their support was essential to its success. They did lead other spontaneous walkouts—among Sacramento hop pickers in 1901, Redlands orange pickers in 1904, and Fresno prune pickers in 1904. Although the press did not report every dispute, the California State Bureau of Labor Statistics found these walkouts common enough to list them in its 1905 report. Growers were also well aware of the spate of strikes. When about two hundred bindlemen struck Fresno raisin grape growers in the summer of 1906, farm leaders, although able to break the strike, began to fear that labor militancy, once confined largely to the Japanese, was gaining momentum.[29]

Angry bindlemen identified many points of leverage. And growers too realized just how open to attack they were at harvest. Hostage to the weather and susceptible to the vagaries of the labor market, they were constantly reminded of their vulnerability. Writing in his memoir, *Fifty Years a Rancher*, C. C. Teague explained that he did "not have an operation as flexible as the average industrial operation." To make matters worse, new industries were emerging every year, increasing the demand for bindlemen in direct competition with agriculture's expanding needs.[30]

Every bindleman with more than one season under his belt knew that agricultural labor was radically different from factory work. Unlike industry, where mechanization, mass-production techniques, and laborsaving devices cut labor demands, intensive fruit and vegetable farming defied mechanization. Except for the wheat harvest and certain aspects of land preparation, it was the sweat and sinews of bindlemen and other hand laborers, not machines, that brought in the harvests. A twenty-five-acre citrus orchard needed about the same number of bindlemen as a two-hundred-acre wheat or corn farm. But it was not just that California's farmers required large numbers of workers, they also required them at exactly the right moment. With perishable crops, even a slight delay in picking was enough to affect quality and marketability. Whether it was peaches or celery, crops had to be picked and packed early enough to prevent spoilage. Hops, which had to be picked and dried at a very specific stage in the growth cycle, could be ruined by just a few hours of hot north wind if left on the vines. Additionally, with new areas opening up to cultivation and growers continually rotating new plants in to replace played out crops (typically a grape grower would have workers removing and replanting 10 percent of his vineyards annually), labor demands were constantly expanding. And, unlike manufacturing industries where lost production could be made up over time, growers prevented from harvesting a single crop might lose their income for an entire year. Under these circumstances, bindlemen understood that agriculture did not have recourse to common anti-union tactics like the lockout. While steel and textile mill operators might close down plants during a dispute, resuming production once matters were settled, growers could not delay production. For all of these reasons, explained California Fruit Growers Association general manager R. I. Bentley before the U.S. Commission on Industrial Relations, he and others "would want to get out of the business" if forced to yield to demands from organized labor.[31]

As things actually worked out, bindlemen realized that those vulnerabilities were more than compensated for by obstacles that made agriculture one of the most difficult of all industries to organize. Because most commercial farms in California were comparatively small, with three of four in 1912 encompassing less than 175 acres (about eighty acres smaller than in 1900) and employing less than a dozen harvest hands, agriculture remained widely dispersed and could therefore absorb and dissipate many traditional tactics of organized confrontation. Strategies that worked in the steel industry, the coal mines, or the textile mills usually failed in agriculture. While bindlemen might set up a picket line around a factory and tie up operations, and they might do the same on a single field, they could not extend their leverage much beyond a few farms; it was virtually impossible to shut down harvest operations that spread out over hundreds of square miles.[32]

Even if they were willing to challenge the agricultural industry, bindlemen then faced the barriers of language and ethnicity. With Japanese and aging Chinese bachelors still holding down the bulk of the jobs, bindlemen also had to consider increasingly large numbers of Sikhs and Mexicans, along with women and children, and sometimes entire families, who were also moving into the fields. Working in the Wheatland, Ukiah, and Pleasanton hop yards, bindlemen were but one part of a labor force that included Indians from neighboring rancherías and citizens from nearby towns. In citrus groves and new farming districts near Los Angeles, crews of "young scholars" from grades six through twelve worked beside bindlemen while gathering the walnut crop (their hands becoming so deeply stained by the brown husks during "hulling" that they could only be cleaned with a mixture of soda, vinegar, and much scrubbing). It was the same story in many other agricultural districts, where the ever changing mixture of peoples added cultural, language, age, and sexual barriers to the already difficult task of class action.[33]

Compounding these obstacles was the highly individualistic attitude of many bindlemen. "We shared the policy of dog-eat-dog with the human pack who preyed upon us, the 'shack' and judge who shook us down for stealing rides, and the farmers who haggled pennies when it came time to pay off and sometimes refused to pay at all," remembered Ralph Chaplin. But despite their anger, discontent, and class consciousness, bindlemen nevertheless lacked the kinds of permanent institutions, fraternal and mutual benefit protective associations, and connections to communities that were essential to sustaining an organized campaign. They were men who, according to the Immigration Commission, dealt "with employers individually, not in groups or through agents." Following the advice of farm labor experts from the University of California, growers kept a lid on discontent by identifying uppity bindlemen and discharging them "before they lower[ed] the morale of other men."[34]

Adding to the difficulties faced by bindlemen was the nature of the fieldwork itself. Average employment in seasonal industries was brief, and harvest work was briefest of all; a bindleman averaged just seven days on the job as compared to ten days in construction, fifteen to thirty days in lumber, thirty days in canneries, and sixty days in mining. Under these circumstances, it was difficult to create a permanent base for organization. How, for example, could organizers collect dues, maintain membership lists, contact members, and perform other important tasks essential to maintaining a union? Among trade union leaders, it was assumed that local unions required stable, geographically concentrated workers and therefore could not easily function among bindlemen and other dispersed workers. Not surprisingly, when the Commission on Industrial Relations considered these matters, it found little basis for union activity among bindlemen, discovering that 65 per cent of the men it interviewed were "absolutely unorganized and knew nothing of any labor organization." In fact, bindlemen were so dispersed that University of Wisconsin professor John R. Commons, after studying the problems of organizing men on the move, lamented in a letter to a colleague that it seemed "almost hopeless to try to maintain a permanent union of itinerant workers."[35]

&

With bindlemen unable to establish a stable base of opposition, growers dictated the conditions of employment and instituted a labor policy based solely on cold calculations that decreased cost and maximized profit. Manipulating the wage structure and developing industrywide pay scales, they extended the workday and the workweek, and continued to hire and fire at will. Adopting wage policies from the citrus industry, they extracted the maximum effort by tying wages to productivity through a wage/piece-rate payment system. To ensure low labor turnover, some even withheld a portion of a picker's paycheck until the end of the harvest and called it a "bonus." Others paid workers in chits and tokens redeemable only at company stores. A few like Rancho Santa Anita owner Lucky Baldwin held field hands under a system of near peonage. When men grumbled and threatened violence because they had not been paid, or had been paid only a fraction of what they were owed, Baldwin gathered up a few hundred dollars in cash and stood outside the ranch store. Threatening to fire them if they persisted, he haggled and stalled and bought their services for little more than a few pairs of boots, groceries, chickens, cheap jewelry, and a couple of silver dollars to buy cheap liquor. Two or three hundred dollars in cash thus distributed could relieve a two or three thousand dollar payroll bill and finance further improvements in his gardens, lawns, vineyards, orchards, winding driveways, and stables full of thoroughbred horses.[36]

Bindlemen understood that when conditions grew intolerable, they had one of three choices: retaliate, work, or quit. Often, they feigned sickness, a strategy that occasionally kept entire crews confined to bunkhouses until a particularly mean foreman was removed. But there were many ways to resist short of violence. By malingering, slowing down, damaging equipment, and, as a last resort, confronting superiors directly, bindlemen fought against speedups and avoided work. As on the wheat farms, retaliation often involved beating up a hated foreman, but on occasion, when pushed too hard, bindlemen would resort to murder. Such was the case on July 29, 1887, when Willows field hand Sam Welling shot I. V. H. Safford and then fled to the Sierra foothills. "What prompted Welling to do the shooting is unknown," reported the *Colusa Sun*. Much more is known about the 1890 murder case involving a field hand named August Koening. A full-bearded, heavy drinking, temperamental German immigrant with deep-set eyes and protruding forehead, Koening exemplified the life of a marginal bindleman. Working sporadically on the Miller and Lux ranches in the San Joaquin Valley in the 1880s, Koening averaged between four and six months' employment but was unable to secure a more stable position. On April 27, 1890, after a night of saloon hopping in nearby Firebaugh, he returned to the Davis ranch, where he had been employed by Miller and Lux, vowing to murder Henry Miller and Davis ranch superintendent E. L. Davis. Disarmed by a laborer, Koening grabbed a shotgun, and unable to find either Miller or Davis, attacked ranch foreman Henry Berger, dropping him dead with a charge of buckshot to the chest. Fleeing the scene with a well-armed posse in pursuit, Koening was discovered hiding in some tall grass at nightfall and wounded by a shot to his head. Transported to Fresno by Constable J. J. Mullery, Koening died the next day in the county jail. "If Henry Miller had been on the Davis ranch yesterday," observed the *Fresno Evening Expositor*, "he would in all probability have been dead today."[37]

Two years later and two hundred miles south, another murder case again exposed the anger and frustration of bindlemen. This case centered on Francisco Torres, a twenty-five-year-old Mexican bindleman, later described by the *Los Angeles Times* as "a low type of the Mexican race, evidently more Indian than white" with "rough oily skin, dark olive complexion . . . rather long arms . . . and about a No. 5 shoe." Employed on the Modjeska ranch in Santiago Canyon about twenty-three miles east of Santa Ana, Torres worked through the summer of 1892 under foreman William McKelvey, a mean and penny-pinching fifty-five-year-old retired sea captain. On Saturday, July 31, McKelvey withheld $2.50 from Torres's weekly paycheck of nine dollars, falsely claiming the deduction was a "poll tax" that Torres owed the county tax collector. When McKelvey refused to pay the balance, Torres quit. What next happened can only be surmised, as there were no witnesses.[38]

According to later newspaper accounts, Torres returned to the ranch the following Sunday morning and found McKelvey in the barn gathering chicken feed. Torres again demanded payment, and when their quarrel turned physical, Torres clubbed McKelvey over the head with a pick handle, crushing his skull; he then stabbed the foreman and hid in the bushes as the sheriff arrived. Torres remained in hiding until McKelvey's body had been removed, then fled into the mountains. A huge manhunt ensued. Torres was eventually captured near Mesa Grande in San Diego County, in possession of McKelvey's wallet and a five-dollar gold piece. Taken by train to the Sycamore Street jail in Santa Ana to await trial, he was greeted by huge crowds of Mexicans and Californios, many of them sympathetic. But on the night of August 20, a group of masked men dragged Torres from the flimsy jail and hung him from a telephone pole at the corner of Fourth and Sycamore streets. At the time of his lynching, a judge had been deliberating a motion to move his case to another jurisdiction, inspiring one member of the lynch mob to hang a sign on the body reading, "Change of Venue."[39]

FIGURE 53. Francisco Torres shortly before he was lynched, 1893. Courtesy of the Bowers Museum of Cultural Art, Santa Ana, California.

The Torres lynching was the last to occur in Orange County. Although an investigation took place, no members of the lynch mob—rumored to include many "prominent citizens"—were ever identified. The lesson was not lost on bindlemen, who, as members of a segregated minority not considered part of the community, knew very well not to trust the justice of "prominent citizens." For some, conflict was inevitable. "The only way to become a good fighter," explained one bindleman in a letter to a radical publication, "is to welcome every opportunity of fighting for your rights."[40]

To advance their course, bindlemen committed acts of sabotage, like loading rocks into boxes of oranges, pulling down large quantities of hops and allowing them to go to waste on the ground, or working slowly. But the majority protested their lot by doing what seasonal workers in other industries did. They became, if provoked, "two-day workers." Writing from a jungle camp just after walking off a job, one bindleman put it this way: "You have a sudden and severe attack of 'wanderlust' . . . and before you realize the fact you are headed for the nearest freight yards . . . and you don't know where you are going to go next or when or why nor where you are going to sleep tonight and don't care a dam either." Hood River Blackie put it more succinctly: "You decide, well, I'm going to quit. I'm not going to do this anymore."[41]

Bindlemen often worked just long enough to build up a small paycheck or stake and fill their stomachs. As the *Pacific Rural Press* explained, "It is a common thing for a man to come along, obtain employment, work 2 or 3 days, demand his pay and leave, without notice, at a critical time." Inventing an excuse for requesting their pay—usually for clothes or medical attention—bindlemen rolled up their bundles and disappeared. "He promptly shakes off the dust of a locality from his feet whenever board is bad, or the boss is too exacting, or the work unduly tiresome, departing for the next job, even if it be 500 miles away," observed one correspondent for *Solidarity*. More commonly, bindlemen faced with intolerable conditions waited until the next payday, drew their wages, and hit the road. "Where the conditions are bad," explained Commission on Industrial Relations investigator Peter A. Speek, "The migratory laborer considers it to be only a temporary job, only for a few days; he expects to find afterwards a better job. After a few days on the job he quits it. He has satisfied his hunger and possibly earned several dollars of money, and he goes. The employers hire new starving." Usually men left alone, but sometimes an entire harvest crew would depart en masse. After losing large numbers of bindlemen during the 1905–6 harvest, the manager of the Indian Hill Citrus Union explained, "They commence to get nervous the last part of the season and want to get into something more steady."[42]

Because bindlemen quit work so frequently, farm economists interested in the problem of labor turnover studied them closely. "As a class they are easily disgusted with poor machinery, and if an implement continually breaks, they are likely to quit without notice," warned Richard Adams in one of his widely cited farm management textbooks. Bindlemen, studies found, tended to leave in larger numbers and with more frequency during good years when jobs were plentiful; during depression years, they were more likely to stay put. They also left more frequently in the spring, when they could easily find work, and less often in the fall, when the harvest season was winding down. In 1901, the California State Bureau of Labor Statistics analyzed job turnover among bindlemen, and found that only one in ten men remained to the end of a job. One in twenty left protesting poor housing; three of ten left because of bad treatment, low wages, and/or "seasonal shiftlessness," meaning they were generally dissatisfied with everything. The remainder gave no clear reason for their departure. "The majority come here and have no food or money," complained an editor for *Pacific Rural Press*, "and about the time you are in the rush of harvest, they either get a thirst spell or a longing for travel, so roll up their blanket (if they are cold blooded enough to possess such an article), draw the few dollars or cents due them and leave."[43]

So great was the turnover among bindlemen that in an attempt to predict behavior, growers tried to measure it. In 1914, Wheatland hop grower E. Clements Horst estimated that for every two bindlemen arriving during the harvest, one departed. In the Napa Valley in 1889, a St. Helena–area wine grape grower found that of forty bindlemen hired on a Friday, only three were still at work by noon on Saturday. Likewise, in 1902, Limoneira Ranch manager C. C. Teague reported that "our crew of men of necessity is constantly changing." Regardless of crop or region, job turnover among bindlemen was so great that growers often debated the problem at their annual conventions. To keep his ninety-three-man crew, the operator of a dried fruit packing plant in Fresno explained to the 1902 California State Fruit Growers Convention that he had to hire forty-one new men each week. "While I need only about fifty men, I had over two hundred names of laborers on my roll during the season," added Fresno raisin grower John S. Dore. "I had to keep my team continually on the road between the ranch and Fresno taking them to and from town." M. E. Angler, who farmed six hundred acres of fruit near Lodi and Manteca, similarly reported that "during the harvest season there was a standing order for men." Countless other growers voiced similar experiences over the years. Losing tolerance for such stragglers, Sacramento Valley fruit grower H. P. Stabler told fellow horticulturalists that he was tired of the way the average field hand worked for five to seven days, then asked for his check "and with a jaunty air . . . rides to town, there to enjoy himself, until moneyless [sic] and hungry he repeats the performance. He is therefore impossible as an orchard hand."[44]

After studying the work habits of bindlemen, one government investigator computed the monthly turnover rate at 245 percent. "Five days is the average that we got out of the laborer," Riverside citrus grower James Mills told the Commission on Industrial Relations. On some fruit ranches, bindlemen seemed to come and go at will. Daily journal entries from Davisville almond farmer George Pierce indicate just how large the problem had become by 1900. To maintain his labor force, Pierce observed that he "went to town in a.m. for more men, got three . . . went to town in p.m. and got more men." Just during the course of a few weeks, he recorded a revolving door of men. "Four new men came at supper time . . . another left before breakfast . . . new man left during the night . . . Joe Morgan quit in a.m. Two others in p.m.," were typical journal entries. The turnover eventually became too much for some growers. "I have tried white laborers, and with unsatisfactory results," explained Vacaville fruit grower A. T. Hatch to the *San Francisco Call*. "One year I used whites exclusively in the harvest time, and found it unprofitable. At least one-third of the force was continually getting locked up in the jail in Suisun for petty misdemeanors, and it was a great deal of trouble to keep a full crew. I was advertising and hunting for help all the time."[45]

Such behavior confirmed something that few agricultural employers wanted to acknowledge. While growers praised the virtues of hard work, bindlemen did not. By packing up and leaving, they rejected both their employer's attitude toward work discipline and their passion for growing crops. What to some seemed like aimless, irresponsible behavior, was, in fact, an ordered response to bad conditions—perhaps the only rational response. This was the conclusion of California Commission of Immigration and Housing investigator Frederick C. Mills, who spent two months traveling disguised as a bindleman in the summer of 1914. Among other jobs, Mills worked for several weeks at the Drake Citrus Association packinghouse in the Tulare County town of Lindsay. After watching a bindleman pick some oranges from the sorting line, smash them to the floor, and walk out of the packinghouse after being admonished by his foreman, Mills wrote in his journal, "It seems to be a characteristic of the American type worker to take no 'lip' from the boss. He is seldom so tied to a job but that he will throw it up if the boss curses him." Hardly demoralized and powerless, such men instead found that the worse off they were, the more freedom they had; with nothing to lose, they lost nothing by leaving. Much to the consternation of many labor organizers, this did not necessarily make them prounion. As the radical labor publication *Solidarity* explained, "The privilege of quitting, is what keeps the scissorbill [a worker who lacked class consciousness] from organizing."[46]

Perpetually broke, always hungry, and constantly facing what Peter A. Speek called an "uncertain, gloomy and almost hopeless future," such men seemed to one newspaperman an "unhappy . . . poor white caste." A life spent stealing rides, drifting between jobs, and living outside mainstream culture imparted to bindlemen a deep resentment of their plight; it molded their attitudes toward employers, religion, labor organizations, and the state, and generated in them an explosive potential. Unleashing a torrent of invective to Speek, one bindleman explained,

> We are nonentities. By constant migration we lose our right to vote. There-
> fore, the parties and politicians do not care for us. They court the labor
> unions, not us migratory laborers. That's why the legislatures do not do any-
> thing for us . . . We are considered to be outside the pale of respectability and
> when we are out of work we are considered almost as criminals. Although we
> are living beings and have the right to life, but legally we are dead.[47]

Reiterating these sentiments in letters to the radical press, other angry and alienated bindlemen nevertheless cautioned against violent retaliation as a remedy for their predicament. "I don't want any revenge," wrote Tyler Williams to the radical publication *Solidarity*. "If I wanted revenge I would burn up half of the box cars and bridges along the pike." Yet some bindlemen could not contain their discontent. In a wrathful poem sent to *Industrial Worker*, Jim Seymour, a frequenter of Chicago's "Bughouse Square" (Newberry Square) who traveled throughout California and the West, wrote:

> You leaches who live off the fat of the land,
> You overhead parasites, look at my hands.
> You laugh at it now, it is blistered and coarse;
> But such are the hands, quite familiar with force.
> And such are the hands that have furnished you drink.
> The hands of the slaves who are learning to think.
> And hands that have red, will crush you as well;
> And cast your damned carcass into hell.[48]

Later commentators would argue that such anger perfectly captured Karl Marx's classic description of the proletariat—men without property who regarded morality, religion, family, and national identity as "so many bourgeois prejudices, behind which lurk in ambush just as many bourgeois interests." Reported the *San Francisco Bulletin*: "Politically they are vassals of discontent, full to the brim with wrath and grumbling."[49]

Surveys confirmed their anger. Four of ten bindlemen questioned by Carleton Parker in his 1914 study of casual labor had no ambition, no plans for the future, no allegiance to law or property rights. Skeptical, embittered, and disillusioned, many advocated "the complete destruction of the present political and economic system." Seven in ten told Parker that they would continue floating between jobs and had no intention of looking for steady work. Country, flag, national loyalty, and political participation meant little (if anything) to them. Four of ten held radical views on political and economic questions, while one of four was indifferent to all matters politic. Harboring deep grievances against growers and maintaining an intense discontent with society in general, many of these men sympathized with critics of large-scale agriculture and voiced strong sympathy for dissident movements. Such men, according to Parker, were anxious and sullenly hostile, "ever . . . ready to take up political or legal war against the employing class." Harassed by police and authorities, ignored by government, forced to break the law constantly, and always on the move, bindlemen embodied class realities that could never have emerged from simply reading Marxist treatises or memorizing revolutionary tracts. Their apparent acceptance of the status quo was, according to one bindleman, a "thin surface over a seething volcano of disgust and discontent with the conditions under which . . . slaves are toiling." Growers feared as much. "They are an uneasy class of people," admitted Santa Clara Valley fruit grower George E. Hyde. One bindleman summarized the discontent in a letter to the *International Socialist Review*: "To understand the class struggle," he explained, "you must ride on top of the boxcars or underneath the boxcars."[50]

As their opportunities shrank and it seemed that bindlemen would never overcome their circumstances, "a grim brooding power" capable of organizing farmworkers moved into the fields, introducing a new radicalism that threatened to reshape labor relations and turn the tables on growers. Developments far from California spurred the change. On January 2, 1905, twenty-six seasoned unionists, socialists, anarchists, and revolutionaries from throughout the country met secretly in a hall on Lake Street in Chicago to discuss how to inject new life into the veins of the moribund American labor movement. Convinced that they could not advance their cause with a labor movement that excluded unskilled workers and immigrants, they called for a more militant organization, one aimed at conducting industrial life on behalf of all workers, regardless of race, sex, or national origin. "We have been naught, we shall be all," they sang. To everyone's surprise, delegates succeeded. In three days of intensive, sometimes acrimonious meetings, they condemned the splintering of the labor movement into craft unions, denounced the American Federation of Labor as the "American Separation of Labor," and adopted a manifesto advocating "one great industrial union embracing all industries . . . founded on the class struggle, and . . . conducted in harmony with the recognition of the irrepressible conflict between the capitalist class and the working class." Calling for a "Continental Congress of the Working Class" to convene in Chicago that summer, attendees chose as chairman William "Big Bill" Haywood, the fiery, dynamic, heavy drinking, one-eyed, gun-toting secretary of the Western Federation of Miners (WFM).[51]

Six months later, on the hot, muggy morning of June 27, Haywood draped his prodigious figure over a podium in Brand's Hall on North Clark Street. Picking up a piece of loose board, he employed it as a makeshift gavel and called to order a miscellany of 203 delegates who reflected every nuance of American radicalism; it was a gathering one attendee later labeled "the greatest conglomeration of freaks that ever met." A commanding speaker with a powerful, entrancing delivery, Haywood drew wild cheers with a rousing speech outlining an extraordinary program of action. "We are here for the purpose of organizing a Labor Organization, an organization broad enough to take in all the working class," he proclaimed. "What I want to see from this organization, is an uplifting of the fellow that is down in the gutter . . . realizing that society can be no better than its most miserable."[52]

A long and heated debate developed over what to call the new organization. Some advocated "The One Big Union," others the "International Workers of the World." Delegates finally settled on the name "Industrial Workers of the World" (IWW). Far more difficult was the matter of the IWW's politics and structure. Delegates drew from lessons learned in strikes at Coeur d'Alene, Leadville, and Cripple Creek, and combined this firsthand knowledge with philosophical ideas from such diverse sources as the Knights of Labor, English Chartists, French syndicalists, and Darwinian scientists. After days of debate, they managed to agree on five key points: first, that a class war existed between workers and their bosses; second, that there was only one crime, and it was being poor; third, that there was no reason for a man, woman, or child to suffer poverty; fourth, that reform politics and political action were useless; and finally, that there was too much "organized scabbery," jurisdictional squabbling, labor autocracy, and hobnobbing between prosperous labor leaders and the millionaires in the National Civic Federation. In an attempt to abolish the wage system and create a new social order, the IWW would organize all workers—skilled and unskilled, young and old, men and women, Italians, Slavs, Finns, Hungarians, Chinese, Japanese, Mexicans, and African-Americans, "timber wolves," dishwashers, and bindlestiffs. So extraordinary were these developments that *International Socialist Review* editor Algie Simons labeled the union "a decisive turning point in American working-class history."[53]

Craft unionists quickly derided the IWW as standing for "I Won't Work," "I Want Whiskey," "Irresponsible Wholesale Wreckers," and "Idle Wonder Workers." Most simply referred to the organization as the Wobblies. One story has the name deriving from the wobbling motion of the boxcars that men rode between jobs, but the most widely accepted had the name originating with a Chinese restaurant owner in Vancouver, British Columbia. Finding it difficult to pronounce "IWW" as he was serving one group, he tried to ask "Are you IWW," but it came out sounding like "All lou eyee wobble wobble?" The name Wobblies stuck.[54]

Bolstered by the remnants of several defunct unions and boasting a dedicated and enthusiastic core of members, the IWW appeared strong at its inception. But, in fact, it was weak, poor, and fragmented. Membership in California was no exception. Many California Wobblies apparently came from among the ranks of Finnish, Russian, and Lithuanian miners and loggers, active in the WFM, who had left Montana and Colorado for the West Coast. Others were perpetual drifters who found their only comfort in the IWW. Two of the most prominent California Wobblies were Joe Ettor, a Brooklyn-born former trade unionist, much-praised street orator, and full-time IWW organizer; and Mortimer Downing, a well-known San Francisco journalist who joined the IWW after meeting several Wobblies on a train to Los Angeles just before the founding convention. Ettor would later be remembered as a leader of the Lawrence, Massachusetts, textile strike of 1912, where he would be arrested, tried, and acquitted of murdering a policeman, while Downing would earn fame as a radical propagandist in numerous court cases well into the 1920s.[55]

A third San Francisco radical was the most formidable and influential of all California Wobblies, George Speed. "Half-scholar, half-agitator," and an excellent speaker, the tall and gaunt Speed had directed contingents of Kelley's Army and Coxey's Army to Washington, D.C., in 1893–94, ran unsuccessfully for the state assembly on the Socialist Party ticket in 1896, and thereafter remained active in the International Workingman's Association, Socialist Party, Socialist Labor Party, and numerous additional radical groups until 1905, when he abandoned the AFL Seaman's Union and joined the Wobblies. With his weather-beaten face and blazing eyes, Speed impressed U.S. senator Frank Walsh in his appearance before the Commission on Industrial Relations as "a true fighter . . . and an old Spartan." Russian-born Wobbly Matilda Robbins called him "the incarnation of the complete proletarian revolutionist," an austere, wise, humorous old bachelor, uncorrupted, and incorruptible, who "knew no life outside of the IWW."[56]

Speed and other San Francisco Wobblies accomplished very little during their first four months other than establishing Local 173, the first IWW local in California, in a storefront south of Market Street. Only loosely affiliated with the national organization, they watched helplessly as organizers moved into the northeastern states, led countless, widely scattered and largely unsuccessful strikes, and launched aggressive incursions against AFL affiliates, particularly in mining and brewing. Unable to mount any organizing activity of their own within the state, they initially looked for guidance outside California, to one of the founders of the IWW, Ben Williams.

Short and frail looking, with thin, drooping shoulders, piercing eyes, a fine nose, and a well-trimmed Vandyke beard flanked by sideburns, Williams had joined the IWW at the 1905 founding convention after several years as a Socialist agitator. At the behest of San Francisco Wobblies, he left Chicago early in November of that year to organize loggers around Humboldt County, in Northern California. But his efforts soon ended in disaster when he was invited to speak to the Eureka Trades Council at the Union Labor Hall. Williams bored and alienated his audience by reciting extracts from the IWW's constitution and attacking the well-regarded local AFL leadership as an "organization of stooges." As a result, Williams was roundly denounced. "He made so many sweeping and rash statements that it is difficult to see how such procedure can gain much sympathy," commented the *Labor News*. "What any local in Humboldt County would have to gain by joining the new organization it is difficult to see."[57]

Following the fiasco at Eureka, Williams returned to Chicago, and the IWW concentrated most of its energies outside of California. Waging struggles among the textile workers, factory hands, streetcar drivers, and miners in cities as widely scattered as Skowhegan, Maine, and Goldfield, Nevada, the IWW established a reputation as a militant defender of the downtrodden. But the union experienced a major setback when William D. Haywood and former WFM president William Moyer were arrested and charged with assassinating former Idaho governor Frank Steunenberg. The court case paralyzed the young organization by sapping meager funds, diverting energy and resources away from organizing activities, and removing its most experienced, popular, and capable leaders. Even more important, the trial tagged the IWW as a violent, antisocial, bomb-throwing organization of desperadoes and anarchists. Dissension further wracked the IWW when an insurgent faction employed extraconstitutional means to purge the entire founding leadership in 1906. Following the coup, the WFM withdrew from the IWW, removing twenty-seven thousand dues-paying members.[58]

With the national organization collapsing into factional strife, California Wobblies were left to their own devices. Many leaders who came to the union from metropolitan industrial unions saw agriculture as an attractive—if difficult—target. With its interlocking complex of banks, chemical companies, machinery manufacturers, packing plants, and marketing cooperatives, the farming industry had become a forty-million-dollars-a-year business, which impressed historian Steven Stoll as "the ultimate city-serving countryside." Because of the perishable nature of crops, urban Wobblies reasoned, farmers were extremely vulnerable. But from their experiences riding the rods, many bindlemen-turned-Wobblies already knew that the nature of seasonal farmwork hindered traditional organizing tactics. So California Wobblies adopted an entirely new and unique approach. Contacting men as they congregated in urban skid rows for the winter, organizers would first convert men to the cause of the IWW, then collect them into so-called mixed locals. These were temporary organizations, part propaganda clubs, part recruiting units, unable to bargain collectively or enforce contracts, which held workers from different industries until they had recruited sufficient numbers. At that point, the mixed locals would be dissolved in favor of appropriate industrial locals. As George Speed explained, the idea at first was: "You establish a nucleus here, and a nucleus there, and they get in touch with other men, they get imbued with . . . ideas . . . sentiment and feeling."[59]

Before Wobblies could implement their strategy of organizing bindlemen into mixed locals, disaster struck. On April 18, 1906, the IWW lost its California headquarters when San Francisco suffered a catastrophic earthquake and fire. Organizing ceased until a new base of operations could be set up in a tent in a vacant lot several weeks later. With the city afloat in unemployed workingmen and twenty-five thousand laborers (most of them Irish and Italian) under the thumb of employers who felt little pressure to hire union workers, San Francisco leader Joe Ettor turned away from bindlemen and instead attempted to exploit the boom in building trades. Eventually arrested after leading several local strikes, Ettor proceeded to languish in jail until George Speed organized mass protest marches down "Newspaper Assassins' Row" (Market Street). Because the jails were in such bad condition, police could not make mass arrests. As a result, the Wobblies gained notoriety for defying authorities, but they achieved little else. When the IWW held its second annual convention in Chicago that summer, California was not represented. With just one local in the state and little to show other than some inroads among San Pedro longshoremen, an unsuccessful strike among San Francisco bakers, and a mass rally against the violence used to defeat the miners in Goldfield, Nevada, the IWW was so weak and disorganized that, in his annual report, IWW secretary-treasurer William Trautmann conceded that Wobblies were in no position to take on California farmers. "The agricultural elements," he said, "are going to be the last and hardest to be organized."[60]

Trautmann did not know exactly how to overcome the obstacles to organizing California farmworkers. But he and other Wobblies did insist that they had an important part to play in their lives, and they were convinced that the time was ripe for action. The rewards could be great, for organized farmworkers were a potentially large force for revolutionary change. Success would require new and innovative techniques, the most important being a method for reaching farmworkers, and a time and place to make their move.

CHAPTER TWENTY-FOUR

I've Been Robbed

The Struggle to Organize Farmworkers

One afternoon in the winter of 1906, a silver-tongued Wobbly named Jack Phelan mounted an improvised platform at the corner of Sixth and Mission streets in the slave market of San Francisco. As usual, hundreds of bindlemen packed the sidewalks. Seeking to gather an audience, Phelan raised his arms and started yelling at the top of his lungs, "I've been robbed! I've been robbed!" Startled by the commotion, men put down their newspapers, paused from their conversations, turned their attention to the cries of distress, and prepared to apprehend the robbers. When the sidewalk filled, Phelan stepped back onto the soapbox and raised his hands as if to thank the assembled mass for coming to his defense. Only then did he reveal his true intentions. "I've been robbed by the capitalist system," he shouted, launching into a tirade against the injustices of society and calling on the assembled bindlemen to join the Industrial Workers of the World.[1]

Union organizers had known for at least a generation that holding down a street corner was one effective way to contact the "true victims" of industrial capitalism. And since orators usually mounted a soapbox, fruit box, packing crate, whiskey barrel, or some other elevated platform in order to see their audience and be heard, the technique became known as "soapboxing" and its practitioners as "soapboxers." So important and accepted was soapboxing that, on many occasions, bindlemen defended it in what came to be known as "free speech fights." The first of these occurred in August 1896, when San Francisco police arrested three Socialist Labor Party (SLP) soapboxers, among them George Speed, for haranguing derelicts, winos, sailors, and bindlemen. While the official reason for the arrests was that the men were too loud and blocked streets and sidewalks, in fact the real reason was the radical nature of the views being espoused. Long dependent on lecture halls and the streets as forums for their message, the SLP would not tolerate any obstruction; to protest the arrest, about one hundred party members stood silently on the same street corner with raised banners proclaiming, "Absolute Silence Will Prevail" and "Please Don't Make Noise." For this,

FIGURE 54. Soapboxer addressing a crowd, San Diego, ca. 1911. Courtesy of the San Diego Historical Society.

they were arrested en masse. In 1897, Oakland Socialist Party members led by writer Jack London went to jail to protest efforts to stifle soapboxing activities in that city. There were free speech fights in Los Angeles in October 1900, San Jose in the autumn of 1903, and again in Oakland in 1905. By 1908, the SLP had become locked into an ongoing, low-grade battle for free speech in a half-dozen cities around the state. That March, the campaign took a dramatic turn when a coalition of Los Angeles Socialists and other radicals were arrested for violating a law against public speaking without a permit. At one point, a long line of men mounted a soapbox one by one, each to be arrested. Each then demanded his own jury trial, a prospect that would have placed such a huge burden on public coffers that the Los Angeles city council instead repealed the ordinance and dismissed all charges against those in jail. "Free Speech Is Won," crowed *Common Sense*, the official publication of the SLP in Los Angeles.[2]

Effective use of nonviolent mass resistance and jail packing made a deep impression on Wobblies who, realizing that they would never attract bindlemen to their cause with traditional organizing techniques, decided to use street speaking as the cornerstone for their plan to build a labor movement among seasonal and transient workers in California. One IWW organizer described the technique as "just like dripping water on a blotter—if you drip enough of it on the center it will soak through clean to the edges." From their street-corner pulpits, Wobblies began recruiting, organizing, and attacking the common enemies of all western workers. One veteran soapboxer put it this way: "We were like old Wesleyan preachers, only we were preaching the Gospel of discontent to a box car congregation."[3]

Soapboxers established their first mixed local in Los Angeles on July 12, 1906; they added a second in September. By the end of the year, Wobblies claimed about six hundred members in California, evenly split between the two Los Angeles locals and the original local in San Francisco. Weak and disorganized, these locals posed little threat to employers, and were nothing more than paper organizations; lacking rent money, hampered by barren treasuries, and hindered by the unrestrained rotation of leaders, they were usually too poor to support even a single soapboxer. With little to show after a year and a half of work, all three shut their doors in spring of 1907 as men departed for the farms, forests, and construction camps. They would only fill up again when men returned to the cities that fall.[4]

The limitations of soapboxing and organizing members into mixed locals provoked extensive debate among national IWW leaders early in 1908, when general executive board members began demanding a more aggressive farm labor organizing campaign. Whatever their backgrounds or racial and ethnic composition, reasoned IWW leaders, bindlemen and other farm laborers lived in rudimentary camps and shared the same dismal conditions and low wages. Whether they picked fruit or drove combines, all wanted clean beds, clean bunkhouses, and decent food; tired of packing bindles from one job to another, they would surely respond to promises of bindle-burning parties and a better life through industrial solidarity. But any labor union hoping to succeed among migrant workers would have to adapt to the realities of life on the move. "Workers on farms and orchards . . . are by the very nature of their work, segregated during the larger part of the year from the workers in the cities," reasoned the *Industrial Union Bulletin*. "Scattered over large districts they seldom have a chance to congregate in large masses; to move them to concerted action seems to be a difficult task." The question was how to capitalize on whatever inroads had been gained by soapboxing.[5]

Wobblies quickly settled on a plan, which, simple as it was, nonetheless amounted to a small revolution. First, they would continue with their soapbox campaign among bindlemen during the off-season in the urban slave markets. Second, they would focus on a common enemy, the employment agent or "shark," whose "untrustworthiness," according to a state investigating commission, was "a matter of common knowledge." Third, from their street-corner pulpits, Wobblies would continue to excoriate the evils of seasonal employment, while in the pages of *Industrial Worker* they would launch a program to help workers find permanent jobs and avoid trouble. Finally, they would establish small IWW locals throughout California's agricultural districts.[6]

Hoping to break the link between farmers, workers, and sharks and allow the IWW to gain control of the flow of labor, San Francisco Local 173 in January 1908, took the unprecedented step of establishing a hiring hall at 510 Larkin Street, where growers and other employers could hire workers. But when IWW correspondent James Palmer wrote to the *Pacific Rural Press* announcing that farm help could be obtained by contacting the office (and a similar facility in Los Angeles), the newspaper advised readers that it knew nothing about the IWW and could not recommend it as a source of labor.[7]

That summer, Wobblies moved into the fields for the first time. H. S. Carroll, a Los Angeles Wobbly and frequent contributor to *Industrial Worker*, established a farmworker local in the town of Holtville, a shipping center for the Imperial Valley cantaloupe industry. From Holtville, Carroll moved through the valley, planting additional locals at El Centro and Brawley. Initially, valley residents were confused by these developments. When the Holtville local opened, for example, hundreds of residents arrived to pay their water bills, thinking that "IWW" stood for the Imperial Valley Water Works. Quickly chastising residents for their mistake, the *Imperial Valley Press* issued a stern warning, labeling the IWW "troublemakers" and "loafing" men.[8]

On June 7, an IWW organizer mounted a soapbox on Main Street in Brawley to address a Sunday evening crowd of about one hundred men and boys. As he called on cantaloupe pickers to demand wages of four dollars a day or let the crop rot in the fields, the city marshal yanked the man from his platform, declaring that he needed to apply for a permit if he wished to continue. The audience began shouting in the speaker's defense, but when he attempted to climb back onto the box and finish his talk, the city marshal drew his gun, swore out twelve deputies, and quickly dispersed the crowd. Angered by their treatment, about sixty unemployed men who had been listening carried the protest to a nearby packing shed owned by L. M. Lyon. After again being scattered by law enforcement, the men threatened to destroy the shed. When a packing shed burned down later that evening, severely injuring two men, the IWW was blamed. Enraged by the incident, the *Imperial Valley Press* wrote:

> If the citizens of this country are the sort of men they are believed to be, the
> disturbers will succeed only in getting themselves in to trouble and jail . . .
> and they will be lucky if nothing worse than jail sentences befall them.
> Organization and peaceable efforts to correct any wrongs which may exist
> will be approved, but plug-ugly tactics and vicious stirring up of strife and
> disorder are not to be tolerated.[9]

As the IWW continued to struggle in the Imperial Valley, it inevitably made contact with Japanese field hands. But within the IWW, there had been considerable disagreement as to whether organizing the Japanese was necessary—or even possible. "It is practically useless, for the present time and under present conditions for the IWW to . . . organize these men," argued George Speed at the union's third annual IWW convention. "We have enough to do . . . and I think it would retard our development." But Spokane organizer J. H. Walsh disagreed. In an article entitled "Japanese and Chinese Exclusion or Industrial Organization," Walsh rebuked Speed and other cautious Wobblies, predicting that because they rarely worked as individuals and were usually bound to labor contractors, Japanese field hands "can be organized as rapidly, if not more so, than any other nationality on earth."[10]

Jumping into the debate, *Industrial Worker* continually reminded unionists who rebelled at the notion of accepting the Japanese as their equals that "a yellow skin is to be preferred a thousand times to a yellow heart." The paper further drew attention to Japanese militancy and solidarity by pointing out their success in the Fresno raisin harvest. Whereas "many [white field hands] will follow the harvest, eat rotten food, and sleep in their master's straw stacks," observed the paper, the Japanese would not tolerate such conditions. "How long it will be before a body of 5,000 American laborers will have the energy and manhood to strike in a body." Some Wobblies went even further. "The Japanese are organized, they are past masters of the art of bringing John Farmer to his knees," added one IWW organizer in Fresno. "My advice is learn the tactics used by the Japanese. Go thou and do likewise."[11]

Had the IWW been able to attract the Japanese—or even form an alliance with them—it would have made for a truly awesome organization. But despite reports to the contrary, few if any Japanese field hands ever joined the IWW. Most had a basic disagreement with the IWW's revolutionary goals. Whereas the IWW aimed to undermine and eventually replace American capitalism, Japanese field hands intended to work within the system. They were doing so well that membership in the IWW offered no practical benefits. They would stick with what they had already achieved under the *keiyaku-nin*.[12]

Failure to incorporate the Japanese left the Wobblies on their own as they launched an organizing campaign early in 1909. Moving into Redlands, they established Local 419 in a storefront office in the heart of the citrus district. Focusing entirely on bread-and-butter issues instead of radical politics, Local 419 leaders vowed to "see if we can't get a bed to sleep in, water enough to take a bath and decent food," arguing that there "was nothing to prevent the men who follow the harvest from raising wages and getting a shorter day." Branch locals in surrounding labor camps concentrated on uniting workers who were scattered over such large distances that they seldom had a chance to come together.[13]

These efforts did not go unnoticed by three conservative California state labor leaders, who now stepped into the picture as the IWW pondered what to do next. Two were Norwegian immigrants, Olaf Tveitmoe and Andrew Furuseth; the third was German-born Paul N. Scharrenberg. Prominent members of a group of San Francisco labor leaders described by Louis Adamic in his book *Dynamite* as "The San Francisco gorillas," the men were living legends: Tveitmoe as the head of the Cement Worker's Union Local 1, editor of *Organized Labor*, and secretary-treasurer to the powerful Building Trades Council; Furuseth as the longtime leader of the socialist-leaning Sailors' Union of the Pacific (SUP), who had long campaigned to protect sailors from shanghaiing and semislavery at the hands of ship captains and owners; and Scharrenberg as secretary and chief lobbyist of the forty-five-thousand-member California State Federation of Labor (CSFL), one of the strongest and most effective state labor federations in the country. Veterans of many strikes, all had experienced the most grinding kinds of labor, Tveitmoe while working as a roustabout, Furuseth and Scharrenberg while sailing the high seas. Given their own backgrounds, the three men were naturally sympathetic to oppressed and unorganized segments of the labor force like farmworkers, a position that was only reinforced by their growing dissatisfaction with AFL president Samuel Gompers's emphasis on crafts rather than industries. Sharing a growing fear of bindlemen acting as strikebreakers, the three men had raised the issue at every CSFL convention, until finally, in 1908, under the impetus of the IWW's efforts, they had convinced the Oakland Labor Council to discuss the issue of organizing farmworkers. Carrying their fight to the AFL national convention that fall, they had elicited pious proclamations from among the rank and file but failed to win over executive council members who, convinced that it would be "impossible to organize permanent unions" among migratory laborers, delegated responsibility to state labor federations that could expend their resources organizing farmworkers.[14]

As the IWW picked up momentum, the three leaders pressed their case at the 1909 annual meeting of the CSFL. Under their prodding, the CSFL executive council in October established a Joint Committee on Migratory Labor, appointed Sailors' Union members J. B. Dale and Edward Thompson organizers, and obtained a federal charter for the United Laborer's Union. "Work is difficult and slow," reported Thompson after initial organizing efforts in Alameda County,

> for the class to which my effort is directed has so long been considered as industrial and to some extent social jetsam that a psychological effect has been produced. They are heterogeneous as to language, intelligence, experience and standards of life; they are hard to approach, suspicious of my notices, heartsore at the failures of the past along lines of organization and doubtful of the efficiency of Unions from the standpoint of the unskilled; and last, and saddest, in many instances they appear satisfied with their sphere and estate.[15]

As the United Laborer's Union stumbled into action during the spring of 1910, Wobblies spread out across the state and established agricultural locals in Redding, Tulare, Sacramento, and Bakersfield. From these bases, a steady stream of organizers went out to work among the migrants. They lectured on the job, sold IWW songbooks, distributed IWW literature, and signed up as many men as possible, then sent the names, initiation fees, and dues to the nearest local. "The harvest is ripe," declared *Solidarity*, urging more men to "get out into the harvest fields, obtain work and carry on the agitation for the One Big Union." True to the IWW's principles, organizers did not discriminate in their efforts to gain support. "We are doing our best to get the slaves organized," reported Holtville Local 437 secretary John R. Boyd,

> and we will get results before long. There is great field work . . . among the Mexicans. My object in writing this is to let the membership know that they may expect great results from the Mexican workers before long . . .
> We held a propaganda meeting in our hall, with about 25 Mexicans present, who listened to Fellow Worker Berrera, and my humble self expound the principles of the one big union. We intend to hold propaganda meetings in Spanish once a week from this time on.[16]

Holding all of these efforts together were the IWW meeting halls. Unique in the annals of the American working class, these institutions served as much more than collective bargaining clubs and places for executive direction of the union. By the summer of 1910, IWW halls were serving as homes to hundreds of bindlemen in every city and major agricultural district of California. "The migratory . . . needed a place to park his 'bindle' and to brew an occasional pot of 'java' in addition to flopping on the floor," recalled IWW organizer and bard Ralph Chaplin in his book *Wobbly*. This was exactly what IWW halls offered. Broad, multidimensional institutions that served as crash pads, mess halls, mail drops, restaurants, and hangouts, IWW halls were invariably located in the poorest sections of town where they provided bindlemen with their only free welcome outside the saloon and the Salvation Army soup line. Many remained open twenty-four hours a day and promised an ongoing card game. A common saying was that IWW halls were a kind of bindleman's lodge and "social substitute for the saloon."[17]

Besides shelter, companionship, and recreation, IWW halls also provided bindlemen with large, well-stocked reading rooms. For men accustomed to spending time each winter keeping warm in public libraries, the lure was almost irresistible, and the IWW advertised them widely in its press. "Come and rest and read with us in a large commodious and comfortable reading room," exclaimed Redlands Local 419 in *Industrial Worker*. In San Francisco, the IWW advertised "a fine reading room and library" at its headquarters on Front Avenue. "Wherever, in the West, there is an IWW local, you will find an intellectual center," observed the radical journalist John Reed, "a place where men read philosophy, economics, the latest plays, novels, where art and poetry are discussed, and international politics."[18]

Of all that they read and discussed, nothing more captivated bindlemen and advanced the cause of industrial unionism than the IWW's own publications. Written not by professional journalists but by fellow workers, Wobbly literature employed appealing language, a distinct point of view, and gritty content. Reading the IWW press, bindlemen acquired a clear image of what not to become, along with a good dose of union lore and tales of heroes and martyrs. Common, everyday dilemmas of a bindleman's life were covered in *Solidarity*, the IWW's official publication. Of even more interest to California bindlemen, though, was *Industrial Worker*. Published in Spokane, Washington, a crossroads on the migratory circuit, and billing itself as "The Spirit of the West," *Industrial Worker* came closer than any other periodical to reflecting the mind and spirit of the average bindleman. A dozen other newspapers in five different languages, including two in Spanish—*Huelga General* (General Strike) and *El Proletario* (The Proletariat)—carried the IWW message to immigrant bindlemen. In addition to these official publications, the IWW "Publishing Bureau" also printed thousands of cheap pamphlets annually. In contrast to the restrained AFL press or lofty Socialist Party publications, popular pamphlets like *Sabotage*, *Direct Action: Tactics and Methods*, and William Trautmann's *Why Strikes Are Lost* were lively reads. Reaching groups that never bothered with the AFL press, these handouts comprised a large chunk of the literature bindlemen found in every IWW hall.[19]

Songs further reinforced the bond between union and bindlemen. As an organizing technique, song was first used in Spokane in 1908, when West Coast organizer J. H. Walsh found himself drowned out by a Salvation Army band while trying to reach bindlemen holed up in the city's slave markets. To compete, Walsh formed his own ensemble and performed such sarcastically revolutionary compositions as Mac McClintock's "Bum Song" and "The Big Rock Candy Mountain." By May 1908, songs had become such a powerful weapon that *Industrial Union Bulletin* reported: "For the past two or three months in our agitational meetings we have had a few songs by some of the fellow workers. It is really surprising how soon a crowd will form in the street to hear a song in the interest of the working class." Later that year, a group led by Richard Brazier (who would become an IWW general executive board member) compiled Wobbly songs into *The Little Red Songbook*. Printed in lots of fifty thousand, it bore the provocative subtitle "Songs to Fan the Flames of Discontent." Most of the songwriters remained anonymous.[20]

Described by folklorist John Greenway as "the first great collection of labor songs ever assembled for utilitarian purposes," the *Songbook* contained thirty-eight compositions that encouraged discontent and rebellion, stirred workers into action, and shocked them out of their apathy and complacency. Often focusing on the troubles and rewards of floating labor, songs spread the philosophy of the IWW to a wide audience and, by capturing much of the spirit, humor, and experiences of migratory and seasonal workers, reinforced the message of class solidarity. Dignifying vagabonds, vilifying law enforcement, and vindicating jungle life, songs included in *The Little Red Songbook* promoted feelings of defiance, strength, pride, and justice. Set to familiar religious melodies, popular ballads, and haunting laments, these compositions frequently involved little more than transforming a Gospel hymn by changing the "I" to "We." No recognized tune was exempt. "Onward Christian Soldiers" might become "Onward One Big Union," while "Marching Through Georgia" became "Paint 'er Red." The popular Wobbly song, "Solidarity Forever," was set to the tune of "John Brown's Body."[21]

Sung with near religious fervor around campfires, Wobbly songs spread rapidly among the floating population and created a sense of unity among widely dispersed bindlemen. Such feelings suggested to some that the One Big Union was right around the corner. "We could practically own California," predicted one Tulare County farmhand during the 1910 alfalfa harvest, if only more organizers would "get out into the harvest fields, obtain work, and carry on the agitation for the One Big Union."[22]

Other bindlemen regarded the IWW's program as a colossal waste of energy and resources. Songs, soapboxing, poems, publications, mixed locals, and slave market agitation, they said, had yielded meager results. Although Wobblies could be found in every town, they held no contracts, were shunned by the Chinese and Japanese, and maintained only the smallest presence in the agricultural districts. Plagued by barren treasuries, incompetent organizers, and anarchistic members who elected new officials weekly, the Oakland and San Pedro locals were in perpetual chaos and offered little hope or inspiration to men returning from a hard summer working in the fields, while San Francisco Local 173 reported half of its three hundred members unemployed and only a few agitators at work, mainly in the building trades. Los Angeles Wobblies were so hated by trade unionists that they were barred from the premises of the city's new AFL "labor temple." San Diego Local 13, which bragged of selling one hundred IWW newspapers per week, nevertheless complained that it was in need of an organizer who would actually leave headquarters and do some organizing. California Wobblies had learned only to attract men during their winter layover and were yet to discover how to sustain an ongoing labor organization. Impatient bindlemen soon began demanding a tangible victory. They found it in Fresno.[23]

ஆ

Often referred to as the "Raisin Capital of the World" and "Queen City of the San Joaquin Valley," Fresno in the spring of 1910 was a bustling city of banks, trolleys, automobiles, and wide boulevards. *Sunset* magazine described it as a place that "has created millionaires and is maintaining them with the prodigality of its wealth and the handsome incomes accruing therefrom." With a population of twenty-five thousand, including large immigrant communities of Armenians, Italians, and Mexicans, Fresno was also a highly stratified labor hub. Huge crews were required to pick, process, and tend the encircling San Joaquin Valley fruit crop. Every August and September, five thousand Japanese and three thousand bindlemen moved in just for the raisin harvest. Packing into an area adjacent to the town's main business district and blending into the edges of Chinatown, bindlemen sustained what the *Fresno Morning Republican* labeled "a whole criminal reservation . . . equal to that of an Eastern city of ten times our population." Here, at various corners along Mariposa, Tulare, and Fresno streets, amid cheap hotels, saloons, brothels, and general stores, Wobblies found an ideal audience for their soapboxing.[24]

Nothing frightened Fresno growers or threatened to undermine their system of racially graduated wage rates more than the possibility of a broad-based union of Asians, Mexicans, and bindlemen. Consequently, when a lone Wobbly had attempted to organize raisin harvesters in the summer of 1908, Fresno Chief of Police William Shaw ordered the man to cease and desist. "We have a large fruit crop on our hands, and it must be cheaply handled," the officer remarked. "If you undertake to organize common labor, we will run you out of town." But the Wobblies did not quit. By fall of 1909, they had established Local 66, rented a union hall, and won a wide following among Mexican railroad workers and white field hands. Late in February 1910, several Wobblies passing through Fresno on their way to Portland reported to *Industrial Worker* that "the local has a hard row to hoe, as this town is certainly a bourgcois controlled place. . . . If I had told the Chief [of Police] that I was an IWW man in making application for the [speaking] permit I would have been driven from the town." As if to prove this statement true, Chief Shaw soon cracked down on Wobbly soapboxers. His actions ignited a fight the likes of which had never been seen before—and has not been seen since—in the farmworker story.[25]

The first skirmish occurred on the evening of April 17, when a man described by the *Fresno Morning Republican* as a "Mexican Socialist" attempted to address the "peons" on the corner of F and Tulare streets in the heart of the slave market. The subject of the man's address was to have been "The Oppressing Powers of the Police," but before he could speak, Police Chief Shaw hauled him off the platform. Whether or not this was Wobbly organizer Frank Little, the tall, muscular, one-eyed half-Indian hard rock miner and Wobbly leader, is debatable, but there is little doubt Little was soon directing IWW actions in Fresno. Personifying the IWW's spirit of militant rebelliousness, physical courage, and proletarian struggle, Little had five months earlier been in Spokane, where J. H. Walsh was trying to break the hold of employment agents on the job market. Despite run-ins with local police, Walsh, Little, and other Wobblies maintained their campaign throughout the winter of 1910 until in March, Spokane city authorities rescinded their ban on street speaking and revoked the licenses of nineteen of thirty-one employment agents. Inspired by the value of direct action and passive resistance, Little headed south intent on carrying the campaign to Fresno.[26]

By early May, Little had whipped Local 66 into fighting shape, and reported to *Industrial Worker*, with some exaggeration, that large numbers of Russians, Germans, Mexicans, Japanese, and Chinese were joining the IWW each day. After securing a permit to speak for two nights (provided he did not verbally attack the police or any governmental body), Little began organizing Mexicans employed by the Santa Fe Railroad east of town. Paid just one dollar a day and required to purchase their supplies at the company store, the workers had quickly become indebted to their employer. Little convinced them to stockpile food and supplies and then stop working. "We have the silent strike on . . . The slave drivers are wild—the slaves won't work as hard as they want them to," he reported to *Industrial Worker*. When the railroads fired many of those involved, Little found himself with a cadre of agitators willing to roam the streets.[27]

At the same time, Wobblies organized a sizable portion of the city's street railway workers and began attacking the city's labor contractors. When a contractor named Silverman had problems recruiting low-paid workers to build a dam east of Fresno, he complained to Chief Shaw. According to the IWW, Shaw supposedly replied, "Take the name of every man who refuses a job and I will put him in jail." By May 28, so many Wobblies were being arrested, threatened, and roughed up by police that *Industrial Worker* reported the confrontation had "come to open war between them and the local police."[28]

On May 29, Little scheduled a well-publicized meeting in Courthouse Park at the end of Mariposa Street. As the first Wobblies mounted their soapboxes to speak, Shaw rescinded their permit. As in other fights, soapboxers then defied authorities by taking the podium and reading from the federal and state constitutions and the Declaration of Independence; Chief Shaw seized the documents and ripped them to shreds. Three days later, a young boilermaker helper named Elmer Shean defied the ban by speaking on the streets of Chinatown and was promptly arrested on a vagrancy charge. Chief Shaw then announced "every permit for speaking on the streets has been canceled . . . and if the Industrial Workers attempt to hold meetings they will be arrested." Furthermore, any man without a job would be arrested on vagrancy charges.[29]

"We are up against a big fight here in the near future," predicted Little. "All fighters must prepare to come to Fresno when the call is sent out." In a June 4 telegram to *Industrial Worker*, Little vowed, "We will go ahead and organize and this fall when the harvest is over, and we can get the men to make the fight, we will take the streets in spite of the police . . . all hobo agitators head this way and get ready to come . . . and help whip the city of Fresno."[30]

ৡ৯

As Little had predicted, agitation slackened during the summer harvest months. A few months later, as Little began planning for the fall campaign, police began arresting Wobblies. On August 24, Little and two other Wobblies were arrested for "creating a disturbance" in front of the Fresno Beer Hall. Three days later, Little wrote to *Industrial Worker* and *Solidarity* from jail, admitting problems organizing bindlemen. As Little languished in jail, more men arrived from the Northwest to take up the fight. In response, Chief Shaw revoked all speaking permits. On Labor Day, he allowed union locals to parade and have a picnic in Zapp's Park, but denied Wobblies the right to march, citing their red flags as unnecessarily provocative. On September 7, the *Fresno Morning Republican* inflamed matters further by reporting that a "disgruntled" and "miscreant" Wobbly had torn the American flag off the flagpole outside the Federated Trades Union Hall.[31]

Throughout all of this, Little continued to plan for the impending battle. "We must prepare to take to the streets, but we have to have outside aid," he wrote to *Solidarity*. "There should be at least 500 men ready to go to jail the day the fight starts. So all rebels who can do so, prepare to come to Fresno County, California, and help us whip the capitalist thugs." Referring to mistakes made in Spokane, Little vowed that no IWW funds in Fresno would be wasted on lawyers and defense funds; all money collected by Local 66 would be used to maintain Wobbly soapboxers, keep the court docket full, and empty Fresno's municipal pocketbook. Veterans of earlier free speech fights in Spokane and Missoula, Montana, would lead the way. *Industrial Worker* endorsed the plan on September 10, concluding that "the only way to prevent the enforcement of this anti-speech law is to go to Fresno and BREAK THE LAW. Break it, smash it into unrecognizable pulp." There was no room for compromise. "The welfare of the IWW west of the Rockies now hinges on this fight . . . We have got to win the streets of Fresno, we have got to show the Bosses that we mean business and that unless we make it stick in Raisin City we are going to have trouble in other California towns. All aboard for Fresno! Free Speech Fight On!"[32]

As these events were unfolding, a contingent of Wobblies arrived from Spokane, ready to enter the fray. One of them, Albert V. Roe, "Agent for I.W.W. Literature," was promptly arrested for selling IWW publications and given thirty days in jail. Another, C. L. "Charlie" Filigno, was arrested for soapboxing. Shortly after his release on September 21, Little headed to Coalinga in southwestern Fresno County to organize oil workers. While he was away, Chief Shaw picked off IWW soapboxers one by one, jailing nearly thirty men in three weeks.[33]

Support for Shaw's actions came from Chester H. Rowell, one of Fresno's preeminent citizens, the editor of the *Fresno Morning Republican*. A leading figure in state politics and the key supporter of Hiram Johnson's nomination for governor, Rowell was also a successful businessman and staunch promoter of the raisin industry. Opposed to labor unions and steadfast in his belief that "the welfare of the whole community" hinged on a successful raisin harvest, Rowell had for years been deeply troubled by the Japanese, whom he labeled "very difficult to handle." Now fearing that bindlemen under IWW leadership might mimic or even unite with the Japanese, Rowell led the charge against the Wobblies.[34]

Rowell's newspaper first featured an item about a Wobbly who refused to pay a restaurant bill on "socialist principles." Another article soon told of a Wobbly, shot while attempting to hold up the train depot at Firebaugh, who "without a doubt was en route to Fresno to join their much talked about war against the city police in an effort to gain what they call 'free speech.'" Rowell's paper also reported Wobblies insulting women, dynamiting construction projects, and stealing chickens, among other things. It was a smear campaign that even growers found excessive. But following Rowell's example, every Fresno newspaper unleashed its wrath on the Wobblies. Carrying rumors of anonymous threats against the city and its public officials, they reported that as many as five thousand bindlemen were on their way to Fresno. Probably the most provocative commentary came from *Fresno Herald and Democrat* editor Paul Vandor: "It is incumbent upon all classes of citizens to aid the police in the suppression of these Industrial Workers of the World if they attempt to disturb the peace of the city," he wrote on October 21. "For men to come here with the express purposes of creating trouble, a whipping post and cat-o-nine tails well seasoned by soaking in salt water is none too harsh a treatment for peace breakers. Indeed such a punishment would prove more efficacious than a term in a dark cell."[35]

Despite inflated newspaper reports and a cartoon in *Industrial Worker* showing the arm of an IWW member bringing a rain of thunder and lightning down on Fresno, Local 66 was finding it difficult to recruit volunteers. Only about three hundred men—not thousands—were in town. About one hundred had set up camp along the railroad tracks south of Fresno, and near Fowler another fifty Wobblies up from Los Angeles had also flopped along the right-of-way. But with more men promised from Portland and Spokane, it seemed only a matter of time before Wobblies took the offensive, flooded the city with men, and choked the courts and jails.[36]

❧

Mass arrests began on the evening of October 14, when thirteen Wobblies, including Frank Little, followed one another onto a soapbox on the corner of I and Mariposa streets and started talking about employment agents and the IWW. As Little urged Fresno police officers to organize and strike for an eight-hour day, he was labeled the "chief agitator of the bunch" and arrested. Seeing him thrown into the tank along with a dozen other speakers—supposedly in violation of a city ordinance prohibiting street speaking—jailed Wobblies broke out singing the "Red Flag." To stop them from singing, jailers turned the prison fire hose on them. After the city closed every meeting in town on October 15, the

IWW moved out of its downtown headquarters into a large tent at Palm and Belmont avenues on the western outskirts of town, where it established facilities to feed and house the stream of men pouring into town. The only condition for aid was that anyone accepting assistance was obliged to speak and risk arrest. Seven more Wobblies mounted the soapbox and were arrested that evening; on October 16, nine more went to jail; the next evening, five more were hauled off. As the arrests mounted, some East Coast Wobblies began questioning the effectiveness of the fight. The *Industrial Worker*, observing the debate over whether or not propaganda battles were useless, reported that "the welfare of the I.W.W. west of the Rockies now hinges on this fight."[37]

Offered bail of $250, none of the arrested Wobblies could raise the funds. Instead, each man demanded a separate jury trial. Managing their own defenses, they challenged as many prospective jurors as was allowed, employed countless delaying tactics, took the witness stand on their own behalf, expounded freely on IWW history and goals before packed courtrooms, and so dragged out each case that Fresno's courts could handle only one or two per day. Although most Wobblies would eventually be convicted and required to serve out their sentence, their trials exacted a huge burden on the city's taxpayers, judges, and businessmen. To make matters worse, none was a compliant prisoner. While in jail, they held propaganda meetings and conducted the business of Local 66. Briefly the city tried to negotiate with the prisoners, hoping for an early end to the battle, but the men unanimously opposed any such deal. As tensions rose and conditions deteriorated, a few men pled guilty and left, but those who resisted accomplished a surprising amount of union business under worsening conditions. "We are not allowed to wash ourselves or use the toilet and we decided in the future not to eat if we didn't get a chance to wash ourselves," wrote Herbert Minderman in a diary confiscated by the police and later published in the *Fresno Morning Republican*.[38]

Sanitation was not the only concern. Locked four to a cell and fed mostly bread and water, the prisoners received far from humane treatment. But when their complaints grew too loud, firemen appeared at the jail and turned 150-pound pressure hoses on the men in their cells. Prisoners tried to protect themselves by erecting a barricade of mattresses, but the hose pressure was so great that it swept the mattresses away and drove the Wobblies against the cell walls. Some men sought refuge by lying flat on the floor, but firemen kept the hoses trained on the men for a half-hour, covering the prisoners in water bruises and stripping them of their clothes. Minderman called this "getting the watercure." On October 20, Minderman wrote: "Hunger don't go through and we got the watercure again for demanding a wash. In our cell was an old miner eighty years old and he was game through the fight. Got bread diet—two fifths of a five cent loaf of bread and two cups of brown beverage was all that we got."[39]

On October 22, Minderman and thirty-three others were moved to the bullpen, a small enclosure without seats, where prisoners were forced to stand. But by ceasing their propaganda meetings, the prisoners negotiated better meals. Recording the ebb and flow of the jail fight, Minderman wrote in his diary on October 27, "Last night some of the men got back their fighting spirit and kicked against the jailor." His entry for dinner that night was, "146 beans, two little potatoes, two fifths of a five cent loaf of bread, one half cubic inch of meat, some-times bone and two cups of brown beverage, and twice a week of raisins." On October 29, he noted: "Three more fighters leave us and we remain with forty-four." November 1: "Motion for hunger strike lost, eleven for with twenty against. Doree organized fourteen men to plead guilty at once and refuse to stay in jail one day longer." On November 2, all but five of fifty-eight men pled guilty and received three-month "floaters," meaning they had to leave town within three hours and not return for the duration of the sentence. The men went immediately to the IWW camp and, as one explained, "postponed the fight and intended to come back if the rank and file of the IWW is willing to fight."[40]

Encouraged by Shaw's rough handling of the prisoners, the *Fresno Morning Republican* on October 22 predicted that the fight would "soon die a natural death." Shaw himself continued making wholesale arrests. At this point, it appeared that the IWW had indeed been defeated. With vigilantes patrolling the railroads to intercept workers arriving by boxcar and the national IWW unable to back the fight with much manpower or money, Local 66 went underground and members stopped carrying IWW literature. Newly arrived Wobblies reported to a coffee shop on I Street and "by handing in a slip of paper purporting to be an order for goods" received directions on how to proceed. After the store owner was discovered, Local 66 began sending all written communications and money orders to a post office box. Meanwhile, IWW organizers traversed the San Joaquin Valley, rounding up men recently released from jail and convincing them to return to Fresno. "As soon as 15 men accumulate," wrote *Industrial Worker*, "we will go at it again."[41]

❦

On November 27, Local 66 sent men back into the streets in force. By now Fresno citizens had grown nearly hysterical. Adding to the panic was the recent mayoral election in Los Angeles, where Socialists and labor unionists had missed electing Job Harriman by just eight hundred votes. With rumors circulating that two hundred Wobblies were on their way into Fresno, it seemed to many that a dangerous radical tide was sweeping through California. Hoping to break the back of Local 66 before the reinforcements arrived, Chief Shaw stepped up mass arrests—but he could not jail Wobblies fast enough. On December 1, he called for a chain gang "as the proper method of getting rid of the Industrial Workers." Shaw next appeared to endorse vigilante action: "Unless something is done immediately," he warned, "the city will be filled to overflowing with these vags."[42]

Meanwhile, Wobblies continued to speak. A dispatch to *Solidarity* from IWW general secretary Vincent St. John seemed to lend support. "If the fight is won it will mean that the IWW will be able to organize the great bulk of the unorganized of the state of California," he wrote. "If the fight is not won now, it means that we will have to make it in the future."[43]

Shaw and other Fresno authorities had assumed that by arresting leaders like Frank Little they could defeat the union, but their assumption was deeply flawed. Neither Little, nor Charlie Filigno, nor Albert V. Roe, nor anyone else had defined leadership positions. No single individual led the group. On December 8, Frank Little was again brought to trial. Conducting his own defense, he astounded everyone present by pointing out that, contrary to popular belief, Fresno had no law prohibiting public speaking. All those imprisoned had been held under the auspices of a police regulation that had been mistaken for a city ordinance. Judge John Briggs was forced to release Little and twenty-four other Wobblies. The remaining thirty men had been arrested on vagrancy charges and remained in jail. Without any law explicitly prohibiting street speaking, Chief Shaw reluctantly ordered his patrolmen to allow Wobblies to speak unmolested.[44]

That night, citizens of Fresno resorted to violence in an attempt to end the battle. Encouraged by Chief Shaw's statement that "if the citizens wished to act they might and he would not interfere," a mob of between five hundred and one thousand men surrounded IWW soapboxers at the corner of Mariposa and I streets, pulled men from soapboxes, chased them down, and beat them severely. Marching on the jail, the mob then roughed-up several Wobblies caught visiting their comrades. Prevented by police from entering the jail, the mob instead marched on the IWW camp outside of town. There, IWW members briefly turned them back but according to the *Fresno Morning Republican*, "the sight of the huge IWW flag which hung over the camp, aroused the mob to uncontrollable fury and the first dash was made for this." Terrorized and outnumbered, the Wobblies quickly fled. As sheriff's deputies stood by, the mob then torched the tent and everything inside, cheering as Wobbly headquarters burned to the ground. Marching back into town, the mob again gathered outside the city jail and demanded that the police turn over all incarcerated Wobblies. Sheriff Robert Chittenden refused, but promised the mob that the Socialist owner of the land where the camp had stood would be prosecuted if the Wobblies were allowed to return. No members of the mob were arrested. On December 11, Sheriff Chittenden announced that Fresno would not permit any "treasonous speeches," warning that "the sooner the I.W.W. learn this the better it will be for them."[45]

News of Fresno's mob action was carried throughout the nation on the Associated Press. Reactions varied. Some viewed the IWW as a bunch of evil malcontents deserving of suppression. Others believed the violence lowered the citizens of Fresno to the level of the IWW. There were sermons advocating suppression of street speaking and there were sermons defending the IWW's right to organize. Republican papers like Michael De Young's *San Francisco Chronicle* praised the Fresno mob for ending the IWW's "agitation." But the rabidly anti-IWW editor of the *Sacramento Bee*, Charles McClatchy, came down hard on the mob, writing: "When the good citizens and the authorities of any city countenance such outrages as those committed by the Fresno mob, the IWW may be said to shine by comparison."[46]

Even Chester Rowell, while still openly hostile to the IWW, nevertheless denounced the mob's rampage as too felonious and violent to stomach. "In fact," he observed, "the most practical objection to the mob is the fact that it defeats its own purpose and makes the effective suppression of the disturbers so much the harder." Certainly the violence only incensed the Wobblies. General Secretary Vincent St. John immediately wired lame-duck Governor James Gillett: "Action of 'respectable mob' will not deter this organization . . . free speech will be established in Fresno if it takes twenty years." Cautioned *Industrial Worker*: "Remember, despite police brutality, don't retaliate in kind."[47]

ℰ𝒶

As more Wobblies were arrested, jail conditions worsened. Minderman wrote in his diary: "Lawyer Moore visits us . . . In regard to the mobbing of our members and the burning of our camp he could not do anything because headquarters did not have the money to meet expenses. We called a meeting but there was so much misunderstanding that we decided to take no action in this matter until we got some better information."[48]

Despite vows not to do so, city officials met secretly with jailed IWW members on December 18 to discuss terms of a settlement. The following day, the prisoners were offered freedom if they would give up the fight. All refused. Meanwhile, Frank Little, now out of jail, established temporary headquarters for Local 66 just twenty miles south of Fresno in the small town of Kingsburg. On December 20, that city's board of trustees enacted its own version of an anti-street-speaking ordinance that read, in part: "It shall be and hereby made unlawful for any person to hold, conduct, or address any assemblage, meeting or gathering of persons, or to make or deliver any public speech, lecture or discourse, or to conduct to take part in any public debate or discussion, in or upon any public park, public street or alley."[49]

More arrests followed in Fresno two days later, filling the bullpen to overflowing. Still unbroken, the prisoners on December 22 protested the manhandling of a drunk by going on a hunger strike. Singing songs and shouting through their cell bars to a large meeting on the street outside, they complained so loudly that jailers again turned the fire hoses on them. After Wobblies continued singing and shouting to the crowd from behind "a fortress of their mattresses," firemen put an end to the protest by using picks to tear away the barrier and then hosing the men full force, leaving them standing knee deep in water throughout the cold winter night.[50]

By early January, most of the jailed Wobblies were ready to quit. Minderman's diary captured their despair. January 1: "Some of the boys lose their courage; there is talk of giving up the fight, because the fight is lost." January 2: "Nobody comes in and the future of the fight looks dark. Murdock puts up a good bluff in the way of speech and that brought back the spirit of the discouraged ones. After he finished his speech, he got a slime cough for an hour and half and it was necessary to call a doctor." One indignity followed another. Men were constantly searched. Those serving a sentence rather than awaiting trial were put to work in the public parks. Some Wobblies argued against jailhouse protest, fearing the watercure. Spirits brightened briefly on January 7 with the news that Spokane Police Chief Sullivan had been killed in an accident. Three days later, conditions in the overcrowded, wet, and frozen jail reached such a bad state that a doctor declared the facility unsanitary. Every prisoner had a cold, several were bedridden, and many verged on pneumonia. By January 12, more than one hundred men ranging in age from twenty-three to forty-five were behind bars. Minderman wrote on January 16: "It looks as though everything is lost. In the evening at our propaganda meeting Filigno and others made good speeches and statements about the way of fighting and cause and effect in fighting and that drove the clouds away."[51]

Just when all seemed lost, *Industrial Worker* editor Ralph Chaplin brought welcome support: "The *Industrial Worker* don't care how the fight started, whether it was called in proper time or not, whether a vote should have been taken to find out our strength for such a fight or how true any of the other objections might be that are being advanced against the fight," he wrote. "WE INTEND TO STICK TO THE BOYS IN JAIL TILL HELL FREEZES OVER." To back up the pledge, the IWW called for volunteers to go to Fresno, join the campaign, and pack the jail. "The only way the hobo can ever make a place for himself in the present system of society," pronounced *Solidarity*, "is to be ready to fight for his rights any old time and place at the drop of a hat." Once again, the popular press fed the hysteria with exaggerated accounts of Wobbly armies on the march. Reporting that upwards of five thousand men were "scheduled to start for Fresno" by boxcar, *The Denver Post* claimed that activists were so determined to get there that they had "announced their willingness to walk."[52]

Men did go to Fresno, but in far smaller numbers than reported—one hundred from Los Angeles, a dozen or so from Chicago, and a handful from scattered locals throughout the state. But their impending arrival took on even more ominous proportions because of events then unfolding in Southern California, where a revolution was brewing along the U.S.-Mexico border. After struggling for decades against dictatorial President Porfirio Díaz, two exiled Mexican brothers, Ricardo and Enrique Magón, raised an army and planned to solve the problem militarily. Calling the Díaz government a bunch of "sneaking, lying butchers," approximately 150 IWW members joined the brothers' band of socialists, mercenaries, adventurers, and Mexican citizens mobilizing at present-day Calexico/Mexicali.[53]

In January, the group crossed into Mexico prepared to spread the revolution, take control of the government, and ultimately redistribute land into the hands of the working classes. The troops were led by Major John Mosby, a onetime Bay Area Wobbly and Marine Corps deserter said to be descendant from Major John Mosby of Civil War fame, and William Stanley, a part-Indian from Canada who had joined the IWW in 1905. In an initial series of skirmishes, the revolutionary army defeated Mexican soldiers, took control of the border, briefly made the Holtville IWW headquarters capital of their new country, and began marching on Tijuana. But Mexican troops quickly rallied against the invaders. Ultimately, Mosby would be arrested, Stanley killed in battle, and the army subdued and imprisoned. Still, residents of Fresno saw these events—especially coming on the heels of the *Los Angeles Times* bombing—as further evidence that Wobblies now would soon bring violent revolution to Raisin City.[54]

Fear of invasion reached a fever pitch in mid-February, when a well-publicized contingent of Wobblies and socialists from Seattle calling themselves the Fresno Relief Brigade headed south to join the struggle. In Portland, 112 men, including thirty-six non-IWW members, paraded through the downtown district for several hours before jumping on a southbound train. When they reached Ashland,

Oregon, city police chased them off the trains and forced them to walk ten miles to the next train stop, but the brigade continued the journey south. *Solidarity* referred to the men collectively as the "Wobbly Train" and described them as "something new in the political history of the United States." Fearing what would happen if the brigade was allowed to reach Fresno, city officials there called on railroad authorities to police trains for agitators. Otherwise, they said, "no city and no railroad is safe." At the same time, Fresno police constructed a "rock pile" by hauling in huge granite blocks from a quarry north of town. The message was clear: Soapboxers caught violating the law could expect to serve a stint breaking rocks. Frank Little mocked the plan, recalling that when Spokane officials had tried a similar program, prisoners had broken all of the sledgehammer handles. Apparently the same thing happened in Fresno, because almost immediately after it was introduced, work on the rock pile ceased. Police blamed too many broken sledgehammers.[55]

On February 6, the Fresno County Sheriff's Office billed the city three hundred dollars for boarding prisoners, and an additional seven hundred dollars for related expenses. As penal costs continued to rise and more Wobblies appeared about to descend on Fresno, city authorities softened their stand and entered into secret negotiations with Local 66. Across the table, Wobblies proved able and realistic negotiators. Local 66 seemed completely unified and sent special communiqués to *Industrial Worker* and *Solidarity* calling for more men and citing the role of free speech fights in the class struggle. "The successful culmination of this fight will have a powerful effect in giving fresh impetus to our daily routine of constructive work and the eight-hour agitation," the committee told *Industrial Worker*. "And the MORE PERSISTENT THE FIGHT IS CONTESTED THE GREATER WILL BE THE EFFECT . . . Whether you like them or not, free speech fights must and will be fought . . . If the IWW wants to survive it will have to fight and fight hard." To *Solidarity*, the committee added, "This fight has now won the distinction of being the best and most classic example of solidarity ever demonstrated on this continent . . . all the more credible when it is remembered that it is fought by 'those ignorant hoboes.'"[56]

❧

On February 12, one hundred prisoners remained in the Fresno jail, many arrested without charge, many more having been incarcerated for more than forty days. On February 19, Fresno's prosecuting attorney met with the prisoners and offered a deal: those pleading guilty would be sentenced to no more than forty days, and those who had been arrested could continue soapboxing in the local park. On February 21, the city offered the IWW a strip of land at K Street near an alleyway where soapboxers could speak. But by then the IWW knew that the fight was won and refused the offer; negotiations continued.[57]

With 115 men in jail on February 22, Sheriff Chittenden refused to accept more prisoners. Still, Police Chief Shaw vowed to arrest street speakers for vagrancy and place them in the county jail over the sheriff's orders. That evening, Chester Rowell urged businessmen meeting in the Chamber of Commerce

Building to form a committee to speak with the IWW. On February 25, a five-member committee visited the jail and spoke with the Wobblies. But just as the two sides were meeting, and again two days later, crowds of several hundred men attacked Wobbly speakers, driving them from their soapboxes, chasing them through the streets, kicking and beating several unmercifully. In one of the IWW's more politically pragmatic moves, *Industrial Worker* tried to assure Fresno citizens that they had nothing to fear. "The impression seems to have gained currency that we are invading Fresno for no other purpose than to make trouble and smash laws," wrote *Industrial Worker*.

> Now to attempt to smash laws founded on social necessity is like trying to sweep back the Pacific with a broom. . . . All citizens must be granted the right to protect themselves for, if not, then there would be no reason for the existence of society or the laws thereof. . . . No, Mr. Taxpayer, we did not come here to smash laws: we only ask that they be upheld. . . . We are ready at any moment to leave you in peace, Mr. Taxpayer, if you will see to it that we are given some guarantee that we shall be left in peace.[58]

On the last day of February, the citizens' committee and city officials agreed to IWW demands. Fearing the Wobbly army was about to invade, municipal authorities revoked the ban on street speaking and began releasing prisoners. The *Fresno Morning Republican* printed the text of the agreement: (1) pardon of all Wobblies convicted and release of those awaiting trial; (2) a permit to speak at K Street, between Mariposa and Fresno streets, and on Tulare Street, between F and G streets in Chinatown; (3) IWW agreement to wire the general headquarters to halt the invasion; (4) those Wobblies released from jail would leave town if they were unable to find work. Three days later, the Wobbly Train reached Chico, but upon learning of the victory, the group disbanded, with only a few men continuing on to Fresno to join the celebration. Others headed to Baja California, to wait out the winter in a warm climate, while others returned to Portland and Seattle. On March 6, Local 66 wired IWW headquarters: "The Free Speech Fight is over, and won . . . Complete victory." On March 9, the mayor of Fresno announced that the city had repealed its ban on street speaking. "Another victory for the militants of the labor movement, the third in a little over a year . . . May there be many more," crowed *International Socialist Review*.[59]

Wobblies won this fight because officials in Fresno, compared to those in Spokane and Missoula, had been relatively restrained. While mobs attacked Wobblies, the general population did not support sustained violence and mass retaliation, and Fresno's progressive leanings and leadership, while hardly sympathetic to the Wobbly cause, had always stood for restraint. Also, the fight had capitalized on two aspects of a bindleman's life that usually impeded organization—migration and poverty. Normally an atomizing tendency, the ability to pack up and travel long distances quickly had become an asset that kept the Fresno jail cells full and soapboxers on the street corners. Besides, for many, jail life was in some ways no worse than life in the jungles and boardinghouses.[60]

The IWW emerged from Fresno as a much-feared radical organization. Newspapers across the country had carried stories of the fight, which revealed a power heretofore unwielded by bindlemen. Although the IWW had failed to achieve its goal of flooding the jail with five hundred men—there were never more than 130 members in jail at any one time—it had shown the power of protest and passive resistance and seemed poised to use propaganda fights as an initial step to organizing farmworkers throughout the state. A month after the free speech fight ended, Local 66 moved into a new hall. "We are holding street meetings twice a week, which are well attended," the local reported.[61]

Later commentators would cite the Fresno free speech fight as a shining defense of First Amendment rights. But for Wobblies, the victory involved nothing so grandiose or abstract. A pivotal episode in the struggle to organize California farmworkers, the Fresno free speech fight illustrated the price to be paid for challenging established authority in rural California. What Wobblies won for six months of struggle was indeed meager—little more than the right to speak on certain designated street corners. They were still faced with the challenge of organizing Fresno's field hands and of establishing an ongoing labor organization. But their sacrifices had not been in vain. With Wobblies apparently poised to follow up on their victory in Fresno and carry their organization into the countryside, Chester Rowell, frightened by prospects of an enlarged IWW on the loose, immediately urged Progressive politicians to take action through labor reform and support for mainstream trade unionism. "If the I.W.W. . . . is to be prevented from growing, union-hating capitalists must learn not to confuse it and its members with those of the trade unions," wrote Rowell in one of his editorials. "The one thing that will prevent the growth of the I.W.W. . . . is the acceptance of the growth of the trade unions as an incontestable fact . . . the Trade union's way is to do business. The I.W.W. is to conduct war."[62]

Shocked out of their lethargy, CSFL leaders accepted Rowell's challenge. Reconsidering and jettisoning failed tactics, they quickly redoubled their efforts among farmworkers. Taking the lead in the fight was an odd labor leader—Carl Browne. A San Francisco Building Trades Union Council member who had once served as a lieutenant in Coxey's Army in 1894, Browne was just as committed to the cause of white labor and just as racist as Tveitmoe, Furuseth, and Scharrenberg, and, like those men, was also sympathetic enough to the cause of the IWW to have assisted the Wobbly Train members when they arrived in Sacramento. Also believing that bindlemen were a huge force of potential scabs waiting in the wings, he joined the four labor leaders in petitioning the AFL executive council for yet another farmworker organizing campaign. "These men are generally getting to believe that not only the world generally but even the trade unionists are the enemies and are therefore learning to hate unionism," Browne argued. "We realize that this means a terrific fight with employers. They will do their utmost to wipe out such organization." AFL executive council members agreed that in the casual worker "lurks a most serious danger . . . to our movement." But as in the past, they left matters up to the state labor federation.[63]

In March 1911, the California State Federation of Labor took action. Shifting J. B. Dale to Fresno, the CSFL promised him a budget of twenty dollars a week;

the AFL pitched in an additional fifteen dollars. With little knowledge of what was required, Dale launched a campaign described by historian Cletus Daniel as "distinguished only by its extraordinary ineptitude." Angry that growers "object to dealing with the business agent from the white, the Caucasian race, yet are ready to deal with the fellow from the others," Dale concocted a plan to enlist white farmworkers and then use the Japanese model to force growers to "deal with the white man, the same as he deals with the Jap, the Chinaman and the Hindu." To this end, he brought in two AFL organizers, P. Sioris and T. C. Seward, installed them as "business agents," then tried to undermine and displace Fresno area *keiyaku-nin*. It took him one month just to secure seven members who could pay the ten-dollar fee required to obtain a local union charter. Attaching them directly to the AFL through the United Laborer's Union of America, Dale declared his organization ready to do business. When no one else joined, he imported unemployed Greek laborers from San Francisco and Sacramento.[64]

Dale managed to place several crews of Greek workers in M. F. Tarpey's raisin vineyards that summer. "There is something peculiarly appropriate in having Greek labor presented to California farmers to do work in a land which has often been spoken of as the Greece of the West," wrote Chester Rowell in one of his editorials. But it soon became apparent that the Greeks could not do the work. Whereas the Japanese averaged sixty-five boxes per day, the Greeks could only pick forty. A week into the harvest, just as Samuel Gompers stopped in town on a statewide speaking tour, Tarpey abruptly fired all of the Greek harvesters and replaced them with Japanese. Other growers who hired Dale's crews promptly followed his example.[65]

After failing at Fresno, Dale abandoned the fields and decided instead to follow the Wobblies into the slave markets during the off-season. Here, he reasoned, he could do the most with his meager twelve-hundred-dollar annual budget. His approach, he later told investigators for the U.S. Commission on Industrial Relations, consisted of meeting field hands "in town, where they are on Sunday." With transferable membership and an initiation fee of just one dollar, Dale's ten Federal Union locals—in Richmond, San Jose, San Francisco, San Rafael, Bakersfield, Eureka, Fresno, Stockton, San Diego, and Sacramento—by the end of the summer claimed a membership of between two thousand and five thousand farmworkers, but these numbers were highly inflated. Other than supplying information about jobs, Dale's locals soon became phantom organizations that conducted no strikes, engaged in no collective bargaining, and did nothing to enhance the union cause or establish AFL credibility among bindlemen and other farmworkers. It was all very discouraging. "Thousands have disappeared after joining, leaving no trace of their whereabouts," admitted Scharrenberg.[66]

Aware of these failures, Gompers vowed in the April 1912 issue of *American Federationist* that "the work will go on" and laid out the main issues as he saw them. First, he conceded that high dues held back organization because seasonally employed laborers could ill afford regular union dues; he also agreed with advocates of industrial organization that workers from other trades and industries would have to bear most of the costs of any organizing drive. Gompers next acknowledged that farmworkers would have to be able to drift between union locals as they migrated with the harvest. He further proposed development of a national union, "which would have the same relationship to the American Federation of Labor as that of the international unions." Fortified by the leadership and resources of the AFL, he argued, such a union might have a fighting chance to succeed where others had failed. But for all his rhetoric, Gompers had not really changed his thinking since the days when he had nixed the Japanese-Mexican Labor Union at Oxnard. Never really believing that farmworkers or other migrant laborers could be organized, Gompers spoke of solidarity with them only to placate the more militant elements of the AFL.[67]

Faced with such double-talk, Furuseth, Tveitmoe, Scharrenberg, and Browne pled for a more effective organizing drive. Rather than concentrating on farmworkers holed up in towns during the off-season, the four unionists advocated a system of paid union organizers who would travel "among their fellows and spread the creed of unionism." Receiving little support from craft unionists and generating little interest among any of the international unions, the idea died when Gompers concluded that the AFL had "given all the attention that has been possible" to organizing farmworkers. As the AFL's confused and largely symbolic adventure among California farmworkers sputtered to a halt, the CSFL could do little more than propose an information agency or state employment bureau. By listing available work and by evaluating conditions of employment, the CSFL hoped to "prevent to a great extent the demoralization and suffering that result when numbers seek employment but are unable to find it." The AFL and CSFL, it turned out, were ideologically, structurally, and financially ill-suited to the task of organizing California farmworkers. Indeed, so disillusioned was Scharrenberg that for the next twenty years he would become a permanent foe of expending any additional money and manpower on something he believed to be a lost cause.[68]

As the AFL and CSFL floundered, Wobblies launched a series of free speech fights the length of the Central Valley, often securing their rights by merely threatening to use Fresno-style tactics. The first of these fights occurred in Porterville early in the summer of 1911. Little is known of this fight other than the fact that Wobblies succeeded in defending their soapboxes. Several weeks later in Stockton, twenty Wobblies jailed on the top floor of the county courthouse for soapboxing activities barricaded themselves behind mattresses and then used tin plates, cups, their voices, and "whatever they could pry loose" to make so much noise that they prevented court from convening; police were forced to release them. A third fight was less successful; on July 9, soapboxers at the corner of Nineteenth Street and Chester Avenue in Bakersfield were promptly arrested, given a "floater," and sent on their way. In November, the entire Marysville IWW local volunteered to go to jail unless police released an imprisoned Wobbly. December saw Wobblies unhappy with their allotted spot on Twentieth Street between L and M streets in the red-light district of Bakersfield move to Sumner and Baker streets, where they were quickly arrested for blocking traffic. Released after a few days in jail, one of the soapboxers returned to the corner of Nineteenth Street and Chester Avenue and was again arrested. Bailed out of jail, he left town, and IWW soapboxing never resumed in Bakersfield.[69]

Widely reported in the press, these fights and others in San Francisco and

Oakland so frightened the *San Francisco Chronicle* that it began referring to the IWW as the "hobo gang." Fearing more confrontations with the "Wobbly menace," employers throughout the state began searching for new countertactics. Undaunted, Wobbly organizers and agitators pressed on, carrying their campaigns for free speech to locations where bindlemen gathered to rest and search for work. Launching what was perhaps the boldest of all attempts to advance the cause of bindlemen, Wobblies ventured into San Diego in 1912. They soon learned a hard lesson.[70]

ॐ

Commentators on the San Diego free speech fight have always dismissed it as irrelevant to the farmworker story. Cut off from the Imperial Valley by the coastal range of mountains and connected to Los Angeles by little more than a spur line of the Santa Fe Railroad, San Diego was an isolated residential alcove, home to some forty thousand residents but lacking anything resembling a farmworker class or a tradition of labor unionism. But this interpretation ignores San Diego's mild climate, which attracted hundreds of wintering bindlemen, and the city's building boom, which brought in thousands more seasonal laborers to lay streetcar lines, build and pave roads, remake the harbor, and work on countless other construction projects. With so many transient workers around, Wobblies found enough converts to form mixed Local 245. In the summer of 1911, most San Diego Wobblies joined the revolutionaries in Baja California, and about one hundred of them were interned by the United States Army after Mexican troops recaptured Tijuana on June 22. Released into San Diego, they immediately gravitated to "Soapbox Row," a square-block area in downtown San Diego, also known as Heller's Corner, where they joined with socialists and other street speakers and held meetings two or three times a week in an attempt to attract bindlemen.

The meetings drew such large crowds that in October 1911, a large group of businessmen invited *Los Angeles Times* owner Harrison Gray Otis and president of the Los Angeles Merchants and Manufacturers Association Felix Zehandlarr to help formulate a plan to forbid street meetings. A month later, the group succeeded in lobbying a reluctant Common Council to ban street speaking within the seven-square-block area where bindlemen congregated. Left unchallenged, the ban would have forced Wobblies to abandon soapboxing not only among casual laborers in San Diego, but also among farmworkers and other transient laborers wherever other municipalities adopted similar measures. With their prime organizing strategy threatened, Wobblies braced for battle. "The chances are strong," predicted the *San Diego Sun*, "that this ordinance will start a fight that will last for a long time and will be bitter all the time."[71]

Quickly aligning with socialists and even some renegade AFL members, Wobblies formed the Free-Speech League and vowed to preserve the gains won in Fresno. When the anti-street-speaking ordinance took effect at 7:30 on the evening of February 8, 1912, a large group of soapboxers were promptly arrested. The following day, Commissioner of Police, Health, and Morals John Sehon ordered a "general roundup of all male vagrants and hoboes" as well as any "crowd" of more than two people. Appalled by the edict, Wobblies declared a free speech fight. *Industrial Worker* urged: "Come on the cushions, ride on top; Stick to the brake beams; let nothing stop."[72]

Determined to head off the influx, Police Chief Keno Wilson entered the fray on February 14 and began intercepting and turning back "undesirables" arriving at Sorrento Train Station just north of town; a mounted posse was assigned to thwart those attempting to walk in by road at San Onofre on the Orange County line. Within two weeks, Wilson had arrested more than two hundred Wobblies and other free speech fighters, keeping them in a jail built to hold sixty. As prison conditions deteriorated, the *San Diego Tribune* dismissed accusations of abuse by claiming that those "howling for mercy against the discomfort of over-crowded jails" had "deliberately created the conditions under which they suffer." Such men, added the *Tribune*, "were not even good enough to be tried for treason . . . They would be better off dead . . . they are the waste material of creation and should be drained off into the sewer of oblivion there to rot in cold obstruction like any other excrement."[73]

By March, the Wobblies seemed on their way to doing in San Diego what they had done in Fresno. With the city and county jails packed, each misdemeanor case requiring a five-day trial, and prosecutors unable to impanel an impartial jury, the legal system soon ground to a halt. So loud were the prisoners and so large were the crowds gathering outside the jail to protest that Chief Wilson complained he was constantly subjected to prisoners "yelling and hollering and telling the jailers to quit work and join the union." But the tide soon turned.[74]

As arrests mounted, the Common Council authorized construction of a temporary stockade to hold overflow from the jails. And on March 22, Chief Wilson began sending his most intransigent prisoners north to Sorrento Station, where they were put on a Los Angeles–bound train and told never to return. When the trains grew crowded, police rounded up Wobblies on sight, gathered them into pens and stockades, and sent them north each night by car and truck. A reporter for the *San Diego Union* described the fate of fifteen men, strung together with clanking handcuffs, who were led slowly down the side stairway of the police station and loaded into a fire department truck in the alley between the station and the jail at 9:30 in the evening. "There was no light, all the jail electronics were switched off, the street lights were out, and clouds obscured the moon," noted the reporter. "Coated, slouch-hatted gunmen sat silent in the truck, silhouetted in the darkness, their rifles pointed upward."[75]

When the number of nightly deportees reached sixty to eighty, authorities abandoned vehicle transportation and began marching men north on El Camino Real to the county line. Turned over to vigilantes, the deportees were first held in a kind of deportation camp for a few hours. Forced to kiss the American flag and sing the national anthem each night, the men were told to leave San Diego under penalty of death, then made to run a gauntlet of club-swinging vigilantes. As each bloodied and exhausted group arrived in Los Angeles, they were met by reporters who conveyed their stories of being beaten, starved, shot at, threatened, and humiliated.[76]

On March 28, sixty-three-year-old Wobbly Michael Hoy died after spending forty days in the city jail. Two days later, police moved in with clubs and broke up his funeral when someone draped a red flag on his coffin. The death led an infuriated Wobbly named Stanley Gue, who had already been arrested once, to appeal for help. "You 50,000 unemployed in San Francisco, come to San Diego," he wrote in *Industrial Worker*. "You 50,000 idle men in Los Angeles, come to San Diego. Come to San Diego a hundred thousand strong. Roads into San Diego guarded by armed deputies."[77]

To head off the invasion of a rumored forty thousand bindlemen, the San Diego County Board of Supervisors on April 4 added forty new mounted deputies, armed them with rifles, equipped them with tents and blankets, and sent them to San Onofre with orders to arrest any Wobblies headed south. Later that day, vigilantes rode north to reinforce the deputies. At about one o'clock on the morning of April 5, several hundred deputies stopped an incoming train, removed 140 bindlemen, and handed them over to the vigilantes. Among the captured was Albert Tucker. In a letter to IWW president Vincent St. John two years later, Tucker recalled: "The moon was shining dimly through the clouds and I could see pick handles, ax handles, wagon spokes and every kind of club imaginable swinging . . . They broke one man's leg, and everyone was beaten black and blue, and was bleeding from a dozen wounds." Chris Hansen, the Wobbly with the broken leg, also wrote to St. John describing the incident. "As I was lying there I saw other fellows running the gauntlet," Hansen recalled. "Some were bleeding freely from cracked heads, others were knocked down to be made to get up and run again."[78]

As it became clear that police were helping the vigilantes and that the violence was being encouraged by the city's two major newspapers—the *Union* and the *Tribune*, both owned by sugar beet capitalist John D. Spreckels—San Diego began to draw overwhelmingly hostile criticism from organized labor and civil liberties groups. On April 14, Governor Hiram Johnson dispatched businessman Harris Weinstock to investigate. Weinstock had played a key role in founding cooperative agricultural marketing associations before moving into government, where he earned a reputation for competence and impartiality; when his hearings convened on April 18 in the grand jury room of the San Diego County Courthouse, Wobblies packed the galleries. The proceedings, unanimously condemned by local officials, were raucous and frequently ugly. Standing on his chair in the back of the room, Thomas Kilcullen, a Wobbly who had been beaten and "deported" by a dozen policemen early in the fight, recognized Assistant Superintendent of Streets Walter Moore, who was then being questioned and shouted, "I know that man. He is one of the vigilantes. I recognize him!" Other Wobblies echoed the accusation. Kilcullen also identified *San Diego Union* reporter Francis Bierman as leader of one of his "deportations." Chaos ensued, and Weinstock was forced to adjourn. On the second day, Weinstock rushed to the police station to rescue a group of Wobblies who were about to be turned over to vigilantes to prevent them from testifying about police assaults and vigilante action. By the time Weinstock wrapped up his investigation on April 20 and headed back to Fresno to write his report, he had amassed forty affidavits along with a great deal of additional evidence, including his own personal experiences with police, Wobblies, and public officials.[79]

When Weinstock released his two-hundred-page report on the San Diego hostilities four days later, it characterized Wobblies as socialists intent on producing a collectivist society and acknowledged the way they had employed nonviolent resistance; the report also criticized their seeming desire to paralyze the industries of the nation and create a society of "thieves, liars, and scoundrels." What most troubled Weinstock, though, was the denial of constitutional rights and the "needless brutality on the part of police officers." Corroborating many of the IWW's charges, an outraged Weinstock singled out the *San Diego Union* and *San Diego Tribune* as voices of repression and vigilante action, and compared San Diego's behavior to the excesses he had witnessed while traveling in Czarist Russia. With few exceptions, wrote Weinstock, San Diego newspapers had been "inclined to inspire young men and boys to the belief that they would be heroes by taking the administration of the law into their own hands."[80]

Turning to the vigilantes, Weinstock summed them up as "a body of men, part of whom were police officers, part constables, and part private citizens," who were far greater criminals than those whom they branded as anarchists. Concluding his report, Weinstock predicted that the tactics employed by the IWW at Fresno and San Diego now menaced the nation at large. To alleviate conditions giving rise to "this new and menacing condition," he recommended state and national labor legislation and called for the state attorney general to instigate criminal proceedings against the vigilantes, as he felt none could reasonably expect justice from San Diego County District Attorney H. S. Utley.[81]

As debate over Weinstock's report raged across the state, Governor Hiram Johnson on May 21 chastised civil authorities in San Diego, defended the right to free speech, and, because constitutional rights had been violated, dispatched state Attorney General Ulysses S. Webb to San Diego to "afford redress to any who have suffered wrong and to mete out equal and exact justice to all." Between one thousand and five thousand people carrying American flags and wearing red, white, and blue bunting greeted Webb at the Santa Fe Railroad station on May 25. "Let us give thanks to God," exclaimed J. R. Gothran, secretary of the Socialist Party of San Diego, "that peace and law may soon be restored in our city." But just two days later, as Webb dined at a beach resort with Spreckels's attorney, H. E. Doolittle, vigilantes surrounded soapboxer A. B. Carson and dragged him down the street screaming, "Kill him, lynch him." More soapboxers were arrested and beaten on June 3, 10, and 23, their attacks culminating in a large and angry meeting led by Wobblies Charles Edward Russell and Mrs. Fremont Older, after which Attorney General Webb threatened to impose martial law.[82]

By October, San Diego's soapbox row was a vacant and lonely place and, according to San Diego free speech leader Laura Emerson, "the sacred spot where so many I.W.W. [men] were clubbed and arrested last winter lies safe and secure from the unhallowed tread of the hated anarchist and in fact, from all other human beings." Unable to recruit new members, an IWW organizer reported from "San Diego (Russia)" to *Industrial Worker* on November 28, 1912, that it was "impossible to hold propaganda meetings here or do very effective work. Not only are the streets denied us but halls as well."[83]

The struggles at Fresno and San Diego had riveted public attention to Wobbly soapboxers. These were, after all, spectacles of unprecedented drama. But ultimately they had changed nothing. To some, San Diego was a great victory; according to ACLU founder Roger Baldwin, it "wrote a chapter in the history of American liberties like that of the struggle of the Quakers for freedom . . . of the militant suffragists to carry their propaganda to the seats of government, and the Abolitionists." But with heavy casualties, at least two dead, hundreds beaten, and many missing in action, there was another perspective as well. If, after seven years of organizing and struggle, the IWW had any lasting impact on California farmers, farmworkers, or bindlemen, it was not evident. As revolutionary bard Joe Hill put it, San Diego was a dubious battle "not worth a whoop in Hell from a rebel's point of view." Profoundly disenchanted by the failure at San Diego, Wobbly publicist Abner Woodruff despaired of ever being able to organize farmworkers and other casual laborers, whom he labeled "almost hopeless." Now, as the IWW began to scrutinize its failures, discontent with soapboxing and propaganda led organizers like John Panzner to call for organizing "the wage slave, not the bourgeois, the street moocher and the saloon soak."[84]

Troubled by these and other developments, Wobblies throughout the fall of 1912 debated how best to proceed. In articles like "Soap-Boxer or Organizer, Which?" the IWW press reviewed the recent free speech fights and concluded that mixed locals in the cities had "never really got much of a foothold among the slaves," and that soapboxing would likely never produce more than a generalized propaganda movement. "If we are to have a strong union," reasoned *Industrial Worker*, "we have to go to the job where the workers are and begin our agitation . . . it is only where we control or are seeking control of the job that we can build up a lasting economic power."[85]

Filling the pages of *Solidarity* with angry letters, Wobblies condemned the strategy of waiting for agricultural workers to blow into town and organize them on the bum. "Organization cannot be accomplished on a street corner," went one common refrain. Too often soapboxers merely pulled off a "few sensational stunts," got the workers excited, recruited them into unions, "made a lot of noise and then went on their way to more virgin fields, leaving behind no organization and nothing but a depleted treasury as the sole evidence of their successful work." Without new tactics that improved conditions, the task of organizing farmworkers seemed to J. S. Biscay "well nigh impossible."[86]

As the debate dragged into the winter of 1912, the California IWW seemed on the verge of disintegration. Beaten, battered, and fragmented, many less patient IWW members turned to the comfort and security of church, family, and ethnic associations. A dejected Ben Williams questioned the IWW's future as a viable labor organization. "We are to the labor movement . . . what the high diver is to the circus," he wrote. "A sensation, marvelous and ever thrilling. We attract crowds. We give them thrills, we do hair-raising stunts and send the crowd home to wait impatiently for the next sensationalist to come along. As far as making industrial unionism fit the everyday life of workers, we have failed miserably."[87]

So great was the sense of failure and so dim were the prospects that many Wobblies quit the movement. Those remaining demanded less sensational and

FIGURE 55. Wheatland hop camp. Note in upper left corner reads, "Durst [Just?] before the riot, 1913." Exhibit from the subsequent murder trial, rescued from the garbage bin after being discarded. Courtesy of Juanita DeValentine/Wheatland Historical Society.

more effective methods, fewer mixed locals, and more functioning industrial unions. Build from the bottom up, the IWW's publications shouted; but the question of how to accomplish that goal remained. Hoping to bring the union to men on the job, many Wobblies now called for a cadre of "walking delegates." First employed by the United Mine Workers Union, which sent organizers out to live and work among the men it was trying to recruit, these types of organizers by 1912 had a long history in the American labor movement. During the spring of 1913, the IWW dispatched groups of these men (known as "camp delegates") into the logging, construction, and farm labor camps throughout the California countryside. Armed with a supply of literature, membership cards, and dues books, delegates hired themselves out and paid their own way with only commissions from the sale of IWW pamphlets to elevate their status. In this way, camp delegates, as historian Melvyn Dubofsky has said, "literally carried a union local under their hats."[88]

Acting only as propaganda agents, camp delegates were not supposed to lead strikes, although strikes might develop, in part as a result of their agitation. But soon they formed into a militant core of mobile agitators. By the summer of

1913, camp delegates had replaced IWW halls and soapboxers as the center of IWW union activity. Because they worked and tramped alongside the men they were recruiting, delegates quickly became well known to bindlemen throughout California.

Increasingly referred to as "job delegates," these men cemented the trust of bindlemen by mingling with them on the job, in boxcars, labor camps, and jungles. Initiating camp cleanups and helping to police the "stick up men" who preyed on bindlemen, they also attacked unsatisfactory working conditions, sometimes calling strikes, or slowdowns. Job delegates also succeeded in getting unionized railway brakemen and conductors to allow card-carrying Wobblies to ride free of charge.[89]

Although job delegates always stressed passive resistance, they spared no effort talking up sabotage. "Grain sacks come loose and rip, nuts and bolts come off wagon wheels and loads are dumped on the way to the barn, machinery breaks down, nobody to blame, everybody innocent," suggested *Industrial Worker*. "Just try a little sabotage on the kindhearted, benevolent boss . . . and see how it works." Armed with a series of editorials describing various methods of sabotage and when they should be employed, job delegates spread the message into the countryside. Men also used song, prose, cartoons, and prominent symbols on posters to reiterate their message that sabotage was not only a valuable nonviolent tactic capable of crippling the agricultural industry, but also a way of awakening a "spirit of revolt." What better way to retaliate against petty growers than to destroy their crops, ruin their orchards, breach their irrigation canals, and pour sand in their water pumps? Destroying agricultural machinery seemed to inspire special glee and one of the IWW's most popular songs, "Ta-Ra-Ra Boom De-Ay," written by Joe Hill:

> I had a job once threshing wheat,
> Worked sixteen hours with hands and feet.
> And when the moon was shining bright,
> They kept me working all the night.
> One moonlight night, I hate to tell,
> I "accidentally" slipped and fell.
> My pitchfork went right in between
> Some cogwheels of that threshing machine.
> Chorus:
> Ta-ra-ra boom de-ay!
> It makes a noise that way.
> And wheels and bolts and hay,
> Went flying every way.[90]

Fearing such incidents, foremen did their best to identify and weed out job delegates, but generally had little success. All that was needed to ignite the deep-seated grievances that many farmworkers felt toward growers was a spark to fire their anger. It was not long in coming. On August 3, 1913, hop pickers on the hot, 640-acre Durst ranch on the edge of the Sacramento Valley farm town of Wheatland revolted when toilets overflowed, drinking water became befouled, a system of wage holdbacks was instituted, and only a third of the twenty-eight hundred hop pickers, including many families and women and children, could get work. After walking out in the largest strike of farmworkers in California history, the pickers gathered with job delegates to debate what to do. At that point, Yuba County sheriff's deputies and the district attorney arrived on the scene. A brief and violent riot broke out, there was a shoot-out, and two hop pickers, the deputy district attorney, and a deputy sheriff died of gunshot wounds; countless other people were injured by twenty rounds fired by various parties; one worker lost his arm to a shotgun blast. After the pickers fled, the National Guard arrived to impose order, and California police conducted a dragnet and arrested dozens of suspects. Two strike leaders were later tried and convicted of murder and inciting a riot and sentenced to twenty years each in San Quentin Prison. During the subsequent decade-long struggle to defend and free them, bindlemen and their allies marshaled their discontent and challenged California agriculture on an industry-wide basis for the first time.[91]

Soon known as "Bloody Sunday," the Wheatland hop riot became what Carey McWilliams termed "California's first farm labor cause célèbre," an unsettling, if perplexing, warning that forever altered how people regarded life and labor on the California landscape. What farmworkers encountered after 1913 severely tested their fortitude, as the rapidly expanding agricultural industry injected into their lives additional opportunities, dilemmas, challenges, and conflicts. Moving far beyond previous protests, strikes, and job actions, the civil disobedience and government suppression that followed closed the formative phase of the farmworker story and opened another even more telling saga. In cotton communities like Pixley and Corcoran, giant labor camps like DiGiorgio, and table-grape centers like Delano and Arvin, farmworkers seeking a better life were pushed to the brink of class warfare. The traditions they formed, the battles they fought in order to improve their lives, the energy they expended attempting to organize a union, and the efforts they made to close the gap between rich and poor and humanize the social system in which they lived, shifted the dynamics of labor relations from the formation of a class to the class struggle. The lessons learned were new ones, and yet they were the same. They infuse the farmworker movement even today.[92]

Reference Matter

Abbreviations Used in Notes

AAAPSS	*Annals of the American Association of Political and Social Science*
AASF	Archive of the Archdiocese of San Francisco, Andrews' Academy, Menlo Park. Copies in the Bancroft Library, University of California, Berkeley; Huntington Library, San Marino, California; and Santa Barbara Mission Archive.
AC	Archives of California, Bancroft Library, University of California, Berkeley. Transcripts of documents in the United States Surveyor General's Office, San Francisco. Originals destroyed in the 1906 San Francisco earthquake and fire.
ACALA	Archival Center, Archdiocese of Los Angeles
ACSCR	American Crystal Sugar Company Records, Minnesota Historical Society, St. Paul, Minnesota
ADCUNR	Alfred Doten Collection, University of Nevada, Reno
AFL	American Federation of Labor
AGFP	Albert Grover Family Papers, Pacific Center for Western Studies, University of the Pacific
AGI	Archivo General de Indias. Originals in Casa Lonja, Seville, Spain
AGN	Archivo General y Pública de la Nación. Originals in the Palacio Nacional, Mexico City, Mexico
AH	*Agricultural History*
AHR	*American Historical Review*
AHS	Anaheim Historical Society
AL	*Antioch Ledger*
ANCRR	Association of Northern California Records and Research, Special Collections, Meriam Library, California State University, Chico
ASBP	Augustus S. Bixby Papers, Huntington Library, San Marino, California
ASC	Abel Stearns Collection, Huntington Library, San Marino, California
ASCHMS	Archives and Special Collections, Haggin Museum, Stockton, California
ASCUCD	Archives and Special Collections, University of California, Davis
ASCUCLA	Archives and Special Collections, University of California, Los Angeles
ASCUCSC	Archives and Special Collections, University of California, Santa Cruz
ASP	Abel Stearns Papers, Huntington Library, San Marino, California
AULHWSU	Archives of Urban and Labor History, Wayne State University, Detroit, Michigan
AWLC	Augustus W. Loomis Collection, California Historical Society
BCL	Butte County Library, Chico, California
BDWP	Benjamin D. Wilson Papers, Huntington Library, San Marino, California
BL	Bancroft Library, University of California, Berkeley

BVVSR	*Buena Vista Viticultural Society Records*, Bancroft Library, University of California, Berkeley
BWC	Ben Walker Collection, Fresno County Historical Society, Fresno, California
CBMM	Charles Bowers Memorial Museum, Santa Ana, California
CCIH	California Commission of Immigration and Housing
CCIHP	California Commission of Immigration and Housing Papers, Bancroft Library
CDFHM	Collection of Documents for the History of Mexico, Archivo General de Mexico, AGN
CH	*California History*
CHDC	California Historical Documents Collection, Huntington Library, San Marino, California
CHQ	*California Historical Quarterly*
CHS	California Historical Society
CHSQ	*California Historical Society Quarterly*
CIR	Commission on Industrial Relations
CIRP	Commission on Industrial Relations Papers, Records of the Department of Labor, Record Group 174, National Archives, Washington, D.C.
CIRPP	Commission on Industrial Relations Papers, State Historical Society, Wisconsin
CJCP	Cave Johnson Couts Papers, Huntington Library, San Marino, California
CKC	Charles Kohler Collection, Bancroft Library
CLDS	Genealogical Society of the Church of Jesus Christ of the Latter-Day Saints, Salt Lake City, Utah, Family History Center, Oakland, California
CDLSA	Church of Latter Day Saints Archives
CLR	*California Law Review*
CMD	California Mission Documents, Santa Barbara Mission Archives
CSA	California State Archives, Sacramento
CSAS	California State Agricultural Society
CSAST	*California State Agricultural Society Transactions*, Sacramento
CSBLS	California State Bureau of Labor Statistics, Sacramento
CSFGCP	*California State Fruit Growers' Convention Proceedings*, Sacramento
CSFGCT	*California State Fruit Growers' Convention Transactions*, Sacramento
CSFGST	*California State Fruit Growers' Society Transactions*, Sacramento
CSFL	California State Federation of Labor
CSL	California State Library, Sacramento
CSU	California State University
CSUC	California State University, Chico
CSUS	California State University, Sacramento
CV	Correspondencia de los Virreyes, Archivo General de la Nación, AGN
DIR	Department of Industrial Relations Records, Bancroft Library, University of California, Berkeley
DJR	Department of Justice Records, Record Group 60, National Archives
DLGD	José de la Guerra Documents, Bancroft Library, University of California, Berkeley
DLGP	José de la Guerra y Noriega Papers, Huntington Library, San Marino, California
DPLHC	Documentos Para la Historia de California, Vallejo Documents, Archives of California, Bancroft Library, University of California, Berkeley
DPLHDM	Documentos Para la Historia de Mexico, AGN
DRMCLJP	Documents Relative to the Missions of California, Lancaster-Jones Papers, Archive of the National Museum of Mexico, Mexico City
DSP	Department of State Papers, Archives of California, Bancroft Library, University of California, Berkeley
DSR	Department of State Records, Record Group 59, National Archives

EBP	Ernest Burgess Papers, Special Collections, University of Chicago
EBWC	Edith B. Webb Collection, Santa Barbara Mission Archives, Santa Barbara, California
EDDMRV	Edward D. Dutra Dredging Museum, Rio Vista, California
EGP	Elviria Gnagi Diaries, Bancroft Library, University of California, Berkeley
EJS	Elizabeth J. Schultz, Anaheim History Room, Anaheim Public Library, Anaheim, California
EPC	Ephemeral Pamphlet Collection, Huntington Library, San Marino, California
FARCSB	Federal Archives and Records Center, San Bruno, California
FCHS	Fresno County Historical Society, Fresno, California
FFLCSF	Frank F. Latta Collection, Sky Farming, Huntington Library, San Marino, California
FHHC	F. Hal Higgins Collection, University of California, Davis, Special Collections and Archives
FMR	*Fresno Morning Republican*
FWP	Federal Writers' Project
FWPC	Federal Writers' Project Collection, Bancroft Library, University of California, Berkeley
GFP	Giles Family Papers, Pacific Center for Western Studies, University of the Pacific, Stockton, California
GHBPS	George and Helen Beattie Papers and Correspondence and Scrapbooks, Huntington Library, San Marino, California
GHM	Gilroy History Museum, Gilroy, California
GHS	Gilroy Historical Society
GLB	Governor's Letter Books, Records of the U.S. Army Continental Commands, 1821–1920, Record Group 393, National Archives
GMC	George McKinstry Collection, California State Library, Sacramento, California
GMP	George McKinstry Papers, Bancroft Library, University of California, Berkeley
GSMIW	Golden State and Miner's Iron Works, Edward D. Dutra Dredging Museum, Rio Vista, California
HAHR	*Hispanic American Historical Review*
HBC	Herbert Bolton Collection, Bancroft Library, University of California, Berkeley
HDBBC	Henry D. Bacon Business Correspondence, Huntington Library, San Marino, California
HDBP	Henry D. Barrows Papers, Huntington Library, San Marino, California
HDC	Henry Dalton Collection, Huntington Library, San Marino, California
HDFP	Henry Delano Fitch Papers, Bancroft Library, University of California, Berkeley
HGP	Hugh Glenn Papers, Bancroft Library, University of California, Berkeley
HL	Huntington Library, San Marino, California
HSSC	Historical Society of Southern California
HSSCAP	*Historical Society of Southern California Annual Publications*
HSSCQ	*Historical Society of Southern California Quarterly*
ICHS	Imperial County Historical Society
ICR	Immigration Commission Reports (also known as the Dillingham Commission Reports), U.S. Senate, *Reports of the Immigration Commission*, 61st Cong., 2nd sess., 1911
ILWUL	International Longshoreman's Union Library, San Francisco
INS	Records of the Immigration and Naturalization Service, Record Group 85, National Archives
ISR	*International Socialist Review*
IUB	*Industrial Union Bulletin*
IW	*Industrial Worker*

JAH	*Journal of American History*
JARH	*Journal of Arizona History*
JARPC	Japanese American Research Project Collection, University of California, Los Angeles
JBC	John Bidwell Collection, California State Library, Sacramento, California
JBP	John Bidwell Papers, Special Collections, Meriam Library, California State University, Chico
JCA	*Journal of California Anthropology*
JDLG	José de la Guerra Papers, Santa Barbara Mission Archives, Santa Barbara mission
JMC	John Marsh Collection, California State Library, Sacramento California
JCGBA	*Journal of California and Great Basin Anthropology*
JCMP	John C. McCubbin Papers, Reedley Historical Society, Reedley, California
JDBSP	James DeBarth Shorb Papers, Huntington Library, San Marino, California
JFE	*Journal of Farm Economics*
JFPP	John Francis Pyle Papers and Diaries, Bancroft Library, University of California, Berkeley
JMC	John Marsh Collection, California State Library
JNH	*Journal of Negro History*
JPHP	John P. Harrington Papers, Smithsonian Institution
JSC	John Sutter Collection, California State Library, Sacramento, California
JSCP	John Sutter Correspondence and Papers, Bancroft Library, University of California, Berkeley
JSDH	*Journal of San Diego History*
JSLS	John Steinbeck Library, Salinas, California
JWHA	John Waterlund Historical Articles on Butte County, Special Collections, Meriam Library, CSU, Chico
LACA	Los Angeles City Archives, City Clerk's Office, City Hall, Los Angeles
LAWC	Lilburne A. Winchell Collection, Fresno County Historical Society, Kearney Park, Fresno
LC	Library of Congress, Washington, D.C.
LFCH	LaFollete Committee Hearings, *Violations of Free Speech and Rights of Labor, Hearings Before a Subcommittee of the Committee on Education and Labor*, U.S. Senate, 76th Cong., 3rd. sess., Pursuant to Senate Resolution 266, A Resolution to Investigate Violations of the Right of Free Speech and Assembly and Interference with the Right of Labor to Organize and Bargain Collectively, Pt. 54, "Agricultural Labor in California," 1940
LH	*Labor History*
LROIACS	Letters Received by the Office of Indian Affairs, 1824–81, California Superintendency, Records of the Bureau of Indian Affairs, Record Group 75, National Archives
LRRST	Letters and Reports Received by the Secretary of the Treasury, Records of the Secretary of the Treasury, Record Group 56, National Archives
MCABHP	Mendocino County American Bicentennial History Project, Mendocino County Museum
MCC	Mother Colony Collection, Anaheim Public Library, Anaheim, California
MCHS	Mendocino County Historical Society, Ukiah, California
MCM	Mendocino County Museum, Willits, California
MCMCF	Mendocino County Museum Clipping File, Mendocino County Museum, Willits, California
MHS	Minnesota Historical Society, St. Paul, Minnesota
MIDRIS	Military Intelligence Division, U.S. Army Records of Internal Surveillance, Record Group 165, National Archives
MNM	Archivo del Museo Nacional, Mexico. Originals in Mexico City

NA	National Archives
NCLCF	Napa County Library Clipping File, Napa County Library, Napa, California
NMHR	*New Mexico Historical Review*
NVWL	Napa Valley Wine Library, St. Helena Public Library, St. Helena, California
NYPL	New York Public Library
NYT	*New York Times*
PBRC	Pierson B. Reading Collection, California State Library, Sacramento, California
PBRP	Pierson B. Reading Papers, Bancroft Library, University of California, Berkeley
PCML	President's Commission on Migratory Labor, Harry S. Truman Library, Independence, Missouri
PCWS	Pacific Center for Western Studies, University of the Pacific, Stockton, California (subsequently the Holt-Atherton Special Collections)
PH	*Pacific Historian*
PHR	*Pacific Historical Review*
PR	Provincial Records, Archives of California, Bancroft Library, University of California, Berkeley
PRP	*Pacific Rural Press*
PSP	Provincial State Papers, Archives of California, Bancroft Library, University of California, Berkeley, California
PSQ	*Political Science Quarterly*
PSTFN	Paul S. Taylor Field Notes, Bancroft Library, University of California, Berkeley
PVHS	Pajaro Valley Historical Society, Watsonville, California
RCDS	Records of the California Department of State, California State Archives, Sacramento
RCIH	Rupert Costo Collection of Indian History, Archives and Special Collections, University of California, Riverside
RN689	U.S. Congress, Joint Special Committee to Investigate Chinese Immigration, *Report of the Joint Special Committee to Investigate Chinese Immigration*, 44th Cong., 2nd sess., 1877.
ROHP	Regional Oral History Project, Bancroft Library, University of California, Berkeley
RVHS	Rio Vista Historical Society, Rio Vista, California
RWDLRDP	Records of the War Department, Letters Received, Dept. of the Pacific, Record Group 98, National Archives
SBMA	Santa Barbara Mission Archives, Santa Barbara, California
SCHMLCSUF	Special Collections, Henry Madden Library, California State University, Fresno
SCHSQ	*Southern California Historical Society Quarterly*
SCM	Sutter County Museum, Yuba City, California
SCML	Special Collections, Meriam Library, California State University, Chico
SCQ	*Southern California Quarterly*
SCUASC	Santa Clara University Archives and Special Collections, Santa Clara University, California
SDEH	*Stockton Daily Evening Herald*
SDHS	San Diego Historical Society
SDI	*Stockton Daily Independent*
SDML	San Diego Mission Library, San Diego, California
SHPL	St. Helena Public Library, St. Helena, California
SHSW	State Historical Society of Wisconsin, Madison, Wisconsin
SI	Smithsonian Institution, Washington, D.C.
SJBHS	San Juan Bautista Historical Society, San Juan Bautista, California
SJPL	San Jose Public Library
SHPL	St. Helena Public Library, St. Helena, California

SP	State Papers, Archives of California, Bancroft Library, University of California, Berkeley
SRCF	Stockton Record Clipping Files, Stockton
SRRP	Survey of Race Relations Papers, Hoover Institution, Stanford University, Stanford, California
SUASC	Stanford University Archives and Special Collections, Stanford, California
SVHS	Simi Valley Historical Society
SVSBCR	Sacramento Valley Sugar Beet Company Records
SWI	*Stockton Weekly Independent*
SWM	*Stockton Weekly Mail*
TC	Taylor Collection, Archives of the Archdiocese of San Francisco, Andrews Academy, Menlo Park
TL	Harry S. Truman Library, Independence, Missouri
TOLP	Thomas O. Larkin Papers, Bancroft Library, University of California, Berkeley
TWNIPCGJB	Thelma Wilson News Items Primarily Concerning General John Bidwell, Meriam Library, California State University, Chico
UCB	University of California, Berkeley
UCDSCA	University of California, Davis, Special Collections and Archives
UCLA	University of California, Los Angeles
UCR	University of California, Riverside
UCRA	Special Collection and Archives of the University of California, Riverside
UCSB	University of California, Santa Barbara
UCSD	University of California, San Diego
UOP	University of the Pacific, Stockton
VCHSQ	*Ventura County Historical Society Quarterly*
VCM	Ventura County Museum, Ventura, California
WHQ	*Western Historical Quarterly*
WLC	William Leidesdorff Collection, Huntington Library, San Marino, California
WLH	*Western Legal History*
WPA	Works Progress Administration, Washington, D.C.
YCL	Yuba County Library, Yuba City, California
YCMA	Yuba County Museum Archives, Yuba City, California

Notes

P R E F A C E

1. Quote from *NYT*, June 11, 1972.

2. Grant McConnell, *The Decline of Agrarian Democracy* (Berkeley, 1953), 1–2; Douglas Sackman, "Foreword," in Carey McWilliams, *Factories in the Field: The Story of Migratory Farm Labor in California* (Boston, 1939 [Berkeley, 1999]), ix–x, xviii, 5; Varden Fuller, "The Supply of Agricultural Labor as a Factor in the Evolution of Farm Organization in California" (Ph.D. diss., UCB, 1939); Lloyd H. Fisher, *The Harvest Labor Market in California* (Cambridge, Mass., 1953); David Vaught, *Cultivating California: Growers, Specialty Crops, and Labor, 1875–1920* (Baltimore and London, 1999). I differ with Paul S. Taylor, "Foundations of California Rural Society," *CHSQ* 24 (Sept. 1945), 193, who sees California farm labor as somehow lying outside the American farm tradition. To the contrary, it is deeply imbedded in that tradition, with roots extending into a system of unfree labor. Although historians have produced major accounts of the building of the transcontinental railroad, the Panama Canal, Hoover Dam, and the Los Angeles Aqueduct, there is no comprehensive account of the emergence of California agriculture or the farm labor class. See Lawrence Jelinek, *Harvest Empire: A History of California Agriculture* (San Francisco, 1979); Richard Steven Street, "Into the Good Land: The Emergence of California Agriculture, 1850–1920," MS (1979), BL; Steven Stoll, *The Fruits of Natural Advantage: Making the Industrial Countryside in California* (Berkeley and Los Angeles, 1998); Claude B. Hutchison, ed., *California Agriculture* (Berkeley and Los Angeles, 1946), 2 vols.

3. Who early farmworkers were, where they came from, what they did, and what happened to them, and a thousand other questions inspire the full spectrum of human emotion—repulsion and admiration, alarm and attraction, inspiration and pity, love and hate, astonishment and contempt, and for a few, mass hysteria. Seen not as a peculiarly California phenomenon but as a phase in the creation of a landless peasantry, and as part of the universal problem of where and how to assemble a labor force, the early history of California farmworkers calls forth such intense emotions, raises such fundamental issues, and provokes such bitter controversy that to attempt to describe it in a way that will engage rather than enrage, and that will have some impact beyond the academy, means to enter, intentionally or not, directly into the farmworker experience—to become part of an ongoing debate. With facts in dispute at each stage in history, and with such an enormous, complicated, controversial, and challenging story to tell, any attempt at presenting a comprehensive scholarly picture of the early years of California farm labor can be overwhelming. See Ronald E. Seavoy, *The American Peasantry: Southern Agricultural Labor and Its Political Economy* (Westport, Conn., 1998); A. Whitney Griswold, *Farming and Democracy* (New York, 1948), vii, 4, 14, 21, 31; William Cronon, *Nature's Metropolis: Chicago and the Great West* (New York, 1991), xvi, 256–57; J. Sanford Rikoon, *Threshing in the Midwest, 1820–1940: A Study of Traditional Culture and Technological Change* (Bloomington and Indianapolis, 1988); Thomas D. Isern, *Bull Threshers and Bindlestiffs: Harvesting and Threshing on the North American Plains* (Lawrence, Kans., 1990); Cecilia Danysk, *Hired Hands: Labour and the Development of Prairie Agriculture, 1880–1930* (Toronto, 1995); David E. Schob, *Hired Hands and Plowboys: Farm Labor in the Midwest, 1815–60* (Urbana and London, 1975); Cindy

Hahamovitch, *The Fruits of their Labor: Atlantic Coast Farmworkers and the Making of Migrant Poverty, 1870–1945* (Chapel Hill, 1997); William H. Friedland and Dorothy Nelkin, *Migrant: Agricultural Workers in America's Northeast* (New York, 1971); Carey McWilliams, *Ill Fares the Land: Migrants and Migratory Labor in the United States* (New York, 1941); Pete Daniel, *The Shadow of Slavery: Peonage in the South, 1901–1969* (London, 1972); LaWanda F. Cox, "The American Agricultural Wage-Earner, 1865–1900," *AH* 22 (Apr. 1948), 95–114; Paul S. Taylor, "The American Hired Man," *Land Policy Review* 6 (spring 1943), 3–17.

4. For the long view, see Barbara W. Tuchman, *A Distant Mirror: The Calamitous Fourteenth Century* (New York, 1978), xiv, xviii; Al Richmond, *A Long View From the Left: Memoirs of an American Revolutionary* (New York, 1973). Herbert Gutman, "Labor in the Land of Lincoln: Coal Miners on the Prairie," in Pete Daniel, ed., *Power and Culture: Essays on the American Working Class* (New York: 1987), 117–212, serves as an example of what Melvyn Dubofsky labels a "monomaniacal" effort at recreating the past "as it actually was."

5. Quote from typed notes, *Watsonville Pajaronian*, June 20, 1878, PVHS.

6. Quotes from Ronald L. Goldfarb, *A Caste of Despair: Migrant Farm Workers* (Ames, Iowa, 1981); Paul S. Taylor, "Migratory Labor and the Body Politic" (Feb. 20, 1951), PCML; McWilliams, *Factories in the Field*, 7; Cletus Daniel, *Bitter Harvest: A History of California Farmworkers, 1870–1941* (Ithaca, 1981), 11; Ernesto Galarza, *Farm Workers and Agribusiness in California, 1947–1960* (Notre Dame, 1977), 4; "The Labor Question," *Kern County Californian*, Jan. 5, 1888. For various other labels, see Truman Moore, *The Slaves We Rent* (New York, 1964); Henry Anderson, *Fields of Bondage: The Mexican Contract Labor System in Industrialized Agriculture* (Berkeley, 1963); Norman Lewis, "Slave-Labourers in the Vineyard," *The Sunday Times Magazine*, Feb. 1, 1970, 18–19; "Our Blue Sky Sweatshops," *Advance* 57 (June 11, 1971), 8–9; Friedland and Nelkin, *Migrant Agricultural Workers*, 174. For the epistemology of despair terminology, see George H. Mead, "The Psychology of Punitive Justice," *American Journal of Sociology* 23 (Mar. 1918), 577–602; Lillian Creisler, "'Little Oklahoma,' or the Airport Community: A Study of the Social and Economic Adjustment of Self-settled Agricultural Drought and Depression Refugees" (M.A. thesis, UCB, 1940), 2; Paul Landis, "Social Aspects of Farm Labor in the Pacific States," *Rural Sociology* 3 (Dec. 1938), 430; Henry Anderson, "Beyond the Bracero System, pt. 2," *Farm Labor* 1 (Oct. 1963); Louisa Shotwell, *The Harvesters: The Story of the Migrant People* (Garden City, N.Y., 1961); Dale Wright, *They Harvest Despair: The Migrant Worker* (Boston, 1965); Tony Dunbar and Linda Kravitz, *Hard Traveling: Migrant Farm Workers in America* (Cambridge, Mass., 1976); Steve Allen, *The Ground is Our Table* (New York, 1966). Describing farmworkers and their environment, University of California, Berkeley, economics professor Paul S. Taylor used the phrases "semi-industrialized rural proletarians" and "open-air food factories." See Paul S. Taylor and Tom Vasey, "Contemporary Background of California Farm Labor," *Rural Sociology* 1 (Dec. 1936), 419; Taylor and Vasey, "Historical Background of California Farm Labor," ibid., 1 (Sept. 1936), 281. This terminology, as well as many other characterizations, has now come under attack by revisionists. Whatever the labels and metaphors—and they have been repeated countless times since the beginning of farm labor in California—farmworkers were undeniably a class systematically manipulated, kept down, and relegated to the fringe; workers set adrift in the congestion of an agricultural labor force expanded and contracted almost at will were excluded from the rights and privileges normally enjoyed by most Americans.

7. Attempting to be systematically comprehensive in my research, I burned many years reading handwritten seventeenth- and eighteenth-century Spanish mission records, only to find, twenty years later, that in the interim most of the relevant documents had been translated and typed up in English. Despite massive documentation and a wide spectrum of books, historians insist farmworkers have suffered from a lack of attention. Devra Anne Weber, "The Struggle for Stability and Control in the Cotton Fields of California: Class Relations in Agriculture, 1919–1942" (Ph.D. diss., UCLA, 1986), 12, introduces an account of farmworkers in the California cotton industry by arguing that farmworkers "have been remarkable mainly by their absence," and makes a similar point in *Dark Sweat, White Gold: California Farm Workers, Cotton, and the New Deal* (Berkeley and Los Angeles, 1994), 2. Sucheng Chan, *This Bittersweet Soil: The Chinese in California Agriculture, 1860–1910* (Berkeley and Los Angeles, 1986), 2, asserts that the story of Chinese farmworkers "has never been properly told," while citing a considerable body of work to the contrary. Salvador Enrique Alvarez, "The Legal and Legislative Struggle of the Farm Worker, 1965-1972," in Octavio Ignacio Romano, ed., *Voices: Readings*

from El Grito. A Journal of Contemporary Mexican American Thought (Berkeley, 1971), 222, argues that "the legal struggles by farm workers . . . have been neither described, documented, nor analyzed." For works stressing irony and paradox, see David Wyatt, *The Fall into Eden: Landscape and Imagination in California* (Cambridge, 1986), xvii, 108, 206–9; Don Mitchell, *The Lie of the Land: Migrant Workers and the California Landscape* (Minneapolis, 1996), 14–16. For Samuel Johnson, see Walter Jackson Bate, *Samuel Johnson* (New York, 1975), xx.

8. In defining class, I do not mean to digress into an abstract discussion of theoretical laws of history. I agree with E. P. Thompson: class is largely determined by the productive relations into which people are born—or enter voluntarily or involuntarily—and it is best understood as it evolves over "a considerable historical period." Quote from E. P. Thompson, *The Making of the English Working Class* (New York, 1963), 10–11. Class consciousness, in Thompson's view, is the mechanism through which experiences are managed: personified in traditions, embodied in value systems, and represented by ideas, institutions, and actions. Following Thompson's definition of class, I also add the salient characteristics binding farmworkers to the means of production, as well as the ties of experience, association, and common interest. By using a class approach, I am not arguing that farmworkers were subjectively aware of their historical role as a force for revolutionary or radical change, although at times this was no doubt true. For views challenging Thompson and stressing Marxian concepts, see Perry Anderson, *Arguments Within English Marxism* (London, 1980), 43; Eric Hobsbawm, "Notes on Class Consciousness," in Hobsbawm, *Workers: Worlds of Labour* (New York, 1984). For a critique of hyperspecialization in working-class history, see Herbert Gutman, *Work, Culture and Society in Industrializing America* (New York, 1976), xii–xiii. For examples of the type of "big history" called for, see Anthony Lukas, *Big Trouble: A Murder in A Small Western Town Sets Off A Struggle for the Soul of America* (New York, 1997); Leon F. Litwack, *Been in the Storm So Long: The Aftermath of Slavery* (New York, 1979); Litwack, *Trouble in Mind: Black Southerners in the Age of Jim Crow* (New York, 1998); Richard White, *"It's Your Misfortune and None of My Own": A New History of the American West* (Norman, Okla., and London, 1991); T. Harry Williams, *Huey Long* (New York, 1970); Scott Berg, *Lindbergh* (New York, 1998). See also George Mosse, *Confronting History: a Memoir* (Madison, Wis., 2000), 53.

9. The key role that Native American wage laborers played in the agricultural workforce will, I believe, emerge as a surprise to scholars and general readers alike, as will the dynamic and pivotal story of mechanized grain farming, the insignificance of farm size, the influence of state laws in controlling and excluding farmworkers, and the importance of "illegal" immigration and homelessness. Slavery, forced labor, coerced labor, peonage, varieties and degrees of free labor, and the creation of a caste system of low-wage workers whose freedom was compromised by debt, physical isolation, and labor contractors are there too, in close proximity, along with racialized notions of work, in far larger doses, over a much longer period, and in far greater variety, than one would like to concede. Likewise, the central importance of white field hands, and in particular families, and on occasion children seeking temporary employment as the harvest swept through their communities, diverges from traditional accounts stressing farm labor as the exclusive domain of oppressed Third World minorities. The account of Chinese farmworkers traces the pattern of their infiltration into California agriculture at a crucial moment, providing a fuller view of their complicated role sustaining the transition from extensive grain farming to intensive fruit and vegetable cultivation, and revealing exactly the process by which they became the ideal by which all subsequent farmworkers were measured and found lacking. The section on Japanese farmworkers explores how labor bosses supplanted the Chinese, built a base of power, launched a wave of strikes, organized the first multiethnic labor union, and proceeded to move up the agricultural ladder, the first, and only, group of farmworkers to do so. A concluding section on bindlemen resurrects their story from the historical dustbin and presents the first comprehensive portrait of the most illusive and transient class to work in the fields. For an overview see, Lamar B. Jones, "Labor and Management in California Agriculture, 1864–1964," *LH* 11 (winter 1970), 23–40.

10. After the introduction, I only occasionally subject the reader to the clutter of references, genuflections to this or that authority, revisions, corrections, and rejoinders to arguments and theses, except in the most general of terms, as broader historical patterns begin and continue to figure in the narrative. Every now and then I relate some point of controversy regarding a particular question as if I were engaged in a discussion with contemporary farmworkers, but I seldom correct or chop logic with various historiographical schools and interpretations.

When I do confront a theory, trend, or dispute, I try to do so as it arises and recurs in the natural chronology of the story.

11. Quote from *Thirty-Sixth CSFGCP* (San Francisco, 1910), 13. Writing a history of the beginning of farm labor in California parallels the way historians of the American West have shifted perspectives away from the "wagon wheels west" movement toward earlier antecedents, stressing conquest, borders, frontiers, and the mixing of diverse groups of people over a long period of time. As I see it, farmworker history, like Western history, followed a kind of historical "path dependence," a concept describing the extent to which previous decisions and developments accumulate upon themselves, locking in certain patterns and behaviors. It is difficult to perceive this process when the story is picked up midpoint, divided into discrete segments, boxed in by one particular crop or time period, or explained through historiographically driven plots holding time constant and treating farmworker history as a monolithic whole. My rejection of such interpretative frameworks in favor of a comprehensive narrative aimed at overcoming disjunction in the farmworker time continuum constitutes another key difference between my approach and that of my predecessors.

12. Quotes from David Brody, *Steelworkers in America: The Nonunion Era, 1880–1920* (Urbana and Chicago, 1998 [1960]), 305; and Melvyn Dubofsky, "Starting Out in the Fifties," *LH* 34 (Aug. 1993), 478. See also Richard White, "History, Rugrats, and the World Championship Wrestling," *Perspectives* 37 (Apr. 1999), 11–13. To achieve power and meaning, I write as "photographically" as is possible. I agree with the critic George Gerbner, who said, "The stories we tell about the world help form the world in which we live." Quotes from Derrick Jensen, "Telling Stories: How Television Skews Our View of Society, and Ourselves: An Interview with George Gerbner," *The Sun* 272 (Aug. 1998), 17. See also Savoie Lottinville, *The Rhetoric of History* (Norman, Okla., 1976), 42; David Carr, *Time, Narrative, and History* (Bloomington, Ind., 1986); Alan Taylor, *William Cooper's Town: Power and Persuasion on the Frontier of the Early American Republic* (New York, 1996); David Harlan, *The Degradation of American History* (Chicago, 1997); William Cronon, "A Place for Stories: Nature, History, and Narrative," *JAH* 78 (Mar. 1992), 1347–79; A. J. P. Taylor, "Fiction in History," *Times Literary Supplement* (Mar. 23, 1973), 327–28.

13. Rudy Calles, *Champion Prune Pickers: Migrant Worker's Dilemma* (Los Alamitos, Calif., 1979), 11–12.

14. Quote from Lincoln Steffens, *The Autobiography of Lincoln Steffens* (New York, 1931), 238. Farmworker history, like all history, leans heavily on documents weighted with crisis and calamity when, in fact, such events were infrequent. See also Brody, *Steelworkers in America*, 347; Alf Ludtke, ed., *The History of Everyday Life: Reconstructing Historical Experiences and Ways of Life*, trans. William Temple (Princeton, N.J., 1995), 12; Bernard Bailyn, *On the Teaching and Writing of History*, ed. Edward C. Lathem (Hanover, N.H., 1994), 52–54.

15. Quote from John Berger and Jean Mohr, *A Seventh Man: Migrant Workers in Europe* (New York, 1975), 8. Many historians believe passionately that understanding the past is a key to understanding the present. This familiar maxim holds even truer for California farmworkers during their formative period. Knowing the meaning of farm labor to millions of people, and their reaction to it in the years before 1913, is essential to appreciating their later insurgencies. Readers seeking insight into modern farm labor relations will find that the root causes of conflict are here, too.

16. Quote from Idwal Jones, *Vines in the Sun* (New York, 1949), 134. See also Clifford Geertz, "Ideology as a Cultural System," in *The Interpretation of Cultures* (New York, 1973). For another example of the need for setting the facts straight, see Joan London and Henry Anderson, *So Shall Ye Reap: The Story of César Chávez and the Farm Workers' Movement* (New York, 1970), a book abounding with astounding claims: for example, the assertion, based on absolutely no evidence, that "the first farm labor 'organizer' in California was an Indian who whispered to another, at some Franciscan mission, 'Let's run away to the hills tonight,'" and the equally ridiculous declaration that "the first farm labor 'sympathizer' was some Franciscan friar who protested that it was not saving souls to put Indians into virtual peonage, laboring in the mission vineyards. There were such organizers and such outside supporters, but their names are irretrievably lost in the past" (p. 19). For an example of factual distortion, see Margo McBane, *The History of California Agriculture: Focus on Women Farm Workers* (Santa Clara, Calif., 1975), wherein a letter from Mrs. Leland Stanford is misquoted as reporting that two thousand tons of hay and alfalfa were destroyed by arsonists during a farm labor dispute in 1898 when, in fact, the letter clearly indicates a far less dramatic figure of three hundred tons

and no labor dispute whatsoever. This error was then picked up and incorporated in Ruthanne Lum McCunn, *An Illustrated History of the Chinese in America* (San Francisco, 1979), 43, and is typical of how such errors have crept into the record and been passed along.

CHAPTER ONE

1. Johann Jakob Baegert, *Observations in Lower California*, trans. M. M. Brandenberg and Carl L. Baumann (Berkeley, 1952), 168–70. For Portolá, see Miguel del Barco, *Historia natural y crónica de la Antigua California* (Adiciones y correcciones a la Noticia de Miguel Venegas), ed. Miguel León-Portillo (Mexico City, 1973), 364; Portolá to de Croix, Feb. 3, 1768, AGN, Californias, 76: exp. 12, fols. 29031. See also Peter M. Dunne, "The Expulsion of the Jesuits from New Spain, 1767," *Mid-America* 29 (Jan. 1937), 3–30.

2. Quote from Benno Ducrue, *Ducrue's Account of the Expulsion of the Jesuits from Lower California (1676–1769)*, ed. and trans. Ernest J. Burrus (Rome, 1967), 66, 68. See also Mary Margaret Downey, "The Expulsion of the Jesuits from Baja California" (Ph.D. diss., UCB, 1940), 31, 37–38, 42–46; Francisco Morales, "Los Franciscanos en la Nueva España. La época de oro, siglo xvi," in Morales, ed., *Franciscan Presence in the Americas* (Potomac, Md., 1983), 77–80; Portolá to de Croix, Loreto, Feb. 3, 1768, in Donald Nuttall, "Gaspar de Portolá: Disenchanted Conquistador of Spanish Upper California," *SCQ* 53 (Sept. 1971), 186; Portolá to de Croix, San Diego, Apr. 17, 1770, in Fernando Boneu Companys, *Gaspar de Portolá, Explorer and Founder of California*, trans. Alan K. Brown (Lérida, Spain, 1983), 107–398.

3. Quote from Bishop Juan de Zumarraga to nephew, Aug. 23, 1539, in Agapito Rey, "Missionary Aspects of the Founding of New Mexico," *NMHR* 23 (Jan. 1948), 23. Although the Jesuits founded sixteen missions, two had been abandoned by 1767. See also John F. Schwaller, *The Church and Clergy in Sixteenth-Century Mexico* (Albuquerque, 1987), 81–109; Robert A. Matter, "The Spanish Missions of Florida: The Friars versus the Governors in the 'Golden Age,' 1606–1690" (Ph.D. diss., University of Washington, 1972), 106–22. For Franciscan work in Mexico, see John Leddy Phelan, *The Millennial Kingdom of the Franciscans* (Berkeley, 1956), 29–28; Erick Langer and Robert H. Jackson, *The New Latin American Mission History* (Lincoln, Neb., 1995). Six dragoons and one of Portolá's officers guarded the Jesuits on the march to Mexico City. A contingent of Jaliscan missionaries had beaten the Franciscans to Loreto by eighteen days. After the Franciscans arrived, the Jaliscans departed for San Blas and Sonora. See Magnus Mörner, ed., *The Expulsion of the Jesuits from Latin America* (New York, 1965). For the pre-Jesuit history of Baja California, see Michael Mathes, "Baja California: A Special Area of Contact and Colonization, 1535–1687," in David Hurst Thomas, ed., *Columbian Consequences: Archeological and Historical Perspectives on the Spanish Borderlands West* (Washington, D.C., 1989), 1: 407–22.

4. Luis Navarro García, *Don José de Gálvez y la comandancia general de las provincias internas del norte de Nueva España* (Seville, 1964),163–69; Herbert I. Priestley, *José de Gálvez, Visitor General of New Spain, 1765–1771* (Berkeley, 1916), 135, 154–57, 279.

5. Before 1769, the term "California" referred only to the peninsula known today as Baja California. As the frontier pushed north, pioneers referred to it first as Nueva California (New California), Alta California (Upper California), and the peninsula as Antigua California (Old California). Around 1880, both terms gave way to Baja California (Lower California) and Alta California (Upper California). See Harry W. Crosby, *Antigua California: Mission and Colony on the Peninsular Frontier, 1697–1768* (Albuquerque, 1994), xv, a magisterial work of great clarity and insight. See also Herbert E. Bolton, ed. and trans., *Palóu's Historical Memoirs of New California* (Berkeley, 1926), 30; Warren L. Cook, *Flood Tide of Empire: Spain and the Pacific Northwest, 1543–1819* (New Haven, 1973), 49; also 44–48; Francisco Javier Clavijero, *Storia della California, opera postuma del Nob. Sig. Abate D. Francesco Clavigero* (Venice, 1789), 4: 20, later published in Mexico as *Historia de la Antigua ó Baja California obra póstuma del Padre Francisco Javier Alegre de la Compañía de Jesús*, trans. Nicolás García de San Vicente (Mexico City, 1852); English version as *The History of [Lower] California*, ed. and trans. Sara E. Lake and A. A. Gray (Stanford, 1937).

6. Spanish explorers had charted the Pacific Coast for the first time on September 28, 1542, when Juan Rodríguez de Cabrillo landed at San Diego, and again on December 15, 1602, when Sebastián Vizcaíno landed at Monterey. See W. Michael Mathes, *Vizcaino and Spanish Expansion in the Pacific Ocean, 1580–1630* (San Francisco, 1968), 167; Mathes, "The Discoverer of

Alta California: Juan Rodríguez Cabrilho or Juan Rodríguez Cabrillo?" *JSDH* 19 (summer 1973), 1–8; Harry Kelsey, *Juan Rodríguez Cabrillo* (San Marino, Calif., 1986).

7. For general studies of the mission phenomenon, see Edward Spicer, *Cycles of Conquest: The Impact of Spain, Mexico, and the United States on the Indians of the Southwest, 1533–1960* (Tucson, 1962), 291; Robert Ricard, *The Spiritual Conquest of Mexico: An Essay on the Apostolate and the Evangelizing Methods of the Mendicant Orders in New Spain: 1523–1572*, trans. Lesley Byrd Simpson (Berkeley, 1966), 3. The classic account of the Spanish mission system is still Herbert E. Bolton, "The Mission as a Frontier Institution in the Spanish American Colonies," *AHR* 23 (Oct. 1917), 42–61. For case studies, see Randall Milliken, "An Ethnohistory of the Indian People of the San Francisco Bay Area from 1770 to 1810" (Ph.D. diss., UCB, 1991), 2, 23, later published as *A Time of Little Choice: The Disintegration of Tribal Culture in the San Francisco Bay Area, 1769–1818* (Menlo Park, Calif., 1995); Steven Hackel, "Indian-Spanish Relations in Alta California: Mission San Carlos Borromeo, 1770–1833" (Ph.D. diss., Cornell University, 1994), 202. For Gálvez, see Gálvez, "Plan para la creación de un Gobierno y Comandancia General," Jan. 23, 1768, in Mario Hernández Sánchez-Barba, *La ultima expansión española en América* (Madrid, 1957), 115; also 114–16; Theodore E. Treutlein, *San Francisco Bay: Discovery and Colonization, 1769–1776* (San Francisco, 1968), 109–17; Henry Wagner, *The Spanish Southwest, 1542–1784: An Annotated Bibliography* (Albuquerque, 1937), 2: 429–32; Luis Navarro García, "The North of New Spain as a Political Problem in the Eighteenth Century," in David Weber, ed., *New Spain's Far Northern Frontier: Essays on Spain in the American West* (Albuquerque, 1979), 201–15. For shifting of Indians between missions, see Bolton, *Palóu's Historical Memoirs*, 1: 38–41, 46–49; Gálvez to Francisco Lasuén, La Paz, Nov. 17, 1768, SBMA; Gálvez to Serra, Santa Ana, July 22, 1768; Gálvez to Palóu, La Paz, Nov. 23, 1768, DRMCLJP, 1: 163–64.

8. Earlier plans of occupation are discussed in Ernest J. Burrus, ed. and trans., *Kino's Plan for the Development of Primería Alta, Arizona, and Upper California: A Report to the Mexican Viceroy* (Tucson, 1961); Charles E. Chapman, *Founding of Spanish California: The Northwest Expansion of New Spain, 1678–1783* (New York, 1916), 14–44; Donald C. Cutter, "Plans for the Occupation of Upper California: A New Look at the 'Dark Age' from 1602–1769," *JSDH* 24 (winter 1978), 79–90.

9. Douglas S. Watson and Thomas W. Temple II, eds. and trans., *The Spanish Occupation of California: Junta Held at San Blas, May 16, 1768* (San Francisco, 1934), 19–23; Peter Gerhard, *The North Frontier of New Spain* (Princeton, N.J., 1982), 297.

10. Crosby, *Antigua California*, 320–43.

11. Ernest J. Burrus, trans. and ed., *Wenceslaus Linck's Diary of His 1766 Expedition to Northern Baja California* (Los Angeles, 1966), 20n, 21, 44; Crosby, *Antigua California*, 350; Clavijero, *History of [Lower] California*, 2: 149–50.

12. David J. Weber, *The Spanish Frontier in North America* (New Haven, 1992), 243. See also Francisco Palóu, *Life of Junípero Serra*, trans. Maynard J. Geiger (Washington, D.C., 1955); Geiger, *The Life and Times of Fray Junípero Serra, O.F.M.*, 2 vols. (Washington, D.C., 1959); Don DeNevi and Noel F. Moholy, *Junipero Serra: The Illustrated Story of the Franciscan Founder of California's Missions* (San Francisco, 1985).

13. Quote from Gálvez to Captain Vicente Vila, Instrucción, Jan. 5, 1769, PSP, 1: 28–37. See also Watson and Temple, *The Spanish Occupation of California*, 21; Zephyrin Engelhardt, *Missions and Missionaries of California: Lower California* (San Francisco, 1912), 1: 335–36, 340. The *San José* sank in 1770, bound for Monterey loaded with supplies. See Michael E. Thurman, *The Naval Department of San Blas: New Spain's Bastion for Alta California and Nootka, 1767–1798* (Glendale, 1967), 53–55. See also Arturo Jiménez-Vera, "Utopia in Baja California: The Dreams of Jose de Gálvez," trans. Ignacio del Río, *JSDH* 18 (fall 1972), 1–13; Harry Crosby, *Doomed to Fail: Gaspar de Portolá's First California Appointees*, Institute for Regional Studies of California, Border Series no. 2 (San Diego, 1989). Agricultural implements comprised a large part of the cargoes on board the supply ships. These included digging bars, pickaxes, shovels, planting poles, and various field implements, as well as various dried seeds and grains. There was also a three-month supply of cheese, olive oil, tallow, jugs of brandy and wine, dried beans and figs, flour, *pinole* (aromatic powder to mix with chocolate), biscuits, *arrobas* (twenty-five pound kegs) of jerked beef, rawhide, and coffee. An incomplete manifest of the *San Carlos* cargo list dated Jan. 5, 1769, much of it intended for the land expedition, is preserved in PSP, 1: 13–21.

14. For the reciprocal relationship between mission building, agriculture, conversion of Indians, and farm labor, see Robert Archibald, *The Economic Aspects of the California Missions*

(Washington, D.C., 1978), 142; Eugene David Burnett, "The Role of Agriculture in the Upper California Mission System as Illustrated at Mission San Diego, 1769–1784" (M.A. thesis, St. Louis University, 1958), 21, 25; Lionel Rideout, "Fermin Francisco de Lasuén and the Economic Development of the California Missions" (M.A. thesis, UCB, 1940), 16–23. For background, see Clarence H. Harding, *The Spanish Empire in America* (New York, 1947).

15. Experiencing a demographic holocaust under the Jesuits, campesinos born on the more prosperous missions had became infected with *mal gálico* (syphilis) and gonorrhea from the Spanish troops. On the poor missions, like San Gertrudis, Los Dolores, and San Luís Gonzaga, the latter two abolished because they were incapable of supporting natives, the number of natives declined because water and arable land were in short supply. On the better missions, like La Purísima and Todos Santos, campesinos benefited from more abundant resources that assured them of at least three meals a day and adequate clothing. At San Borja mission, in the middle of the Baja California desert, the padres often dispatched campesinos along with other mission Indians to scavenge for food, returning in relays every three or four weeks to attend mass and live and work around the mission. Wherever they were, campesinos suffered from epidemics of measles and other diseases for which they lacked immunity. Well fed or not, they died out at a frightening rate, declining from about forty thousand in 1697, when the Jesuits had arrived, to about seven thousand in 1768, when the Franciscans took control. See Gálvez to Serra, Nov. 23, 1768; Gálvez to Serra, July 22, 1768, DRMCLJP, 1: 163–64, 200–203; Gálvez to Lasuén, Feb. 1769; Palóu to Juan Andrés, Loreto, Nov. 24, 1769 [describing the syphilis infection at Todos Santos mission], SBMA; Bolton, *Palóu's Historical Memoirs*, 1: 38–41, 85–86, 119. Population figures are from Weber, *The Spanish Frontier*, 241. For another demographic assessment, see Ignacio del Rio Chávez, *Conquista y aculturación en la California Jesuítica, 1697–1768* (Mexico City, 1984), 224–26. For a far more severe demographic assessment showing unintended genocide, see Robert H. Jackson, "Epidemic Disease and Population Decline in the Missions of Baja California," *SCQ* 63 (winter 1981), 310, calculating that the Indian population dropped from sixty thousand in 1697 to twenty-one thousand in 1762, and 12,300 in 1775. See also Homer Aschmann, *The Central Desert of Baja California: Demography and Ecology* (Berkeley, 1959), 145, 148, 187, 251. Palóu to Rafael Verger, June 13, 1772, CDFHM, 1, expresses fear that the Indians would die out. See also Informe General, CV, 172, no. 699, par. 14, for an overview of diseases among Baja California Indians. Gálvez to Council of the Indies, Dec. 18, 1773, Guadalajara 418, AGI, reports on the failure of plans to reduce Baja California Indians to organized town dwellers. For shifting Indians about, see Gálvez to Serra, July 22, 1768, DRMCLJP, 1: 163–64.

16. Quote from Miguel Venegas, *Empressas Apostolicas de los Misiónes de la Compañia de Jesus de la Provincia de Nueva España Obras en la Conquista de Californias . . . por el Padre Miguel Venegas de la Misma Compañia de Jesus, Sabado, 7 de Noviembre de 1739*, HL [incomplete copy], HBC [complete copy], párrafo 519; also 516, 523. The best scholarly account of the Cochimíes is Sigismundo Taraval, *The Indian Uprising in Lower California, 1734–1737*, trans. Marguerite Eyre Wilbur (Los Angeles, 1931), 38. For the Cochimí boys sent to Guadalajara, see Padre Francisco María Piccolo to Gen. Ambriosio Odón, May 17, 1702, in Francisco María Piccolo, *Informe del estado de la Nueva Cristianidad de California, 1702 [y otros documentos]*, ed. Ernest J. Burrus (Madrid, 1962), 100–104. Guaycuras—according to Jacobo Baegert, the French-born Jesuit missionary serving at San Luis Gonzaga mission from 1751 to 1768—were "stupid, awkward, rude, unclean, insolent, ungrateful, mendacious, thievish, abominably lazy, great talkers to their end, and naive and childlike so far as intelligence and actions are concerned . . . unreflecting people, without worries, unconcerned, a people who possess no self-control but follow, like animals in every respect, their natural instincts." As for the Pericú groups, who constantly attacked and defended themselves against the Guaycuras, Rivera and other veterans of the peninsula regarded them with equal contempt. With a bloody record of distressing encounters with Europeans, a "rebellious," belligerent nature, and "turbulent dispositions," Rivera dismissed them as too independent-minded to serve with Serra and Portolá. Quotes from Baegert, *Observations in Lower California*, 43, 80, 133. To these characteristics, Padre Sebastián de Sistiaga, the Oaxacan-born Jesuit at Santa Rosalía and San Ignacio missions from 1728 to 1747, added cowardice, "sloth," "abhorrence of all labor," and excessive conceit. See Sebastián de Sistiaga to Esteban Rodríguez, Mar. 6, 1731, AGN, Historia, 308: 488. See also Palóu to Rafael Verger, San Francisco Javier mission, June 13, 1772, CDFHM, 1, expressing fear that the Indians would die out. For an overview of diseases among Baja California campesinos, see Informe General, CV, 172, no. 699: 14. The failure to reduce Baja California Indians to organized town dwellers is dis-

cussed in José de Gálvez to Council of the Indies, Madrid, Dec. 18, 1773, Guadalajara 418, AGI. For shifting Indians about, see Gálvez to Serra, Real de Santa Ana, July 22, 1768, DRMCLJP, 1: 163–64; Robert Wauchope, ed., *Handbook of Middle-American Indians* (Austin, 1966), 4: 53–55; Ernest Burrus, ed. and trans., *Jesuit Relations: Baja California, 1716–1762* (Los Angeles, 1984), 111–48. For the Pericú group, see Barco, *Historia natural y crónica de la Antigua California*, 171, 440, which gives the figure of three thousand Pericú. See also *Descripción breve de la California, su situación, extensión, costas, etc. [sic] con otras noticias que pueden conducir para el conocimiento de ellas*, AGI [transcripts], BL, which was probably written by a Dominican missionary of the post-Jesuit period; Clavijero, *The History of Lower California*, 89–101.

17. The most detailed retracing of the trek up the Baja California peninsula is Harry Crosby, *King's Highway in Baja California: An Adventure into the History of and Lore of a Forgotten Region* (San Diego, 1974). For specific details of the journey, see Donald Eugene Smith and Frederick J. Teggart, eds., *Diary of Gaspar de Portolá During the California Expedition of 1769–1770* (Berkeley, 1938), 1: 21–89. See also Herbert E. Bolton, ed. and trans., *Fray Juan Crespí, Missionary Explorer on the Pacific Coast, 1769–1774* (Berkeley, 1927). A figure of forty-two Cochimí campesinos is given in José Cañizares, "Diario ejecutado por Tierra desde el parage de Villacata á este puerto de San Diego," MS (July 3, 1769), BL; also Virgina E. Thickens and Margaret Mollins, trans., "Putting a Lid on California: An Unpublished Diary of the Portolá Expedition by José de Cañizares," *CHSQ* 31 (spring 1952), 109–15; Hubert H. Bancroft, *History of California* (San Francisco, 1886), 1: 132. See also Peter Gerhard and Howard E. Gulick, *Lower California Guidebook: A Descriptive Traveler's Guide with Route Maps, Illustrations, Bibliography and Index* (Glendale, 1956), 93.

18. Burrus, *Wenceslaus Linck's Diary*, 56–58; Barco, *Historia natural y crónica de la Antigua California*, 353.

19. Quote from Richard Pourade, *The Call to California* (San Diego, 1968), 71. Modern maps of Baja California designate the burial site as Valladares. The most comprehensive account is Harry Crosby, "*El Camino Real* in Baja California: Loreto to San Diego," *JSDH* 23 (winter 1977), 1–45. See also Engelhardt, *Missions and Missionaries of California*, 1, chs. 5–6. Serra would carry a copy of Linck's diary with him when he followed Portolá. See Geiger, *Junípero Serra*, 1; 223.

20. Junípero Serra, "Notas de 1776," MS (1776), SDML, describes campesinos dying along the way. See also Bancroft, *History of California*, 1: 133–34. Although it is assumed that deserting campesinos made their way back to their original missions, there is no record indicating any survived the dangerous return trek.

21. Quote from Portolá to de Croix, San Diego, July 4, 1769; also Feb. 11, 1770, in Companys, *Gaspar de Portolá*, 393–94, 320–21. For a succinct narrative that well describes conditions on the rainy night when the expedition arrived at San Diego, see Miguel Costansó, "Diario Histórico de los Viajes de mar y tierra hechos al norte de California," MS (1776), BL. For a translation, see Miguel Costansó, *The Portola Expedition of 1769–1770: Diary of Miguel Costanso*, ed. and trans. Frederick J. Teggart (Berkeley, 1911).

22. Portolá to de Croix, San Diego, July 4, 1769; Feb. 11, 1770, in Companys, *Gaspar de Portolá*, 320–21, 393. For planning, see Watson and Temple, *The Spanish Occupation of California*, 19–23. Failing to consider Baja California field hands, London and Anderson, *So Shall Ye Reap*, 6, as well as many other commentators, mistakenly assert that the Indians of Alta California were the first farmworkers.

23. By some accounts there were forty-six campesinos on the second expedition. See Francisco Palóu, *Life and Apostolic Labors of the Venerable Fray Junípero Serra*, ed. and trans. C. Scott Williams (New York, 1913), 72. Of about 219 members of the two "Sacred Expeditions" who started by land and sea, 126 survived the journey, although figures are imprecise. See also Bolton, *Palóu's Historical Memoirs*, 1: 295; Antonine Tibesar, ed. and trans., *Writings of Junípero Serra* (Washington, D.C., 1955), 1: 59–61. At least two campesinos originated at Nuestra Señora de Guadalupe mission, where they had departed with pack animals on April 13. Campesinos also seem to have served in a military capacity; on May 26 they seized one of two Indians seen trailing the expedition, tied him up, and brought the bruised and terrified man to be blessed, fed, and interrogated by Serra himself.

24. Quote from Serra's diary in Winfred E. Wise, *Fray Junípero Serra and the California Conquest* (New York, 1967), 44. See also Bolton, *Palóu's Historical Memoirs*, 1: 53–54. Pourade, *Call to California*, 79, describes the three desertions. For an analysis of the reasons why cam-

pesinos died along the way or deserted, see Padre Rafael Verger's thoughts as described in DeNevi and Moholy, *Junípero Serra*, 105–6.

25. For the general state of affairs during the first few days after arriving in San Diego, see Portolá to de Croix, San Diego, July 4, 1769, in Companys, *Gaspar de Portolá*, 393–94; also 320–21. Engelhardt, *Missions and Missionaries*, 2: 16, tallies the death of the five campesinos. In all, the combined camps of the Rivera and Portolá expeditions comprised some eighty-six campesinos, two military officers, a sergeant, two padres, thirty-five soldiers, between seven and nine muleteers, a ship's mate, and several "man servants," including an Indian altar boy for Serra. For a partial enumeration of articles taken from each mission, see Bolton, *Palóu's Historical Memoirs*, 1: 53–54. Lashed to the backs of 163 mules and horses, the expedition brought a vast array of provisions—canvas tents, muskets, gunpowder, lances, extra boots, and ammunition for every soldier, packsaddles, branding forceps, leather bags, and hundreds of head of cattle—both to augment the food supply along the way and to furnish breeding stock for the proposed missions and settlements in Alta California. Serra also carried with him from Santa María mission a chalice and other religious articles, including sacred vestments, silver cups, crosses, a large image of Nuestra Señora de los Dolores, a small crib with a statue of the infant Jesus, sacramental linen, a copper print of the Virgin Mary and Saint Joseph, silk and gauze garments, a copper-plated stand for the baptismal font, three small bell towers, and a bake-iron for making altar breads.

26. Crespí's diary in Bolton, *Palóu's Historical Memoirs*, 2: 104, says, "Only fourteen of the forty-four who started with the first expedition and some twelve who went with the second reached San Diego." Bancroft, *History of California*, 1: 132–41, 165–68, also cites these numbers. DeNevi and Moholy, *Junípero Serra*, 99–105, claim that twenty-seven of the Baja California Indians survived, and that ninety-three started north (thirteen of fifty-one Indians surviving the Portolá march), but cite no sources. DeNevi and Moholy may be also counting the Indian servants assigned to Serra. Various other accounts state that a total of ninety-one campesinos left from Baja California, and that forty-nine departed on the Rivera y Moncada expedition. However, the usually reliable Engelhardt, *Missions and Missionaries*, 1: 14, 16, asserts that only fourteen campesinos came north with Rivera, and twelve with Portolá, apparently counting only the survivors. My estimate that there were twenty-seven Baja California field hands in Alta California in 1770 is based on figures in Bolton, *Palóu's Historical Memoirs*; Bancroft, *History of California*, 1: 165, 167–68, 175–77; Chapman, *A History of California*, 222–23. The accounting is as follows: twenty-six survivors from the original eighty-six; minus one killed in the attack on the San Diego mission; six who died of sickness that winter; two who went south with Rivera's resupply expedition to Mexico on Feb. 11, 1770; ten dropped off by the ship *San Antonio* on March 19, giving a total of twenty-seven. However, Bancroft's account can be interpreted as indicating that the ten field hands were those left behind when the second Monterey expedition departed on April 17. This would lower the total Baja California campesino force to seventeen. Another accounting discrepancy may be caused by the presence of three Baja California Indian "boy servants," one of whom was killed in the August 15 attack, who seem to have been included in some lists but not others. I regard these calculations as rough estimates. See Street, "First Farmworkers, First *Braceros*: Baja California Field Hands and the Origins of Farm Labor Importation in California Agriculture, 1769-1790," *California History* 125 (winter 1996–97), 306–21, 381–83. During December 1770, Padre Rafael Verger, newly elected as head of the Franciscan missionaries at the College of San Fernando, Mexico City, examined the reasons so few campesinos survived the trek north. He discovered that five on the Portolá expedition had died of starvation; having been forced to shift for themselves, they had received a little nourishment which "in truth was more water than gruel." This was the reason nine others had deserted. Because of what happened to them, and because of the deaths of their comrades, Verger recommended to Viceroy Marqués de Croix a number of changes in rules governing the treatment of campesinos assigned to future expeditions. I have not located the archival documentation for this matter. See DeNevi and Moholy, *Junípero Serra*, 106. For one campesino who accompanied an expedition along the length of the Santa Clara Valley and the east side of San Francisco Bay to near the Sacramento-San Joaquin Delta in the spring of 1772, see Lowell J. Bean, ed., *The Ohlone Past and Present: Native Americans of the San Francisco Bay Region* (Menlo Park, Calif., 1994), 6.

27. Quotes from Portolá's journal, July 28, 1769, in Companys, *Gaspar de Portolá*, 375; also 399; Peter Browning, ed., *The Discovery of San Francisco Bay: The Portolá Expedition of 1769–1770*;

The Diary of Miguel Costansó (Lafayette, Calif., 1992), 139. The twenty-seven campesinos who constituted the first farmworkers in California are not the ones commemorated in paintings and other idyllic depictions of mission agriculture. There is not a single sketch of them. That they were "foreign" laborers who traveled long distances across borderlands and worked far from home has been entirely omitted from the mission story, and from the farmworker story as well. Modern updates of Bolton, which at least mention campesinos, are John Francis Bannon, *The Spanish Borderlands Frontier, 1513–1821* (New York, 1970), 49–54; Crosby, *Antigua California*, 390–93. A painting of San José del Cabo by Ignacio Tirsch may depict campesinos in 1767. See Doyce B. Nunis Jr., *The Drawings of Ignacio Tirsch, Jesuit Missionary in Baja California*, trans. Elsbeth Schultz-Bischof (Los Angeles, 1972), 47. For campesinos on Rivera's return trip to Baja California in February 1770, see Palóu, "Relación de la Vida etc. de Junípero Serra," MS (1787), xix, 94, BL; Palóu, "Noticias de [Nueva] California," MS [copy] (Mexico City, 1857 [San Francisco, 1974]), 2: 245–46; Portolá to de Croix, Feb. 11, 1770, AGN.

28. According to Bancroft, *History of California*, 1: 168, Portolá recovered one of three deserters. For mulatto *arrieros* who deserted, and for food resources, see 162. See also Browning, *Discovery of San Francisco Bay*, 141; Portolá to de Croix, June 15, 1770, AGN; Pedro Fages and Costansó to de Croix, June 13, 1770, MNM.

29. For campesinos acting as translators and teachers, see DeNevi and Moholy, *Junípero Serra*, 105–6.

30. For early planting and descriptions of starvation, see Tibesar, *Writings of Junípero Serra*, 1: 227, 297, 367; 3: 145; Herbert E. Bolton, ed. and trans., *Font's Complete Diary: Chronicle of the Founding of San Francisco* (Berkeley, 1933), 177–78; 301–3. For irrigation as early as 1773, see F. E. Green, "The San Diego Old Mission Dam and Irrigation System," MS (1934), 16, Junípero Serra Museum Archives, SDML [copy in SBMA]; Lasuén, Informe de la Misión de San Diego, Dec. 31, 1779, AGN [copy in SBMA]; Herbert E. Bolton, ed., *Anza's California Expeditions* (Berkeley, 1930), 4: 303. Padre Rafael Verger, head of the college of San Fernando in Mexico City complained in a letter to Viceroy Antonio María Bucareli y Ursúa, Dec. 25, 1772, AGI, Chapman doc. no. 1939, HL, that "what is lacking is hands to cultivate and work the fields because the soldiers do not want to help in any way in this task."

31. Quote from Engelhardt, *Missions and Missionaries*, 2: 131.

32. Quote from Bucareli to Julián de Arriaga, May 27, 1774, Chapman doc. no. 2625, HL.

33. Quote from Tibesar, *Writings of Serra*, 2: 141; 3: 299. See also "Anza's Return Diary," in Bolton, *Anza's California Expeditions*, 2: 110, 224; Verger to Bucareli, Dec. 25, 1772, AGI, Chapman doc. no. 1939, HL. The food crisis is described in Serra to Palóu, Monterey, Aug. 18, 1772, in Maynard Geiger, ed., *Palóu's Life of Junípero Serra* (Washington, D.C., 1960), 124–26; Fages to the Viceroy, Monterey, June 26, 1772, Californias, 66, AGN; Padre Francisco Pangua, Informe del estado las misiones de Monterey, Mexico, Dec. 9, 1776, Californias, 72, AGN [transcript in SBMA]. See also Augusta Fink, *Monterey County* (Fresno, 1978), 45; Engelhardt, *San Diego Mission* (San Francisco, 1920), 103. Because of their critical importance to early mission life, campesinos soon became the center of considerable debate over their treatment. It is often assumed that controversy over farmworkers was a modern phenomenon originating in farmworker strikes of the early twentieth century and the well-publicized plight of Dust Bowl refugees in the 1930s.

34. Representación of Serra to Bucareli, Mexico, Mar. 9, 1773, SBMA [copy], unfolds the original petition. Serra's Representación of Mar. 13, 1773, ibid., contains a request for peons, farm families, and artisans, as well as thirty-two points covering every phase of mission activity. Acting head of the missions, Palóu, recommended that twenty-five families travel north from the Baja California missions "of their own free will" in 1772. The following year Serra endorsed the idea because of the need for laborers, and also because Alta California natives found it strange "to see all these men [Baja California campesinos] without any women among them." Ten Baja California campesino families walked north from San Fernando de Velicatá mission in July 1773. One woman was left at San Diego mission, six families left at San Gabriel mission, and the rest marched to San Luis Obispo mission. See Francisco Palóu, *Noticias de la Nueva California* (San Francisco, 1874), 1: 240, 245–46, 250, 256–60, 261; and Bolton, *Palóu's Historical Memoirs*, 1: 298–303, reporting that the arrival of the Baja California field hands at San Gabriel mission was greeted like the second coming of the "Sacred Expedition" of 1769. See also Tibesar, *Writings of Serra*, 1; 310–11; Palóu to Gov. Felipe de Barri, July 20, 1773, AGN, Californias, 66: 398. Serra, "Report on the Missions," May 2, 1773, doc. no. 336, J. S. C. from A. S.

Taylor published notes, SBMA, reports padres at San Antonio mission plowing and planting with the help of two Baja California campesinos.

35. Serra to Bucareli, May 21, 1773, SBMA, describes labor shortages and other problems at length, as does Palóu to Bucareli, "Report on the State of the Missions," San Carlos, Dec. 10, 1773, in Bolton, *Palóu's Historical Memoirs*, 3: 213–38. See also Steven Hackel, "Land, Labor, and Production: The Colonial Economy of Spanish and Mexican California," in Richard J. Orsi and Ramón A. Gutiérrez, eds., *Contested Eden: California Before the Gold Rush* (Berkeley, 1998), 114.

36. Palóu to Serra, San Carlos, Nov. 26, 1773, DRMCLJP, 2: 78–86, reports ten Cochimí families and twelve Cochimí boys traveled north. Besides the padres, and some settlers, Bancroft, *History of California*, 2: 194–96, mentions twenty-five native families from the northern missions. Bancroft also asserts that one family remained at San Diego mission. My tally of field hands in the July–Sept. expedition to San Diego and San Gabriel is from Palóu to Serra, San Carlos, Nov. 26, 1773, DRMCLJP, 2: 78–86. Baja California campesinos played an especially important role training the first native converts at San Luis Obispo mission in 1773–74.

37. Quote from Palóu to Bucareli, Dec. 10, 1773, SBMA. Serra to Bucareli, Monterey, Feb. 5, 1775, ibid., also refers to the Baja California field hand families at San Gabriel mission.

38. For various aspects of the program to import Baja California field hands, see "Decision of His Excellency and the Royal Council," Mexico, May 6, 1773, in Bolton, *Palóu's Historical Memoirs*, 3: 37–55; Juan José Echeveste, "Regulations for the Peninsula of California and the Establishments of Monterey," Mexico, May 24, 1773, ibid., 57–77; "Opinion of the Fiscal," Mexico, June 14, 1773, ibid., 78–89; Bucareli to Del Campo Viergol, Mexico City, Aug. 4, 1773, in Bucareli, Provincias Internas 113, AGN; Serra to Bucareli, Mar. 13, 1773, "Report on the General Condition and Needs of the Missions of Upper California," in Tibesar, *Writings of Serra*, 1: 295–327.

39. Tarabal may or may not have come north from Santa Gertrudis mission with the Sacred Expedition in 1769. In some accounts his name is Taraval. Biographical information on Tarabal is from Engelhardt, *San Gabriel Mission and the Beginnings of Los Angeles* (San Gabriel, 1927), 17–19, 24. For his wife, listed as a *madrina* (godmother) in the baptismal registry of San Gabriel mission, see San Gabriel mission, "Libro Primero en que se Assientan las Partidas de los Bautismos de los Gentiles q[u]e se Christianan en Esta Misión de San Gabriel Archangel," 1771–95, entry 13 SBMA [copy].

40. Bancroft, *History of California*, 1: 221, states Tarabal deserted with his parents in August, not in October, with a Cochimí boy, but cites no source. Chapman, *A History of California*, 298–99, claims Tarabal escaped with his wife and brother, but also fails to cite a source. Hildegarde Hawthorne, *California Missions: Their Romance and Beauty* (New York, 1942), 66, asserts that Tarabal "sneaked away under cover of night with two other natives," but cites no documentation. Based on the accounting in Palóu to Bucareli, Dec. 10, 1773, SBMA, describing five Baja California Indian families and a number of single Baja California campesinos at San Gabriel mission, one might conclude that Tarabal fled with his wife and one of the single men. See also Theodore Hittell, *History of California* (San Francisco, 1885–97), 1: 362.

41. For Tarabal and Anza, see "Anza's Diary from Tubac to San Gabriel, 1774," in Bolton, *Anza's California Expeditions*, 2: 57–96, 157; 115–17, 121; "Díaz's Diary from Tubac to San Gabriel, 1774," ibid., 2: 270–88; "Garcés's Diary from Tubac to San Gabriel, 1774," ibid., 2: 325–47. The importance of friendly tribes in permitting the crossing and protection of the expedition is covered in Jack D. Forbes, *Warriors of the Colorado: The Yumas of the Quechan Nation and Their Neighbors* (Norman, Okla., 1965), 149–50, 156–57. See also Scott J. Maughan, "Francisco Garcés and New Spain's Northwest Frontier, 1768–1781" (Ph.D. diss., University of Utah, 1968), 105, 108, 117. The expedition consisted of thirty-four men—Anza, twenty troopers, five Indian muleteers, four Indian laborers and interpreters, one soldier from California, Padre Francisco Garcés, Díaz, and Tarabal—along with sixty-five head of cattle and 140 horses.

42. Bolton, *Font's Complete Diary*, 118n1; 129; 130n1 [quote], 140–43, 146, 478. The March 10 camp is near the present-day junction of Highways 78 and 86, at the southwest end of the Salton Sea. Deserted today, San Sebastián is called Harper's Well. Information on landmarks is from Mildred Hoover, Hero Rensch, and Ethel Rensch, *Historic Spots in California*, rev. ed. (Stanford, 1966), 107.

43. Quote from Bolton, *Anza's California Expeditions*, 1: 151–52; and "Garcés's Diary from Tubac to San Gabriel, 1774," 2: 321–22; 5: 117, citing Anza to Bucareli, Santa Olaya [on the Colorado River], Feb. 28, 1774. See also Elliott Coues, ed. and trans., *On the Trail of a Spanish Pioneer: The Diary and Itinerary of Francisco Garcés on His Travels through Sonora, Arizona, and Cal-*

ifornia, 1775–1776 (New York, 1900), 204-5n. For a discussion of the controversy over the actual route, see Engelhardt, *Missions and Missionaries of California*, 2: 135-37; 666-67. See also Finbar Kenneally, ed. and trans., *Writings of Fermín Francisco de Lasuén* (Washington, D.C., 1965), 1: 49-50.

44. Quote from Engelhardt, *Missions and Missionaries*, 3; 193. See also Harlan Hague, *The Road to California: The Search for a Southern Overland Route, 1540–1848* (Glendale, 1978), 58-67; Richard Pourade, *Anza Conquers the Desert* (San Diego, 1971), 1-63; Charles E. Chapman, *The Founding of Spanish California: The Northward Expansion of New Spain, 1687–1783* (New York, 1916), 415. Tarabal is mentioned in a number of letters written by Bernardo Urrea, Captain at Altar, in the *legajo*, or bundle of documents, in the Archivo General de Mexico, Provincias Internas, but for some reason is ignored in Bolton, ed., *Guide to Materials for the History of the United States in the Principal Archives of Mexico* (Washington, D.C., 1913 [1977]), 132, describing these letters as "of little interest." See also John L. Kessell, "The Making of a Martyr: The Young Francisco Garcés," *NMHR* 45 (July 1970), 181-96.

45. Quote from Bolton, *Font's Complete Diary*, 512; also 84. See also Chapman, *A History of the Spanish Period*, 316, 340-41. In an otherwise well-researched treatment, Francis F. Guest, *Fermín Francisco De Lasuén, 1736–1803: A Biography* (Washington, D.C., 1973), 353, omits Tarabal from his summary assessment of the work of Anza and Rivera y Moncada's expeditions. Tarabal's sojourn can be followed in John Galvin, ed. and trans., *A Record of Travels in Arizona and California, 1775–1776* [Daily Record of Garcés] (San Francisco, 1965), vi; (Dec. 5, 1775), 15; (Dec. 18), 21; (Dec. 19), 22, 24; (Feb. 14, 1776), 29; (Mar. 4, 1776), 35; (Feb. 29), 29; (Feb. 29), 34; (Mar. 4), 35; (Mar. 17), 37; (Apr. 13), 44; (Apr. 26), 45; (Apr. 27), 47; (Apr. 30), 47; (May 3), 50; (May 6), 55; (May 7), 56; (May 30), 60; (July 25), 81. See also Coues, *On the Trail of a Spanish Pioneer*, 82-88, 106-10; Bolton, *Font's Complete Diary*, 512. During spring 1781, field hands from the Sonoran missions were among a large party of soldiers, colonists, and animals who traveled from the Altar Valley to Caborca, and from there made their way north by a different route, a new southwestern trail that had opened up after Tarabal, Garcés, and Anza crossed the Colorado River near its junction with the Gila River at Yuma. Following the Yuma massacre, Spain abandoned the Yuma crossing, closed the Sonoran trail, and henceforth relied entirely on sea routes to resupply the missions. After the massacre, only a few field hands traveled north via the sea route, as the slow and fragile transports, struggling to tack against the prevailing winds and currents, were used mainly for delivering food, tools, artisans, colonists, and Spanish officials. See Miguel Costansó, "Report to the Viceroy, Sept. 5, 1772," in Bolton, *Anza's California Expeditions*, 5: 8-11. For the founding of the Yuma outposts, see Richard Yates, "Locating the Colorado River Mission San Pedro y San Pablo de Bicuñer," *JARH* 13 (summer 1972), 123-30. For the Yuma massacre, see Kieran McCarthy, ed. and trans., "The Colorado Massacre of 1781: Maria Montielo's Report," ibid., 16 (fall 1975), 221-25. The definitive account is Mark Santiago, *Massacre at the Yuma Crossing: Spanish Relations with the Quechans, 1779–1782* (Tucson, 1998), 25-27, 76-166, esp. 168-69. Aspects of Tarabal's travels can also be gleaned from Raymund F. Wood, "Francisco Garcés, Explorer of Southern California," *SCQ* 51 (Sept. 1969), 189, 193-97; Engelhardt, *Missions and Missionaries*, 2: 134-37, 192-93, 195; 3: 198-99; Frank F. Latta, "Indian Buckaroos," MS (n.d.), 2, FFLCSF. Tarabal is also mentioned as a *padrino* (male sponsor) for a baptism at San Gabriel mission in Baptismal Registry, San Gabriel mission, Apr. 7, 1776, entry 271, SBMA, transcript, Thomas W. Temple Collection, Chancery Archives, Los Angeles, vol. 5.

46. Ynez Viole O'Neill, "Padre Serra Plans the Founding of Mission San Juan Capistrano," *CHSQ* 56 (spring 1977), 47, translates a list of supplies that includes Baja California field hands "who . . . came up . . . of their own free will . . . assigned to this mission for its inception and for its agriculture." See also Bancroft, *History of California*, 1: 201. It is impossible to tabulate the exact number of Baja California field hands who traveled north between 1769 and 1820.

47. Never viewed as a people born out of exploration and colonization, and as trailblazers who ventured into and confronted unknown territory, early farmworkers are usually seen as people with a short recent history. An exception to the omission is Harlan Hague, "Guides for the Pathfinders: The Indian Contribution to the Exploration of the American West," *Pacific Historian* 26 (fall 1982), 54-55, 58, 62-63. For Baja California campesinos doubling as trailblazers on Portolá's expedition to San Francisco Bay, see Browning, *The Discovery of San Francisco Bay*, xxi-xxxi, 191. For campesinos as translators, see Palóu, "Vida," xxii, 105-6; Palóu, *Noticias*, 2: xxi, 261-63.

48. Braceros derived their name from the Spanish term for arm, *brazo*. Hence braceros were, literally, strong-armed men. Considered the standard account of the beginning of farm labor importation programs, Otey Scruggs, "The First Farm Labor Program, 1917–1921," *Arizona and the West* 2 (winter 1960), 320–23, establishes the World War I era as the beginning of government-sponsored bracero programs but does not consider the arrangement under which Baja California campesinos came north. Some writers have suggested that labor importation first began on an organized basis with the recruitment programs of the sugar beet companies around the turn of the century. See for example, Theresa Wolfson, "People Who Go to the Beets," *The American Child* 1 (Nov. 1919), 220.

CHAPTER TWO

1. Maynard J. Geiger, *Mission Santa Barbara, 1782–1965* (Santa Barbara, 1965), 98. See also Geiger, *The Indians of Mission Santa Barbara in Paganism and Christianity* (Santa Barbara, 1982).

2. Quote from Franklin Carter, ed. and trans., "[August B.] Duhaut-Cilly's Account of California in the Years 1827–28," *CHSQ* 8 (winter 1929), 329. Other references to Baja California campesinos are few and far between. There is some information supplied by Plácido Ortiz, an alleged witness to the 1783 murder of Santa Clara mission neophyte Sixto Antonio. See Fages to Francisco González, Mar. 12, 1786, AC, 23: 34–35. See also Bolton, *Palóu's New California*, 3, 19, 51. By the 1820s, Baja California campesinos had become such a rare sight that Duhaut-Cilly may have recorded one of the last remaining in Alta California.

3. For Baja California field hands serving as interpreters, see Serra, memo, June 22, 1774, in Tibesar, ed., *Writings of Serra*, 2: 89, referring to Cypriano Rivera, who as a child had accompanied Serra north. Married to a twelve-year-old Indian girl at San Carlos mission in November 1772, Rivera also guided search parties. See Serra to Fernando Rivera y Moncada, July 31, 1775, in ibid., 4: 425. For the flogging of one campesino, see Serra to Neve, Jan. 7, 1780, in ibid., 3: 409. For the switch in recruiting from Baja California to the mainland of New Spain, see Virginia M. Bouvier, *Women and the Conquest of California, 1542–1840: Codes of Silence* (Tucson, 2001), 56–57. For a group of five Baja California campesinos serving as the core group in the founding of Santa Clara mission, see Joseph Rosario of San Francisco Borja; Anecleto Valdez of San Francisco de Velicatá; Plácido Ortiz of San Ygnacio; Francisco Gragiola of San Ygnacio; and Esteban of San Francisco Borja, in "Libro de Casamientos, 1778–1863," vol. 1, SCUASC. Baja California campesinos were involved in three of the first nine weddings at Santa Clara mission and four of the first eleven at San Francisco mission. See also Diego and Tomás de la Peña Noboa, "Padron de los Indios Neofitos de esta Misión de la S. M. Santa Clara de Thamien existentes en 31 del mes de Diciembre del 1873," DPLHDM, segundo serie, tomo 2, doc. 33.

4. Quotes from Bolton, *Font's Complete Diary*, 195; padres Juan Martín and Juan Cabot, Respuesta [reply], Apr. 15, 1814, SBMA. See also Francis F. Guest, "The Indian Policy under Fermín Francisco Lasuén, California's Second Padre President," *CHSQ* 45 (Sept. 1966), 266–67; Kenneally, *Writings of Lasuén*, 1: 211; Charles Francis Saunders and F. Smeaton Chase, *The California Padres and Their Missions* (Boston, 1915); Racine McRoskey, *The Missions of California* (San Francisco, 1914); John Steven McGroarty, *Mission Memories* (Los Angeles, 1929).

5. Native peoples varied more widely among themselves than did the Franciscan missionaries, Spanish administrators, and the racially mixed lot of colonists who accompanied them. Each of their tribes or groups had clearly defined territories determined by the quantity and productivity of resources. Guarding, and if necessary, fighting over their territories, California Indians prospered, achieving the highest population density of any native peoples in North America. They had a culture devoid of carts, wheels, and guns, did not write, kept rock pictographs, used shell money, smoked tobacco in clay pipes, hunted with bows, arrows, snares, and traps, danced to rattles and the rhythm of pebble-filled gourds, had their own distinct religion, lived in conical, hemispherical, and wedge-shaped tule and wooden structures, and enjoyed such pleasures as hallucinogenic drugs and the daily ritual of relaxing in their *temescal*, or village sweat house. They also used plants extensively as medicine, traded over long distances with neighboring tribes, and had an extensive and imaginative oral literature of legends, myths, songs, genealogy, and historical accounts. All had creation myths and innumerable hero symbols. Especially trained bards and storytellers preserved this oral tradition by committing it to

memory and passing it along to subsequent generations, while shamans acted as middlemen between the people and the mystical, interceding to fight off illness, deflect storms, and assure good harvests. Indians had plenty of raw material for housing, weapons, tools, utensils, and clothing. From herds of elk, antelope, and deer they derived hides and venison. Summer-browned hills and lush riverbanks yielded crops of sweet clover, lettuce, bulbs, tubers, pine nuts, grapes, berries, tobacco, fruits, and innumerable seeds. Rivers were choked with fish, especially salmon during the spawning run. Seashores and bays abounded with seals, abalones, mussels, clams, oysters, beached whales, and other marine life. Ducks and geese darkened the skies with their huge numbers as they flocked to the marshlands, wetlands, and estuaries everywhere. Most California natives also had at least one nearly inexhaustible source of food that they gathered, processed, and stored much like wheat, corn, barley, and other cultivated crops: the oak tree acorn. Of some twenty different species of oak, natives derived most of their acorns from the blue oak, maul oak, black oak, and most importantly the valley oak, the heaviest producer, which grew throughout the valleys and into the foothills of the Sierra Nevada. Although Indians liked certain oak acorns more than others, accessibility and quantity, not quality, usually determined which acorns they harvested. Every third year beginning in September, California Indians could reap a bumper crop from the valley oaks, and they would spend much of the fall harvesting a year's supply, often deriving as much as five hundred pounds of acorns from a single tree. Storing huge quantities of the acorns inside dwellings or in elevated granaries, they devoted considerable amounts of time to processing the crop. They would first shell them and then grind them into a flour, place the flour in baskets or sand-lined depressions, and then pour hot water through the flour to leach out the tannic acid. Next they cleaned the flour, roasted it, and stored it away. For meals, they either baked the acorn flour tortilla-style on hot flat stones, or boiled it with tree fungi, clover, and lily pond roots. Adding mushrooms for additional flavor, they drank the mush or ladled it out with a wooden spoon. So important was acorn flour to Indian survival that tribal territory was often defined according to the distribution of oaks; what little conflict occurred between California natives often involved disputes over control of acorn gathering grounds. For many years the standard work on the California Indians was A. L. Kroeber, *Handbook of the Indians of California* (Washington, D.C., 1925), passim, and esp. 880–83. Superseding it is William C. Sturtevant, gen. ed., *Handbook of North American Indians: California*, ed. Robert F. Heizer (Washington, D.C., 1978), and more recently, Julia G. Costello and David Hornbeck, "Alta California: An Overview," in David Hurst Thomas, ed., *Columbian Consequences: Archeological and Historical Perspectives on the Spanish Borderlands West* (Washington, D.C., 1989) 1: 303–33, esp. 305, from which much of my account of Alta California Indians is drawn. Compared to native peoples of the eastern United States, California Indians had little tradition of organized warfare and no tradition of confederation necessary for unified resistance to intruders. See James Robert Moriarty III, "Accommodation and Conflict Resolution among Southern California Indian Groups," *SCQ* 56 (summer 1974), 109–22. For observations of Indian homes, see Stephen V. Powers, *The Tribes of California* (Washington, D.C., 1877 [Berkeley, 1976]), 370. For a modern analysis of the Los Angeles tribes, see William McCawley, *The First Angelinos: The Gabrielino Indians of Los Angeles* (Banning/Novato, Calif., 1995). For medicine among interior tribes, see George W. Stewart, "Yokut Indians of the Kaweah Region," *Sierra Club Bulletin* 12 (1927), 393; José Longinos Martínez, *California in 1792: The Expedition of José Longinos Martínez*, trans. Lesley Byrd Simpson (San Marino, 1938), 33–34. For warfare among interior tribes, see Steven R. James and Suzanne Graziani, "California Indian Warfare," *Contributions of the University of California Archeological Research Facility No. 23* (Mar. 1975), 95–97. For clashes between the Yokut and Chumash, consult Stephen Bowers, "The Santa Barbara Indians," MS (1879), 535, Southwest Museum Library. For protoagricultural trends, see Lowell J. Bean and Harry W. Lawton, "Some Explanations for the Rise of Cultural Complexity in Native California with Comments on Proto-agriculture and Agriculture," in Henry T. Lewis, ed., *Patterns of Indian Burning in California: Ecology and Ethnohistory* (Ramona, Calif., 1973), v–vii; Harry W. Lawton, "Agricultural Motifs in Southern California Indian Mythology," *Journal of California Anthropology* 1 (spring 1974), 53–79. See also Malcolm Margolin's excellent *The Ohlone Way: Indian Life in the San Francisco–Monterey Bay Area* (Berkeley, 1978). Outside the coastal strip where Spanish colonizers first encountered them, Eastern Mono and Yuma tribes did practice protoagriculture, increasing natural yields of seed plots through a form of irrigation along the Colorado River. See Martin A. Baunhoff, "Ecological Determinants of Aboriginal Populations," *University of California Publications in American Archeology and Ecology No. 49* (May 1963), 163–67; Robert F. Heizer and Albert B. Elsasser, *The Natural World of the California Indian* (Berkeley, 1980), 93, 100; Thomas Blackburn, *December's Child: A Book of Chumash Oral Narratives Collected by J. P. Harrington* (Berkeley, 1975), 276.

6. Quotes from Serra, "Report on the Missions," May 2, 1773, doc. no. 336, from A. S. Taylor published notes, SBMA. Of rapes by Spanish soldiers, Serra writing to Bucareli on April 22, 1773, lamented, "It is as though a plague of immorality had broken out." Quote from Tibesar, *Writings of Serra*, 1: 341; also May 21, 1773, 363. See also Bancroft, *History of California*, 1: 180–82, 189n. For events at San Francisco de Asís mission, see Edward D. Castillo, "Neophyte Resistance and Accommodation in the Missions of Alta California," in Howard Benoist and Matia Carolina Flores, eds., *The Spanish Missionary Heritage of the United States: Selected Papers and Commentaries from the November 1990 Quincentenary Symposium* (San Antonio, 1993), 60–75. For San Luis Obispo mission, see Engelhardt, *Missions and Missionaries*, 2: 230–31. For the grisly episode at San Gabriel mission, see Engelhardt, *San Gabriel Mission*, 6–7. Florence C. Shipek, "California Indian Reactions to the Franciscans," *The Americas* 41 (Apr. 1985), 480–93; Castillo, "The Native Response to the Colonization of Alta California," in David Hurst Thomas, ed., *Columbian Consequences: The Spanish Borderlands in Pan-American Perspective* (Washington, D.C., 1989), 3: 384–86; both Shipek and Castillo are critical of missionary recruitment and conversion. See also Mariano G. Vallejo, "Notas Históricas Sobre California" (Historical and personal memoirs relating to Alta California), trans. Earl R. Hewitt, MS (1874), 1: 15, BL; George R. Phillips to author, "Comments and Analysis," Feb. 20, 1996; Edward D. Castillo to author, "Comments and Analysis," Feb. 19, 1996, author's possession; Christopher Reynolds, "Patience of a Saint," *San Diego Union*, Aug. 17, 1987; Douglas Monroy, "The Creation and Re-creation of Californio Society," in Orsi and Gutiérrez, *Contested Eden*, 179; Rupert Costo and Jeannette Henry Costo, eds., *The Missions of California: A Legacy of Genocide* (San Francisco, 1987), ix, 3, 92–93, 187; Jack D. Forbes, *Native Americans of California and Nevada* (Healdsburg, Calif., 1957); Edward D. Castillo, ed., *Native American Perspectives on the Hispanic Colonization of Alta California* (New York, 1992), 423; *Seattle Times*, Sept. 14, 1987; Greg Critser, "The Million-Dollar Canonization," *California Magazine* 10 (Aug. 1985), 115; Carey McWilliams, *Southern California Country: An Island on the Land* (New York, 1946), 29; Lucia Norman Heaven, *A Popular History of California from the Earliest Period of its Discovery to the Present Time* (San Francisco, 1883), 11; Donald Bahr and Susan Fenger, "Indians and Missions: Homage to and Debate with Rupert Costo and Jeannette Henry Costo," *Journal of the Southwest* 31 (fall 1989), 300–21. Curt Gentry, *The Last Days of the Late, Great State of California* (New York, 1968), 141, asserts that "it was the Franciscan padres who started it all by keeping their Indian converts in virtual slavery." Hittell, *History of California*, 1: 563–65, describes mission farmwork as a "slavish kind of existence." Edward J. Wickson, *Rural California* (New York, 1923), 61, characterizes mission farm labor as "near slavery." For a Chicano scholar's views, see Juan Gómez-Quiñones, "The Origins and Development of the Mexican Working Class in the United States: Laborers and Artisans North of the Rio Bravo, 1600–1900," in Elisa Frost, Michael Meyer and Josefina Vazquez, eds., *Labor and Laborers through Mexican History* (Tucson, 1979), 463, 473–75, 516–17. See also the legal briefs, papers, testimony, and documents prepared during the 1950s and 1960s for the Indian Claims Commission and deposited in RCIH, UCRA; and Jack Norton, *Genocide in Northwestern California* (San Francisco, 1979). For a stimulating discussion of advocacy in the Indian interpretation of mission farm labor and a view of such history as yet another example of "white over red, of European dominance over aboriginal culture . . . not only justified but glorified in the name of religion," see James Sandos, "Junípero Serra's Canonization and the Historical Record," *AHR* 93 (winter 1988), 1266–69.

7. Sabine MacCormick, "The Heart Has Its Reasons: Predicaments of Missionary Christianity in Early Colonial Peru," *HAHR* 65 (Aug. 1985), 443–66; Clement W. Meighan, "Indians and the California Missions," *SCQ* 69 (fall 1987), 187–201; Ricard, *The Spiritual Conquest of Mexico*, 284–90; Robert H. Hoover, "Spanish-Native Interaction and Acculturation in the Alta California Missions," in Thomas, ed., *Columbian Consequences: Archeological and Historical Perspectives*, 1: 397. Some natives were amazed by cows and cow's milk; astounded by the sight of friars shepherding herds of cattle (natives having no domesticated animals); bewildered by the huge oxen and carts they pulled; baffled by the absence of women; mystified by Spanish boats moving under full sail; fascinated by strange things such as guns, metal, and horses; puzzled by cheese (which they mistook for the brains of dead men); confused by their first sight of a Spaniard's eyes seen magnified behind spectacles (*Cuatro ojos, cuatro ojos*, or "four eyes," children

cried); and delighted by pieces of red cloth, red being a color that Indians found only on scalps of woodpeckers and on a few spring flowers. Whatever the path onto the missions, the reasons natives acquiesced were never simple, often overlapped, changed over time, varied among the different tribes and missions, usually occurred in waves, seldom involved entire villages, and consisted mainly of family units trickling in to each mission. Quotes from Alfred Robinson, *Life in California, also Including Boscana's Chinigchinich* (Santa Barbara, 1970), 19; Serra to Bucareli, Aug. 24, 1774, in Tibesar, *Writings of Serra*, 2: 139; for references to the Spanish as mules, see 67, 87. For prohibitions on force in conversion as late as the 1790s, see Gov. Diego de Borica to commandant of San Francisco, Monterey, June 9, 1796, PSP, 12: 86; José D. Argüello to Borica, San Francisco, Mar. 30, 1798, 27: 97. The cheese reference is in Vicente P. Gómez, "Lo Que Sabe de California," MS (1877), 53–54, BL. For food, conversion, and the reference to exiles, see Pedro Fages, *A Historical, Political, and Natural Description of California by Pedro Fages, Soldier of Spain, Dutifully Made for the Viceroy*, ed. and trans. Herbert Priestley (1775 [Berkeley, 1937]), 43–44, 64–65. For Yolstamal Indians amazed by the sight of horses, see Felipe de Goycoechea quoted in Henry Raup Wagner, "The Last Spanish Exploration of the Northwest Coast and Attempt to Colonize Bodega Bay," *CHSQ* 10 (winter 1931), 344.

8. Indians attracted by persuasion, gifts, and recruiting are described in Charles Wilkes, *Narrative of the United States Exploring Expedition* (New York, 1844), 5: 183; Goycoechea to Fages, Santa Barbara, June 27, 1787, PSP, 7: 58; José de Jesús Vallejo, "Reminiscencias Históricas," MS (1877), 27, BL. For hiring gentiles to sow wheat and work at Santa Cruz mission in September 1791, see Cora Miranda Older, *California Missions and Their Romances* (New York, 1938), 185. Employers usually negotiated with chiefs to obtain workers, who were paid in grain, blankets, and clothing, although pay varied between missions.

9. Quote from Tibesar, *Writings of Serra*, 3: 127. For *entradas*, see Bolton, *Font's Complete Diary*, 365–72; Juan Crespí, "Diary Kept during the Exploration That Was Made to the Harbor of Our Padre San Francisco," in Bolton, *Juan Crespí*, 279, 293–98. For baptism of the sick during one *entrada*, see Serra, baptismal entry for Miguel Gregorio, May 9, 1775, San Carlos Borromeo mission baptism no. 0350, Archive of the Diocese of Monterey, San Carlos Borromeo mission Baptismal Registry, 1770–1896 (microfilm 0913159), CLDSA. See also Milliken, "An Ethnohistory of the Indian People of the San Francisco Bay Area from 1770 to 1810," 2, 23. Typical conversion techniques are outlined in Padre Juan Amoros, entries in San Rafael mission Baptismal Registry, entries 331, 325, 385, 444, 463, AASF [copies in SBMA and BL]. For the preponderance of child baptisms in the early years, see Baptismal Registry, San Juan Capistrano Mission Archives. See also Coues, *On the Trail of a Spanish Pioneer*, 272–74; Crespí, "Diary Kept during the Exploration that Was Made to the Harbor of Our Padre San Francisco," in Bolton, *Juan Crespí*, 293–95, 372; Ramon A. Gutiérrez, *When Jesus Came, the Corn Mothers Went Away: Marriage, Sexuality, and Power in New Mexico, 1500–1846* (Stanford, 1991), 93. Padre Gerónimo Boscana, "Chinigchinich: An Historical Account of the Origin, Customs, and Traditions of the Indians of Alta-California," in Robinson, *Life in California*, 70; Kenneally, *Writings of Lasuén*, 2: 202; Bernadine Richman, *California under Spain and Mexico, 1535–1847* (Boston, 1911), 254.

10. Percentages of natives employed in various tasks are extrapolated from Santa Cruz mission information in Robert H. Jackson, "Population and the Economic Dimension of Colonization in Alta California: Four Mission Communities," *Journal of the Southwest* 33 (fall 1991), 387–439. For native craftsmen, see Mardith Schuetz-Miller, *Building and Builders of Hispanic California, 1769–1850* (Los Angeles, 1994), the first work to credit the role played by native skilled craftsmen in building colonial structures. In 1825, at Santa Cruz mission, 31 percent of 227 native laborers worked on textile looms, and another 10 percent worked as artisans or apprentices. See Padre Luis Gil y Taboada, Dec. 31, 1825, Santa Cruz, DPLHC.

11. The principal scholar of the California missions, Zephyrin Engelhardt, and the former mission Indian Lorenzo Asisara conclude that farmwork was the principal task of mission Indians. See Engelhardt, *The Missions and Missionaries*, 2: 279, 376–81; and Lorenzo Asisara, "Narrative of a Mission Indian," in E. S. Harrison, *History of Santa Cruz County*, trans. from an interview by E. L. Williams (San Francisco, 1892), 47. See also Gary Coombs and Fred Plog, "The Conversion of the Chumash Indians: An Ecological Interpretation," *Human Ecology* 5 (June 1977), 309–28.

12. Quote from Georg Heinrich F. von Langsdorff, *Voyages, and Travels in Various Parts of the World, During the Years 1803, 1804, 1806, and 1807* (London, 1814), 2: 193. For the first irriga-

tion canal and systems, see Informe de la Misión de San Antonio, 1773; Informe de la Misión de Santa Clara, 1777, SBMA; Fages, in Priestly, *A Description of California*, 56–57; Felipe de Neve to Bucareli, Monterey, June 6, 1777, Provincias Internas 121, AGN; Engelhardt, *Mission San Carlos* (San Francisco, 1927), 243–45; also 87–89. For mission gardens and garden walls, see Isaac Mylar, *Early Days at Mission San Juan Bautista* (Watsonville, Calif., 1929), 20; Decision of the United States Land Commission, Mar. 18, 1865, in Book A, Patents, 182–83, Santa Barbara County Recorder's Office; Mariano Guadalupe Vallejo, "Ranch and Mission Days in Alta California," *Century Magazine* 19 (Dec. 1890) [article written by Charles Shinn from material dictated by Guadalupe Vallejo], 188–89; Anthony Soto, "Mission San Luis Rey, California—Excavations at Sunken Gardens," *The Kiva* 26 (winter 1961), 34–43.

13. Quotes from Bolton, *Font's Complete Diary*, entry of Feb. 13, 1776, 1: 240; Serra to Bucareli, Aug. 24, 1774, in Tibesar, *Writings of Serra*, 2: 145; also 177, 203, 295; 3: 99. Reporting on Indian field hands at San Carlos mission on June 21, 1774, Serra described how "from the labor of their hands we can boast of fields of wheat, corn, beans, peas, and a garden chock-full of cabbage, lettuce and all kinds of vegetables." See Serra to Bucareli, June 21, 1774, ibid., 2: 79. Both baptized and nonbaptized field hands worked the grain and sardine harvest. The last request for Baja California campesinos apparently came in December 1816, when Padre Mariano Payeras, who had become president of the missions, asked for twenty laborers from Mexico to cultivate vines. See *California Farmer*, Mar. 21, 1862; Bancroft, *History of California*, 1: 613–14.

14. For the shifting of Indian farmworkers from older to newer missions during the 1770s, see Kenneally, *Writings of Lasuén*, 2: 88, 231. For the 1780s, see Lasuén, Informe de la Misión de San Diego, Dec. 31, 1780, SBMA. For the 1790s, see Lasuén to Borica, May 5, 1797, PSP, 7: 27–31. Primitive grain production techniques, methods of the sixteenth century in Rome and ancient Iberia, provided little relief from physical labor and kept field hands constantly occupied. Because the padres seldom if ever rotated crops to limit soil exhaustion, and because they did not make extensive use of fertilizers or allow fields to remain fallow, field hands were constantly compensating for exhausted soil by clearing and planting new plots of virgin land. Better or improved seed stock and grain varieties would have diminished the dependence on labor and virgin land, but the missionaries never employed them. Consequently, grain production remained extremely uneven. If the locusts, birds, fungus, rodents, and drought spared the wheat fields, the padres could expect a wheat seed-to-harvest ratio ranging from as little as 1:1 on the poorest missions in the worst years early in the mission era, to 1:22 and higher on the best missions during the most favorable growing seasons late in the mission era. Ratios were better for corn—as low as 1:40 in bad/early years to as high as 1:192 in good/later years. An average yield of wheat seed sown to seed harvested for the years 1785–1821 is calculated at 1:15 in Archibald, *Economic Aspects of the California Missions*, table 17, 169–70. This meant that for the principal crop, close to 7 percent of all the harvest had to be saved for replanting and could not be consumed. Confirmation of these figures is found in José Señán, "A Further Report to the Commissioner, Nov. 9, 1822," 163–64, TC, which also reports that "most of the cultivated fields may be described as little better than mediocre." Figures for five missions are in Robert H. Jackson, "The Changing Economic Structure of the Alta California Missions—A Reinterpretation," *PHR* 61 (Aug. 1992), 394–95, 404–11, app. 1, giving generally higher harvest-to-seed ratios. For the year 1791, see Lasuén, "Estado de las misiones de la Nueva California sacado de los Informes de sus Ministros en fin de Diciembre del año 1791 en California y Costa N.O.," 1: 330, Museo Naval, Madrid, giving figures as 1:17 for wheat; 1:24 for barley; 1:97 for maize; 1:111 for corn. For Soledad mission, see the highly variable harvest-to-seed ratios for the years 1792–1832 in table 1, Paul Farnsworth and Robert H. Jackson, "Cultural, Economic, and Demographic Change in the Missions of Alta California: The Case of Nuestra Señora de la Soledad," in Erick Langer and Robert H. Jackson, eds., *The New Latin American Mission History* (Lincoln, Neb., 1995), 121. Evidence for lack of fertilization from harvest-to-seed sown ratios at five missions is in Jackson and Edward Castillo, *Indians, Franciscans, and Spanish Colonization: The Impact of the Mission System on California Indians* (Albuquerque, 1995), 20. Sierra Gorda farming experiences from Edith B. Webb, *Indian Life at the Old Missions* (Los Angeles, 1952), 52–53. By forcing field hands to rely so much on wheat, the padres committed a fundamental error, since many of the cool and foggy mission farms were poor places to grow wheat and were far better suited to maize and barley. So backward, technologically stagnant, and dependent on virgin land, good weather, and abundant labor were the padres that when drought struck and crops shriveled in the summer of 1778, all they could do was stare toward heaven, organize elaborate

religious ceremonies, make "ceaseless petitions for rains," and beg superiors in Mexico for supplies of corn and tools. Quote from Fages, Informe General Sobre las Misiones, 1778, Bancroft Collection, nos. 6–12, BL [copy in SBMA].

15. Mission Indian field hands used tools such as broad and stubbing hoes, shovels, hoeing spades, pickaxes, mattocks, hatchets, shears, weed hooks, and flails. See padres José Antonio Murguía and Thomas de la Peña, Informe de la Misión Santa Clara, Dec. 30, 1777; Padre Vicente Fuster, Informe de la Misión de San Diego, Mar. 20, 1777; Lasuén, Informes de la Misión de San Diego, Dec. 31, 1778, Dec. 31, 1780, Dec. 31, 1781, Dec. 31, 1784; Lasuén, Inventorio de la Misión de San Diego, May 4, 1783, AGN [copies in SBMA].

16. Quote from James Douglas, "Journal [From Columbia to California in 1840]," MS (n.d.), BL. During the first few years, field hands may have lacked teams of oxen and had to lash their plow beams to mules, the only draft animals available. See Tibesar, *Writings of Serra*, 1: 367; Serra, Representación, May 21, 1773, SBMA. Employing one hundred plowmen in the 1820s, San José mission often set them all to work preparing the same field. For *la cruzada*, see Lasuén, Informe de la Misión de San Diego, Dec. 31, 1779, SBMA.

17. John Marsh to Hon. Lewis Cass, 1842, in *History of Monterey County with Illustrations Descriptive of Its Scenery, with Biographical Sketches* (San Francisco, 1881), 38. A survey of farm labor and agriculture for the years 1772–1773 is in Palóu to Bucareli [on the State of the Missions], San Carlos, Dec. 10, 1773, in Bolton, *Palóu's Memoirs*, 3: 213–38, esp. 217. For San José mission, see Trowbridge Hall, *California Trails, Intimate Guide to the Old Missions* (New York, 1920), 204–5, whose account is based on an interview with a mission foreman cited in Robinson, *Life in California*, 43.

18. Quote from Edwin Bryant, *What I Saw In California* (Philadelphia, 1848), 294–95. See also Eugene Duflot de Mofras, *Exploration of the Territory of Oregon, and California . . .* , ed. and trans. Marguerite E. Wilbur (1844 [Santa Ana, 1937]), 2: 251–54; Engelhardt, *Missions and Missionaries*, 2: 260–61; Padre Luis Antonio Martínez to Gov. Pablo Vicente Sola, San Luis Obispo, Sept. 14, 1816, SBMA; Andrevitch Choris, "Port San Francisco and Its Inhabitants," in August C. Mahr, ed., *Visit of the "Rurik" to San Francisco in 1816* (1822 [Stanford, 1932]), 95; Engelhardt, *San Gabriel Mission*, 144; Paul H. Kocher, *Mission San Luis Obispo de Tolosa: A Historical Sketch* (San Luis Obispo, 1972), 29–30.

19. The mill had a grindstone that could not increase or decrease its speed and could only make exactly the same number of revolutions as the waterwheel. Because larger waterwheels did not make the grindstone revolve quickly enough to function properly, the Santa Cruz mill wheel, in contrast to most large-diameter waterwheels of the times—with boards on their periphery and gears to adjust the drive power—was extremely inefficient.

20. Quote from von Langsdorff, *Voyages*, 2: 169. See also Luis Antonio Martínez to Governor Sola, Sept. 14, 1816, SBMA; Choris, "Port San Francisco and Its Inhabitants," in Mahr, *Visit of the "Rurik,"* 95; Engelhardt, *San Gabriel Mission*, 144; Kocher, *Mission San Luis Obispo*, 29–30.

21. Metates were rough, curved grindstones shaped on an inclined plane and resting on three feet. For *tahonas* and *querns*, see Informe de la Misión San Antonio, 1810, Fábricas [buildings]; Informe de la Misión de San Gabriel, 1815, Fábricas; Informe de la Misión Santa Cruz, 1816, SBMA. For women grinding corn and making adobe bricks, see Goycoechea to Borica, Santa Barbara, Dec. 14, 1798, AC [copy in SBMA], 10: 71–80. For nursing mothers, see Padre Esteban Tapis to Lasuén, Santa Barbara, Oct. 30, 1800, Provincias Internas 216, AGN. For estimates of quotas, see Geiger, *The Indians of Mission Santa Barbara in Paganism and Christianity*, 34. Although women shouldered all kinds of other duties—washing and sewing clothes, weaving cloth, hauling firewood, mixing sand, straw, and manure as members of tile and adobe brick manufacturing crews, even traveling to remote camps to cook for field hands—they seldom toiled in the fields. This represented a major change for recently converted native women, who shifted from vital work at the center of tribal life to sedentary chores. Except for light hoeing duties and those occasions when they helped to gather cut grain stalks or pick up grain from the threshing corral floors, most women remained cloistered in the mission compound. For the San Gabriel mission mill, see Webb, *Indian Life*, 130; Bancroft, *History of California*, 1: 618.

22. Quote from Carter, "Duhaut-Cilly's Account," 237. See also Helen Pruit Beattie, trans., "José del Carmen Lugo, Life of a Rancher," *HSSCQ* 32 (Sept. 1950), 228; Padre Francisco Pangua, Informe del estado las Misiones de Monterey, Dec. 9, 1776, Californias, 72, AGN [copy in SBMA]; Bancroft, *California Pastoral* (San Francisco, 1888), 351, 357–58, 445; John Bidwell,

Echoes of the Past About California (Chico, 1891), 43–44; Engelhardt, *Missions and Missionaries*, 2:280–81.

23. By the early 1820s, Massachusetts harvesters using cradles were cutting grain at the rate of two or three acres per day. See William T. Hutchinson, *Cyrus Hall McCormick: Seed-Time, 1809–1856* (New York, 1930), 1: 71–2.

24. Carter, "Duhaut-Cilly's Account," 237; Howard S. Russell, *A Long Deep Furrow: Three Centuries of Farming in New England* (Hanover, N.H., 1976), 399; Hall, *California Trails*, 204–5; Anna B. Lincoln Ellis, "A 'Mystery Mission,'" *Noticias* 42 (fall 1979), 1–8, in Francis Weber, ed., *El Camino Real: A Documentary History of California's Estancias* (Hong Kong, 1988), 15–16.

25. Assuming a harvest rate of one half-acre per man per day based on Leo Rogin, *The Introduction of Farm Machinery and its Relation to the Productivity of Labor in the Agriculture of the United States during the Nineteenth Century*, University of California Publications in Economics, vol. 9 (Berkeley, 1931), 125–26, San Francisco de Solano mission's three-thousand-bushel crop in 1833 required four hundred "man days" to harvest. Assuming an average workweek of thirty-six hours, San Francisco de Solano mission would employ 152.5 men for one thirty-six-hour week to harvest its crop, half that number if operations were stretched over two weeks, and so on.

26. Nowhere in any of the histories of the California wine industry is there a reference to mission Indian field hands. The document establishing San Juan Capistrano mission as the birthplace of winemaking in California is Padre Pablo de Mugártegui to [Síndico of the College of San Fernando], Mar. 15, 1779, DRMCLJP, 2 [copy in SBMA]. Serra to Lasuén, Dec. 8, 1781, San Carlos, hints that vines were also planted at San Diego in 1779. For plantings in 1781, see Lasuén, Informe de la Misión de San Diego, Dec. 31, 1781, AGN [copy in SBMA]. The implication that these plantings were done by six Baja California field hands is in Engelhardt, *San Juan Capistrano: The Jewel of the Missions* (Los Angeles, 1922), 19. The most succinct discussion of when and where Indians and padres harvested and produced the first California vintage is Roy Brady, "The Swallow that Came from Capistrano: How the Vine Really Got to California and Who Really Made the State's First Wine," *New West* 4 (Sept. 24, 1979), 55–60. Likely sources of cuttings were the Baja California missions of San Javier, San José de Comondú, La Purísima, and San Ignacio, which had substantial vineyard and winemaking operations. For the vat at San Fernando mission, see Norman Neuerburg, "Biography of a Building: New Insights into the Construction of the Padre's Dwelling, an Archeological and Historical Resume," *SCQ* 79 (fall 1997), 292–94.

27. For the status of winemaking on five of the southern missions, see Lasuén, Biennial Reports, 1797, 1798, Feb. 20, 1799, San Carlos, SBMA. For the northern missions, see Biennial Reports, 1809, 1810, Padre Esteban Tapis, San Luis Rey, May 25, 1811. See also Edith B. Webb, "Agriculture in the Days of the Early California Padres," *The Americas* 4 (Jan. 1948), 330–35. Vine numbers at the *La Viña Madre* are from Hugo Reid to Abel Stearns, June 1, 1844, ASP. Even though the padres drank wine themselves, traded it, served it at mass, shipped it to their superiors as evidence of their accomplishments, and made a powerful grape-based brew known as *aguardiente*, Indians could not—under penalty of the lash—taste even a drop beyond that given at communion. For liquor, see padres Juan Martín and Juan Cabot, Respuesta no. 17 (1814), San Miguel mission, Apr. 15, 1814, SBMA; Padre Narciso Durán, Respuesta no. 18 (1814), San José mission, Nov. 1, 1814, trans. Francis Florence McCarthy, SBMA. The description of field hands stomping out the vintage is from Carlos N. Híjar, "California in 1834: Recollections," MS (1877), BL; Col. Agoston Haraszthy citing Mariano Guadalupe Vallejo as his source in CSAST, 1858, 312; John A. Waddell, "Some Memories of Early College Days in Santa Clara," MS (n.d.), SCUASC; Padre Narciso Durán to Gov. José Figueroa, June 17, 1833, SBMA. Winemaking techniques at La Soledad mission are described in Alonso de Herrera, *Agricultura General que trata de la Labranza del Campo y Sus Particularidades . . .* (Madrid, 1777), 2: SBMA [copy in EBWC], whose soiled and well-worn pages suggest that Padre Antonio Jayme, the winemaker at La Soledad mission, followed these procedures closely during his tenure from 1796 to 1821.

28. Charles F. Saunders and St. John O'Sullivan, *Capistrano Nights* (Los Angeles, 1929), 73–74. See also California Olive Industry, *Proceedings of the Third Annual State Convention* (Sacramento, 1893), 226–28. In 1868, when Elwood Cooper, "Father of the California olive industry," planted olive orchards at Santa Barbara he did so using slips (cuttings) taken from olive trees that Alta California natives had planted at Santa Barbara, San Fernando, and San Diego missions in the early 1800s. Following standard farming practices of the time, they

would have prepared deep and wide holes and filled the bottoms with straw. After waiting a year for the straw to "rot and mix," they split the cuttings at the base, inserted a stone in the split (to promote the spread of roots), and watered the young trees for the next few years.

29. Herrera, *Agricultura General*, 3: 166; Engelhardt, *San Diego Mission*, 154; Bancroft, *History of California*, 2: 418n10; Elwood Cooper, "The Olive in California," *The Californian* (Jan. 1892), in EBWC.

30. Roberta S. Greenwood and N. Gessler, "The Mission San Buenaventura Aqueduct with Particular Reference to the Fragments at Weldon Canyon," *Pacific Coast Archeological Society Quarterly* 4 (winter 1968), 61–87; Fred C. Hageman and Russell C. Ewing, *An Archeological and Restoration Study of Mission La Purísima Concepción* (Glendale, 1980); Soto, "Mission San Luis Rey," 34–40.

31. Dorothy E. Brovarney, "Cañada Larga: History and Preservation of the San Buenaventura Aqueduct," *Ventura County Historical Society Quarterly* 32 (spring 1987), 3–33; Engelhardt, *San Gabriel Mission*, 112. Acreage figure for 1834 from Adams, "Historical Background of California Agriculture," in Claude B. Hutchison, *California Agriculture*, 10; Jackson and Castillo, *Indians, Franciscans, and Spanish Colonization*, 114–23; F. E. Green, "The San Diego Old Mission Dam and Irrigation System" (ms). At San Luis Obispo mission, field hands shaped hundreds of tons of stone into beautiful, terraced ponds, elaborate stairways, and fountains that foreign visitors likened to those of Versailles. Natives not only built these facilities, they used and enjoyed them. Bathing in San Luis Obispo mission's pools in the evenings and washing their clothes in the pools on Saturdays, they kept the upper pools and gardens supplied with water by means of a crude chain pump, the first such pump in California. Two strong-legged men turned the clumsy apparatus in two-hour shifts, twice each day. See Kocher, *Mission San Luis Obispo*, 29–30; Engelhardt, *Mission San Luis Obispo* (Santa Barbara, 1933), 51, 57; Carter, "Duhaut-Cilly's Account," 228.

32. Julia D. Costello and Robert L. Hoover, eds., "The Brick and Tile Kiln," *Excavations at Mission San Antonio, 1976–1978*, Institute for Archeology Monograph No. 26 (Los Angeles, 1985), 122–45.

33. Julio César, "Recollections of My Youth at San Luis Rey Mission," ed. and trans. Nellie Van De Grift Sanchez, *Touring Topics* 22 (1878), 42–43; Raymundo Carrillo to Gov. José Joaquín Arrillaga, Santa Barbara, Oct. 13, 1802, Provincias Internas 216, AGN; Goycoechea to Borica, Dec. 14, 1798, PSP, 17: 70; Antonio Grájera to Borica, San Diego, Mar. 21, 1799, 17: 191; Harrison Rogers, first journal, Jan. 9, 1827, MS, MHS; Serra to Lasuén, Dec. 8, 1781, SBMA; Alexander Forbes, *California: A History of Upper and Lower California* (London, 1839), 158–59. See also Francis Florence McCarthy, *History of Mission San Jose California, 1797–1835* (Fresno, 1958), 73. The only book on the San Jose mission, McCarthy's study is strewn with racist assumptions, and must be used with care. For a devastating critique, see Edward D. Castillo, "The Language of Race Hatred," in Lowell J. Bean, ed., *The Ohlone, Past and Present: Native Americans of the San Francisco Bay Region* (Menlo Park, Calif., 1994), 271–95.

34. For watchmen, see Webb, *Indian Life*, 89. Webb's notes and research materials in SBMA do not disclose the information upon which she based this particular piece of information. For bird-catchers, see Padre Vicente de Santa Maria to Lasuén, Sept. 3, 1795, SBMA.

35. Padres José Maria Real and John Nobli, Inventorio, San José, 1850, trans. Norman Neuerburg, ACALA, gives a detailed accounting of living quarters as they existed at the height of the mission era. See also Geiger, *Mission Santa Barbara*, 42; James J. F. Deetz, "Archaeological Investigations at La Purisma Mission," *Archaeological Survey Annual Report* 5 (1963), 144–61. Square footage comparison from Philip D. Morgan, *Slave Counterpoint: Black Culture in the Eighteenth-Century Chesapeake and Lowcountry* (Chapel Hill, N.C., 1998), 111.

36. For San Antonio mission, see Robert Hoover, "Mission San Antonio de Padua in California," *Archeology* 32 (1979), 56–58; Donald M. Howard, "Excavations at Tes-haya: The Indian Rancheria at Mission San Antonio de Padua," *Monterey County Archaeological Quarterly* 2 (1972), 1–11; Padre Randolf, "Report of the Excavations of the Indian Dwellings at Mission San Antonio de Padua," MS (1956), San Antonio Mission Archives. For one of the earliest, if not *the* earliest, view of field hands, see José Cardero, "Vista del Presidio del Monte Rey," Museo Naval, Madrid, copy in the Robert B. Honeyman Collection, BL, depicting work outside the walls of the presidio of Monterey near San Carlos mission in 1791. I am indebted to Professor Donald C. Cutter for a copy of the Museo Naval view and for his confirmation of my suspicion that this is the earliest image of mission field hands in Alta California.

37. Florence C. Lister and Robert H. Lister, "A Descriptive Dictionary for 500 Years of Spanish Tradition Ceramics," *Society for Historical Archaeology Special Publication No. 1* (1977), 27; Ronald V. May, "An Analysis of Certain Ceramics from the San Buenaventura Mission," in R. S. Greenwood, *The Changing Faces of Main Street* (Ventura, 1976), 233; Hoover and Costello, *Excavations at Mission San Antonio*, 20, 32–33, 37, 41, 66, 68, 72, 80, 84.

38. For quarters at the missions, see Edwin Bryant, *Rocky Mountain Adventures* (New York, 1889), 310–11; Maynard J. Geiger, *Franciscan Missionaries in Hispanic California* (San Marino, 1969), 68; typewritten notes by Edith Webb, "Pages from the History of Mission San Luis Obispo," for *California History Nugget* (Jan. 1938), EBWC; Engelhardt, *Mission Santa Barbara* (San Francisco, 1923), 77. For *estancias*, see Padre Juan Cabot, San Miguel mission, to Gov. José M. Echeandía, Nov. 26, 1827; Fages, Informe General Sobre Misiones, 1787, SBMA [copy]; Padre Antonio Peyri to Governor Echeandía, Oct. 8, 1827, SP, Missions, 5: 205; Kocher, *Mission San Luis Obispo*, 30–31; William R. Cameron, "Rancho Santa Margarita of San Luis Obispo," *CHSQ* 36 (Mar. 1957), 1–24; Phil Brigandi, "The Outposts of Mission San Luis Rey," *San Diego History* 45 (spring 1999), 1–5; Don C. Meadows, "From Missionaries to Marines: Rancho Santa Margarita y Las Flores," *Los Angeles Corral of Westerners Brand Book No. 13* (Los Angeles, 1969); Gloria Brooks Forsyth, "The Lost Chapel of Cieneguita," *Noticias* 7 (spring 1961), 11–17; George W. Beattie, *California's Unbuilt Missions* (n.p., 1930); J. M. Carrillo, *The Story of Mission San Antonio de Pala* (Balboa Island, Calif., 1959).

39. Paso Robles *estancia* of San Miguel mission held more than 190 field hands as late as 1839. See William Hartnell, "Diario, informe, y borradores de correspondencia," MS (1877), BL. For field hands at Rancho San Antonio de Pala of San Luis Rey mission, see Annual Reports, San Luis Rey mission, SBMA. For San Gabriel mission, see L. T. Burchman, *California Range Land* (Davis, 1981), 120. See also Francis Weber, *El Caminito Real: A Documentary History of California's Estancias* (Hong Kong, 1988), v; J. J. O'Keefe, *The Buildings and Churches of the Mission Santa Barbara* (Santa Barbara, 1886), 17, 31.

40. For field hands on La Puente, see Padre José Zalvidéa to Faustino Solá, May 16, 1816, AASF. For San Pablo y San Pedro, see Steve Deitz, "Report of Archeological Investigations at Sanchez Adobe Park Historic District," MS (n.d.), 31–35, San Mateo Parks and Recreation Department, Redwood City, Calif.; George W. Hendry and Jacob N. Bowman, "The Spanish and Mexican Adobe and Other Buildings in the Nine San Francisco Bay Counties, 1776 to about 1850," 7 vols. (1940–45), pts. 5–6: 487, 490, 497, 499, 501, 503. For Paso Robles, see William Hartnell, "Diario, informe, y borradores de correspondencia." San Diego mission's field hands also migrated, living in their rancherías for much of the year, then traveling to the mission to work at various farm tasks and to receive religious instruction. See also Paul G. Chace, "A Summary Report of the Costa Mesa Estancia," *Pacific Coast Archaeological Society Quarterly* 2 (spring 1966), 30–37; Roberta S. Greenwood and Robert W. Browne, "The Chapel of San Gertrudis," ibid., 4 (winter 1968), 61–87; Frank M. Stanger, "The Hospice or Mission San Mateo," *CHSQ* 23 (Sept. 1944), 253; Maynard J. Geiger, "New Data on the Building of Mission San Francisco," ibid., 46 (Sept. 1967), 202.

41. One task followed another. Plowmen were busiest in October and November, when in rapid succession, they tilled huge acreages following the first rains, then worked frantically while planting wheat into early December. Spring was usually devoted to plowing fields and planting corn, often two different varieties (yellow and "small" or white corn), and perhaps barley. Field hands labored longest and hardest in July, August, and September, when the grain, corn, fruit, and grape harvests all overlapped. But they always had something to do. They pruned fruit trees in December and January and mucked out the *zanjas* (irrigation canals) in April. In the fall, after the maize and corn harvest, they helped vaqueros drive herds of cattle into the harvested fields to feed on the stubble. For the December and January wheat planting schedules, the spring corn planting regime, and fall harvest and threshing, see the Santa Cruz Mission Account Book, HSSC, Loomis House, Los Angeles. See also Fernando Librado, "Padre Rosales," interview, [ca. 1908], JPHP; Padre José Señán to Don José de la Guerra, Jan. 28, 1817 [copy in BL]; Señán to Sola, Jan. 2, 1817, TC.

42. Bancroft, *California Pastoral* (San Francisco, 1888), 357, 445; Palóu, "Estado de las misiones de la nueva California sacado de los Informes," Dec. 31, 1784, SBMA; Waddell, "Some Memories of Earlier College Days in Santa Clara." For wheat, corn, and barley, see Annual Reports, San Gabriel mission, AGN. For corn, see Annual Reports, San Diego mission. Like modern farmworkers, mission field hands were often distinguished by their dress and certain

physical characteristics. They received, along with everyone else, the standard mission uniform—baggy, bluish woolen pantaloons cut a few inches above the ankle and tied around the waist with a thick cord, sandals, hats, a short tunic, and a *frazada* (heavy blanket) with a slit cut through it Mexican serape style. Besides going shirtless, men sometimes also discarded their hats, pants, and sandals, and worked only in diaperlike *taparabos*. Additionally, their feet and ankles were sometimes scarred by carelessly swung hoes, machetes, and axes, and their hands often bore telltale scars, usually near the small of the finger, where the sickle made a slice. Thus, almost from the very beginning, California farmworkers were marked by many of the traits that commonly identify people as campesinos—as men of the fields. Quote from Robert F. Heizer, ed., *The Indians of Los Angeles: Hugo Reid's Letters of 1852* (Los Angeles, 1968), 86, letter no. 19, "New Era of Mission Affairs." See also padres Juan Martín and Juan Cabot, Respuesta no. 36 to Interrogatorios of Oct. 1812, San Miguel mission, Apr. 15, 1814; padres Luis Antonio Martínez and Antonio Rodríguez, Respuesta no. 32, San Luis Obispo mission, Apr. 12, 1814, SBMA. For going about naked, see "Relación del viaje hecho por las goletas Sutil y Mexicana en el año de 1792," MS (Madrid, 1802), n.p. This has recently been translated and annotated in Donald C. Cutter, *California in 1792: A Spanish Naval Visit* (Norman, Okla., 1990), 134. For general appearance, see Cardero, "Vista del Presidio de Monte Rey." For gardens, see Thomas Brown, "Mission Era Gardens and Landscapes," in Nicholas M. Magalousis, ed., *Early California Reflections* (San Juan Capistrano, 1987), 9–28, Orange County Public Library; Norman Neuerburg, *The Decoration of the California Missions* (Santa Barbara, 1987), 3.

43. Quote from Kenneally, *Writings of Lasuén*, 1: 168. See also Geiger, *The Life and Times of Junípero Serra*, 2: 191–201; Daniel Garr, "A Frontier Agrarian Settlement: San José de Guadalupe, 1777–1850," *San Jose Studies* 2 (Nov. 1976), 94–97. Given a yoke of oxen, a mule, two horses, some cows, sheep, and goats, some corn for planting, a daily soldier's ration and ten pesos per month, each settler also received a cattle brand, a town lot measuring 137 ½ by 137 ½ feet, and a plot of land about 184 ¼ by 184 ¼ yards. See Leonard McKay, ed., *Clyde Arbuckle's History of San José* (San Jose, 1986), 10–22; Ralph Rambo and Clyde Arbuckle, *Santa Clara County Ranchos* (San Jose, 1968); W. F. James and G. H. McMurray, *History of San Jose* (San Jose, 1933); Eugene T. Sawyer, *History of Santa Clara County, California, with Biographical Sketches* (Los Angeles, 1922). Harvest statistics for 1781 are from Felipe de Neve, Sept. 1782, quoted in Edwin A. Beilharz, *Felipe de Neve: First Governor of California* (San Francisco, 1971), 165.

44. Becoming permanent fixtures in the pueblos, rented mission field hands planted and harvested nearly twelve thousand bushels of maize and wheat for Los Angeles farmers in 1784. For rented mission Indians working for Fages in 1790, see Fages to Castro, letters from Apr. to Sept., 1790, DSP, San José, 1: 28–40. For Los Angeles, see Ruth Emily Baugh, "The Geography of the Los Angeles Water Supply" (Ph.D. diss., Clark University, 1929), 13; Greg Layne, *Annals of Los Angeles: From the Arrival of the First White Men to the Civil War, 1769–1861* (San Francisco, 1935), 7; Howard J. Nelson, "The Two Pueblos of Los Angeles: Agricultural Village and Embryo Town," *SCQ* 59 (spring 1977), 1–11; J. M. Guinn, *A History of California and an Extended History of Los Angeles and its Environs* (Los Angeles, 1915), 75. Thomas Workman Temple II, "Se Fundaron un Pueblo de Españoles," *HSSCAP* 15 (1931), 69–98. For the composition of the Los Angeles settlers, see Temple, "First Census of Los Angeles," ibid., 16 (1931), 148–49. For San José, see Oscar O. Winther, "The Story of San Jose, 1777–1869," *CHSQ* 14 (winter 1935), 3–27, 147–74. See also "Settlement in Alta California Before 1800" (M.A. thesis, UCB, 1931), 80–82.

45. Quote from Krill Timofeevich Khlebnikov, "Memoirs of California . . . ," ed. Anatole G. Mazour, *PHR* 9 (spring 1940), 325. The stereotype that the Californios had an unusually deep aversion to labor is debunked in David J. Weber, "Here Rests Juan Espinosa: Toward a Clearer Look at the Image of the 'Indolent' Californios," *WHQ* 10 (Jan. 1979), 61–68, which advances a view of them as people willing to take chances, come to California, and work hard as the one act that most quickly elevated them from the bottom to the top of the social ladder. See also Weber, "'Scarce More than Apes': Historical Roots of Anglo-American Stereotypes of Mexicans," in *New Spain's Far Northern Frontier: Essays on Spain in the American West* (Albuquerque, 1979), 293–307. For Branciforte, see Francis Florian Guest, "The Establishment of the Villa Branciforte," ibid., 41 (winter 1962), 29–50; Guest, "The Foundation of the Villa de Branciforte," ibid., 46 (Dec. 1967), 307–35; Garr, "Villa Branciforte: Innovation and Adaptation on the Frontier," *The Americas* 35 (July 1978), 95–109. For rented field hands working with gentiles at San Francisco in 1794, see Sal to Arrillaga, Apr. 30, 1794, PSP, 12: 73. For field hands rented

from Santa Cruz mission to residents of Villa de Branciforte for 1.5 reales per day to clear and plant land, see Santa Cruz Mission Account Book, HSSC [copy in Saint Mary's College Archives, Moraga, Calif.]. For one transaction, see receipt for $485 for a Soledad mission neophyte employed at Monterey, n.d., PSP, Presidio, 2:29. For field hands rented to presidios, see Ramón Olbés, "Lista de los Neofitos de la Misión de S[an]ta Cruz que son congregados en d[ic]ha Misión," TC. See also Donald Howard, *California's Lost Fortress: The Royal Presidio of Monterey* (Monterey, 1976), 30. For wages charged for field hands rented out with equipment and/or animals (mules and oxen), see Presidio Account Book, signed by José Francisco Ortega, Monterey, Dec. 31, 1788, AASF [copy in SBMA]. For general rental arrangements, see "Libro de quentas que esta Misión de Santa Barbara tiene con la Habilitacion de este presidio de el mismo nombre y otros various particulares," Santa Barbara mission, 1794–1805, SBMA; Santa Barbara Mission Account Book, 1805–7; La Purísima Mission Account Book, 1806–34, trans. Lewis G. Thomas and Elmira Osuna, Berkeley, 1938, WPA Project, 143, SBMA. Wages for field hands rented to presidio farmers are listed in Borica to commandant of San José presidio, Dec. 23, 1795, PR, 2:147. Production statistics from Francis F. Guest, "Municipal Institutions in Spanish California, 1769–1821" (Ph.D. diss., USC, 1961), 262, 267. See also Howard J. Nelson, *The Los Angeles Metropolis* (Dubuque, Iowa, 1983), 133. Never consulted about being rented, mission field hands were never paid any of the wages they earned. Cheap and efficient, they helped Los Angeles to achieve agricultural self-sufficiency by 1786, when Spain discontinued financial support, and to produce by 1790 some forty-five hundred bushels of grain, and seventy-eight hundred bushels six years later. They also briefly sustained a scheme to develop a commercial hemp industry. Grown in small quantities on a few northern missions as early as 1791, hemp was an essential fiber used to make rope, netting, sacks, and bags. About 1795, Mexico began subsidizing hemp prices and production increased significantly. Hoping that the crop would became a major export for the struggling pueblo farmers, Governor Borica ordered settlers at San José to begin growing the crop on a large scale. Field hands rented from Santa Clara and San José missions harvested 560 pounds of hemp in 1796. Because the northern missions lacked the expertise and climate required for large-scale production, the industry never prospered. Hoping to expand production, Spanish authorities dispatched an experienced hemp farmer north from San Blas to Monterey in 1801. But in 1804 most of the San José hemp crop was lost in a warehouse fire, and the following year poor weather cut yields to 150 pounds. See Lasuén to Padre Tomás Pangua, Dec. 16, 1793, San Diego, in Kenneally, *Writings of Lasuén*, 1; 328–29; Sanford A. Mosk, "Subsidized Hemp Production in Spanish California," *AH* 13 (Oct. 1939), 171–75; Joaquín Sanchez to Arrillaga, Aug. 30, 1805, San José, AC: 11: 1, 184. During the summer of 1807, when residents of San José could not bring in their large wheat and hemp crops, Governor Arrillaga allowed them to travel into the San Joaquin Valley and solicit labor from pagan Indians in the village of Cholvon. Working for wages of thread, needles, glass beads, and blankets, the Cholvon Indians brought in the harvest and returned to their home, only one of them having converted and received baptism. See Arrillaga to commandante of San José, July 23, 1807, Archives of the City of San Jose, doc. 21, San Jose Historical Society; Aug. 17, 1807, doc. no. 22; Sept. 4, 1807, doc. no. 24; Sept. 5, 1807, doc. no. 25. Cholvon people apparently continued helping with the harvests well into 1810, with many converting at San José mission. To tend and harvest their hemp crop, *pobladores* around Los Angeles obtained crews of field hands from San Gabriel and San Juan Capistrano missions, paying the padres with future earnings, goods, or some combination of the two. As hemp production increased from 1,800 pounds in 1806 to 220,000 pounds in 1810, a figure exceeding the total production of the preceding two decades, more and more field hands moved from the missions onto the pueblo hemp farms. This had unintended consequences. Deprived of spiritual guidance, rented mission field hands tended to become independent, turn away from the church, ignore the padres, and "devolve into paganism." When this problem became acute in 1810, Padre José Suñer of San Juan Capistrano mission stopped supplying field hands to Los Angeles hemp growers. Had hemp growing not collapsed the following year, when the Mexican government stopped buying it and Governor Arrillaga restricted hemp production to the needs of the province, farmers would have had no other choice than to hire gentile Indians from the ranchería of Yang-Na, paying them a large part of their grain crop. For the program of renting out mission field hands for hemp culture, see Don José del Carmen Beattie, "Life of a Rancher," 226. See also Juan Bandini, "Historia de Alta California," MS (1877) 115–16, BL; Bancroft, *History of California*, 2: 90–91; Engelhardt, *San Juan Capistrano: The Jewel of the Missions*, 50–53; Governor Arrillaga to Tapis, Oct. 5, 1810,

SBMA; Viceroy José de Iturrigaray to Arrillaga, Dec. 4, 1805, Mexico, AC: 12; 74; Arrillaga to Sánchez, Feb. 22, 1811, Monterey, AC: 26: 12; Governor Arrillaga to Tapis, Monterey, Oct. 5, 1810, AASF [copy in SBMA]. For the original petition by Los Angeles hemp growers for mission laborers, see Tapis, "Parecer sobre Repartimientos de Indios Trajabadores," Oct. 5, 1810, San Francisco, BL. See also Hackel, "Indian Spanish Relations in Alta California: Mission San Carlos Borromeo, 1770–1833," 59–82, esp. 83; Robert H. Jackson to author, "Comments and Analysis," Feb. 22, 1996, author's possession.

CHAPTER THREE

1. Quotes from Guest, *Fermín Francisco De Lasuén*, 251–55, 260–63, 273; see also 219, 254–55, 259–60, 289. La Pérouse's statements have been translated, interpreted, and presented slightly differently by various scholars. For two other versions, see Charles N. Rudkin, ed. and trans., *The First French Expedition to California: Lapérouse in 1786* (Los Angeles, 1959), 55–56, 64–65, 68; John Dunmore, ed., *The Journal of Jean-François de Galaup de la Pérouse, 1785–1799*, 2 vols. (London, 1994), with an excellent index.

2. Quotes from Malcolm Margolin, ed., *Monterey in 1786: The Journals of Jean François de La Pérouse* (Berkeley, 1989), 34–35, 57, 70, 79, 81–82, 85, 89–90. Church historians attempting to undermine La Pérouse argue that he was a follower of the Enlightenment and a strong believer in the rights of man with a robust anticlerical bias. And there is some truth to this accusation. La Pérouse believed in reason and the superiority of his own culture, and these values certainly shaped his thinking. But they did not cause him to falsify information in order to undermine the Spanish. Reporting what he found, La Pérouse faithfully collected facts, attempted to "see things as they are," and moved on. The specific details of his journals, not his philosophical asides, give power and veracity to his reports. Had he been an acid-tongued Protestant, his observations could simply have been dismissed. But La Pérouse was a world-renowned explorer, well educated and trained in diplomacy, who arrived at his conclusions with such anguish that he was difficult to discredit. For La Pérouse, see Jean François de La Pérouse, *A Voyage Round the World Performed in the Years 1785, 1786, 1787, and 1788 by Bousole and Astrolabe* (Paris, 1797), 2: 247–83.

3. Quotes from Marguerite E. Wilbur, ed., *Vancouver in California, 1792–1794, the Original Account of George Vancouver* (Los Angeles, 1953–54), 42; also 41, 43, 148–49; Margolin, ed., *Monterey in 1786*, 33 [Otto von Kotzebue]; Choris, "Port San Francisco," in Mahr, *The Visit of the 'Rurick,'* 99; also 93, 95, 97, 101, 103; Harrison G. Rogers, first journal, Dec. 2, 1826, MHS; James O. Pattie, *Personal Narrative of James O. Pattie*, ed. William Goetzmann (1831 [Philadelphia, 1962]), 194–95, 202. For a cautionary note on Pattie's recollections, see Richard Bateman, *American Ecclesiastes: An Epic Journey Through the Early American West* (New York, 1984). Although Bateman shows that Pattie was not kept in a dungeon in San Diego as he claimed, that he was no hero of any Indian scrapes, and that he often embellished some facts and forgot others, Bateman does not challenge his characterizations of mission farm labor. The reference to "vassalage" is in Gov. Felipe Neve to Bucareli, Oct. 30, 1775, AC, 22, 147–49. See also Neve's correspondence of July 4, 1780, summarized in Galindo Navarro, Sept. 20, 1781, Californias, 1, 2, AGN. For Neve's administration and the context and background of his accusations, see Beilharz, *Felipe Neve*, 2, characterizing Neve as a highly intelligent, excessively strong-willed individual who was forever battling Serra. Charges of slavery began even before missions were planted in Alta California. After four months surveying the Jesuit missions of Baja California, Gálvez found that there was no way field hands could escape what he characterized as the "insupportable slavery under which they all groaned." See Gálvez to de Croix, Nov. 23, 1768, Guadalajara 416, AGI. See also Khlebnikov, "Memoirs," 332; Robinson, *Life in California*, 18. Travelers' impressions of mission farm labor as cruel, tyrannical, and "slavelike" are discussed in Arrillaga to Iturrigaray, Nov. 3, 1804, Provincias Internas 216, AGN. See also Richard H. Dana, *Two Years Before the Mast*, ed. John Haskell Kemble (Los Angeles, 1964), 1: 84; William H. Davis, *Seventy-Five Years in California* (San Francisco, 1929), 11. One of the most famous and troubling accusations of slavery during the first generation came not from hostile government officials or inquisitive foreigners, but from one of the padres. After six months helping to found San Miguel mission in 1797, Padre Antonio de la Concepción Horra suffered a breakdown, returned to Mexico, and in September, wrote a long letter to the viceroy. Condemning his immediate superior, Padre Buenaventura Sitjar, of San Antonio mission, as a man of barbaric incompetence, Horra asserted that Sitjar, as well as other padres, were running a sham operation.

Field hands and other native laborers, Horra claimed, were really little more than forced laborers who spent days in the stocks for the most trivial reasons and were "treated with so much cruelty that they are kept whole days without a drink of water." Declared insane and deported back to his native Spain, Horra became stranger and more erratic, and after innumerable public disturbances, fled to Madrid, where he died a lunatic priest in exile, an example of the only type of missionary capable of condemning, questioning, or challenging the forced farm labor system on the missions, and the price paid by any padre brave or crazy enough to raise such issues. This set in motion the biggest controversy of the decade, as the viceroy ordered Governor Borica to investigate the charges, point by point. Joining the controversy, Lasuén wrote a "Refutation of Charges," 130 paragraphs long, in which he defended in great detail those aspects of mission life that had come under attack. Not surprisingly, the viceroy exonerated the missionaries. In doing so, he ignored information in the contrary opinions of Borica, his successor, Arrillaga, and most of the presidio commanders, who, when interviewed by Mexican officials, conceded that mission field hands were vassals, birth to death, with no hope of ever owning anything, no chance of escaping the will of others, no incentive to work or to improve their lives. Quote from Antonio de la Concepción Horra to the viceroy, July 12, 1798, Provincias Internas 216, AGN. See also Buenaventura Sitjar to Lasuén, Jan. 31, 1799; Borica to Azanza, Sept. 13, 1797; Dec. 31, 1798; Argüello to Borica, Dec. 11, 1798; Hermenegildo Sal to Borica, Dec. 15, 1798; Goycoechea to Borica, Dec. 14, 1798, AGN. Church historians dismiss Horra's claims on the grounds he was a "mental case." But Lasuén, who had succeeded Serra as head of the missions, clearly thought Horra normal enough at first, which is why he assigned him the important task of helping to found a mission. Perhaps as a rationalization for what would be done to Horra, Lasuén later recalled certain "eccentric" actions and "ill humor" that indicated he was "mentally deranged." Quotes from Kenneally, *Writings of Lasuén*, 2: 103–4, 110; also 41–42, 47–49. See also Lasuén's "Refutation of Charges," June 19, 1801, 194–234, SBMA. See also César, "Recollections of My Youth," 42; José María Amador, "Memorias sobre la Historia de California," MS (1877), 77, 93–94, 98–99, BL.

4. Jackson and Castillo, *Indians, Franciscans, and Spanish Colonization*, 50; Edward D. Castillo, "The Other Side of the 'Christian Curtain': California Indians and the Missionaries," *The Californians* 10 (Sept.–Oct. 1992), 8–17, esp. 15; Sherburne F. Cook, *The Conflict Between the California Indian and White Civilization* (Berkeley, 1976), 101; Douglas Monroy, *Thrown Among Strangers: The Making of Mexican Culture in Frontier California* (Berkeley, 1990), 52, 54, 58; Richard Rodriguez, *Days of Obligation: An Argument with My Mexican Father* (New York, 1992), 116. An opposing view asserts that field hands, particularly those born on the missions, enjoyed and appreciated their lives, and felt no impending sense of doom. "The Indian learned to live a regular and orderly life . . . under a benevolent and paternalistic regime . . . and . . . received other social and economic gains in the form of social security," wrote the historian of Santa Barbara mission. Field hands felt rewarded by their tasks, which "challenged their inherent desire to excel in feats of skill." They thrived on the rivalries and comradeship that developed among competing crews of harvesters and plowmen, and appreciated being taught "the great lesson from Christian teachers that things did not only grow, but that man could cultivate and multiply their growth." Quotes from Geiger, *Indians of Mission Santa Barbara*, 30, 39. See also Webb, *Indian Life at the Old Missions*, 56.

5. Quote from Travis Hudson, ed., *Breath of the Sun: Life in Early California As Told By a Chumash Indian, Fernando Librado, As Told to John P. Harrington* (Banning, Calif., 1979), 47. See also Antonio Peyri and Francisco Suñer, Respuesta no. 19, Dec. 12, 1814; Juan Martín and Juan Cabot, Respuesta no. 19, Apr. 15, 1814, SBMA; Alice Hartman, "Bells of Camino Real," MS (n.d.), BL; clipping, *San Francisco Bulletin*, Nov. 5, 1859, Bancroft Scrapbooks, BL.

6. Marjorie Tisdale Wolcott, ed., *Pioneer Notes from the Diaries of Judge Benjamin Hayes, 1849–1875* (Los Angeles, 1929), 122–23; St. John O'Sullivan, *Little Chapters About San Juan Capistrano* (Los Angeles, 1929), 32; M. R. Harrington, "The San Fernando Bells Ring Again," *Masterkey* 20 (spring 1948), 64–66; Marie T. Welsh, *The Mission Bells of California* (San Francisco, 1934), 147; Webb, "Bells," MS (n.d.), 24–25; Webb, "Bell Towers," MS (n.d.), 6, EBWC.

7. Working schedules can be traced in Antonio Grájera to Borica, Mar. 21, 1799, PSP, 17: 191. A workday of four to six hours is reported in Bolton, *Font's Complete Diary*, 179–80, entry for Jan. 5, 1776; Reply of Tapis to Lasuén, Oct. 30, 1800, Provincias Internas 216, AGN. A workday that did not exceed five hours, and often did not amount to four, is described in Gregorio Fernandez to Lasuén, Nov. 11, 1800; Señan and Vicente de Santa María to Lasuén, Oct.

21, 1800, AGN. The discrepancies may reflect seasonal fluctuations caused by peaks and valleys in the labor required to tend and harvest the various crops and handle other mission duties. At San Antonio mission field hands had breakfast before mass.

8. Quote from Geiger, *The Indians of Mission Santa Barbara*, 32. "The missions were the original sin of farm labor in California," United Farm Worker Union leader César Chávez was fond of saying. "They made us what we are, and they locked us out of what we might become." César Chávez, interviews by author, Greenfield, Calif., Aug. 7, 1979; Calexico, Calif., Nov. 17, 1980, author's possession. See also Chumash Indian CheeQweesh Auh-Ho-Oh, in Christopher Reynolds, "Patience of a Saint," *San Diego Union*, Aug. 17, 1987; Monroy, "The Creation and Re-creation of Californio Society," 179; Costo and Costo, *The Missions of California*, ix, 3, 92–93, 187; Forbes, *Native Americans of California and Nevada*; Castillo, *Native American Perspectives on the Hispanic Colonization of Alta California*, 423. Serra is compared to Hitler in *Seattle Times*, Sept. 14, 1987. CSU, Northridge, Chicano history professor Rudy Acuña's statement describes Serra as a "brutal sadist" in Greg Critser, "The Million-Dollar Canonization," *California Magazine* 10 (Aug. 1985), 115. For popular opinions, see McWilliams, *Southern California Country*, 29; Lucia Norman Heaven, *A Popular History of California from the Earliest Period of its Discovery to the Present Time* (San Francisco, 1883), 11. See also Donald Bahr and Susan Fenger, "Indians and Missions: Homage to and Debate with Rupert Costo and Jeannette Henry," *Journal of the Southwest* 31 (fall 1989), 300–321. As with African Americans damaged and burdened with the legacy of their servitude in the antebellum South, Native Americans and Mexican Americans struggling with the onus of field labor turn to the historical record and cite their "enslavement" in briefs and appeals calling for respect, understanding, acknowledgment of past wrongs, remedial legislation, and financial compensation. Rebutting the enslavement thesis, mission defenders note that the effective military guard overseeing some fifteen thousand mission Indians in 1800 was only 372 men, including sixty invalids; twenty years later, on San Antonio mission, just six soldiers and two padres directed more than thirteen hundred Indians; and on San Buenaventura and La Purísima missions, for example, the ratios of padres to Indians were 1 to 788 and 1 to 760, respectively. As late as 1830, neophytes and gentile Indians outnumbered priests, soldiers, and settlers ten to one. Such a small number of Spaniards could hardly compel anything from such a large number of natives, so the argument goes. Ratios are established by measuring an average of two padres against the peak Indian population. For La Purísima and Santa Inés, see Roberta S. Greenwood, "Obispeño and Purísmeño Chumash," in Kroeber, *Handbook of North American Indians*, 8: 521; Campbell Grant, "Eastern Coastal Chumash," ibid., 518. A mean population at Santa Barbara and San Buenaventura missions can be calculated from Cook, *Conflict*, tables 1, 2. When compared to the 1:800 ratio of padres to Indians in colonial Mexico, the Alta California missionaries appeared to have enjoyed a far more favorable ratio. Forbes, *California: A History of Upper and Lower California*, 200–201, gives the ratio of non-Indian to Indians as follows: fifteen thousand Indians and thirteen hundred non-Indians in 1801; 18,683 Indians and 4,342 non-Indians in 1831. Figures for 1770–1820 are from Peter Gerhard, *The North Frontier of New Spain* (Norman, Okla., 1993), 309.

9. Report of Governor Borica, June 30, 1797, in Enrique Florescano and Isabel Gil Sánchez, eds., *Descripciones económicas regionales de Nueva España: Provincias del Norte, 1790–1814* (Mexico City, 1976), 47; Andres Quintana and Antonio Rodríguez, "Annual Report to Padre Presidente Tapis," Dec. 31, 1810, SBMA. Although field hands had no legal say in any aspect of their lives and work, it would be too strong to assert, as many have said, that they were slaves in the strict sense of the word—property, chattel, like field hands on an Alabama cotton plantation, seized, shackled, and shipped across an ocean, branded, and placed on the auction block to be bought and sold, like furniture or some other item. They were comparable to slaves mainly in four respects: they could not leave; they underwent a restructuring of beliefs; they were disciplined, at times whipped and shackled; and no matter how diligently they applied themselves they could not reap the rewards of their own labor, could not enjoy the most basic benefits of liberty, could not acquire wealth, achieve social standing or independence. Unlike slaves, their status as unfree laborers was supposedly temporary; they would supposedly regain their freedom once they had served out their "sentence" and completed their "rehabilitation." And at worst, the padres were men of great frugality, charity, determination, and sacrifice, hardly driven by capitalistic goals. These differences have led scholars to search for an appropriate analogy in the experiences of inmates in what social psychologist Irving Goffman calls a "total institution"—a place where a large number of people are cut off from their society for a long period of time in an "enclosed,

formally administered round of life." Prisons and mental institutions are two such places. People there follow a plethora of rules, regulations and customs, are constantly checked, and are subjected to a completely integrated system of control and a hierarchy of superiors. Dominated and managed, they have little say in the circumstances of their lives, can not leave, work for others, and have their values, customs, and culture shredded by those who lord over them. This is the situation that is often forced on colonized people and people in remote work camps and company towns. It is also the course that mission field hands, faced with no alternatives, tolerated as best they could. Quote from Irving Goffman, *Asylums: Essays on the Social Situation of Mental Patients and Other Inmates* (New York, 1962), 6–7. See esp. George H. Phillips, "Indians in Los Angeles, 1781–1875: Economic Integration, Social Disintegration," *PHR* 43 (fall 1980), 451, which skillfully expands on the concept and applies it to the California missions. See also Howard Lamar, "From Bondage to Contract: Ethnic Labor in the American West, 1600–1890," in Steven Hahn and Jonathan Prude, eds., *The Countryside in the Age of Capitalist Transformation: Essays in the Social History of Rural America* (Chapel Hill, N.C., 1985), 293–326.

10. Quote from Report of Gov. Borica, June 30, 1797, in Florescano and Sánchez, *Descripciones económicas*, 47. Some scholars use *monjería* rather than *monjerío*. See Randall Milliken, "An Ethnohistory of the Indian People of the San Francisco Bay Area from 1770 to 1810" (Ph.D. diss., UCB, 1991), 153. I follow Webb, *Indian Life*, 321; and Bouvier, *Women and the Conquest*, 263. See also José María Lugo, "Vida de un Ranchero," MS (1877), 22, 100, BL; Amador, "Memorias," 90; Kenneally, *Writings of Lasuén*, 2: 206–7. Construction sequence from Geiger, "The Buildings of Mission San Gabriel: 1771–1828," *SCHSQ* 50 (spring 1968), 33–36; Robert H. Jackson, *Indian Population Decline: The Missions of Northwestern New Spain, 1687–1840* (Albuquerque, 1994), 132–33, table 3. Women's quarters averaged a space of two by seven feet per person. See also Webb, "Monjerios, Dormitorios, Infirmaries," 8, EBWC.

11. Quotes from Apolinaria Lorenzano, "Memorias de la Beata," MS (1787), 7–8; Eulalia Pérez, "Una Vieja y Sus Recuerdos," MS (1877), 16 and 20, BL; "Font's Complete Diary of the Second Anza Expedition," in Bolton, *Anza's California Expeditions*, 4: 270, and 181–82. See also Engelhardt, *San Francisco or Mission Dolores* (Chicago, 1924), 141. For a published version of the Eulalia Pérez memoir, see Nellie Van der Grift Sánchez, trans., "Keeper of the Keys: The Recollections of Señora Eulalia Pérez, Oldest Woman in the World, of Life at Mission San Gabriel," *Touring Topics* 21 (Jan. 1929), 24–25.

12. Only the most loyal and trusted Indians served as vaqueros. Fages to Lasuén, Monterey, Aug. 20, 23, 1787; 6: 65–66; Fages to José Antonio Romeu, May 28, 1791, AC, 10: 149–51; Antonio Olivera, "List of Those Who Ride Horses at the Mission," Mar. 4, 1818; Francisco González de Ibarra to José de la Guerra, July 11, 1821, DLGP; Pablo Vicente de Solá, "Regulations on the use of horses," Jan. 7, 1818, PR, 12: 143–45. See also Case for the Stealing of Horses, Rafael Gomez, Counselor, Apr. 21, 1831, PR, 73: 2–3 [copy in Agricultural History Center, University of California, Davis]. For disarming of field hands, see Circular from Vicente de Sarría, July 22, 1824, AASF, 4, pt. 2 [copy in BL].

13. Neuerburg, *Decoration of California Missions*; Neuerburg, *The Architecture of Mission la Purísima Concepción* (Santa Barbara, 1987); Neuerburg, "Painting in the California Missions," *American Art Review* 6 (1977), 72–88; Neuerburg, "The Changing Face of Mission San Diego," *Journal of San Diego History* 33 (winter 1986), 32–45; Neuerburg, "New Light on the Church of Mission San Buenaventura," *VCHSQ* 28 (1983), 237–55.

14. At San Gabriel mission the *campanario* (belfry) was a massive, upward-curving buttress attached to the rear of the church, its six arched spaces, each of a different size, fitted to a specific bell. On San Buenaventura mission the bell tower was a soaring structure, the second and third stories each slightly smaller than the other, with ornamental finials on the four corners of the upper tiers and a lovely dome capping the upper tier. Even the much less majestic bell towers at San Francisco de Asís and San Francisco missions, their lines enriched by decorative molding and tile work, displayed elements of beauty seldom found elsewhere in the missions. See Edward Vischer, *Missions of Upper California* (San Francisco, 1872); *San Francisco Chronicle*, Aug. 28, 1884; Charles Franklin Carter, *The Missions of Nueva California* (San Francisco, 1900); Rexford Newcomb, *The Old Mission Churches and Historic Houses of California* (Philadelphia, 1925); Baegert, *Observations in Lower California*, 143–45; Harriet Rebecca Piper Forbes, *California Missions and Landmarks: El Camino Real* (Los Angeles, 1925); Paul Elder, *The Old Spanish Missions of California* (San Francisco, 1973); Kurt Baer, *Architecture of the California Missions* (Berkeley, 1958), 44–51; John A. Berger, *The Franciscan Missions of California* (New York, 1948).

15. Quote from Robinson, *Life In California*, 18, 31. See also Engelhardt, *Mission San Francisco*, 118; Engelhardt, *Santa Barbara Mission*, 85, 119; Engelhardt, *San Luis Rey Mission: The King of the Missions* (San Francisco, 1921), 30. A typical arrangement consisted of workrooms, storerooms, dormitories, guardhouses, infirmaries, schools, communal kitchens, *monjeríos*, and miscellaneous buildings. For a schematic layout, see Costello and Hornbeck, "Alta California: An Overview," in Thomas, *Columbian Consequences*, 2: 312, fig. 19-4.

16. Frances Rand, *The Architectural History of Mission San Carlos Borromeo* (Berkeley, 1921), 22–23; Bancroft, *History of California*, 1: 203; 2: 120; Tapis to Lasuén, Oct. 30, 1800, doc. no. 368, SBMA.

17. For gatekeepers, see Tapis to Lasuén, Oct. 30, 1880, Provincias Internas 216, AGN; Encarnación Pinedo, "Early Days at Santa Clara," *The Owl* (Apr. 1934), SCUASC.

18. The use of mirrors to spy on natives at San Gabriel mission is described in a sign hung in the church sacristy. The advice to kiss the Bible is in DSP, Benecia Prefecturas y Juzgados, 1804, 1: 23, BL. Roll calls and the requirement to kiss the Bible are described in Engelhardt, *Missions and Missionaries*, 2: 255. For the use of confessions, see Madison S. Beeler, ed., "The Ventureno Confesionario of José Señan," *University of California Publications in Linguistics No. 47* (Berkeley, 1967), 4, 27; Harry Kelsey, ed., *The Doctrina and Confesionario of Juan Cortés* (Altadena, Calif., 1979), 110, 120; Edward D. Castillo, "The Native Response to the Colonization of Alta California," in Castillo, *Native American Perspectives*, 424–25.

19. George W. James, *Picturesque Pala* (New York, 1923), 55–59; Señán to José de la Guerra, Mar. 15, 1819, JDLG; Webb, *Indian Life at the Old Missions*, 270–72.

20. Vallejo, "Ranch and Mission Days in Alta California," 183–92; Nellie van der Grift Sánchez, *California and Californians: Spanish Period* (Los Angeles, 1932), 1: 436.

21. Serra, Representación to Bucareli, Mar. 13, 1773, in Bolton, *Palóu's Historical Memoirs*, 3: 2–36; Decision of the Royal Council of War and Exchequer, May 6, 1773, in ibid., 3: 37–55; Serra to Bucareli, Aug. 24, 1774, in Tibesar, *Writings of Serra*, 2: 136–47; employment record, José de Santa Ana Avila, 1794–1805; employment record, Tomas Espinosa, La Purísima Mission Account Book, 1806–34, trans. Lewis G. Thomas, 59, 87; "Libro de quentas que esta Misión de Santa Barbara tiene con la Habilitación de este presidio de el mismo nombre y otros varios particulares, 1794–1805," SBMA; Engelhardt, *Missions and Missionaries*, 2: 445–46. Pay for one *mayordomo* is listed as twelve *piastres*, two bulls, lard, and some grain in Anatole G. Mazour, ed., "Memoirs of California by T. H. Khlebnikov," *PHR* 9 (May 1940), 314. I use the Spanish version, *mayordomo*, rather than the Anglicized, majordomo.

22. Quote from Pablo Tac, "L'evangelizzazione e i costumi degli Indi Luisenos secondo la narrazione di un chierico indigeno" [Rome, ca. 1835], 19–20, Biblioteca dell' Archiginnasio di Bologna, Mezzofanti Collection, original trans. Carlo Tagliavini, copies with additional editing by Maynard Geiger in BL and SBMA, English translation in Minna Hewes and Gordon Hewes, ed. and trans., "Indian Life and Customs at Mission San Luis Rey: A Record of California Indian Life Written by Pablo Tac, an Indian Neophyte," *The Americas* 9 (1952), 87–106. Tac's document dates from between 1834, when he arrived in Rome and began to study grammar, rhetoric, humanities, and philosophy, and 1840, when he died from smallpox. A view of *mayordomos* as hated tyrants, apparently confusing them with *alcaldes* and *regidores*, is in James A. Lewis, "Preconception and Reality," in Costo and Costo, *Missions of California*, 89.

23. Quote from Benjamin D. Wilson, Ranch Journal, "Observations," BDWP, cited in Robert Glass Cleland, *Pathfinders* (Los Angeles, 1929), 386–87; Sheldon Jackson, *A British Ranchero in Old California: The Life and Times of Henry Dalton and Rancho Azusa* (Glendale and Azusa, Calif., 1977), 81. I have not discovered any other references to the incident, and I have not been able to establish a date. See also Hugo Reid, letter no. 19, "New Era in Mission Affairs," in Susanna B. Dakin, *A Scotch Paisano: Hugo Reid's Life in California, 1832–1852, Derived from His Correspondence* (Berkeley, 1939), 270–72, describing the work of Claudio López, *mayordomo* of San Gabriel mission (ca. 1826), and assigning him credit for most of the agricultural accomplishments usually attributed to the "half-mad" Padre Zalvidea.

24. Baegert, *Observations in Lower California*, 122; Barco, *Historia natural y crónica de la Antigua California*, 120, 260.

25. Quote from Margolin, *Monterey in 1786*, 89. On the origins and development of the *alcalde* system, see Engelhardt, *Missions and Missionaries*, 2: 34; Lugo, "Vida de un Ranchero," 225–26; Bancroft, *History of California*, 1: 585; Beilharz, *Felipe de Neve*, 64–65, 95–96.

26. Quotes from Tac, "Indian Life," 19; Hugo Reid, letter no. 19, "New Era in Mission Af-

fairs," in Dakin, *Scotch Paisano*, 272. For the observations of a British naval officer, see Barry M. Gough, ed., "The Views of Lieutenant George Peard, R.N., on Alta California, 1826 and 1827," *SCQ* 56 (fall 1974), 218. At San Luis Obispo and San Carlos missions, *alcaldes* believing themselves above punishment used their authority to commit numerous crimes. At San Carlos mission, one *alcalde* used his position to engage in adultery and to supply women to soldiers. For abuses at San Carlos and San Luis Obispo missions, see Serra to Lasuén, Aug. 16, 1779; and Serra to Rafael Verger, Aug. 15, 1779, in Tibesar, *Writings of Serra*, 3: 349–51, 365. For a persuasive argument that the padres used the *alcalde* system to incorporate Indian leadership into the mission society and social order, not as a way to destroy native authority, see Hackel, "Indian-Spanish Relations in Alta California," 166–216, esp. 190.

27. George H. Phillips, "The Alcaldes: Indian Leadership in the Spanish Missions of California," in *The Struggle for Political Autonomy: Papers and Comments from the Second Newberry Library Conference on Themes in American History*, Occasional Papers in Curriculum Series, no. 11 (Chicago, 1989), 83–87. For dress and staffs, see Serra to Lasuén, Mar. 29, 1779, in Tibesar, *Writings of Serra*, 3: 295.

28. For flogging, see Tibesar, *Writings of Serra*, 3: 409. For abusive behavior, see Kenneally, *Writings of Lasuén*, 1: 168–69. For housing, food, and privileges, see Annual Report, San Antonio de Padua mission, 1779, AGN; Carmel Mission Account Book of Planting and Harvest, 1777–1787?, CLDSA. For riding, see César, "Recollections of My Youth," 42.

29. Quote from Juan B. Alvarado, "Historia de California," MS (1876), 1: 68–69; also 2: 23, BL. For *alcaldes* feeding men in the fields, see Dakin, *Scotch Paisano*, 279, Hugo Reid, letter no. 20. According to Serra, one of the *alcaldes* at San Gabriel mission, in addition to his duties as a foreman, also acted as a pimp, "supplying women to as many soldiers as asked for them." See Serra to Neve, Monterey, Jan. 7, 1780, in Tibesar, *Writings of Serra*, 3: 415.

30. Quotes from Robinson, *Life in California*, 18; also 25–26, 44–46; Frederick W. Beechey, *Narrative of a Voyage to the Pacific and Beerings Strait . . . in the Years 1825, 26, 27, 28* (London, 1831), 2: 31–32. See also Mofras, *Exploration*, 340–47, Jan. 18–27, 1842, entries for his visit to San Luis Rey mission.

31. Quote from Maynard Geiger and Clement W. Meighan, eds. and trans., *As the Padres Saw Them: California Indian Life and Customs as Reported by the Franciscan Missionaries, 1813–1815* (Santa Barbara, 1976), 109–10. See also Francis F. Guest, "The California Missions Were Far From Faultless," *SCQ* 76 (fall 1994), 236–44; Solá, Manifesto, Monterey, June 2, 1816, SBMA. For the custom of punishing and disciplining mission Indians, see Pedro Borges, *Métodos Misionales en la cristianización de América, Siglo 17* (Madrid, 1960), 119–36. For the pervasive use of force in seventeenth-century Europe, see Lawrence Stone, *The Crisis of the Aristocracy, 1558–1641* (London, 1967), 20.

32. As for the custom of branding as a form of punishment, a practice commonly used to mark thieves and other criminals in Europe and America at this time, the only evidence that the padres ever employed this punishment comes from Robert B. Forbes, the captain of an American trading ship, who during a visit to the San Francisco Bay in 1825 claimed to have witnessed padres converting Indians by sending soldiers and ranchers "into the field to catch them with lasso, and mark them with the cross." Quote from Robert B. Forbes, *Personal Reminiscences* (Boston, 1878), 95–96. Some interpret the term "mark" as referring to imprinting the idea of Christianity on them. The only other report of branding, Wilson, "Observations," appears to describe reprisals against Indian stock raiders after the mission era.

33. Whipping practices were arbitrary and subject to the whims of *mayordomos*, *alcaldes*, *regidores*, and other figures of authority. See Lorenzo Venancio [Asisara], "Early Indian Life (1819) [1877]," trans. E. L. Williams, in Francis Weber, ed., *Holy Cross Mission: A Documentary History of Santa Cruz* (Hong Kong, 1981), 22; Tapis to Lasuén, Oct. 30, 1800, Provincias Internas 216, AGN; Solá, Manifesto, June 2, 1816, AGN [copy in SBMA]; photo of *la disciplina*, SBMA.

34. For the punishment of a field hand who threw a stone at a padre, see Arrillaga to Manuel Rodríguez, Loreto, Feb. 16, 1805, AC, 26: 260–61. For the murder case, see governor to the commander at Santa Barbara, Nov. 18, 1796, 23: 360, AC. For head thumping, see Padre Tomás de la Peña to Lasuén, Nov. 25, 1786, Provincias Internas 1, AGN. For an Indian whipped for breaking a wine barrel, see Hudson, *Breath of the Sun*, 18.

35. Borica to commander of the presidio of San Francisco, Feb. 25, 1795, AC, 25: 46; Arrillaga to Rodríguez, Feb. 16, 1805, AC, 26: 260–61, ; Asisara, "Narrative," 47; Harrison Rogers,

first journal, Dec. 10, 1826; Jan. 3, 1827; Thomas Blackburn, "A Manuscript Account of the Ventureno Chumash," *UCLA Archeological Survey Reports* 5 (1963), 146; Serra to Lasuén, Aug. 16, 1779; Serra to Neve, Jan. 7, 1780, in Tibesar, *Writings of Serra*, 3: 365–76, 412; Juan Bojorges, "Recuerdos Sobre la Historia de California," MS (1877), 9, BL; Hudson, *Breath of the Sun*, 17. Women were never whipped in public, but in an enclosed and somewhat removed place so that their cries would not cause the men to revolt. See Margolin, *Monterey in 1786*, 89. For dress, see Phillips, "Indian Paintings from Mission San Fernando: An Historical Interpretation," *JCA* 3 (summer 1976), 96–114.

36. Quote from Hudson, *Breath of the Sun*, 17. For general punishments, see José de Zúñiga to Fages, San Diego, Feb. 12, 1790, AC, 5: 212; Fages to Romeu, Monterey, May 31, 1791, AC, 6: 142; Rodríguez to governor, San Diego, Dec. 19, 1798, AC, 10: 70; Azanza to Borica, Mexico, Mar. 28, 1799, AC, 10: 222–24; Kenneally, *Writings of Lasuén*, 2: 217.

37. Bancroft, *History of California*, 2: 358.

38. Quote from Mariano G. Vallejo to Gov. José Figueroa, confidential memo, May 6, 1833, DPLHC, 2: 140. For a full discussion of punishment on the missions of Baja California, see Miguel Venegas, *Empressas Apostolicas*. See also Michael Mathes, ed., *Obras Californianas del Padre Miguel Venegas*, index by Vivian C. Fisher and Moisés Coronado (La Paz, Baja California, 1979).

39. Quote from Francis F. Guest, "An Enquiry into the Role of the Discipline in California Mission Life," *SCQ* 71 (spring 1989), 37–38. See also Richard L. Carrico, "Spanish Crime and Punishment: The Native American Experience in Colonial San Diego, 1769–1830," *WLH* 3 (winter–spring 1990), 32–33.

40. Quotes from Amador, "Memorias," 90. For whippings, see Lugo, "Vida de un Ranchero," 227; Lorenzano, "Memorias de la Beata," 13–14; Fages to P. Matias, June 11, 1785, AC, 23: 52; Harrison Rogers, first journal, Dec. 14, 1826; Edward D. Castillo, "An Indian Account of the Decline and Collapse of Mexico's Hegemony over the Missionized Indians of California," *American Indian Quarterly* 13 (fall 1989), 391–408.

41. Quotes from J. M. Guinn, *Historical and Biographical Record of Southern California* (Chicago, 1902), 41. For punishment for infanticide, see Hugo Reid, letter no. 19, "New Era in Mission Affairs," in Heizer, *Indians of Los Angeles*, 87.

42. Quote from Respuesta, 1814, Santa Cruz, SBMA. For angry Indian testimonies, see Catherine S. Saubel, "The Serra-Mission Atrocities"; Maurice Magante, "Torture and Punishment"; Eva Kolb, "The Children Starved"; in RCIH. Testimonies by Asisara, Tac, Librado, and César all describe abusive whippings. For a contrary view, see Kenneally, *Writings of Lasuén*, 1: 130. For a full discussion of this issue from the church perspective, see Francis F. Guest, "Cultural Perspectives on California Mission Life," *SCQ* 65 (spring 1985), 1–65. The truth of individual incidents often took years to emerge. This is what happened in the case of Sixto Antonio, an incompetent Indian irrigator on Santa Clara mission. Thumped with a cane by Padre Tomás de la Peña in July 1783 for failing to attend to his work, Antonio bled slightly from a head wound, seemed to recover, but died soon thereafter. The matter lay dormant for a year until Plácido Ortiz, a campesino brought up from Baja California, accused Padre Peña of murdering Antonio, along with three other mission Indians. Receiving the charges, Captain Nicolás Soler, adjutant inspector of the California presidios, was forced to investigate. A foe of the missions, Soler amplified the charges with claims that Padre Peña was crazy. Repeating accusations that the padre had often whipped other field hands with two hundred lashes after exhausting himself by administering kicks and other blows, Soler eventually complained to mission head Francisco Palóu, forcing him to travel to Santa Clara mission in October 1783. After hearing extensive testimony, Palóu agreed that Antonio had indeed been struck by Peña with a hoe for wasting water. But Palóu also concluded that the blow caused Antonio little damage and was not the cause of the field hand's death, which Palóu attributed to diseases that struck large numbers of Santa Clara mission Indians that year. Nevertheless, Peña was tried twice in rapid succession in April and May 1786, the second time by Governor Fages himself. Fages found Peña guilty of murder, but was so angered with two of the native witnesses, as well as with Plácido Ortiz, all of whom had committed perjury, that he arrested them and sentenced them to ten years in the Monterey Presidio. Allowed to leave Alta California and return to Mexico, Peña was declared innocent on April 8, 1795, after the three Indian conspirators—kneeling before the assembled citizens of San José and the entire community of Santa Clara mission—repudiated their false testimony, begged pardon for their crimes, and were released

from prison. See Miguel de la Grua Talamanca y Branciforte to Governor Borica, Oct. 8, 1795, AC, Mexico City, 7: 308–14. For the accusations against Peña, see Fages to Gonzáles, Mar. 12, 1786, AC, 23: 34–35. See also Erick Langer and Robert H. Jackson, "Colonial and Republican Missions Compared: The Cases of Alta California and Southeastern Bolivia," *Comparative Studies in Society and History* 30 (1988), 286–311, esp. 303. For the judgment of the viceroy and the viceregal decrees of innocence, see the fiscal to the viceroy, Feb. 26, 1795, AC, 23: 34–35. For the investigation by Fages, see Palóu to Jacobo Urgate y Loyola, Jan. 24, 1787, AC, 23: 35. Peña's account of his encounter with Sixto Antonio as well as information on the trials is in Peña to Lasuén, Nov. 25, 1786, AC: 35. For Ortiz, see Kenneally, *Writings of Lasuén*, 1: 110, 113, 122, 130. For contradictions in the testimony and more on the nature of the charges against Peña, see Fages to commandant general of the Internal Provinces, n.d., 1786, AC, 22: 352, esp. Peña to Lasuén, Nov. 1786; Mugártegui to the fiscal, College of San Fernando, Oct. 26, 1791, both in Provincias Internas 1, AGN. The Indians had apparently concocted the charges after Peña had discovered evidence that Plácido had absconded with supplies while managing the mission storehouse.

43. Geiger, *The Indians of Mission Santa Barbara*, 32. See also Tapis to Lasuén, Oct. 30, 1800, Provincias Internas 216, AGN; Goycoechea to Borica, Dec. 14, 1798, AC, 10: 71–80; Kocher, *Mission San Luis Obispo*, 28.

44. Quotes from Tapis to Lasuén, Oct. 30, 1800, California Mission doc. no. 368, SBMA; Padre Pedro Cabot to Padre José Señán, Respuesta, Feb. 26, 1814, SBMA [copy]; Margolin, *Monterey in 1786*, 85; von Langsdorff, *Narrative*, 60. The following accounts describe food supplies as adequate: Amador, "Memorias," 188; Serra to padre guardian, Monterey, June 14, 1774, in Tibesar, *Writings of Serra*, 2: 68–75; Alice Eastwood, ed., "Menzies' California Journal," *CHSQ* 2 (winter 1924), 359. An unbelievable eight pounds of food each day per Indian, excluding fruit, is cited in Tapis to Lasuén, Oct. 30, 1800, Provincias Internas 216, AGN. For works questioning the adequacy of food supplies, see Ann Stodder, *Mechanisms and Trends in the Decline of the Costanoan Indian Population of Central California* (Salinas, 1986), concluding that malnutrition contributed to population collapse and caused lowered birthrates among women; Robert H. Jackson, *Indian Population Decline*, 128–32, esp. table 3.8. Peasants in Spain consumed 4 to 4.7 *fanegas* (about 1.5 bushels) of grain per person per year; those in England consumed between 3.7 and 5 *fanegas* of wheat; mission Indians consumed between 1.6 and 4.5 *fanegas* of grain. The amount of grain consumed can not be calculated by dividing production by population because not all grain went to Indians. Large amounts were reserved for seed, and given to the military and to settlers. See also Lasuén, Refutation of Charges, June 19, 1801, in Tibesar, *Writings of Lasuén*, 2: 203–4. Throughout the early mission era field hands periodically suffered from food shortages and feigned hunger in order to engage in traditional hunting and gathering. As varied and abundant as their diet sounded, it did not provide field hands everything they needed. While some field hands may have suffered from malnutrition, it is impossible to settle claims about whether or not their diet made them susceptible to disease and figured in their birth- and death rates. There is ample evidence from the padres themselves that some meals caused sickness and were prepared under unsanitary conditions and eaten on old surfaces "so . . . dirty that with a knife one could scrape up the . . . grease." There is also some evidence that a few padres abused their control over meals, dispensing food to children as if they were common pets. On Sunday evenings at San Gabriel mission in January 1827 the clerk for the Jedediah Smith fur trapping party observed one padre throwing oranges "among the young squaws to see them scuffle for them, the activist [*sic*] and strongest would get the greatest share." Quotes from Bolton, *Font's Complete Diary*, 241, entry for Feb. 18, 1777; Harrison Rogers, first journal, Jan. 7, 1827. Children of field hands at San José mission suffered an even more degrading experience. Reporting on what happened to them, the English explorer Frederick Beechey recalled how a padre amused himself by tossing pancakes to the children, who stood gape-mouthed around his table.

> For this purpose, he had every day two piles of pancakes made of Indian corn; and as soon as the *olla* was removed, he would fix eyes upon one of the boys, who immediately opened his mouth, and the padre, rolling up a cake would say something ludicrous in allusion to the boy's appetite, or to the size of his mouth, and pitch the cake at him, which the imp would catch between his teeth, and devour with incredible rapidity, in order that he might be ready the sooner for another, as well as to please the padre, whose amusement consisted in a great measure in witnessing the sudden disappearance of the cake. In this manner, the pile of cakes were gradually distributed among the boys, amidst much laughter, and occasional squabbling.

Quote from Beechey, *Narrative*, 2: 33–34; also 20–21. Such groveling may have been no more than a daily diversion. But the willingness of the sons and daughters of field hands and other native laborers to fight, beg, and perform for food may also suggest that they were hardly content with their food rations. Containing what one anthropologist called "lower-quality" calories with far less quantities of vitamins and minerals than the native foraging diet, the mission diet supplied field hands an energy value of about 2,320 calories per day (plus or minus 20 percent), far below the modern minimal daily requirement of three thousand calories. It is quite possible that native field hands and their children—who were considerably smaller than the Spaniards and may not have needed the three thousand–calorie minimum—survived on barely adequate, unbalanced rations. Field hands got approximately 1,405 of those calories from mission gruel, but the nutritional value of their meals ranged widely from a high of around two thousand calories at Santa Cruz mission to a low of 715 at San Antonio mission. Calorie information from Cook, *Conflict*, table 2, 37, 40–48, 50. The mobile kitchen anecdote is from Hudson, *Breath of the Sun*, 3.

45. Ample food supplies are described in Padre Ramón Oblés, Respuesta, 1813 SBMA [copy]. For reports of food shortages after 1800, see Mariano Payeras to Governor Solá, Aug. 5, 1821, AASF, 4: 76; Zalvidea to Gov. José María Echeandía, July 15, 1826, AASF, 5: 25; Governor Argüello to de la Guerra, Apr. 21, 1820, DLGD, 4: 136. See also David Huelsbeck, ed., *Lost and All But Forgotten: Archeology and History at the Santa Clara Mission Site* (Salinas, 1996), maintaining that wild foods were not an important element in the diet of mission laborers. Overturning this view, discovery of pieces of pottery, along with animal bones and other items, excavated in a seven-by-seven-foot pit dug for a clogged swimming pool drain at the Santa Clara University in August 2000, revealed how mission Indians there supplemented their diet by foraging. See "Construction yields 200–year old Native American site," press release, Santa Clara University, Aug. 15, 2000. See also Padre Pedro Cabot to Lasuén, Respuesta, Feb. 26, 1814, SBMA, describing "days of slaughter." The main benefit field hands derived from all of this slaughter was meat, steady and at times wasteful quantities of it. This went to the cooks, who boiled the bones and meat scraps in soup pots, set aside choice cuts for immediate use, and laid out the long strips on racks in the sun to be made into *carne seca* (dried meat). Additionally, field hands enjoyed meals supplemented by the hard fat gathered from about the kidneys and loins and stored in skin bags or bladders to be used in cooking beans and lean meat, as well as tongues and occasionally the bullock's head, all of which were considered delicacies to be used in special meals, barbecues, and Sunday feasts. For slaughtering practices, see Vallejo, "Ranch and Mission Days," 187. For meat drying practices, see Anna Packman, *Early California Hospitality* (San Francisco, 1929), 116; Packman, *Leather Dollars* (San Francisco, 1932), 64. For a story about barbecuing bullock's heads, see William Maxwell Wood, *Wandering Sketches of People and Things in South America, Polynesia, and California* (New York, 1849), 284. See also James Steele, *Old California Days* (New York, 1912), 116–17; Steele, *A Sojourn in California*, 52. One measure of the extent and daily availability of these supplies can be seen in the ratios of animals to people. In 1800, for example, there were 3.97 head of cattle and 6.2 sheep to each mission Indian. In 1810, the ratio increased to 6.2 head of cattle and 8.4 sheep to each native. By 1821, the ratios had risen to 7.3 to 1 and 9.12 to 1. Ratios also rose both as the size of herds grew and as the high death rate, low birthrate, and large numbers of Indians running away stagnated the native population. Cattle and sheep ratios are based on tables 15 and 21 in Archibald, *Economic Aspects of the California Missions*.

46. These foods added about 840 additional calories to the daily food intake. For milk rations, see Geiger, *Indians of Mission Santa Barbara*, 32. Dietary comparisons are based on Richard Herr, *Rural Change and Royal Finances in Spain at the End of the Old Regime* (Berkeley, 1989), 190–95; Henri Sée, *Economic and Social Conditions in France During the Eighteenth Century* (New York, 1912), 21, 37; Geroid T. Robinson, *Rural Russia Under the Old Regime* (New York, 1967), 94–95; G. E. Fussell, *The English Rural Labourer* (London, 1949). Kitchen caption from San Juan Bautista mission from Ruben G. Mendoza, "The Old Mission's History" (1997), http://archaeology.monterey.edu/mendoza1/SJBHistory1.html. Questions of hunger and famine are hardly settled. See, for example, Phillip L. Walker, Patricia Lambert, and Michael J. DeNiro, "The Effects of European Contact on the Health of Alta California Indians," in Thomas, *Columbian Consequences*.

47. Quote from Mariano Payeras to Padre Josef Vinals, July 2, 1806, DPLHDM, primera serie, 2, AGN [copy in SBMA]. For epidemics in 1806–7, see Payeras to Padre Thomas de la

Peña, Mar. 1, 1806, DPLHDM, primera serie, 2 [copy in SBMA]; Tapis, "Noticia de las Misiónes," 1805–6, Mar. 13, 1807, SBMA; Lorenzano, "Memorias de la Beata," 7. Rosemary Valle, "Medicine and Health in the Alta California Missions" (Ph.D. diss., UCB, 1973), 144, suggests that scarlet fever was present on the missions.

48. For lighting, see Engelhardt, *Missions and Missionaries*, 2: 558. For pollution and sanitation, I have followed the ideas advanced in Iris Engstrand, as well as interviews with Rev. Francis Guest, Doyce B. Nunis Jr., John Johnson, and David Hornbeck, in Steiner, "The Serra Report," in Costo and Costo, *Missions of California*, esp. 199; Johan Huizinga, *The Waning of the Middle Ages* (New York, 1969). Smallpox does not seem to have appeared before 1822, due mainly to quarantine measures and inoculation.

49. For San Francisco de Asís mission's polluted water supply, see Guest, "The California Missions Were Far From Faultless," 288–89. For the drain at San Antonio mission, see "Se ha abierto un zanjón," Informe, 1827, SBMA.

50. Quote from Payeras to the College of San Fernando, Feb. 2, 1820, SBMA. For foreign observations, particularly of the extent of syphilis, see William Shaler, *Journal of a Voyage Between China and the Northwestern Coast of America in 1804 by William Shaler* (Claremont, Calif., 1935), 57–59; George Simpson, *Narrative of a Journey round the World, during the Years 1841 and 1842* (London, 1847), 1: 317; Abel Du Petit-Thouars, *Voyage of the Venus: Sojourn in California*, trans. Charles N. Rudkin (Los Angeles, 1956), 85. For missionary concerns about the ravages of syphilis, see Fages, "Sobre Puntos del gobernador de la Península de California," Monterey, Feb. 26, 1791, AC, 6: 154; Ramón Abella to Solá, Jan. 29, 1817; Sarría to Solá, June 28, 1815, SBMA.

51. Death, disease, and epidemics among field hands are extrapolated from general reports on the native populations described in José María Benites, Expediente on Diseases of the Indians, Jan. 1, 1805, which is probably the most complete report; Ramón Olbés to minister of foreign relations, Respuesta, Dec. 31, 1813; Sarría to Solá, June 28, 1815; Abella to Solá, Jan. 29, 1817; Payeras to Baldomero López, July 26, 1820, trans. Zephyrin Engelhardt; Zalvidea to governor, Dec. 3. 1832, SBMA. Compounding the high rate of sickness were the lingering effects of syphilis and gonorrhea, especially as they affected births. In the initial infectious stage, one in three fetuses aborted. In the latter stage, pregnancies came to full term, but infected infants were doomed to suffer from congenital syphilis leading inevitably to death. A side effect for wives and other women infected by gonorrhea was sterilization. Causing pelvic inflammation and 60 to 70 percent sterility, gonorrhea also invoked spontaneous abortion. Fetuses surviving to birth were often blind. See David E. Stannard, "Disease and Infertility: A New Look at the Demographic Collapse of Native Populations in the Wake of Western Contact," *Journal of American Studies* 24 (Dec. 1990), 337–40; Serra to Bucareli, Apr. 22, 1773, in Tibesar, *Writings of Serra*, 1: 341; Serra to Bucareli, May 21, 1773, in ibid., 363; Rosemary K. Valle, "Prevention of Smallpox in Alta California During the Franciscan Mission Period," *California Medicine* 119 (spring 1973), 73–77.

52. Figures for San Carlos mission are from Sherburne Cook and Woodrow Borah, "Mission Registers as Sources of Vital Statistics: Eight Missions of Northern California," in Cook and Borah, *Essays on Population History: Mexico and California* (Berkeley, 1979), 3: 226, 246. Mortality rates at San Gabriel mission are estimated at twice that of births in Taboada and Zalvidea to Padre Presidente, Respuesta, June 28, 1814, Article 15, SBMA. For general mortality rates, see Cook, "Population Trends Among the California Indians," *Ibero-Americana* 14 (Berkeley, 1940), 1–48. For 1813 and 1815, see Geiger and Meighan, *As the Padres Saw Them*, 78. The ratio of death- to birthrates in 1831 varied among the missions, being much higher at San José, San Juan Bautista, San Fernando, and San Miguel missions than at San Luis Rey mission. See Estado de las Misiones de Alta California, 1831, SBMA. For San José mission, see Milliken, "An Ethnohistory of the Indian People of the San Francisco Bay Area," 254, 371–86. For a comparison with death rates among other populations, see Jackson, "La dinámica del desastre demográfico de la población india en las misiones de la bahía de San Francisco, Alta California, 1776–1840," *Historia Mexicana* 40 (spring 1991), 204–5.

53. For infant mortality among the Chumash, see John Johnson, "Chumash Social Organization: An Ethnohistoric Perspective" (Ph.D. diss., UCSB, 1988), table 5.3 and 5.4; Johnson, "Chumash Population History," in Sally McLendon and John Johnson, *Cultural Affiliation and Lineal Descent of Chumash Peoples in the Channel Islands and Santa Monica Mountains* (New York and Santa Barbara, 1998), ch. 7, tables 7-8, 7-15, 7-22; Cook and Borah, *Essays on Population History*, 3: 210–29, 232–38. For comparative figures from Texas, see Mardith Schultz Miller,

"The Indians of the San Antonio Missions, 1718–1821" (Ph.D. diss., University of Texas, Austin, 1980), 175–76. For Europe, see Olwen Hufton, *Europe: Privilege and Protest* (Ithaca, 1980), 38; Fernand Braudel, *The Structure of Everyday Life: The Limits of the Possible*, trans. Siân Reynolds (New York, 1979), 84.

54. Quote from padres Juan Martín and Juan Cabot, Respuesta, Apr. 15, 1814, SBMA. For chapels in hospitals, see Mariano Payeras, Biennial Report to Solá, San Gabriel mission, May 4, 1819, SBMA. For male/female ratios and death rates, see Cook, *Conflict*, 10. See also Robert H. Jackson, "Patterns of Demographic Change in the Missions of Central Alta California," *JCGBA* 9 (spring 1987), 257–58.

55. Virginia Maria Bouvier, "Women, Conquest, and the Production of History: Hispanic California, 1542–1840" (Ph.D. diss., UCB, 1995), 363–69.

56. Quotes from Robinson, *Life in California*, 31; Thomas Jefferson Farnham, *Life and Adventures in California* (New York, 1846), 110–11. See also Charles B. Churchill, "Thomas Jefferson Farnham: An Exponent of American Empire in Mexican California," *PHR* 60 (Nov. 1991), 517–37. One ironic benefit of the high death rates among the wives and children of field hands was the way it eased the pressure on mission agriculture by creating a population with a high ratio of workers and a low one of dependent children and aged parents. Geiger, *Indians of Mission Santa Barbara*, 32, asserts that at Santa Barbara mission, "the old, the children and the infirm . . . constituted two-thirds of the mission community," and that "only one-third of the Indians . . . produced but that all ate." See also J. N. Bowman, "The Resident Neophytes (Existentes) of the Missions, 1769–1834," *HSSCQ* 40 (June 1958), 145–46, which convincingly presents the thesis that the demographics of death produced a higher ratio of workers to dependents.

57. Quotes from Pablo Tac, "Conversion of the San Luisenos of Alta California," 19–20.

58. Quote from Asisara, "Narrative," 47. See also Lorenzo Asisara, "Muerte del Padre Andrés Quintana," in Amador, "Memorias," 90; César, "Recollections of My Youth," 42; Baldomero López to Lucas Alaman, July 5, 1825, AASF, 3: (2), 141–48; Interrogation of Toypurina, Jan. 3, 1786, in Provincias Internas 120, AGN [copy in BL]; statement by a Santa Barbara neophyte in Maynard Geiger, ed. and trans., "Fray Antonio Ripoll's Description of the Chumash Revolt at Santa Barbara in 1824," *SCQ* 52 (winter 1970), 355. See also Hackel, "Land, Labor, and Production," 124.

59. Quote from von Kotzebue, "From Oonalashka to California," in Mahr, *The Visit of the "Rurick,"* 62–63.

60. Quote from Tapis to Lasuén, Respuesta, Santa Barbara mission, Oct. 30, 1800, Provincias Internas 216, AGN.

61. Carter, "Duhaut-Cilly's Account," 317.

62. Language and religion are discussed in Goycoechea to Borica, Dec. 14, 1798, AC, 10: 71–80, reporting that the padres did not require field hands to speak Spanish, and that Goycoechea did not know if they understood the Catholic religion. Tapis to Lasuén, Santa Barbara mission, Oct. 30, 1800, Provincias Internas 216, AGN, agrees with Goycoechea on language but not religion. Señán and Vicente de Santa María to Lasuén, Oct. 21, 1800, Provincias Internas 216, AGN, reports that the missionaries addressed field hands in Spanish, allowing them to reply in their own language. Spanish words incorporated into the Indian language are well summarized in George Harwood Phillips, *Indians and Intruders in Central California, 1769–1849* (Norman, Okla., 1993), 100–101.

63. Quotes from Owen F. da Silva, ed., *Mission Music of California, A Collection of Old California Mission Hymns and Masses* (Los Angeles, 1941), 30–31; César, "Recollections of My Youth," 42–43. "They had no more idea that they were worshiping God, than an unborn child has of Astronomy," recalled Hugo Reid. Quote from Hugo Reid, letter no. 17, "Conversion," in Heizer, *The Indians of Los Angeles*, 74. Pérez, "Una Vieja y Sus Recuerdos," 20, doubts the effectiveness of religious conversion. "Causa criminal contra indio Silverio . . . de San Luis Obispo por haver cometido el delito de homicidio," Monterey presidio, 1796, Californias 65, AGN, agrees. Narciso Durán to Padre Presidente, Respuesta, San José mission, Nov. 1, 1814, trans. Francis F. McCarthy, Articles 7, 8, and 11, doc. no. 644, SBMA, reports few Indians speaking Castilian. See also Martha Voght, "Shamans and Padres: The Religion of the Southern California Mission Indians," *PHR* 36 (winter 1967), 363–73; Constance G. DuBois, "The Religion of the Luiseno Indians of Southern California," *University of California Publications in American Archeology and Ethnology* 8 (Berkeley 1908), 74–76; A. L. Kroeber, "A Mission Record of the California Indians," ibid., 95. "Contestación al interrogatorio del año 1811," SBMA, notes

most field hands had only a superficial knowledge of Spanish. For an exploration of incomplete conversion, see Jorge Kor de Alva, "Spiritual Conflict and Accommodation in New Spain: Toward a Typology of Aztec Responses to Christianity," in George Collier et al., *The Inca and Aztec States, 1400–1800: Anthropology and History* (New York, 1982). For native cremation ceremonies applied to Christian burial rites, see Kroeber, *Handbook of California Indians*, 556–67. See also Engelhardt, *Missions and Missionaries*, 2: 253; Ramón A. Gutiérrez, *When Jesus Came, the Corn Mothers Went Away: Marriage, Sexuality, and Power in New Mexico, 1500–1846* (Stanford, 1991), 92–94. Guest, "Cultural Perspectives on California Mission Life," 25, maintains that "the church effected an almost complete separation . . . from . . . aboriginal culture. The missionaries performed a kind of surgical operation on Indian society, cutting off one member after another." See also Engelhardt, *Mission Santa Inéz Virgen y Mártir and Its Ecclesiastical Seminary* (Santa Barbara, 1932), 14–15.

64. Quote Geiger and Meighan, *As The Padres Saw Them*, 48. For one Indian punished for practicing his native religion, see the case of Tomás, July 1926, Santa Inéz mission, miscellaneous legal documents dealing with military, civil, and criminal cases, Los Angeles and Santa Barbara, 1815–33, DLGD. Artifact data from Paul Farnsworth, "The Economics of Acculturation in the Alta California Missions: A Historical and Archeological Study of Mission Nuestra Señora de la Soledad" (Ph.D. diss., UCLA, 1987), 105, 610–11, shows that natives there retained 30 to 45 percent of their material culture. See also Arthur Woodward, "An Early Account of the Chumash," *The Masterkey* 8 (July 1934), 122. For evidence that field hands did not completely surrender their language and religion, and essential elements of their culture, see Tapis and Cortes to Goycoechea, Respuesta, Santa Barbara mission, Oct. 30, 1800; Lasuén, Contestación, 1811; Juan Amorós, Respuesta no. 14, San Carlos mission, Feb. 3, 1814, SBMA; William E. Hartnell, Instructions, San José mission, Aug. 28, 1839, 7: 42; Garcia Diego to Figueroa, Santa Clara mission, Sept. 21, 1833, AC, DSP, Missions, 2: 78.

65. Even on the verge of death, native beliefs held such strong sway over one thirty-five-year-old San Juan Capistrano mission Indian that he refused, even as he lay on his deathbed, to confess and accept the Holy Sacrament, angrily declaring that he would not do so because, "If I have been deceived whilst living, I do not wish to die in the delusion!" Quotes from Padre Gerónimo Boscana, *Chingichngsh: A Revised and Annotated Version of Alfred Robinson's Translation of Padre Gerónimo Boscana's Historical Account of the Belief, Usages, Customs and Extravagances of the Indians of this Mission of San Juan Capistrano Called the Acagchemen Tribe*, annotated by John P. Harrington and reprinted with a new preface by William Bright (1846 [Banning, Calif., 1978]), 80–81, 89. I have used the more common spelling of *Chinigchinich* (also spelled *Chungichnish* and *Chingichnich*). A slightly different translation ["Having lived deceived, I do not want to die deceived"] is in Henry Reichlen and Paule Reichlen, "Le Manuscript Boscana de la Bibliothèque Nationale de Paris: Relation sur les Indiens Acâgchemem de la Mission de San Juan Capistrano, Californie," *Journal de la Société des Américanistes* 60 (1971), 266–67. See also Francisco A. Lomelí, "Fray Gerónimo Boscana's '*Chingichngsh*': An Early California Text in Search of a Context," in María Herrera Sobek, ed., *Reconstructing a Chicano/a Literary Heritage: Hispanic Colonial Literature of the Southwest* (Tucson, 1993), 118–39; Lowell Bean and Sylvia Vane, "Cults and their Transformations," in Heizer, *Handbook of North American Indians*, 669, suggests that *Chinigchinich* may have evolved from sporadic contact between natives and Christian survivors of shipwrecks and runaway seamen, possibly on Santa Catalina Island or near Long Beach.

66. Richard B. Applegate, "The Datura Cult Among the Chumash," *JCA* 2 (summer 1975), 7–17; Blackburn, *December's Child*, 8–88; Lesley B. Simpson, trans. and ed., *Journal of Jose Longinos Martinez: Notes and Observations of the Naturalist of the Botanical Expedition in Old and New California and the South Coast, 1791–1792* (San Francisco, 1961), 56; Ramón Olbés and Marcos Amestoy, Respuesta, Oct. 6, 1812, SBMA; John Willoughby, *Division of Labor Among the Indians of California*, U.C. Archeological Survey Reports, no. 60 (Berkeley, 1963), 57; Fages, *Breve descripción histórica, política y natural de la Alta California, 1770–1774*, ed., Andres Henestrosa (1775 [Mexico City, 1973]), 66; Miguel Costansó, "Diario Histórico," xxviii–xxix, BL.

67. Nothing so repulsed and repelled the padres as certain "obscene" dance rituals in which a single man wearing only a loincloth and body paint chanted and sang to an assembled throng. "During the last part . . . of the song," remembered the Chumash Indian Fernando Librado, "he was trying to persuade someone to come over to lick his penis. But by the time of the last verse of the song, he had lost all hope and so did it himself . . . When he finished he

squatted down and defecated amid the people." Another ritual dance performed by natives from several tribes at Santa Barbara mission also involved defecation as part of a story involving a contest between Coyote and the Devil. Quote from Travis Hudson, Thomas C. Blackburn, Rosario Curletti, and Janice Timbrook, eds., *The Eye of the Flute: Chumash Traditional History and Ritual as Told by Fernando Librado "Kitseput" to John P. Harrington* (Banning and Santa Barbara, 1981), 86; also 88–90.

CHAPTER FOUR

1. James A. Sandos, "Levantamiento! The 1824 Chumash Uprising Reconsidered," *SCQ* 67 (spring 1985), 109–33; Thomas Blackburn, ed., "The Chumash Revolt of 1824: A Native Account," *JCA* 2 (summer 1975), 223–27; Travis Hudson, "The Chumash Revolt of 1824: Another Native Account From the Notes of John P. Harrington," *JCGBA* 2 (spring 1980), 123–26; Jack Holterman, "The Revolt of Estanislao," *The Indian Historian* 3 (winter 1970), 43–54.

2. Antonio Ripoll to Padre Sarría, "Levantamiento de los Indios," Santa Barbara, May 5, 1824, TC; Engelhardt, *Santa Barbara Mission*, 121, 123. For another reprint of the Indian message to Ripoll, see Gary B. Coombs, "With What God Will Provide: A Reexamination of the Chumash Revolt of 1824," *Noticias* 26 (summer 1980), 21–29.

3. Quote from Ripoll to Sarría, May 5, 1824, SBMA. As part of a general disarmament order, the president of the missions required Ripoll to collect all weapons, including the "chopping knives" and machetes normally controlled by field hands. For the disarmament order, see circular from Sarría to missions, July 22, 1824, AASF [copy in BL]. Some of the best evidence for the participation of field hands in the revolt comes from the Santa Barbara mission Indians themselves. After looting the mission storerooms and arming themselves, they fled deep into the Central Valley. Encamped in the interior, they sent a message back to Padre Ripoll stating: "We shall maintain ourselves with what God will provide us in the open country." They could do this, they said, because they were a broad cross section, "soldiers, stonemasons, carpenters, etc." The key to the message was the abbreviation "etc.," and the emphasis on the wide range of skills they possessed, an indication that many different segments of the mission community had fled, including field hands. Another part of the message also reinforces the interpretation that field hands were a significant part of the revolt. In this section the rebels assured Ripoll that they intended "to provide for ourselves by our work," an indication that the field hands among them would cultivate land and grow crops necessary for survival. Quotes from Geiger, "Fray Antonio Ripoll's Description of the Chumash Revolt," 352. See also Engelhardt, *Santa Barbara Mission*, 120–38; Geiger, *Mission Santa Barbara*, 86–89.

4. Quote from John C. Ewers, ed., *Adventures of Zenas Leonard, Fur Trader* (Norman, Okla., 1959), 122. Within a few years of their discovery, an epidemic swept through the area and killed all of the Chumash fugitives. See Sherburne F. Cook, "The Epidemic of 1830–1833 in California and Oregon," *University of California Publications in American Archeology and Ethnology* 48 (1955), 303–26. The reference to gold and silver is questionable. If true, it certainly refers to church relics not coins, as the California economy was based almost entirely on barter. Mission inventories do not mention any stockpile of gold and silver. Figures on those remaining free are from Cook, *Conflict*, 60, table 3.

5. Quote from Geiger, *Mission Santa Barbara*, 89. When Kumeyaay villagers attacked San Diego mission on August 15, 1769, killing one colonist and wounding a padre and three others, the only field hands present were Baja California field hands, who defended the mission, the padres, and themselves. Mission Indian field hands may have been among a handful of runaways who joined one thousand Kumeyaay, burned San Diego mission, and killed a padre and two colonists on Nov. 4, 1775. As for a plot nine years later at San Gabriel mission, when a group of Gabrielino Indian men and their leader, a female shaman named Toypurina, were arrested for conspiring to kill the priests and soldiers, there is scarce indication that field hands were involved, although it seems likely that they must have known of the plot. See Engelhardt, *San Diego Mission*, 1–12; José Francisco Ortega, "Account of Insurrection," Nov. 30, 1775, PSP, Benicia Military, 1: 1; Thomas W. Temple III, "Toypurina the Witch and the Indian Uprising at San Gabriel," *The Masterkey* 32 (1958), 136–52; Edward Castillo, "The Other Side of the 'Christian Curtain,'" 8–17.

6. Bancroft, *History of California*, 2: 146, concludes the plot was nothing more than a rumor. See also 147n.

7. Quote from Engelhardt, *San Antonio de Padua, the Mission in the Sierras* (Santa Barbara, 1930), 105. These observations are confirmed in Monterey, "Diarios de Sucesos, 1800–1802," MS (n.d.), 30, BL, finding Pujol's intestines "black and putrid." See also Bancroft, *History of California*, 1: 147n; Kenneally, *Writings of Lasuén*, 2: 254; Henry Harris, *California's Medical Story* (San Francisco, 1932), 24, 27–28.

8. The 1801 incident can be followed in Padre Antonio de la Toba to Lasuén, San Gabriel mission, Apr. 26, 1801, Missions, 1, second series, AGN. In padres Juan Martín and Pedro Martínez to José Raymundo Carrillo, San Gabriel mission, Apr. 27, 1802, AC, Missions, 11: 205–6, BL, the two poisoned padres asserted that the natives were innocent. José Raymundo Carrillo to Arrillaga, Monterey, June 5, 1802, AC, Missions, 11: 203, asserts that the Indians concocted their story to increase their standing among fellow natives and recommends punishing them with a whipping. Concurring with the padres, Lasuén attributed the poisoning to spoiled or contaminated mescal (a liquor made from the maguey plant). Guest, *Lasuén*, 322, makes the case for lead residue poisoning.

9. Quotes from Bancroft, *History of California*, 2: 345; Castillo, "The Native Response to the Colonization of Alta California," in Thomas, *Columbian Consequences*, 1: 383; Engelhardt, *San Diego Mission*, 162–93n, citing the burial record, entry no. 2143, July 1812, written by Padre Gerónimo Boscana at San Diego mission; Proceedings of the 1811 cases, PSP, 49: 2–7; Engelhardt, *San Diego Mission*, 163–64. Panto did not receive the last rites. See also Doyce B. Nunis Jr., ed., *Hispanic California Revisited: Essays by Francis F. Guest, O.F.M.* (Santa Barbara, 1996), 285–86. For a revisionist interpretation based on a questionable reading of the evidence effectively disputed by Nunis, see Carrico, "Crime and Punishment: The Native American Experience in Colonial San Diego, 1769–1830," 21–22. See also Nunis, "The 1811 San Diego Trial of The Mission Indian Nazario," *WLH* 4 (winter–spring 1991), 52. The two-hundred-lash figure apparently originated in prosecuting Judge Don Domingo Carillo's tally of the total of all lashings Nazario claimed to have ever received from Panto over a period of several years. See also Summary Transcript of Trial Proceedings, Dec. 18, 1811, San Diego mission, AC, PSP, 49: 2–7, BL [copy in Santa Barbara Trust for Historic Preservation]. Although Bancroft, *California Pastoral*, 187, is sometimes cited as evidence for the death-by-poisoning thesis, Bancroft in fact only writes that Panto was "supposed to have been poisoned by his cook." For bitter broom, see Peter Raven, *Native Shrubs of Southern California* (Berkeley, 1964), 883.

10. Edward Castillo, ed. and trans., "The Assassination of Padre Andrés Quintana by the Indians of Mission Santa Cruz in 1812: The Narrative of Lorenzo Asisara [1877]," *CH* 68 (fall 1989), 117–25, is questioned by Nunis, "To the Editor," ibid., 70 (summer 1991), 207–12. Castillo's response follows on 213–15. Bancroft, *California Pastoral*, 162–68, contains the standard account. See 592–600, for the first translation of the Asisara dictation, minus the sexual references. See also Lorenzo Asisara, "Muerte del Padre Andrés Quintana," in Amador, "Memorias," 58–79, 90–113; Francis J. Weber, *California Catholicism* (Los Angeles, 1975), 73–74, citing a manuscript account by José Eusebio Galindo, "Apuntes para la Historia de California," MS (1877), 63–64, BL. While Asisara asserts that natives at Santa Cruz mission were "severely treated by the padres" and often received "fifty lashes on the bare back" with a rawhide lash, he also says that he personally never received anything stronger "except for a few slaps for forgetfulness." Quotes from Venancio [Asisara], "Early Indian Life," in Francis J. Weber, *Holy Cross Mission*, 22. Asisara mentions a rawhide lash not a horsewhip as claimed in some accounts. He also states that natives often received fifty lashes on the bare back.

11. Quotes from Castillo, "Assassination," 117–25. For a recent publication of the Asisara dictation, see Malcolm Margolin, ed., *The Way We Lived: California Indian Stories, Songs and Reminiscences* (Berkeley, 1981 [1993]), 160–63. Introducing this account, Margolin ignores the controversy surrounding it, writing that it "captures something of the fear-soaked, perverse, nightmarish quality that pervaded this and, one suspects, other missions." In Cook, *Conflict*, 130–31, Lorenzo Asisara is presented as Lorenzo Asesara. There are other mutations too numerous to recount. Bancroft, *History of California*, 2: 388n44, asserts that in addition to his cruelty, Quintana was murdered for seducing an Indian woman. See also Death Register, Oct. 13, 1812, Santa Cruz mission, SBMA.

12. The episode has a vast folklore and numerous mutations. Williams, "Fate of Fray Andrés Quintana" [1877], in Weber, *Holy Cross Mission*, 18–20, has Quintana being hung from a tree. "Reflections of a Tragedy" [the condensed interview and recollections of Santa Cruz native Justiniano Roxas, ca. 1875], ibid., 42–43, holds that after Quintana was hanged, the pear tree

"withered immediately," and is the source of the leprosy legend. This version has the plot being uncovered several years later by a *mayordomo* lying down to rest for dinner on a distant cattle ranch where, feigning sleep, he overheard several Indians talking of the night they killed Quintana. For the fate of the murderers, see Older, *California Missions and Their Romances*, 189. According to Simpson, *Narrative*, 105–6, Quintana died at the hands of a jealous husband who took revenge on the padre for having an affair with his wife. There are many other versions. Contrary to legend, all four assassins survived their punishment. See Nunis, *Hispanic California Revisited*, 131–32. Questioned about the assassination while imprisoned in the San Francisco presidio on November 21, 1820, a field hand known only as Alberto confessed that he had refused to join the conspiracy and ran away following the murder. See Bancroft, *History of California*, 1: 389n. A dying field hand at San Luis Obispo mission also confessed to being involved in the assassination. See Mariano G. Vallejo, "Historia de California," MS (1877), ii, 12–14, BL. These later confessions suggest that a much larger number of field hands knew of the plot and murder, possibly participated in it, and kept quiet. Alvarado, "Historia de California," 1, 103–7, reports that in the San Ramon Valley soon after Quintana's murder (and by implication as part of the revolt against the padres), eight hundred Indians attacked an expedition from San José mission, killing the padre. This was later covered up by the missionaries.

13. Quote from "The Death of Padre Quintana," in Margolin, *The Way We Lived*, 162. The contradiction between the alleged cruelty of Padre Quintana and the fact that he was murdered after arising in the middle of the night to minister to a dying man is noted in Gerald Hurley, "Mission of the Holy Cross," *The Antonian* (Feb. 1939), in Weber, *Holy Cross Mission*, 132. Recalling the assassination fifty-seven years after the fact, Asisara clearly got some details wrong. For example, Asisara states that Quintana was strangled on a Saturday evening, but Oct. 11, 1812, was a Sunday, indicating that Asisara slightly corrupted his dates. The date of the murder, for example, was Oct. 12, a Monday. For the misdating, see Nunis, "To the Editor," 237n32. There are numerous discrepancies concerning the numbers, names, and sentences of the conspirators that can not be resolved. In general, however, the Asisara account is accurate. For the missionary view, see José María Estudillo to Padre Marcelino Marquínez, Oct. 15, 1812, California Historical Documents Collection, HL; Estudillo to Arrillaga, Oct. 23, 1812, PSP, Benecia Military, 44: 21. Although Quijano's autopsy has been labeled the first official autopsy ever performed in California, it appears that distinction belonged to the Pujol case, which predated that of Quintana by eleven years. For Quijano, see Robert Moses, "Manuel Quijano and the Waning of Spanish California," *CH* 67 (June 1988), 79–93. Documentation from the formal investigation and trial was sent to Mexico and apparently lost. See Report of Solá to Viceroy Felix M. Calleja, June 21, 1816, in Engelhardt, *Missions and Missionaries*, 3: 14–16. Solá's report is dismissed by Castillo, "Assassination," 125, as a piece of collusion between the Franciscans and the civil government. Various details, often contradictory, are also found in Juan B. Alvarado, "Historia de California," 1: 98–100, which is the source of details about Cárlos Castro.

14. Quotes from Castillo, "Other," 15. For another version of the protest incident, see Antonio María Osio, *The History of Alta California: A Memoir of Mexican California*, ed. and trans. Rose Marie Beebe and Robert M. Senkewicz (Madison, Wis., 1996), 67. The stone-throwing incident is in Arrillaga to Antonio Rodríguez, Loreto, Feb. 16, 1805, AC, 26: 260–61. For abortion, see Solá to viceroy, Monterey, Apr. 3, 1818, PR, 9: 176; Khlebnikov, "Memoirs of California [1829]," 315; Hugo Reid, letter no. 19, "New Era in Mission Affairs," in Dakin, *A Scotch Paisano*, 274; Marcos Briones to Hermenegildo Sal, San Luis Obispo, Jan. 8, 1797, in Sherburne F. Cook, ed. and trans., "Colonial Expeditions to the Interior of California: Central Valley, 1800–1820," *Anthropological Records* 16 (May 1960), 241. When disciplined, field hands could take their punishment stoically, refusing to let their tormentors see any pain or fear. On San Gabriel mission in January 1827, for example, six field hands accepted their public whippings without protest. But one of them who, according to a witness, "did not like to submit to the lash," was knocked down by the commandant, tied, and severely whipped, "then chained by the leg to another Ind. who had been guilty of a similar offense." On several missions, *alcaldes* were afraid to discipline or chastise such quarrelsome, aggressive, and difficult to control field hands, citing their "bad dispositions." Other field hands, when whipped, would frequently laugh as the blows were delivered. Commenting on such responses, church scholars cite them not as examples of resistance but evidence that whippings were so mild, light, and painless as to be a joke. Quote from Harrison Rogers, first journal, Jan. 3, 1827. Contradicting the claim that such punishment was easy to take, the church scholar of San Gabriel mission once argued that

natives "would take care [not to laugh too much?] lest the whole number without any deduction would be inflicted." If whippings were laughing matters, what would be the point of taking care not to laugh excessively? What would be the point of whipping to exact discipline? See Engelhardt, *San Gabriel Mission*, 354.

15. Edward Castillo, "Neophyte Resistance," in *The Spanish Missionary Heritage*, 60–75; Castillo, "Resistance and Social Control in the Alta California Missions," 73–86, in Castillo and Robert H. Jackson, *Indians, Franciscans, and Spanish Colonization: The Impact of the Mission System on California Indians* (Albuquerque, 1995); Norman Neuerburg, "Indians As Artists In California before and after Contact with the Europeans," in Román Piña Homs, ed., *Les Illes Balears i America* (Palma, Spain, 1992), 43–66, quote 47, a revised version of Georgia Lee and Norman Neuerburg, "The Alta California Indians as Artists Before and After Contact," in *Columbian Consequences*, 1: 467–80; Neuerburg, "Indian Pictographs at Mission San Juan Capistrano," *The Masterkey* 56 (1982), 55–58.

16. Quotes from Hudson, *Breath of the Sun*, 18. Fernando Librado, who told this story to anthropologist John P. Harrington, was a master storyteller and apparently managed to embellish many facts. Claiming a birth date of 1804, he may have been born as late as 1838, or possibly sometime in between. A cautionary note in citing Librado as a source is found in John R. Johnson, "The Trail to Fernando," *JCGBA* 4 (summer 1982), 132–38. I am indebted to Michael Mathes for correcting my translation of Librado's joke.

17. Anastacio Carrillo to José de la Guerra, Los Angeles, Aug. 5, 1821, DLGP; Hewes and Hewes, "Indian Life and Customs at Mission San Luis Rey," 97; Tapis and Juan Cortes, Respuesta, Oct. 30, 1800, answer no. 10, SBMA.

18. Governor to Lieutenant Gonzalez, Monterey, Sept. 9, 1785, 23: 33; Fages to commander of the Monterey presidio, San Gabriel mission, Jan. 11, 1787, 4: 156–57; Fages to Borica, Monterey, Jan. 16, 1799, AC, 16: 115.

19. Quote from Wilbur, *Vancouver in California*, 41–42, 148–49. For the case of one "incorrigible," see Goycoechea to Fages, Santa Barbara mission, Oct. 22, 1788, AC, 4: 301. For injuring cattle, mares, and colts, see Arrillaga to the commander of the San Francisco presidio, Monterey, Mar. 20, 1794, AC, 22: 364; Fages to the commander general of the internal provinces, San Diego mission, Mar. 17, 1786, AC, 22: 351; Felipe de Neve, Instruction, no. 4, Saucillo, Sept. 7, 1782, Guadalajara, 283, AGI.

20. Quotes from Kenneally, *Writings of Lasuén*, 2: 202, 207–8; also 107–8, 120; padres Luis Antonio Martinez and Antonio Rodríguez to Señán, San Luis Obispo mission, Article 5, in Francis J. Weber, ed., *Mission in the Valley of the Bears: A Documentary History of San Luis Obispo* (Hong Kong, 1981), 24; Padre José Altimira to Don Luis Argüello, Oct. 18, 1823, CHDC. See also Señán and Vicente de Santa María to Lasuén, San Buenaventura mission, Oct. 21, 1800; Lasuén to Señán, San Carlos mission, June 19, 1801, both in Provincias Internas 216, AGN.

21. I have extrapolated statistics on runaway field hands from general figures. The investigation of the San Francisco de Asís mission mass escape is in José Pérez Fernández to Borica, San Francisco de Asís mission, Sept. 13, 1795, AC, 7: 361–62. For Santa Cruz mission, see Robert H. Jackson, "Patterns of Demographic Change," 259. For the 1780 escape, see Serra's breakdown in Serra to Lasuén, Jan. 12, 1780, in Tibesar, *Writings of Serra*, 3: 421. See also Serra to Lasuén, Dec. 22, 1781, PSP, Benecia Military, 3:27; Cook, *Conflict*, 58–61, 70, 399–446, esp. tables 3 and 4. Cook's claim that 15.6 percent of San Carlos mission neophytes fled is questioned in Hackel, "Indian-Spanish Relations," 123–27, app., 347–67. Hackel proposes a figure of 4.5 percent (including both temporary and permanent fugitives) and finds that fugitivism declined during the nineteenth century. Population figures from Robert H. Jackson, *Indian Population Decline*, 114–15.

22. Padre Taboada, Dec. 31, 1825, Santa Cruz mission, DPLHC, C-B 50, 2: 607–9. San Fernando mission seems to have had a low rate of runaways. For comparisons with American slave runaways and terminology, see John Spencer Bassett, ed., *The Southern Plantation Overseer As Revealed in His Letters* (Northampton, Mass., 1925), 263.

23. The best data on the motivations of escaping field hands comes from the testimony of twenty-three voluntarily returning members of a July 1796 mass escape of two hundred natives from San Francisco de Asís. Interrogated by the presidio commander and three soldiers, their responses are found in Argüello, Relación, San Francisco de Asís, Aug. 9, 12, 1791, PSP, 16: 71–74; "En cumplimiento de superior orden del Señor Gobernador y Comandante Inspector Don Diego de Borica su fecha de 21 de Julio de 1791 para que declaren los indios cristianos huidos de

la Misión de San Francisco," San Francisco presidio, Joséf Argüello, Joaquin Fico, Claudio Galindo, Joséf Miranda, and José Gonzalez, Californias 65, AGN. For one particularly lucid explanation of why a San Antonio mission field hand ran away from the floggings and "oppression" in the hope of farming independently, see Echeandia to *alcalde* of Monterey, January 17, 1831, DSP, 9: 49.

24. Quote from von Langsdorff, *Voyages and Travels*, 2: 171. For mission Indians joining those whom they were sent to bring back, see José Pérez Fernández to Borica, May 3, 1795; Antonio Dantí to Borica, San Francisco de Asís mission, May 3, 1795, Californias 65, AGN. The stories about fleeing after being locked in collars and hitched to plows are from Florence C. Shipek, "California Indian Reactions to the Franciscans," *The Americas* 41 (winter 1985), 487; Rosalie Robertson, "The 'Crying Rock'—Where They Killed the Children," MS (n.d.), RCIH. I have been unable to confirm these claims. For well-cared-for but ill Indians who fled, see Francis F. Guest, "The Indian Policy Under Fermín Francisco de Lasuén, California's Second Padre President," *CHSQ* 45 (spring 1963), 209. See also Kenneally, *Writings of Lasuén*, 2: 205; also 203, 215, 401–3, 410–14.

25. Large quotes from Bancroft, *History of California*, 2: 331; Kenneally, *Writings of Lasuén*, 2: 203; also 6 and 412. See also Harrison Rogers, first journal, Nov. 30, 1826. "Wayward sheep" reference from Serra to Rivera y Moncada, July 24, 1775, in Tibesar, *Writings of Serra*, 2: 285–87. Figures from Cook, *Conflict*, 61–62, table 4; Cook, *Population Trends among the California Mission Indians*, Ibo-America, no. 17 (Berkeley, 1940), 27–28. There is no way of knowing whether or not field hands escaped more or less frequently than other natives. I assume that in any group of runaways, field hands were probably present. When possible, I identify groups that were entirely composed of field hands.

26. José de Zúñiga to Fages, San Diego mission, Feb. 12, 1790, AC, 5: 212; Fages to José Antonio Romeu, Monterey, May 31, 1791, AC, 6: 142; Carter, ed., "Duhaut-Cilly's Account," 214–15. After they wandered about the vicinity of San Pablo, living off the land and the cattle they killed, a ranchero captured two of them, and unable to catch the third, shot him as he fled.

27. Cook, *Conflict*, 60, table 3.

28. Borica, "Castigos que han de sufrir los indios cristianos y gentiles," Monterey, Aug. 26, 1797, Californias 65: 77–79, AGN; Geiger, "Fray Antonio Ripoll's Description of the Chumash Revolt," 352. Although the fate of the San Diego escapees is unknown, it is unlikely that they succeeded.

29. Quote from Kenneally, *Writings of Lasuén*, 1: 152. Escape statistics for field hands who remained at large (as opposed to those who fled and were recaptured or voluntarily returned) are extrapolated from general estimates and are discussed in Cook, *Conflict*, 58–59. For attempts to recapture runaway field hands, see José Fernandez Perez to Borica, San Francisco de Asís mission, May 29, 1795, AC, 7: 489–90; Borica to Amador, Monterey, July 21, 1797, AC, 24: 118. For voluntarily returning field hands, see padres José de la Cruz Espí and Martín de Landaeta to Argüello, San Francisco de Asís, July 26, 1797, AC, 9: 89; Argüello to Borica, San Francisco presidio, May 28, 1798, AC, 10: 109–10.

30. Harrison Rogers, first journal, Nov. 30, 1826.

31. Quote from María Solares, interview [a Chumash Indian, who described herself as *una esclava de la misión*—"slave of the mission"], JPHP, National Anthropological Archives, SI. See also Carobeth Laird, *Encounter with an Angry God: Recollections of My Life with John Peabody Harrington* (Banning, Calif., 1975), 16–18. For punishment of pagan Indians harboring *huidos* (runaways), see Borica to Sanchez, Monterey, Feb. 11, 1795, AC, 24: 43.

32. Quote from Durán to Ignacio Martínez, San José mission, May 16, 1827, AASF.

33. Quote from Neve, "Instruction . . . for Don Pedro Fages," no. 5, Sept. 7, 1782, Guadalajara 283, AGI, in Beilharz, *Felipe de Neve*, 160–61, trans. Beilharz [copy in Provincias Internas 120, AGN].

34. Quote from Arrillaga, "Instructions to Presidio Commanders," Dec. 22, 1806, San Diego, PSP, 19: 109.

35. Commander of Santa Barbara presidio to Arrillaga, Feb. 19, 1811, PR, 11: 44–47; Jacobo Ugarte y Loyola to Fages, Arispe, Dec. 12, 1787; Fages to Lasuén, Monterey, June 15, 1788, SBMA.

36. Quote from Narciso Durán to Commandant Martínez Nov. 7, 1828, San José mission, copy in SBMA. See also Kenneally, *Writings of Lasuén*, 2: 217; Bancroft, *History of California*, 2: 136–37.

37. For punishments of runaway field hands, see Borica, "Castigos que han de sufrir," Californias 65: 77–79, AGN; "Causa criminal . . . por el cabo de la escolta Marcos Briones en ocho . . . [handwriting unclear]," Monterey presidio (n.d.), 1796, AGN; Tapis to Lasuén, Santa Barbara mission, Oct. 30, 1800; Gregorio Fernández, Purísima Concepción mission, Nov. 1, 1800, Provincias Internas 216, AGN. Although some foreign travelers would later claim that padres went even further and branded the cross on recaptured runaway field hands, there is little basis for believing these reports, or the probably fraudulent and definitely lurid accusations of Russian fur trapper Vassilli Tarakanoff. Captured and held for more than one year at San Fernando mission (or possibly Santa Barbara mission), Tarakanoff later wrote a lurid and often-cited account suggesting that when it came to dealing with runaways the padres were sadists, or at least tolerated sadism. According to Tarakanoff, at some point in his stay he watched in horror as a group of recaptured natives was brought back to the mission bound with rawhide ropes. "Some were bleeding from wounds, and some children were tied to their mothers," he recalled. "The next day we saw some terrible things. Some of the runaway men were tied on sticks and beaten with straps. One chief was taken out to the open field and a young calf that had just died was skinned and the chief was sewed into the skin while it was yet warm. He was kept tied to a stake all day, but he died soon and they kept his corpse tied up." See Vassili Petrovitch Tarakanoff, *Statement of My Captivity Among the Californians*, trans. Ivan Petroff, notes by Arthur Woodward (Los Angeles, 1953), 14–18. For the claims of branding, see Robert B. Forbes, *Personal Reminiscences* (Boston, 1878), 95–96; B. D. Wilson, "Observations on Early Days in California and New Mexico," *HSSCAP* (1934), 90.

38. Quote from Durán to Martínez, Nov. 7, 1828, San José mission, SBMA. See also Marion Lydia Lothrop, "The Indian Campaigns of General M. G. Vallejo, Defender of the Northern Frontier of California," *Quarterly of the Society of California Pioneers* 9 (Sept. 1932), 165n, 170. For failing to return from the *paseo*, see Lasuén to Fages, Sept. 6, 1787, Kenneally, *Writings of Lasuén*, 1: 152.

39. Quotes from Carter, ed., "Duhaut-Cilly's Account," 215; "Pioneer," *Santa Clara News*, Nov. 13, 1869, in Pomponio Collection, Marin County Historical Society. See also Bancroft, *History of California*, 2; 537–38; Cook, *Conflict*, 1, 74–79. The most comprehensive account is Alan Brown, "Pomponio's World," *Argonaut* 6 (1975), 1–20. For the story of one *huido alcalde* who cut off his heel to slip out of shackles at San Carlos mission, see Estéban de la Torre, "Reminiscences, 1815–1848" in Galindo, "Apuntes para la historia de California."

40. Sebastián Rodríguez, report, May 26 to June 9, 1828, in Sherburne F. Cook, ed. and trans., "Expeditions to the Interior of California: Central Valley, 1820–1840," *Anthropological Records* 20 (Feb. 1962), 186; Juan Coluco, interview, JPHP. For smuggling food to runaway field hands at San Francisco mission, see Padre José Viader to Argüello, May 30, 1823, TC; Ignacio Martínez to Argüello, Apr. 1, 1823, DSP, 10: 82. For a tabulation of runaways to 1817, see Cook, *Conflict*, 61, giving a figure of 3,205 from fifteen missions; from that he extrapolates the figure of 4,060 for nineteen missions.

41. Quotes from Tapis to Arrillaga, Santa Barbara mission, Mar. 1, 1805, SBMA; also R. Abella to Solá, San Francisco de Asís mission, Jan. 29, 1817, AASF, fol. 3 (1): 125; Francisco González and Domingo Carranza to Borica, Santa Cruz mission (n.d.), 1798, AASF.

42. Statistical analysis derived from Archibald, *Economic Aspects of the Missions*, table 15, "Mission Population 1785–1821," 154. For population decline on one mission, see Geiger, *Indians of Mission Santa Barbara*, 15–18.

43. Robert H. Jackson, "Disease and Demographic Patterns at Santa Cruz Mission, Alta California," *JCGBA* 5 (spring–summer 1983), 33–57, argues the need for labor provided a major incentive for large-scale gentile (pagan) recruitment.

44. Padre L. A. Martínez to Solá, San Luis Obispo mission, May 30, 1816; Sarría to Solá, May 30, 1816 [protesting the use of soldiers in the cause of forced labor and conversions], AASF [copies in SBMA and BL]; Padre Juan Amorós to Solá, San Rafael mission, Sept. 26, 1819, SBMA. For mission expeditions bringing back runaways, rebels, and others, see Governor Arrillaga to presidio commander, San Diego mission, Dec. 22, 1806, PSP, 19: 109; Padre L. A. Martínez to Solá, San Luis Obispo mission, May 30, 1816; Padre Juan Amoros to Solá, San Rafael mission, Sept. 26, 1819; Amorós to Argüello, Apr. 10, 1823; Padre Altimira to Señán, San Francisco de Asís mission, July 10, 1823 [charging the padres at San José mission with forcibly seizing natives)], SBMA; Juan Bandini, "Apuntos para la Historia de Alta California," MS (1878), 6, BL.

45. Quote from Engelhardt, *San Miguel Archangel: The Mission on the Highway* (Santa Barbara, 1929), 10. See also Cook, *Conflict*, 200–201; table 2, 245–48; Bancroft, *History of California*, 2: 45–57; Padre Juan Martín, "Visita a los gentiles tularenos, 1804," MS (1815), 6: 85–89, SBMA; Juan Martín to Señán, San Miguel mission, Apr. 26, 1815, SBMA; Herbert I. Priestley, "Franciscan Exploration," MS (n.d.), BL.

46. Two of the most famous or infamous recruiting expeditions are described in Pedro Muñoz, diary, Sept. 21–Nov. 2, 1806, in Cook, "Colonial Expeditions," 248–52; Joaquin Piña, diary, May 26–June 1, 1829, in ibid., 177–78. Information on natives kidnapped for field labor on the pueblos is in Echeandía, June 15, 1826, DSP, 1: 146, which permits San José residents to "induce" the gentiles of the Tulares to come and work during the harvests. Echeandía, Oct. 23, 1829, DSP, 7: 240, contains some evidence that kidnapped children were put to work in the harvests at San José mission.

47. Quotes from William H. Davis, *Sixty Years in California*, ed. Harold Small (San Francisco, 1889 [1994]), 9; Beechey, *Voyage*, 2: 18.

48. Quote from Ygnacio Vallejo to Governor Borica, San José, Sept. 1, 1797, AC, 8: 341–42. See also Vallejo to Borica, San José, July 1, 23; Aug. 30; Sept. 26, 1797, AC, 8: 333–35, 337, 345. Hermenegildo Sal to Gabriel Moraga, comisionado del pueblo de San José, Monterey, Sept. 10, 1796, Archives of the City of San José, doc. no., 54, San José Historical Society.

49. Quote from Carter, ed., "Duhaut-Cilly's Account," 242–43. Typical wages were the equivalent of a cotton (shirt) and *manta* (blanket) per month, and daily rations of meat and boiled maize. See Bancroft, *History of California*, 1: 614n27. See also Robert Smile, *The Sonoma Mission: San Francisco de Solano* (Fresno, 1975), 28–29.

50. For payment methods, see Viceroy Venadito to Solá, Dec. 15, 1819, SBMA. For the type of society sustained by this labor system, see José Bandini, *A Description of California in 1828* (Berkeley, 1951), 9. See also John R. Johnson, "The Indians of Mission San Fernando," in Doyce B. Nunis Jr., ed., "Mission San Fernando Rey de España, 1797–1997: A Bicentennial Tribute," *SCQ* 89 (fall 1997), 252.

51. Quote from Padre Vicente de Santa María to Lasuén, San Fernando mission, Sept. 3, 1795, SBMA. For uppity gentile field hands and for the attempt to regulate Indian-white relations, see William Marvin Mason, "Fages' Code of Conduct toward the Indians, 1787," *JCA* 2 (summer 1975) 94–98.

52. Quote from padres Toboada and Zalvidea to Señán, Respuesta of June 28, 1814, SBMA; also in Engelhardt, *San Gabriel Mission*, 105. See also Lesley Byrd Simpson, ed., *The Letters of José Señán, O.F.M., Mission San Buenaventura, 1796–1823*, trans. Paul D. Nathan (Ventura, Calif., 1962), 2; Padre Alonso Isidro Salazar, Representación to Viceroy Branciforte, Mexico, May 11, 1796; Señán, Representación to Viceroy Branciforte, Mexico, May 14, 1796, SBMA.

53. Figures from Señán, "Estado de las Misiones de Alta California sacado de los informes de las Misiones en fin de Deciembre de 1821," SBMA. There is some archeological evidence in the excavation of the vineyardist's house at San Antonio mission that hispanicized natives by the early 1800s had taken over supervisory positions. Information from Robert Hoover, California State Polytechnic University, San Luis Obispo, to author, May 3, 1993, author's possession.

54. Vallejo, "Ranch and Mission Days," 187; Titus F. Cronise, *The Natural Wealth of California* (San Francisco, 1868), 35–54.

55. Quote from Padre Mariano Payeras to Padre Guardian José Gasol, La Soledad mission, June 26, 1822, in Donald Cutter, ed. and trans., *Writings of Mariano Payeras* (Santa Barbara, 1995), 322. See also Bancroft, *History of California*, 2: 458–77; Adele Ogden, "Hides and Tallow: McCulloch, Hartnell and Company, 1822–1828," *CHSQ* 6 (Sept. 1927), 255–56.

56. C. Alan Hutchinson, "The Mexican Government and the Mission Indians of Upper California," *The Americas* 21 (Apr. 1965), 346–48; Engelhardt, *Missions and Missionaries*, 3: 379–402.

57. "Plan for the Administration of the Missions in the Territories of Upper and Lower California. Proposed by the Junta de Fomento of that Peninsula," Mexico City, Apr. 6, 1825; "Final Opinion," May 15, 1827, in Keld J. Reynolds, ed. and trans., "Principal Actions of the California Junta de Fomento," *The Americas* 25 (Dec. 1946), 303–8, 360.

58. For details of events at San Juan Capistrano mission, see Corporal Hilario Machado to Echeandía, Jan. 22, 1826, SP, 1: 494–97; Report of Capt. Juan M. Estudillo to Echeandía, Apr. 25, 1827, San Diego mission, DSP, 2: 20–25. Scholars often cite a strike by Chinese field hands in Kern County in 1884 as the "first" farm labor strike in California. For vaqueros, mule-

teers, and artisans petitioning for freedom at San Buenaventura mission, see Petition to Echeandía, Oct. 23, 1826, San Buenaventura mission, Californias 18, AGN.

59. Quote from Echeandía to commandants of San Diego, Santa Barbara, Monterey, and the Padre Prefect, July 25, Californias 18, AGN. For developments in 1826, see Angustias de la Guerra Ord, "Occurrences in California," MS (1877), 52–54, BL; Antonio Maria Osio, "Historia de California," MS (1877), 119–20, BL; Bancroft, *History of California*, 3: 101–4, 308. For Mexican opinion at this time, see Carlos María Bustamante, "Medidas para la pacificacíon de la America Mexicana, 1820," MS (n.d.), 1, BL; Tadeo Ortiz de Ayala, *Resumen de la Estadística del Imperio Mexicano* (Mexico City, 1822), 30.

60. David Hornbeck, "Economic Growth and Change at the Missions of Alta California, 1776–1846," in Thomas, *Columbian Consequences*, 1: 423–33; Monroy, *Thrown Among Strangers*, 69; Jackson, "The Changing Economic Structure of the Alta California Missions," 387–415.

61. Quote from Beechey, *Narrative*, 2: 582–83.

62. Quote from Informe, 1826, in *Boletín del Archivo General de la Nación*, 30 (1959), 252. For similar developments at San Juan Capistrano mission, where the Indians would not obey, refused to work, and declared themselves to be free, see Capt. Juan M. Estudillo to Echeandía, Apr. 25, 1827, San Diego mission, DSP, Missions, 2: 20–25, BL [copy in SBMA]. My thanks to Padre Virgilio Biasiol for the original document and translation. See also Lisbeth Haas, *Conquests and Historical Identities in California, 1769–1936* (Berkeley and Los Angeles, 1995), 38.

63. George Tays, "Revolutionary California: The Political History of California During the Mexican Period, 1822–1846" (Ph.D. diss., UCB, 1932), BL; Manuel P. Servin, "The Secularization of the California Missions: A Reappraisal," *SCQ* 47 (June 1965), 133–49.

64. Durán to Figueroa, July 3, 1833, SBMA. On the basis of these observations, Durán concluded that emancipation would in fact result in slavery and begged Figueroa to reconsider his plans for secularization. See also C. Alan Hutchinson, "The Mexican Government and the Mission Indians of Upper California," 335–62; Michael C. Neri, "Narcisco [*sic*] Durán and the Secularization of the California Missions," *The Americas* 32 (Jan. 1977), 411–29.

65. Quotes from Robinson, *Life in California*, 88; Durán to Figueroa, July 19, 1833, SBMA. See also Durán to Figueroa June 17, 1833; Capt. Pablo de la Portilla to Figueroa, Feb. 10, 1833, SBMA.

66. Quotes from Figueroa to minister of foreign relations, July 20, 1833, DPLHC. Argüello to Figueroa, Sept. 27, 1833, DPLHC, gives slightly different numbers, reporting that at San Diego mission only two of fifty-nine heads of families left the mission under Figueroa's emancipation offer, but were joined by fourteen from San Dieguito, while at San Luis Rey mission out of 108 families none desired emancipation, although four married men did not completely dismiss the offer. These efforts resulted in two pueblos, Las Flores at San Luis Rey mission, and San Dieguito at San Diego mission.

67. Quote from Hutchinson, *Frontier Settlement in Mexican California: The Híjar-Padrés Colony and Its Origins, 1769–1835* (New Haven, 1969), 238. See also Figueroa to minister of foreign relations, July 20, 1833, DPLHC; Engelhardt, *Missions and Missionaries*, 3: 481. Of the unwillingness of field hands to leave San Diego and San Luis Rey missions, Engelhardt, *San Juan Capistrano*, 111, argues, "This proves that the convert Indians had received fair and kindly treatment . . . otherwise it is incomprehensible why they did not quickly grasp the chance to be free to go wherever they pleased."

68. Quotes from Figueroa to Vallejo, Aug. 17, 1833; Portilla to Figueroa, Sept. 21, 1833, DPLHC. See also Engelhardt, *San Juan Capistrano*, 112, 131; Bancroft, *History of California*, 339.

69. Engelhardt, *Mission San Juan Capistrano*, 116–17. Relations between field hands and the *mayordomo* are summarized in Agustín Sánchez to Alvarado, ca. 1836–38, AC, SP, Missions, 11: 632.

70. Durán to Figueroa, July 22, 1833, SBMA. For the situation on the *estancias* of Pala and Agua Caliente at San Luis Rey mission, see Portilla to Figueroa, Jan. 23, 1835, SP, Missions, 11: 47–49, 52.

71. Quotes from Hudson, *Breath of the Sun*, 91; Portilla to Figueroa, San Luis Rey mission, Dec. 20, 1834, DSP, Missions, 11: 658–61. For field hands meeting secretly and demanding the removal of abusive *mayordomos* at San Gabriel mission, see Juan Bandini to William Hartnell [probably June 1839], DSP, Missions, 11: 150–53, BL [copy in SBMA]. For congregating, see Simpson, *Narrative*, 1: 353, describing natives "whose . . . mischief . . . was forced into full play by a sense of . . . injustice and inhumanity."

72. Figueroa report from Santa Barbara mission, Oct. 5, 1833, DSP, Missions, 2: 72.

73. Durán, "Crítica sobre las Prevenciones de Emancipación," MS (1833), entry of July 16, 1833, BL; "Reglamento Provisional para secularización de las Misiones de la Alta California," Aug. 9, 1843, SBMA.

CHAPTER FIVE

1. Quotes from Robert Ryal Miller, *Juan Alvarado: Governor of California, 1836–1842* (Norman, Okla., 1998), 29; Alvarado, "Historia de California," 3: 6–7. See also Bancroft, *History of California*, 3: 331–32; 4: 53. There are several slightly different translations of Alvarado's statement. John Walton, *Storied Land: Community and Memory in Monterey* (Berkeley, 2001), 93, finds in the momentary indecision of the few who hesitated evidence less of passivity than receptivity to new ideas and a mulling over of their choices. I see it as evidence of fear and confusion.

2. Quotes from Durán to Figueroa, July 19, 1833, AASF; Durán to Figueroa ["vagabonds"], Aug. 6, 1833; Durán to Figueroa ["no Padre"], July 22, 1834, San Gabriel mission, SBMA. See also Durán to Figueroa, June 17, 1833; José Altimira to Argüello, Oct. 4, 1834, SBMA. Violence, threats, and revenge against padres at San Gabriel mission are described in Pérez, "Una Vieja y Sus Recuerdos," 14–15. Field hands at San Gabriel mission refusing to work "on account of lack of clothing" are described in William Hartnell to Alvarado, June 17, 1839, DSP, Missions, 11, 69.

3. Quote from Pablo de la Portilla to Governor Figueroa, Dec. 20, 1834, DSP, Missions, 11: 658–61. The San Luis Rey mission field hands eventually planted fifty *fanegas* of wheat, but in March 1835 they again refused to work unless a new *mayordomo* was appointed. See Portilla to Figueroa, Mar. 23, 1835, ibid., 47–49, 52. Hittell, *History of California*, 2: 190, translates the Portilla quote as, "We are free. It is not our pleasure to obey. We do not choose to work." For stealing grapes at Santa Clara, see Wilkes, *Narrative of the United States Exploring Expedition*, 5: 206–7. For attempts to remove *mayordomos*, see Juan Bandini to Governor Alvarado, ca. 1839, DSP, Missions, 150–53.

4. For an example of a native laying claim to land at Santa Barbara mission, see Francisco Massili land claim, witnessed by Padre Antonio Jimeno, Victor Lino, and Octavio Gutiérrez, *alcaldes*, Oct. 3, 1849, SBMA. The beginning of a barrio of field hands along the lower reaches of the Ventura River near San Buenaventura mission is described in John Johnson, "The Chumash Indians After Secularization," in Benoist and Flores, *The Spanish Missionary Heritage of the United States*, 143–64. For Pueblito de las Flores, see Terry E. Stephenson, "Forster vs Pico," *SCQ* 18 (winter 1936), 25. For emancipation, see Proceedings by Urbano, Odon, and Manuel, natives of San Fernando, petitioning for a tract of land named *Escorpion*, Expediente 461, Book 5: 320–27; Samuel to Gov. José Manuel Micheltorena, Apr. 21, 1843, Expediente 461, Book 5: 187–88; Proceedings in relation to one league of land in the San Fernando mission, granted to Joaquin, *alcalde*, and forty companions," Expediente 576, Book 5, 633–35, CSA; Bancroft, *History of California*, 4: 350, 369–71.

5. The battle with Pío Pico can be followed in the petition of Pablo Apis, Diego Peyri, Ygnacio Atulo, Guillermo Apis, José Miguel Gapala, Agustin Talle, and Leon Nojú to Figueroa, Aug. 1, 1838, DSP, Missions, 1: 652–53; Engelhardt, *San Luis Rey Mission*, 103; Bancroft, *History of California*, 3: 623–25n17. See also Joaquin de los Ríos to governor, Nov. 15, 1840, DSP, Missions, 10: 117–22. The analysis of Pico's *pueblo libre* plan is from Padre Francisco Ibarra to Prefecto Durán, Feb. 13, 1840, SBMA.

6. Quotes from Joseph J. Hill, *The History of Warner's Ranch and its Environs* (Los Angeles, 1927), 124–31, 151–52; Charles F. Lummis, "The Exiles of Cupa," *Out West* 16 (May 1902), 472; Lummis, "The Last Eviction," ibid., 17 (Nov. 1903). See also A. R. Johnson, diary, ibid., 17 (June 1903), 746, remembering how field hands had been "stimulated to work by three dollars per month and repeated floggings." As late as the 1860s, Indians were still on the property. Having driven off Warner in an uprising in which four of their leaders were later arrested and executed, they concluded a treaty with the U.S. Army troops sent to suppress them, and remained on the land through various sales and subdivisions until 1903. In that year U.S. Supreme Court judge and former governor John G. Downey, the latest in a long line of proprietors, evicted them. They eventually settled in the Pala Valley, just ten miles away, but not before they kept title to their land and continued their old ways longer than any other group of former mission field hands. See also Lorrin L. Morrison, *Warner: The Man and the Ranch* (Los Angeles, 1962), 20–22, 39.

7. Quote from Hudson, *Breath of the Sun*, 19. For San Gabriel mission, see Jackson, *A British Ranchero in Old California*, 83. For gambling, see Unknown to Hugo Reid, Feb. 10, 1844, DSP, Los Angeles, 8: 120. For field hands deserting San Juan Capistrano mission after failing in their petition for a new administrator, see José Delfin, Petition to Alvarado, Apr. 8, 1839, ibid., Missions, 4: 34–37. For travelers' descriptions of field hands guarding orchards, stomping out small quantities of wine, and plowing fields with crooked branches tipped with flat iron plates, see Herman Leader, ed., "A Voyage from Columbia to California in 1840: The Journal of Sir James Douglas," *CHSQ* 8 (June 1929), 111–12; Wilkes, *Narrative of the United States Exploring Expedition*, 5: 206–7.

8. Quote from Engelhardt, *Missions and Missionaries*, 4: 113. For another report on Santa Barbara mission, see Simpson, *Narrative of a Journey*, 1: 386. See also George Harwood Phillips, "Indians and the Breakdown of the Spanish Mission System in California," *Ethnohistory* 21 (fall 1974), 259–60, 268; Daniel Garr, "Planning, Politics and Plunder: The Missions and Indian Pueblos of Hispanic California," *SCQ* 54 (winter 1972), 291–312; Engelhardt, *San Luis Rey Mission*, 100–107, 122–23; C. Alan Hutchinson, *Frontier Settlement*, 255–60. For whipping at San Luis Rey, see W. H. Emory, *Notes of a Military Reconnaissance, from Fort Leavenworth, in Missouri, to San Diego, in California, Including Parts of the Arkansas, Del Norte, and Gila Rivers*, 30th Cong., 1st sess., 1846, S. Doc. 7, 116–17.

9. The story of Rogerio Rocha illustrates the trajectory of life for those who obtained land grants after secularization. Born at San Fernando mission in 1824, he lived as a young adult on land granted San Fernando mission Indians in 1843. Establishing an adobe and working a small orchard and field on twelve acres along Pacoima Creek, he lived comfortably, not knowing that in 1846 Governor Pío Pico sold all of the San Fernando mission lands to Eulogio de Célis. Patented in 1873, the land was sold two years later to G. K. Porter, a local real estate dealer and rancher, and Edward Maclay, a former California state senator. Attorneys for Porter and Maclay evicted Rocha, his wife, and three elderly women during a storm in 1886. Homeless, and stranded with their meager possessions, the old wife contacted pneumonia and died, and Rocha retired to a small hut in the mountains, where he died in 1904. See Engelhardt, *San Francisco Rey*, 96; "Golden Secret of His Grave: Aged San Fernando Mission Indian Buried," Grace Nicholson Papers, Addenda, Indian Scrapbook, 2: 123, HL. Stealing a horse with the idea of returning to his native ranchería, one old man could not resist the temptation of first riding up to Governor Alvarado as he inspected San Juan Capistrano mission. Defiant, unafraid, embittered by his life on the missions, the old man had nothing to lose, and so he gave Alvarado a last piece of his mind. "I am not an animal," he told the governor. "You can do two things with me; either order me to be shot . . . or give me liberty . . . for me it is all the same. I . . . shall have to die soon anyway. You know that it matters little to me whether I die to-day or to-morrow." Quote from Engelhardt, *Missions and Missionaries*, 4: 156–57; Engelhardt, *Mission San Juan Capistrano*, 123, both apparently citing Alvarado to Hartnell, Aug. 1939, SP, Missions. I have not been able to locate this letter. See also Alvarado, "Historia," 4: 59; Bancroft, *History of California*, 4: 57n26.

10. Quote from Robert F. Heizer and Alan F. Almquist, eds., *The Other Californians: Prejudice and Discrimination Under Spain, Mexico, and the United States to 1920* (Berkeley, 1971), 17–18. Freedom eventually came to most field hands in 1840. Touring the missions on assignment for the territorial government in March, settler and rancher William Hartnell heard numerous complaints and recorded them both in his diary and official report. Before resigning in disgust, he found many emancipated Indians living at San Buenaventura mission. At Soledad, Santa Cruz, San Francisco de Asís, and San Rafael missions those Indians who had not been emancipated petitioned for their freedom and distribution of remaining property. Those at Santa Cruz mission in particular complained of abuses by administrators. After achieving their freedom, many remained close by, living in mission dormitories, farming former mission lands both as individuals and communally. At San Rafael mission it was the "old Christians," those who had been on the mission for many years, who cried strongest and loudest for freedom. By the end of the year it appears that Indians still living at San Rafael mission had achieved their freedom. However, following their emancipation, most there decided to leave. See William Hartnell, "Diario, Informe, y Borradores de Correspondencia," and José Anzar and Andrés Pico, "Inventario de los muebles raices semovientes en la Mision de S[an]ta Cruz por la comisión nombrada p[o]r el Exc[elentísi]mo S[eñ]or Gobernador," BL; Annual Report for 1840, Mission San Rafael, SBMA; Edna Kimbo, Robert H. Jackson, and Mary Ellen Ryan, "Como la Sombra Huye la

Hora: Restoration Research, Santa Cruz Mission Adobe, Santa Cruz Mission State Historic Parks and Recreation" (unpublished MS, California Dept. of Parks and Recreation, 1985), 64–69, 104, 112–13, 137–56. See also Susanna B. Dakin, *Lives of William Hartnell* (Stanford, 1949), 213–29, 232; Alvarado, "Historia de California," 4: 144–45; Juana Machado, "Los Tiempos Pasados de la Alta California," MS (1878), 11–17, BL; Bancroft, *History of California*, 3: 614–15; 4: 67–77. Trading stolen horses is described in Robert Glass Cleland, *This Reckless Breed of Men: The Trappers and Fur Trappers of the Southwest* (Albuquerque, 1976), 270, 308–10. For the development of the ranchos, see David Hornbeck, "Land Tenure and Rancho Expansion in Alta California, 1784–1846," *Journal of Historical Geography* 4 (winter 1978), 371–90.

11. Quote from Durán to Figueroa, July 3, 1833, SBMA. See also Simpson, *The Letters of José Señán*, 2; C. Alan Hutchinson, "The Mexican Government and the Mission Indians of Upper California, 1821–1835," 350–51.

12. Agricultural statistics are from 1836. See J. A. Wilson, *History of Los Angeles County, California* (Oakland, 1880), 64; Léonce Jore, "Jean Louis Vignes of Bordeaux, Pioneer of California Viticulture," trans. L. Jay Oliva, *SCQ* 45 (winter 1963), 296; Cleve E. Kindall, "Southern Vineyards: The Economic Significance of the Wine Industry in the Development of Los Angeles, 1831–1870," *HSSCQ* 41 (June 1959), 30–31; Marguerite Eyer Wilbur, trans. and ed., *Duflot de Monfras' Travels on the Pacific Coast* (Santa Ana, 1937), 2: 185.

13. Quote from Emory, *Notes of a Military Reconnaissance*, 122. For the planting of one hundred thousand vines by 1833, see *Alta California*, Feb. 2, 1862. The number of mission field hands in 1830 is estimated at 104, and the number of gentile field hands at 157 in W. N. Charles, "Transcription and Translation of the Old Mexican Documents of the Los Angeles County Archives," *HSSCQ* 20 (June 1938), 84. For Vignes and field hands employed in the early Los Angeles wine industry, see Jean Luis Vignes [Misc. Notes], MS (n.d.), BL; Irving McKee, "Jean Louis Vignes: California's First Professional Wine Grower," *Wine Review* 16 (July and Sept. 1948), 12, 18; Gómez, "Lo Que Sabe Sobre Cosas de California," BL. For an overview of agriculture in Los Angeles at this time, see Howard Nelson, "The Two Pueblos of Los Angeles: Agricultural Village and Embryo Town," *SCQ* 59 (spring 1977). For the developing wine industry, see, Iris Ann Wilson, "Early Southern California Viniculture, 1830–1856," *SCQ* 39 (Sept. 1957), 242–50. Wages are from 1842 and are cited in Wilbur, *Duflot de Mofras' Travels*, 2: 186.

14. Quote from Engelhardt, *Missions and Missionaries*, 4: 110. Farm labor force numbers are extrapolated from the Census of 1836, 3: 514–32, LACA, which counted 223 mission Indians in Los Angeles, 533 in the district, and thirty-two gentiles. The census of 1836 also listed sixty-five farmworkers, presumably all of them natives. For a discussion of census figures and some convincing recalculations, see Hackel, "Land, Labor, and Production," in Orsi and Gutiérrez, *Contested Eden*, 136. For living conditions of the mission Indians, see *Ayuntamiento* Minutes (May 23, 1846), 2: 726–27, LACA [transcripts and copies in BL]; "Petition of the Indians Addressed to the Second Constitutional Alcalde," in *Ayuntamiento* Minutes (Apr. 27, 1838), 1: 487. Translations can be found in "Excerpts from the Archives of the *Ayuntamiento*, City of Los Angeles, California, 1832–1847," Misc. MS Collection 100, box 117, ASCUCLA. For the two communities, see Bernice E. Johnston, *California's Gabrielino Indians* (Los Angeles, 1962), 103; W. W. Robinson, *The Indians of Los Angeles: Story of the Liquidation of a People* (Los Angeles, 1952), 16–17. For the *zanja* laborers, see Vincent Ostrom, "The Los Angeles Water Supply," *Water and Politics* (Los Angeles, 1953), 3–26. For Wolfskill, see his son-in-law's account, H. D. Barrows, "William Wolfskill, the Pioneer," *HSSCAP* 5 (1902), 292–93; and the more extensive account in the *Wilmington (California) Journal*, Oct. 29, 1866. In William Wolfskill's vineyard, native men planted thirty-two thousand vines between 1838 and 1846. Their labor was no doubt one reason why Los Angeles wine production jumped to twenty-four thousand gallons in 1841, and Wolfskill alone was able to produce 180 casks (twenty-eight hundred gallons) of wine and an equal amount of *aguardiente* in 1846.

15. For arrests of drunken Indian field hands, see *Ayuntamiento* Minutes (Jan. 28, 1836), 2: 104–5, LACA [copies in BL]. For self-government among field hands, see *Ayuntamiento* Minutes (Mar. 11, 1838), 2: 185, ibid. For the petition against Juan Domingo, see "Petition of the Indians addressed to the Second Constitutional *Alcalde*," in *Ayuntamiento* Minutes (Apr. 27, 1838), 1: 487; (June 2, 1838), 2: 435. Census of 1844, 3: 603–26, LACA, counted 650 mission and pagan Indians in Los Angeles. About 210 could have worked as field hands. See Marie E. Northrop, ed., "The Los Angeles *Padrón* of 1844," *HSSCQ* 7 (Dec. 1960), 360–417. Hackel, "Land, Labor, and Production," 136, recalculates the number of Indians in Los Angeles in 1844,

finding that about 377 Indians lived in town, considerably less than the often cited figure of 650. Hackel estimates about 339 were laborers and concludes that the total number of Indians increased by roughly 50 percent, not the 300 percent suggested by Monroy, *Thrown Among Strangers*, 128; and Phillips, "Indians in Los Angeles," 436. The arrest policy for vagrancy can be followed in *Ayuntamiento* Minutes (Jan. 12, 1844), 2: 544–45, LACA; "1846 Verbal Transactions of the Second Justice's Court," Copy Book of Legal Cases in Los Angeles, 1840–1850, 1: 9–10, 18–19, 27, HL.

16. For field hands under custody of private citizens, see "1846 Verbal Transactions of the Second Justice's Court," Copy Book of Legal Cases in Los Angeles, 1840–1850, 1: 23–28, LACA. For farmers allocating field hands to clean the *zanjas*, see Bancroft, *California Pastoral*, 357. For vagrancy arrest orders, see Order issued by Jimeno Casarin, secretary to Governor Alvarado, AC, n.d., 11: 53, BL.

17. Quote from Pío Pico to William Hartnell, San Luis Rey mission, June 5, 1839, DSP, Missions, 11: 334–41; also SBMA. See also Jessie D. Francis, "An Economic and Social History of Mexican California, 1822–1846" (M.A. thesis, UCB, 1935), 503; Padre José Abella to José de la Guerra, San Luis Obispo mission, June 17, 1838, DLGP.

18. Quote from *Ayuntamiento* Minutes (Feb. 19, 1846), in W. W. Robinson ed., "The Indians of Los Angeles as Revealed by the Los Angeles City Archives," *HSSCQ* 20 (Dec. 1938), 167–68. See also Francisco Figueroa and Luis Vignes, Petition (Feb. 19, 1846), 1: 527–30; *Ayuntamiento* Minutes (May 12, 1845), 2: 287; (June 7, 1845), 2: 799–801; (Dec. 22, 1845), 2: 845–55; (Feb. 14, 1846), 1:37, LACA. Criminal problems, especially the growth of prostitution, can be seen in a survey of Criminal Cases in Los Angeles and Santa Barbara, 1830–1847, California Documents Collection, HL. Concerned with the increasing use of alcohol, citizens also appealed to Pío Pico, who had been declared governor following the overthrow of Governor Micheltorena in February 1845. Immediately issuing a Proclamation on Viticulture, Pico prohibited people from buying grapes or wine from Indians who, besides drinking in excess, apparently had been stealing grapes and making wine on the sly, and thus undermining local winemakers and not paying the required taxes. For Pico's edict, see Pío Pico, Proclamation on Viticulture, Sept. 6, 1845, California Mission doc. no. 3996, DSP, Angeles, 10: 259–60 [copy in SBMA].

19. *Ayuntamiento* Minutes (May 2, 1846), 2: 717; (May 9, 1846), 1: 721–22; (May 23, 1846), 2: 726–27, LACA. For the destruction of Pueblito, see Common Council Minutes (Oct. 30, 1847), 4: 497; (Nov. 8, 1847), 4: 507–8; (Nov. 20, 1847), 4: 510, LACA. Boys "unable to do a man's work" were excluded from laboring on the *zanjas*. But as in mission days, children did play an important role in viticulture. Armed with hats full of stones and slings, they spent most of each September, morning to night, watching over the crops from scaffolding erected in the middle of each vineyard. Their chief task consisted of firing their rocks at blackbirds, crows, and various animals that in some years could destroy half the harvest. Quote from Stephen C. Foster, circular, "Committee on Water Supply for the Year 1848," Feb. 4, 1848, LACA, 4: 533. For more on children, see Briton C. Busch, ed. and intro., *Alta California, 1840–1842: The Journal and Observations of William Dane Phelps, Master of the Ship "Alert"* (Glendale, Calif., 1983), 320, entry for Sept. 14, 1842. Field hands, said one who claimed to have seen them close up, were caught in "absolute vassalage, even more degrading, and more oppressive than that of our slaves in the south." They would "for many years, be as little expensive [*sic*] to the farmers of that country, as slave labor, being procured for a mere nominal consideration." Quote from Lansford W. Hastings, *The Emigrant's Guide to Oregon and California* (Cincinnati, 1845), 103, 132–33. Hastings's guide contains innumerable errors and exaggerations and should be used with care. However, his descriptions of field hands are consistent with the observations of others. For an analysis of Hastings's reliability and unreliability as an observer, see Thomas F. Andrews, "The Controversial Hastings Overland Guide: A Reassessment," *PHR* 37 (Feb. 1968), 21–34. See also Charles Camp, ed., *James Clyman: American Frontiersman, 1791–1881 . . . His Own Reminiscences and Diaries* (San Francisco, 1928), 186, observing how field hands were "kept in a state of slavery having or receiving no compensation for their labor except a scanty allowance of subsistence."

20. W. W. Robinson, *Ranchos Become Cities* (Pasadena, 1939), 11; Robinson, "The Dominguez Rancho," *HSSCQ* 35 (Dec. 1935), 345; Bancroft, *History of California*, 1: 609–11, 659–56.

21. Quotes from Monroy, "The Creation and Re-Creation of California Society," in Orsi and Gutiérrez, *Contested Eden*, 177; G. W. Beattie, "Life of a Rancher," 187, 216–17. Many years later, after the United States took control of California, many rancheros would lose title to

their lands, in part because of their casual mapping practices. See also Nellie Van de Grift Sánchez, *Spanish Arcadia* (Los Angeles, 1929), 185–97; W. A. Hawley, *The Early Days of Santa Barbara* (Santa Barbara, 1920), 94–100; Lillian Charlotte Lederer, "A Study of Anglo American Settlers in Los Angeles County Previous to the Admission of California to the Union" (M.A. thesis, USC, 1927), 38–46; Gerald Geary, *The Secularization of the California Missions, 1810–1846* (Washington, D. C., 1934). See also Terry Stephenson, *Don Bernardo Yorba* (Los Angeles, 1941), 27; Bruce Conde, "Santa Ana of the Yorbas," *HSSCQ* 21 (May 1939), 78. See also M. R. Harrington, trans., "Will of Don Tomás Yorba Year 1845," *HSSCQ* 33 (Mar. 1951), 30–33; Stephenson, "Tomás Yorba, his wife Vicenta, and his Account Book," ibid., 23 (Sept. 1941), 138, 144, 148, 150.

22. Paul Bryan Gray, *Forster vs. Pico: The Struggle for the Rancho Santa Margarita* (Spokane, 1998), 52–53.

23. Gregg Layne, "The First Census of the Los Angeles District: Padrón de la Ciudad de Los Angeles y su jurisdicción año 1836," *HSSCQ* 18 (Sept.–Dec. 1936), 38–40; original census, 59–60. Holding all of this together on several ranchos was a class of Indian women, often under the direction of the ranchero's wife. Working in the kitchens and around the house as servants and cooks, Indian women servants planted and tended gardens between chores chopping wood and washing clothes. Watching them at work during a visit to California in 1834, the American traveler Edwin Bryant was struck by the multiplicity of roles that certain Indian women played on the ranchos. They milked cows and made dairy products for sale and trade, cleaned house, cooked for large families and numbers of men, and carried out myriad other activities. While the men "are employed in attending to herds of cattle and horses, and engaged in their other amusements," recalled Bryant, "the women . . . superintend and perform most of the drudgery appertaining to housekeeping, and the cultivation of the gardens." Quote from Edwin Bryant, *What I Saw In California* (1846 [Santa Ana, 1936]), 448. See also Híjar, "Recuerdos," 9; Lugo, "Vida de un Ranchero," 76–77; Juan Bandini to Eustace Barron, Dec. 8, 1828, ASP; Henry Dalton, diary, Apr. 23, 1845, 1: 8, HDC.

24. Quote from Salvador Vallejo, "Notas Históricas Sobre California," MS (1874), MSS C-D 22, BL. See also Alice M. Cleaveland, "The North Bay Shore, During the Spanish and Mexican Regimes" (M.A. thesis, UCB, 1932), 120, 130–31; B. G. Rousseau, "Early History of the City of Vallejo," *Overland Monthly* 81 (Aug. 1923), 20–21; Thomas Savage, "Documentos Para la Historia de California," MS (n.d.), AC, 2: 6–7; Myrtle M. McKittrick, *Vallejo, Son of California* (Portland, Ore., 1944), 83, 91–93, 336.

25. Quoted in Engelhardt, *Missions and Missionaries*, 4: 136.

26. Quote from Simpson, *Narrative*, 177–78. For military-like organization on Rancho Azusa, see Henry Dalton, diary, Mar. 18, 1845, HDC. See also Sanchez, *The Spanish Period*, 432–35; Híjar, "Recollections," 15–17, 35; E. J. Pleasants, "A Visit to Santiago Canyon," *Orange County History Series* 1 (1931), 141–42; W. W. Robinson, *The Story of the San Fernando Valley* (Los Angeles, 1961), 17.

27. Archaeological exploration confirms that Indian field hands on several ranchos continued manufacturing countless implements, including their own pottery. As for wages and compensation, in at least one case they received nothing. When Indians on Rancho San Bernardino finished the season, Tiburcio Tapia refused to pay them and drove them from his property. See Roberta S. Greenwood, "The California Ranchero: Fact and Fancy," in *Columbian Consequences*, 451–65; Gerald Smith, *The Indian Slave Trade along the Mojave Trail* (San Bernardino, 1965), 5–10.

28. Robert W. Brackett, *A History of the Ranchos: The Spanish, Mexican and American Occupation of San Diego County and the Ownership of the Land Grants Therein* (San Diego, 1939), 2–3. For Cañada de Santa Ana, see "Life of a Rancher," 451–65. Debt peonage on San Luis Rey mission can be followed in José Antonio Pico, "Account Book for the year 1847 [with a fragment from 1845]," MS, signed by J. B. Charbonneau, *alcalde*, discovered at San Juan Capistrano mission, trans. St. John O'Sullivan, SBMA.

29. Quote from Mexican Archives, Monterey County, 1835–46, 12: 681; 11: 195, Monterey County Historical Society [copies courtesy Gary S. Breschini], index Monterey Public Library. The documents do not say whether or not the Santa Clara mission *mayordomo* was replaced. John Walton, *Storied Land*, 96–97, 128, makes more extensive use of these sources. See also David Langum, *Law and Community on the Mexican California Frontier: Anglo American Expatriates and the Clash of Legal Traditions, 1821–1846* (Norman, Okla., 1987), 10.

30. For Fort Ross, see James Clifford, *Routes: Travel and Translation in the Late Twentieth Century* (Cambridge, Mass., 1997), 299–343. Russian agronomists raised that first orchard from seedlings grown from the pits of peaches brought from Peru on the schooner *Chirikov*. Seedlings and cuttings for pear, olive, grape, fig, and cherry trees were carried north from the California missions, principally Carmel, and from trade ships, mainly from Peru and Chile. As ties deepened, more natives relocated their rancherías closer to the fort in order to maximize contact with their family members, supply colonists with food, and earn more income as seasonal wage laborers and field hands. Because the Russians were uninterested in converting anyone to their beliefs, Kashaya Pomo enjoyed the benefits of a flexible system of rewards and constraints that left their culture intact, even as they adopted Euro-American food habits like bread and flour. Although outlying tribes raided stock, local Pomo and Russian settlers rarely fought. Probably the worst incident occurred in 1832, when a settler killed a Kashaya Pomo woman and her settler husband, apparently mistaking the couple for stock raiders. In retaliation local Pomo settled the score by attacking herds and killing several horses, but they spared the settlers. See P. A. Tikhmenev, *A History of the Russian-American Company*, ed. and trans. Richard A. Pierce and Alton S. Donnelly (Seattle, 1978), 139–40, 418–19; Bickford O'Brien, ed., *Fort Ross: Indians-Russians-Americans* (Jenner, Calif., 1980), 9; Diane Spencer-Hancock and William E. Pritchard, "Notes to the 1817 Treaty between the Russian American Company and Kashaya Pomo Indians," *CH* 59 (fall 1981), 306–13. For an excellent bibliography with materials on Fort Ross, see W. Michael Mathes, *La Frontera Ruso-Mexicana: Documentos Mexicanos para la historia del establecimiento ruso en California, 1808–1842* (Mexico City, 1990), 27–44. See also Robert Oswalt, *Kashaya Texts* (Berkeley, 1964), 269. See also Helen Pruit Beattie, "José Carmen Lugo," 185–236; Roy Elmer Whitehead, *Lugo: A Chronicle of Early California* (Redlands, Calif., 1978), 13–37; George William Beattie, "San Bernardino Valley before the Americans Came," *CHSQ* 12 (June 1933), 11–124; George P. Hammond and Dale L. Morgan, *Captain Charles M. Weber, Pioneer of the San Joaquin and Founder of Stockton, California* (Berkeley, 1966).

31. Quote from José Figueroa, "Diary of an Expedition to Fort Ross, Led by General Figueroa," MS (Aug. 9–Sept. 12, 1834), entry for Aug. 23, BL. For sentries, see Nicholas Del Cioppo, ed. and trans., "Diary of Padre Mariano Payeras: Travels of the Cañon Fernández de San Vicente to Ross," MS (n.d.), 2, BL. See also James R. Gibson, *Imperial Russia in Frontier America* (New York, 1976), 130. That Ross was really a very modest fort better referred to as Colony Ross is the point of E. Breck Parkman, "Fort and Settlement: Interpreting the Past at Fort Ross State Historic Park," *CH* (winter 1996–97), 354–69, 387–89. I have followed its official title of Fort Ross. See also "The Russian Colonies in California: A Russian Version"; E. O. Essig, "The Russian Settlement at Ross"; Adele Ogden, "Russian Sea-Otter and Seal Hunting in the California Coast, 1803–1841," in *CHSQ* 12 (Sept. 1933), 189–239; Papers Concerning Fort Ross, California, 1927–48, 9 folders [E. O. Essig comp.], BL. Kostromitinov farm has not yet been uncovered, although most archaeologists place it on or near Willow Creek, the first tributary upstream on the Russian River. The Khlebnikov farm was located near the present-day town of Bodega. Chernykh farm was located on Coleman Valley Road near present-day Occidental. See E. Breck Parkman to author, June 24, 26, 2002, author's possession.

32. According to one observer, as many as 150 Indians would be rounded up, marched off to Fort Ross, sent out to the various farms, and forced to work in the fields for as long as six weeks without rest or compensation. During one particularly gruesome roundup in 1838, Fort Ross settlers trooped inland forty-three miles and attacked a ranchería, tying up seventy-five men, women, and children. Driven to the fort like cattle, they were immediately kept under surveillance by sentinels as they gathered and threshed grain. Becoming increasingly belligerent, many refused to work and began stealing large amounts of wheat. After raiding parties swept in, burned several fields, and killed as many as one hundred head of cattle, the Russians, now fearing famine, retained large amounts of food normally sent to their trappers. They also purchased additional foodstuffs from San Francisco de Solano mission, and from at least one local Indian chief, Camillo Ynitia of Olompali, a coastal Miwok village located on the road from San Rafael mission to Francisco de Solano mission. Although the Russians abandoned Fort Ross in 1841 when the sea otter population collapsed, they probably could not have continued much longer. Unable to round up Indians and force them to work, the Russians could not grow the crops necessary for sustaining their fur hunting operations. Quote from Vassili Petrovich Tarakanoff, "Statement of Vassili Petrovich Tarakanoff, a Hunter in the Employ of the Russian American Company," *Morskoi Sbornik*, trans. Ivan Petroff, MS (Nov. 1852), 4–5, BL. Roundup

figures and attacks are described in Gibson, *Imperial Russia*, 128–31. Harsh treatment of native field hands is described in Del Cioppo, ed. and trans., "Report to Mariano G. Vallejo: Confidential Information Concerning the Ross Settlement, 1833," MS (1979), 6, BL [copy in California Dept. Parks and Recreation, Sacramento].

33. George D. Lyman, *John Marsh, Pioneer: The Life Story of a Trail-blazer on Six Frontiers* (New York, 1931), 220, 291; Emily June Ulsh, "Doctor John Marsh, California Pioneer, 1836–1856" (M.A. thesis, UCB, 1928); Flora Loretta De Nier, "Robert Livermore and the Development of Livermore Valley to 1860" (M.A. thesis, UCB, 1926); Charles L. Camp, ed., *George C. Yount and his Chronicles of the West, Comprising Extracts from His "Memoirs" and from the Orange Clark "Narrative"* (Denver, 1966), viii, 123, 128–29, 143.

34. Quotes from John Bidwell, "Address" [delivered to the Society of California Pioneers on November 1, 1897], *Quarterly of the Society of California Pioneers* 3 (Mar. 31, 1926), 9–10; Edwin Gudde, trans., "Edward Vischer's First Visit to California," *CHSQ* 19 (Sept. 1939), 6–8; Mary E. Bucknall, *Early Days* [In the Napa Valley] (San Francisco, ca. 1900), BL. See also Mariano Guadalupe Vallejo, "Historical and Personal Memoirs Relating to Alta California," trans. Earl R. Hewitt, MS (1877), 4: 23, BL; Theodore T. Johnson, *Sights in the Gold Region and Scenes by the Way* (New York, 1849), 143; Wallace W. Elliot and Co., *History of Fresno County, California, with Illustrations* (San Francisco, 1882), 184; Wallace Smith, *Garden of the Sun: A History of the San Joaquin Valley, 1772–1939* (Los Angeles, 1939), 76–107, 552–53.

35. Quote from Richard Dillon, *Captain John Sutter: Sacramento Valley's Sainted Sinner* (New York, 1967), 89; also 15–91. See also the reminiscences of Maximo in "An Aged Indian Chief," *Sacramento Daily Record Union*, May 25, 1885; Nunis, "A Mysterious Chapter in the Life of John A. Sutter," *CHSQ* 38 (Dec. 1959), 321–27; John A. Hawgood, "John Augustus Sutter: A Reappraisal," *Arizona and the West* 4 (winter 1962), 345–56; Richard Peterson, "Sutter and the Indians," *The Californian* 3 (Mar.–Apr., 1985), 24–27; Patricia Nelson Limerick, *Something in the Soil: Legacies and Reckonings in the New West* (New York, 2000), 128; Robert Dawson and Gray Brechin, *Farewell, Promised Land: Waking from the California Dream* (Berkeley, 1999), 35; Marguerite E. Wilbur, ed. and trans., *A Pioneer at Sutter's Fort, 1846–1850: The Adventures of Heinrich Lienhard* (Los Angeles, 1941), 3; Donald Dale Jackson, *Gold Dust: The Saga of the Forty-Niners* (New York, 1980), 7–8, 10–12, 34, 240–41, 333; James P. Zollinger, *Sutter: The Man and His Empire* (New York, 1939), 6–9, 104; Howard R. Lamar, "John Augustus Sutter, Wilderness Entrepreneur," in Kenneth N. Owens, ed., *John Sutter and a Wider West* (Lincoln, Neb., 1994), 26–50.

36. For gifts, contracting through native headmen, and initial contacts, see John Sutter to John Marsh, Oct. 7, 1840, JMC; John C. Frémont, *Memoirs of My Life* (Chicago, 1887), 1: 351; Wilbur, *A Pioneer at Sutter's Fort*, 7, 86. Miwok headmen included Anashe, the principal headman; Maximo, who had been in the business of supplying field hands to San José mission after secularization; Narciso, a former San José mission neophyte and village chieftain; Rufino, another Miwok headman; and Simplon, another headman who would become *alcalde* of field hands at Sutter's Fort. More than one generation before the appearance of the Chinese crew bosses who are traditionally described as the first farm labor contractors, these *capitanos* were fulfilling that function. Maximo's career and relationship with Sutter can be followed in "The Dead Chieftain," *Sacramento Daily Record Union*, May 25, 1886. For Narciso, see Vallejo, "Historical and Personal Memoirs," 4: 28; Sutter to Gov. Juan B. Alvarado, n.d., 1841, DSP, 17: 33. For Simplon, see Thomas H. Thompson and Albert A. West, *History of Sacramento County, California, with Illustrations* (Oakland, 1880), 35. For Rufino, see Sutter et al., *New Helvetia Diary: A Record of Events kept by John A. Sutter and His Clerks at New Helvetia, California, From September 9, 1845, to May 25, 1848* (San Francisco, 1939), 2, 9, 33–34; Albert L. Hurtado, *Indian Survival on the California Frontier* (New Haven, 1988), 48–49. For Eusebio, see Joseph Warren Revere, *Tour of Duty in California* (New York, 1849), 155; Sutter to Leidesdorff, June 1, July 22, 1846, WLC.

37. Acting in his self-appointed role as a kind of marriage broker who had initially banned the practice of polygamy, Sutter catered to his headmen by lining up all the Indian men and women in rows opposite one another, having the women step forward and select the husbands they wanted, prohibiting all the chiefs from taking more than one wife, and then, to accommodate his headmen, exempting them from the ban. See Sutter, *New Helvetia Diary*, 5–6. For relationships with other headmen, see Mayo E. Wheeler, "John A. Sutter, a California Pioneer; an Historical Sketch and Collection of Correspondence" (M.A. thesis, UCB, 1924), 426; Edwin G. Gudde, ed., "The Memoirs of Theodore Cordua, the Pioneer of New Mecklenburg in the Sacramento Valley," *CHSQ* 12 (Dec. 1933), 309; Joseph T. Downey, *Filings from an Old*

Saw: Reminiscences of San Francisco and California's Conquest, ed. Fred B. Rogers (San Francisco, 1956), 19.

38. Quotes from Helen Putnam Van Sicklen, ed., *A Sojourn in California by the King's Orphan: The Travels and Sketches of G. M. Waseurtz Sandels, a Swedish gentleman who visited California in 1842–1843* (San Francisco, 1945), 72–73; Busch, *The Journal of William Dane Phelps*, 208. For Phelps, see also Webfoot [William D. Phelps], *Fore and Aft; Or, Leaves from the Life of an Old Sailor* (Boston, 1871), 258. For polygamy, see John A. Sutter, "Personal Reminiscences of General John Augustus Sutter," MS (1876), 38–39; also 44–46, BL.

39. Sutter to Lt. Henry Halleck, Dec. 20, 1847, MS, 50–51, GMP; "The Launch of a Tug Boat," *Sacramento Daily Union*, Sept. 29, 1862; Sutter, "Personal Reminiscences," 44–46. Field hands did feel a heightened loyalty to Sutter after Oct. 15, 1840, when the angry chief of the Yalecumnes abandoned his men working in the fields and stormed into Sutter's Fort reporting that a band of San José mission Indians had attacked his ranchería, dashing out the brains of old women and murdering five Yalecumnes. Promising to take action, Sutter assembled a force of white men and Indians and tracked down and executed by firing squad fourteen of the San José mission Indians deemed responsible for the violence. Sutter to José de Jesús Vallejo, Oct. 15, 1840, JSC; Sutter to Pierson B. Reading, May 10, 11, 1845, PBRC; Sutter to Marsh, May 17, 1845, JMC. See also Dillon, *Captain Sutter*, 105.

40. E. Gould Buffum, *Six Months in the Gold Mines* (Philadelphia, 1850), 54–55; Samuel C. Upham, *Notes of a Voyage to California* (Philadelphia, 1878), 318–20; Hipolite Ferry, *Description de la Nouvelle Californie* (Paris, 1850), 97; Marvin Brienes, "East of Sutter's Fort: Block K-L28-29 in Sacramento, 1840–1955" [Report prepared for Sutter Community Hospitals, Sacramento City Planning Division, 1983]. Like much of the material at Fort Sutter, the cannon had been obtained in 1841 along with livestock and other property and equipment at small cost from the Russians when they abandoned Fort Ross.

41. Quote from Wilbur, *A Pioneer at Sutter's Fort*, 68; also 7. For huts, see Busch, *The Journal of William Dane Phelps*, 199, 208. For destruction of the dance house, see Sutter, *New Helvetia Diary*, 123. For disease and medical care, see Sutter to Larkin, Nov. 5, 1845, TOLP; John Williams to Thomas Larkin, July 28, 1847, in George P. Hammond, ed., *The Larkin Papers* (Berkeley, 1951–68), 6: 241; Halleck to Sutter, Aug. 16, 1847, GLB.

42. Quote from Wilbur, *A Pioneer at Sutter's Fort*, 3; also 77. Limerick, *Something in the Soil*, 138, labels this part of "a long-running tradition in the battles that punctuated the invasion and conquest of North America." For military expeditions, see Sutter to Pierson B. Reading, May 8, 11, 1845, PBRC; Wilkes, *Narrative of the United States Exploring Expedition*, 182–83.

43. Bells or drums sounded throughout the day. Called here, dispatched there, assembled for lunch, dismissed for afternoon labor, summoned again for the evening meal, field hands heard bells well into the night as a soldier patrolling the fort struck a small hand bell at half-hour intervals while calling out, "All is well." For the bulldog, see Erwin G. Gudde, *Sutter's Own Story* (New York, 1936), 55; clipping, *San Francisco Argonaut*, n.d., Bancroft Scrapbooks, BL. For medical care and disease, see Fred Blackburn Rogers, ed., *Marius Duvall, A Navy Surgeon in California, 1846–1847: The Journal of Marius Duvall* (San Francisco, 1957), 17. For bells and drums, see John Yates, "Sketch of a Journey in the Year 1842 from Sacramento California through the valley by John Yates of Yatestown," MS (n.d.), BL; Sutter, "Personal Reminiscences," 45.

44. Quotes from Sutter to Suñol, May 19, 1845, JSC; Marsh to Suñol, June 16, 1845, JMC. See also Francis, "A History of Mexican California," 507, which compares Sutter's rental arrangement with the practice whereby slave owners in the antebellum South sent slaves "down river." Nothing more clearly demonstrated Sutter's power to do as he wanted with natives than his custom of presenting young Indian girls as gifts to friends. And nothing more clearly demonstrated his own personal proclivities than the special girls' room he kept next to his chambers where, according to his overseer, Sutter maintained a "large number of Indian girls," many as young as ten years of age, who were "constantly at his beck and call." See Sutter to Leidesdorff, Apr. 17, May 11, 1846, WLC; Wilbur, *A Pioneer at Sutter's Fort*, 76–77; John Chamberlain, "Memoirs of California Since 1840," MS (1877), BL. A few rented field hands ran away even before departing, or they bided their time, waiting for a chance to escape from their new employers, quietly slipping off a month or two into their work. For the income Sutter achieved by renting labor to Leidesdorff to reduce part of his $2,198.10 debt, see "Account of William A. Leidesdorff," Aug. 1, 1844, to Jan. 27, 1846; Sutter to Leidesdorff, May 11, 1846, WLC. Sutter's

rental arrangements can be followed in Sutter to Suñol, June 18, 29; Aug. 30, 1844; June 14, 1845, JSC; Sutter to Marsh, May 17, 1845, JMC; Sutter to Henry Delano Fitch, Apr. 17, 1846, HDFP.

45. Sutter to Leidesdorff, July 31, 1845, WLC. The necklaces and pay arrangements are described in Sutter, *New Helvetia Diary*, 27; Sutter, "Personal Reminiscences," 41; Bryant, *What I Saw In California*, 267–68. For clothing, see Sutter to Leidesdorff, July 31, 1845, WLC; Donald Jackson and Mary Lee Spence, eds., *The Expeditions of John Charles Frémont* (Urbana, Ill., 1970–73), 1: xix–xx, 654–55, 664.

46. Quotes from Camp, *James Clyman*, 173–74; Hans Jørgen Uldall and William Shipley, comps., "Nisenan Texts and Dictionary," *University of California Publications in Linguistics* (Berkeley, 1966), 46: 67. Feeding arrangements are similarly described in Wilbur, *A Pioneer at Sutter's Fort*, 7, 68; Benjamin Barney, *Across the Plains by Prairie Schooner* (Eugene, Ore., 1924), 11–12. Visitors who did not understand that the Indians considered sweet clover, grasshoppers, and acorn meal as treats were disgusted to see Sutter turning Indians loose to "graze."

47. For winemaking and distilling, see Sutter to Marsh, Oct. 7, 1845, JSCP; Yates, "Sketch of the Sacramento Valley," 15. Although Julian Dana, *Sutter of California: A Biography* (New York, 1934), 203–4, asserts Sutter planted his first wheat crop in Mar. 1845, William Dane Phelps, visiting Sutter on Apr. 6, 1842, found Sutter had already planted three hundred acres of wheat. See Busch, *The Journal of William Dane Phelps*, 283. As roustabouts or general workers, Sutter's Indians handled a great deal of "set-up work"—cutting out brush, chopping and rolling logs, grubbing out stumps, lopping off small trees and shrubs, and piling refuse in heaps for burning. This process was generally known as "smacking smooth" or "smacking clear." The best information on day-to-day farmwork is Seymour Dunbar, ed., *The Fort Sutter Papers, Together with Historical Commentaries Accompanying Them, Brought Together in One Volume for Purposes of Reference*, 39 vols. (n.p., 1922). The original materials, collected by Captain Edward Kern at Sutter's Fort, with his annotations and editorial commentaries, are in HL. Because the valley floor was not heavily forested or overgrown with brush, sod-busting work and rough plowing absorbed far more time than set up work. Field hands usually tackled this task in the spring, after being instructed by Sutter's overseers in the complicated tasks of hitching and directing teams and guiding plows. At peak times, they ran thirty plows simultaneously with fresh oxen to pull them each morning, a sod-busting regimen made even more strenuous because at first Sutter lacked the ponderous but effective heavy plows employed by American farmers at that time. Because their initial cuts did little more than skip across the thickly interwoven roots and "devil's shoe-strings," native prairie breakers had to struggle mightily to rip open the matted grasslands, often making many passes before they could finish-plow and plant. Furthermore, the constant need to resharpen their plow tips required them to make innumerable trips back to the blacksmith shop at the fort. See Sutter, "Reminiscences," 46. For blacksmith activities required to maintain and repair plows and farm tools, see Sutter, *New Helvetia Diary*, 14–18, entries for Nov. and Dec. 1845; and 18–25, entries for Dec. 15, 1845, to Feb. 1, 1846. For more information on work, see Sutter to Leidesdorff, Aug. 8, 1844, WLC; various materials relating to agriculture in the Charles Weber Collection, BL. Men also cut, split, and hauled huge quantities of wood for an enormous fence, three miles in length and the longest such fence in California, which was necessary to protect Sutter's wheat field from marauding animals and livestock. More commonly, they secured crops against cattle and horses by cutting deep ditches around their fields, another backbreaking task. But even as some crews were establishing grainfields and surrounding them with fences and ditches, others were planting a ten-acre irrigated garden beside the American River. See Sutter, *New Helvetia Diary*, viii, and entries of Oct. 13, Nov. 18, 1845, summer 1846, and throughout spring 1847; Joseph Henry Jackson, *Anybody's Gold: The Story of California's Mining Towns*, intro. Wallace Stegner (San Francisco, 1970), 13, 15.

48. For aspects of harvesting, see Wilbur, *Duflot de Mofras' Travels*, 2: 251–54; Sutter, "Personal Reminiscences," 43; Sutter, *New Helvetia Diary*, 50–96; Sutter to Leidesdorff, Sept. 10, 1847; Sutter to Leidesdorff, Oct. 13, 1847, WLC.

49. Bryant, *What I Saw In California*, 245–46, 267–68. See also Thompson and West, *History of Sacramento County*, 37–38; Sutter, *New Helvetia Diary*, June 30, 1847; Dana, *Sutter*, 264, 274.

50. In desperation Sutter wrote to Thomas O. Larkin, the U.S. counsel at Monterey: "If I could get these machines before next harvest about month of June it would safe [*sic*] me Thousands of Dollars." In all likelihood Sutter, Larkin, and Captain Phelps were the only people in California who knew of the value of the recent inventions, with Phelps perhaps the only one who had seen them. But Larkin, with his eye on the bottom line and Sutter's mounting debts,

refused to help. This directly affected Sutter's field hands. Quotes from Sutter to Larkin, [July 23], 1845, TOLP; Reuben L. Underhill, *From Cowhands to Golden Fleece: A Narrative of California, 1832–1858* (Stanford, 1939), 38–50. For population figures, see [George McKinstry], Nov. 1846 [Population Enumeration of the Sacramento Valley], MS, 12–15; Sutter to Halleck, Dec. 20, 1847, MS, 14–15, GMP; reprinted in Thompson and West, *History of Sacramento County, California*, 191.

51. Heavy implements with curved blades attached to a long-handled pole, scythes were so massive that they could have been used as coulter blades mounted in front of the plow blade to cut the ground in advance of a plowshare. To use a scythe properly, a laborer gripped the pole with both hands and swung it in a long, lazy arch, clipping the grain stalks just above the ground. One native, a six-and-a-half-foot-tall, heavily muscled, tireless old man named Laban, earned Sutter's respect for being the only Indian who could wield a scythe. Working steadily, he could cut two or three acres per day, compared to about three-quarters of an acre with a sickle. See Dana, *Sutter*, 203, 285. Harvest speed estimates are based on William T. Hutchinson, *Cyrus Hall McCormick*, 1: 71–72.

52. The harvest is described in detail in John Bidwell, *Life in California Before the Gold Discovery* (Palo Alto, Calif., 1966), 29–30; Bidwell, "Dictation Material" [1895], typescript, 59, SCML. This typescript is nearly the same as the "Dictation" [1891], BL, but has different pagination and lacks Bidwell's handwritten corrections.

53. Quotes from Sutter, "To Mechanics" [dated Feb. 1847], *California Star*, Apr. 3, 1847, Bancroft Scrapbooks, BL; Sutter, "Personal Reminiscences," 43. For manufacturing iron plows, see Sutter to Larkin, New Helvetia, Nov. 5, [Dec.], 1845, TOLP; Dana, *Sutter*, 287, 280.

54. For cradles, see Thomas H. Thompson and Albert A. West, *History of Yuba County, California* (San Francisco, 1879), 30. Sutter did not indicate the make of his cradles or his fanning mill, which most likely arrived with the overland wagon trains of 1846. Sutter's first cradlemen were not Indians but Mormon immigrants and had apparently used cradles before. For the 1847 harvest, see Sutter, *New Helvetia Diary*, 90–91; Milo Milton Quaife, ed., *Echoes from the Past, by General John Bidwell; In Camp and Cabin by Rev. John Steele* (Chicago, 1928), 43–44, 82–83; Sutter's reminiscences reprinted in *The Argonaut*, n.d., clipping, Bancroft Scrapbooks, BL; Sutter to Leidesdorff, New Helvetia, Sept. 10, Oct. 13, 1847 [complaining of lack of field hands], WLP. Compared to farmworkers in the vineyards of Los Angeles, those at Sutter's Fort lived a life of comfort and leisure. Although they occasionally fought and gambled, they did not engage in tumultuous drunken brawls among themselves, did not stab and murder one another by the dozens, did not regularly drink themselves into a stupor and pass out in the dust. For Anashe's ranchería, see Bryant, *What I Saw*, 344. For the Lower Cosumnes natives, see George F. Wyman, deposition, San Francisco, Sept. 6, 1853, in Transcript of Proceedings in Case no. 523, Hicks and Martin, Claimants, v. the United States, Defendant, for the Place Named "Cosumnes," U.S. Land Claims 240, n.d.: 28, BL; Sutter, deposition, San Francisco, Sept. 14, 1853, in ibid., 34; Sutter, *New Helvetia Diary*, 25, 43, 61–62, 90, 96–98, 111, 124–25, 128.

55. John Sutter to [unknown], New Helvetia, May 18, 1845, published in the *California Farmer*, Mar. 13, 1857; Sutter to Larkin, July 22, 1845, TOLP; John Hawgood, "The Pattern of Yankee Infiltration in Mexican Alta California," *PHR* 27 (Feb. 1958), 27–38.

56. Quotes from John Bidwell, "A Journey to California," in Nunis, *The Bidwell-Bartleson Party: 1841 California Emigrant Adventure* (Santa Cruz, 1991), 61; Reading to brother, Feb. 7, 1844, PBRC. For Lassen, see R. J. Swartzlow, *Lassen: His Life and Legacy* (Chico, Calif., 1964), 16, 20, 24, 26; Frémont, *Memoirs of My Life*, 1: 473. See also Josiah Belden, *Josiah Belden, 1841 California Overland Pioneer: His Memoir and Early Letters*, ed., Doyce B. Nunis Jr. (Georgetown, Calif., 1962), 54, 58, 88. For Euro-American field hands on Rancho de los Putos, see John R. Wolfskill, deposition, in U.S. District Court Records, United States v. Wolfskill, 1854, Case No. 232, Records of the Northern District, San Francisco, 34–34, CSA; Ellen L. Wood, "Samuel Green McMahan," *CHSQ* 23 (Dec. 1944), 289; Tom Gregory, *History of Sonoma County* (Los Angeles, 1911), 1: 490. Like Bidwell and Reading, Lassen had also worked briefly at Sutter's Fort and, upon settling on a Mexican land grant farther north, relied on nearby Indians to plant cotton, wheat, and vine cuttings from Los Angeles, and over the next few years build a store, adobe cabin, blacksmith shop, gristmill, and bunkhouse. Among settlers, there was a debate over whether or not Indians were equal to black slaves. One prevailing argument held that Indian labor was "about half as good . . . as Missouri Negroes." Quote from "Letter of Dr. John Marsh to Hon. Lewis Cass," *CHSQ* 22 (Dec. 1943), 316, 318, 320, widely reprinted, for example,

in the *Contra Costa Gazette*, Dec. 21, 1867. See also *History of Monterey County California, with Illustrations* (San Francisco, 1881), 35–39; *Overland Monthly* 38 (Feb. 1890), 216; Robert Semple, "Sketch of the Country," in Lansford W. Hastings, *A New History of Oregon and California* (Cincinnati, 1849), 154. Marsh, who housed an entire tribe of Coastal Miwoks at Los Méganos, bragged that it was not long before he had "the whole tribe for willing serfs." Quote from Essex [John Marsh] to editor, *New Orleans Picayune*, Feb. 1846; also Richard Fulton to Marsh, June 12, 1843, JMC. See also Forbes, *History of Upper and Lower California*, 173; John T. Hughes, *California, Its History, Population, Climate, Soils, Productions, and Harbors* (Cincinnati, 1848), 79; Lyman, *John Marsh*, 291; Gertrude Steger, "A Chronology of the Life of Pierson B. Reading," *CHSQ* 22 (Dec. 1943), 365–71.

57. Underhill, *From Cowhides*; Dwight L. Clarke, *Stephen Watts Kearney, Soldier of the West* (New York, 1961); Ferol Egan, *Frémont, Explorer for a Restless Nation* (New York, 1977); *California Star*, Dec. 11, 1847; Neil Harlow, *California Conquered: The Annexation of A Mexican Province, 1846–1850* (Berkeley, 1982), 276, 292–95.

58. Quotes from *California Star*, Feb. 20, Jan. 16, 1847. See also Senate, *Messages from the President . . . Communicating Information Called for by . . . the Senate . . . Relating to California and New Mexico*, 31st Cong., 1st sess., 1850, serial 557, 334–35; Delilah Beasley, "Slavery in California," *JNH* 3 (Jan. 1918), 36.

59. Quote from James Rawls, *Indians of California: The Changing Image* (Norman, Okla., 1984), 85. See also *California Star*, Sept. 18, 1847. See also Filipa Osuna de Marrón, "Reminiscences," interview by Thomas Savage, Jan. 26, 1878, BL, describing native field hands picking corn, beans, and other crops, and later being arrested and executed for allegedly plotting against San Diego mission administrators.

60. Sutter to Mason, July 12, 1847, in *Messages from the President*, 351; Mason to Sutter, July 21, GLB; *California Star*, July 24, 1847; unidentified clipping, n.d., Bancroft Scrapbooks, BL; Charles White to R. B. Mason, July 16, 1848, AC. See also Camp, *George Yount*, 152; Dillon, *Captain Sutter*, 271–74; Bancroft, *History of California*, 5: 568, 610. Kidnapping had by this time grown into a major criminal pursuit, with perhaps as many as one-fifth of the Indian population forcibly removed during the early 1840s. Understandably, in the early months of military rule, it was important for commanders to assert control over this case as it was a widely reported crime that threatened to incite an Indian rebellion. For kidnapping in 1846, see J. W. Revere, *A Tour of Duty in California* (New York, 1849), 88, 114. For the activity of Antonio and Victor Castro, "the Castro brothers," two notorious kidnappers who sold Indian children to ranchers around San Pablo, see Vallejo to Governor, 1836, DPLHC, 3: 112.

61. Quotes from Halleck to Sutter, Halleck to Vallejo, Aug. 16, 1847; also Mason, "Proclamation," Sept. 6, 1847; "Circular to Indian Agents and Others," Sept. 6, 1847, GLB; *California Star*, Sept. 18, 1847; also Dec. 11. A final edict, issued on Nov. 29, promised severe punishment to anyone selling liquor to Indians and held Indians to be competent witnesses in trials to prosecute all who violated the edict. See Ellison, *A Self-Governing Dominion*, 141. Mason and other authorities had two goals. They wanted to thwart Indian stock raiders and keep field hands at work. To accomplish this, they kept up a constant stream of ever more detailed edicts concerning Indian behavior. See Sherman to John Burton, Sept. 6, 1847, in *Messages from the President*, 347–48. See also Fernando F. Fernandez, "Except a California Indian," *SCQ* 50 (June 1968), 161–75.

62. William T. Sherman to John Burton, Sept. 6, 1847, Charles Weber Collection, BL; J. D. Stevenson to C. S. Foster, Feb. 24, 1848, LACA, 2: 672.

63. Quotes from Bryant, *What I Saw*, 435; *California Star*, Dec. 11, 1847, Bancroft Scrapbooks, BL.

64. Quotes from Richard B. Mason to adjutant general, Washington, D.C., Aug. 17, 1848, also known as "Mason's Report," in Rodman Paul, ed., *The California Gold Discovery, Sources, Documents, Accounts and Memoirs* (Georgetown, Calif., 1967) 95–96; Jacques A. Moerenhaut, *The Inside Story of the Gold Rush*, trans. and ed. Abraham P. Nasatir (San Francisco, 1953), 3. See also Larkin to Charles Oliver Sterling and John S. Williams, July 28, 1848, TOLP. See also Dillon, *Captain Sutter*, 295; Edward G. Buffum, *Six Months in California*, 83; Sutter, "The Discovery of Gold in California," *Hutching's Illustrated California Magazine* 2 (Nov. 1857), 197; James H. Carson, *Recollections of the California Mines: An Account of the Early Discoveries of Gold, with Anecdotes and Sketches of California Miner's Life, and a Description of the Great Tulare Valley* (Oakland, 1950), 5; Henry Dalton to [unknown], Oct. 16, 1848, HDC.

65. By fleeing the farms, natives had introduced into agriculture a new concern—really a whole new kind of problem. They created what was in effect the first farm labor shortage. See Sutter, *New Helvetia Diary*, 45–46; Dana, *Sutter*, 336, 339, 359; Bancroft, *History of California*, 7: 103; Sutter notes in clipping, *San Francisco Argonaut*, n.d., Bancroft Scrapbooks, BL; Gudde, "The Memoirs of Theodore Cordua," 136; Chester S. Lyman, "Conditions in California in 1848, A Letter to 'The Friend,' Honolulu, from Chester Smith Lyman," *CHSQ* 13 (spring 1934), 177; John C. Frémont, "Geographical Memoir Upon Upper California," S. Doc. 148, 30th Cong., 1st sess., 1848, 22. Henry Dalton persuaded his field hands to stay with him through February 1849 by promising to finance their expedition to the gold fields. See Jackson, *A British Ranchero*, 131.

66. Quote from James Delavan, *Notes on California and the Placers: How to Get There and What to do Afterwards, by One Who Has Been There* (New York, 1850 [1956]), 54. See also James Sandos, "Between Crucifix and Lance: Indian-White Relations in California, 1769–1848," in Orsi and Gutiérrez, *Contested Eden*, 201; William Cronon, George Miles, and Jay Gitlin, eds., *Under an Open Sky: Rethinking America's Western Past* (New York, 1992), 16; Ruby Johnson Swartzlow, "Peter Lassen: Northern California's Trail-Blazer," *CHSQ* 18 (Dec. 1939), 297; T. Vogel-Jorgensen, "Peter Lassen of California," mimeo (1966), trans. Helge Norrung, 23, 24, 72, Red Bluff Public Library; Charles Alexander, *The Life and Times of Cyrus Alexander*, ed. George Shochat (Los Angeles, 1967), 44–45, 61, 85; John Yates, *A Soldier's Sketch of the Sacramento Valley in 1842* ed., Ferol Egan (Berkeley, 1971), 17, 20–21.

67. Green and other proslavery farmers claimed that the state was full of poison oak and only could be worked with black field hands, as they were known to tolerate poison oak better than white men. See also Walter Colton, *Three Years in California* (New York, 1850), 374. For the convention, see C. A. Duniway, "Slavery in California after 1848," *American Historical Association Annual Report for 1905* (1905), 1: 244; Lucille Eaves, *A History of California Labor Legislation* (Berkeley, 1910), 91–94; Cardinal L. Goodwin, *The Establishment of State Government in California, 1846–1850* (New York, 1914), 110–12; Harlow, *California Conquered*, 338–42.

68. Quotes from J. Ross Browne, *Debates in the Convention of California on the Formation of the State Constitution in September and October, 1849* (Washington, D.C., 1850), 43–44, 45–47, 53, 65, 67, 72–73; also 49–50, 63–68, 146–47, 294, 297–98, 333, 338–40. The Constitutional Convention also denied blacks the right to vote, hold public office, testify in court against whites, serve on juries, attend public schools, or homestead public land. See Richard Griswold del Castillo, *The Treaty of Guadalupe Hidalgo: A Legacy of Conflict* (Norman, Okla., 1990); Heizer and Almquist, *The Other Californians*, 95–104, 115–17; Robert R. Miller, *Juan Alvarado: Governor of California, 1836–1842* (Norman, Okla., 1998), 128, 137. See also Gordon M. Bakken, "Constitutional Convention Debates in the West: Racism, Religion, and Gender," *WLH* 3 (summer–fall 1990), 236; McWilliams, *California: The Great Exception*, 48; Delilah L. Beasley, *The Negro Trail Blazers of California* (Los Angeles, 1919), 60; Kenneth G. Goode, *California's Black Pioneers: A Brief Historical Survey* (Santa Barbara, 1974), 77–78; Eugene H. Berwanger, *The Frontier Against Slavery: Western Anti-Negro Prejudice and the Slavery Extension Controversy* (Urbana, Ill., 1967), 69; Goodwin, *The Establishment of State Government*, 120–27.

69. Quotes from Bancroft, *History of California*, 4: 698; Thomas Knight, "Statement of Early Events in California, of a Pioneer of '45,'" MS (1879), 16, BL.

70. Quotes from *Alta California*, May 28, 1850, in Robert F. Heizer, ed., *Collected Documents on the Causes and Events in the Bloody Island Massacre of 1850* (Berkeley, 1973), 18; also 42–45; Nathaniel Lyon to E. R. S. Canby, May 22, 1850, RWDLRDP, in Robert F. Heizer, ed., *The Destruction of the California Indians: A Collection of Documents from the Period 1847 to 1865 in which Are Described Some of the Things that Happened to Some of the Indians of California* (Santa Barbara, 1974), 245. Arrested for their inhumane treatment of field hands, both Kelseys were later released. For the Kelseys, see Alan Rosenus, *General M. G. Vallejo and the Advent of the Americans: A Biography* (Albuquerque, 1995), 56; "The Four Kelsey Brothers," *Sonoma County Historical Society Journal* 2 (June 1964), 13; ibid., 3 (Mar. 1964), 5–8; ibid., 3 (June 1965), 7–8; ibid., 3 (Sept. 1965), 8–9; "The Recollection of Nancy Kelsey," *San Francisco Examiner*, Feb. 5, 1893. For their slaving operations, see Cook, *Conflict*, 305, 311; L. L. Palmer, *History of Napa and Lake Counties* (San Francisco, 1881), 59. There are many versions of the murder and massacre. Some accounts have Kelsey and Stone dying by rifle fire. One has an Indian woman administering the coup de grâce to Kelsey by stabbing him in the heart, retaliation for killing her son, a young boy murdered for stealing wheat to feed her. See Hurtado, *Indian Survival*, 102–4; Max Radin, ed., "The Stone and Kelsey 'Massacre' on the Shores of Clear Lake in 1849: The Indian View-

point, by William Ralganal Benson," *CHSQ* 11 (Sept. 1932), 266–71; Aurelius O. Carpenter and Percy H. Millbery, *History of Mendocino and Lake Counties* (Los Angeles, 1910), 125.

CHAPTER SIX

1. Jackson, *Gold Dust*, 140–42; William Kelly, *An Excursion to California over the Prairie, Rocky Mountains, and Great Sierra Nevada. With a Stroll through the Diggings and Ranches of that County* (London, 1851), 2: 37, 53, 151–53; Buffum, *Six Months in the Gold Mines*, 98–99, 144–46; William Taylor, *California Life Illustrated* (New York, 1861), 48–49.

2. For prices of fruit and vegetables, see James L. Tyson, *Diary of a Physician in California, Being the Results of Actual Experience, Including Notes of the Journey by Land and Water* (New York, 1850), 9–10, 61–64, 73–75, 78–79, 81. For cattle, see Robert Glass Cleland, *The Cattle on a Thousand Hills: Southern California, 1850–1880* (San Marino, Calif., 1941), 102–10. See also James M. Jensen, "Cattle Drives from the Ranchos to the Gold Fields of California," *Arizona and the West* 2 (Dec. 1960), 341–52. So great were the opportunities for profit that, according to one popular story, an enterprising woman actually sold the pears from her trees before they were picked, indeed before they had even grown into edible fruit. While her fruit was still in blossoms, she made labels, wrote the owner's name on each one, and tied the labels to branches. The idea was that the owner would have the right to pick whatever resulted, or did not result, from the chosen blossom. See Elizabeth L. Guinn, *Records of a California Family* (San Diego, n.d.).

3. Paolo Sioli, comp., *Historical Souvenir of El Dorado County, California, with Biographical Sketches* (Oakland, 1883), 110–11; unidentified clipping, Nov. 12, 1848, in Dudley T. Ross, ed., *The Golden Gazette: News from the Newspapers* (Fresno, 1978), 5; Katherine Coman, *Economic Beginnings of the Far West* (New York, 1912), 2: 291; William to Sarah Dressler, July 20, 1851; Mar. 14, May 1, 1852, William Dressler Papers, BL.

4. For a settler trading his pistols to a Spaniard for a yoke of oxen to plow his first crop of vegetables, see John Horner, "Looking Back," *Improvement Era*, 1905, 29, Mission Peak Heritage Foundation Archives, Fremont, Calif. For daily diet, see Vardis Fisher and Opal Laurel Holmes, *Gold Rushes and Mining Camps of the Early American West* (Caldwell, Idaho, 1968), 137; Samuel E. Giddings, "The Foundations of Placer County Horticulture" (M.A. thesis, CSUS, 1969), 1–45; Ruby A. Ferguson, "The Historical Development of the Russian River Valley, 1579–1865" (M.A. thesis, UCB, 1925), 122–24.

5. For an overview, see Rodman Paul, "The Beginnings of Agriculture in California: Innovation vs. Continuity," *CHQ* 52 (spring 1973), 16–27. For the beginning of the dried tree fruit industry see, Robert Couchman, *The Sunsweet Story: A History of the Establishment of the Dried Tree Fruit Industry in California and of the Fifty Years of Service of Sunsweet Growers, Inc.* (San Jose, 1967), 7–9. For the "Spud Rush," see Margaret Koch, *Santa Cruz County: Parade of the Past* (Fresno, 1973), 22. For agricultural patterns near the mines, see *Sacramento Union*, Feb. 26, June 25, Oct. 8, 1859; *North San Juan Hydraulic Press*, May 19, 1860; Thompson and West, *History of Yuba County*, 131; Elliot and Moore, *History of Monterey County*, 44; *Alta California*, Nov. 14, 1851, in Ross, *Golden Gazette*, 41; *CSAST, 1858*, 169–70; Wilson Flint, "Textile Fibers of the Pacific States," *CSAST, 1864–65*, 284–85; W. H. Mackie, *Soil Survey of the Pajaro Valley, California*, U.S. Dept. of Agriculture, Bureau of Soils (Washington, D.C., 1910), 62–64, 103; Ernest Seyd, *California and Its Resources* (London, 1859), 125–26. Along the Feather River near present-day Yuba City, George Briggs settled on Park's Bar and Foster Bar roads, about five miles from present-day Marysville, planted watermelons, and earned such high profits from his first crop that he was able to import fruit trees from Oregon and begin transforming his "Water-Melon Ranch" into California's finest orchard. While melon and potato entrepreneurs appeared to do particularly well, often earning overnight fortunes, farmers who grew anything—onions, barley, turnips, radishes, cabbages, carrots, squash, celery, peas, beans, corn—seemed to prosper. A grower with just an acre and a half of tomatoes could expect to earn a profit of eighteen thousand dollars. A quarter-acre of turnips easily fetched three thousand dollars. But even if all a grower had to offer was a water pail full of fresh garden greens he could not, according to one story, get down a street in Sacramento without café owners waving bids of ten dollars. So profitable were vegetables that, according to another story, a prostitute/farmer of renown who kept a garden patch behind her cribs netted fifty thousand dollars, retired from her profession, and opened a small restaurant. The prostitute story is in James R. Garniss, "Reminiscence," MS, [1849–50], 17, BL. For the eighteen-thousand-dollar tomato crop, see *San Francisco Herald*, Aug. 1, 1850. One orchard, planted in 1853 and containing

eighteen thousand fruit trees with 250 different varieties, grossed two hundred thousand dollars in 1856. See Charles D. Ferguson, *California Gold Fields* (Cleveland, 1948), 33; Belinda Desmond, "History of the City of Marysville, California, 1852–1859" (Ph.D. diss., Catholic University, 1962). For garden crops yielding more than three thousand dollars an acre, see *Sacramento Transcript*, Oct. 14, Nov. 29, 1850; *San Francisco Picayune*, Oct. 28, 1850.

6. Quote from Bayard Taylor, *El Dorado, or Adventures in the Path of Empire* (New York, 1850), 1: 218; 2: 47, 123. For Old Zwart, see Edward Wilson, *Travels in California* (Boston, 1852); Wilson, *The Golden Land* (New York, 1852); Charles D. Ferguson, *California Gold Fields* (Cleveland, 1948); Daniel Woods, *Sixteen Months at the Gold Diggings* (New York, 1851), 71; also 57; Peter H. Burnett, *An Old California Pioneer* (Oakland, 1946), 201–2; Edwin Bryant, *What I Saw In California* (New York, 1848 [1967]), 36, entries for Oct. 25, 1846; Theodore Johnson, *California and Oregon; Or Sights in the Gold Region, and Scenes by the Way* (Phil., 1850 [1865]), 118–19, 123–25; Frederick J. Teggert, ed., "Diary of Nelson Kingsley, a California Argonaut of 1849," *Academy of Pacific Coast History Publications* 3 (Dec. 1914), 237–413. For a list of delta farmers along with descriptions of Indian field hands, see Cadwalader Ringgold, *A Series of Charts, with Sailing Directions, Embracing Surveys of the Farallones, Entrance to the Bay of San Francisco . . . with additions* (Washington, D.C., 1852). Even the crudest contemporary maps of California instantly reveal why delta-area farmers were well placed. The coastal mountains that walled off the western side of the Central Valley were breached only in one place, at the Carquinez Straits, on the north end of San Francisco Bay. This outlet, constricted on the north by the Montezuma Hills and on the south by the Mount Diablo range, was so narrow that it caused the entire drainage from sixty thousand square miles of the interior valley to slow and back up for miles before finally pushing its way through a channel into the bay. Merging here, twenty-two million acrefeet of water from the state's two major rivers, the Sacramento and San Joaquin, as well as smaller rivers like the Cosumnes and Mokelumne, created a huge delta, twenty-four miles across at its widest point, and forty-eight miles along its north-south axis. So packed with organic matter was delta soil that when dry it would catch fire and burn. See John Thompson, "The Settlement Geography of the Sacramento-San Joaquin Delta, California" (Ph.D. diss., Stanford University, 1957), 185–210; Stanley W. Cosby, *Soil Survey of the Sacramento-San Joaquin Delta Area, California*, U.S. Dept. of Agriculture, Bureau of Plant Pathology, and University of California Agricultural Experiment Station, Bulletin no. 21, series 1935 (Washington, D.C., 1941), 43; Harold Gilliam, "San Joaquin County—The Conquest of the Delta," *San Francisco Chronicle*, Dec. 7, 1952; Richard Dillon, *Delta Country* (San Rafael, 1986), 54–68.

7. Quote *Alta California*, Nov. 30, [1849?], Bancroft Scrapbooks, BL. See also Ralph Raven [George Payson], *Golden Dreams and Leaden Realities* (New York, 1853), 79; William S. M'Collum, *California as I Saw It*, ed. Dale Morgan (Los Gatos, Calif., 1960), 125; Robert G. Cleland, ed., *Apron Full of Gold: The Letters of Mary Jane Megquier from San Francisco, 1849–1859* (San Marino, Calif., 1949); J. S. Holliday, *The World Rushed In: The California Gold Rush Experience* (New York, 1981), 53; John J. Werth, *A Dissertation on the Resources and Policy of California* (Benicia, 1851), 71–74; Franklin Street, *California in 1850* (Cincinnati, 1851), 42. Comparative wage rates from David Schob, *Hired Hands and Plow Boys: Farm Labor in the Midwest, 1815–1869* (Urbana, Ill., 1975), 69–71. See also William Shaw, *Golden Dreams and Waking Realities* (London, 1851), 170–77; Robert Hernandez Cornejo, *Los Chilenos en San Francisco de California* (Valparaiso, Chile, 1930), 1: 92. Even after the initial lure of gold had dissipated, no job paying less than three dollars a day interested former gold miners. In their diaries and letters home, miners made no secret of their feelings. "Found work at eighteen dollars a week. Rather low wages but better than lying still . . . I wish I could get some job steady for all summer . . . Done nothing today," wrote one newcomer while holed up in a cheap, crowded San Francisco boardinghouse. "Had a place on a farm offered me at forty dollars, but I think I can do better if I stay here a spell longer." Another confided in his diary: "Agriculture . . . will continue for some time to come as of secondary consideration. Men will not submit to its toils while they can gather a harvest of gold." Quotes from George F. Shaw, diary, MS (1855), entry for May 15, 1855, CHS; Walter Colton, *Colton's Traveler and Tourist's Guide Book* (New York, 1854), 227. See also *California Assembly Journal, Document No. 19* (Sacramento, 1855), 7; James Mason Hutchings, diary, MS (1855), 179, BL; unidentified clipping, [*Sacramento Union*], ca. 1858, MCMCF; Frank Marryat, *Mountains and Molehills* (San Francisco, 1855), 63. The farm labor shortage of 1850 was significant because it was the first of dozens of subsequent labor shortages that would afflict California agriculture and because unlike most later ones, it was quite real and threaten-

ing and not solely the exaggeration of farmers seeking to flood the labor market and thereby insulate themselves from wage pressures and unionizing activity. I computed the number of farmworkers employed at this time from House, *Seventh Census of the United States, 1850,* 32nd Cong., 2nd sess., Misc. Doc., 1853, 119–20, 127–28, 146–47, 727–28, 761–62, 928, 967, 976. Since there were 1,486 people listed as farmers, and 872 farms, I calculated the farm labor population by subtracting the number of farms from farmers to get an estimated farm labor force of 614. This was obviously not an adequate number for spring plowing, planting, and land clearing, not to mention the summer and fall harvests, or for farming operations thereafter. The 1850 census is highly suspect, and survey information did not differentiate between farmers and farm laborers until 1860. Hence, quantitative assessments are open to considerable debate. On this matter, see David Hornbeck and Mary Tucey, "The Submergence of a People: Migration and Occupational Structure in California in 1850," *PHR* 46 (Aug. 1977), 478. For similar problems using the 1852 state census, see Dennis Harris, "The California Census of 1852: A Note of Caution and Encouragement," *Pacific Historian* 28 (summer 1984), 59–64. Patterns of agricultural diversification can be seen in Alan Bowman, *Index of the California Census of 1850* (Berkeley, 1972), showing that most farms in addition to a wheat field had a garden, cows, and fruit trees or a vineyard of some sort. For the number of farmers, see J. D. B. DeBow, *Statistical View of the United States, Compendium of the Seventh Census* (Washington, D.C., 1854), 201–2.

8. Bidwell to James W. McCorkle, Dec. 20, 1851, enclosed in McCorkle to Luke Lea, Feb. 6, 1852; Bidwell to James W. McCorkle, Dec. 20, 1851, enclosed in McCorkle to Luke Lea, Feb. 6, 1852, LROIACS. A singularly capable and appealing person described by immigrants from the southern states as having certain aspects of "the better plantation owners back home," Bidwell had clerked for Sutter at Bodega Bay, where he supervised the transfer of all Russian property, including Fort Ross. Becoming a naturalized Mexican citizen in 1844 and promoted to foreman of Hock Farm in 1845, he soon became bookkeeper and general manager for Sutter's entire operations. After acquiring two land grants—one of two leagues, for Rancho Colus, in present-day Colusa County, which he later sold for two thousand dollars, the other for Rancho Ulpinos, in present-day Solano County, near Rio Vista, which he also sold—Bidwell obtained Rancho Chico, a twenty-two-thousand-acre grant of land along Chico Creek, in present-day Butte County, where he proceeded to hire local Mechoopda Indians to clear undergrowth and plant saplings and vines. Shocked by their appearance, the New York-born Bidwell described the Mechoopdas as completely naked, "almost wild as deer," and not being accustomed to clothing, given to removing their pants and shoes at the end of each workday, and carrying them to work the following day. Bidwell got them to abandon their naked ways, integrate seasonal farmwork into their hunting-gathering routine, and learn to plow fields and harvest and thresh wheat. By the second year he had taught them to dry fruit and make wine. According to one widely circulated rumor, the Mechoopdas worked so well because the daughter of their tribal chief had become Bidwell's temporary wife. This union, if true, placated hostility and protected Bidwell from raids by neighboring tribes. Quotes from Doyce B. Nunis, ed., *The Bidwell-Bartleson Party: 1841 California Emigrant Adventure* (Santa Cruz, 1991), 61; F. S. Clough, *The House on Fifth and Salem* (Chico, Calif., 1978), 44. The marriage rumor is from Henry Azbill, "Some Aspects of Mechoopda Indian Culture on John Bidwell's Rancho del Arroyo Chico," interview, 1966, 3, 267, ANCRR; and Maggi Ramsland, "Nopani, Unsung Heroine," *Butte County Bugle* 1 (Mar. 1973), which is apparently based on the Azbill interview. See also Rockwell Hunt, *John D. Bidwell, Prince of California Pioneers* (Caldwell, Idaho, 1942), 140, 163, 359; Charles C. Royce, ed., *John D. Bidwell, Pioneer, Statesman, Philanthropist* (Chico, Calif., 1906), 55–56, 61. For the Mechoopdas, see Dorothy Hill, "Indians of Chico Rancheria; An Ethnohistoric Study" (M.A. thesis, CSUC, 1974), x, 27–33. There is no doubt that very early during his work Bidwell exploited field hands, although in later years he remarked that his Mechoopdas were not very profitable to him and that he had employed them because "idle Indians are a nuisance." An even hand and "a kind of parental protection" were Bidwell's slogans regarding how to treat Mechoopdas. Having observed firsthand the way Sutter, Marsh, and other rancheros had handled Indians, he knew the benefits that Anglo and Hispanic settlers derived from their labor, as well as the general sentiment to impose controls guaranteeing their continued usefulness. These were the views and experiences he carried into politics when he was elected to the state senate. See Royce, *John D. Bidwell,* 55–56, 61; Rosena A. Giles, "More Than Three Quarters of A Century Ago," GFP; Annie H. Currie, "Bidwell Rancheria," *CHSQ* 36 (Dec. 1957), 313–25. See also Bidwell to McKinstry, Nov. 4, 1848, GMP.

9. Original copy in Old Bill File, CSA. See also California Senate, *Journal of the Senate*, 1st sess. (Sacramento, 1850), 217, 223–24, 228–29, 257, 366–67, 369, 384. For Bidwell, see Michael J. Gillis and Michael F. Magliari, *John Bidwell and California: The Life and Writings of a Pioneer, 1841–1900* (Spokane and San Francisco, 2002), ch. 6.

10. With minor variations, growers faced with labor shortages would, on countless occasions over the next century and a half, look to government action to prime the supply of farm labor artificially. For background, see Chauncey Shafter Goodrich, "The Legal Status of the California Indian: Introductory," *CLR* 14 (1926), 89–93; George C. Mansfield, *History of Butte County* (Los Angeles, 1918), 52, 137–40. For Brown, see *History of Contra Costa County, California, Including its Geography, Geology, Topography, and Biographical Sketches of Early Prominent Settlers and Representative Men* (San Francisco, 1882), 515–31. For Douglas, see [W. F. Wallace], ed., *History of Napa County: Comprising an Account of Its Topography, Geology, and Biography of Its Pioneers and Principal Inhabitants* (Oakland, 1901), 96; California Assembly, *Journal of the Assembly*, 1st sess. (Sacramento, 1850), 1284. See also *An Illustrated History of San Joaquin County, California, Together with Glimpses of Its Future Prospects* (Chicago, 1890), 47.

11. Quotes from California Legislature, *Statutes of California Passed at the First Session of the Legislature: 1849–1850* (Sacramento, 1850), 408–10. Carey McWilliams claimed that the law was "designed to preserve the substance, if not the form, of peonage" and that it also created "an open season on Indians in California." Quote from McWilliams, *Southern California*, 43. See also Fernandez, "Except a California Indian: A Study in Legal Discrimination," 161–75. For Bidwell, see John Bidwell, "Recollections," MS (1897), JBP; Cora E. Cody, "John Bidwell: His Early Career in California" (M.A. thesis, UCB, 1927), 148.

12. Quotes from *Statutes of California: 1849–1850*, 408–10. See also Heizer and Almquist, *The Other Californians*, 47. The comparison with the black codes is in Rawls, *Indians of California*, 107–8. The 1850 act is reprinted in Edward C. Ord, *The City of Los Angeles and the City of Saints, or a Trip to Los Angeles and San Bernardino in 1856* (Los Angeles, 1978), 37–39.

13. Quotes from *Statutes of California, 1849–1850*, 409. See also S. Garfield and F. A. Snyder, *Compiled Laws of the State of California* (Benicia, 1853), 647–50.

14. Quote from McWilliams, *California: The Great Exception* (New York, 1949), 150. See also Walter Van Tilburg Clark, ed., *The Journals of Alfred Doten, 1849–1903* (Reno, 1973), 1: 361; Clifford E. Trafzer and Joel R. Hyer, eds., *Exterminate Them! Written Accounts of the Murder, Rape, and Enslavement of Native Americans During the California Gold Rush* (East Lansing, Mich., 1999), 18–20; Taylor, "Foundations of California Rural Society," 196–97. Some historians argue that the 1850 law was not enforced, that its effects were minimal at best. Certainly there is ample evidence that Indians went about their business as they liked. During this time Indian vagrants were seen drifting about the countryside on their own, unmolested even in farm country. They continued working for wages, usually at between four and five dollars a day. And they continued to refuse to work for wages, begging passersby for coins and handouts when they met on the byways. To such natives, the law was meaningless; it never intruded into their lives. See Hurtado, "California Indians and the Workaday West: Labor, Assimilation, and Survival," *CH* 119 (spring 1990), 10.

15. Producing 57,366 gallons of wine, Los Angeles became the leading wine-producing area in the country, the "City of Vines," where the road passing from the city to San Pedro crossed so many vineyards that it was sometimes called "Vineyard Lane." The best listing of Los Angeles winemakers at this time is Ernest P. Peninou and Sidney S. Greenleaf, *A Directory of California Wine Growers and Wine Makers in 1860, with Biographical and Historical Notes* (Berkeley, 1967), 12–30. See also Brian McGinty, *Strong Wine: The Life and Legend of Agoston Haraszthy* (Stanford, 1998), 312–13; "California Wine," *California Farmer*, Oct. 3, 1856; Mrs. A. S. C. Forbes, "Los Angeles When it Was 'The City of Vines,'" *HSSCAP* 15 (1932), 337; Iris Higbie Wilson, *William Wolfskill, 1798–1866: Frontier Trapper to California Ranchero* (Glendale, 1965), 168. Carefully cutting free clusters of table grapes weighing up to three pounds each, crews of Indians placed them in large, wicker baskets, piled them on wagons, and hauled them off to packing sheds. There workers spread the grapes on clean white sheets, trimmed the clusters, carefully placed them in redwood crates, placed a sheet of blotter paper between every layer, and then added a layer of sawdust to protect them against the rough ocean voyage north to San Francisco. With the table grape harvest well under way, other men moved into winemaking. Adding a sense of urgency to the harvest, the Gold Rush promised unbelievable profits. For the harvest, see William P. Blake, "Geologic Report," in *Report of Explorations and Sur-*

veys to Ascertain the Most Practicable and Economical Route for a Railroad from the Mississippi River to the Pacific Ocean, 33rd Cong., 2nd sess., 1857, S. Doc. 78, 5: pt. 2, 77–78. For packing techniques, see Julius Froebel, *Seven Years' Travel in Central America, North America, Northern Mexico, and the Far West of the United States* (London, 1859), entries for Sept. 7–30, 1854. See also Arpad Haraszthy, "Wine Making in California," *Overland Monthly* 7 (Dec. 1871), 491–92; ibid., 8 (Jan. 1872), 34–41, 105–9, 393–98; John Steven McGroarty, ed., *History of Los Angeles County* (Chicago, 1923), 1: 178; Walter Colton, *Three Years in California and a Selection of . . . Letters from Monterey* (Stanford, 1949), 355–56; Jesse B. Schilling, "Brief Economic History of the California Wine-Growing Industry," mimeo (n.d.), 2, Wine Institute, San Francisco. For fresh grape sales, see Andre W. McKee, "Agriculture, The Grapes and Wine Culture of California," in *United States Patent Office Reports* (Washington, D.C., 1858), 340.

16. Quote from Minutes of the Los Angeles Common Council, Aug. 16, 1850, 1: 60, 68, LACA; see also Oct. 7, 1850, 1: 87; Nov. 27, 1850, 1: 111; Sept. 22, 1852, 1: 264; Guinn, *Historical and Biographical Record of Los Angeles* (Chicago, 1901), 148; *Los Angeles Star*, Apr. 3, Nov. 20, 1852; Benjamin Hayes, "I Know the 'Californians' Well," MS (Jan. 14, 1853), Benjamin Hayes Scrapbooks, BL.

17. Quote from Newmark, *Sixty Years in Southern California*, 30. See also *Los Angeles Star*, July 17, 1852; Jan. 15, Apr. 2, June 18, Oct. 2, Dec. 3, 1853; Jan. 4, 18, 1855; Oct. 23, 1858; Oct. 1, 29, 1859. Negro Alley got its name one morning in 1832 when Don José Antonio Carrillo posted signs proclaiming the narrow alley southeast of the town plaza (that was then occupied by dark-skinned Angelinos) as Calle de Los Negroes. As the strip of adobe brothels, saloons, and boardinghouses grew, the name stuck, becoming synonymous with the area's other title as "the wickedest street on earth." See John D. Weaver, *Los Angeles: The Enormous Village, 1781–1981* (Santa Barbara, 1980), 29–30. To grow and flourish, the auction system required a peculiar environment with plenty of cheap liquor, a lot of destitute natives, a place where they could congregate and carouse, farms that were not too far away, and a police force willing to round up men for drunkenness, vagrancy, and the slightest violation of obscure city statutes. These were all found in abundance around the "vile little dump" of asphaltum-roofed mud huts that constituted the city of Los Angeles. Organized around a single church, the city at this time prefigured such wild places as Abilene, Dodge City, and many other tough western cow towns of the American West. Here men went around armed to the teeth. Liquor flowed freely. Gunshots rang out daily. Fights occurred nightly. Of this state of affairs a Massachusetts minister who witnessed five months of barbaric behavior and ten murders in a fortnight just outside the door to his home could only say, "This is nominally a Christian town, but in reality heathen." Similarly, the editor of the *Los Angeles Star* admitted, "There is no country where . . . human life is of so little account. Men hack one another in pieces with pistols and other cutlery." Los Angeles, in short, was full of the kinds of dangers and temptations that would get natives in trouble, land them in jail, place them on the auction block, and make them easy pickings. Quotes from James Woods, diary, Apr. 29, 1855, in Lindley Bynum, ed., "Los Angeles in 1854–55, the Diary of Rev. James Woods," *HSSCQ* 25 (1941), 82–84; *Los Angeles Star*, Feb. 28, 1853. See also John and LaRee Caughey, *Los Angeles: Biography of a City* (Berkeley, 1977), 115; John Caughey, *The Pueblo Water Right of Los Angeles, Historically Considered* (Los Angeles, 1969), 87–98; Ludwig Louis Salvator, "A Flower from the Golden Land," *Touring Topics* 21 (Feb. 1929), 41; Leonard Pitt, *The Decline of the Californios* (Berkeley, 1966), 156–60; William H. Brewer, *Up and Down California in 1860–1864* (1865 [New Haven, 1974]), 12–15. Patrolled by packs of barking dogs, the street was sometimes invaded by groups of well-armed Anglos who stumbled about peppering the adobe walls or the doors and windows and even the dogs with pistol shots. In constant fear of robbers, store owners always packed weapons and were ready if an emergency arose to defend themselves on the spot. Not surprisingly, Negro Alley accounted for an excessively large proportion of the town's murders each year. But by far the pleasures and diversions of Negro Alley outweighed its dangers. With no other place to go, native field hands tasted the pleasures of Negro Alley as often as possible. See Guinn, *Historical and Biographical Record of Los Angeles*, 310; Guinn, "The Passing of the Old Pueblo," *HSSCAP*, 5 (1901), 117; *Los Angeles Star*, Mar. 31, 1855.

18. Quotes from *Los Angeles Star*, Dec. 3, 1853; July 10, 1852; John R. Bartlett, *Personal Narrative of Explorations and Incidents in Texas, New Mexico, California, Sonora, and Chihuahua* (New York, 1854), 2: 82–84.

19. Quote from *Los Angeles Star*, Dec. 3, 1853. For typical newspaper reports, see May 17,

1851; June 18, 1853; Jan. 11, 1855; Jan. 11, Oct. 18, 1856; Apr. 4, 1857; Oct. 23, 1858. For kickbacks to *alcaldes*, see Minutes of the Los Angeles Common Council, Oct. 2, 1850, 1: 87; Nov. 27, 1850, 1: 111; Sept. 22, 1852, 1: 264, LACA. Producing about nine million pounds of grapes, most for wine, Los Angeles in 1854 shipped more than fifty thousand pounds of fresh grapes north to San Francisco, no small feat when done entirely with sailing ships. For Los Angeles agriculture at this time, see Julius Froebel, *Seven Years' Travel in Central America, Northern Mexico, and the Far West of the United States* (New York, 1854).

20. Horace Bell, *Reminiscences of a Ranger, Or Early Times in Southern California* (Los Angeles, 1853 [Santa Barbara, 1929]), 33–36. For the report of a ranch manager sent to pick up field hands, see Charles Henry Brinley to Abel Stearns, Aug. 30, 1852, ASP.

21. Field hands supposedly could escape auction. All they had to do was pay off their fines. On this basis, some observers of the Southern California farm labor scene think that native men must have willingly accepted their role as field hands, that their work in the vineyards and on the farms was a conscious act reflecting a reasoned decision to make the best of a bad situation. But the interpretation stretches the truth. See *Los Angeles Star*, Nov. 20, 1852; J. J. Warner, Benjamin Hayes, and J. P. Widney, *An Historical Sketch of Los Angeles County* (Los Angeles, 1876), 81. Census information from Maurice H. Newmark and Marco R. Newmark, *Census of the City and County of Los Angeles for 1850* (Los Angeles, 1929), 70–72, 115.

22. Quote from Harry Carr, *Los Angeles, City of Dreams* (New York, 1935), 95–96. For the town itself, see Guinn, "Los Angeles in the Adobe Days," *HSSCAP* 4 (1899), 49–53. For planting patterns, see Laurence L. Hill, *La Reina—Los Angeles in Three Centuries* (Los Angeles, 1929), 20–23; unidentified newspaper clipping, "W.H.S.," Apr. 25, 1864, Bancroft Scrapbooks, BL.

23. Quote from *Los Angeles Star*, Sept. 7, 1853. For the log and chain arrangement, see Bell, *Reminiscences of a Ranger*, 38. See also J. Ross Browne, "Conditions of the California Indians, 1856–57," LROIACS; Browne, "The Indian Reservations in California," *Harper's Magazine* 13 (Aug. 1861), 315; Robinson, *The Indians of Los Angeles*, 1–3.

24. Quotes from Bartlett, *Personal Narrative*, 2: 82; *Los Angeles Star*, Jan. 4, 1853; *Alta California*, Mar. 31, 1853. For befouled water sources, see *Los Angeles Star*, June 16, 1855; Henry D. Barrows, "Water for Domestic Purposes versus Water for Irrigation," *HSSCAP* 8 (1911), 208n. Also useful is 1860 MS Census, Los Angeles County, LACA, 30–5, 57, 113–14. Natives who were married and had grown daughters might benefit from money that women earned as house servants, cooks, and laundresses. But adult single men had only two choices—starve or work. Joseph Lancaster Brent found dead and wounded men everywhere. Estimating that fifty people had been killed, he personally counted thirteen corpses. "These all had their heads smashed beyond recognition, which is the sign manual of Indian murder," he observed. Quote from Joseph Lancaster Brent, *The Lugo Case: A Personal Reminiscence* (New Orleans, 1926), 7–8. The former mission field hands were from the Luiseño tribe. For the game of *peón*, see DuBois, "The Religion of the Luiseno Indians of Southern California," 167–68; *Southern Californian*, Nov. 16, 1854, HL. Newspapers simply noted the stabbings and killings in hundreds of cryptic reports. "An Indian named Bacilio was found dead near the zanja . . . this morning," stated the *Star* after one particularly grisly night of fighting. "Justice Dryden and a jury sat on the body; verdict, death from intoxication, or the visitation of God." Bar proprietors ignored the antiliquor laws. Continuing to sell liquor and offer cockfighting and *peón*, they simply paid their fines out of their very considerable profits. See *Los Angeles Star*, July 10, Aug. 14, 1852; Dec. 3, 1853; Mar. 31, 1855; Minutes of the Los Angeles Common Council, May 21, 1851, 1: 164–65, LACA; *Southern Californian*, Nov. 16, 1854; *Alta California*, Nov. 13, 1851, Bancroft Scrapbooks, BL.

25. Quotes from *Los Angeles Star*, Jan. 4, 1853; June 20, 1860; Bell, *Reminiscences*, 35–36. Sundays were the worst. "Each Sunday morning," reported the *Star*, "our streets are filled with drunken . . . filthy drooling beasts, in human shape, at one hundred. Who knows or where they procure the rotgut stuff that makes them thus." See *Star*, Oct. 9, 1852; Mar. 31, 1855; Lanier Bartlett, *On the Old West Coast* (New York, 1953); Benjamin S. Harrison, *Fortune Favors the Brave: The Life and Times of Horace Bell* (New York, 1953).

26. Quote from Capt. Edward Otho Cresap Ord to Maj. W. W. Mackall, Aug. 9, 1856, RWDLRDP. See also Edward C. Ord, *The City of Angels*, 13, 23–24, 27, 32–34.

27. Quotes from Hubert H. Bancroft, "Personal Observations During a Tour Through the Line of Missions of Upper California," MS (1874), 46; Cave Johnson Couts to Don A. Hollister, Rancho Guajome, Jan. 10, 1861, CJCP; also Augustus S. Ensworth to Couts, Jan. 10, 1861. For indenture, see "Indenture wherein Jesus Delgado and Paula Delgado bind an Indian child

Sasaria to Isidora Bandini de Couts," San Luis Rey, Jan. 25, 1854; "Indenture wherein Indian woman Jacinta binds over her son to Isidora Bandini Couts," San Diego County Justice of the Peace, San Luis Rey, Aug. 13, 1866; "Judgment rendered by Willima Caswell Ferrell, Justice of the Peace, in case of Cave Johnson Couts vs. Francisco, an Indian Boy," San Diego County, May 6, 1858, SDHS; Couts to Benjamin Wilson, May 7, 1854, BDWP. When Couts was absent from Rancho Guajome, native field hands would often go on drunken sprees. Returning unexpectedly, he once caught them in the act. "I found that there was a general drunk and the family were in such a grand scare I found some difficulty to induce them to open the doors to let me in," he related in a letter to another ranchero. But field hands did not end their drunkenness with his arrival. On the following evening they returned to drinking liquor, and, in their stupor and celebration, set the smokehouse on fire and burned all of the rancho's bacon supply. Quote from Couts to John Forster, Santa Margarita, Feb. 23, 1870, CJCP. For others who ran away, see "Servants, 1853–57," ledger entries 2543-19; "Servants, 1864–69, Guajome," ledger entries 2543-46; "Guajamito account book and journal, 1854–64," ledger entries 2543-16, CJCP. For Couts and Rancho Guajome, see Paul Bryan Gray, *Foster vs. Pico: The Struggle for the Rancho Santa Margarita* (Spokane, Wash., 1998), 110–12; Richard Pourade, *The Silver Dons* (San Diego, 1963), 21; Iris Wilson Engstrand and Thomas L. Sharf, "Rancho Guajome: A California Legacy Preserved," *JSDH* 20 (winter 1974), 1–14; Engstrand and Mary F. Ward, "Rancho Guajome: An Architectural Legacy Preserved," ibid., 1 (fall 1995), 251–83; Floyd Sorensen Jr., "Cave Johnson Couts and La Adobe Casa del Rancho Guajome," *Brand Book Number Two* (San Diego, 1971), 96–108; Lyle C. Annable, "The Life and Times of Cave Johnson Couts, San Diego County Pioneer" (M.A. thesis, CSU, San Diego, 1965).

28. Quote from Horace Bell, "Reminiscences of a Ranger . . . newspaper clippings from the *Los Angeles Morning Republican*," MS (n.d.), BL. See also Henry Dalton, "Indian Books—Wages and Accounts for Indian Employees on Azusa Ranch, 1857–1862," HDC.

29. Quote from Monroy, *Thrown Among Strangers*, 242–43. See also Robert C. Gillingham, *Rancho San Pedro: The Story of a Famous Rancho in Los Angeles County and of Its Owners, the Dominguiz Family* (Los Angeles, 1961), 225; Abel Stearns, account books, ASP; account book for Rancho Santa Ana del Chino, various entries 1840–59, California Historical Documents, HL; Don Meadows, "Bernardo Yorba Hacienda of Rancho Canada de Santa Ana," MS (n.d.), CBMM. Although the Mormons who settled in the San Bernardino Valley in the fall of 1851 cleared, plowed, planted, and harvested their fields on their own, they did resort to hiring Indians for the onerous task of digging an irrigation canal. See Edward Leo Lyman, *San Bernardino: The Rise and Fall of a California Community* (Salt Lake City, 1996), ix, 63–66, 73–77, 199–230.

30. Quotes from *Napa Reporter*, Dec. 20, 1858, NCLCF; Jacob D. B. Stillman, *The Gold Rush Letters of J. D. B. Stillman* (Palo Alto, 1967), 63; Sherburne F. Cook, *Conflict*, 57. The Fresno auctions are further described in *Marysville Weekly Express*, Mar. 5, 1859, FCHS. The opprobrious term "digger Indians" was applied to San Joaquin Valley tribes because of their use of branches to dig for roots.

31. Quote from E. A. Stevenson, agent for Nome Lackce Reservation, in Robert F. Heizer and Alan F. Almquist, eds., *The Other Californians: Prejudice and Discrimination Under Spain, Mexico, and the United States to 1920* (Berkeley, 1971), 42. See also Peter Campbell to commissioner of Indian Affairs, June 1, 1851, LROIACS; *Sacramento Union*, Sept. 13, 14, 1854; *Alta California*, Oct. 2, 1854; *Humboldt Times*, May 5, 1855.

32. Kidnapping grew into a small industry. The Berryessa family, whose founder Nicolas Antonio went north with Anza in 1776 and eventually acquired vast acreage around Clear Lake and the present-day counties of Santa Clara, Napa, Alameda, and Sonoma, was a prime example of old, established Californios who not only kidnapped field hands and used them on the family farm, but additionally resold them in a kind of retail operation that sent large gangs to other ranches throughout the state. See *Sacramento Union*, May 20, 1857; *Alta California*, Apr. 7, 1855, Bancroft Scrapbooks, BL; Brewer, *Up and Down California*, 493; L. L. Palmer, *History of Mendocino County* (San Francisco, 1880), 168; Col. T. J. Henley enclosures and memo to secretary of Indian Affairs, Oct. 14, 1854; Robert White to T. J. Henley, May 13, Aug. 9, 1855, LROIACS; *San Francisco Bulletin*, June 1, 1860, Bancroft Scrapbooks, BL.

33. Quotes from *Sacramento Union*, July 31, 1860; also Sept. 13, 14, 1854; Aug. 31, 1862; *Marysville Appeal*, Dec. 6, 1861; also Oct. 21, 1861; *San Francisco Bulletin*, cited in *Hutching's California Magazine* 5 (1860), 48; *Alta California*, Jan. 17, 1858; *Ukiah Herald*, cited in *Alta California*, Aug. 31, 1861. The *Butte Record*, May 23, 1857, reported on a Mexican "who has been in the habit

of stealing Indian children and selling them to Mexican rancheros in Southern California." See Isaac Cox, *Annals of Trinity County* (1858 [Eugene, Ore., 1940]), 102; also 112–14; H. C. Bailey, "California Indian Slave Trade of Pioneer Days," *San Francisco Chronicle*, Sept. 19, 1897, reprinted as Henry Clay Bailey, "Indian Life in the Sacramento Valley," *San Bernardino County Museum Quarterly* 7 (fall 1957), 17.

34. Quotes from Senate, 32nd Cong., 2nd sess., 1853, S. Doc. 57, 5–10; Vincent Geiger to Henley, Sept. 24, 1857, LROIACS; also Henley to Manypenny, Oct. 15, 1854, reporting from the northern Sacramento Valley that slave catchers "infested this portion of the country stealing Indian children to be sold as servants." William Scott's testimony, taken in Cloverdale, Mar. 2, 1860, Indian War Files.

35. Quotes from Lynwood Carranco and Estle Beard, *Genocide and Vendetta: The Round Valley Wars of Northern California* (Norman, Okla., 1981), 40; George Gibbs, "Journal of the Expedition of Colonel Redick McKee, United States Indian Agent, through North-Western California, Performed in the Summer and Fall of 1851," in Chad L. Hoopes, *Lure of Humboldt Bay Region* (Dubuque, Iowa, 1971), 231; *Butte Record*, May 23, 1857. See also Heizer, *Destruction of the California Indians*, 232–33; Franklin A. Buck, *A Yankee Trader in the Gold Rush: The Letters of Franklin A. Buck*, ed., Katherine A. White (Boston, 1930), 117–18; Sherburne F. Cook, *Conflict*, 57. For the trauma of kidnapping, see Simmon Storms to Henley, June 20, 1856, LROIACS. Kidnapped native children were no less devastated, no less psychologically and physically damaged, than the children of black slaves who were ripped from their families and sold "down the river" in the antebellum American South.

36. Quote from *Marysville Herald*, Nov. ?, 1856, in Robert F. Heizer, ed., *They Were Only Diggers: A Collection of Articles from California Newspapers, 1851–1866, On Indian and White Relations* (Ramona, Calif., 1974), 72. See also *California Statutes, 1854* (Sacramento, 1855), ch. 12; U.S. Dept. of the Interior, Office of Indian Affairs, *Report of the Commissioner for 1858* (Washington, D.C., 1858), 9–11; *San Francisco Bulletin*, June 29, 1857.

37. Quote from John Bidwell to Sen. J. W. McCorkle, Dec. 20, 1851, in McCorkle to Luke Lea, Feb. 6, 1852, LROIACS, cited in Hurtado, "'Hardly a Farm House—A Kitchen without them': Indian and White Households on the California Borderland Frontier in 1860," *WHQ* 13 (July 1982), 245.

38. Estimate of available "working hands" is in E. F. Beale, "Recommendations on Federal Indian Assistance for California Indians, 1852," in Beale to Luke Lea, Nov. 22, 1852, LROIACS. Hurtado, "California Indians and the Workaday West," 10, concluded that the 1850 law was not enforced much, citing examples of Indian field hands hiring out on their own, and coming and going as they pleased. For the Bell Ranch, see Washington Township Research Committee, *History of Washington Township* (Stanford, 1950), 168–69.

39. Mrs. Josephine H. Blacow (Horner's only surviving daughter), interview, 1952; John M. Horner, "Adventures of a Pioneer," 665; various materials in Boxes 15–16, FHHC; Annaleone D. Patton, *California Mormons by Sail and Trail* (Salt Lake City, 1972), 85–89; John S. Sandoval, "First Farmer of California," *Westways* 41 (Aug. 1949), 8–9; *California Farmer*, Jan. 27, Feb. 2, May 17, 1854; *National Intelligencer*, Mar. 6, 1851; Washington Township Research Committee, *History of Washington Township*, 132, 167; M. W. Wood, *History of Alameda County, California* (Oakland, 1883), 817, 879–80; Horner, "Adventures of a Pioneer," MS (1904), 665, Mission Peak Heritage Foundation Archives, Fremont.

40. The Moores were not related. See "Extension of Patent and the Granting of a New Patent," *Scientific American* (Jan. 5, 1853), 141, FFLCSF; Joseph Hutchinson, "California Cereals," *Overland Monthly* 2 (July–Aug. 1883), 145; typed notes on *California Farmer*, May 25, 1854, FWPC. Mormon field hands using cradles to harvest the 1852 wheat crop in San Bernardino engaged in contests to see who could cut and bind the most grain and acquire the title of "champion cradler." See Lyman, *San Bernardino*, 75–76. According to F. Hal Higgins, "Mule Train Ranching in the West," MS (n.d.), 2, FHHC, the introduction of cradles on Horner's ranch allowed a cradleman to do the work of six Indians with reaping hooks. Higgins based his account on an interview with James Patterson's eighty-year-old son, Eddie.

41. Quote from typed notes, *California Farmer*, Aug. 3, 1854, FWPC. See also Patton, *California Mormons*, 89; Sketch and notes by Albert Horner; Reminiscences of Robert Horner (1930), FHHC; Robert Terry, "The Combined Harvester-Thresher," *Implement and Tractor* 64 (Aug. 1949), 45–46.

42. Quote from Clark, *The Journals of Alfred Doten*, 1: 616; also 429. The machine cost

twelve thousand dollars. See also F. Hal Higgins, "John M. Horner and the Development of the Combined Harvester," *AH* 32 (Jan. 1958), 14–17; Frank F. Latta, "Combined Harvester," MS (n.d.), FFLCSF. Experiments continued into 1862–69. H. H. Thurston and D. J. Marvin built a combine on the Thurston ranch near Stockton and won a prize at the San Joaquin Valley District Fair in 1863. Marvin patented the combine in 1864, and in 1867 began manufacturing the machine. For a combine chronology, see F. Hal Higgins, "Mule Train Ranching in the West," MS (n.d.), 3–5, FHHC.

43. Quotes from Bayard Taylor, *At Home and Abroad* (New York, 1862), 51; John Bidwell to Sen. J. W. McCorkle, Dec. 20, 1851, in McCorkle to Luke Lea, Feb. 6, 1852, LROIACS. For Pierson B. Reading's natives see 1852 MS Census, Shasta County, Schedule I, RCDS. See also W. J. Pleasants, *Twice Across the Plains, 1849–1856* (San Francisco, 1906), 107; Helen D. Crystal, "The Beginnings of Vacaville" (M.A. thesis, UCB, 1933), 170, 183; *Sacramento Union*, Feb. 26, June 25, Oct. 8, 1859, California Scrapbooks, HL; Jose Noriega, deposition, Petition no. 213, U.S. Supreme Court, Appellants v. Alice Marsh, JMC. For Yount's field hands, see Richard Henry Dana, *Two Years Before the Mast*, ed. John Haskell Kemble (Los Angeles, 1964), entry for Dec. 21, 1859: 2, 444–45. For Marsh's natives, see Abby Marsh to parents, Oct. 19, 1851, Amos Tuck Papers, JMC. For Knight's Valley, see typed notes, "The Farm of Thomas Knight," *CSAST, 1858*, FHHC.

44. Quote from Sutter to Henley, Feb. 9, 1856, LROIACS. For Lupilloni ranch field hands, see R. G. Bailey to C. E. Mix, Nov. 4, 1858. See also Sim Moak, *The Last of the Mill Creeks and Early Life in Northern California* (Chico, 1923), 9; *Sacramento Union*, Apr. 13, July 10, 1852.

45. Charles A. Baker, "Don Enrique Dalton of the Azusa," *HSSCAP* 10 (1917), 17–35; Frank P. Brackett, *History of Pomona Valley, California, with Biographical Sketches of the Leading Men and Women of the Valley Who have been Identified with its Growth and Development from the Early Days to the Present* (Los Angeles, 1920); Henry Dalton, rancho journal, Mar. 18, 1845, HDC. Before leaving for Rancho Azusa, the Cahuillas required a personal invitation from Dalton's foreman, who traveled south to their ranchería a few weeks before the harvest. Bearing presents, including stovepipe hats adorned with red ribbons, blue coats with pants trimmed in red, and yards of brightly colored calico cloth, he advised the chief that his help was needed for picking grapes and making wine. A few days later, the chief arrived. For the next few days Dalton entertained him, honoring and generally bestowing a royal welcome on him and his men, as he often did with other visitors. This arrangement ensured that field hands would remain to finish the grape harvest. And it also provided a reserve supply of laborers who, upon completing work at Rancho Azusa, traveled into the pueblo of Los Angeles to assist in Dalton's vineyards. Thus, while most of the other grape growers of Los Angeles struggled to round up extra hands on the auction block, the Cahuillas provided Dalton with a ready supply of reliable labor. For the arrangements with Dalton, see Jackson, *A British Ranchero in Old California*, 168–69, 194–95. For the location of the Indian village, see Plan of Azusa Homestead, HDC. For the Temecula and San Bernardino field hands, see Dorothy M. Day, "Azusa: A Rancho That Became a City" (M.A. thesis, Clark University, 1944), copy in Azusa Public Library.

46. For the Paiutes, see Gae Whitney Canfield, *Sarah Winnemucca of the Northern Paiutes* (Norman, Okla., 1983), 6–9; Knight, "Statement of Early Events in California,"15–16. The Paiutes repeated the journey in 1852.

47. Quotes from Honoria Toumey, *History of Sonoma County* (Chicago, 1926), 1: 123. See also J. Ross Browne, *Crusoe's Island: A Ramble in the Footsteps of Alexander Selkirk, with Sketches of Adventure in California and Washoe* (New York, 1867), 285; Browne, *Report of the Debates in the Convention of California*, 63–68; California Legislature, *Statutes of California*, 1st sess., ch. 133 (Sacramento, 1850), 408–10.

48. 1852 MS Census, San Joaquin County, Schedule I; Jack D. Forbes, *Native Americans of California and Nevada* (Healdsburg, Calif., 1969), 50; Bayard Taylor, *El Dorado, Or Adventures in the Path of Empire* (New York, 1850), 123; Esther Bouton Black, *Rancho Cucamonga and Doña Merced* (Redlands, Calif., 1975), 233; Baldwin [Balduin] Mollhausen, *Diary of a Journey from the Mississippi to the Coasts of the Pacific with a United States Government Expedition* (London, 1858), entry of Mar. 18, 1854, BL.

49. For agricultural accounts omitting or diminishing the role of natives, see Walton Bean, "James Warren and the Beginnings of Agricultural Institutions in California," *PHR* 13 (Dec. 1944), 361–75; Margaret E. Trussell, "Land Choice by Pioneer Farmers: Western Butte County, Through 1877" (Ph.D. diss., University of Oregon, 1969), 220, 226–28, 234; William F. Heitz,

Wine Country: A History of Napa Valley, The Early Years: 1838–1920 (Santa Barbara, 1990), 23; Charles L. Sullivan, *Napa Wine: A History* (San Francisco, 1994), 17–29; Frank Adams, "Historical Background of California Agriculture," in Claude B. Hutchison, ed., *California Agriculture*, 30. One exception is Jim Gerber, "The Origins of California's Export Surplus in Cereals," *AH* 67 (fall 1993), 44, 51, 55.

50. R. V. P. Steele [Latley Thomas], *Between Two Empires: The Life Story of California's First Senator* (Boston, 1969), 248, 285; Paul W. Gates, "The Frémont-Jones Scramble for California Land Claims," *SCQ* 65 (spring 1974), 13–20; Gates, "Adjudication of Spanish-Mexican Land Claims in California," *The Huntington Library Quarterly* 21 (May 1958), 213–18; Gates, "Carpetbaggers Join the Rush for California Land," *CHQ* 56 (summer 1977), 98–127; David A. Williams, *David C. Broderick: A Political Portrait* (San Marino, Calif., 1969), 50. An Indian agent observing conditions around Santa Rosa in Northern California in 1851 tried to explain the situation to his superiors. Natives were caught under a new and disturbing force that seemed to be enveloping the agricultural districts. An awful attitude toward farm labor relations appeared to be developing. Everywhere field hands were kept "perfectly under control," he said. They were "always treated," he said, "as péons, and inculcated [with] the idea of their obligation to labor." See George Gibbs, "Journal of the Expedition of Redick M'Kee, United States Indian Agent, Through Northwestern California in the Summer and Fall of 1851," in Henry Rowe Schoolcraft, *Archives of Aboriginal Knowledge: Containing All . . . of the Indian Tribes of the United States* (Phil., 1860), 3: 100–102.

CHAPTER SEVEN

1. L. J. Rose Jr., *L. J. Rose of Sunny Slope, 1827–1899, California Pioneer, Fruit Grower, Wine Maker, Horse Breeder* (San Marino, Calif., 1959), 54–55. See also Thomas A. Garey, *Orange Culture in California, with appendix on grape culture by L. J. Rose* (San Francisco, 1882), 222–24, 227; L. J. Rose, "Gringo Grandees," MS (n.d.), HL.

2. Quotes from *El Clamor Público*, Oct. 16, Dec. 1, 1855; *Los Angeles Star*, Jan. 4, Dec. 3, 1853; Jan. 4, 18, 1855; also Mar. 17, 1855. It was a different story on a chilly November afternoon a few months later when John Rains, owner of Rancho Cucamonga, was shot by an assassin hiding in ambush along the San Bernardino Road southeast of the Rancho Azusa ranch house. One week later, searchers led by Rancho Azusa field hands discovered Rains's wagon deep in a ravine, and a few days after that, they found his harness in a tree, and nearby his bloodstained hat, overcoat and body. He had been "lassoed," dragged from his wagon by his right arm, which was torn from the socket, and the flesh "mangled from the elbow to the wrist." Robbery was immediately ruled out as a motive because Rains still had his money and jewelry. Although suspicion at first fell on Rains's wife as either an assassin or conspirator, attention soon focused on a native field hand named Manuel Cerradel. Charged with the crime, he was given a hasty trial, convicted of the murder, and sentenced to ten years in prison. But as he was being transported to a ship for the journey north to San Quentin Prison, vigilantes intercepted the guard detail. Overpowering the deputies, they seized Cerradel, hanged him on the spot, then threw his body in the ocean. Quote from *Los Angeles Star*, Nov. 28, 29, 1862. See also Henry Dalton, diary, Mar. 3, 1861; Nov. [n.d.], 1862, HDC; George W. Beattie and Helen P. Beattie, *Heritage of the Valley* (Pasadena, 1939), 149. Esther B. Black, *Rancho Cucamonga and Doña Merced* (Redlands, Calif., 1975), 27, 30, 32, 52–53, 65–66, 77, claims to have uncovered the real murders.

3. For the smallpox epidemic, see Laura King, "Reminiscences of San Gabriel," *HSSCAP* 9 (1920), 59; *Los Angeles Star*, Jan. 31, Feb. 21, Mar. 7, 1863.

4. Quotes from Henry Dalton, diary, 2: 28 [Nov. 24, 1861]; also many other entries, HDC; J. Browne, *Crusoe's Island*, 284. Dalton's ledger entries listed each Indian, if not by his surname, then by some prominent characteristic: *pelón*, the bald one; and *Juan viejo*, John the old one; by task: *irrigador*, irrigator; or by relation: *Hermano de Flores*, brother of Flores. Account books at Rancho Azusa recorded the transactions of Juan Durán, who purchased twenty bottles of *aguardiente* during October 1858, his first month at the ranch. The only other items Durán purchased were two blankets. But the liquor-debt system also affected a woman in charge of ironing, the washerwoman, and seamstress, all of whom accumulated debts by purchasing *aguardiente*. See Henry Dalton, diary, 2: 10, 38–40; Dalton, Indian books, Dec. 1856 to Sept. 1858, 1: 1, 26, 66, 83, 85, as well as entries in vols. 3, 5, 7, HDC.

5. Dalton, daily diary, 2: 1 [Oct. 1861?]; Dalton, "Indios que se han hido," Indian books, 2–4.

Debts ranged from six reales to eighty-six pesos. Owing thirty pesos and four reales to various people when he began working for Dalton, *mayordomo* Martin Duarte managed to clear his obligations, take a mare, and start a new account. But he could not climb out of debt. Paid eighteen pesos per month, Duarte never covered his expenses. He purchased necessities like soap, shirts, candles, cigars, handkerchiefs, socks, shoes, as well as *aguardiente*. After two months—including several days when his pay was docked because he was "*borracho y fallo*" (falling down drunk) and could not perform his duties—Duarte owed about twenty-two pesos. When he went on a long binge and was fired or quit working in mid-September 1858, his debt from two years of labor was fifty-eight pesos. Quote from Dalton, Indian books, 2: 12 [Jan. 12, 1857]. For labor turnover, see Dalton, daily diary, 2: 10 [n.d.]. For Indian alcoholism, see also William B. Taylor, *Drinking, Homicide, and Rebellion in Colonial Mexican Villages* (Stanford, 1979).

6. Quotes from *Los Angeles Star*, Jan. 4, 1855; also Dec. 3, 1853; *Los Angeles Semi-Weekly News*, Feb. 11, 1869. See also Stephen Powers, *The Tribes of California* (Washington, D.C., 1877), 15–17.

7. Quotes from George B. Ironside to Benjamin Wilson, Apr. 11, 1869, BDWP; *Los Angeles Star*, Dec. 12, 1868. John Frohling's wife put it this way: "The Indians . . . disregarded the necessary work, let the ground crack after irrigating and heeded no persuasion, only merry play, dance, feast, steal chickens, do nothing until the last cent was gone." Quote from Mrs. Amelia John Frohling, "Stirring Days of City's Birth Told by One of Early Pioneers," MS (n.d.), MCC. For population figures, see 1860 MS Census, Los Angeles County, Schedule A, 30, 32, 35, RCDS; U.S. Dept. of Interior, Office of Indian Affairs, *Annual Report of the Commissioner of Indian Affairs to the Secretary of Interior in the Year 1869* (Washington, D.C., 1870), 194–95; *Annual Report . . . 1871* (Washington, D.C., 1872), 329. Agricultural statistics from Matthew Keller, "Report to California Growers and Vintners," *Wilmington (California) Journal*, Apr. 20, 1867, EPC. For the marginalization thesis, see Jerard D. Wagers, "History of Agricultural Labor in California Prior to 1880" (M.A. thesis, UCB, 1957), 63, 77. Native field hands in Los Angeles deteriorated to such an extent that their plight gave rise to yet another of the many myths obscuring early farmworkers. It is that the Los Angeles story encapsulated a larger, statewide trend. According to this version of events, natives disappeared from farms everywhere in California during the 1860s. From then on, they never figured prominently in the farmworker story. Swallowed whole, this interpretation has gone unchallenged and projected a false portrait of what actually happened. It has the same defect as so many other stories told about early California farmworkers, the same weakness that surfaces in anecdotes concerning other downtrodden classes in history, and from all labor history that is read backwards from the present rather than as it actually unfolded. It is too neat, too simple, too logical, and like most such fables rests on a foundation of apparent fact or evidence. Demographic data in particular seems to lend credence to the tale. Relying on information tallied by census takers during the federal survey in 1860, scholars note that the largest concentrations of natives were found not in farming districts but near mining communities. Since the fertile interior valleys were supposedly the center of agriculture and since the census figures suggest relatively few natives resided there, some have concluded that outside of Los Angeles, natives worked at other tasks. They were draymen, muleteers, guides, stock tenders, even miners. They did not comprise a significant part of the farm labor force or make an important contribution to the new agricultural industry. Another version of native irrelevance to farming is less complicated. In this unfolding of events, natives vulnerable to hostile white settlers and farmers were slaughtered by the thousands all over the state. This systematic extermination of Indian farmworkers, occurring simultaneously with their devastation by disease and liquor, has been called their "second genocide," and it supposedly further depleted the supply of farm laborers. Contemporaries lent considerable support to this tale of tragic disappearance by chronicling in bloody detail the sorry story of native field hands or potential field hands who were being shot, chased out, maimed, and killed under various pretexts, all the time, everywhere. My assessment that natives were still the principal field hands at this time runs contrary to Hurtado, *Indian Survival*, 159, 165–67; and Hurtado, "'Hardly a Farm House,'" 245–70, maintaining that racist assumptions prevented many Gold Rush farmers from hiring natives.

8. For the genocide theme, see Lynwood Carranco and Estle Beard, *Genocide and Vendetta: The Round Valley Wars of Northern California* (Norman, Okla., 1981), 35–156; Costo and Costo, *The Missions of California*, 64. Death figures from Anthony J. Bledsoe, *Indian Wars of the Northwest: A California Sketch* (1885 [Oakland, 1956]); Cook, *Conflict*, 3–5, 262–63, 272, 277, 350–57, 379–82.

9. Quote from Clark, *The Journals of Alfred Doten*, 1: 361.

10. For field hands stealing threshed oats and digging up potatoes, see *Sacramento Union*, Nov. 8, 1858. For stealing sacked wheat, see *Red Bluff Beacon*, Aug. 25, 1858. For threshing out and packing off wheat, see July 24, 1862. "A worse set of vagabonds cannot be found bearing the human form," wrote Hinton Rowen Helper, a North Carolina author of popular tracts who went to California during the Gold Rush. "Partially wrapped in filthy rags, with their persons unwashed, hair uncombed and swarming with vermin, they may be seen loitering about the kitchens and slaughterhouses waiting to seize upon and devour like hungry wolves such offal or garbage as may be thrown to them." Quote from Hinton Rowan Helper, *Dreadful California: Being a True and Scandalous Account of . . . the Golden State*, ed., Lucius Beebe and Charles M. Clegg (New York, 1948), 152 [originally published as *The Land of Gold: Reality Versus Fiction* (1855)].

11. A crucial fact of agricultural industrialization is that people in distress, whose ranks are supposedly too depleted to provide all of the required labor for an industry, may nevertheless play an essential role in certain specific areas and key functions. They may appear to be finished, but in reality they are not, and may have an impact disproportionate to their numbers. It is exceedingly possible that this is what was happening with native field hands. Their massive population decline may not have occurred so precipitously that it prevented them from providing labor essential to the success of certain crops and agricultural regions. Despite their dire straits, their relocation to reservations, their dislike for farmwork, and their considerable efforts to avoid it, natives seem to have continued working on farms in large numbers for at least a generation after the Gold Rush. Furthermore, the places where farmworkers labored then do not necessarily correspond to the centers of farmwork today or even a decade after the Gold Rush. My criticism of census sampling techniques and skewed conclusions is based from a sample drawn from the 1860 MS Census returns from Alameda, Sacramento, San Joaquin, San Mateo, Santa Clara, and Sonoma counties, Records of the Bureau of the Census, RG 29, NA.

12. Quote from J. Ross Browne, *The Coast Rangers*, 35–36. A journalist visiting natives on Tejon Reservation in the Tehachapi Mountains in 1882 found them to be "happy, tolerably thrifty and very comfortable people, as civilized as a good many who came in emigrant ships from Europe to New York." Quote from Charles A. Nordhoff, *California for Health, Wealth, and Residence* (New York, 1882), 142. For forcible removal, see *Mariposa Gazette*, ca. 1858, Hayes Scrapbooks, BL. See also Frank F. Latta, *Handbook of Yokuts Indians* (Santa Cruz, 1977), 673. For the evolution of the reservation system, see Henry Ellison, "The Federal Indian Policy in California, 1846–1860" (Ph.D. diss., UCB, 1918), 323–43, 341–42. See also Thomas J. Henley to George Manypenny, Aug. 28, 1854; Vincent E. Geiger to A. B. Greenwood, Oct. 12, 1859, LROIACS. For an analysis of opposition to the reservations on the grounds that they would remove needed cheap labor, see Henley to Manypenny, Dec. 18, 1855. A balanced and nuanced account of the origins of the reservation system in California is George Harwood Phillips, *Indians and Indian Agents: The Origins of the Reservation System in California, 1849–1852* (Norman, Okla., 1997), the middle volume in Phillips's projected trilogy on Indian-white interaction in the California interior; see esp. 132–54.

13. Quote from R. G. Bailey to C. E. Mix, Nov. 4, 1859, LROIACS. Other than for a brief period on Tejon Reservation, agricultural production alone never supported the Indians, who rapidly learned that no matter how diligently they applied themselves, their exertions were doomed to failure, and that simply to survive they would often have to leave in order to gather wild food. See also Jack Forbes, *Native Americans of California and Nevada* (Healdsburg, Calif., 1969), 64; Petition, Tehama County Citizens to Secretary of the Interior, n.d., Office of Indian Affairs; J. Y. McDuffie to Hon. A. B. Greenwood, Oct. 18, 1859, in Heizer, *Destruction of the California Indians*, 137–42. Rawls, *Indians of California*, 154–58, 171, estimates that 20 percent of California's approximately fifty thousand Indians resided on reservations.

14. Annie R. Mitchell, *Jim Savage and the Tulareño Indians* (Los Angeles, 1957), 16; Mitchell, "Major James D. Savage and the Tulareños," *CHSQ* 28 (Dec. 1949), 223–24; "Princeton Woman Furnishes Much Historical Data on Life of James Savage," Princeton, Ill., *Bureau County Record*, July 17, 1929; *Sacramento Union*, Aug. 12, 1852; James O'Meara, "A White Medicine Man," *The Californian* 5 (Feb. 1882), 150; Robert Eccleston, *The Mariposa Indian War, 1850–1851, Diaries of Robert Eccleston: The California Gold Rush, Yosemite, and the High Sierra*, ed. C. Gregory Crampton (Salt Lake City, 1975), 106, 120.

15. Quotes from newspaper clippings, Anonymous to O. M. Wozencraft, May 9, 1852, *Alta California*, May 31, 1852, Steamer ed.; "Observer" to editors, Apr. 30, 1852, *San Joaquin Republi-*

can, May 8, 1852; anonymous to editors, May 1, 1852, *San Joaquin Republican*, May 8, 1852, Lilbourne Winchell Clipping File, "Material Relating to James Savage," BL.

16. Quotes from Maria Lebrado, interview by Carl P. Russell, Feb. 1928, Yosemite Museum, Yosemite National Park; H. B. Edwards to Edward Beale, Sept. 20, 1853, LROIACS. See also M. B. Lewis to T. J. Henley, May 8; Nov. 14, 15; Dec. 27, 31, 1858; Jan. 8, 15, 1859.

17. R. G. Bailey to C. E. Mix, Nov. 4, 1858; P. T. Herbert to Henley, Dec. 1, 1858; statement of J. L. Clapp in J. Ross Browne to Charles H. Mix, Nov. 1, 1858; Browne to J. W. Denver, Jan. 18, 1859; Browne to A. B. Greenwood, Nov. 5, 1859; Browne to Greenwood, Nov. 15, 1859; Citizens of Tehama County to Secretary of the Interior, 1859, LROIACS; M. R. Morgan to W. W. Mackall, Sept. 1, 1857, RWDLRDP; Norman E. Berg, *History of Kern County Land Company* (Bakersfield, 1978), 2–4; Helen S. Giffen and Arthur Woodward, *The Story of El Tejon* (Los Angeles, 1942), 48–49; S. T. Harding, *Water in California* (Palo Alto, 1960), 145; unidentified newspaper clippings, Sept. 1863, Beale Memorial Library Special Collections, Bakersfield, Calif.; typewritten notes, "Work for the Indians," *SDI*, Dec. 9, 1862, FFLCSF.

18. Thomas E. Ketcham to Drum, Nov. 4, 1862; Capt. Charles Douglas to Drum, Jan. 19, 1863; W. P. Melendy to George Hansen, Oct. 19, 1862, RWDLRDP; William B. Secrest, "Jarboe's War," *The Californians* 6 (Nov.–Dec. 1988), 16, 18. Reservation Indians also went to work as field hands on commercial farms because many subagents were greedy and unscrupulous individuals who found it convenient and profitable to order natives to toil on their own private farms.

19. Quote from Sutter to Henley, Feb. 9, 1856, LROIACS. See also Sutter to Henley, Dec. 1, 1856; Henley to Sutter, Dec. 4, 1856; Henley to Manypenny, Dec. 4, 1856; J. Y. McDuffie to A. B. Greenwood, Oct. 1859. Saved from bankruptcy, Sutter was able to economize on his labor costs, continue farming, and stay in business for a decade until an arsonist burned him out. But his field hands hardly benefited. See Sutter's reminiscences in *Santa Cruz Sentinel*, July 17, 1875.

20. Quote from John W. Caughey, ed., *The Indians of Southern California in 1852, The D. B. Wilson Report* (San Marino, Calif., 1952), 16, 21–23. On large vineyards around Los Angeles, pruning crews began each year by shaping each vine to a height of about six feet. To accomplish that, they removed huge quantities of vine canes. Separating them into two groups, they cut those with the thickest shoots into thirty-inch lengths, tied them together in bundles of one hundred, piled the bundles onto carts, transported them to the nursery, laid the butt ends of the bundles in shallow trenches, and partially covered them in wet sand to preserve them until the following spring when they hauled them out and planted them. The remainder they heaped into huge piles and burned, later mixing the ashes with seaweed and scattering the material beneath the vines as fertilizer. Men found pruning to be monotonous but pleasant, not the hot, sweaty, stoop labor of harvest time, and performed it with little supervision or interruption, enjoying the work in the mild, sunny, winter climate. For pruning, see H. D. Barrows, diary, Jan. 9, 1857, HDBP; Ord, *The City of Los Angeles and the City of Saints*, 32; William Marsh to Benjamin Wilson, Lake Vineyard Ranch, July 13, 1854, BDWP. On year-round employment, see the B. D. Wilson report in *Los Angeles Star*, Feb. 12, 1868.

21. Quote from Joseph E. Pleasants, "Los Angeles in 1856," *Touring Topics* 22 (Jan. 1930), 37. See also J. Albert Wilson, *History of Los Angeles County* (Oakland, 1880), 53; H. D. Barrows, diary, Jan. 7, 1857.

22. Land clearing remained a particularly grueling task. While the soil about Los Angeles was deep and fertile, the desertlike surface was thickly covered with chaparral, cactus, elders, sagebrush, and large weeds. Natives had to grub all of this out by the roots, pile the debris, and burn them. They started in the spring, first plowing and leveling the land, then using heavy metal bars to punch foot-deep holes on six-foot spacings in the soft, wet earth. After the rains ended, they planted the grapevine cuttings, one thousand vines per acre. Hand watering them throughout the summer, they eventually cut in irrigation ditches. For planting in general, see R. J. Swartzlow, *Lassen: His Life and Legacy* (Chico, Calif., 1964), 16–22; Irving McKee, "Vallejo: Pioneer Sonoma Wine Grower," MS (n.d.), 4–14, Wine Institute, San Francisco. For planting practices and costs, see Charles Kohler, "Wine Production in California," MS (1886), 8, CKC. For snakes, see Augustus Bixby, diary, ca. 1863, ASBP. Fences were built by driving posts into the earth every two feet, then weaving long brush branches and vines between them to form highly durable barriers that protected some vineyards and orchards without repair for twenty years. To protect wheat fields crews ran miles of standing post fences, sometimes called the "close stake fence." This required them to sink eight-foot poles two feet into the ground every four feet and then connect them with poles lashed horizontally between them about four feet

above ground. These fences mainly kept out cattle, and little else. When a denser barrier was needed, field hands built fences with poles lashed horizontally every eight inches between posts. Many crews were kept constantly employed not only building the fences, but repairing them. Furthermore, fences were essential because the state legislature, dominated by cattle interests, had passed the so-called No-Trespass Act, whereby farmers who had their unfenced crops trampled and eaten by stray cattle were denied the right to sue for damages. Making the matter even more burdensome was the fact that barbed wire, which later revolutionized fencing practices and eliminated the open range, was still to be invented, while traditional fencing materials were unavailable. See Dalton, ranch diary, Dec. 26, 1867; *CSAST, 1864–65*, 68; J. S. Silver, "Farming Facts for California Immigrants," *Overland Monthly* 1 (Apr. 1865), 176; *Millennial Star*, Mar. 1, Sept. 25, 1852; *Southern Vineyard*, Apr. 8, 1858, HL; *List of Acts Passed by the Legislature of the State of California at Its First Session* [in 1849 and 1850] [San Jose, 1850], no. 53, 328–29. Board fences were also out of the question, as lumber in 1859 cost thirty dollars per thousand board feet. On Rancho Azusa fencing costs per mile ran as follows: brush fence, $231; loose stone fence, $324; close stake fence, $792; tight board fence, $1,841; and brick and mortar walls, $2,053. For estimates of costs, see J. W. Osborne to Hobbs, Gilman and Co., Dec. 21, 1859, ASC.

23. Henry D. Barrows, "Story of an Old Pioneer," *Los Angeles World*, Oct. 7, 1887; clippings, *Los Angeles Star*, Nov. 20, 1852; Apr. 7, 1855, Hayes Scrapbooks, BL; unidentified newspaper clipping, n.d., Bancroft Scrapbooks, BL; Charles Kohler, "Wine Production in California," 3. For production figures, see Froebel, *Seven Year's Travel in Central America, North America, Northern Mexico, and the Far West of the United States*, entry for Sept. 7.

24. Quote from Newmark, *Sixty Years in Southern California*, 203. For more on treading, see *Los Angeles Star*, Oct. 24, 1857; Louise Lenz, ed., "Memories of Caroline Van der Leck Lenz," *HSSCQ* 36 (summer 1954), 197–98; John W. Caughey, ed., "The Jacob Y. Stover Narrative," *PHR* 6 (summer 1937), 176–77.

25. Quote from Barrows, "Letter from Los Angeles," *San Francisco Daily Evening Bulletin*, Oct. 24, 1859. See also *Cozzens' Wine Press*, Jan. 20, 1859; E. H. Rixford, *The Wine Press and the Cellar* (San Francisco, 1883), 23; Albert J. Wilson, *History of Los Angeles County* (Oakland, 1880), 65.

26. Upkeep expenses from Agoston Haraszthy, *Grape Culture, Wines, and Wine Making; with Notes upon Agriculture and Horticulture* (New York, 1862), 151–52. In the 1860s, winemakers about Los Angeles paid $1,604.56 in wages and materials to plant one hundred acres of vines; they would invest another $4,019.64 to prune, train, and irrigate them for the first three years. The first year's one hundred-acre crop brought in between twenty-thousand and thirty-three thousand dollars, providing an average winemaker with a nice profit that *California Farmer* estimated at fifteen to forty cents per gallon. With such good margins and a steady demand, winemakers continued to expand production. Profits estimated in *California Farmer*, Sept. 5, 1856, were calculated at sixty cents to produce one gallon of wine, and sales of wine at seventy-five cents to one dollar a gallon at the vineyard. According to another estimate, a winemaker with a one hundred-acre vineyard planted to one thousand vines per acre could expect to harvest ten pounds of grapes per vine for a total yield of one million pounds. With twelve pounds of grapes required to make one gallon of wine, the vineyardist could produce 833 gallons of wine per acre, and at forty cents per gallon, could gross $33,320. See Augustus S. Bixby, diary, n.d. Profits were even larger for fresh fruit, with Wolfskill netting one hundred dollars from each of his thirty-two bearing orange trees, and making even more from his nursery business, which supplied most of the state's citrus. See also Caughey, *The Indians of Southern California in 1852*, 16, 21–23. The three main wineries were those operated by the Sainsevan brothers, Kohler and Frohling, and Matthew Keller. See Matthew Keller, "The Grapes and Wine of Los Angeles," in *U.S. Patent Office, Report, Agriculture 1858* (Washington, D.C., 1858), 344–45; Peninou and Greenleaf, *Directory of California Wine Growers . . . in 1860*, 12–29, 40–43. Farmers in California required one farmworker for every two farmers. In Ohio and Illinois the ratio was three farmers to one farmworker; in Indiana four to one. Farmer to farmworker ratios from Paul W. Gates, ed. and intro., *California Ranchos and Farms, 1846–1862, Including the Letters of John Quincy Adams Warren of 1861, being Largely Devoted to Livestock, Wheat Farming, Fruit Raising, and the Wine Industry* (Madison, Wis., 1967), 62–63; F. D. Calhoon, *49er Irish: One Irish Family in the California Mines* (Hicksville, N.Y., 1977), 13–14; Seth Smith to father, July 9, 1850; Apr. 24, 1851; Seth to Asa Smith, May 27, 1851; Seth Smith to father, Oct. 9, 1853, Seth Smith Papers, BL. San Fernando mission information from H. M. Butterfield, "Early Days of Califor-

nia's Pear Industry," *The Blue Anchor*, n.d., in Butterfield, *History of Deciduous Fruits in California* (Sacramento, 1938), 5. Many of my generalizations about labor requirements derive from a sample analysis of farms in Franklin, Georgiana, and Union townships, in Sacramento County. See 1860 MS Census, "Census of the U.S. Population." Farmer to farmworker ratios are probably on the low side because census figures did not include those employed as field hands on reservations. Since there were 21,687 farmers at this time it is likely that the farm labor force at peak harvest was considerably larger than the number that has been generally acknowledged.

27. Regarding opium, the *Mining and Scientific Press* observed, "There is probably no crop which offers to the capitalist so profitable a return for the money invested, just the crop to afford employment for families where there are large numbers of children too young for field hands." Quote from "Culture of the Poppy for Opium," Feb. 12, 1870, 102. See also "Opium Culture—A New Branch of Industry," *California Mail Bag*, June 1871, xvii; Ernest Seyd, *California and Its Resources* (London, 1859), 125–26; Brewer, *Up and Down California in 1860–1864*, 178, 188, 300. One large orchard planted with 250 different varieties of fruit in 1853 sold every piece of fruit it produced in 1856, grossing more than two hundred thousand dollars. For various aspects of agriculture, see "The Farm of Thomas Knight," *CSAST, 1858*, 11–12; Jan Otto Broek, *The Santa Clara Valley, California: A Study in Landscape Changes* (Utrecht, 1932), 55–60; "J.W.R." in *San Joaquin Republican*, Mar. 3, 1852, FCHS; Clyde Arbuckle, *Santa Clara County Ranchos* (San Jose, 1968), 19, 21, 24–25, 30; unidentified newspaper clipping, "When Santa Clara Was Young," n.d., Mrs. Fremont Older Scrapbook, SJPL; Malcolm Rohrbough, *Days of Gold: The California Gold Rush and the American Nation* (Berkeley, 1997), 167. For experiments with various crops, see John E. Bauer, "California Crops that Failed," *CHSQ* 45 (Mar. 1966), 41–68. For canning, see CSBLS, *Fourth Biennial Report, 1889–90*, 93. For dried fruit using a lye solution and burning sulfur process, see Couchman, *Sunsweet Story*, 14–15. For the Sonoma fair, see "Sonoma County Fair—No. 2," *Alta California*, Oct. 16, 1862. For the vegetable and fruit trade between Hood and San Francisco, see John Leale (with interpretations by Marian Leale), *Recollections of a Tule Sailor* (San Francisco, 1939), 36, 65.

28. For labor costs at Rancho Cucamonga, see Black, *Rancho Cucamonga*, 259.

29. Quotes from *Sacramento Standard*, n.d., in *Alta California*, Mar. 17, 1860; California Legislature, Joint Committee on the Mendocino War, *Majority and Minority Reports* (Sacramento, 1860), 11. See also clipping, *San Francisco Bulletin*, June 29, 1857, Bancroft Scrapbooks, BL; *Marysville Herald*, Nov. 1856, in Heizer, *They Were Only Diggers*, 72; various clippings from *California Farmer* in the editorial offices of *California Farmer*, San Francisco and Concord, Calif. For lingering proslavery sympathies, see B. D. Wilson, "Narrative of B. D. Wilson," 69, GHBPS.

30. Quotes from "An Act Amendatory of an Act entitled, An Act for the Government and Protection of Indians, passed April twenty-second, one thousand eight hundred and fifty," in Trafzer and Hayer, *Exterminate Them!* 157; *Sacramento Union*, Dec. 4, 1861. For details of the law, see also California State Senate, *Journal of the Senate, 1860* (Sacramento, 1860), 196; *Statutes of California Passed at the Eleventh Session of the Legislature, 1860* (Sacramento, 1860), ch. 231: 196–97. For lobbying, see *San Francisco Bulletin*, June 29, 1857; U.S. Dept. of the Interior, Office of Indian Affairs, *Report of the Commissioner . . . for . . . 1858* (Washington, D.C., 1860), 9–11; typed notes, *Tulare Times*, n.d., 1860, FFLCSF. For Warner, see Lillian A. Williamson, "New Light on Warner," *HSSCAP* 13 (1924), 21. For the role of Rep. Lewis Burson of Humboldt County, see *Journal of the Assembly of California*, 11th sess. (Sacramento, 1860), 196, 469, 631, 702; Pamela A. Conners, *The Chico to Round Valley Trail of Tears* (Willows, Calif., 1993), 8.

31. Quote from *Humboldt Times*, Feb. 23, 1861, in *San Francisco Bulletin*, Mar. 2, 1861. *Marysville Appeal*, Mar. 22, 1861.

32. Quote from *Sacramento Union*, July 31, 1860; also Feb. 4, 1861. See also *Marysville Appeal*, Jan. 4, 1861, in Heizer, *Destruction of the California Indians*, 240. Considerable dispute surrounds the three years that native field hands were subjected to the revised law. Estimates of how many Indians were involved range from a few hundred to many thousands. In some places, entire communities of farmers became dependent on entire communities of indentured field hands. For example, in Calpella Township, a small farming settlement near Ukiah in Mendocino County, 308 out of 782 people listed in the 1860 census were Indian "apprentices" who were "bound over to sundry citizens" and "employed on farms as servants or laborers." Quotes from 1860 MS Census, Mendocino County, Calpella Township, MCM. I have unsuccessfully searched for the Indian Indenture List, originally in the Eureka Courthouse, Humboldt County, now lost, but possibly in the Robert Heizer Papers, BL.

33. Quotes from Indenture of La-Ache, also known as "Jack," to Ira McCray, Oct. 11, 1862, FCHS. See also 1860 MS Census, Sonoma County, Healdsburg Township, Healdsburg County Library; *Sacramento Daily Union*, Feb. 4, 1861, list of indentures "to be used in ranching, farming and housework" in Tehama County; *Red Bluff Independent*, n.d., in *Marysville Appeal*, Jan. 4, 1861; *Columbia Times*, Jan. 10, 1861.

34. Quotes from *Marysville Appeal*, Dec. 6, 1861; clipping, *Sacramento Union*, Aug. 31, 1862, Bancroft Scrapbooks, BL; *San Francisco Alta California*, Oct. 5, 1862. See also U.S. Interior Dept., Office of Indian Affairs, California Superintendency, *Report of the Commissioner of Indian Affairs for the Year 1861* (Washington, D.C., 1862), 149; indenture papers of Frederico, minor child, to Joseph Smith, Dec. 16, 1861; indenture papers of Dolores Rosario, a minor child, to Hannah Schiller, Feb. 11, 1867, SDHS. For naming practices, see "Among the Diggers Thirty Years Ago," *Hutchings' Illustrated California Magazine* 32 (Apr. 1898), 395.

35. Quotes from *Sacramento Union*, July 15, 1862; also Feb. 4, 1861, Hayes Scrapbooks, BL; Bailey, "Indian Life in the Sacramento Valley," 18; Helen M. Carpenter, "Among the Diggers of Thirty Years Ago," *Overland Monthly* 21 (Apr. 1893), 389–99.

36. Elijah Renshaw Potter, "Reminiscence of Early History of Northern California and the Indian Troubles," MS (1878), 8–9, BL; Robert A. Anderson, *Fighting the Mill Creeks: Being a Personal Account of Campaigns Against Indians of the Northern Sierras* (Chico, Calif., 1909), 80, 84–85; *Alta California*, Oct. 5, 1862. One visitor who witnessed the particularly "shameful and horrible crimes" committed against kidnapped Indian boys fleeing the farms in the northern counties later related the following story:

> Some time in February last, a man named L—who has a . . . ranch . . . had an Indian boy, whose family lived within a mile of his place. L—'s boy would occasionally run off to visit his relations. This incensed L—so much, that he went down one morning and slaughtered the whole family—of about six persons—boy and all. He then made a rude raft of logs, put the victims on it, marked it to W. H. Mills—who was known to be opposed to indiscriminate slaughter of the Indians—and started the bodies down the river.

Quote from *San Francisco Bulletin*, June 1, 1860.

37. Quotes from Edward Dillon to Capt. C. S. Lovell May 31, 1861, RWDLRDP; U.S. Dept. of the Interior, Office of Indian Affairs, *Report of the Commissioner of Indian Affairs for 1862* (Washington, D.C., 1863), 315; also *Report for 1861*, 149–50; *Sacramento Union*, May 4, 1862; also Aug. 31, 1861.

38. Quotes from California Legislature, *Report of the Joint Select Committee Relative to the Chinese Population of the State of California*, in Appendix to Legislative Journals, 1862, no. 23 (Sacramento, 1863), 5, 6, 10.

39. "Good Haul of Diggers—One White Man Killed—Thirty-eight Bucks Killed, Forty Squaws and children Taken," reported the *Humboldt Times*, of Apr. 11, 1863. See also *Fourteenth Session of the California State Legislature, 1863* (Sacramento, 1864), 743; Albert Grover to James Grover, Apr. 7, 1863, AGFP. For comparison with the Black Codes, see Litwack, *Been in the Storm So Long*, 373.

40. For background, see *California Farmer*, May 29, 1857; California State Agricultural Society, *Official Report of the Third Annual Fair* (Sacramento, 1856), 6.

41. Annie E. Bidwell, "The Mechoopdas, or Rancho Chico Indians," *Overland Monthly* 27 (Jan.-June 1896), 205; William Dunstone, *History of Wyandotte* (Dunstone, Calif. 1884), 12; John R. Tubbesing, "Economics of the Bidwell Ranch: 1870–1875" (M.A. thesis, CSUC, 1978), 14; *CSAST, 1858*, 218–19; J. M. Cunnard to Bidwell, July 26, 1862, JBP; *Marysville Appeal*, Feb. 9, 1860. Gentle people, the Mechoopdas were willing to labor for wages of cloth, beads, and food. According to Bidwell, the men could plow furrows a mile or two long and straight as a surveyor's line, using as their instruments nothing more than two poles and a plow. They were particularly adept at handling and caring for horses. These skills proved especially valuable during the grain harvest when they would back up wagons exactly to where they were needed to catch grain from the loaders. Mechoopda women also provided essential labor. Many worked in the gristmill and those that did not were kept busy sewing flour sacks throughout the winter and spring. They also spent weeks in the fields gathering wheat seeds after the harvest. Tossing them in shallow woven trays, they separated the seeds from the chaff, producing seeds so clean and free of weeds that Bidwell used them to plant the next year's crop. The best

and worst of these workers were regularly identified by foremen who issued written reports to Bidwell. Those who malingered or did not meet Bidwell's somewhat arbitrary production standards had their wages docked. But men and women who were especially diligent and productive could not win raises. Loyalty and hard work kept them constantly fed and regularly employed. But it never earned any additional rewards. See Michele Shover, "John Bidwell: A Reconsideration," in *Ripples Along Chico Creek: Perspectives on People and Times* (Chico, 1992), 109; *Yreka Semi-Weekly Union*, Sept. 28, 1864; Charles L. Stilson, diaries, Nov. 1865 to July 1866, Northeastern California Collection, SCML; J. F. Eddy to Bidwell, May 17, 1863; John Bidwell to Annie Bidwell, Dec. 22, 1868, JBP.

42. Michele Shover, "Bitter Moments and Sweet Memories," *The Diggins* 30 (winter 1989), 70–71; WPA, *California, A Guide to the Golden State* (Hastings, N.J., 1939), 466; *Marysville Appeal*, Feb. 9, 1860; Harry L. Wells, *History of Butte County, California* (San Francisco, 1882), 206. After Bidwell died, his wife deeded the ranchería to those Indians remaining on the ranch. But following her death, the ranchería deteriorated. By the 1930s, it was nothing more than a desolate, weed-choked tract of weather-beaten shanties organized around a crumbling little church.

43. Pierson B. Reading to Mrs. Elizabeth Lee, Feb. 23, 1856; *Reading Ranch Journal*, Aug. [n.d.], 1854, PBRC; Fannie Reading to grandmother, Jan. 1, 1857, PBRP; Rosena A. Giles, "More than three Quarters of a Century Ago," GFP. Butte County information from 1860 MS Census, Butte County, Schedule A, 21, 27, 35, 37–39, 46, 59, RCDS.

44. Quote from L. V. Bogy in U.S. Office of Indian Affairs, *Report of the Commissioner of Indian Affairs, 1867* (Washington, D.C., 1868), 117. See also *Sacramento Union*, July 17, 1865; N. G. Taylor in U.S. Office of Indian Affairs, *Report of the Commissioner of Indian Affairs, 1868* (Washington, D.C., 1869). "A good many . . . have heretofore been induced to retain their camps in squads of half a dozen to a dozen families on certain ranches," reported the *Ukiah Herald*, "so that the owners could have the benefit of their labor, making them such remuneration as the Indians would accept." Quotes from *Sacramento Union*, Sept. 23, 1861, citing the *Ukiah Herald*, n.d.; and *Pacific Echo*, July 4, Aug. 2, 1862. For a sample of wage variations, see Cronise, *The Natural Wealth of California*, 386.

45. Quotes from *San Francisco Bulletin*, Oct. 21, 1861; Juan Bandini, diary, 1: Mar. 16, 1880; May 28, 1881, trans. Margaret Gaffey Mel, Juan Bandini Papers, HL. See also Doris and Clyde Foster, "One Hundred Years of History at Foster's Hogue Ranch," *Madera County Historian* 1 (Oct. 1961), 3, 6; WPA, "Indians in California Agriculture," in *Documentary History of California Agriculture*, MS (1939), 13, BL; Ida May Shrode, "The Sequent Occupation of Rancho Azusa de Duarte, a Segment of the Upper San Gabriel Valley of California" (Ph.D. diss., University of Chicago, 1948), 70; Michael Forbes to Stearns, July 29, 1873, ASP.

46. 1852 MS California Special Census, Yolo County, Sutter County, Schedule I, RCDS; H. B. Edwards to E. F. Beale, Sept. 20, 1853; Sutter to Henley, Feb. 9, 1856; J. Ross Browne and E. F. Beale to Luke Lea, Apr. 2, 1857, LROIACS; Frank Laloguna, "Wheat in Tehama County," MS (1968), Tehama Public Library, 2; Frank A. Speth, "A History of Agricultural Labor in Sonoma County, California" (M.A. thesis, UCB, 1938), 18.

47. Quote from *Sacramento Union*, Aug. 19, 1865.

48. Quotes from Henry Gandt, May 22, 1863, JBP; Juan Forster to Cave Couts, Dec. 27, 1863, CJCP; J. Ross Browne, *The Coast Rangers* (Balboa Island, 1959), 38.

49. Quote from William H. Boyd and Glendon J. Rogers, eds., *San Joaquin Vignettes, The Reminiscences of Captain John Barker* (Bakersfield, 1955), 34. See also John Barker clipping file, BWC; Charles W. Clough and William B. Secrest, *Fresno County—The Pioneer Years: From The Beginning to 1900* (Fresno, 1984), 1; 258–59.

50. Quote from *Sacramento Union*, July 22, 1858, CSL. See also *Nevada Journal*, May 31, 1861. For grasshopper feasts, see *Marysville Appeal*, Aug. 31, 1861. For a description of the use of sulfured rags and burning dung, see Dalton, diaries, July 10, 13, 15, 1870.

51. Quotes from Frank F. Latta, "Sky Farmers' Homes," MS (n.d.), 1; Latta, "The Story of Henry Hammer," MS (n.d.), 3, FFLCSF. Another form of abuse greeted natives around San Juan Bautista, a small farm-town fifty miles south of San Jose. Congregating in a run-down ranchería near the juncture of the San Juan and Hollister roads at a place called, not surprisingly, "Indian Corners," they had to rely on the women of the ranchería to make ends meet by washing clothes for town residents in the San Juan Creek. This was humiliating to them, particularly on Saturday mornings when the women would load their laundry into baskets and carry them on their heads single file along the main road into town. Unemployed most of the

year, except for the odd jobs, the men could only find work cutting, binding, and threshing grain during July and August, a task they performed well. "Some of these men were large, strong, and of fine physique," recalled one farmer. "They were excellent workers at the harvest." But they also consumed large amounts of alcohol. As soon as they started working, natives started drinking. Stumbling down the town streets on their way home, they invariably ran into hostile whites, often with deadly consequences. Arguing with some white man or committing no greater crime than crossing too close or failing to obey an order, numerous drunk, unarmed harvesters were shot dead and their murderers acquitted, invariably by claiming self-defense. This bothered no one. So callous were the farmers of San Juan Bautista that after one drunk harvester, a big man named Frank, tottered out of town and got run over by a Southern Pacific train near Pescadero Creek, the engine—locals joked—was acquitted on grounds of self-defense. Quote from Isaac L. Mylar, "Indian Women Did the Washing in Primitive Style," *Watsonville Pajaronian*, n.d., PVHS.

52. Quote from Benjamin Arthur, deposition, Round Valley, Feb. 28, 1860, Indian War Files, CSA; also William T. Scott, deposition, Cloverdale, Mar. 2, 1860. Forced to sleep in the open and worked unmercifully, the men grumbled and once even threatened to run away. When this happened, Hall whipped them. See Mrs. Estle Beard, interview, Round Valley, Aug. 22, 1981, author's possession.

53. Quote from G. W. Gillette, "Some of My Indian Experiences," *HSSCQ* 6 (1904), 158–60. Wage rates are from E. K. Dunlap, testimony taken by A. B. Chapman in Philip Sichel v. Maria Merced W. de Carillo et al., Apr. 1866, Santa Clara County Superior Court, copy in San Bernardino County Museum. For an account of payday on Rancho Azusa that resembles one at Rancho Cucamonga, see C. B. Glasscock, *Lucky Baldwin* (New York, 1933) 247–49.

54. Quote from *Sacramento Union*, Aug. 19, 1865. See also G. M. Hanson to John Bidwell, Sept. 28, 1863, JBP; Robert J. Chandler and Ronald J. Quinn, "Emma Is a Good Girl," *The Californians* 8 (Jan.–Feb. 1991), 34–38; *California Police Gazette*, Sept. 26, 1865. Wage information from Benjamin Hayes, "I Know the 'Californians' Well," MS (n.d.), Hayes Scrapbooks, BL.

55. Quote from *Monterey Gazette*, Nov. 28, 1867 [copy supplied by Dennis Copeland], California History Room, Monterey Public Library. See also Copeland to author, Mar. 16, 2002, author's possession; Jail Register, 1850–1872, entry no. 558, Indian, José Laurencio ["Laruinso"], May 13, May 15, Aug. 15, 1867; José Morales, May 27, 1868 [copies supplied by Graham Blake]. Although Walton, *Storied Land*, 127–28, locates these documents in Colton Hall Museum, I found them in the California History Room, Monterey Public Library. For the 1866 shooting incident, see C. Alan Hutchinson, *Manifesto to the Mexican Republic* (Berkeley, 1978), 97.

56. Calculated from 1860 MS Census, Schedule A, particularly Yuba, Tulare, Calaveras, and Sutter counties. See also Bob Powers, *South Fork Country* (Los Angeles, 1980), 26; Bruce Levene et al., *Mendocino County Remembered: An Oral History* (Mendocino, 1976), 1: 89; H. B. Sheldon, U. S. Office of Indian Affairs, *Report . . . 1884* (Washington, D.C., 1884); Alvin F. Aggen et al., "Mechanization of Lima Bean Threshing: Joe Terry Is Interviewed by Wallace Smith," *Ventura County Historical Society* 25 (spring 1980), 5.

CHAPTER EIGHT

1. Quote from Alfred Doten, journals, Book no. 22, July 19, 1860, ADCUNR.

2. Ibid.

3. Quote from Clark, *The Journals of Alfred Doten*, 1: 550. See also Doten to Rock, Aug. 17, 1860, ibid.

4. For the view of agriculture as an industry built in "occupied territory" entirely on the backs of poor, powerless, people of color, see Ronald B. Taylor, *Chavez and the Farm Workers* (Boston, 1975), 19; Edna Bonacich, "Asian Labor in the Development of California and Hawaii," in Lucie Cheng and Bonacich, eds., *Labor Immigration under Capitalism: Asian Workers in the United States before World War II* (Berkeley, 1984), 151; Daniel, *Bitter Harvest*, 26; Chan, *Bittersweet Soil*, 272; Sucheng Chan, Douglas Henry Daniels, Mario T. Garcia, Terry P. Wilson, eds., *Peoples of Color in the American West* (Lexington, Mass., 1994), 7.

5. Quote from *Country Gentleman*, July 27, 1854. Yields varied according to location from ten bushels per acre in Tulare County and fourteen bushels in Stanislaus to the fantastic thirty and forty bushel-per-acre yields in virgin river bottomlands. See John S. Hittell, *Resources of California . . .* (San Francisco, 1863), 172–73; California Senate, *Annual Report of the Surveyor*

General of California for 1855, 6th sess. (Sacramento, 1856), 78. For the beginnings of the wheat industry, see Kenneth A. Smith, "California: The Wheat Decades" (Ph.D. diss., USC, 1969), 42–50. Production figures for 1852–59 are in *CSAST, 1859*, 325.

6. Quote from J. P. Munro-Fraser, *History of Santa Clara County, California* (San Francisco, 1891), 23. For farming patterns, see 1860 MS Census, Alameda County, showing that of 892 farmers, 418 grew wheat, most of them more than one hundred bushels; and 1870 MS Census, San Joaquin County, showing that of 250,000 acres of fenced land, 117,0000 were planted to wheat, and the remainder to barley, hay, and fruit. Production information is highly unreliable. Other than Gov. John Bigler's reference to exports of wheat and flour totaling one million dollars in 1855, there are no export statistics until 1856, when *Commerce and Navigation*, Apr. 4, June 6, July 25, Aug. 15, 1856, reported exports of 33,088 bushels of wheat and 114,572 barrels of flour valued at $1,106,869. See Charles H. Shinn, "Early Horticulture in California," *Overland Monthly* 6 (Aug. 1885), 128; *California Farmer*, Jan. 11, 1856. For poorly ground flour, see typed notes, *SWI*, Sept. 14, 1861, FFLCSF. For grasshopper infestations, see *California Farmer*, June, July, Aug. 1855. For dirty wheat acquiring a bad reputation and fetching low prices in Southern California, compared to cleaner wheat produced in the northern part of the state, see C. R. Johnson to Stearns, July 21, 1856, ASP. For general developments, see R. H. Allen, "The Spanish Land-Grant System as an Influence in the Agricultural Development of California," *AH* 9 (July 1935), 133–34. For local developments, see Will Green, *History of Colusa County* (San Francisco, 1880), 23, 60; Curtis and Connover to Kenady and Hopkins, Sept. 20, 1860, Curtis and Hopkins Papers, HL.

7. Quote from Horace Davis, "Wheat in California," *Overland Monthly* 1 (Nov. 1868), 442. For the American-born, see John S. Hittell, "The Mining Excitements of California," *Overland Monthly* 2 (Apr. 1869), 415; Edwin S. Holmes, *Wheat Growing and General Agricultural Conditions in the Pacific Coast Region of the U.S.*, U.S. Dept. of Agriculture, Bureau of Statistics, Misc. Series, Bulletin no. 20 (Washington, D.C., 1901), 17–19. In these circumstances, men abandoned their promise never to resume the mundane life they had left behind. Facing starvation, those who had been field hands and had come west to escape the drudgery of their work now reassessed their vows. Once hostile to their former profession, they fell back on it as a means of survival. Hoping to purchase a ship's passage to the East Coast or simply remain in California until their fortunes improved, they drifted into the fields in such large numbers that they offset the declining supply of Indians. Some found work through newspaper advertisements and employment agencies. Others were sought out by farmers who put the word out that they needed help or drove into town seeking field hands. Many field hands learned of work through a relative. Often they joined friends from back home who had been working on a particular farm and had notified them that a farmer was looking for men. Most men simply showed up, following word-of-mouth information or a hunch. Crews often consisted entirely of men who had crossed the plains by wagon train together and who had remained together while working in the diggings and after. For newcomers joining relatives and friends, see John Perry, interview, Mar. 23, 1930, Manteca, Calif., FFLCSF; Susan Folger Gardner, diary, Jan.–Apr. 1853, Perkins Library, Duke University, Durham, N.C. For local employment agencies, see *Napa County Reporter*, Feb. 6, 1869, NCLCF.

8. The Greeks, Portuguese, and Italian sailors had jumped ship; stranded, they were looking to just get through the year. The Mexicans and Chileans had escaped their bosses and went to work on the wheat farms after being brought to California under contract, and were often referred to by farmers as "Spaniards." The Irish and German dockworkers were seeking relief from their periodic unemployment and hoped to earn a stake and shelter to get them through the winter. For Italians, see Mariano Guadalupe Vallejo, "What the Gold Rush Brought to California," in Valeska Bari, ed., *The Course of Empire, First Hand Accounts of California in the Days of the Gold Rush of '49* (New York, 1931), 5–6. For Chileans, see Cornejo, *Los Chilenos en San Francisco*, 92; Steve Giaboci, "Chile and Her Argonauts in the Gold Rush, 1848–1856" (M.A. thesis, CSU, San Jose, 1967). For the Portuguese, see Alvin Ray Graves, "Immigrants in Agriculture: The Portuguese Californians, 1850–1970's" (Ph.D. diss., UCLA, 1977), 50–51. For Portuguese sailors buying land and settling down after a year in the fields, see Washington Township Research Committee, *History of Washington Township*, 18. For Italians, see Hans Christian Palmer, "Italian Immigration and the Development of California Agriculture" (Ph.D. diss., UCB, 1965), 137. For Irish, see Calhoon, *49er Irish*, 13–14.

9. Quote from unidentified newspaper clipping, FFLCSF. Clark, *Journals of Alfred Doten*,

1: 555, contains one of the earliest uses of this term. Doten also refers to bindlemen as "stragglers." See also 1: 339, 364, 402, 412, 420–21, 423. For bindlemen in the early 1860s, see unidentified newspaper clipping, Doten to Plymouth Rock, Aug. 17, 1860, ADCUNR; Henry Brooks, "A Few Words about 'Pile' Making," *California Mountaineer* 1 (Jan. 1861), 130–31; *San Francisco Bulletin*, July 7, 1862, Bancroft Scrapbooks, BL; *CSAST, 1863*, 81. For tramping laborers of the previous decade, see Edward F. Beale to Luke Lea, Nov. 22, 1852, LROIACS; H. D. Barrows, diary, Dec. 12, 1854; Jan. 20, 1855, HDBP; *Napa Reporter*, Jan. 23, 1858; July 2, 1859; *Sacramento Weekly Union*, Dec. 4, 1858; William Perkins, *Three Years in California: William Perkins' Journal of Life at Sonora, 1849–1852* (1924 [Berkeley, 1964]), 103; Raven, *Golden Dreams and Leaden Realities*, 79; William M'Collum, *California As I Saw It*, ed. Dale Morgan (Los Gatos, Calif., 1960), 125. Bindlemen were not always treated well by the steamship companies, concerns that preferred carrying bulk goods. The routine for getting ashore could be a rugged one for a lone farmhand. As a boom swung the gangway toward a "brush landing"—literally a tangle jutting out from the riverbank—the chief mate would call out, "You get off here, mister," and the unsuspecting laborer would be motioned out onto the gangway. Close behind him and politely carrying his belongings would be a deckhand—a big one. Seeing that there was nothing on which to step but the uninviting mass of brush, the laborer would try to get back. This was where the deckhand came in. Planting his large foot in the seat of the victim's pants, he sent the laborer overboard—frequently to disappear to his armpits in the brush—then tossed his belongings after him. Quote from Jerry MacMullen, *Paddle-Wheel Days in California* (Stanford, 1944), 91–92. See also Thelma White, *Glenn County Sketchbook*, ed. Dorothy J. Hill and Lois H. McDonald (Chico, Calif., 1995), 117; Helen Hohenthal, "A History of the Turlock District" (M.A. thesis, UCB, 1939), 55.

10. Frank Gilbert and Harry L. Wells, *History of Butte County, California* (San Francisco, 1882), 221.

11. Quote from Clark, *Journals of Alfred Doten*, 1: 399. Because horses were so essential to operations, bindlemen and former gold miners spent much of their time tending to their needs, driving the animals between pastures, feeding them, maintaining their stables, and ministering to animals that were injured or in labor. Periodically throughout the year men would also "rat proof" fields, poison squirrels, kill coyotes that were raiding the henhouses, and round up rabbits "for tamale purposes." Sometimes they accomplished this by hunting the varmints and shooting them with shotguns. But because that was so expensive and time-consuming they more commonly rid their farms of pests by spreading out pieces of chicken bait soaked in strychnine or phosphorus. Whenever coyotes raided henhouses and killed prize laying hens, men would rescue what remained of the bodies, gather up other food scraps, soak them in the poison of choice, strychnine again being a favorite, and distribute the scraps to the affected areas. In this way they poisoned entire local populations of mice, coyotes, foxes, crows, other birds, and squirrels. They also inadvertently killed plenty of dogs and even some cattle as well. Much of their work away from the wheat fields centered on producing their own food. On many farms they tended hogs. Feeding them refuse and scraps, they raised animals of huge proportions that sometimes became wild and mean, often inflicting serious injuries on careless men. One hog accident, described in detail in the *Marin Journal*, occurred on the Mattone ranch in western Marin County.

> The men on the premises had been pressing grapes for wine, and had thrown out the pomace to the hogs on the place. The brutes ate the refuse of the grapes voraciously, and straightway devils entered into the herd of swine; in other words, they became fighting drunk. While in this condition a large boar, which hitherto had been very peaceable, attacked old Antonio Boccaglio, knocking him down, biting him and lacerating his side fearfully with his projecting tusks. Dr. Proctor was hastily summoned from Petaluma and attended to his injuries. The hog had to be shot.

Quote from undated clipping, *Marin Journal*, ca. 1862, Marin County Historical Society. Besides raising hogs, field hands maintained gardens, built and serviced chicken coups, fed and milked cows, broke young heifers to milking, churned butter, made cheese, raised and slaughtered pigs, branded cattle, picked fruit, gathered eggs, pruned trees, hauled produce to town and sometimes peddled it as well. Because of the incessant activity, their few surviving diaries tended to be cryptic catalogs of endless tasks and challenges.

12. Doten continues:

Assisted at the castrating . . . greased his penis with some lard—tied a string tightly about the scrotum, just above the stones—cut a slit on each side, pressed out the stones, and put on clamps . . . castrated three boars . . . took 11 baskets of peaches down to Alviso . . . made two grain forks . . . suckered peach trees . . . went up to repair the windmill . . . went down the well and fixed the pump . . . cleaned up the places where the machines & grain sacks had stood . . . killed and dressed the scrub sow . . . burning brush, cutting wood & splitting out posts.

Quotes from Clark, *Journals of Alfred Doten*, 1: 251, 304, 308, 310, 317, 320, 328, 355, 359, 380, 381–82, 384, 401, 404, 407, 468, 558, 605, 621, 629. See also Julian Dana, *The Sacramento, River of Gold* (New York, 1939), 183; many entries in John Francis Pyle, diaries, JFPP; Elvira Gnagi, diaries, EGP; William Carey Bailey, diary; Orlando Brown, travel diary, CHS. During the spring, men repaired equipment, built grain bins, sewed grain sacks, mended fences, ditched around wheat fields, dug and cleaned wells, erected barns and blacksmith shops, fixed wagons, plows, and other tools, and so on. At other times they would drive into town to obtain supplies, sweep the bunkhouse, build roads, cut rails and posts for fences, and perform numerous duties associated with maintaining what was otherwise completely raw land. Often they would be deployed as if they were troops. "Morning a young man by the name of Melchoir came to work at $1.00 per day," read Doten's log, "set him to trimming and suckering the apple trees—Set Barney to sewing the rest of the cloth for the fly roof of the dairy—Had Thomas whitewashing, and Israel hoeing—PM, Mark came over with his horse harnessed in the old milk wagon, and rode up to MV with him." Quote from Clark, *Journals of Alfred Doten*, 1: 399.

13. Quote from Richard Henry Dana, *Two Years Before the Mast* (Boston, 1911), 489. In the Santa Clara Valley they could not go more than a day without breaking their plows on tough old roots—"Devil's shoe strings," they called them. Spending excessive amounts of time taking plows in for repair, men were literally worn out, and when they finished in March they spoke of never feeling the same again. See Dudley Chase, "Western Agricultural Improvements," *Overland Monthly* 4 (Feb. 1870), 149–50; *CSAST, 1859*, 236; *CSAST, 1860*, 233; Henry Mills, interview, Dec. 1936, FFLCSF; Horace Davis, "California Breadstuffs," *Journal of Political Economy* 2 (Sept. 1894), 600; John Hyde Braly, *Memory Pictures, An Autobiography* (Los Angeles, 1912), 127; Latta, "Seed Spreader Disc Cultivator of Valley Origin," *Fresno Bee*, July 9, 1933, BWC.

14. Quotes from "Labor Omnia Vincit," *Napa Reporter*, Nov. 9, 1872, NCLCF; Clark, *Journals of Alfred Doten*, 1: 555, 370. See also newspaper clipping, Doten to Plymouth Rock, Aug. 17, 1860, ADCUNR; *CSAST, 1863*, 81.

15. Quote from *California Farmer*, June 15, 1854. As they spread throughout the wheat districts, mechanical harvesters enlarged the acreage that could be cultivated, becoming far more common much earlier in California than in any other wheat-growing district, although not without some initial trepidation on the part of their owners. An old Californio like Los Angeles ranchero Antonio María Lugo still preferred traditional cradles and scythes. Upon seeing his first reaper, he could only curse it as an evil aberration of the American newcomers, then point his finger at it and exclaim: "The Yankee is but one finger shy of the devil!" But this was far from typical. Quote from Henry D. Barrows, "Don Antonio Maria Lugo: A Picturesque Character of California," *HSSCAP* 3 (1894–96), 32. McCormick reapers employed a serrated, rectilinear (back and forth) cutting blade that lay parallel to the ground and snipped the wheat scissorlike, while Hussey mowers employed a rotary cutter. See also Douglas Hurt, *American Farm Tools: From Hand Power to Steam Power* (Manhattan, Kans., 1982), 41–42; Eliza Farnham, *California, In-Doors and Out; Or, How We Farm, Mine, and Live Generally in the Golden State* (New York, 1865), vi; Latta, "The Reaper," MS (n.d.), FFLCSF. Unlike the introduction of mechanical tomato harvesters, no controversy surrounded the introduction of mechanical reapers. See for example Edward H. Hall, *The Great West* (New York, 1864), 78; U.S. Bureau of Labor Statistics, "Mechanization of Agriculture as a Factor in Labor Displacement," *Monthly Labor Review* 3 (Oct. 1931), 24–25. On small farms, recently cleared and hacked from stands of timber, cradles still proved useful for harvesting between protruding stumps. They were otherwise useless on large wheat farms. At an average rate of two acres per day, 4,464 cradlers and 8,928 binders—who gathered and tied the bundles of cut grain—would have taken about twenty-eight days to cut California's 1860 wheat crop of 250,000 acres. They would have required another month to cut the barley. Data for cradlemen extrapolated from 1860 figures as follows: 250,000 acres divided by twenty-eight days is 8,928 acres per day, divided by two acres

per day average harvest with the cradle is 4,464 cradlers per day times two binders is 8,928 binders, for a total of 13,392 field hands. See William T. Hutchinson, *Cyrus Hall McCormick*, 1: 71–72, 325, 377, 471n; *Marysville Appeal*, Dec. 12, 1860. Wheat growers used many different versions of these machines including the Manny reaper, and one built by Ogg Shaw. See "Harvesting Machines," *PRP*, Mar. 4, 1871. Sales figures from *California Farmer*, Aug. 22, 1856; June 24, 1859; June 22, July 20, 1860; Aug. 4, 1862. For the labor shortage of 1862, see *San Francisco Bulletin*, July 7, 1862; Clark, *Journals of Alfred Doten*, 1: 664. For custom reaper operators charging two dollars an acre see, ibid., 613. Hundreds of reapers and mowers were lost in shipwrecks while in transit. Although farmers in the eastern United States purchased reapers for $125 to $150, in California the more "refined" machines sold for $350 to $650, with those manufactured in California selling for about $250. Freight costs from the East Coast added about forty to one hundred dollars to the cost of each reaper and mower. There was also considerable difference in prices among models, with McCormick reapers costing twenty-five dollars more than others. Prices from *CSAST, 1858*, 64, 124–25; *CSAST, 1859*, 235; *CSAST, 1861*, 137; *CSAST, 1864–65*, 17; Butte County, Assessor, Assessment of Real and Personal Property, 1858–59, Butte County Assessor's Office, Oroville [James Morehead's reaper on his Llano Seco Ranch near Chico was assessed at seventy-five dollars in 1861]; *Los Angeles Star*, Apr. 13, 1861. For reaper sharing, see Clark, *The Journals of Alfred Doten*, 1: 366–71, 551. For group purchases, see 546. For the general trend, see Alan Olmstead, "The Mechanization of Reaping and Mowing in American Agriculture, 1833–1870," *Journal of Economic History* 35 (June 1975), 334. For cradles, see George Emerick, interview, in Levene, ed., *Mendocino County Remembered*, 1: 129.

16. Extrapolated from Donald P. Greene, "Prairie Agricultural Technology, 1860–1900" (Ph.D. diss., Indiana University, 1957), 257–58; "Good Binders Help the Threshers," *American Thresherman* 25 (June 1922), 5; Clark, *The Journals of Alfred Doten*, 1: 551. See also Graeme R. Quick and Wesley F. Buchele, *The Grain Harvesters* (St. Joseph, Mich., 1978), 11, 39, 43–57; Hurt, *American Farm Tools*, 47–49; Leo Rogin, *The Introduction of Farm Machinery*, 102–3. Dick Meister and Anne Loftis, *A Long Time Coming: The Struggle to Unionize America's Farm Workers* (New York, 1977), 5, mistakenly assert that "the use of harvesting machines meant that only a relatively few workers were needed." Although Paul A. David, "The Mechanization of Reaping in the Ante-Bellum Midwest," in Henry Rosovsky, ed., *Industrialization in Two Systems* (New York, 1966), 3–39, 23–27, claims that only about 50 percent of the wheat crop in the Midwest was harvested with machines by 1860, in California the evidence suggests that nearly 100 percent was being cut with machines by that date. See Merrill Denison, *Harvest Triumphant: The Story of Massey-Harris* (New York, 1949), 78–79; Clark, *The Journals of Alfred Doten*, 1: 368–69, 420; *California Farmer*, Aug. 22, 1856; "Monitor Number 2 Notice," advertisement, July 4, 1868, ibid.; Thomas Ogg Shaw, advertisement, *Napa Pacific Echo*, July 4, 1862, NCLCF. The general goal of custom operators and farm owners alike was to keep their machines running for at least five years, and ten years if possible, a time sufficient to pay off loans and interest rates and earn a substantial return on investment. For these reasons, reaper drivers had to be proficient at making repairs.

17. Because sweep arms did not allow drivers to sit on the machine, McCormick quickly modified the apparatus, creating a so-called pigeon wing sweep arm (so-named for its resemblance to a pigeon wing) that allowed drivers to remain seated. By 1864, two-thirds of all McCormick harvesters had "pigeon wing" sweep arms. Simple, sturdy, and lightweight, these machines came with a warranty and cost two hundred dollars, a price that most farmers could afford. Improved machines would further widen the swath cut, move with less horsepower, and be pushed rather than pulled so as to eliminate the trampling of the grain before it was cut. Because they delivered the grain far to the left so that the reaper could pass between the shocks and the standing grain, the machine could harvest a field without binders and stackers. A variant arrangement, known as a "dropper," allowed the driver to depress the rear of the reaper gavel table at regular intervals, allowing the grain to slide backward onto the ground. These machines reduced the number of men by roughly two-thirds. See Clark, *Journals of Alfred Doten*, 1: 419; "Harvesting Machines," *PRP*, Mar. 4, 1871; Merritt Finley Miller, *The Evolution of Reaping Machines*, U.S. Dept. of Agriculture, Office of Experiment Stations, Bulletin no. 103 (Washington, D.C., 1902), 31–33; Wallace Smith, *Garden of the Sun: A History of the San Joaquin Valley, 1772–1939* (Los Angeles, 1939), 222; Latta, "The Story of Henry Hammer," MS (1929), FFLCSF; Higgins, "83 Years of Equipping California Farms," MS (n.d.), FHHC; *Napa Pacific Echo*, July 4, 1862, NCLCF. At the rate of about fourteen acres per day, 637 self-rake

harvesters would have required twenty-eight days to cut the 1860 wheat crop. Computation of the number of self-rake reapers as follows: 250,000 acres divided by twenty-eight days is 8,928 acres per day divided by fourteen acres per day average reaper rate totals 637 reapers. See Clarence H. Danhof, "Agricultural Technology to 1880," in Harold F. Williamson, ed., *The Growth of the American Economy* (New York, 1951), 146; Rogin, *Introduction of Farm Machinery*, 126–28. A harvest rate of twenty acres per day is described in Clark, *Journals of Alfred Doten*, 1: 375. Like yields, harvest speed varied widely with crops, crews, and terrain.

18. Quote from C. L. Brace, *The New West* (New York, 1869), 231. See also F. Hal Higgins, interview by author, Mar. 23, 1970, Davis, Calif., author's possession; Clark, *Journals of Alfred Doten*, 1: 364–66; Arthur Domonoske, "Recollections," interview, n.d., FHHC; Lauren Dennen, interview, in Levene et al., *Mendocino County Remembered*, 1: 119; Arnold P. Yerkes and L. M. Church, *Cost of Harvesting Wheat by Different Methods*, U.S. Dept. of Agriculture, Bulletin no. 627 (Washington, D.C., 1918), 11; M. L. Wilson and H. E. Murdock, *Reducing Wheat Harvest Costs* (Bozeman, Mont., 1924), 11. To the casual observer, shocks seemed to be nothing more than little piles of bundled hay, although boosters of California agriculture tended to use more flowery phrases and military terms, sometimes describing them as looking "like crowded encampments." But shockers actually had a clear idea of how each shock should be constructed, and why. The patterns varied with circumstances. Thick or thin stands of wheat affected the distance between the piles left by the binder, and therefore the number of bundles that could be carried a reasonable distance. In some fields shockers simply stood up pairs of inward-leaning bundles, but more commonly in creating their shocks they employed one of three stacking arrangements—an H-shaped pile, with two bundles in the center, and three on each side, all parallel; a round pile, with eight bundles arranged around two in the center; and oval or oblong piles, with four bundles in the center, and three on each side. Besides the reaper driver, a harvest crew required six other men. During 1860, according to the six-man-per-crew average, 3,826 men would have bound and gathered the California wheat crop, but the number was probably considerably larger. When drivers are included, a minimum of 4,463 men would have been involved in bringing in the harvest. Those men comprised at least 45 percent, probably more, of the 10,421 field hands listed in the census that year. Their numbers call into question the accuracy of census figures and suggest that the farm labor force was considerably larger. Computation of harvest labor requirements for self-rake reapers for the 1860 wheat crop as follows: 637 reapers per day multiplied by six binders equals 3,822 binders, plus 637 reaper drivers for a total of 4,459 field hands. For a ten-man crew, see Clark, *Journals of Alfred Doten*, 1: 375; Marvin McKinley, *Wheels of Farm Progress* (St. Joseph, Mich., 1980), 4; John F. Steward, *The Reaper: A History of the Efforts of Those Who Justly May Be Said to Have Made Bread Cheap* (New York, 1931), 49–51, 237–56, 268–343; Rogin, *Introduction of Farm Machinery*, 107–9. On some reapers, binders rode on an attached platform, where they lifted the grain from the box, tied it in bundles with straw and twine bands, then dropped it on the ground. Davis, "Wheat in California," 449; Clark, *Journals of Alfred Doten*, 1: 551. See also Thomas D. Isern, *Bull Threshers and Bindlestiffs: Harvesting and Threshing on the North American Plains* (Lawrence, Kans., 1990), 45–50. Old bindlemen recalled some of the finer points of shock construction. They usually lifted bundles by the tie and carried one in each hand. If mustard was growing in the field, they would spend a lot of time pulling it out of their bundles. When setting the first bundles, it was necessary to plant them firmly on the ground and not leave them tipsy on the standing stubble. Next a shocker would wrap his wrists and arms around the bundles and hold them tightly against his body with the heads up and butts down. Then he planted them down hard, using the weight of his body to set them firmly. Shocking freshly cut grain that was still slightly green was simple, as bundles fit together easily. But if the grain had lain in the field for a day or two in a dry wind, the bundles would be stiff and the shocker had to push on them with considerable force to get them to stand solidly together. See Yerkes and Church, *Cost of Harvesting*, 13.

19. Quotes from Clark, *Journals of Alfred Doten*, 1: 364–66, 375, 618. See also 1: 551; Doten to Rock, June 3, 1857, ADCUNR. As they worked, wheat harvesters also hunted. Seeing large numbers of rabbits in the standing grain, they often stopped the reaper, fetched a couple of rifles or shotguns, and then beat the grain. As the rabbits were flushed out, the men shot them on the run. Marveling at the size of the animals, they would skin and dress them and that night enjoy a rabbit stew.

20. Dalton, diary, Sept. 21, 1860, HDC, lists the cost of his thresher at five thousand dollars, but this may be a misprint of five hundred dollars. On the other hand, Philip Hefner's thresher

in Butte County was assessed at only two hundred dollars in 1859. See Butte County, Assessment of Real and Personal Property, 1858–59. See also F. T. Gilbert, *History of San Joaquin County* (San Francisco, 1881), 115; Edward Carpenter, "The Groundhog Thresher: An Enigma," *Wisconsin Magazine of History* 37 (summer 1954), 217–18; Quick and Buchele, *The Grain Harvesters*, 58–59. Expenses for one threshing job on Doten's farm were listed as follows: "David & horses 52 ½ days with thresher at 3.50 per day $183.75—Per contra—clipping 100 acres at $2.00 per are $200.00—Threshing 1109 bushels wheat at 6 cts per cwt $66.54—straw-hauler 2 days work at $1.50 per day $3.00—Balance due W & J $85.79, for which I gave my note." See Clark, *Journals of Alfred Doten*, 1: 625. See also Carolyn B. Crosby, journal, July 25, 27, 1857, Utah State Historical Society. For the introduction of threshers, see also Francis M. Lyman to Amasa M. Lyman, Jan. 13, 1853, GHBPS. For horsepower, see Reynold M. Wik, "Steam Power on the American Farm, 1830–1880," *AH* 25 (fall 1951), 181–85.

21. Five thresher crews handled the entire Sonoma County grain crop in 1860. The census reported only one reaper working in the county. See also Clark, *Journals of Alfred Doten*, 1: 423, 558, 605, 621, 665. Although the *Alta California*, May 19, 1860, estimates threshing costs at "less than the interest on the machine," this does not seem possible. C. L. Brace, *New West*, 32, reports threshers charging forty dollars per day, plus nine cents per bushel, and threshing about nine hundred bushels per day. That would yield a fantastic income of $121 per day. However, no other source mentions a daily fee other than what was charged for the actual threshing. Around San Bernardino, the fee for harvesting ten acres of barley was two bushels per acre for cutting and five bushels per acre for threshing, with meals provided by the farmer. See Francis M. Lyman to Amasa M. Lyman, Jan. 13, 1853, GHBPS. Saturdays and Sundays were tamer around the Mormon community of San Bernardino in the mid-1850s, where crews were treated to a Saturday evening meal prepared by a farmer's wife, and a large, Sunday-morning breakfast. See Edward W. Lyman, *San Bernardino: The Rise and Fall of a California Community* (Salt Lake City, 1996), 208–9.

22. Quote from Clark, *Journals of Alfred Doten*, 1: 555.

23. Timothy Parson, "Building Good Wheat Stacks," *American Thresherman* 28 (June 1925), 4; C. M. Hennis and Rex E. Willard, *Farm Practices in Grain Farming in North Dakota*, U.S. Dept. of Agriculture, Farmers Bulletin no. 757 (Washington, D.C., 1919), 13. At first men pitched bundles in haphazard fashion, but as the rack grew in size, they attempted to build up the sides and layer in the bundles with bundle butts facing out.

24. *California Farmer*, Mar. 1, Apr. 12, Aug. 2, 23, 1861; Hurt, *American Farm Tools*, 42–43; Merritt Finley Miller, *The Evolution of Reaping Machines*, 25–26; Paul W. Gates, *The Farmer's Age: Agriculture, 1815–1860* (New York, 1960), 286.

25. Driving big threshers, the popular Pitts-Carey sweep (developed by Hiram Pitts) better utilized the strength of the horses, but had considerable shortcomings. Isern, *Bull Threshers*, 20–22; Thomas B. Keith, *The Horse Interlude* (Boise, 1976), 30; George F. Wright, ed., *History of Sacramento County, California* (Oakland, 1880), 220; Floyd Clymer, ed., *Album of Historical Steam Traction Engines* (Los Angeles, 1949), 128.

26. Quote from Davis, "Wheat in California," 449. For the musical metaphor, see Herbert Quick, *The Hawkeye* (Indianapolis, 1923), 251.

27. Quote from Clark, *Journals of Alfred Doten*, 1: 370, 422–23, 556. Because the slightest breeze always obscured one side of the thresher, men changed sides frequently. See Rogin, *The Introduction of Farm Machinery*, 187.

28. Quote from Clark, *Journals of Alfred Doten*, 1: 364. See also notes on the *Northern Enterprise*, Nov. 20, 1869, in TWNIPCGJB, 2. Speed of threshing lowered the labor cost per bushel of grain. But cost per bushel had more than accounting significance. The individual field hand was the actual unit and the variables in cost were productivity and wages. The goal was to multiply productivity in relation to wages. By raising the pace of production, mechanization enormously increased the yield factor in the labor cost calculation. For the thesis that mechanization reduced labor demands, see Meister and Loftis, *Long Time Coming*, 5.

29. Quote from Fannie Reading to mother, July 8, 1864, PBRP.

30. Quote from Royce, *John Bidwell*, 55–56. See also Hall, *The Great West*, 78, 87.

31. Quotes from Clark, *Journals of Alfred Doten*, 1: 308, 423, 551–52, 554.

32. Quotes from Samuel Bowles, *Our New West* (Hartford, Conn., 1869), 439; Davis, "Wheat in California," 449. For men kicked by horses, see Clark, *Journals of Alfred Doten*, 1: 614. For men kicked to death by mules, see Justus H. Rogers, *Colusa County, its History Traced*

from a State of Nature through the Early Period . . . with a Description of its Resources, Statistical Tables, etc., also Biographical Sketches . . . (Orland, Calif., 1891), 139.

33. Quote from *Napa Pacific Echo,* July 19, 1862, NCLCF.

34. Quote from Rogers, *Colusa County,* 153. Higgins, interview by author, Davis, Calif., Mar. 12, 1970. For a man caught in a belt and horribly mangled, see Washington Township Research Committee, *History of Washington Township,* 70. For a boy who caught his foot in a thresher and had his leg amputated at the knee joint, see Amasa Mason Lyman, journal, Aug. 12, 15, 18, 1853; Andrew Jensen, "Manuscript History of San Bernardino, California," drawn largely from Richard R. Hopkins; *San Bernardino Branch Record,* Aug. 13, 1853, CLDSA.

35. Quotes from Latta, interview, citing personal interviews with early farmworkers, Pescadero, Mar. 12, 1978, author's possession; Clark, *Journals of Alfred Doten,* 1: 330. Although the tendency among writers has been to link harsh conditions exclusively to minority groups, this is obviously not true. Later farmworkers had no monopoly on hard labor. See also Perkins, *Three Years in California,* 103; Raven, *Golden Dreams and Leaden Realities,* 79; M'Collum, *California As I Saw It,* 125.

36. As Doten put it: "As for a place to sleep, haystacks and straw piles lay round loose, everywhere, and constitute the sleeping accommodations of all the harvest hands." Quotes from Clark, *Journals of Alfred Doten,* 1: 306, 330, 555, 608; also 552.

37. Quotes from Clark, *Journals of Alfred Doten,* 1: 469, 558; also 612.

38. Quote from Rogers, *Colusa County,* 118. See also Clark, *Journals of Alfred Doten,* 1: 321, 368, 423, 556, 621. With few possessions, grain harvesters were in constant need of supplies— clothes, boots, gloves, socks, handkerchiefs, jackets, tobacco, and other sundry materials. But while living a crude existence far removed from the nearest towns, they were not isolated. Traveling peddlers covering a wide area did a thriving business supplying them with various items. And foremen, as well as key field hands, were ever on the move transporting materials about, shifting wagons and teams between farms, delivering grain to shipping and storage points, picking up seed and grain sacks in town, and taking horses and equipment to the blacksmith shops. Through these and other activities, they maintained human contact, spread news, and minimized the boredom of their daily routine. See Richardson Wright, *Hawkers and Walkers in Early America: Strolling Peddlers, Preachers, Lawyers, Doctors, Players, and Others from the Beginning to the Civil War* (Philadelphia, 1927); Thelma B. White, *Glenn County Sketchbook,* ed. Dorothy J. Hill and Lois H. McDonald (Chico, Calif., 1995), 75–79; traveling peddlers photographs, Paradise Historical Society, Paradise, Calif.

39. Quotes from Clark, *Journals of Alfred Doten,* 1: 555; for bar fights, 320, 349; going to town, 612; Isaac Mylar, "The Streets of San Juan in its early Days," *Watsonville Pajaronian* [ca. 1913], PVHS. Alfred Doten described one such meeting at San Jose that attracted two thousand people at the end of the threshing season in September 1860. Located in a "fine evergreen grove," the meeting featured "plenty of preachers" but made "few converts . . . although they tried hard to bring them by the score." Quotes from Clark, *Journals of Alfred Doten,* 1: 404, 558; also 324, 543.

40. On John Bidwell's Butte County farm, field hands could drink in a bar located in the first floor of Bidwell's two-story adobe residence. But those who gambled and caused a nuisance were not tolerated. Foremen thrashed them with a stick and chased them off. Most left quietly, but some took considerable offense at their treatment. Told to clear out, one particularly raucous bunch of Bidwell's field hands did so with drawn pistols. Mounting their horses, they cursed and fired shots at the ranch from a distance to punctuate their anger. See Bidwell to Annie K. Bidwell, July 30, 1888, JBP.

41. Quotes from Clark, *Journals of Alfred Doten,* 1: 349, 370–71, 610–12, 627. Another incident in a Vacaville tavern developed when a bully, David Gordon, stumbled into a saloon where William Byron was playing billiards. After some words, Gordon turned to leave and Byron smashed a pool cue over his head. As Byron raised the cue for a second blow, Gordon shot him in the stomach, followed him out the backdoor, and overtaking him near Putah Creek, shot him four more times, killing him on the spot. Apparently believing Gordon had been provoked, a jury convicted Gordon only of manslaughter. He served a short prison sentence. After getting out of jail, he left California for Missouri, where he murdered another field hand and was sentenced to death. Apparently hostilities spilled over into the countryside. For example, on May 12, 1866, while hauling threshed barley five miles southeast of Denverton in the Sacramento Valley near present-day Fairfield, William Westphal abandoned Fritz Polzing after he had fallen out of the grain wagon and been run over by its rear wheels. Claiming

the accident had killed Polzing, he informed Polzing's wife, then took her to the scene. But Polzing was not dead. Discovering him alive and propped up on one elbow motioning for water, Polzing's wife walked a short distance toward a nearby creek. When she looked back she saw Westphal strike Polzing three times on the head with an axe. "I will fix you out this time," he said. Westphal must have known that Polzing was a much hated man. Or else he himself had plenty of friends and clout in the community. After a short and sensational trial, he was found not guilty. See also *History of Solano County . . . Illustrated* (San Francisco, 1879), 144. For the float, see Isaac Mylar, "The Streets of San Juan in its early Days," *Watsonville Pajaronian*, n.d., PVHS. See also Rogers, *Colusa County*, 111.

42. Quote from Clark, *Journals of Alfred Doten*, 1: 555; also 556, 613, 625. See also Charles Nordhoff, "California," *Harper's Magazine* 45 (July 1872), 255–67.

43. Quote from Clark, *Journals of Alfred Doten*, 1: 330.

44. Quotes from C. F. Menefee, *Historical and Descriptive Sketch Book of Napa* (Napa, 1873), 217–18; *CSAST, 1863*, 81, 170–71.

45. *California Farmer*, Dec. 19, 1867; Jan. 9, 1868; Clark, *Journals of Alfred Doten*, 1: 553.

46. Quotes from Rogers, *Colusa County*, 159; Clark, *Journals of Alfred Doten*, 1: 423; also 643, 369–70. See Dalton, diary, Mar. 3, 1861; Nov. 3, 1862; Rogers, *Colusa County*, 119, 130, 140, 175, 188, 190, 212–13, 245 [Thomas Neilson suicide by laudanum poisoning, July 29, 1869; Myron Haines, by drowning, Dec. 2, 1872; John Gifford suicide, Aug. 9, 1874; Lafe Grigsby, by ingesting powdered glass, Dec. 8, 1879; A. B. Woods, by gunshot, Feb. 4, 1882; James Drake, by laudanum, Apr. 16, 1882; Lee Powell, by gunshot, May 12, 1885; J. D. Fisher, by gunshot, June 20, 1885; Martin Sullivan, by laudanum, Aug. 1, 1888; unknown, from morphine, July 25, 1889]; Latta, "The Lucky Irishman," MS [Grover Savage suicide] (n.d.), 6, FFLCSF.

47. Latta, "Combined Harvester," 7–8, FFLCSF; Wallace Smith, *Garden of the Sun*, 231. For Cook's Napa Valley combine, see *CSAST, 1868–69*, 115–16. See also Higgins, "The Michigan-California Combine Link," MS (n.d.); Albert Horner, hand-drawn sketch of his father's push combine (n.d.); Higgins, "Mule Train Ranching in the West," MS (n.d.), 2, FHHC. For the Michigan antecedents, see Lucius Lyon to Hiram Moore, May 4, 1839; contract of Aug. 6, 1841; Lyon to commissioner of patents, Aug. 7, 1841; and Lyon to Arthur Bronson, Aug. 15, 1841, copies in FHHC, describing the very first combine experiments in Michigan; Michele Shover, "Bitter Moments," 71–90; *CSAST, 1885*, 112–13; Higgins, "The Moore-Hascall Harvester Centennial Approaches," *Michigan History Magazine* 14 (fall 1930), 415–37; Higgins, "California Invented the 'Pusher' Combine," *California Farmer*, Jan. 1, 1952, 28–29, FHHC.

48. Quote from *California Farmer*, Aug. 13, 1868, FHHC. See also Higgins, "The Farm Machine in the Sacramento Valley," *Wagon Wheels*, 13 (Feb. 1967), n.p., FHHC.

49. Quotes from *California Farmer*, July 22, 29, 1869. Some historians have seen this simply as a criminal act of lawlessness. Others interpret it as a violent political act aimed at resisting the introduction of new machinery. Still others argue that it was an attempt at collective bargaining by riot. But the most likely explanation is that bindlemen, in choosing to burn the machine, were not blindly flailing away at the object of their loathing. If the Monitor No. 2 and similar machines could have been prevented or eliminated by some other means (by agreement, for instance, between field hands and farmers) there might have been no need to resort to violence. But in the absence of trade unions and other peaceful mechanisms of action or communication, bindlemen with grievances against the perceived threat posed by Monitor No. 2 took the only action available to them. See *Dewey's Mining and Scientific Press*, July 31, 1869; Higgins to Miss Pearl Carlisle, Mar. 17, 1954, Mission Heritage Foundation Archives; Higgins, "John M. Horner and the Development of the Combined Harvester," *AH* 32 (Jan. 1985), 14–15; Higgins, "Mule Train Ranching in the West," MS (n.d.), 2, FHHC.

50. McWilliams, *Factories in the Field*, 81–92, coined the term "factory farming" when discussing the sugar beet industry. But as the Monitor episode clearly shows, nothing could be more inaccurate. It was in the wheat industry of the 1860s that field hands first experienced such conditions. My definition of industrialized working conditions stresses that point in the farmworker story when regimented, factory-like conditions, including dangerous and complicated machinery and an industrial work ethic, came to the wheat fields.

51. Quote from George Ohleyer to *PRP*, Aug. 11, 1894. See also *CSAST, 1868–69*, 11–12; Michael F. Magliari, "California Populism, A Case Study: The Farmers' Alliance and People's Party in San Luis Obispo County, 1885–1903" (Ph.D. diss., UCD, 1992), 111, citing *Paso Robles Record*, Mar. 22, 1902. Editorial, *California Farmer*, July 29, 1869; also editorials and advertise-

ments, Aug. 12, 1869. See also Eugene W. Hilgard, *The Agriculture and Soils of California*, U.S. Dept. of Agriculture, Annual Report for 1878 (Washington, D.C., 1879), 498.

CHAPTER NINE

1. Quotes from "Caspar T. Hopkins Autobiography," MS (ca. 1885), MSS C-D 762, BL; California Immigrant Union, *All About California* (San Francisco, 1870), 8ff. See also Richard J. Orsi, "Selling the Golden State: A Study in Boosterism in Nineteenth-Century California" (Ph.D. diss., University of Wisconsin, 1973), 381–415; *CSAST, 1868–69*, 11–12; *CSAST, 1870–71*, 17–18.

2. Quote from California Immigrant Union, *All About California*, 53–54. See also Caspar T. Hopkins, *Common Sense Applied to the Immigrant Problem* (San Francisco, 1869), 5–6, 12–13, 21–22; Edward Young, "Special Report on Immigration," in U.S. Bureau of Labor Statistics, *Report* (Washington, D.C., 1872), 183.

3. Quote from *Napa County Reporter*, Feb. 6, 1869, NCLCF. See also advertisements in various issues thereafter.

4. With very little prospect of work, and benevolent relief associations and soup kitchens unable to handle requests for assistance, unemployed men congregated in Sacramento, Napa, Marysville, Stockton, and dozens of other towns. Packing the boardinghouses and cheap hotels, they guarded their meager savings, if they had any, or borrowed on credit. More than seven thousand unemployed men piled up just in San Francisco. Desperate and seeking a way to survive, all faced the same choice: how to weather the next year. While most of these men also had an aversion to farm labor, they did not intend to starve. See Ira B. Cross, *A History of the Labor Movement in California* (Berkeley, 1935), 60–62; *Springfield (Massachusetts) Republican*, Feb. 12, 1870; *San Francisco Evening Bulletin*, Jan. 12, 22; Mar. 13, 31, 1870.

5. Quote from NIBS, "A Few Words to the Unemployed," *PRP*, Mar. 18, 1871.

6. Quotes from NIBS, "A Few Words to the Unemployed." See also John Hays, "A New View of the Labor Question," *Overland Monthly* 6 (Feb. 1871), 141–47.

7. Quotes from Steven V. Powers, *Afoot and Alone: A Walk from Sea to Sea* (Hartford, Conn., 1872), 304; Mary Cone, *Two Years in California* (Chicago, 1876), 132. Computations from 1870 MS Census, Alameda, Sacramento, San Joaquin, San Mateo, Santa Clara, and Sonoma counties, as follows: 9,114 field hands, of which 3,683 were American-born; 3,418 were Canadian-born; 1,552, Chinese; 17, Mexican; 444, "Other." Since the census was taken in June, it underrepresented certain farmworkers, particularly those harvesting wheat, wine, raisins, and table grapes, activities that did not begin until late July and peaked in August and September.

8. Quotes from Menefee, *Historical and Descriptive Sketch Book*, 217; "Condition of Farm Laborers," *Napa Reporter*, Nov. 9, 1872, NCLCF. See also Nordhoff, "California," 255–67; Cross, *A History of the Labor Movement in California*, 61–63, 68–72; Henry George, *Our Land and Land Policy, National and State* (New York, 1871), 24–26.

9. Quotes from Menefee, *Historical and Descriptive Sketch Book*, 217–18; *San Francisco Evening Bulletin*, Apr. 14, 1877; *PRP*, June 2, 1877; "Labor, A Many Sided Question," Feb. 7, 1874; also Feb. 23 and Mar. 23, 1878; Cone, *Two Years in California*, 132. See also RN689, 796; remarks of John W. Strong, *CSAST, 1872*, 307; Rodman Paul, *Mining Frontiers of the Far West, 1848–1880* (New York, 1963), 39; Bancroft, *Popular Tribunals* (San Francisco, 1887), 2: 704.

10. Quotes from unsigned handwritten note, "California, 1876: The Chinese Necessity. Why We Need Them," Bancroft Scrapbooks, BL; Nordhoff, "California," 252–67. See also *PRP*, Mar. 23, 1878.

11. Quotes from *Marysville Appeal*, Aug. 27, 1879, California Scrapbooks, CSL; also Aug. 7, 1877; Rogers, *Colusa County*, 166, 168, 207; *Gilroy Advocate*, Nov. 17, 1877, GHS. See also typed notes, *Tuolumne City News*, Jan. 25, Oct. 18, 1868, FFLCSF.

12. Quote from *San Francisco Morning Chronicle*, Sept. 5, 1875.

13. Quote from *CSAST, 1887*, 738. See also *CSAST, 1880*, 231; *CSAST, 1870–71*, 84–85; *CSAST, 1874*, 201; *CSAST, 1886*, 189; John Lee Coulter, "Agricultural Laborers in the United States," *AAAPSS* 40 (Mar. 1912), 43–44.

14. Quotes from *Napa Reporter*, Nov. 7, 1863, NCLCF; George, *Our Land and Land Policy*, 19, 75. See also George, *Progress and Poverty: An Inquiry into the Cause of Industrial Depressions, and of Increase of Want with Increase of Wealth, The Remedy* (New York, 1879), 237, 266, 395–96, 408–10; *CSAST, 1870–71*, 82–85; *CSAST, 1874*, 201; *CSAST, 1880*, 229; Henry George Jr., *The Life of Henry George: The Complete Works of Henry George* (Garden City, N.Y., 1911),

1: 193–94; 9: 197; Edward J. Rose, *Henry George* (New York, 1968); Charles A. Barker, *Henry George* (New York, 1955), 131–40; Barker, "Henry George and the California Background of Progress and Poverty," *CHQ* 24 (June 1945), 97–115; Robert Heilbroner, *The Worldly Philosophers* (New York, 1953), 155–63. Writing in *Overland Monthly*, George argued in his first published essay that the impending completion of the transcontinental railroad would bring wealth to a few and poverty to many. That view was strengthened in 1870, when as editor of the Oakland *Daily Transcript*, he learned of the enormous increase in the cost of neighboring agricultural land, partly occasioned by railroad building, and argued that with population growth, "land grows in value, and the men who work it must pay more for the privilege." Too much went to land speculators, like railroads, which acquired the land as a subsidy, he argued, and too little went to the field hands, like bindlemen, whose sweat and muscle brought in the harvest. "On the land we are born, from it we live," George wrote in 1871, "to it we return again—children of the soil as truly as the blade of grass or the flower of the field." See George, "What the Railroad Will Bring Us," *Overland Monthly* 1 (Oct. 1868), 297–306.

15. Warren P. Tufts et al., "The Rich Pattern of California Crops," in Claude B. Hutchison, *California Agriculture*, 114. By 1889, wheat farmers were harvesting more than forty million bushels and cultivating 2.75 million acres of land, statistics that made California the second leading producer of wheat in the country. Sutter died impoverished in a Washington, D.C., hotel in 1880 while petitioning Congress for money he claimed the government owed him for his services during the Mexican War. See Hurtado, *Indian Survival*, 217.

16. Production is difficult to measure because it was variously given in centrals, bushels, and tons of two thousand pounds, although when wheat was loaded on board ships the ton changed to 2,240 pounds. Also, figures often contradict one another, as in 1898, when different sources reported production as low as 12,224,000 and as high as 21,150,000 bushels of wheat. Cited figures from Wickson, *Rural California*, 97, 100, 126–27, 130, 132, 136–37, 142. For wheat prices, see Albert Montpellier, "Diagram Showing the Fluctuation in the San Francisco Wheat Market, According to the Monthly Average Quotations, from January 1864 to September 1874, the quotations being to the nearest 1/10 of a cent per pound," July 1876, JBP. See also Davis, "California Breadstuffs," 530–32, app., table 3, 608; table 6, 611; Smith, "Wheat Decades," 10.

17. James Gray, *Business Without Boundary: The History of General Mills* (Minneapolis, 1954), 107–8; Herman Stern, *Flour Milling in America* (Westport, Conn., 1963), 172; W. A. Starr, "Abraham Dubois Starr: Pioneer California Miller and Wheat Exporter," *CHSQ* 27 (Sept. 1948), 193.

18. Descriptions of wheat growers as "sandlappers," "bonanza farmers," and "sky farmers" have both embellishments and deletions but contain more truth than illusion. The term "bonanza farmers" was particularly appropriate in describing those men, who, in their monomania for wheat and efforts to squeeze the last ounce of profit from the land, established agricultural enterprises of vast size, productivity, and impact on the environment. Similarly, the term "sky farmers" demonstrated exactly the way these men worked under wide-open skies. As for the expression "sandlappers," it well captured those people daring enough to attempt dry grain farming on sandy land previously devoted only to grazing cattle. See Latta, "Large-Scale Sky Farmers," MS (n.d.), FFLCSF; *Fresno Weekly Expositor*, July 10, 1872. See also Effie E. Marten, "The Development of Wheat Culture in the San Joaquin Valley, 1846–1890" (M.A. thesis, UCB, 1922). Local developments can be followed in Hittell, *Resources of California*, 162; Brace, *The New West*, 349. For the British trade, see Rodman W. Paul, "The Wheat Trade Between California and the United Kingdom," *Mississippi Valley Historical Review* 45 (Dec. 1958), 391–97; Morton Rothstein, "American Wheat and the British Market" (Ph.D. diss., Cornell University, 1960), 303–4. See also Charles A. Nordhoff, *California for Health, Pleasure, and Residence: A Book for Travelers and Settlers* (New York, 1873), 183. Maintaining production at this high level until well after the turn of the century, wheat and barley growers would not only require the labor of tens of thousands of field hands, they would need them to appear—and disappear—almost instantly. "When our haying commences, it is quick," one farmer told the Joint Committee to Investigate Chinese Immigration in 1877. "It has got to be cured. Our grain is the same way." Quote from RN689, 304. For the relationship between farm location and shipping points, see Margery Saunders, "California Wheat, 1867–1910: Influence of Transportation on the Export Trade and the Location of Producing Areas" (M.A. thesis, UCB, 1960), 3, 47. For the San Fernando Valley, see Remi Nadeau, "When Wheat Ruled the Valley," *Westways* 55 (Apr. 1963), 18–21; Jackson Mayers, *The San Fernando Valley* (Los Angeles, 1976), ch. 9. For Tulare, see Annie R. Mitchell, *A Modern History of Tulare County* (Visalia, Calif., 1974), 38–40.

19. Quotes from Solomon P. Elias, *Stories of Stanislaus: A Collection of Stories on the History and Achievements of Stanislaus County* (Modesto, 1924), 19. For one part of the Sacramento Valley wheat industry, see U.S. Bureau of the Census, *Industry and Wealth at the Ninth Census* (Washington, D.C., 1872), 3: 104–5, 346, showing that in Sacramento County, Franklin Township, the number of farms devoted to grain growing at this time increased from sixty-six to 101, while diversified farms decreased from eighty-two to thirty. For Mitchell's farm, see *Weekly Northwest Miller*, Mar. 4, 1881.

20. Quotes from *CSAST, 1880,* 231. See also *CSAST, 1886,* 194; Daniel Meissner, "Bridging the Pacific: California and the China Flour Trade," *CH* 76 (winter 1997–98), 86–87; Rodman Paul, "The Great California Grain War," *PHR* 27 (summer 1958), 401; Gerald D. Nash, "Henry George Reexamined: William S. Chapman's Views on Land Speculation in Nineteenth Century California," *AH* 33 (July 1959), 133–37.

21. Quote from "The Bloomfield Ranch," *Gilroy Advocate-Leader,* June 3, 1876, GHS. See also Dana, *Sacramento River,* 183; Edwin E. Wilson and Marion Clawson, *Agricultural Land Ownership and Operation in the Southern San Joaquin Valley* (Berkeley, 1945), 13–14. Sacramento Valley data from *Sacramento Union,* Feb. 8, 15, 22, 1873. Fresno-area data from Paul E. Vandor, *History of Fresno County, with Biographical Sketches* (Los Angeles, 1919), 1: 168, estimating the average bonanza wheat farm at three thousand acres. Smith, *Garden of the Sun,* 170, puts the average San Joaquin Valley bonanza farm at ten thousand acres. Production estimates from "Old Timer," *Chico Enterprise,* Jan. 19, 1936, JWHA. Moving out onto these farms must have surely been a daunting journey for unemployed men. There were no hills, only a wide golden sea of grain. The land was big and depopulated. "Wheat, wheat, wheat," wrote Nordhoff, "nothing but wheat is what you see on your journey as far as the eye can reach." Quote from Nordhoff, *California for Health,* 131, 182–84.

22. Nordhoff, *California for Health,* 187; *Sacramento Daily Union,* May 24, 1877; California Legislature, Assembly, *Biennial Report of the State Board of Agriculture for the Years 1870 and 1871,* 20th sess. (Sacramento, 1874), app., 2: 22–23; Bancroft, *History of California,* 7: 27–28; "Fresno County—20 years, 1856–1976," *Fresno County History Essays,* 2 (July 1976), 1–2.

23. Alan L. Olmstead and Paul Rhode, "An Overview of California Agricultural Mechanization, 1870–1930," *AH* 62 (summer 1988), 103. For the Stockton gangplow, see Latta, "Stockton Gang Plow Invented Near Manteca," *Fresno Bee,* July 2, 1933, BWC; U.S. Patent Office, "Gang-Plow," Patent No. 46,164: Jan. 31, 1865; clippings, *SDI,* Oct. 30, Nov. 1866, FFLCSF. Because implement makers produced so many patents for gangplows or multibottom plows (one of every four patents for gang- or multibottom plows between 1859 and 1873 was for a California device), field hands throughout the wheat era would be exposed to the very latest and most modern plowing and planting devices.

24. For men finding work on plow teams, see letter to the editor, *PRP,* Mar. 18, 1871; Hohenthal et al., *Streams in A Thirsty Land,* 87. See also Ester R. Cramer, *La Habra: The Pass Through the Hills* (Fullerton, Calif., 1969), 106–8, 112–13. For a report that one man with a Challenge gangplow pulled by eight horses plowed more land than fifty men and fifty single share plows pulled by one hundred horses, see *CSAST, 1866–67,* 71, 192. For similar comments, see *CSAST, 1868–69,* 214; Rogin, *Introduction of Farm Machinery,* 204, 222, 424. Equipped with box seeders on the front, or end-gate, sprocket-driven broadcast seeders on the rear, and followed by harrows that covered the seed with soil, Stockton gangplows dramatically increased the amount of land one man could work. About 6,670 men would have been required for two months to put in the 1873 wheat crop using two-share gangplows and broadcast sowing devices. But with heavy rains often stopping the work, they most probably would have worked twice as long, probably until March of the following year. Calculation of planting crews as follows: 2,000,000 acres divided by 300 (2 months x 150 acres) totals 6,666.67 men. The military analogy is from Frank Norris, *The Octopus* (New York, 1901), 127–28. My acreage estimate is based on California Legislature, Assembly Journal, *Biennial Report of the Surveyor General of the State of California from August 1, 1873, to August 1, 1875,* 21st sess. (Sacramento, 1875), app., 2: 26–27, which sets the acreage in 1873 at 2,128,165 acres.

25. Charles A. Nordhoff, *Northern California, Oregon, and the Sandwich Islands* (New York, 1874), 8; Cronise, *Natural Wealth of California,* 386; George H. Tinkham, *A History of Stanislaus County* (Los Angeles, 1921), 235; Justus Rogers, *Colusa County,* 136, 292; E. W. Hilgard, "The Agriculture and Soils of California," in U.S. Dept. of Agriculture, *Report of the Commissioner of Agriculture for the Year 1878* (Washington, D.C., 1879), 497. Combination gangplows

and seeders tilling forty acres a day are described in L. D. Brackett, *Our Western Empire* (Philadelphia, 1882), 585–90. Although gangplows were in use in the Midwest at this time, very few were imported to California. See also Douglas L. Meikle, "James Oliver and the Oliver Chilled-Plow Works" (Ph.D. diss., Indiana University, 1958), 166–67. Plowing costs are in Hohenthal, "History of Turlock," 49. Wages of $2.50 a day are reported in John Bidwell, diary, Jan. 11, 1870, JBP; see also Jan. 10, 19; Feb. 10, 1870. For a report of three hundred gangplows of four shares in the Sacramento Valley, see *Marysville Appeal*, Dec. 29, 1871. For harrows, see Latta, "The Seed Broadcaster and the Disc Harrow," MS (n.d), 5, FFLCSF. For gangplows being used to clear land for planting grapevines, see *Fresno Weekly Expositor*, Mar. 12, 1873. Snapped in the ring on the near side of the bit of the lead horse or mule, the jerk line passed through swing rings, back along the team, and, on many teams, through a swing ring on the front of the plow to prevent it from becoming fouled in turning. When the plowman wanted to turn right he called "Gee," and jerked the line so that when the lead horse heard the word and felt the jerk, it threw its head back and moved right. When the plowman wanted to turn left, he pulled on the line and called "Haw." After a few weeks training, the "Gee" and "Haw" strap was removed from the bit and would only be used if the horses became stubborn or needed another lesson. At this point, plowmen said the horse had been "broken to the word," meaning no lines were required for control. For driving plow teams, see Latta, "Tommy Dragoo and the Long-Line Hitch," MS (n.d), 12, 15, FFLCSF; Henry F. Blanchard, *The Improvement of the Wheat Crop of California*, U.S. Dept. of Agriculture, Bureau of Plant Industry, Bulletin no. 178 (Washington, D.C., 1910), 8–9; Ralph, May, and Jim Runkle, "The Runkle Family," interview, Oct. 14, 1974 [transcribed Mar. 9, 1991], 2–3, SVHS; Ann F. Scheuring, ed., "Tillers: An Oral History of California Agriculture," MS (1982), 96; *CSAST, 1893*, 15.

26. Quote from Nicholas W. Hansen, *As I Remember* (Willows, Calif., 1936), 136. See also unidentified newspaper clippings, BWC; "The Great Grain Seeder," *California Farmer*, Nov. 6, 1873; Charles A. Nordhoff, *California for Travelers* (New York, 1873), 184; Latta, "The Long-Line Plow Team," MS (n.d.), 1–6, FFLCSF. To the usual dangers, later plowmen added valley fever spores, asbestos, and anthrax. Soil in portions of Los Angeles, Orange, San Diego, Kern, and Ventura counties had become polluted with anthrax in summer 1872, after Basque sheep owners near Bakersfield had imported infected sheep from France and proceeded to graze them in the San Fernando Valley and the Ventura plains. Within six weeks, half of the flock died and large portions of the grazing land became infected, and as the result of further grazing, many areas in the surrounding counties also became infected. By 1894, more than one hundred sheepherders had become infected, mostly through skinning diseased animals. The first field hands to contact anthrax were Amos Miller and Ed Jewett, who had been plowing east of Ventura when both suffered slight abrasions and were inoculated with the virus in December 1902. Given the usual treatment—injections of carbolic acid, deep incisions swabbed with mercuric bichloride, and doses of quinine—both men survived. See "Strange Cases of Poisoning," *Ventura Free Press*, Dec. 12, 1902. For background, see Cephas L. Bard, "The Ravages of the Bacillus Anthracis in California," *Southern California Practitioner* 2 (Apr. 1894), 1–13.

27. Quote from Smith, *Garden of the Sun*, 554. Author unknown.

28. Carl Meyer, interview, n.d., Tehama County Library; M. L. Wilson and H. E. Murdock, *Reducing Harvesting Costs on Montana Dry Lands*, Montana Extension Service, Bulletin no. 71 (Bozeman, Mont., 1924), 15; Yerkes and Church, "Cost of Harvesting Wheat," 17. Self-rakers in 1870 cost about two hundred dollars, self-binders about three hundred dollars. See *PRP*, Mar. 4, 1871. Among field hands there were few, if any, objections to the new technology. Wire-binding reapers multiplied labor output far beyond that of previous years, while considerably easing work. Field hands on John Bidwell's farm liked to use self-binders because they saved time, allowing them to cut his crop one or two weeks early, before the hottest weather arrived. They would then stack it and thresh it later. Still the mechanisms never really caught on. See Arthur Domonoske, "Recollections of the Big Change from Stationary Threshers," interview, n.d., FHHC; "California Grain Growing," *PRP*, Sept. 8, 1883; G. W. Faulkner, diary, entry for June 1882, cited in "Farm Life in 1882: Excerpts from the Diary of G. W. Faulkner," *VCHSQ* 7 (Nov. 1956), 16. Binder drivers kept oilcans at the ready to lubricate squeaky parts and bearings. There were thirty or more spots to oil, and some of them, such as the pitman arm, had to be greased many times during the course of the day, almost continuously if the field was extremely dusty and dry. Drivers also had to make sure that the bullwheel that drove the knotting mechanism functioned properly. On muddy, sandy, or bumpy ground, the

wheel would sometimes slip, and the binder would kick out untied bundles. To remedy this, binder men would mount a wine barrel on a frame atop the binder. When slippage occurred, they filled the barrel with water as needed, thereby providing extra weight and traction and eliminating the problem. See F. M. Redpath, "Cradle to Combine," MS (n.d.), 5, Kansas State Historical Society, Topeka, Kans.; "An Early Binder Engine Experience," *American Thresherman* 16 (Feb. 1914), 70–71. For snakes, see Clark, *The Journals of Alfred Doten*, 1: 333. "I mowed over one once with a scythe, and came near stepping directly upon him before he sprung his rattle," recalled Doten. "We used to kill at least a dozen snakes a day. . . . When we were spreading the hay, mornings, under every cock of it, we would find snakes that had crawled under, during the night." See also Powers, *South Fork Country*, 26.

29. Twine binders were considered superior because men could cut grain when it was "in the dough" rather than when it was "dead ripe." This increased the yield, as the wheat kernels would not dry out and lose weight. With twine binders, men could also cut grain earlier and end their harvest sooner, thereby avoiding some of the hottest weather, or early rains. This allowed them to commence threshing as soon as possible. Additionally they were relatively inexpensive, costing between $150 and $175, and were particularly well-suited to small farms where a farmer and a few men needed only to cut between eight and ten acres a day. See I. N. Hoag, "Mistakes in Wheat Culture and Harvesting in California," *CSAST, 1879*, 130; *PRP*, June 1, 1895; *Paso Robles Moon*, Apr. 15, July 15, 1893; George W. Hendry, *Cereal Hay Production in California*, University of California, College of Agriculture, Agricultural Experiment Station, Bulletin no. 394 (Berkeley, 1925), 46. Experiments showed that twine binders increased grain yields by 1.4 bushels per acre, and wheat hay yields up to 10 percent compared to a header cutting wheat when it was "dead ripe." See F. B. Swingle, "The Invention of the Twine Binder," *Indiana Magazine of History* 10 (Sept. 1962), 35–41. Invented in 1849 by George Esterly of Wisconsin, headers were shipped west in the early 1850s by clipper ships. The most popular model was the Haines Illinois header, which cost two hundred dollars. Santa Clara farmer E. Peck won prizes at the 1858 and 1859 California state fairs for headers built by San Francisco manufacturer Thomas Ogg Shaw, who is credited with also building the first steel plow and reaper in California. Virtually all headers used in California after 1860 were manufactured in the state. By 1863, Marysville manufacturer Treadwell and Company was building three different models. By 1866, headers were being used throughout the Central Valley. Modifications never stopped. In the San Joaquin Valley opposite the Livermore pass where strong west winds blew the grain away from the header spout, farmers added a second draper to run above the grain and hold it against the lower draper until it was delivered into the wagon. See Latta, "The Header Wagon," MS (n.d.), 1; "The Grain Header," MS (n.d.), 3–4; and "The Story of Henry Hammer," MS (n.d.), 28, FFLCSF; Hohenthal, "Turlock," 51; *History of Kern County, California, with Illustrations, Descriptive of its Scenery, Farms, Residences, Public Buildings, Factories . . . From Original Drawings, with Biographical Sketches* (San Francisco, 1883), 73; Rogin, *Introduction of Farm Machinery*, 106; Smith, *Garden of the Sun*, 228–29; F. Hal Higgins, "1860–90: Headers Came West," MS (n.d.), FHHC. Headers never became popular in the Midwest, where the humid environment made it too risky to harvest the crop before the wheat heads were dead ripe.

30. Half standing, half sitting on a small, thirty-inch-diameter cast-iron seat, the header puncher braced his feet against the foot stirrups and simultaneously controlled the horses with long reins and steered the header by means of a tiller extending forward from the rear wheel between his knees, all the time regulating the height of the sickle while guiding the header around the field. Good header punchers achieved a happy medium, cutting as little straw as possible while not clipping the grain heads too severely. Work often continued long after dusk, as punchers usually had to remove the conveyor canvases and roll them up to keep them dry and prevent the dew from dampening and shrinking them. Header drivers had the same general maintenance concerns as binder drivers, but generally started their cutting much later than binder drivers, preferring to have the grain hard and dead ripe, rather than when the heads had just turned yellow and the straw was still slightly green. Header drivers often tied a sheepskin over their iron seats when they became too hot to sit on. Headers were often cooperatively owned by four or five growers who used them first to cut their crops and then hired them out to other farms. See Otto Hughes, interview, in Levene, *Mendocino Remembered*, 1: 214. Domonoske, "Recollections"; *History of Kern County*, 73; Latta, "The Grain Header," 2–4; typed notes, *SDI*, Sept. 13, 1861, FFLCSF; Andrew Heidrick, "Recollections of Dr. Glenn, His Times

and Machines," interview, Woodland, Calif., Oct. 1946, 5, FHHC; "California Grain Growing," *PRP*, Sept. 8, 1883.

31. Some crews used special "dump wagons" activated by a lever that tipped up the hinged wagon box and dumped out the grain. For dump barges, see *Gilroy Advocate-Leader*, June 25, July 15, 1876, GHS. Several other modifications considerably improved header wagons, the most important being the "goose neck" drop axle, which lowered the wagon to less than two feet off the ground and reduced the length and height of the header conveyor.

32. Latta, "Originator of Grain Header was Unknown Pioneer Valley Rancher," *Fresno Bee Republican*, July 16, 1933, BWC. Header rates from *Marysville Appeal*, June 23, 28, 1872; May 31, 1877; William H. Brewer, "Report on the Cereal Production of the United States," in *Tenth Census of the United States, 1880: Production of Agriculture, General Statistics* (Washington, D.C., 1880), 456–57. Bayless ranch data from William S. Cornelius, "The Wheat Harvest of 1884 on the Glenn Ranch," interview, n.d., ANCRR. Alexander Lovell "Dick" Richards is misidentified as Lowell A. Richards in Stoll, *Fruits of Natural Advantage*, 28. See Latta's recollections in Latta, "Large-Scale Sky Farmers," MS (n.d.), 2; Latta, "The Dick Richards System," MS (n.d.), 1, FFLCSF.

33. Crews sometimes found it easier to use a binder to cut the threshing circle, later moving in with the header. See Dick Richards, records, [ca. 1876], FFLCSF. See also *PRP*, Jan. 4, 1879; Feb. 1, 1879; Sept. 8, 1883; Domonoske, "The Illustrations Remind Me," *Colusa County, California . . . With Historical Sketch . . .* (San Francisco, 1880 [1973]), xvi; Rogin, *Introduction of Farm Machinery*, 177; typed notes, *PRP*, 1875, FHHC; *Fresno Weekly Expositor*, July 10, 1872.

34. Quote from Clark, *The Journals of Alfred Doten*, 1: 559. Around 1854 or 1855 farmers in the Mormon community of San Bernardino began threshing with at least five steam engines. Moving them from one small family-owned field to another, crews would charge two bushels per acre to cut a field, and five bushels for threshing, in addition to being fed by the farmer. Earning $2.25 per day, women worked on these crews, along with young men. Soon threshers spread north to the Sacramento Valley. When a crew moved an engine built by the Union Iron and Brass Factory into a Yolo County wheat field in 1857, it earned front-page headlines. See Carolyn B. Crosby, journal, July 25, 27, 1857, Utah State Historical Society, Salt Lake City. See also *PRP*, Apr. 17, 1880; Sept. 2, 1882; *San Luis Obispo Reasoner*, Aug. 2, 1894; Hurt, *Farm Tools*, 67–70; Higgins, "83 Years Equipping California Farms," 231, FHHC; John Muir, "Notes on Childhood," John Muir Papers, PCWS; *Marysville Appeal*, July 26; June 11, 1874. By 1880, about 80 percent of California's wheat was being threshed by steam power. See Brewer, "Cereal Production," 435; Carleton E. Watkins, Greenfields Ranch Album, Photo no. 82, LC. For an engine built in the Napa Valley shop of Moody, Ulrich and Smith, see *Napa County Reporter*, May 16, 1874. For descriptions of some of the first steam-powered threshers, see *Tuolumne City News*, June 12, 1868. Threshing rates are given in *California Farmer*, Aug. 22, 1856. The reference to ninety threshers at work in Colusa County is from Rogers, *Colusa County*, 209.

35. Costs from *Whittier News*, June 27, 1903; miscellaneous records, Steele Family Papers, 16: 56, 190, 210, 394, BL; *PRP*, Sept. 2, 1882. F. S. Bagnall, "Fifty Years Ago," MS (1938), SVHS.

36. Quotes from *Napa County Reporter*, Sept. 7, 1872, NCLCF; *Gilroy Advocate*, Aug. 11, 1877. A typical notice in the *Napa County Reporter*, July 13, 1872, read:

THE VIBRATOR THRESHING MACHINES, against which many have had strong prejudices, has now been thoroughly tested in our country, so far has given almost perfect satisfaction. Mr. J. H. Bostwick, of Berryessa, has had one at work on his ranch in that valley for some time, and it did so well that Mr. John Lawley purchased one to take to his ranch in the same valley. He says he does not care for a better machine. He commenced work with his machine Thursday.

See "Local Happenings," *Napa Daily Journal*, Sept. 27, 1900; "Harvesting in Berryessa," *Napa Daily Register*, July 31, 1880, NCLCF.

37. *Paso Robles Record*, July 13, 1895; Augustus Keyser, et al., eds., *Creston, 1884–1984* (Creston, Calif., 1984), 19. For threshing outfits working on twenty-eight different farms in thirty-one days, see *Marysville Appeal*, Sept. 30, 1870; July 9, 13, 1879; Aug. 29, 1884. For a crew taking forty-four jobs in fifty days and threshing twenty-six thousand sacks, see *PRP*, Oct. 13, 1877.

38. Quote from *Napa County Reporter*, July 30, 1870, NCLCF. See also Bob Powers, *South Fork Country*, 110.

39. Quote from *Santa Rosa Daily Republican*, Oct. 6, 1877. See also William C. Shipley,

Tales of Sonoma County (Santa Rosa, 1965), 3–4; "The Harvest in Napa Valley," *Napa Daily Register*, July 27, 1880, NCLCF.

40. Quote from *Napa Daily Journal*, Aug. 28, 1900, NCLCF. When approaching bridges, crews always experienced a moment of fear. To minimize these dangers, some outfits traveled with a wagon full of three-inch-thick planks that they laid crosswise in front of their rigs as they inched forward. Nevertheless, many drivers and engineers went down with their engines when they broke through a wooden bridge designed only for light wagons. See clippings, *Napa Daily Journal*, Sept. 15, Nov. 17, 1900, NCLCF, listing claims against Napa County for damages caused when a threshing engine fell through a bridge; and Ranch Ledger, Sept. 5, 1874, Durham Ranch Records, SCML. See also I. N. "Jack" Brotherton, *Annals of Stanislaus County: River Towns and Ferries* (Santa Cruz, 1982), 12.

41. For Cone, see Gary Burchfield, *Cone Ranch* (Red Bluff, 1968), 14. For Glenn, see clipping, *California Patron* (n.d.), FHHC; Higgins, "Dr. Glenn's Million Dollar Wheat Crop," *PRP*, Oct. 26, 1946; *Northwestern Miller*, Feb. 23, 1883; Street, "Dr. Glenn: 'Wheat King,'" in Richard Hilkert and Oscar Lewis, eds., *Breadbasket of the World: California's Great Wheat-Growing Era: 1860–1890* (San Francisco, 1984).

42. Street, "The Murder of Hugh Glenn," *Sacramento Magazine* 11 (July 1985), 49–54; Jimmy V. Allen, "Hugh Glenn" (M.A. thesis, CSUS, 1970); Rogers, *Colusa County*, 387–89.

43. For men arriving at Jacinto, see *San Francisco Chronicle*, July 17, 1879. For estimates of the size of Glenn's labor force, see *Marysville Appeal*, Feb. 7, 1875; Aug. 9, 1877. Payroll figures from Charles D. McCormish and Rebecca T. Lambert, *History of Colusa and Glenn Counties, California* (Los Angeles, 1918), 211. See also the reminiscences in *Oakland Tribune*, July 16, 1950, FHHC.

44. Quote from Albert Webster, "A California Wheat-Harvest," *Appleton's Journal* 23 (Aug. 1880), 453. See also *Willows Journal*, July 26, 1879; Powers, *South Fork Country*, 24; invoice book, receipts for food purchases, Sept. 12, Nov. 27, 1884, HGP.

45. Quote from *History of Colusa County, California*, xviii.

46. Latta, "The Dick Richards System."

47. Quote from Frank F. Latta, interview by author, Pescadero, Apr. 17, 1979, author's possession. See also *History of Kern County, California*, 73; Webster, "A California Wheat-Harvest," 452; Nicholas Hansen, "Reminiscences," *Wagon Wheels* 1 (Feb. 1955), 12.

48. See Isern, *Bull Threshers and Bindlestiffs*, 102–3; Latta, handwritten notes, FFLCSF.

49. Mrs. Edward H. Connor, ed., "Tales of Sonoma County, by Dr. William C. Shipley, originally published in the *Healdsburg Tribune* in 1938," *Sonoma County Historical Society Quarterly* [n.v.] (June 1965), Sonoma County Historical Museum, Healdsburg, Calif.; *PRP*, Oct. 13, 1877. See also Ernest B. Ingles, "The Custom Thresherman in Western Canada," in David C. Jones and Ian McPherson, eds., *Building Beyond the Homestead: Rural History on the Prairies* (Calgary, 1985), 138–39.

50. G. F. Connor, *Science of Threshing: Treating the Operation, Management and Care of Threshing Machinery* (St. Joseph, Mich., 1906), 153–56; F. N. G. Kranich, "The Care and Handling of Separators," *American Thresherman* 13 (Aug. 1910), 74–76, 78.

51. Brewer, "Cereal Production," 457; Domonoske, "Recollections."

52. Quote from *Willows Journal*, July 26, 1879. See also Higgins, "Centennials," 17; Gilbert, *History of San Joaquin County*, 55; *Tehama County, California* (San Francisco, 1880), 129.

53. Quote from *History of Colusa County*, xvii–xviii. See also *History of Kern County*, 74; Cornelius, "The Wheat Industry."

54. Quote from Webster, "A California Wheat-Harvest," 453. A spring-eye needle had one side of the eye cut out with a spring inserted in the opening, so that pressure from a loop of twine caused it to open and allow the loop to enter the eye. The front end of the eye had a sharp cutting edge to sever the twine and remove the needle.

55. Latta, "The Dick Richards System," 3; F. T. Gilbert, "Electric Elevator," in *History of San Joaquin County*, 32; George H. Tinkham, *History of San Joaquin County, California with Biographical Sketches* (Los Angeles, 1923), 319; Powers, *South Fork Country*, 110.

56. Typed notes, "Overhiser's Improved Hay and Grain Elevator," *SDI*, Aug. 11, 1866, FFLCSF; *Marysville Appeal*, June 10, 1877; *PRP*, Aug. 27, 1889; clipping, "Falls Under Heavy Load of Hay," *FMR*, n.d., BWC; Domonoske, "Recollections." A favorite trick was to dump an entire hay-fork load on the head of an unsuspecting crewman. Sometimes the oddest incident could lead to near catastrophe. When Kern River thresherman and local historian Bob Powers asked a straw buck to toss a canteen full of water twenty feet up to him on the stack,

723

Notes to Pages 197–199

the toss came up short, fell back, hit the rump of one of the straw-buck horses, and so frightened the team that it took off running. Pulling the cable attached to the rake, the team propelled a load of grain to the top of the stack where it hit the stops with a loud crash. Still attached to the cable, the stacker horses lunged forward again and again, only to be violently yanked backward six feet when the fork hit the stops. As this was happening the men on the stack feared that the entire derrick would fall apart and collapse on them. Eventually the horses calmed down and were subdued. At this point the man who had called for the canteen looked over the now peaceful scene and said, "All I wanted was a drink of water." Quote from Powers, *South Fork Country*, 28.

57. Latta, "The Derrick, Hay Fork, and Divided Net," MS (n.d.), 4–6; "Hay Mucker's Hay Rides," MS (n.d.), 1; "Rolling Net," MS (n.d.), 4–6, FFLCSF. In most operations men simply rolled the header load directly to the thresher.

58. The divided net quickly replaced the rolling net as the standard apparatus for stacking cut grain. See Latta, "Originator of Grain Header was unknown Pioneer Valley Farmer," *Fresno Bee*, July 16, 1933; Latta, "Valley Pioneer Invented Divided Net, Hay Derrick," MS (July 23, 1933), BWC. For the Jackson self-feeder, see Rogin, *Introduction of Farm Machinery*, 190; *Tehama County, California*, 129; *Supplement, History of Colusa County*, xvii.

59. For hours, see Latta, "Henry Hammer"; *Napa Daily Journal*, July 10, 1891, NCLCF. For the Acme stacker and costs, see *PRP*, Nov. 26, 1887. A common assumption was that six men and ten horses could stack one hundred tons a day.

60. Quotes from letter to editor, *PRP*, Mar. 18, 1871; Kirby Brumfield, *This Was Wheat Farming* (Seattle, 1968), 68. See also Heidrick, "Recollections." Of their workday, Simi Valley field hands Ralph and Jim Runkle recalled: "Get up at 4 A.M., feed the mules hay and grain. Brush them and harness them, clean out the stables. Go in for breakfast about 6 A.M. Leave barn at 6:30, work till 11:30. Unhook the animals and come in for lunch. Work from 1 until about 5 P.M. Dinner at 6 P.M. Then go back out and curry the mules again. We didn't need a lot of entertainment." Quote from Jim and Ralph Runkle, interview, 1981, SVHS.

61. Lillie Dunlap Schwartzbach, "Family Life in Early Orange County," interview by Ann L. Spencer, July 18, 1985, Orange County Pioneer Council and CSU, Fullerton, Oral History Program, 4, CSU, Fullerton; Latta, "Hay Muckers' Hay Rides."

62. Powers, *South Fork Country*, 25. See also Webster, "A California Wheat Harvest," 453.

63. Quote from Latta, "Sky Farming," 4–5. One particularly infamous meat burner named Bob Bodley earned quite a reputation while working on the McCabe ranch near the town of Newman on the west side of the San Joaquin Valley. Recalled Frank Latta:

> Cooking hadn't always been Bob's occupation and it was the unanimous opinion of the crew that he never should have changed occupations. As a general thing, Bob's cooking was edible, except that he had a bad habit of picking his nose . . . when [he] was making biscuits. But once in a while he would turn out a masterpiece. Once Bob baked a batch of biscuits that were as hard as chunks of concrete and just as waterproof and enduring. Another time he baked a pumpkin pie that certainly never has had an equal. It was as tough as, and very little thicker than a piece of rubber and canvas belting and the crust was vulcanized to the tin pie plate. It was impossible to cut it.

Quote from Latta, "Bob Bodley, Meat Burner," MS (n.d.), FFLCSF.

64. Quotes from Latta, "Hay Muckers' Hay Rides," 2; *History of Kern County*, 73. See also Chester Gillespie, interview, in *Hollister Evening Free Lance*, ca. 1972, Hollister Historical Society, Hollister, Calif.; Latta, "The Story of Henry Hammer," 31; Hohenthal, "Turlock," 57. For a fictional account of a cook crew, see C. M. Harger, "The Mistress of the Cook Shack," *Outlook* 88 (Sept. 1907), 209–13. The first portable cookhouse on T. L. Reed's ranch north of Reedley in 1888 is described in John C. McCubbin, "First Eating Places," MS (n.d.), JCMP.

65. Traveling over a huge swath of territory as part of Greene's custom threshing business, so the story goes, they moved so far and so fast that the locations of the farm kitchens on the morning and evening of the same day were often many miles apart. This was a matter of great concern because Greene's men, like most wheat threshers, expected as part of their employment to receive a hearty lunch. But after they lost too much time commuting to and from meals, Greene began to consider ways to eliminate the problem. Proposing to build a mobile cookhouse that would allow the owner of a threshing outfit to feed his men and remove this responsibility from the farmer, he decided he could do so by charging an additional one cent per

bushel for threshing. But when he suggested the idea to fellow farmers and discussed the advantages and disadvantages of running a cook wagon, he found only two farmers would agree to the scheme. Convinced of the wisdom of his scheme, he built his cookhouse and used it throughout the harvest. Other farmers quickly recognized its value. Within a few years threshing crews throughout the state were being fed by cook wagons. See Higgins, "The Harvest Cook Wagon Started in '76," MS (n.d.), 1–2, FHHC. See also H. F. Harris, *Health on the Farm* (New York, 1911); "A Cafeteria on Wheels" (n.d.), Kern County Museum, Bakersfield, Calif.; *Modesto Herald*, July 18, 1878. For the portable bunkhouse, see typed notes on the *Northern Enterprise*, Oct. 31, 1873, in TWNIPCGJB, 1. See also Nordhoff, "California," 255–67.

66. Quotes from Nathan A. Cobb, "The California Wheat Industry," in New South Wales Dept. of Agriculture, *Miscellaneous Publications No. 519* (Sydney, Aust., 1901), 19; *Supplement, History of Colusa County, California*, xviii. See also Otto Hughes, interview, in Levene, *Mendocino County Remembered*, 1: 216; McCormish and Lambert, *History of Colusa and Glenn Counties*, 211. With its system of lights "that turn night into day," one Ventura County cookshack was described by the local newspaper as making "a magnificent showing" and furnishing "a night scene worth going miles to see." Quote from "County's Threshers," *Oxnard Courier*, Oct. 4, 1902.

67. Quote from Cobb, "The California Wheat Industry," 19. See also Katherine Nichel, comp., *Beginnings in the Reedley Area: A Treasury of Historical Accounts 'till 1913 Written by Pioneers of the Reedley Area* (Reedley, Calif., 1916), 81; *History of Kern County*, 74; Domonoske, "Recollections." Besides food, harvest and threshing crews could also count on being provided with certain amenities, for example, "thunder mugs," one under the edge of every bed for "nighttime purposes," one or two blankets, and if the farmer was conscientious, a collection of crudely constructed but well-ventilated outhouses. As for lodging, careless men sleeping and smoking in barns presented such a high fire hazard, and were responsible for burning down so many buildings, that many wheat farmers deemed it necessary to provide bunkhouses not so much for humanitarian reasons but simply to protect their property. See Rogers, *Colusa Sun*, 157, reporting a barn fire on Grand Island in which one man died. For "thunder mugs," see Latta, "Ranch Pets," MS (n.d.), FFLCSF.

68. Quote from Webster, "A California Wheat-Harvest," 453. See also *Sacramento Daily Record Union*, Aug. 2, 1879. It was not uncommon for some crews to conclude after dusk and to finish by moonlight, particularly if they were preparing to shift to a new location. See letter to editor, *PRP*, Mar. 18, 1871.

69. Quote from Isidore Goumaz to sister, Apr. 14, 1871 [English translation from the original version], *Wagon Wheels* 25 (Sept. 1975), 18, original in Colusa Historical Society. For general wage data on the 1870s, see Nordhoff, *California for Health*, 183; Cone, *Two Years in California*, 132; Domonoske, "Recollections." For food and candy, see invoice book, receipts for steam candy, June 1885, Jacinto Pay Receipts, 1882–1904, HGP. Because they were more skilled and had more responsibilities, thresher tenders generally earned four dollars per day, as did the crew foreman. Among the best-paid men, wagon makers earned up to fifty dollars a month, while engineers on the big engines operating the threshers topped the list at sixty dollars per month. One exception to the $1.15 to $1.50 per day general pay schedule for threshermen and harvesters came during the fall of 1872, when threshing crews around Chico Township refused to work for less than $3.50 per ten hours. Although the local wheat farmers complained, they paid the rate. It was one of the few known examples of wage setting by threshing crews at the time. At the lower end of the pay scale were Chinese vegetable gardeners, stable bucks, laborers, pitchers, and straw or hay bucks, all of whom received ten dollars a month. See time book, June 19–Oct. 14, 1876, E. W. Chapman Ranch Records, Madera County Historical Society, Madera, Calif. For the 1872 season, see "Old Timer," *Chico Record*, Feb. 9, 1936, JWHA. For the 1880s, see Andrew Cullers to David Coverstone, Mar. 31, 1886, HM 16845, Miscellaneous Collection, HL; Poso Ranch Threshing Records, Aug. 1885, Miller and Lux Correspondence, HL, both listing a rate of $1.50 per day, or twenty-five to thirty dollars a month; time book, Mudd Ranch, Aug. 1888. While the story of life in wheat camps marks the beginning of an important theme in farmworker history, it has never been told. This omission has distorted all accounts of California farmworkers because, in discussing labor camps, commentators always pick up the narrative much later. Citing public outcry and protests against decrepit and unsanitary housing and the failure of state efforts to regulate and improve camps on the big fruit and hop farms around the turn of the century, activist writers draw ammunition supporting the claim that farmworkers have always lived in abysmal conditions, that farmers have never cared for or

properly sheltered them, and that the agricultural industry had a callous attitude toward farm-worker housing almost from its inception. For a photograph, see Carleton E. Watkins, Green-fields Ranch, Camp no. 36, headers at dawn, 1888, Tenneco West.

70. Rogers, *Colusa*, 292; *California Farmer*, Jan. 18, 1872; *San Francisco Chronicle*, July 17, 1879; *Colusa* (Colusa, 1891), 311; Hansen, *As I Remember*, 137, 166; Heidrick, "Recollections."

71. Quote from Anna Morrison Reed, "Opening Address," *CSAST, 1887*, 15. For conditions on large farms, see Carleton E. Watkins, "The Creasey Farm," LC; Cone, *Two Years in California*, 132; Latta, interview.

72. Clippings, *Marysville Appeal*, May 14, June 3, 1874; June 3, 1875, Tehama Scrapbook, CSL; *Whittier News*, Aug. 5, 1893; *Whittier Register*, May 24, 1895; Latta, "McCabe and Garzas Ranch," FFLCSF.

73. Quotes from typed notes, *Sacramento Bee*, June 18, 1890, FWP, "Source Material Gathered on Migratory Farm Labor," BL.

74. Quote from Hansen, *As I Remember*, 161–62. See also Meyer, interview.

75. Quote from Latta, "Hay Muckers' Hay Rides," 1–2, FFLCSF. See also Latta, "Sky Farmer's Homes," FFLCSF; W. J. Duffy, *The Sutter Basin and Its People* (Davis, 1972), 97. For bunkhouses, see *Sacramento Daily Record-Union*, Aug. 2, 1879.

76. Latta, "Old Scratch," MS (n.d.), 3, 5, FFLCSF.

77. Quote from ibid.

78. Quotes from Rogers, *Colusa County*, 249; also 247. On Apr. 15, 1889, Kern was sentenced to twelve years in Folsom Prison. See also Latta, "Sky Farmers," 3, FFLCSF.

CHAPTER TEN

1. Hoag and others like him are described as tenants in the *Marysville Appeal*, Apr. 4, 1875; Aug. 9, 1877. But the issues of July 27, 1879; Oct. 12, 1880; and Apr. 25, 1882, use the term "renters." See also Donald Houghton, interview by author, Feb. 12, 1986, author's possession. Typically Hoag and others paid all costs and turned over half of their crop to Glenn before expenses. The Monitor consisted of three small threshers bolted together: a forty-one-inch stroke Nichol and Shepherd vibrator; a forty-inch Buffalo Pitts, and a forty-inch Geyser. The Monitor also had a Jackson feeder that eliminated the need for hand feeding.

2. Quote from *PRP*, July 26, 1875; *Willows Daily Journal*, Oct. 15, 1917. Considerable controversy surrounds this episode. For a detailed treatment, see Richard Steven Street, "Mystery Achievement," *California Farmer* 266 (Sept. 1, 1987), 8–9, 12. For Hoag, see unidentified newspaper clipping, "Old Timer," Jan. 19, 1936, JWHA, Book 1; Amanda Hoag, "Autobiography," MS (n.d.), Colusa Historical Society. See also *PRP*, July 26, 1875; May 6, 1876. Another treatment, although slightly confused, is Higgins, "Dr. Glenn's Million-Dollar Wheat Crop," ibid., Oct. 26, 1946. Hoag's record was a remarkable achievement at a time when, in the Ohio River Valley, nine hundred bushels was considered the upper limits of threshing in a twelve-hour period.

3. Sima Baker and Florence Ewing, *The Glenn County Story, Days Past and Present* (Willows, Calif., 1968), 59–61; "California Harvest Scene—Dr. Glenn's Farm in Colusa County," *Wagon Wheels* 1 (Aug. 1951), 1–4; Higgins, "Honest Heritage," *Implement Record* [n.v.] (Apr. 1947), 23–24, FHHC; *Sacramento Bee*, Mar. 7, 1957.

4. The painting was not without its flaws. Foreground figures were somewhat large and sticklike, and Hill took the liberty of moving the sun around so it rose in the north and therefore sculpted the scene with a soft, golden light that hit men and machines at a perfectly impossible angle. He also moved the Sutter Buttes fifty miles north. See Domonoske, "Recollections," 3; "Harvest Scene," *PRP*, Apr. 1, 1876; Donald Houghton, interview by author, Jan. 8, 1985, San Francisco; Dr. Joseph Baird, interview by author, Tiburon, Calif., Mar. 23, 1985, both in author's possession. There is some evidence that in hiring Andrew Hill, Hoag mistook him for the far more famous landscape painter Thomas Hill. On the basis of the painting, Hill's reputation soared. He won more commissions and an armful of medals, including one from the California State Agricultural Society. See also Peter H. Hassrick, *The Way West: Art of Frontier America* (New York, 1997), 142–43; "Andrew P. Hill, Artist and Photographer," *California Country Journal* 5 (June 30, 1899), 37; Victoria T. Olsen, "Pioneer Conservationist A. P. Hill: 'He Saved the Redwoods,'" *The American West* 14 (Sept.–Oct. 1977), 32–40.

5. For Moran, see Carol Clark, *Thomas Moran: Watercolors of the American West* (Fort Worth, Tex., 1980); Thurman Wilkins, *Thomas Moran: Artist of the Mountains* (Norman, Okla.,

1966). For Hahn, see Marjorie Arkelian, "William Hahn: German-American Painter of the California Scene," *American Art Review* 4 (Aug. 1977), 109; Jeanne Van Nostrand, *The First Hundred Years of Painting in California, 1775–1875* (San Francisco, 1980), 72, 102; H. Armour Smith, *William H. Hahn: Painter of the American Scene* (Yonkers, N.Y., 1942). For the background to Hahn's threshing painting, see William Hahn Scrapbook, Rostow Collection, Oakland Museum.

6. In its longest run, which lasted three hours before they had to move to a new set, the Thompson crew threshed 664 sacks of grain. See *Modesto Herald*, Aug. 22, Sept. 12, 1878.

7. Quote from *Willows Journal*, July 26, 1879. Although the new engine had arrived in 1878, Glenn did not employ it to any great extent because heavy rains in the northern Sacramento Valley caused extensive damage to his crop. Glenn alone lost twenty thousand sheep and several thousand acres of grain in the flood. Scrambling to salvage everything they could, field hands and wheat growers alike were in no mood or inclination to push for a new threshing record. For the catastrophe of 1878, see clipping, Old Timer, "Floods, Failing Ground, End Prosperous Era for Farmers," *Chico Enterprise*, Feb. 23, 1936, JWHA. For Enright, see Munro-Fraser, *History of Santa Clara County, California*, 186; Latta, "Enright's Steam Engine," MS (n.d.), FFLCSF. For building the Missouri Chief, see clipping, *Colusa Sun*, July 26, 1879, Willows Library. See also Higgins, "Mule Train Ranching in the West," MS (n.d.), 10, FHHC, which gives the date of the world-record threshing as July 8.

8. Quote from *Willows Daily Journal*, July 26, 1879. See also *Colusa Sun*, July 26, 1879; *PRP*, July 26, 1879; Higgins, "What It Took to Raise a Million Bushels of Wheat," MS (n.d.), FHHC. During threshing, the crew shut down the thresher three times, the first time for nearly an hour when a piece of iron dropped into the cylinder and broke some teeth; the second for just a few minutes, also from a piece of iron that did no damage; and the third time for a half hour, when the lagging on the cylinder pulley came loose from its guides and the steam engine had to be repositioned in order to reset the belt. The *Willows Daily Journal* described these efforts as "an impossibility to do in so short a time, after looking at the enormous amount of machinery to be moved." Quote from *Willows Daily Journal*, July 26, 1879. See also Baker and Ewing, *Glenn County Story*, 58.

9. Quotes from *Colusa Sun*, Oct. 2, 1880; "Nick Hansen's Reminiscences," *Wagon Wheels* 1 (Aug. 1951), 6. See also Higgins, "Honest Heritage," *Implement Record* [n.v.] (Apr. 1947), 66, FHHC; Rogers, *Colusa*, 179, 202; *PRP*, Oct. 9, 1880.

10. Quotes from Rogers, *Colusa County*, 129, 179; also 153, 178; *Napa County Reporter*, July 13, 1872, NCLCF. See also "Vaca Valley Ablaze," *San Francisco Call*, June 18, 1895, and accompanying drawing. There was considerable debate over new steam-boiler models and inherently unstable designs such as Enright's triple-return boiler, which was said to burn too hot and could not be controlled. See various clippings, FHHC; Powers, *South Fork Country*, 111–12; Hansen, *As I Remember*, 154–55; Latta, interview; Domonoske, "Recollections." Explosions also occurred when threshers hit a bunch of smutty wheat, threw up a cloud of black dust, and a spark ignited the cloud in a ball of fire. And there were plenty of close calls when the steam pressure kept building, the pressure release valve stuck, the emergency engine whistle shrieked madly, and everyone started backing away from the engine, then suddenly turned on their heels and broke into a sprint. Of the new triple-return boiler, the *Willows Journal* observed,

> It is not in favor with engineers. There is too much fire surface. We doubt very much whether the straw burners can ever be as safe as wood or coal burning engines. The flames cannot be kept uniform and hence must often have a too intense heat. This variation of heat will cause the water to rise and fall so that the engineer is sometimes at fault about the amount of water in the boiler.

Quote from *Willows Journal*, July 26, 1879.

11. Quote from *Napa County Reporter*, June 27, 1868, NCLCF. See also *Stanislaus County Weekly News*, July 30, 1886.

12. Every thresherman had a story about a boiler explosion. Recalling their close calls and the carnage of a particularly ghastly steam engine accident that they had witnessed, old-time threshers would spin out the most extraordinary and detailed accounts of narrow escapes and men they had known who had died or been maimed in these accidents. Press accounts went further. Full of gory details, they took considerable pains identifying the jobs of those killed and injured and how they died, for example, water monkeys who were scalded, pitchers who

were crushed under equipment, thresher tenders decapitated by flying debris, and so on. For various accidents, see Powers, *South Fork Country*, 28; *PRP*, July 15, 1886; Rogers, *Colusa*, 153; Nathan C. Sweet, "An 1876 Harvest," *Madera County Historian* 1 (Apr. 1961), 3; "Accidents," *Napa Daily Journal*, July 6, 1900; "About the Town and County," July 7, 1900; "Reed & Co. take their Separator and Working Crew To Suisun," Aug. 8, 1900, NCLCF. For county hospitals full of maimed threshermen, see *Modesto Herald*, Aug. 1878. For One Armed Hughson, see Hohenthal, "History of Turlock," 56.

13. Quote from "Fatal Accident at Elmira," *San Francisco Call*, June 7, 1895.

14. Quote from Latta, "The Story of Henry Hammer," 30, FFLCSF. For heat, see Mary Agnes Crank, "Ranch Life 50 Years Ago," James Crank Papers, HL; Mark Twain, *Roughing It* (New York, 1872), 412; William Brewer, Sunday evening notes, May 12, 1861; notes from June 15, 1862; Apr. 5, 1862, William Brewer Field Notes, BL. See also "Great Heat Makes California Still More Like Hell," *Solidarity*, Aug. 12, 1925. Terminology borrowed from Wallace Stegner, *Beyond the Hundredth Meridian: John Wesley Powell and the Opening of the West* (Boston, 1953).

15. Quote from "Stockton Notes," *PRP*, July 31, 1886. For men dropping dead from heat, see Rogers, *Colusa*, 174. For a discussion of heat and farmwork compared to conditions in the eastern United States, see *Kern County Californian*, Sept. 3, 1887.

16. Quote from "Died from Overheating," *Chico Enterprise*, June 30, 1876. See also "Harvesting in Colusa—Seven Deaths from Overheating," June 16, 1876. Michael Magliari provided these newspaper clippings. See also Rogers, *Colusa County*, 146, 203.

17. Quote from Latta, "The Story of Henry Hammer," 30. See also *Supplement to History of Colusa County*, xvii; time book, E. W. Chapman ranch, June 19–Oct. 14, 1876, Madera County Historical Society.

18. For problems with flies, gnats, and heat, see Arthur B. Domonoske, address to Willows Chamber of Commerce [a reminiscence], Aug. 16, 1947, FHHC; clippings, *Marysville Appeal*, June 3, 1872; May 14, June 3, 1874, Tehama Scrapbook, CSL.

19. *Sacramento Daily Union*, Aug. 21, 1879, lists the average workday for a threshing crew on the Glenn ranch at an unbelievable sixteen hours. That would mean men worked about ninety-two hours per week, with a half-day (eight hours) on Saturdays, compared to the average sixty to sixty-six-hour workweek in the Midwest, and the seventy- to eighty-hour workweek for threshers elsewhere. See U.S. Dept. of Labor, Bureau of Labor Statistics, *History of Wages in the United States from Colonial Times to 1928*, Bulletin no. 499 (Washington, D.C., 1929), 159–60, 225, 253–54, 448. See also Hohenthal, "History of Turlock," 58–61. In late June, near Woodland, a score of men from Sonoma Valley employed by the threshing outfit of a Mr. Kennedy was passing through a fruit ranch owned by a Mr. N near Cashville. Seeing a lush crop on the trees, the men proceeded to help themselves to Mr. N's crop. "His wife went to the men and interposed an objection, but they intimated that she might go where the woodtick diggeth," reported the *Woodland Mail*. "The lady was greatly offended and her husband took action." Soon warrants were issued against the entire crew, and officers went to the ranch of William Hatcher, where the crew had set up. "They were greatly disturbed by the prospect of arrest and begged to be allowed to go," reported the *Mail*. "They say that they did not intend to insult Mrs. Nutting, and would apologize, in addition to paying twenty dollars for the stolen fruit. This being satisfactory to all parties, the men were not jailed." Quote from *Woodland Mail*, June 29, 1889, cited in "Saucy Pilferers Dealt With," *PRP*, July 13, 1889.

20. Quote from Richard Gird, journal, n.d., 31–32, HL. Men often received their wages at the office in back of the camp store, their money being brought out to the farms and camps in a large sack or satchel containing as much as eighty thousand dollars in twenty-dollar gold pieces. See Cornelius, "Wheat Harvest of 1884," 2; *PRP*, Aug. 12, 1882; Jacinto Post Office Quarterly Records, Oct. 1–Dec. 21, 1881, HGP. For parallel developments among canalers, see Peter Way, "Evil Humors and Ardent Spirits: The Rough Culture of Canal Construction Workers," *JAH* 79 (Mar. 1993), 1398, 1412.

21. Clipping, *Oakland Tribune*, July 14, 1946; Cornelius, "Harvest of 1884," 2; Valeda Hoag, "Recollections," FHHC.

22. Higgins, "Reflections on Dr. Glenn," *The Observer* 1 (June 19, 1968) 1–5; Heidrick, "Recollections," 2. Card sharks are described in Latta, "The Lucky Irishman," 1–6, FFLCSF. For a field hand shot and killed by the saloon keeper at Jacinto on August 26, 1874, and a Spaniard stabbed in a saloon in Princeton on September 16, 1874, see Rogers, *Colusa County*, 140–41.

23. Rensch et al., *Historic Spots in California*, 97.

24. Quotes from Rogers, *Colusa County*, 154, 163; Elias, *Stories of Stanislaus*, 297. See also Tinkham, *History of Stanislaus County*, 101; Heidrick, "Recollections," 2; Hansen, *As I Remember*, 141; "Willows, Its Story," *Wagon Wheels* 2 (Apr. 1982), 3–6; Higgins, "Honest Heritage," FHHC.

25. Quotes from John C. McCubbin, "The Rise and Fall of Traver," MS (n.d), JCMP; Latta, "Hay Muckers' Hay Rides," 7–8; Elias, *Stories of Stanislaus*, 293; also 271–73, 294–97. "None of these statements made in this story are for effect," wrote Latta. "Stanislaus and Merced County Inquest reports, read by one with an understanding of conditions on the Front [Front Street], will furnish several hundred specific illustrations, all supported by sworn statements and all more sordid than anything I have presented in this sketch." I have not consulted the Merced County Inquest Reports, 1870–1880, presumably in Merced County Court House, Merced, Calif.

26. Quote from Rogers, *Colusa County*, 253.

27. Quotes from ibid., 255; also 126, 257, 259; Latta, "Lou McElvaney," 1–2; clipping, U. G. Knight to editor, *Gustine Standard*, n.d., FFLCSF. See also Latta, "Fred Buchanan"; "Firebaugh Murder Ends in Drunken Row," *Visalia Times Index*, [ca. 1881], Visalia Historical Society, Visalia, Calif.; "The History of Turlock," *Stockton Record*, n.d., SRCF; Hohenthal, "History of Turlock," 59.

28. Quotes from Latta, "Hills Ferry," 4; U. G. Knight [saloon murder story] to *Gustine Standard*, n.d., FFLCSF. Latta attributes the "sordid, dirty hole" quote to William Brewer while serving on the 1864 survey of California. According to Latta, town founder Jesse Hill became so disgusted with Hills Ferry that "he stated that he never wanted to see the place again" and left for Santa Maria, never to return. See also Brotherton, *Annals of Stanislaus County*, 41–44.

29. L. C. Branch, *History of Stanislaus County* (San Francisco, 1881), 227–29; Latta, "Ah Gun" [who ran a "Sporting House" in Newman], 8; Latta, "Lou McElvery" [the Pink House], 2.

30. Quotes from Latta, "Hills Ferry," 4, FFLCSF; *San Francisco Morning Chronicle*, Oct. 21, 1883. See also *Fullerton Tribune*, Aug. 12, 1893.

31. For rolling drunks, see Latta, "Rolling Rooms," 1, FFLCSF. See also John C. McCubbin, "The Rise and Fall of Traver," *Fresno Republican*, Mar. 5, 1923, BWC; Alan F. Patterson, *Land, Water, and Power: A History of the Turlock Irrigation District, 1887–1987* (Spokane, 1989), 33–34; Kathleen Small, *History of Tulare County* (Chicago, 1926), 1: 187, 404; Archie E. Marston, "Chowchilla Beginnings," *Madera County Historian* 2 (Apr. 1962), 1–3. Men generally would accumulate a stake of $150 before going to town for their periodic binge. See Latta, "Hundred and Fifty Dollar Stake Men," 1–2, FFLCSF. For a divorce case arising out of the tradition of field hands going on a binge, see Susan v. Nicholas Dodge, Case no. 2829, Santa Clara County Municipal Court, testimony of Deborah McGowan, Santa Clara County Court Records, Santa Clara, Calif.

32. Elias, *Stories of Stanislaus*, 293–317; Smith, *Garden of the Sun*, 257–58; Rogers, *Colusa County*, 184. "There were plenty of killings that never went to trial," recalled one old field hand of the violence among threshers around Willows. "I can recall eight or nine in our community. Everybody knew who did most of them, but minded their own business because each man had usually settled his own problem by killing the man he thought needed killing to settle a personal score of some kind—gambling, women, stealing, etc." Quote from Heidrick, interview. While not as violent as their counterparts in Hills Ferry, field hands in the nearby town of Newman were just as rowdy. Fighting, playing cards, and engaging in "general debauchery," they "renewed their youth and spirits," and "blew their pile" to the limits of their endurance and pocketbooks. Some of their antics were as strange as they were pathetic. One unfortunate victim of their pranks was a field hand named Jimmy Murphy. A native of Ireland, Murphy had come to California with a troupe of Irish singers. Something went wrong in San Francisco, and the troupe broke up. Unable to find work, Murphy drifted from one job to another. Eventually settling on fieldwork, he lived on a farm outside Newman, and spent most of his free time drinking in town. One day, while on one of his periodic drinking binges, Murphy fell into a horse trough in front of the Elkhorn Saloon. Dozens of field hands, local barflies, and pimps witnessed the indignity, and from then on they made it a favorite outdoor sport to push Murphy into any one of the three other horse troughs every time they could get him near one. Jimmy Murphy became known as "Horse Trough Murphy," and any greenhorn field hand near a horse trough was certain to get a dunking. See Latta, "Horse Trough Murphy," MS (n.d.), 1–2, FFLCSF. Field hands in Newman were always pulling tricks like that on their pals. But they did not limit their pranks and mischief to their own kind. Anyone who crossed their

path was fair game. Because they were so wild and unpredictable, ladies absolutely would not dare to walk down the streets near the saloons and whorehouses. Even after the worst drunks had passed out and been removed from the sidewalks and placed in rolling rooms, women would not go near this part of town. The saloon strip was forbidden territory to all but the roughest sorts. If a woman was in a general store and wanted to drive her buggy just one block to another business and had to pass by the saloons, she would not take a direct route but instead followed a circuitous path to her destination. If she was walking, she would stroll three blocks out of her way just to avoid Front Street, where all of the threshers congregated in one of five saloons known collectively as "The Dirty Five." This area was known, appropriately, as "No Ladies Land." Any woman seen there was assumed to be either a prostitute or dance hall girl, and could expect rough treatment. Quote from Latta, "Lou McElvaney," 1–2. See also Latta, "No Ladies Land," MS (n.d.), 1–5; "'Whitey' Evans, Front Street Casualty," 1; "Jerky Johnny and His Delirium Tremens," 1–3; "Alcohol Bill," 1–5; U. G. Knight to editor, *Gustine Standard*, n.d., all in FFLCSF.

33. *Stanislaus County Weekly News*, July 30, 1886; *PRP*, Aug. 12, 1882.

34. Quote from Latta, "Hay Muckers' Hay Rides," 6–9. See also Higgins, "Reflections on Dr. Glenn"; Mike Cahn, interview, n.d., FHHC.

35. Old Timer, "Many Large Ranch Houses Built During Prosperity of Seventies," *Chico Record*, Feb. 16, 1936, JWHA. Yanked out of court and packed into header wagons, the men would be hauled back to work, the cost of their fines deducted from their next paychecks. Back in their bunkhouses, they slept off their carousing and went to work the next day. They followed this routine until late September, sometimes early October, when the last of the threshing finished and sheep were turned into the fields to graze on the stubble. At this time, they always faced a crisis. Most had worked little more than four months during the harvest season. If they had not gambled or blown their earnings, they had by now accumulated $200 to $250. This was their "stake." It was never enough. Consequently, during the winter men had to take whatever work they could find. See *Sacramento Daily Record-Union*, Aug. 21, 1879; *San Francisco Chronicle*, July 17, 1879; Domonoske, interview; U. G. Knight to editor, *Gustine Standard*.

36. Quote from statement of James Jenkins in "Conditions of the Labor Market as reported by the Committee of the Labor Council," *First Biennial Report*, CSBLS, 1883–84, 142.

37. C. A. Havens account with C. G. Austin Jr., Nov. 5, 1889, SVHS; Pat Havens, interview by author, Mar. 12, 2002, Simi Valley, Calif.

38. Quotes from anonymous photograph, FCHS. See also Street, "Annual Rabbit Slaughter," *History of Photography* 8 (Apr.–June 1988), 103–5; Edwin M. Eaton, *Vintage Fresno* (Fresno, 1965), 20–21; William J. Browning, "Personal Recollections After More Than 60 Years," interview by F. F. Latta, 1938, 24–25, FFLCSF. For a detailed description of rabbit drives and goose slaughters, see "'Rabbit Bill' Browning, King of the Jackrabbit Hunters, Has Trapped Animals Since 1880," *Shafter Progress*, Feb. 12, 1937, Shafter Public Library. See also "Tomorrow's Rabbit Drive," *Oxnard Courier*, May 3, 1902. See also Charles Clough, *Madera: The Rich, Colorful and Exciting Historical Heritage* (Madera, Calif., 1968), 32; Mary Agnes Crank, "Ranch Life 50 Years Ago"; Langston C. Winston to Henry Douglas Bacon, Nov. 19, 1881; Winston to Bacon, Nov. 22, 26, 1881, Henry D. Bacon Business Correspondence, HL; William J. Browning, "Personal Recollections after more than 60 Years," interview by F. F. Latta, 1938, 23, FFLCSF. "I probably had more to do with the reduction of the large number of jack rabbits that over-ran the San Joaquin Valley than all other agencies," asserted Browning. "It began on April 25, 1880, in the Woods field at the Canal Farm of Miller and Lux at Los Banos." Browning goes on at length about the history of this practice. See also John C. McCubbin, "Jack Rabbits," MS (n.d.), JCMP.

39. Quote from William S. Cornelius, "Herding Wild Geese on the Dr. Hugh Glenn Ranch in Glenn County during the 1880s together with an account of Dr. Glenn's Murder," interview by Hector Lee, Nov. 1949, ANCRR, Oral History Program, SCML. "I remember one instance . . . when . . . one of the cooks went out to empty the dishwater after washing dishes and was shot down," recalled Cornelius. "Now, nobody knew who killed him. He was killed dead. He was killed from a goose herder's gun, from stray bullets." See also "Colusa County Waterfowl's Paradise," MS (n.d.), Colusa County Historical Society; Hansen, *As I Remember*, 154; *San Francisco Daily Call*, Oct. 14, 1883; *Sacramento Union*, Feb. 24, 1883; *Oakland Tribune*, Jan. 13, 1883. When he bought David Bayliss's wheat crop in 1879, Glenn had to pay an additional $909.45 to keep the geese off those fields. On another occasion, he paid four men $425 for six months of goose herding on his French Crossing and Dry Creek ranches. Goose herd-

ing wages of one dollar a day from Jacinto daybook, Apr. 9, 1883, HGP. Most goose herders used 45/60 and 45/70 Winchester 16-gauge shotguns. One man loaded shells for ten to twelve herders, who protected about fifteen hundred acres, and each goose herder was required to pick up all expended shell casings and return them to the shop for reloading. On the largest farms single men worked out of "goose cabins" and "goose shacks" mounted on sleds and pulled into the middle of fields by teams of eight to ten mules. Known as "cabin herders," they received food and shells twice a week. Each had a dog, but no horse, and was assigned to keep geese and ducks away from a 160-acre tract. See Stephen G. Hurst, *California I Love You* (Marysville, 1959), 203; *San Francisco Morning Call*, Oct. 14, 1883. Goose herders would also cut off the breast meat, boil it up, and feed it to their dogs. But on Sundays they would always take an especially fat goose that they had shot to the camp cook. Recalled one former goose herder: "He'd cook that goose nice and fix it up nice and bring it to the long tables in the room where we ate." Quote from William S. Cornelius, "Herding Wild Geese." See also *PRP*, Dec. 23, 1882.

40. *San Francisco Morning Chronicle*, Oct. 14, 1883; *Marysville Appeal*, May 12, 1887; *1878 Colusa County Directory*, 61–62; Green, *History of Colusa*, 59; *Chico Enterprise*, June 8, 1882; invoice book, monthly purchases, n.d., HGP; Bidwell, diary, Jan. 10, 19; Feb. 10, 1870, JBP. In 1877, Glenn employed one hundred men to cut seven thousand cords of wood. Although he needed large quantities of wood to heat his farm buildings, Glenn sold most of it to river steamers docking at Jacinto, and to a Sacramento brickyard where it was used to fire kilns. For hand gleaning, see Latta, "The Story of Henry Hammer," 31.

41. Quotes from Latta, "That Nightmare, Straw Hauling," MS (n.d.), 47–48, 51, FFLCSF. When the straw was all gathered, the piles would be set afire, reddening the skies and covering the whole country with a smoky haze. Occasionally the straw would be saved and used to cover muddy roads.

42. For halfway houses, see Guy Crow, "Coming of the Railroad and the Birth and Naming of the Town of Berendo," *Madera County Historian* 5 (Apr. 1965), 2. See also *Paso Robles Record*, Sept. 21, 1895; Linda A. Young, "Homesteaders in the Shandon Valley," *La Vista* 3 (June 1972), 4–34.

43. Quote from *San Francisco Morning Call*, Dec. 9, 1880. McCubbin, "Rise and Fall of Traver," JCMP, apparently cribbed from the *Call* in his more extensive report on grain hauling in Traver. See also *Marysville Appeal*, Dec. 10, 1873; Aug. 4, 1876; *Stanislaus County Weekly News*, Aug. 1, 1886; clipping, *Oakland Tribune*, July 21, 1880, FHHC; *Marysville Appeal*, Aug. 1, 1882; Hansen, *As I Remember*, 156; *Colusa County Directory, 1893* (Colusa, 1893), 8; Mitchell, *A Modern History of Tulare County*, 40; Marston, "Chowchilla Beginnings," 5; Meyer, interview; Latta, "Tommy Dragoo and the Long-Line Hitch," MS (n.d.), 1–2; U. G. Knight to editor, *Gustine Standard*, n.d., FFLCSF.

44. Latta, "Death of Will," FFLCSF; Rogers, *Colusa County*, 245; E. E. Dodds to Abner Dodds, Sept. 26, 1891, Simi Land and Water Company Collection, SVHS.

45. Quotes from *Napa County Reporter*, Sept. 7, 1872, NCLCF; Rogers, *Colusa County*, 245–46; also 123, 142. Headlines from Oct. 12, 19, 1872, ibid.; *Chico Enterprise*, June 30, 1876; "A SINGULAR AND FATAL ACCIDENT," unidentified clipping, *Vacaville Record*, n.d., Vacaville Museum. For one man loading wheat after breaking his arm and another falling and being crushed when the wagon passed over his head, legs, and arms, see *Modesto Herald*, Aug. 14, 22, 1878. For a rope coil accident, see July 18, 1878. See also Latta, "Indian Joe and Early Roads," MS (n.d.), 2; Latta, "Tommy Dragoo and the Long-Line Hitch," 3–8, 15–16, FFLCSF; "Load Falls on Man," *Oxnard Courier*, Oct. 16, 1903; Apr. 28, 1905.

46. Many wheat threshers worked on farms where growers maintained effective systems of surveillance. Those on Bidwell's farm found themselves closely watched by superintendents, and informed on by a network of spies, including an Indian who circulated among the men joking with them and gathering information. Hundreds of men lost their jobs as a result of this system until a field hand wrote Bidwell informing him of the practice. See anonymous to General Bidwell, Nov. 28, 1881, JBP. See also Cornelius, "1884 Harvest"; statement of Huram Miller, in Governor Waterman Pardon Files, 2–3, File no. 5385, CSA.

47. Quotes from *PRP*, Aug. 29, 1885; *San Francisco Morning Call*, Oct. 14, 1883. For crop descriptions, see *Marysville Appeal*, Apr. 25, 1885; *Oakland Tribune*, Feb. 19, 1883. During September and October, as they struggled to move hundreds of thousands of sacks of wheat to steamboats lining the Sacramento River, men returning to Jacinto overheard Glenn cursing them for their complaining manner and slothfulness. Particularly galling was Glenn's threat to

hire Chinese field hands. Asked if he was afraid that his men might revolt, he supposedly proclaimed loudly, "I am always fixed for them." See People v. Huram Miller, Superior Court of Colusa County, Feb. 1883, testimony of Miller, 210, File no. 10873, Bin 2811, CSA.

48. Quote from testimony of Miller, 2–3, in Waterman Pardon Files, CSA.

49. Quote from testimony of Miller in Waterman Pardon Files, CSA. See also Allen, "Hugh Glenn."

50. The manslaughter explanation is too pat, too much an after-the-fact rationalization by local historians who have a stake in preserving Glenn's reputation. It strains credibility to believe that Miller just happened to be walking around with a loaded shotgun, that he was shielding his face from a stiff north wind and almost ran into Glenn, that Glenn and he exchanged words, that Glenn had seized the muzzle of the loaded shotgun, that a struggle occurred, that in the struggle Miller saw Glenn reach into his pocket and heard him say, "I'll fix you," and that Miller had instinctively fired his shotgun without taking aim, somehow hitting Glenn in the back of the head. See People v. Miller, testimony of Miller, 261–62; testimonies of J. D. Thornton and H. B. Wilson, 132–34, 142; testimony of Mrs. J. T. Higel, 141; testimony of Constable Charles Ayers, 161; testimony of Paul Maupin, 167, CSA. The manslaughter/self-defense thesis is in White, *Glenn County Sketchbook*, 180–84. Lying on his face in the dusty street with one hand still in his pants pocket, Glenn had a silver-dollar-sized hole in his head. His blood and brains leaked into the dust. Apparently aware that he was mortally wounded, he remained conscious but unable to move or speak. See Richard Steven Street, "The Murder of Hugh Glenn," *Sacramento Magazine* 11 (July 1985), 49–54.

51. Quote from Miller testimony, Waterman Pardon Files, CSA. See also Rogers, *Colusa County*, 197.

52. Various unidentified newspaper clippings, FHHC. See also *Willows Journal*, Feb. 18, 1883.

53. Street, "The Murder of Hugh Glenn," 49–54; People v. Miller, testimony of Dr. L. P. Tooley, 162; Rogers, *Colusa County*, 202.

54. For Glenn's combines, see *Marysville Appeal*, June 11, 1882; clipping, *Chico Record*, n.d., JWHA; "Complete Harvesters," *PRP*, July 2, 1881.

55. Glenn had begun upgrading his equipment in 1881 by having Sacramento agricultural implement wizard A. J. Cunningham build new boilers for his two Enright engines, directing him to use steel, not iron, because while more expensive, it lasted longer. See James King to Glenn, Jan. 12, 1881, HGP. For a discussion of Glenn's use of a Shippee combine and then a Matteson and Williamson Queen Model combine, see Higgins, "Bonanza Wheat Farming," typescript, 1; "Honest Heritage," *Implement Record*, 86, FHHC.

56. When a farmer was asked how he was going to harvest his grain, he would reply, "By stationary" (meaning with a stationary thresher) or "By traveler" (meaning with a combined harvester and thresher). Higgins, "Luke's Recollections of 40 Years in Combines," MS (n.d.), FHHC. As of 1868 there were about twenty experimental combines scattered through California's wheat districts. See *CSAST, 1868–69*, 115–16. Experimental combines were still regarded as novelties in 1874. See *Sacramento Union*, June 15, 1874. As late as 1880 the U.S. Census reported "comparatively few" combines were at work. See U.S. Dept. of Commerce, Bureau of the Census, *Tenth Census of the United States: 1880, Production of Agriculture* (Washington, D.C., 1883), 3: 458.

57. Most accounts estimate costs at around $1.75 per acre. For a typical modification, see D. H. Fuller, "The Gaines Combined Header and Thrasher," *PRP*, n.d., FHHC. See also Cobb, "The California Wheat Industry," 1328–31; Jacob Price to editor, "A Visitor in the Valley Grain Fields," *PRP*, July 7, 1877, contains an extensive firsthand description and comparison of the various combines. See also "The 'Houser' Combined Header and Thresher," *PRP*, Mar. 28, 1885. For the merger of the two combine companies, see "Concentrating Harvester Manufacture," *SDI*, Oct. 15, 1885. See also "History Gives Description of Bidwell's Famed Rancho Chico," *Chico Record*, Feb. 9, 1936, JWHA; typed notes, *Stanislaus News*, n.d., FFLCSF. For the first combine in Colusa County, see Rogers, *Colusa County*, 250. The September 20, 1882, California State Fair trial is described in typed notes, "Trial of Combined Harvesters," *PRP*, Sept. 29, 1883, FHHC.

58. Quote from Higgins, "Mule Skinner Language Bit, Blistered and was Deep Purple," MS (n.d.), FHHC.

59. *Benicia Evening News*, July 15, 1886, FFLCSF; Branch, *History of Stanislaus County*, 208; Higgins, "California Invented the 'Pusher' Combine," *California Farmer*, Jan. 15, 1952, 28–29.

60. Quote from Latta, "The Dick Richards System," 5, FFLCSF.

61. Quotes from "The Shippee Combined Harvester Improved," *PRP*, Apr. 11, 1885; "No More Headers," ibid., Mar. 29, 1884. The twenty- to forty-acre per day figure is from clipping, *San Joaquin Valley Argus*, ca. Mar. 1878, FFLCSF. Harvest rates varied according to the size of the cutting bar and the density and dryness of the wheat. See also Hugh M. Hoyt Jr., "The Wheat Industry in California, 1850–1910" (M.A. thesis, CSUS, 1953), 60–61. See also Bancroft, *History of California*, 7: 28; *CSAST, 1893*, 363; *CSAST, 1894*, 100, 119, 124, app.; Alfred Bannister, "California and Her Wheat Culture," *Overland Monthly* 12 (July 1888), 68. Surviving production records identify the three categories of expenses: materials, seeds, sacks, and equipment; rent or mortgage payments; plowing, seeding, harrowing, harvesting, and threshing. These later expenses amounted to between 30 and 40 percent of the total costs. And of these production costs, harvesting and threshing were by far the largest. They not only amounted to a very considerable sum, they were the only ones wheat farmers could influence, and that combines might reduce drastically. To them, the advantages of the new technology were too great to ignore and they enthusiastically embraced combines. The best analysis is "Wheat Growing in California," *PRP*, July 21, 1888. See also Portia Kellogg, "An Analysis of the Economic Causes of the Rise and Decline of Wheat Growing in the Great Central Valley of California" (M.A. thesis, USC, 1926), 89; Hoag, "Mistakes in Wheat Culture and Harvesting in California," 128. For a detailed breakdown of costs, see "Combined Harvesters 'Not In It,'" in Latta, "The Dick Richards System," 10–11.

62. Quote from *Sacramento Bee*, July 1, 1889. The *Bee* also reported wages at $3 to $3.50 per day, and as high as $5 for combine drivers. See also Scheuring, "Tillers," 96; Old Timer, "Harvesters Revolutionize Grain Cutting," *Chico Record*, Apr. 19, 1936, JWHA, which puts combine costs at one dollar an acre. See also *PRP*, July 11, 1879; "The Shippee Combined Harvester," ibid., Sept. 19, 1883; "Combined Harvesters," ibid., Feb. 28, 1885; "Cost of Wheat," ibid., Apr. 17, 1886; Davis, "Wheat in California," 61–62; Joseph Hutchinson, "California Cereals," 145. Colusa profit calculations as follows: Plowing and seeding: $1.19. Cutting and threshing by combine: $1.50. Bags: seventy-five cents. Hauling to warehouse: $1.10. Rental of land: $3.35. Freight to tidewater: $1.90. Weighing and loading charges: thirty-five cents. See Rogers, *Colusa County*, 308–9.

63. As late as 1884, there were ninety stationary threshing machines running in Colusa County in the northern Sacramento Valley, each averaging eight hundred sacks per day, and just three or four combines. Four years later, combines gathered only about 15 percent of the California wheat crop. See "The Harvest," *PRP*, Aug. 18, 1888. For traditional threshing outfits, see *Napa Daily Journal*, Oct. 7, 1891, describing Alexander and Imrie's threshing crew working eighty-seven consecutive days in the Napa and Sonoma valleys. See also *PRP*, July 21, 1883. For threshers in Colusa County, see Domonoske, "Recollections." See also "Mammoth thresher purchased by F. Tombs, Dry Creek. Largest thresher in county," *Healdsburg Enterprise*, July 18, 1888. Combine adoption statistics from Olmstead and Rhode, "An Overview of California Agricultural Mechanization, 1870–1930," 107. One reason why so few field hands worked with combines in some wheat growing areas was that the machines did not perform well in hilly or rough territory. Trying to operate them in the Montezuma Hills east of Fairfield, men were injured when the top-heavy machines toppled over or their cutting bars snagged on stumps and boulders, bringing the combines to a sharp halt and sending men tumbling headlong into the machinery. Not until 1893 would Holt Manufacturing Company make a successful hillside combine. Another reason for their limited involvement was that combines did not work well in tight fields. Unable to maneuver into corners, combines left so much grain still standing that farmers preferred to use small headers to cut the standing grain, then pitch it into the combines. Then there was the matter of their cost. Selling for fifteen hundred to two thousand dollars each, combines were too expensive for most small-scale farmers. Thus, at first, only field hands on the largest bonanza farms even saw or worked with the new contraptions. For more on comparative costs, see Joseph Hutchinson, "California Cereals," 145–47. For twenty combines operating on thirty thousand acres of land farmed by the '76 Land and Water Company, see newspaper clipping, *Traver Advocate*, ca. 1889, Madera County Historical Society. See also *History of Kern County*, 74. Not until the late 1880s would combines be able to raise and lower their wheels on one side or another to function on hillsides or adjust the height of the cutting bars so that they no longer snagged on obstructions. See Steele Family Papers, 16: 190, 210, 219; *PRP*, June 1, 1895; *Paso Robles Moon*, Aug. 5, 1893; Joseph A. McGowan, *History of*

the Sacramento Valley (New York, 1961), 1: 250; Rogin, *Introduction of Farm Machinery*, 147–48; Marion N. Jewell, "Agricultural Development in Tulare County, 1870–1900" (M.A. thesis, USC, 1950), 22.

64. Field hands on small farms in the Napa, Sonoma, Pajaro, and Salinas valleys still had little if any contact with combines. Such farms were usually below the threshold governing adoption of combines. Well into the twentieth century, men working on diversified farms or on wheat farms under 160 acres still used headers to cut the grain and then helped stationary thresher crews bring in the harvest. A general rule of thumb was that farmers with more than 160 acres always had at least four horses or mules that could be diverted from plowing and wagon work into pulling a combine or grain wagon, while those below that size usually lacked the necessary animals. The threshold of 160 acres and four horses is described in "The Centennial Harvester," *PRP*, July 20, 1878. For headers, see "Stockton Notes," Aug. 11, 1883; typed notes, *Watsonville Pajaronian*, July 20, 1882, PVHS; typed notes, *Gilroy Advocate*, July ?, 1882, GHS. See also clippings, *Visalia Weekly Delta*, Aug. 21, 1886; Aug. 17, 1891, Tulare County Historical Society; Mitchell, *Modern History of Tulare*, 40.

65. Quote from McGowan, *History of the Sacramento Valley*, 1: 252. For the Thompson road steamer, see *PRP*, Jan. 14, 1871. For one of the earliest road steamers, see typed notes, *Los Angeles Star*, Aug. 4, 1860, FFLCSF. For the Hyde steam wagon, see *Marysville Appeal*, Sept. 3, 1871.

66. Quotes from *Kern County Courier*, Mar. 20, 1875; *Marysville Appeal*, June 3, 1874. See also June 23, 1872; June 3, 1873; June 23, Sept. 3, 1878; Sept. 16, 1881; Feb. 23, 1900. Traveling around for a week by buckboard, Hyde examined each farm to determine which was best adapted for his new contraption. Agreeing to bring his steam plow to Kern Island Farm, he had to delay work until the railroad bridge across the Kern River was reinforced to bear the weight of his machine and the railroad flatcars upon which it rested. See *Kern County Weekly Courier*, Jan. 2, 9, 1875; Latta, "Billy Carr and the Steam Plow," MS (n.d.), 1–6, FFLCSF.

67. The extent to which wheat harvesting depended on animal power could be seen in Colusa County, which in 1879 had a horse population of 10,369. Mules, which did most of the work, were too numerous to count. See also *PRP*, June 12, 1880.

68. Higgins, "Berry's Self-Propelled Combine," MS (n.d.), FHHC. Berry also suspended a header from the right side of the frame, hinged the separator on the left side with wheels to support it, connected the two with a draper and self-feeder mechanism, added a bench and a large straw rack over the front wheels, and hinged the entire apparatus in the middle so it would bend like a V when moving over uneven fields. He then connected the front drive wheels to the boiler power drive by means of a specially designed differential, and used a separate steam pipe from the boiler to convey power to a small engine that ran the separator and cutting bar. As no one had ever attempted such a feat, failure would impede further efforts. When Berry prepared to run the machine, field hands joined other skeptics and bet it would never thresh even a bushel of wheat. See "New California Harvester," *PRP*, Aug. 7, 1886; clippings, *Tulare Register*, Aug. 8, 9, 1886, Tulare County Historical Society; Mitchell, *Modern History of Tulare*, 39. Latta, "The Stockton Berry Steam Harvester," 2–4; "Self-Propelled Harvester Originated Here," *Lindsay Gazette*, Apr. 25, 1930, FFLCSF. Compared to other steam combines that field hands would see and work on, Berry's was better designed and constructed, and from the beginning, it performed extremely well. Because it was hinged rather than rigid, drivers had no difficulty following the contours of the land, including even the so-called hog wallows, without missing any of the grain. The only problem was the clutch. Constant turning wore it out before the harvest finished, and as a result Berry devised a stronger differential and clutch mechanism, almost identical to those on modern tractors, consisting of heavy gears in a cast-iron box filled with oil. To the men who helped assemble the new differential it became known as the "Jack in the Box." Although Berry failed to patent the device, thereby giving away what may have been the most valuable feature of this entire machine, he soon had plenty of orders. See Floyd Clymer, ed., *Historical Steam Traction Engines* (New York, 1965), 23, 31; "Auto-Motive Combined Harvester Used in Lindsay District," *Fresno Bee*, Aug. 6, 1933; George Berry to editor, *PRP*, Nov. 20, 1886; Higgins, "Straw-Burners on Combines," typed notes on Byron Jackson machinery catalog (n.d.), FHHC.

69. Quote from Smith, *Garden of the Sun*, 236. See also Latta, "Auto-Motive Combined Harvester," 8; Rogers, *Colusa County*, 307–10; clipping, *Woodland Mail*, Aug. 3, 1889, Yolo Historical Society; "More About Steam Harvesting," *PRP*, Aug. 10, 1889; Domonoske, "Recollections." Within a few months field hands encountered another consequence of the new inven-

tion, when Berry reversed the steering mechanism on his machine, converted it to a tractor, fixed huge lanterns front and rear, hitched his steam wagon to five Stockton gangplows, and began plowing day and night. Two crews, each working twelve-hour shifts, kept the road locomotive busy until they had plowed 160 acres in twenty-four hours. After they finished, they replaced the plows with a seeder and harrow and planted 450 acres a day, yet another record, at a cost of thirty-five cents an acre. For all its success, however, the machine proved too heavy for most farms. Packing the moist soil so hard that the marks of the wheels remained in the ground several years thereafter, Berry's steam plow and others like it quickly retired from plowing. See "Berry's Improved Harvester," *PRP*, Sept. 29, 1888; *CSAST, 1888–89*, 236; Latta, "Auto-Motive Combined Harvester," 2, FFLCSF; Brooks Gist, *Tales By The Campfire* (Tulare, Calif., 1974), 88; *Marysville Appeal*, Feb. 20, Mar. 9, Nov. 16, 1889. For one of the earliest efforts at steam plowing, see Higgins, "Locher's Steam Plow Stirred Butte County in 1869," FHHC. For the first public trial of a steam plow, see *California Farmer*, Feb. 11, 1869.

70. Edward A. Pomeley, "Development of Mechanical Power for Agriculture," in Louis B. Schmidt and Earle Dudley Ross, eds., *Readings in the Economic History of American Agriculture* (New York, 1925), 368; Latta, "The Haskall & Moore Combine," 4, FFLCSF; "California Combined Harvesters," *PRP*, Feb. 19, 1898; "Best's Steam Engine," ibid., Aug. 24, 1889; George E. Walsh, "Steam Power for Agricultural Purposes," *Harper's Weekly* 45 (June 1, 1901), 567; Smith, *Garden of the Sun*, 237; Cobb, "California Wheat," 1328–29; Reynold Wik, "Steam Power on the American Farm, 1830–1880" *AH* 25 (Oct. 1951), 186. One of the first crews to run the machines on a large scale worked on A. H. Wolfsen's ranch, fourteen miles west of Corcoran. Living in a camp described as resembling a small town and "equipped with every convenience," fifty-two men operated five steam-powered combines, threshing and cutting Wolfsen's six-thousand-acre crop at the incredible rate of two hundred acres per day. Some crews harvested and threshed at an even greater pace. For Wolfsen's men, see *FMR*, July 27, 1929, BWC. See also Smith, *Garden of the Sun*, 223. Although crews on steam-powered combines were smaller than those using horses, overall expenses were often much higher. The most careful study calculated costs for one day of operation for one steam combine at sixty-six dollars. At one-thousand bushels per day, this brought the cost of harvesting, cleaning, and bagging down to about three cents per bushel, not including bags. But even at that rate, contract crews using horse-powered combines on small San Joaquin Valley wheat farms often did better. One study of crews using horse-powered combines in 1888 found that on farms producing eighteen bushels per acre, they brought in grain at about .097 cents per bushel, while another study of steam combines in 1893 found that on farms producing fifteen bushels per acre, steam combines harvested and threshed at $1.75 per acre and brought in the crop at .116 cents per bushel. For costs per day, see Cobb, "California Wheat," 19. Cobb's calculations did not take into account using the steam traction engine for spring plowing. For costs in 1888, see Alfred Bannister, "California and Her Wheat Culture," *Overland Monthly* 12 (July 1888), 65–70. For costs in 1893, see *CSAST, 1893*, 363. Men worked with steam-powered combines for only a brief period lasting from the mid-1880s until about 1912, when gasoline-powered engines replaced them. When asked about their work on both steam- and horse-powered combines, most field hands expressed satisfaction, especially if they were old enough to recall an earlier era in wheat harvesting. To them, mechanization was an overwhelmingly positive step, infinitely preferable to hand and stoop labor. "They were entering the riding-working age when it became the ambition of everyone to sit down while they worked, and of many to sit down, period," recalled one bonanza wheat farmer. Quote from Latta, "The Dick Richards System."

71. *CSAST, 1891*, 183; *PRP*, Jan. 25, 1890; Davis, "California Breadstuffs," 534. Given an average yield of thirteen bushels per acre, it cost most farmers seventy-seven to eighty cents to produce one central of wheat, leaving just fifty-six cents to pay their taxes, clear their mortgage debts, buy supplies, make improvements, and earn a profit. At that price, many wheat farmers could no longer meet expenses. With yields declining and farmers doing nothing to restore the fertility of the land, there was no reversing the process. A few hoped that the Southern Pacific would save them by pushing a line to New Orleans, thus allowing them to ship wheat out of the Gulf of Mexico and thereby overcome their high transportation costs. Some hoped that a canal dug across the Isthmus of Panama would bring them back into competition on the world market. But most wheat farmers saw the end was near. The worse off among them suddenly told their combine crews that they would feed them, but that they had no money to pay them. Men would have to take promissory notes or work at considerably re-

duced rates. On some wheat farms, combine drivers and crewmen were ordered simply to stop harvesting. A few never received what they were due for the season's work. "We threshed for bacon and beans," one old field hand recalled. "But we got no goddam measly paycheck all that season." Quote from Latta, interview. See also Domonoske, "Recollections"; Hoag, interview. A large contingent also found continuous work on header crews and stationary threshing outfits drifting in a triangular-shaped circuit through eastern Oregon, Lovelock, Nevada, and the Central Valley of California, and on farms around Oxnard, Delano, Fresno, and Sonoma, where steam-driven combines never gained a foothold. Just as hot and exhausting as ever, their work acquired one additional danger: electrocution. Transporting their hay derricks, crews were always tangling them in power lines. Those not fried instantly in at least one case met their end when the apparatus fell on them as they foolishly attempted to untangle the mess. For irrigated wheat farming, see *CSAST, 1894*, 188; Victor M. Cone, *Irrigation in the San Joaquin Valley*, U.S. Dept. of Agriculture, Office of Experiment Stations, Bulletin no. 239 (Washington, D.C., 1911), 17. For the general state of the industry, see Starr, "Abraham Dubois Starr," 200; Davis, "California Breadstuffs," 534. For the triangular circuit, see Latta, "Hay Mucker's Union and Windy Red," MS (n.d.), 1–2, FFLCSF. For the persistence of header crews and stationary threshing operations, see "Agricultural Co.'s Extensive Business," *Oxnard Courier*, June 13, 1903. See also "Fire at Coalinga Burns Harvester," *FMR*, June 9, 1918. For electrocution of wheat threshers, see "Two Farm Workmen Are Electrocuted," *FMR*, May 8, 1918.

72. For good descriptions of lima bean threshing, see Wallace Smith, "Mechanization of Lima Bean Threshing," *VCHSQ* 25 (spring 1980), 3–16; "Announcement of a Successful Lima Bean Thresher," Charles Outland Indices of Early Ventura County Newspapers, Agriculture, 1871–1915; *Ventura Free Press*, Nov. 24, 1883; "Harvesting Beans," Nov. 16, 1884; also Mar. 25, Oct. 17, 1890 [describing the first "all bean train that ever left California"]; "Colonia Cullings," Sept 6, Oct. 16, 1895; "Ventura's Bean Crop," Aug. 8, 1902; *Oxnard Courier*, Sept. 20, Oct. 4, 1902; *Hueneme Herald*, July 1894, VCM.

73. The decline of the wheat industry is described in *CSAST, 1884*, 206–7; Bannister, "California Wheat and Her Culture," 68; Mansel G. Blackford, *The Politics of Business in California, 1890–1920* (Columbus, Ohio, 1977), 3 12.

74. Higgins, "From Bonfires to Wind machines," MS (n.d.), FHHC; *California Farmer*, Mar. 4, 1859; *Amador Ledger* [Spring 1876], Amador-Livermore Historical Society.

CHAPTER ELEVEN

1. Quote from Augustus W. Loomis, "How Our Chinamen Are Employed," *Overland Monthly* 2 (Mar. 1869), 232–34.

2. Quotes from ibid., 232; Davis, "Wheat in California," 450; Bentham Fabian, *The Agricultural Lands of California* (San Francisco, 1869), 6. "Visit the rural districts at harvest time," Loomis urged,

> and when you perceive how large a portion of the binders who follow the reaping machines are Chinamen, you will exclaim: 'Well, if white labor is as difficult to be obtained as is reported, and as indeed it must be, since wages are so high, what would these farmers do but for the Chinamen? But for them a large portion of the grain must be wasted in the field, our farmers would have to reckon up their loses rather than their profits, and our State would be materially deficient in that which she is beginning to count upon as a prominent branch of trade and revenue.'

See Loomis to unknown, in "Chinese in California," 2, correspondence for 1860, AWLC, describing a trip to Oakland where Loomis found Chinese using their experience as "hoeing hands" tending strawberry and raspberry plants. See also various clippings, Horace Davis Scrapbooks, BL; Theodor Kirchhoff, *Californische Kulturbilder* (Cassel, Germany, 1886), 336–76; Brace, *The New West*, 231; typed notes, "The Harvest in Santa Clara," *Mariposa Mail*, July 31, 1868, FFLCSF. For those employed by the Anaheim Union Water Company, see Minutes of the Anaheim Union Water Company, Jan. 16, Feb. 13, Mar. 13, Apr. 10, July 24, Aug. 7, 1869, MCC. See also Charles Rinehart, "A Study of the Anaheim Community with Special reference to Anaheim's Development" (M.A. thesis, USC, 1932). For Chinese in the Pajaro Valley, see typed notes, *Watsonville Pajaronian*, July 15, 1869, PVHS.

3. Quotes from Corinne K. Hoexter, *From Canton to California: The Epic of Chinese Immi-*

gration (New York, 1976), 96. Some historians have argued that the Chinese set the stage for all subsequent developments—from low pay and reliance on labor contractors to dependence on immigrant workers and playing one group against another. Although the interpretation has received considerable endorsement, it achieved its widest acceptance among Marxist scholars claiming that the Chinese allowed farmers to develop their own "special adaptation of the concept of imperialism." Rather than participating in the physical seizure of foreign lands, farmers used the Chinese to reverse the process and farm their land with foreign workers. Quotes from Kushner, *Long Road to Delano*, 9; Cook, *Conflict*, 315–16; also 61. See also Marten, "The Development of Wheat Culture in the San Joaquin Valley," 12; David Selvin, *Sky Full of Storm: A Brief History of California Labor* (San Francisco, 1975), 9, 36; B[ertram] Schrieke, *Alien Americans: A Study of Race Relations* (New York, 1936), 23. With the Chinese pouring into the state by the tens of thousands after the Gold Rush, the theory of early dominance seems founded in hard numbers and on the logical assumption that the Chinese were so ill-prepared to do much other than grub work that they had to move immediately into agricultural labor. But like so many ideas that have been advanced about farmworkers, this one is mostly erroneous and largely derived from later events. See McWilliams, *Factories in the Field*, 66; Fuller, "The Supply of Agricultural Labor," 198–203; WPA, "Documentary History of the Chinese in California Agriculture," MS (1939), BL; Thomas W. Chinn, Him Mark Lai, and Philip C. Choy, eds., *A History of the Chinese in California: A Syllabus* (San Francisco, 1969), 57; Stewart H. Holbrook, *Machines of Plenty* (New York, 1955), 83; Anna M. Strong, *My Native Land* (New York, 1932), 81.

4. Quotes from Charles V. Gillespie to Thomas O. Larkin, Mar. 6, 1848, TOLP; *Alta California*, Nov. 4, 1848. See also John C. Hough, "Charles H. Brinley: A Case Study in Rancho Supervision," *HSSCQ* 40 (June 1958), 174–79.

5. Although somewhere between two thousand and three thousand Chinese arrived by 1851, they were not from the right class. Many congregated in the cities, taking up jobs as servants, cooks, laundrymen, laborers, fishermen, barbers, grocers, and merchants. Contemporaries state emphatically that very few of them had any impact on the Gold Rush farm labor force, that only a tiny number of the first wave of Chinese immigrants became agricultural workers, and that most regarded farmwork as a considerable step down in status from what they aimed to attain. If they exerted any influence, it was by their absence. See Mary Coolidge, *Chinese Immigration* (New York, 1909), 198–200.

6. Herbert Wung, interview, Feb. 22, 1924; Dr. Lew and Seto More, interview, Mar. 6, 1924, SRRP; Kil Zo Young, "Chinese Emigration into the United States, 1850–1880" (Ph.D. diss., Columbia University, 1971), 54–56; Peter Ward Fay, *The Opium War, 1840–1842* (Chapel Hill, N.C., 1975); Frederick E. Wakeman Jr., *Strangers at the Gate: Social Disorder in South China, 1839–1861* (Berkeley, 1966), 58, 109–11. In 1852, 20,026 Chinese arrived, two thousand of them in just one forty-eight-hour period. Explaining immigration, most accounts stress the Opium War, the T'aip'ing Rebellion, the Red Turbans uprisings, the Punti-Hakka feuds, overcrowding, crop failures, floods, and countless other natural disasters that pushed peasants out of the countryside. Yong Chen, "Internal Origins of Chinese Emigration to California Reconsidered," *WHQ* 28 (winter 1997), 521–46, questions the "push" factors, seeing Chinese immigration primarily as a flight from poverty and hunger, as well as the "pull" of California, and the substantial commercial contacts that developed between the Pearl River Delta and California.

7. Quote from unidentified clipping, Bancroft Scrapbooks, BL. See also *Alta California*, Apr. 27, 1851; William Speer, *An Humble Plea Addressed to the Legislature of California in Behalf of the Immigrants from the Empire of China* (San Francisco, 1856), 12.

8. Quote from James H. Carson, "Tulare Plains," *San Joaquin Republican*, Mar. 3, 1852. For delta farmers supporting Chinese contract labor, see *Alta California*, Feb. 4, 1852. Land was first sold in chunks of 160 acres, and then in tracts of 320 and 640 acres. See Cadwalader Ringgold, *A Series of Charts, with Sailing Directions, Embracing Surveys of the Farallones, Entrance to the Bay of San Francisco* (Washington, D.C., 1852), 39.

9. Quotes from "Minority Report of the Select Committee on Senate Bill no. 63, an act to enforce contracts and obligations to perform work and labor," in California Legislature, *Senate Journal, 1852* (Sacramento, 1852), 671–72; California Legislature, *Journal of the California Assembly, 1852* (Sacramento, 1852), 15; *Alta California*, Mar. 10, 16, 1852; also Mar. 8. Endorsing the bill, Lt. Gov. John McDougal declared that the Chinese would do especially well since they were people "to whom the climate and the character of these lands are peculiarly suited." One commentator has termed these importation schemes "an abortive Chinese bracero program."

See H. Brett Melendy and Benjamin F. Gilbert, *The Governors of California: Peter H. Burnett to Edmund G. Brown* (Georgetown, Calif., 1965), 40.

10. *San Francisco Morning Herald*, Mar. 12, 1852; California Legislature, *Senate Journal*, 1852, 373–78.

11. Construction techniques are described in "Miscellaneous Report of O. P. Beasley, on the Reclamation of Swamp Lands," Annual Report of the Surveyor General for the Year 1860, *Appendix to Assembly Journals*, 12th sess. (Sacramento, 1860), 54–55. See also California State Commissioner of Public Works, "Report . . . to the Governor of California, 1894," California Senate and Assembly, *Appendix to the Journals of the Senate and Assembly*, 31st sess. (Sacramento, 1895), 14; I. N. Hoag, "Farmer's Gardens," *CSAST, 1870–71*, 339–40; Josiah B. Greene, *Evidence Taken Before the Swamp Land Committee* (Sacramento, 1861), 2; Dana, *The Sacramento*, 160–62.

12. For Chinese on the Jones ranch, see Smith, *Garden of the Sun*, 222; Latta, "Stockton Gang Plow Invented Near Manteca," *Fresno Bee*, July 2, 1933, FFLCSF. For Chinese in the San Joaquin Valley, see Franklin Tuthill, *History of California* (San Francisco, 1866), 375. For Chinese working on the Hill vineyard, see the recollections of John Hill in RN689, 796–97. Farm labor figures computed from 1860 MS Census, Sacramento, Yuba, and San Joaquin counties. Oddly, despite their work in the grain fields, census takers found no trace of the Chinese in San Joaquin County. Nor did census enumerators discover any Chinese field hands in Sacramento or Yuba counties, two other prime farming districts.

13. Quote from typed notes from *California Farmer*, May 25, 1854, FWPC; *California Farmer*, Apr. 26, 1855. For reclamation companies planning to import Chinese, see *Alta California*, Dec. 10, 1856.

14. Quote from California Legislature, Assembly, *Legislative Report of the Select Committee to whom was Referred Assembly Bills Numbers 206, 207, and 208, with Reference to Foreign Miners, Assembly Document Number 19*, 2nd sess., 1855 (Sacramento, 1856), 7.

15. Quote from Amalie Hammes Frohling, "Stirring Days of City's Birth Told by One of the Early Pioneers," MS (1914), 5, 8, MCC, EJS. See also Lucile Dickson, "The Founding and Early History of Anaheim, California," *HSSCAP* 11 (1919), 30. Chinese are mentioned in the Los Angeles Vineyard Society Minutes, July 23, 1859 [translations by Elizabeth J. Schultz], MCC, EPS. For reaction to and evaluation of the Los Angeles Vineyard Society's project, see *Sacramento Union*, Mar. 19, 1859; *California Farmer*, Dec. 23, 1859. For a detailed account of expenses incurred by the Los Angeles Vineyard Society, including labor costs, between Sept. 1857 and Sept. 1859, see *Southern Vineyard*, Dec. 22, 1859, HL. See also *Anaheim Centennial History* (Anaheim, 1976), 34, describing thirty Chinese "imported" from San Francisco around this time, each given a town lot. Mildred Yorba MacArthur, *Anaheim: The Mother Colony* (Los Angeles, 1959), 30, 82–83, claims seven hundred Chinese were employed, but provides no documentation. Although the society's ledgers do not identify the nationalities of the eighty-eight men employed at wages of between eighteen and thirty-five dollars per month, it is likely that many, if not most, of the eighteen-dollar workers were Chinese, and furthermore that they were responsible for planting most, if not all, of the society's eight thousand grapevines.

16. Quotes from California Legislative, *Assembly Journal, 1862* (Sacramento, 1862), app., no. 23: 10; *Alta California*, Oct. 13, 1865; also Oct. 26; typed notes and clippings, *Pajaro Times*, Apr. 28, 1866; Aug. 18, 1866, PVHS. See also July 28, Aug. 18, 1866. The 1861 legislative hearings on Chinese labor are reported in a clipping, *San Francisco Bulletin*, May 6, 1861, Bancroft Scrapbooks, BL. Horrific headlines in the Oct. 12, 1865, *Alta California*, disclosed the fate of one crew. Headed into the delta packed tightly into the forward below-decks steerage or "China hold" of the California Steam Navigation Company steamer *Yosemite*, they were scalded to death and dismembered when the boiler exploded just as the *Yosemite* left the dock at Rio Vista. Only as a kind of afterword to an account of the deaths of thirteen American passengers and the rescue of a baby from the river did the *Alta California* observe that "there were twenty-nine Chinamen killed by the explosion, all of whom were buried at Rio Vista." Whom they left behind, the horrifying details of their deaths, in short, all the information provided in gruesome detail about the other casualties was omitted from the news account. It was typical of the anonymous status accorded Chinese field hands as they dispersed into farming districts. See *Solano Press*, Oct. 25, 1865; MacMullen, *Paddle-Wheel Days in California*, 91–92. For an earlier report of a drowning, see *Mariposa Chronicle*, Jan. 20, 1854. See also wage books, Sept. 9, Oct. 2, 1864, BDWP.

17. Quote from *Monterey Gazette*, May 25, 1866; see also Apr. 6, May 4. For the agreement

bringing the Chinese to San Antonio, see signed agreement between Luco and Ah Yuk, lease book, Monterey County, Book A, Mar. 1866, 216, Monterey County Clerk's Office, Salinas, Calif.

18. Quotes from *Solano Press*, Sept. 4, 1866; typed notes from *SDI*, Sept. 11, 1866 [citing the *Monterey Gazette*]; typed notes, *The Mariposa Mail* [apparently citing the *San Jose Mercury*], July 31, 1868; *Tuolumne City News*, Aug. 14, 1868, FFLCSF. Figures from 1870 MS Census, Yuba, Monterey, Santa Cruz, Sonoma, and Solano counties. See also clippings, *Monterey Gazette*, Aug. 24, 1866; *Watsonville Pajaronian*, July 15, 1866, PVHS; "A Movement in the Right Direction," *San Francisco Bulletin*, Mar. 30, 1867. The stories gave the impression that there were far more Chinese field hands around than the twenty-eight men in the Pajaro Valley and the 120 total in the two counties of Santa Cruz and Monterey, who would be counted a few years later when the census takers came through. For rock walls, see Curtis Wolfe and Steve Grootveld, "The Rock Walls of Tehama County," *Wagon Wheels* 22 (Feb. 1972), 6–9. For Los Angeles, see *Los Angeles Star*, Dec. 12, 1868. For Lake County, see unidentified newspaper clipping, Mar. 30, 1863, Bancroft Scrapbooks, BL.

19. Quote from Brace, *The New West*, 208, 211; also 231. On one large farm, Brace discovered that forty of the sixty field hands were Chinese. See also Ellen R. Wood, "Californians and the Chinese: The First Decade" (M.A. thesis, UCB, 1972); *Red Bluff Triweekly Independent*, Feb. 11, 1862, Red Bluff Public Library.

20. Quotes from clipping, *St. Helena Star*, n.d., NVWL; Beatrice Rodriguez, interview by Hazel Clymer, July 10, 1981, Ventura County Museum. Often characterized as filthy, opiated, dull-witted heathens, fond of eating mice, rats, and cats, the Chinese came under attack merely for the way they grappled with pronouncing common English phrases. "All right," according to one scornful report was "oh lie." When a Chinese field hand said "thank you," another derisive observer claimed, it became "san-ky-u." Likewise, if something went "haywire," a Chinese farmhand would say it was "hey-why-a." See typed notes on *SDI*, Nov. 1, 1866; Latta, "The Ju Jung Boys," MS (n.d.), FFLCSF. See also Limin Chu, "The Images of China and the Chinese in the *Overland Monthly*, 1868–1875, 1883–1935" (Ph.D. diss., Duke University, 1966), 426; *Red Bluff Triweekly Independent*, Feb. 11, 1862, Red Bluff Public Library.

21. In a typical encounter with Chinese miners, a newspaper correspondent found one group "inhabiting close cabins, so small that one . . . would not be of sufficient size to allow a couple of Americans to breathe in it. Chinamen, stools, tables, cooking utensils, bunks, etc., all huddled up together in indiscriminate confusion, and enwreathed with dense smoke, presented a spectacle." Quote from Otis Gibson, *The Chinese in America* (Cincinnati, 1877), 234. See also Rodman Paul, *California Gold* (Lincoln, Neb., 1947), 130, 320; Eve Armentrout-Ma, "Chinese in California's Fishing Industry, 1850–1941," *CH* 60 (June 1981), 152; Arthur McEvoy, "In Places Men Reject: Chinese Fishermen at San Diego, 1870–1893," *JSDH* 23 (Dec. 1977), 14; Patricia A. Etter, "The West Coast Chinese and Opium Smoking"; and William S. Evans, "Food and Fantasy: Material Culture of the Chinese in California and the West, circa 1850–1900," in *Archeological Perspectives in Ethnicity in America: An Afro-American and Asian Culture History*, ed. Robert L. Schuyler (Farmingdale, N.Y., 1980), 89–101; Paul M. Ong, "Chinese Labor in Early San Francisco: Racial Segregation and Industrial Expansion," *Amerasia Journal* 8 (Feb. 1981), 69–92. Getting a handle on the number of Chinese field hands in the 1860s is complicated because their numbers change with each passing year. Published census data giving the 11 percent figure is from Bureau of the Census, *Ninth Census of the United States: Statistics of the Population, 1870* (Washington, D.C., 1872), 1: 15, 722–23, 799; 3: 826–30. The 18-percent figure, and the percentages of Chinese working as field hands, are computed from 1870 MS Census, Alameda, Sacramento, San Joaquin, San Mateo, Solano, and Sonoma counties, revealing 1,552 farm laborers out of 8,763 were Chinese. After Tehama County, the largest percentage of Chinese involved in farm labor was San Mateo County, with 34.7 percent. After that the percentages in five other counties were as follows: Sacramento, 19.5; Alameda, 18.1; Solano, 17.7; Santa Clara, 9.5; Sonoma, 8.9; and San Joaquin, 3.1. "Unspecified" rural workers were not included in this sampling. My total from the manuscript census is slightly lower than that of Sucheng Chan, *Bittersweet Soil*, 305, who gives a figure of sixteen hundred Chinese field hands out of nine thousand (apparently rounded-off), but also gives the same 18-percent figure. Subtracting the 1,552 Chinese field hands computed from the manuscript census from the published figure of 1,637 suggests that there were only eighty-five Chinese among the 7,231 farmworkers remaining in the other counties, a dubious number. I computed the Tehama figures using manuscript census

data from five of nine Chinese market gardens employing field hands, one of them employing fourteen, another employing twenty-three, and three others employing thirty-nine each for a total of 154, which is 52 percent of Tehama's Chinese population of 289 men and five women. I did not use the Tehama County figures in adjusting the overall estimate of the percentage of field hands who were Chinese. These and other instances, especially where newspapers report Chinese but census enumerators do not, have convinced me that there were probably many more Chinese and many more field hands at work than were ever counted.

22. Within Sacramento County, Chinese laborers concentrated in the fruit- and vegetable-growing district reclaimed from the swamplands of Georgiana and Franklin townships in the northern delta; from Freeport south to Sherman Island, the Chinese accounted for seven of ten, and four of ten field hands, respectively. In the hop-growing district of Center Township along the American River, nine of ten field hands were Chinese. In San Mateo County, the Chinese concentrated on truck farms in First Township, where half of all field hands were Chinese. In Alameda County, the Chinese comprised seven out of ten field hands in Washington Township, a fertile swath of alluvial soil between the salt marshes of San Francisco Bay and the coastal foothills, where John M. Horner had established his farming operations. The exact percentages of Chinese field-workers were as follows: Washington Township, 67; Georgiana Township, 72; Franklin Township, 39; First Township, 48. Census material, both published and manuscript, is very inaccurate and only moderately useful for quantitative assessments. For example, it fails to record as farmworkers the large numbers of Chinese who migrated in and out of San Francisco under contract for specific harvest jobs, and it also misses field hands employed early or late in the season, such as mustard harvesters or orchard pruners. Not only were such field hands missed, they were probably tallied as urban workers, if they were tallied at all. There is ample evidence that Chinese field hands were present in some areas even though census enumerators found none. See, for example, Ping Chiu, *Chinese Labor in California, 1850–1880; An Economic Study* (Madison, Wis., 1963), 75, 81, 84–86; Karen Lea Reed, "The Chinese of Tehama County, 1860–1900: With Particular Attention to the Anti-Chinese Movement" (M.A. thesis, CSUC, 1977), 27–29, app. B, 106. Percentages of Chinese working as field hands in six agricultural counties were as follows: Sacramento, 19.1; San Joaquin, 3.1; San Mateo, 34.1; Santa Clara, 9.5; Solano, 17.7; and Sonoma, 8.9. Computed from 1870 MS Census, Alameda, Sacramento, San Joaquin, San Mateo, Santa Clara, Solano, Sonoma, and Tehama counties; Bureau of the Census, *Ninth Census of the U.S.: 1870*, 1: 799. In San Mateo County, there were 180 Chinese and 146 Irish field hands. But when all European and U.S.-born field hands were counted in these counties, they vastly outnumbered the Chinese, constituting between 75 and 80 percent of all farmworkers. Using similar figures, Chan, *Bittersweet Soil*, 303–4, describes Chinese field hands as "ranked first" in Alameda, San Mateo, and Sacramento counties, an unfortunate choice of words giving the misimpression that they were the prime group of farmworkers when they were not.

23. Quote from L. W. Wigmore in Lotus Singleton, "Childhood Memories of Our Chinese Cooks," *Wagon Wheels* 22 (Feb. 1972), 8–9. Later commentators would assert that the Chinese by this time comprised 90 percent of the farm labor force, and that from this dominating position they passed on a "legacy of peonage," stimulated the growth of large-scale, industrialized agriculture, "perpetuated land-monopoly," and caused farming to develop along "undemocratic lines." See Schrieke, *Alien Americans*, 23; McWilliams, *Factories in the Field*, 60–67, 70–71; Taylor, "Foundations of Rural Society," 218–21; Fisher, *Harvest Labor Market*, viii, 7, 20; Chiu, *Chinese Labor in California*, 81–87; Daniel, *Bitter Harvest*, 27–28; Majka and Majka, *Farm Workers*, 10. Census figures are somewhat inadequate. For farm cooks, see H. [Horace] A. Van Coenen Torchiana, *California Gringos* (San Francisco, 1930), 24; Orville Foster, "The Men of Miller-Lux," *Old West* (summer 1973), 32–34, 58–60; Henry S. Brooks, "At Don Ignacio's," *Overland Monthly* 12 (Dec. 1888), 593; photo album, George West Collection, ASCHMS; J. Ross Browne to A. B. Greenwood, Nov. 5, 1859, LROIACS; plot record, Stockton Rural Cemetery, Book 13, Stockton, Calif.; Latta, "Jo Woo"; and "No Sabe Style," FFLCSF; time book and payroll, July 1908, Miller and Lux Collection, BL.

24. George F. Emery, "Vornon; or, Mulberry Trees," *Overland Monthly* 3 (Aug. 1869), 186; Anna G. Murphy, "Some of Jon'than's New Ideas," ibid., 9 (June 1887), 645; Charles S. Greene, "Camping in Mendocino," ibid., 22 (Oct. 1883), 343; *1878 Colusa County Annual Supplement to the Weekly Colusa Sun*, Jan. 1, 1878, FFLCSF; *St. Helena Star*, Dec. 9, 1892.

25. Quote from John Dong, interview, "John Dong: Cowell Ranch Cookhouse," MS (1967),

ASCUCSC, 10–11. See also pay ledgers, June 21, July 19, 1873; Jan. 2, 1874, Durham Ranch Records, SCML.

26. Latta, "Jo Woo," MS (n.d.), FFLCSF; Mrs. James Franklin Morehead, interview by Susan Book and Dorothy J. Hill, Sept. 12, 1973, 1–4; Mrs. Peggy Morehead Travis, ibid., Oct. 3, 1973, 1–2; Elysa Brookes, ibid., Nov. 25, 1973, 5, ANCRR; Clark, *The Journals of Alfred Doten*, 1: July 23, 1862, 665; also 663; William Turner Ellis, *Memoirs: My Seventy-two Years in the Romantic County of Yuba, California* (Eugene, Ore., 1939), 12–13; stage fare for Gee Lee to Firebaugh, Miller and Lux [Firebaugh] Ledger, Apr. 1885–Feb. 1895, Miller and Lux Collection; ledger entries, 1874, Durham Ranch Records, SCML.

27. Adele Chauvet, interview, Alameda, Mar. 23, 1975, courtesy William Heintz, Sonoma, copy in NVWL; Frank Weston, interview, n.d., Colusa County Historical Society, cited in White, *Glenn County Sketchbook*, 132; obituary for Young Moon, *Santa Rosa Press Democrat*, Feb. 17, 1937.

28. Clark, *The Journals of Alfred Doten*, 1: 663. See also Frank Hinckley, diary, Feb. 2–3, Apr. 18, 1881, Frank Hinckley Papers, HL. See also the descriptions of Anaheim farm cooks Ah Chow, Ah Yin, and Ah Ying in "Census of the U. S. Population," 1880 MS Census, Los Angeles County, Records of the Bureau of Census, RG 29, NA; and L. W. Wigmore, interview, in Singleton, "Childhood Memories," 22; William C. Shipley, "Tales of Sonoma County," 56 (June 1965), originally published in the *Healdsburg Tribune* in 1938, ed. Edward H. Connor, Sonoma County Historical Society, Sonoma.

29. Quoted in Latta, "Jacobs Ranch Cook," MS (n.d.), FFLCSF. See also Alice Arnold Borgstrom, interview, June 19, 1979, VCM. For a fictionalized account, see Horace A. Vachell, "The Consequence of Quong Wo," *Overland Monthly* 14 (Nov. 1894), 504–8. See also Edith Parker Hinckley, *Frank Hinckley: California Engineer and Rancher, 1838–1890* (Claremont, 1946), 110, 121–22; Glenn Kennedy, *It Happened in Stockton, 1900–1925* (Stockton, 1967), 39; Bruce Levene, ed., *Mendocino County Remembered*, 1: 52; Chester Bishop, interview by Mendocino County American Bicentennial Project, 1976, Mendocino County Museum/Mendocino County Historical Society; Juan Bandini, diary, 2: June 13; Oct. 7, 13; Nov. 21, 1883; Apr. 3; July 27, 28, 30; Aug. 3; Sept. 2, 8, 1885, Juan Bandini Papers, HL.

30. Quotes from Clark, *The Journals of Alfred Doten*, 1: 663; Mary Agnes Crank, "Ranch Life Fifty Years Ago;" *SDI*, Oct. 23, 1876. See also 1870 MS Census, San Joaquin and Sacramento counties, Records of the Bureau of Census, RG 29, NA; Dorothy J. Hill, "Wong Gee: 60 Years at the Morehead Ranch," ANCRR; Wong Gee to Mrs. Morehead, July 13, 1915, James C. Morehead Collection, SCML; Helen Gage, "Memoirs," *Diggings* 24 (spring 1980), 5–7; Billie Chinaman, paycheck, May 16, 1901, Chinese Pay Stubs, FFLCSF.

31. Quote from David Igler, *Industrial Cowboys: Miller and Lux and the Transformation of the Far West, 1850–1920* (Berkeley, 2001), 133. See also 1900 MS Census, Fresno County, Records of the Bureau of Census, RG 29, NA; Wong Gee to Frank Morehead, July 13, 1915, Morehead Ranch Papers; Dorothy J. Hill, "Wong Gee, 60 Years at the Morehead Ranch"; Mrs. James F. Morehead, interview by Susan Book and Dorothy J. Hill, Sept. 12, 1973, SCML; Chester Bishop, interview.

32. "The Chinese as Agriculturalists," *Overland Monthly* 4 (June 1870), 526–32. Although hardly widespread, the examples of Chinese immigrants working as field hands at this early date modify Chan's thesis in *Bittersweet Soil*, 80, 87–88, that "the first Chinese to engage in agriculture in California were independent owner-operators or small-scale tenants and not farm laborers." It appears that both developments proceeded in parallel. The evidence, I believe, shows a process whereby the Chinese simultaneously became truck farmers and field hands employed on truck farms. See also Robert F. Spier, "Food Habits of Nineteenth-Century California Chinese," *CHSQ* 37 (Mar. 1958), 79–84; and (June 1958), 129–36; Clotilde Grunsky Taylor, *Stockton Boyhood, Being the Reminiscences of Carl Ewald Grunsky Which Covers the Years 1855 to 1877* (Berkeley, 1959), 82–83; typed notes, *SDI*, Nov. 6, 1866, FFLCSF.

33. Owen Clarke Treleavan, "Poison Jim Chinaman," *Overland Monthly* 74 (July 1919), 40–45; "A Prosperous San Juan Mongolian," *Watsonville Pajaronian*, Jan. 4, 1900; Isaac Mylar, "Tribute to 'China Jim,'" [ca. 1920], ibid., SJBHS; "Dodge and Millard Employed Twenty Chinese," *Santa Cruz Sentinel*, Oct. 21, 1865, ASCUCSC.

34. "Upwards of 400,000 pounds of mustard seed," *Salinas Index*, Sept. 28, 1876; "Yellow Mustard on David Jacks' Ranch," ibid., Aug. 11, 1887, JSLS; clipping, *Watsonville Pajaronian*, Jan. 4, 1900, PVHS; "The Yellow Mustard Fields," *San Francisco Chronicle*, Dec. 25, 1882. My

thanks to Sandy Lydon, Cabrillo College, Aptos, for sharing his ideas on the mustard workers. The San Juan Bautista Historical Society was unable to locate the photograph of Poison Jim that appears in Mylar, *Early Days at Mission San Juan Bautista*, 177. Chu, "The Images of China and the Chinese in the Overland Monthly, 1868–1875, 1883–1935," 414, describes how, during 1866–1867, when stock and crops died off in the San Juan Valley, Poison Jim brought a dozen large freight wagons full of supplies south from San Jose to rescue poor whites and Indians from starvation.

35. Strawberries sold for as much as eight cents per pound, and as little as five cents, sums that leave "a very handsome margin for profit to the producer." Quote from *Santa Clara Agriculturalist*, cited in "Strawberries in California," *PRP*, May 27, 1871. See also clipping, *Alta California*, n.d., Bancroft Scrapbooks, BL. The area produced roughly one-fifth of all the produce sold in San Francisco, as well as one-seventh of the fruit.

36. Clipping, *Alta California*, n.d., Bancroft Scrapbooks, BL. Farming analysis from *Hare's Guide to San Jose* (San Jose, 1872), 75; Santa Clara County, Leases, Book A, 648; Book B, 75, 116, 106, 118, 353; Deeds, Book U, 263; miscellaneous Records, Book C, 220, 271; Miscellaneous Records, Book D, 14, 43, Santa Clara County Recorder's Office, San Jose. Market estimates are from Francis J. Weber, *The Observation of Benjamin Cummings Truman on El Camino Real* (Los Angeles, 1978), 84. See also Nordhoff, *California for Health*, 66, 124, 186. *Santa Clara Agriculturalist* in "Strawberries in California" estimated three hundred acres were in production and that they "furnished most of California's strawberries." The *Agriculturalist* reported income of two hundred to three hundred dollars per acre, and as much as four hundred dollars. The labor force estimate is computed as follows: three hundred acres at six men per ten acres totals 180 harvesters. Other sources give far higher labor force estimates, for example, Gloria Sun Hom, *Chinese Argonauts: An Anthology* (Santa Clara, 1971), 7, claiming that strawberry picking required three Chinese per acre. That would have meant a harvest labor force in 1868 of nine hundred men. Hom also states that one man could care for two acres of strawberries, presumably during the off season. That would have meant there were 150 Chinese farmers in the valley. Computed according to the six extra men and six regular men per ten-acre figure given by the *Santa Clara Agriculturalist*, the harvest labor force would have been about 372 men. The percentage of Chinese in the county population is computed from Bureau of the Census, *Ninth Census: 1870*, 1: 15; Bureau of Census, *Tenth Census: Production of Agriculture, 1880*, 382.

37. Quote from Santa Clara County, Leases, Book D, 35; also 66. Kee doubled as a labor contractor and charged a 10-percent commission. Employment arrangements described in Ralph F. Rambo, *Remember When* (San Jose, 1965), 18. Number of field hands computed from the 1870 MS Census, Santa Clara County. Pickers were organized into teams of five or six and worked on a piece-rate basis. Although some were paid according to the number of boxes packed, most earned two cents per pound—a relatively small proportion of overall harvest costs of ½ cent per pound for rail or boat transportation; ¼ cent for shipping to San Francisco; and eight cents for commission sales charges. The work required attentiveness; workers could never overfill the eight- to ten-pound boxes without squishing the berries and had to stack boxes on wagons in such a way that the berries would not be squashed during the bumpy wagon ride to the rail line or to Alviso wharf for shipment by boat to San Francisco. For contract labor migration, see Sing-Wu Wang, *The Organization of Chinese Emigration, 1848–1888: With Special Reference to Chinese Emigration to Australia* (San Francisco, 1978), 313. Harvest procedures from Stephen Wilhelm and James E. Sagen, *A History of the Strawberry* (Berkeley, 1974), 175–76. By the late 1870s, there were about eight hundred pickers and 150–200 growers. For the late 1880s, see *Pen Pictures from the Garden of the World, or Santa Clara County* (Chicago, 1888), 183.

38. Quotes from newspaper clipping, *Alta California*, [May ?, 1871], Bancroft Scrapbooks, BL; Ben Brooks, *The Chinese in California: To the Committee on Foreign Relations of the U.S. Senate* (San Francisco, 1878), 13–14, BL. Labor requirements are given in *PRP*, Apr. 14, 1877.

39. Quote from Forrest Crissey, *Where Opportunity Knocks Twice* (Chicago, 1914), 27–28; also 33, 54–58, 119–20.

40. Haraszthy grew grapes unsuccessfully at San Francisco de Asís mission, and then at Crystal Springs in San Mateo, correctly attributing the latter two failures to excessive summer fog. He purchased The Vineyard Farm for $11,500. See Paul Frederickson, "Haraszthy in San Francisco and San Mateo," *Wines and Vines* 28 (July 1947), 15; Frederickson, "Haraszthy's Early Years in Sonoma," ibid., 28 (Aug. 1947), 17–18.

41. Originally planted in 1832 or 1834 by a Sonoma Valley Indian trying to establish a home-

stead after secularization, the property had subsequently been taken over by Vallejo's brother, Salvador, transferred about 1842 to a Mexican soldier named Damaso Rodriguez, sold to Jacob Leese in 1846, expanded by Benjamin Kelsey in 1850 and Joseph Wardlow in 1852, and purchased by Julius Rose in 1853. For Julius Rose, see *California Farmer*, June 29, 1854; Nov. 7, 1856; Julius K. Rose, deposition, Apr. 28, 1858, in U.S. v. Agoston Haraszthy, U.S. Circuit Court, Old Circuit Court, Civil Cases, RG 21, FARCSB. See also Brian McGinty, "A Vintage Life," *HSSCQ* 41 (Dec. 1959), 375–83.

42. Brian McGinty, *Strong Wine: The Life and Legend of Agoston Haraszthy* (Stanford, 1998), 272, 297–98, 313; Peninou and Greenleaf, *A Directory of California Wine Growers and Wine Makers in 1860*, 1, 4, 6–7, 12, 30, 32, 39, 45, 48.

43. For experimentation with various types of labor, see *San Francisco Examiner*, Sept. 2, 1867. For Haraszthy's views on labor, see Arpad Haraszthy, "The Haraszthy Family," MS (1886), 2, 5–6. 16, BL; Arpad Haraszthy, "Early Viticulture in Sonoma," in *Sonoma County and Russian River Valley* (San Francisco, 1888), 77–78. There is some evidence from the dates supplied by the Wine Institute that Ho Po may have been a contractor from a later period, ca. 1868–72, and not the first China boss at Buena Vista. For Ho Po, see the photos in Theodore Schoenman, ed., *The Father of California Wine, Agoston Haraszthy; Including Grape Culture, Wines, and Winemaking* (Santa Barbara, 1979), 48; Harvey Hansen et al., *Wild Oats in Eden: Sonoma County in the Nineteenth Century* (Santa Rosa, 1962), 86.

44. Numbers of Chinese employed from *BVVSR*, 1864, 7, BL; *CSAST, 1866–67*, 447. See also Rockwell D. Hunt, ed., *California and Californians* (New York, 1926), 2: 526; Agoston Haraszthy to O. C. Wheeler, Oct. 31, 1858, *CSAST, 1858*, 243–44. McGinty, *Strong Wine*, 301, calculates that the Chinese planted 16,850 vines on eight-foot spacings covering twenty-five acres.

45. As a means of hyping vintages, embellishing labels, and selling wine, Chinese cave digging is regularly offered to visitors to Buena Vista Winery, who are shown the pick marks "made by Chinese excavators patiently chipping away" inside the storage caves. Because it is so similar to well-known stories about Chinese laborers hanging from wicker baskets over thousand-foot-high cliffs while cutting a railroad route through the Sierra Nevada, the propaganda about the Chinese being adept cave diggers at Buena Vista makes perfect sense to most visitors. However, the real story is more elaborate. Quote from tour leader, Buena Vista Winery, July 3, 1990; *Buena Vista Winery* (Sonoma, 1987), 2.

46. *Sonoma Democrat* quoted in *Alta California*, Dec. 6, 1857; Agoston Haraszthy to O. C. Wheeler, Oct. 31, 1858, *CSAST, 1858*, 311–29, 243. The wine cellar held about forty thousand gallons. While it is highly probable that the Chinese were responsible for much of the tunneling, it is unclear whether or not they did it all, and to what extent others were involved.

47. "Great Vineyards in Sonoma," *California Farmer*, Sept. 7, 1860.

48. *CSAST, 1860*, 78. Krug had lived with Haraszthy for a time in Sonoma and owned a vineyard there before moving to the Napa Valley. See Brian McGinty to author, July 1, 2002, author's possession. For Krug, see Krug to editor, *St. Helena Star*, May 18, 1885. Maintaining wines at a year-round temperature of between 56.5 and 58.5 degrees Fahrenheit, the Chinese cellars were so ideal for aging and protecting wine that Buena Vista uses them even today. Evidence on tunnel size and that the Chinese blasted as well as dug with hand tools is from *Alta California*, July 23, 1863.

49. *By-Laws and Prospectus of the Buena Vista Vinicultural Society* (San Francisco, 1863), 11, 13, 17–24; *Reports of the Board of Trustees and Officers of the Buena Vista Vinicultural Society* (San Francisco, 1864), 8–10, BL; Arpad Haraszthy, "Early Viticulture in Sonoma," 78, reprinted in *San Francisco Merchant* 20 (1888), 113–14; "Great Vineyards in Sonoma," *California Farmer*, Sept. 7, 1860; Haraszthy, "Wine Presses—No. 2," *California Wine, Wool, and Stock Journal* 1 (1863), 113–16. Beginning in 1859, the Chinese probably worked with the first redwood wine vats in the Sonoma Valley, possibly the first in the state, which were used to store white grapes before pressing, and to ferment both white and red wine. The Chinese laboriously steam-cleaned the vats in order to remove any unpalatable resins from the wood. For steaming, see Arpad Haraszthy, "Wine-Making in California," *Harper's New Monthly Magazine* 29 (1864), 23.

50. Stoll, *The Fruits of Natural Advantage*, omits Buena Vista from his account of agricultural modernization. Haraszthy and Buena Vista would seem the logical starting point for any such account. See McGinty, *Strong Wine*, 333, 398. For Chinese in Haraszthy's Sonoma Tule Land Company operation, see *California Farmer*, Oct. 12, 1860.

51. *Southern Vineyard*, Oct. 11, 1859, HL; Agoston Haraszthy, *Grape Culture, Wines, and*

Wine-Making (New York, 1862), xv–xxii; *CSAST, 1866–67*, 447; *BVVSR*, 1864, 7; Haraszthy to governor, in *California Farmer*, Feb. 21, 1862.

52. Quote from *Alta California*, July 23, 1863. Planting techniques from ibid., July 23, 1863; Arpad Haraszthy, "Wine-Making in California," *Harper's Magazine* 29 (June 1864), 23–24. See also George Husmann, *American Grape Growing and Wine Making* (New York, 1866), 30–31. For Haraszthy's ideas on hillside planting, see Agoston Haraszthy, "Report on Grapes and Wine in California," *CSAST, 1858*, 314. Haraszthy's costs for establishing a one-hundred-acre vineyard were in order of importance: $892.68 for eighteen men to lay out, stake, and dig holes, and plant the vines; $255 for horses and feed; $231.60 for six men with nine horses for deep tillage and six horses for shovel plowing; $170 for the land; $30 for a blacksmith; and $55.36 miscellaneous expenses for a total cost of $1,634.64. See Haraszthy, *Grape Culture and Wine-Making*, 154, 118–120; Arpad Haraszthy, "Wine-Making in California," *Overland Monthly* 7 (1871), 23–24. During winter 1864–65, the Chinese participated in a huge planting experiment. Convinced that he could make more and better wine by planting his vines four feet on center, rather than the eight feet initially employed, Haraszthy devised a technique to cut the standard distance in half through a system of "layering." Sending Chinese crews into one of his vineyards, he directed them to dig holes adjacent to vines, bend 260,000 canes (branches) down into the holes and cover them with soil, leaving two buds exposed to the sunlight. Receiving food and nutrition from the mother plant, the layered vines quickly sent down roots, while the two buds grew into new canes. That winter, after the layered vines had established good roots, the Chinese went through the new vineyards cutting the layered vines free. Neighbors were aghast, believing that it was necessary to leave eight feet between vines so two-horse plows could work the soil. But the newly layered vines yielded a smaller, far more intense, slightly stressed crop that made better wine than grapes grown on traditionally spaced vines. See Agoston Haraszthy, "Best Modes of Cultivating the Grape in California as Established by Observations Made in Europe, and Practical Experiments in California, by Col. A. Haraszthy, Manager of the Buena Vista Vinicultural Society's Vineyards in Sonoma," *California Rural Home Journal*, Feb. 15, 1866, reprinted in *CSAST, 1864–65*, 290–95; *Hyatt's Hand-Book of Grape Culture* (San Francisco, 1867), 74–79; Buena Vista Viticultural Society, *Reports* (1865), 4, 7.

53. For picking, see Frederick Whymper drawing (pen, pencil, and wash on cream paper), Oct. 21, 1864, courtesy Brian McGinty, Scottsdale, Arizona, and Frank Bartholomew, Sonoma, original in the Haraszthy Villa, Buena Vista Vineyards, Sonoma, noting, "Chinamen picking the grapes and filling boxes with them not baskets. A white man or two may be looking on directing the operations." Story from Jones, *Vines in the Sun*, 46, a work that should be used with great caution. For the Chinese role in a drainage project, see *California Farmer*, Oct. 12, 1860.

54. Daily harvest figures from Arpad Haraszthy, "Later Triumphs," *Overland Monthly* 8 (Jan. 1872), 41. Two Chinese at work filling wine bottles at Buena Vista, ca. 1872, are recorded in Eadweard J. Muybridge, "Buena Vista Vineyard, Sonoma—Bottling Wine," stereographic photograph no. 1106, n.d., BL. Average field hands at Buena Vista earned between eighteen and twenty dollars per month plus board, or more commonly, a dollar a day if they provided their own food and housing. That was much less than the thirty-five dollars a month plus fifteen dollars board, or two dollars a day and no board, which Haraszthy paid to white laborers. The Chinese apparently preferred the dollar-a-day wages without board, learning to economize on food and housing by pooling resources and providing for themselves. But that was not the only advantage they presented to growers like Haraszthy. Perhaps more important, they were easy to manage and kept to themselves, seldom mixing with Sonoma's white population, never causing even the slightest trouble. One wine industry historian claimed that the Chinese at Buena Vista were "in many respects the American counterpart to the pre-1848 serf and agricultural field labor of eastern Europe." Quote from Vincent P. Carosso, *The California Wine Industry: A Study of the Formative Years, 1830–1895* (Berkeley, 1951), 71. White wage rates from U.S. Dept. of Agriculture, Division of Statistics, *Wages of Farm Labor in the United States, Results of Eleven Statistical Investigations, 1866–1899* (Washington, D.C., 1901), 10; Haraszthy, *Grape Culture and Wine-Making*, 119–20; speech delivered at Petaluma, Aug. 30, 1860, in *Alta California*, Sept. 1, 1860.

55. Quote from clipping, *Sacramento Union*, July 17, 1865, Bancroft Scrapbooks, BL. Work output computed from figures in Arpad Haraszthy, *Grape Culture and Wine-Making*, 114–20. See also *CSAST, 1858*, 311–29. The figure of twenty-five hundred vines that a man could supposedly top (prune) is unbelievable, and most certainly a misprint of 250 vines, a somewhat more realistic but still large figure. The only other explanation is that it refers to the number of

vine canes cut or that it refers to a procedure known as "opening up the vines," wherein men pulled leaves and canes to allow more light to reach the fruit.

56. Quotes from Agoston Haraszthy, "Introductory Address to the Sonoma County Agricultural and Mechanical Society, 1860," *CSAST, 1860*, 21–22; "A Flying Visit to Sonoma," *Alta California*, Sept. 12, 1866; Victoria Post Ranney, Gerald J. Rauluk, and Carolyn F. Hoffman, eds., *The Papers of Frederick Law Olmstead: The California Frontier, 1863–1865* (Baltimore, 1990), 5: 8. In his address, Haraszthy claimed to hire Chinese at eight dollars per month and board, but this is probably a misquote by the reporter. See also *Alta California*, Sept. 2, 1860; May 4, 1867; "President's Opening Address," *California Farmer*, Oct. 3, 1862.

57. Quote from Agoston Haraszthy, "Introductory Address," 21–22. For protection of his Chinese laborers, see "A Notable Gorham Accession, With a Reason," *San Francisco Examiner*, Sept. 2, 1867. See also *BVVSR*, 1865, 7–8; *Alta California*, Apr. 13, 1865; Haraszthy, "Report on Grapes and Wine of California," in *CSAST, 1858*, 198–99.

58. Quote from "The Vine Clad Homes of Old Sonoma," *Alta California*, May 20, 1870. For Chauvet, see "Heart Ailment Claims Life of Young Moon," *Santa Rosa Press Democrat*, Feb. 17, 1937; Hazen Cowan, interview by William Heintz, Nov. 27, 1971; Carrie Burlingame, ibid., June 21, 1972 [copies in the Depot Museum, Sonoma County Historical Society]; Adele Chauvet, ibid., Nov. 17, 1972 [copies at Geyser Peak Winery and Napa Wine Library, St. Helena], courtesy William Heintz, Sonoma. See also Albert Snell, "Viticulture in California, 1870–1900, a Chapter in the Economic History of California" (M.A. thesis, UCB, 1929), 4; William F. Heintz, "The Role of Chinese Labor in Viticulture and Wine Making in Nineteenth Century California" (M.A. thesis, CSU, Sonoma, 1977); *Report of the California State Board of Agriculture 1911* (Sacramento, 1911), 185.

59. Quote from "The Chinese Population in California," *San Francisco Bulletin*, May 6, 1861, Bancroft Scrapbooks, BL. See also *History of Sonoma County*, 365; 1870 MS Census, Sonoma County; *California Farmer*, Oct. 12, 1860; Mar. 15, 1861. Vineyard acreage figures certainly suggest that the Chinese had some effect. From 150 acres in 1857, vineyard plantings approached six hundred acres per year in 1859–60, with Haraszthy's Chinese still leading all others by adding 223 acres.

60. Quote from Agoston Haraszthy, "Introductory Address," 21–22. After briefly acknowledging Chinese cave diggers, wine lore drops them from the picture to go on at great length about Haraszthy the heroic, selfless figure, man of vision, and restless genius, first to banish the inferior Mission grape and import and plant fine European grape varieties on a large scale, California's pioneer champagne-maker, the Johnny Appleseed of wine, an innovator who overcame the shortage of imported oak casks by substituting redwood storage tanks, the man who brought winemaking out of the dark ages and into the light of twentieth-century business methods. The story then passes to the American, Italian, French, and German pioneers, with the Italians quickly accorded unusual honors. It is as if the Chinese had no hand in any of this, as if Haraszthy accomplished everything himself. This tale of steadfast heroism always includes descriptions of the social event of 1864, an elaborate vintage ball in which Haraszthy and his wife entertained lavishly, and is capped with Haraszthy's banishment as manager of Buena Vista in 1868 by the impatient, shortsighted financial backers who had bought the winery from him five years earlier, and by his mysterious demise on July 6, 1869, in a Nicaraguan jungle, where, according to legend, he fell into a stream filled with alligators and was eaten alive or drowned while attempting to scout a location for a sugar processing plant. See California Wine Association, untitled pamphlet (San Francisco, 1896), 2, Wine Literature Collection, ACSUCD; "A Trip to Sonoma Valley," *California Wool and Stock Journal* (May 1863); Joan Marie Donohoe, "Agoston Haraszthy: A Study in Creativity," *CHSQ* 48 (June 1969), 157; *Sacramento Bee*, Apr. 2, 1961; J. S. Hittell, *The Commerce and Industries of the Pacific Coast* (San Francisco, 1882), 243. As late as two years before his death, Haraszthy himself had made a point of emphasizing his indebtedness to the Chinese, the central role they played at Buena Vista, and the costs and problems incurred by hiring them.

61. McGinty, *Strong Wine*, 429–31, 436–38, 470–72, 527nn18–19, 742. Although between one hundred and two hundred Chinese field hands worked at Buena Vista, the 1860 census strangely does not record any of them, further illustrating the fallacy of drawing too many conclusions from census data. Leon D. Adams speculated in an interview that as a last resort the Chinese may have been involved in setting up a steam engine and running a system of pipes and flexible hoses among the vines to pump in experimental applications of carbon bisulfide

and potassium sulfocarbonate, two extremely toxic, highly explosive chemicals introduced from France in a desperate attempt to kill phylloxera. I have not verified this practice. See Adams, interview by author, Nov. 13, 1978, Sausalito, author's possession. After the phylloxera catastrophe, Buena Vista's land remained bare for thirty years. The tunnels fell into disrepair, and during the 1906 earthquake they partially collapsed. Thereafter the role that the Chinese played in establishing Buena Vista and laying the foundations for the Northern California wine industry were forgotten. My account of the last years of Chinese labor at Buena Vista is based on an interview with Frank H. Bartholomew, who purchased Buena Vista in 1941 and rehabilitated it before selling it to Racke International in 1973, Sonoma. See Bartholomew, interview by author, Mar. 10, 1974, Sonoma, author's possession. See also handwritten research notes apparently taken from Agoston Haraszthy's account book, now missing, attached to Arpad Haraszthy, "Haraszthy Family," MS (n.d.), BL.

62. Quote from "The Chinese in California," *Nation*, Oct. 14, 1864, Bancroft Scrapbooks, BL. See also *San Joaquin Republican*, Mar. 3, 1852, describing Chinese field hands as "sober, quiet, industrious, and inoffensive." For praise of their self-sufficiency, opposition to begging, and diligence, see Clark, *The Journals of Alfred Doten*, 1: May 19, 1857, 361. See also *Oakland Daily Transcript*, July 15, 1869; *Los Angeles Star*, Dec. 12, 1868, carrying these themes forward.

63. Brace, *The New West*, 218.

CHAPTER TWELVE

1. Leland Stanford to Andrew Johnson and James Harlan, Oct. 10, 1865, H. S. Crocker and Co., HL; Wesley Griswold, *The Work of Giants: Building the First Transcontinental Railroad* (New York, 1962), 123, 160–61; George Stewart, *Donner Pass* (New York, 1954), 47; E. L. Sabin, *Building the Pacific Railway* (Philadelphia, 1919), 111; Maury Klien, *Union Pacific: Birth of a Railroad, 1862–1893* (Garden City, N.Y., 1987), 1: 219; Alexander Saxton, "The Army of Canton in the High Sierra," *PHR* 35 (June 1966), 141–52; typed notes, *SDI*, Jan. 7, 1862; Oct. 31, 1866, FFLCSF.

2. Sylvia Sun Minnick, *Samfow: The San Joaquin Chinese Legacy* (Fresno, 1988), 35–52; Tinkham, *History of San Joaquin County*, 161; Taylor, *Stockton Boyhood*, 58–59.

3. Chinese headed to the islands around the present-day towns of Walnut Grove, Rio Vista, Courtland, and Isleton and found employment restoring levees on Grand and Sherman islands, building new ones on Grizzly Island, and tending and harvesting fruit for white and Chinese farmers in Sacramento County. For Chinese reclamation workers on Grizzly Island, see Betham Fabian, *Agricultural Lands of California*, 27; Joan Frost, *A Brief Pictorial History of Grizzly Island* (San Francisco, n.d.); "Ledger," 508, GSMIW. For Sherman Island, see Marsden Manson, "The Swamp and Marsh Lands of California," *Transactions of the Technical Society of California* 5 (Dec. 1888), 89. For Chinese gardeners near Rio Vista, see "Industrial Condition of the State," *Alta California*, July 12, 1869. The 1870 census counted 622 Chinese field hands in Franklin and Georgiana townships alone. Percentages of farmworkers who were Chinese in Sacramento County broke down as follows: Franklin Township, 39; Georgiana Township, 72. See 1870 MS Census. For Roberts and early reclamation work, see Paul W. Gates, "Public Land Disposal in California," *AH* 49 (Jan. 1975), 158–78; J. Ross Browne, "Reclamation and Irrigation," *CSAST, 1872*, 401; J. P. Whitney, *Fresh Water Tide Lands of California* (Cambridge, Mass., 1873). For contemporary thinking on nature and reclamation, see Donald Worster, *Nature's Economy: A History of Ecological Ideas* (Cambridge, Mass., 1977), 1–55.

4. Tide Land Reclamation Company, "Certificate of Incorporation," June 9, 1869, Articles of Incorporation File no. 10011, CSL; "Off for the Swamplands," *Sacramento Bee*, Oct. 20, 1871. See also Richard H. Peterson, "The Failure to Reclaim: California Swamp Land Policy and the Sacramento Valley, 1850–1866," *SCQ* 56 (spring 1974), 45–60. For prevailing engineering concepts, see "Reclamation of Swamp Land by Steam Power," *Mining and Scientific Press*, Mar. 20, 1869. China bosses have been described with a variety of phrases—as "High Bossee Men," as a skilled hierarchy, an oligarchy, a semiprofessional clique of foremen, villainous dealers in human flesh who kept their workers under their thumb, the Chinese California equivalent of Mexican compradores, Greek *koumbaria*, and Italian padrones who kept workers in debt bondage, part of a power structure that had, at its base, a tradition of leadership by men who interceded between workers and employers. For a comparison with compradores, see Chan, *Bittersweet Soil*, 344–50, 406. For background on compradores, see Yen-p'ing Hao, *The Comprador in Nineteenth Century China: Bridge between East and West* (Cambridge, Mass., 1970), 2.

For Mexican, Italian, and Portuguese padrones, see Gunther Peck, *Reinventing Free Labor: Padrones and Immigrant Workers in the North American West, 1880–1930* (Cambridge, U.K., 2000). The key role of labor contractors has been attributed to the Japanese and placed much later in the farmworker story—usually after the turn of the century—but under China bosses, immigrant workers for the first time exerted some influence over the terms of their employment and developed a rudimentary form of collective bargaining. When the Chinese were but a dim memory, farmworkers would look back on the boss system with some regret. Living under the thumb of mean contractors, contemporary farmworkers would see China bosses as the original brokers of human muscle and flesh and would have great cause to regret that they had ever run afoul of such men. And so, quite rightly, their view of labor contractors is that they have always been a tool of growers, and that the plight of California farmworkers could never improve until these men were eliminated, their power broken, and their role replaced with a union hiring hall. See Ronald B. Taylor, *Chavez and the Farm Workers*, 19.

5. Donald Alvord, interview, June 9, 1979, VCM; James Lance, "Labor Under Industrialized Agriculture," *Industrial Pioneer* 2 (May 1924), 15; Nicholas Russell [Nikolai Konstantinovich Sudzilovskii], *Around California in 1891*, ed. Terence Emmons (1893–94, n.p. [1999, Stanford]), 41; testimony of E. Clements Horst, CIR, *Final Report of the United States CIR* (Washington, D.C., 1915), 5: 4928, 4950. For the impact of duty, tradition, and obligation, see Kung-chuan Hsiao, *Rural China: Imperial Control in the Nineteenth Century* (Seattle, 1967), 26–29, 43–83. The exploitative nature of Chinese contractors in other industries is stressed in Robert A. Nash, "The 'China Gangs' in the Alaska Packers Association Canneries, 1892–1935," in *Life, Influence and the Role of the Chinese in the United States, 1776–1960* (San Francisco, 1976), 257–83; Jack Masson and Donald Guimary, "Asian Labor Contractors in the Alaskan Canned Salmon Industry, 1880–1937," *LH* 23 (summer 1981), 377–97.

6. Quotes from RN689, 437, 440, 443; also 441, 436. As was true elsewhere in California, white laborers were in short supply around the delta and generally would not work for less than three dollars a day; they had to be fed and housed and proclaimed an especially intense aversion to "muck work"—like toiling waist deep in slimy mud under a burning sun. "It is a class of work that white men do not like," Roberts told the congressional committee investigating Chinese immigration. See also Nordhoff, *Northern California, Oregon, and the Sandwich Islands*, 130, 138; Israel C. Russell, *Rivers of North America* (New York, 1898), 144. Not all of the Chinese who worked for Roberts obtained their jobs through contractors. Many, in fact, seem to have drifted onto Twitchell Island on their own.

7. For the first Chinese reclamation workers on Sherman Island, see "Industrial Condition of the State," *Alta California*, May 17, 1869, which gives costs for Chinese laborers raising forty-seven miles of levees on Sherman Island at fifteen to twenty-five cents per cubic yard. See also Sept. 6, 1869; "Tule Reclamation" (letter to editor), Oct. 15, 1869. Twitchell Island land moving contracts were for eight hundred thousand cubic yards of earth at rates from nine to 25 cents per cubic yard, including brush removal.

8. Chinese gangs and tent camps are described in *PRP*, Apr. 26, 1873; RN689, 437. Information on the work day is extrapolated from "Rules of the Vorden Ranch," MS (n.d.), Pieter Van Löben Sels Papers, copy courtesy Mrs. Carl Van Löben Sels, Courtland, Calif.

9. "Repairing Levees," *San Francisco Bulletin*, Mar. 6, 1879, Bancroft Scrapbooks, BL. "We witnessed many gangs of Chinamen . . . in all 250, making levees or embankments." Quote from *PRP*, Apr. 26, 1873.

10. Tide Land Reclamation Company, *Fresh Water Tide Lands of California* (San Francisco, 1869, and edition of 1872), 21, quoting the *San Francisco Daily Herald*, July 10, 1869. Tule knives are described in U.S. Dept. of Agriculture, "Reclamation of Swamp and Overflow Lands in California," *Report of the Commissioner of Agriculture for the Year 1872* (Washington, D.C., 1874), 186.

11. "Reclamation of Swamp Land," *Mining and Scientific Press*, Mar. 20, 1869; J. J. Peatfield, "Dredging on the Pacific Coast," *Overland Monthly* 24 (Sept. 1894), 315, 322, which contains a sketch of Chinese wheelbarrow gangs. After the mid-1870s the men would switch their wheelbarrows from the inside of the levee to the outside. See also Friedrich Ratzel, *Die Chinesische Auswanderung* (Breslau, 1893), 246.

12. Quote from Pieter Van Löben Sels MS.

13. It had cost Roberts about $7.61 an acre to reclaim Twitchell Island's 3,680 acres, far below the twelve-dollars-per-acre costs commonly cited for Sherman Island and other areas of the delta. See "Reclamation," *SDI*, July 1, Sept. 11, 1876; *Illustrations of Contra Costa County, Califor-*

nia, with Historical Sketches (Oakland, 1879 [1952]), 8; Minutes, Pierson Reclamation District, Feb. 26, 1909, Pierson Reclamation District Papers, ASCUCD. Roberts sold Twitchell Island in June 1870 for sixty-eight thousand dollars, or about twice what Tide Land Reclamation had paid the Chinese to reclaim it. Reclamation costs computed as follows: sixty-eight-thousand-dollar sale price for Twitchell Island, minus forty thousand dollars profit, gives a twenty-eight thousand dollars investment in raw swampland and Chinese labor, divided by 3,680 acres equals $7.61 per acre reclamation costs. See "Agricultural Notes—Grain from Sherman Island," *PRP*, July 8, 1871; Sacramento County, Swamp Land Clerk (Grove Johnson), in Board of Supervisors, "Journal of Swamp Land Business," 1: Meeting of June 8, 1870, 604, EDDMRV.

14. "Industrial Condition of the State," *Alta California*, Dec. 6, 1869; May 30; June 6, 13, 1870; Jan. 23, 1871; I. N. Hoag, "Farmers Gardens," *CSAST, 1870–71*, 343–44; A. J. Wells, "Tilling the Tules," *The American Monthly Review of Reviews* 30 (Sept. 1904), 313–14.

15. Quote from RN689, 440. The drowning episode is described without documentation in Dana, *The Sacramento River*, 169. For an account of four Chinese who drowned while attempting to fill a levee break on Roberts Island, see *SDI*, Dec. 17, 1885. Drowning victims are also recorded in the Stockton Rural Cemetery, Death Registers A, B, C, D, Stockton. Because the Chinese were by far the largest single expense of reclamation, landowners kept extremely close tabs on them. Seventy-five percent of the $350,000 spent by the Glasgow-California Land Reclamation Company, Ltd., to reclaim the southern portion of Roberts Island between July 1, 1877, and Jan. 31, 1879, went to employ four thousand Chinese; 10 percent for white laborers; another 10 to 13 percent for miscellaneous services; and less than 2 percent for dipper dredges. See Swamp Land (Reclamation) District no. 303, "Sworn Estimate on Statement of Engineer," May 14, 1879, 3, EDDMRV. For thirteen hundred Chinese employed on Roberts Island, see "Reclamation of Roberts Island," *Alta California*, Nov. 14, 1875; "San Joaquin—Extensive Reclamation Enterprise," *PRP*, Mar. 6, 1875; "A New Dredging Machine," Nov. 18, 1876; "Reclamation Enterprise," *AL*, Mar. 13, 1875; "Gigantic Enterprise," *SDI*, Sept. 25, 1875. For scraper crews, see "Roberts Island," *SDI*, Aug. 21, 1874; Sept. 22, 1877; typed notes "Reclamation," *SDI*, Nov. 10, 1876, FFLCSF. For Whitney, see Richard A. Miller, *Fortune Built by Gun: The Joel Peter Whitney Story* (Walnut Grove, Calif., 1969). See also *An Illustrated History of San Joaquin County, California* (Chicago, 1890), 111. For scrapers, see James Porteous Collection, FCHS; Latta, "Self-Propelled Harvester Originated Here," *Lindsay Gazette*, Apr. 25, 1930. Scholars have questioned reports that three thousand Chinese were employed by "Land Hog" Williams. Such numbers would only have been necessary if Williams had been trying to raise his peat walls as fast as possible, in which case the men would not have been needed for very long. See "Reclamation of Union Island," *SWI*, July 1, 1876. Scoop dredges were not built until July 1869, when they were used on Bradford and Jersey Islands. For dredges in the delta, see John Thompson and Edward A. Dutra, *The Tule Breakers: The Story of the California Dredge* (Stockton, 1983), 30, 33, 38, 41, the definitive account. For "suction dredgers" on Union Island, see "About the Tule Lands," *SDI*, Sept. 19, 1876; "Reclamation Works," ibid., Oct. 11, 14 1876; "Tule Reclamation," *The Engineer*, Nov. 1, 1876; "Swamp Land Reclamation in San Joaquin," ibid., Dec. 2, 1876; C. H. Kluegal, "Field Notes Book no. 1" (June 1878), 10, California State Dept. of Engineering, Sacramento. Because many levees built by the Chinese on Twitchell, lower Brannon, and Andrus Islands were laid out on surfaces unaltered except for some brush removal (with, as the editor of the *Sacramento Union* put it, "a sublime disregard for any unity of plan or action, and in many cases with the smallest consideration for the most ordinary principles of hydraulic engineering"), they failed soon after Roberts sold the land, and the Chinese had to be called in to rebuild them. Quote from "Reclamation," *Sacramento Union*, Nov. 2, 1874. For a comparison between dredging and peat-block building, see "Industrial Conditions of the State," *Alta California*, June 23, 1873. On the edges of the delta, where horse-drawn scrapers could be used to push alluvium and clay into barriers, Chinese crews raised strong levees extremely cheaply and with little or no supervision. They performed these duties with such efficiency around the mouth of Cashe Slough near Rio Vista that their barriers withstood all subsequent floods and never had to be rebuilt. See "Reclamation of Marsh Lands in California," *PRP*, May 30, 1885; "Reclamation," *SDI*, Nov. 11, 1876; "Repairing Levees," *San Francisco Bulletin*, Mar. 6, 1879, Bancroft Scrapbooks, BL.

16. John Leale (with interpolations by Marian Leale), *Recollections of a Tule Sailor* (San Francisco, 1939), 36, 46–48.

17. Quote from RN689, 442–43. Few Chinese could write their names in English. Most

placed an X-mark opposite their pay receipt. See Roberts Island Reclamation Pay Receipts, "Receipt for Labor," Oct. 25, 1884, San Joaquin County Probate Receipts Collection, ASCHMS; clipping, *San Francisco Bulletin*, Nov. 30, 1877, Bancroft Scrapbooks, BL. Piece-rate payment was to have profound and lasting consequences for farmworkers, agricultural labor relations, and farm owners for generations to come, since the arrangement ensured that no matter how hard they worked, or whether or not they malingered, every Chinese field hand was an efficient worker. See Pieter Van Löben Sels MS.

18. Quote from Pieter Van Löben Sels MS. See also Dana, *The Sacramento River*, 169. It is not quite true that the Chinese stoically accepted mistreatment. They were famous for regularly fudging the results of their excavation pit work. Knowing the schedule for measuring the dirt column used in evaluating their pits, and wishing to receive as much money as possible, field hands went to great pains to leave their pyramid at the highest point of ground before they dug it. But there is also evidence from a few years later that they tricked foremen and engineers whenever possible by sneaking out to the pits at night to perform an "operation." The men would carefully pile on and tamp down extra layers of dirt, and in this way the following morning the column would be higher and the pit would appear deeper and thus be worth more. When discovered, workers would be fined and disciplined. Accepting the judgment, and never making a fuss, they behaved, according to one farmer, "like naughty but good children." Quote from Pieter Van Löben Sels MS. My estimate of the reclamation labor force is based on Roberts's testimony that in 1876 he had "three or four thousand [Chinese] employed, mostly under contract." But there are numerous other references to gangs of several hundred to several thousand Chinese reclamation workers, for example the four thousand Chinese hired by the Glasgow-California Land Reclamation Company over a two-year period between 1877 and 1879, and two hundred Chinese and forty Hawaiians hired by Robert Kercheval to expand his levees. See RN689, 437; Nordhoff, *Northern California, Oregon, and the Sandwich Islands*, 130; Swampland Reclamation District no. 303, "Sworn Statement of Engineer," May 14, 1879, EDDMRV.

19. Sylvia Sun Minnick, *Samfow*, 68; unidentified clipping, Mar. 21, 1878, Bancroft Scrapbooks, BL; "Insurrection on Union Island," *SDEH*, Mar. 21, 1878; also Mar. 22, 23, 1878. One part of the farmworker legend holds that Chinese reclamation hands received but a tiny and disproportionate fraction of what they earned, that they were "exploited." The one thousand Chinese who rebuilt Union Island levees for "Land Hog" Williams after he purchased the island from Roberts received fifteen cents a cubic yard of dirt. But they created fields that would soon produce 26.6 bushels of wheat per acre and net Williams a handsome profit of seventeen thousand dollars per acre. With the money earned by their labor, they were barely able to survive, while wealthy George Roberts and "Land Hog" Williams lived in the lap of luxury. Roberts himself is partially responsible for generating this particular legend. Testifying before a senate committee investigating Chinese immigration, he said of his Chinese field hands: "I think they are much better than slaves or negroes . . . They are more reliable." From that statement historians have cast the Chinese working for Roberts and other delta land magnates as plantation workers of the worst kind, people under the control of a man who used them much as a southern slave owner used black workers. And there are certain similarities. Chinese field hands reclaimed some thirty thousand to forty thousand acres for Roberts, playing the same role that blacks played in reclaiming bottomlands for sugarcane and rice farmers in Mississippi, Arkansas, Georgia, South Carolina, and Louisiana. But it does not necessarily follow that they were not free or that they earned Roberts a fortune. Chinese reclaimed land at the rate of between six and twelve dollars an acre. Roberts purchased that land at between one and four dollars, and sold it at between twenty and one hundred dollars an acre. Thus Roberts supposedly earned somewhere between $120,000 and $160,000 on the low side and $2.78 million and $3.72 million on the high side. In addition, Roberts also earned money from crops grown on his reclaimed swamps. Hence the picture of the lord riding to riches on the backs of a peasant labor force. Quote from RN689, 442; also 437, 440. See also data compiled from San Joaquin County Deeds, Book A of Deeds, Book 39: 355; Thompson, "The Settlement Geography of the Sacramento-San Joaquin Delta," 226–32, app. A, 472–73. The problem with this analysis, like so much else about California farmworkers, is that in its blind rush to judgment it fails to factor in all of the variables, or even to give a close accounting of events. Roberts himself left no record of his profits, but it is known that he suffered many setbacks from cracked levees and flooded crops. Whether due to these failures or because of mismanagement or the highly risky and speculative nature of his enterprise or all three, he lost all of his land, except

for Twitchell Island, which he somehow managed to hang on to out of sentimental attachment as his first reclamation project. Cheap and abundant Chinese laborers thus allowed Roberts to bring thousands of acres of swampland into productive use. But it does not follow that by their sweat and blood, they allowed him to amass a fortune. Chan, *Bittersweet Soil*, 185–86, discusses the matter at length. Never able to repay his debts, "Land Hog" Williams eventually went bankrupt. For Roberts see Dillon, *Delta Country*, 98–99.

20. The Chinese never patented their tule shoes. Nor did they try to limit or control their use. This is why, when celery growers around La Cienega in Los Angeles began using the contraptions and called them "peat shoes" in the early 1900s, no one questioned their claims and they took full credit. See Rogers, "The Delta Story," *Stockton Record*, July 16, 1951, SRCF; Nordhoff, *Northern California, Oregon, and the Sandwich Islands*, 131; "The Flooded Plains," *Alta California*, Feb. 24, 1878, Bancroft Scrapbooks, BL. For the La Cienega story, see Arthur Inkersley, "Celery-Growing in the Peat Lands of California," *Overland Monthly* 46 (Aug. 1905), 101–6; Fern Coleman, "History of the Celery Industry," *Orange County History Series* 3 (Apr. 1939), 101–5.

21. Quotes from RN689, 40, 271; also 295.

22. E. G. Nourse, *The Chicago Produce Market* (New York, 1918), 76; Jessie Boyd, "Historical Import of the Orange in Southern California" (M.A. thesis, UCB, 1922), 82–83; Leonard M. Davis, *From Trail to Rail! 1869–1909* (Roseville, Calif., 1969); "The Transportation of Fresh Meats and Fruits Etc., Through Long Distances—The Davis Refrigerated Car," *Scientific American* 23 (Nov. 12, 1870), 312; A. W. McKay et al., "Marketing Fruits and Vegetables," *USDA Yearbook for 1925* (Washington, D.C., 1926), 683, 691.

23. Quote from Higgins, "The Pacific Fruit Express," MS (n.d.), FHHC. For descriptions of departing fruit trains, see *Winters Advocate*, July 1, 1876, Yolo Historical Society. For the impact of the railroad on agriculture in Placer County, see Giddings, "Foundations of Placer County Horticulture," 50, 75; Bessie P. Bennet, "The Economic Development of Southern California with Special Reference to Transportation, 1870–1885" (M.A. thesis, UCB, 1927), 65; Margaret Ann Laughlin, "The California-Oregon and Oregon-California Railroad" (M.A. thesis, CSUS, 1964); Guy Crow, "The Coming of the Railroad," *Madera County Historian* 5 (Apr. 1965), 1–2; Osgood Hardy, *March of Industry* (New York, 1929), 81–82; Chan, *Bittersweet Soil*, 170; Gilbert, *History of San Joaquin County*, 132; Higgins, "How the Railroads Brought California Fruits to Market," unidentified clipping; "Cold Storage," *Pacific Fruit Grower*, Nov. 1887; "Shipping Fruit East," ibid., Feb. 1888, FHHC; *Sacramento Record-Union*, June 8, 1892; *Sacramento Bee*, Feb. 18, 1895; *PRP*, Dec. 7, 1901.

24. For some of the first reports of China bosses outside of the delta, see Bidwell, diary, Oct. 12, 1874, JBC; typed notes, *PRP*, Aug. 28, 1873; Aug. 30, 1884, WPA Material, BL. See also Mrs. G. W. Aiken, "The Labor Question," *CSAST, 1902*, 393; *Proceedings, CSFGCP, 1907*, 68–69. For the efficiency of Quong Yuen Long Company, see Leonard M. Davis, *Newcastle, Gem of the Foothills: A Pictorial History of Newcastle, Placer County, California, from its Formative Years to the Present* (Newcastle, Calif., 1993), 32. Bosses had innumerable opportunities for profit. They boarded laborers in the backs of shops and businesses, operated stores that stocked goods, foods, and supplies, supplied them with opium, and provided various mail drops and letter-writing services. Together with fees they collected for obtaining jobs, these various sundry expenses allowed bosses to earn substantial incomes. For China bosses running stores catering to field hands, see Jean C. Gilbert, "Tsuda Grocery: A History," *Sierra Heritage* 8 (May–June 1989), 47–49; Nordhoff, *California for Wealth*, 190, 212–13; Robert F. Spier, "Food Habits of Nineteenth Century California Chinese," *CHSQ* 37 (June 1958), 130; Spier, "Food Habits," ibid. 37 (Mar. 1958), 79–83. Scattered records indicate that a small-town boss netted between two hundred and six hundred dollars a year, with the more successful bosses pulling in as much as fifteen hundred dollars. Figures for larger China bosses in major cities are unavailable, but there is no reason their figures would not have been proportional. For the prosperity achieved by Sin Si Wau, a prosperous Anaheim China boss, see Anaheim City Tax Ledgers, 1876–80, MCC, showing Wau accumulated property valued at eleven hundred dollars by 1880. For Chinese bosses acting as subagents, see the reference to Sin Tin Wo in the *Anaheim Gazette*, Oct. 23, 1875. See also Ng Yee Yick habeas corpus case no. 10988, June 6, 1894, U.S. District Court of Northern California, Admiralty Case Files, 1851–1943, FARCSB. On the job, bosses also had many opportunities to make money. For example, when Chinese field hands went to work on a hop ranch, began grubbing out scrub oak for a hillside vineyard, or started cleaning and excavating canals and ditches before planting row crops, they typically earned a

contractor a bonus of twenty-five cents per man, even larger bonuses of fifty cents to one dollar on certain fruit farms if the fruit was ripening too fast. Although they never actually performed farm labor, bosses always received a daily wage, usually $1.25 to $1.50 a day, in addition to other sources of income. Paid a lump sum, bosses could skim something off the top without challenge. Even if men objected to conditions, bosses seldom worried that men would leave their jobs, as duty and obligation mandated that they fulfill their responsibilities. See Walter Allen, diary, Nov. 3, 11, 14, 31, 1879, Walter Allen Papers, HL. Field hands supplied bosses with numerous other nonmonetary benefits, most important among them status. Contracting conferred respect and standing. When China bosses died, their funerals were often elaborate affairs, complete with musicians, priests, caskets mounted on wagons, and elaborate graveside feasts in which the clothing and bed on which the contractor died were burned. Perhaps the greatest nonmonetary reward, besides the rank contracting bestowed on them, was the opportunity to marry. China bosses were part of the rare minority who were able to break free from the bachelor society and raise a family. As members of the merchant class, bosses became some of the few Chinese who traveled between California and their native land, and in a few cases brought their mothers and fathers over from their home villages. For funerals, see *Anaheim Gazette*, July 27, 31, 1890; May 20, 1897. For marriage and family information, see ibid., Oct. 8, 1896; *Anaheim Cemetery Records, 1867–1902* (Orange County, 1983), 5: pt. 1: 110, 124, 160, 481; MacArthur, *Anaheim: The Mother Colony*, 165.

25. The Anaheim Union Water Company paid the $158 transportation costs. See Minutes of the Anaheim Union Water Company, Jan. 16, Feb. 13, Mar. 13, Apr. 10, July 24, Aug. 7, 1869, MCC. See also Charles Rinehart, "A Study of the Anaheim Community with Special reference to Anaheim's Development" (M.A. thesis, USC, 1932). For Chinese in the Pajaro Valley, see typed notes, *Watsonville Pajaronian*, July 15, 1869, PVHS.

26. Quote from *Santa Cruz Sentinel*, May 28, 1870. For Bidwell's Chinese, see Bidwell, diaries, Jan. 11, Feb. 8, 1870, JBP. For Chinese at Red Mountain Vineyard, see Irene D. Paden, "Tullock & Knight's Ferry," MS [notebook] (n.d.), Irene D. Paden Papers, PCWS. For Schell, see "Abraham Schell," *Stanislaus Stepping Stones* 14 (winter 1990), 739–43. Having accumulated a considerable fortune driving sheep and cattle overland to California during the Gold Rush, Flint and a dozen other entrepreneurs led by E. H. Dyer raised $250,000 in capital and established the California Sugar Beet Company at Alvarado. Because the soil around the Alvarado plant was unsuitable for growing beets, Flint grew much of the crop on his San Juan Bautista farm, then shipped it north for processing at Alvarado. For the Chinese at Flint's ranch, see 1870 MS Census, San Benito County. For an account erroneously placing the first Chinese sugar beet workers two years later and a hundred miles north in the Sacramento Valley, see Chinn, Lai, and Choy, *A History of the Chinese in California*, 57. For beet harvest techniques, see R. A. McGinnis, *Beet-Sugar Technology* (New York, 1951), 7–8. For the Alvarado factory, see *History of Alameda County* (Oakland, 1883), 822–23, 880–81.

27. My calculations of the percentage of the farm labor force consisting of Chinese in Select townships are as follows: Alameda County, Washington Township, 67 percent; San Mateo County, First Township, 48; Santa Clara County, Santa Clara Township, 22, San Jose Township 13. Many Chinese who doubled as reclamation workers and hunted up other jobs as salmon canners and roustabouts were not counted as farm laborers.

28. Evidence for Chinese grape picking in the Napa Valley in 1871 comes from a reference to the previous year's harvest in the *San Francisco Wine Dealer's Gazette*, Mar. 1872. For cotton, see *History of Kern County*, 112. For the Ventura canal, see *Ventura Signal*, Apr. 14, 1871. For West Side Canal builders, see Latta, "Fresno Scraper," *Fresno Republican*, July 9, 1933. For hop pickers near Watsonville, see typed notes, *Watsonville Pajaronian*, Oct. 5, 1871, PVHS.

29. For the Coe ranch incident, see *History of Santa Clara County, California, Including Its Geography . . . Illustrated* (San Francisco, 1881), 237. Coe's operations are described in Elma Glover, *Santa Clara County* (San Jose, 1888), 14; *PRP*, Feb. 15, 1873.

30. Quotes from Rose, *Sunny Slope*, 81–82.

31. On December 21, two white men set fire to a bunkhouse in the Red Bluff Chinatown. See *Red Bluff Independent*, Dec. 21, 1871. For the Red Bluff murder, see *Tehama Independent*, May 25, 1872.

32. Quote from *Napa County Reporter*, Oct. 5, 1872, NCLCF. For a report of what may be the first strike by Chinese field hands, see *PRP*, Nov. 9, 1872. For Bakersfield, see W. Harland Boyd, *A California Middle Border: The Kern River Country, 1772–1880* (Bakersfield, 1972), 96.

For San Mateo, see Gilbert Richards, *Crossroads, People, and Events of the Redwoods of San Mateo County* (San Mateo, 1973), 106. For Los Angeles, see "Daily Occurrences at Rancho Azusa," 104–5, Oct. 7, 8, 9, 10, 15, 1872. For St. Helena, see *Napa County Reporter*, Sept. 7, 1872, NCLCF. For the Sacramento Sugar Beet Company, see Nordhoff, *California*, 90, 212–13, 220. Chinese are identified as the first sugar beet workers in Gibson, *The Chinese in America*, 57, 98. Chinese were barred from the beet-processing factory, where jobs went only to white workers, Mexicans included.

33. Quotes from Henry George, "The Chinese of the Pacific Coast," *New York Tribune*, May 1, 1869, in A. M. Winn, *Valedictory Address, January 11, 1871, at Excelsior Hall, San Francisco, to the Mechanics' State Council of California* (San Francisco, 1871), 13–19; George, *Progress and Poverty*; George, *Our Land and Land Policy*, 14, 17, 25, 27.

34. George, *Our Land and Land Policy*, 27; John Hayes, "One of Our Farming Counties," *Overland Monthly* 11 (Sept. 1873), 239. For Chinese docility and refusal to strike, see Brooks, *The Chinese in California*, 14; RN689, 767, 1201–2.

35. For Miller and Lux, see Lilbourne S. Winchell, *History of Fresno County, and the San Joaquin Valley* (Fresno, 1933), 110; "Statement of Expenses from 8/19/73–9/17/73" and "Chinamen—Big Jim Gangs No. 1 & 2, for March 1873," FFLCSF. For Butte County, see Old Timer, "Butte County Towns Spring Up In Wake of Grain Raising," *Chico Record*, Feb. 2, 1873, JWHA. For an account of what may be the second strike by Chinese field hands, see *PRP*, Aug. 28, 1873.

36. For Chu Muk, see Axel Wiederstrum, interview, Apr. 1975, San Francisco Maritime Museum, San Francisco. For Sisson and Wallace, see "Correspondence, The American Chinaman," *Alta California*, Sept. 12, 1869. See also Nordhoff, *Northern California, Oregon, and the Sandwich Islands*, 130, 143–44; Chinese Account Book, December 1888, G. W. Patterson Ranch Records, Mission Peak Heritage Foundation Archives [copies]. For crews of one thousand men, see *PRP*, Aug. 28, 1873; Aug. 30, 1884.

37. The standard dollar-a-day wage is described in John H. Strong, letter to the editor, *CSAST, 1872*, 307; also 257–58; Peter C. Y. Leung, *One Day, One Dollar: The Chinese Farming Experience in the Sacramento River Delta, California* (Taipei, 1985), 33. For variations, see Herd Ranch Time Book, Dec. 1888, HGP; Miller and Lux Chinese pay stubs to Su Shimm, May 4, 1875; Sam Fram, June 4, July 16, 1875; Ah Him, Aug. 23, 1875, FFLCSF. For developments in La Grange, see Elias, *Stories of Stanislaus*, 213. Savings and expenses computed from CSBLS, *First Biennial Report, 1883–84*, 166–67. The 20 to 30 percent figure is in Special Committee on Chinese Immigration, *Chinese Immigration; Its Social, Moral, and Political Effect*, Report to the California State Senate, Appendix to the Journals, California Legislature, 22nd sess. (Sacramento, 1878), 3: 271. A deviation from the dollar-a-day rate is in Sweet, "An 1876 Harvest," 1, describing Chinese ranch hands earning $1.50 during the wheat harvest.

38. Quotes from Tom Yuen, interview, in Victor Nee and Bret Nee, *Longtime Californ': A Documentary Study of an American Chinatown* (New York, 1974), 21; Chung Sun to C. O. Cummings, in *Watsonville Pajaronian*, Nov. 9, 1871, PVHS, cited in Sandy Lydon, *Chinese Gold: The Chinese in the Monterey Bay Region* (Capitola, Calif., 1985), 134–35.

39. Based on no documentation, McWilliams, *Factories in the Fields*, 79, claimed that in one year the Chinese sent back more than ten million dollars. Figures of five to ten million dollars in savings sent home are mentioned in clippings, *San Francisco Call*, Oct. 18, 1879; *San Francisco Chronicle*, Apr. 27, 1873; Mar. 15, 1879; *San Francisco Bulletin*, Aug. 7, 1879, Bancroft Scrapbooks, BL, but seem largely designed to support anti-Chinese sentiments. For the myth that the Chinese were sending home millions of dollars, see typed notes, *Gilroy Advocate-Leader*, July 12, 1873, GHM. For an estimate that field hands living on eight to ten dollars a month sent half of their wages back home, see CSBLS, *First Biennial Report, 1883–84*, 10–11, 166–67, tables 36–37. For one individual case, see *SDI*, Oct. 23, 1876. See also Rose Hume Lee, *The Chinese in the United States of America* (Hong Kong, 1960) 22; Young, "Chinese Emigration into the United States," 192–95.

40. Quotes from Yee Ah Chong, interview by Ronald Limbaugh, 1978, PCWS; Brooks, *The Chinese in California in California*, 15, BL; Benjamin Brooks, *Opening Statement before the Joint Committee of the Two Houses of Congress on Chinese Immigration* (San Francisco, 1876), 14; Grant W. Heil, ed., "California in the 80's As Pictured in the Letters by Anna Seward," *VCHSQ* 24 (winter 1979), 3. For a fire at a stable quarters, see *St. Helena Star*, Oct. 15, 1880. See also clippings, *Marysville Appeal*, May 14, June 3, 1874, Tehama Scrapbook, CSL; *CSAST, 1872*,

307; *PRP*, July 27, 1872; July 27, 1877; Rose, *Sunny Slope*, 162; Dalton, "Daily Occurrences at Rancho Azusa," diary, Jan. 27, 1874, HDC.

41. Martha W. Furrer, interview, June 23, 1981; William P. Clark, interview, Oct. 12, 1979, VCM. The China camp on the three-thousand-acre G. W. Patterson ranch near Fremont consisted of at least one dozen wood-slat cabins arranged on a service road south of the main ranch house. See Dr. Robert Fisher, interview by author, Fremont, Dec. 12, 1982, author's possession. For the China camp at Patterson ranch, see various deeds, checks to "Hock John," and "Ah Sing," and the "China Account," G. W. Patterson Ranch Records, Mission Peak Heritage Foundation Archives [copies]; Fisher, interviews by author, Fremont, Dec. 8, 14, 1982, author's possession. See also *Ventura Free Press*, Sept. 15, 1877; Heil, "California in the 80's As Pictured in the Letters by Anna Seward," 3; RN689, 437, 443, 570, 579–80, 591, 1094; Margaret Jennings, "The Chinese in Ventura County," *VCHSQ* 29 (spring 1984), 14, 21, 27.

42. Quote from clipping, *PRP*, Aug. 30, 1884, Scheter Files, ILWUL.

43. Quote from unidentified newspaper clipping, Bancroft Scrapbooks, BL. For a hatchet attack, see *St. Helena Star*, Nov. 17, 1893. For the Nom Kee murder, see Ronald H. Limbaugh and Walter A. Payne, *Vacaville: The Heritage of A California Community* (Vacaville, 1978), 131. For the Ing Cue incident, see *Napa Register*, Nov. 14, 1890, NCLCF. For Chinese farm labor in the transition period, see Wagers, "History of Agricultural Labor in California Before 1880," 86–87; Mary Coolidge, "Chinese Labor Competition," *AAAPSS* 34 (Sept. 1909), 124–25; J. R. Dodge, "Chinese Labor in Agriculture," U.S. Dept. of Agriculture Reports, 41st Cong., 2nd sess., , 1870, H. Doc., 572–76.

44. Quotes from Chester Rowell, "Chinese and Japanese Immigration," *AAAPSS* 34 (Sept. 1909), 4; "The Labor Problem," *Kern County Californian*, Jan. 5, 1888; *PRP*, Feb. 11, 1888.

45. Quote from Alice Prescott Smith, "The Battalion of Life, One Woman's Land Army and Its Work in the West," *Sunset* 41 (Nov. 1918), 30.

46. Quote from L. C. Lee, interview, June 1924, SRRP.

47. See also H. P. Stabler, "California Growers and the Labor Question," *CSFGCT, 1902*, 269; *San Francisco Chronicle*, May 31, 1877; farmer near Reedley, interview, Sept. 6, 1928, PSTFN; L. C. Lee, interview.

48. Quotes from Brace, *The New West*, 313; McWilliams, *Factories in the Fields*, 67. See also Richard and Maisie Conrat, *The American Farm: A Photographic History* (San Francisco and Boston, 1977), 191; Martin, "The Development of Wheat Culture in the San Joaquin Valley," 93.

49. For Culp, see J. P. Munro-Fraser, *History of Santa Clara County, California* (San Francisco, 1881), 272, 303. For the Gilroy tobacco industry, see Marjorie Pierce, *East of the Gabilans: The Ranches, the Towns, the People—Yesterday and Today* (Santa Cruz, 1976), 97, 153; Pat Snar, "Tobacco Culture in Gilroy and the Consolidated Tobacco Company," MS (n.d.); "Culp's Patent," *Gilroy Advocate*, Jan. 20, 1873; "Tobacco Statistics," ibid., Apr. 19, 1873; "Organized," ibid., Apr. 20, 1873; "The American Tobacco Company," ibid., Apr. 27 1873; "Progress of the Tobacco Enterprise," ibid., Aug. 9, 1973, GHM.

50. For Chinese tobacco workers, see typed notes, *Gilroy Advocate*, Apr. 27, 1872; Apr. 19, Sept. 27, 1873; Jan. 9, Apr. 16, 1875; Sept. 20, 1929, GHM. For labor contractors in San Francisco, see Pat Snar, interview, GHM, Apr. 6, 1993, author's possession. See also "Chinese Cigar Makers," *California Weekly Leader*, May 7, 1875, GHM.

51. For Ah Tyng and Ah Quin, see typed notes, *Gilroy Advocate*, Jan. 9, 1875; Mar. 15, 1873, GHM; see also May 31, 1873. After they went to work at San Felipe Ranch and on nearby tobacco farms, men remained there under the direction of several field bosses. They rarely came into town. According to local newspapers, they settled comfortably into "China houses" and bunkhouse communities. They began working immediately in January 1872, as it was absolutely essential for them to plant seeds and raise hundreds of thousands of young tobacco seedlings. Their work was very labor intensive, as the Chinese had to nurture the young plants carefully through late frosts by warming the outdoor growing beds with large sprinklings of rotting hay. Thereafter they were employed on a nearly year-round basis.

52. Typed notes, *Gilroy Advocate*, June 7, Aug. 9, Sept. 13, 1873, GHM.

53. Ibid., Jan. 3, 1874; Mar. 12, May 14, 1875, GHM.

54. Ibid., May 31, 1873.

55. Quote from "Farmers Club," *Napa County Reporter*, Nov. 16, 1872, NCLCF. See also clipping, *The Argonaut*, Dec. 29, 1877, Horace Davis Scrapbooks, BL; typed notes, *Oroville Weekly Union*, Jan. 31, 1863; *Mariposa Gazette*, Sept. 22, 1866, FFLCSF; Mark Twain, *Roughing*

It, 391; T. W. Whaun, interview, Mar. 5, 1924, SRRP; Ella Cain, *The Story of Early Mono County: Its Settlers, Gold Rushes, Indians, Ghost Towns* (San Francisco, 1961), 60–70; Howard Clark Bald, "Reminiscences of Early Ojai," *VCHSQ* 23 (fall 1977), 13; Richard B. Haydock, Reminiscences, interview, n.d., VCM.

56. Quotes from typed notes, Latta, "China Songs," FFLCSF. See also Stuart C. Miller, *The Unwelcome Immigrant: The American Image of the Chinese, 1785–1882* (Berkeley, 1979), 7, 15; Elmer Sandmyer, *The Anti-Chinese Movement in California* (Urbana, Ill., 1939), 26, 47. For Chinese binding but not threshing wheat, see Frank Hinckley, diary, June 27, July 30, 1873, Frank Hinckley Collection, HL.

57. Quote from *Napa County Reporter,* Jan. 24, 1874, NCLCF. Discussing how the violence had followed an invasion of grasshoppers, the *St. Helena Star* could not resist editorializing: "'Can't the Chinese be trained to eat the grasshoppers?' is the question which agonizes the heart of one section of the Great West; while another is riven with anguish over the dread inquiry, 'Can't they train the grasshoppers to eat the Chinese?'" See ibid., Nov. 19, 1874.

58. Quote from Latta, "Dead Chinese," FFLCSF. See also T. M. Whaun, interview, Mar. 5, 1924, SRRP. Although threatened with death and made the butt of jokes, Chinese field hands did not flee. Early the following year they were reported hoeing and planting castor beans at Rancho Azusa. Later in the year, they were spotted picking cotton around Los Angeles, drilling a five-hundred-foot-deep water well thirty strong on the McClung ranch in the southern San Joaquin Valley, working in the orange groves about Anaheim, building irrigation canals in Ventura County, weeding fields on Rancho Chico, and picking grapes and stripping Turkish tobacco again at Rancho Azusa. Hardly the dominant group in any of these operations, they often worked in conjunction with remnants of the Indian labor force, white field hands, and Mexicans, although each group usually performed a different task. Nevertheless the Chinese seemed to stand out, and their performance continued to win support and attract attention. For Rancho Azusa, see "Daily Occurrences at Rancho Azusa," Jan. 24, 30, 31; Oct. 14, 15, 16, 17, 1874. For the McClung ranch, see McClung Ranch Photograph no. 63, Carleton E. Watkins Album, Tenneco West Archives, Bakersfield. The Ventura County canal work is described in Minutes of the Farmer's Canal and Water Company, June 2, 1874, VCM. For Chinese working at Rancho Chico, see Bidwell, diary, Sept. 21, 1874, JBP. For Sonoma, see "Industrial Survey of Sonoma County," *CSAST, 1874,* 390. In the cotton fields, white men out-picked the Chinese, gathering twice as much cotton per day, or so said a reporter for *Overland Monthly.* But in the long run the Chinese supposedly proved to be more productive, owing to their "patience and steadfastness." In the citrus orchards they apparently were the epitome of efficiency as they worked without complaint, trudging down the rows with wicker baskets full of fruit suspended from long bamboo poles resting on one shoulder as if, said one observer, they were still in the Flowery Kingdom. "The Chinaman cannot be classified as a rapid worker, but he begins his work with rather a delicate motion which is kept up continuously throughout the day and is just the same night as in the morning," was a fairly typical evaluation. "For work like picking and packing fruit this characteristic is a valuable one, as haste cannot be used if best results are to be obtained." This perception would be repeated endlessly. The Chinese made superior hop pickers because they were shorter than whites and had a better disposition than Indians. Quotes from John L. Strong, "Labor in Cotton Culture," *Overland Monthly* 13 (July 1874), 19; Gregory, *History of Solano and Napa Counties,* 130. The bamboo pole incident is in Ida M. Shrade, "The Sequent Occupation of The Rancho Azusa de Duarte, a Segment of the Upper San Gabriel Valley of California" (Ph.D. diss., University of Chicago, 1948), 81. The hop picking comparison is in "China vs. Indian Hop Picking," *PRP,* Sept. 13, 1875. John Hayes, "One of Our Farming Counties," *Overland Monthly* 11 (Sept. 1873), 239, claims Chinese can't milk cows.

59. For problems with white tramp labor, see "Tramps, Tramps, Tramps," *Napa County Reporter,* Jan. 24, 1874, NCLCF; Menefee, *Historical and Descriptive Sketchbook,* 217–18. For the general "difficulty of getting hired help," see *PRP,* Feb. 7, 1874.

60. Quote from *Kern County Californian,* Jan. 5, 1888. For Chinese binding wheat by moonlight, see Hinckley, *Frank Hinckley,* 89. Chinese binding wheat by moonlight also occurred in the delta that summer when hundreds of white men employed by George D. Roberts quit after just two or three days on the job. Forced to keep a steamer constantly ready delivering men "of all nations" as fast as the ship could make the round trip to Stockton, Roberts at this point turned to China bosses. Contracting to obtain several hundred men, Roberts hired them to shock and bind his crop at so much per acre. Because it was extremely hot and the men would

have to put up several hundred acres of cut grain, their bosses decided to do the work by moonlight. Within a few days they had finished. "They did the work well and faithfully, and of course we abandoned white labor," explained Roberts several years later. From that point forward China bosses did everything except run the threshing machine on Roberts's grain farms. Quote from RN689, 439–40. For the prohibition on operating threshing machines, see Domonoske, "Recollections," 9.

61. Cone, *Two Years in California*, 140, 185; *PRP*, Oct. 7, 1876. See also Morley, "The Chinese in California as Reported by Henryk Sienkiewicz," 308–9; Wallace Smith, "Another Eden," *VCHSQ* 17 (fall 1971), 18.

62. Quotes from typed notes, *Anaheim Gazette*, Jan. 9, 1875; Feb. 12, 1876, MCC. For more on Chinese contractors in Anaheim, see ibid., Oct. 16, 23, 27, 1875; Feb. 12, 1876; *Anaheim Business Directory, 1876* (Anaheim, 1876).

63. Cone, *Two Years in California*, 140, 185; *Anaheim Gazette*, Mar. 13, 27; July 17, 1875. About 125 of Anaheim's 750 residents were Chinese. The canal project followed passage on May 16, 1874, of the Bush Act, a law that allowed farmers to form irrigation districts. The water was initially allocated to citrus farmers in northeast Fullerton, where groundwater had fallen to one hundred feet below the surface.

64. *Anaheim Gazette*, Nov. 13, 20; Dec. 4, 1875; Apr. 22, 1876, MCC. For an excellent history, see Roger G. Hatheway and Tori Zimmerman, with contributions by Jim Sleeper, *The Anaheim Union Water Company—Cajon Canal*, Civil Works Projects in Southern California, U.S. Army Corps of Engineers (Los Angeles, 1989), 14–17. Less reliable is Pamela Hallan-Gibson, *Golden Promise: An Illustrated History of Orange County* (Santa Ana, 1986), 84–86; and Virginia Carpenter, *Placentia: A Pleasant Place* (Santa Ana, 1977), 32, 42.

65. *St. Helena Star*, July 29, Aug. 26, 1875; Kay Archuleta, *The Brannan Saga* (San Jose, 1977), 68–69.

66. For Chinese crews on John Lewelling's winery on Spring Street in St. Helena, see *St. Helena Star*, July 29, 1875. See also Charles Sullivan, *Napa Wine*, 44; RN689, 1201; Bidwell, diary, Apr. 1876, JBC. Indian wages are in Durham Ranch Records, ledger, Feb. 28, Apr.–Sept. 1874, SCML. Information on the fruit dryer in "Rancho Chico Fruit Dryer," *Chico Evening Record*, July 25, 1878; "The Fruit Dryer," *Chico Enterprise*, July 26, 1878, in Royce, "In Memoriam John Bidwell," all in SCML. Tubbesing, "Economics of the Bidwell Ranch," 14, 34, 40–43, 220, counts sixty-one Chinese, eleven Indians, and 346 white field hands employed on Bidwell's farm.

67. Chinese at Natomas are described in George Husmann, *Grape Culture and Wine-Making in California: A Practical Manual for the Grape-Grower and Wine-Maker* (San Francisco, 1888), 226–33. See also Frona E. Wait, *Wines and Vines of California* (San Francisco, 1889), 198.

68. Quote from *Marin Journal*, Mar. 30, 1876, Marin County Historical Society, San Rafael. See also *Alta California*, Mar. 17, 19, 1876.

69. RN689, 40, 59–68, 129–40, 159–76, 185–87, 198–207, 214–15, 295; "A Resident to Editor," *Healdsburg Enterprise*, Feb. 8, 1876. For developments in San Francisco, see *Alta California*, Mar. 23, 1876.

70. Richard H. Dillon, *The Hatchet Men: San Francisco's Chinatown in the Days of the Tong Wars* (New York, 1962), 98–101.

71. Quote from ibid., 101. See also Brooks, *The Chinese in California*, 14–15. For the "cubic-air law," see *Alta California*, Mar. 12, 1876. The "antiqueue" ordinance is described in "Scraps on Chinese Immigration," *San Francisco Bulletin*, Apr. 18, 1876, Bancroft Scrapbooks, BL. Men arrested in the cubic-air raids are described in Board of Supervisors, *San Francisco Municipal Reports for Fiscal Years 1875–1876 and 1876–1877* (San Francisco, 1878), 237, 358. For the law prohibiting Chinese from reclamation projects, see *Statutes of California, 1875–1876* (Sacramento, 1876), 747.

72. For aspects of the anti-Chinese campaign in the farming districts, see *PRP*, Mar. 25, 1876; "The Chinamen," *Napa Register*, Mar. 25, 1876, NCLCF; "A Resident," *Healdsburg Enterprise*, n.d., Healdsburg Museum. See also Chan, *Bittersweet Soil*, 370–71; Lydon, *Chinese Gold*, 119–22.

73. Quote from typed notes, *Gilroy Advocate-Leader*, July 1, 1876, GHM. For more on "bummers," see Dillon, *The Hatchet Men*, 109. See also typed notes, *Watsonville Pajaronian*, June 2, 1876, PVHS; *Healdsburg Enterprise*, June 3, 1876, Healdsburg Museum; *San Francisco Bulletin*, July 14, 1876. In September 1876, largely under the order's pressure, the Consolidated Tobacco Company of Gilroy fired all of its Chinese, although Chinese field hands continued working on the tobacco farms around town. See *Gilroy Advocate-Leader*, Sept. 8, 1876.

74. For the "Great Gospel Swamp," see Patricia Lin, "Perspectives on the Chinese in Nineteenth Century Orange County," *Journal of Orange County Studies* 3/4 (fall 1989–spring 1990), 35; Don Meadows, *Historic Place Names in Orange County* (Balboa Island, 1967), 67; Ellen K. Lee, *Newport Bay: A Pioneer History* (Fullerton, 1973), 30.

75. Quote from Henryk Sienkiewicz, *Orso*, foreword by Carey McWilliams (San Francisco, 1939), 9. For his treatment of the Chinese, see Sienkiewicz, *Portrait of America: Letters* (New York, 1959). See also Stephen Gould, *An Illustrated History of Modjeska, Sienkiewicz, and Salvator: The Polish and German Speaking Writers of Los Angeles and Orange County from 1870 to 1910* (Hollywood, 1994), viii, 1, 17–19; Milton L. Kosberg, "The Polish Colony of California, 1876–1917" (M.A. thesis, USC, 1952).

76. Like many China bosses, Sin Si Wau seems to have prospered. His property was worth $1,075 in 1876–77, and $610 the following year. See Anaheim City Tax Records, 1876–78, MCC; *Business Directory of the Town of Anaheim* (Anaheim, 1876); death notice, *Anaheim Gazette*, July 24, 1889; Frank Raiche, "Anaheim's Chinatown," in *Orange County California: Cities and Towns*, WPA, Orange County Historical Research Project No. 3105 (Santa Ana, 1935). For the other contractors, see *Anaheim Gazette*, Oct. 27, 1875; *Anaheim Business Directory*, 1876. For See Yup, see Jan. 9, 1875. For the Gee Wau Company, see Feb. 12, 1876. For Tin Wo, see Oct. 16, 23, 1875. For Raine, see *Los Angeles City and County Directory, 1883–84* (San Francisco, 1884), 438; *History of Orange County, California . . .* (Los Angeles, 1911), 59.

77. For treatment of the Chinese in Anaheim, see Leo J. Friis, *When Anaheim Was 21* (Santa Ana, 1986), 6. For tensions in the Gospel Swamp area, see Esther R. Cramer et al., eds., *A Hundred Years of Yesterdays: A Centennial History of the People of Orange County and Their Communities* (Santa Ana, 1988), 105; Leo J. Friis, *Orange County Through Four Centuries* (Santa Ana, 1965), 63–64.

78. Quote from *Anaheim Daily Gazette*, Sept. 2, 1876, MCC.

79. Quotes from A. P. Dietz to editor, *St. Helena Star*, Sept. 15, 1876; also Sept. 8, 1873. For hop pickers working for Charles Story, see Sept. 1, 1876. For Chinese workers in the Simpson Thompson nursery south of Napa City at Suscol, see Jan. 5, 1877. For tramp laborers, see "Tramps," *Napa County Reporter*, Dec. 23, 1876, NCLCF. See also *San Francisco Chronicle*, Sept. 1, 1876, Bancroft Scrapbooks, BL. For the incident on Grand Island, see Rogers, *Colusa County*, 154.

80. Quote from *St. Helena Star*, Sept. 15, 1876. See also Norton King, *Napa County, An Historical Overview* (Napa, 1967), 61; Heintz, "The Role of Chinese Labor in Viticulture and Wine Making."

CHAPTER THIRTEEN

1. Samuel E. Becker, *Humors of a Congressional Investigating Committee: A Review of the Report of the Joint Special Committee to Investigate Chinese Immigration* (Washington, D.C., 1877), 1–36.

2. RN689, vi, 47, 50, 62, 439–40, 768–69, 786–89, 901–3; Coolidge, *Chinese Immigration*, 97; Brooks, *Opening Statement before the Committee of the two Houses of Congress on Chinese Immigration* (San Francisco, 1876), 14, BL; Dillon, *Hatchet Men*, 101–3; John L. Levinsohn, *Frank Morrison Pixley of the Argonaut* (San Francisco, 1989); Samuel V. Blakeslee, "Address on Chinese Immigration," MS (1877), BL.

3. S. E. W. Becker, clipping, *The Catholic World* (1876), Bancroft Scrapbooks, BL; Brooks, *The Chinese in California*, 21–22.

4. Quotes from RN689, 72, 272, 436, 667, 767–69, 778, 786–87, 1201–2; *Chinese Immigration and Its Social, Moral, Political, and Economic Effect: Report to the California State Senate* (Sacramento, 1878), 40; Dillon, *Hatchet Men*, 101, 109; Brooks, *Opening Statement*, 15; F. Hal Higgins, "Chinese Farm Labor in 1876," MS (n.d.), FHHC. See also Wen Hwan Ma, *American Policy Toward China as Revealed in the Debates of Congress* (Shanghai, [1916]), 63–66; Oliver P. Morton, *Views of the Late Oliver P. Morton on the Character, Extent, and Effect of Chinese Immigration to the United States*, 45th Cong., 2nd sess., 1878, S. Misc. Doc. 20. See also Coolidge, *Chinese Immigration*, 96–108.

5. RN689, 768–69. See also vi, viii, 40, 271, 436–43, 569–85, 620–24, 766–69, 771, 786–87, 778, 799–801, 1033–34, 1067, 1075, 1199, 1201–2; *NYT*, Feb. 28, 1877. While the hearings were in session in San Francisco two Chinese were badly beaten, two others shot or stabbed to death,

and a Chinese laundry and match factory attacked by mobs. See Augustus Layres, *Both Sides of the Chinese Question, or Critical Analysis of the Evidence for and Against Chinese Immigration, as Elicited before the Congressional Commission* (San Francisco, 1877), 8.

6. For reaction and subsequent developments, see clippings, *San Francisco Bulletin*, Nov. 16, 1876; *Nevada Transcript*, Nov. 17, 1876; *Alta California*, Nov.14, 15, 19, 1876; *Santa Cruz Courier*, Nov. 24, 1876, Bancroft Scrapbooks, BL; *New York Herald*, Oct.1, 1876; *St. Helena Star*, Dec. 22, 1876.

7. Clipping, *San Francisco Chronicle*, May 31, 1877, Bancroft Scrapbooks, BL. "Men who own and . . . cultivate tracts . . . in the Sacramento and San Joaquin Valleys," continued the *Chronicle*, "have no sympathy with white labor, nor any other interest connected with the laborer than to obtain the greatest amount of work at the lowest market price." Commenting on the circumstances propelling men into anti-Chinese agitation, John Bidwell denied that poverty or unemployment were involved, instead emphasizing character defects. See clipping, *Chico Enterprise*, Mar. 23, 1877, JWHA.

8. White unemployment figures statewide are from *San Francisco Evening Bulletin*, Apr. 14, 1877. See also *Healdsburg Enterprise*, Feb. 8, 1877, Healdsburg Museum. Unemployment figures for San Francisco are from Bancroft, *Popular Tribunals* (San Francisco, 1887), 2: 704. For white tramps, see *PRP*, Jan. 30, June 30, 1877.

9. Quotes from *Butte Record*, Mar. 24, 1877, in "In Memoriam John Bidwell," comp. Charles Royce, clippings and documents concerning John Bidwell, JBP. For the Simpson Thompson incident, see *St. Helena Star*, Jan. 5, 1877. A native of Bucks County, Penn., Thompson had founded his nursery in 1852; in 1856 he was joined by his two sons, James and Thomas. See William F. Heinz, *California's Napa Valley: One Hundred Sixty Years of Wine Making* (San Francisco, 1999), 24. For the incidents at Bidwell's rancho, see *Chico Enterprise*, Mar. 2, 9, 1877, BCL; *Butte Record*, Feb. 10, 1877. Bidwell's payroll from January through November 1877 totaled $46,727 of which $4,179 went to the Chinese; $37,646.20 to whites; and $4,902 to Indians. See also Hunt, *Bidwell*, 215–16; *Chico Enterprise*, Dec. 14, 1877, BCL. Bidwell describes threats in "Dictation Material," [1891], 5, BL. In Bidwell, "Address," Jan. 12, 1878, CSL, he claims he employed no more than twelve Chinese at this time, although he may be referring only to permanent employees. Violence was not exclusively caused by whites. On June 12, 1877, a Chinese field hand was found murdered in his cabin on the east side of the Sacramento River south of Colusa. "A hatchet had done the deadly work," wrote the *Colusa Sun*. The implication was that a fellow Chinese had committed the murder. Quote from Rogers, *Colusa County*, 137. In December 1876, a Chinese field hand was murdered on the Rancho Tapo in Simi Valley and an Indian arrested and sentenced to five years in prison for the crime. No motive was given. See Charles Outland, Indices of Early Ventura County Newspapers, 1871–1915, Simi Valley and Las Posas Ranchos, VCM.

10. The Lemm ranch incident is in Mansfield, *History of Butte County, California*, 274–75; clipping, *Chico Enterprise*, Mar. 16, 1877, in "In Memoriam John Bidwell," comp. Charles Royce comp., JBP. For Nord, "58,000 Chinese Once Employed by Contractors in California," *Chico Record*, Feb. 4, 1937, JWHA.

11. Quote from *Oroville Mercury*, in Stephen G. Hust, *This My Own, My Native Land* (Yuba City, 1956), 152. Bidwell's activities in the Lemm ranch massacre can be traced in Bidwell, diary, Mar. 9–10, 12, 14, 27, 31, 1877, JBC.

12. Quote from *Chico Enterprise*, Mar. 30, 1877. See also Michele Shover, *Chico's Lemm Ranch Murders and the Anti-Chinese Campaign of 1877* (Chico, 1998), 35–38.

13. Bidwell, diary, Apr. 4–5, 9, 11, 16–18, 1877.

14. "The most pitiable was Mrs. Stainbrook, hardly more than a girl and a child at her breast," wrote Stephen Hust. "She sobbed as if her heart was broken." Quotes from Stephen J. Hust, "Persecution of Orientals is Key to Valley's Mass Murder," *Marysville Independent Herald*, June 14, 1951, YCMA, which reprints much information and is the fullest account. See also Bidwell, diary, Mar. 9–10, 12, 14, 27, 31; Apr. 4–5, 9, 11, 16–18, 1877.

15. "It is doubtful that they felt anything but contempt when the murders departed the Oroville train station for San Quentin Prison," wrote Hust. "Humans are strange creatures and these calloused murders, strangely enough, were dear to their own. . . . Had their victims been white men, they would have been hanged. In fact they would have been undoubtedly accorded that special type hanging termed lynching." Quote from Hust, "Persecution of Orientals." See also *Chico Enterprise*, May 15, 17, 22, 28, 1877.

16. *Healdsburg Enterprise*, Aug. 9, 1877. For developments at Rancho Chico, see *Chico Enterprise*, Oct. 12, 19; Dec. 14, 1877, BCL; Bidwell, address, Jan. 12, 1878; Bidwell, dictation material [1891], 36, BL; typed notes, *PRP*, Dec. 8, 1877, FHHC. For Colusa, see Rogers, *Colusa County*, 161, for a petition circulated to remove the Chinese from the county.

17. Quote from clipping, *San Francisco Examiner*, Aug. 28, 1888, Bancroft Scrapbooks, BL. See also Lee Chew, "Biography of a Chinaman" ["A Chinese Immigrant Makes His Home in America"], *Independent* (Feb. 19, 1903), 417–23, reprinted on www.historymatters.gmu.edu/text/1650a-chew.html; *NYT*, Mar. 17, Aug. 16, 1869; Nov. 5, 1876; John H. Kimble, trans., "Andrew Wilson's Jottings on Civil War California," *CHSQ* 37 (Dec. 1953), 209, 212–14; Hoexter, *From Canton to California*, 138–39; Dorothy J. Perkins, "Coming to San Francisco by Steamship," in Genny Lim, ed., *The Chinese American Experience* (San Francisco, 1984), 26–33; Collin H. Dong, "The Saga of the Dong Family," MS (July 4, 1971), 5, PVHS.

18. Quotes from *New York Herald*, Oct. 15, 1870; statement carved into the wall above a bunk bed at Angel Island Immigration Station in San Francisco Bay by an anonymous immigrant, Angel Island State Park, photograph by the author, translation by Charles A. Litzinger. See also Him Mark Lai, Genny Lim, and Judy Young, eds., *Island: Poetry and History of Chinese Immigrants on Angel Island, 1910–1940* (San Francisco, 1980). For Jewish immigration, see Irving Howe, *World of Our Fathers* (New York, 1976), 29–53. Understanding that exhausting labor awaited them, only the hardier peasants traveled east. The aged and ill, the very young, and the unambitious stayed home. And those who did come often did so after being well informed of what to expect. The huge investment and need to borrow heavily for the trip reinforced the sense of caution, helping to further weed out the weak and unambitious. This selectivity provided agriculture with the hardiest, most adventuresome, and desperate of China's masses. See Lai Chun-Chuen, *Remarks of the Chinese Merchants of San Francisco, upon Governor Bigler's Message* (San Francisco, 1855), 3, 6, BL.

19. Quotes from Wong Sam and Associates, *An English-Chinese Phrase Book* (San Francisco, 1875), 13–22, 52–56, 108–28, 155, 219, 232, BL.

20. Albert S. Evans, "From the Orient Direct," *Atlantic Monthly* 25 (June 1869), 543–47; J. Ross Browne to Secretary Guthrie, Aug. 1, 1854, LRRST; Gunther Barth, *Bitter Strength: A History of the Chinese in the United States, 1850–1870* (Cambridge, Mass., 1964). For Chinese San Francisco, see Yong Chen, *Chinese San Francisco, 1850–1943: A Trans-Pacific Community* (Stanford, 2000), 52–53. For the stoning of a Chinese field hand, see *San Francisco Evening Bulletin*, June 15, 1870.

21. Quotes from Loomis, "Chinese in California: Their Sign-Board Literature," *Overland Monthly* 2 (Aug. 1868), 152–55; "The Old East in the New West," ibid., 1 (Oct. 1868), 364. See also Thomas B. Wilson, "Old Chinatown," ibid., 68 (Sept. 1911), 231–32. Unlike enclaves of European immigrants, where other groups intermingled, San Francisco's Chinatown was almost totally Chinese. See Thomas W. Chinn, Him Mark Lai, and Philip C. Choy, eds., *A History of the Chinese in California: A Syllabus* (San Francisco, 1969), 10; Huie Kin, *Reminiscences* (Beijing, 1932), 25, 28; Lee Chew, "The Life Story of a Chinaman," in Hamilton Holt, ed., *The Life Stories of Undistinguished Americans as Told by Themselves* (New York, 1906), 298; Minnick, *Samfow*, 196.

22. Percentages of field hands who immigrated under the auspices of the Six Companies computed from RN689, 29–33, 44, 175–76. See also Dr. Lew Seto More, Dr. Park, and Miss Raushenbauch, interviews, Mar. 6, 1924, SRRP.

23. Chung Kun Ai, *My Seventy-Nine Years in Hawaii* (Hong Kong, 1960), 16, recalls that $120 would be repaid on a sixty-dollar loan. For a suicide caused by debt, see Clough, *The House on Fifth and Salem*, 64–65, describing a cook who hung himself after being visited by two countrymen demanding that he return to China to fulfill his obligation to those who had paid his passage. See also Rogers, *Colusa County*, 229; Sing-Wu Wang, *The Organization of Chinese Emigration, 1848–1888: With Special Reference to Chinese Emigration to Australia* (San Francisco, 1978), 38–40, 87, 312–13.

24. Coming on the end of the long eastern crossing, the trip must surely have been uncomfortable and disorienting. Those headed for Marysville, Chico, Oroville, Stockton, Isleton, Walnut Grove, Red Bluff, Princeton, Jacinto, and Sacramento had the easiest journey, traveling most of the way by boat, or after a brief layover, a series of boat rides. Stepping off the docks, they had only a short stroll to reach Chinatown. Railroad lines carried others south to Salinas, Santa Cruz, and Watsonville, and north to Santa Rosa, St. Helena, Vacaville, Winters, Tehama, and Vina. In these towns men also had an easy walk from the train depot into Chinatown. But

men headed to Knight's Ferry, Bakersfield (which had two Chinatowns, one downtown, one on the outskirts of town), Gilroy (where a Chinatown grew up along Monterey Street between Seventh and Ninth streets near the cigar factories), Los Angeles (where the Chinese took over Negro Alley), and a dozen other towns arrived by circuitous routes combining long and exhausting boat or train trips, or both, followed by a dusty wagon ride. Those headed to Patterson and Newman on the west side of the San Joaquin Valley surely had the worst experiences. They had first to reach Stockton, then take a paddle-wheel steamer up the San Joaquin River. See Minnick, *Samfow*, 77; Him Mark Lai and Philip P. Choy, *Outlines: History of the Chinese in America* (San Francisco, 1973), 116; *Salinas Democrat*, Feb. 14, 1891; George Chu, "Chinatowns in the Delta: The Chinese in the Sacramento-San Joaquin Delta, 1870–1960," *CHSQ* 49 (Mar. 1970), 29–30; John W. Stephens, "A Quantitative History of Chinatown, San Francisco, 1870 and 1880," in *The Life Influence and Role of the Chinese in the United States, 1776–1960* (San Francisco, 1976), 71–88. Credit-ticket system statistics are from 1873 to 1876.

25. Charles C. Dobie, *San Francisco's Chinatown* (New York, 1936), 124; William Hoy, *The Chinese Six Companies* (San Francisco, 1942), 8.

26. Quote from typed notes on *Mariposa Gazette*, Sept. 8, 1866, FFLCSF.

27. Quotes from "Life History and Social Document of Andrew Kan," Aug. 22, 1924, SRRP.

28. Quotes from ibid.; Ginn Wall, in Nee and Nee, *Long Time Californ'*, 27. Songs told of sad failure. "My life's half gone, but I'm still unsettled. I've erred, I'm an expert at whoring and gambling. Syphilis almost ended my life. I turned to friends for a loan, but no one took pity on me. Ashamed, frightened—Now, I must wake up after this long nightmare." Quote from Marlon K. Hom, ed. and trans., *Songs of the Golden Mountain: Cantonese Rhymes from San Francisco Chinatown* (Berkeley, 1987), 294.

29. Quote from Chinese Six Companies, "To the American Public," Apr. 1, 1876, in Gibson, *The Chinese in America*, 300. See also Stanford Lyman, *Chinatown and Little Tokyo* (New York, 1986), 171–72.

30. Unidentified newspaper clipping, "Sam Low Goes to Ancestors—Last Representative of Once Flourishing Colony Passes," ca. 1935, MCC; WPA, "Sam Law, Pioneer Chinaman," *Pioneer Tales* (Orange County, 1934), 1; Loomis, "The Chinese in California," 3, 12. Return statistics computed from Gibson, *The Chinese in America*, 19–20, 36–37, 300; Stanford Lyman, "The Structure of Chinese Society in Nineteenth-Century America" (Ph.D. diss., UCB, 1961), 22–24. Between 1850 and 1882, about 330,000 Chinese arrived, while 150,000 or 47 percent, returned home. Field hands can not be separated out from the larger population.

31. Quote from *St. Helena Star*, Jan. 12, 1894. See also Jan. 24. For the funeral of Anaheim labor contractor Sin Si Wau, see Patricia Lin, "Perspectives on the Chinese in Nineteenth-Century Orange County," 33. See also *San Francisco Evening Bulletin*, June 29, 1861; newspaper clipping, *Watsonville Pajaronian*, June 19, 1913, PVHS; typed notes, *SDI*, Nov. 1, 1866; Dec. 28, 1885, FFLCSF.

32. For burial bricks, see Ernest Otto, "Old Santa Cruz," *Santa Cruz Sentinel*, Nov. 22, 1943. Common grave memorial marker, Stockton Rural Cemetery, trans. Charles A. Litzinger, CSU, Bakersfield. For burials and shipment of bodies home, see typed notes, *Gilroy Advocate*, July 12, 1873, GHM; *Pacific Echo*, Sept. 6, 1862, NCLCF; *St. Helena Star*, Apr. 23, 1885; "The Immigrant Chinese," *Hanford Sentinel*, Mar. 1983, special ed.; Loomis, "Chinese Baked Meats," *Overland Monthly* 3 (July 1869), 21–29; Tinkham, *History of San Joaquin County*, 163. For exhumation, see *St. Helena Star*, Feb. 9, 1894, describing a ten-dollar fee issued by the town to remove the bones of Lee Fee Nang, a fifty-five-year-old man killed by a train.

33. Quotes from Huie Kin, *Reminiscences*, 27; Six Companies, "To the American People," Apr. 1, 1876, in Gibson, *Chinese in America*, 300.

34. Quote from Nee and Nee, *Longtime Californ'*, 27. See also Lai Chun-Chuen, *Remarks of the Chinese Merchants of San Francisco, upon Governor Bigler's Message* (San Francisco, 1855), 3, 6, BL.

35. Quotes from *Fresno Republican*, May 11, 1899. "Occasional groups of Chinese women, sometimes leading quaint little children, and all in gorgeous silken and embroidered attire, were of great interest and wonder," the *Republican* added. "Strange things were whispered of these slim creatures with shining bare heads and impassive, painted faces." Most of these women apparently were prostitutes. See also William Henry Bishop, *Old Mexico and Her Lost Provinces—A Journey in Mexico, Southern California, and Arizona By Way of Cuba* (New York,

1883), 161; Latta, "Jo Woo," 1, FFLCSF; Ernestine Winchell, "Across the Tracks," *FMR*, Aug. 31, 1930, Fresno Scrapbooks, BL.

36. Quotes from Jim Sleeper, *Turn the Rascals Out! The Life and Times of Orange County's Fighting Editor, Dan M. Baker* (Trabuco Canyon, Calif., 1973), 80–81; Latta, "Jo Woo," FFLCSF; *Weekly Calistogian*, June 25, 1880. Old field hands remembered how rooms were so crowded in some boardinghouses that they slept on beds nailed one above another, like shelves onto the walls. Sometimes rooms would be so packed that men slept in shifts. See Nee and Nee, *Longtime Californ'*, 69–70; typed notes, *Watsonville Pajaronian*, Nov. 26, 1896, PVHS, describing Chinese living in the storeroom of the Kuhlitz building on lower Main Street; *Anaheim Gazette*, Sept. 12, 1874, describing the Sam Lee laundry and boardinghouse in Santa Ana.

37. Mrs. Leland A. Chow, "Chinese in Kern County," interview, 1972, Special Collections, CSU, Bakersfield; Axel Wiederstrum, interview; White, *Glenn County Sketchbook*, 137; *St. Helena Star*, Apr. 27, 1883; *Weekly Calistogian*, June 25, 1880; Helen Rocca Goss, *Life and Death of a Quicksilver Mine* (Los Angeles, 1958), 72.

38. Because the settlement was said to have the same relationship to Watsonville that Brooklyn had to Manhattan, it became known as Brooklyn. See Lydon, *Chinese Gold*, 192. Following a fire that destroyed their Market Street Chinatown in January 1870, the San Jose Chinese regrouped to Vine Street adjacent to the Guadalupe River, only to return to the old Market and San Fernando streets quarters a decade later, which came to be known as Ah Toy Alley. Following yet another fire on May 4, 1887, they settled near Hobson and San Pedro streets in an area later called "Big Jim's Chinatown," where many found employment under a boss known as Chin Shin, and referred to by whites as Big Jim. Heinlenville extended from the block formed by Sixth, Taylor, Seventh, and Jackson streets, and centered on Cleveland Street, an unincorporated alleyway cutting through the area from north to south. About four thousand Chinese resided in Heinlenville. See *San Jose Weekly Mercury*, Jan. 20, 1870; Glory Anne Laffey, "The San Jose Chinatowns," MS (July 1979), 7, San Jose Historical Museum. Of the protective fence at San Jose, the *Kern County Californian* wrote:

> They claim that these measures are taken simply as means of protection against the attacks of hoodlums and the lawless elements of society, but the officers believe that the design is mostly to sequester themselves from police scrutiny and that they may pursue their deviltry unmolested by official indifference [*sic*]. It is a serious obstacle to the efficient operation of the fire department, and constitutes a nursery for all kinds of infectious diseases and a hatchery of crime.

See *Kern County Californian*, July 14, 1888.

39. Quotes from *Salinas Democrat*, Feb. 14, 1891; *Santa Ana Evening Blade*, May 24, 1906. Salinas Chinatown layout from 1880 MS Census, Monterey County. Lease arrangements in Chama Zamora and Chin Yik lease, Monterey County Lease Books, Book B, May 23, 1874: 454, Monterey County Recorder's Office. In Salinas, Chinese field hands occupied a wedge-shaped block of frame tenement houses and stores, literally "on the other side of the tracks," where the Southern Pacific Railroad line intersected North Main Street. St. Helena doctors complained that the Chinese refused to boil water, simply dipping a bucket into the nearest river or water source. After finding "very foul cess-pools, closets, and drains in the very heart of town," with tenement houses and pigpens side by side and the inhabitants of both "gloriously mixed," St. Helena Board of Health investigators recommended stringent measures designed to clean up the Chinese quarters. Oxnard businessmen continually harped on Chinese laundries whose "stagnant water standing about . . . is liable to breed pestilence." Quotes from *St. Helena Star*, May 8, 1884; *Ventura Signal*, Oct. 15, 1875; Aug. 23, 1884. Chinese field hands living in Watsonville attracted especially vitriolic attacks. Reporting on garbage disposal practices in the local Chinatown, the *Watsonville Pajaronian* went into great detail about how "this delectable sink hole of barbarism and multitudinous stinks . . . poisons the balmy breeze for twice its area around with opium, hog flesh, dead fowls." The smell, continued the newspaper, was "only second to the howling, and wrangling, and fighting of Chinamen and the lowest greasers and Indians." When the Chinese struck back at the criticism by heaping their garbage in the street and burning it, the newspaper described seeing "the green, and black oily smoke rolled up toward the starry vault of heaven and the evening zephyrs gently wafted it to all parts of our beautiful town." To survive, added the paper, citizens gasped and clawed at their handkerchiefs, remarking "whew" and thinking of suicide. "The stench was fearful, and in less than four min-

utes the streets were deserted even by the dogs, and a few belated buzzards, flying but a short distance over town, caught a breath of it and with despairing squawks fell dead upon the earth." Quotes from typed notes, *Watsonville Pajaronian*, Sept. 3, Oct. 1, 1874, PVHS.

40. Quote from Russell [Sudzilovskii], *Around California in 1891*, 40–41. See also Stephen Gould, "Tustin's Chinatown," *Orange Countiana* 1 (1973), 23–29.

41. Ng Yee Yick Habeas Corpus Case no. 10988, June 6, 1894, U.S. District Court of Northern California, Admiralty Case Files, 1851–1934, FARCSB; "Chinese Laborers Reported Ill," *Sacramento Bee*, Dec. 6, 1918; Jennings, "The Chinese in Ventura County," 4; Latta, "Jo Woo," FFLCSF; George Oelkers "Memoirs," MS (n.d.), 2, MCC.

42. Quote from Clara H. Hisken, *Tehama, Little City of the Big Trees* (New York, 1948), 26. See also Rosena A. Giles, "Early Chinese in California," GFP; Thompson and West, *History of Sacramento County*, 220; *Stories of the Sacramento River Delta*, n.d., 14, Pamphlet Collection, BL; Michele Shover, "Chico's Mystery Tunnel," *Diggings* 33 (spring 1989), 15–17; Edith Bartholomew, "Valley Chinatowns," *Wagon Wheels* 22 (Feb. 1973), 30; "Napa's Chinatown," *Napa Register*, Feb. 21, 1962, NCLCF; Ronald Limbaugh, ed., "Yee Ah Chong Remembers Vacaville Chinatown: An Oral Account of Life in a Town-Within-A Town," *CH* 63 (summer 1984), 247.

43. Quotes from Rogers, *Colusa County*, 157, 172. See also Levene, *Mendocino Remembered*, 1: 52; *Memorial and Biographical History of the Counties of Merced, Stanislaus, Calaveras, Tuolumne, and Mariposa California*, 138–39; Minnick, *Samfow*, 43, 159, 166–69; Lydon, *Chinese Gold*, 279–80, 295–96, 301; "A Big Blaze, Chinatown in Flames," *St. Helena Star*, Aug. 14, 1884, is an account valuable for listing various stores, their owners, and calculating the loss; also July 8, 1887; July 22, 1898; *Red Bluff People's Cause*, Aug. 7, 1886; Margaret Koch, *Santa Cruz County: Parade of the Past* (Fresno, 1973), 215; Charles P. Owen, "The Chinatowns of San Jose," *San Jose Mercury Herald*, Feb. 25, 1917; *Chico Enterprise*, Nov. 11, 1887; David G. Gawrosch, "The Chinatown Fire," in Hom, *Chinese Argonauts*, 98–100. For the Colusa Chinatown fire, see *Colusa Sun*, July 12, Aug. 18, 1877; Jan. 13, 1879. At least one Chinatown was burned as a matter of public policy. After two decades of accusations that it was an unhealthy eyesore, a purported case of leprosy served as pretext for residents of Santa Ana to burn their Chinatown and move seven hundred Chinese out beyond the Santa Ana River. See Derek Kakuda, "Chinatown in Anaheim: 1870–1940," MS (n.d.), MCC; Mary Lou Begert, "The Chinese in Anaheim, 1860–1935" (M.A. thesis, CSU, Dominguez Hills, 1993). For their part, Chinatown landlords seldom gave such matters a second thought. Most treated Chinese field hands as easy marks. When they poured into the neighborhoods, real estate values fell and frequently new owners took over. These were often other immigrants, for example, Italians and Germans in Stockton. Ignoring whatever housing regulations existed, they seldom made repairs or improvements, and in the continuing housing shortage and wrath against Chinese immigrants, charged outrageous rents and still kept their buildings full. In some instances, they received a kickback from the boardinghouse manager based on the number of borders. For hovels where men were stuffed into every nook and cranny from cellar to garret, landlords were not shy about charging Chinese an average of 20 percent more per room than English-speaking tenants. See Thomas A. McDannold, "Development of the Los Angeles Chinatown: 1850–1970" (M.A. thesis, CSU, Northridge, 1973); 37–54; Edwin R. Bingham, "The Saga of the Los Angeles Chinese" (M.A. thesis, Occidental College, 1942), 21–33; Tinkham, *History of San Joaquin County*, 161; typed notes, *SDI*, Dec. 13, 1867, FFLCSF.

44. For Bakersfield, see Chow, interview. For Heungshan and T'oishan differences, see Chu, "Chinatown in the Delta," 22–30; 1880 MS Census, Union Township, giving a breakdown of 105 Heungshan Chinese out of 545. For Stockton, see Minnick, *Samfow*, 77.

45. Quote from Darrell Conard, "Big Steer Tells About Old Cow Outfits: Cattle Industry Did Not Really Develop Here Till After 1900," *Red Bluff Daily News* (ca. 1956), in Henry Albert Schafer Scrapbook, SCML. For tongs, see Dr. More, Dr. Park, and Miss Raushenbauch, interviews; Chinese tong members, interviews, Jan. 7, 1925; letter by C.O.M., Dec. 14, 1913, Segregation Folder, SRRP; Barth, *Bitter Strength*, 77–80, 86–90, 100–103. From tongs proliferated a bewildering variety of other social, political, and economic organizations. Priests came immediately after the population grew large enough to support them. Local parishes emerged to coordinate the activities of the different village and district groups. Joss Houses or God Houses—large two-story temples filled with carvings and images, covered in gold leaf, with a sanctuary usually located on the second floor, and "finely fitted up with many gew gaws"—developed as both social meeting halls and chapels. Downstairs in Watsonville's Brooklyn temple, the local

tong maintained a hostel during the harvest season where field hands could sleep if they had no other place to stay. Quote from *St. Helena Star*, Mar. 13, 1884. For priests and Joss Houses, see Reuben Ibanez, ed., *Historical Bok Kai Temple in Old Marysville, California* (Marysville, 1967); *Napa Register*, Mar. 13, 1884, NCLCF. For tongs and the hostel in the Brooklyn temple, see Lydon, *Chinese Gold*, 266–68, 296, 203. For the Sam Yip Company clubhouse in Bakersfield, see handwritten notes on the *Kern Standard*, Feb. 11, 1899, FFLCSF.

46. With little prospect of marrying, bachelor Chinese were, in the words of a Cantonese rhyme, womanless men, "pathetic . . . lonely bachelors stranded in a foreign land." Quote from Hom, *Songs of the Golden Mountain*, 90. Figures from Lucie Cheng Hirata, "Chinese Immigrant Women in Nineteenth Century California," in Carol Ruth Berkin and Mary Beth Norton, eds., *Women of America: A History* (Boston 1979), 234; also 225–26; Hirata, "Free, Indentured, Enslaved: Chinese Prostitutes in Nineteenth-Century America," *Signs: Journal of Women in Culture and Society* 5 (fall 1979), 4–6, 13–14. For efforts of a San Francisco mission worker to free a Chinese prostitute from a Bakersfield brothel, see *Fresno Republican*, Jan. 6, 8, 29, 1901. With Chinese women utterly subordinate to men, they were in no position to oppose deals whereby they would be sold into the sex trade. Procurers specializing in obtaining prostitutes kidnapped young women from peasant families, and when necessary, lured or bought them, paying as little as fifty dollars, then reselling them in California for three to twenty times that amount. For many rural families, selling daughters into the sex trade became a common method whereby they avoided the expense of supporting daughters and needed income. Even after going to work, prostitutes continued sending earnings to their families, most of them under condition of debt bondage. Many young women came "voluntarily," receiving free steerage and an advance of four hundred dollars. In exchange for four-and-a-half years' service, they had to work 320 days a year, and could be docked an extra year for failing to live up to their contracts. Some arrived after being deceived by promises of marriage to wealthy men. Unable to read or write, they signed contracts with their thumbprints, and once in California found themselves sold to the highest bidder, used as sex slaves or concubines, then cast off to a brothel. Under such circumstances, many prostitutes were beaten and abused or became addicted to opium. A few committed suicide by overdosing on drugs, slitting their wrists, drowning themselves in the Sacramento River, or throwing themselves off a bridge. Unlike men who died in California, few prostitutes ever had their bones returned home; many were simply discarded on the streets. Occasionally a mission worker would attempt to gain custody of a Chinese girl, then lose custody to agents of the tongs, who would grab the girl and spirit her away. Chinese prostitution even had its defenders, among them the *San Francisco Evening Post*, which condemned efforts to free Chinese prostitutes from their slavelike status on the grounds that they had been born into slavery and thus should remain there. See Joyce Mende Wong, "Prostitution: San Francisco Chinatown, Mid- and Late Nineteenth Century," *Bridge: An Asian American Perspective* (winter 1978), 25–26; G. B. Densmore, *The Chinese in California: Description of Chinese Life in San Francisco: Their Habits, Morals, and Manners* (San Francisco, 1880), 84; *Census of the United States, 1900*, 1: 495.

47. Quote from Judy Yung, *Unbound Feet: A Social History of Chinese Women in San Francisco* (Berkeley, 1995), 29. The source of my tabulation of Chinese brothels in San Francisco, Chen, *Chinese San Francisco*, 77–79, 83, views encounters with prostitutes in a broad context. See also Peggy Pascoe, "Gender Systems in Conflict: The Marriages of Mission-Educated Chinese American Women, 1874–1939," in Ellen Carol DuBois and Vicki L. Ruiz, eds., *Unequal Sisters: A Multicultural Reader in U.S. Woman's History* (New York, 1990), 143. For Stockton, see Minnick, *Samfow*, 182. For the Market Street houses of prostitution, see Sanborn Map, 1883, map 16. For arrests, see typed notes *SDI*, Oct. 11, 1861, FFLCSF. For a Chinese house of prostitution, see *SWM*, Oct. 17, 1885. See also Herbert Asbury, *Barbary Coast: An Informal History of the San Francisco Underground* (New York, 1933), 176–77. Traveling into Marysville, Sacramento, and Watsonville on Saturday nights, Chinese men found sex with prostitutes in a distinct subsection of Chinatown, as did those visiting Fresno, where numerous signs solicited them as they walked along the main thoroughfare. In Stockton, men looked for sex in a section that ran through the middle of Market Street and extended around the corner to Hunter Street. But field hands did not always find their prostitutes in Chinatown. Those working in the delta could find comfort at landings between Whiskey Slough and Holt Station. Apparently many field hands had favorite prostitutes. Every so often they would fight over a woman, and the resulting melee, especially when someone was shot or stabbed, won headlines in the pages of

the local press. See Charles Morley, trans., "The Chinese in California as Reported by Henryk Sienkiewicz," *CHSQ* 34 (Dec. 1955), 307; Warren S. Thompson, *Growth and Changes in California's Population* (Los Angeles, 1955), 49. For one shooting, see *Fresno Republican*, Sept. 5, 6, 16, 1899. For the *Republican's* fight with the *Post* over Chinese prostitution, see ibid., Aug. 2, 1899. For Chinese prostitution along the main thoroughfare leading west through the Fresno Chinatown, see ibid., July 6, Sept. 19, 1899; May 2, 1900; July 6, 1904; Chester H. Rowell, "A Brief Account of the Life of Chester H. Rowell" MS (n.d.), Chester Rowell Papers, BL.

48. Quote from T. M. Whaun, interview, Mar. 5, 1924, SRRP. For a general picture of gambling, see Gibson, *The Chinese in America*, 15–16; Stewart Culin, "The Origin of Fan Tan," *Overland Monthly* 28 (Aug. 1896), 153–55. For personal reminiscences and observations, see Lew Chew, "Life Story of a Chinamen," 294.

49. Quotes from Frank Raiche, "Anaheim's Chinatown," in *Orange County, California: Cities and Towns*, WPA, Orange County Historical Research Project no. 3105 (Santa Ana, 1935), 1; *St. Helena Star*, Mar. 8, 1889. See also *Napa County Register*, July 29, 1887, NCLCF.

50. Quote from *St. Helena Star*, Nov. 2, 1883. The Feb. 12, 1886, issue counted seven Chinese gambling houses in Sonoma. For gambling in the Brooklyn Chinatown of Watsonville, see *Watsonville Pajaronian*, Feb. 12, 1891; Nov. 2, 1893; June 21, 1894; Luke P. Cikuth, "The Pajaro Valley Apple Industry, 1890–1930," interview, by Elizabeth S. Calciano, 1968, 131, ASCUCSC. For Colusa, see Rogers, *Colusa County*, 162. For violence arising out of gambling, see *St. Helena Star*, Sept. 20, 1876; *Anaheim Gazette*, July 21, 1877; Dec. 22, 1879. For arrests, see typed notes, *San Andreas Independent*, Mar. 7, 1857, FFLCSF; *Anaheim Gazette*, Dec. 27, 1879; May 22, 1889.

51. Quote from *Fresno Morning Expositor*, Oct. 25, 1895, Fresno Scrapbooks, FCHS. When policemen knocked down the guard posted outside one gambling establishment on October 25, 1895, they were surprised to find a locked, steel-sheathed door bolted from the inside. After failing to bash it in, they gave up and arrested the doorkeeper and another man on charges of vagrancy. During all of this, the large crowd inside could be heard shouting and betting as if nothing had happened.

52. *Fresno Republican*, Oct. 8, 1899; Dec. 8, 9, 13, 15, 30, 1898; Sept. 15, 16, 1899; Oct. 26, 1901. To get around the iron doors, police sometimes entered through a backdoor. A newspaper account of one such raid in St. Helena began:

> Descent was made by town Marshall A. L. Spurr and Ed Kenyon assisted by a large posse of citizens. Suspicion was attracted to the house on Main Street kept by Hop Hung, by its being closed and dark while its fellows were all brilliantly lighted. The building was broken into from the rear and officers and assistants rushed in. Here they found a large number of Chinese playing the game and arrested 13 of them, though a large number escaped upstairs on the roof . . . about 50. . . . They were all searched and articles taken, including $143.35. Of this $95.65 was found on Ah Shuey who appeared to be dealer and treasurer of the institution and $41.10 on Ah Hoy. The prisoners were escorted uptown by 100 or more white citizens (who gathered to see the fun) and were all locked up in jail.

All were tried and convicted, the gambling den owner fined thirty dollars, and each gambler thirteen dollars. Four of the men could not raise any money and served two weeks in jail. Because fines increased upon subsequent arrests, it was common for habitual gamblers to give police a different name each time they were caught in the hope that they would slip through unrecognized as prior offenders. Quote from *St. Helena Star*, Aug. 3, 1883. See also Aug. 10, Nov. 26, 1883; Jan. 7, July 29, 1887; Mar. 8, 1889. For Stockton, see typed notes, *SDI*, Sept. 21, 25, 1885; Oct. 8, 1885, FFLCSF. For the arrest of thirty-six Chinese for gambling in Colusa, see Rogers, *Colusa County*, 162. For the arrest of sixteen men, all of whom were given one hundred days or one hundred dollars' bail and paid the bail, see Sheriff's Booking Log, 2: Feb. 5, 1886, Ventura County Sheriff's Booking Logs, 1873–1900, VCM.

53. Eugene Block, "Combating the Drug Evil in San Francisco," *Overland Monthly* 60 (July 1912), 69–78; Block, "Fighting the Opium Ring," ibid., 68 (Aug. 1911), 184–91. For arrests, see *St. Helena Star*, Dec. 18, 1885; Feb. 21, 1886, listing three opium dens in operation in Sonoma; Apr. 30, 1897, for suicide by eating opium; June 6, 1890, describing a fight in which an opium smoker was shot, apparently as an innocent bystander as the result of a tong war. Prices from Chen, *Chinese San Francisco*, 87, 294. Estimate of percentage of men using opium is from Yee Ah Chong, interview. See also Ernest Otto, "Old Santa Cruz," *Santa Cruz Sentinel*, Sept. 5, 1943; Tom Lee, interview, ca. 1924, SRRP; *Watsonville Pajaronian*, Mar. 14, 1889; *Ventura Vidette*,

Mar. 6, 1891, VCM. There are good descriptions of opium smoking in L. N. Wisser, interview by Derek Kaduda, n.d., Biography File, MCC; *Napa Register*, Apr. 30, 1886, NCLCF. For a raid, see clipping, *Watsonville Pajaronian*, n.d., citing the *Salinas Index*, PVHS. Occasionally a man would overdose on opium, fall into a creek, get fished out, and, "hopelessly crazed," be sent to an asylum to recuperate. See "City and County," *Riverside Citrograph*, Sept. 2, 1893. For descriptions of the opium smoking ritual, see *Fresno Republican*, Nov. 20, 1904; Russell [Sudzilovskii], *Around California in 1891*, 41–42. For an overview of opium use, see John Helmer, *Drugs and Minority Oppression* (New York, 1975).

54. Quote from *Riverside Press*, May 10, 1897; Harry Lawton, "Riverside's Pioneer Chinese," Feb. 11, 1959, *Riverside Daily Press*, Riverside Public Library, Local History Room.

55. Quotes from *Fresno Daily Evening Expositor*, Sept. 14, 1894, Fresno Scrapbooks, FCHS. See also Oct. 5, 1897; *FMR*, Mar. 5, Oct. 8, 1899. Lottery ticket sales figures from ibid., Dec. 3, 1899; Oct. 5, 1901.

56. Quote from Diane Mei Mark and Ginger Chih, *A Place Called Chinese America* (Dubuque, Iowa, 1982), 52. For *jinshanzhuang*, see Madeline Y. Hsu, *Dreaming of Gold, Dreaming of Home: Transnationalism and Migration Between the United States and South China, 1882–1943* (Stanford, 2000), 36–40. See also Lyman, *Little Chinatown*, 123; Robert Culin, "Customs of the Chinese in America," *Journal of American Folklore* 6 (July–Sept. 1890), 191–93; "The Sound of Slippers," in Paul Radin, ed., *The Golden Mountain: Chinese Tales Told in California*, coll. and trans. John Lee (Taipei, 1971), 5; Sam and Associates, *An English-Chinese Phrase Book*, 13–22, 52–56, 108–28, 155, 219, 232, BL.

57. Ng Yee Yick, habeas corpus case, June 6, 1894, Habeas Corpus Case Files, no. 109888. See also Dong, "The Saga of the Dong Family," 6–7, describing the family stores in Gonzales and Salinas.

58. Quotes from clipping, *Fresno Weekly Republican*, [ca. 1883], BWC; *St. Helena Star*, Feb. 13, 1889. See also Loomis, "Holiday in the Chinese Quarter," *Overland Monthly* 2 (Feb. 1869), 148–49, 151.

59. Quotes from *St. Helena Star*, Feb. 13, 1880; also Feb. 11, 1881; June 14, 1889; *Winters Express*, Feb. 15, 1896.

60. Quote from *Ventura Free Press*, Feb. 10, 1905. See also *SWM*, Nov. 14, 1885; "Orientals Celebrating New Year's," *Oxnard Courier*, Jan. 26, 1906, VCM; typed notes, *San Andreas Independent*, Jan. 31, 1857, FFLCSF.

61. Frederick Shearer, ed., *The Pacific Tourist* (New York, 1879), 279; Zhang Yinhuan, *Sanshou riji* (Journal of the sojourn to three continents) (Beijing, 1896), 1: 74, JARPC; M. von Brandt, *Chinese Pigtails and What Hangs Thereby* (New York, 1900), 4; RN689, 640.

62. Quotes from Chew, "The Life Story of a Chinaman," in Hamilton Holt, ed., *The Life Stories*, 298; Crissey, *Where Opportunity Knocks*, 27; also 33–34. See also RN689, 38–39; Augustus W. Loomis, "Chinese in California," MS (n.d.), 3, 12, AWLC; "Interviews with Two Chinese," Nov. 21, 1924; "Report on Fresno, California: The Chinese," Feb. 12, 1924; Herbert Wung, interview, Feb. 22, 1924, SRRP.

63. Nee and Nee, *Longtime Californ'*, 16; also 13, 21, 26–29, 72; Paul C. P. Siu, "The Sojourner," *American Journal of Sociology* 58 (July 1952), 35–36.

64. Quote from old Chinese saying cited in Gordon Chan, interview, Oct. 23, 1988, San Anselmo, author's possession. See also Charles Morey, ed. and trans., "Chinese in California," *CHSQ* 34 (Dec. 1955), 308–9; Cikuth, "The Pajaro Valley Apple Industry," 127, 131.

CHAPTER FOURTEEN

1. Joseph McGie, *Gridley Centennial Pictorial History Book* (Oroville, Calif., 1970), 14; various unidentified newspaper clippings, Gridley Public Library. See also Richard J. Vieira, "Gridley, California: The Evolution of a Mid-Sacramento Valley Farm Community" (M.A. thesis, CSUC, 1968), 56–59.

2. Quotes from *San Francisco Daily Morning Call* cited in *Healdsburg Enterprise*, Nov. 22, 1877, Healdsburg Museum; *San Francisco Daily Morning Call*, Aug. 20, 1877. See also Aug. 9. For the arson campaign, see McGowan, *History of the Sacramento Valley*, 326–27. For other threats, see *PRP*, June 30, 1877; unidentified newspaper clippings, n.d., 1: 71, Horace Davis Scrapbooks, BL; Howard Clark Bald, interview, VCM.

3. Quote from *San Francisco Daily Morning Call*, Aug. 20, 1877. For the capitulation of delta

farmers, see *St. Helena Star*, Sept. 7, 1877. Chan, *Bittersweet Soil*, 373–74, does not mention the capitulation, citing it as evidence of growers protecting the Chinese rather than of caving in to anti-Chinese agitation.

4. Quote from "Chinese Cheap Labor," *Anaheim Daily Gazette*, Aug. 10, 1877. See also "A Matter of Self-Preservation," Aug. 10, 1877, including Citizens to Mr. Raine & Co., and Citizens to Mr. Sin Se Wo [Sin Si Wau]; Aug. 4, 7, 11, 1877.

5. Quote from "Vineyard Men and Employers of Chinese Generally," *Anaheim Review*, Aug. 16, 1877, MCC. Sin Si Wau lost three hundred dollars, the amount he had advanced to his men for food, clothing, and transportation to the hop fields.

6. Quote from "Conflict of Races," *Anaheim Daily Gazette*, Aug. 19, 1877. See also Aug. 17, 18, 1877. The August 18 issue offered a fifty-dollar reward for information leading to the arrest and conviction of those who wrote the threatening letter.

7. Law enforcement authorities searched for the Chinese hop picker who had done the shooting, but never found him. "The Mongol could not be found," reported the *Anaheim Daily Gazette*. Quotes from "Santa Ana Items," *Anaheim Daily Gazette*, Aug. 17, 21, 26, 1877. See also Aug. 25, 28; Sept. 7, 1877.

8. Quote from *Santa Cruz Sentinel*, Jan. 5, 1878. For Kearney see Frank M. Fahey, "Denis Kearney: A Study in Demagoguery" (Ph. D. diss., Stanford University, 1956), 68–69. For aspects of the anti-Chinese campaign, see Minutes of the Marysville City Council Meeting, Oct. 2, 1876, Yuba County Recorder's Office.

9. Quote from Wallace Irwin, *Chinatown Ballads* (New York, 1934), 13. A reporter for the *Alta California* who ventured into the Napa countryside to observe Kearney's men discovered a mass of drunken, shiftless fugitives from the law, social misfits, former gold miners, and poor bachelors with no future whose "demoralization . . . [was] the result of a long train of circumstances running through the course of many years." Observed the reporter: "Wages have been so high, that farmers could not afford to employ them, except for a few months of seeding and harvesting." Consequently the men when not working, which was most of the time, traveled about the countryside denouncing Chinese field hands for taking their jobs, while spending their idle hours "in intoxication as the most agreeable pastime." Quote from *Alta California*, Sept. 10, 1877. See also Aug. 20, 1877; clipping, *San Francisco Chronicle*, May 31, 1877, Bancroft Scrapbooks, BL; *PRP*, June 2, 1877.

10. Quotes from *Grange Proceedings, 1877* (Sacramento, 1878), 48, 55; ibid., *1878* (Sacramento, 1879), 28.

11. For the conflict between the Grange and farm elite, see Gerald Prescott, "Farm Gentry vs. the Grangers: Conflict in Rural California," *CHQ* 56 (winter 1977–78), 339. For farmers defending Chinese field hands, see Lydon, "The Anti-Chinese Movement in Santa Cruz County, California: 1859–1900," in Thomas W. Chinn, ed., *The Life, Influence, and the Role of the Chinese in the United States, 1776–1960* (San Francisco, 1976), 219–42; clipping, *The Argonaut*, Dec. 29, 1877, Horace Davis Scrapbooks, BL.

12. Quotes from *CSAST, 1878*, 124; clipping, *San Francisco Post*, Oct. 12, 1877, Bancroft Scrapbooks, BL.

13. For the myth that the Chinese were driven out of the fields, see McWilliams, *Factories in the Field*, 77; Nee and Nee, *Longtime Californ'*, 52–54. A contrary view is in Chan, *Bittersweet Soil*, 77, 370–74; Eve Armentrout Ma, "Chinatown Organizations and the Anti-Chinese Movement, 1882–1914," in Sucheng Chan, ed., *Entry Denied: Exclusion and the Chinese Community in America* (Philadelphia, 1991), 165. For the Chinese exodus from the mining districts, see U.S. Dept. of Commerce, Bureau of the Census, *Tenth Census of the U.S. Population, 1880* (Washington, D.C., 1883), 51, 382, 565; *Twelfth Census of the U.S. Population, 1900* (Washington, D.C. 1902), 11, 75–80.

14. For typical tenant arrangements in Yuba County, see Edward Woodruff vs. North Bloomfield Mine Company et al., Circuit Court of the United States for the Ninth Circuit and the State of California, 1883 [briefs] 19; 7761–62, 7474–76 [a detailed portrait of Shanghai Bend truck gardens near Yuba City]; 21: 7462, 8471–72, 8497–99, 8646–47; 22: 9292, YCL/SCM; Chinese Account Book, December 1888, noting sixteen Chinese workers employed by Chinese tenants; Chinese Account Book, 1892, summarizing tenant arrangements, including crops grown, G. W. Patterson Ranch Records; George C. Roeding to Siu Look, Lease of Dec. 6, 1921, agreement for one year to raise truck crops on 9.218 acres at forty dollars an acre, California Nursery Records, Mission Peak Heritage Foundation Archives.

15. Leasing arrangements for peanuts, orchards, and strawberries in Sonoma are described in *St. Helena Star*, July 17, 1883. For Chinese field hands employed by Chinese tenants, see Colusa County Leases, Book A, 82, 162, Colusa County Recorder's Office; Sacramento County Leases, Book B, 95, Sacramento Museum and History Commission. For delta potato loaders, see MacMullen, *Paddle-Wheel Days*, 92–93.

16. Quote from *Ventura Signal*, Apr. 14, 1877, VCM. For a crew of thirty to forty Chinese hop pickers on Owen Tuttle's Pajaro Valley farm, see typed notes, *Watsonville Pajaronian*, Sept. 27, 1877, PVHS. For Chinese in the Santa Clara berry industry, see *PRP*, Apr. 14, 1877.

17. *Salinas Index*, Apr. 12, June 21, Aug. 9, 1877.

18. David Jacks lease with Sam Kee, Jan. 1877, David Jacks Collection, HL. Leases laid out very specific duties. Typically men had to have the land "perfectly clear of brush and trees and in good farming condition" within sixteen months. This involved more than merely chopping down trees, requiring men to "clear said land root and branch of all brush and trees." For this work, their bosses obtained the land rent-free during the following four years, and as usual, obtained rights to sell all of the firewood that field hands cut. Quote from Rafael Estrada lease with Jim Kee, Monterey County Leases, Book B, July 3, 1882: 572.

19. Bardin lease with Jim Sing, Monterey County Leases, Book C, Mar. 23, 1888: 167; David Jacks leases with O. Jim, A. Len, and Cong Sue Kee, Jan. 1885, Jacks Collection, HL.

20. Quote from Gibson, *Chinese in America*, 55. See also *San Francisco Post*, Oct. 12, 1877, reporting Chinese farmworkers in Alameda County receiving seventy-five cents per day; clipping, *The Argonaut*, Dec. 29, 1877, Horace Davis Scrapbooks, BL.

21. *Santa Cruz Sentinel*, Nov. 28, 1874; May 6, 1875; Oct. 14, 1876; *Salinas Index*, Nov. 15, 1877; typed notes, *Watsonville Pajaronian*, May 6, 1875; June 6, 1876, PVHS. For a typical contract, see the agreement between Ah Dong and John T. Porter, May 1879, John T. Porter Collection, CHS.

22. Quotes from typed notes, *Watsonville Pajaronian*, June 20, 1878, PVHS. See also Schwartz, *Seasonal Farm Labor*, 103–4. Perhaps someone had concluded by this time that long-handled hoes could not be employed among the thick sugar beet foliage, and that the only way to thin out unwanted plants and weeds was to squat down low to see what had to be chopped out. It is not clear whether or not the Chinese decided on their own to cut the handles off hoes, or if they were acting on suggestions from factory owners seeking greater efficiency, or some combination of the two. Whatever the reasons, it seems possible that sugar beet thinning may have been the first agricultural task to require farmworkers to use the short-handled hoe, that the tool may have been in use by the mid-1870s at Soquel, and that Chinese field hands could have been the first to experience its painful and crippling effects. There is no evidence that growers imposed the tool on the Chinese, or that any inhuman motives lurked behind its introduction. Eventually the short-handled hoe was employed in thinning asparagus, cabbage, and most other row crops. To use it, a field hand stooped over, twisted to one side, and faced across a row, chopping out unwanted plants and weeds and pulling them away with a free hand while sidestepping down a furrow. To best use the tool, men often had to crawl between the plants. This was as exhausting as it was threatening to their health. Beet thinners used short-handled hoes for eight hours a day, often on piece-rate, so much per row, for several months at a time. They worked in two or three cycles for each crop—early weeding, summer plant thinning, and a later combined thinning and weeding operation. See Agnes Benedict, "Barefoot Boy," *Survey* 58 (Apr. 15, 1927), 89–90; Marcia H. McClain, "The Distribution of Asparagus Production in the Sacramento-San Joaquin Delta" (M.A. thesis, UCB, 1954), 54–57. Short-handled–hoe work was so awful and debilitating, and had such a well-earned reputation for ruining backs and hips, tearing ligaments, rupturing discs, creating arthritic joints, and crippling workers early in life, that Mexican field hands would later call it "the man killer." Unable to pass a field of beets or lettuce without first thinking that someone had earlier tediously thinned the plants, farmworker organizers labeled the short-handled hoe an inhumane tool, symbolic of the dark ages of farm labor relations, evidence that farmers did not give a damn about their workers. Eventually the short-handled hoe would become a principal grievance of farmworker organizers and a major rallying cry among urban supporters, and they would succeed in banning it from the fields. But even while it was being used, as well as long after it had been banned, the tool would serve as a powerful symbol of oppression. See Jacques Levy, *Cesar Chavez: Autobiography of La Causa* (New York 1975), 73–76; *Stockton Record*, Apr. 1, 1971, SRCF; *San Francisco Chronicle*, May 4, July 14, 1973; *El Malcriado*, Jan. 13, 1975; various materials in short-handled-hoe file, California Rural Legal Assistance Field Office Archives,

Oceanside, Calif.; Ralph Abascal, interview by author, Jan. 12, 1991; Jose Padilla, interview by author, Jan. 12, 1991, San Francisco, author's possession.

23. Great Western Sugar Company, *Información Acerca del Trabajo y Sueldo de Betabeleros* (ca. 1920), ACSCR; John W. Mamer, "The Generation and Proliferation of Agricultural Hand-Labor Saving Technology; a Case Study in Sugar Beets" (Ph.D. diss., UCB, 1958), 22–29, 39, 51–55.

24. During the spring, China bosses swung into action. "CHINESE HELP FURNISHED," read one offer in the *St. Helena Star*. "San Sing, at Ginger's China Store, St. Helena, will furnish all kinds of help . . . at Yountville, Oakville, Rutherford, St. Helena, Calistoga, Pine Flat, or any of the surrounding country. Good at cheap prices." Quote from clipping, *St. Helena Star*, July 27, 1877, NVWL. For Kong Sam Kee, see Robert Louis Stevenson, *The Silverado Squatters* (New York, 1883 [1996]), 99–100. For the Chinese in Ventura County at this time, see *Ventura Signal*, Oct. 5, 1878, VCM.

25. Quote from *St. Helena Star*, Aug. 30, 1878. For the influx of Chinese, see ibid., June 7, 1878; "How Not to Do It," *Napa Register*, Apr. 29, 1878, NCLCF; clipping, *San Francisco Post*, May 10, 1878, Horace Davis Scrapbooks, BL.

26. Many Chinese also found work excavating wine cellars. As usual, their role would not be revealed until a tunnel collapsed or there was an accident. When this happened, the *St. Helena Star* would succinctly report how one Chinaman had been killed, and several injured, while digging this or that wine tunnel. The dead would not even rate obituaries. But while newspapers still tended to ignore the Chinese, tramp laborers did not. As the number of Chinese grew, so too did the efforts to have them removed. Shortly after a jury acquitted hoodlums of assaulting Chinese field hands in nearby Vallejo, white laborers in St. Helena formed a chapter of the Workingman's Party, and on June 7, Denis Kearney himself addressed them at a picnic. But after delivering his message that "the Chinese must go," he departed the valley, and hardly anything more was said on the issue. Wages at the Charles Krug winery are in *St. Helena Star*, Jan. 5, 1877. For the tunnel accident at Charles Lemme's winery just east of St. Helena on June 7, which killed one Chinese field hand and badly injured several others, see June 8, 1877. For the arrival of Chinese hop pickers from San Francisco, see Aug. 30, 1878. For Denis Kearney and anti-Chinese sentiments, see June 4, 1878; clipping, *San Francisco Post*, June 7, 1878, Horace Davis Scrapbooks, BL. For events in Vallejo, see *Vallejo Chronicle*, May 3, 1878. For Chinese diggers at Beringer Winery, see Sullivan, *Napa Wine*, 59–60. When Beringer Winery began excavating its wine cellar, the Chinese presumably handled much of the work; while no published documentation describes excavation work, it was considered such a well-established fact that a state historical landmark eventually commemorated their role. See State Historical Landmark at the winery. For the Beringer Winery, see *St. Helena Star*, Mar. 2, Aug. 31, 1877; Feb. 6, Oct. 4, 1878.

27. Quote from *Western Broker* cited in "Wine Making in California," *San Francisco Merchant* 17 (June 10, 1887), 53; "Napa Valley," *San Francisco Chronicle*, Oct. 15, 1883, Street Scrapbook, CSL.

28. Quote from H. Shewin, "Observations," *Overland Monthly* 7 (Jan. 1886), 97. For the comparison to mules, see *St. Helena Star*, Feb. 2, 1886. See also Marcia Wilcox, "Blue Gowns and Gold Hills," MS (Feb. 1951), Napa County Historical Society; Wait, *Wines and Vines*, 19. The Chinese stereotype is fully described in Edward Roberts, "California Wine-Making," *Harper's Weekly* 33 (Mar. 9, 1889), 197–200.

29. *St. Helena Star*, Aug. 30, 1878; Husmann, *Grape Culture and Wine-Making in California*, 217.

30. Quote from Thomas Hardy, "California Vineyards," *San Francisco Merchant*, Aug. 14, 1885, which reports "two old Chinamen" working in the cellar at Gundlach and Co. Winery, who, when questioned, replied "No savee."

31. Drawing, "The Vintage in California—At Work at the Wine Presses," *Harper's Weekly* 22 (Oct. 5, 1878), 77–78. In 1873, *Harper's* had commissioned Frenzeny and Jules Tavernier to illustrate scenes of the American West, and Frenzeny had spent most of 1874 traveling by railcar and working with Tavernier on a series of wood-block drawings that won such acclaim that he spent most of 1877 traveling with Buffalo Bill's Wild West Show. For Frenzeny, see Robert Taft, *Artists and Illustrators of the Old West, 1850–1900* (Princeton, N.J.: 1953), 115–16, 347; Patricia Trenton and Peter H. Hassrick, *The Rocky Mountains: A Vision for Artists in the Nineteenth Century* (Norman, Okla.: 1983), 243–47.

32. Hillside wineries worked as follows: Using gravity to send fermented juice flowing

down pipes from third-floor crushing rooms to second-floor fermenting rooms and first-floor aging cellars, "cellar rats" shoved debris, stems, and leaves along chutes from the conveyor dump site to pomace piles further down the hillside. For production information, see *Annual Report of the State Board of Viticultural Commissioners, 1887* (Sacramento, 1888), 18–20. For further details of harvesting, see sections in the valuable but overlooked Thomas Hardy, *Notes on the Vineyards of America and Europe* (Adelaide, Aust., 1885), American chapters reprinted in *Wines and Vines*, Sept. 1966–Sept. 1968. For hillside construction, see Wait, *Wines and Vines*, 21.

33. Quotes from "John Chinaman in the Wine Press," *San Francisco Call*, Oct. 14, 1878, Bancroft Scrapbooks, BL; *Sonoma County Tribune*, Sept. 20, 1891. When the editor of the *Cloverdale Reveille* learned that *Harper's Weekly* was planning another story on the valley, he reviewed the entire episode. See *Cloverdale Reveille*, May 20, 1882. Chinese field hands themselves never received any criticism. Wine industry spokesmen reserved most of their anger and strongest language for the artist who featured the Chinese in his drawing.

34. For arson at Grigsby's winery, see "Incendiarism," *St. Helena Star*, Nov. 15, 1878. After surviving the attacks at the Grigsby winery, Chinese field hands did not fare so well. They could not escape the anti-Chinese forces now building strength. Already the state had passed a law requiring Chinese bone pickers in cemeteries to receive permits from county health officials before they could exhume bones for shipment back to China; they also had to enclose remains in a metal casket, an expensive requirement, and pay a ten dollar fee. Entitled "An Act to Protect Public Health from Infection Caused by Exhumation and Removal of the Remains of Deceased Persons," the new law at least partially reflected a common belief that the practice of sending bones of dead field hands back home was yet another measure of the disdain the Chinese felt for California. But it had other goals as well. By further complicating the practice of shipping bones back home, opponents hoped to create an obstacle that might impede men from immigrating. See McGowan, *History of the Sacramento Valley*, 1: 326–27; "Taxing the Chinaman's Hope of Heaven," *San Francisco Evening Bulletin*, Mar. 9, 1878; *Debates and Proceedings of the Constitutional Convention of the State of California* (Sacramento, 1880–81), 1: 140; *Alta California*, Oct. 3, 1879.

35. Quotes from "Threatening Letters" and "Was Rape Intended," *Napa County Reporter*, Jan. 3, 1879; also Jan. 24, 1879. Desperate and hungry, the tramps had just taken to the road— had been forced to tramp, it was reported, because they had lost their jobs, were addicted to liquor, and could not find other work. Many were known as thieves; others fought with police and were arrested and jailed in every town they hit. Immediately the Napa press speculated that they were up to no good and were there to dislodge the Chinese and take their jobs. For Krug, see *St. Helena Star*, Oct. 3, 1879. See also "What Chinese Cheap Labor Means," *San Francisco Bulletin*, Nov. 22, 1878, Bancroft Scrapbooks, BL.

36. Quote from *Santa Cruz Sentinel*, Mar. 15, 1879. For comparison of Chinese field hands to black slaves, see *San Francisco Chronicle*, Mar. 6, 1879. For fights between farmers and tramps, see Clough and Secrest, *Fresno County*, 1: 139. For distrust and dislike of tramp field hands as "anything but reliable," see *PRP*, Apr. 19, 1879. With tramps overrunning rural districts, many farmers feared that they might have to actually employ tramps in place of the far more reliable and peaceable Chinese. But most remained adamantly opposed to the anti-Chinese movement. When Denis Kearney made a stop in Santa Ana and insulted locals for hiring Chinese, several farmers sent hefty foremen to pay Kearney a visit, and Kearney made a hasty retreat.

37. Quote from *Colusa Sun*, Oct. 24, 1879. See also *St. Helena Star*, Aug. 15, 1879; Elmer C. Sandmeyer, *The Anti-Chinese Movement in California* (Urbana, Ill., 1939), 68–73. Of 2,346 votes in Monterey County, only one favored continued Chinese immigration.

38. Quote from clipping, *San Francisco Bulletin*, Aug. 18, 1880, Bancroft Scrapbooks, BL. Quantitative analysis of the Chinese in Santa Clara Township, Santa Clara County, from 1880 MS Census, Santa Clara County; *Statistics of the Population of the United States, Tenth Census, 1880*, 382; *Tenth Census: Report on the Production of Agriculture*, 34–35.

39. Quote from *Pen Pictures from the Garden of the World, or Santa Clara County*, 183. See also Gibson, *Chinese in America*, 57, 98. For the stereotype of Chinese docility, see Daniel, *Bitter Harvest*, 27–28.

40. Statistical information from Taylor and Vasey, "Historical Background of California Farm Labor," 284; Lloyd H. Fisher, "The Harvest Labor Market in California," *Quarterly Journal of Economics* 65 (Nov. 1951), 392–415.

41. Unidentified newspaper clippings, Yolo County Archives; Edward J. Wickson, *Califor-

nia Illustrated: Vacaville Early Fruit District (San Francisco, 1888), 16, 23, figs. 2333, 2356, 2388; W. R. Nutting, "Peach Gathering, Henry Bassford's Orchard," photograph, in H. R. Nutting Collection, VM.

42. Quantitative analysis for Sacramento, San Joaquin, Colusa, Yuba, and Solano counties from 1880 MS Census; Chiu, *Chinese Labor*, 76. For Napa and Sonoma, see Chinn, Lai, and Choy, *A History of the Chinese in California*, 21. For Fresno County, see "Recapitulation for California," *Directory of Grape Growers, Wine Makers* (Fresno, 1891). See also McGowan, *History of the Sacramento Valley*, 1: 244. In the Napa Valley, Chinese field hands apparently were expendable enough to be employed on some of the first crews spraying an extremely toxic chemical, carbon bisulfide, to combat a phylloxera infestation in vineyards just north of St. Helena. For Napa, see Heintz, *Wine Country*, 165. For Chinese moving from land clearing into binding wheat in the Salinas Valley, see *Santa Cruz Sentinel*, July 24, 1880. For Southern California, see Juan Bandini, diary, 1: Mar. 5, Apr. 25, 1880, trans. Margaret Gaffey Mel, HL; Walter C. Allen, diaries, Jan. 24; July 10, 26, 28, 29, 31; Aug. 3, 4, 5, 6, 7; Oct. 25, 29, 30; Nov. 23, 24, 25; Dec. 4, 6, 8, 9, 10, 11, 15, 18, 20, 21, 22, 23, 1880, Walter Allen Papers, HL. In the southern San Joaquin Valley around Bakersfield, the Chinese dominated the unpleasant task of cleaning irrigation canals. For Bakersfield canal cleaners, see Time Book for Wages, July–Sept. 1880, China labor; Wages, Canal Excavation and Cleaning, East Ditch, West Side Ditch, Jewett Farm and Cotton Ranch, July–Sept. 1880, FFLCSF.

43. *St. Helena Star*, Sept. 3, 24, 1880.

44. Quote from Woodruff et al. v. North Bloomfield, 19: 7462; also 7761–62; 21: 84976–79, for land clearing, canal building, and farmwork near Marysville.

45. William H. Nicholson, daily journal [June?], 1888, HL; J. E. Pleasants, *History of Orange County* (Los Angeles, 1902), 2: 84. Prices ranged widely. For example, dried apricots sold on the Los Angeles market varied from four and one-half cents per pound in the 1890s to almost fourteen cents per pound in 1906. See *Whittier Register*, June 30, 1899; *Fullerton Tribune*, Mar. 24, 1899; Earl C. May, *The Canning Clan: A Pageant of Pioneering Americans* (New York, 1937), 197–204, 223–39; Isador Jacobs, "Relations Between Fruit Grower and Canner," *CSFGCP, 1906*, 250–51. Within a few years of their entry into fruit drying, Chinese field hands acquired a reputation as superior workers. Sitting at long tables in the shade of some palm thatching or canvas, they would receive their supply of apricots and plums and lay them out in piles. Using a special cot-knife or plum-knife with a wide, slanting blade that came to a sharp point at the end of a half-moon cut in the center of the blade, they picked up the fruit in one hand, cupped it between thumb and forefinger, fit the half-moon-shaped blade into the stem end of the cot, made a swift, semicircular cut, then turned the fruit, slid the pit through and into a can, then placed the fruit faceup on a redwood tray, the rows barely touching but never overlapping. If the fruit was mushy or overripe, men did not use their knives and simply pushed the pit out the bottom. On some farms they left the fruit to dry in the sun, but when consumers balked at the sight of the product, farmers introduced artificial fruit dryers. Stacking the cut fruit over a pit or "sulfur house" filled with powdered sulfur, the Chinese then lit the sulfur, and after "bleaching" the fruit, removed it, and placed it out in the sun to dry over three to seven days. They then culled out any darkened fruit, sorted it, and covered it with fine canvas. Heaping it into piles, they would later turn it and allow it to "sweat" for ten days to two weeks, until the fruit was pliable and ready for market. See *Fullerton Tribune*, June 9, 1894; July 24, 1902.

46. Quote from clipping, *PRP*, July 30, 1881, Horace Davis Scrapbooks, BL. "The Chinaman comes to the ranch when he is wanted, does the work required, and then disappears from the district and gives no trouble. From the standpoint of capitalism, this is, of course, ideal. The laborer is a perfect machine." Quote from Sidney L. Gulick, *The American Japanese Problem* (New York, 1914), 36. See also G. H. Hecke, "The Pacific Coast Labor Question from the Standpoint of a Horticulturalist," *Thirty-Third CSFGCP, 1907*, 68–69; Chan, *Bittersweet Soil*, 159; Donald Pflueger, *Glendora, The Annals of a Southern California Community* (Los Angeles, 1951), 122; Henry M. Page, *Pasadena, Its Early Years* (Pasadena, 1964), 66; Arthur T. Johnson, *California, An Englishman's Impressions of the Golden State* (London, 1913), 206.

47. Quotes from Walter C. Allen, diaries, Jan. 4, 6, 8, 13, 15; Feb. 5, 1881; Mar. 15, 18, 21; July 7, 8; Oct. 22; Dec. 2, 9, 11, 1881. See also Jan. 1, 10, 11, 13, 28, 29, 31; Feb. 3, 4, 14, 16, 17; Mar. 14, 17, 18, 26, 29, 30, 31; Apr. 1, 2, 5, 7, 15, 16, 25, 30, Walter Allen Papers, HL.

48. For kinship migration to Chinese tenant farms, see Jessie Juliet Knox, "A Chinese Horace Greeley," *Oakland Tribune Magazine*, Dec. 3, 1912; newspaper clippings, miscellaneous ma-

terials, and family records, Chew Family Papers, in possession of Miss Mansie Condit Chew, Oakland, courtesy William Heintz. The Anaheim incident is described in *Anaheim Gazette*, Dec. 10, 1881.

49. Arthur Amos, "Hop Growing on the Pacific Cost of America," pts. 1–4, *Journal of the Board of Agriculture* 19 (May, June, July, Aug. 1912), 89–98, 187–95, 293–300, 378–88; Flint, "Hops," CSAS, *Report, 1905* (Sacramento, 1906), 60–62; Hubert Parker, *The Hop Industry* (London, 1934), 79–82; *PRP*, June 3, July 8, 1882. Crop failures in England and Germany sent the price of hops up from fifteen to forty-five cents per pound to $1.10. For hop pickers, see Daniel Flint, "Hop Culture in California," *PRP*, June 1881, Scheter Files, ILWUL. For hops, see Sonoma County Leases, Book D, 284. For specifics of hop production on a 580–acre farm run by Ah Wing and Hong Tong Vey in Suisun Township, Solano County, see "Census of Productions of Agriculture," 1880 MS Census, Solano County.

50. Quote from Calhoun "Cal" Collins, *The McKittrick Ranch* (Bakersfield, 1958), 59; also 60–63.

51. Quote from Collins, *McKittrick Ranch*, 59. See also Watkins, "Irrigating on Panama Ranch" [Watkins no. 402]; "Jackson Ranch: Irrigating Alfalfa from the Ditch to the Check," [Watkins no. 663]; "Jackson Ranch: Irrigating Alfalfa; Filling a Check," [Watkins no. 662] Photographic Views of Kern County, California, Tenneco West Archives, Bakersfield. A few irrigators worked entirely on their own, stoking and tending steam-powered, coal-fired pumps that ran day and night pumping water at the McClung ranch headquarters. See Watkins, "Boiler Tender—McClung Ranch," [Watkins no. 618]; "Kern Island Dairy: Dairy House," [Watkins no 183] Photographic Views of Kern County, California, LC. Taking great pride in their work and shouldering considerable responsibilities, they were hardly the cheap and docile laborers of popular history folklore. See also Hugh Jewett, "Reminiscences: Yellow Sam," BL; Bishop, *Old Mexico and Her Lost Provinces*, 408.

52. Watkins Albums, James ranch [Watkins no. 322], Alfalfa Equipment; Lakeside Ranch [Watkins no. 108], Alfalfa Mowing; Stockdale Ranch [Watkins no. 48] Chinese Alfalfa Stacking; Bellvue Ranch [Watkins no. 18] Chinese Stackers and Derrick; Collins ranch [Watkins no. 221], LC; George G. Carry to Alex Mills, July 26; Nov. 24, 28, 1888, Miller and Lux Correspondence, FFLCSF. See also *History of Kern County*, 112.

53. Quote from Flint, "Hop Culture." See also *Salinas Index*, June 23, 1881, praising Chinese field hands because they did "not get drunk and leave their employers in the lurch."

54. Quotes from clippings, *PRP*, July 30; J. W. Gally to editor, Dec. 10, 1881 ["teat"]; Judge W. C. Blackwood, "Our Fruit Interests and the Labor Question," Dec. 24, 1881, Scheter File, ILWUL.

55. *St. Helena Star*, Dec. 12, 13, 1881; Jan. 12, 1882; *Napa County Register*, Mar. 10, Apr. 21, Oct. 13, 1882, NCLCF; *St. Helena Star*, Mar. 11, 1882. The Occidental Winery "cellar rats" were not the only Chinese who resorted to violence. Two sensational murder cases had occurred in 1878. On Aug. 2, Ah Chow, a Chinese field hand, murdered an Italian and dumped his body in the Sacramento River near Grime's Landing. Ah Chow was quickly arrested. On October 21, a Chinese field hand named Lang killed a sheepherder named John Maginley on Brim's ranch, near Freshwater. "The Chinaman first tried to use a hatchet on his victim, but was prevented by by-standers," reported the *Colusa Sun*. "He finally succeeded in plunging a knife into the heart of Maginley. The murderer then fled." In neither case did the newspapers provide any explanation for the violence. See Rogers, *Colusa County*, 168–69. Such cases made growers especially nervous as other Chinese confronted growers over wages, dickered over working conditions, and bargained over the terms of their employment throughout the winter and well into spring. Although none resorted to murder or violence, their conduct was such that growers now became convinced that they were up to no good, and that they were intent on taking advantage of the growing shortage of labor.

56. Quotes from *St. Helena Star*, Mar. 31, 1882; McGowan, *History of the Sacramento Valley*, 1: 327. For conflicts, see Walter S. Allen, diary, Mar. 9, 1882, Walter Allen Papers, HL. For a shortage of men, see *Weekly Calistogian*, Feb. 10, 1882.

57. This was Wing's last act of defiance in 1882. Nothing more was noted of the case until Jan. 2, 1891, when the *San Francisco Chronicle* reported that Wong Ah Wing, confined at San Quentin for a twenty-two-year term, was found dead in his cell, apparently of epilepsy. See *San Francisco Chronicle*, Jan. 2, 1891; *St. Helena Star*, Jan. 3, 1891.

58. *Congressional Record*, 47th Cong., 1st sess. (1882), 2551–52; memorandum, Apr. 1, 1882, in

Notes from the Chinese Legation in the United States to the Department of State, 1868–1906 (microfilm, reel 1), NA; David L. Anderson, "The Diplomacy of Discrimination: Chinese Exclusion, 1876–1882," *CH* 57 (spring 1978), 44; Rogers, *Colusa County*, 190.

59. Quotes from act of May 6, 1882, Sections 4, 12, 15, *United States Statutes at Large*. See also *St. Helena Star*, Apr. 21, May 19, 1882; Roderick D. McKenzie, *Oriental Exclusion: The Effect of American Immigration Laws, Regulations, and Judicial Decisions Upon the Chinese and Japanese on the American Pacific Coast* (Chicago, 1928); Note from the Chinese Legation in Washington to the Secretary of State, June 18, 1882, in *Notes from the Chinese Legation*. See also Lucy E. Salyer, *Laws Harsh as Tigers: Chinese Immigrants and the Shaping of Modern Immigration Law* (Chapel Hill, N.C., 1995).

60. Quote from *St. Helena Star*, Sept. 24, 1882. For the *City of Sydney* incident, see Petition for Habeas Corpus, In re: Ah Tie, no. 2876, Old Circuit Court, Civil Cases, Common Law Series, RG 21, FARCSB; *San Francisco Morning Call*, Aug. 19, 1882. For the reaction of anti-Chinese organizations, see Ira B. Cross, ed., *Frank Rooney, Irish Rebel and California Labor Leader* (Berkeley, 1931), 360, 384, 460, 526–36. A few Chinese even went so far as to call for retaliation against the United States.

61. Quotes from Jones, *Vines in the Sun*, 5; *PRP*, Sept. 9, 1882. For predictions, see *Napa Register*, Oct. 5, 1883. See also *St. Helena Star*, Aug. 5, 1882; Rose Hum Lee, *The Chinese in the United States of America* (Hong Kong, 1960), 22. Modern farmers would uncritically accept this version of events, and one of them, a grape grower near Calistoga in the Napa Valley, would supply the popular wine writer Idwal Jones with one of the more colorful and enduring stories about the aftermath of the new law. Recalling the so-called exodus of Chinese from his father's vineyard, he told Jones: "It was a dark night, and I stood by the gate of the farm, watching them go by, on foot, on horseback, some riding in laden wagons, others pushing hand carts; and the parade was lighted by lanterns at the end of poles . . . We were all sad at their going." Quote from Jones, *Vines in the Sun*, 5. Scholars have also asserted that the new law "involuntarily weaned" growers from the "Chinese teat," which supplied "more than 50 percent of the agricultural labor force in California and as much as 75 percent of the specialty-crop workers." Quotes from Monroy, *Thrown Among Strangers*, 251; R. Douglas Hurt, *American Agriculture: A Brief History* (Ames, Iowa, 1994), 186.

62. Sandmeyer, *Anti-Chinese Movement in California*, 96; Stuart Creighton Miller, *The Unwelcome Immigrant: The American Image of the Chinese, 1785–1882* (Berkeley and Los Angeles, 1969), 3. Admissions dropped to 8,031 in 1883, and 4,009 in 1884. Between 1881 and 1890, 61,711 Chinese were admitted to the United States, and another 14,799 between 1891 and 1900. See Lee, *Chinese in the United States*, 22; *San Francisco Post*, Apr. 22, 1882; Christian G. Fritz, "A Nineteenth-Century 'Habeas Corpus Mill': The Chinese before the Federal Courts in California," *American Journal of Legal History* 32 (fall 1988), 347–72.

63. *San Francisco Evening Bulletin*, Oct. 29, 1883; Peter C. Leung, "When A Haircut was a Luxury: A Chinese Farm Laborer in the Sacramento Delta," *CH* 64 (summer 1985), 212.

64. Quote from *PRP*, Nov. 18, 1882. For Chinese working for fruit merchants, see Aug. 26, 1882. For hop picking, see Sept. 9, 1882. For land clearing in Napa, see *Weekly Calistogian*, Feb. 10, 1882. For the Berryessa Valley, see *Napa Register*, Jan. 22, 1883.

65. For general developments in the wine industry, see Carosso, *California Wine Industry*, 143–44; *First Annual Report of the Board of State Viticultural Commissioners* (Sacramento, 1881), 9. For Napa and Sonoma, see *St. Helena Star*, Apr. 2, 1880; Aug. 24, 1884; *Russian River Flag*, Feb. 26, 1880. Planting figures from the *Healdsburg Enterprise*, Jan. 26, 1882, claim two hundred million acres of vines were planted between 1880 and 1882. But this is obviously a typographical error. For the state's largest wine-making operation, James DeBarth Shorb's fifteen-million-gallon Los Angeles winery, see Shorb to Sen. William M. Gwin, Sept. 20, 1881; Shorb to Evan J. Coleman, Oct. 25, 1881, JDBSP.

66. Quote from *San Francisco Chronicle*, Oct. 2, 1883. For Chinese blackberry pickers, see *Napa Register*, July 24, 1883. For Chinese arriving for spring planting, see *St. Helena Star*, Mar. 23, 1883. For Chinese in the grape harvest, see Sept. 29, 1883. For Chinese at the Charles Krug winery, see Oct. 19, 1883.

67. Planting figures from Charles Wetmore, *Second Annual Report of the Chief Viticultural Officer of the State Viticultural Commissioners of California, 1885* (Sacramento, 1885), 42. Because men working on the one-hundred-thousand-acre Joseph Cone ranch east of Red Bluff were so far away from farm headquarters, they frequently deviated from their normal pattern of feeding

and housing themselves and instead received all the required tools, animals, and food from farmers. As usual, the amount of their pay for such work was fixed on a piece-rate basis. A China boss would bid on a project, estimating so much per acre. At about a penny per running foot for wall construction, Chinese gangs had to work long hours to make ends meet. Many lived in tents besides the walls they were building, moving on as they completed sections. But after completing their walls, the men did not move on. About one hundred found permanent work as cooks, field hands, and wood choppers on the Cone ranch, where they also raised vegetables and sold them to whites. Another five hundred were employed on the ranch during the harvest season. For Chinese land clearing and farm labor in the northern Sacramento Valley, see Steve Muir, "Joseph Cone in Tehama," MS (1970), 23; Gary Burchfield, "Cone Ranch," MS (1969), 14; Curtis Wolfe, "The Chinese Rock Walls of Tehama County," MS (1969), Tehama Public Library; Curtis Wolfe and Steve Grootveld, "The Chinese Rock Walls of Tehama County," *Wagon Wheels* 22 (Feb. 1972), 6–9.

68. Karen Lea Reed, "The Chinese of Tehama County, 1866–1900, with Particular Attention to the anti-Chinese Sentiment" (M.A. thesis, CSUC, 1977), 52; Rogers, *Colusa County*, 199; Darrell Conard, "Big Steer Tells About Old Cow Outfits: Cattle Industry Did Not Really Develop Here Till After 1900," *Red Bluff Daily News*, n.d., in Henry Albert Schafer Scrapbook, Tehama Public Library.

69. Quote from Joaquin Miller, *Sacramento Record-Union*, July 3, 1886; also June 5, 1875. A good overview is Fern Hill, "Vina," *Chico Enterprise-Record*, Feb. 16, 1948. The structure of the Vina Chinatown can be gleaned from bill of sale, "Miscellaneous Records," Book F, 63, Tehama County Recorder's Office, Red Bluff. The sales transactions are in "Deeds," Book R, 132–37. Various aspects of the Gerke ranch are described in E. J. Lewis, *History of Tehama County* (San Francisco, 1880), 25–26.

70. *Memorial and Biographical History of Northern California* (Chicago, 1891) 268; Bancroft, *History of the Life of Leland Stanford* (Oakland, 1952), 147–51; Meyer, interview; Larry E. Moulton, "The Vina District, Tehama County, California: Evolution of Land Utilization in a Small Segment of the Middle Sacramento Valley" (M.A. thesis, CSUC, 1969), 1–29.

71. Quote from Francis Leninger, interview by author, Vina, Sept. 22, 1979; Pinky O'Brien, interview by author, Vina, Nov. 2, 1972, author's possession; notes taken by Father Anselm during an interview with Colonel F. T. Robson June 1955, both in Vina Archives, Our Lady of New Clairvaux Monastery, Vina.

72. After China bosses concluded a deal to supply Vina foremen with most of their field hands, 230 "rather industrious" Chinese men marched into the scrub brush and pine stands and in January 1872 began hacking clear a one-thousand-acre swath of land. *Sacramento Record-Union*, Jan. 27, 1882, Stanford Family Scrapbooks, SUASC.

73. From these quarters they commuted to the ranch each morning at 5:30 A.M. Assembling on the main street, they would climb into wagons for the short ride to work. But many simply walked to the ranch or rode bicycles. Frank Carpenter, "Carpenter's Letter, A Visit to Senator Stanford's Great Ranch in Northern California and a Look at Its Wonders," *Cleveland World* [May 1893], Stanford Family Scrapbooks, SUASC.

74. The French were housed in two-story bunkhouses complete with large porches and balconies where they retained their own native language and customs and lived much as they had in the Old World. See John S. Hittell, *The Commerce and Industries of the Pacific* (San Francisco, 1882), 244; Bancroft, "Leland Stanford," MS (1877), 374, BL; Rose, *L. J. Rose of Sunny Slope*, 105; Joseph E. McConnell, "The Stanford Vina Ranch" (M.A. thesis, Stanford University, 1961), 14–20, 33. Sources differ as to the number of European workers but generally agree that there were between fifty and seventy in residence.

75. *Sacramento Record-Union*, Jan. 27, 1882; *Red Bluff Sentinel*, Dec. 25, 1883; Elizabeth Gregg, "The History of the Famous Stanford Ranch at Vina, California," *Overland Monthly* 52 (Oct. 1908), 336–37.

76. Clippings, *Sacramento Record-Union*, Mar. 25, 1882; Apr. 1, 1887, Stanford Family Scrapbooks, SUASC; *Red Bluff Sentinel*, Dec. 25, 1883; *San Francisco Examiner*, Apr. 6, 1890.

77. Leninger, interview; *Napa County Register*, Oct. 5, 1883; *Ranch Field Fireside*, Nov. 1, 1884; Thomas W. Chinn, ed., *Bulletin of the Chinese Historical Society of America* 7 (Apr. 1972), 6–7.

78. Husmann, *Grape Culture and Wine-Making in California*, 216–17, 226–27. The strike is reported in "Natomas Vineyards," *Napa County Register*, Oct. 5, 1883, NCLCF.

79. Quote from *Napa Register*, June 22, 1883. See also Oct. 5, 1883.

80. Walter Allen, diaries, Apr. 9, May 11, 1883. Also Jan. 31; Feb. 1, 26, 27, 28; Apr. 9, 12; May 10, 11, 12, 21, 22, 23, 24, 25, 26, 28, 29, 30, 31; June 1, 11, 12, 13, 14, 25, 16, 18, 19, 20, 21, 22, 23; July 16, 17, 18, 19, 20, 30, 31; Aug. 1, 2, 3, 4, 20, 21, 22, 23, 24, 25, 27, 28, 29, 30, 31, Walter Allen Papers, HL.

CHAPTER FIFTEEN

1. Quote from Braly, *Memory Pictures*, 151. Chinese field hands had done this eleven years earlier, when twenty of them moved into the Francis T. Eisen vineyards and spent six weeks hand-picking larvae from the vines and stomping them under foot, thereby saving Eisen's crop and, some said, also saving the raisin industry in its infancy. See Wallace Elliot, *History of Fresno County, California, with Illustrations* (San Francisco, 1882), 211; Vandor, *History of Fresno County with Biographical Sketches*, 1: 190–91; John Steven McGroarty, *Fresno County California* (Fresno, 1916), Pamphlets Collection, BL.

2. Braly, *Memory Pictures*, 149–52.

3. George Thompson to *Marysville Appeal*, Feb. 11, 1911; Ernest E. Sowell, "Purple Gold: The Birth of California's Thompson Seedless Grape and Raisin Industry," MS (n.d.), William Thompson Collection, Memorial Museum of Sutter County, Yuba City; Snell, "Viticulture in California from 1870 to 1900," 6–79.

4. Refusing to bleach his raisins, as did other growers seeking high prices, Onstott sold his raisins to the eastern market for seven and a half cents a pound and his operation grew rapidly in size. See Carol Withington, "The Thompson Seedless," *Sutter County Historical Society News Bulletin* 19 (Jan. 1980), 11–23; Peter Delay, *History of Yuba and Sutter Counties* (Los Angeles, 1924), 371–72, 388, 393.

5. "The Goodman Vineyard," *Fresno Republican*, June 28, 1884; *Imperial Fresno: Resources, Industries, and Scenery, Illustrated and Described* (Fresno, 1897), 13–15; Charles C. Colby, "The California Raisin Industry—A Study on Geographical Interpretation," *Annals of the Association of American Geographers* 14 (June 1924), 49–108. For packing sheds see, H. E. Jacob and J. R. Herman, "Harvesting and Packing Grapes in California," University of California, College of Agriculture *Bulletin No. 390* (Berkeley, 1925), 11–12, 24. Climate information from U.S. Dept. of Agriculture, *Weather Bureau, Climate Summary of the United States: Section 17—Central California* (Washington, D.C., 1934), 17. Despite Fresno's boom, the largest raisin vineyard in California in 1882 was owned by R. B. Blowers and Sons of Woodland. See ledger, June 1900, R. B. Blowers and Sons Papers, BL.

6. Quote from *Fresno Weekly Republican*, n.d., BWC. Not all of the colonies survived. Buying up 240 acres of Washington Colony, William Hall established the Montecito Vineyard, turned over operations to his wife, and promptly retired to San Francisco. See also Virginia Thickens, "Pioneer Agricultural Colonies of Fresno County," *CHSQ* 25 (Mar.–June 1946), 175; Frank Pixley, "An Idyl of the Tulare Lake Land," in *Secure a 20-Acre Home in the Tulare County* (San Francisco, 1885), 32; H. S. Drake, *Lindsay-Strathmore Land Development Directory* (Lindsay, Calif., 1929); Arthur Maas and Raymond L. Anderson, *And the Desert Shall Rejoice: Conflict, Growth, and Justice in Arid Environments* (Cambridge, Mass., 1978), 157; C. A. Rohrabacher, *Fresno County, California: A Descriptive, Statistical and Biographical* (Fresno, 1890), 47–48, 61–62; *Fresno County, California, Its Offering for Settlement* (San Francisco, 1886), FCHS; A. B. Butler, "California and Spain," *California—A Journal of Rural Industry* 3 (Mar. 15, 1890); clipping, *Fresno Expositor*, n.d., FCHS. A common calculation held that a twenty-acre vineyard of raisins would yield about four thousand boxes, each weighing twenty pounds. With prices ranging from two to three dollars per box for the twenty-year period between 1783 and 1893, a grower could gross between eight thousand and twelve thousand dollars. With cultivation costs (labor, taxes, insecticides, etc.) at about eighteen hundred dollars per acre, an enterprising farmer could expect a net profit of $6,200 to $10,200 for the harvest. With yields increasing year after year, prospective raisin growers saw a bright and profitable future. My hypothetical calculations are based on common assumptions at the time and are designed to identify the entrepreneurial mind-set of people going into the raisin business. Picking, packing, and marketing generally ran forty to fifty dollars per ton; a typical grape crop produced about two tons per acre. See *Fresno County, California—Where Can Be Found Climate, Soil, and Water, the Only Sure Combination for the Vineyardist* (San Francisco, 1887), 65, 71, BL. For at least twenty years, industry leaders like Gustav Eisen claimed that profits of $200 to $250 per acre were common on the smaller vineyards.

7. Generally a farmer purchased land for a 25-percent down payment, with the remainder payable over three years at an 8-percent interest rate. While some farmers got through the lean years by intercropping vegetables (planting between the young vines) and supplementing their diets with a few chickens, cows, rabbits, and other animals, many raisin farmers lacked the capital necessary even for that meager program. They survived the early years by hiring themselves out as farmworkers. Faced with these challenges, hard work only went so far. Long before the first harvest, labor costs mounted. Even the smallest raisin growers could not plant and prune their vineyards by themselves. On a hypothetical twenty-acre vineyard, periods of intense activity requiring massed, gang labor followed by periods of inactivity. During January and February workers had to prune the grapevines, carefully selecting which canes (long wooded shoots) to lop off, which to keep, and which to cut short as spurs. Small crews did the work, gathering up the huge piles of canes, burning them, and then plowing the ash into the ground when they had finished. During March field hands had to begin irrigating. To protect the grapes from mildew, crews periodically sprayed the vines with sulfur dust. Using portable backpacks with a kind of bellows blower operated by flapping one arm on the bellows lever, and using the free hand to direct a spray hose toward the grapevine, sulfur dusting was a truly odious business, always commenced early in the morning before any breeze kicked up; at the end of the day men left the vineyards with watery eyes and running noses, covered head to foot in the yellow, itchy dust. See E. J. Wickson, *California Fruits and How to Grow Them: A Manual of Methods Which Have Yielded Greatest Success, with the List of Varieties Best Adapted to the Different Districts of the State* (San Francisco, 1912), 355–69; Gustav Eisen, *The Raisin Industry: A Practical Treatise on the Raisin Grapes, Their History, Culture and Curing* (San Francisco, 1890), 170–80; *PRP*, June 3, 1871; Aug. 27, 1892; C. F. Dowsett, *A Start in Life: A Journey Across America. Fruit Farming in California* (London, 1891), 83–93; Timothy Paige, *Farming That Pays* (San Francisco, 1891), 11, Beinecke Library, Yale University; Thomas Forsyth Hunt, "Suggestions to the Settler in California," University of California College of Agriculture Agricultural Experiment Station *Circular No. 210* (Mar. 1919), 4–5; Thomas Forsyth Hunt, *How Can a Young Man Become a Farmer?* (paper presented at the San Jose Meeting of the Patrons of Husbandry of California, Oct. 21, 1913), BL; Charles Colson, diary, Sept. 30, 1878, Charles Colson Collection, HL.

8. With mature vines averaging five to six tons per acre or more, but occasionally yielding up to thirteen tons, a husband and wife could, through diligent, dawn-to-dusk work, harvest between fifty and one hundred trays of grapes and lay them on trays in the sun to dry. A man and wife harvesting two thousand pounds of grapes per day would require about three months to harvest the crop. They would then have to return to the vine rows and turn every tray, wait another ten days, and then finally load all of the dried grapes into field boxes and haul them to their sheds. See Eisen, *Raisin Industry*, 180; Albert J. Winkler, *General Viticulture* (Berkeley, 1974), 192, 612; Earl Pomeroy, *The Pacific Slope: A History of California, Oregon, Washington, Idaho, Utah, and Nevada* (New York, 1965), 171; *Fresno County, California—Where Can Be Found Climate, Soil, and Water, the Only Sure Combination for the Vineyardist* (San Francisco, 1887), BL.

9. For the early Chinese, see *Fresno Weekly Evening Expositor*, Dec. 25, 1895, Fresno County Scrapbook, 1: 253–5; Aug. 19, 1891, ibid., 1: 163, describing Sing Long Chung Kan Kee Company; May 14, 1873; Mar. 8, 1876, ibid., 1: 3–4, SCHMLCSUF; Moses J. Church, "Irrigation in the San Joaquin Valley," dictation material, May 3, 1883, 7–8, BL; C. E. Grunsky, "Water Appropriation from Kings River," in U.S. Dept. of Agriculture, Office of Experiment Stations, *Report of Irrigation Investigations in California*, Bulletin no. 100 (Washington, D.C., 1901), 259–325; June English, "Leaves From the Past: Chinese Pioneers of Fresno County," *Ash Tree Echo* 8 (Jan. 1973), 20–37. Chinese had also planted thousands of fruit trees and grapevines and established a thriving truck farming business. For vineyard work, see Edith C. Meyer, "The Development of the Raisin Industry in Fresno County, California" (M.A. thesis, UCB, 1931), 53. Raisin production went from eighty thousand pounds in 1882 to eight hundred thousand in 1884, and reached seven million pounds in 1887. For pruning, see Frank H. Ball, "My Work in the Raisin Vineyard," *California, A Journal of Rural Industry* 2 (July 1890), 12; Franklin P. Nutting, interview, 1955, ROHP, 7. For one Chinese field hand employed year-round on a twenty-acre colony vineyard, see C. C. Smith, testimony to the Fresno Board of Trade, Nov. 23, 1887, in M. Theo Kearney, *Fresno County, California: The Land of Sunshine, Fruits, and Flowers* (Fresno, 1893), 15.

10. Rohrabacher, *Fresno County*, 47–48; Eisen, "The Raisin Industry of Fresno," *California —A Journal of Rural Industry* 1 (Feb. 1890), 1–8.

11. Clippings, *Fresno Weekly Expositor*, n.d., FCHS; *Stockton Daily Evening Herald*, n.d., Bancroft Scrapbooks, BL; Bishop, *Old Mexico and Her Lost Provinces*, 392–94.

12. Often workers stacked trays by the "roof" method. Rather than placing one tray on top of another, they created two piles of trays, each about three feet high, with empty trays between full ones to admit plenty of air. Ball, "My Work in the Raisin Vineyard," 12; T. C. White, interview, in *Fresno Weekly Evening Expositor*, May 19, 1892, Fresno County Scrapbooks, 1: 196–99, SCHMLCSUF; White, "Raisin Drying, Packing, and Preparing for the Market," in Board of State Viticultural Commissioners of California, *Report of the Sixth Annual State Viticultural Convention, Mar. 7–10, 1888* (Sacramento, 1888), 17–34; White, "The Raisin Grape," *Proceedings of the Twelfth California State Fruit Growers Convention, Nov. 5–8, 1889*, in State Board of Horticulture, *Annual Report for 1889* (Sacramento, 1890), 433.

13. Eisen, *The Raisin Industry*, 142, 148, 180, 186. Eisen reports that a good picker could fill fifty trays each day, and that most crews could usually turn twenty acres of grapes per day. However, he does not specify how many men worked in an average tray turning crew. See also Mary F. Austin, "Raisin Making," *Fresno Republican Directory, 1881* (Fresno, 1881), FCHS.

14. Quote from "A Word on Vineyard Labor," *Fresno Republican*, Nov. 4, 1883. The strike is described in "Viticultural Notes," *Napa County Register*, Oct. 5, 1883, NCLCF.

15. Quote from William Henry Pinckney, interview by Richard C. Bailey, Oct. 1951, Bakersfield, in W. Harland Boyd, John Ludeke, and Marjorie Rump, eds., *Inside Historic Kern: Selections from the Kern County Historical Society's Quarterly, 1949–1981* (Bakersfield, 1982), 126. Offering a piece of advice that gained absolutely no support, the newly elected president of the California State Agricultural Society called upon farmers to encourage their sons to become farmworkers. Although the record does not specify how the society responded, it is likely that it was with befuddlement. Other than to fill in at an odd spot or as a way to learn the business, no farmer wanted his sons working in the fields. See Hugh LaRue, "Opening Address," *CSAST, 1882*, 20.

16. Quote from Pinckney, interview. See also Melton McClanahan, "Early Negro Settlers," ibid., 123; CSBLS, *First Biennial Report, 1883–84*, 22; Wallace Morgan, *History of Kern County* (San Francisco, 1884), 93; Eugene W. Hilgard, "Cotton in California," *California Cultivator* 40 (June 5, 1913), 691; Ray Barry, ed., "Negroes in California Agriculture," in FWP, "Documentary History of Farm Labor in California Agriculture," MS (1939), 2, BL.

17. Quote from *Fresno Weekly Expositor*, Nov. 5, 1883. Although some agricultural leaders still hoped to attract field hands from the influx of immigrants drawn in by the California Immigrant Union and Southern California Immigration Association, many now rejected any such deals. When the San Luis Obispo Immigration Association later attempted to transport black field hands from Texas, the editor of the *Santa Ana Standard*, a former southerner, prayed for destruction of the city. "The sooner a gentle earthquake takes her in the better, for it wouldn't be half as bad a calamity as a nigger colony. Santa Ana Valley wants white men for settlers, and has no use for any kind of valley-tanned, copper-tinged, or crow-colored savages from any country, and least of all does she want niggers." Quote from clipping, *Los Angeles Times*, Jan. 22, 1885, California Scrapbooks, HL. See also Bancroft, "Isaac DeTurck Statement," MS (Sept. 1883), Isaac DeTurck Papers, BL.

18. Quotes from *PRP*, Oct. 6, Nov. 3, 1883; clipping, *San Francisco Call*, Nov. 1, 1883, Bancroft Scrapbooks, BL.

19. Quotes from *Sacramento Bee*, Sept. 22, 1887. See also June 25, 1886; Sept. 22, 1887; Jan. 3, 1889. On Mar. 5, 1892, the *California Fruit Grower* noted that many farmers provided better accommodations for their animals than for their harvesters. See also *CSAST, 1886*, 201.

20. Quote from W. J. Sanborn, "Labor and Statistical Problems of the Farm," in CSBLS, *First Biennial Report, 1883–84*, 172; also 10–11. Small-scale, diversified growers would have to regard field hands as their equals and treat them "as fellow creatures who are capable of being our own equals—capable of some day filling the positions we now occupy—not as slaves but as free men," advised the editor of the *Pacific Rural Press*. Quote from *PRP*, Oct. 6, Nov. 3, 1883. See also *Sacramento Bee*, Apr. 17, 1885; June 5, 25, 1886; unidentified clipping, 1889 ["help their neighbors"], Bancroft Scrapbooks, BL; Reed, "Opening Address," 15, 40.

21. W. C. Blackwood, "A Consideration of the Labor Problem," *Overland Monthly* 3 (May 1884), 455; J. H. Durst, "Exclusion of the Chinese," *North American Review* 134 (Sept. 1884), 257, 261–62, 265. For rejection of diversification, see Hugh LaRue, "Opening Address," *CSAST, 1883*, 18. "An interesting feature of those fruit-drying days," recalled an old-timer many years later, "was

to see the many hands employed in the orchards and on the ranch, line up in single file on Broadway at the Bidwell office on Saturday nights, to receive the weekly pay. Sometimes the line of workers would be more than a block long." Quote from Old Timer, "Floods, Failing Ground, End Prosperous Era For Farmers," *Chico Record*, Feb. 23, 1936, JWHA. For the fruit drying house, see Bidwell, diary, Aug. 29, 1874, JBP. For glowing descriptions of children working on farms, see Oscar T. Shuck, comp., *The California Scrapbook* (San Francisco, 1869), 480, BL.

22. Eugene W. Hilgard, *Report on the Physical and Agricultural Features of the State of California with a Discussion of the Present and Future of Cotton Production in the State* (San Francisco, 1884), 74; *Second Annual Report of the Chief Viticultural Officer of the State of California, 1884* (Sacramento, 1885), 27; *PRP*, Oct. 6, Nov. 3, 1883; editorial, ibid., Sept. 8, 1883; *Placer Herald*, May 29, 1886.

23. *PRP*, Sept. 8, Oct. 6, Nov. 3, 1883.

24. Quote from *PRP*, Nov. 3, 1883. See also June 9, 1884.

25. Quote from *Lakeport Bee-Democrat*, n.d., in *St. Helena Star*, Apr. 17, 1884. White field hands generally earned $1.75 to $2 a day with board, or $30 to $45 a month when hired on that basis. See also Woodruff et al. v. North Bloomfield, 19: 7462.

26. Quotes from *St. Helena Star*, Apr. 14, 28, 1884. Reports of higher wages in Napa and Lake counties run counter to many other reports that still listed wages at one dollar a day. For general reports, see CSBLS, *First Biennial Report, 1883–84*, 167; *CSAST, 1872*, 252–58; Husmann, *American Grape Growing and Wine Making*, 168; *San Francisco Wine Merchant*, Aug. 14, 1885. Just how high wages rose could be seen in an advertisement running in the *Star* during October. "GRAPE PICKERS," the ad announced. "Any person wishing to engage Chinamen to pick grapes at $1.15 per day can be accommodated by applying immediately at Yung Him's Employment Office, Rutherford, California." Never before had China bosses demanded such wages in the Napa Valley. Quote from *St. Helena Star*, Oct. 2, 1884; also June 9, Oct. 11, 1884; Sept. 17, 1886.

27. For Chinese at Bidwell's ranch, see "The Army Worm," *Chico Daily Enterprise*, July 3, 1884; "After Beets," ibid., July 7, 1884; Bidwell, diary, July 6–9, 1884, JBP. For hop pickers in Mendocino, see *St. Helena Star*, Sept. 18, 1884.

28. Quote from *Anaheim Gazette*, Aug. 2, 1884, referring to wages paid to Wau's men working as *zanjeros* on the Cajón Ditch. For other Chinese contractors, see *Business Directory of the Town of Anaheim* (Anaheim, 1878). For the strike in Kern County, see *PRP*, Aug. 28, 30, 1884. Some commentators have mistakenly identified this as the first recorded farm labor strike. See Kushner, *Long Road to Delano*, 6.

29. For uppity Chinese dismissed for rudeness, see Bandini, diary, Apr. 25, 1885, HL. For the hop boycott, see *Wheatland Graphic*, Mar. 27, 1885. See also "California Vineyard," *San Francisco Merchant* 14 (Aug. 14, 1885), 40. For land clearing in Knight's Valley, see *Weekly Calistogian*, Feb. 23, 1885; *St. Helena Star*, Feb. 26, 1885. For land clearing around Gridley, see *Gridley Herald*, Feb. 13, 1885. For general land clearing in the northern Sacramento Valley, see Ed Schirmer, interview, Aug. 14, 1928, Tehama Public Library. For Monterey, see Robert L. Balzer, *This Uncommon Heritage: The Paul Masson Story* (Los Angeles, 1970), 30. For land clearing and picking citrus in San Bernardino, see Hinckley, diary, Feb. 27; Mar. 2, 3, 4, 1885; Hinckley, *Frank Hinckley*, 108. For land clearing around Newcastle, see *Newcastle News*, July 11, 1888; *PRP*, Mar. 13, 1886; Mar. 11, 1893; Harry E. Butler, "History of the English Colony," MS (1948), 5, Harry Butler Biographical Letter File, California Room, CSL; "Immigrant Labor in the Fruit Industries of the Newcastle District," *ICR* 24: 417; May W. Perry, "Stewart's Flat and Penryn," *Placer Nugget* (Oct. 1964), 4–5; Leonard Davis, *Newcastle, Gem of the Foothills*, 30–32; Gilbert, "Tsuda Grocery: A History," 47–49. By 1890, the Chinese had cleared about eight thousand acres around Newcastle.

30. Quotes from *Sonoma Index-Tribune*, July 11, 1885; Sept. 19, 1885.

31. In another attack, two Chinese field hands stabbed and killed a half-blind Chinese field hand on John Dowdell's hop farm. Stealing his life's savings, they fled to Los Angeles. By the time law enforcement authorities tracked them down and brought them back to Napa one year later, all of the witnesses had left. With no one able to identify them at the preliminary hearing, they were released. See *St. Helena Star*, Oct. 31, 1890; Sept. 14, 1894; Jan. 18, Nov. 22, 1895; *Napa Register*, Nov. 22, 1895; Rogers, *Colusa County*, 130. For an attack on Chinese field hands on the Osborne farm in the Alexander Valley, see *Healdsburg Tribune*, Sept. 27, 1889.

32. For a Chinese field hand killed by an infuriated steer, see unidentified newspaper clip-

ping, June 17, 1889, Mrs. Sarah Steel Scrapbook, Colusa County Historical Society, Colusa. For a man hurt when a log rolled on him while cutting wood, see *St. Helena Star*, Jan. 29, 1885. For death under a shifting pile of potatoes, see *SDI*, Aug. 30, 1887.

33. Quotes from *St. Helena Star*, June 12, 1884; Jan. 29, 1885; *Kern County Californian*, Dec. 24, 1887; Rogers, *Colusa County*, 250.

34. Quote from "An Aged Chinaman's Awful Fate," *St. Helena Star*, Apr. 23, 1885. For wagon accidents, see June 16, 1893; *Ventura Free Press*, Jan. 26, 1887.

35. Quote from *St. Helena Star*, July 1, 1887. For loss of work due to weather and other interruptions, as well as some idea of how many days per year permanent field hands worked, see Walter Allen, diary, Dec. 6, 1879; Jan. 22, 1880; July 10, 1880; Oct. 29, 1880; Jan. 8, 15, 27, 28, 31; Feb. 3, 4; Mar. 26, 29, 30; Apr. 5, 7, 15, 16; May 19, 24, 27, 28, 31; June 1, 2, 4, 15; Dec. 15, 1881; Oct. 3, 4, 5, 1883; Frank Hinckley, diary, July 13, 14, 25; Dec. 20, 22, 1884; Feb. 24, 25, 26; Mar. 3, 4; Apr. 13, 14, 15, 16, 17, 20, 21, 1885.

36. Quote from Rogers, *Colusa County*, 214; also 216. At his trial on September 16, Van Weizer pled guilty to the shooting and was sentenced to life imprisonment. For Ventura, see *Ventura Signal*, Jan. 8, 1885. For Chico, see A.M.E. Episcopal Church to Mayor Bidwell, May 15, 1885, JBP. For Modesto and Stockton, see *SWM*, Nov. 28, 1885. For Calistoga and Knight's Valley, see "Threatening Letters," *Napa Register*, Aug. 25, 1885, NCLCF.

37. Quote from *St. Helena Star*, Oct. 18, 1885.

38. Quote from ibid., Dec. 4, 1885. For the incident with juveniles, see Oct. 23, 1883. About six hundred people probably lived in the St. Helena Chinatown, although some estimates range up to three thousand.

39. Quotes from *St. Helena Star*, Dec. 4, 1885; CSBLS, *Second Biennial, 1885–86*, 47. See also *St. Helena Star*, Feb. 16; Dec. 18, 1885.

40. Quotes from *St. Helena Star*, Dec. 11, 1885; Feb. 5, 1886, which also contains a brief account of the origins of Chinatown. See also Feb. 12, 19, 1886. Chinatown would remain in St. Helena for another sixteen years. Frustrated with the failure to remove the Chinese, local bully and anti-Chinese zealot Tony McGinnis entered a Chinese cabin on New Year's Eve and celebrated the holiday by knocking out six Chinese. Shortly thereafter he skipped town. For the incident, see Jan. 7, 1886. The Anti-Chinese League quietly negotiated with the Chinatown owner and eventually bought the property for sixteen hundred dollars.

41. "The Wickersham Tragedy," in *An Illustrated History of Sonoma County, California* (Chicago, 1889), 272–75. This was not the first murder case involving supposedly loyal Chinese cooks. For a Chinese cook accused of poisoning a family on the Welsh farm near St. John south of Willows and setting a barn fire that killed two boys on July 19, 1875, see Rogers, *Colusa County*, 146.

42. *St. Helena Star*, Apr. 30, 1886; *Russian River Flag*, Jan. 27; Feb. 3, 17; Mar. 31, 1886; Rogers, *Colusa County*, 220.

43. Quote from *Napa Register*, Feb. 12, 1886, NCLCF. For Sonoma, see *Sonoma Index-Tribune*, Feb. 20, 1886. While many Napa Valley Chinese lost work, and a few were physically assaulted by drunken men near Oakville, opposition to them was mostly verbal. Despite calls for boycotts of Chinese goods and employers of Chinese labor, large numbers of the anti-Chinese faithful continued patronizing Chinese vegetable peddlers on a daily basis, much to the consternation of other members of the local anti-Chinese movement. For an assault on a Chinese field hand, see *St. Helena Star*, Feb. 26, 1886. For Chinese thieves, see Mar. 9, 1886. For anti-Chinese advocates patronizing Chinese vegetable peddlers, see Mar. 26, 1886.

44. Quote from F. Hal Higgins, "John Chinaman was a California Farm Hand," MS (n.d.), FHHC. See also "Siskiyou County Used to Have a Bounty on Chinamen," notes dated Sept. 1955, from interview with an old-timer.

45. For Stockton see *SDI*, Jan. 1, 15, 20, 24, 25, 28; Feb. 5, 6, 7, 12, 17, 19, 1886; *SWM*, Jan. 9, 1886. For Turlock, see Hohenthal et al., *Streams in a Thirsty Land*, 57.

46. For Chico, see Bidwell, address, Feb. 22, 1886, JBC; Hunt, *Bidwell*, 213–23; *Butte Record*, Feb. 26, 1886; *Chico Enterprise*, Jan. 29; Feb. 5, 12, 1886; Chinese Consulate General to Bidwell, Feb. 27, 1886, JBP.

47. Quote from Charles J. McClain, *In Search of Equality: The Chinese Struggle against Discrimination in Nineteenth-Century America* (Berkeley, 1994), 176. The Chinese consul general in San Francisco frantically telegraphed Gov. George Stoneman, only to receive a noncommittal reply. For Stoneman's refusal to intervene, see House, *Foreign Relations of the United States*, 49th

Cong., 2nd sess., 1886, H. Doc., 1: 158. Because the Chinese protested so much, the captain of the ship *Knight*, which was about to tow the barge, at first refused $125 from the vigilantes to cover the cost of taking the Chinese out of the area. Eventually he agreed to load them on board among the bags of wheat he was carrying, as much to protect them as for the money, leaving three or four field hands behind to settle matters in the community. The best accounts of this episode are in the *Sacramento-Record Union*, Feb. 19, 23, 1886; *Wheatland Graphic*, Feb. 27, 1886.

48. *Marysville Daily Appeal*, Jan. 28, Feb. 26, 1886; *Wheatland Graphic*, Feb. 27; Mar. 6, 1886.

49. The *Chico Enterprise* described Cheng Ping as a slender, distinguished-looking, English-speaking man with "a very intelligent air about him." Quote from Feb. 19, 1886. See also *Sacramento Record-Union*, Feb. 23, Mar. 13, 1886; In re: Baldwin, 192–96, File 3989, FARCSB. Some accounts give Ping's first name as Ching, not Cheng.

50. *San Francisco Bulletin*, Mar. 18, 1886; *San Francisco Morning Call*, Mar. 19, 1886.

51. S. G. Hilborn to Atty. Gen. A. H. Garland, Apr. 5, 1886, Dept. of Justice, Year File 980–84, no. 2498, DJR; *Sacramento Record-Union*, Mar. 17, 18, 19, 1886.

52. *San Francisco Morning Call*, Mar. 31, 1886; *San Francisco Evening Post*, Mar. 30, 1886. In the Harris case, McAllister claimed that the court had simply ruled that ordinary criminal acts under prevailing notions of federalism were the exclusive realm of the states and could not be prosecuted as violations of the Thirteenth, Fourteenth, and Fifteenth amendments. Labeling this as tortured and specious logic designed to salvage an unconstitutional law, former U.S. attorney general A. L. Hart, now representing Baldwin and the Nicolaus vigilantes, concluded his rebuttal by asserting that if McAllister's logic was accepted then every crime against Chinese immigrants would have to be tried in federal court.

53. Quotes from *San Francisco Evening Post*, Mar. 30, 1886; In re: Baldwin, 192–93. See also *San Francisco Morning Call*, Apr. 1, 1886. Sawyer argued that treaty provisions provided ample basis for the federal government to protect Chinese rights not only against unfriendly state legislation but also against individuals. By guaranteeing the Chinese the right to pursue a lawful vocation, treaties conveyed a large array of rights and privileges that, by implication, could be used to fight boycotts and various other coercive measures they encountered.

54. "I can imagine no case that so urgently requires prompt action," wrote Sawyer. "This whole coast is inflamed by active men who are organizing to perpetuate similar outrages. If there is any law making such action criminal, it ought to be authoritatively declared." Quote from Lorenzo Sawyer to Garland, Apr. 5, 1886, Dept. of Justice, year file 980–84, no. 2497, DJR. See also Brief on Behalf of Petitioner, case file, Baldwin v. Franks, 120 United States Reports, 678, 682–83; Brief for Respondent, 15–33, U.S. Supreme Court Records and Briefs, Records of the U.S. Supreme Court, RG 267, NA.

55. Quotes from Hunt, *Bidwell*, 221. For splits within the anti-Chinese movement, see *Wheatland Graphic*, Mar. 6, 1886. For the State Non-Partisan Anti-Chinese Organization, see *PRP*, Mar. 13, 1886.

56. Quote from Hunt, *Bidwell*, 281; also 216 and 222. On Mar. 20, an angry letter attacking Bidwell appeared in the *Butte Record*. "As defender of the heathen you put yourself forward," the writer began. "You think of nothing but yourself. The many poor young white girls, who are looking for a living and cannot get it because of these Mongolians, never enter into your thoughts." Quote from *Butte Record*, Mar. 20, 1886.

57. Bidwell, dictation (1891), 51; *Colusa Sun*, Mar. 13, 1886; *Chico Enterprise*, Mar. 3, 1886; *PRP*, Mar. 27, 1886; *Butte Record*, Apr. 3, 10, 1886; Andrew Cullers to David Coverstone, Mar. 31, 1886, Misc. Collection, HL.

58. Quote from Hunt, *Bidwell*, 223. See also *Butte Record*, Apr. 10, July 31, 1886; Bidwell, diary, Mar. 5, 10, 15, 1886, JBP. Bidwell also fired one field hand who would not attend meetings of his Committee of One Hundred, dismissed a machinist who was anti-Chinese, and used his influence to retaliate against other leaders in the anti-Chinese movement, including a local photographer whose photographs Bidwell supposedly excluded from an exhibition because of the photographer's anti-Chinese activities. For a cautionary note on using Rockwell Hunt's work, see Michael J. Gillis and Michael F. Magliori, *John Bidwell and California: The Life and Writings of a Pioneer, 1841–1900* (Spokane, Wash., 2003), 20–23.

59. *Chico Enterprise*, May 7, 21, 28, 1886; *Red Bluff People's Cause*, June 15, 1886. Newspaper accounts identify an H. J. Burns, but I believe this is William J. Burns.

60. For anti-Chinese meetings, see *St. Helena Star*, Apr. 2, 1886. For Stockton, see *SDI*, May 9, 1886. For Santa Rosa, see Ruth Habert, "Chinese of Santa Rosa Township and Santa

Rosa" (Dec. 16, 1970), NVWL. Many of the Santa Rosa Chinese fled south to find work in the vineyards and wineries near Glen Ellen. The move is described in *Sonoma Index-Tribune*, Mar. 13, 1886.

61. CSBLS, *Second Biennial Report, 1885–86*, 44–47, 53–54. For the thesis that Chinese now controlled all farm labor, see McWilliams, *Factories in the Field*, 66. For contemporary comments on the CSBLS investigation, see *St. Helena Star*, Feb. 12, 1886. See also "A Scholar Traces China's Vinous Past," *Wines and Vines* 55 (Sept. 1974), 52–53. For the importance of Asian agricultural laborers after this point, see E. G. Mears, *Resident Orientals on the American Pacific Coast* (Chicago, 1928), 238.

62. Quotes from CSBLS, *Second Biennial Report, 1885–86*, 64; also 42–47; *CSAST, 1886*, 201. See also H. Shewin, "Observations," *Overland Monthly* 7 (Jan. 1886), 97; G. H. Hecke, "The Pacific Coast Labor Question from the Standpoint of a Horticulturalist," 68–69.

63. Quotes from *ICR*, 24: 208; L. C. Forrest, "Recollections of Over 50 Years Packing Citrus Fruit," *California Citrograph* (Oct. 1943). See also E. B. Norman, "Reminiscences of Early Days of Citrus Marketing in Duarte," *California Citrograph* (Feb. 1940); CSBLS, *Second Biennial Report, 1885–86*, 53–54. For complaints, see "The Packing of Fruit," *San Francisco Call*, June 8, 1895. As always, Euro-American field hands still predominated, and in some places like the Yulupa Valley northwest of Sonoma, completely dominated farmwork. For white field hands in the Yulupa Valley, see *Santa Rosa Daily Republican*, Oct. 6, 1886.

64. Patience and agility were very important, as packers had to stand at long tables removing raisins from large "sweat boxes" and carefully fitting them into smaller boxes. Eliminating small or imperfect raisins, packers cut stems from bunches, sorted the bunches according to quality, packed the raisins in five-pound layers, pressed them flat, and placed a fancy paper wrapper on top, repeating the process three more times to produce twenty-pound shipping boxes. See Eisen, "The Raisin Industry of Fresno," *California—A Journal of Rural Industry* 1 (Feb. 1, 1890); "Who Grew the Raisin?" ibid., 3 (Apr. 12, 1890); "Woman Horticulturalist," ibid., 3 (May 24, 1890); Vandor, *History of Fresno County*, 1: 191; "Successful Women Farmers of California," *San Francisco Bulletin*, Dec. 25, 1904, Harriet Williams Russell Strong Collection, HL. According to the *San Francisco Merchant*, even Miss Austin could not "keep it up as her Chinamen can." Quote from "A Talk with Miss Austin," *San Francisco Merchant* 13 (Mar. 14, 1885), 365–68. See also James E. Ayers, "The Central California Colony," *Fresno Past & Present* 7 (Apr. 1965), 2. Production statistics from *History of Fresno County*, 206. For packing, see Belle A. Kandarian, *Fifty Years in Fresno: The Life Story of Belle A. Kandarian* (New York, 1963), 39–41; Leroy Chaddock, "Fifty Years as a Raisin Packer," MS (1943), 36, SCHMLCSUF; W. B. West, "California Raisins," *CSAST, 1880*, 188–89; *California Fruit Grower*, Oct. 26, 1889; Sept. 10, 1892.

65. Quotes from Frank P. Nutting, interview, 22–23; *Fresno Weekly Evening Expositor*, Oct. 15, 1891, 1: 167; also Sept. 28, 1891, 1: 165–67, Fresno Scrapbook, FCHS. See also A. B. Butler, "California and Spain," in *California—A Journal of Rural Industry* 3 (Mar. 15, 1890); Chaddock, "Fifty Years as a Raisin Packer," 41–42; Bernard Marks, *Small Scale Farming in California: The Colonization System of the Great Valley of the San Joaquin in Central California* (San Francisco, 1890), 29, BL; Kandarian, *Fifty Years in Fresno*, 39–48. Many packers shifted between cannery work and packing vegetables and fruit on the coast, and packing fresh Muscat table grapes, plums, peaches, and other fruit around Fresno. Most of Fresno's Chinese were relegated to "out-of-town work," either in the vineyards or in the smaller sheds run by growers like Minnie Austin. Of their work packing fruit, the *Pacific Rural Press* wrote that the Chinese "by tact peculiar to themselves mainly, seem to have reduced it to a science." Equally important, Chinese packers also assembled their own fruit boxes. Whatever savings in wages they provided was secondary to their efficiency and attention to detail. These qualities were essential and irreplaceable components not only to the raisin industry, but also to an expanding fruit industry, now packing much of its harvest for sale outside of California. Particularly in packing Bartlett pears, no one could compete with the Chinese, who earned praise as extremely skilled, careful, and fast workers who devised special techniques. For example, to prevent pears from bruising they developed the "China pack," wrapping each pear in tissue paper that was carefully folded into a point so that, upon opening a box of pears, a merchant could immediately display a box for sale. According to the *Pacific Rural Press*, Chinese labor was "the only body of people who understand how to pack fruit for eastern shipment." Quote from *PRP*, June 10, 1893; also Mar. 6, 13, 1886; "Orchards and Orientals," *Oakland Tribune*, June 2, 1952.

66. Quotes from *PRP*, Mar. 6, 1886; *PRP* quoted in Speth, "Agricultural Labor in

Sonoma," 56; George D. Kellogg to P. J. Healey, Apr. 26, 1886, in *California State Board of Horticulture, Biennial Report, 1885–1886* (Sacramento, 1887), 426. See also *CSAST, 1886*, 201.

67. Quotes from *PRP*, Mar. 20, Apr. 10, 1886.

68. Nutting, "Mr. Gibbs in the Cutting Shed on the E. R. Thurber Ranch"; "Packing Fruit at L. L. Hatch's Ranch, Upper Vaca Valley"; "H. Bassford Fruit Packing Shed"; "Peach Gathering, Henry Bassford's Orchard"; "Chinese Houseboys in front of the Fred Buck Ranch," photographs, all in Nutting Collection. Chinese field hands are also described in Wickson, *California Illustrated: Vacaville Early Fruit District*, 16, 23, and 127, and their higher wages on 46. A figure of "several hundred" Chinese is given by the *Vacaville Reporter* in Wickson, ibid., 154.

69. One of the central myths of farmworker history holds that by this time most of the state's fruit and vegetables were being harvested and processed by migrating hordes of field hands. But if Nutting's images are any indication, around Vacaville and probably elsewhere, a more complex situation prevailed in which various groups worked together, each one handling a distinct segment of the harvest. For family labor in the harvest, see dozens of oral histories of Vacaville residents, Vacaville Museum. "All of the people interviewed for our local history series have memories of working in the fruit sheds as children, cutting apricots for ten to twelve hours a day." Quote from Sabine Goerke-Shrode, interview by author, Vacaville, Aug. 10, 1998, author's possession.

70. P. W. Butler, "Peach Culture," *Official Report of the Tenth CSFGCP, Nov. 20–23, 1888* (Sacramento, 1889), 71–74. See also *PRP*, Dec. 20, 1890; George D. Kellogg, "Fruit Packing, Marketing, and Transportation," *Twenty-Seventh CSFGCP, Dec. 2–5, 1902*, in California State Board of Horticulture, *Eighth Biennial Report for 1901–2* (Sacramento, 1903), 304–8.

71. Quote from Wickson, *Vacaville Early Fruit District*, 128; see also 119, 127. For dried fruit, see Couchman, *Sunsweet Story*, 19.

72. Quotes from Wickson, *Vacaville Early Fruit District*, 127, 129. Confirmation of the importance of child labor in the fruit-drying yards is found in hundreds of entries in Luther Harbison, ledgers, Luther Harbison Collection, Vacaville Museum. For typical entries, see Helen Harbison, June 14–15, 17, 20, 27, 28, 1899. Paid 15 cents a box, a six-year-old girl earned 50 cents on July 14; 85 cents on July 15; 50 cents on July 17; 25 cents on July 20; 50 cents on July 27; and $1.50 on July 28.

73. Quotes from *PRP*, Mar. 27, May 15, Apr. 24, 1886; also Mar. 6, 13; Apr. 3, 10; clipping, *Vacaville Reporter*, ca. 1887, Vacaville Museum. See also *Solano Republican*, Apr. 16, 1886.

74. Quotes from clipping, *PRP*, Feb. 2, 1886, Napa Scrapbook, CSL; unidentified newspaper clipping, Feb. 27, 1886, Scientific Scrapbook, CSL. See also Lydon, *Chinese Gold*, 123–25; F. Hal Higgins, "John Chinaman was a California Farm Hand," MS (n.d.) 3, FHHC.

75. Quote from typed notes, *Watsonville Pajaronian*, Apr. 8, 1886, PVHS. See also *St. Helena Star*, Mar. 26, 1886. The Placer County labor force divided up in countless ways, large and small. For example, Newcastle grower George Kellogg got through most of the year with four men to help him farm thirty acres of peaches. But during the 1885 harvest, Kellogg required ten additional men for three weeks to pick and pack his crop. See George D. Kellogg to P. J. Healey, Apr. 26, 1886. See also *California Fruit Grower*, Apr. 11, 18, 25; May 2, 1891, containing a detailed description of thirty-nine Newcastle District fruit ranches. Around Tehama, where anti-Chinese sentiments had almost completely disappeared, the main threat to Chinese field hands was not hostile whites but other Chinese. Here the source of violence was a confrontation between the Hop Sing Company and tenant farmer Lui Hing over title to five hundred acres near Vina on Deer Creek. Joseph Leininger, one of the largest ranchers in the area, had first leased the land to the Hop Sing Company in 1879. Then without notice he suddenly sold it to Lui Hing in February 1886. Almost immediately after purchasing the property, Hing attempted to force all of the Hop Sing field hands off his land. When they refused to leave, Hing drew a revolver. Fights broke out, Hing shot and killed one of the Hop Sing field hands, and order was only restored after the sheriffs arrived. Eventually a court decided the matter, ruling that Hing was indeed the new owner. See *Red Bluff Sentinel*, Feb. 13, 20, 1886. One of the first signs of a decline in anti-Chinese activities came in Stockton, where public sentiment was acutely divided and Chinese field hands had many defenders among prominent farmers, civic leaders, and newspaper editors. Defending the Chinese and praising them for their keen dedication and hard work, and knowing that the area lacked the manpower to replace them, many Stockton farmers refused to fire their Chinese cooks and field hands, even after many whites applied for their jobs. See *SDI*, Mar. 7, 1886; *CSAST, 1886*, 200–201.

76. Quote from clipping *Sacramento Record-Union*, ca. 1886, Stanford Family Scrapbooks, SUASC. See also F. T. Robson, "The Famous Stanford Vina Ranch," MS (1955); "The Vine and Wine at Stanford-Vina Ranch," MS (1955), Robson Scrapbook, Herbert Kraft Library, Red Bluff. Vina labor force estimates from *Red Bluff People's Cause*, Aug. 28, 1886. Almost twice as many Chinese departed from San Francisco in 1885 and during the first half of 1886 as in the previous years. Departure figures from *LFCH*, 1982I, table 8.

77. Quote from *St. Helena Star*, Dec. 24, 1886. For Chinese in the Pajaro Valley strawberry industry, see typed notes, *Watsonville Pajaronian*, Apr. 8, 22, 1886, PVHS; Harrison, *History of Santa Cruz County*, 30. For Chinese in Vaca Valley orchards, see clipping, *Vacaville Judicion* [probably 1885–86], Vacaville Public Library; "Letter from Vaca," *Solano Republican*, Apr. 16, 1886. For a railroad car full of Chinese arriving in the Napa Valley grape and hop harvests under contract from Sacramento China bosses, see *St. Helena Star*, Sept. 24, 1886. For two hundred Chinese pickers arriving in Sonoma in one week, see *Sonoma Index-Tribune*, Sept. 25, 1886; *San Francisco Merchant*, Sept. 25, 1886.

78. For the Dowdell farm incident, see *St. Helena Star*, Jan. 21, 1887. Ruling in the Baldwin decision, Supreme Court Chief Justice Morrison R. Waite declared Section 5519 far too broad and released Baldwin and the other Nicolaus defendants from prosecution. Despite treaty obligations guaranteeing their safety, Chinese field hands were now left unprotected by the federal government. For the Nicolaus case, see Baldwin v. Franks, 120 U.S. Reports (Washington, D.C., 1887), 678, 682–707; *San Francisco Evening Post*, Mar. 22, 1887; *Alta California*, Mar. 10, 1887; note left by Chinese Minister Chang Yin-huan at the Dept. of State, Mar. 18, 1887, in House, *Papers Relating to the Foreign Relations of the United States*, 50th Cong., 2nd sess., 1889, H. Doc., 1: 368–69. Even such strong supporters of severe restrictions on Chinese immigration as the *Sacramento Record-Union* described the Supreme Court decision as injecting new life into the anti-Chinese movement. See *Sacramento Record-Union*, Mar. 9, 1887.

79. Quote from *San Francisco Morning Chronicle*, May 22, 1887. Although wounded in the shoulder and slammed to the floor, Weaver claimed to have barricaded himself and the two children in the kitchen. As Hueng put his rifle aside and began chopping down the door, Weaver somehow managed to grab Hueng's rifle and chase him off with a carving knife. Hueng then fled the scene, and took a boat across the river to Chico. At that moment one of the daughters slipped out of a window and ran for help to St. John, about two miles south of Hamilton City. See *Chico Record*, July 16, 1887; Colusa Coroner's Office Registry of Deaths, Colusa County Clerk's Office, Colusa. See also Rogers, *Colusa County*, 231–32.

80. *Chico Record*, Apr. 15, 16, 23, citing *Colusa Herald*; May 7, 22, 23, 28; June 4, 1887; *Sacramento Bee*, May 26, 1887; People v. Ho Ah Hueng, Superior Court of Colusa City, Colusa County Clerk's Office.

81. *San Francisco Morning Chronicle*, May 25, 1887; *San Francisco Examiner*, May 24, 1887; *Sacramento Bee*, May 22, 26, 1887; *Chico Record*, July 16, 29, 1887; Rogers, *Colusa County*, 233.

82. Fearing the worst, the sheriff attempted to protect Hueng by a subterfuge, or so he later claimed. Ordering the jail surrounded by the local National Guard unit and most of his deputies, he hid Hueng in a secret basement cell, brought a closed carriage to the jail door, covered a deputy in a heavy coat, loaded him quickly into the carriage as if he were Hueng, and sped away with the guard and most of the mob following. The sheriff then left the jail dark, unprotected, and unlocked—as if no one was there. But at 12:30 A.M., an armed mob discovered the secret basement cell, stormed into the jail, dragged Hueng out, and hung him from a pole at the train depot. Hardly anyone objected. At the inquest, the coroner condemned the jury, hailed the lynching as a vindication of Mrs. Billiou's honor, praised the mob for overturning the injustice of the jury's verdict, and ruled that Hueng had met his death "by the hands of unknown persons." Even happier at the outcome, the *Marysville Appeal* celebrated the lynching as a fine public event that should be repeated regularly to present Chinese field hands with "an impressive object lesson." However, a year later the *Appeal* and everyone else involved in the case would have to reconsider their positions when Billy Weaver, having survived what some called an attempt at drowning himself in Stony Creek, committed suicide by slitting his throat, an action many took as evidence indicating his guilt and largely verifying Hueng's account. Quotes from *Chico Enterprise*, July 15, 1887; also July 22; *Chico Record*, July 23, 1887; Rogers, *Colusa County*, 235. See also Coroner's Report on Ho Ah Hueng, "a.k.a. Hong Di," Colusa County Clerk's Office; *Chico Enterprise*, July 15, 1887. For Weaver's suicide, see Raymond H. West, *The Story of St. John: The Ghost City of Glenn County* (n.p., n.d.), 14.

83. Note from the Chinese foreign office to the British minister at Peking, Aug. 3, 1886, in Notes from the Chinese Legation in the U.S. to the Dept. of State, 1868–1906, DSR; Note left at the State Dept. by the Chinese minister, Mar. 13, 1887, *Papers Relating to the Foreign Relations of the United States*, 1: 366. For labor in sugar beets, see *Sacramento Bee*, May 24, 1888.

84. Quote from clipping, *Winters Express*, Aug. 13, 1887, Yolo County Historical Society.

85. Quotes from *St. Helena Star*, Sept. 30, 1887; Jan. 6, 1888. At Inglenook Winery, the beautiful European chateau-style winery that millionaire Finnish sea captain and fur dealer Gustav Niebaum was establishing in the Napa Valley, Chinese worked in the vineyards, and in virtually every other aspect of Inglenook's operations—growing vegetables to feed workmen, milking and feeding cows and making cheese in the dairy, caring for horses, and when Niebaum began "estate bottling" his vintage, entirely taking over that task as well as many aspects of cellar work. For the Harris murder, see Rogers, *Colusa County*, 236, 239. Ying was tried and convicted of murder on December 10, and sentenced to fourteen years' imprisonment. For developments in Napa County, see "Napa Vineyards," *San Francisco Merchant* 19 (Oct. 28, 1887); Tom Parker, *Inglenook Vineyards: 100 years of Fine Winemaking* (Rutherford, Calif., 1979), 54–55; Inglenook Vineyard Accounting Sheets, Sept. 2–27, 1886; Inglenook Time Book, Oct. 1888; Inglenook Pay Roll of Employees of Inglenook Wine Cellar, 1888, Inglenook Vineyards Collection. For Chinese digging wine cellars at Jacob Grimm's vineyard, see Sullivan, *Napa Wine*, 159.

86. Quotes from *Traver Advocate*, n.d., cited in "Chinese Grape Pickers," *San Francisco Merchant* 21 (Oct. 12, 1888), 29; J. W. Sallee, "The Pomological Society," *Rural Californian* 10 (Nov. 1887), 256. See also *Sacramento Bee*, Sept. 2, 1887; Feb. 23, Apr. 19, 1888; *Sonoma Index-Tribune*, Mar. 3, 1888.

87. Quote from *Kern County Californian*, Jan. 5, 1888.

88. Quotes from *Sacramento Bee*, Sept. 22, 1887; see also Feb. 23, Mar. 28, 1888; Thomas Bayard to W. L. Putnam, Sept. 13, 1888, in C. Tansill, *The Foreign Policy of Thomas J. Bayard* (New York, 1940), 171. For treaty developments, see Michael Hunt, *The Making of a Special Relationship: The United States and China to 1914* (New York, 1983), 105; *Papers Relating to the Foreign Relations of the United States*, 1: 354–55; Lucy E. Salyer, *Laws Harsh as Tigers: Chinese Immigrants and the Shaping of Modern Immigration Law* (Chapel Hill, N.C., 1995), 18–23.

89. Flint is sometimes spelled Flynt. See also typed notes on Judge William C. Blackwood, "Labor Problems," *California Fruit Grower*, June 2, 8, 1888, in Ray Barry, ed., "Labor in the Peach Industry," WPA, "Documentary History of California Agriculture," MS (1939), 48, BL; B. N. Rowley to Bidwell, Apr. 24, 1888, JBP.

90. For Spreckels, see William W. Cordray, "Claus Spreckels of California" (Ph.D. diss., USC, 1955), 83, 102–3; Jacob Adler, *Claus Spreckels: The Sugar King in Hawaii* (Honolulu, 1966), 24; Stephen Birmingham, *California Rich* (New York, 1980), 59–70. For the importance of the factory, see Phil Francis, *Beautiful Santa Cruz County* (San Francisco, 1986), 108. The factory produced one thousand tons of raw sugar per year but shipped it to San Francisco for refining. See War Food Administration, *Beet Sugar Factories of the United States* (Washington, D.C., 1943), 2, ACSCR; George W. Shaw, "The California Sugar Industry," Univ. of Calif. Agricultural Experiment *Station Bulletin No. 149* (Sacramento, 1903), pt. 1: 10–11.

91. Quote from typed notes, *Watsonville Pajaronian*, Mar. 8, 1888, PVHS. See also Feb. 2, 23; Mar. 8, 23; Apr. 5, 12, 26.

92. Typed notes, *Watsonville Pajaronian*, June 20, July 12, 26; Aug. 9, 1888, PVHS; Lydon, *Chinese Gold*, 185–91; Bette Brown, "Cabrillo Professor Reviews Chinese Era in Pajaro Valley," *Watsonville Register-Pajaronian*, Apr. 30, 1977. One minor obstacle stood in the way of the move. Before the Chinese finally pulled up stakes, they would have to consult with Vice Consul F. A. Bee and the head of the Chinese Six Companies. Visiting Watsonville the two leaders inspected the new site and promptly endorsed the move. With that, the Chinese put their buildings on skids and began hauling them down Union Street and across the river. "The old Chinese quarters look desolate since the removal of the Mongolians," commented the *Watsonville Pajaronian*, which bragged to its readers that the episode was "the first time in the history of the Pacific slope where Chinese have been removed from a community of their own consent." But in fact nothing of the kind had happened. Far from being forced out, the Chinese had moved only after being dealt with as equals during three months of negotiations. Watsonville's citizens considered them so important that they even paid their moving expenses and their first three months rent. Within four years, the Chinese had their main street illuminated by electricity. Quotes from typed notes, *Watsonville Pajaronian*, Sept. 20, Apr. 26, 1888,

PVHS. One newspaper story claimed that several old Chinese actually rode inside the buildings, either too scared to leave or too ill to leave. Within a few months, the Chinese had erected two rows of neat buildings along a street laid out by Porter himself, completing their move early in September. When they dragged their last building into place, they had created an entirely new Chinatown along what was now called Brooklyn Street. See also typed notes, *Pajaro Valley Times*, June 16, 1892, PVHS.

93. Francis, *Beautiful Santa Cruz County*, 167; J. S. Coates, "Official Occupants of the Old Custom House," *Game and Gossip* 13 (1946), 4–7. In Bakersfield, business leaders and leaders of the local Chinese community also discussed moving their Chinatown, but for entirely different reasons. See *Kern County Californian*, May 25, 1889.

94. Quotes from *Sacramento Bee*, Jan. 3, 1889.

95. Quotes from *Kern County Californian*, Jan. 5, 1888. "The small orchardist with a big family need not fear a scarcity of labor," predicted the *Sacramento Bee*, "while the man whose vineyards and orchards extend over hundreds of acres will forever be in hot water." See Mar. 1, 1888; also Apr. 26, June 21, 1888; Jan. 10, 1889. For more on restructuring, see *Weekly Independent Calistogian*, Jan. 13, 1888. For improving working conditions, see *Sonoma Index Tribune*, June 23, 1888; *PRP*, Feb. 11, 1888.

96. *Sacramento Record-Union*, Aug. 8, 1888, cited in "Indian Hop Pickers," *PRP*, Aug. 18, 1888.

97. Quote from *PRP*, Apr. 28, 1888. For Baldwin's scheme, see typed notes, "How Carolina Negroes are Shipped Here by Wholesale to Work on Farms," *San Francisco Chronicle*, Apr. 16, 28, 1888, in FWP, "Source Material Gathered on Migratory Farm Labor," BL. See also "Vineyard Help," *Napa Register*, May 11, 1888, citing *St. Helena Star*, May 4, 1888.

98. *PRP*, May 19, 26, 1888. See also *California Fruit Grower*, June 23, 30; July 7, 21, 1888; "Labor for Vineyards," *San Francisco Merchant*, June 8, 1888; *St. Helena Star*, June 15, 1888.

99. *PRP*, Apr. 21, 28; June 9; July 21, 1888. St. Helena school district figures from *Napa Daily Journal*, Oct. 13, 1891, NCLCF.

100. "The Grape Harvest," *PRP*, July 21, 1888. The image is an engraving "made directly from a photograph . . . last year." For boys imported to break the Roseville strike, see *Sacramento Bee*, July 30, 1888. For State Board of Trade plan, see Mar. 7, 1889. See also *California Fruit Grower*, Aug. 11, 1888; *Kern County Californian*, Aug. 25, 1888.

101. Quotes from *Sacramento Bee*, Apr. 19, 26, July 30, Aug. 18, 1888; *Chico Chronicle*, Aug. 11, 1888. See also *California Fruit Grower*, Aug. 17, 1888; "Boys as Fruit Harvesters," *PRP*, Aug. 17, 1889; *San Francisco Examiner*, Apr. 6, 1890.

102. Quotes from "The Boy Experiment," *PRP*, Aug. 25, 1888; *California Fruit Grower*, July 11, 1888; *Sacramento Bee*, July 2, 16, 1888. See also *Kern County Californian*, Sept. 1, 1888.

103. Quote from "Vacaville Notes," *PRP*, Aug. 4, 1888. The three-quarters figure is from *Sacramento Bee*, Sept. 29, 1887. See also Charles Fell, "Recollections of Boyhood on a Ranch Southwest of Chico," interview by Dorothy Hill, Mar. 12, 1974, 8, ANCRR, describes family labor in the northern Sacramento Valley. For Vacaville, see "Life on a Fruit Ranch," *Solano Republican*, Feb. 5, 1892.

104. Quote from Everett "Joe" Delano Chavez, interview, n.d., SVHS. See also *Ventura Signal*, Mar. 22, 1884; Mar. 28, 1885, Charles F. Outland Indices to Early Ventura County Newspapers, Agriculture, 1871–1915, VCM.

105. Quotes from *Chico Enterprise* in *Sacramento Bee*, Nov. 22, 1888.

106. Quotes from "Hop Picking," *PRP*, July 18, Aug. 4, 1888; also June 9, 1888. Boys employed in the fruit drying yards on the William Pleasants ranch in Pleasants Valley are described in Wickson, *California Illustrated, The Vacaville Fruit District of California* (San Francisco, 1888), 53, 60–61. See also J. M. Gwinn, *History of California and an Extended History of its Southern Coast Counties* (Los Angeles and Chicago, 1907), 312.

107. Gunther Peck, *Reinventing Free Labor: Padrones and Immigrant Workers in the North American West, 1880–1930* (Cambridge and New York, 2000), 2–3; Hans Christian Palmer, "Italian Immigration and the Development of California Agriculture," 137, 141, 144, 149–55; Graves, "Immigrants in Agriculture: The Portuguese Californians, 1850–1970s," 50–62; *ICR*, 24: 22, 30, 33, 36–39, 187, 199n, 217, 233; *Napa Register*, Sept. 17, 1886, NCLCF; John Koren, *The Padrone Bands*, U.S. Bureau of Labor, Bulletin no. 9 (Washington, D.C., 1897), 113–29.

108. Quote from Bishop, *Old Mexico and Her Lost Provinces*, 359–60. See also Charles L. Sullivan, *Like Modern Edens: Winegrowing in Santa Clara Valley and Santa Cruz Mountains, 1798–1981* (Cupertino, Calif., 1982), 24–28; *ICR*, 2: 459.

109. Quote from Frank Norris, "Italy in California," *The Wave* 15 (Oct. 24, 1896), 8–9. See also Alberto Pecorini, "The Italian as an Agricultural Laborer," *AAAPSS* 33 (Mar. 1909), 380–90. Asti proved very prosperous, paying dividends of five dollars per share in 1896. Nearly all of the vineyardists worked at Asti for at least five to seven years and saved seven hundred to eight hundred dollars, most of which they sent home or reinvested in Asti. Every Saturday night, Alfredo Sbarboro, Andrea Sbarboro's eldest son and a cashier with the Italian American Bank, traveled to Asti to collect weekly deposits. Merging with the California Wine Association in 1901, Italian Swiss expanded and became Italian Swiss Colony, one of the most successful winemaking enterprises in the state. For the founding of Italian Swiss Colony, see Arthur Inkersley, "The Vintage in California and Italy," *Overland Monthly* 114 (Oct. 1909), 408; misc. notes, Italian Swiss Colony File, CHS; "A Pleasing Celebration," *Alta California*, Oct. 12, 1885; E. Peixotto, "Italy in California," *Scribner's* 48 (July 1919), 75–85; Andrea Sbarboro, "Memories," MS (Jan. 1, 1911), BL. Sbarboro restricted membership to Italians, although he initially hired Swiss workers because an Italian-Swiss investor was on the board of directors. Membership was permanent and all members had to be U.S. citizens. See also Sbarboro, "Wines and Vineyards of California," *Overland Monthly* 25 (Jan. 1900), 65–76, 95–96; *Sixth Annual Report, The Italian-Swiss Agricultural Colony* (San Francisco, 1887); M. B. Leverick, "A Man With Three Thousand Monuments," *Sunset* 30 (Jan. 1913), 93–94; C. Dondero, "Asti, Sonoma County, an Italian-Swiss Agricultural Colony," *Out West* 17 (July–Dec. 1902), 253–66; Edmund A. Rossi, "Italian-Swiss Colony, 1949–1989: Recollections of a Third-Generation California Winemaker," interview, 1990, ROHP.

110. Quote from *Marysville Appeal*, July 10, 1888, cited in *PRP*, July 18, 1888. Of the Italians and Portuguese working in the Santa Clara Valley, one grower said: "It was more inconvenient to obtain them than it had been to obtain the Chinese, because they were not organized into groups, did not remain on the ranch as the typical Chinese had done, and were not so skillful in their work." Quote from *ICR*, 24: 200. For Indians and whites, see Mary Peet, *San Pasqual: A Crack in the Hills* (San Diego, 1949).

111. *Alta California*, Oct. 2, 1888; *San Francisco Chronicle*, Oct. 2, 1888.

112. *Alta California*, Oct. 5, 10, 1888; *San Francisco Morning Call*, Oct. 12, 13, 1888; In re: Chae Chan Ping, 36 Federal Reporter, 431, 433–36; Circuit Court [old federal] of Northern California 1888; Brief of George Hoadly and James C. Carter, 14, 20, in Case File, Chae Chan Ping v. United States, 130 U.S. Reports, 581, U.S. Supreme Court Records and Briefs; Sawyer to Matthew Deady, Oct. 18, 1888, Matthew Deady Papers, Oregon Historical Society, Portland, Ore.

113. Quote from *San Francisco Evening Bulletin*, Oct. 15, 1888. See also Shih-Shan Henry Tsai, *China and the Overseas Chinese in the United States, 1868–1911* (Fayetteville, Calif., 1983), 90–91; Hudson N. Janisch, "The Chinese, the Courts, and the Constitution: A Study of the Legal Issues Raised by Chinese Immigration, 1850–1902" (J.S.D. diss., Univ. of Chicago, 1971), 699–751; Milton Konvitz, *The Alien and the Asiatic in American Law* (Ithaca, 1946), 1–22.

114. McClain, *In Search of Equality*, 195–97; Memorandum of July 8, 1889, in Notes from the Chinese Legation.

115. Referring to experiences the previous year, a few growers told a meeting of the Labor Committee of the State Board of Trade how they "could have made thousands of dollars more if they could have found help to gather it," then predicted that they would now have to prepare for similar problems. Also speculating on the effects of the Scott Act, the *Sacramento Bee* predicted that by ending the labor surplus that had long held down wages and contributed to abysmal farm labor housing, the Scott Act would force growers for the first time to improve working conditions and raise pay simply to attract harvest hands. Quotes from *Sacramento Bee*, Feb. 28, 1889; see also Jan. 3, Mar. 28, 1889; *St. Helena Star*, Jan. 18, 1889; *California Farmer*, Feb. 2, May 25, 1889; *PRP*, Feb. 2, 23, 1889; Frank Hinckley, diary, Feb. 20, 22, 23, 1889.

116. Although Ping held a return certificate, Field decided that he held it "at the will of the government, revocable at any time, at its pleasure." The only rights created by previous treaties that Ping could possibly claim were property rights. Quote from Chinese Exclusion Case, *Chae Chan Ping v. United States*, 130 U.S. Reports (Washington, D.C., 1889), 581, 609, see also 600–10.

C H A P T E R   S I X T E E N

1. Quotes from *California Fruit Grower*, July 16, 1889; advertisement, *Marysville Daily Appeal*, July 25, 1889; lease with Rosalie L. Younger, 1890, Santa Clara County, "Leases," Book F,

519. For the profanity arrest, see *St. Helena Star*, Sept. 13. See also "Ventura Notes," *PRP*, July 13, 1889; *Independent Calistogian*, Aug. 1, 14, 1889.

2. Quote from *Kern County Californian*, Dec. 8, 1889. "There seems to be a growing disposition to substitute white labor for the Chinese," observed the *St. Helena Star* during the September grape harvest. Quote from *St. Helena Star*, Sept. 6, 1889. See also *San Francisco Merchant* 22 (Sept. 8, 1889), 3.

3. *California Fruit Grower*, Aug. 23, 1890; "Grape Pickers Wanted," ibid., Sept. 6, 1890; *PRP*, Dec. 6, 1890; unidentified clipping, Fresno County Scrapbooks, 1: 163–64, SCHMLCSUF. For efforts to replace Chinese with white field hands in Sonoma, see *Santa Rosa Daily Republican*, Sept. 2, 1890. For Tehama, see *San Francisco Examiner*, Apr. 6, 1890. See also *Sacramento Bee*, Mar. 18, 1891. *PRP*, Aug. 1, Sept. 5, 1891; *Fresno Weekly Evening Expositor*, Aug. 19, 1891; also Sept. 3, 1891; *California Fruit Grower*, Sept. 19, 1891; July 18, Sept. 10, 1892.

4. Quote from L. E. Rickseller to *Santa Rosa Daily Republican*, Sept. 10, 1890. See also Speth, "Agricultural Labor in Sonoma," 55, 60–61; *Sonoma County Daily Republican*, Sept. 10, 1890. For the end of organized efforts to employ children in the Napa Valley hop harvest, see *St. Helena Star*, Aug. 31, 1894. See also *Rio Vista Sacramento River News*, Dec. 19, 1890, in River News-Herald Library, Rio Vista, Calif.

5. Following the precedent of other communities, Gird offered Oxnard an outright gift of land. One week after signing a contract, Oxnard brought in a German architect and began laying out the factory beside seven artesian wells whose aggregate flow of two million gallons provided water for the plant. See Stephen E. Graves, "The Life of Richard Gird in Chino," *Pomona Valley Historian* 5 (Jan. 1969), 29–36. Passage of the McKinley Tariff Act in 1890— which provided a federal bounty of two cents per pound on all domestically produced sugar and allowed for free importation of beet seed and sugar processing machinery—had provided a rich opportunity. See Margaret Palmer Dennis, "The History of the Beet Sugar Industry in California" (M.A. thesis, USC, 1937), 15, 18, 21–29, tables 1, 2; Street, "Into the Good Land: The Emergence of California Agriculture, 1850–1920," MS (1978), 261–63, BL.

6. Quote from entry of Apr. 14, 1891, California, no. 1, typewritten entries by Dan Gutleben, taken from the Lewis L. Ware Scrapbooks, Philadelphia Memorial Library, ACSCR. For the incident at Chino, see *Chino Valley Champion*, Apr. 24, 1891; *St. Helena Star*, Apr. 24, 1891, which congratulates the vigilantes for removing the menace; Richard Gird to editor, *Chino Valley Champion*, Apr. 16, 1891; Gird, diary, entries for Apr. 1891, Richard Gird Papers, HL. The mob is described as composed of "local growers" in Anthony Lehman, "The Sugar Beet Builds a Business," *Pomona Valley Historian* 5 (Apr. 1969), 77–79. For another version of the incident, see Adolph Whitney, *History of Chino Valley* (Chino, 1962), Chino Valley Historical Society; *Chino Valley Champion*, Nov. 6, 1987; Gerald F. Brown, Clara Ebeling Brown, Mary Ruth Wagner, and Alice B. Reher, interviews by Phyllis Outhier, Chino Valley Historical Society, n.d., in Outhier to Jennifer Fukunaga, Chino Branch Library, copy to author, n.d. [May 2, 1998], author's possession. California's Exclusion Act forbade all Chinese except elected government officials from entering the state and required all Chinese in California within one year to obtain an identification certificate with their photograph or face deportation. For the state exclusion law, see Act of Mar. 20, 1891, *Statutes California, 1891*, ch. 140 (Sacramento, 1891), 185–92; *Sacramento Bee*, May 15, July 15, 1891; Sandmeyer, *The Anti-Chinese Movement in California*, 102–3.

7. Quote from "Still a Mystery," *Vacaville Reporter*, June 15, 1895; also July 30, 1891. For the incident with the dog, see *St. Helena Star*, May 8, 1891.

8. Quotes from *Vacaville Reporter*, July 9, 23, 1891; *St. Helena Star*, n.d.; *Sacramento Bee*, Sept. 30, 1891; *Wheatland Four Corners* in *PRP*, Aug. 15, 1891; also Sept. 2. The Lovdal brothers hop yards were the largest in the world; the Menke yards were nearly as large. For a Chinese farm cook falsely arrested for stealing a farmer's wallet, see *St. Helena Star*, Aug. 14, 1891. During July and August the Chinese poured into the vineyards at Vina five hundred strong. With thirty-nine hundred acres, Vina was still the largest vineyard in the state, and its labor demands —135 men for a few weeks during pruning, and seven hundred to bring in the harvest—typified in microcosm what was happening throughout California. Extrapolating those figures and applying them to the state, William H. Mills, a land agent and Southern Pacific Railroad employee, told the State Agricultural Society that California's two hundred thousand acres of bearing vineyards would need about thirty-five thousand harvesters. The calculation yielded a land-to-person ratio of about one person for every six acres. "It would be impossible to have the labor of nine men available for a few months in the vintage season for one man who might

find steady employment," concluded Mills. But in fact that was actually what the grape industry in 1891 required. This realization would soften considerably the anti-Chinese movement. Quote from William H. Mills, "Annual Address," *CSAST, 1891*, 200. See also "Vina," *Sacramento Union*, Sept. 23, 1891.

9. Quotes from *Sacramento Bee*, Sept. 30, 1891.

10. Quotes from *St. Helena Star* in *Napa Daily Journal*, Oct. 8, 1891, NCLCF; "Chinese Fruit Buyers," *Vacaville Reporter*, July 2, 1891.

11. *St. Helena Star*, Feb. 5, 9, 12; Oct. 21, 1892.

12. Quotes from *California Fruit Grower*, Sept. 12, 1891; June 18, 1892. See also Clough and Secrest, *Fresno County*, 1: 333; U.S. Dept. of Agriculture, Misc. Series, *Report No. 4* (Washington, D.C., 1892), 53–54. Schwartz, *Seasonal Farm Labor Market*, 5, 15, 35, identifies this as the first attempt at wage fixing.

13. Quote from Inkersley, "Celery Growing in the Peat Lands of California," 104. Having pioneered the transcontinental shipment of fruit, Earl Fruit was expanding operations, building a series of icing stations throughout the state and moving into vegetable growing on a huge scale. See also Lin, "Perspectives on the Chinese in Nineteenth-Century Orange County," 35; Friis, *Orange County Through Four Centuries*, 103–4. Although celery was a new crop, men—dressed in slickers and rubber boots—quickly worked out an efficient routine. Using a light, four-wheeled, highly modified potato-digger, one man would guide a team of horses that pulled the machine forward, while another tended a long, sharp, horizontal knife. Fixed to an adjustable bar, the knife could be lowered and raised according to soil conditions, cutting the celery roots just below ground level. Big-footed dobbin horses were used extensively to pull equipment and fitted with special "peat shoes" to prevent them from sinking into the mud. Trailing behind the horse-drawn cutting machine, six or seven Chinese gathered the celery. After trimming the tops, they packed the celery in crates and placed the crates in furrows. Crews following behind loaded the crates onto wagons and hauled them out of the fields. Working incessantly, Chinese celery workers never rested, "stopping only now and then to roll a cigarette." Quote from Coleman, "History of the Celery Industry," 98–103.

14. Quotes from "War in the Peatlands," *Anaheim Gazette*, Apr. 6, 1893, in Leo J. Friis, *Kleinigkeiten* (Santa Ana, 1975), 30–31.

15. Quote from Mr. J. D. Price, interview by Chloe Holt, Garden Grove, Dec. 17, 1924, SRRP. See also McWilliams, *Ill Fares the Land: Migratory Labor in the United States* (New York, 1941 [1992]), 89.

16. Select Committee on Immigration and Naturalization, *Chinese Immigration*, Report no. 4048, 51st Cong., 2nd sess., 1890, H. Doc., 252, 277, 295, 315, 323, 342; Note from Minister Tsui to Secretary Blaine, Apr. 12, May 5, Nov. 7, 1892, *Notes from the Chinese Legation; San Francisco Evening Bulletin*, Sept. 10, 23, 1892; *San Francisco Morning Call*, Sept. 14, 20, 1892.

17. Quote from typed notes, *Watsonville Pajaronian*, Mar. 30, 1893, PVHS. Some sources like the *Sacramento Bee* claimed that representatives of the Chinese Six Companies were threatening to kill or severely punish anyone caught violating their edicts and registering. See also Apr. 26, 1893; Tsui Kuo-yin to Walter Gresham, Mar. 13, 21 1893, in House, *Foreign Relations of the United States*, 53rd Cong., 2nd sess., 1893, H. Doc., 1: 245–47; *Oriental*, Mar. 24, 1893; *San Francisco Morning Call*, Apr. 1, 1893. According to the Dept. of Treasury, 13,342 Chinese had registered by May 5, while 93,445 had not, with about one in ten unregistered Chinese being members of the exempt classes. See House, Committee on Foreign Affairs, *Report to Accompany House Resolution 3687*, 53rd Cong., 1st sess. , 1893, 2.

18. *SWM*, Jan. 22, 1894; *Sacramento Bee*, Apr. 26, May 10, 1893.

19. Quote from typed notes, *Watsonville Pajaronian*, May 25, 1893, PVHS. See also "The New and Monstrous Anti-Chinese Bill," Ng Poon Chew Collection, Asian American Studies Library, UCB.

20. *Watsonville Pajaronian*, Apr. 11, May 25, 1893.

21. *NYT*, May 6, 11, 1893.

22. Quotes from Fong Yue Ting v. United States, 149 U.S. Reports (Washington, D.C., 1893), 737; also 698–760, U.S. Supreme Court, Records and Briefs; *Sacramento Bee*, May 17, 1893. Although it is unclear how deeply field hands comprehended the ruling, there is no doubt that through information passed along by the Six Companies they understood that Chief Justice Melville Fuller, and justices David Brewer and Stephen Field, strongly dissented from the majority opinion.

23. Quote from typed notes, *Watsonville Pajaronian*, May 13, 1893, PVHS. For estimates of registration, see Jan. 4, 11; Feb. 22, 1894; *Ventura Weekly Free Press*, May 19, 1893. See also *Sacramento Bee*, July 15, 1893; *St. Helena Star*, Dec. 15, 1893.

24. Quotes from Lydon, *Chinese Gold*, 250–52. See also Judy Yung, *Unbound Voices*, 37–39. District and circuit courts in San Francisco heard about ten thousand habeas corpus cases. These records, transcripts of interrogations, and other supporting documents contain photographs, and offer a vast and rich snapshot of life in China and Chinese immigration to California. See Larisa K. Miller, "From Courtroom to Research Room: Studying the West in Federal Court Records," *WLH* 10 (spring–summer, 1997), 34; Christian G. Fritz, *Federal Justice in California: The Court of Ogden Hoffman, 1851–1891* (Lincoln, Neb., 1991), 210.

25. For the proportion of Chinese working as farmhands, see the computations in Chan, *Bittersweet Soil*, 378–81. For one unsuccessful habeas corpus hearing for a merchant who was denied reentry, see Ham Tung habeas corpus case, Habeas Corpus Case File no. 10932, Apr. 1894. See also Haiming Liu, "The Trans-Pacific Family: A Case Study of Sam Chang's Family History," *Amerasia Journal* 18 (1992), 1–34; Waverly Lowell, "Chinese Immigration and Chinese in the United States: Records in the Regional Archives of the National Archives and Records Administration," National Archives and Records Administration, *Reference Information Paper No. 99* (1996), Chinese Arrival Case Files, San Francisco District Office, INS; Yung, *Unbound Voices*, 11, 15, 32–56; "Angel Island Immigration Station: Interviews with Chris Chow, Mr. Yuen, Ira and Ed Lee," 1977, Asian American Resources Oral History Project, 21, BL.

26. Smuggling costs from *Sacramento Bee*, Mar. 2, 1901. The Ensenada route is described in Oct. 25, 1901; see also July 24; Nov. 12, 1901. Chinese dumped overboard weighted with rocks are described in Alma Pixley Dean, "The Chinese in Early Orange County, California," interview, 1986, 4, CSU, Fullerton. Marooned Chinese are described in L. Clifford Fox, "Pursuing the Smuggler," *Overland Monthly* 61 (June 1913), 531–41. See also F. B. Worley, "Five Hundred Chinese Refugees," ibid., 81 (Mar. 1918), 290–94.

27. For fifty-six "Asiatics" lost in the desert between San Felipe and Mexicali, see *Holtville Tribune*, Oct. 6, 10, 1915, bound volume, Imperial Valley Historical Society, Pioneer Museum, Imperial, Calif. [originally researched in the old museum]. For the route from San Felipe, see Philip L. Fradkin, *A River No More: The Colorado River and the West* (New York, 1981), 328. For aspects of the smuggling operation, see *El Centro Progress*, Feb. 2, 1915, San Diego State University, Calexico Campus Library. See also Erika Lee, "At America's Gates: Chinese Immigration During the Exclusion Era, 1882–1943" (Ph.D. diss., UCB, 1998), ch. 5; "Seattle Smugglers," *San Francisco Call*, June 20, 1895.

28. Quote from *Oxnard Courier*, Apr. 12, 1902, VCM. See also *Sacramento Bee*, May 16, Aug. 1, 1889; James G. Blaine to Ryan, Oct. 22, 1890; Ryan to Blaine, Nov. 1, 1890, *Papers Relating to Foreign Relations of the United States*, 1: 655–56; "Chinese Labor," *Mexican Financier* 8 (1886), Edward L. Doheny Papers, Occidental College Special Collections, Los Angeles.

29. Samuel Reznick, "Unemployment, Unrest, and Relief in the United States during the Depression of 1893–1897," *Journal of Political Economy* 61 (Aug. 1953), 324–45; Charles Hoffmann, *The Depression of the Nineties, an Economic History* (Westport, Conn., 1970); Julian Ralph, *Our Great West: A Study of the Present Conditions and Future Possibilities of the New Commonwealths and Capitals of the United States* (New York, 1893), 307.

30. Quotes from "City and County," *Redlands Citrograph*, Sept. 2, 1893, Heritage Room, A. K. Smiley Library, Redlands; *Sacramento Bee*, Sept. 27, 1893. For unemployed men soliciting farmwork, see H. A. Pellet to Jane Stanford, July 10, 15, 1893, Jane Stanford Papers, SUASC.

31. Quote from *Los Angeles Times*, Aug. 14, 1893. See also *Fresno Weekly Evening Expositor*, Aug. 15, 17, 22; Sept. 9, 1893, Fresno County Scrapbook, 1: 168–71, SCHMLCSUF. For the situation on Fourth Street and the surrounding orchards and hop fields, see *Sacramento Bee*, Aug. 16, 1893, reporting "The road and the various wayside resorts contain many people in search of employment"; see also Sept. 20, 23, 27, 1893; *San Francisco Morning Call*, Sept. 22, 1893. For white laborers offering to replace Chinese for the same wages, see *Redlands Citrograph*, Sept. 9, 1893. Near Pomona, large numbers headed for the Chino sugar beet refinery. Establishing temporary camps, they had nowhere to go following the harvest, and seemed an incredible sight to a reporter for the *San Francisco Examiner*, who wrote a long account of their plight.

> Just outside the factory gates there is a motley collection of tents and shanties built of corn stalks, burlap bags, bed comforters, dry goods boxes, and oil cans. Mexicans, Dutch-

men, Frenchmen, and even Americans, two and three families . . . often huddled in one
little 12 x 12 cornstalk shack. They come here prepared to live hard and close in order
that they may carry away with them at the end of the campaign a few eagles with which
to bluff the gaunt wolf from the door next winter. Life . . . with its broad contrasts, its
comedy and tragedy, is epitomized here in Chino.

Quote from entry for Oct. 7, 1893, Ware Scrapbooks, General, no. 1, ACSCR.

32. Quotes from Chan, *Bittersweet Soil*, 378, 386; McWilliams, *Factories in the Field*, 74; *St.
Helena Star*, Aug. 25. See also Sept. 1; C. T. McEachran to editor, Sept. 8, 1893. See also "The
Unemployed, Proceedings of Company A, First Regiment," MS (1893), SHSW; FWP, "Oriental Labor Unions" (Oakland, 1939), 1, BL; Sucheng Chan, *Asian Americans: An Interpretative History* (New York, 1991), 51; Chu, "Chinatowns in the Delta," 21.

33. Quotes from Sullivan, *Napa Wine*, 112; *PRP*, Aug. 26, 1893. See also McWilliams, *Factories in the Field*, 75; *St. Helena Star*, Aug. 25, Sept. 1, 1893.

34. Quotes from McWilliams, *Southern California: An Island on the Land*, 90–91; Glendora
Citrus Association, *50 Year History, 1895–1945* (Glendora, 1946), 1. See also Charles Carlson, di-
ary, Feb. 4, Sept. 30, 1878; Jan. 18, 21, 1888; notes by Carlson's daughter, Alice Mary Carlson,
photocopy of typewritten manuscript, Charles Carlson Collection, HL; Harry W. Lawton, "A
Brief History of Citrus in Southern California," in Esther H. Klotz, Harry W. Lawton, Joan
H. Hall, eds., *A History of Citrus in the Riverside Area* (Riverside, 1969 [1989]), 10–11; Riverside
Municipal Museum, *Life in Little Gom-Benn: Chinese Immigrant Society in Riverside, 1885–1930*
(Riverside, 1991), 10; *Riverside Press and Horticulturalist*, July 18, 1878; Harry Lawton, "River-
side's Pioneer Chinese," Feb. 10, 1959, *Riverside Daily Press*; "The Great Fire of 1893," Feb. 11,
1959, Riverside Public Library, Local History Room.

35. Visiting growers and packers in Crafton late in August, unemployed men demanded jobs,
insisted that the Chinese must go, and physically prevented Chinese field hands from departing from trains arriving at Mentone. See "City and Country," *Redlands Citrograph*, Sept. 2, 1893.

36. Quotes from McWilliams, *Factories in the Field*, 77; McWilliams, *Southern California:
An Island on the Land*, 90.

37. "No Chinamen allowed to Stop at Mentone," and "Mentone & Crafton Chinese asked
to Leave," Sept. 2, 1893; "The Mongol Must March—Redlands Chinese Evicted by Legal
Methods," "Committee of Riverside to study how Redlands deports Chinese," "Praise for Redlands over Chinese excitement," and "Chinese Flee Redlands," Sept. 9, 1893, *Redlands Citrograph*. See also *Los Angeles Times*, Aug. 14, Sept. 3, 1893; *Riverside Press*, Sept. 1–7, 1893.

38. Quote from *Los Angeles Times*, Sept. 3, 4, 1893. See also "The Mongol Must March,"
Sept. 9, 1893; "Redlands Chinamen ordered deported by Judge Ross," and "Thirteen Chinese
leave Redlands," Sept. 16, 1893, *Redlands Citrograph*; Edith Parker Hinckley, *On the Banks of
the Zanja* (Claremont, 1951), 94.

39. Quotes from McWilliams, *Factories in the Field*, 76; Lawrence E. Nelson, *Only One
Redlands: Changing Patterns in a California Town* (Redlands, 1963), 138–39.

40. "Redlands Chinaman Ordered Deported by Judge Ross," *Redlands Citrograph*, Sept.
16, 1893. After enduring similar harassment around Anaheim, Chinese field hands were threatened outside Planter's Hotel on the evening of August 31 by a crowd of unemployed men and
curious boys, but never attacked. Chinese field hands were well regarded by most Anaheim
citizens, who would have nothing to do with mob action. When speakers urged bystanders to
kick out the Chinese, a deputy sheriff and several officers appeared and quickly disbanded the
gathering. Nevertheless, Anaheim's Chinese took no chances. "All the Chinese houses were
closed early in the evening, and the lights were out and the doors barred," reported the *Anaheim Gazette* of the events on Saturday evening. "The heathen had a good scare, but doubtless
breathed easier Sunday morning when they awoke and found themselves alive and well and
their houses still standing over them," Quote from *Anaheim Gazette*, Aug. 31, 1893. See also
T. M. Whaun, interview, Mar. 5, 1924, SRRP.

41. *Selma Weekly Enterprise*, Aug. 17, Sept. 8, 1893, Selma Public Library, Selma, Calif. In
some accounts Vinzent is spelled Vincent.

42. Ibid., Sept. 15, 21; Oct. 5; Dec. 5, 1893. When the Chinese sued the town for inadequate
police protection, the *Selma Enterprise*, heretofore silent on the issue, editorialized that there
"should be as little delay as possible in removing from among us by legal process these expensive and troublesome Chinese," while businessmen suggested that the town should refuse to

grant any licenses to Chinese establishments. Finally, on Dec. 1, the city attorney laid the four-month-old dispute to rest. Selma could not discriminate against any racial group, he explained, "for all must be treated alike."

43. *California Fruit Grower*, Aug. 26, 1893; *Fresno Weekly Expositor*, Aug. 15, 17, 22; Sept. 9, 1893, Fresno County Scrapbook, 1: 168–71, SCHMLCSUF; *Sacramento Daily Record-Union*, Aug. 15, 16, 21, 1893; *Sacramento Bee*, Aug. 23, 1893.

44. *Sacramento Bee*, Aug. 23; Sept. 13, 20, 27, 1893; *San Francisco Morning Call*, Sept. 22, 1893; *PRP*, Sept. 16, Nov. 17, 1893. Various other groups also tried to remove the Chinese. For example, on the afternoon of August 18, Perch Cox, described by newspapers as a book agent in Stockton, organized a mass meeting of some two hundred unemployed men. Convening them in Hunter Square, Cox whipped them up with some hot speeches and vowed to march on the Chinese quarters that evening "to tell the Chinese to leave Stockton." That evening, with the local police on alert to prevent him from entering Chinatown, Cox attempted to further inflame his followers, but could manage only a pitiful candlelight speech from a rickety pine table. Quotes from typed notes, *SDI*, Aug. 19, 1893, FFLCSF. See also Clough and Secrest, *Fresno*, 1: 333–34; *Los Angeles Times*, Aug. 15, 19; Sept 1, 2, 1893; *San Francisco Morning Call*, Sept. 22, 1893.

45. Quotes from *PRP*, Sept. 16; Oct. 7, 1893; *Los Angeles Times*, May 17; Aug. 17, 26, 1893. For the agricultural press, see *PRP*, June 10; Sept. 16, 1893. See also Robert J. Pitchell, "Twentieth Century California Voting Behavior" (Ph.D. diss., UCB, 1955), 113–14; Donald E. Walters, "Populism in California, 1889–1900" (Ph.D. diss., UCB, 1952), 142.

46. Quotes from typed notes, *SDI*, Aug. 20, 23, 1893, FFLCSF. See also June 12, 1901. Both the *Los Angeles Times* and *San Francisco Call* inaccurately reported that Stockton residents had participated in the anti-Chinese campaign. For an excellent discussion of Chinese laborers in the asparagus industry, see Minnick, *Samfow*, 182–84. Quickly learning how to cut asparagus spears just below the soil surface with a notched blade on the end of a three-foot-long steel pole, they tended the crop daily, discovering that by only harvesting between January and June they could eliminate the need to replant the crop each year. Following these cultural practices growers were soon producing bumper harvests, and as supplies outstripped demand, the Hick-mott Company built what would be the first of several factories to sort, cut, pack, and cook the excess "gras," as the vegetable was known locally.

47. Quote from *Santa Rosa Democrat* in *St. Helena Star*, Sept. 8, 1893. For the view that the Chinese could more easily survive unemployment than white field hands, "whose entire stake is in the country and whose families form a permanent and desirable part of our population," see *Red Bluff People's Cause*, Sept. 2, 1893. In the hop fields southwest of Sacramento, growers hired 125 unemployed white men, who almost immediately struck for a raise from $1.10 to $1.35 per one hundred pounds. But with so many other unemployed men available, the strikers lacked leverage, and within a few days all but forty-five returned to work. See *Sacramento Bee*, Sept. 20, 1893.

48. Quotes from clippings, *San Francisco Morning Call*, Feb. 1, 1894; *San Francisco Chronicle*, Feb. 1, 1894, Stanford Family Scrapbooks, SUASC. See also David Starr Jordan, *The Days of a Man* (New York, 1922), 1: 497–98; *San Francisco Star News*, cited in *Sacramento Bee*, Jan. 1, 1894. Sentiment against the Chinese at Vina continued to worsen. In 1898, when the vineyard manager leased the grape crop to a China boss, white field hands refused to work. Blaming Mrs. Stanford, they destroyed all of the vineyard tools and plows, then set fire to three hundred tons of hay and alfalfa, along with several barns. To calm them, Mrs. Stanford herself late in August traveled to Vina. Going among the men she urged calm, broke the contract with the Chinese, fired the vineyard manager, fired all of the Chinese, and hired three hundred white pickers. See Jane Stanford to Mary Hopkins, Aug. 29, 1898, Jane Stanford Papers, SUASC.

49. For Rivera, see *Sacramento Bee*, Mar. 14; May 16, 1894. For Anaheim, see *PRP*, Mar. 3, 1894. For the wage situation, see Apr. 7, 1894. For Chinese in the packing sheds, see Evelyn Hollinger, *La Verne: The Story of the People Who Made a Difference; A History of La Verne, California, 1837–1987* (La Verne, 1989), 109. See also Ella Cain, *The Story of Early Mono County; Its Settlers, Gold Rushes, Indians, and Ghost Towns* (San Francisco, 1961), 60–70.

50. For Dowdell, see *St. Helena Star*, Mar. 23, 1894. For Coxey's Army in California, see Carlos Schwantes, *Coxey's Army: An American Odyssey* (Lincoln, Neb., 1985), 99; Donald L. McMurry, *Coxey's Army: A Study of the Industrial Army Movement of 1894* (1929 [Seattle, 1968]), xiii, 14–15, 127–28, 130–31, 148, 196–97, 243, 260; Henry Frank, "The Crusade of the Unem-

ployed," *Arena* 10 (July 1894), 239, 243–44; Lucy G. Barber, *Marching on Washington: The Forging of an American Political Tradition* (Berkeley and Los Angeles, 2002), 16–43.

51. Quotes from *Vacaville Reporter*, May 21, 1894; also May 16, 21.

52. Quote from *Sacramento Bee*, May 23, 1894. See also *Vacaville Reporter*, May 21, 23, 25, 28, 29, 1894.

53. So many men were in jail at one time that ten managed to break out, and six were able to make a clean getaway. But by the end of the month, these activities apparently had established Vacaville's reputation as a tough town where Chinese field hands were able to go about their business free of attacks and harassment. See Limbaugh and Payne, *Vacaville*, 134–35.

54. Quote from *St. Helena Star*, June 15, 1894.

55. Quotes from *Sacramento Bee*, May 23, 1894; also May 9; *Winters Express*, July 7, 1894, Yolo County Historical Society. Chinese domination of fruit growing in the northern Sacramento Valley is described in "A Menace to the Fruit Industry," *PRP*, Mar. 2, 1895; "Review of the Dried Fruit Market," ibid., July 20, 1895.

56. Quote from *Sacramento Bee*, Aug. 22, 1894. See also "Cooly Contract Labor," *San Francisco Call*, June 8, 1895.

57. Quote from Con Nevin, "The Pleasanton Hop Company," *Pleasanton Times*, Aug. 13, 1910. See also J. E. McGown, *Progressive Pleasanton, 1902* (Pleasanton, 1902), 1–6, Amador-Livermore Valley Historical Society, Pleasanton; "Agriculture long a part of city's history," *Amador Valley Times*, Sept. 12, 1982; "Cooly Contract Labor," *San Francisco Call*, June 8, 1895.

58. Quote from "Cooly Contract Labor." See also *Sacramento Bee*, Aug. 22; Sept. 19, 1894.

59. Quote from ibid.

60. Quote from *PRP*, Nov. 17, 1894.

61. Quotes from *PRP*, July 20, 1895. See also *Watsonville Pajaronian*, May 25, 1893; Feb. 28, May 9, 1895; Mar. 12, 1896; *Salinas Index*, June 27, 1895. For the Cleveland administration, see Roy L. Garis, *Immigration Restriction: A Study of the Opposition to and Regulation of Immigration into the United States* (New York, 1927), 294–302. Chinese field hands and their bosses flourished despite the brutality. Even while they were being abused, maimed, and driven out, they continued to use their intimate knowledge of agriculture and their contacts with farmers to identify trends, spot opportunities, seize the initiative, move in, and take over. When no one else would do a job, they always made themselves available. When they could not handle all the tasks on a farm, they often shared responsibilities with crews of Indian and Mexican field hands. For evidence suggesting that the Chinese had mastered the intricacies of grapevine pruning, see E. H. Bauman to Leopold Justi, Jan. 21, 1905, Leopold Justi Collection, BL. For the importance of Chinese field hands to several Fresno vineyards, see *Fresno Republican, Imperial Fresno* (Fresno, 1900), 13–15. For Chinese working with Indians and Mexicans in Los Angeles vineyards, see Black, *Rancho Cucamonga*, 260. There was plenty of work for everyone, regardless of race, including Indian field hands who continued to troop into the Napa Valley from Lake County to pick hops. During August 1895, Chinese hop pickers in the Sonoma Valley worked for the rock-bottom rate of sixty cents per one hundred pounds after growers fixed wages. For wage fixing in the Sonoma hop industry, see *Napa Daily Journal*, Aug. 21, 1895, NCLCF.

62. Quotes from *Salinas Index* in Lydon, *Chinese Gold*, 311–12. See also Margaret Tynan lease, Mar. 30, 1895, Santa Cruz County, "Leases," Book 3: 368; *Watsonville Pajaronian*, Mar. 12, 1896; *Salinas Index*, June 27, 1895.

63. *Salinas Index*, Feb. 20; Mar. 19; Aug. 6, 13; Sept. 10; Dec. 3, 1896. "The beet payday last week was a giant and twenty-dollar pieces crowded each other in Watsonville," reported the Jan. 21, 1897, *Watsonville Pajaronian*. "There was about as much money paid out here that payday as the railroad company pays out monthly at its big shop center, Sacramento; and the next day will be about as large." Quote from Herbert Myrick, *The American Sugar Industry* (New York, 1907), 44.

64. *Watsonville Pajaronian*, Sept. 20, 1900; *PRP*, Mar. 27, Oct. 30, 1897; Feb. 12, 1898; *Salinas Evening-Democrat*, Dec. 29, 1897; Jan. 5, 12, 14; Apr. 15; June 11, 1898; Frederick de L. Booth-Tucker, *A Review of the Salvation Army Land Colony in California* (New York, 1903), 18–25; H. Rider Haggard, *The Poor and the Land* (London, 1905), 36–66; John E. T. Milsaps, diary, 3, Jan. 5, 6; Apr. 15, 1898, John Milsaps Collection, Houston Public Library, Houston, Tex.

65. Quote from "Not Employing Chinese: Union Sugar Company of Santa Maria Want White Labor," *Oxnard Courier*, Apr. 22, 1899, citing a Santa Maria newspaper.

66. Quote from *Watsonville Pajaronian*, Sept. 20, 1900. Federal manuscript census information from Lydon, *Japanese in the Monterey Bay Region: A Brief History* (Capitola, Calif., 1997), 28. See also *Salinas Index*, Feb. 2, 1899. For a Chinese beet contract for 297 acres, see Wing Tai Chung lease, Monterey County, "Leases," Book D, Dec. 1899: 398.

67. Quote from *Watsonville Register*, June 25, 1901, in "Sugar Beet Harvester," *Oxnard Courier*, June 29, 1901.

68. Quote from *Watsonville Pajaronian*, Jan. 21, 1897, cited in Myrick, *American Sugar Industry*, 44; typed notes on A. W. Tate, "Development of the Apple-Drying Industry in the Pajaro Valley," *Watsonville Pajaronian*, Sept. 5, 1918, PVHS. Living in giant bunkhouses, barns, and shacks beside their dehydrators, most worked at coring and peeling apples that failed to meet the grade as fresh fruit. Placing each apple onto a spindle, they turned a crank causing a series of knives to skim the surface of the apple, thus removing the skin. After removing the apple from the spindle, they cut out the core, saving it and the peel in bins for making vinegar. At this point in the process, cutters sliced and washed the apples, spread them in a single layer on large wooden trays, then stacked the trays in the sulfur room for an hour or so before removing them and placing them in the kilns for another six or eight hours. See Lydon, *Chinese Gold*, 219, 396–409. Tramping through the Pajaro Valley in 1912, British journalist Arthur T. Johnson reported that "the Chinese possess and work practically every one of its fifty-seven apple evaporating furnaces. . . . They also hold the apple canneries and vinegar factories." See Johnson, *California: An Englishman's Impressions of the Golden State* (London, 1913), 206–7.

69. Quote from Chester Bishop, interview, n.d., MCABHP. See also the edited version in Levene, *Mendocino County Remembered*, 1: 60. See also *St. Helena Star*, May 1, 1896. Yet for all their willingness, the Chinese were hardly acquiescent. Using their unity and organization to defend wage gains, a crew of forty Chinese pickers employed on John Sheenan's Sonoma County hop ranch walked out of the fields in September, obtaining a raise in wages from one cent per pound of hops to 1.5 cents per pound. See *Sonoma County Tribune*, Sept. 4, 1896. For Indian hop pickers, see *Napa Register*, Sept. 18, 1896. For the events in Riverside, see *Riverside Press*, Feb. 29, 1896. See also Harry Lawton, "Riverside's Pioneer Chinese," *Riverside Daily Press*, Feb. 10, 1954, Riverside Public Library, Local History Room.

70. Quote from *Winters Express*, June 25, 1897; *Fresno Daily Evening Expositor*, Aug. 28, 1897; see also July 2; *California: A Journal of Rural Industry* 14 (Apr. 12, 1890), 12–23; *PRP*, June 10, 1893; and account books, 1890–1893, R. B. Blowers Papers, BL. Advertisements, *PRP*, June 26; July 3, 17, 1897; *Davisville Enterprise*, July 30, 1898; *Newcastle News*, July 30, 1902. At the center of hop production in the Sacramento Valley, E. C. Horst, P. C. Drescher, and D. P. Durst (a.k.a., the "Hop King"), grew eleven hundred acres of hops, about 15 percent of the state's total. Much valued by British brewers, their hops required substantial investments in the rich alluvial soil of the Bear River bottomlands, as well as hop kilns, warehouses, large baling presses, and elaborate trellises. Harvest labor requirements were extraordinary; hops had to be picked during a three-week window, usually from mid- to late August, when the crop achieved the proper ripeness. Wheatland hop industry information from James Parsons, "The California Hop Industry: Its Eighty Years of Development and Expansion" (M.A. thesis, UCB, 1939), 28, 111; *PRP*, Aug. 30, 1902; *Sacramento Bee*, Aug. 21, 1902; "Immigrants in Industries," *ICR* 24: 157–58; *CSAST, 1891*, 196–97; testimony of E. C. Horst, in CIR, *Final Report*, 5: 4931; Records of Deeds received, Dec. 16, 1915, Durst Bros. Hop Ranch Papers, SCML.

71. Quotes from unidentified newspaper clipping, FHHC; *CIR*, 5: 4920; *Maywood Colony Advocate*, Nov. 1, 1899. Holdbacks and bonuses are described in *Davisville Enterprise*, July 30, 1898; *PRP*, Sept. 2, 1899; Aug. 30, , Sept. 6, 1902.

72. Quote from *St. Helena Star*, Feb. 17, 1899 see also May 8, 1897. For mixed crews at this time, see farm labor force calculations from LFCH, pt. 3: 223; pt. 54: 19883; Alvin H. Thompson, "Aspects of the Social History of Agricultural Labor in California, 1885–1902" (M.A. thesis, UCB, 1953), 236–38.

73. Fred B. Palmer, *My Eighty Years in Pomona* (Pomona, 1968).

74. Quotes from *St. Helena Star*, Nov. 12, 1897; Chloe Holt, "A Sketch of the Orientals in Orange County," MS (Feb. 23, 1925), SRRP. Census figures and other data from Chan, *Bittersweet Soil*, 77, 313–14, 386, 391–99; U.S. Dept. of Commerce, Bureau of the Census, *Twelfth Census of the United States, 1900* (Washington, D.C., 1902), 2: xxii; U.S. Dept. of Commerce, Bureau of the Census, *Thirteenth Census of the United States, 1910* (Washington, D.C, 1913), 161; Lee, *Chinese in the United States*, 22, 116.

75. McWilliams, *Factories in the Field*, 90; Chinn, *A History of the Chinese*, 21; Chan, *Bittersweet Soil*, 313–14, table 29, 381; Speth, "Agricultural Labor in Sonoma," 52; 1900 MS Census.

76. Quote from Harry Butler, "A History of the First Malaria Mosquito Control Campaign in the United States, at Penryn, California, 1910," MS (Apr. 15, 1945), 1–3, Harry Butler Biographical Letter File, CSL. See also William B. Herms, *Malaria: Cause and Control* (New York, 1913), 65–67, 89–91, 95–96; Harold Farnsworth Gray and Russell E. Fontaine, "A History of Malaria in California," in California Mosquito Control Association, Inc., *Proceedings and Papers of the Twenty-Fifth Annual Conference, June 30, 1957*, reprint in CSL; W. F. Snow, "Co-Operative Farm Sanitation," California State Commission of Horticulture, *Thirty-Eighth CSFGCP, Dec. 6–9, 1910* (Sacramento, 1911), 164–73.

77. Dillon, *The Hatchet Men*, 111–16, 126–27, 214, 250; Minnick, *Samfow*, 205, 229–34. According to the *Sacramento River News*, tong hatchet men began using Isleton as a refuge from police raids in San Francisco and other urban areas. See Apr. 13, 1894.

78. Quote from Wallace L. Ware, *The Unforgettables* (San Francisco, 1964), 70–72. See also *Fresno Republican*, Apr. 16, 20, 23; June 22, 1899. Arrested and shipped back to Santa Rosa, they claimed innocence, their alibi being that they been playing fan-tan in a Chinese laundry in Sausalito. When police searched them, they found peanuts in Park's coat pockets. Placing the men on board a Santa Rosa–bound train, the authorities were able to break their alibi and hold them for trial when the peanut concessionaire on the train identified Park, and conductor and brakeman confirmed that the three had been on board their train the previous day. See Ware, *Unforgettables*, 70–72.

79. Ware, *Unforgettables*, 72–76.

80. Quotes from Rogers, *Colusa County*, 157, 258; also 175–77, 184, 222. For context, see McKenna, *Homicide, Race, and Justice*, 18–23.

81. Quotes from "Vicious Gambling Among Oriental Farmworkers," *San Francisco Chronicle*, Jan. 15, 1919, Pamphlets on the Japanese, BL; Ronald Takaki, *Strangers from a Different Shore: A History of Asian Americans* (New York, 1989), 131; "General Summary of the Oriental Situation in California Agriculture," MS (n.d.), 2, SRRP; Allyn C. Loosley, "Foreign-Born Population of California, 1848–1920" (M.A. thesis, UCB, 1928), 34. Desperate, hungry, and without children to support them in their old age, a few old Chinese did something they had never done before and which was extremely uncharacteristic—they stole. Most commonly, they poached firewood or fuel. To supplement their diet, they would also nab poultry and pigs from farms or fruit from orchards. When they were captured and brought to trial, their emaciated and "toothsome" appearance so alarmed authorities that they usually dropped the charges. This was clearly the case in St. Helena. Arrested for snatching hens from chicken coops on John Dowdell's farm, an old field hand named Doo On was found to be in such pitiful health that he was acquitted. The court then sentenced him to "several good meals." For the incident, see *St. Helena Star*, Feb. 17, 1899.

82. Quote from *St. Helena Star*, Sept. 25, 1896; "Chinese Laborers Reported Ill," *Sacramento Bee*, Dec. 6, 1918.

83. More than five hundred found employment cultivating, harvesting, and sacking potatoes, beans, onions, and asparagus with just one tenant farmer, Chin Lung, a Stockton-based Chinese entrepreneur. Known as the Chinese "Potato King," Lung leased thousands of acres of land throughout the delta. For the decline of Chinese field hands in the Napa Valley, see "Vineyards of California," *Pacific Wine and Spirit Review* 48 (Aug. 31, 1905), 51; Charles Forni, interview, Feb. 13, 1974; Carl Dressel, interview, June 21, 1972; William Lyman, interview, Mar. 29, 1973, all with William Heintz, courtesy William Heintz. Information on Chinese field hands in the delta from 1900 MS Census, Contra Costa and San Joaquin counties; "Chin Lung—Potato King," *Stockton Daily Evening Record*, n.d., SRCF; Minutes, Pierson Reclamation District, Feb. 26, 1909, Pierson Reclamation District Papers, reports pay of six cents per yard of fill.

84. Quote from "Chinese Help," *River News*, Feb. 19, 1915. See also Christopher Yip, "Locke, California, and the Chinese-Americans" (M.A. thesis, UCB, 1977); Frank Lortie, "Historical Sketch of the Town of Locke," MS (State Department of Parks and Recreation, Sacramento, 1980), 6–8.

85. Chu, "Chinatowns in the Delta," 22, 31; Leung, "When a Haircut was a Luxury," 213; Chan, *Bittersweet Soil*, 209–10, 397.

86. Daniel Arreola, "Locke, California: Persistence and Change in the Cultural Landscape of a Delta Chinatown" (M.A. thesis, CSU, Hayward, 1975).

87. George Kagiwada, "Report on Locke: A Historical Overview and Call for Action," *Amerasia* 9 (spring 1982), 57–78; Jean Rossi, "Lee Bing, Founder of California Historical Town of Locke," *PH* 20 (winter 1976), 351–66. In some accounts the Sze Yup are described variously as Sze Yip and Sze Yup. Similarly Zhongshan Chinese are also identified as Huengshan or Chungshan Chinese.

88. Quoted in Allen Castle, "Locke: A Chinese Chinatown," *PH* 24 (spring 1980), 1. For a biased but rare firsthand account, see Esther A. Thomas, "A Chinese Town on the Sacramento," *Missionary Review of the World* 57 (1934), 407–8. See also Sally Ooms, "The Effects of Change and Intervention on the Chinese Town of Locke, California" (M.A. thesis, USF, 1980); Chan, "The Significance of Locke in Chinese American History," in Jeff Gillenkirk and James Motlow, eds., *Bitter Melon: Stories from the Last Rural Chinese Town in America* (Seattle, 1987), 18.

89. Ralph Weitz, "The California Canned and Dried Fruit Industries, with Special Reference to their Dependence upon Exporting" (M.A. thesis, UCB, 1925); *ICR*, 24: 251–52. For Chinese cannery workers in Fresno, see "A Humming Bee-Hive of Industry: The Tenney Canning Company," *Fresno Daily Evening Expositor*, June 22, 1896, FCHS. Comparative pay figures from CSBLS, *Fourth Biennial Report, 1889–90*, 90–92, 97–101. The Isleton asparagus cannery was built by Chinese entrepreneur Tom Foon. Branching out from his tomato canning operation at Alviso, Foon hired famed industrial designer William de Back to build the first plant to can green asparagus successfully, which until then had been packed while white. By 1920 standards, the plant and the work was truly fantastic. Most of the asparagus came from two thousand acres Foon leased on nearby Sherman Island. Receiving boxes of asparagus from the fields, cannery workers stacked them in two rows, with the delicate tips or spears pointing to the center of the box. Placing the asparagus onto a conveyor belt, they again made sure that the tips all faced in one direction. Farther down the packing line, where the asparagus dropped through six or seven sizing slots, cutters bundled the asparagus ends so that they could cut the thick butt ends to length with large, hinged knives. Cookers toughened the asparagus enough to survive the canning process by placing it in wicker baskets and blanching it in hot water, then dousing the asparagus in tubs of cold water. At the canning station, trimmers cut out bruises or discolored spots and sorters removed pieces too small for canning, setting them aside for "soup cuts." Next canners placed the asparagus in square cans and sent them to cookers. Square cans were used to prevent the asparagus from rotating inside the cans and breaking off their tips. Finally "cappers" soldered the cans shut and men pasted labels on the cans by hand. Later in the season, trimmers would cut the asparagus short to eliminate the tough butt ends, and peal it to make it more tender. The work was inherently messy, with men standing in trimmings and squashed asparagus all day, struggling not to slip on the slick floors. See *San Jose Mercury*, Feb. 15, 25, 1931; *San Francisco Examiner*, Feb. 25, 1931; J. C. Wright, "Thomas Foon Chew—Founder of Bayside Cannery," in Hom, *Chinese Argonauts*, 27–29. On Andrus Island across the river from Walnut Grove, 140 asparagus cannery workers, eighty-six of them married, lived in a single large bunkhouse with three cooks and three waiters, their own dishwasher, and at least one man who did odd jobs around the bunkhouse. Two other asparagus cannery communities existed on Roberts Island. One consisted of seventy-six men, three quarters of them over fifty years of age. The other was comprised of forty-seven men in their fifties, sixties, and seventies. Like their counterparts on Andrus Island, they lived in a gigantic bunkhouse and were tended to by a staff of cooks, laundrymen, and waiters. Although census takers failed to note whether or not the Roberts Island men were married, it would seem logical that like their counterparts on Andrus Island many of them also supported families. See 1910 MS Census, Sacramento County, Georgiana Township [Andrus Island] and San Joaquin County, O'Neal Township [Roberts Island].

90. Quote from Sec. of Treasury Metcalf to Assistant Sec. of Treasury Lawrence Murray, Oct. 1, 1904, "Chinese Segregated Files," File 12811, Records of the INS, RG 85, NA. See also Chinese Chamber of Commerce et al. to Sec. of Commerce and Labor, Jan. 27, 1909, Subject Correspondence, File 52366/14, INS. See also Mary Bamford, *Angel Island: The Ellis Island of the West* (Chicago, 1917); Connie Young Yu, "Rediscovered Voices: Chinese Immigrants and Angel Island," *Amerasia Journal* 4 (spring 1977), 123–39; Nee and Nee, *Longtime Californ'*, 14–15.

91. "Chinese American Community," *Oxnard Press-Courier*, Sept. 24, 1948, ACSCR; "How Uncle Sam Watches the Immigration and Catches the Smuggler," *San Francisco Call*, Jan. 28, 1900; Elliot A. P. Evans and David W. Heron, "Isla de Los Angeles: Unique State Park in San

Francisco Bay," *CH* 66 (Mar. 1987), 37; Thomas B. Wilson, "The Chinese Character," *Overland Monthly* 107 (June 1911), 658; Frank B. Lenz, "The Americanized Student," ibid. 119 (Apr. 1917), 285.

92. Lai et al., *Island: Poetry and History of Chinese Immigrants on Angel Island*, 16–17, 22–23, 27; Lai, "Island of Immortals: Angel Island Immigration Station and the Chinese Immigrants," *CH* 57 (spring 1978), 88–103; Rogers, *Colusa County*, 229; Keith Power, "Ellis Island of the West," *San Francisco Chronicle*, Nov. 25, 1974.

93. Quote from Lai et al., *Island: Poetry and History of Chinese Immigrants on Angel Island*, 60. See also Bruce Koon, "Ellis Island of the West—The Chinese Experience," *San Francisco Chronicle*, Aug. 31, 1980, quoting the same poem. See also Connie Young Yu, "Rediscovered Voices: Chinese Immigrants and Angel Island," *Amerasia Journal* 4 (spring 1977), 123–39. Angel Island shut its doors in 1940.

94. Quotes from Stabler, "Discussion of the Labor Question," 276, 278, 395; *Los Angeles Times*, Mar. 2, 1902. For the debate over the Chinese and who would replace them, see Wylie Giffen, interview, in Myer, "Fresno Raisin Industry," 53; G. H. Hecke, "Pacific Coast Labor," *CSFGCT, 1908* (Sacramento, 1908), 69; CSBLS, *Fifteenth Biennial Report, 1910*, 47; ICR, 24: 108; Rowell, "Chinese and Japanese Immigration," *AAAPSS*, 4. While some later commentators on Chinese farm labor would recall them as laborers who did not compete with others and did not lower labor costs, others characterized them as a class that depressed wages. See Coolidge, "Chinese Labor Competition on the Pacific Coast," 341–50; Carl C. Plehn, "Labor in California," *Yale Review* 4 (Feb. 1896), 409–25. For burning of the Santa Ana Chinatown as a "public nuisance," see *Santa Ana Evening Blade*, May 24–25, 1906.

CHAPTER SEVENTEEN

1. Quote from Will Irwin, "The Japanese and the Pacific Coast," *Collier's Magazine* 90 (Oct. 19, 1907), 17–19. The essay, complete with photographs, was the last of a three-part series. See also ibid. (Oct. 5, 1907), 13. For an attack on Irwin's essay, see the *Vacaville Reporter*, Oct. 19, 1907. See also *FMR*, Jan. 1, 12; Sept. 13, 1907; "Japanese in Agriculture," *ICR*, 23: 67; "Race Relations Report: California, the Japanese," pt. 2: 1, 6, 10; "Report on Fresno, California, the Armenians," pt. 1: 11, SRRP.

2. For Japanese shipped in from Los Angeles and Sacramento by railcar, see *Sacramento Bee*, July 20, 1901. See also *Fresno Weekly Evening Expositor*, Oct. 26, 1897, Fresno County Scrapbook, 1: 202, SCHMLCSUF; *California Fruit Grower*, Oct. 7, 1899. Piece rates described in "Immigrants in Fresno County, California," *ICR*, 24: 573–75, 591, 635, 586. For the pattern of Japanese infiltration into the fields, see CSBLS, *Thirteenth Annual Report, 1907–8*, 141–42, 201; CSBLS, *Fourteenth Annual Report, 1909–10*, 268; Meyer, "The Raisin Industry" 54–55; *California Fruit Grower*, Apr. 18, 1903; Kiyoshi K. Kawakamiu, "The Japanese on Our Farms," *Forum* 50 (July 1913), 82–83.

3. Quotes from Mrs. G. W. Aiken, "The Labor Question," *CSFGCT, 1902*, 394; Frank Smith, "Report on the Japanese," MS (n.d.), SRRP; *FMR*, Aug. 31, 1899, Fresno County Scrapbooks, 1: 172, SCHMLCSUF. See also Bessie Ezaki, interview, in Yoshiro Tajiri Hasagawa and Keith Boettcher, eds., *Success Through Perseverance: Japanese-Americans in the San Joaquin Valley, Fresno County* (Fresno, 1980), 154, and the full interview in the California History Room, Fresno Public Library.

4. For the invention and consequences of the seeder, see E. Leroy Chaddock, "Fifty Years a Raisin Packer," MS (1943), 83–89, SCHMLCSUF; James Madison, "Raisin History," MS (July 5, 1914), 6, BWC; *California Fruit Grower*, Nov. 28, 1903; *PRP*, May 23, 1903; *FMR*, Aug. 5, 1907; Meyer, "The Raisin Industry," 71–74; Simon W. Hatheway, *The Evolution of the Not-A-Seed Raisin* (Fresno, 1906), Franklin P. Nutting Papers, BL. For piece rates, see A. B. Butler, "California and Spain," *California: A Journal of Rural Industry* 1 (Mar. 1890), 8; Eisen, *The Raisin Industry*, 42, 180; Aiken, "The Labor Question," 394; "Immigrants in Fresno County, California," *ICR*, 24: 586; *PRP*, Sept. 1, 1900; McCubbin, "How the Work is Done," MS (n.d.), JCMP. Harvest rates did not specify the number of men in a crew. The phenomenal increase in acreage harvested was due in part to increased efficiencies, but also no doubt, to larger crews.

5. Yuji Ichioka, *The Issei: The World of the First Generation Japanese Immigrants, 1885–1924* (New York, 1988), 91–92, gives a low estimate, stating that by 1909 about thirty thousand out of 119,611 field hands were Japanese, with six thousand working in sugar beets. Of 54,463 farm-

workers on 2,369 farms surveyed by the CSBLS in 1909, 47.4 percent (25,826) were white, 41.9 percent (22,811) Japanese, 3.8 percent (2,091) Chinese, 3.4 percent (1,847) Mexicans, 1.9 percent (1,033) Indians, 1.4 percent (732) "Hindus" (Indian Sikhs and Punjabis), and 0.2 percent (82) "other." See CSBLS, *Fourteenth Annual Report, 1909–10*, 266–70, app. B. Ratios are from H. A. Millis, "Some Economic Aspects of Japanese Immigration," *American Economic Review* 5 (Dec. 1915), 794–95. See also Ichihashi, *Japanese in the United States*, 176–77; Iwata, "Japanese Immigrants in California Agriculture," 27.

6. For Japanese excluded from certain jobs, see *ICR*, 1: 61, 68, 70; 5: 18; 23: 61; 24: 20–23, 199–201. For independent farm labor markets based on ethnic composition, see Schwartz, *Seasonal Farm Labor*, 21; *CIR*, 5: 4940–41. See also Sidney Gulick, *The American Japanese Problem* (New York, 1914), 317; Edward K. Strong, *Japanese in California* (Stanford, 1933), 104–5; See also CSBLS, *Fifteenth Annual Report, 1910*, 48; Meyer, "Raisin Industry," 54–55; J. C. Trombetta, "Report on Japanese in the Delta," in "Japanese in the United States," Yamoto Ichihashi Papers, SUASC; Melvyn Sanguinetti, "Immigrant Japanese in the Fruit and Vegetable Industry," 4, SRRP.

7. Quote from J. H. Walsh, "Japanese, Chinese Exclusion or Industrial Organization," *Industrial Union Bulletin*, Apr. 11, 1908. Loftis and Meister, *Long Time Coming*, attribute the beginning of labor militancy to the Industrial Workers of the World. Philip Taft, *Labor Politics American Style—The California Federation of Labor* (Cambridge, Mass., 1968), attributes these developments to the American Federation of Labor, a dubious if not ridiculous assertion. See also Ray Barry, "Contract Labor in California Agriculture," in WPA, "Documentary History of Farm Labor in California Agriculture," MS (1939), 16, BL; Ko Murai, ed., *Zaibei Nihonjin Sangyo Soran* (Los Angeles, 1940), 1, JARPC.

8. For crop disasters, see Doi Yataro, *Yamaguchi-ken Oshima-gun Hawai Imishi*, trans. Tasura Namura (Tokuyama, 1980), 17–20, JARPC. For the Hawaii phase, see Hilary Conroy, *The Japanese Frontier in Hawaii, 1868–1898* (Berkeley, 1953); Hilary Conroy, "Robert Walker Irwin & Systematic Immigration to Hawaii," in Conroy and T. Scott Mikakawa, eds., *East Across the Pacific* (Santa Barbara, 1972), 40–55. Those in the small, conservative, tradition-bound, southwestern agricultural prefectures of Kumamoto, Hiroshima, and Yamaguchi, as well as peasants on Kyushu Island, comprised the bulk of the immigrants. For a good description of distress among the peasant class, see *Japan Weekly Mail*, Dec. 20, 1884, in Nippi Jiji, *Golden Jubilee of the Japanese in Hawaii, 1885–1935* (Honolulu, 1935). For rural society in the Meiji era, see Peter Duus, ed., *The Cambridge History of Japan: Twentieth Century* (New York, 1988), 2: 541–57. See also Ichioka, *The Issei*, 45.

9. Quote from "Life History of Sakoe Tsuboi," May 9, 1924, SRRP. See also "Life History of a Japanese Man, aged 22," trans. Masao Dodo, Santa Paula. For conditions leading to immigration, see Yoshida Yosaburo, "Sources and Causes of Japanese Emigration," *AAAPSS* 34 (Sept. 1909), 379–87; Alan Moriyama, "The Causes of Emigration: The Background to Japanese Emigration to Hawaii, 1885 to 1894," in Lucie Cheng and Edna Bonacich, eds., *Labor Immigration Under Capitalism: Asian Workers in the United States Before World War II* (Berkeley, 1984), 250–54; Azusa Tsuneyoshi, "Meiji Pioneers: The Early Japanese Immigrants to the American Far West and Southwest, 1880–1930" (Ph.D. diss., Northern Arizona University, 1989), 180–33; Hart H. North, "Chinese and Japanese Immigration to the Pacific Coast," *CHSQ* 28 (Dec. 1949), 343–44; Tsuyashi Matsumoto, "Reminiscences," Tsuyashi Matsumoto Papers, JARPC. Immigration expenses from Paul R. Spickard, *Japanese Americans: The Formation and Transformation of an Ethnic Group* (New York, 1996), 12.

10. *ICR*, 23: 29; 24: 6–8, 317; Wakayama-Ken, *Wakayama-Ken Imin Shi* (History of Japanese immigration from Wakayama prefecture) (Wakayama-Ken, 1957), 305–6, copy in JARPC; Sidney L. Gulick, *The American-Japanese Problem*, 322; Yamato Ichihashi, *Japanese in the United States* (Stanford, 1932), 87–88; Tadashi Fukutake, *Japanese Rural Society* (Ithaca, 1967), 6, 7, 39, 40, 42, 47; Yoshiko Kasahara, "The Influx and Exodus of Migrants among the 47 Prefectures in Japan, 1920–1935" (Ph.D. diss., University of Michigan, 1957), 1–12; interviews with Issei conducted by the Japanese-American Research Project, UCLA, showing one in four immigrants intended to stay. Compared to other immigrant groups, Japanese field hands were both better educated, with an average of an eighth-grade education, and financially secure, arriving with an average of $21.57 each, a sum that placed them alongside Dutch, Scotch, English, and French immigrants. See also *ICR*, 1: 13, 99; 2: 106; John P. Irish, "Reasons for Encouraging Japanese Immigration," *AAAPSS* 34 (Sept. 1909), 75. Average age of Japanese farm laborers in Monterey

County in 1900 was twenty-seven, compared to fifty-four for Chinese. See Lydon, *The Japanese in the Monterey Bay Region*, 28.

11. Quotes from Bill Hosokowa, *Nisei: The Quiet Americans, The Story of a People* (New York, 1969), 48; clipping, *San Francisco Call*, June 25, 1902, Pamphlets on the Japanese, BL. See also Tohru Takanoshin, "The Story of a Japanese Emigrant: The Life Story of Domoto Takanoshin," *The East* 5 (Mar.–Apr. 1969), 3–9.

12. Quote from "Life History of a Japanese Immigrant," interview no. 285, SRRP. Unable to speak English, ignorant of American culture, and coming from a feudal society, Japanese immigrants often were further disoriented by the sights and smells of the city. Quickly they learned certain key words like "hot," "work," and "drink water"—survival English. Meals became adventures. Most had never seen a tomato. To buy eggs, one man who could not easily make himself understood resorted to squatting, cackling like a hen, and dropping a rock as if laying an egg. Some men never quite adapted. Language and egg anecdote from Hosokowa, *Nisei*, 77–78. See Hisaakira Kano, *Tunnels Under the Pacific* (New York, 1919), 19–21; Katayama Sen, *To-Beiannai* [Guide to America] (Tokyo, 1901), 2, 5, 14, 67–78; *Sacramento Bee*, May 30, 1900; June 28, 1902; *ICR*, 23: 3–4, 17–18; U.S. Census Bureau, *Thirteenth Census of the United States* (Washington, D.C., 1910), 1: 141; North, "Chinese and Japanese Immigration to the Pacific Coast," 343–50; Yasuo Wakatsuki, "Japanese Emigration to the United States, 1866–1924," in Donald E. Fleming, ed., *Perspectives in American History* (New York, 1979), 12: 401–4, 452–53, 494, 510; "Life Before Evacuation," in "Biography of a Nisei Celery Grower from Venice," MS (n.d.), Carey McWilliams War Relocation Material, Claremont College Archives and Special Collections, Claremont, Calif.

13. Chotoku Toyama, "The Japanese Community in Los Angeles" (M.A. thesis, Columbia University, 1926), 6; Michinari Fujita, "The History of the Japanese Association in America" (M.A. thesis, Northwestern University, 1928), 54, 57; J. C. Trombetta, "Report on the Japanese in the Delta"; "Economic Status of the Japanese in Walnut Grove," Ichihashi Papers, SUASC. For guidebooks, see Henry (Yoshitaka) Kiyama, *The Four Immigrants Manga: A Japanese Experience in San Francisco, 1904–1924*, trans. and intro. Frederick L. Schodt (Berkeley, 1998); Shimizu Tsuruzaburō, *Beikoku rodo benran* (Labor handbook for America) (San Francisco, 1903); Kawamura Tetsutaro, *Saikin katsudo Hoku-Bei jigyo annai* (Guide to current jobs in North America) (Tokyo, 1906), JARPC.

14. For Japanese in the Vaca Valley in 1887–88, see *PRP*, May 19, 1888; *ICR*, 24: 197; *Winters Express*, May 12, 1888; Limbaugh and Payne, *Vacaville*, 136; Toyoji Chiba, "Truth of the Japanese Farming in California," in *California and the Oriental: Japanese, Chinese, and Hindus* (Sacramento, 1920), 218.

15. Yoneda Landing is today called Ward's Landing. For Japanese in Solano County in 1889, see Robert A. Wilson and Bill Hosokowa, *East to America: A History of the Japanese in the United States* (New York, 1980), 60. For Japanese field hands in Santa Cruz, see Lydon, *The Japanese in the Monterey Bay Region*, 26. For Japanese in Sonoma, see Speth, "History of Agricultural Labor in Sonoma," 62–63a. For the thirty Japanese in Vacaville, see Zai Bei Nihonjin-Kai, *Zai Bei Nihonjin-Shi* (History of the Japanese in America) (San Francisco, 1940), 773, JARPC. The sequence of harvests in the Vaca Valley is described in William A. Bowen, "Evolution of a Cultural Landscape: The Valley Fruit District of Solano County, California" (M.A. thesis, UCB, 1963), 111; Karen Nolen, ed., *Solano's Gold: The People and Their Orchards* (Vacaville, 1999).

16. Quotes from *Vacaville Reporter*, June 26, 1890; Cikuth, "The Pajaro Valley Apple Industry," 136–37.

17. Quotes from *Sacramento Bee*, May 20, 1891. See also *Vacaville Reporter*, May 28; June 4, 14, 15, 1891; *California Fruit Grower*, June 13, 1891.

18. Quote from Daniel Flint, "The Hop Industry in California," *CSAST, 1891*, 197. For Japanese working in hops, see *Sacramento Bee*, Sept. 30, 1891. For Japanese in pears near Marysville and Biggs, see Japanese Association of Marysville, *History of the Japanese in the Big Four* (Marysville, 1939), 49. For men seeking out relatives, see Mrs. Fumi Nakajima, interview, in Hasagawa and Boettcher, *Success Through Perseverance*, 195. Perhaps the most impressive demonstration of Japanese grit and character at this time occurred in October, when fifteen Japanese field hands finished picking raisin grapes near Fresno. Walking along the railroad tracks south two hundred miles to Riverside, the men took more than two weeks to reach their destination. Although they probably could afford train tickets, they apparently walked to save money because they were unsure whether they would obtain work. Immediately employed in

the citrus orchards and packing plants, some of these same men camped in tents under a eucalyptus tree at the corner of Magnolia and Adams streets. They would remain there for more than a decade. Local residents later referred to them as the "Gum Tree" Japanese. See Roy Ito, "The Japanese in the Inland Empire," MS (n.d.), 1, Archives and Special Collections, University of California, Riverside.

19. Prior to arriving in Watsonville, Kimura may have been secretly connected with the U.S. Navy. See typed notes, Sazukō Kimura obituary, ca. 1900, *Watsonville Pajaronian*, PVHS; Ichihashi, various notes on visit to Watsonville, 1908; Ichihashi, "Supplementary Report on Japanese in Watsonville," 8–9, in "Japanese in the United States," Ichihashi Papers, SUASC. According to Ichihashi, outsiders did not receive club privileges and remained in boardinghouses, but anyone could join the club by paying the five-dollar annual fee. See Ichihashi, *Japanese in the United States*, 173. For the first Japanese contractors in the Pajaro Valley, see *Watsonville Pajaronian*, Feb. 28; May 9, 1895. For 1896, see Lydon, *Japanese in Monterey*, 27–28. For the Japanese in the Pajaro Valley, see *PRP*, May 22, 1896; Apr. 10, 1897; "Note and Comment," May 1, 1897. For Kimura, see Shinichi Katō, ed., *Beikoku Nikkeijin Hyakunen Shi* (The hundred-year history of the Japanese in America) (Los Angeles, 1961), 421–22; Kō Murai, ed., *Zaibei Nihonjin Sangyō Sōran* (A compendium of Japanese agriculture in America) (Los Angeles, 1940), 897. *Keiyaku* means contract, *nin* means person, so the term literally referred to a "contract person."

20. Quote from Ichihashi, "Supplementary Report on the Japanese in the Watsonville District," 8, Ichihashi Papers, SUASC.

21. Ichihashi, *Japanese in the United States*, 172–73, contains a condensed version of his field notes and other material in his papers, but curiously omits the names of the various clubs as well as many important details including the discovery that 150 women belonged to the clubs. Dates for the clubs were: the Higashi (1899); the Hirabayashi (1902); the Matsuaka (1903). Matsuaka is also spelled Matsuoka. Membership figures were: Higashi, 140; Hirabayashi, 120; Matsuaka, 130. See Ichihashi, "Supplementary Report on the Japanese in the Watsonville District," 9, Ichihashi Papers, SUASC. For *keiyaku-nin* shipping men to the fields in wagons, see typed notes, *Watsonville Pajaronian*, May 20, 1896, PVHS. The first *keiyaku-nin* in Watsonville was probably Kōzaburō Baba, who began work in 1890. According to Karl G. Yoneda, *Ganbatte: Sixty-Year Struggle of a Kibei Worker* (Los Angeles, 1983), 24, Baba organized the Japanese Labor Union in 1892. Its purpose was to "control the Japanese workers under contract, to maintain the rake-off system, and to pit the Japanese against other ethnic workers. The word 'union' was actually a camouflage to ward off growing anti-Japanese sentiments in the Winters and Vacaville area where Japanese workers were first employed as field hands." Baba appears again in 1903 as a leader in the Oxnard sugar beet strike. See also Masakazu Iwata, *Planted in Good Soil: A History of the Issei in United States Agriculture* (New York, 1992), 1: 387.

22. Quote from Lydon, *Japanese in Monterey*, 27. One aspect of their work that delighted growers, besides the ease and convenience the *keiyaku-nin* provided, was their attention to certain details of the modern farm labor regimen. Sugar beet harvesting required crew bosses to constantly supervise men. Easier said than done, many non-Japanese contractors were inattentive, but not the *keiyaku-nin*. "This may seem a small affair," explained the *Pacific Rural Press*, "but cheapness and speed of work depend upon . . . the greatest economy of time in every operation." Quote from *PRP*, Dec. 4, 1897.

23. Quote from David Mas Masumoto, *Country Voices: The Oral History of a Japanese American Family Farm Community* (Del Rey, Calif., 1987), 9. For *keiyaku-nin* taking telephone orders, see *ICR*, 24: 17–18; also 158–59, 227–28; H. A. Millis, "Some Economic Aspects of Japanese Immigration," 796. See also Isamu Nodera, "A Survey of the Vocational Activities of Japanese in the City of Los Angeles" (M. A. thesis, USC, 1937), 57, 63; *San Francisco Chronicle*, May 30, 1910. See also Millis, *The Japanese Problem in the United States* (New York, 1915), 111; Fisher, *Harvest Labor Market*, 20; Tsuyoshi Matsumoto, "History of Resident Japanese in Southern California," MS (n.d.), trans. Togo Tanaka, Japanese Evacuation and Resettlement Study Collection, BL; Loretta Balcom, "Comparative Study of the Japanese," Dec. 29, 1923, SRRP. For *keiyaku-nin* shifting men about, see CSBLS, *Fifteenth Annual Report, 1910*, 47. Although Ichioka, *Issei*, 81, claims growers did not pay fees for providing men, S. Hori to C. L. Lesnold, Dec. 17, 1914; and S. Hori to Lesnold, Dec. 18, 1914, French-Glenn Papers, describe fees of seven dollars per man paid to Hori and Company for field hands supplied to farmers around Willows. Employment estimates from *ICR*, "Japanese and other Immigrant Races in the Pacific Coast and Rocky Mountain States," 10: 590.

24. Quote from *Vacaville Reporter*, July 16, 1892. For Japanese around Colusa in 1893, see the *Colusa Sun*, cited in *Red Bluff People's Cause*, July 6, 1893. For Japanese field hands arriving at Florin in 1894, see *ICR*, 25: 405; Wilson and Hosokowa, *East to America*, 61. For Japanese in Chico, see *Sacramento Bee*, May 9, 1894. For Japanese in the Sacramento hop harvest, see ibid., Aug. 22, 1894.

25. For the system that distributed immigrants to *keiyaku-nin* and the various statistical breakdowns of where men went to work, see "Whites Driven Out," *San Francisco Call*, June 6, 1895; "Cooly Contract Labor," ibid., June 8, 1895; Ichioka, *The Issei*, 57–80. For one *keiyaku-nin*, see Yokoyama Gennosuke, *Kaigai Katsudo no Nihonjin* (Active Japanese Abroad), trans. Tatsuro Nomura (Tokyo, 1906), 13–18, JARPC. For another, see Kesa Noda, *Yamato Colony, Livingston, California* (Livingston, 1981), 4. For commission arrangements and finder's fees, see Miki Saito to Takahira, Jan. 26, 1905, Japanese Foreign Ministry Archival Documents, JARPC. For a general discussion of the movement of Japanese from labor contractors to landowners, see J. W. Jenks and W. J. Lauck, *Immigration Problems* (New York, 1913), 247–49. See also Iwata, *Planted in Good Soil*, 1: 221–481. For *keiyaku-nin* working out of the Tokyo Club and gambling houses in Sacramento, see Robert I. Okazaki, interview by Joe Grant and Japanese American Citizens League interview, 1967, JARPC.

26. For repayment schedules, see Wakayama-Ken, *Wakayama Ken Imin Shi*, 128–31. For the profits of Japanese farm labor contracting, see Edwin Hiroto, interview by Grant and Japanese American Citizens League, n.d.; Okazaki, JARPC. For shifting men, see Soichi Nakatani, interview, in Cheryl L. Cole, "A History of the Japanese Community in Sacramento, 1883–1972" (M.A. thesis, CSUS, 1973), 149.

27. Quotes from *Sacramento Bee*, Jan. 27, 1897; Cikuth, "The Pajaro Valley Apple Industry," 134. See also Yamato Ichihashi, interview by Mr. [Francisco] Palomares, in "Efficiency of the farm hands by nativity," Ichihashi Papers, SUASC.

28. Quotes from *Sacramento Bee*, Jan. 27, 1897; *PRP*, Sept. 21, 1895. See also Gulick, *American Japanese Problem*, 29–30; Gregory, *History of Sonoma*, 130; Kaizo Naka, "Social and Economic Conditions among Japanese Farmers in California" (M.A. thesis, UCB, 1913), 26–28; Mrs. C. C. Violett, interview, Garden Grove, Dec. 16, 1924, no. 274 (13), SRRP. On May 27, 1901, the *Sacramento Bee* observed that the Japanese were "willing to labor for such small pay that they are actually displacing Chinese." For Florin, see May 1, 1913. For Japanese working for seventy-five cents per day without board at Monte Rio while Chinese worked for ninety cents, see *PRP*, Apr. 10; May 1, 1897. For undermining whites and Chinese in the Santa Clara Valley, see Apr. 7, 1894. For the daily figure, see *ICR*, 24: 18, 27, 41, 63, 158–60, 220–22; Millis, *Japanese Problem in the United States*, 111. For the bilingual functions of *keiyaku-nin*, see Secretary, Japanese Association, interview, Garden Grove n.d., doc. no. 274-A; W. S. Cairns, interview, Feb. 11, 1925, doc. no. 83, in "Interviews with Farm Workers," SRRP. For more information on *keiyaku-nin*, see advertisement by the Japanese Contracting Department, 530 Pine Street, San Francisco, in clipping, *Japan Tribune*, Apr. ?, 1901, Pamphlets on the Japanese, BL.

29. Quote from "Coolies on Strike," *San Francisco Call*, June 12, 1895. For Fujimoto, see "Whites Driven Out," ibid., June 6, 1895. Often greeted with ugly racial slurs and taunted while disembarking at railroad stations, they were called "Yellow Jap," "Almond-eyed heathen," "Buddha-head," and much more. Entering white-owned barbershops they would be told, "We don't cut animal's hair." Mistaken for Chinese, they would be asked to speak "Chink talk" and make "Chop-Suey." Quotes from Minoru Ino, "My Life History," MS (Apr. 12, 1926), 3–4; "Life History of Sakoe Tsuboi," 3, SRRP; Kazuo Ito, *Hoku-Bei Hyakunen Sakura* (Hundred-year-old cherry blossoms in North America) (Seattle, 1969), 893–94, hereafter cited as *A History of the Japanese in North America* (1973 ed.), 93, 95, 99, 100, 127, 129, 130; Shiki Ito, "My Sixty-Four Years in America," in East Bay Japanese for Action, ed., *Our Recollections* (Berkeley, 1986), 125. See also Kiyoshi Kawakami, "How California Treats the Japanese," *The Independent* 74 (May 8, 1913), 1020; Eileen Sunada Sarashn, ed., *The Issei: Portrait of a Pioneer, An Oral History* (Palo Alto, 1983), 64, 67.

30. "Hordes of Japanese," *San Francisco Call*, June 1, 1895; "Pleasanton Inquiry," June 5, 1895.

31. Quotes from "Japanese Are Agitated," *San Francisco Call*, June 13, 1895.

32. Quotes from "Whites Driven Out," *San Francisco Call*, June 6, 1895; "Pleasanton Inquiry," ibid., June 5, 1895. One contractor agreed to work the beet fields for fifteen dollars an acre, receiving five dollars after the first hoeing, three dollars after the second, and if the crop produced more than eight tons per acre, receiving one dollar a ton for each extra ton of beets.

A similar contract between Sato and A. R. Downing paid Sato fifteen dollars an acre, of which four dollars were withheld until thirty-six days after the harvest, with the balance of eleven dollars paid at the end of the harvest.

33. Quote from "Whites Driven Out." Later that day, local notary public A. C. Vandervoort testified that the Japanese "buy cheap wine by the gallon and get drunk as lords. As a result there are frequent brawls among themselves in their quarters." At this time, the term coolies was synonymous with Chinese labor.

34. "The idea in making these contracts so early," wrote the *Call*, "is that, as all the coolies in the state are engaged for the season, to wait much longer would make it impossible for the Fresno patrons of cheap labor to secure the required help." Quote from "Imported Jap Laborers," *San Francisco Call*, June 11, 1895. "When I gave an order on May 27 for a lot of men they were not in San Francisco," Fujimoto told the commissioners. "I waited two weeks for the men to arrive. I am not a partner in the boardinghouse. I don't write to Japan for laborers." Quote from "Whites Driven Out." See also "Cooly Contract Labor," *San Francisco Call*, June 8, 1895.

35. Quotes from "Imported Jap Laborers."

36. Quotes from "Coolies on Strike." Sato gave inconsistent testimony. Claiming to have earned twenty-two dollars in his first job providing two men to cultivate twenty acres of sugar beets over four months at $1.10 a day, he supposedly earned $1.50 a ton on 340 tons of beets, which would have meant a net loss of eight hundred dollars. Questioned further he claimed that nine men he had employed picking peas near Hayward the following spring had gone on strike because they could not earn more than sixty cents a day. His next contract in April or May 1894 was for eighty acres of sugar beets. Producing only ten tons to the acre, Sato had employed sixty men for two months, and thirty men for three months and twelve days, again losing money on the contract, paying his men only sixty-seven cents per day. Confronted with figures showing a loss of $3,664.20, Sato, according to the *San Francisco Call*, "gave a very flimsy story of forty-eight of his men running away without their money." Shown that even when making allowances for those men, he still lost two thousand dollars, he claimed that storekeepers in Pleasanton had covered his expenses, only to be confronted with testimony from the storekeepers that neither had advanced him either money or credit. "He said all the Japs are dissatisfied with the way the white men are beating them and are now anxious to go to the orchards," reported the *Call*. "If he were not in debt there he, too, would go to the fruit orchards."

37. So incendiary were the commission hearings that one Japanese newspaper, *Shinseikai* (The New World), denounced the entire proceedings and demanded the removal of hostile and biased personnel. Another, the *So Ko* (San Francisco Times) roasted the Japanese witnesses who cooperated with the commission. Charging that Shiono's testimony had been coerced and labeling most of it a fabrication, if not entirely false, the newspaper claimed that commissioners had threatened to send Shiono to San Quentin Prison if he did not cooperate. Quotes from "Japanese Are Agitated," *San Francisco Call*, June 13, 1895; "More Jap Certificates," ibid., June 16, 1895. So concerned were members of the Japanese community that they met the steamer *Mexico* on June 15, when it arrived from British Columbia. Prevented from boarding, they slipped around to the steerage, endeavoring to instruct passengers before they were run off the deck. "The guarantee that he will be cared for if sick is really a dead letter because so far as can be learned the Japs who have become ill here have had to foot the bills themselves," observed the *Call*. "The guarantee of all the work the cooly [*sic*] wants is likewise of little use, as the poor fellow as a rule falls into the hands of a contractor who keeps him busy at from 40 to 80 cents a day." See also "Cooly Help from Japan," *San Francisco Call*, June 15, 1895; *So Ko*, June 11, 1895, in ibid., June 14, 1895.

38. Quote from "Vacaville Japanese," *San Francisco Call*, June 18, 1895. The *Call* estimated that there were between six hundred and eight hundred Japanese and about fourteen hundred Chinese laborers harvesting the early cherry and apricot crops around Vacaville.

39. Quotes from "Inquiry at Vacaville," *San Francisco Call*, June 19, 1895; "Methods of Japanese Immigration," *Vacaville Reporter*, June 22, 1895.

40. Quote from "Vacaville Japanese," *San Francisco Call*, June 18, 1895. See also CSBLS, *Seventh Biennial Report, 1895–96*, 101–26.

41. Quotes from *Vacaville Reporter*, July 9; Nov. 2, 1895.

42. Quotes from *PRP*, Sept. 21, 1895; "Cooly Contract Labor," *San Francisco Call*, June 8, 1895.

43. Quote from *Sacramento Bee*, Jan. 13, 27, 1897. See also *PRP*, Apr. 10, 1897; *Watsonville Pajaronian*, Apr. 29, 1897.

44. For Charlie Mura, see C. C. Teague to Charlie Mora [*sic*], Sept. 29, 1902, C. C. Teague Papers, BL. For Hori and Company, see J. Kubota to C. L. Lesnold, Dec. 17, 18, 1914, French-Glenn Records, BL. For Mr. Kawamoto, see Meyer, "Raisin Industry," 54–55. For Yoneda, see Akiji Yoshimura, "A Brief History of the Japanese in Colusa County," *Wagon Wheels* 19 (Sept. 1969), 6. See also *ICR*, 24: 27, 590–91; Mary G. Luck, "Labor Contractors," in Emily H. Huntington, ed., *Doors to Jobs: A Study of the Organization of the Labor Market in California* (Berkeley, 1942), 308; CSBLS, *Ninth Annual Report, 1900*, 23. An estimate of three-hundred *keiyaku-nin* is given in T. Iyenaga and Kennosuke Sato, *Japan and the California Problem* (New York, 1921).

45. Quote from Ichihashi, *Japanese in the United States*, 174. See also Ichihashi, notes on the Santa Clara Valley, Ichihashi Papers, SUASC.

46. Large quote from Takeuchi Kōjirō, *Beikoku Seihokubu Nihon Iminshi* (History of Japanese immigrants to the Pacific Northwest of America) (Seattle, 1929), 33, JARPC. Small quote from Kawamura Tetsurarō, *Saikin Katsudo Hokuo Bei Jigo Annai* (Guide to current jobs in North America) (Tokyo, 1906), 83, JARPC. Both translations courtesy Tatsuro Nomura. See also Wilson and Hosokowa, *Nisei*, 54, 73; Fisher, *Harvest Labor Market*, 27. Both Rokki Jihōsha, *Sanchubu to Nihonjin* (The Rocky Mountain region and the Japanese) (Salt Lake City, 1925), 75; Washizu Bunzo [Shakuma], "Rekishi Inmetsu no Tan," MS (1922), pt. 4, in Oka Shigeki Papers, JARPC, describe the general techniques for milking laborers. For profits see Hiroto, interview.

47. Just as white migrants were known as bindlestiffs, so too did Japanese migrants at this time became known as *buranke-katsugi*, or men who shouldered blankets. See Ichioka, *Issei*, 83; Lydon, *Japanese in Monterey*, 26. Although the evidence is fragmentary, there were plenty of examples of *keiyaku-nin* bolting with wages: Abe Kumakichi, a strawberry contractor operating near Glendale who fled with a fifteen-hundred-dollar payroll; Fujiwara Kumataro, a hop contractor supervising sixty men in Sonoma, who deserted with two thousand dollars; and Komoto and Tachimi, two Hanford contractors supervising fifty grape pickers, who stole a fifteen-hundred-dollar payroll. "There were many such cases," recalled one Japanese store owner. Quote from Mrs. Kamikawa, interview, in Hasagawa and Boettcher, *Success Through Perseverance*, 645. Cases of *mochinige* are reported in *Shin Sekai*, Aug. 15, Sept. 9, 26, 1906; Sept. 16, 1907, JARPC. For a contractor who ran a restaurant in Hamilton City and "skipped out after the last campaign, leaving several debts behind him . . . a total of about $480," see E. C. Hamilton to E. A. Pardee, Oct. 5, 1909, SVBCR, SCML. *Keiyaku-nin* absconding with wages are also described in Tetsutaro, *Saikin Katsudo Hokubi Jigyo Annai*, 141; Ito, *A History of the Japanese in North America*, 376–77. See also CSBLS, *Thirteenth Annual Report, 1907–8*, 218; CSBLS, *Fifteenth Annual Report, 1911–12*, 52. Six Japanese employment agencies shut down for questionable practices are described in Robert Devlin, "Report of U.S. Attorney at San Francisco, relative to Board of Police Commissioners decision to refuse licenses to Japanese Employment Agencies," July 16, 1907, File no. 17971/256–59, DSR. See also *San Francisco Chronicle*, Apr. 18, 1908; *San Francisco Call*, Apr. 17, 1908.

48. Quote from Mike Masaro Iwatsubo, interview, in Hasagawa and Boettcher, *Success Through Perseverance*, 590. See also Iwaka, interview, in Cole, "Japanese in Sacramento," 29, 149; "Life Before Evacuation," in "Biography of a Nisei Farmer"; Timothy J. Lukes and Gary Y. Okihiro, *Japanese Legacy: Farming and Community Life in California's Santa Clara Valley* (Cupertino, Calif., 1985), 21; Akemi Kikumura, *Through Harsh Winters: The Life of a Japanese Immigrant Woman* (Novato, Calif., 1981), 30–31.

49. Quotes from J. Vance Thompson to George Bell, 1916, in "IWW Investigation," Simon J. Lubin Correspondence, BL; "Discussion of the Labor Question," *CSFGCT, 1902*, 396–97. Bicycle arrest and riding data from Riverside Police Court Docket Records, 1907–13, Riverside Municipal Archive, Riverside, Calif.; Mitsuru Inaba reminiscences in George Ringwald, "The Japanese-Americans—2," *Riverside Press Enterprise*, Aug. 15, 1966. See also *Vacaville Reporter*, Apr. 21, 1900. For more on the use of bicycles in the harvest, see *ICR*, "Japanese and Other Immigrant Races in the Pacific Coast and Rocky Mountain States," 24: 227–28; Blas Coyazo, interview by Robert Gonzales, Redlands Oral History Project, Apr. 28, 1994, 8; Joe Herrera, ibid., Apr. 13, 1994, 21, A. K. Smiley Public Library Heritage Room, Redlands.

50. Quote from Ichihashi, "Supplementary Report on the Japanese in the Watsonville District," 3, Ichihashi Papers, SUASC. For San Jose, see Patti Jo N. Hirabayashi, "San Jose Nihonmachi" (M.A. thesis, CSU, San Jose, 1977), 8, describing eleven boardinghouses, three bathhouses, and five pool halls in the San Jose Japantown in 1910. Ichioka, *Issei*, 154–55, identifies seventy-eight boardinghouses in Los Angeles in 1915. For Sacramento, see *ICR*, 23: 45–46,

249–53, identifying thirty-seven Japanese boardinghouses in Sacramento. For Marysville, see Strong, *Japanese in California*, 104–5, describing boardinghouses as labor supply stations. For Marysville boardinghouses catering to men from specific prefectures, see Sadao Sud Itamura, "The Settlement Pattern of the Japanese in the Yuba-Sutter Area of California" (M.A. thesis, CSUS, 1971), 30, 34. For Los Angeles boardinghouses, see William M. Mason and John A. McKinstry, *The Japanese of Los Angeles* (Los Angeles, 1969), 19. For Japantowns in Watsonville and Salinas, see Lydon, *Japanese in Monterey*, 30–31. See also Mrs. Fumi Nakajima, interview, in Hasagawa and Boettcher, *Success through Perseverance*, 179. For a tabulation of Japanese businesses in Isleton, see Ichihashi, "Economic Status of Japanese in Isleton," Ichihashi Papers, SUASC. Ichihashi, "Supplementary Report on The Japanese in the Watsonville District," 2–3, finds one of four Japanese businesses in Watsonville's Japantown were boardinghouses.

51. Millis, *Japanese Problem*, 57; Claude Midkiff, interview, n.d., Glendale Historical Society; CSBLS, *Fifteenth Annual Report, 1911–12*, 607, 616, 625; *ICR*, 24: 188; State Office of Historic Preservation/Cathy Ariki, *Ethnic Minority Cultural Resource Survey: Walnut Grove* (Sacramento, 1979), 2; *Sacramento Bee*, Oct. 15, 1915; *Sacramento Union*, Oct. 7, 1915; N. T. Novell, "Part Played by Japanese in Sugar Beets," 10, SRRP.

52. Quotes from Mrs. C. C. Violett, interview by Chloe Holt, Garden Grove, Dec. 16, 1924, SRRP; Washizu Bunzo [Shakuma], "Rekishi Inmetsu no hata" [A history of people on the verge of annihilation] pt. 17 (1922), Oka Shigeki Papers, JARPC. See also Kikumura, *Through Harsh Winters*, 30; Ito, *A History of the Japanese in North America*, 293, 294, 299; Archie McDonald, *The Japanese Experience in Butte County, California* (Chico, Calif., 1993), 15. Steven Misawa, ed., *Beginnings: Japanese Americans in San Jose* (San Jose, 1981), 12, asserts that later generations could not possibly understand camp conditions at this time.

53. Quotes from *Shin Sekai*, Oct. 17, 1900; Yoshimura Daijirō, *To-Bei Seigyō no Tebiki* (A guide to further training in America) (Osaka, 1903), 120; George W. Moore, interview by Chloe Holt, Smeltzer, Feb. 16, 1925, SRRP. Camp size data from *ICR*, 24: 226, describing Japanese camps in Rialto, Highgrove, and Riverside.

54. Mrs. Kozo Kamikawa, interview, in Hasagawa and Boettcher, eds., *Success Through Perseverance*, 658. See also various interviews with Japanese, California History Room, Fresno County Public Library.

55. Quotes from Bunzo, "Rekishi Inmetsu no Tan," pt. 17. See also Mr. Gotto, interview, in Hasagawa and Boettcher, *Success through Perseverance*, 20.

56. Quote from *Vacaville Reporter*, June 9, 1892.

57. For fights over thefts, see *San Jose Mercury*, Feb. 3; and Dec. 11, 1905. For bandits and robbers, see clippings, FMR, Feb. 17, 27, 1899; *Fresno Daily Evening Expositor*, Feb. 17, 1899; Clough and Secrest, *Fresno*, 1: 243.

58. Quotes from Ito, *A History of the Japanese in North America*, 435, 442, 250–51, 280; Mr. Kitahara, interview, in Hasagawa and Boettcher, *Success Through Perseverance*, 782. See also Gotto, interview, 20; James Kashitawa, diary, June 1–29, 1906, Labor Archives and Research Center, CSU, San Francisco.

59. For data on the Sacramento Japanese, see Sacramento Betsuin, "Kakocho, 1900–1902" (Book of the deceased). For Fresno death data, see *Shin Sekai*, Sept. 1, 1908. This list, compiled by the Japanese Association of Fresno, identifies 182 laborers who died between 1898 and 1907 but does not enumerate the causes. For Sacramento Japanese from Aichi prefecture, see Mizutani Bangaku [pseud.], *Hokubei Aichi Kenjinshi* (Publication of the Japanese from Aichi prefecture in North America) (Sacramento, 1920), 451–55. For the Japanese Consular data, see "California, Number of Japanese deaths by Causes, 1906–1913," in Japanese Foreign Ministry Archival Documents, JARPC, which contains information on 3,836 Japanese who died in California between 1906 and 1913. For the Butte County cases, see Butte County Infirmary, Patient Registers, 3–4: 1898–2872, Oroville, Calif., SCML. Of these cases, the youngest was eighteen years of age, all but five under age thirty. For gonorrhea cures, see *Shin Sekai*, June 8, 1914. For Solano County, see Rosalie S. (Neall) Cunningham and Dolores (Vega) McLean, *Solano County Cemeteries: Some Early Deaths and Burials in the Vacaville and Elmira Areas of Solano County, California* (Fairfield, Calif., 1989); Cunningham, "Solano County Cemeteries: Vacaville-Elmira," MS (1986), Solano County Genealogical Society Office, Vacaville; Records of the Matt Stewart Funeral Home, Vacaville Museum.

60. Yonez Yoshido, tape-recorded speech, Japanese Citizens League dinner, Nov. 12, 1969, Turlock Public Library; "Life History of a Japanese Man, aged 22, Santa Paula," interview no.

323 (19), trans. Mosao Dodo, SRRP; Tsuyosh Matsumoto, "Reminiscences," MS (n.d.), JARPC. Immigration statistics from Ichihashi, *Japanese Immigration*, 9–12. For the drowning suicide, see Butte County Coroner's Inquisitions, 1896–1913, SCML. For the slashing, see Butte County Infirmary, Patient Registers. For the Vacaville suicide and bunkhouse arson, see "Body Found in Tree," *Vacaville Reporter*, Oct. 17, 1910.

61. *Marysville Buddhist Church, Seventy-Fifth Anniversary* (Marysville, 1968), 68; Takashi Tsujita and Karen Nolen, *Omi i de: Memories of Vacaville's Lost Japanese Community* (Vacaville, 2001), 16–17; Itamura, "Settlement Pattern of Japanese in Yuba-Sutter," 35–40; Lydon, *Chinese Gold*, 449–50; Raymond Hillman and Leonard A. Covello, *Cities and Towns of San Joaquin County since 1874* (Fresno, 1985), 214; Wong, "The Japanese in Riverside," 23–25, 33, 120–26, 137; *ICR*, 23: 251; U.S. Census, 1900, Butte County [copy in Meriam Library, CSUC]. For a list of businesses in Stockton's Japantown, see J. C. Trombetta, "Delta Japanese," 5, Ichihashi Papers, SUASC. For Watsonville, see Yamato Ichihashi, "Supplementary Report on the Japanese in the Watsonville District," 2–3.

62. Quotes from C. H. Tavenner, "Tokio of America," *Fresno Tribune*, Sept. 7, 1907, cited in *Vacaville Reporter*, Sept. 14, 1907; Yoshimura, "A Brief History of the Japanese in Colusa County," 7–8. See also Marcia Jeffers, *Research Report: From Rising Sun to Golden Hills, The Japanese-American Experience in Solano County* (Vacaville, 1988).

63. Quotes from Nihon Gaimushō, *Nihon Gaikō Bunsho: Tai-Bei Imin Mondai Keika Gaiyō* (Japanese diplomatic documents) (Tokyo, 1972), 210; *Watsonville Pajaronian*, May 18, 1905; Millis, *Japanese Problem*, 72.

64. Itamura, "Settlement of Japanese in Yuba-Sutter," 44; and Coleman, "History of Celery," 103, have good descriptions of bathhouses. For trips to Fresno bathhouses, see Mrs. Kazu Kamikawa and George Hasegawa, interviews, in Yoshiro and Boettcher, *Success Through Perseverance*, 266, 644, 659.

65. Ito, *A History of the Japanese in North America*, 293–94, 301; J. Vance Thompson, memo, "I.W.W. Investigation," 1916, in J. Vance Thompson to George Bell, Simon J. Lubin Correspondence, BL.

66. Yuji Ichioka, "Ameyuki-san: Japanese Prostitutes in Nineteenth-Century America," *Amerasia* 4 (spring 1977), 6–7; Takaki, *Strangers*, 185. San Francisco had forty-one Japanese-operated pool halls, Sacramento, twenty-one; Stockton and Vacaville, six; Fresno, nineteen; and Los Angeles, twenty-five. Field hands could hardly miss pool halls sporting such elaborate names as the Imperial Pool Hall, National Pool Hall, and Miyako Pool Hall. Many no doubt chose those pool halls named after specific geographical areas in Japan—men from Wakayama prefecture frequented the Kinokuniya Pool Hall, those from Kumamoto prefecture liked the Higoya Pool Hall, while field hands from Kagoshima prefecture went to Nankaiya Pool Hall. For many field hands, pool halls bearing the names of home villages proved irresistible, for example the Tawara Pool Hall in Los Angeles, named after a fishing village in Wakayama prefecture that sent hundreds of men to California. Figures on pool halls are from 1912 and come from Shin Sekai Shimbunsha, *Panama Taiheiyō Bankoku Dai-Hakurankai* (San Francisco, 1912), app., "Zaibei Nihonjin Jūsho Seimei Roku," 16–20, 53–54, 84–85, 123, 128–29; Hohenthal et al., *Streams in a Thirsty Land*, 110–11; Mrs. Masako Inada, interview, in Hasakawa and Boettcher, *Success Through Perseverance*, 178; *Vacaville Reporter*, Sept. 14, 1907.

67. Quote from *Nihon Gaiko Bunsho: Tai-Bei Imin Mondai Keika Gaiyō* (Tokyo, 1972), 213. See also *Shin Sekai*, Oct. 23, 1908; *FMR*, July 1, 1908; Aug. 5, 7, 29; Sept. 15, 1909; Yee Ah Chong, "The Chinese in Vacaville" interview by Ronald H. Limbaugh, 1977, Oral History Project, Vacaville Museum; Women's Occidental Board of Foreign Missions, *Twenty-Sixth Annual Report* (San Francisco, 1899), 85. Japanese figures from Mutsu Hirokichi to Komura Jutaro, Aug. 11, 1898, Japanese Foreign Ministry Archival Documents.

68. Quote from Tsuruzaburō Shimizu, *Beikoku Rōdō Benran* (Labor handbook for America) (San Francisco, 1903), 261–62, JARPC. See also "Debauchery and Gambling—What Did You Come to America For?" *Shin Sekai*, June 12, 1908.

69. Quote from Mojiro "Charlie" Hamakawa, interview by Newton Wallace, *Winters Express*, May 22, 1975. Fresno gambling figures from *FMR*, June 10, 1908. Lottery information from Dec. 5, 1899; Oct. 5, 1901, listing the names of eleven gambling operations and twenty-five businesses selling lottery tickets. Figures from Watsonville from Irwin, "Japanese and the Pacific Coast," 18–19. See also "Vicious Gambling Among Oriental Farm Laborers," *San Francisco Chronicle*, Jan. 15, 1919, Pamphlets on the Japanese, BL.

70. Explanations of the preoccupation with gambling are from *Nichibei Shimbun*, Aug. 20, 1913; and Sashihara Hideo, "Zaibei Dōhō to Hanzai," *Beikoku Bukkyō*, Feb. 1, Mar. 1, and Apr. 1, 1914. See also Stewart Culin, "The Gambling Games of the Chinese in America," *Publications of the University of Pennsylvania, Philology, Literature and Archeology* 1 (1891), 1–17. For a raid, see *San Jose Mercury*, July 12, 1908. For fights with professional gamblers, see Oct. 14, Nov. 24, 1909.

71. "I sort of understand their thinking," recalled a Japanese farmer, "because their outlook . . . was so bleak that they thought the chance they had of getting out of this doldrum was by striking it rich gambling." Quote from Masaru Iwatsubo, interview, in Hasakawa and Boettcher, *Success Through Perseverance*, 589. See also Shigeo Uota, interview, 301.

72. Quote from *Vacaville Reporter*, July 18, 1903. For a drunken brawl, see *San Jose Mercury*, May 28, 1895. For an inebriated field hand in a train station, see Nov. 8, 1902. For the shooting of a boardinghouse proprietor by an unknown assailant, see Feb. 6, 1908. For a large "jui jitsu fight," see Apr. 26, 1908. For a riot and knife fight caused by field hands resisting a "press gang," see Oct. 6, 1908; Mar. 20, 1909. For Hanford, see the *St. Helena Star*, Feb. 12, 1897.

73. For Chinese and Japanese crews in the Pajaro Valley berry fields, see 1900 MS Census, Monterey County.

74. *Shin Sekai*, Feb. 4, 1900. For developments elsewhere, see Masakkazu Iwata, interview, 1966; Ayaka Takahashi, interview, 1968; Charles Kamayatsu, interview, 1965, JARPC. See also Huntington, *Doors to Jobs*, 308; Lowenstein, "Strikes and Strike Tactics," 19.

75. Quotes from *Davisville Enterprise*, Aug. 15, 1901; *Los Angeles Times*, Mar. 2, 1901. For wage setting in the hop industry, see *Sacramento Bee*, July 7, 1901. See also Michael Kazin, *Barons of Labor: The San Francisco Building Trades and Union Power in the Progressive Era* (Urbana, Ill., 1987), 53–56. "United action wanted to settle the Indian wages question," proclaimed the *Inyo Register*, justifying its action on the grounds that the Indians would only waste their higher wages by buying whiskey, getting drunk, and brawling among themselves. Quote from July 18, 1901.

76. Quote from *Sacramento Bee*, July 7, 1901. After boxcars full of fruit began to stack up and rot on the Embarcadero, Port Costa became choked with wheat and fruit, and the American Can Company shut down canning operations, farmers sent emissaries to San Francisco to demand mediation so that their vital "road to market" would be kept open. Fearing that the lockout would mortally wound organized labor in the city, teamsters devised new tactics designed to disrupt the entire state economy, punish outside parties, and bring pressure against the Employer's Association. In support of them, the San Francisco labor council called a sympathy strike. Quote from *San Francisco Argonaut*, Aug. 5, 1901. See also Robert M. Robinson, "San Francisco Teamsters at the Turn of the Century," *CHSQ* 35 (June 1956), 147; Paul N. Scharrenberg, "Reminiscences," oral memoir by Corinne L. Gilb and Robert E. Burke, Jan. 1955, 52–53, ROHP.

77. *Sacramento Bee*, July 13, 16, 30; *Sacramento Record-Union*, Sept. 1, 1901; *Oakland Tribune*, Sept. 9, 1901.

78. For Pierce, see *Woodland Democrat*, July 3, 1913; Pierce obituary, *Davis Enterprise*, Mar. 14, 1930. Tacking two large sheets of canvas onto a sixteen-foot sled pulled by a single horse, they knocked the almonds out of Pierce's trees onto the canvas by hitting branches with twenty-foot-long poles. After each tree had been "knocked," they then lifted the canvas and emptied the almonds into a sled. One man then sacked the almonds and dropped off the sacks. Teamsters then loaded and hauled them back to Pierce's sheds. For harvest methods, see Pierce, "Gathering Almonds, 1901," Pierce, account book, 121, 144. For Kubo, see Pierce, daily journal, Aug. 7–13, 1901; *Davisville Enterprise*, Aug. 15, 1901; Nov. 21, 1901; Pierce, daily journal, Aug. 13–Sept. 13, 1901; Aug. 18–Sept. 18, 1901; Aug. 13–Sept. 13, 1903. Wing Hai's Chinese worked so well that Pierce hired all labor through him in 1902 and 1903. Unable to secure Chinese field hands through Wing Hai in 1904, Pierce feigned vulnerability and sold his entire crop to Kubo, who agreed to pick and haul the crop to the Davisville Almond Grower's Association for $250 and the remaining proceeds. Well aware that spring hailstorms had ruined 75 percent of his crop, Pierce thus managed to exact a profit and strike back at Kubo all in one stroke. For all of his work, Kubo netted just $185. After paying his crews, Kubo had nothing left.

79. Aiken, "The Labor Question," 394; "Discussion of the Labor Question," 396; "The Grape Growing Industry in the United States," *ICR*, 24: 447. For the labor bureau, see poster, "Call for Convention of Fruit Growers," Jan. 15, 1901, Kearney Papers; *California Fruit Grower*, Mar. 9; May 25, 1901.

80. Quote from *PRP*, Aug. 24, 1901. See also FWP, "Oriental Labor Unions in California

Agriculture," MS (1939), 10, 14, BL; Lowenstein, "Strike and Strike Tactics," 14, 20; Cikuth, "Pajaro Valley," 124; Barry, "Contract Labor in California Agriculture," 26–28; *PRP*, Aug. 24, 1901; *San Francisco Examiner*, Aug. 8, 1901.

81. Quote from *PRP*, Jan. 2, 1902. See also *Sacramento Bee*, June 11, 1902; *San Francisco News*, Feb. 16, 1902. Although 5,269 Japanese arrived in 1901, many came with false passports. See *Sacramento Bee*, May 30, 1900; June 28, 1902; Ichihashi, *Japanese in the United States*, 3–4; U.S. Dept. of Commerce and Labor, *Bulletin of the Bureau of Labor No. 47* (Washington, D.C., 1903), 761, 836–37. The thesis that increased numbers of immigrants bolstered the bargaining power of *keiyaku-nin* is advanced in Melvin Sanguinetti, "Importance of the Japanese in the Fruit and Vegetable Industry," 5, interview no. 330, SRRP. For Japanese around Newcastle, see *California Fruit Grower*, Apr. 11, 18, 25; May 2, 1891; J. M. Francis, "Statements of Fruit Ranch Owners of Placer County," no. 10, comp. T. G. Chamberlain, June 1916, Elwood Mead Papers, BL. Most of the immigrants from Hawaii had signed a contract with a middleman, immigration company, or big city innkeeper in Japan. A typical arrangement involved a loan of two hundred yen, paid back over a three-year period at 80 percent interest. In return, the men received the necessary passports, documents, paperwork, and western clothing, and were taught the stories most suitable to the immigration inspectors. They also received steamship tickets along with thirty dollars in "show money," which they gave back to emigration company officials shortly after arrival. Life on the plantations was hard, and after years of laboring on isolated sugar plantations, where their food, housing, and recreation was controlled totally by plantation owners, many Issei yearned for a better existence. As residents of an American territory, they would not be subject to restrictive immigration laws and could easily move to the mainland. Measuring wages in Hawaii against those in California, they calculated they could at least double their income and jumped at the chance to re-emigrate. Those unable to scrape together the funds again turned to familiar immigration companies such as the Japanese Boardinghouse Keepers Association, which dispatched agents to Honolulu and advertised the higher California wages in the local Japanese press. "GREAT RECRUITING TO AMERICA," shouted one advertisement in the *Hawaiian-Japanese Chronicle*.

> Through an arrangement made with Yasuwaza of San Francisco we are able to recruit laborers to mainland and offer them work. The laborers will be subjected to no delay upon arriving in San Francisco, but can get work immediately through Yasuwaza. Employment offered in picking strawberries and tomatoes, planting beets, mining and domestic service. Now is the time to go! Wages $1.50 a day. *Tokujiro-Inoya-Niigata Kejin*—care of the Nishimura Hotel.

Quote from clipping, *Hawaiian-Japanese Chronicle*, Mar. 22, 1905, JARPC. See also Alan Takeo Moriyama, *Imingaisha: Japanese Emigration Companies and Hawaii, 1894–1908* (Honolulu, 1985), 134, 202, app. 15; *San Francisco Call*, June 11, 1895; Wakayama-Ken, *Wakayama Ken Imin Shi*, 128–31, 276–80; Saitō Miki to Komura Jutarō, May 28, 1902, enclosed in Alex Center to H. Hockfield Co., n.d., Japanese Foreign Ministry Documents.

82. Quote from *Sacramento Bee*, June 28, 1902. See also Moriyama, *Imingaisha*, 134–35.

83. Quotes from *ICR*, 15: 754–55; *Watsonville Pajaronian*, Sept. 20, 1900. See also Ichihashi, *Japanese in the United States*, 229, 232; Ito, *A History of the Japanese in North America*, 27, 33, 38; *Sacramento Daily News*, [Ōfu Nippō], Sept. 9, 1909, Pamphlets on the Japanese, BL. In 1907 authorities refused to license six Japanese employment agencies on the grounds that they engaged in questionable practices. See Robert Devlin, U.S. Attorney at San Francisco, "Report relative to the Board of Police Commissioners decision to refuse licenses to Japanese Employment agencies," July 16, 1907, File no. 17971/256–59, DSR; CSBLS, *Thirteenth Annual Report, 1907–08*, 218.

84. Quotes from Stabler, "California Fruit Grower," *Twenty-Seventh CSFGCT . . . 1902*, 270; George Hecke, "The Pacific Coast Labor Question from the Standpoint of a Horticulturalist," *Official Report of the Thirty-third CSFGC . . . 1907* (Sacramento, 1908), 67. For Hecke, see *Who's Who in America* (Chicago, 1926), 14: 923. Hecke's work and writing can be followed in the George Hecke Papers, ASCUCD.

85. Quote from clipping, *Vacaville Reporter*, n.d., Vacaville Public Library.

86. Quotes from *PRP*, July 26, 1902; also Aug. 30; Sept. 6, 1902. For the strike, see *Marysville Daily Appeal*, Aug. 20, 1902; also Aug. 21, 23. See also *Sacramento Record Union*, Aug. 20, 22, 1902; *Sacramento Bee*, Aug. 21, 1902.

87. Quote Mrs. S.M.S., interview by Chloe Holt, Santa Ana, n.d., doc. no. 274-A (23), SRRP. See also Fisher, *Harvest Labor Market*, 28–29; Gulick, *American Japanese*, 14, 30; John Modell, "Japanese American Company Union," *PHR* 38 (May 1969), 197; *ICR*, 1: 67; 2: 109; 25: 109, 374, 598; CIR, *Final Report of the Commission on Industrial Relations* (Washington, D.C., 1916), 4940–41.

88. *California Fruit Grower*, Apr. 18, 1903. See also H.S., "California," *New Republic* 1 (June 1913), 550–52; Mrs. G. W. Aiken, "Labor Question," *CSFGCT, 1902*, 395; Chester Rowell, "Chinese and Japanese Immigration," 5.

89. *ICR*, 25: 374. For a fictional account, see Wallace Irwin, *Seed of Sun* (New York, 1921), 242–43, 246. See also Andrea Sbarbora, interview, "Life of an Italian American Pioneer," n.d., 261, ROHP.

90. Quote from *Marysville Record Union*, ca. Sept. 1902, Tehama Public Library. See also Thompson, "Social History of California Agriculture," 276–78; Mr. Righter, "Discussion of the Labor Supply," *CSFGCT, 1902*, 278.

91. Quotes from *Red Bluff Union* in *Sacramento Bee*, Sept. 1, 1902; "Discussion of the Labor Question," *CSFGCT, 1902*, 395. See also Nankashū Nihonjin Shichijūnen Shi Hankō Iin Kai, *Nankashū Nihonjin Shichijūnen Shi* (The seventy-year history of the Japanese in Southern California) (Los Angeles, 1960), 195. *Sacramento Bee*, Sept. 10, 12; Oct. 14, 1902; *Sacramento Record Union*, Dec. 22, 27, 1902.

92. Quote from R. L. Adams, *Farm Management: A Text-Book for Student, Investigator, and Investor* (New York, 1921), 518; Adams, "Farm Labor Problems," R. L. Adams Collected Papers, BL. See also "Final Report from the Office of the State Farm Labor Agent," and "Notes Secured from Mr. L. B. Landsborough, Manager of A. B. Humphry's Orchard" (Jan. 4, 1924), by V. S. McClatchy, SRRP; Adams, *Managing Western Farms and Ranches: A Series of Monographs* (Berkeley, n.d.), 2, Giannini Foundation Library, UCB; typed notes from Simon J. Lubin, Mar. 1927, WPA material, BL; Stabler, "The California Fruit-Grower and the Labor Supply," 269.

93. Quote from clipping, *PRP*, n.d., FHHC. See also CSBLS, *Twelfth Annual Report, 1906*, 68; *PRP*, Feb. 28, 1903; C. C. Teague, *Fifty Years a Rancher: The Recollections of half a century devoted to the citrus and walnut industries of California* (Los Angeles, 1944), 150; *CSFGCT, 1911* (Sacramento, 1912), 12; Frank App and Allen G. Waller, *Farm Economics: Management and Distribution* (New York, 1938), 655; Fisher, *Harvest Labor Market*, 93.

94. Quotes from "Discussion of the Labor Question," *CSFGCT, 1902*, 396–97; also 268–81. For Pajaro Valley growers petitioning Congress to amend the Chinese Exclusion Act on the grounds that they only had two-thirds of the necessary laborers, see S. W. Coffman, "Memorial to Congress," 272–73. See also *Sacramento Record Union*, Dec. 27, 1902.

95. Quotes from *Placer County Republican*, Mar. 11, 1903. See also Lincoln Steffens, "California and the Japanese," *Colliers* 57 (Mar. 25, 1916), 2; *Newcastle News*, Mar. 11, 1903.

CHAPTER EIGHTEEN

1. Quote from George W. Shaw, *The California Sugar Industry, Part 1: Historical and General*, University of California Agricultural Experiment Station, Bulletin no. 149 (Sacramento, 1903), 37. See also Thomas J. Osborne, "Claus Spreckels and the Oxnard Brothers: Pioneer Developers of California's Beet Sugar Industry, 1890–1900," *Southern California Historical Quarterly* 54 (summer 1972), 119; Diane LeDesma, "The Oxnard Brothers and the Beet Sugar Factory," MS (1981), 3–7, VCM; Dan Gutleben, "The Oxnard Beet Sugar Factory, Oxnard, California," MS (1942), 4, ACSCR. Production statistics from *Oxnard Courier*, Sept. 11, 1903. The Oxnard refinery was second only to the Spreckels sugar beet factory in size. See also William J. May, "The Great Western Sugarlands: History of the Great Western Sugar Company" (Ph.D. diss., Univ. of Colorado, 1982), 4; Torstein A. Magnuson, "History of the Beet Sugar Industry in California," *HSSCAP* 11 (1918), 68–79; Federal Trade Commission, *Report on the Sugar Beet Industry in the United States* (Washington, D.C., 1917), 26–27.

2. Vera Bloom, "Oxnard . . . A Social History of the Early Years," *VCHSQ* 4 (Feb. 1959), 17; Richard B. Haydock, "By All Means, Reminiscent," ibid., 11 (Feb. 1966), 4–5; Raymond G. Cushman, "The Geography of Sugar Beet Growing in California" (M.A. thesis, UCB, 1951); "Co-operation With Growers in Sugar Manufacturing," *California Citrograph*, Dec. 1915; Dennis, "The History of the Beet-Sugar Industry in California."

3. "Work Being Done on the Experimental Farm," *Oxnard Courier*, June 9, 1900; "Of In-

terest to Beet Growers," Jan. 13, 1900; Jan. 10, 1908; Sept. 11, 1903 [production statistics]; Lyman H. Andrews, "The Relation of the Sugar Beet Root System to Increased Yields," *Facts About Sugar*, Feb. 15, 1929, ACSCR.

4. *Oxnard Courier*, special issue, Dec. 1905, reports that during the 1905 campaign the factory paid out eight hundred thousand dollars for beets and $253,300 for factory labor. When fuel, factory wages, lime rock, and field labor were factored in, some sources put the amount contributed to Oxnard at over four million dollars annually. See also Jan. 13, Feb. 3, 1900; Oct. 11, 1902; "Oxnard Fifty Years Ago," *Oxnard Press-Courier*, Sept. 25, 1948. Contract provisions from Agreements Between L. A. Wilson and American Beet Sugar Company, Jan. 3, 1902; B. F. Barr and American Sugar Beet Company, Nov. 28, 1902, Oxnard Season, 1902, ACSCR. The town was being referred to as Oxnard years before its formal naming. See Charles Johnson, Ventura County Museum librarian, interview by author, Mar. 29, 2002, author's possession.

5. "Fruit Workers: A Large Number of them Camped Near Saticoy," *Oxnard Courier*, July 15, 1899; also June 28, 1899; "An Important Enterprise for Oxnard," May 26, 1900; "Oxnard's Second Beet Sugar Campaign," Aug. 18, 1900; "Sugar Factory Working Smoothly," Aug. 25, 1900; "Great Campaign of 1901," Nov. 9, 1901; Dec. 4, 1901; "Beneficial Influence of Sugar Beet Culture," Mar. 8, 1902; Oct. 4, 1902; Dec. 4, 1908; Madeline Mieda, "Hueneme as Grain Port," *VCHSQ* 3 (Feb. 1958), 20; "Labor Exchange," *IW*, July 1, 1906.

6. "Juan S. Mauri Drowned at Sugar Factory," *Oxnard Courier*, Aug. 7, 1903. For the other accidents, see Aug. 12, 1899; Sept. 8, 1900; Sept. 21, 1901; June 27, 1903; Sept. 22, 1905; "Drowned in Sewage Canal," *Ventura Free Press*, Aug. 14, 1903. During the processing campaign, the average workday was twelve hours. Wages for unskilled labor averaged twenty cents an hour.

7. Bloom, "Oxnard . . . A Social History of the Early Years," 18–19; Ralph, May, and Jim Runkle, "The Runkle Family," 11, 14. For a murder, see *Oxnard Courier*, Mar. 23, 1906. See also Gilbert Cuevas Garcia, "The Oxnard Area: An Analysis of the Changing Pattern of Land Use" (M.A. thesis, CSU, Northridge, 1972); Howard Gregor, "Changing Agricultural Patterns in the Oxnard Area of Southern California" (Ph.D. diss., UCLA, 1950); John H. LeResche, "The Lower Ventura Valley, California: A Study in Changing Occupancy" (M.A. thesis, UCLA, 1951); E. Enderlein, "Sugar Beets at Oxnard," *Sunset* 9 (1902), 114.

8. Quote from entry of Mar. 18, 1898, Lewis L. Ware Scrapbooks, Oxnard, no. 10, Dan Gutleben copies from the Philadelphia Memorial Library, ACSCR. See also Coletha Nicholson Lehmann, "I Remember Those Things," *VCHSQ* 18 (summer 1978), 38; W. H. Hutchinson, *Oil, Land, and Politics: The California Career of Thomas Robert Bard* (Norman, Okla., 1956), 2: 96; *Oxnard Courier*, Mar. 22, Apr. 4, 1902; Mar. 23, 1906; "Free Reading Room for Factory Men," Aug. 14, 1903.

9. Quotes from "Work in the Beet Fields: Difficulty of Securing Competent Beet Thinners," *Oxnard Courier*, Apr. 29, 1899; "White Labor Cheaper," May 20, 1899, citing *Riverside Enterprise*; "Chinese Labor," Feb. 4, with photos; "Free Labor Bureau," Mar. 11, 1899, citing *Ventura Independent*; Mar. 18, 1899; June 3, 1899, citing the *Ventura Free Press*. See also "Hobo Problem: The Oregon Sugar Company Has Solved It," July 8, 1899. An "experienced crew of Chinese" arrived from Visalia in July to take over soldering operations for incompetent white workers at the local cannery but remained in the cannery. For the Visalia crew, see July 15, 1899. See also entries for May 18, 1899; Aug. 4, 1899; Dec. 7, 1901, Ware Scrapbooks, ACSCR.

10. Headlines from *Oxnard Courier*, Dec. 9, 1904. Quote from Bloom, "Oxnard: A Social History of the Early Years," 19. See also William T. Dagodag, "A Social Geography of La Colonial: A Mexican-American Settlement in the City of Oxnard, California" (M.A. thesis, San Fernando Valley College, 1967), 5.

11. *Oxnard Courier*, Mar. 22, Apr. 4, 1902; Feb. 10, Mar. 26, 1906. The Laborer's Headquarters is described in Feb. 2, 1906. See also "Chinamen on the Move," Aug. 7, Oct. 11, 1903; Nanka Nikeijin Kaigisho, *Nan Kashu Nihonjinshi* (History of the Japanese in Southern California) (Los Angeles, 1956), 54; Kashiwamura Kazusuke, *Hoku-Bei Tosa Taidan* (A broad survey of North America] (Tokyo, 1911), 223–24, JARPC.

12. At least one contractor, Sakukō Kimura, had come to Oxnard from the Pajaro Valley after more than a decade in the contracting business. Another, Charles Yamashita, was involved in a sensational murder. A cross-eyed *keiyaku-nin* with a shady reputation, Yamashita handled gangs on the Patterson ranch, the experimental farm run by the American Beet Sugar Company, and other large sugar beet growing operations, first gaining notoriety in a boxing contest with a Mexican contractor who defeated him easily. He apparently did better at manhandling

field hands. Flush with money, he soon took up with Nora Price, a beautiful twenty-seven-year-old mulatto prostitute from Texas. Spending huge sums of money on her, Yamashita then got deeply into debt and, unable to pay his bills, skipped out with his crew's wages. Arrested several months later in Riverside and brought back to Oxnard, he returned five hundred dollars to the Lehmann and Waterman ranch, his largest debtor, then prepared to resume contracting. Now broke, he was rejected by Price and grew jealous of her when she took another lover. One night, after being told that she "didn't want any such a cross-eyed Oriental specimen prowling about her lodgings," Yamashita followed her home, and failing to win back her affection, became enraged, shot her in the stomach, and fled, never to be seen again. Price died the following day. Quote from "A Tragedy in the Tenderloin," *Oxnard Courier*, Mar. 22, 1902.

13. Quotes from *Oxnard Courier*, May 17, 1900; "Will Handle Men by the Thousand," Mar. 15, 1902. Percentages computed from 1900 MS Census, Twelfth Census: Ventura County. See also N. T. Nowell, "Part Played by Japanese in Sugar Beets," interview no. 332, n.d., 10, SRRP.

14. Quote from Thomas Pecha, "The Culture of the Sugar Beet," *Beet Sugar Gazette*, in *Oxnard Courier*, Sept. 30, 1904. Plowing crews consisting of ten men who lived in a "boarding-house on wheels" while working in the fields. Deploying an engine on one side of the field, they ran a long cable to the other side, attached the cable to a plow, and pulled the plow through the field, breaking virgin ground to a depth of two feet at the heretofore unheard-of rate of fifteen to twenty acres per day. After that they shaped furrows then used new beet-seed drills to plant four rows at a time, about eighteen to twenty-two inches apart. For plow crews using stationary steam engines and cables, see "Steam Plow at Chino," *Oxnard Courier*, June 10, 1904. See also "Steam Plows Now at Work," Nov. 16, 1901.

15. Quotes from House, *Hearings on the Investigation of the American Sugar Refining Company and Others*, 62nd Cong., 2nd sess. 1912, 7864–65, 2533. See also *Oxnard Courier*, Apr. 5, 1902. For hand labor, see Mamer, "The Generation and Proliferation of Agricultural Hand Labor-Saving Technology," 22–23, 28–29, 39, 51–55. See also A. W. Skuderna, comp., *Practical Farming Hints* (Denver, 1924), 5; Schwartz, *Seasonal Farm Labor*, 103–4; "Clean Fields Produce Good Stands," *The Sugar Beet*, n.d., 10, ACSCR.

16. Quote from "Oxnard Beet Tops," *Oxnard Courier*, May 24, 1902. See also entry for Aug. 4, 1889, Ware Scrapbooks, California no. 7, ACSCR.

17. "Patent Beet Thinner," *Oxnard Courier*, Mar. 15, 1902; "The Culture of the Sugar Beet," Sept. 30, 1904.

18. For beet plows, see picture, "The Eifler and Nauman Beet Plow," *Oxnard Courier*, June 6, 1902; "Test of New Beet Plow," ibid., June 13, 1903; "A New Riding Beet Plow," ibid., Aug. 9, 1903; "Another Beet Puller Invented," ibid., July 18, 1903; "Improvement on Eifler Beet Plow," ibid., Nov. 6, 1903. For traditional beet plows and methods, see "Harvesting Sugar Beets," *Napa Daily Journal*, Sept. 24, 1897, NCLCF.

19. Quote from WACC advertisement, *Oxnard Courier*, Oct. 4, 1902. One of many myths surrounding WACC is that it was the creation of "a number of prominent Jewish businessmen and bankers in Oxnard." See Tomás Almaguer, *Racial Fault Lines: The Historical Origins of White Supremacy in California* (Berkeley, 1994), 189–90. In fact, WACC had a rather complicated history and went through several changes. See, for example, *Oxnard Courier*, Feb. 28, 1903. So important was the Bank of A[chilles]. Levy to the early lima bean industry in Ventura County that it was known as the "Bank that beans built." See Ernie Volz, interview, 1986, SVHS.

20. "Interesting to Farmers," *Oxnard Courier*, Apr. 12, 1902. See also "Brief Mention," Apr. 5, 1902; "Flurry Over Beet Thinning," Apr. 26, 1902.

21. "The contracting company took up a number of these farmers, especially on the Las Posas, and helped them through in order that labor might not get the better of farmers. On other contracts of their own, where farmers brought in other labor, paying from $1 to $2.50 extra per acre, they refunded the difference to the farmers." Quotes from "Interesting Data From The Farmers," *Oxnard Courier*, May 24, 1902.

22. Quotes from "Labor Is In Great Demand," *Oxnard Courier*, Oct. 11, 1902; "Expert Agriculturalist with Contractors," ibid., June 21, 1902. For a contractor skipping town with six hundred dollars in wages, see "Leaves Friends in the Lurch," ibid., Aug. 23, 1902. Production figures from "Slicing Completed," ibid., Nov. 29, 1902. Herz is misidentified as Merz in Juan Gómez-Quiñones, *Mexican American Labor, 1790–1990* (Albuquerque, 1994), 77.

23. "Howell-Bryson," *Oxnard Courier*, Nov. 29, 1902; "Changes in Contracting Company," ibid., Dec. 6, 1902. See also Takaki, *Strangers*, 198.

24. *Oxnard Courier*, Feb. 28, 1903; Kashiwamura Kazusuke, *Hoku-Bei Tosa Taidan*, 223; Nanka Nikkeijin Shogyo Kaigisho, *Nan Kashu Nihonjinshi*, 54–55.

25. WACC's arrangement with the American Beet Sugar Company may be the earliest example of a "sweetheart" contract arrangement in which a grower brought in one union to subvert another. Sweetheart deals would figure prominently in farmworker organizing struggles of the early 1970s. The standard account of the 1903 Oxnard strike is Tomás Almaguer, "Racial Domination and Class Conflict in Capitalist Agriculture: The Oxnard Sugar Beet Workers' Strike of 1903," *LH* 25 (summer 1984), 325–50. I discussed this strike at length in an exchange of letters with Almaguer while reviewing a draft of his essay in 1982. My analysis, derived from a reading of every Ventura County newspaper available in both the Ventura County Museum and the American Crystal Sugar Company records at the Minnesota Historical Society, as well as the Dan Gutleben Scrapbooks, which Almaguer did not employ, turned up vast amounts of new information on the causes of the strike, life and labor in the Oxnard sugar beet fields, various forms of contractor exploitation, violent conflict with workers over wages, violence between strikers and nonstrikers, and the *keiyaku-nin*, including one Pajaro Valley contractor who was probably the father of Japanese labor contracting. My research also uncovered the earliest reference to the infamous short-handled hoe. Whereas Almaguer saw the strike as a case study in his account of white racism, I evaluate it within the context of Japanese farm labor history, especially the growing power of the *keiyaku-nin*. I take up the debate over the strike and demonstrate how a more careful reading of Oxnard newspapers uncovered information that Almaguer missed in "The 1903 Oxnard Sugar Beet Strike: A New Ending," *Labor History* 39 (May 1998), 193–99.

26. Espinosa is described in "Mexican Independence Day," *Oxnard Courier*, Sept. 7, 1901; "Patent Beet Thinner," ibid., Mar. 15, 1902. See also Mar. 27, 1902; Feb. 28, 1903. For biographical information on Inosuke Inose, see Fu Inshi [pseud.], *Zaibei Seikō no Nihonjin* (Tokyo, 1904), 156–68, JARPC.

27. Quote from Yamaguchi to editor, "Communication from the Union," *Oxnard Courier*, Mar. 28, 1903. See also *Los Angeles Herald*, Mar. 29, 1903; advertisement for Joe Baba, *Oxnard Courier*, Jan. 6, 1905. Baba operated out of the Japanese boardinghouse on Saviers Road. See also Kaigisho, *Nan Kashu Nihonjinshi*, 53; Kazusuke, *Hoku-Bei Tosa Taidan*, 223–25; Yuji Ichioka, "A Buried Past: Early Issei Socialists and the Japanese Community," *Amerasia Journal* 1 (July 1971), 3.

28. Quotes from editorials, *Oxnard Courier*, Mar. 7, 28, 1903. See also Jan. 13, Feb. 3, Mar. 24, May 19, Sept. 8, 1900; June 28, 1902; Sept. 18, 29, 1903. For a railroad strike by Mexicans, see Louis B. Perry and Richard S. Perry, *A History of the Los Angeles Labor Movement, 1911–1941* (Berkeley, 1963), 71.

29. Quote from John Murray, "A Foretaste of the Orient," *ISR*, 4 (Aug. 1903), 73–74. Murray, a socialist, spoke at several meetings, and participated in many events. For Driffill, see entries for Nov. 24; Dec. 2, 11, 1897; Jan. 7, 1898; Aug. 15, 17, 1899, Ware Scrapbooks, California, no. 7, ACSCR. Driffill is identified as a major in most correspondence until 1898 and a colonel beginning in 1899, but no reason for the promotion is given. For more biographical information, see *Oxnard Courier*, special issue, Dec. 1905. See also FWP, "Organization of Mexicans," MS (1938), 6–7; FWP, "Oriental Labor Unions and Strikes in California Agriculture," 11–13; N.T. Nowell, "Part Played by Japanese in Sugar Beets," interview no. 332 (fall 1924), 10, SRRP.

30. Founded in 1881 and led by Samuel Gompers for all but one of its first forty-two years, the AFL was well established in certain industries and had expanded its membership from 256,000 in 1897 to slightly more than twelve million in 1914. For the AFL in the steel industry, see David Brody, *Steelworkers in America: The Non-Union Era* (Cambridge, Mass., 1960).

31. Quotes from *AFL Convention Proceedings, 1894* (Washington, D.C., 1894), 25; Alexander Saxton, *The Indispensable Enemy: Labor and the Anti-Chinese Movement in California* (Berkeley and Los Angeles, 1995), 271. See also Samuel Gompers, *Some Reasons for Chinese Exclusion: Meat vs. Rice, American Manhood Against Asiatic Coolieism, Which Shall Survive?* (New York, 1902), 25; Arthur Mann, "Samuel Gompers and the Irony of Racism," *Antioch Review* 13 (1953), 203–14; Philip S. Foner, *History of the Labor Movement: The Policies and Practices of the American Federation of Labor, 1900–1909* (New York, 1965), 3: 268, 272.

32. Quote from *Organized Labor*, May 13, 1905; also Jan. 13, 1906. "It would be the height of inconsistency for our movement to unionize the Chinese against whom we have declared," wrote Gompers to an AFL official. See Gompers to Jere L. Sullivan, June 24, 1903, AFL Cor-

respondence, AFL-CIO Headquarters, Washington, D.C. See also Ira B. Cross, *History of the Labor Movement in California*, 17, 73, 86–99.

33. The AFL issued 1,700 federal charters to unions between 1901 and 1914. Federal unions were basically recruiting organizations. Rejecting any such radical notions as an eight-hour day, the Gilroy Labor Union of Packers seemed flexible and nondoctrinaire, and soon began demanding wages of $1.50 a day and a workday from 7 A.M. to 6 P.M., with an hour off for lunch and overtime paid at the rate of twenty cents per hour. The Santa Clara union had been formed on Mar. 17, 1902, by H. Ryan, after "two years of preparation." Quote from *PRP*, Mar. 28, 1903. See also February 28; May 16; June 13, 1903; *California Cultivator*, Sept. 4, 1903; CSBLS, *Twelfth Annual Report, 1906*, 183–85, 200; *American Federationist* 8 (Nov. 1901), 485; CIR, *Final Report*, 5: 4972–77; Kenneth A. Smith, "Industrial Relations in the California Fruit and Vegetable Canning Industry" (M.A. thesis, UCB, 1949), 86; Lowenstein, "Strikes and Strike Tactics," 98; William O. Weyforth, *The Organizability of Labor* (Baltimore, 1913), 22–23.

34. Widely regarded as "the citadel of the open shop," Los Angeles under the thumb of *Los Angeles Times* publisher Harrison Gray Otis and the Merchants and Manufacturers Association held union membership to less than one-third that of San Francisco. But while the Los Angeles labor movement remained weak and paled in comparison to its counterpart in San Francisco, it had gathered momentum after 1901, when the thriving construction market provided a base for socialist-leaning unions among building tradesmen and metal craftsmen. See Grace H. Stimson, *Rise of the Labor Movement in Los Angeles* (Berkeley, 1955), 143–46, 172–94, 217, 269, 331; Robert E. Knight, *Industrial Relations in the San Francisco Bay Area, 1900–1918* (Berkeley, 1960) 369–89; Perry and Perry, *A History of the Los Angeles Labor Movement*, vii, 21, 215; Walton Bean, *Boss Ruef's San Francisco* (Berkeley, 1952), 12–14, 26; Ralph E. Shaffer, "Radicalism in California, 1869–1929" (Ph.D. diss., UCB, 1962), 143, 152, 161. Murray would win a seat on the Los Angeles City Council in 1913. See also CSBLS, *Tenth Annual Report, 1901*, 67–77; CSBLS, *Twelfth Annual Report, 1906*, 183–85; CSBLS, *Thirteenth Annual Report, 1907*, 163–82; CIR, *Final Report*, 5: 4857, 4878; John A. Fitch, "Transgressor," *Survey* (Sept. 26, 1914), 632–33.

35. Murray, "Foretaste," 76–77, argues that Wheeler actually played the key role organizing JMLA. Maintaining that there was little support among white businesses, Almaguer, *Racial Fault Lines*, 194, is contradicted by "Beet Thinners Organize," *Ventura Free Press*, Mar. 6, 1903. "The union has the sympathy of the greater part of the residents of Oxnard and especially of the merchants who are willing to see the trade of hundreds of employees who work in the beet fields . . . instead of going to the favored few," reported the newspaper. For a circular soliciting beet workers and supporting their opposition to scrip payment arrangements, see "Dissertation on Contract Wages," *Oxnard Courier*, Nov. 1, 1902. For biographical information on Wheeler, see *The People*, Sept. 23, Dec. 16, 1900, Kangaroo ed.

36. Quotes from "The Japs and Mexicans," *Oxnard Courier*, Mar. 7, 1903; "Oxnard Has Labor Troubles," *Ventura Independent*, Mar. 5, 1903.

37. Quote from "Oxnard Has Labor Troubles," *Ventura Independent*, Mar. 5, 1903.

38. Quote from "Mexican's Rash Suicide," *Oxnard Courier*, Mar. 21, 1903. For information on Mexican children working in the fields, see "Says the Census Was Not Stuffed," ibid., June 6, 1903. Murray, "Foretaste," ibid., 76, 78, describes the differences between Mexican and Japanese field hands in Oxnard. Statistics from 1900 MS Census, Ventura County.

39. Overcoming huge linguistic, cultural, and other barriers, Lizarras united two ethnic groups in the first effective interracial farm labor union in California agriculture. See Kazusuke, *Hoku-Bei Tosa Taidan*, 223–5; Kaigisho, *Nan Kashu Nihonjinshi*, 53. See also *Oxnard Courier*, July 12, 1902; Feb. 7, 14; Mar. 7, 1903; *San Francisco Examiner*, Mar. 27, 1903; *Ventura Free Press*, Mar. 6, 1903; *Ventura Weekly Democrat*, Feb. 27, 1903; Stuart M. Jamieson, *Labor Unionism in American Agriculture*, U.S. Bureau of Labor Statistics, Bulletin No. 836 (Washington, D.C., 1945), 53–54; also Jamieson, "Labor Unionism in American Agriculture" (Ph. D. diss., UCB, 1943).

40. Quotes from Mrs. Reginald Shand, interview, Moorpark, Calif., Aug. 25, 1960, Thomas Bard Collection, HL; W. W. Brown, journal, Oct. 5, 1901, VCM; *Oxnard Courier*, Feb. 11, 1910. See also "The Officers Taboo Promiscuous Shooting," *Oxnard Courier*, June 13, 1903.

41. For the headlines, see *Oxnard Courier*, July 7, 1900; July 26, 1901; June 14, July 12, Oct. 4, Nov. 15, 1902; Dec. 4, 1904; Sept. 1, 1905. For general accounts of violent events in Sonoratown and the vicinity, see Sept. 7, 1901; Sept. 13, Nov. 1, 1902; May 16, 1903. For the Avila murder case, see "Fiendish Murder Perpetrated," July 12, 1902. For Mexicans robbing and attacking a

farmer, see "Shot By A Bean Thief," Oct. 4, 1902. For two labor contractors in a shooting affray that injured a woman, see Sept. 23, 1905.

42. For one "reliable" contractor involved in civic activities, see "Mexicans to Celebrate Here," *Oxnard Courier*, Sept. 13, 1902. For a contractor absconding with a payroll, see "Leaves Friends in the Lurch," ibid., Aug. 23, 1902. The amount of money that Mexican farm labor contractors handled, and the way it made them a target for robbers, can be seen in "Two Contractors Robbed and Beaten," ibid., Nov. 8, 1902.

43. "The Japs and Mexicans," *Oxnard Courier*, Mar. 7, 1903; *Oakland Tribune*, Apr. 21, 1903.

44. Quote from "The Japs and Mexicans," *Oxnard Courier*, Mar. 7, 1903. Lizarras and Yamaguchi to editor, "Communication," Mar. 28, 1903, stresses "beet thinners . . . have not asked for a raise in wages, but only that the wages not be lowered." The class conflict theme, developed initially in Murray, "Foretaste," 73–74, and then Foner, *History of the Labor Movement in the United States*, 3: 276–77, is picked up and advanced in Almaguer, *Racial Fault Lines*, 192, and then accepted as gospel in Takaki, *Strangers*, 198. Others also follow Almaguer, for example, Gómez-Quiñones, *Mexican American Labor*, 76–77.

45. Quote from *Ventura Daily Democrat*, Mar. 1, 1903. See also Murray, "Foretaste," 73.

46. Quote from "Riot Monday in Chinatown," *Oxnard Courier*, Mar. 28, 1903, a review of the entire strike. All that in fact happened was that as groups of union members had marched into the fields to set up picket lines, wrote their demands on plain brown paper, tacked them to poles and fences, and called upon men to join the strike, nonunion workers had walked out, swelling the ranks of the JMLA. As evidence of their support, strikers wore white union buttons sporting the acronym J.M.L.A. in black letters over an insignia of a red rising sun and a pair of clasped hands. That, in brief, was the first "violence" and "Jap trouble" of the Oxnard sugar beet workers strike. "Jap trouble" phrase from "Oxnard," *Ventura Free Press*, Mar. 15, 1903. See also *Oakland Tribune*, Apr. 1, 1903; WPA, FWP, "Organization of Mexicans," MS (1938), 6, BL.

47. Quote from "Trouble with the Laborers," *Oxnard Courier*, Mar. 14, 1903. See also "Oxnard," *Ventura Free Press*, Mar. 13, 1903.

48. Quote from Murray, "Foretaste," 72; also 73–76. No beet hand or his family went hungry during the strike or lacked the necessities of life; and none, certainly, lived any worse than they had grown accustomed to during ordinary periods of unemployment in the off-season.

49. Quote from ibid., 75. Ventura County's Santa Clara Valley should not be confused with the Santa Clara Valley south of San Francisco.

50. Quotes from "Parade and Union Meeting," *Oxnard Courier*, Mar. 28, 1903.

51. Quotes from "Parade and Union Meeting," and "Large Acreage of Beets," *Oxnard Courier*, Mar. 21, 1903. See also Gómez-Quiñones, "First Steps: Chicano Labor Conflict and Organizing, 1900–1920," *Aztlán* 3 (spring 1972), 24–26.

52. Quote from "Parade and Union Meeting," *Oxnard Courier*, Mar. 28, 1903.

53. Ibid.

54. Quote from *Ventura Daily Democrat*, Mar. 27, 1903. See also *Ventura Free Press*, Mar. 27, 1903; *Los Angeles Herald*, Mar. 27, 1903. For the arrests see Murray, "Foretaste," 74, 76.

55. Quote from "Peace and Harmony Reign After Bloody Affair at Oxnard," *Ventura Free Press*, Mar. 27, 1903, which contains the most detailed description of the violence.

56. Quote from ibid. For a description of men escaping through railroad car windows, see Murray, "Foretaste," 77.

57. This version of events did not become clear until eyewitness testimony was taken at the coroner's inquest beginning Mar. 26. See "Inquiry into the Cause of Louis [*sic*] Vasquez death a Farce," *Ventura Independent*, Apr. 2, 1903. Earlier, more confused versions of events appear in "Five Men Victims of a Resort to Gun Play," *Oxnard Courier*, Mar. 28, 1903; *Los Angeles Herald*, Mar. 25, 1903. See also Gómez-Quiñones, *Mexican American Labor*, 77. In some accounts Hawkins is identified as Hankins; Ogas as M. Ogaz. Many other names have multiple spellings, for example, Lizarras as Lizarraras.

58. Quote from "Peace and Harmony Reign After Bloody Affair at Oxnard," *Ventura Free Press*, Mar. 27, 1903. See also *Los Angeles Times*, Mar. 28, 1903; *Los Angeles Herald*, Mar. 24, 1903. Luis Vásquez is sometimes referred to as Louis.

59. Quote from "Great Excitement," *Oxnard Courier*, Mar. 28, 1903.

60. Quote from ibid. See also *San Francisco Call*, Mar. 24, 25, 1903; *San Francisco Examiner*, Mar. 26, 1903; *Santa Barbara Morning Press*, Mar. 24, 1903.

61. "Intense Excitement," *Ventura Fee Press*, Mar. 27, 1903.

62. Quotes from *Los Angeles Times*, Mar. 24, 1903; "The Situation at Oxnard," *Ventura Independent*, Mar. 26, 1903. See also "Sheriff Arrives," *Oxnard Courier*, Mar. 28, 1903; Murray, "Foretaste," 72.

63. Quotes from "Attempt at Compromise," *Oxnard Courier*, Mar. 28, 1903; *Ventura Daily Democrat*, Mar. 26, 1903. See also *Los Angeles Times*, Mar. 26, 27, 1903.

64. Quote from Lizarras and Yamaguchi to editor and "After Arnold," *Oxnard Courier*, Mar. 28, 1903. See also "Intense Excitement," *Ventura Free Press*, Mar. 27, 1903; *Ventura Daily Democrat*, Mar. 31, 1903.

65. Quotes from "Take A Crew Out," *Oxnard Courier*, Mar. 28, 1903. See also "Small Satisfaction," ibid., and "Shephard to the Rescue," *Ventura Free Press*, Mar. 27, 1903.

66. Quote from "More Quiet Tuesday," *Ventura Free Press*, Mar. 27, 1903. See also *Oakland Tribune*, Apr. 11, 1903.

67. Quote from "Vásquez Inquest," *Oxnard Courier*, Apr. 4, 1903.

68. "Harping on this line became monotonous to the jury," explained the *Ventura Independent*, "a monotony occasionally relieved by Juror [T. B.] Gosnell's impatient exclamation, 'Try the dead man for awhile' and 'what about the man shot in the hip.'" Quote from "At Inquest Arnold is Exonerated," *Ventura Independent*, Apr. 2, 1903.

69. Quote from ibid.

70. "Jury Rejects Inspired Evidence," *Ventura Independent*, Apr. 2, 1903. See also *Ventura Daily Democrat*, Mar. 31, 1903; *Los Angeles Times*, Apr. 1, 1903; *Los Angeles Times and California Mirror*, Apr. 4, 1903. The shooting could easily have been a botched attempt at robbery, as foremen and contractors carrying payrolls were frequently targeted.

71. "Incorporation the Subject," *Oxnard Courier*, Apr. 4, 1903; see also "Roosevelt in Oxnard," May 16; "Wonder Store Again Opened," July 18; "Oxnard Troubles to be Compromised," *Ventura Independent*, Apr. 2, 1903.

72. "More Beets than Ever," "Peace and Work Once More," and "Have Come to Terms," *Oxnard Courier*, Apr. 4, 1903.

73. Ichioka, *Issei*, 98. For an argument that "seasonal farm workers as a general proposition have been impassive," see Fuller, *Labor Relations*, 42. An argument asserting this was a harvest strike, when in fact it was over beet thinning, is found in *Golden Lands, Working Hands* (California Federation of Teachers, Sacramento, 1998), video, an otherwise excellent presentation.

74. Quote from "The Labor Situation," *Oxnard Courier*, Mar. 28, 1903.

75. Clearly the JMLA was functioning as a true labor union, with the Japanese branch reaping most of the benefits. For Yamaguchi, Otomo, and contract statistics, see "Work of Japanese Labor Association," *Oxnard Courier*, Apr. 18, 1903.

76. Quote from *Oakland Tribune*, Apr. 20, 1903; see also Apr. 1, 21.

77. Quote from *San Francisco Examiner*, Mar. 26, 1903. See also Jamieson, *Labor Unionism in American Agriculture*, 62–65; WPA, FWP, "Unionization of Farm Labor, 1903–1930," MS (1938), 4, BL.

78. Quote from Samuel Gompers to Lizarras, May 15, 1903, AFL-CIO Correspondence, Washington, D.C. See also Murray, "Foretaste," 78. Even before the JMLA became the SBFLU and applied for AFL membership, the *Oxnard Courier* found it "incredible" that the AFL would consider gathering "into its fold an organization of Japanese and Mexican aliens." See Apr. 4, 1903. Karl G. Yoneda, *Ganbatte: Sixty-Year Struggle of a Kibei Worker*, intro. Yuji Ichioka (Los Angeles, 1983), 24, identifies Baba as the president of the SBFLU. At the very moment Lizarras was writing to Gompers, AFL cooks and waiters in Sacramento were boycotting hotels and restaurants employing "oriental help."

79. "We are going to stand by men who stood by us in the long, hard fight which ended in a victory over the enemy. We therefore respectfully petition the AFL to grant us a charter under which we can unite all the Sugar Beet & Field Laborers of Oxnard without regard to their color or race." Quote from Lizarras to Gompers, June 8, 1903, AFL-CIO Correspondence, Washington, D.C. See also Murray, "Foretaste," 78, which reprints the letter.

80. Quotes from Lowenstein, "Strike and Strike Tactics," 22–23, 97–98; *American Labor Union Journal*, June 25, 1903. See also *AFL Convention Proceedings, 1903* (Washington, D.C., 1904), 103–4; WPA, FWP, "Unionization of Migratory Labor," 4. Looking at these same facts, David Montgomery, *The Fall of the House of Labor: The Workplace, the State, and American Labor Activism, 1865–1925* (Cambridge, Mass., 1987), 86, claims: "So many Japanese field workers

sought to join the American Federation of Labor . . . that the Los Angeles Council was tempted to let them in."

81. Quote from Andrew Furuseth to Frank T. Morrison, June 12, 1903, AFL-CIO Correspondence, Washington, D.C. Except for a few local members in Los Angeles and Oakland, California labor leaders opposed organizing the Japanese with a vehemence that made their national leaders look timid. For Furuseth, see Hyman Weintraub, *Andrew Furuseth, Emancipator of the Seamen* (Berkeley, 1959), 113. California State Federation of Labor, *Proceedings of the 9th Annual Convention* (San Jose, 1908), 13–14, 49, 55, 90, advocates exclusion not organization of Japanese laborers. See also WPA, FWP, "The Migratory Agricultural Worker and the AFL to 1938 inclusive," MS (1939), 2, BL; *San Francisco Chronicle*, Aug. 14, 1908.

82. "Paid His Men Off With Bullets," *Oxnard Courier*, May 16, 1903.

83. For the labor shortage, see "Sugar Factory to Start Up," *Oxnard Courier*, May 16, 1903; see also "Busy Harvest Days Begun," June 20; "Shortage of Help to Handle Fruit," July 11; "Progress of Beet Harvest," July 18.

84. For the campaign to clean up Oxnard, see "The Officers Taboo Promiscuous Shooting," *Oxnard Courier*, June 13, 1903. See also "Japanese Gambling Joint Raided," July 4; "Constant Disturbance Injuring Business," Oct. 30.

85. "Deputy Sheriff Russell's Terrible Fight for Life," *Oxnard Courier*, July 11, 1903.

86. Quote from "John Inose Shot by Unknown Person," *Oxnard Courier*, Aug. 14, 1903. See also "Attempted Murder: A Jap is Shot Tuesday Night in Oxnard," *Ventura Free Press*, Aug. 14, 1903.

87. For the harvest, see "Beet Tonnage is Picking Up," *Oxnard Courier*, Aug. 14, 1903; see also "Second Campaign at the Factory," October 20; "Factory Will Run Several Weeks Yet," Oct. 9; "The 1903 Sugar Campaign," Oct. 16; "Resume of the Crop Harvest," Nov. 13. For Tomiyama Company, see Tomiyama Company advertisement, Oct. 30.

88. Quotes from Joe Baba advertisement, *Oxnard Courier*, Nov. 27, 1903; "Japanese to Farm on Co-Operative Plan," ibid., Dec. 25, 1903. See also Joe Baba advertisement, "Japanese Contractor," ibid., Jan. 6, 1905.

89. Quote from "Japanese to Farm on Co-Operative Plan," *Oxnard Courier*, Dec. 25, 1903. See also Almaguer, *Racial Fault Lines*, 202.

90. Manufactured by the American Beet Harvester Manufacturing Company, the beet topper and puller was expected to be on the market the following year. For experiments, see "Beet Topper and Puller," *Oxnard Courier*, Sept. 16, 1904. For the Japanese in the western sugar beet industry, see *ICR*, 1: 61, 68, 70.

91. "Wm. Suytar Fatally Shot," *Oxnard Courier*, Sept. 23, 1904.

92. Quotes from "Reliable Help," ibid., Aug. 11, 1905; advertisement, "Japanese General Contractors," ibid., Dec. 29, 1905; Feb. 2, 1906. See also "Labor Bureau to be Established Here," ibid., May 26, 1905; Bloom, "Oxnard," ibid., 19.

93. Quote from *Oxnard Courier*, Mar. 23, 1906. Angered by the murder, the city launched a furious vendetta in "the tenderloin district." Routing out the "opium joints" and closing down every Chinese crib, authorities took their revenge, even though there was no evidence that Japanese or Chinese field hands had been involved in the murder.

CHAPTER NINETEEN

1. *Vacaville Reporter*, Sept.19, 1903. "I have no love for the Japanese," Loomis-area fruit grower Lee Tudsbury stressed after years of wrestling with *keiyaku-nin*, "but they are certainly good horticulturists." Quote from Lee Tudsbury, interview, Nov. 11, 1924, no. 40, in Eliot Mears, "102 Interviews with Employers of Farm Workers," SRRP.

2. *CSFGCT, 1901* (Sacramento, 1902), 395; *CSFGCT, 1903* (Sacramento, 1904), 217–21; *California Fruit Grower*, Dec. 20, 1902; *PRP*, Dec. 27, 1902; H. P. Stabler, "California Fruit Growers and Labor," 268–69; *Sacramento Record Union*, Dec. 22, 1902; George W. Pierce, daily journal, Feb. 3–Mar. 24, 1903.

3. Eleven additional labor agents joined them, barnstorming Ohio, Pennsylvania, and other states. See *California Fruit Grower*, Jan. 31; Feb.7, 28, 1903. The July 25, 1903, issue reprints a union circular advising against immigration to California.

On ranches and fruit farms Chinese and Japanese were employed for years until the past year when their places were taken by white persons for less pay than received by the

Asiatics. Ranch hands are compelled to sleep out of doors and furnish their own bedding, and when the fruit season is over are discharged, the managers of these places knowing that a fresh lot of victims can be secured next season.

See also "Discussion of the Labor Question," *CSFGCT, 1902*, 275–80; *Davisville Enterprise*, Mar. 14, 1903; *Orchard and Farm*, Apr. 15, 1903; *PRP*, Feb. 14, 1903; unidentified newspaper clippings, 4, 5, 20, 28, California Pamphlets Collection, BL.

4. Quote from Michael Kazin, *Barons of Labor: The San Francisco Building Trades and Union Power in the Progressive Era* (Urbana and Chicago, 1987), 162–70. See also *PRP*, Feb. 4, 13, 1904; "Report of the Committee on Farm Labor," *CSFGCT, 1903*, 89–92; "Report of the Committee on Farm Labor," *CSFGCT, 1904* (Sacramento, 1904), 219–21. For efforts to close schools during the grape harvest, see *Healdsburg Enterprise*, Sept. 19, 1903.

5. Quotes from *CSFGCT, 1902*, 280–81; also 89–90. See also "Report of the California Employment Committee," in California Commissioner of Horticulture, *First Biennial Report, 1903–4* (Sacramento, 1905), 387–88.

6. Quote from *PRP*, Aug. 15, 1903. See also *California Cultivator*, Sept. 4, 1903; "Oriental Labor Unions and Strikes in California Agriculture," 10–11.

7. Quote from "Report of the California Employment Committee," *Proceedings of the Thirtieth Annual Convention of the California State Fruit Growers*, Dec. 6–9, 1904, in California Commissioner of Horticulture, *First Biennial Report for 1903–1904* (Sacramento, 1905), 387–88.

8. *Marysville Daily Appeal*, July 20, 22, 23, 24; Oct. 14, 15, 19, 22; Nov. 6, 1904; July 20, 1906. Mug shots of Hankins taken by Marysville photographer Clara Smith after his arrest are in Arne Svenson, *Prisoners* (New York, 1997), 44. Hankins was paroled Oct. 26, 1914, after serving his sentence. See arrest record, Claude F. Hankins, no. 937, July 20, 1904, Marysville Police Logbook, 1895–1908, courtesy Arene Svenson. Hankins died in 1965, of congestive heart failure, near Seattle, after working without incident as a merchant seaman. See Coroner's Report no. 1879, State File no. 7289, May 11, 1965, King County, Wash. Children continued to provoke headlines for their criminal activity. On Aug. 25, 1907, two boys from San Francisco who arrived in town on the "hop train special" were arrested for stealing clothes from a store in Yuba City. One was acquitted, the other fined thirty dollars and sentenced to thirty days in the county jail. See *Marysville Daily Appeal*, Aug. 25, 27, 1907.

9. On Feb. 6, 1905, the burglar pled guilty and received a sentence of sixty days in county jail. See "Burglar Captured," *Marysville Daily Appeal*, Nov. 3, 1904; "Black Sharkey Held," ibid., Nov. 5, 1904; "Charge Reduced," ibid., Feb. 6, 1905.

10. Quotes from Report of the Indian Hill Citrus Union for 1903–1904, Special Collections, California History Room, Pomona Public Library; clipping, *California Fruit Grower*, Aug. 15, 1903, FHHC; clipping, *Los Angeles Times*, n.d., Harris Weinstock Scrapbooks, Harris Weinstock Papers, BL. See also *ICR*, 24: 374; CSBLS, *Twelfth Biennial Report, 1905–6*, 68.

11. *ICR*, 1: 33, 67; 2: 108–10; 24: 27, 234–37; Paul S. Taylor, *Mexican Labor in the United States: Imperial Valley, California*, University of California Publications in Economics (Berkeley, 1930), 5–6; Noritake Yagasaki, "Ethnic Cooperativism and Immigrant Agriculture: A Study of Japanese Floriculture and Truck Farming in California" (Ph.D. diss., UCB, 1982), 15; Kawamura Tetsutarō, *Saikin Katsudō Hoku-Bei jigyō annai* (Guide to current jobs) (Tokyo, 1906), JARPC.

12. Quote from Otis B. Tout, *The First Thirty Years, Being An Account of the Principal Events in the History of Imperial Valley, Southern California, 1901–1931* (Holtville, Calif., 1931), 5; see also 28, 50.

13. Taylor, *Mexican Labor in the United States: Imperial Valley*, 5, establishes 1904 as the date that Japanese field hands moved into the Imperial Valley melon industry. Beginning in 1903, entrepreneurs had planted a few acres of cantaloupes in the Coachella Valley, and following a successful harvest, extended the industry south into the upper end of the Salton Basin in 1904. Although aphid infestations damaged the 1904 crop, several farmers near Brawley became interested. Planting their crops early in winter, they directed field hands to place glassine paper covers over each cantaloupe plant to create small tents and further protect the crops with long windbreaks of tough wrapping paper held in place by rows of stakes and arrowweed brush. With better transportation, packing, cooling, and shipping, growers believed that the valley could supply the nation with cantaloupes when none had ever been available. For the early cantaloupe industry, see B. A. Harrigan, "Cantaloupes," MS (n.d.), Pioneer Museum, Imperial County Historical Society. See also Tout, *The First Thirty Years in Imperial Valley*, 178;

William C. Smith, "Interview with Dr. E. E. Chandler," Aug. 23, 1924; E. E. Chandler to George Gleason, May 2, 1924, William C. Smith Papers, Special Collections, University of Oregon, Eugene.

14. Quote from *Oakland Tribune*, Aug. 31, 1905. See also Claude Midkiff Recollections, MS (n.d.), Glendora Historical Society, Glendora, California; *ICR*, 24: 26; *California Fruit Grower*, Mar. 28, 1903; Mar. 3, 1906.

15. Quote from Cikuth, "The Pajaro Valley Apple Industry," 127–28. See also reminiscences contained in unidentified newspaper clippings, "Americanization in Hawaii Sugar Plantation Interference," June 27, 1920; "Won—But What Did They Win?" July 3, 1920, Chester Rowell Papers, BL; Lydon, *Japanese in Monterey*, 28.

16. "The school census of Oxnard is reduced at least 150 by reason of the employment of some six or seven hundred Japs at labor that should be done by as many American laborers, and among whom we could at least count upon 150 families to support." Quote from "Jap vs. White Labor Killing San Dimas," *Oxnard Courier*, May 12, 1905.

17. For the peach strike, see Irwin, "Japanese and the Pacific Coast," 17–18. For the walnut strike, see *PRP*, Oct. 13, 1906. See also Coolidge, *Chinese Immigration*, 385; S. S. Schwartz to Atlanta and St. Andrews Railway Company, n.d.; Atlanta and St. Andrews Bay Railway Company to J. C. Horton, Apr. 17, 1906, Justice Dept. Records, File no. 50-162-8, RG 60, NA; Zaibei Nihonjin, *Zaibei Nihonjin Shi* (San Francisco, 1940), 166, JARPC; CSBLS, *Twelfth Annual Report, 1905*, 69, 73. CSBLS studied 147 farms. The word *"cholo,"* popular in the vernacular of the 1840s, originally referred to Mexican immigrants who arrived in Texas a generation after the first immigrants. In the late nineteenth century, wealthier elements used the term to disassociate themselves from the rest of the Mexican community, to draw a distinction between old families and immigrants, between *gente decente* and *cholos*. For the etymology of the term *"cholo,"* see Gómez-Quiñones, *Mexican American Labor*, 27, 43, 76. The term was also applied by the United Fruit Company to workers on its Guaymí banana plantation in Central America. See Philippe I. Bourgois, *Ethnicity at Work: Divided Labor on a Central American Banana Plantation* (Baltimore, 1989), 120–59, arguing that the term was a form of "conjugated oppression."

18. Quote from *San Jose Mercury*, Dec. 6, 1906, San Jose Museum. Apparently the anti-Japanese scheme did not have the support of growers around Saratoga and Cupertino; they told a reporter for the *San Francisco Chronicle* that while they paid high rates to the Japanese, they found them dependable and believed that "if they employed white labor there would soon be a prune picker's union." See *San Francisco Chronicle*, Oct. 9, 1906.

19. Limbaugh and Payne, *Vacaville*, 139–40; *Vacaville Reporter*, Dec. 29, 1906, reprinting excerpts from CSBLS, *Twelfth Biennial Report, 1905–6*; G. H. Hecke, "Pacific Coast Labor," *CSFGCT, 1906* (Sacramento, 1907), 69; *San Francisco Chronicle*, Oct. 9, 1906. Following a series of sensational articles repeating these themes in the San Francisco and Sacramento newspapers, including one comparing Vacaville to a Tokyo suburb, *Collier's Weekly* sent Will Irwin to investigate. His story cemented the view of *keiyaku-nin* as "devious Orientals" and Japanese field hands as a militant, ambitious, and dangerous threats to white labor. See Irwin, "The Japanese and the Pacific Coast," 17–19. The essay was not enough to cause growers to embrace immigration restriction. They may not have liked the Japanese, but they also could not do without them. Whenever legislators vowed to exclude the Japanese, Vacaville growers rose up in protest, claiming that if the Japanese were banned, "the great fruit and wine industries are threatened with disaster." Quote from *PRP*, Dec. 15, 1906.

20. CSBLS, *Eleventh Biennial Report, 1904*, 75–76; *Twelfth Report, 1905*, 65; Walter MacArthur, "Opposition to Oriental Immigration," *AAAPSS* 34 (Sept. 1909), 223–30; *Proceedings of the Asiatic Exclusion League* (San Francisco, 1908), 55, Asiatic Exclusion League Collection, Labor Archives, CSU, San Francisco. See also David Brudnoy, "Race and the San Francisco School Board Incident: Contemporary Evaluations," *CHQ* 50 (Sept. 1971), 295–312; Kazin, *Barons of Labor*, 164–69.

21. Quotes from letter to editor, *San Francisco Chronicle*, Jan. 2, 1907; Abiko Kyūtarō to Tadasu Hayashi, Feb. 15, 1907, *Nihon Gaikō Bunsho, 1907* [Japanese Foreign Ministry Documents] (Tokyo, 1961), 90: 3, 331–32, Asian American Studies Center, UCLA. See also "Labor on the Pacific Coast," *California Fruit Grower*, Jan. 5, 1907; Roger Daniels, *The Politics of Prejudice* (New York, 1968), 26–38.

22. *California Fruit Grower*, May 4, Aug. 10, 1907; "To the Congress," *CSFGCT, 1907* (Sacramento, 1907), 65–66; G. H. Hecke, "The Pacific Coast Labor Question from the Standpoint

of a Horticulturalist," *CSFGCT, 1906,* 68–69 [copy in Hecke Papers, ASCUCD]; Minami Kashu Doho Taikai to Hayashi, Feb. 20, 1907, *Nihon Gaikō Bunsho, 1907,* 90: 3, 343.

23. Quotes from Irish to *Fresno Republican,* n.d., John P. Irish Papers, SUASC; *CSFGCT, 1907,* 69–70, 92. As the crisis unfolded, *keiyaku-nin* hoped that growers might succeed in petitioning President Roosevelt for amendments to the law, obtain quotas large enough to protect crops, and secure admission of Japanese under the same conditions as European immigrants. See Col. John P. Irish, "Labor in Rural Industries," typescript, Irish Papers; Ichioka, *Issei,* 71–72. Growers naturally desired any policy that would flood the farm labor market and undermine Japanese militancy, although this sentiment was never explicitly stated. Understanding the realities of immigration politics, growers had to be careful. By explicitly calling for a glutted farm labor market, they would have undermined their cause and given restrictionists ammunition to hold fast. Oddly, growers counted on support from *keiyaku-nin* who, without a continual stream of their countrymen, feared that it was only a matter of time before they would be out of business. They had become "cunning—even tricky," as one grower put the matter, a "pest in the shape of cheap labor." According to the newly elected president of the California Almond Growers Association, Japanese field hands did not belong "either by training or instinct to the purely servant class" and "their labor cannot be classed as cheap labor." Rejecting the proposition that only people capable of rapid assimilation should be admitted into the United States, John P. Irish asked fruit growers to "imagine a crop three times as large as that of 1907." Where would growers find enough reliable white labor to harvest? Time was of the utmost importance, he noted, as "the fruit of the tree and vine does not wait for a crew to go off to town Saturday night and get drunk and straggle back Monday and Tuesday, and some of them not at all." Quotes from CSFGC, *Annual Report, 1907* (Sacramento 1908), 58.

24. Quotes from Hecke, "Pacific Coast Labor Question," 68; Irish, "Labor in the Rural Industries of California," in *CSFGCT, 1907,* 64. After the harvest season, fruit growers gathered in Sacramento and assessed the situation at their annual convention. To a man, they confessed at being perplexed by the behavior of field hands. Worried about the future, growers unfolded stories of labor unrest, labor shortages, and odd behavior. One distraught raisin farmer explained how he had tried to pacify a mob enraged over his use of Chinese field hands in his 320-acre vineyard. Offering to hire all the white men who wanted to work, he discovered that half showed up drunk, and that the others refused to do the work. Even though he employed two cooks and furnished new bunks, at the end of the first day of harvesting only three men remained on his ranch. "How can you survive conditions like that?" he asked. "We have come to the determination that if the whites will not harvest our crops we must go out and seek those who will." See also *CSFGCT, 1902,* 274; CSFGC, *Proceedings, 1917* (Sacramento, 1918), 78.

25. Quotes from *California Fruit Grower,* Aug. 27, 1907; Irish, "Labor in the Rural Industries of California," in *CSFGCT, 1907,* 64.

26. Quote from Irish to editor, *FMR* [1910], Irish Papers, SUASC.

27. Quotes from *ICR,* 24: 235; typed notes, Barry, "Labor in California Sugar Beet Crop." CSBLS found that 641 of 642 permanent positions were held by white workers. Studying 2,393 harvest hands on 117 farms in Napa and Sonoma counties in 1907, the bureau found that 51 percent were white and 49 percent "Oriental." Expanding its study the following year, the Bureau of Labor Statistics investigated 4,102 farms, including 1,733 operated by Japanese. Scattered across 697,236 acres in thirty-six counties and growing almost every crop, these farms employed 80,984 field hands, including 9,458 women. On the white farms employing 63,198 people, 53.4 percent of the labor was white, 36.4 percent Japanese, and 10.2 percent Chinese, Mexicans, Hindus, and Indians. But on Japanese farms employing 17,784 people, 96 percent of the labor was Japanese. Together, these figures suggested that white and Japanese field hands each furnished about half of the state's farm laborers. Additionally, in interviews throughout California, field agents for the U.S. Immigration Commission observed again and again how "white men do not particularly object to the character of the work" and "white ranchers in this district employ white men in preference to Mexicans or Japanese," and so on. See CSBLS, *13th Biennial Report, 1907–8,* 119, 267, 270.

28. Described in Lanier Bartlett, "An Immigrant in the Land of Opportunity," *World's Work* 17 (Apr. 1909), 1137–39, as a man "more Teuton than Latin in appearance—a big, short-necked, round-headed, broad shouldered, bluff-mannered man of middle age"—Segundo Guasti concluded that he could grow grapes without irrigation, much as vineyardists did in Italy, after traveling to the Cucamonga Desert, digging below the surface layer of decomposed granite,

and finding damp loam. With a force of sixty-five mule teams, each pulling a Fresno scraper, he proceeded to clear the brush and level the land. He had to organize huge rabbit drives to prevent the animals from devouring his vineyards, and succeeded in keeping them out only by erecting a fence at a cost of four thousand dollars. See *The Californians*, 7 (May/June 1987), 35; James D. Hofer, "Cucamonga Wines and Vines: A History of the Cucamonga Pioneer Vineyard Association" (M.A. thesis, Claremont Graduate School, 1983), 5, 41–42; Jim Cavener, "Historic Old Guasti Plaza," *Rancho Cucamonga Magazine* (Dec. 13, 1989), 2–5; Marcia Stumpf, *Growing Up in Guasti* (Cucamonga, 1999), 3–9; *Ontario Daily Report*, Nov. 3, 1913.

29. Quotes from Jack Blue, "The good old days of wine and roses," *Cucamonga Sun-Telegram*, Feb. 13, 1979; Bartlett, "An Immigrant in the Land of Opportunity," 1137–39. Completely self-sufficient, Guasti boasted its own power plant, refrigeration room, and barrel manufacturing operation capable of producing two hundred oak or redwood barrels per day. Married couples lived in neat, clapboard cottages, each equipped with a cellar and gable roofs. Unmarried, white single men occupied two dormitories equipped with showers, indoor plumbing, and tub baths. An artesian well, 450 feet, furnished pure water to the community and allowed the permanent residents to irrigate truck gardens and fruit trees.

30. Antonio Perelli-Minetti, interview, "A Life in Winemaking," 1968, ROHP; Baudelio Sandoval, interview by Carlos Arturo Castaneda, Apr. 13, 1978, Upland Public Library. For company towns in the American West, see James B. Allen, *The Company Town in the American West* (Norman, Okla., 1967). See also unidentified newspaper clippings, "Segundo Guasti" and "Leader in Wine Industry Dies," Ontario Public Library, Model Colony History Collection, Ontario, Calif.; unidentified newspaper clipping, "Artistic Church at Guasti Modeled After Famous Church Near Turin, Italy," Guasti Plaza Archives.

31. Quote from Pierre Biane, interview by author, Brookside Winery, May 17, 1974, author's possession. See also *Ontario Record*, Oct. 7, 1909; Harry Bachigalupi, interview by author, San Bruno, Calif., May 12, 1977, author's possession; various materials, Model Colony History Room, Ontario Public Library; Ontario Museum of History and Art, Ontario, Calif. Even when crews were packing boxes for the fresh fruit market, the boxes could be stacked in the gondolas, quickly hauled to a shady siding, kept out of the sun, and transferred to boxcars. After the harvest, Guasti's permanent employees disassembled the railroad tracks, stacked them on flatcars, and hauled them out of the vineyards so that plow crews and pruning crews could cultivate and tend the vines. When the 1906 earthquake shattered wine tanks and the wine industry of Northern California, the Italian Vineyard Company laid more track, planted another one thousand acres of grapevines, and went on making wine by the trainload. Pushing his industrialized operations to the limits, Guasti increased production, demanding maximum efficiency from machines and field hands alike. By 1909, his self-contained operation ranged from barrel making to marketing agents in Chicago, New Orleans, and New York. Guasti made so much money that year that the onetime fry cook dined on plates of gold. For the Great Western Vineyard Company, see McCubbin, "Wahtoke," in Nichel, *Beginnings in the Reedley Area*, 21–22. For El Pinal, see Teiser and Harroun, *Winemaking in California*, 150.

32. Quotes from H. A. Millis, "East Indian Immigration to the Pacific Coast," *Survey* 28 (June 1, 1912), 379–86; "The Hindu, the Newest Immigration Problem," ibid., 379–86; Herman Scheffauer, "The Tide of Turbans," *Forum* 43 (June 1910), 616–18; *Organized Labor*, July 24, Nov. 6, 1909. For the beginning of Sikh labor, see Bruce La Brack, *The Sikhs of Northern California, 1904–1975* (New York, 1988), 105; Sucheta Mazumdar, "Punjabi Agricultural Workers in California, 1905–1945," in Cheng and Bonavich, *Labor Immigration*, 550–67.

33. Pierce, daily journal, May 15–July 29, 1907; "Hired Help," Pierce, account book, 1907: 155, Pierce Family Papers, UCDSCA. See also Rajani Kanta Das, *Hindustani Workers on the Pacific Coast* (Berlin, 1923), 6.

34. Quote from *San Jose Mercury*, Sept. 1, 1907. Of the 30,824 Japanese who departed Japan, 30,226 were admitted to the United States.

35. Quotes from partially dated clipping, *California Fruit Grower*, 1907, FHHC; CSBLS, *Fifteenth Biennial Report, 1910*, 48.

36. Quote from David Vaught, "'An Orchardist's Point of View': Harvest Labor Relations on a California Almond Ranch, 1892–1921," *AH* 69 (fall 1995), 579. See also Pierce, account book, "Almonds," 1907, 116; Pierce, daily journal, July 21, 1907, Pierce Family Papers, UCDSCA. Late in November, the Japanese encountered yet another threat to their power and position when Vacaville farmer C. M. Hartley replaced his Japanese with a crew of Sikhs, again hired at

$1.25 a day without board. Fortunately for the Japanese, the Sikhs did not work very well. Although a tough lot, many of them having served in the British military, they were unfamiliar with orchard culture and did more damage than good. Within a week, they were gone, and the Japanese were back on Hartley's farm. But nothing would ever be the same. About three hundred Sikhs settled around Vacaville. Several hundred were also reported hoeing fields and picking fruit near Newcastle, east of Sacramento. Some worked the first season for as little as fifty cents a day. See Limbaugh and Payne, *Vacaville*, 140; Dhan Gopal Mukerji, *Caste and Outcast* (New York, 1923), 269–77; CSBLS, *Thirteenth Biennial Report, 1907–8*, 141–42, 218; *ICR*, 24: 118.

37. Quote from *Sacramento Bee*, Jan. 27, 1908. See also McWilliams, *Factories in the Field*, 139–40; *Sutter County Farmer*, Jan. 10, 31; Feb. 7, 14, 1908; *Sutter County Independent*, Jan. 30, 1908.

38. Quote from Dr. E. E. Chandler, interview, Aug. 23, 1924; E. E. Chandler to George Gleason, May 2, 1924, William C. Smith Papers, Special Collections, University of Oregon, Eugene. See also Joan M. Jensen, *Passage from India: Asian Immigrants in North America* (New Haven, Conn., 1988), 36–37, 40.

39. Quote from Ichihashi, *Japanese in the United States*, 174.

40. Quotes from Chester H. Rowell, "Chinese and Japanese Immigration," 5; *ICR*, 24: 8–9, 242, 598; *IW*, Apr. 22, May 20, 1909; CSBLS, *Fifteenth Biennial Report, 1911*, 48; clippings, *FMR*, Feb. 24, May 30, 1910, BWC. See also Charles W. Blanpied, *A Humanitarian Study of the Coming Immigration Problem on the Pacific Coast* (San Francisco, 1913), 44, 47, 62–63; A. E. Yoell, "Oriental vs. American Labor," *AAAPSS* 34 (Sept. 1909), 28; WPA, FWP, "Oriental Labor Unions," 5; *San Francisco Chronicle*, May 30, 1910; *PRP*, June 11, 1910; Sept. 16, 1911. For Orange County, see *Orange County Tribune*, Jan. 29, Feb. 12, 1908. For the Sonoma hop harvest, see CSBLS, *Thirteenth Biennial Report, 1907–8*, 136. For *keiyaku-nin* around Watsonville in 1908, see Ichihashi, *Japanese in the United States*, 173.

41. Repelled by the dry, barren environment, extreme isolation, and crude, frontier conditions, hundreds of men would arrive on supply trains, look around at the heat and the desert, and leave. See Tout, *The First Thirty Years in Imperial Valley*, 104–5, 170, 176.

42. Quote from "Labor Situation," *Imperial Valley Press*, June 13, 1908. See also *Los Angeles Times*, June 11–12, 1908. Although the *Times* reported that six thousand field hands were needed, less than half that number were actually required. Some Japanese field hands may have been part of two groups of Okinawans who had been shipped to the Esperanza mine in Mexico in 1904 and 1907, and left that "living hell" for California by way of El Paso, Texas. See Ichioka, *Issei*, 70.

43. Quote from "Labor Situation."

44. Quote from "Trouble Makers." For events in Imperial Valley, see newspaper clippings in "Anti-Japanese Riots in California," Pamphlets on the Japanese, BL; *ICR*, 24: 233.

45. "Fire at Meloland," *Imperial Valley Press*, June 13, 1908.

46. Quote from *PRP*, July 4, 1908. See also J. H. Walsh, "Japanese, Chinese Exclusion or Industrial Organization," *IUB*, Apr. 11, 1908.

47. Pierce, daily journal, Jan. 9, 10; Mar. 14; May 21; June 28; Aug. 4–Sept. 9, 1908; "Shaam Singh account"; Feb. 26; Aug. 6–Sept. 5, 1909; Aug. 3, 1910; "Hindu Gang No. 2," Aug. 17, 1913; Feb. 5; May 26; June 8; Aug. 8; Dec. 25, 1914; "Indar Singh and Kalla Singh," Apr. 16; Aug. 16; Dec. 19, 1915; Jan. 22; Mar. 6; Aug. 1; Dec. 26, 1916; "Anokh Singh," Dec. 9, 1918; Pierce, time book, Aug. 1913, Pierce Family Papers, UCDSCA.

48. According to the U.S. Immigration Commission, it soon became an almost universal policy "to discriminate against the East Indian in wages." In these circumstance, Sikhs and other East Indians often fell back on their own culture for guidance. Working eleven hours in the fields, they refused to abandon their religion. On a haying crew, one man would act as an *imam* (priest); climbing atop some bale of hay, he would read from the Koran five times a day. Because the men took fifteen-minute breaks for each reading, growers somewhat disliked the disruptive effects of Muslim traditions. At least one grower, familiar with Muslim religious practices, offered his East Indian crew a fifteen-cent-per-day bonus if they would only pray three times. See *ICR*, 3: 333; Mukerji, *Caste and Outcast*, 269–77; 1910 MS Census, Monterey County.

49. As often as not, Indian Sikhs could not alter the circumstances of their work. Cutting and boxing asparagus near Isleton for ten cents a box, they worked from 4:30 A.M. until 7 P.M. So exhausted were the men in the evening after working in asparagus or yanking old grape vines out of the fields around Fresno at two cents a vine that all they could do was bathe, eat

dinner, and drink themselves into a stupor (despite prohibitions against use of liquor). See Willard Schurr, "Hindus in Los Angeles"; J. M. Hamer, interview July 8, 1924; Inder Singh, interview, May 31, 1924, William C. Smith Papers, Special Collections, University of Oregon, Eugene.

50. The SVSBC was originally known as the Alta California Sugar Company. Funded by J. G. Hamilton, after whom Hamilton City was named, the company had opened for business at Hamilton City on Mar. 3, 1908. Construction of the $2.2 million sugar beet processing factory had begun in 1906. From the beginning the company had struggled to round up enough men to thin its fields and harvest its crop. See E. C. Hamilton to E. A. Pardee, July 30, 1908; Manager's Annual Report to Board of Directors, 1908; Annual Report of the Agricultural Department, SVSBCR, SCML; *ICR*, 1: 67; 2: 109; *IW*, June 3, 1908.

51. *Shin Sekui*, June 9; Aug. 11, 13, 22, 1908; *FMR*, Aug 31, 1908; Shakai Bunko, *Zai-Bei Shakaishugisha Museifushugisha Enkaku* (A History of Japanese Socialists and Anarchists in America) (Tokyo, 1964), 1: 213, 230–42, JARPC, which is particularly valuable for its use of secret reports from the Japanese Ministry of Home Affairs.

52. Bunko, *Zai-Bbei Shakaishugisha Museifushugisha Enkaku*, 213, 217, 237, 248–54, calculates membership at two thousand. Itō Banshō [pseud.], *Fukei Jiken no Shinsō* (Facts about the Lèse-majesté Incident) (Fresno, 1912), 126, JARPC, gives a membership of one thousand. CSBLS, *Thirteenth Biennial Report, 1907–8*, 201, estimates about one thousand Japanese lived around Fresno and could not handle the harvest. CSBLS, *Fourteenth Biennial Report, 1908–9*, 268, estimates about five thousand Japanese converged on Fresno in 1910 from all parts of the state during the raisin grape harvest. Fresno Labor League also translates to Fresno Labor Society.

53. *FMR*, Aug. 29, 31, 1908

54. Quotes from ibid., Oct. 13, Sept. 8, 1908.

55. Ibid., Sept. 14, 1908; Robert Clark, "The Labor History of Fresno, 1886–1910" (M.A. thesis, CSU, Fresno, 1976), 143. If the Fresno Labor League did contract with any ranch, it is not known. It did achieve its main purpose—protecting the $1.65-per-ton wage rate, and preventing *keiyaku-nin* from underbidding one another.

56. Sympathetic to radical labor organizations, the league attacked capitalism, militarism, and dangerous working conditions. The league also called for the public ownership of land and urged the "workers of the world" to unite. This did not win many friends among well-established members of the Japanese community. See Bunko, *Zaibei Shakaishugisha Museifushugisha Enkaku*, 230–34, 248–54; Ichioka, "A Buried Past: Early Issei Socialists and the Japanese Community," *Amerasia Journal* 1 (July 1971), 10–18; *IW*, May 20, June 10, 1909.

57. Quotes from *Annual Report of the Commissioner of Immigration, 1907* (Wash., D.C., 1907), 146ff, in Note Z, Ichihashi Papers, SUASC. For "illegal" Japanese immigration, see Elliot G. Mears, *Resident Orientals on the American Pacific Coast* (Chicago, 1928), 409; Jean Pajus, *The Real Japanese California* (Berkeley, 1937), 15. Of the 3,275 Japanese who immigrated in 1909, 3,111 were admitted.

58. Quote from "Testimonial Meeting . . . IWW Hall," Mar. 4, 1924, SRRP. See also Millis, *Japanese Problem*, 117, 119; *ICR*, 24: 591; 25: 37. For Kawamoto, see clipping, *FMR*, Sept. 18, 1912, BWC. For Japanese moving into pruning, see Myer, "Fresno Raisin Industry," 54. For quantitative data from 1910, see Gulick, *American-Japanese*, 322. For tainting of farmwork, see Millis, "Some Economic Aspects of Japanese Immigration," 795. For Fresno *keiyaku-nin* acting as contractors for Indian Sikhs, see *FMR*, Aug. 23; Sept. 3, 13, 1910.

59. Quote from *Vacaville Reporter*, June 3, 1910. See also *FMR*, May 30, 1910; California Senate, *Journal of the Senate* (Sacramento, 1910), 39. I failed to find any portion of the Mackenzie report in the California State Archives or the papers of Franklin Hichborn, Bureau of Governmental Research, UCLA. A summary is printed in *PRP*, June 11, 1910.

60. Walled off from Los Angeles and the Pacific Coast by rugged mountains, and from the east by the Sonora Desert, the Imperial Valley was still a remote place of dust, heat, few roads, and crude towns. Getting there by train took an entire day. And once in the valley, a cotton picker could look forward to a crude existence at best. See John Turner, *White Gold Comes to California* (Bakersfield, 1981), 30; Steven John Zimrick, "The Changing Organization of Agriculture in the Southern San Joaquin Valley, California" (Ph.D. diss., Louisiana State University, 1976); Robert L. Finley, "An Economic History of the Imperial Valley of California to 1971" (Ph.D. diss., University of Oklahoma, 1974), 22; Bryan T. Johns, "Field Workers in California Cotton" (M.A. thesis, UCB, 1948), 17–18.

61. Quote from *Imperial Valley Press*, Aug. 6, 1910. For early cotton growing in the valley, see William I. Darnell, "The Imperial Valley: Its Physical and Cultural Geography" (M.A. thesis, CSU, San Diego, 1959), 90–95. For isolation, see "Imperial Valley First," *Valley Grower*, n.v. (summer 1982), 38. See also Mr. L. C. Lee, interview, El Centro, Calif., June 1924, File B46, William C. Smith Papers, Special Collections, University of Oregon, Eugene. For importing Mexican cotton pickers, perhaps the first such proposal, see *Imperial Daily Standard*, Sept. 19, 1908.

62. Quotes from *Imperial Valley Press*, Sept. 3, 1910. Should any shortage of laborers appear, the paper reported, "it is known that if necessary carloads of Hindus now located in the San Joaquin Valley may be shipped in here on short notice . . . they are more reliable . . . than the Southern Negroes." See also May 28, Oct. 15, 1910.

63. Quote from *Holtville Tribune*, Sept. 26, Oct. 21, 1910, in bound volumes, Imperial Valley Historical Society [old location]. See also Aug. 6, Sept. 3, 1910; *San Francisco Chronicle*, May 30, 1910; Taylor, *Mexican Labor: Imperial Valley*, 6–7, 11, 16–17, 26. "They pick very clean cotton but only about 40 to 70 pounds a day . . . their wages barely pay for what they eat. They do not like the work . . . no more Indians will be sent here." Quote from *Imperial Valley Press*, Oct. 29, 1910; also Oct. 15.

64. Quote from *Imperial Valley Press*, Sept. 3, 17, 1910. See also O. F. Cook, *Results of Cotton Experiments in 1911*, U.S. Dept. of Agriculture, Bureau of Plant Industry Circular No. 96, July 1912; James H. Street, *The New Revolution in the Cotton Economy: Mechanization and Its Consequences* (Chapel Hill, N.C., 1957), 37, 107–8, 117–18.

65. Quote from E. C. Hamilton to J. A. Graves, Feb. 23, 1910, SVSBCR. See also Hamilton to E. A. Pardee, Feb. 10, 1910; E. J. Preyed to Pardee, Apr. 3, 1910, SVSBCR. "I am sorry to have to say that these fields, except where they were replanted, or for some reason worked the third time, before planting, are very weedy and the contractor and the sub-contractors have good reason for complaining," wrote SVSBC president Hamilton to his foreman. Quote from Hamilton to Pardee, Mar. 28, 1910.

66. Preyed to Pardee, Apr. 3, 1910; E. C. Hamilton to Pardee, Mar. 31, 1910; manager to Pardee, Apr. 12, 1910, SVSBCR.

67. Quote from E. C. Hamilton to Pardee, Mar. 28, 1910, SVSBCR.

68. Quote from Robert Kibby, "Hamilton City, Its Story as Told by Ernest C. Hamilton," *Orland Unit*, Feb. 14, 1958. Beet thinning rates were much higher than the fifteen cents per one thousand feet (the equivalent of $2.25 to $2.75) or $1.50 per day plus free firewood, water, and tents that SVSBC offered. See also telegram, Pardee to SVSBC, Mar. 10, 1910; manager to Pardee, Apr. 12, 1910; Preyed to Pardee, May 2, 1910; secretary to Hamilton, May 18, 1910, SVSBCR.

69. Quotes from Hamilton to J. A. Graves, Apr. 7, 1910; secretary to Hamilton, May 18, 1910, SVSBCR. Eventually the *cholos* arrived by railroad at a total round-trip fare of twenty-five hundred dollars.

70. Quote from *Monterey Cyprus*, June 1, 1910. As they scaled the agricultural ladder some unscrupulous Japanese contractors were not above exploiting their positions of trust and authority, and resorting to fraud. This was apparently the case around Woodland, where a few Japanese contractors employed by SVSBC apparently began diverting carloads of SVSBC sugar beets to rival sugar beet companies. It was easy enough to do. With hundreds of carloads of beets shipped out daily and Japanese contractors handling everything, no one would miss ten or fifteen carloads sent south to Spreckels rather than to Woodland. The only reason the company was able to uncover the fraud was that so many contractors appeared to be making so much money beyond what they would earn hiring and supervising men that it became apparent that they were up to something. This so infuriated and concerned one SVSBC field supervisor that he made arrangements with station managers to notify the company any time a load of sugar beets was diverted. See A. M. Gelston to William C. Baker, Feb. 6, 1915; Baker to Gelston, Feb. 8, SVSBCR. "We had to secure this labor, though we had to secure them at the eleventh hour," reported one company official. "It was necessary to offer them somewhat more than they were getting on railroads and other places and this additional money was the only chance for us to get them away from works where they were at that time engaged." Quotes from Preyed to Pardee, May 2, 9, 1910, SVSBCR. The wisdom of this decision quickly became apparent. Marching into the sugar beet fields early in May, Japanese crews made short work of the thinning. Within ten days they finished their hoeing and moved on. Still reeling from their action, SVSBC officials

wondered what else they could do. Briefly they considered recruiting people from the eastern states, but with the sugar beet harvest about to begin, they rejected the idea as too little too late—and possibly too provocative toward the Japanese. "This labor question is a serious one in our locality, and is bound to continue so for some time to come," lamented the SVSBC secretary. Quote from secretary to E. C. Hamilton, May 18, 1910, SVSBCR.

71. E. C. Hamilton to Pardee, Oct. 15, 1911; Hamilton to Mr. Nicholson, May 13, 1910; secretary to J. G. Hamilton, May 18, 1910, SVSBCR.

72. E. C. Hamilton to E. A. Pardee, Feb. 15, 1911, SVSBCR.

73. Quotes from E. C. Hamilton to Pardee, Feb. 15, 1911, SVSBCR. See also E. C. Hamilton to Mr. H. C. Shay, Mar. 21, 1912.

74. Quote from E. C. Hamilton to Pardee, Feb. 15, 1911, SVSBCR.

75. Quotes from "Agricultural News Notes of the Pacific Coast," *California Cultivator*, Nov. 7, 1912; "Agricultural News Notes of the Pacific Coast," *Ibid.*, Nov. 21, 1912. Strikebreaking data and anti-Japanese violence are described in Paul G. Williamson, "Labor in the California Citrus Industry" (M.A. thesis, UCB, 1947), 38–39; *ICR*, 24: 229. Apparently prepared for what happened in Lindsay, the Japanese lay low, and when feelings calmed down, returned to town; within a few days they were all back at work. For the Japanese in San Juan, see Lydon, *Japanese in Monterey*, 31–32. Lydon located a cluster of Korean field hands in the San Juan Valley. Lydon to author, Nov. 6, 1996, author's possession.

76. Quote from Ben Walker, interview, Dec. 23, 1927, Ichihashi Papers, SUASC. Wage data from Naka, "Social and Economic Conditions Among Japanese Farmers in California," 34–35; Gulick, *American-Japanese*, 30, 318; Millis, *Japanese Problem*, 117–19; *ICR*, 24: 35–38.

77. The Japanese Association figures are slightly suspect, and could only have been earned by a field hand working seven days a week at the extremely high wage rate of three dollars a day, a figure achieved for only a few months during sugar beet thinning and raisin harvesting. The U.S. Immigration Commission noted that the Japanese not only advanced their wages, they now earned more than whites for the same work, averaging $1.49 a day without room and board vs. $1.38 for whites. But when room and board were included, their daily wages dropped below those of whites, averaging $1.54 compared to $1.80. See Senate, *Abstract of the Report on Japanese and Other Immigrant Races in the Pacific Coast and Rocky Mountain States* (Washington, D.C., 1911), 55; Saku Taro Otsuki, "Economic Conditions of the Japanese Farmers in California" (M.A. thesis, Columbia University, 1923), 11–12, 25; Emil T. H. Bunje, *The Story of Japanese Farming in California* (Berkeley, 1937), 25; R. L. Adams and T. R. Kelley, *A Study of Farm Labor in California* (Berkeley, 1918), 2. Growers calculated fifteen to thirty cents a day for boarding the Japanese and sixty cents a day for whites. Considerable discrepancies exist regarding wage rates. For example, Japanese employed on farms around San Jose earned eighty cents to $1.75 a day, including lodging. Food costs were calculated at twelve to fifteen dollars a month. See *ICR*, 24: 35, 37–38, 41, 43; Iwata, *Planted in Good Soil*, 2: 163–64, 182.

CHAPTER TWENTY

1. Quote from Ronald Tobey and Charles Wetherell, "The Citrus Industry and the Revolution of Corporate Capitalism in Southern California, 1887–1944," *CH* 124 (spring 1995), 6. For the citrus machinery industry, see Vincent Moses, "A Citrus Monopoly in Riverside, 1900–1936," ibid., 111 (spring 1982), 27–35. For citrus labels, see Gordon T. McClelland and Jay T. Last, *California Orange Box Labels: An Illustrated History* (Santa Ana, 1985); Pat Jacobsen, *Millennium Guide to Fruit Crate Labels: A Price Guide and Collector's Reference* (Weimar, Calif., 2000), which is definitive and goes far beyond its title. For a citrus community, see Mark Echeverri, "Pomona, California: The Early Years, 1875–1920" (Ph.D. diss., Claremont Graduate School, 1980), 164–95. See also Jesse E. Boyd, "Historical Import of the Orange Industry in Southern California" (M.A. thesis, UCB, 1922).

2. The delay in planting citrus outside of the missions was due in part to the padres, who refused to distribute seedlings to private ranchos. Although the citrus boom of the 1870s was largely a response to a national market, orange fever was also inspired when Wolfskill began realizing upwards of one thousand dollars per acre selling oranges in San Francisco during the 1850s. See McWilliams, *Southern California*, 213–14; Esther H. Klotz, Harry W. Lawton, and Joan H. Hall, eds., *A History of Citrus in the Riverside Area* (1969 [Riverside, 1989]), 6–23; Joan H. Hall, *A Citrus Legacy* (Riverside, 1992), 19, 30–34, 103–7; W. A. Spaulding, *The Orange: Its*

Culture in California (Riverside, 1922); Herbert J. Weber, "History and Development of the Citrus Industry," in Leon Batchelor and Herbert J. Weber, *The Citrus Industry* (Berkeley, 1948), 3: 1–39; J. J. Warner, "The Orange Tree in Los Angeles," *Los Angeles Star*, Aug. 30, 31, 1871.

3. For Sunkist, see Josephine K. Jacobs, "Sunkist Advertising" (Ph.D. diss., UCLA, 1966); Rahno M. MacCurdy, *The History of the California Fruit Growers Exchange* (Los Angeles, 1925), 60–63, 82; H. E. Erdman, *The California Fruit Growers Exchange: An Example in Cooperation in the Segregation of Conflicting Interests* (New York, 1933); Albert J. Meyer, "History of the California Fruit Growers Exchange, 1893–1920" (Ph.D. diss., Johns Hopkins University, 1950), 151–83. Sunkist membership figures and statistics are from 1910–11. See also Kevin Starr, *Inventing the Dream: California Through the Progressive Era* (New York, 1985), 140–47. For the citrus belt, see Clifford Zierer, "The Citrus Fruit Industry of the Los Angeles Basin," *Economic Geography* 32 (Jan. 1934). For one company, see Lorne Allmon, *The Story of Samuel B. Hampton and the California Citrus Industry, 1887–1918* (Riverside, 1994); articles of incorporation, Corona Foothill Lemon Company, June 6, 1911, CSA.

4. Quote from Douglas Peters to Duarte Monrovia Fruit Growers Exchange, June 6, 1911, Duarte Monrovia Fruit Growers Exchange Records, HL. See also A. C. Huff to R. O. Simpson, Oct. 24, 1913; Mary Bennett to gentlemen, Feb. 26, 1910; A. R. Parrish to secretary, Oct. 16, 1911.

5. Morrison G. Wong, "The Japanese in Riverside, 1890 to 1945: A Special Case in Race Relations" (Ph.D. diss., UCR, 1977), 36–37; Claude Midkiff Recollections; *ICR*, 24: 26; *California Fruit Grower*, Mar. 28, 1903; Mar. 3, 1906.

6. Quote from Report of the Indian Hill Citrus Union, 1905–6, Indian Hill Citrus Company Records. The Japanese comprised ten out of thirteen citrus pickers near Rialto, one of two near Highgrove, eight of ten near Colton, and six of ten near San Dimas. Around Pomona, the Japanese picked all of the citrus grown by the Indian Hill Citrus Union. Even where they were not a majority, Japanese field hands constituted such a large proportion of the citrus labor force that it was impossible to bring in the crop without them. See *ICR*, 24: 20–23, 26; 25: 33, 41 218, 226, 229, claims three of ten citrus laborers were Japanese, compared to the six of ten figure in Saku T. Otsuki, "Economic Conditions of the Japanese Farmers in California" (M.A. thesis, Columbia University, 1923), 9–12, 25. In Riverside the breakdown was as follows: Japanese, 1,460; White, 650 plus; Mexican, 255 plus; Other, 35. This was a considerably higher ratio of Japanese to the total number of farm laborers. See also Sanguinetti, "Immigrant Japanese," 4; H. B. Ainsworth to Duarte-Monrovia Fruit Growers Exchange, Apr. 16, 1912, Duarte-Monrovia Fruit Exchange Records. In 1915 members of the California Fruit Growers Exchange employed about twenty-five thousand citrus pickers. See William W. Cumberland, *Cooperative Marketing: Its Advantages as Exemplified in the California Fruit Growers Exchange* (London, 1917), 23–24. For Pomona, see Report of the Indian Hill Citrus Union for 1911–12. Statewide, the Japanese made up seven of ten citrus pickers in 1915. White workers handled most of the supervisory jobs, skilled teamstering, construction, and packinghouse work involving lifting, packing, and box building, as well as pruning, nursery, and irrigation. Some citrus communities remained off-limits to the Japanese. In Corona, forty-five miles southeast of Los Angeles, one resident recalled in an oral memoir: "A Jap came here from L.A. and rented a building on W. Sixth Street to start a pool hall and an employment agency. He never got his stuff unloaded at the depot. Corona was a white man's town. The first foreigner to come to Corona was an Italian, no objection was made to him, at least he was a white man." Quote from C. T. Songer, "Reminiscences of Early Corona," MS (1965), Corona Public Library.

7. Reports of the Manager of the Indian Hill Citrus Union, 1908–9, 1910–11; Minute Book no. 2 of the Board of Directors of the Indian Hill Citrus Union, 173, Indian Hill Citrus Company Records; E. C. Eckmann and C. J. Zinn, *Soil Survey of the Pasadena Area, California*, U.S. Dept. of Agriculture (Washington, D.C., 1919), 18; Maude W. Glasby, "The Largest Lemon Ranch," *Sunset* 15 (June 1905), 199–200; "Average Profits," *Pacific Fruit Grower* (July 1887), BL; "Cost of Producing Oranges and Lemons in California," *California Citrograph* (Aug. 1924); E. M. H., *Ranch Life in California* (London, 1886), 166–67; K. MacRae, "Citrus Facts as Viewed by a Grower," *California Citrograph Supplement to the Riverside Enterprise*, May 20, 1915; Charles C. Teague to Guy L. Hardison, Mar. 18, 1902; to C. P. Collins, Dec. 1, 1902; to W. A. Hardison, June 13, 1902, Teague Papers, BL.

8. Teague, *Fifty Years a Rancher*, 3, 24, 30, 46; Dean Hobbs Blanchard, *Of California's First Citrus Empire: A Rainbow Arches from Maine to Ventura County*, ed. Grant Heil (Pasadena, 1983); James Roy Fraysier, "Place of the Lemon: A History of the Limoneira Ranch" (M.A.

thesis, Pepperdine College, 1969); Gladys Caroline Emerson, "Geographical Aspects of the Development of the Limoneira Company, Santa Paula, California" (M.A. thesis, UCLA, 1968).

9. Limoneira Company journal, no. 1, 1893 to 1899, Limoneira Company Records, Santa Paula, Calif.; Laura Turner, "Citrus Culture: The Mentality of the Orange Rancher in Progressive Era Northern Orange County" (M.A. thesis, CSU, Fullerton, 1996); *The Home of the Lemon: A California Story in a Few Words with Illustrations* (Los Angeles, 1905), 1–2, VCM.

10. In 1907, Teague constructed a similar dormitory for ninety-six white men, along with twenty-three bungalows and a cluster of apartments for married foremen and permanent employees. Located north of the big packing shed, it had electricity, hot and cold running water, and indoor toilets. See Richard G. Lillard, "Agricultural Statesman: Charles C. Teague of Santa Paula," *CH* 115 (Mar. 1986), 7; Margo McBane, "The Role of Gender in Citrus Employment," ibid., 124 (spring 1995), 70–73; Crissey, *Where Opportunity Knocks Twice*, 177–79; J. D. Culbertson, "Housing of Ranch Labor," *First Annual Report of the California Citrus Institute* (San Bernardino, 1920), 98. For estimates of Limoneira's labor force, see Teague, *Fifty Years a Rancher*, 30, 47–53. For housing, see Limoneira Company Records, Limoneira Company Archives; Blanchard, *Of California's First Citrus Empire*, 110–13, 107, 120, 131, 145–46; J. D. Culbertson, interview by A. D. Shamel, 1918, A. D. Shamel Papers, UCRA; various materials, especially glass plate photographs, A. D. Shamel Collection, Riverside Museum; George Clements, speech to the Southern California Economic Conference, "A Brief History of California's Agricultural Labor," Nov. 4, 1935, George Clements Papers, ASCUCLA; G. Harold Powell, *Annual Report of the General Manager of the California Fruit Growers Exchange*, 1920–21, n.p., Sunkist Records Center, Ontario, Calif.

11. Profit and loss statement, Season 1909–10, "Disbursements," in Minutes, Oct. 30, 1910, Azusa Foothill Citrus Company Collection, Azusa-Pacific College Archives, Azusa, Calif. See also Fred Card, *Farm Management* (New York, 1913), 278; Mr. Righter, "Discussion of the Labor Supply," *CSFGCT, 1902*, 278; CIR, *Final Report*, 5: 4957–58; Robert G. Cleland, *The Place Called Sespe* (Chicago, 1940); *California Citrograph* (Mar. 8–23, 1918). For ten Italian families recruited to teach the Chinese how to pack lemons at the Arlington Heights Fruit Company in Casa Blanca, see *Corona Daily Independent*, Feb. 8, 1972; Stanley Reynolds and Fred Eldridge, eds., *Corona, California: Commentaries* (Los Angeles, 1986), 41–43, Corona Public Library. For the C. W. Leffingwell ranch, see Hermon Brannon, interview by Mitch Haddad, Apr. 15, 1970, CSU, Fullerton; *Fullerton News*, June 7, 1906; "How They Do It on the Leffingwell Ranch," *Whittier News*, Aug. 19, 1903; C. W. Leffingwell, "Leffingwell Rancho: From Trees to a Community of Homes," MS (1955), HL; A. D. Shamel, "Housing Employees of California's Citrus Ranches," *California Citrograph* (June 1918); Charles Greene and Henry Greene, *Greene and Greene: The Architecture and Related Designs of Charles Sumner Greene and Henry Mather Greene, 1894–1934* (Los Angeles, 1977), 146–47. For the Sargent brothers ranch east of Whittier, see *Orange County Tribune*, Nov. 30, 1910.

12. Quote from A. D. Shamel, "Housing the Employe[e]s of California's Citrus Ranches," *California Citrograph* (Mar. 1918). When married families were employed, companies often gave rebates on half of the December rent at large Christmas parties in order to cut turnover and promote loyalty. See also Labor Camp Report no. 103, "The A. F. Call Estate," Folder CAA-CAG, DIR; Thomas A. Robertson, *A Southwestern Utopia: An American Colony in Mexico* (Los Angeles, 1964), 26–63; Patricia Havens, *Simi Valley: A Journey Through Time* (Simi Valley, 1997), 147–50; Thomas A. Patterson, "Recollections of the Sinaloa Ranch," MS (1979), 2, SVHS; Crane S. Miller, "The Changing Landscape of the Simi Valley, California, from 1795 to 1968" (M.A. thesis, UCLA, 1968); Luis Cruz, interview by Helen Ritter, Apr. 3, 1979, Corona Public Library; Alexandra Minna Stern, "Buildings, Boundaries, Blood: Medicalization and Nation-Building on the U.S.-Mexico Border, 1910–1930," *Hispanic American Historical Review* 79 (1999), 41–81; Tom Patterson, "Martinez Camp once was a thriving community of citrus workers," *Riverside Press Enterprise*, Mar. 21, 1982.

13. Quote from A. D. Shamel, "Housing the Employe[e]s of California's Citrus Ranches," *California Citrograph* (Feb. 1921), describing the Chase plantation. See also Shamel, "It Pays to be Decent" (Dec. 1921); *Celebration in Honor of the Eighteenth Birthday of Ethan Allen Chase* (Riverside, 1912); Ethan Allen Chase, diary, Apr. 10, 1906, Ethan Allen Chase Collection, Riverside Municipal Museum. To eliminate turnover, Mexican families were always preferred over single men. "By this means comparatively little friction ever occurs between the different employees on the ranch," explained Limoneira assistant ranch manager J. D. Culbertson in an

interview with Shamel. Quote from A. D. Shamel, "Housing Employe[e]s of California's Citrus Ranches," *California Citrograph* (May 1918).

14. Quote from unpaginated draft, Adams, "Farm Management," in R. L. Adams Collected Papers, BL. See also CSBLS, *Fifteenth Biennial Report, 1911*, 12, 48; Adams, *Farm Management Notes*, 531–35; *California Fruit Grower*, Jan. 17, 1903. Citrus costs from Cumberland, *Cooperative Marketing*, 187; J. Eliot Coit, *Citrus Fruits: An Account of the Citrus Fruit Industry with Special Reference to California Requirements and Practices and Similar Conditions* (New York, 1917), 162–63.

15. Quote from Mr. Righter, "Discussion of the Labor Supply," *CSFGCT, 1902*, 278. "Horses were cared for better than the men," he added. Dozens of similar observations, persuasive through their repetition, point to one conclusion: housing for many Japanese field hands, despite their reputation for making the best of bad circumstances, was often terrible, and growers admitted as much. But perhaps the most indisputable evidence came from the California Bureau of Labor Statistics. Conducting the most extensive early investigation of farm labor camps, the bureau concluded that one in five was "very bad," and that the rest were barely habitable. See also E. Clements Horst, "What is Wrong with the Farmer?" *San Francisco News*, Sept. 15, 1930, FHHC; clippings, *San Francisco Call*, Dec. 4, 1901; *Stockton Record*, Jan. 26, 1900; *Salinas Journal*, May 25, 1901; *Oakland Tribune*, Sept. 23, 1901; *Santa Ana Register*, Nov. 4, 1910; clipping, *Sacramento Union*, Jan. 29, 1910; clipping, *San Francisco Bulletin*, May 27, 1911, Harris Weinstock Scrapbooks, BL; WPA, FWP, "Living Conditions of Farm Workers," in source material gathered on migratory farm labor (Oakland, 1938), BL; George B. Hodgkin, "Survey of the Labor Situation," *California Citrograph* (Aug. 17, 1920), FHHC; "Labor Market in the Orange Industry," CIRPP.

16. Quote from "The Citrus Situation in California," *California Citrograph* (Dec. 1915). See also *IUB*, Jan. 11, 1908; Chaoi Vasquez, interview by Ronald Banderas, June 2, 1971, CSU, Fullerton; L. F. Laverly to A. T. Blair, Jan. 28, 1911, Duarte-Monrovia Fruit Exchange Business Records.

17. Quote from Teague, *Fifty Years a Rancher*, 65. Setting the fires upwind, they let the smoke drift over their orchards, fueling the fires with cuttings from the previous year's pruning. See also Robert W. Durrenberger, "Climate as a Factor in the Production of Lemons in California" (Ph.D. diss., UCLA, 1956), 1–34; Tom Patterson, "The Great Freeze of 1913," in Klotz, Lawton, and Hall, eds., *A History of Citrus in the Riverside Area*, 56–59; Robert G. Cleland, *The Irvine Ranch of Orange County* (Los Angeles, 1952), 117–19; Floyd Young, "Frost Warning in the Early Days," *Pomona Valley Historian* 5 (Oct. 1969), 171–74; Frank Palmer, "Eleven Years in an Orange Grove," excerpts from a diary, 1891–1901, ibid., 1 (Apr. 1965), 55–61; "Frost Insurance in the Limoneira Groves," *California Citrograph*, Dec. 1915; "Frost Protection," May 1916; J. E. Adamson, "Fighting the Frost," Oct. 1916; "To Fight or Not to Fight Jack Frost," Jan. 18, 1919; J. E. Adamson, "Does Citrus Orchard Heating Pay?" Oct. 1928; Glasby, "The Largest Lemon Ranch," 200; Langston C. Winston to Henry D. Bacon, Nov. 19, 1881, HDBBC; *CSFGCT, Mar. 1911* (Sacramento, 1912), 119–23; H. J. Weber, "A Study of the Effects of Freezes on Citrus in California," U.S. Dept. of Agriculture, Agriculture Experiment Station *Bulletin No. 304* (Washington, D.C., 1919), 245–321; Everett "Joe" Delano Chavez, interview, n.d.; Natalie Gamino Duncan, interview, n.d., SVHS; *Riverside Daily Press*, Jan. 9–12, 1913, Riverside Public Library, Local History Room; Street, "Into the Good Land," 176–80.

18. Quote from J. A. Stromquist, "California Oranges," *Industrial Pioneer* 1 (Mar. 1921), 24–25. See also John Delgado, "Men at Work," MS (Oakland, 1938), WPA, FWP, Northern California, BL.

19. *Fullerton News*, June 7, 1906; F. G. Webber, "Careful Handling of Lemons from Tree to the Car," *California Citrograph*, May 1923; Victor Salandini, "A Story of Orange Picking," Victor Salandini Papers, AULHWSU.

20. Quote from Frank App and Allen G. Waller, *Farm Economics: Management and Distribution* (New York, 1938), 658–59. For Powell, see H. Vincent Moses, "'The Orange-Grower is Not a Farmer': G. Harold Powell, Riverside Orchardists, and the Coming of Industrial Agriculture, 1893–1930," *CH* 124 (spring 1995), 22–37.

21. For Powell, see Vincent Moses, "The Flying Wedge of Cooperation: Harold Powell, California Orange Growers and Corporate Reconstruction of American Agriculture" (Ph. D. diss., UCR, 1996), 538–39; H. Harold Powell, *Letters from the Orange Empire*, ed., Richard G. Lillard (Los Angeles and Redlands, 1996). Crop loss figures from *New York Fruitman's Guide*, June 27, 1907; *Pacific Fruit World*, Mar. 2, 1908. See also J. Parker Whitney, "Oranges and Iron

Fingers: The Time-Honored Custom of Wrapping Fruit by Hand Revolutionized by a Mechanical Invention," *Sunset* 24 (Jan. 1910), 113–14; MacCurdy, *History of the California Fruit Grower's Exchange*, 52; Grace Larsen, "The Economics and Structure of the Citrus Industry," *CH* 74 (spring 1995), 41.

22. For labor modernization, see R. L. Adams, *Managing Western Farms and Ranches: A Series of Monographs* MS (College of Agriculture, Berkeley, n.d.), Giannini Foundation Library, 1; Card, *Farm Management*, 159–62, 281. See also *CSFGCT, 1908*, 57, 100. For similar policies applied to vineyard work, see H. E. Jacob and J. R. Herman, "Harvesting and Packing Grapes in California," University of California, College of Agriculture, *Bulletin No. 390* (Berkeley, 1925), 10. See also Henry Ramsey, "What System of Paying Pickers results in Least Fruit Injury?" *California Citrograph*, July 1921.

23. Quote from "Teach Pickers How," *California Cultivator*, Sept. 8, 1917.

24. Quotes from Shamel, "Housing Employe[e]s of California's Citrus Ranches," *California Citrograph* (May 1918); Peter Dreher, Report for 1904–5, "Annual Reports of the Secretary of the San Antonio Fruit Exchange," Pomona Public Library; Cramer, *La Habra*, 156. The admonition to handle lemons as if they were eggs is also in Teague, *Fifty Years a Rancher*, 30. There is some evidence that clippers were first introduced by the Chinese at a time when California citrus "experts" were still describing the proper method for twisting oranges free from their stems. See Vincent Moses, "New Exhibit Unearths Story of Riverside's Chinatown," *Riverside Museum Bulletin* 37 (July/Aug. 1985), 3. See also Coit, *Citrus Fruits*, 279; F. A. Little, "Proper Method of Picking Oranges," *California Citrograph* (Jan. 1919); F. G. Webber, "Careful Handling of Lemons from Tree to Car" (May 1923); H. G. Easton, "Careful Handling of Oranges," Dec. 1923; "Raise Grades through Care in Handling Fruit," Dec. 1925; "Lemon Pickers More Careful," July 1918. Statistics from C. S. Milliken, "Some Lemon Picking Records," June 1916; H. C. Harris to A. T. Blair, Feb. 13, 1911, Duarte-Monrovia Fruit Exchange Papers.

25. "Canterbury's Picking Sack is Boon to Citrus Grower," *California Citrograph*, Jan. 24, 1916, FHHC; clipping, *Redlands Facts*, ca. 1915, A. K. Smiley Library, Redlands; Coit, *Citrus Fruits*, 281; clipping, *California Cultivator*, Aug. 25, 1928, PSTFN; C. C. Teague to Ira White, Dec. 6, 1902, Teague Papers, BL.

26. Quote from Minutes of the Covina Orange Growers Association, Apr. 7, 1934, Covina Citrus Growers Association Records, HL. Foremen took great care to keep boxes clean and free of debris that might scar and nick fruit, and not to fill them so full that when stacked the bottom of the boxes rested on the fruit rather than on the boxes. See also E. B. Norman, "Reminiscences of Early Days of Citrus Making in Duarte," *California Citrograph*, Oct. 13, 1939; Blaz Coyazo, interview by Robert Gonzales, Apr. 28, 1994, 7, Redlands Oral History Project, A. K. Smiley Public Library Heritage Room.

27. Quote from F. G. Webber, "Careful Handling of Lemons from the Tree to the Car," *California Citrograph*, May 1923. See also G. Harold Powell, *Letters from the Orange Empire* (Los Angeles, 1990), 70; C. F. Warren, *Farm Management* (New York, 1919), 332; Coit, *Citrus Fruits*, 281.

28. Quotes from E. B. Hodgkin, "Reducing Labor Costs," *California Citrograph*, Sept. 1921; F. A. Little, "Proper Method of Picking Oranges," ibid., Jan. 1919; Henry Ramsey, "What System of Paying Pickers Results in Least Fruit Injury?" ibid., July 1921. See also F. O. Wallschlaeger, "Oranges in Cost of Production of Citrus Fruits Since 1910," ibid., Aug. 1921; C. S. Milliken, "Some Lemon Picking Records," ibid., June 1916. Fruit picked on a piece-rate basis typically had a much greater rate of decay than citrus harvested by men paid on an hourly basis. See Mr. F. A. Edinger, interview, Hood, Calif., Dec. 13, 1924; Ernest B. Gammon, president, Sacramento County Farm Bureau, interview, n.d., SRRP; E. B. Mittleman, "Gyppo System," *Journal of Political Economy* 31 (Dec. 1923), 840–51; "Lemon Pickers," *California Cultivator*, Feb. 28, 1920; Schwartz, *Seasonal Farm Labor*, 77, 83.

29. Quote from H. O. Easton, "Reducing Labor Costs," *California Citrograph*, Dec. 1923. See also "Lemon Picking, Handling, Packing Considered at Club Meeting," ibid., July 1929; "Raise Grades through Care in Handling Citrus Fruit," ibid., Dec. 1925; F. G. Webber, "Careful Handling of Lemons from Tree to Car," ibid., May 1923. Wages were twenty-eight cents an hour, with a bonus of six cents an hour. Because these wages are from a later period, I have not incorporated them into my analysis. Wage and bonus data cited is from Indian Hill Citrus Union, Minute Book of the Directors of the Indian Hill Citrus Union, MS (n.d.), 173; Report of the Indian Hill Citrus Union for 1908–9, Indian Hill Citrus Company Records.

30. Roy J. Smith, "Methods of Paying Citrus Pickers," *California Citrograph*, Aug. 1942; Coit, *Citrus Fruit*, 282. The same differences also held for workers in table grape vineyards. A slow worker in an old vineyard with poor quality fruit might pick and pack only ten boxes a day, while a fast one in a young orchard might pick and pack sixty. See Jacob and Herman, "Harvesting and Packing Grapes in California," 23. Resourceful growers often pitted crews against one another, with those showing the best overall speed and quality of work receiving a bonus. See Sunkist Growers Association Meeting, Dec. 20, 1921; Jan. 3, 1922; Jan. 16, 1922, Sunkist Growers Association Collection, HL; wage records, Azusa-Foothill Citrus Company Collection, HL; R. L. Adams, "Farm Labor Situation in California," *Transactions of the Commonwealth Club of California* 13 (May 1918), 82.

31. Quotes from Report of the Indian Hill Citrus Union, 1909–10, Indian Hill Citrus Company Records; Mr. M. B. Allen, interview, Garden Grove, Jan. 5, 1925, SRRP. Walking from row to row behind the pickers, scanning trees to see that no "shiners" had been overlooked, *keiyaku-nin* continued to garner approval. Other groups, by some accounts, would sit in the shade for ten or fifteen minutes and smoke when their boss was not looking. See U.S. Dept. of Agriculture, Bureau of Plant Industry, "The Decay of Oranges While in Transit from California," *Bulletin No. 123* (Washington, D.C., 1908) 15–16, 26, 39; *CSFGCT, 1911*, 67.

32. For the results of better techniques, see clipping, *Redlands Daily Review*, Mar. 27, 1907, G. Harold Powell Family Papers, ASCUCLA.

33. O. E. Bremner, *Destructive Insects and their Control* (Sacramento, 1910); Alexander Craw, *Destructive Insects, Their Natural Enemies, Remedies, and Recommendations* (Sacramento, 1891); Harry S. Smith, Henry J. Quayle, and E. O. Essig, "Protecting Plants from their Enemies," in Claude B. Hutchison, *California Agriculture*, 239, 245; H. E. Bishop, "Establishing the Orange Industry," *Orange County Historical Series* 1 (1931), 111–12; George F. Johnson, "The Early History of Copper Fungicides," *AH* 9 (Apr. 1935), 67–79.

34. Orchardists calculated it cost ten to twenty dollars per acre to protect gross profits of one hundred to seven hundred dollars an acre. See *PRP*, Mar. 10, 1900; C. W. Woodruth, "Directions for Spraying the Codling Moth," University of California, Agricultural Experiment Station, *Bulletin No. 155* (1904), 6–15; Woodruth, "The Insecticide Industries of California," *Journal of Economic Entomology* 4 (Aug. 1912), 358; A. Freeman Mason, *Spraying, Dusting, and Fumigating of Plants: A Popular Handbook on Crop Protection* (New York, 1929), 12; Samuel T. Maynard, *Successful Fruit Culture: A Practical Guide to the Cultivation and Propagation of Fruits* (New York, 1905); E. J. Wickson, "Cost of Planting and Care of Trees and Vines to Bearing Age," MS (Division of Rural Institutions, n.d.), Giannini Foundation Library; Rollin La Follette, "Pest Control on the Leffingwell Rancho," *California Citrograph*, June 1918. On Limoneira Ranch, crews mounted special tanks on mule-drawn wagons. Connected to a spraying device, the rear wheels of the wagon powered the spray pump and propelled the poison past baffles in a mixing tank out through an adjustable nozzle. See W. A. Spaulding, "Early Chapters in the History of California Citrus Culture," Jan. 1922; J. R. La Follette, "The Use of Towers in Spraying," Oct. 1924. The drenching of orchards in lead arsenate, Paris green, and who knows what else certainly had some effect on citrus pickers working in the early morning, when the leaves were still damp and the orchards had recently been sprayed. See James Whorton, *Before Silent Spring: Pesticides and Public Health in Pre-DDT America* (Princeton, 1974), 176–212; William Haedden, "Arsenical Poisoning of Fruit Trees," *Journal of Economic Entomology* 2 (June 1909), 242; E. D. Ball, "Is Arsenical Spraying Killing Our Fruit Trees," *Journal of Economic Entomology* 2 (Apr. 1909), 142–48; E. D. Ball, E. G. Titus, and J. E. Greaves, "The Season's Work on Arsenical Poisoning of Fruit Trees," *Journal of Economic Entomology* 3 (Apr. 1910), 187–97; Daily Application Charts, Spraying, Patton Grove, San Marino, Pasadena Orange Growers Association, HL; C. C. Teague to R. C. Allen, Apr. 8, 23; Aug. 13, 1902; to W. F. Stearns, Apr. 30, 1902; to Southern Refining Company, June 5, 1902; to E. W. Jones, July 2, 1902; to W. H. Volck, July 5, 1902; to A. P. Samuel, July 14, 1902; to F. Kahles, July 24, 1902; to S. L. Gross, Sept. 10, 1902; to S. F. Vest, Sept. 17, 1902, Teague Papers, BL.

35. Braun Corporation, *School of Fumigation . . . Held at Pomona, California, August 9–13, 1915* (Los Angeles, 1915); R. S. Wolgum, "Recent Results in the Fumigation of Citrus Trees with Liquid Hydrocyanic Acid," *Journal of Economic Entomology* 12 (Feb. 1919), 117–18; Wolgum, "Hydrocyanic-Acid Gas Fumigation," U.S. Dept. of Agriculture, Bureau of Entomology, *Bulletin No. 90* (Washington, D.C., 1911), 1–2; Teague to E. W. Jones, July 2, 1902, Teague Papers, BL; "How Fumigation Tents Were Applied and Withdrawn in 1891," *California Citro-*

graph, Apr. 1921; H. J. Quayle, "Liquid Hydrocyanic Acid," Dec. 1917; Quayle, "Fumigation in Tulare County in 1915," *California Citrograph*, Feb. 1916, Harris Weinstock Scrapbooks, BL.

36. Quote from Kazuo Miyamoto, *Hawaii: The End of the Rainbow* (Rutland, Vt., 1964), 219–20. See also Robert Higgs, "Landless by Law: Japanese Immigrants in California Agriculture to 1941," *Journal of Economic History* 38 (Mar. 1978), 205–25.

37. Quote from *Santa Cruz Surf*, Jan. 26, 1907. See Ichioka, *Issei*, 52–53. See also *ICR*, 23: 79; 24: 179–80, 186, 203, 285–87, 299–300; Zaibei Nihonjin Rengō Kyōgikai, *Zaibei Nihonjin Rengō Kyōgikai Hōkokusho* (The United Japanese Deliberative Council of America: Report) (San Francisco, 1907), 20.

38. Quote from "Oriental and Agriculture," n.d., SRRP. To be eligible for marriage, farmers had to earn an annual profit of four hundred to five hundred dollars and have savings of at least one thousand. See Nagai Matsuzō to Chinda Sutemi, June 17, 1902, enclosure, "Geisai no Shikaku," Japanese Foreign Ministry Archival Documents, JARPC. After 1915, the Japanese government allowed field hands to summon a wife, provided they had eight hundred dollars in savings. Of the 490 Japanese immigrants surveyed by the Immigration Commission, only ten had gone into business immediately upon arrival, while another eighteen had immediately become farmers. Of the remainder, 259 worked their way up from the ranks of field hands, while 103 had been railroad section hands, four had been sawmill workers, fifty-four domestic servants, and forty-two had begun in other occupations. Few began with any amount of money of consequence. See *ICR*, 1: 80; 24: 762–69, 798–801, 822–23, 830–31, 838–39, 996–1001; Ichihashi, *Japanese Immigration*, 162–63. See also Barry, "Contract Labor," in *Documentary History*, 18; H.S., "California," *New Review* 1 (June 1913), 550; McDonald, *The Japanese in Butte County*, 37.

39. Iwata, *Planted in Good Soil*, 154; Ichioka, *Issei*, 121; Gulick, *American Japanese*, 319; Yoell, "Oriental vs. American Labor," 34–36. For farming companies composed of men from the same prefectures pooling resources to lease land, and for sharecroppers forming farming companies, see Lukes and Okihiro, *Japanese Legacy*, 30–31. See also Robert Higgs, "The Wealth of Japanese Tenant Farmers in California, 1909," *AH* 53 (Apr. 1979), 488–93. For long-term contracts, see Statement of Harry Butler, no. 31, SRRP; T. G. Chamberlain, "Fruit Ranching Conditions in the Placer County Fruit Belt," 13, Elwood Mead Papers, BL; Ichihashi, "Supplementary Report on the Japanese in the Watsonville District," 5, Ichihashi Papers, SUASC.

40. Quotes from *Sacramento Bee*, Apr. 11, 1905; "Statements of Fruit Ranchers of Placer County," comp. T. G. Chamberlain, June 1916, statement of E. S. Birdsall, no. 77, Mead Papers, BL; *Vacaville Reporter*, Nov. 12, 1909. See also Chamberlain, "Fruit Ranching Conditions in the Placer County Fruit Belt," June 1916; Chamberlain to Prof. Morgan, June 15, 1916, Mead Papers, BL; "Immigrant Labor in the Fruit Industries of the Newcastle District," *ICR*, 24: 414, 419–22. Leases usually required Japanese farmers to ship fruit under the label of the lessee; they often had to agree to hire the landlord at so much per week or month. Technically speaking, this was not a lease arrangement. Essentially the Japanese were managers who paid handsome rents and assumed all the risks. Orchard leasing tended to be risky business, with losses two of three years. See also Roy McCallum, interview, Nov. 12, 1924, no. 41, in "Interviews with Employers of Farm Workers," SRRP.

41. Yamoto Ichihashi, *Japanese in the United States* (Palo Alto, 1932), 179–81; California State Board of Control, *California and the Oriental* (Sacramento, 1922), 48, 101–2. Ichihashi asserts that men from one particular province in Japan dominated orchard leasing, possibly because of their traditional "love of adventure and speculation." He does not name the province. See Ichihashi, *Japanese in the United States*, 183–87. For Japanese leases and farming companies based on kin and prefectural ties in the Pajaro Valley strawberry industry, see Kazuko Nakane, *Nothing Left in My Hands: An Early Japanese-American Community in California's Pajaro Valley* (Seattle, 1985), 27, 38–43, 66. The debate over exactly how much orchard land the Japanese controlled around Vacaville can be followed in Takashi Tsukita and Karen Nolan, *Omo i de: Memories of Vacaville's Lost Japanese Community* (Vacaville, 2001), 12–13; Limbaugh and Payne, *Vacaville*, 136–41; CSBLS, *Twelfth Biennial Report, 1906*, excerpts reprinted in *Vacaville Reporter*, Dec. 29, 1906. By 1910, the Japanese rented 16 percent of the raisin vineyards around Fresno. See "Immigrant Labor in the Orchards and Vineyards of Fresno County," *ICR*, 24: 508; Iwata, *Planted in Good Soil*, 372–73; Ichihashi, "Japanese Agriculture in Fresno County," and "Japanese farm acreage by type of farming in Fresno County," Ichihashi Papers, SUASC; *Vacaville Reporter*, Oct. 19, 1907.

42. Quote from Bunje, *The Story of Japanese Farming in California*, 18. See also Ichihashi, *Japanese in the United States*, 183; notes on Kinji Ushijima, Ichihashi Papers, SUASC.

43. *San Francisco Chronicle*, Mar. 8, 13, 1909; Jan. 6, Apr. 7, Dec. 15, 1910; Jan. 25, 1912; Nov. 20, 1919; Mar. 27, 28, 29, Apr. 18, 1926; July 1917; K. K. Kawakami, *The Real Japanese Question* (New York, 1921), 45; William J. Rogers, "The Delta Story," *Stockton Record*, July 4, 1951, SRCF; George Shima to Hiram Johnson, Feb. 11, 1911, Hiram Johnson Papers, BL.

44. Quote from clipping, *San Francisco Chronicle*, June 25, 1912, George Shima Collection, San Joaquin Valley Historical Society, Lodi, Calif. The *Byron Times* wrote of him in 1910: "As our personal friend, we are always glad to say pleasant things about him, because he is a most deserving and successful man—the kind that is usually to be found in the lead along the march of progressive accomplishment and success." Years later he told one interviewer that he had lived in California so long that he felt "more at home here than in Japan" and explained to another that his success masked failures, and that he had really only hit it big once every ten years or so, "but people think every year is big." Quotes from "The Famous California Potato King," *Byron Times*, 1908–9, special booster ed., San Joaquin Delta Collection, PCWS; "Visit with Mr. George Shima, 'Potato King' of California," interview, July 14, 1924, 1–3, SRRP; clipping, *Stockton Record*, Apr. 27, 1975, SRCF. See also Edwin Cox, "Farm Tenancy in California," *Transactions of the Commonwealth Club of California* 11 (Dec. 1916), 445–46. Success did not insulate Shima from racism. When he purchased a home in Berkeley, newspapers announced, "Jap Invades Fashionable Quarters," and protestors led by a professor of classic literature ordered him to move to an "Oriental" neighborhood. Shima stayed, sending his children to school at Vassar, Harvard, and Stanford. See J. M. Bigger, interview, Dec. 3, 1924, SRRP; Kiyoshi K. Kawakami, *Asia at the Door: A Study of the Japanese Question in the Continental United States, Hawaii, and Canada* (New York, 1914), 45, 99; Ikeda Nobumasa, *Ijinden Bunko: Ushijima Kinji* (Great men biographical series: George Shima) (Tokyo, 1941), JARPC.

45. Bureau of the Census, *Chinese and Japanese in the United States, 1910*, Bulletin No. 127 (Washington, D.C., 1914), 44; Ichihashi, *Japanese in the United States*, 184; Yuji Ichioka, "Japanese Immigrant Response to the 1920 California Alien Land Law," *AH* 58 (Apr. 1984), 158, table 1; *Nichibei Nenkan*, 1911, no. 7: 130–31; 1914, no. 10: 120–21; Masakazu Iwata, interview by Manki Matsumoto, Los Angeles, 1972, tape, JARPC.

46. Naka, "Japanese Farmers," 28–97; Jean Pujas, *Real Japanese California* (Berkeley, 1937), 52–53; Masakazu Iwata, "The Japanese Immigrant in California Agriculture," *AH* 36 (Jan. 1962), 25, 30; *ICR*, 2: 374; "Japanese Association of America to Woodrow Wilson," [ca. 1916], 5, Ichihashi Papers, SUASC. In their drive to acquire land, the Japanese could be both persistent and ruthless. Most landowners knew this to be true, but in 1916, muckraking journalist Lincoln Steffens explored the issue of Japanese farming for *Collier's Magazine*. Encountering a group of *keiyaku-nin* who had harvested one woman's fruit farm for years, Steffens learned how every summer the *keiyaku-nin* had visited her and offered to buy her entire crop while it was still on the trees, always for about half its value. "She'd reject his offer and go on with her preparations to handle her fruit with her own [Japanese] labor," wrote Steffens.

> A day or two before the time to begin to harvest the little businessman would come back, renew his offer, raising his price, perhaps, a little—a very little. Considering it preposterous, she would again refuse. The next day all her workers would quit: a strike, a labor strike called by a businessman. She understood: she'd hunt up the smiling bidder and take his best bid. And he would turn in with 'her' labor and take in the fruit—and the profit.

It was a common tactic, with *keiyaku-nin* dropping hints that they might refuse to work after the first of the year if a farmer did not meet their request. Left in a quandary as to how they would prune their orchards, and fearing they would be boycotted and lose their crops, growers sensed a good deal and capitulated. Quote from Lincoln Steffens, "California and the Japanese," *Colliers* 57 (Mar. 25, 1916), 2. See also James D. Phelan to Woodrow Wilson, Apr. 20, 1912, James D. Phelan Papers, BL; clipping, *Winters Express*, n.d., in Proceedings of the Asiatic Exclusion League, Apr. 1908, Asiatic Exclusion League Collection, Labor Archives, CSU, San Francisco; G. H. Hecke, "Pacific Coast Labor," *CSFGCT, 1907*, 70; Charles F. Lambert, "Sacramento Valley Irrigation and Land," oral memoir by Willa Baum, 1957 77, 88, ROHP, BL; *California Fruit Grower*, Apr. 18, 1903.

47. Quotes from *Placer County Republican*, Apr. 28, May 12, June 30, 1910; *PRP*, May 14, 1910. See also Testimony of Ivan H. Parker, in House Committee on Immigration and Naturalization, *Japanese Immigration Hearings*, 66th Cong., 2nd sess., 1921, 322–24.

48. Quote from Ben Walker, interview, Dec. 23, 1927, Ichihashi Papers, SUASC. Rubbish

paraphrase from Mark Twain, *Roughing It* (New York, 1872). See also Bunje, *The Story of Japanese Farming in California*, 44–52, BL; Edna Sunada Sarasohn, ed., *The Issei: Portrait of a Pioneer, An Oral History* (Palo Alto, 1983), 87; Carol Mita, "Through a Rural Child's View," MS (1975), 1–3, University of Wisconsin; F. H. King, *Farmers of Forty Centuries* (New York, 1927), 57–63; John P. Irish, *Japanese Farms in California* (Oakland, 1919); Kashū Nichonjin Chūō Nōkai, *Rōnō Konshinkai Kinen* (Conference of experienced farmers) (San Francisco, 1909), i–ix, 1–10, 23, 77, 128, 147–166, JARPC.

49. Quotes from Crissey, *Where Opportunity Knocks Twice*, 22; also 125–30; California State Board of Control, *California and the Oriental: Japanese, Chinese, and Hindus: Report of the State Board of Control of California to Gov. Wm. D. Stephens* (Sacramento, 1920), 207. While the average California farm of two hundred acres was worth forty-two dollars an acre, Japanese farms, while only about fifty-seven acres in size, were valued at $141 per acre. Similarly, on the farms investigated by the CSBLS, Japanese crops were valued at $79.91 per acre, while overall the average value of crops was $40.15 per acre, a difference reflecting the high returns and expenses of intensive farming. The other characteristic of Japanese farms was their size. In 1910, when 38.9 percent of California farms were one hundred acres or larger, 42.6 percent of Japanese farms were nineteen acres or smaller. See Ichihashi, *Japanese in the United States*, 190; H. A. Millis, *The Japanese Problem in the United States* (New York, 1915), 137; *ICR*, 23: 89.

50. Irish, "Orientals in California," *Overland* 78 (Apr. 1920), 333; Japanese Citizen's League, "History of the Japanese People in the San Gabriel Valley and Pomona," Japanese Evacuation and Resettlement Collection, BL; clippings, *San Francisco Chronicle*, May 30, 1910, JARPC; "Rich Soils of the River Islands Won by Hard Toil" and "Sacramento is Center for Prosperous Farming Region," Jan. 15, 1919, Japanese Pamphlets Collection, BL; George E. Hanson, "The Early History of Yuba River Valley" (M.A. thesis, UCB, 1924), 27–31; Mita, "Through the Depression," 1–3; Mr. S. Nitta, interview, 1924, SRRP; Toyoji Chiba, "Truth about Japanese Farming in California," in *California and the Oriental*, 240–46; J. C. Trombetta, "Delta Japanese," 4, Ichihashi Papers, SUASC [also in SRRP]. The figures for Japanese farming around Vacaville range from one-third to three-fifths of the valley's fifteen thousand acres of orchard land. The one-half figure is from Labor Commissioner W. W. Stafford's report, cited in *Vacaville Reporter*, Dec. 29, 1906. See also Tsujita and Nolan, *Omo i de*, 14, 18.

51. For Santa Clara Valley clusters see *ICR*, 24: 445–49. For Cortez Colony, see Valerie J. Matsumoto, *Farming the Home Place: A Japanese American Community in California, 1919–1982* (Ithaca, 1993). In Florin, the Japanese established themselves by accepting $4.50 a week for jobs that the Chinese had done for seven dollars. See *Sacramento Bee*, May 11, 30, 1900; Feb. 28, May 11, 27, July 5, 10, 12, 21, 22, 1901; Jan. 14, 20, Feb. 10, Mar. 2, 1902; Pujas, *Real Japanese*, 51–52; Horace F. Chansler, "The Assimilation of the Japanese in and Around Stockton" (M.A. thesis, UOP, 1932); *ICR*, 2: 401–6; Mr. Ishikawa, interviews, Dec. 16, 1924; C. E. Lewis, Dec. 16, 1924, in "Interviews with Employers," SRRP.

52. For Kyūtarō, see Toshio Yamamura, "Abiko Kyūtarōwo Oboete," Aug. 3, 1956, Shigeki Oka Papers, JARPC; *Japanese-American News, 1903–1919*; Yokoyama Gennosuke, *Kaigai Katsudo no Nihonjin* (Active Japanese abroad) (Tokyo, 1906), 1–46, JARPC; Mr. Fishikawa, interview, Dec. 16, 1924, no. 73, SRRP. For a very fine history of the colony, see Kesa Noda, *Yamato Colony, 1906–1960* (Livingston-Merced, 1981). See also Japanese Association of America to Woodrow Wilson, [ca. 1916], 12, Ichihashi Papers, SUASC.

53. Central Japanese Association Minutes, Mar. 24, Apr. 16, 1923; Central Japanese Association Records; Minutes, Central Japanese Farmers Association of Turlock, Feb. 12, 1916; Dec. 12, 1921, Turlock Farm Corporation Records; Proceedings of the Central Japanese Agricultural Association Records, Jan. 13, 1909, Central Japanese Agricultural Association Records; Records of the Associated Japanese Sugar Beet Growers of Southern California; *History of the Southern California Flower Market* (Los Angeles, 1952), JARPC; W. L. Jackson, "The Importance of the Los Angeles Labor Market," *California Cultivator*, n.d., FHHC; F. M. Hudson, interview, June 27, 1924, SRRP; Michinari Fujita, "The Japanese Associations of America," *Sociology and Social Research* 13 (Jan.–Feb. 1929), 286–89.

54. Roger Daniels, *The Politics of Prejudice: The Anti-Japanese Movement in California and the Struggle for Japanese Exclusion* (Berkeley, 1962 [1977]), 58–67; McWilliams, *Brothers Under The Skin* (Boston, 1964), 154; Madelon Berkowitz, "The California Progressives and the Anti-Japanese Agitation" (M.A. thesis, UCB, 1966); Thomas A. Bailey, "California, Japan, and the Alien Land Legislation of 1913," *PHR* 1 (Mar. 1932), 36–59; Spencer C. Olin Jr., "European Im-

migrant and the Oriental Alien: Acceptance and Rejection by the California Legislature of 1913," *PHR* 35 (Aug. 1966), 303–16. Indian Sikhs used similar methods of evasion, including marriage to Mexican women.

55. Gulick, *American-Japanese*, app. B, 317; CSBLS, *Thirteenth Biennial Report, 1907–8*, 270. Ninety-six percent of the field hands on Japanese farms were Japanese.

56. Quote from *Sacramento Bee*, May 1, 1913, in Susan McCoin Kataola, "Issei Women: A Study in Subordinate Status" (Ph.D. diss., UCLA, 1977), 38. Other than the long voyage east to California and use of photographs, the proxy arrangement did not differ significantly from the customary system of marriages arranged between families in Japan for centuries. See also Masami Kakaghi, "A Study of Marriage and Family Relationships Among Three Generations of Japanese-American Family Groups" (M.A. thesis, USC, 1964); Paul Spickard, *Japanese Americans: The Formation and Transformations of an Ethnic Group* (New York, 1996), 32–34; Harry Kitano, *Japanese-Americans—The Evolution of a Subculture* (Englewood Cliffs, N.J., 1969), 62–65; Elliot G. Mears, *Resident Orientals of the American Pacific Coast: Their Legal and Economic Status* (Chicago, 1928), 342–43. For picture brides obtained without photographs, see Hasagawa and Boettcher, *Success through Perseverance*, 588. Figures for women are from 1908 to 1924.

57. Quotes from "Immigrant Labor in the Fruit Industries of the Newcastle District," *ICR*, 24: 427–28. One picture bride later recalled how she had shared quarters with a young boy and elderly man who stretched a heavy rope across the middle of the room and hung their clothes and blankets on it to provide a modicum of privacy. "What an inappropriate life for a bride and groom!" she later recalled. Another picture bride remembered her farmhouse as a place where the wind "blew in with a weird whistle through the cracks in the board walls." Quotes from Chieko Sano, "Recollections," in East Bay Japanese for Action, ed., *Our Recollections* (Oakland, 1979), 179; Kazuo Ito, *Issei: a History of Japanese Immigrants in North America* (Seattle, 1973), 260, 498. By 1920, the number of Japanese women in California had grown to 22,193, and the ratio of Japanese men to women had narrowed from 24 to 1 to 1.9 to 1. Ratios from V. S. McClatchy, "Picture Brides and their Successors," *Sacramento Bee*, Nov. 28, 1921; T. Iyenaga, *Japanese and the California Problem* (New York, 1921), 113. Because most men had left when they had been in their 20s and 30s, they were almost always much older than their young brides. For each, there almost always came an awkward moment when the farmers appeared at the dock to greet and claim their wives. Because many farmers had forwarded photographs of themselves as young men or had sent retouched images that eliminated facial blemishes and bald spots, they often presented quite a shocking figure to brides expecting attractive, urbane gentlemen. All too often, the farmers in these first meetings turned out to bear little resemblance to the individuals portrayed in exchanged photographs. Some farmers, in fact, were so unattractive that their brides refused to accept them and demanded to be shipped back home. Other men became abusive or proved to be such disappointments that brides deserted them and ran off with younger men after living with their new husbands for just a short time. But even for women who had known their husbands before coming to California, the period of separation produced such changes in both that they often barely recognized one another. Other picture brides discovered to their astonishment that they had married sharecroppers who had passed themselves off as landowners. See Fujita Kiyuko, "'Zairyū Fujin ni Atau' wo Yomite," *Shin Sekai*, Sept. 8–10, 1912; *Nichibei Shimbun*, Sept. 12, 1912; *Shin Sekai*, Apr. 17, 18, May 3, 1908; Tom Toshimi Shimasaki, interview, in Hasagawa and Boettcher, *Success Through Perseverance*, 216; Cikuth, "Pajaro Valley," 124–25; *ICR*, 24: 449; U.S. attorney general to secretary of state, July 31, 1908; memorandum, Division for Eastern Affairs, Oct. 7, 1908, File no. 14932; Mr. MacMurray, memorandum, Nov. 20, 1914; "The Picture Bride Question and the Japanese Question," memorandum, Division for the Eastern Affairs, Nov. 19, 1919, File no. 711.94/310; memorandum, Division for Eastern Affairs, Mar. 18, 1921, File no. 811.5294/352, State Department Records, RG 59, NA; Darrell H. Smith and J. Guy Herring, *The Bureau of Immigration* (Baltimore, 1924), 27.

58. Quotes from "Statements of Fruit Ranch Owners of Placer County," comp. T. G. Chamberlain, June 1916, Mead Papers, BL; Konrad Bercovici, "The Japanese in the United States," *The Century* 110 (Sept. 1925), 606; also 608. See also Peter B. Kyne, *The Pride of Palomar* (New York, 1921); V. S. McClatchy, *Japanese Immigration and Colonization*, Skeleton Brief, 67th Cong., 1st sess., Doc. 55, 1921, 14. Whereas there were no Japanese children in 1900, by 1910 there were 4,502 native-born children in the United States. See Ichihashi, *Japanese in the United States*, 164. See also Sandra Uyeunten, "Struggle and Survival: The History of Japanese Immigrant Families in California, 1907–1945" (Ph.D. diss., UCSD, 1988), 64–88.

59. Quotes from Ito, *Issei*, 442. See also 250–51, 255, 280–82; Yukiko Hanawa, "The Several Worlds of Issei Women" (M.A. thesis, CSU, Long Beach, 1982), 86. Wives cooking for harvest crews are described in J. C. Trombetta, "Report on the Japanese in the Sacramento Delta," Ichihashi Papers, SUASC. For the issue of women working on Sundays, particularly in the Los Angeles flower industry, see Nanka Kasho Kumiai, *Nanka Kasho Kumiai Shi* (Los Angeles, 1933), 28; Nanka Chuo Nihonjin Kai et al., "Take Sundays Off," pamphlet, July 1920, JARPC. For women working seven days a week, see George Abe, interview, in Hasagawa and Boettcher, *Success through Perseverance*, 6; Mr. Goto, interview, 20, copies in California History Room, Fresno Public Library.

60. Quote from "Japanese Woman Hangs Herself," *Oxnard Courier*, Dec. 8, 1905.

61. Rapid progress in learning English is described in *ICR*, 24: 58–62. See also Iwata, *Planted in Good Soil*, 1: 165, 182–83; "Economic Status of the Japanese in Walnut Grove," Ichihashi Papers, SUASC.

62. Quote from McWilliams, *Factories in the Field*, 111.

CHAPTER TWENTY-ONE

1. Quotes from Fred Thompson, interviews by author, Mar. 23, 24; June 5, 1973, Chicago, author's possession. Thompson did not give a date for his sojourn. I place it in early April 1923. For agriculture around Lindsay, see William Wilcox Robinson, *The Story of Tulare County and Visalia* (Los Angeles, 1964). For the citrus belt circuit, see A-Number 1, The Famous Tramp [Leon Ray Livingston], *The Wife I Won* (New York, 1915), 14–15. For the orange harvest in Lindsay, see F. C. Mills, "The Orange Industry of Central California," typescript (1914), CCIHP; "The Labor Market in Tulare," 9, CIRP, SHSW. See also "Labor in Tulare," 1–3; "Notes on the Labor Complaints and Claims in Los Angeles" handwritten (Oct. 7–8, 1914), CIRPP.

2. Quotes from Thompson, interviews. Later in the month Thompson was arrested in Marysville and convicted on criminal syndicalism charges. He spent four years in San Quentin. After prison, he became a radical labor activist and historian of western migrant workers. For biographical information on Thompson, see Kenneth Allsop, *Hard Travellin': The Hobo and His History* (New York, 1976), 301; Dave Roediger, comp. and ed., *Fellow Worker: The Life of Fred Thompson* (Chicago, 1993), 54–55; Franklin Rosemont, "Fred Thompson, 1900–1987: Wobbly and Scholar," *Labour* 20 (1987), 7–11. Bindlemen employed in the orange groves around Lindsay toiled like bees. Working in ten- to twelve-hour shifts, they packed seventy-five-pound boxes of oranges at 4 ½ cents a box, graded them at twenty-five to thirty cents an hour, nailed them together at two cents each, or picked them for two to three dollars a day. See Jack Gaveel, "Sunny California—Land of Romance and Unemployment," *Industrial Pioneer* 1 (Feb. 1921), 9. See also A. L. Evans, "Lindsay, the Hub of the Citrus Industry of Interior California," *California Citrograph*, Feb. 1916; "Lindsay Packing House Co. Adds $30,000 in Machinery," ibid., Mar. 1923. Lindsay had fourteen packinghouses lined up along the Santa Fe Railroad tracks, one of which packed twenty-two carloads of oranges per day, largest capacity of any citrus packinghouse in the world.

3. Quotes from Morrison Swift, *What a Tramp Learns in California: Social Danger Line* (San Francisco, 1896), 1–2, in Pamphlets by Bay Area Authors Collection, BL; *Napa Calistogian*, in *Napa Register*, Sept. 28, 1893, NCLCF; typed notes on *Oxnard Courier*, May 18, 1899, Ware Scrapbooks, ACSCR; John T. Bramhall, "The Orient in California," *World Today*, n.v (Apr. 1911), Scheter Files, ILWUL. Contemporaries estimated that about two hundred thousand bindlemen circulated throughout the western states from British Columbia to Mexico.

4. Quotes from H. A. Van Coenen Torchiana, *California Gringos* (New York, 1930), 23. Large quote from *PRP*, Mar. 5, 1881. Small quotes beginning with "transient cattle" from *Hanford Sentinel* in *PRP*, Oct. 5, 1895; *Oakland Tribune*, Aug. 31, 1905; Gaveel, "Sunny California," 9; "American Tramps," *PRP*, Nov. 10, 1888; *Sacramento Bee*, Jan. 10, 1889; "Idle Men Told to Leave Marysville, or Get Busy," *Marysville Evening Democrat*, Oct. 24, 1909; Allan Pinkerton, *Strikers, Communists, Tramps, and Detectives* (New York, 1878), 39. See also Adams, *Farm Management: A Textbook*, 520–21; Adams, *Farm Management Notes*, 300. Bindlemen held down roughly half of the state's harvest jobs. In some areas, like the rice industry of the northern Sacramento Valley, bindlemen dominated harvest work completely. Of the field hands at Vina, one employee observed that, after the Chinese had been dismissed, "nearly all belong to that class of workmen which you find in California who drift along from place to place, working all along

the coast from Los Angeles to Seattle and not caring for a home of their own." Quote from Frank Carpenter, "Carpenter's Letter, A Visit to Senator Stanford's Great Ranch in Northern California and a look at its wonders," *Cleveland World*, May 23, 1893, Stanford Family Scrapbooks, 3: 121, SUASC. For whites in the rice harvest, see "A Pioneer in California Rice Growing," *Pacific Rice Grower*, Mar. 1919. For strychnine, see *Chicago Tribune*, July 12, 1877. For shotguns, see *Napa County Reporter*, Sept. 27, 1889, NCLCF. For rock piles, see "A remedy for the Tramp Evil," *Napa Register*, Jan. 18, 1895, NCLCF. For "shiftlessness," see CIR, *Final Report*, 23: 4959. For studies of "feeblemindedness," see Carleton Parker, "The California Casual and his Revolt," *Quarterly Journal of Economics* 30 (Nov. 1915), 1101–26; Parker, "Preliminary Report on Tentative Findings and Conclusions in Investigation of Seasonal, Migratory and Unskilled Labor in California" (Sept. 1, 1914), 4, CIRP; Nels Anderson, *The Hobo: The Sociology of the Homeless Man* (Chicago, 1961), 126–25; Alice W. Solenberger, *One-Thousand Homeless Men: A Study of Original Records* (New York, 1911), 36.

5. Quotes from Jack London, "The Tramp," *Wilshire's Magazine* 6 (Apr. 1904), 190–91. For London's life on the road, see London, "The Tramp," ibid. (Feb. 1904), 72–74; Richard Etulian, ed., *Jack London, On the Road* (Logan, Utah, 1979). Bindlemen had many other chroniclers. One close student was Josiah Flynt Willard. An alcoholic fan of wanderlust, Willard produced a prolific body of accounts of the secrets of a "blowed-in-the-glass-stiff." As a group, Willard found bindlemen afflicted with defects and idiosyncrasies that made them unfit for normal society. See Josiah Flynt Willard [Josiah Flynt], *Tramping with Tramps: Studies and Sketches of Vagabond Life* (New York, 1900); Willard, *My Life* (New York, 1908); Edward A. Steiner, *From Alien to Citizen: The Story of My Life in America* (New York, 1914), 53–208. Another who conducted an "experiment in reality" by tramping as a bindleman in 1891 was sociologist Walter Wyckoff. See Walter Wyckoff, *The Workers: An Experiment in Reality: The West* (New York, 1898), 303. See also Johnson, *California*, 59–60; also 206; William Staats, *A Tight Squeeze; Or, the Adventures of a Gentleman Who on a Wager of Ten Thousand Dollars, Undertook to Go from New York to New Orleans in Three Weeks without Money as a Professional Tramp* (Boston, 1879), 23–26; J. J. McCook, "Leaves from the Diary of a Tramp," *The Independent* (Nov. 21, 1901–June 1902), series of nine articles, John James McCook Social Reform Papers, Antiquarian and Landmarks Society, Hartford, Conn.; Charles E. Adams, "The Real Hobo; What He Is and How He Lives," *Forum* 33 (1902), 438–39; clipping, *FMR*, ca. 1890, BWC; "Make them Work," *Napa Weekly Register*, Sept. 20, 1889, NCLCF; "Treatment of Migratory Workers," *Solidarity*, Dec. 2, 1925. Residents of some migratory centers would acknowledge the work that bindlemen performed and the role that they played bringing in the crops. In the little agricultural community of Reedley, bindlemen were even honored every August beginning in 1911 with a "hobo party," although none was ever invited or attended. Dressing in ragged pants and old shirts, local residents carrying canes and bundles wrapped in red bandannas camped out on a beach along the Kings River, told stories, played games, shared "mulligan stew," and generally conducted themselves as roving, bumbling, disheveled, and impudent, happy-go-lucky, Jack Wanderlust hobo adventurers. For the hobo party, see Nickel, *Beginnings in the Reedley Area*, 217. See also Coulton Waugh, *The Comics* (New York, 1947), 38; "Wild West," *Atlantic Monthly* 36 (Dec. 1920), 785–88; Harry Beardsley, "Along the Main Stem with Red," doc. no. 145, EBP.

6. Quotes from CIR, *Final Report*, 5: 4928; *Solidarity*, Mar. 6, 1915. For an estimate that there were about three million migrants in 1920, see Shelby M. Harrison et al., *Public Employment Offices: Their Purpose, Structure and Methods* (New York, 1924), 434–35, 528, 555–57. A figure of 3.5 million a decade earlier is in Parker, *The Casual Laborer and Other Essays* (New York, 1920), 17, 19. A figure of three million in 1915 is in CIR, *Final Report*, 5: 4933. Eric H. Monkkonen, *Police in Urban America, 1860–1920* (New York, 1981), finds that as many as one in five American workers passed the night at one time or another as indigent or homeless "guests" of local police departments. McCook, "A Tramp Census and Its Revelations," *Forum* 15 (1893), 760; and Edmund Kelly, *The Elimination of the Tramp* (New York, 1908), 1, give the figure of one to six out of every one thousand Americans tramping in search of work. The four-million figure is from Ed Boyce to Samuel Gompers, Mar. 16, 1897, in Samuel Gompers, "An Address to the Western Federation of Miners, in Convention Assembled, June 1897," 1–2, AULHWSU. For a review of figures cited in the labor press, see Michael Davis, "Forced to Tramp: The Perspective on the Labor Press, 1870–1900," in Monkkonen ed., *Walking to Work: Tramps in America, 1790–1935* (Lincoln, Neb., 1984), 141–70. Studying jailhouse lodging figures, John C. Schneider, "Omaha Vagrants and the Character of Western Hobo Labor, 1887–1913," *Nebraska History*

63 (summer 1982), 255–72, postulated that up to one-fifth of the labor force wandered in search of work. The population was so highly mobile that, within a decade, a hypothetical city of 363,000 residents would have at least 690,000 people pass through it, stay awhile, and move on. Hundreds of thousands of casual laborers circulated in numerous crisscrossing, branching, and overlapping migratory routes. Traveling throughout the northeastern states, one group of transient workers spent the winter cutting ice on frozen lakes and shoveling snow and coal, then shifted to railroad construction during the spring, and finished the year by laying pipe, working as steersmen on keelboats in the rivers and canals of the northeast, then heading south to drill for oil in Texas or load bananas in New Orleans. Within a single state like Michigan, men moved ceaselessly from lumber mills in Saginaw to ship caulking in Detroit to work as deckhands on vessels plying the Great Lakes. Along the Atlantic Coast, men traveled from Florida to New Jersey and sometimes as far north as Maine, picking various crops along the way. Still others shifted between jobs as "boomers" (bridge builders), "gandy dancers" (railroad tie tampers), "jerries" and "snipes" (railroad hands), "bridge snakes" (structural-steel workers on bridges), "skinners" (mule drivers), "diamond cutters" (ice-cutters), "splinter bellies" (rough carpenters), and "pearl divers" (dishwashers). For various migrant streams and groups, see Hahamovitch, *The Fruits of their Labor*; Paul S. Taylor, "Migratory Labor in the United States," *Monthly Labor Review* 44 (Mar. 1937), 538–39; William Dimmit, "An Organized Harvest," *Industrial Pioneer* 1 (Sept. 1921), 3; Jules Tygiel, "Tramping Artisans: Carpenters in Industrial America, 1880–90," *LH* 22 (summer 1981), 348–76; Douglas Lamar Jones, "The Strolling Poor: Transiency in Eighteenth-Century Massachusetts," *Journal of Social History* 8 (spring 1974), 28–54; numerous newspaper clippings, Migratory Labor Folder, Edwin Witte Papers, SHSW.

7. Quote from Hamlin Garland, *A Son of the Middle Border* (New York, 1917), 174. For pay rates and working conditions, see United States Industrial Commission, *Report* (Washington, D.C., 1900–1902), 10: 851; 11: 81. For one variant route, see "The Vagrant Potato Pickers," *Literary Digest* 47 (Oct. 4, 1913), 607. See also Harold Briggs, "Early Bonanza Farming in the Red River Valley of the North," *AH* 6 (Jan. 1932), 26–37; John Lee Coulter, "Industrial History of the Valley of the Red River of the North," *Collections of the State Historical Society of North Dakota* 3 (1910), 529–672; O. E. Baker, comp., "A Graphic Summary of Seasonal Work on Farm Crops," U.S. Dept. of Agriculture, *Yearbook, 1917* (Washington, D.C., 1918), 556–57, figs. 23–26; Don D. Lescohier, *Harvest Labor Problems in the Wheat Belt*, U.S. Dept. of Agriculture, Bulletin No. 1020 (Washington, D.C., 1922), 1. See also Rikoon, *Threshing in the Midwest*, 54, 87, 95–96. For internal migration, see Stephen Thernstrom and Peter Knights, "Men in Motion: Some Data and Speculations about Urban Population Mobility in Nineteenth-Century America," *Journal of Interdisciplinary History* 1 (fall 1970), 7–35; Sumner H. Slichter, *The Turnover of Factory Labor* (New York, 1919). While a few men drifted all the way from Oklahoma into Alberta, Canada, most adhered to more restricted regional circuits. Following the winter wheat harvest belt, working only in spring wheat, or shifting from the strawberry crop along the Gulf Coast into southwest Missouri for the potato harvest, then on to Kansas and North Dakota for the wheat harvest, and finally east to pick apples and peaches before returning to Texas, such men seemed to Kansas governor Lorenzo Lewelling much like the vagabonds of Elizabethan England and prerevolutionary France. For the Midwest, see Allen G. Applen, "Migratory Harvest Labor in the Midwestern Wheat Belt, 1870–1940" (Ph.D. diss., Kansas State University, 1974); J. A. Huffman to Lorenzo D. Lewelling, Dec. 6, 1893; G. H. Fish to Lewelling, Dec. 9, 1893, Lorenzo D. Lewelling Papers; Governor Lewelling, Executive Proclamation, Dec. 4, 1893, in *Topeka Daily Capital*, Dec. 5, 1893, all in Kansas State Historical Society, Topeka.

8. Quotes from *Solidarity*, Mar. 6, 1915; London, "The Tramp," 142. See also Ernestine Winchell, "Evolution of the Hitch-Hiker," *FMR*, Dec. 7, 1930, Fresno Scrapbooks, BL. For the potter's field, see Johnson, *California*, 60; "Buried in Potter's Field," *Marysville Daily Appeal*, Aug. 7, 1913.

9. John N. Webb, "The Migratory-Casual Worker," in WPA, Division of Social Research, *Research Monograph No. 7* (Washington, D.C., 1937), x–xi; J. Forbes, "The Tramp, or, Caste in the Jungle," *Outlook* 98 (Aug. 19, 1911), 869–75; E. Lamar Bailey, "Tramps and Hoboes," *Forum* 26 (Oct. 1898), 218. The history of the word "hobo" is vague. Josiah Flynt, "The American Tramp," *Contemporary Review* 60 (Aug. 1891), 254, contains one of the earliest uses of the term. See also Charles Ely Adams, "The Real Hobo: What He Is and How He Lives," *The Forum* 33 (June 1902), 440. For "California blankets," see William Haywood to migrants, *Solidarity*, Nov. 28, 1914.

10. Quotes from Anderson, *The Hobo*, 87; Ben L. Reitman, "The American Tramp," MS (n.d.), 3–9, [inconsistent pagination], Ben Reitman Papers, Special Collections, University of Illinois, Chicago Circle. See also J. H. Russell, *Cattle on the Conejo* (Pasadena, 1957), 32; *Chicago Evening American*, Jan. 7, 1935; "How to Tell a Hobo from a Mission Stiff," *Survey* 31 (Mar. 21, 1914), 781; J. Kenney, "Migratory Workers," *Solidarity*, June 17, 1925; *Napa Reporter*, Sept. 20, 1889; "Make them Work," *Napa Weekly Register*, Sept. 20, 1889; ibid., Sept. 2, 1899; "A Tramp Takes a Tumble," *Napa Daily Journal*, Apr. 8, 1900, NCLCF; clipping, *Chicago Daily Socialist*, Nov. 24, ?, John Murray Papers and Scrapbooks, BL; "Hobo Ace," doc. no. 46; and "Classification of Homeless Men," doc. no. 78, EBP. Hoboes, itinerant workers, and bindlemen were thus defined by their relationship to the economy and labor market. They had no strong passion for traveling, and accepted it for the work opportunities it brought. On the other hand, tramps and bums were addicted to the road and resembled today's skid row derelicts. This was also true of the various other homeless elements—skid row "down-and-outs," who according to one observer constituted "the lowest scale of the social order . . . vagrant . . . degenerate . . . usually old . . . stinking . . . lazy as the devil," and alcoholic; the "ding bats," "swill buzzards," and "home guards," who scavenged garbage piles and just seemed to ooze along; the "haybags," those female bums who traded sex for booze; and "stump bums," so called because they were usually amputees given to begging. Quotes from Howard M. Bahr, *Skid Row: An Introduction to Disaffiliation* (New York, 1973); Towne Nylander, "The Migratory Population of the United States," *American Journal of Sociology* 30 (Sept. 1924), 130–36; Richard Wakefield and Paul H. Landis, "Types of Migratory Farm Laborers and their Movement into the Yakima Valley, Washington," *Rural Sociology* 3 (June 1938), 133–44; Orlando Lewis, "The American Tramp," *Atlantic Monthly* 101 (June 1908), 745; A-Number 1 [Leon Ray Livingston], *Mother Declasse of the Hoboes and other Stories* (Erie, Penn., 1918), 43–4; John S. Gambs, *The Decline of the I.W.W.*, Columbia University Studies in History, Economics and Public Law, no. 361 (New York, 1932), 112; E. Hofer, "The Tramp Problem," *Overland Monthly* 23 (June 1894), 628–32. See also Wyckoff, *The Workers: The East* (New York, 1897); Wyckoff, *The Workers: The West*; Wyckoff, *A day with a tramp, and other days* (New York, 1901).

11. Quotes from *IW*, Apr. 15, 1909; CIR, *Final Report*, 5: 4939. Between jobs, a twenty-four-year-old Danish-immigrant bindleman sat down with Commission on Industrial Relations interviewer Peter A. Speek and outlined a portion of his California travels after three weeks in San Francisco's Barbary Coast. "He left for the South to pick oranges," wrote Speek. "Put to work by police on street cleaning in a small town. Worked a day then told to get out of town. No trial. Went to Los Angeles. A job for the city, pick and shovel, $2.25 a day, 8 hours. Worked five months. Quit—too hot. Went sailing." Quotes from Peter A. Speek, "Report on the Psychological Aspect of the Problem of Floating Laborers (An Analysis of Life Stories)" (June 25, 1915); "Interview No. 3, Jungle, Redfern, South Dakota" (July 10, 1914), CIRPP. During a rainy week while stranded in Calipatria, a bindleman named James Fay, who had been on the road for twenty years, penned an "absolutely truthful" account of his employment over the previous twelve months. During that time he had worked in Oklahoma, Kansas, Iowa, Montana, Idaho, Washington, Oregon, and California at twenty different jobs ranging from threshing and logging to "mucking" and harvesting potatoes. His longest job, laying pipe, lasted thirty-three days, his shortest just one day. He was fired three times (for union activity, refusing to work on Sunday, or working too slow) and quit three times (because of a rotten camp, low wages, and a strike) and never earned more than $1.50 a day. See James Fay, "A Migratory Worker's Diary," *Industrial Pioneer* 2 (Feb. 1924), 29. See also Jesse W. Dee Jr., *Flophouse* (Francestown, N.H., 1948), xix, 47; James E. Keenan, "The Wail of the Bindle Stiff," *Solidarity*, Aug. 4, 1917; Charles Craig, interview, 1982, CSU, Fullerton. For itinerant workers in the American West, see David M. Emmons, *The Butte Irish: Class and Ethnicity in an American Mining Town, 1875–1925* (Urbana, Ill., 1989); William C. Robbins, *Hard Times in Paradise: Coos Bay, Oregon, 1850–1986* (Seattle, 1988).

12. Quotes from Parker, *Casual Laborer*, 59, and 69–74, 17. See also Joyce Kornbluh, ed., *Rebel Voices: An I.W.W. Anthology* (Ann Arbor, 1972), 405; CIR, *Final Report*, 5: 4933; *Solidarity*, Dec. 5, 1914. Work itineraries traced in Robert Blaine, E. S. Carey, John J. Conner, Otto Eiser, and Frank Johnson files, MIDRIS.

13. Quotes from J. Kenney, "Migratory Workers," *Solidarity*, June 17, 1925; Richard Wormser, *Hoboes: Wandering in America, 1870–1940* (New York 1994), 18. See also Don D. Lescohier, "Farm Labor Problem," *Journal of Farm Economics* 3 (Jan. 1921), 11; "Red," *Oxnard Courier* n.d., Coroner's Record of Violent Deaths, VCM. One of two was under thirty years of age;

one of three between thirty and forty years of age; and eight of ten under forty years. One of twenty was a widower, divorced, or otherwise separated from their wives and children. See Parker, "Statistical Tables from the Life History Schedules Selected at Random Among Casual Laborers in California," in California Commission of Immigration and Housing (CCIH), *Report on Unemployment* (Sacramento, 1914), 47–53; Speek, "Preliminary Report on the Psychological Aspect of the Problem of Floating Laborers," 7–8, CIRP. See also CIR, *Final Report*, 5: 4933–34; Parker, *Casual Laborer*, 74–76; *Solidarity*, Nov. 21, Dec. 5, 1914; *ICR*, 24: 72, 74, disclosing that 1,036 of 1,621 migrants surveyed by the Immigration Commission in 1911 were single. Comparative data from W. Jett Lauck and Edgar Sydenstricker, *Conditions of Labor in American Industries: A Summarization of the Results of Recent Investigations* (New York, 1917), 296.

14. Parker, *Casual Laborer*, 71, 116–17. There is some evidence that their lack of job skills may have been more pronounced. Studying skill levels among bindlemen, the CCIH discovered that all berry pickers contacted by the commission were unskilled, and that 95 percent of all beet workers, 96 percent of all fruit pickers, and 99 percent of grape pickers also lacked skilled trades to fall back on. See CCIH, *First Annual Report* (Sacramento, 1914), 31, table 1; CIR, *Final Report*, 5: 4933. Had they worked steadily, bindlemen would have earned $6.37 a week (37.5 hours at seventeen cents an hour) for an annual salary of between $325–$350 a year, about that of Chicago slaughterhouse workers. As far as wages were concerned, California bindlemen were not unusually worse off than other itinerant workers. About one-quarter of all workers in twelve other basic American industries earned less than four hundred dollars a year, and half less than six hundred dollars a year. See Parker, "The California Casual and His Revolt," 113, 117; Rexford G. Tugwell, "The Casual of the Woods," *Survey* 44 (July 3, 1920), 472; Bellamy Partridge, *Fill 'Er Up* (New York, 1952), 193.

15. Quote from typed notes, "Farm Labor," *California Citrograph*, July 1917, FHHC.

16. Quote from Parker, *Casual Laborer*, 72. Identifying those forces pushing and pulling workers onto the road has always provoked considerable debate and conjecture. See Stuart A. Rice, "Vagrancy," *Proceedings of the National Conference of Charities and Correction* (1914), 461–62. For a view stressing certain social pathologies, see Ben Reitman, "Wanderlust, The Tramps' Disease," MS (n.d.), Reitman Papers, Special Collections, University of Illinois.

17. Quotes from grave marker, Caliente, Nevada, cemetery; Hood River Blackie [Mr. Ralph Goodings], interview by Lisbeth M. Scott, 1981, 12, California State Railroad Museum, Sacramento. For laziness as a leading cause of tramping, see *PRP*, Mar. 17, 1883. William D. Haywood, "To Migratory Workers," *Solidarity*, Nov. 28, 1914, stressed how the ranks of casual laborers were swelled by men traveling west with high hopes who soon found themselves stranded, friendless, and homeless. "You can not freeze to death in California, you can not starve to death in California," one bindleman told an investigator for the CCIH. Quote from CCIH, *Report on Unemployment*, 8, 47–49.

18. Quotes from *Napa Weekly Register*, Sept. 20, 1899, NCLCF; CIR, *Final Report*, 1: 157; Gaveel, "Sunny California," 6. See also Parker, *Casual Laborer*, 71, 116–17. For bindlemen flocking into California from Rocky Mountain mining camps, see *Sacramento Bee*, Nov. 1, 1893. For a group of stranded circus acrobats who delighted everyone by practicing their acts in the orchards during the Santa Clara Valley harvest, see C. E. "Swede" Righter, *From Farm Boy to World Traveler: An Autobiography*, MS (Nov. 20, 1973), 12, Stanford University Library. Between 1900 and 1910 California received 775,000 newcomers—immigrants and migrants from other states. For migration to California, see Frank L. Beach, "The Transformation of California" (Ph.D. diss., UCB, 1963), 13, 18–19, 29, 32, 45–59, 64. Not all bindlemen were social outcasts. Some had lived successfully for many years as small farmers. Serving as elders in their local church, and pillars of their communities, they were pushed into the migratory circuit by mounting debts, declining markets, and poor harvests. For such men, tramping was a way station in life, not a final stop. For a farmer turned itinerant worker who exemplified this type of bindleman, see Joseph Warren Matthews, diary, 1869–1900, Joseph Warren Matthews Papers, BL.

19. Men could find only 2,251 jobs in the lumber industry in January, compared to 9,855 jobs in July. Data on manufacturing employment from U.S. Dept. of Commerce, *Statistical Abstract of the United States: 1916* (Washington, D.C. 1917), 264. For more systematic analysis, see Lauck and Sydenstricker, *Conditions of Labor in American Industries*, 150, 173; Speek, "Notes on the Situation of Migratory Laborers and Unemployment in California" (Oct. 3, 1914), CIRPP; Speek, "Report on My General Impressions and Observations on the Pacific Coast" (Sept. 25, 1914), CIRP.

20. Quotes from Parker, *Casual Laborer*, 80; Charles Ashleigh, "The Floater," *ISR* 15 (July 1914), 35. For first-person analysis, see "The Bindle Stiff," *Defense News Bulletin*, May 1, 1918; James E. Keenan, "The Wail of the Bindle Stiff," *Solidarity*, Aug. 4, 1917.

21. For field hands tramping the roads, see Thelma White, "Up and Down the River Shorty," *Wagon Wheels* 22 (Sept. 1972), 35; Latta, "Dan Hart: Patriarch of the Bindle Stiffs," MS (n.d.) 1, FFLCSF. Unlike their counterparts in Canada who bought cheap tickets on harvest "excursion cars" holding fifty-six men in groups of four on seats that folded into beds, California bindlemen never rode in passenger cars. They referred to this derisively as "riding the cushions." For Canadian bindlemen, see John Herd Thompson, "Bringing in the Sheaves: The Harvest Excursionists, 1890–1929," *Canadian Historical Review* 59 (1978), 469–70; George V. Haythorne, "Harvest Labor in Western Canada: An Episode in Economic Planning," *Quarterly Journal of Economics* 47 (May 1933), 533. For train riding in the American West, see Clark C. Spence, "Knights of the Tie and Rail—Tramps and Hoboes in the West," *WHQ* 2 (spring 1971), 5; Henry Osborne to Peter A. Speek, June 27, 1914, CIRP; CIR, *Final Report*, 23: 4959.

22. Quotes from *San Francisco Chronicle*, Dec. 19, 1892; Ashleigh, "The Floater," 35; *IW*, Mar. 18, 1909.

23. Charmian London, *The Book of Jack London* (New York, 1921), 1; 153–56; *Solidarity*, Jan. 16, 1915; *IUB*, May 23, 1908; typed notes, *Imperial Valley Press*, Dec. 7, 1901, Ware Scrapbooks, General, no. 11, ACSCR; Len DeCaux, *Labor Radical: From the Wobblies to the CIO: A Personal History* (Boston, 1970), 42; O. F. Lewis, "Concerning Vagrancy," *Charities* 21 (Jan. 23, 1909), pt. 2: 714.

24. Quotes from Swift, *What a Tramp Learns in California*, 2–3. See also George Underwood, "Memories of the Jungles," interview by Eugene Nelson, July 1971, Sebastopol, Calif., author's possession; Ralph Chaplin, *Wobbly: The Rough and Tumble Story of an American Radical* (Chicago, 1948), 88; Speek, "The Psychology of Floating Workers," *AAAPSS* 69 (Jan. 1917), 77–78; Gaveel, "Sunny California," 9. Bindlemen were full of stories about their bindles. A favorite tale, often told, modified, and embellished, concerned the time one bindleman stole his own bindle. It seems that after the man got off a northbound train in Newman, an old bindleman immediately stashed his bindle under the platform at the depot, then moseyed across the street to make his rounds in the saloons. After tossing back several beers, the man missed his bindle, and immediately began accusing everyone of stealing it. "He searched under several of the saloons and their board sidewalks, around the gutters, horse troughs and hitching racks and finally gave it up, retreating across Front Street, under the hitching rack and across the railroad right of way toward the depot," recalled San Joaquin Valley historian Frank Latta. "As he was passing the loading platform he spotted a roll of blankets. By this time he was desperate at the thought of spending the night in a railroad culvert with no bindle, so he decided to steal the roll. He hung around the depot for a half-hour, feeling as guilty as a man can and that everyone in town was watching him. Finally he screwed up courage, stepped in, grabbed the roll and wobbled around the corner of the platform to the warehouse to . . . hide until he could sober up some more and catch another freight." Quote from Latta, "Blanket Roll Thief," 1, FFLCSF.

25. Henry McGuckin, "Recollections of a Wobbly," MS (n.d.), 60, AULHWSU; statement of James J. McCunnigle, Dec. 12, 1915, Ford-Suhr Prison Papers, CSA.

26. Quote from Spence, "Knights of the Tie and Rail," 9. See also Ashleigh, *The Rambling Kid* (London, 1930) 15, 112–13; William Davis, *Autobiography of a Super Tramp* (New York, 1917); Stewart H. Holbrook, *The Story of American Railroads* (New York, 1947), 391–92; Edward Abbey, "Hallelujah, on the Bum," *American West* 7 (July 1970), 13; DeCaux, *Labor Radical*, 41, 44; Bill Quirke, "Job Hunting via Box Car," *Hobo News*, Sept. 17, 1921; Jim Burke, "Memories of the Rails," interview, Feb. 5, 1977, author's possession, courtesy of the Hobo Foundation. Bindlemen always avoided jumping for the step or ladder on the rear end of a boxcar. If they did not follow these rules, they would swing around and get pried loose, certainly ending up beneath the wheels. For this reason bindlemen always jumped for the step on the front end of a boxcar. Many bindlemen stumbled into a switch in the dark or hit some other unforeseen obstacle while running. Later they would be picked up along the right-of-way, a bloody, mangled mess. If they miscalculated, they might take a bad fall but would not be cut to shreds. London, "Holding Her Down," *Cosmopolitan* 93 (June 1907), 142–50.

27. Quotes from London, "Hoboes that Pass in the Night," *Cosmopolitan* 44 (Dec. 1907), 195; Leon Livingston, *Life and Adventures of A Number 1, America's Most Celebrated Tramp* (Cambridge Springs, Penn., 1910), 23; also 33–34. Men riding the blinds were relatively safe.

However, if discovered by the crew they might be sprayed by a hose, hit with coal chunks, or doused with shovels full of hot ash. More commonly, they would be hauled into the engine tender and forced to stoke the fire until the next stop, then given the boot. Trainmen checked the blinds at every division point, so the possibility of being discovered was great when the train was stopped. Men who rode the blind baggage swallowed dust and ashes from the train engine, and when the engine took on water on the fly, were showered by a freezing spray. See Glen Mullin, "Adventures of a Scholar-Tramp," *Century Magazine* 105 (Feb.-Mar. 1923), 507; T. Joseph Nylander, "The Casual Laborer of California" (M.A. thesis, UCB, 1922), 7, 33; Ashleigh, *Rambling Kid*, 113–14; Holbrook, *Railroads*, 391; Merle Lovell "Riding the Blinds" (Aug. 4, 1940), Todd-Sonkin Material, Folklore Archives, LC. Bindlemen generally avoided flatcars, which lacked shelter, riding them only as a last resort. Cattle cars were also to be avoided for obvious reasons, while gondolas were second in popularity because, while providing windbreaks, they offered little protection from rain and cold and tended to leave men dirty from their usually unpleasant contents. Riding refrigerator cars, experienced bindlemen ensured against being locked inside by fixing the car lid so that it could not close on them after they dropped inside. See Loren Eiseley, *All the Strange Hours: The Excavation of a Life* (New York, 1975), 49–51; Flynt, *Tramping*, 359–60; Craig, interview; Hood River Blackie, interview, 70; Fred Maloy, diary, Oct. 27, 1933, Fred Maloy Papers, BL. Many bindlemen found a comfortable spot in the oblong battery box that held batteries to power the train's lights. Located halfway back on Pullman coaches, empty battery boxes made secure nests. Crawling inside, a resourceful bindleman pulled the door shut from the inside and kept it from flapping by means of a piece of stiff wire with a screw-eye fastened to a staple or screw head on the outside of the box. The box was very cramped. "M ol' spine had sprung a reverse curve, like a croquet wicket," explained Glen Mullin, a veteran bindleman, after riding hunched in a battery box from Chicago to Los Angeles on the Golden State Limited. Quote from Glen H. Mullin, *Adventures of a Scholar Tramp* (New York, 1925), 123–24, 132. Riding a slow freight or "rattler" was not difficult, but "holding down a cannon ball"—a speedy passenger train—required both ability and fortitude. One unpleasant riding spot was the deck or roof on top of a passenger car or mail car. One San Francisco–bound bindleman riding the top of a coach highballing west out of Cheyenne endured a shower of cinders from the engine that "cut through his clothes like bullets" and lacerated his neck and face. As the engineer increased speed, the train rolled and lurched violently, and the bindleman wound his arms and legs around a stovepipe and hung on for dear life. "His coat-tails flapped so hard that he saw he must lose them, but dared not loosen his grip upon the pipe to tuck them under him, and they were shortly torn off like leaves whipped from a limb by a terrific storm," wrote Allan Pinkerton, apparently from close personal contact and observation in his book *Strikers, Communists, Tramps, and Detectives*. "The lighter cinders passed over him, but the heavier ones pelted him like the fiercest hail, burned his clothes, cut his arms, legs and face, and beat upon the poor fellow's head remorselessly. So great was his actual physical suffering, and so terrible his fear . . . that when . . . he was let down more dead than alive, his hair turned grey, and he looked more like an old man of sixty than a lad of nineteen as he was." Quote from Pinkerton, *Strikers, Communists, Tramps, and Detectives*, 65; also 41. See also Wormser, *Hoboes*, 24–25; Roger Bruns, *Knights of the Road: A Hobo History* (New York, 1980); Roger Bruns, *The Damndest Radical: The Life and World of Ben Reitman, Chicago's Celebrated Social reformer, Hobo King, and Whorehouse Physician* (Urbana and Chicago, 1987), 11. Bindlemen seeking to move as quickly as possible found a train standing on a siding and quietly slipped beneath the Pullman cars, into the car's undercarriage. Once there, they found a place to wedge themselves. One popular location was in among the round, two-inch diameter iron bracing rods running lengthwise 18 inches below the car's belly. Only the most experienced and crazy men ventured here. Many bindlemen considered riding the rods the true test of manhood. Most avoided them. Better to miss a train than ride the rods. To assist in riding the rods, some bindlemen carried a ten-inch-long piece of board with a groove down the center. This device was known as "a tramp's ticket." By shoving it into the yard-long lateral strut parallel with the cross-section and the axles, bindlemen created an improvised, very painful seat that kept them perched perilously a few inches below paying passengers and a few inches above the rails. See Fred Maloy, diary, Oct. 24, 1933, Fred Maloy Papers, BL. For the best description of a man using a "tramp's ticket," see "Dangerous Ride," *Sacramento Daily Union*, May 3, 1871. Riding the "trucks"—the maze of brake beams, struts, and springs holding the wheels to the tracks—was also something that only the most experienced bindlemen attempted. A man had to know exactly what he was doing. But even then he could easily be cut to pieces. When a bindleman crawled over the brake beam across the axle and into a truck, he usually had only a minute or two, and once inside, if he discovered that he had made a mistake and there was no place to ride, he was in big trouble. Bindlemen were thumped off the trucks by stones, suffocated while crossing long sections of dusty roadbeds or tunnels, or smashed to bits after falling asleep and tumbling beneath the wheels. For all of these reasons, no one ever rode the trucks unless he was desperate and really wanted to get somewhere or make time. For a bindleman discovered in the trucks while a train stood at a siding in Middletown, Napa County, see "Bounced," *Napa Daily Journal*, Sept. 25, 1890, NCLCF. For the romanticization of "riding the rods," see Hood River Blackie, interview, 38. See also William Z. Foster, *Pages from a Worker's Life* (New York, 1939), 117–9; "Boy Tramp," doc. no. 39; "Boy Eighteen, On Way Home," doc. no. 92, EBP.

28. London, *The Road* (New York, 1907), 36; also 37–52; Tom Kramer, *Waiting for Nothing* (New York, 1935), 149–54.

29. Quote from *Napa Daily Journal*, Oct. 20, 1895, NCLCF.

30. Quote from *Sacramento Bee*, Nov. 1, 1893, cited in *Journal of the Knights of Labor*, Dec. 28, 1893. See also Ben L. Reitman and Bertha Thompson, *Sister of the Roads: The Autobiography of Box-Car Bertha* (New York, 1937); Charles Craig, interview.

31. Locked from the outside, refrigerator car doors sometimes swung shut when the train jerked and swayed and were occasionally locked by yardmen unaware that anyone was inside. Afraid of being arrested or beaten up, inexperienced bindleman often kept quiet. Then on the road the reefer would develop a "hot-box" (overheated wheel bearing) or a "pulled lung" (wrecked coupling) and would be set out on a siding. The bindleman inside, not knowing what all the switching was about, would make no noise that might attract attention. Hearing the train whistle, he might try to get out, and if the car was at some frequented spot, he was not so bad off; at worst he was slugged or thrown in jail. But if the car happened to be on a desert siding, miles from nowhere, the unfortunate bindleman froze or starved to death. He would not be discovered until the contents of the reefer were unloaded or trainmen and car inspectors noticed a foul smell, sometimes weeks later, and discovered the dead bindleman inside. See Holbrook, *Railroads*, 391–92; "Tramping," *Industrial Pioneer*, Sept. 1921, 43; London, "Hoboes that Pass in the Night," 192; Foster, *Pages from a Worker's Life*, 117; DeCaux, *Labor Radical*, 59; Walter Nef, "Job Control in the Harvest," *ISR* 17 (Sept. 1916), 143; Hood River Blackie, interview, 39.

32. Quote from *Vallejo Chronicle*, cited in *Napa Register*, Dec. 22, 1893, NCLCF. See also J. Forbes, "Caste in the Jungle," *Outlook* 98 (Aug. 19, 1911), 870; A-Number 1, The Famous Tramp, *From Coast to Coast with Jack London* (New York, 1917), 126; "Pioneer Hobo, age 51, Perhaps Dying," doc. no. 13; "Anemic Man," doc. no. 14, EBP. To depart from a moving railcar, a bindleman had to thrust his body forward in the direction the train was going. The goal was to create as much space as possible between his body and the train, and to gain backward momentum while he swung free from the car, as if intending to strike the ground with the back of his head. The whole effort was to overcome as much as possible the primary forward momentum the train imparted to his body. When his feet hit the ground, his body would be tilted backward at an angle of 45 degrees. In this position, he did not pitch immediately forward onto his face. Instead, he hit, bounced, his body rose to the perpendicular, inclined forward, and he began running. If the train had been moving too fast, he eventually wound up on his stomach, skidding through the weeds and gravel. See London, "Some Adventures with the Police," *Cosmopolitan* 44 (Mar. 1908), 421.

33. Quotes from "Laborer is Killed in Train Accident," *FMR*, Sept. 4, 1917. See also "Is Crushed Under Wheels of Train," ibid., Sept. 9, 1917.

34. Quote from "Fearfully Mangled Body Found Today," *Marysville Daily Democrat*, Aug. 31, 1906. See also Richard Reinhardt, "Out West with Rowdy Brakemen," *American West* 7 (May 1970), 29–40; Josiah Flynt, *My Life* (New York, 1908), 101–19.

35. Quote from Spence, "Knights of the Tie and Rail," 11.

36. See also Duvall brothers, "Freight Train Blues" (Aug. 7, 1940), 48B1 ; "Hobo Bill's Last Ride" (Aug. 14, 1940), 53A1, Todd-Sonkin Field Notes, Folklore Archives, Library of Congress. Statistics from Allsop, *Hard Travellin'*, 141; Foster, *Pages from a Worker's Life*, 111–12, 115–16, 120; F. V. Whiting, "Trespassers Killed on Railways—Who Are They?" *Scientific American* 73 (May 11, 1912), 303–4; Orlando F. Lewis, "Vagrant and the Railroad," *North American* 185 (July 19, 1907), 607–8.

37. For the ride from Corcoran, see Fred Maloy, diary, Oct. 27, 1933, Fred Maloy Papers,

BL. For the Shasta Limited, see Ashleigh, *Rambling Kid*, 182. Crossing the Imperial Valley could be a problem. If a man missed the 8:45 A.M. train out of El Centro, he walked north to Imperial or the next junction and camped beside a cantaloupe shed. It took E. F. Lefferts two days to get from Brawley to Redlands, a distance of 170 miles. He had to skirt Colton, fifty miles south of Los Angeles, but the ride to Bakersfield was both easy and scenic. Just south of Fresno, he had to walk around the yards again, but it was easy enough to catch the same train pulling out bound for Madera, Sacramento, Tracy, or Oakland. For the trip across the Imperial Valley, see E. F. Lefferts, "Taking a Vacation in Southern California," *IW*, June 17, 1909. For Needles to San Francisco, see H. Roger Grant, ed., *Brownie the Boomer: The Life of Charles P. Brown, an American Railroader* (DeKalb, Ill., 1991), 171. For speedy train riding, see "Boston Jack," *Napa Register*, Aug. 13, 1886, NCLCF. See also Apr. 1, 1909; H. S. Corrall to IW, "Sunny California, Land of Slaves," June 10, 1909; J. Kenney, "Migratory Workers," *Solidarity*, June 17, 1925; A-Number 1, *The Ways of the Hobo* (Erie, Penn., 1915), 60–62, 80; J. Vance Thompson to Simon J. Lubin, Feb. 14, 1918, in "IWW Investigation," Simon J. Lubin Papers, BL.

38. Bindlemen would hear that a boxcar on a siding in Indio was full of canned hams from Norway, break in, find nothing but soda crackers, and be pursued up and down the line by railroad bulls intent on rounding up anyone packing a bedroll. See Hood River Blackie, interview, 8; Lewis, "The Vagrant and the Railroad," 603–13; Charles Craig, interview; Burke, interview; R. W. Clark to William Weir, May 18, 1912, Northern Pacific Company Records, MHS.

39. For fires, see "Up Valley News" and "Barns, Fences, and Stubble Destroyed at Larkmead Station," *Napa Register*, Sept. 27, 1889, NCLCF; *Ventura Free Press*, Jan. 28, 1887; *Napa Daily Journal*, Aug. 1, 1890; "Calistoga News," Nov. 26, 27, 1892 [Hooper fire]; "Local Happenings," Feb. 2, 1900, "Barns Burning," Oct. 3, 1900, ibid., NCLCF; *PRP*, Aug. 18, 1888 [Richards fire]; "Work of Tramps," *San Francisco Call*, June 6, 1895.

40. Quote from "Tramps," *Vacaville Reporter*, July 26, 1889. See also DeCaux, *Labor Radical*, 46; "Tramping," *Industrial Pioneer* (Sept. 1921), 43; John Greenway, *American Folksongs of Protest* (Philadelphia, 1953) 199; Allsop, *Hard Travellin'*, 165.

41. Quote from "Hoboes Housed," *Napa Register*, Dec. 22, 1893, NCLCF. See also Richard Brazier, "The Story of the IWW's 'Little Red Songbook,'" *LH* 9 (winter 1968), 93; Anderson, *Hobo*, 26; "Local Happenings," Jan. 28, 1900; "Hoboes Run In," Feb. 20, 1901, *Napa Daily Journal*. Bindlemen often shed blood in their encounters with police. All that was required for a bindleman to collect a clubbing or worse was for police to be stumped by some unsolved burglary or boxcar pilfering or to receive complaints that men had begged food or money in town. This was excuse enough for police to seize the first bindlemen they saw, "beat the b'jeezuz out of the boozers," and toss everyone in jail. See *Napa Daily Journal*, Sept. 26, 1894; Feb. 24, Oct. 4, 1895, NCLCF.

42. This was not the policy in Yuma, Arizona. Astride a major east–west railroad spur, Yuma police frequently raided the camps where bindlemen rested beside the rail lines. Describing one big sweep on a winter evening in January 1911, the *Yuma Sentinel* reported how "local officers rounded up all the hoboes and idle stragglers they could find in town, to the number of about thirty," then notified the men to get jobs or move along. Quote from *Yuma Sentinel*, cited in *Brawley News*, June 11, 1911. See also John A. Fitch, "Old and New Labor Problems in California," *Survey* 32 (Sept. 19, 1914), 610; Vernon H. Jensen, "Labor Relations in the Douglas Fir Lumber Industry" (Ph.D. diss., UCB, 1939), 38.

43. Quotes from *Santa Rosa Daily Republican*, Oct. 6, 1886; Dan Buckley, interview, in Hyman Weintraub, "The IWW in California, 1905–1931" (M.A. thesis, UCLA, 1947), 279. For Colton, see Foster, *Pages from a Worker's Life*, 110–11; A-Number 1, *The Wife I Won*, 22. For Rutherford, see *Napa Register*, Oct. 4, 1889, NCLCF.

44. Hohenthal et al., *Streams in a Thirsty Land*, 55.

45. Quotes from "Warning to Vags," *Napa Register*, Mar. 11, 1893, NCLCF; also "War on the Vags," ibid., Apr. 24, 1893; *Sacramento Bee*, Feb. 5, 1902. So great was the fear of bindlemen and other outsiders that they formed the majority of those charged with intoxication and disturbing the peace. Arrest statistics for Pomona from Echeverri, "Pomona, California: The Early Years, 1875–1920", 249, table 22. Bindlemen arrested as vagrants supposedly were entitled to legal consul and trial by jury. But this seldom happened. Shortly after the state vagrancy law was enacted, bindlemen arrested for vagrancy in San Francisco so clogged the courts and cost the city so much money by demanding jury trials that county judges denied them and others arrested for petty offenses their right of jury trails. Although the decision was appealed, California Superior Court

justices turned down the plea, and rural communities tacked on a series of ordinances strengthening the vagrancy statute. One Pomona judge received a rebuke from the Los Angeles County Board of Supervisors for excessively punishing bindlemen arrested for vagrancy. See Stuart Queen, *The Passage of the County Jail* (Menasha, Wis., 1920), 3; "Be Ware," *Napa Weekly Register*, Sept. 20, 1889, NCLCF; letter from the Los Angeles County Board of Supervisors to Erastus Barnes, Sept. 21, 1893, Los Angeles County Board of Supervisors, Old Doc. 477ιT, LACA.

46. *Pomona Daily Times*, Jan. 25, 1888; Oct. 16, 1888. For trial by jury, see "Every Variety of the Law Defier," *Fresno Daily Evening Expositor*, Apr. 6, 1888, Fresno County Scrapbook, SCHMLCSUF; "Not Entitled Jury Trials," *Napa County Reporter*, July 13, 1888, NCLCF. For examples of vagrant bindlemen released on a "floater," see "M. Mahon Must Answer for Crime," *Marysville Daily Appeal*, Nov. 10, Dec. 7, 1906; "Will Steal Anything He Can get His Hands On," Jan. 22, 1906; "City Court Notes," *Marysville Daily Democrat*, July 22, 1901.

47. Quote from Ben Reitman, "The American Tramp," MS (n.d.), Ben Reitman papers, Special Collections, University of Illinois. See also *Napa Daily Journal*, Oct. 8, 1891; "Insane Tramp," Jan. 25, 1895; "Committed to the Asylum," Jan. 31, 1895, NCLCF; Speek, "Report on Interviews with Unemployed Migratory Workers in the Streets and Public Parks in San Francisco" Oct. 4, 1914, CIRP.

48. "Idle Men Told to Leave Marysville, or Get Busy," *Marysville Daily Appeal*, Sept. 24, 1909; *Napa Daily Journal*, July 31, 1890; Jan. 6, 1900; Jan. 13, 22, 1901, NCLCF. See also Nels Peterson, interview, Feb. 23, 1978; Sam Krieger, interview, Sept. 24, 1987, Deborah Shaffer Papers, SHSW; Testimony of William Grannat, in Unites States v. William D. Haywood et al., IWW Collection, AULHWSU.

49. Quotes from "McCoy Cleans City of Undesirables," *Marysville Daily Appeal*, Nov. 9, 1911; "Vacation Time Fills the Jail," ibid., Oct. 3, 1913. For Marysville, see Queen, *Passage*, 7. An air of desperation pervades the Marysville police logs, as men waiting for the harvest apparently had little or no resources to carry them through the next weeks. See arrest records of W. F. Spencer, no. 920, Oct. 18, 1903; Tom Kelley, no. 1109, Sept. 19, 1905; Ed Skur, no. 1032, Jan. 23, 1906; Ed Brown, no. 1034, Feb. 9, 1906; Thomas Gordon, no. 1052, July 13, 1906; Frank Curry, no. 1126, Aug. 24, 1907, Fred Roland, no. 1127, Sept. 8, 1907, Marysville Police Logbook, 1895–1908, courtesy Arne Svenson; Ashleigh, *Rambling Kid*, 111; Nils H. Hansson, "The Promised Land," *ISR* 15 (Dec. 1914), 357.

50. Quotes from *Napa Register*, Sept. 20, 1889, NCLCF; also Mar. 20, 1889; Jan. 25, 1895; *Pomona Daily Times*, Jan. 1, 1889; *Sacramento Bee*, Apr. 27, 1896.

51. Quote from *Sacramento Bee*, Feb. 5, 1902; see also Feb. 8, 1902.

52. Quote from "Chain Gang Has Been Put to Work," *Marysville Evening Democrat*, Oct. 21, 1909.

53. Quote from Ashleigh, "The Floater," 35. See also Queen, *Passage*, 1, 7, 41–55. For more information on bindlemen arrested for vagrancy, see *Industrial Pioneer*, Mar. 18, 1909; CIR, *Final Report*, 5: 4982–84; CSBLS, *Twelfth Biennial Report, 1905–6*, 29; *Fourteenth Biennial Report, 1909–10*, 359–70; *Fifteenth Biennial Report, 1911–12*, 665–68; "Report of Visit to Police Court," doc. no. 50, EBP; William M. Dufus, "Labor Market in Harvest Fields of the Middle West" (Dec. 1, 1914), 33, CIRP; various arrest cases from Marysville Police Logbook, 1895–1908.

54. Quotes from CIR, *Final Report*, 5: 4928; *San Luis Obispo Breeze*, cited in *Sacramento Bee*, Feb. 8, 1902. See also *Brawley News*, Jan. 9, 1911.

55. Quote from Queen, *Passage*, 3; also 4, 6, 8, 14.

56. County vagrancy arrest statistics from CSBLS, *Twelfth Biennial Report, 1905–6*, 29–34. For the seasonal patterns of vagrancy arrests, see CSBLS, *Fourteenth Biennial Report, 1909–10*, 384. See also CSBLS, *Fifteenth Biennial Report, 1911–12*, 48; Anderson, *Hobo*, 26, 163–65.

57. "Fight on Wheels," *Napa Daily Journal*, July 29, 1890, NCLCF. See also Ashleigh, "The Floater," 37.

58. Quote from "Boy Tramp," doc. no.110, EBP. In 1907, Southern Pacific had seventy-five policemen operating just in San Francisco and Oakland. See Foster, *Pages*, 106–7. Some through their tenacious pursuit of men and their ability to shake down men boosted their incomes by forty to seventy dollars a month, not to mention payment in kind extracted from bindlemen along the way. See Peter A. Speek, "Report on the Transportation of Laborers" (July 15, 1915), 5–6, CIRPP.

59. Eiseley, *All the Strange Hours*, 9; Flynt, *Tramping for Life*, 303–4; Anderson, *Hobo*, 155–57; G. R., "Tramping the Northwest," *Industrial Pioneer* 1 (Sept. 1921), 43–44; Fred Winstead,

"Tightline," ibid., 3 (July 1923), 23; Gregory R. Woirol, *In the Floating Army: F. C. Mills on Itinerant Life in California, 1914* (Urbana, Ill., 1992), 102–3.

60. When confronted by a bindleman well ensconced in the trucks of a boxcar, shacks devised a devilish revenge. Standing on top of a boxcar, they would tie a length of rope to a railroad spike, drop it down the forward end of the boxcar until it began skipping along the ties, then play it out so that it bounced off the railroad ties and slammed into the wheels and undercarriage where the bindleman was riding. With the train speeding along, the spike destroyed everything it came in contact with, smashing rods and riders alike. Any bindleman hit by the weapon would either be killed outright or knocked to the tracks and run over. The only way a man could escape was by jumping out from beneath the train far enough to clear the rails, a leap that was nearly impossible to make. See Nylander, "California Casual," 57; M. M. Snow, *Nine Thousand Miles on a Pullman* (New York, 1898), 138–45; Rogers, *Colusa County*, 225.

61. Quote from McGuckin, "Recollections of a Wobbly," 71, 74. See also Charles B. George, *Forty Years on the Railroad* (Chicago, 1887), 230–31; Allsop, *Hard Travellin'*, 141; A-Number 1, *Coast to Coast*, 42–44; "Monika Songs," in George Milburn, *The Hobo's Hornbook* (New York, 1930), 25–37.

62. Quotes from "Robbery in Yuba City," *Marysville Daily Democrat*, July 22, 1901; William Dimmit, "An Organized Harvest," *Industrial Pioneer* 1 (Sept. 1921), 3. See also "Stole Money," *Napa Daily Journal*, Oct. 3, 1900, NCLCF; Chaplin, *Wobbly*, 87–90; Howard W. Odum, *Rainbow Round My Shoulder* (Indianapolis, 1928), 226–27; Underwood, interview; Kent L. Steekmesser, "Sontag and Evans: Outlaws or Outraged?" *The Californians* 1 (Jan.–Feb. 1983), 6–13; "University of Iowa Student," doc. no. 58, EBP.

63. "Killed While Asleep," *Oxnard Courier*, Nov. 24, 1904.

64. So extraordinary was the sight of elderly bindlemen that when journalists encountered them in their camps they invariably lingered behind to interview them and listen to their stories. Many were hollow shells. Apparently well, they excused themselves from a bunkhouse dinner or card game, laid down a bindle, and died from no apparent cause. See Johnson, *California*, 59–61; *IW*, June 10, 1909; Coroner's Records, various death entries, VCM; "An Old Timer: The Story of a Migratory Worker," *ISR* (Aug. 1914), 87–88; Thompson, "Housing," 1–3; Parker, "Preliminary," 4, CIRP; "Pioneer Hobo," doc. no. 13; "Anemic Man," doc. no. 14, EBP.

65. Parker, *Casual Laborer*, 75; Anderson, *Hobo*, 125–26; Solenberger, *One-Thousand Homeless Men*, 36; Rogers, *Colusa County*, 138, 145; Speek, "Preliminary," 9; *Napa Daily Journal*, Aug. 12, 1897, NCLCF.

66. Quotes from B. S. Warren, "Preliminary Memorandum Relative to Spread of Disease by Floating Laborers in the United States," 1–3, CIRPP. Exact figures: 54.9 percent in fair to bad physical condition; 21.4 percent unclean in their clothes or body. Some bindlemen were crippled and otherwise marked by an accident incurred riding trains or working seasonal industries. Handicaps ranged from broken bones that never quite mended to horrible, disfiguring scars that made them freaks and kept them on the move. See Parker, "Statistical Tables," in CCIH, *Report on Unemployment*, 47–53; CIRP, *Final Report*, 5: 4233–44. For a particularly moving description of a bindleman with a "melted face," see Hood River Blackie, interview. See also Gunther Peck, "Mobilizing Community: Migrant Workers and the Politics of Labor Mobility in the North American West, 1900–1920," in Eric Arnesen, Julie Greene, Bruce Laurie, eds., *Labor Histories: Class, Politics, and the Working-Class Experience* (Urbana and Chicago, 1998), 175–76.

CHAPTER TWENTY-TWO

1. Quotes from London, "Hoboes," 193. See also G. R., "Tramping the Northwest," 43; George Underwood, interview; Hood River Blackie, interview; Arthur Johnson, *California*, 59–60; Gladys B. Kahl, "The Old Country Tramp," *For the Record* (1967), Merced County Historical Society.

2. Quote from Hood River Blackie, interview, 5. See also CSBLS, *Third Biennial Report, 1885*, 205.

3. Quotes from Swift, *Tramp California*, 3; Thompson, interview. See also Kemp, *Tramping*, 132; "Industrial Union of Harvest Hands," *IW*, July 1, 1909; *Solidarity*, June 16, 1915; J. Kenney, "Migratory Workers," *Solidarity*, June 17, 1925; "Twenty Four," doc. no. 7, EBP. Chinese proverb from John Gardner and Francesca Reese, *Know and Listen* (New York, 1980), 13.

4. Dreams from T-Bone Slim "Tightline," *Industrial Pioneer* 2 (July 1923), 12. For Kearney,

see Vandor, *History of Fresno County*, 1: 218–25; William E. Smythe, "A Benefactor of the State," *Out West* 25 (Aug. 1906), 146–50. For overviews, see Albert Croutch, "Housing Migratory Agricultural Workers in California, 1913–1948" (M.A. thesis, UCB, 1948); WPA, FWP, "History of Living Conditions Among Migratory Laborers in California" (Oakland, 1938), BL. For discussion of the location of a labor camp, see R. B. M. to J. J. Roupe, Dec. 13, 1912, Tapo Citrus Association Records, SVHS.

5. Kearney's name was pronounced "Karney." His first name was Martin. A tall, stately Englishman of somewhat mysterious origins, Kearney was described variously as the son of a Liverpool dockworker and a highborn "remittance man." He did not mix with the men. See Schyler Rehart and William K. Patterson, *M. Theo Kearney, Prince of Fresno* (Fresno, 1988); *FMR*, Mar. 2, 1899; Mar. 28, 1908; *San Francisco Chronicle*, Sept. 29, 1895; Vandor, *History of Fresno*, 1: 218–24; Smith, *Garden of the Sun*, 518–23; Mabelle Selland, "Kearney Landmarks in Kearney Park other than Mansion and Servants Quarters," mimeo (Apr. 1977), FCHS.

6. *FMR*, July 6, 1919; clipping, *Fresno Evening Democrat*, Mar. 7, 1903; Edwin M. Eaton, "The Kearney Estate," *Fresno Home Life* (Jan.–Feb. 1960); M. Theo Kearney, notebooks, 1900–1903, M. Theo Kearney Collection, BL; M. Theo Kearney, *Fresno Vineyard, Situated in Easterby Rancho, Fresno County, California, Incorporated December 17, 1880* (Fresno, 1880), 1–2; Benjamin Bencomo, "M. Theo Kearney," MS (Nov. 17, 1978), author's possession.

7. Quote from E. C. Hamilton to Shay, Mar. 21, 1912, SVSBCR.

8. Arriving in San Francisco in the early 1850s, both Miller and Lux found work as butchers, quickly rose to independent proprietors, and over the next thirty years used legal and extralegal means and state and federal land and water laws to amass an empire three times as big as the state of New Jersey and twice the size of the kingdom of Belgium. See David Igler, *Industrial Cowboys: Miller and Lux and the Transformation of the Far West, 1850–1920* (Berkeley, 2001), 1–18, now the standard work. See also Edward Treadwell, *The Cattle King: A Dramatized Biography* (New York, 1931), 322–26; William D. Lawrence, "Henry Miller and the San Joaquin Valley" (M.A. thesis, UCB, 1933); various clippings, Miller and Lux Collection, Ralph Milliken Museum, Los Banos.

9. Quotes from Miller, "Management of Miller and Lux Ranches," MS (n.d.), Miller and Lux Records, BL. See also Viola Jean Dunn, "Miller and Lux: A Contribution Toward A History," MS (Jan. 1970), 37, CSU, San Jose, Special Collections; Michael Belloumini, "The Great Miller and Lux Empire," MS (Apr. 22, 1968), 26–27, Cecil Tracy, interview, Beale Memorial Library, Bakersfield; William Henry Pinckey, interview by Richard Bailey, Oct. 1951, Kern County Museum. It was often said that Miller and Lux's empire was so large that one could ride on horseback from Canada to Mexico and every night sleep on one of their ranches. Number of bindlemen from Bancroft, *Chronicles of the Builders of the Commonwealth* (San Francisco, 1890), 381.

10. Quote from Henry Miller to P. H. Pat Henry Turner, Dec. 18, 1909, Miller and Lux Records, BL. See also Miller to Turner, May 13, 1909; Nov. 5, 11; Dec. 16, 1910.

11. Belloumini, "Miller and Lux," 28, Julio Fannuchi, interview.

12. For the Great Western Vineyard Company, see John C. McCubbin, "Wahtoke," in Nichel, *Beginnings in the Reedley Area*, 21–22; John C. McCubbin, *The McCubbin Papers: An early history of Reedley and the "76" Country* (Reedley, Calif., 1988), ed. Kenneth Zech, 150 [map], 155–56; various articles in JCMP.

13. Quote from *California Fruit Grower*, Mar. 5, 1912. See also *ICR*, 24: 39; CIR, *Final Report*, 5: 4933–42; CCIH, *Final Report, 1914* (Sacramento, 1914), 18; CCIH, *Annual Report, 1926* (Sacramento, 1927), 17; letter to editor, *Country Gentleman*, Feb. 2, 1918; B. S. Warren, "Sanitation of Labor Camps, Housing and Living Conditions: A Critical Study of the Report on the Wheatland Hop Fields Riot" (Sept. 8, 1914), 1–3, CIRPP. For the views of bindlemen, see "An Old Timer," 87–88.

14. Quotes from typed notes, *Technical World*, n.d., 812–13, in WPA, FWP, "Source Material Gathered on Migratory Labor," BL; CSBLS, *Fifth Biennial Report, 1910*, 12; CIR, *Final Report*, 5: 4937. See also clipping, *California Fruit Grower*, Jan. 17, 1903, FHHC; clipping, *San Francisco Bulletin*, May 27, 1911, Weinstock Scrapbooks, BL.

15. Quote from John S. Hare, undated correspondence [ca. 1904], Rancho Tapo Records, SVHS. Rancho Tapo was a remnant of the original De la Guerra ranch. It extended for twenty-five square miles over the Tapo Valley. The camps were Orchard Ranch; Hill Camp; Home Camp; Hoffmayer Camp; Valley Camp; Upper Camp; Lower Camp; Hare Camp; the

Hare Barn; the Stud Barn; the Big Barn on the Hill Ranch; and the Adobe Ranch Camp. See Charles F. Outland, Index of Ventura County Newspapers, 1871–1915, Simi Valley, VCM.

16. Quote from Adams, *Farm Management: A Textbook for Students, Investigator and Investor* (New York, 1921), 519–21. See also Warren, *Farm Management*, 333; Adams, "Value of Board as Part of Wages," typescript, 17–21; unpaginated draft, Adams, "Farm Management," Adams Papers, BL.

17. Quote from Arthur S. Crites, *Pioneer Days in Kern County* (Bakersfield, 1951), 159. See also *Oakland Tribune*, Aug. 31, 1905; Adams, "Farm Management," 299, 531–35; Adams, *Managing Western Farms*, 15–17; Adams, *Farm Management: A Textbook*, 520–21.

18. Quotes from Gaveel, "Sunny California," 8–9; "Industrial Union of Harvest Hands," *IW*, July 1, 1909. See also J. H. Walsh, "A Field for Organizers," *IUB*, May 23, 1908; Fred Mann, "The Harvest Drive is on Again," *Industrial Pioneer* 2 (July 1925), 3; Report on Special Investigation to George Bell, San Francisco, May 30, 1917, in "Investigation of IWW," Lubin Papers, BL.

19. *Santa Rosa Daily Republican*, Nov. 3, 1880; John Fulkerson Jr., "The Building of Somis," *VCHSQ* 1 (Oct. 1966), 24; Gudde, *California Place Names*, 141; Johnson, *California*, 264–65; Walter Packard, "Land, Water, and Power Development in California, Greece, and Latin America," interview by Alan Temko, 1970, 70, ROHP; "Recital of Hobo and Private Police," doc. no. 59, EBP; Nylander, "California Casual," 33; "Happy Life of a Harvest Hand," *IW*, July 8, 1909; "Simple," ibid., Mar. 18, 1909.

20. Quotes from O. W. Sewell, "Gleanings Along the Road," *IUB*, Oct. 5, 1907; June 24, 1909. See also "On the Spot," *Railroad Magazine* 39 (Feb. 1946), 89–92; Carleton H. Parker, "Preliminary Report," 8.

21. Quote from Hood River Blackie, interview, 61. See also Forbes, "Caste in the Jungle," 869–70, 874; Will Irwin, "Japanese and the Pacific Coast," 18; William W. Aspinwall to John James McCook, June 10, 1893, Social Reform Papers of John James McCook, Antiquarian and Landmarks Society, Inc., of Connecticut.

22. For raids on jungle camps, see "Thieving Tramps," *Napa Daily Journal*, June 10, 1894. NCLCF. Usually the man in charge of food was the "bull cook," who frequently served also as camp mayor. Crimes included lighting a fire that might attract police, "hijacking" (robbing men) as they slept, failing to clean utensils, and not respecting others. For the structure of jungle camps, see Harry Kemp, "The Lure of the Tramp," *Independent* 70 (June 1, 1911), 1270; Charles Grant, "Life in the Jungles," *IW*, Mar. 18, 1909; "Out in the Jungles," Apr. 1, 1909; *Solidarity*, Nov. 28, 1914; Report of J. Vance Thompson, Aug. 18, 1915, in George Bell to Hiram Johnson, Aug. 20, 1915, Ford-Suhr Prison Papers, CSA.

23. Monkkonen, *Walking to Work*, 238; Chaplin, *Wobbly*, 90; Anderson, *Hobo*, 20; Ashleigh, *Rambling Kid*, 183, 191; Greenway, *American Folksongs*, 197; Freeman Hubbard, *Railroad Avenue* (New York, 1945), 308–34, 347, 359, 363; Hood River Blackie, interview, 65.

24. Of a bindleman's slang, the use of the final "g" in "ing" endings to most words was especially tricky. Sentences having two present participles ending in "g" often dropped the second "g." Even their cussin' was original. Interspersed among such slang, bindlemen injected hundreds of vivid and original words. See John Steinbeck to Mavis McIntosh, Feb. 4, 1935, in Elaine Steinbeck and Robert Wallstem, eds., *Steinbeck: A Life in Letters* (New York, 1975), 105; Fred Thompson to author, Mar. 28, 1973, author's possession; Stewart H. Holbrook, "Wobbly Talk," *The American Mercury* 7 (Jan. 1926), 62–64; Willard, *Tramping*, 383; Holbrook, *Railroads*, 397; Chaplin, *Wobbly*, 180; London, *Coast*, 17; "The Revolutionist," *ISR* 9 (Dec. 1908), 429–30.

25. Quote from Josiah Flynt, "Homosexuality Among Tramps," in Havelock Ellis, ed., *Studies in the Psychology of Sex* (1910 [New York, 1936]), 2: 360. For carnal relations with animals, see Crites, *Pioneer Days*, 159–60. See also Frank C. Laubach, *Why There Are Vagrants: A Study Based Upon an Examination of One Hundred Men* (New York, 1916), 13–14. Of one hundred men in New York City's Municipal Lodging House, the author classified twenty-four as "perverts."

26. For homosexuality at this time, see David F. Greenberg, *The Construction of Homosexuality* (Chicago, 1997), 393–416, which gives the prison statistics. See also "Sex and the Single Man," in Allsop, *Hard Travellin'*, 212–25; Thomas Minehan, *Boy and Girl Tramps of America* (New York, 1934).

27. Quotes from "College Man," doc. no. 30; "Chronic Drinker," doc. no. 31; "Cases of Disease," doc. no. 87; "Boy Tramp," doc. no. 110, EBP. See also Tully, *Beggars of Life*, 130–31; Ben Reitman, "Following the Monkey," MS (n.d.), 80–82; Parker, *Casual Laborer*, 73–75; Anderson, *The Hobo*, 144–49; Jim Tully, *Beggars of Life* (New York, 1924); Monkkonen, *Walking to Work*, 14.

28. Quote from John Worby, *The Other Half: The Autobiography of a Tramp* (New York, 1937), 28. See also William Edge, *The Main Stem* (New York, 1927), 119, 125–27; Nels Anderson, "The Juvenile and the Tramp," *Journal of Criminology and Criminal Law* 14 (Aug. 1922), 306. Original folksong from John Greenway, *American Folksongs of Protest* (New York, 1970), 203–4.

29. Quote from arrest record of W. F. Spencer, no. 920, Oct. 18, 1903, Marysville Police Logbook, 1895–1908. See also Anderson, *The Hobo*, 67–68, 102, 134–35; Parker, *Casual Laborer*, 73, 118.

30. Quote from "Skat, You're It, Says the Police Judge," *Marysville Evening Democrat*, Aug. 25, 1909. See also Parker, "Statistical Tables from Life History Schedules Selected at Random Among Casual Laborers in California," in CCIH, *Report on Unemployment*, 57–58; Luther Fry, "Migratory Workers in Our Industries," *World's Work* 40 (Oct. 1920), 600–610.

31. Quote from *Napa Daily Journal*, July 23, 1895, NCLCF. For bindlemen fighting with Italians, see "A Street Fight," Mar. 28, 1901.

32. "Robbery in Yuba City," *Marysville Daily Democrat*, July 22, 1901; Thompson, interview.

33. Forbes, "Caste in the Jungle," 874; A. E. Holt, "Bos," *Survey Graphic* 60 (Aug. 1928), 456–59; Walter Packard, "Land, Water and Power," interview, 70.

34. Nicholas V. Lindsay, "Rules of the Road," *American Magazine* 74 (May 1912), 54–59; "Signs," *School Arts* (1922), 546–47, IWW Collection, AULHWSU; Wormser, *Hoboes*, 44; Holbrook, "Wobbly Talk," 62–4; Latta, "A-Number 1," 5, FFLCSF.

35. Quote from Quizzy, "Life on a Fruit Ranch," *Solano Republican*, Feb. 5, 1892. See also Arthur L. Sueur, "Observations on the Migratory Worker," *Solidarity*, Mar. 6, 1915; Fry, "Migratory Workers," 601–5; 609–10; unidentified newspaper clippings, Stuart Jamieson Field Notes, Jamieson Papers, BL; CSBLS, *Thirteenth Biennial Report, 1907–8*, 119.

36. "Vacation Time Fills the Jail," *Marysville Daily Appeal*, Oct. 3, 1913. The terms "skid" or "skidder" were logging jargon designating a logging truck. When Seattle was a cluster of ramshackle buildings, Henry Yesler had a lumber mill there. Logs were skidded down a skidway from the forested hills to Yesler's mill; the original skidway is now Yesler Way. The area grew up as one of the rowdier sections of town rife with saloons, flop houses, and brothels frequented by loggers, and became known as "skid row" or "skid road." Thanks to Lillian Ashworth for this information. See also Samuel Wallace, *Skid Row as a Way of Life* (Totowa, N.J., 1965), 13, 17; Kenneth T. Jackson, "The Bowery: From Residential Street to Skid Row," in Rick Beard, ed., *On Being Homeless: Historical Perspectives* (New York, 1987), 68–79; Keith A. Lovald, "From Hobohemia to Skid Row: The Changing Community of the Homeless Man" (Ph.D. diss, University of Minnesota, 1960).

37. W. S. Goodrich to Lubin, July 21, 1915, CCIHP; Willard, *Tramping with Tramps*, 107; *Opening Statement of George F. Vanderveer, Council for the Defense, in the Case of USA vs. William D. Haywood et al.* (Chicago, 1919), 15, 46, SHSW; Jesse W. Dees, *Flophouse* (Francestown, N.H., 1948), xxv; Donald Bogue, *Skid Row in American Cities* (Chicago, 1963), 404; Sara Harris, *Skid Row, USA* (New York, 1956); "A Voice from the Jungles," *Solidarity*, June 3, 1911; Chaplin, *Wobbly*, 87–91, 166; CIR, *Final Report*, 5: 4121, 4187, 4933–34; *IW*, July 8, 1909; J. Kennedy, "Migratory Workers," June 17, 1925; Fry, "Migratory Workers," 610; "To the President and Members of the Board of Trustees," Mar. 26, 1915, in J. F. Douglass et al., sample copy, John R. Commons Papers, SHSW.

38. CCIH, *Annual Report, 1919* (Sacramento, 1919), 33; "Cannon Ball Chop Shop," *IW*, Apr. 1, 1909; *Solidarity*, Dec. 5, 1914; George Hegen, "Exploitation," MS (n.d.), 23, Ralph Chaplin Collection, Washington State Historical Society; Holbrook, *Holy Old Mackinaw—A Natural History of the American Lumberjack* (New York, 1939), 194–207; Ashleigh, *Rambling Kid*, 128–30, 191–92; Harry Beardsley, "Along the Main Stem with Red," doc. no. 145, EBP.

39. Quote from *San Francisco Opinion*, in *John Swinton's Paper*, Nov. 4, 1883. For a similar statement see, Ralph Chaplin, "Reminiscences," MS (n.d.), Ralph Chaplin Collection, Washington State Historical Society. San Francisco's flophouse district was one of four distinct areas of San Francisco, the other three being the financial district, Chinatown, and the Barbary Coast. See also Charles Lockwood, "South of the Slot," *San Francisco Examiner and Chronicle* (June 10, 1979), 78; Jules Tygiel, "Housing in Late-Nineteenth-Century American Cities: Suggestions for Research," *Historical Methods* 12 (spring 1979), 93.

40. Quote from Peter A. Speek, "Report on Interviews," Oct. 4, 1914, CIRP. See also *PRP*, Mar. 20, 1897; Margaret Cooper, "Growth of San Francisco" (M.A. thesis, UCB, 1928), 154. The thirty thousand to forty thousand figure is from Parker, *Casual Laborer*, 80. An excellent overview is Alvin Averbach, "San Francisco's South of Market District, 1850–1950: The Emergence of a Skid Row," *CHQ* 52 (fall 1973), 196–223, esp. 204.

41. Flynt, *Tramping*, 299; Nylander, "California Casual," 47; Wallace, *Skid Row*, 70; Alice C. Williard, "Reinstatement of Vagrants through Municipal Lodging Houses," *Proceedings of the National Conference of Social Work* (1903), 408; "Life in Fresno Lodging Houses, 1896," *Fresno Daily Evening Expositor*, July 7, 1896, Fresno County Scrapbook, 1870–99, FCHS; Speek, "Report on Cheap Lodging Houses in the Cities" (July 25, 1915), typescript, 1–8, CIRPP.

42. Quotes from Martin F. Schmidt and Dee Brown, *The Settler's West* (New York, 1974), 62; J. Vance Thompson, "Report of Investigator of Commission of Immigration and Housing of California on Conditions at Marshall Hotel, Now Being Used by the City Authorities for Housing the Unemployed," MS (n.d.), 1–3, CIRPP.

43. Quote from Len DeCaux, *Labor Radical*, 56. See also Grant, *Brownie the Boomer*, 208–9; Len DeCaux, interview, 1985, Oral History Program, ASCUCLA.

44. Nylander, "The California Casual," 47; Solenberger, *One-Thousand Homeless Men*, 314–15; "BMR-Hotel: For Men Only," *IW*, Mar. 25, 1909.

45. Quote from Harry Beardsley, "Along the Main Stem with Red," doc. no. 145, EBP. See also *IW*, Mar. 25, Apr. 1, July 15, 1909; John J. Morris, "The Migratory in the Winter Time," *Solidarity*, Dec. 9, 1925.

46. Edwin A. Brown, *"Broke," the Man without a Dime* (Chicago, 1913); Edward A. Steiner, *From Alien to Citizen: The Story of My Life in America* (New York, 1914), 53–208; Speek, "Report on the Unemployed in San Francisco" (Oct. 4, 1914), CIRPP.

47. Curt Gentry, *Madams of San Francisco: An Irreverent History of the City by the Golden Gate* (New York, 1964), 167, 185–88, 206. Information on the Chinese houses of prostitution comes from the years 1909–12. Information on the Municipal Crib is from 1904.

48. Ibid.

49. William H. Davies, *Autobiography of a Super-Tramp* (New York, 1917); Vachel Lindsay, *Handy Guide for Beggars* (New York, 1916); Tracy McGregor, *Twenty Thousand Men* (Detroit, 1922); Edward T. Devine, "The Shiftless and Floating City Population," *AAAPSS* 10 (Sept. 1897), 149–64.

50. Efforts by San Francisco workingmen at establishing a labor exchange in 1868 described in California Labor Exchange, *Facts About California* (Sacramento, 1868), BL. See also A. A. Hoffmayer to William Leiserson, June 17, 1917, CIRPP.

51. Quotes from Anderson, *Milk and Honey Route* (New York, 1931), 57; Peter A. Speek, "Report on the Psychological Aspects of Floating Laborers [An Analysis of Life Stories]" (June 25, 1915), 104–13; interview no. 3, Jungle, Redfern, South Dakota (July 10, 1914), CIRPP. See also Wallace, *Skid Row*, 60; George Orwell, *Down and Out in Paris and London* (New York, 1933), 126; Dees, *Flophouse*, 47; Nylander, "California Casual," 13; "Transient Dreamer," doc. no. 5; "Boy in Teens," doc. no. 6; Beardsley, "Along the Main Stem," doc. no. 145, EBP.

52. Quote from McWilliams, *Factories in the Field*, 37. See also "Dictation and Biographical Material on the Life of Henry Miller," Miller and Lux Records, BL.

53. Quotes from Paul P. Parker, "Along the Dirty Plate Route," *California Folklore Quarterly* 3 (Jan. 1944), 16; Latta, "The Dirty Plate Route," MS (n.d.), FFLCSF. See also Miller to J. H. Vandiveer, Jan. 9, 1906, Miller and Lux Records, BL.

54. Quote from Joseph Warren Matthews, undated letter [Mar.–Apr. 1899], Joseph Warren Matthews Papers, BL. Because those arriving early gained little and might be required to chop or carry wood, men often hid under a culvert or down in a ditch until suppertime. Straggling along a road, they timed their arrival at the dining hall just as the "flunky" began whanging away at the triangle dinner gong. See "Hospitality of Henry Miller," *Bakersfield Morning Echo*, Dec.14, 1912; CIR, *Report*, 6: 4367; H. A. Van Coenen Torchiana, *California Gringos* (New York, 1930), 54; Paul Miller, "Management of Miller and Lux Ranches in California, Nevada, and Oregon," MS (n.d.), CHS; various clippings, Miller-Lux Land Records and Correspondence, Archives and Special Collections, Main Library, California State University, Fresno.

55. Quotes from Smith, *Garden of the Sun*, 555; Parker, "Along the Dirty Plate Route," 16.

56. Quote from "Nipped a New Coat," *Marysville Daily Appeal*, Dec. 3, 1905. For the "flim flam" incident, see "Worked A Flim Flam," Sept. 20, 1902. For the boot episode, see "Plucky Capture," *Napa Daily Journal*, Jan. 12, 1901. For the Palace Hotel incident, see "Bothersome Tramps," *Napa Register*, Sept. 20, 1889. For thievery, see "Thieving Tramps," *Napa Daily Journal*, June 10, 1894, NCLCF; "Idle Men Told to Leave," *Marysville Daily Democrat*, Sept. 24, 1909; "Vacation Time," Oct. 3, 1913. For the general atmosphere of restlessness, see Ashleigh, *Rambling Kid*, 92.

57. "Tramps, Tramps, Tramps," *Napa County Reporter*, Jan. 24, 1874, NCLCF.

58. For the Chinese restaurant incident, see typed notes on the *Selma Irrigator*, Feb. 16, 1889, FFLCSF. For stealing from Chinese graves, see Tinkham, *San Joaquin County*, 163. For stealing a cripple's blankets, see "Charged with Stealing Cripple's Blankets," *Marysville Daily Appeal*, Dec. 20, 1905.

59. "Forged A Check and is in Jail," *Marysville Daily Appeal*, July 14, 19, 1906.

60. "Begging as a Fine Art," *Nation* 79 (Apr. 12, 1904), 516–17; "Beggars and their Ways," *NYT*, Dec. 3, 1882; "Mendicants in the Metropolis," *Harper's Weekly* 40 (1896), 302.

61. Quotes from *Fresno Weekly Expositor*, Mar. 1, 1882; Foster, *Pages from a Worker's Life*, 133. See also "The Tramp," *Napa Register*, Sept. 20, 1889, NCLCF; *San Francisco Examiner*, cited in *Napa Daily Journal*, Feb. 8, 1894; London, *The Road*, 21; Irving Goffman, *The Presentation of Self in Everyday Life* (New York, 1956), ch. 2; Harvey Zorbaugh, *The Gold Coast and the Slum* (Chicago, 1929), 164. Sometimes bindlemen were unmasked midway through their lies. After entering a Napa house in December 1876, a "rough-looking fellow" brought a woman to tears and obtained some bread and meat by telling her a tale of woe about being without food and shelter. But just after the woman's husband arrived, the bindleman cut off his story and walked off with his food without even answering the husband's question about why he was there. As he left, he was observed throwing the food into the gutter. "We warn our citizens," wrote the *Napa Reporter*. "Give them food if you can afford it, for it would be wrong to turn a hungry man from your door unfed, and there are some good honest men who are compelled by misfortune or otherwise to beg; but give them no money." Quote from "Tramps," *Napa Reporter*, Dec. 23, 1876, NCLCF. See also "Ungrateful Wretches," Nov. 18, 1878; A-Number 1, *The Wife I Won*, 14–16.

62. Quotes from Righter, *Farm Boy to World Traveler*, 13; Mary Pollock Daily, interview, n.d., SVHS.

63. Quote from "Free Labor Bureau," *San Francisco Call*, June 22, 1895.

64. Efforts by the federal government to provide employment information are described in William Leiserson, *Adjusting Immigrant and Industry* (New York, 1924), 31, 35–40, 51; Shelby M. Harrison et al., *Public Employment Offices: Their Purpose, Structure, and Methods* (New York, 1924) 22–26, 550–51; Udo Sautter, *Three Cheers for the Unemployed: Government and Unemployment before the New Deal* (New York, 1991).

65. Quotes from Speek, "Report on my general impressions and observations on the Pacific Coast" (Sept. 25, 1914), CIRP; clipping, *San Francisco Bulletin*, Jan. 24, 1914, Wheatland Hop-Field Riot Scrapbooks, BL. See also *Sacramento Bee*, Mar. 28, Apr. 25, 1889. For Napa, see "Be Ware," *Napa Weekly Register*, Sept. 20, 1889. See also Harvey Osborne to Peter A. Speek, June 27, 1914, CIRP; Simon J. Lubin to R. H. Durst, June 11, 1914, Lubin Papers, BL; Peter A. Speek, "Preliminary Report on the Psychological Aspect of the Problem of Floating Laborers" (June 25, 1915), CIRPP.

66. Quote from Wallace E. Smith, ed., additions by Alvin F. Aggen and others, "Mechanization of Lima Bean Threshing," *VCHSQ* 25 (spring 1980), 5. See also W. J. Duffy, *Sutter Basin and Its People* (Davis, Calif., 1972), 97; "A Pioneer in California Rice Growing," *Pacific Rice Grower* (Mar. 1919); Hood River Blackie, interview, 46–47.

67. The total number of labor agencies in California is estimated in Parker, "Preliminary Report on Tentative Findings and Conclusions in Investigation of Seasonal, Migratory and Unskilled Labor in California" (Sept. 1, 1914), 2; Parker, "A Report on Employment Agencies in California" MS (n.d.), 1–3; Speek, "Employment Offices in the State of California" (Dec. 4, 1914), CIRPP. Along Howard Street in San Francisco, between Third and Fourth streets, there were seven employment agencies, with a dozen others scattered throughout the area, all easily reached by a short walk from the railroad yards south of Bryant Street. Bindlemen hoping to ship out did not visit labor agencies but rather gathered along the piers at the first glimmer of dawn, ten times as many as were needed, submitting to a boss stevedore who would climb up on a podium and pick a crew by pointing and shouting: "You, and you, and you." Growing desperate, some men who had worked as sailors moved into a seaman's boardinghouse. Signing over most of their savings to the house master, they would be housed until they had spent all of their money and turned to "crimps," middlemen between the ships' captains and boardinghouse masters, who charged men five dollars for each job, and loaned money at exorbitant interest rates. No matter how much they hated the system of predawn shape-ups, boardinghouse masters, and crimps, bindlemen seeking work on the docks or in ships had few alternatives. Sometimes they had no choice at all. Loaded with cargo and ready to sail, shippers with short crews turned to "man-

catchers" who, for thirty-five to fifty dollars a head, prowled the dives and saloons, got their victims drunk or slipped them a "mickey," and hauled them off to impatient captains. Many skid-row joints were made to order for man-catchers, and as a rule, the police never interfered with their trade. Quote from Ashleigh, *Rambling Kid*, 18–19. See also Weintraub, "IWW in California," 4–7; Paul S. Taylor, *The Sailors' Union of the Pacific* (New York, 1923), 26. Crimps ran a loan business on the side. For the crimp system, see Hyman Weintraub, *Andrew Furuseth*, 6.

68. For men crowding around job boards, see *IUB*, Jan. 11, 1908. See also Edmund W. Bradwin, *The Bunkhouse Man: A Study in the Camps of Canada, 1903–1914* (New York, 1928), 51. See also J. Nelson Dispatch Sheet to John Sweet and Son, Martinez, Apr. 3, 1907, Rough and Ready Labor Agency; Murray and Ready Labor Agency advertisement, ca. 1907, Pat Jacobsen Collection of Fruit Crate Label Art, Weimar, Calif. Apparently the service was so satisfactory that during an average year employment agencies provided 250,000 different jobs on farms and various industries. Most of those jobs came through a few very large labor agencies. Leading the way was the firm of Murray and Ready, headed by H. R. Ready. Operating for eighteen years in San Francisco, Murray and Ready placed sixty thousand men each year, while the firm of Meyers and Young, also of San Francisco, sent men to jobs not only in California but as far away as Washington and Idaho. Although the 250,000 figure seems large, it is not, and refers to the total number of individual jobs, many of them lasting just a few days. Statistics on jobs provided by labor agencies from Hugh Hanna, *Administration of Labor Laws on the Pacific Coast*, U.S. Department of Labor, Bulletin no. 211 (Washington, D.C., 1917), 17–20. For Murray and Ready, see "Industrial Union of Harvest Hands," *IW*, July 1, 1909; Coolidge, *Chinese Immigration*, 387.

69. Quotes from Ashleigh, "The Floater," 37; J. A. Stromquist, "Industrial Union in Sunny California," *IW*, July 1, 1909; see also July 23, 1910.

70. Quote from CIR, *Final Report*, 5: 4924. See also Wide Awake Agency to Charles L. Leonard, Feb. 12, 1920, French-Glenn Records, BL. For men finding work by following rumors, see Thompson, *The I. W. W.: Its First Fifty Years* (Chicago, 1955), 47. Fees in Fresno from CSBLS, *Fifteenth Biennial Report, 1911–12*, 542. Fifty-one percent of the bindlemen studied by the Commission on Industrial Relations used private employment agencies. See CIR, *Final Report*, 5: 4933. See also typed notes on Charles H. Forster, "Despised and Rejected: Hoboes of the Pacific Coast," *Survey* (Mar. 20, 1915), 671–72. Wages for field hands in Los Angeles in 1906 are from CSBLS, *Twelfth Biennial Report*, 179. So popular were labor agents that when orange and olive picking began in Redlands and Moreno Valley in Southern California during January 1908, hundreds of riotous bindlemen crowded the labor agencies along First and Second streets in Los Angeles hoping to snag some work. Later that year, when tramp author Morrison Swift applied at a reliable employment office in San Jose, the agent told him that a dozen "good, strong, clean, temperate men" had been waiting for the past ten days just to obtain a harvest job. Quote from Swift, *Tramp California*, 1–2. The situation in Los Angeles is described in Reiss and Allen, "Olive Picking in California," *IUB*, Jan. 11, 1908. Fee schedules from Stromquist, "Industrial Union." See also "Imperial Valley Swindle," *Solidarity*, July 22, 1916; United States v. William D. Haywood et al., 10549–54, Aug. 7, 1918, in IWW Collection, AULHWSU.

71. Quotes from *IUB*, Feb. 27, 1909; *Songs of the Workers* (New York, 1956), app. A. For fee splitting, see CIR, *Final Report*, 5: 4939. The joke is in J. C. Cohanan to editor, *IW*, Mar. 18, 1909. See also Mar. 25, June 3, 1909. The joke is repeated in *Solidarity*, June 16, 1915. Abuses are analyzed in Frank B. Sargent, *Statistics of Unemployment and the Work of Employment Offices*, U.S. Dept. of Labor, Bulletin no. 109 (Washington, D.C., Oct. 15, 1912) [1913], 36; "Notes on the Labor Complaints and Claims in Los Angeles" (Oct. 7–8, 1914), CIRPP. For boarding agencies, see William Haber, "The IWW: Their Activities During the War" (M.A. thesis, University of Wisconsin, 1921), 28. See also Haywood to migratory workers, *Solidarity*, Nov. 28, 1914. Sent to nonexistent jobs on distant farms or to farms that had already concluded their harvest, unfortunate bindlemen had little recourse. Stranded without work, they could not afford to return and exact revenge. Nor could they demand a refund. Most simply looked for work on their own initiative. Labor agents, it was often said, always had one crew going to a job, one leaving it, and one on the job.

CHAPTER TWENTY-THREE

1. Quote from "Death of an Unknown Tramp," *Napa Daily Journal*, Aug. 10, 1897, NCLCF.
2. "An Old Timer," 87–88; Fry, "Migratory Workers," 605; California State Board of Hor-

ticulture, *Biennial Report, 1901–2* (Sacramento, 1902), 274; *Oakland Tribune*, Aug. 31, 1905; Speek, "Life Histories of 25 Native and Foreign-Born Unemployed, Floating Laborers," MS (n.d.), CIRPP; CIR, *Final Report*, 5: 4941–42, 4976; Spencer C. Olin Jr., *California's Prodigal Sons: Hiram Johnson and the Progressives, 1911–1917* (Berkeley, 1968), 28, 198; Parker, *Casual Laborer*, 102, 113; Henry T. McGuckin, *Memoirs of a Wobbly* (Chicago, 1987), 89–90.

3. Quote from *Sacramento Bee*, Jan. 27, 1897; also Nov. 17. See also Daniel, *Bitter Harvest*, 258–61, 284–85; Earl C. Crockett, "History of California Labor Legislation, 1910–1930" (Ph.D. diss., UCB, 1931), 1–12; Clara M. Beyer, "History of Labor Legislation in Three States," in U.S. Dept. of Labor, Women's Bureau, *Bulletin of the Women's Bureau No. 66* (Washington, D.C., 1929), 120–29.

4. Quote from clipping, *San Francisco Bulletin*, Feb. 13, 1914, Wheatland Scrapbook, BL. When California extended the eight-hour law to children in 1901, agriculture was again excluded. Beginning during California's territorial days and continuing during the first decade of statehood, California officials had used laws to control Indian field hands and provide growers with a docile labor force. Now, a half-century later, politicians considerably amplified these policies, broadening them beyond one specific ethnic group to cripple not only bindlemen but the entire farmworker class. See California Legislature, *Statutes of California, 1901* (Sacramento, 1901), ch. 109, sections 1–7, CSL; CSBLS, *Tenth Biennial Report*, 32, 39, 149–50. See also Austin P. Morris, "Agricultural Labor and National Labor Legislation," *CLR* 54 (Dec. 1966), 1939–89; Beverly Tangri, "Federal Legislation as an Expression of United States Public Policy toward Agricultural Labor, 1914–1954" (Ph.D. diss., UCB, 1967).

5. William Deverell, *Railroad Crossing: Californians and the Railroad, 1850–1910* (Berkeley, 1994), 149–70; *The Railroad Is an Issue in Politics* (San Francisco, 1898); Curtis E. Grassman, "Prologue to California Reform: The Democratic Impulse, 1886–1898," *PHR* 42 (Nov. 1973), 518–36; W. W. Hutchinson, "Prologue to Reform: The California Anti-Railroad Republicans, 1899–1905," *SCQ* 44 (Sept. 1962), 175–218.

6. Jack W. Bates, "The Southern Pacific Railroad in California Politics" (M.A. thesis, UOP, 1942); Bean, *Boss Ruef's San Francisco*; Walters, "Populism in California, 1889–1900."

7. Ralph Shaffer, "A History of the Socialist Party in California" (M.A. thesis, UCB, 1955), 151–67, 192–209; James Weinstein, *The Decline of American Socialism* (New York 1969), 11–16, 23, 43–44; David A. Shannon, *The Socialist Party of America* (Chicago, 1967), 1, 32, 37, 39, 40, 43.

8. "The Man with the Hoe," *San Francisco Examiner*, Jan. 15, 1899. Frank Norris modeled the character of Presley in *The Octopus* after Markham. See also William Le Stiger, *Edwin Markham* (New York, 1933); Louis Filler, *The Unknown Edwin Markham: His Mystery and Significance* (New York, 1966); Markham, *The Man With the Hoe: Collected Poems* (New York, 1899); Ralph Hancock, *Fabulous Boulevard* (New York, 1949); Robert V. Hine, *California's Utopian Colonies* (New York, 1953); Howard Quint, "Gaylord Wilshire and Socialism's First Congressional Campaign," *PHR* 26 (Nov. 1957), 327–40; Starr, *Inventing the Dream*, 207–81; Miriam deFord, *Uphill All the Way* (Yellow Springs, 1956), 1–17.

9. Gov. George C. Pardee, the former mayor of Oakland whose limited and largely unsuccessful reform proposals between 1902 and 1906 caused Southern Pacific Railroad to oppose his renomination for governor, never gave a thought to bindlemen. Nor did his successor, Gov. James N. Gillett. Busy carrying on the work of business-oriented Republican politicians, Gillett was an especially unsavory character, openly referred to as the "Southern Pacific Railroad's governor." Unpopular even with his own party, Gillett was elected only because William Randolph Hearst's third-party effort, the Independent League, pulled enough votes away from the Democrats to give him the election in 1907. So corrupt and riddled with graft was Gillett's administration that historian Kevin Starr characterized it as setting "new records for influence-peddling and outright bribery." Quote from Kevin Starr, *Inventing the Dream*, 205. See also Edward F. Staniford, "Governor in the Middle" (Ph.D. diss., UCB, 1955); Alice M. Rose, "The Rise of California Insurgency: Origins of the League of Lincoln-Roosevelt Republican Clubs, 1900–1907" (Ph.D. diss., Stanford University, 1942). Even those progressive reformers concerned with a wider agenda who gathered regularly at the Commonwealth Club in San Francisco to discuss issues of the day, hardly gave a thought to bindlemen. See Albert H. Clodius, "The Quest for Good Government in Los Angeles, 1890–1910" (Ph.D. diss., Claremont Graduate School, 1953), 401–2.

10. George E. Mowry, *The California Progressives* (Berkeley, 1951 [1963]), 87, 96–97, 128–34, 143–45; Spencer C. Olin Jr., "Hiram Johnson: The California Years, 1911–1917" (Ph.D. diss.,

Claremont Graduate School, 1964); Miles C. Everett, "Chester Harvey Rowell, Pragmatist and California Progressive" (Ph.D. diss., UCB, 1965). Wasting little time, Johnson called a special election on October 10, 1911. Voters passed all but one of twenty-three measures. So great was the discontent with the status quo that the Socialist candidate, J. Stitt Wilson, received 47,819 votes, effectively taking enough votes away from Johnson's Democratic opponent to ensure Johnson's election. Johnson won with 177,191 votes to Bell's 154,835.

11. Quotes from Walton Bean, *California: An Interpretative History* (New York, 1968), 326. See also Crockett, "The History of California Labor Legislation," 285; also 7, 8, 12, 32, 33, 286–90; John L. Shover, "The Progressives and the Working Class Vote in California," *LH* 10 (fall 1969), 584–602. Early in Johnson's administration, a small group of Progressives began examining the labor requirements of commercial agriculture. Academics looked to Belgium and Germany, which met seasonal labor fluctuations by redistributing employment more evenly throughout the year, delaying public building projects until the slack season, and encouraging private industry to undertake winter projects. Some investigators resurrected calls for restructuring agriculture, in particular reducing farm size and diversifying production. The California State Bureau of Labor Statistics had repeatedly called for "cutting up the large holdings, putting small farms on the market at reasonable figures," and "making an especial endeavor to attract men with families who can raise crops" in order to produce "some radical change in the present system." Lending support to such an approach, investigators with the U.S. Depts. of Agriculture and Labor pointed to the effects of diversification on intensive cultivation. Comparing the labor demands of two farms, researchers found that on one 115-acre cotton farm a grower had little work seven months out of the year, hired one man for two months, and then needed several dozen men to pick his crop over a period of two months. By way of contrast, another grower with 150 acres who planted thirty acres of cotton, forty of corn, twenty-five of oats, twenty-four of wheat, twenty-five of sorghum, and a small truck garden, was able to get through the year with a handful of full-time hired hands. From these and other studies, Progressives understood that farmers who raised six or seven different crops of fruit, vegetables, and grain rather than one large cash crop could either eliminate or drastically reduce migration and create a stable community of permanent workers. But it was one thing for a handful of academics and bureaucrats to recognize the need for change, quite another to propose and enact laws or programs that might help integrate bindlemen and other farmworkers more fully into society. Quotes from CSBLS, *Tenth Report, 1901,* 15; CSBLS, *Twelfth Report, 1906,* 69. See also Don Lescohier, *Labor Market* (New York, 1923), 6, 244, 282, 285, 288, 301; CIR, *Final Report,* 5: 4967; *ICR,* 25: 52; "Labor Market in Sonoma and Mendocino Counties," in "Labor Market in Certain Agricultural Sections and Industries of California," 17, CIRP; George W. Milas, "Hiram Johnson's Campaign for the Governorship of California, 1910" (M.A. thesis, Stanford University, 1949), 1–54.

12. Simon Lubin's Russian immigrant father David established the department store chain. See Simon Julius Lubin (1876–1936), *Addresses in Memoria* (1936); Lubin to Blaustein, Aug. 23, 1912, Lubin Papers, BL. In May 1907, State Labor Commissioner W. V. Stafford opened a free public employment bureau to help the unemployed in San Francisco find work following the 1906 earthquake and fire. Although hundreds of men found employment through the bureau, most found their own jobs. See Christopher Morris Douty, *The Economics of Localized Disasters: The 1906 San Francisco Catastrophe* (New York, 1977), 188–90.

13. Although Lubin initially rejected the idea of placing the word "housing" in the commission title, the committee report overturned his opposition. After placating the California State Federation of Labor by inserting an amendment banning the new commission from inducing or encouraging immigration, the California Commission of Immigration and Housing (CCIH) came into being. The CCIH had little impact until 1913. Only then would the commission assume a different function, launching the first statewide attack on rural squalor. See Mitchell, *Lie of the Land,* 44–45, 51–56; CCIH, *First Annual Report* (Sacramento, 1912), 7; Paul N. Scharrenberg, "Reminiscences," interview by Corinne L. Gilb and Robert E. Burke, 1955, 67, ROHP.

14. Quote from Knight, *Industrial Relations in the San Francisco Bay Area,* 242. See also Norris Hundley Jr., "Katherine Philips Edson and the Fight for California Minimum Wage, 1912–1923," *PHR* 29 (Aug. 1960), 271–73; Alexander Saxton, "San Francisco Labor and the Populist and Progressive Insurgencies," ibid., 34 (Nov. 1965), 421–38; Gerald D. Nash, "The Influence of Labor on State Policy, 1860–1920," *CHSQ* 92 (Sept. 1963), 241–57; Herbert Croly to

Chester A. Rowell, Sept. 10, 1914, Chester Rowell Papers, BL; Franklin Hichborn, *The Story of the Session of the California Legislature of 1910, 1911, and 1913* (San Francisco, 1911–14), 128, 347; Robert G. Cleland, *California in Our Time* (New York, 1947), 89–90. Campaigning in the citrus districts, Johnson reminded growers how he had supported tariff restrictions to keep out cheap foreign lemons, that he had also supported regulation of Southern Pacific's shipping rates. For the rural basis of Progressive support, see Michael Rogin, "Progressivism and the California Electorate," *JAH* 55 (Sept. 1968), 297–314. See also William Deverell and Tom Sitton, eds., *California Progressivism Revisited* (Berkeley, 1994), 1–7, 61–69, 100, 129–30; Mowry, *California Progressives*, 143; Olin, *California's Prodigal Sons*, 58–71.

15. Quote from California Legislature, *Assembly Journal, Mar. 27, 1911* (Sacramento, 1912), 25, 62. For commentaries on the exclusion of farmworkers, see *Labor Clarion*, Feb. 24, 1911; Mar. 3, 17, 24, 1911; Feb. 7, 1913. See also Mowry, *California Progressives*, 144; CSBLS, *Fifteenth Biennial Report, 1910–11*, 62, 72; *San Francisco Chronicle*, Mar. 12, 1913, Weinstock Scrapbooks, BL; G. H. Hecke, "California Farming and the Eight-Hour Day," *PRP*, June 20, 1914, Wheatland Scrapbooks, BL; C. C. Teague to Harry Chase, Apr. 3, 1902; Teague to Captain Daniels, Apr. 5, 1902; Teague to R. C. Allen, Sept. 1, 1902, Teague Papers, BL; "Eight-Hour Day," *Child Labor Bulletin* 2 (Feb. 1914), 40–54. When organized labor attempted to amend the eight-hour law and extend it to canneries, growers again defeated the effort. See also California Legislature, *Assembly Journal, Jan. 25, 1913* (Sacramento, 1913), 245.

16. Quotes from clipping, *Fresno Bee*, Jan. 26, 1914, BWC; Scharrenberg, "Reminiscences" 59–60. For the petition presented by the California State Fruit Growers Association, see California Legislature, *Assembly Journal, January 14, 1913*, 114–15. See also clippings, *San Francisco Chronicle*, Apr. 3, 1913; May 26, 1913; editorial dated Jan. 26, 1914, Wheatland Scrapbooks, BL; George E. Farrand, "The Workman's Compensation Insurance and Safety Act," *California Citrograph*, n.d., George P. Clements Papers, ASCUCLA; Industrial Accident Board of California, *Program for Workman's Compensation Legislation* (Sacramento, 1914), 2; Herbert Croly to Chester Rowell, Sept. 10, 1914, Rowell Papers, BL. For revisions of the law in 1915, 1919, 1921, 1923, 1925, and 1927 that continued the policy, see A. J. Pillsbury, "An Adventure in State Insurance," *American Economic Review* 9 (Dec. 1919), 684–86; U.S. Dept. of Commerce and Labor, Bureau of Labor, *Review of Labor Legislation*, Bulletin no. 97 (Nov. 23, 1917), 904–9; Frank J. Greede, "Changes in Workman's Compensation," *California State Bar Journal* 32 (July 1927), 14–18; "Farmers Covered by Compensation Law," *Monthly Labor Review* 25 (Dec. 1927), 85.

17. Quote from William Baker to Mr. Pardee, Aug. 10, 1914, SVSBCR, SCML. See also Pardee to Baker, Aug. 10, 1914.

18. Daniel, *Bitter Harvest*, 11, 83, advances the "powerless" theme. For the counterculture of transient life, see Ralph Chaplin, *Wobbly*, 90

19. Archie Green, "Labor and Folk History," untranscribed tape-recorded speech, AULHWSU; Hood River Blackie, interview, 32; "Overland's Delight," in Henry H. Knibbs, *Songs of the Outlands: Ballads of the Hoboes and other Verse* (New York, 1914), 26.

20. Quote from Matt Valentine Huhta, a.k.a. T-Bone Slim, *One Big Union Monthly* (Apr. 1920). I deal with songbooks in Chapter 24. See People's Songs, *Hard Hitting Songs for Hard Hit People*, preface by John Steinbeck (New York, 1940); "Monika Songs," in Milburn, *The Hobo's Hornbook*, 25–37.

21. Quote from *IUB*, Apr. 4, 1908. For the origins of the song, see Greenway, *American Folksongs of Protest*; "Birth of a Song Hit," *One Big Union Monthly* (Mar. 1938). See also Carl Sandburg, *The American Songbag* (New York, 1927); Milburn, *Hobo's Hornbook*; Joyce L. Kornbluh, ed., *Rebel Voices: An I. W. W. Anthology* (Ann Arbor, 1968), 71–72. Of other workers, only coal miners developed a similar, thick musical heritage. But unlike coal miners, who sang in meadows, homes, and on Sunday in churches with their families nearby, bindlemen sang in the jungles to themselves or to one another. Just as the mark of coal dust was upon the songs of coal miners, the mark of the open road was stamped on the songs sung by bindlemen. Unlike coal miners, who played fiddles, drums, horns, and washboards, bindlemen outside of the rescue missions seldom played musical instruments. One exception was the harmonica. All that was required to ready a harmonica was to tap it against a thigh to knock out the debris and pocket fuzz. Men played all kinds of sounds on harmonicas—lean, modest, sounds; gentle or biting songs; or harmonic tunes with longing cords—forming different tones by arching or cupping a palm over the instrument, making it wail like a bagpipe, swell like an organ, or shriek like a lonesome train whistle. They could recreate the chugging of a slow freight or the

sound of wheels moving over tracks at sixty miles per hour. Rhythms alone conveyed state of mind. If they lost or broke a harmonica, they could easily buy a new one. See George Underwood, interview; "Harmonica," July 28, 1940; Field Notes 30BZ, Aug. 3, 1940, Todd-Sonkin Field Notes, Folklore Archive, Library of Congress; Harry Beardsley, "Along the Mainstem with Red," doc. no. 145, EBP. See also Bill Querke, "Job Hunting via Box Car," *Hobo News* (Sept. 1921), 12; Woody Guthrie, *Bound for Glory* (Garden City, N.Y., 1943), 32; Chaplin, *Wobbly*, 90; Gibbs M. Smith, *Labor Martyr: Joe Hill* (New York, 1969), 16–42; Greenway, *American Folksongs*, 121; George G. Korson, *Coal Dust on the Fiddle: Songs and Stories of the Bituminous Industry* (Hatboro, Penn., 1965), 17, 20, 285.

22. Quotes from Spence, "Knights," 15; also Stegner, "Depression Pop," 52.

23. Wallace Stegner, "Depression Pop," *Esquire* (Sept. 1975), 52. See also Allsop, *Hard Travellin'*, 166; Nels Anderson, *Men on the Move* (Chicago, 1938), 37; Knibbs, *Songs of the Outlands*, 26, 50–52; *Hobo Ballads* (Cincinnati, n.d.), 8, SHSW.

24. Quote from G. Wallace Lockhart, *On the Trail of Robert Service* (New York, 2000), 22. See also James MacKay, *Vagabond of Verse* (Edinburgh, 1996); Robert Service, *The Spell of the Yukon* (Newark, N.J., 1922), 15.

25. Quote from Hill to *Solidarity*, Nov. 29, 1914. See also Smith, *Joe Hill*, 52–53; Philip S. Foner, *The Case of Joe Hill* (New York, 1965), 9–13, 16–18, 23–24; Wallace Stegner, "Joe Hill: The Wobblies' Troubadour," *New Republic*, Jan. 6, 1948. For the San Pedro docks see ibid., Aug. 15, 1912.

26. Quotes from *Songs of the Workers* (New York, 1956), app. A.

27. Hill's funeral in Chicago attracted thirty thousand mourners. His ashes were divided up and spread on three continents, every state but Utah, and a half dozen different countries. Whether or not Hill was a crook and migrant yegg as Wallace Stegner and John Greenway assert, or a true labor martyr, can not be established. See Elizabeth Gurley Flynn, *Rebel Girl* (New York, 1955), 192; Gunlög Fur, "The Making of a Legend: Joe Hill and the I.W.W.," *Swedish-American Historical Quarterly* 40 (spring 1989), 101–13; Wallace Stegner, "I Dreamed I Saw Joe Hill Last Night," *The Pacific Spectator* (Jan. 1947), 184–87, in Stegner Collection, Hoover Institute, Stanford University; Joe Hill, "The Tramp," in Kornbluh, ed., *Rebel Voices*, 223–24. For Hill himself, see Joe Hill in *IW*, May 25, 1911. For fictional treatments, see Barrie Stavis, *The Man Who Would Not Die* (New York, 1954); Wallace Stegner, *The Preacher and the Slave* (Boston, 1950).

28. Quotes from Chaplin, *Wobbly*, 90. See also Cross, *History of the Labor Movement in California*, 229; Robert H. Bremner, *From the Depths: The Discovery of Poverty in the United States* (New York, 1969), 259.

29. *PRP*, Feb. 28, 1903; Dec. 22, 1906; CSBLS, *Twelfth Biennial Report, 1905–6*, 183–85; *Sacramento Bee*, July 16, 30, 1901; *Sacramento Union*, Sept. 1, 1901; William O. Weyforth, *The Organizability of Labor*, Johns Hopkins University Studies in Historical and Political Science, no. 2 (Baltimore, 1913), 35: 50–51; *Thirty-Sixth CSFGCP*, 12; Morin, *Organizability of Farm Labor*, 58; Herbert Myrick, *The Hop: Its Culture and Cure, Marketing and Manufacture* (New York, 1899), 42, 162.

30. Quotes from Teague, *50 Years a Rancher*, 150. These imperatives were as true for cotton farmers in the Imperial Valley as for avocado growers in San Diego, whose industry was struggling to establish itself at this time. Specializing in an odd, green fruit originally known as the "*ahuacate*" but also commonly known as the "alligator pear," Southern California avocado growers were just beginning to build a lucrative business when they confronted the labor equation. Because it was difficult to see the mature, green-colored fruit amid all of the plant's green leaves and dense foliage, growers hired only the most experienced pickers, usually at high wages. During the first large harvest, crews snipped avocados with a long stem attached, but the stem often fell off before the fruit fully ripened, rendering the fruit worthless. If crews pulled avocados without stems, the tissue around the stems could be damaged and the fruit could bruise or rot. Growers devised all sorts of harvest contraptions in an attempt to find an efficient middle ground. Some crews used little cans with notches on one side that were attached to a long pole; the trick was to place the notch on the stem so that the fruit fell into the can. But this process, besides being slow, damaged too many avocados that were not caught and fell to the ground. Next crews began using clippers attached to long poles. Activating the clipper by means of a sash cord running through guides to the tip of the pole, the picker dropped the clipped fruit into a large funnel that led the avocado into a canvas chute where it

slid into a canvas bag that held up to ten avocados. But this, too, proved tedious, and eventually growers resorted to the standard orange picking technique of snipping the stems close and dropping the fruit into modified Canterbury picking sacks, then dumping them into boxes for transport to a packing plant. The avocados were then packed into single-layer, thirteen-pound boxes and shipped rock hard to ripen in a few days at room temperature. For avocados, see Street, "Marketing California Crops at the Turn of the Century," *SCQ* 61 (winter 1979), 239–53; Cramer, *La Habra*, 144. See also Stoll, *The Fruits of Natural Advantage*, xii.

31. Quotes from CIR, *Final Report*: 5: 4913, 4915. For farm size, characteristics, and comparisons with farms in the midwestern corn and wheat belt, see Oliver E. Baker, "The Agricultural Regions of North America," *Economic Geography* 2 (Oct. 1926), 459–93; (Jan. 1927), 50–86; (July 1927), 309; (Oct. 1927), 447–65; 4 (Jan. 1928), 44–73; (Oct. 1928), 399–433; 5 (Jan. 1929), 36–69; 6 (Apr. 1930), 166–90.

32. One of the myths of agricultural history is that large farms, remnants of the gigantic Mexican land grants, were characteristic of commercial farming, a phenomenon that by concentrating large numbers of workers in one place should have made them easy to organize. In fact, nothing could be further from the truth. Few early twentieth-century farming operations corresponded to the original Mexican land grants. Even when a vineyard or orchard occupied old rancho land, it usually covered only a small portion of the original grant. For farm size, see *Thirteenth Census of the United States*, 6: 134. For the elements influencing labor unions, see Jack Barbash, *The Practice of Unionism* (New York, 1956), 17; Harland Padfield and William Edwin Martin, *Farmers, Workers, and Machines* (Tucson, 1965), 6; Wallace, *Skid Row*, 79; Roger Burach and Patricia Flynn, *Agribusiness in the Americas* (New York, 1980), 151; Thorstein Veblen, "Farm Labor and the I.W.W.," in *Essays in Our Changing Order* (New York, 1934), 330; Helen B. Lamb, "Industrial Relations in the Western Lettuce Industry" (Ph.D. diss., Radcliffe College, 1942). Organizing problems are also discussed in *IUB*, Jan. 4, 1908.

33. "This was really an honorable sign which distinguished those who picked walnuts from those who did not," recalled Simi Valley resident Ross Harrington of her stained hands. Quote from Ross Harrington, interview, n.d., SVHS. "It was with great reluctance," observed the *Orange County Tribune*, "that some of them returned to school, with their nutstained hands, after a week or more of walnut harvesting vacation." Quote from *Orange County Tribune*, Oct. 28, 1908. Around La Habra, bindlemen using twenty-six- to thirty-two-foot-long poles slapped down the ripened walnuts, but within a few years, Mexican families replaced bindlemen. Paid forty cents a sack, they pooled their wages, earning eight to ten dollars a day during the two-month harvest, enough money, it was claimed, to survive the whole year in a Mexican village. See *Orange County Tribune*, Oct. 5, 1908. In Simi Valley, local workers and Mexicans from Los Angeles split the work, with large numbers of school children engaged in the harvest. Since they received more per gunnysack for clean walnuts, many children hulled the walnuts while picking. Green hulls left in the sack took up too much space and resulted in a lower payment. See Virginia Barnes, Lorine Willard, interviews, n.d., SVHS. See also Nietta Eaves, "In Hop-Picking Time," *Cosmopolitan* 16 (Nov. 1893), 27–35; Con Nevin, "The Pleasanton Hop Company," *Pleasanton Times*, Aug. 13, 1910; *PRP*, July 14, 1894; *California Fruit Grower*, Aug. 31, 1895; Annie M. MacLean, *Wage-earning Women* (New York, 1910), 109–11; "Immigrant Labor in California Agriculture Industries," *ICR* 24: 573–600; photographs from the Pleasanton Hop Company, 1898–99, Amador Valley Historical Society. Working in the fields around Santa Barbara, women and children so impressed farmer-turned-writer Horace Vachnell that after returning to England he could not forget their appearance. "The faces of the men and women—ay, and the children—shocked me," he wrote in *The Procession of Life*. "The sun seemed to have sucked from them the good red blood as it sucks the sap from the grass." Quote from Horace A. Vachnell, *The Procession of Life* (New York, 1899), 34.

34. Quotes Chaplin, *Wobbly*, 89; Immigration Commission, *Report*, 24: 6; App and Waller, *Farm Economics*, 194, 655. See also *CSFGCT, 1886*, 201. For delta islands, see Bouldin Island Quadrangle, SE 4/Rio Vista 15' Quadrangle N 380–W12130/7.5, U.S. Dept. of the Interior, Geological Survey, Topographic Map, 1931, 1952, 1968 revisions, Holland Land Company Scrapbooks, UCDSCA. For Teague, see Teague to F. M. Vaill, Apr. 2, 1902, Teague Papers, BL. Drifting from one job to another, bindlemen learned of necessity to form quick friendships of convenience, not to become too attached to anyone, and not to expect to see a workmate after the job was finished. Even on a job in which men worked together for weeks, crew members sleeping in adjoining bunks did not learn one another's names.

35. Quotes from CIR, *Final Report*, 5: 4933; also 4941; John R. Commons to Henry Pauley, Apr. 6, 1915, John R. Commons Papers, SHSW. Several concepts borrowed from *IW*, July 1, 1909. Of all workers in the country, bindlemen seemed to present the greatest obstacles. Even when discontented bindlemen avoided surveillance, mounted an organized challenge, and engaged with the industry's pathological hostility to unions, they found it so difficult to exploit their leverage over perishable crops that government bureaucrats and academics despaired that bindlemen could ever be organized. Turnover made it impossible to maintain permanent unions. See also John Fulkerson Jr., "The Building of Somis," *VCHSQ* 12 (Oct. 1966), 27; "University of Iowa Student," doc. no. 58, EBP; Anderson, *The Hobo*, 20; Chaplin, *Wobbly*, 90. Contemporaries discuss obstacles to organizing farmworkers in London, "The Tramp," *Wilshire's Magazine* 6 (Mar. 1904), 142; *Solidarity*, Jan. 3, 1913; Hoxie, *Trade Unionism in the United States* (New York, 1917), 148. For length of work, see Parker, *Casual Laborer*, 74–76. See also Weyforth, *The Organizability of Labor*, 91,152, 250–52.

36. *ICR*, 24: 33; Harry Schwartz, *Seasonal Farm Labor in the United States* (New York, 1945), 107; Schwartz, "Organizational Problems of Agricultural Labor Unions," *JFE* 23 (May 1941), 456–66; Lamar B. Jones, "Labor and Management in California Agriculture," *LH* 11 (winter 1970), 23–40; C. B. Glasscock, *Lucky Baldwin: The Story of an Unconventional Success* (New York, 1933), 247–48.

37. Quotes from Rogers, *Colusa County*, 235; *Fresno Evening Expositor*, Apr. 28, 1890. Koening's work record is in Miller and Lux Ledger, Apr. 1885–Feb. 1895, 54, FFLCSF. See also Rogers, *Colusa County*, 124. For the issue of violence in the American West, see Richard Maxwell Brown, *No Duty to Retreat: Violence and Values in American History and Society* (Norman, Okla., 1994), 87–127; Clare V. McKanna Jr., *Homicide, Race and Justice in the American West, 1880–1920* (Tucson, 1997), 3, 17.

38. Quote from *Los Angeles Times*, Aug. 3, 1893.

39. Quote from *Santa Ana Standard*, Aug. 27, 1892; also Sept. 10; *Santa Ana Weekly Blade*, Aug. 3, 25, 1892; also Aug. 11, 18. The ranch was owned by Helena Modjeska, the acclaimed Polish actress. For the Modjeska ranch, see Marion Moore Coleman, *Fair Rosalind: The American Career of Helena Modjeska* (Cheshire, Conn., 1969), 841–69. See also Jean Riss, "The Lynching of Francisco Torres," *Journal of Mexican American History* 1 (spring 1971), 90–112, the definitive account. For lynchings, see McWilliams, *Southern California*, 6–61.

40. Quote from *Solidarity*, Feb. 18, 1911. See also *IW*, June 18, Sept. 9, 1910.

41. Quotes from *IW*, Sept. 9, 1910; Hood River Blackie, interview. See also Swift, *Tramp California*, 6; *ICR*, 24: 16; CSBLS, *Thirteenth Biennial Report, 1907–8*, 127–29, 137–38; James Elliot, "Cause of Fresno Indictments," *Defense News Bulletin*, Dec. 15, 1917; Parker, *Casual Laborer*, 74, 76. For labor turnover in the lumber industry, see Vernon H. Jensen, *Labor and Lumber* (New York, 1945), 114. See also Ashleigh, "The Floater," 37.

42. Quotes from editorial, *PRP*, Oct. 1, 1881; *Solidarity*, Nov. 21, 1914; also Jan 16, 1915; Speek, "Report on Interviews" (Oct. 4, 1914), CIRP; Report of the Indian Hill Citrus Union, 1908–9, Pomona Public Library. See also Swift, *Tramp in California*, 6; Peter A. Speek, "The Psychology of the Floating Laborer," *AAAPSS* 69–71 (1917), pt. 1: 73. See also *Sacramento Bee*, Aug. 23, 1893.

43. Quotes from Adams, *Farm Management: A Textbook for Students*, 520–21; Parker, *Casual Laborer*, 74, 76; *PRP*, Aug. 29, 1914. See also CSBLS, *Twelfth Biennial Report, 1905–6*, 72.

44. Quotes from C. C. Teague to F. M. Vaill, Apr. 21, 1902, Teague Papers, BL; "Discussion of the Labor Question," 395–98; Stabler, "The California Fruit-Grower and the Labor Supply," 270; Mr. M. E. Angler, interview, in Sanguinetti, "The Importance of Japanese in the Fruit and Vegetable Industry," interview no. 330, SRRP. See also "Make Them Work," *Napa Weekly Reporter*, Sept. 20, 1889, NCLCF. For their tendency to "leave in the lurch," bindlemen earned a bad reputation as people who "every year go around the circle on the brake beam." Quote from CIR, *Final Report*, 23: 4959; also 4927–28. See also "Cooly Contract Labor," *San Francisco Call*, June 8, 1895.

45. Quotes from CIR, *Final Report*, 5: 4956; Pierce, daily journal, Aug. 2–11, 1900, George W. Pierce Family Papers, UCDSCA [disk copy]; "A Serious Charge," *San Francisco Call*, June 1, 1895. See also Parker, *Casual Laborer*, 71, 78–79.

46. Quote from Frederick C. Mills, record [daily journal], May 24, 1914, in Woirol, *In the Floating Army*, 30–31; Sin Bad to editor, *Solidarity*, Jan. 16, 1915. See also Mills, "The Orange Industry of Central California"; and "A Supplementary Report Concerning Orange Picking

Conditions," CCIH. For transience as strategy, see Patricia Cooper, "The Traveling Fraternity: Union Cigar Makers and Geographic Mobility, 1909–1919," *Journal of Social History* 17 (winter 1983), 127–38; Richard A. Raja, "A Dandy Bunch of Wobblies: Pacific Northwest Loggers and the Industrial Workers of the World, 1900–1930," *Labor History* 37 (spring 1996), 208. See also CIR, *Final Report*, 5: 4925; Lloyd Fisher, *The Harvest Labor Market in California*, 7–9; Harry Schwartz, *Seasonal Farm Labor in the United States* (New York, 1945); Carl C. Taylor, *Trends in the Tenure and Status of Farm Workers in the United States Since 1880* (Washington, D.C., 1948), 25–34; Varden Fuller, interview by author, Occidental, Calif., July 23, 1979, author's possession; *Solidarity*, Jan. 16, 1915; Jack Kenney, "Migratory Workers," June 17, 1925; George Holmes, "IWW and Early TUUL," interview, Stuart Jamieson Notes, Stuart Jamieson Papers, BL.

47. Quotes from Speek, "Report on Interviews with Unemployed Migratory Workers in Public Parks of San Francisco," 2 (Oct. 4, 1914), CIRPP [copy in CIR]. See also *Solidarity*, Mar. 6, 1915.

48. Quote from Jim Seymour to editor, *IW*, May 11, 1913; Tyler Williams, "Special to Solidarity," *Solidarity*, June 3, 1919. See also St. John to editor, Oct. 11, 1913, ibid.; anonymous ditty, IWW Collection, AULHWSU; Harry Beardsley, "Along the Main Stem with Red," doc. no. 145, EBP; Mortimer Downing, "California Agriculture," *Industrial Pioneer* 1 (Aug. 1921), 28; Stegner, "Depression Pop," 154; "The Boe's Lament," in *Hobo Ballads*, 8, People's Song Book Collection, AULHWSU.

49. Quotes from Speek, "Preliminary Report on the Psychological Aspect of the Floating Laborers" (June 25, 1915), 9, CIR; Sidney G. P. Coryn, "The Japanese Problem in California," *AAAPSS* 34 (Sept. 1909), 48; Karl Marx and Friedrich Engels, *The Manifesto of the Communist Party* (New York, 1932), 12–17; *San Francisco Evening Bulletin*, May 19, 1880. See also "Agricultural Proletariat," *Defense News Bulletin*, Jan. 5, 1918; Foster, *Pages*, 106–7; Chaplin, *Wobbly*, 89; *Solidarity*, Aug. 24, 1914; J. Kenny, "Migratory Workers," ibid., June 17, 1925; *PRP*, Mar. 20, 1897; George Underwood, interview; CSBLS, *Sixteenth Report, 1914*, 20–23; 144–45, 153.

50. Quotes from Parker, *Casual Laborer*, 72, 76, 87; CIR, *Final Report*, 5: 4962; also 4933–34; R. L. H., "California Fields," *Solidarity*, Feb. 27, 1915; letter to editor, *ISR* 12 (Feb. 1912), 65. Interview statistics came from a sample of 222 men. One of five men interviewed refused to furnish any information whatsoever. "The laborers can have no love for the country or village in which they work, when the spirit that meets them seems to be that amusement is vice, and the characteristics of the country instead of being freedom and generosity are intolerance and loss of liberty," observed the *California Citrograph*. See "Farm Labor," July 1917. See also Sin Bad to editor, *Solidarity*, Jan. 16, 1915; Tugwell, "Casual," 472; Parker, "Statistical Tables," in *Report on Unemployment*, 47–53; Speek, "A Plan of Investigation of the Life and Labor of Common or Unskilled Laborers" MS (n.d.), CIRPP; Chaplin, *Wobbly*, 89; William D. Haywood, "To Migratory Workers," *Solidarity*, Nov. 28, 1914.

51. Quotes from Melvyn Dubofsky, *We Shall Be All: A History of the Industrial Workers of the World* (New York, 1969), 290; IWW, *Proceedings of the First Convention of the IWW* (Chicago, 1905) 5–6, 299; William D. Haywood, *Bill Haywood's Book: The Autobiography of William D. Haywood* (New York, 1929), 178. See also Selig Perlman, "A Plan of an Investigation of the IWW and the Unskilled and Floating Labor" (Jan. 13, 1914), CIRP; CIR, *Final Report*, 5: 4945; Harvey Duff, *The Silent Defenders: Courts and Capitalism in California: A Brief History of the Struggle . . . and Exposé of the Sacramento Frame-Up and Conviction* (Chicago, 1919), 4, SHSW; Paul F. Brissenden, *The I.W.W.: A Study of American Syndicalism* (New York, 1919), 56–57, 137; Vincent St. John, *The I.W.W.: Its History, Structure, and Methods* (Chicago, 1917), 3; Fred Thompson, interview by author and Robert Halstead, Chicago, Apr. 23, 1973, author's possession [copy in SHSW]; Luke Grant to Samuel Gompers, July 8, 1905, quoted in Foner, *History of the Labor Movement*, 4: 39, 560n.

52. Quotes from Joseph Conlin, *Big Bill Haywood and the Radical Union Movement* (Syracuse, 1969), 91, 118; IWW, *Proceedings of the 1906 IWW Convention* (Chicago, 1906), 5, 7; also 153–57. Present were such disparate personalities as Lucy Parsons, widow of executed anarchist Albert Parsons; Eugene Debs, Socialist candidate for president of the United States; Daniel DeLeon, the sharp-tongued leader of the Socialist Labor Party; Father Thomas Hagerty, the tall, black-bearded Catholic priest who was Haywood's old drinking partner; and seventy-five-year-old Mary Harris "Mother Jones," the white-haired, grandmotherly organizer of Appalachian coal miners. Dominating the conference were members of the Western Federation of

Miners (WFM), badly mauled from bloody confrontations with mine owners at Cripple Creek, Colorado, along with several associated unions, who comprised more than half of all delegates and nine of ten convention votes. Sixty-one delegates represented no group at all. Seventy-two belonged to labor unions but did not attend as official representatives. There was also a large contingent described by delegate George Speed as "would-be craft union leaders, who were ambitious to get back in the game, for possible personal gain or emolument." See also Melvyn Dubofsky, "The *Industrial Union Bulletin*: An Introduction and Appraisal," *LH* 12 (spring 1971), 289; Robert E. Doherty, "Thomas J. Hagerty, the Church, and Socialism," ibid., 3 (winter 1962), 53; Conlin, *Bread and Roses Too: Studies in the Wobblies* (Westport, Conn., 1969); Salvatore Salerno, *Red November, Black November: Culture and Community in the Industrial Workers of the World* (Albany, 1989); Patrick Renshaw, *The Wobblies: The Story of Syndicalism in the United States* (Garden City, N.Y., 1967).

53. Quotes from Melvyn Dubofsky, *"Big Bill" Haywood* (New York, 1987), 38; Algie Simmons, "I.W.W.," *ISR* 6 (Aug. 1905), 65–77. See also Phil Mellinger, "How the IWW Lost Its Western Heartland: Western Labor History Revisited," *WHQ* 27 (fall 1996), 303–9; Philip S. Foner, ed., *The Letters of Joe Hill* (New York, 1963), 27; Peter Carlson, *Roughneck: The Life and Times of Big Bill Haywood* (New York, 1983), 178; "The I.W.W. Preamble," in Brissenden, *The I.W.W.*, 350; Charles A. Madison, *American Labor Leaders* (New York, 1962), 282; David Brundage, *Making of Western Labor Radicalism: Denver's Organized Workers, 1878–1905* (Urbana and Chicago, 1994), 2–3; Ferdinand Marais, "Workers Arise and Seize the Earth," *ISR* 15 (Oct. 1914), 218–19; David Montgomery, "The 'New Unionism' and the Transformation of Workers' Consciousness in America, 1909–1922," *Journal of Social History* 7 (summer 1974), 510.

54. To further its goals, the IWW set initiation fees at one dollar. Dues would be even lower, about twenty-five cents per month, sometimes forgotten or forgiven during organizing drives. Members would be able to freely transfer between jobs and locations. Even immigrants with paid-up union cards in their country of origin would be eligible for immediate membership. Soon the IWW acquired a spate of nicknames. For the universal transfer system, see *IW*, July 8, 1909. See Thompson and Patrick Murfin, *The I.W.W.: Its First Seventy Years, 1905–1975* (Chicago, 1976); Kenneth Allsop, *Hard Travellin'*, 304.

55. Many of the first California Wobblies could be found frequenting such hangouts as the big shack on Market Street known as the St. Helena Vegetarian Café, haunted by IWW member Edward Morgan, a "dreary apostle of pure reason," who liked to harangue people as they arrived for lunch, and the nearby Liberty Bookstore, where the redheaded anarchist single-taxer William Horr and his Marxist buddy William McDevitt promoted the IWW to anyone who would listen. One California Wobbly later recalled arriving in San Francisco by side-door Pullman in 1900 wearing a "three-button cut-away and stiff hat"—the standard outfit for a "gentleman of the road." For Downing, see Mortimer Downing, interview, cited in Weintraub, "IWW," 17n, 281–83. For the St. Helena Vegetarian Café crowd, see Lucy Robbins Lang, *Tomorrow is Beautiful* (New York, 1948), 42–43, 85; *Oakland World*, May 1, 1909. San Francisco radicals included such fringe groups as the "Gruppo Anarchico Volonld," with its library and reading room on Stockton Street, and the Union of Russian Workers, a foreign-language federation affiliated with Russian Marxist revolutionaries. For Finnish, Russian, and Lithuanian miners and loggers from Montana and Colorado, see Weintraub, "IWW," 18–19; 276; St. John, *The I.W.W.*, 1–18; Brissenden, *The I.W.W.*, 191–212; Justus Ebert, *The Trial of a New Society* (Chicago, 1913), 23–61 [for Ettor, see 40]. With four hundred members, the Journeymen Tailor's Protective and Benevolent Union of San Francisco, headed by George Nesbit, was the only California labor organization at the IWW's first convention. See IWW, *Proceedings of the First IWW Convention*, 8. For Ettor, see André Tridon, *The New Unionism* (New York, 1913), 11.

56. Quotes from Frank Walsh, "Impressions of the Witnesses and their Testimony," *Solidarity*, July 31, 1915, Exhibit F, DJ File 150139–46, RG 60, in Lubin to Gregory, Nov. 26, 1915, Lubin Papers, BL; Matilda Robbins, "My Story" MS (n.d.), 61–3, Matilda Robbins Collection, AULHWSU. For Speed, see Joan London, *Jack London and His Times: An Unconventional Biography*, 71–72, 76–77, 80–81, 86, 181–83, 188; Harry Beardsley, "Along Main Stem with Red," doc. no. 145, EBP; Joseph Noel, *Footloose in Arcadia* (New York, 1940), 24; Sharon Smith, "Intellectuals and the Industrial Workers of the World" (M.A. thesis, University of Wisconsin, 1963), 52–53; Weintraub, "IWW," 293; George Speed, "52 Years of Work Seeking One Big Union," *IW*, July 5, 1924.

57. Quotes from CIR, *Final Report*, 5; 4940, 4946–47; *Labor News* Nov. 11, 1905, quoted in

Daniel Cornford, *Workers and Dissent in the Redwood Empire* (Philadelphia, 1987), 149. Williams was described by historian Melvyn Dubofsky as looking "like a soft-grained American version of Lenin and other Bolshevik revolutionaries." Second in importance only to Vincent St. John in shaping the IWW's formative years, Williams had led a peripatetic existence. Born in the slate-quarry town of Monson, Maine, in 1877, he had moved to Nebraska after his father had deserted the family in 1888. Running a small print shop with his half brother, he worked as an apprentice printer, becoming radicalized by the Farmer's Alliance and Populist Party movements. By age twelve, he was reading the works of Karl Marx, Edward Bellamy, and Thomas Huxley. After briefly attending Tabor College in Iowa, he became interested in socialism and began lecturing widely for the Socialist Labor Party. Quote from Dubofsky, *We Shall Be All*, 145. Biographical information on Williams from *Solidarity*, May 28, 1915; Ben Williams, "American Labor in the Jungle: The Saga of One Big Union," MS (n.d.), 25, AULHWSU; 112; Kornbluh, ed., *Rebel Voices*, 51; Mrs. Rose Williams, interview, in Warren R. Van Tine, "Ben Williams: Wobbly Editor" (M.A. thesis, Northern Illinois University, 1967), 7; also 33-34; Williams to editor, *IUB*, Apr. 16, 25, 1908; CIR, *Final Report*, 5: 4945.

58. J. Anthony Lukas, *Big Trouble: A Murder In A Small Western Town Sets Off A Struggle For The Soul of America* (New York, 1997), 232-33, 242, 380, 484, 511-68, 666, 690-92, 748; Dubofsky, *We Shall Be All*, 96-119. Williams became IWW unofficial chairman in 1908, and from 1909 until 1917 served as editor of *Solidarity*, the official publication of the IWW. Haywood was acquitted on July 27, 1907. See Dubofsky, *We Shall Be All*, 120-32. For developments in the Pacific Northwest, see Jensen, *Labor and Lumber*, 119-21. For leadership of the spontaneous Tacoma smelter strike, see J. H. Walsh to *IUB*, May 4, June 8, Aug. 24, 1907. For a successful strike by Portland streetcar drivers, see *IUB*, Apr. 13, 1907. For leadership in an unsuccessful spontaneous strike of mill workers in Portland, see *IUB*, Sept. 14, 1907. Williams became enveloped in IWW internal politics and was elected to the general executive board in 1907. Convinced that factory workers constituted a better base for organization than western bindlemen and other seasonal workers, he urged the IWW to concentrate less on California and more on settled workers in the urban Northeast.

59. Quotes from Stoll, *The Fruits of Natural Advantage*, xiii; "Industrial Union of Harvest Workers," *IW*, July 1, 1909; CIR, *Final Report*, 5: 4940, 4946-47. Although I do not employ the term, this new configuration would eventually be known as "agribusiness." See Street, "Into the Good Land," 425-80, BL; Osgood Hardy, "Agricultural Changes in California, 1860-1900," in American Historical Association, Pacific Coast Branch, *Proceedings* (1929), 216-30; George Robertson, "Statistical Summary of the Production and Resources of California," in California State Board of Agriculture, *Fifty-Eighth Annual Report for 1911* (Sacramento, 1912), 90-91, 145, 159; CSFGCP, *Thirty-Eighth Convention*, 88; Claude B. Hutchison, *California Agriculture*,158. For discussions of mixed locals, see *IUB*, Sept. 14, 1907; Apr. 4, May 9, 1908; J. A. Stromquist, "California Oranges," *Industrial Pioneer* (Mar. 1921), 26; Brissenden, *IWW*, 161-62; Ed White, "The IWW and the American Frontier" (M.A. thesis, Stanford University, 1970), 18-19, 21, 26. Speed believed in adapting to individual circumstances and conditions, and discarding obsolete practices. This ability to mutate and meet challenges head-on led the IWW to reconsider the task of organizing seasonal workers. Unlike the settled, family-oriented, foreign-born toilers in the steel mills, coal mines, and textile mills of the Northeast, loggers, construction hands, wage slaves, shovel stiffs, bindlemen, and migrant farmhands were never in one place long enough to sustain industrywide unions. Experience had demonstrated that it was nearly impossible for organizers to reach widely scattered field hands or escape the watchful eye of growers.

60. Quotes from *Proceedings, Second IWW Convention, 1906* (Chicago, 1906), 309. See also Brissenden, *I.W.W.*, 134-35; Speed, "52 years of Work." For San Pedro, see *IUB*, May 18, 1907. For Italian bakers in San Francisco, see *IUB*, Sept. 14, Oct. 5, 1907. For support in San Francisco for the Goldfield strikers, see *IUB*, Mar. 16, May 11, Dec. 21, 1907. By June, Ettor had organized hundreds of Italian workers into Building Construction Union No. 501, the first IWW industrial local in California. As reconstruction of San Francisco proceeded following the earthquake and fire, new materials and structural methods called for reinforced concrete and steel buildings, providing plenty of work for Olaf Tveitmoe's Cement Worker's Union and members of the Building Trades Council, but little opportunity to unskilled workers affiliated with the IWW. So poor and disorganized were California Wobblies that when the IWW held its second annual convention in Chicago in June, no California local was represented.

CHAPTER TWENTY-FOUR

1. Quote from Fred Thompson, interview by author, Chicago, Aug. 3, 1973, expanding on a previous interview with Joyce Kornbluh, Oct. 16, 1963, author's possession.

2. Quotes from *Los Angeles Common Sense*, Feb. 8,15; also Mar. 14, 21; June 20, 27; July 18, 25; Aug. 8, 1908. See also Grace H. Stimson, *Labor Movement in Los Angeles*, 324; London, *Biography*, 135–36; Joseph Noel, *Footloose in Arcadia* (New York, 1940), 34; "A Notable Triumph of Free Speech in Los Angeles," *Arena* 11 (Oct. 1908), 350–51; *San Francisco Call*, Aug. 16, 17, 30, 1896; *IUB*, Mar. 14, 1908; *Los Angeles Socialist*, July 9, 1904; Mar. 28, 1903. Orators of every stripe had been operating in California ever since the Gold Rush, shouting their message to passersby, transients, labor unions, fellow agitators, students—in fact, to anybody who would listen to them expound on anything from Jesus Christ and German literature to the popular sciences and pork chops. Appearing with a Bible, a human skull, a suitcase full of literature, men screamed, stomped about, writhing and spouting scripture, preaching whatever they chose to promote. See Noel, *Footloose*, 34; Elizabeth Gurley Flynn, *I Speak My Piece: Autobiography of "The Rebel Girl"* (New York, 1955), 164; Justus Ebert, *The IWW in Theory and Practice* (Chicago, n.d.), 47; Ashleigh, "The Floater," 38; McGuckin, "Recollections," 55–56; Miriam deFord, *They Were San Franciscans* (Caldwell, Idaho, 1941), 138.

3. Quotes from Allsop, *Hard Travellin'*, 319; Joe Hill to E. A. Vanderleith, n.d., Frank Walsh Papers, Manuscript Division, NYPL. A variety of approaches was required. Wobblies first had to attract an audience. Often this called for theatrics. One soapboxer, known as Lone Wolf and described by West Coast bindleman Henry McGuckin as "a very ugly person," with a bullet-shaped head, a long neck, a big nose and mouth, and large eyes "that stood so far out you would wonder why they didn't fall out completely," would drop to his knees whenever a policeman appeared and launch into a lecture on the police so vitriolic that it drove them away or resulted in his arrest. Once a crowd had formed, a speaker had to be heard. Some of the best soapboxers achieved their prominence in part because they possessed the great, booming voices necessary for reaching large, outdoor audiences. "Through sheer effort of projecting your voice into outdoor space, over the noises of the street and without the aid of mechanical amplification, you imported a physical force to the qualities of passion and conviction," recalled professional revolutionary Al Richmond of his soapboxing days. "You had to speak from your guts . . . to launch the words on a trajectory that reached to the periphery of the crowd and beyond." Holding an audience was the third element in successful soapboxing. To keep the soapbox for half an hour, Wobblies did not make half-hour speeches, but rather ten three-minute talks. Masters of "lecturing on the run," they captured an audience by projecting a powerful sense of authority and a command of their subject. Quotes from McGuckin, "Recollections," 59–60; Al Richmond, *A Long View From the Left*, 89–90. Ralph Chaplin claimed that good IWW leaders "could always attract a larger crowd to our educational meetings than any professor in town." Quote from Chaplin, *Wobbly*, 181. Adept Wobblies like Fred Thompson could contend with Sky Pilots and attract crowds with speeches on everything from Victor Hugo and Herbert Spencer to Marx to Carlyle. "I just moved around, soapboxing and organizing, living on next to nothing, a can of beans and a loaf of bread," Thompson recalled many years later. See Thompson, interview. Ballad singers and "patters" with their street-corner parodies and radical, antipapal satirical monologues were early antecedents to soapboxers. See E. P. Thompson, *Making of the English Working Class*, 712. See also Barrie Stavis, *The Preacher and the Slave* (Boston, 1950), 11–12; Ashleigh, *Rambling Kid*, 95, 184; Anderson, *Hobo*, 216, 220; W. Z. Foster, *Pages from a Worker's Life* (New York, 1939), 269–70; Lucy Robbins Lang, *Tomorrow Is Beautiful* (New York, 1948), 85–86; Emma Goldman, *Living My Life* (New York, 1931), 1: 446–47; David Saposs, *Left Wing Unionism: A Study of Radical Policies and Tactics* (New York, 1926), 158; William McEven, "A Survey of the Mexicans in Los Angeles" (M.A. thesis, USC, 1914), 69–70; J. C. Cohanan to editor, *IW*, Mar. 18, 1909; "Labor Exchange," July 1, 1909; Feb. 5, Apr. 30, 1910; Sept. 4, 1913; *IUB*, July 25, 1908; *Solidarity*, Dec. 3, 1910; Jan. 20, Apr. 27, 1912; *San Francisco Chronicle*, July 26, Aug. 16, 1911; Warren K. Billings, interview by Corinne Gilb, 1959 , 156, ROHP; "Soapboxer, Scientific Bent," doc. Z; "Single Tax Advocate," doc. no. 24; "Co-Operative Movements," doc. no. 61; "Charts," doc. no. 21; "Soap-Boxer," doc. no. 12; "Borrowed," doc. no. 60; "Notes on Talks by the Soapbox," doc. no. 26, EBP; clipping, *San Francisco Labor Clarion*, Sept. 2, 1910, Ira B. Cross Papers, BL; Grant S. Youmans in William D. Haywood, Letters Relating to Free Speech Fights, CIRP.

4. According to Brissenden, "IWW," 9, CIRPP, Los Angeles mixed Local 12 had two

hundred members at this time. See also William Trautmann's report in *IUB*, Oct. 7, 1907; Feb. 1, 1908.

5. Quotes from *IUB*, Jan. 4, 1908.

6. Quotes from CCIH, *Report on Unemployment to his Excellency Governor Hiram W. Johnson* (Sacramento, 1914), 9; CSBLS, *Seventeenth Biennial Report, 1914*, 9–10, 33–39. The California Bureau of Labor Statistics found that fifty-two of eighty-one licensed employment agencies were "of doubtful honesty." See also "Employment Agency Man Held for Fraud," *San Francisco Examiner*, May 13, 1921; Speek, "Notes on Investigation," Aug. 10–13, 1914, CIRP. There were 247 licensed employment agencies in California in 1913.

7. *PRP*, Jan. 18, 1908; *IUB*, Mar. 16, 1907; J. H. Walsh to G. E. B., Mar. 9, 1907; Jan. 4, 1908; "To Agricultural Workers," May 30, 1908; *IW*, Mar. 18, Apr. 1, June 3, 1909; "Notes," Section 50, FWP Source Material on Agriculture, 50, BL; Hyman Weintraub, "The IWW in California: 1905–1931" (M.A. thesis, UCLA, 1947), 64; Chaplin, *Wobbly*, 149–50; Joseph Conlin, *Bread and Roses Too: Studies of the Wobblies* (Westport, Conn., 1969), 74.

8. J. C. McKeigan, "Statement from Local 419," *IUB*, Feb. 20, 1909; *IW*, Apr. 8, 1909; E. F. Lefferts to editor, May 1, 20, 1909; H. S. Corral, "Sunny California, Land of Slaves," June 10, 24, July 8, 1909. Located on the west side of Pine Street, near some chicken yards and pigpens just north of the railroad yards, Local 437 had twenty-six members who congregated in an adobe house measuring about sixty feet long by twenty-five feet wide. With a dirt floor, arrow-weed thatched roof, two windows, stove, dishes, several tables, and about a dozen cots, Local 437 could house up to nine men, most of whom had usually just left a train from Arizona and needed a place to flop. Providing board for three dollars a week, the adobe hall afforded considerable savings over the going rate of $7.50 in town. A favorite pastime for Local 437 members, according to one local resident, was to cut out one side of a five-gallon tin, fill it with water, place dimes and nickels on the bottom, wet the ground, and connect it with an electric wire. Curious children seeking to pluck out coins would be shocked. See statement of Mobley Meadows, n.d., Herb Hughes Scrapbook, ICHS.

9. Quote from *Imperial Valley Press*, June 13, 1908. See also *IUB*, Jan. 4, 1908. Water Works story from *IW*, Feb. 12, 1910, cited in Weintraub, "IWW in California," 23.

10. Quotes from testimony of George Speed, CIR, *Final Report*, 5: 4941, 4947–48; *Proceedings of the Third IWW Convention, 1907* (Chicago, 1907), report no. 7: 9.

11. *IW*, May 20, Apr. 22, 1909. For racial prejudice in the Sailors' Union, see Philip S. Foner and Daniel Rosenberg, *Racism, Dissent, and Asian Americans* (Westport, Conn., 1993), 109–10. W. F. Townsend, a Wobbly who later turned state's evidence during the criminal syndicalism trials of World War I, claimed that more than one thousand Japanese carried IWW membership cards at this time. For this inflated estimate, see *San Francisco Examiner*, May 13, 1923. See also *IW*, Apr. 22, 1909; May 18, 1911; Jat Fox, "The Jap Question Not Yet Solved," *The Syndicalist* (June 1, 1913), 1; Albert Grundstrom, interview, in Weintraub, "IWW in California," 297. For an example of one local of Chinese lumber workers in Vancouver, B.C., consult "Testimonial meeting on the Oriental, the IWW Hall," Mar. 4, 1924, B5, Folder 16, SRRP.

12. Japanese field hands, particularly those affiliated with socialist and anarchist groups, seem to have been receptive enough for *Industrial Union Bulletin* to report: "Japanese workmen already hold cards in the IWW, and more are coming." Quotes from *IUB*, Apr. 11, 1908; May 20, 1909.

13. "These serve as meeting places for the union, as a 'jungle' to eat in, away from the bulls, and in a pinch, as shelter at night," reported *Industrial Worker*. "Those members who work in the town or the neighborhood hold the charter the year-round and on the arrival of strangers at harvest or crop time it is only necessary for them to transfer and be in good standing." Quotes from *IW*, July 8, 1909; also Apr. 22. Opening in December at the start of the orange picking season and closing in June, Local 419 recruited mostly bindlemen and, wherever possible, Mexicans. On July 8, 1909, *IW* reported: "The industrial unions in California are sending out voluntary organizers into the farming country with good results, unions should be started in farming communities where there are enough people who have steady jobs to warrant it." See also "Industrial Union of Harvest Workers," *IW*, July 1, 1909; Nov. 14, 1912; Weintraub, "IWW in California," 22; Paul N. Scharrenberg, "Minority Report," Paul N. Scharrenberg Papers, BL.

14. Quotes from *Organized Labor*, Jan. 20, 1906; May 13, 1905. All three shared many characteristics—the same quick wit and rugged appearance, Furuseth somewhat sterner and lean-faced, deeply furrowed, with penetrating eyes, a high-pitched voice, and a beak nose "like the

prow of a Viking ship," making him resemble Scrooge in *A Christmas Carol*; Tveitmoe a muscular, six-foot-tall, "somewhat menacing" figure once described by the *San Francisco Chronicle* as "the stormy petrel of labor circles"; and Scharrenberg, chisel-featured, and politically connected. Jack London used Furuseth as a character in his novel *The Sea Wolf*. Tveitmoe would later be arrested, tried, and convicted of illegal transportation of dynamite and served two months in San Quentin (1912–13) before his case was dropped for lack of evidence. These fears, however, did not lead them to break with the long tradition of virulent racism then prevalent among union leaders who maintained two seemingly contradictory impulses—that of inclusiveness and a faith in class solidarity, and an exclusiveness and deeply felt fear and hatred that branded Asian workers as threats to white working-class life. Tveitmoe, who served as the first president of the Asiatic Exclusion League, told delegates to the 1906 meeting of the California State Federation of Labor "that this nation cannot exist one-third yellow, one-third black, one-third Caucasian . . . any more than it could exist half free and half slave." Determined to maintain the labor movement as a Caucasian preserve and bulwark against the incursions of inferior people who could live, as Patrick McCarthy once said, "on the smell of an oily rag," these men had no intention of organizing Japanese, Chinese, or Indian Sikh field hands. When they spoke of a farmworker union, they meant a union of "white" farmworkers, of bindlemen. Quotes from Louis Adamic, *Dynamite: The Story of Class Violence in America* (New York, 1931 [1963]), 206–9; also 202, 217; *San Francisco Chronicle*, Mar. 10, 1923; Paul S. Taylor, *The Sailors' Union of the Pacific* (New York, 1923), 175. For Tveitmoe, see Richard H. Frost, *The Mooney Case* (Stanford, 1968), 39, 55; Irving Stone, *Clarence Darrow for the Defense: A Biography* (New York, 1941), 269; Franklin Hichborn, *Story of the Session of the California Legislature of 1911* (San Francisco, 1911), 344; Samuel Gompers, *Seventy Years of Life and Labor: An Autobiography* (New York, 1925), 1: 166; 2: 60, 154; Grace Stimson, *The Rise of the Labor Movement in Los Angeles* (Berkeley, 1955), 334, 341, 354, 388; Lang, *Tomorrow Is Beautiful*, 42, 45–46, 61, 150; Helen Valeska Bary, "Labor Administration and Social Security: A Woman's Life," interview, 1974, 26–35, ROHP; Ira B. Cross Papers, Carton 3, Folder 91, BL. For Furuseth, see *A Symposium on Andrew Furuseth* (New Bedford, Mass., 1949); London, "Tramp," 71–72; Knut Gjerst, *Norwegian Sailors in American Waters* (Northfield, Minn., 1933) 172; Weintraub, *Andrew Furuseth: Emancipator of the Seamen* (Berkeley, 1959), 1–3, 10, 27, 46, 48, 50–51, 84, 218n; Arnold Berwick, *The Abraham Lincoln of the Sea: The Life of Andrew Furuseth* (Santa Cruz, 1993). For the Sailors' Union of the Pacific, see J. Bruce Nelson, "Maritime Unionism and Working-Class Consciousness in the 1930s" (Ph.D. diss., UCB, 1982), 91–127. See also Robert V. Ohlson, "The History of the San Francisco Labor Council, 1892–1939" (M.A. thesis, UCB, 1941), 66–67, 194–95. The leadership of the AFL was also reluctant to antagonize American farmers, with whom it hoped to align, particularly in its campaign promoting the union label. For the question of organizing farmworkers, see Lewis Lorwin, *The American Federation of Labor: History, Politics, and Prospects* (Washington, D.C., 1933), 67, 110–11; *American Federationist*, 15 (July 1908), 546; Robert E. Knight, *Industrial Relations in the San Francisco Bay Area, 1900–1918* (Berkeley, 1960), 275; David Selvin, *Sky Full of Storm: A Brief History of California Labor* (San Francisco, 1975), 23–25; Cross, *History of the Labor Movement*, 229; Austin Lewis, "A Drift in California," *ISR* 11 (Nov. 1911), 272–74.

15. Quote from CSFL, *Proceedings of the Eleventh Annual Convention* (San Francisco, 1910), 52. See also AFL, *Twenty-ninth Convention Proceedings* (Toronto, 1909), 229–31; AFL, *Thirtieth Convention Proceedings* (St. Louis, 1910), 178, 181, 186, 215, 243–44; AFL, *Thirty-First Convention Proceedings* (Atlanta, 1911), 69–71; AFL, *Thirty-Second Convention, 1912* (Seattle, 1913), 88–89, 196, 346–47, 377; CSFL, *Proceedings of the Twelfth Annual Convention* (San Francisco, 1911), 67. See also CSFL, *Proceedings of the Tenth Annual Convention* (San Francisco, 1909), 45–47; "Migratory Workers," *Survey* 27 (Dec. 16, 1911), 1381; Gompers, *Labor and the Employers* (New York, 1920), 42, 145, 162; *American Federationist*, 15 (July 1908), 546; *Labor Clarion*, Sept. 3, Oct. 1, Dec. 24, 1909; CSFL, "Minutes of the Executive Council," Oct. 8, 1909; "Unions Pledged to Assist Organizing of Migratory Labor," Oct. 1909; Paul N. Scharrenberg to Andrew J. Gallagher, May 4, 1910, San Francisco Labor Council Records, BL.

16. Quotes from John R. Boyd to *IW*, Dec.1, 1910 [Bob Halstead notes]; Bob Halstead notes from *Solidarity*, Aug. 13, 1910. See also Dubofsky, *We Shall Be All*, 293; P[aul] F. Brissenden, "A Report on the IWW in California" (Aug. 1914), 9, Folder, Labor Unions, General, CIRPP.

17. Quotes from Chaplin, *Wobbly*, 173; J. C. Cohanan, to *IW*, Mar. 18, 1909; J. S. Biscay, "Job Organization," *Solidarity*, Jan. 10, 1913. See also J. H. Walsh to *IUB*, May 18, 1907; Bris-

senden, *The IWW*, n.d., 307, 313–14; Frank Bohn, "Is the IWW to Renew?" *ISR*, 11 (July 1911), 44; Parker, *The Casual Laborer*, 115; Kornbluh, *Rebel Voices*, 69; Dubofsky, *We Shall Be All*, 293. Entering a hall in the evening, bindlemen usually encountered several men crowded around a small stove. There might be a mulligan stew simmering in a pot, the odor filling the room. As one group tended the stew, another might be arguing some philosophical point while a musically inclined bindleman played the piano. All around, tired, shabbily dressed men just off the trains would be sitting in a crowded outer room, eyeing passersby. Others would be stretched out in a back room, having parked their bindles or unrolled them to sleep on the floor. Still others would be settled into the most comfortable chairs, their feet propped up on a pot-bellied stove, whiling away the hours discussing national affairs or their last barroom encounter with a choice circle of friends. Without permanent addresses, such men often bought money orders and mailed them to the next IWW hall for safekeeping rather than packing cash with them as a precaution against the robbers and professional gamblers who infested the jungles. Men also often left their bindles and other property in a baggage room, and used the washroom—with tubs, washboards, a clothesline, and other utensils—to "boil out" and dry various garments of a "hobo's wardrobe." There was always a card table in full operation. Saturday night "smokers"— including boxing matches and other amusements—were also common. On such occasions, IWW halls would be so crowded that police officers had difficulty getting everyone out before the 1 A.M. curfew. Traditionally these smokers would feature a quartet singing labor songs. But IWW halls also held regular Sunday open forums, Tuesday evening "educational meetings," and Thursday evening lectures by prominent radicals on such topics as "Direct Action" and "Improved Machinery and Unemployed." Most were free, although lectures by prominent radical feminist Elizabeth Gurley Flynn cost ten or fifteen cents. These were always well attended. See Richard Brazier, "The Story of the IWW's 'Little Red Songbook,'" *LH* 19 (winter 1968), 93–95; Chaplin, *Wobbly*, 134, 138, 173–75; *IW*, Mar. 18, 1909; June 30, 1917 [photographs]; Weintraub, "IWW in California," 12–14; J. S. Biscay, "Job Organization in the West," *Solidarity*, Jan. 10, 1913; Sin Bad to ibid., June 16, 1915; Parker, *The Casual Laborer*, 106, 115–16; Conlin, *Bread and Roses*, 79; Ashleigh, *Rambling Kid*, 121–22; Thompson, *IWW*, 45–48; Robert L. Tyler, "Rebels of the Woods: A Study of the I.W.W. in the Pacific Northwest" (Ph.D. diss., University of Oregon, 1953), 31, 19–20, 26; Donald M. Barnes, "The Ideology of the Industrial Workers of the World, 1905–1921" (Ph.D. diss., Washington State University, 1962), 78; Brissenden, *The I.W.W.*, 161–62; Foner, *History of the Labor Movement*, 4: 149.

18. Quotes from *IW*, Apr. 1, 1909; Parker, *The Casual Laborer*, 115–16. See also *IW*, Apr. 29, 1909; Mar. 12, 1910; Sept. 13, 1919; Manuel Gamio, *Mexican Immigration to the United States: A Study of Human Migration and Adjustment* (New York, 1929 [1971]), 129; Lescohier, "IWW in Westlands," *IW*, Aug. 12, 1916; Flynn, *I Speak My Piece*, 183; Smith, *Hill*, 9. The IWW libraries were based on an idea that traced back to 1898, when labor leader Frank Roney had recognized the value of providing a reading room for "thinking workers" in Vallejo. See Cross, *Frank Roney*, 551.

19. Black headlines in almost every issue warned of some "frame up." Prose was peppered with the slang of the road. Humorous, witty, catchy poems filled every issue with fallen heroes and the spirit of brotherhood and social justice. Lively visual material conveyed messages succinctly. Well-drawn cartoons, as good as any appearing in the comic pages of big dailies, glorified and mocked workers, reinforced stereotypes, depicted snakelike employers, and framed issues vividly, presenting them in simple terms rather than sophisticated rhetoric. Too dumb to see his exploitation, despite his regular disillusionment and poverty, "Mr. Block," the square-headed cartoon character drawn by Minneapolis illustrator Ernest Riebe, was the most famous of all Wobbly characters. "His head is made of lumber and solid as a rock," wrote Riebe. "He is a common worker and his name is Mr. Block." Quote from *Songs of Workers: To Fan the Flames of Discontent* (Chicago, 1973), 36. See also *IW*, Mar. 18; Apr. 1, 1909; July 23, Oct.1, 1910; Feb. 2, 1911; Apr. 24, 1913; Chaplin, *Wobbly*, 195–96; Thomas H. McEnroe, "The Industrial Workers of the World: Theories, Organizational Problems, and Appeals, as revealed in the Industrial Worker" (Ph.D. diss., University of Minnesota, 1960), 62–63; "Vincent," *Solidarity*, Oct. 1, 1913; Nov. 28, 1914, announcing a twenty-four-page booklet of Mr. Block cartoons available for fifteen cents; Clarence Schettler, *Public Opinion in America* (New York, 1960), 192–210. See especially Franklin Rosemont, "A Short Treatise on Wobbly Cartoons," in Kornbluh, *Rebel Voices*, 425–43; Rosemont, "Introduction," in Ernest Riebe, *Mr. Block* (Chicago, 1984); Douglas Haller, "IWW Cartoonist Ernest Riebe" (M.A. thesis, Wayne State University, 1982). Columns such as

"News from the Jobs" reported on wages, working conditions, and hours, by issuing specific warnings such as "Rotten Job" and "Lousy Grub." One typical report warned, "The Dutch Kid's Camp is No. 4 Garbage rotten at $1.50 per. This is a gypo layout. All the slaves have humps on their backs from hurry. I got canned for selling some Wob papers." Quotes from Jim Seymour, "The Dishwasher," *IW*, May 11, 1913; Nov. 28, 1914; Stewart Holbrook, "The Last of the Wobblies," *American Mercury* 42 (Apr. 1946), 65. See also *IW*, Mar. 18, Apr. 1, July 1, 1909; July 23, Oct.1, 1910; Feb. 2, 1911; Dec. 14, 1912; Apr. 24, 1913; T-Bone Slim, "Mysteries," July 23, 1921; Oct. 1, 1913; "Weakness of the Western Wobbly," *Solidarity*, Jan. 16, 1915 [Cynicism]; Dec. 14, 1911 [Gorky]; Trautmann, "The Structure of Industrial Unionism," *IUB*, Jan. 1908; Austin Lewis, "Drift in California," 12.

20. Quote from "The Value of Music in IWW Meetings," *IUB*, May 16, 1908. Further demonstrating the value of song, Walsh one month later led a group of nineteen singing Wobblies east by boxcar to the IWW convention in Chicago. Known as the "overalls brigade" because they all dressed in black overalls and jumpers, black shirts, and red ties, Walsh's gang fed themselves and raised funds on their "side door journey" by selling literature and holding propaganda meetings, literally singing their way across Montana. Arriving in Chicago two weeks later, Walsh acknowledged that his singing might not have been as "scientifically revolutionary as some would like, but it certainly has its psychological effect upon the poor wage slave that . . . has starvation army dope poured into the ears about five times a week." See also J. H. Walsh, "Developments in Spokane, *IUB*, Apr. 4, 1908; *IUB*, Oct. 24, 1908; Foster, *Pages*, 109.

21. All of its songs were tough, humorous, and skeptical. Many, like "Hallejulah I'm a Bum," "Where Is My Wandering Boy Tonight," and "Gila Monster Route," dealt with migration, riding trains, and jungle camps. Others, like "Long-Haired Preacher," ridiculed Salvation Army preachers in four easily recalled stanzas:

> I don't care if it rains or freezes,
> I'll be safe in the arms of Jesus.
> I can lose my shirt and britches,
> He'll still have us sons-of-bitches.

Third IWW Songbook; *Songs of Workers: To Fan the Flames of Discontent* (Chicago, 1973); Joe Hill to *Solidarity*, Feb. 13, 1911; Nov. 28, 29, 1914; Preston, "Shall This Be All?" *LH* 10 (summer 1971), 441; Brazier, "Little Red Songbook," 99; *IW*, Apr. 8, 1909; Mar. 6, 1913; *San Francisco Bulletin*, Jan. 3, 1914, Wheatland Scrapbooks, BL; Parker, "Preliminary Report on the IWW," 3, CIRPP; Cornelia Parker, *An American Idyl: The Life of Carleton H. Parker* (Boston, 1919), 78; Harvey O'Conner in Staughton Lynd, ed., "Personal Histories of the Early CIO," *Radical America* 5 (May–June 1971), reprinted as *Personal Histories of the Early CIO* (Cambridge, Mass., 1971), 4; Donald E. Winters Jr., *The Soul of the Wobblies: The IWW, Religion, and American Culture in the Progressive Era, 1905–1917* (Westport, Conn., 1985), 37; Ashleigh, "Floater," 37; Foner, ed., *Letters of Joe Hill* (New York, 1965), 10–17.

22. Quote from *IW*, Aug. 13, 1910. See also B. F. Weber, "In Defense of Mexicans," *IUB*, Jan. 8, Feb. 15, 1908.

23. *IW*, June 16, 1910; J. Vance Thompson to Bell, June 18, 1917, "IWW Investigation: IWW 1912," Simon J. Lubin Correspondence, BL; David A. Carter, "The Industrial Workers of the World and the Rhetoric of Song," *Quarterly Journal of Speech* 66 (fall 1980), 365; Archie Green, "John Newhouse: Wobbly Folklorist," *Journal of American Folklore* 73 (July–Sept., 1960), 189; Conlin, *Bread and Roses Too*, 67; Chaplin, "Why I Wrote 'Solidarity Forever,'" *American West* 5 (Jan. 1968), 19–27, 73; Smith, *Hill*, 3, 17–18, 41; Thompson, *IWW: First 50 Years*, 38–39; Kornbluh, *Rebel Voices*, 65. "The AFL," wrote *Industrial Worker*, "with its over two million members has no songs, no great poetry, and no prose. The IWW has a vast wealth of both, rising out of the toil and anguish of the disinherited." Quote from *IW*, May 27, 1916. Andrew Rolle, *A History of California* (New York, 1969), 519, puts membership at one thousand in twelve locals but provides no documentation. Weintraub, "IWW in California," 23; also 17–19, 117, 281–83, puts the 1910 membership at eleven locals in eight cities. *IW*, Apr. 13, 14, 1910, lists eight locals. See also Feb. 12; Mar. 12; July 9, 16, 25; Aug. 6, 1910. Knight, *Industrial Relations in the San Francisco Bay Area*, 267, lists two hundred members in Oakland and San Francisco in 1911. Brissenden, *I.W.W.*, 113–255, details the internal factional struggles of 1905–8. I estimate paid membership of five hundred to one thousand in eleven locals. Membership figures compiled from J. C. Cohanan to editor, *IW*, Mar. 18, July 1, 1909; Jan. 29, Feb. 5, Apr. 30, 1910; *Solidarity*, Aug. 13, 1910;

Warren K. Billings, interview. For internal strife, see William Trautmann's Report in *IUB*, Oct. 19, 1907; Feb. 1, 1908.

24. Quotes from William D. Robertson, "Empire Building Irrigation," *Sunset* 24 (Mar. 1910), 351; *FMR*, Nov. 25, 1900. See also Paul N. Beringer, "Fresno the Paradise of the Industrious Man of Small Means," *Overland Monthly* 52 (Dec. 1908), 562–72; L. Teague, "The Fresno Vineyards," ibid. (Dec. 1908), 573–78; G. H. Rothe, "Fresno City and Country," *Grizzly Bear* 19 (June 1916), 14–16; Charles C. Colby, "The California Raisin Industry—A Study in Geographical Interpretation," *Annals of the American Association of American Geographers* 14 (June 1924), 49–108.

25. Quote from *Solidarity*, Mar. 11, 1911; *IW*, Mar. 5, Oct. 19, Dec. 24, 1910. See also Dubofsky, *We Shall Be All*, 179.

26. Quote from *FMR*, Apr. 17, 1910. See also *Oakland World*, Dec. 31, 1910; Mr. Hubert Phillips, interview by RCB, Ichihachi Papers, SUASC; White, "IWW and the American Frontier," 74. For biographical material on Little, see James P. Cannon, *Notebook of a Labor Agitator* (New York, 1958), 32–36; Little to *IW*, June 10, 1909. For the Spokane campaign, see Tyler, "Rebels of the Woods," 34–35, 39; Flynn, *I Speak*, 95–96; Flynn, "Latest News from Spokane," *ISR* 10 (Mar. 1910), 828; Dubofsky, *We Shall Be All*, 175–76; Gregory R. Woirol, ed., "Two Letters on the Spokane Free Speech Fight: A Document Note," *Pacific Northwest Quarterly* (1986), 68–71. For employment agents, see *IW*, Mar. 25, Apr. 29, June 3, 1909; *IUB*, Feb. 27, Mar. 18, June 3, Aug. 5, 1909; Feb. 13, 1910; Fred Heslewood, "Barbarous Fresno," *ISR* 10 (1910), 711. At one point, police raided IWW halls, closed the offices of *Industrial Worker*, and arrested hundreds of bindlemen, among them Frank Little. Hauled into court, Little was asked by the presiding magistrate what he had been reading when arrested. "Reading the Declaration of Independence," he replied. To this the magistrate pronounced: "Thirty days." Released in December 1910, he would be lynched in August 1917, when Montana vigilantes left his body dangling from a railroad trestle outside of Butte, Montana.

27. Quote from *IW*, May 21, 1910. See also Martin Dodd, "The IWW, Fresno, and the Free Speech Fight of 1910–11: A Case Study in Hobo Activism" (Senior Thesis, CSU, Fullerton, 1974), 52–53.

28. Quotes from *IW*, May 28, June 11, 1910; also Apr. 19, 23; E. Flatwith, "Barbarous Fresno," *People's Paper*, cited in *Solidarity*, Dec. 31, 1910; Mar. 11, 1911.

29. Quotes from E. Flatwith, "Barbarous Fresno."

30. W. F. Little to *IW*, June 10, Oct. 19, 1910. Also May 21, 28; June 4; Sept. 1; Dec. 29, 1910. In some accounts, Shean is listed as Shoen. See also *FMR*, May 26, 1910. For the IWW in Fresno, see Fred Thompson to Ted Lehmann, May 31, 1971, Thompson Papers, AULHWSU; *Solidarity*, Aug. 4, 1917; Dec. 17, 1910; *Oakland World*, Dec. 31, 1910; Daniel O'Regan to Charles McCarthy, Nov. 10, 1914, CIRP; CIR, *Final Report*, 5: 5004; George Holmes, interview, "The IWW and Early TUUL," Stuart Jamieson Notes, 1–2, Stuart Jamieson Papers, BL. According to Dubofsky, *We Shall Be All*, 118, 150, 186–87, Little arrived in March. *FMR*, Oct. 20, 1910, reports that his brother, W. F. Little, was in town.

31. Quotes from *Solidarity*, Aug. 27, 1910. See also Aug. 13, 1910; *FMR*, Aug. 13, 26, 1910; Ted Lehmann, "The Fresno Free Speech Fight" (Unpublished seminar paper, CSU, Fresno, 1971), 12. While in jail, Little remained defiant. Ordered to rake leaves in the courthouse square, Little refused and was thrown in "the tank"—a hot, dark iron cell measuring seven by seven feet—and placed on a bread and water diet. After appeals from IWW leaders, he agreed to rake leaves for the remaining sixteen days of his sentence. Also arrested was Frank's brother, W. F. Little, whose crime was to question the validity of the arrests. Quickly tried and acquitted by a jury, W. F. Little upon his release from jail telegraphed IWW national secretary Vincent St. John for help. *Industrial Worker* reported: "F. E. Little sentenced before a perjured jury to 25 days in jail. A police conspiracy to get organizer Little out of town." Quote from *IW*, Sept. 3, 1910.

32. Quotes from *Solidarity*, Aug. 27, 1910; *IW*, Aug. 13, 10, 17; Sept. 3, 1910. See also *FMR*, Sept. 3, 7, 9, 1910.

33. Quotes from *IW*, Aug. 13; Oct. 8, 19, 1910. Shaw quoted from Wobbly newspapers to support his actions, at one time citing *Industrial Worker's* vow "to show the Bosses that we mean business and that unless we make it stick in the Raisin City we are going to have trouble in other California towns." See also Kornbluh, *Rebel Voices*, 96; Minutes, Board of Trustees, Fresno County, Oct. 3, 1910, City Clerk's Office, Fresno. For Filigno, see Helen C. Camp, *Iron in Her Soul: Elizabeth Gurley Flynn and the American Left* (Pullman, Wash., 1995), 24.

34. In one editorial, Rowell endorsed importing twenty-five hundred to three thousand Greeks to "do away with the Japs altogether." Quotes from *FMR*, Jan. 16, 1911. See also ibid., May 30, 1910; Rowell to W[ylie] M. Giffen, Dec. 10, 1909, Chester Rowell Papers, BL; Frank Van Nuys, "A Progressive Confronts the Race Question: Chester Rowell, the California Alien Land Act of 1913, and the Contradictions of Early Twentieth-Century Racial Thought," *CH* 73 (spring 1994), 2–13. Once referred to as "the most brilliant and most versatile genius in our progressive movement in this state," Rowell made his reputation upon becoming editor in 1898 by campaigning against M. Theo Kearney's arrogant leadership of the Raisin Association. Over the next twelve years, he developed a reputation as a fighting editor while expanding the *Republican's* circulation from three thousand to thirteen thousand. Taking the lead in modernizing Fresno, he worked to overturn years of weak, corrupt, and shoddy, municipal government and used his paper to attack the railroad attorneys, brewery officers, racetrack operators, brothel owners, pimps, gamblers, and saloon owners whom he claimed were the real powers in town.

35. Quotes from *FMR*, Sept. 27, 30; Oct. 13, 1910; Nov. 9; Jan. 16, 1911; *IW*, Oct. 26, 1910; Chester Rowell, "IWW Not Condoned" and "A Calamity," Chester H. Rowell Papers, BL. The whipping quote is cited secondhand in most sources as the *Fresno Herald and Democrat*, in *IW*, Oct. 26, 1910. Labeling the IWW "a dangerous body of men" unworthy of sympathy, Rowell set them off from Socialists, who, he reasoned, elected candidates and followed traditional forms of political protest and therefore did not pose much of a threat. From this premise, Rowell concluded that as far as the IWW was concerned, free speech was not an unconditional right. Therefore, draconian measures might be necessary. See also Miles C. Everett, "Chester Harvey Rowell, Pragmatic Humanist and California Progressive" (Ph.D. diss., UCB, 1966), 188–97, 381–82; editorials, *FMR*, May 21, 1903; Feb. 8, 1909; Mar. 6, 1910; Fred Thompson to Ted Lehmann, May 31, 1911, Fred Thompson Papers, AULHWSU; V. A. Pipkin, interview, cited in Lehmann, "Fresno Free Speech Fight," 18–19; George Holmes, interview, "IWW and Early TUUL," 1–2, Jamieson Notes, Stuart Jamieson Papers, BL.

36. *FMR*, Oct. 18, 1910; *IW* Oct. 1, 1910 [cartoon]; also Oct. 8, 19. Adding to the impending sense of disaster and general fear that extremist elements were on the prowl was the October 1 bombing of the *Los Angeles Times* building, which killed twenty innocent bystanders. The explosion so alarmed Fresno citizens that on October 12, growers obtained an injunction against AFL-affiliated organizers and met with local businessmen to discuss vigilante action against the "undesirable characters" flooding into town.

37. Quote from *IW*, Oct. 19, 1910. See also Philip S. Foner, ed., *Fellow Workers and Friends: I.W.W. Free-Speech Fights as Told by Participants* (Westport, Conn., 1981), 77; *FMR*, Oct. 14, 19, 1910; *Solidarity*, Dec. 17, 1910; *IW*, Oct. 26, 1910. Joe Hill supposedly participated in the Fresno fight. But the only evidence for this came from a speech given by Wobbly Ted Fraser at a meeting in London, England, in which he claimed to have fought alongside Hill at Spokane and Fresno. Richard Brazier, who definitely was at Spokane, doubted that either Fraser or Hill were present there or at Fresno. For Fraser's statement, see *Solidarity*, Jan. 9, 1915. For Brazier's statement, see Brazier to Fred Thompson, Dec. 21, 1966, Fred Thompson Papers, AULHWSU.

38. Quotes from Herbert Minderman, "The Fresno Free-Speech Fight," CIRPP; *FMR*, Oct. 20, 1910. With so many men in jail, the Fresno press believed the fight would "soon die a natural death." Spirits would sink further when W. F. Little was jailed for drunkenness, an arrest that would shortly result in his resignation from Local 66. But Wobblies remained defiant, condemning their trials as "star chamber" proceedings. Each dark, iron cell measured seven feet two inches wide, six feet nine inches wide, and eight feet four inches tall.

39. Quotes from Herbert Minderman, "The Fresno Free-Speech Fight"; *FMR*, Oct. 20, 1910. See also Dodd, "The I.W.W., Fresno, and the Free Speech Fight," 72.

40. Minderman, "The Fresno Free-Speech Fight"; *FMR*, Oct. 29, Nov. 3, 1910; also Nov. 30; Fresno Municipal Court (Police Court) Records, Oct. 24, 1910, Fresno.

41. Quotes from *FMR*, Oct. 29, 1910; *IW*, Nov. 17, 24, 1910; Minderman, "Fresno Free Speech."

42. Quote from *Solidarity*, Nov. 19, 1910.

43. Quote from Lehmann, "Fresno Free Speech Fight," 18–19.

44. By December 5, there were fifty-five Wobblies awaiting trial in the one-room bullpen. Morale remained high, and prisoners held daily meetings. See Dodd, "The IWW, Fresno, and the Free Speech Fight," 84–86; O'Reagan to McCarthy, Nov. 10, 1914, CIRP.

45. Quotes from *FMR*, Dec. 10, 11, 1910; Vincent St. John to mayor of Fresno, Dec. 9, 15,

1910; Lehmann, "Fresno Free Speech Fight," 18–19; William Normart, interview, cited in Ronald Genini, "Industrial Workers of the World and their Fresno Free Speech Fight, 1910–1911," *CHQ* 57 (spring 1974), 108. See also Edward Delaney and M. T. Rice, *The Bloodstained Trail* (Chicago, 1927), 57. According to the *FMR*, most mob members were working-class people; however, the *Republican* also reported that businessmen and members of the middle class led the mob. That members of the working class were involved in the attack seemed obvious to the *Oakland World*. "Even their own class went back on them, and wanted them to get off the soap-box and go to work . . . That is just about the psychology of the average working man." Quote from *Oakland World*, Jan. 7, 1911.

46. Quotes from *FMR*, Dec. 10, 12, 1910; *Sacramento Bee*, Dec. 10, 1910; *San Francisco Star*, Dec. 17, 1910.

47. Quotes from *FMR*, Dec. 12, 1910; "Organization," and "IWW Not Condoned," Rowell Papers, BL; *IW*, Dec. 22, 1910.

48. Quotes from *FMR*, Dec. 11, 1910. See also Minderman, "Fresno Free Speech Fight."

49. Quote from Foner, *IWW*, 187.

50. To further curb Wobbly agitation, Fresno passed a new ordinance. Similar to one enacted in Los Angeles, it prohibited standing in public places, doorways, or streets so as to obstruct businesses. It also made downtown Fresno off-limits to public speaking. With a free hand to suppress the IWW, Fresno on December 23 had eighty-two Wobblies packed into the jail bullpen. Minderman left this account in his diary:

> We decided to go on a hunger strike because no food at all was better and healthier than water and bread. . . . For supper we sing the red flag and other songs and that brought some spectators to the jail. . . . Every time the spectators leave, we start to raise hell again until there were some others. . . . The sheriff orders the speakers to stop this . . . we got the watercure. . . . There are two sewer holes in the bull-pen and the water flows into them as fast as they put it in. This lasts for two hours—then the fire department came. . . . Every time the stream struck a man his body was paralyzed where the stream struck. Schultz got the stream on his head and was lifted from the floor and then dropped down. The top of his hat was torn off and his eye badly hurt. It is a wonder that nobody was killed.

51. Quotes from Minderman, "Fresno Free Speech." Analyzing the county jail records, Fresno historian Ted Lehmann found many prisoners using such creative aliases as world heavyweight boxing champion John L. Sullivan and *Los Angeles Times* publisher Harrison Gray Otis. See Lehmann, "Fresno Free Speech Fight," 25.

52. Quotes from *IW*, Jan. 26, 1911; also Dec. 29, 1910; *Solidarity*, Feb. 18, 1911; also Mar. 11. See also *FMR*, Dec. 19, 20, 24, 1910; Jan. 11, Feb. 13, 1911. The *St. Louis Globe Democrat* reported that one hundred IWW members

> left their quarters at 3 o'clock yesterday afternoon to march on Fresno, California, and take part in the free-speech fight there by the Industrial Workers of the World. When the army reaches Kansas City the number will be enlarged to about 200. By picking up the unemployed along the route, the marchers expect to number more than a thousand when they reach Fresno. They say . . . the city of Fresno will be unable to provide for them should they be arrested, and this would cause the taxpayers to protest at the expense of feeding them.

See *FMR*, Feb. 21, 1911; *San Francisco Call*, Dec. 23–25, 1910; *IW*, Jan. 5, 1911; Delaney and Rice, *The Bloodstained Trail*, 57; Weintraub, "IWW in California," 49–53; Minderman, "Fresno Free Speech."

53. After struggling for decades against Porfirio Díaz, the Magón brothers aimed at solving Mexico's problems through revolution. See *NYT*, Feb. 8, Apr. 3, 8, 10, 1911; George Bucklin, "Mobley Meadows was a Valley Hero," *San Diego Union*, n.d.; "Dreams of a Socialist Republic," Richard Emerson Memoir (n.d.), both in Hughes Scrapbooks, ICHS; Stimson, *Labor Movement in Los Angeles*, 321.

54. *FMR*, Feb. 18, 1911; *IUB*, Feb. 27, 1909; *IW*, June 8, 22; July 6, 1911; Lowell Blaisdell, *The Desert Revolution* (Madison, Wis., 1962), 42–43. The latest and best treatment is Lawrence D. Taylor, "The Magónista Revolt in Baja California: Capitalist Conspiracy or *Rebelion de los Pobres*?" *Journal of San Diego History* 45 (winter 1999), 2–31.

55. Quotes from *FMR*, Feb. 14, 21, 1911; also Feb. 18. "We later gained the support and sym-

pathy of the citizens and press, we succeeded in advertising the Industrial Workers of the World as never before had been done, we were a great factor in winning the fight in Fresno, the trip was a school to us and the lessons learned there will be no doubt reflected and mirrored in the future work of the organization," recalled one of the Wobbly Train members. "Tis hoped we made REVOLUTIONISTS." Quote from Charles P. Le Warne, "On the Wobbly Train to Fresno," *LH* 14 (spring 1973), 264–89. A report on the trip over the signatures of five leaders appears in *IW*, Apr. 6, 1911. A slightly different version by one of the five, E. M. Clyde, appears in *Solidarity*, Apr. 8, 1911. See also *Seattle Daily Times*, Feb. 16, 17, 1911; *Portland Morning Oregonian*, Feb. 17, 18, 1911; *Tacoma Daily Ledger*, Feb. 18, 1911.

56. Quotes from *IW*, Feb. 16, 1911; *Solidarity*, Feb. 18, 1911. A brief flurry of activity surrounded disclosure in the *Fresno Morning Republican* that Frank Little had received thirty dollars per week as an organizer; this so infuriated a number of men that they asked to be released from jail and were granted their wish. The IWW promptly denied that Little was being paid, and described the money as a "jungle fund."

57. One prisoner, Frank Lefferts, decided to make it as unpleasant as possible for his jailers. Taking off his heavy boots, he spent the whole night pounding on the bars with his boots, making it impossible for anyone in the vicinity to sleep. "He was put in a cell by himself . . . but he kept up the racket," reported Daniel O'Regan, an investigator for the Commission on Industrial Relations.

> Ed Jones, the jailor, warned him to be quiet or some extreme measures would have to be taken with him. Lefferts told him to go ahead, so Jones tied him . . . then took off one of Leffert's socks and put it in his mouth as a gag. The severity of this punishment can be understood by one who is familiar with the rank and file of I.W.W.'s and knows how rarely they bathe. In a short time the gag was removed and Lefferts [was] asked if he'd behave. He said he would and give no trouble afterwards.

Quote from Daniel O'Regan, "Free Speech Fights of the I.W.W.'s," MS (n.d.), 15–16, CIRPP [copy in IWW Collection, AULHWSU].

58. Quote from *IW*, Mar. 2, 1911. One reporter for the *San Francisco Call* found Fresno Wobblies so fascinating and bewildering in their tactics, goals, and behavior that he headlined one article as if describing a religious crusade: "Hundreds in Jail and More to Seek Martyrdom." Quote from *San Francisco Call*, Mar. 2, 1911. Until negotiations began, the city would continue making arrests, understanding that, if the situation deteriorated, the mayor "had no doubt 2000 men, or as many more as necessary, could be sworn in as special police, who would be very glad to serve without pay." Quote from *FMR*, Feb. 22; also Feb. 17, 26, 28, 1911. See also Foner, *Fellow Workers and Friends*, 78; Minderman, "Fresno Free Speech."

59. Quotes from *FMR*, Mar. 2, 1911; *IW*, Mar. 6, 1911; "Solidarity Wins in Fresno," *ISR* 11 (Apr. 1911), 634–36. One part of the Wobbly Train continued on when the train fares were paid by the manager of the May Roberts Theatrical Company. Hired to attend each of her shows as part of an advertising ploy, the men found their journey easy enough and so appreciated it—especially after their ordeal in the Siskiyou Mountains—that they gave May Roberts a photo album with all of their pictures. Near Sacramento they learned of the victory. See *IW*, Feb. 26, 28, 1911. Dubofsky, *We Shall Be All*, 188, incorrectly reports that settlement terms were not announced. Commenting on the fight, the *San Francisco Call* described it as "one of those strange situations which crop up suddenly and are hard to understand, some thousands of men, whose business is to work with their hands, tramping and stealing rides, suffering hardships and facing dangers—to get into jail. And to get into that particular jail." Quote from *San Francisco Call*, Mar. 2, 1911. See also Brissenden, "A Report on the IWW in California," Aug. 1914, CIRPP; Le Warne, "On the Wobbly Train to Fresno," 289.

60. During World War I the IWW's *Defense News Bulletin* recalled Fresno this way: "By placing in jail the advocates of industrial unionism, no doubt, the master class believed by so doing that it would intimidate others. But did it? The members rolled in by the hundreds to take the place of their fellow workers." Quote from O. P. McVay, *California News Bulletin*, Jan. 26, 1918. See also Elizabeth Gurley Flynn, *Memories of the Industrial Workers of the World* (Chicago, 1977), 5; Brissenden, "A Report on the IWW in California" (Aug. 1914), 10, CIRPP. Total costs for the fight ranged from six hundred to one thousand dollars, but these figures did not specify whether they referred to national IWW costs or those of Local 66. See *IW*, Feb. 26, 28, 1911; Press Committee, "Solidarity Wins in Fresno," *ISR* 11 (Apr. 1911), 10. See also Dodd,

"The IWW, Fresno, and the Free Speech Fight," 36, 41; Gordon Shriver, "The Fresno Free Speech Fight, 1910–1911" MS (n.d.), Woodward Pamphlet Collection, SCHMLCSUF.

61. Quote from *Solidarity*, Apr. 29, 1911; also May 2, 1911.

62. Quotes from Mark Leier, "Solidarity on Occasion: The Vancouver Free Speech Fights of 1909 and 1912," 23 *Labour/Le Travail* (spring 1989), 39; Rowell, "Invasion Collapses," Rowell Papers, BL. See also Tom N. McInnis, "Kansas City Free Speech Fight," *Missouri Historical Review* 53 (Apr. 1990), 253–69; McGuckin, "Recollections," 55–56; Brissenden, *I.W.W.*, 261, 365; *San Francisco Chronicle*, Dec. 27, 1913; *Labor Clarion*, May 12, 1913; Richard Frost, *The Mooney Case* (Stanford, 1968), 12; Ashleigh, "Floater," 38; W. F. Little to *IW*, June 10, 1909; Mar. 12, 1912; *Solidarity*, Mar. 11, 1911; Grant S. Youmans in William D. Haywood, "Free Speech Fights, Letters Relating to," CIRP. Departing Fresno, one bindleman added another verse to the old favorite "Hallelujah, I'm a Bum," singing:

> Springtime has come,
> and I'm just out of jail.
> Without any money,
> without any bail.

Quote from Patrick Renshaw, *The Wobblies: The Story of Syndicalism in the United States* (Garden City, N.Y., 1967), 89. Of the Fresno fight, Austin Lewis wrote: "But from the point of view of the migratory workers, the . . . fight was a distinct gain . . . The Fresno local of the organization grew in power and importance . . . large numbers were brought into contact with the propaganda and the Industrial Workers, and . . . their . . . ideas became widely known throughout the rural districts of the state." Quote from Austin Lewis, "Movements of the Migratory Unskilled in California," *New Review* 2 (Aug. 1914), 461. For similar assessments, see *IW*, May 18, 1911; Fred Thompson, "First Forty Years," ibid., July 14, 1945; *Solidarity*, Apr. 29, 1911; Weintraub, "IWW in California," 64, 130–32, 137–39; Dubofsky, *We Shall Be All*, 189. For a positive spin on the Fresno fight, see Foner, *History of the Labor Movement*, 4: 186–89. Vaught, *Cultivating California*, 126, questions the prevailing orthodoxy regarding what the IWW "won" at Fresno. Along these lines it should be noted that Frank Little, despite his minor leadership role, gained fame as yet another Wobbly apostle who went on to fight battles elsewhere.

63. Variously described as "somewhat of a demagogue," "an eccentric publicist," and an unprincipled opportunist who managed to affiliate with most of the radical movements between the late 1870s and World War I, Browne had taken part in Denis Kearney's Workingman's Party, edited its official publication, *Open Letter*, served as Kearney's private secretary, and in 1894, had helped organize the California contingent of Coxey's Army. For Carl Browne, see Shaffer, "Radicalism in California," 15–17; Carl Browne, *When Coxey's Army Marcht on Washington* (San Francisco, 1944); various materials in Jacob S. Coxey Papers, 1874–1976, Massillon Museum, Ohio Historical Society, Columbus, Ohio. For the effect of the Fresno fight on AFL and CSFL efforts to organize farmworkers, see Frank Little to editor, *IW*, July 30, 1910; Speed, "52 Years Ago."

64. Quotes from Daniel, *Bitter Harvest*, 79; *Report of the Proceedings of the Thirtieth Annual Convention of the AFL, New Orleans, Nov. 14–26, 1910* (Washington, D.C., 1910), 178; also 69, 147, 186–87, 215, 243, 266–67, 276; Andrew Furuseth to Gompers, May 27, 1911, in *San Francisco Bulletin*, May 27, 1911. See also Ira Cross, "Labor Notes," Cross Papers, BL.

65. CIR, *Final Report*, 5: 63, 4974, 4978; *PRP*, Sept. 9, 11, 16, 1911; *FMR*, Aug. 30; Sept. 1, 7–9, 12, 18, 19; Oct. 13, 1911; *Solidarity*, July 29, 1911; *California Fruit Grower*, Sept. 30, 1911.

66. Quotes from CIR, *Final Report*, 5: 4977, 4978–79; also 4945, 4973, 4977; CSFL, *Proceedings of the Fourteenth Annual Convention* (San Francisco, 1913), 78; *Labor Clarion*, Oct. 3, 1913. About two hundred farmworkers were in, of all places, Oakland. Figures from Phillips Russell, "The Class War on the Pacific Coast: An Interview with O. A. Tveitmoe," *ISR* 13 (Sept. 1912), 236–38. See also Austin Lewis, "Organization of the Unskilled," *New Review* 1 (Dec. 1913), 463; Lewis, "Organization of the Unskilled," ibid. (Nov. 1913), 873–72; Ione Wilson, "The IWW in California with Special Reference to Migratory Labor" (M.A. thesis, UCB, 1946), 8; Schwartz, *Seasonal Farm Labor*, 93; Knight, *Industrial Relations in San Francisco Bay Area*, 276.

67. Quotes from *American Federationist*, Apr. 1912; AFL, *Report of the Proceedings of the Thirty-First Annual Convention*, Nov. 13–25, 1911 (Washington, D.C., 1911), 70; also 71. See also Gompers, *Labor and the Employer*, 163; Foner, *History of the Labor Movement*, 3: 221.

68. Quotes from AFL, *Report of the Thirty-Second Annual AFL Convention*, 29; also 182,

384; *American Federationist*, Mar. 1914. See also Lorwin, *The AFL*, 110–11; Kenneth A. Smith, "Industrial Relations in the California Fruit and Vegetable Canning Industry" (M.A. thesis, UCB, 1949), 90. For Scharrenberg's later thinking, see *LFCH*, pt. 49: 17946.

69. McGuckin, "Recollections," 55–56; *IW*, Nov. 20, 30, 1911; Jan. 13, 27; Feb. 1; July 1, 29; Oct. 7, 1912; George Speed, "52 Years of Work Seeking One Big Union," July 16, 1924; Boyd, Ludeke, and Rump, *Inside Historic Kern*, 98; Weintraub, "IWW in California," 32–37. Curiously, when orange pickers at Lindsay struck spontaneously to restore wages from four to five cents a box in June 1911, the IWW did not become involved. See "Agricultural News Notes of the Pacific Coast," *California Cultivator* 36 (June 1911), 693n. Perhaps inspired by these efforts, the Socialist Party at its April 1912 San Francisco convention for the last time focused its attention on migrant farmworkers. Job Harriman, the state's leading Socialist, formed a committee to study the matter.

70. Quotes from Foner, *Fellow Workers*, 123–24; clipping, *San Francisco Chronicle*, [ca. May 25, 1912], FHHC. In January 1912, San Francisco Local 173 launched a free speech fight after being denied permits to hold public street meetings, defying the order without problems. Also denied a permit, members of Oakland Local 174 on March 9 were driven from their Ninth and Broadway soapboxing spot and, after fighting a running battle over several blocks, were beaten unmercifully as they sought haven in their Hamilton Hall headquarters. See *Oakland World*, May 25, 1912; *California Social Democrat*, May 11, 1912. See also Richard C. Miller, "Otis and His Times: The Career of Harrison Gray Otis of Los Angeles" (Ph.D. diss., UCB, 1961); Knight, *Industrial Relations*, 267; Shaffer, "Radicalism in California," 226; A. Tucker to Vincent St. John, Sept. 2, 1914, CIRP.

71. Quote from *San Diego Sun*, Jan. 9, 10, 1912. See also Foner, *History of the Labor Movement*, 4: 194. Meeting on Friday evenings, Local 245 listed headquarters at 752 Fifth Avenue with C. B. Wolfe as president. Additional locals included mixed Local 13, and Public Service Local 378. According to one Wobbly, "about half of the 250 insurrectos . . . in Tia Juana are members of the I. W. W." Quote from F. G. Peterson to *IW*, June 8, 1911. See also *IW*, July 26, 1947. Climate alone made the city an attractive destination for bindlemen. See *San Diego Tribune*, Jan. 11, 1912; Col. George Ruhlen, interview by Fred Hastings, Apr. 12, 1961; Eugene Skinner, ibid., Mar. 24, 1959, both in San Diego Historical Society, Junípero Serra Museum and Library. See also James Mills, "Comes the Revolution," *San Diego Magazine* 11 (Oct. 1959), 74–75; Margaret Secor, "San Diego Looks At the Maderista Revolution in Mexico," *Journal of San Diego History* 18 (summer 1972); clipping [*IW*], "The IWW," File 268.5, San Diego Historical Society, Junípero Serra Museum.

72. Quote from *IW*, May 1, 1912. See also Charlotte Benz Villalobos, "Civil Liberties in San Diego: The Free Speech Fight of 1912" (M.A. thesis, CSU, San Diego, 1966), 17.

73. Quotes from *San Diego Sun*, Jan. 3, 1912; *San Diego Tribune*, Mar. 4, 1912. For Sehon, see Carl H. Heilborn, ed., *History of San Diego County* (San Diego, 1936), 278; Don Stewart, *Frontier Port* (Los Angeles, 1965), 77–79; Richard F. Pourade, *History of San Diego: Gold In the Sun* (San Diego, 1965), 5: 42–43, 90. For Wilson, see A. E. Jensen, "Keno Wilson—A Lawman's Lawman," *San Diego Historical Society Quarterly* 8 (Oct. 1962), 5–14; biographical material in Keno Wilson Papers, San Diego Historical Society, Junípero Serra Museum.

74. On the evening of March 10, Wilson summoned the fire department and ordered firefighters to turn their high pressure hoses on a crowd gathering outside. "For a full hour hundreds packed themselves in a solid mass . . . bending themselves to the terrific torrent that poured upon them they held their ground until swept from their feet by the irresistible flood," reported the *Oakland World*, Mar. 11, 1912.

75. Quote from *San Diego Union*, Apr. 5, 1912.

76. Robert W. Diehl, "To Speak or Not to Speak: San Diego" (M.A. thesis, University of San Diego, 1976), 108–12; Kate Haurshan Taylor, "A Crisis of Confidence: The San Diego Free Speech Fight of 1912" (M.A. thesis, UCLA, 1966).

77. Quotes from San Francisco Labor Council, Special Investigating Committee, *San Diego Free Speech Controversy* (San Francisco, Apr. 25, 1912), 8, SHSW; *San Diego Tribune*, Mar. 4, 1912; *IW*, Apr. 4, 11, 1912. Resorting to hit-and-run tactics, protestors regrouped, dispersed, and then regrouped again, outmaneuvering the fire department, pulling so many alarms all over the city that the police had to station an officer at each alarm box in the downtown area. See also Hartwell S. Shippey, "The Shame of San Diego," *ISR*, 12 (May 1912), 718–22.

78. Quotes from A. Tucker to Vincent St. John, Sept. 21, 1914; Chris Hansen to St. John,

n.d., CIRP. Julius Tum's ordeal is described in *San Francisco Bulletin*, May 16, 1912. Anti-IWW journalist Walter Woelke, "I.W.W." *Outlook* 51 (July 6, 1912), 531, summarized the action this way: "Thus did San Diego, having given its money to mark the historic highway [El Camino Real] with the symbols of love and charity, teach patriotism and reverence for the law to the travelers thereon." Mills, "Comes the Revolution," 74–75; Shippey, "The Shame of San Diego," 718–22; "A. R. Sauer's Biography," San Diego Historical Society, Junípero Serra Museum. Vigilantes were also busy in the city, where six masked men sprang from the bushes and kidnapped Abraham R. Sauer, the sixty-five-year-old owner and editor of the weekly *San Diego Herald*, as he returned home. Dragging him off the front of his porch, they forced Sauer into a car, and sped away just as his wife and children ran to the porch in their nightclothes. About twenty miles outside of town, the vigilantes yanked Sauer from the car, shoved him under a tree, placed a noose around his neck, and threw one end of the rope over a branch. Pulling the rope tight, they lifted Sauer's body from the ground for several moments, lowered Sauer back to the ground, and then forced him to promise to never return to San Diego. Released, he phoned his family and fled by train to Los Angeles, returning to San Diego several days later. He never divulged the names of the vigilantes. Before his abduction, he had come very close to naming names when he wrote: "The personnel of the vigilantes represents not only the bankers and merchants but has as its workers leading church members and bartenders. The chamber of commerce and the real estate board are well represented. The press and the public utility corporations, as well as members of the Grand Jury are known to belong." Quote from *San Diego Sun*, Apr. 6, 1912.

79. With a hand in every aspect of San Diego's economic life, Spreckels had the most to lose from any Wobbly activity, and pushed hard for repressive measures. Wobblies involved with the Magón insurrection had stopped work trains building Spreckels's railroad eastward on the Mexican side of the border and confiscated supplies. Wobblies had also begun organizing conductors and motormen employed on his streetcar line. Out of perhaps two thousand employees, only the print shops on his newspapers were organized, and he intended to keep it that way. For Spreckels, see H. Austin Adams, *The Man: John D. Spreckels* (San Diego, 1924), 77–78, 81–83; *San Francisco Bulletin*, May 23, 1912; James R. Moriarty III and Elaine P. Lamb, "The Railroad and the Revolutionaries" MS (n.d.), 2–10; "Spreckels Biographies No. 1," San Diego Historical Society, Junípero Serra Museum; Oscar W. Cotton, *The Good Old Days* (New York, 1962), 96–97. Repression intensified after the evening of May 7, when Joseph Mikolash was killed in a shootout that left two policemen wounded outside IWW headquarters. Played up in the press as further evidence of the threat that the IWW posed, the shooting inspired a massive dragnet and general mobilization scheme, wherein fifteen hundred armed vigilantes could be summoned within minutes after hearing the riot whistles from the new electric power plant. So determined to eliminate the IWW were San Diego authorities that they denied permission for the funeral, forcing Wobblies to hold services in Los Angeles. One week later vigilantes attacked anarchist Emma Goldman and her lover Ben Reitman as they arrived in San Diego. Barely making it off the railroad platform, they were greeted by a mob screaming: "Give us that anarchist; we will strip her naked; we will tear out her guts." That evening vigilantes kidnapped Reitman from the Grant Hotel. Reitman later recalled: "With a lighted cigar they burned the letters I.W.W. on my buttocks; then they poured a can of tar over my head and in the absence of feathers, rubbed sage brush on my body. One of them attempted to push a cane up my rectum . . . another twisted my testicles . . . then they let me go." Shipped north by train, Reitman arrived in Los Angeles pale and terrified, with a mass of wounds and grotesque letters branded on his flesh. He would never fully recover from the physical and emotional scars. Quotes from Goldman, "Outrage of San Diego," *Mother Earth* (San Diego ed.) 7 (June 1912), 115–22; Reitman, "The Respectable Mob," ibid., 112. Neither Goldman nor Reitman were Wobblies. See Emma Goldman, *Living My Life* (New York, 1934), 495, 500–501; *IW*, June 6, 1912; *San Francisco Call*, May 14, 1912; Richard Drinnon, *Rebel in Paradise: A Biography of Emma Goldman* (Chicago, 1961), 135–36; Charles Forward, interview by Sylvia Arden, Apr. 29, 1975, San Diego Historical Society, Junípero Serra Museum. The irony of Goldman and Reitman's treatment is that, while San Diego authorities held Goldman and Reitman in fear, most Wobblies merely regarded them with disdain as "parlor radicals." See Cheryl Turner, "The San Diego 'Free Speech Fight': A Threat to Property" (M.A. thesis, UCB, 1972). Back in Los Angeles two days later, Reitman attempted to tell his story to a mass meeting protesting the San Diego outrage, but only elicited ridicule from the audience. See Reitman, "Following the Monkey," MS (n.d.), 285, Reitman Papers, Special Collections, University of Illinois. There were

two versions of the Mikolash shooting. One account had two officers watching IWW head-quarters and upon approaching being fired upon by two men. As the officers returned fire, their assailants disappeared, but a wild man, Joseph Mikolash, ran out of the IWW hall with an ax and hit one of the officers over the eye. Wounded in the stomach and legs, Mikolash managed to crawl two blocks away before a private citizen found him and called police. The IWW version called the incident murder. According to the IWW, police officers had followed Mikolash to the IWW hall from a street meeting where they had already beaten him. In a deathbed statement, Mikolash said that the policemen had pursued him to give him more of the same. He had been standing in the IWW hall doorway when a policeman had flashed a light in his eyes and ordered him outside. But before he could comply, the officer opened fire, wounding him mortally. At this point Mikolash grabbed the ax lying just inside the doorway and hit the officer. There had been no mysterious gunmen, and the wounded policeman had actually been wounded by the one who had been hit by the ax. See *San Diego Sun*, Mar. 19, 23; Apr. 19; May 8, 10, 18, 1912; *San Diego Union*, Apr. 20, May 9, 1912; *San Diego Tribune*, Apr. 22, 1912; *Solidarity*, June 1, 1912; *IW*, Apr. 4, 1912; Mills, "Comes the Revolution," 74; Villalobos, "Civil Liberties in San Diego," 83; George Waddel Brooks, interview by Edgar F. Hastings of the San Diego Historical Society, Sept. 7, 1960; Bert Shankland, interview by Robert Wright of the San Diego Historical Society, Nov. 24, 1972, Junípero Serra Museum. In some accounts, Mikolash is identified as Mikloasek.

80. Quote from *Report of Harris Weinstock, Commissioner to Investigate the Recent Disturbances in the City of San Diego and the County of San Diego, California, to His Excellency Hiram H. Johnson, Governor of California* (Sacramento, 1912), 11–19; also 3–4, 7–8.

81. Weinstock reported to Governor Johnson,

Your commissioner has visited Russia and while there . . . heard many horrible tales of high-handed proceedings and outrageous treatment of innocent people at the hand of despotic tyrannic Russian authorities. Your commissioner is frank to confess that when he became satisfied of the truth of these stories as related by these unfortunate men it was hard for him to believe he was still not sojourning in the "land of the free and home of the brave." Surely these American men, who, as the overwhelming evidence shows, in large numbers assaulted with weapons in a most cowardly and brutal manner their helpless and defenseless fellows, were certainly far from "brave" and their victims far from "free."

Quote from *Report of Harris Weinstock*, 7–8. See also San Francisco Labor Council, Special Investigating Committee, *San Diego Free Speech Controversy*, 1–10. A list of twenty-four alleged vigilantes including bank executives, realtors, constables, and police officers appeared in *Mother Earth* (San Diego ed.) 8 (June 1912), 108.

82. Quotes from *San Francisco Bulletin*, Apr. 21, 1912; *San Francisco Call*, May 22; June 3, 1912; also May 20, 25, 28, 1912; *San Francisco Bulletin*, May 20, 1912; also May 28; *America, A Catholic Review-of-the-Week* 7 (May 25, 1912), 158; *San Diego Tribune*, June 7, 1912. See also *San Diego Sun*, June 22, 1912; Selig Perlman and Philip Taft, *History of Labor in the United States, 1896–1932* (New York, 1935), 4: 242; San Francisco Labor Council, Special Investigating Committee, *San Diego Free Speech Controversy*, 1–10.

83. Gradually the free speech fighters in San Diego were released from jail. E. E. Kirk and Harry McKee, Wobbly lawyers, were sentenced to six and three months in jail, respectively, and a three-hundred-dollar fine for each. Defiant, McKee told the court just before he was sentenced: "We are not defeated . . . We are triumphant no matter what sentence your honor may inflict." Quotes from *Solidarity*, Aug. 24, 1912. See also Albert Tucker to Vincent St. John, Sept. 21, 1912; Chris Hansen to St. John, CIRP; *IW*, Oct. 17, 1912. The sentences were upheld by the higher courts, and Governor Johnson refused to issue any pardons, fearing that "the anarchy of the IWW and their brutality are worse than the anarchy of the vigilantes." Quote from Hiram Johnson in J. Stitt Wilson to Hiram Johnson, Aug. 1, 1913, CIRP. As the vigilantes were being reigned in, John Spreckels and *Los Angeles Times* owner Harrison Gray Otis, along with John Sehon, concocted the most preposterous accusations. Claiming to have evidence that Wobblies armed with guns and dynamite were engaged in "a criminally treasonous" conspiracy to create a new government in the Southern California region, Sehon asserted that Wobbly armies at that moment were congregating across the nation, preparing "to overthrow the Government and take possession of all things." Although the federal grand jury refused to believe the fabrication, Spreckels, Otis, Sehon, and a committee of five hundred San Diego business-

men continued to press for federal suppression. Comparing the California labor situation to Chicago in 1894, when Pres. Grover Cleveland had dispatched troops to put down the Pullman strike, prominent Republican National Committee member F. W. Eastabrook suggested to Pres. William Taft that "it is time that vigorous action, whenever opportunity occurs, should be taken to stamp out the revolutionary methods of this anarchistic organization" and "crush out the methods of this [IWW] organization." Such action, he stressed, would guarantee California's vote for Taft in the November presidential election and work to the detriment of Governor Johnson. Although President Taft on September 7 asked Atty. Gen. George Wickersham to show the "strong hand of the United States in a marked way so that they shall understand that we are on the job," Wickersham concluded that the IWW posed no threat, and refused to intervene. Quotes from F. W. Eastabrook to Charles Hillers, Sept. 5, 1912; Charles H. DeLacour, Sept. 5, 1912; Taft to Wickersham, Sept. 7, 1912; DJ File 150139-29; Wickersham to Taft, Sept. 16, 1912; and C. D. Hillers, Sept. 16, 1912, DJ File 150139-31, Records of the Dept. of Justice, RG60, NA. See also John Sehon to Wickersham, May 2, 1912, and Wickersham's reply, May 6, 1912, DJ File 150139-10; Rep. J. C. Needham to Wickersham, May 4, 1912; Wickersham's reply, May 6, 1912, DJ File 150139-12; James W. Wedham to Wickersham, May 5, 1912, and Wickersham's reply, May 6, 1912, DJ File 150139-11; Wickersham to McCormick, May 6, 1912, DJ File 150139-13; Wickersham to Sen. John D. Works, May 9, 1912, DJ File 150139-14, RG60; Wickersham to Taft, Sept. 16, 1912; and C. D. Hillers, Sept. 16, 1912, DJ File 15039-31; Charles DeLacour to Wickersham, Nov. 22, 1912, with marginal note by W. R. H., DJ File 15039-35; Senator Works to Wickersham, May 2, 1912; Wickersham's reply, May 6, 1912, DJ File 150139-10, RG 60; *IW*, June 6, 1912; Foner, *History of the Labor Movement*, 4; 203; William Preston, *Aliens and Dissenters* (Cambridge, Mass., 1963), 52–53; *San Francisco Call*, June 4, 1912; *IW*, June 20, 1912. On September 21, the San Diego Grand Jury indicted six Wobblies charged with carrying firearms into Mexico. These men had been arrested the previous month in El Cajon, a small city a few miles east of San Diego. They allegedly had dynamite in their possession. Chief Wilson at first declared that they were headed to Baja California to join the revolution there. Later he claimed that one of them confessed that the group's plan was to blow up the newly built Spreckels Theatre. On this pretext, police raided IWW headquarters in San Diego and arrested seven more Wobblies. This second group was released the following day when no evidence could be found to link them with the El Cajon Wobblies. The alleged bomb-carriers were then turned over to Federal authorities. See *San Diego Sun*, June 6, Aug. 23, 1912; *San Diego Union*, Aug. 23, 1912; *San Diego Evening Tribune*, Aug. 24, 1912.

84. Quotes from San Francisco Labor Council, Special Investigating Committee, *San Diego Free Speech Controversy*, 8–9; Joe Hill to E. A. Vanderleith, n.d., Frank Walsh Papers, Manuscript Division, NYPL; Abner Woodruff, *The Evolution of American Agriculture* (Chicago, 1916), 74–75, SHSW; W. I. Fisher, "Soap-Boxer or Organizer, Which?" *IW*, June 6, Aug. 15, 1912. See also IWW, *Twenty-Five Years of Industrial Unionism* (Chicago, 1930), 20; Mary Anderson Hill, "The Free Speech Fight at San Diego," *Survey* 28 (May 4, 1912), 192–94. During the city elections of 1913, the Socialists decided that they would not run a candidate for mayor, and instead concentrated on a successful effort to defeat Comm. of Morals John Sehon. However, the ordinance restricting street speaking still remained on the books. In 1915, free speech forces in conjunction with the Open Forum finally forced repeal of the ordinance and voted Dist. Atty. Harold Utley out of office. He was reelected a few years later and remained district attorney until his death in 1922. Chief Keno Wilson lost his job on January 17, 1917, when the new chief made him acting sergeant, then demoted him to patrolman a month later. Wilson never again regained his status in the police department, and retired as a desk sergeant in 1926. Abraham Sauer continued his weekly publication until his death on May 3, 1933. Ernest Kirk, sentenced to six months in jail on conspiracy charges, set up a small library, desk, and office in the corridor outside his private cell, and from this temporary office launched what would become San Diego's first law school. Spreckels continued expanding his empire until his death on June 7, 1926. See Foner, *History of the Labor Movement*, 4: 204; Pourade, *History of San Diego*, 5: 173; Jensen, "Keno Wilson," 50–54; San Francisco Labor Council, Special Investigating Committee, *San Diego Free Speech Controversy*, 4–8; *IW*, June 6, 1912; May 16, 1912, reprinting *Organized Labor*. An angry Chris Hansen, recovering in the hospital from his beating by vigilantes, vowed that if he ever participated in another free speech fight "it will be with machine guns and aerial bombs." Quotes from *IW*, Aug. 18, 1912; Tucker to St. John, Sept. 2, 1914; Hansen to St. John, n.d., CIRP.

85. Quotes from *IW*, Dec. 26, 1912. See also W. I. Fisher, "Soapbox or Organizer, Which?" June 6, 1912; Nov. 14, 1912.

86. Quotes from *IW*, Jan. 15, June 16, July 2, 1910; July 20, 1911; Dec. 28, 1911; June 6, Dec. 26, 1912; also "Some Weaknesses of the Western Wobbly," June 16, 1915; Jack Kenney, "Migratory Workers and the IWW," *Solidarity*, June 17, 1925; J. S. Biscay, "Controlling Migratory Jobs," Jan. 3, 1913; Biscay, "Job Organization in the West," Jan. 10, 1913; "Job Delegate an Objective," Nov. 28, 1914; *Voice of the People*, Oct. 23, 1913; Conlin, *Bread and Roses*, 6. See also Ben Williams, "Saga of the One Big Union," AULHWSU; Delany, *Bloodstained Trail*, 54; Foner, *History of the Labor Movement*, 4: 118; Austin Morris, "Movements of Migratory Unskilled in California," *New Review* 2 (Aug. 1914), 463; Jamieson, Notes, Box 1, Folder 20, p. 3, citing "Agriculture: The World's Basic Industry," 61.

87. Quote from Dubofsky, *We Shall Be All*, 288. So insignificant were agricultural workers within the ranks of the IWW that they were not even noted in a breakdown of membership made by Secretary-Treasurer Vincent St. John. See also Brissenden, *The I.W.W.*, 297, 309–10; Louis Levine, "The Development of Syndicalism in America," *PSQ* 28 (1913), 478.

88. Quote from Dubofsky, *We Shall Be All*, 293. See also *IW*, Feb. 1, 1912; *Solidarity*, May 3, 1912; *Proceedings of the Tenth IWW Convention*, 64; Brissenden, "A Report on the IWW in California," Aug. 1914, "Unions in General" Folder, 8, CIRPP; "Building the IWW," *Industrial Pioneer* 1 (Sept. 1923), 39–41; Anderson, *The Hobo*, 234; James Lynch, "The First Walking Delegate," *American Federationist* (Sept. 1901), 347; George Holmes, interview, 1–2, IWW and early TUUL, Box 1, Folder 2, Jamieson Notes, Jamieson Papers, BL. The first walking delegates in California were probably the secretaries for the Carpenter's Eight-Hour League. During the 1860s they traveled about the city inspecting jobs to make sure that only union men of the proper craft were employed. Although they acquired a reputation as petty grifters and despots who thrived in certain East Coast construction industries, walking delegates had also become an important part of the San Francisco building trades, where they acted more like labor policemen who enforced union rules, collected information from shop stewards, and earned a reputation as corrupt and brutal business agents who went about browbeating employers and workers alike, often receiving kickbacks from employers for keeping men in line. See also Leroy Scott, *The Walking Delegate* (New York, 1905), a working-class novel about insurgent ironworkers in New York.

89. Quote from William Dimmit, "An Organized Harvest," *Industrial Pioneer* 1 (Sept. 1921), 3–4. See also Barnes, "Ideology of the IWW," 239; *Solidarity*, Dec. 17, 1910; Nov. 28, 1914; Feb. 10, 1915; Tim, "The Job Delegate," June 4, 1919; *IW*, May 27, 1909; CIR, *Final Report* 1: 29; 5: 4941, 4945–46, 5004; W. J. Harju, *John Klim Hutter* (Palo Alto, 1974), 258; Vernon H. Jensen, "Labor Relations in the Douglas Fir Lumber Industry" (Ph. D. diss., UCB, 1939), 43.

90. Quotes from *IW*, May 28, 1910; Sin Bad, "Some Weakness of the Western Wobbly," *Solidarity*, Jan. 16, 1915; *IW*, June 3, 1909; Rodiger, *Fellow Worker*, 55; Barrie Stavis and Frank Harmon, eds., *Songs of Joe Hill* (New York, 1960), 22–23. See also *IW*, Mar. 13, 1913; Ben H. Williams, "Sabotage," *Solidarity*, Feb. 25, 1911; Frank Bohn, "Some Definitions: Direct Action—Sabotage," ibid., May 18, 1912; Oct. 3, 1914; CIR, *Final Report* 5; 4240–44; Elizabeth Gurley Flynn, *Sabotage: The Conscious Withdrawal of the Worker's Industrial Efficiency* (Cleveland, 1915), 5.

91. Parker, *The Casual Laborer*, 89, 172; Street, "Wheatland: Birth of the Farm Labor Movement," *Sacramento* 10 (Dec. 1984), 38–42, 63–65; "A Report to His Excellency Hiram W. Johnson, Governor of California, by the Commission of Immigration and Housing of California on the Causes and All matters Pertaining to the So-Called Wheatland Hop Fields' Riot and Killing of August 3, 1913, and Containing Certain recommendations as a Solution for the Problems Disclosed," in Parker, *The Casual Laborer and Other Essays*, app., 171–99; "Report on the Wheatland Hop-Field Riot," CIRPP.

92. Quote from McWilliams, *Factories in the Field*, 162.

Acknowledgments

Many people and institutions helped me during the long genesis of this book. Formulating and teaching an illustrated undergraduate lecture course at Stanford University, I was able to test some of the design on students. Their responses and suggestions helped me reshape the presentation, as did the questions and encouragement from audiences at several lectures I delivered at academic meetings throughout California. The invitation to lecture at the Changing Faces of Rural California conferences at the University of California, Davis, in 1998, 1999, and 2000, and the opportunity to lecture at the Center for U.S-Mexico Studies at the University of California, San Diego, in the spring of 1999, and the challenge of delivering the Davies Forum Lectures at the University of San Francisco in 2001 in conjunction with an exhibition of my farmworker photography, all forced me to further rethink large parts of the project.

When I began writing this history in 1972, I envisioned a one-volume treatment, finished in ten years. Thirty years later, the study filled three volumes and led me into the biography of two of the principal photographers of California farmworkers. A fellowship from the University of Wisconsin launched the initial phase of research. The James D. Phelan Award for Literature from the San Francisco Foundation funded further research into the emergence of California agriculture and produced a manuscript, *Into the Good Land: The Emergence of California Agriculture, 1850–1920*. A fellowship from the Henry E. Huntington Library allowed me to probe materials in Southern California. Grants and awards from the Dwight D. Eisenhower Library, Harry Truman Library-Institute, Franklin D. Roosevelt Library, John F. Kennedy Library, Boston, Sourisseau Academy, and the Minnesota Historical Society all helped me to fully exploit widely dispersed archival collections. A John Simon Guggenheim Memorial Fellowship provided a year of uninterrupted writing during which I completed volume one and the photographic book. Stints at the U.S.-Mexico Center, University of California, San Diego, the Stanford Humanities Center, and the Stanford history department provided a robust and supportive environment while I shifted from commercial agricultural photography to academe and worked on the latter stages of the project. On many levels, Stanford University remains among the most momentous experiences of my intellectual life, affirming and broadening my conviction that there is room in scholarship to reach a wider audience. Plenty of people told me the project was too big and ambitious in its scope, but colleagues at Stanford accepted the design matter-of-factly, offered constructive suggestions and, in one big intellectual brawl at the Stanford Humanities Center, argued with great passion over which photographs should appear on the cover.

My fifty-five-thousand-mile journey in search of information took me to twenty-two states, Spain, Mexico, and the U.S. Virgin Islands, and ranged from large, well-known research libraries to the back of a Chinese cemetery outside French Camp, near the Sacramento-San Joaquin Delta. There a single black marble tombstone marks a common grave, standing as a monument to that time in California history when gangs of Chinese laborers, including many who died in the act, transformed the delta swampland into one of the richest and most productive agricultural regions in the world. Along the path of my journey, so many people, archivists, librarians, and complete strangers assisted me in so many different ways that relating their contributions to my scholarship would amount to a book in itself. For the help and guidance I received on my research journey, I extend thanks and appreciation to: Mary Carr, AFL-CIO/George Meany Archives; Cynthia Ostle, Amadore-Livermore Valley Historical Society; Anahid Nazarian, American Zoetrope Research Library; Steve Cavin, American Academy of Franciscan History; Jane K. Newell, Mother Colony Collection, Anaheim History Room, Anaheim Public Library; James H. Nottage, Autry Museum of Western Heritage; Robert Becker, Leslie Clarke, Malca Chall, Mrs. Alma Compton, Suzanne Gallup, James D. Hart, James Kantor, Paul Machlis, Irene Moran, Erica Nordmeier, and Bill Roberts, The Bancroft Library; Don Donofro and O. G. Wilson, Bank of America Archives; Armand J. Labbe, The Bowers Museum of Cultural Art; Danette Cook Adamson, Special Collections, California State Polytechnic University, Pomona; Luis Bloch, California State Bureau of Labor Statistics; Pierre Biane and Nancy Farris, Brookside Vineyards; Terry Mangon, California Historical Society; Lisa Christiansen, California History Center/DeAnza College; John F. Burns, Joseph Samora, David Snyder, and Genevieve Troka, California State Archives; Ellen Harding, Gary F. Kurutz, Mary Weinstein, and Sibylle Zemitis, California State Library; Bill Jones, Special Collections, Meriam Library, California State University, Chico; Walter Gray III, California State Railroad Museum; Melissa Heyman, Campbell Historical Museum; Albert M. Tannler, University of Chicago Archives and Special Collections; Jennifer Fukunaga, Chino Valley Historical Society; C. Daniel Elliot, Levi D. Phillips, A. I. "Dick" Dickman, Donald Kunitz, and John Skarstad, Archives and Special Collections, University of California, Davis; Graham Blake, Colton Hall Museum; Richard Johnson, Colusa County Historical Society; Gloria Scott, Heritage Room, Corona Public Library; Tricia Saxton, Cucamonga Vineyards; Kathy Barnes, Bill Michael, Eastern California Museum; Dorothy Haase, Fillmore Historical Society; Barbara Blankman, First American Title Insurance Archives; Kevin O'Brien, Freedom of Information Division, FBI; Ben Bencomo, Ronald Noricks, Nate Orgill, and Diane Seeger, Fresno County Historical Society; Ray Silva, Bill Secrest, and Keith Boettcher, Fresno County Library, California History Room; Susan Voss, Pat Snar, Gilroy Historical Museum; Jean Coffey, Special Collections, Henry Madden Library, California State University, Fresno; Clarke Pauley and Maria Gonzalez, Guasti Plaza/The Italian Vineyard Company, Ontario; Susan Benedetti, Raymond Hillman, Tod Ruhstaller, and Barry J. Ward, the Haggin Museum; Dave Henderson, Haraszthy Cellars; Hannah Clayborn, Healdsburg Museum; Bill George, Alan Jutzi, and Jennifer Watts, the Huntington Library, San Marino, California; Mary Ann Bamberger, Special Collections, University of Illinois, Chicago Circle; Joe Anderholt and Lynn Bogdan, Imperial Valley Historical Society; K. J. Iwagaki, Japanese American Resource Center/Museum; Jeff Nickell and Carola Rupert, Kern County Museum; Galen Beery, the Historical Society of La Verne; Myra Manfrina, Lompoc Valley Historical Society; Jerry Kearns, Gail French, Library of Congress; Cathy Kobiachi, Mary S. Pratt, Carolyn Cole, Los Angeles Public Library; Lila Lee, Mendocino County Historical Society; Mary Beth Shaw, Mendocino County Museum; Andrea Morris Metz, Merced County Historical Society; June Erreca, Ralph Milliken Museum, Los Banos; Marilyn Ziebarth, Minnesota Historical Society; Robert Fisher, Mission Peak Heritage Foundation; Mona Gudgel, Monterey County Historical Society; Dennis Copeland, Monterey Public Library; Joseph E. Howerton, National Archives; John H. Cahoon, William M. Mason, Natural History Museum of Los Angeles; Ann Reinert, Nebraska State Historical Society; Rafael Rodriguez, Niebaum-Coppola Estate Winery; Terry Carter, Model Colony History Room, Ontario Public Library; Karen Joseph, Raymond Hoffman, Pajaro Valley Historical Association; Susan Hutchinson, David Streeter, Pomona Public Library Special Collections; James Hofer, University of Redlands Special Collections and Archives; Vincent Moses, Marvin Powell, Kevin Hallaran, Riverside Museum; William Swafford, Riverside Public Library; Coleen Frandsen, Reedley Historical Society; Steve Helmich, Jim Henley, Nikki Pahl, Sacramento Museum and Historical Commission; Cindy Krimmel, Chris Travers, San Diego Historical Society; Iris Engstrand, University of San Diego; Jeffrey Burns, Archives of San Francisco Diocese of the Catholic Church; Robert Bonta, Valarie Franco, Medora Johnson, San Joaquin County Historical Society; Ann F. Whitesell and Leslie Masunaga, History Museums of San Jose; Michael Redmon, Santa Barbara Historical Society; Virgilio Biasiol, Crescencia Olmstead, and Maynard Geiger, O.F.M., Santa Barbara Mission Archives; Wyman Spaulding and Debby Burns, Santa Paula Historical Society; Patricia Havens, Bill Appleton, Simi Valley Historical Society and Museum; Heritage Room, A. K. Smiley Public Library; Quentin R. Carter, Solano Community College; Mrs. Carolyn A. Wallace, the Southern Historical Collection, University of North Carolina; Polly Armstrong, Margaret Kimball, Grace Morledge, Patricia Palmer, Sarah Woodward, Stanford University Archives and Special Collections; Michael J. Hart, Sunny Slope Water Company; Kristen Childs, Jean Gustin, and Julie Starke, Community Memorial Museum of Sutter County; Faye Dudden, Syracuse University Archives; Dolores Nariman, Title Insurance and Trust Company, Los Angeles; Ellen Gorelick, Annie R. Mitchell, Tulare County Historical Society; Dace Taube, University of Southern California Archives; Sabine Goerke-Shrode, Vacaville Museum; James E. Kern, Vallejo Naval and Historical Museum; Robin Inglis, Vancouver Spanish Pacific Historical Society; Charles Johnson, Ventura County Museum; Elaine

Miller, Lynette Miller, Washington State Historical Society; Dennis East, Beverly Fodell, Thomas Featherstone, Philip Mason, Warner Pflug, Urban and Labor History Archives, Wayne State University; Merriam Griffith, Juanita DeValentine, Mildred Philips, Wheatland Historical Society; Jeff Edwards, Wild Horse Ranch, Porterville; Eileen M. Colla, Wine Institute; Marilyn Thompson, Yolo County Archives/Records Center; Barbara Beroza, Yosemite Museum; Linda Eade, Yosemite Research Library.

I also owe a debt of gratitude to Carl Abbott, Sarah Burns, Covello Photography, William Cronon, Melvyn Dubofsky, Dan Gerawan, Robert Hoover, "Turpie" Jackson, David Johnson, Marcel Jojola, Don Johnson, Michael Magliari, Phil Martin, Michael Mathes, Margo McBane, John Nopel, Richard J. Orsi, Steve Pavich, R. H. Powell, Glenn Price, Morton Rothstein, Chris Schneider, John Scott, Katherine Tachau, Mrs. Carl Van Löben Sells, David J. Weber, and countless others with whom I corresponded and talked during the long genesis of this project. Frank F. Latta and F. Hal Higgins, pack rats and pioneer historians, each left behind massive archives studded with gems of information, which I acknowledge in countless notes throughout this work. I met both men toward the end of their lives, and marvel at the extent of their collections and the huge debt that all historians of California and the American West owe these two men.

My work would have taken forever had it not been for the support of Thomas McCormick, whose friendship predates the beginning of this book; Doyce B. Nunis Jr., also known as "Editor Nunis," another whose support and encouragement was unwavering; Kevin Starr, who never doubted my sanity or tried to warn me off; and Jacqueline Jones, whose remarkable work on the laboring classes furnished a powerful example for my own effort.

I also owe a debt to three men who, regrettably, died before I finished this undertaking. Wallace Stegner gave me a view of history and the greatest book on the American West, *Angle of Repose*. Fred Thompson reeled off countless stories, as his wife fed me Swedish pastries, during numerous interviews at the beginning of this project. Paul S. Taylor instilled in me a sense of academe and an admiration for a marriage that unified love and work; I treasure the ideas, contacts, photographs, interviews, and the many wonderful encounters in his cluttered third-floor office.

At a critical juncture, the manuscript grew legs and ran off in all directions, and I had to call in an old editor-friend, Greg Critser, to hack away at the underbrush and reestablish some boundaries. Alexandra Russell left her marks on every page of the manuscript, much to the reader's benefit. The manuscript would have been a third-again as big had they not intervened. My editor at Stanford University Press, Norris Pope, has always been good-humored and supportive as the book expanded. I appreciated his critical reading of the manuscript, and I pray that in its ultimate form the book met his expectations. Anna Eberhard Friedlander directed the publication process for Stanford University Press, and Matt Stevens patiently pruned my writing and saved me from innumerable errors.

Material pertaining to the early years of the farmworker saga is ever expanding. In addition to excellent materials in all of the usual archives, even more can be found off the main path in the form of seminal and original academic studies, a wealth of newspaper accounts, work chronologies, company records, police files, personal papers, government studies and investigations, and the assorted files of a surprisingly large number of people who took it upon themselves to clip and compile substantial, specialized archives.

As the notes suggest, I have drawn heavily on the pioneering work of several generations of scholars who populate the Notes. I am indebted to them for sharing their work and blazing out paths. For providing ideas, information, and materials I thank: Tomás Almaguer, Edward Castillo, Sucheng Chan, Ping Chiu, Sherburne Cook, Cletus Daniel, Lloyd Fisher, Varden Fuller, Ernesto Galarza, Matt Garcia, Paul Gates, Gilbert González, James Gregory, Ramón Gutiérrez, Lisabeth Haas, Cindy Hahamovitch, Yuji Ichioka, Thomas Isern, Masakazu Iwata, Robert H. Jackson, Stuart E. Jamieson, Lawrence Jelenik, Joan M. Jensen, Karen Leonard, Sandy Lydon, Phil Martin, Linda and Theo Majaka, Brian McGinty, Don Mitchell, Gary Okihiro, Carleton E. Parker, James Rawls, Marc Reisner, Sandy Rikoon, Douglas Sackman, Walter J. Stein, Steve Stoll, Arne Svenson, Ronald Takaki, Daniel Rothenberg, David Vaught, David Weber, Devra Weber, and Greg Woirol. While sometimes diverging from their views, I acknowledge their role laying the foundation upon which subsequent study can be constructed.

I thank Leon Litwack for instilling in me a love of history, David Johnson for encouraging the historian's craft, and Charles Litzinger, James Reichart, and Tanamura Namura for translating Chinese and Japanese sources.

I must acknowledge Carey McWilliams, who gave me my first opportunities to write for *The Nation* and an appreciation for the power of language; his book *Factories in the Field: The Story of Migratory Farm Labor in California*, though flawed, dated, and fodder for graduate students and academic entrepreneurs, still captures the essence of what is important and remains a powerful indictment of race and class in California agriculture.

Earlier versions of various chapters appeared briefly elsewhere in different guise. For permission to reprint this material, I thank the editors of *American History Illustrated*, *American Heritage*, *California History*, *California Living/San Francisco Examiner Magazine*, *The Chronicle of Higher Education*, *History of Photography*, *Journal of the West*, *Labor History*, *Pacific Historical Review*, *Sacramento*, *San Diego*, *Southern California Quarterly*, and *West/San Jose Mercury News Magazine*.

Index